APB No.	Date Issued	Title
21	Aug. 1971	Interest on Receivables and Payables
22	Apr. 1972	Disclosure of Accounting Policies
23	Apr. 1972	Accounting for Income Taxes—Special Areas
24	Apr. 1972	Accounting for Income Taxes—Equity Method Investments
25	Oct. 1972	Accounting for Stock Issued to Employees
26	Oct. 1972	Early Extinguishment of Debt
27	Nov. 1972	Accounting for Lease Transactions by Manufacturer or Dealer Lessors
28	May 1973	Interim Financial Reporting
29	May 1973	Accounting for Nonmonetary Transactions
30	June 1973	Reporting the Results of Operations
31	June 1973	Disclosure of Lease Commitments by Lessees

SFAC No.

Financial Accounting Standards Board (FASB),
Statement of Financial Accounting Concepts (1978–85)

1	Nov. 1978	Objectives of Financial Reporting by Business Enterprises
2	May 1980	Qualitative Characteristics of Accounting Information
3	Dec. 1980	Elements of Financial Statements of Business Enterprises
4	Dec. 1980	Objectives of Financial Reporting by Nonbusiness Organizations
5	Dec. 1984	Recognition and Measurement in Financial Statements of Business Enterprises
6	Dec. 1985	Elements of Financial Statements (a replacement of *FASB Concepts Statement No. 3*, incorporating an amendment of *FASB Concepts Statement No. 2*)

SFAS No.

Financial Accounting Standards Board (FASB), *Statements of Financial Accounting Standards (1973–88)*

1	Dec. 1973	Disclosure of Foreign Currency
2	Oct. 1974	Accounting for Research and Development Costs
3	Dec. 1974	Reporting Accounting Changes in Interim Financial Statements (an amendment of *APB Opinion 23*)
4	Mar. 1975	Reporting Gains and Losses from Extinguishment of Debt
5	Mar. 1975	Accounting for Contingencies
6	May 1975	Classification of Short-Term Obligations Expected to Be Refinanced
7	June 1975	Accounting and Reporting by Development Stage Enterprises
8	Oct. 1975	Accounting for the Translation of Foreign Currency Transactions and Foreign Currency Financial Statements
9	Oct. 1975	Accounting for Income Taxes—Oil and Gas Producing Companies (an amendment of *APB Opinions 11* and *23*)
10	Oct. 1975	Extension of "Grandfather" Provisions for Business Combinations (an amendment of *APB Opinion 16*)
11	Dec. 1975	Accounting for Contingencies—Transition Method (an amendment of *FASB Statement 5*)
12	Dec. 1975	Accounting for Certain Marketable Securities
13	Nov. 1976	Accounting for Leases
14	Dec. 1976	Financial Reporting for Segments of a Business Enterprise
15	June 1977	Accounting by Debtors and Creditors for Troubled Debt Restructurings
16	June 1977	Prior Period Adjustments
17	Nov. 1977	Accounting for Leases—Initial Direct Costs
18	Nov. 1977	Financial Reporting for Segments of a Business Enterprise—Interim Financial Statements
19	Dec. 1977	Financial Accounting and Reporting by Oil and Gas Producing Companies
20	Dec. 1977	Accounting for Forward Exchange Contracts
21	Apr. 1978	Suspension of the Reporting of Earnings per Share and Segment Information by Nonpublic Enterprises
22	June 1978	Changes in the Provisions of Lease Agreements Resulting from Refundings of Tax-Exempt Debt
23	Aug. 1978	Inception of the Lease
24	Dec. 1978	Reporting Segment Information in Financial Statements that Are Presented in Another Enterprises's Financial Report
25	Feb. 1979	Suspension of Certain Accounting Requirements for Oil and Gas Companies (an amendment of *FASB Statement 19*)
26	Apr. 1979	Profit Recognition on Sales-Type Leases of Real Estate (an amendment of *FASB Statement 13*)
27	May 1979	Classification of Renewals or Extension of Existing Sales-Type or Direct Financing Leases (an amendment of *FASB Statement 13*)
28	May 1979	Accounting for Sales with Leasebacks (an amendment of *FASB Statement 13*)
29	June 1979	Determining Contingent Rentals (an amendment of *FASB Statement 13*)
30	Aug. 1979	Disclosure of Information about Major Customers (an amendment of *FASB Statement 14*)
31	Sept. 1979	Accounting for Tax Benefits Related to U.K. Tax Legislation Concerning Stock Relief
32	Sept. 1979	Specialized Accounting and Reporting Principles and Practices in AICPA Statements of Position and Guides on Accounting and Auditing Matters (an amendment of *APB Opinion 20*)
33	Sept. 1979	Financial Reporting and Changing Prices
		Illustrations of Financial Reporting and Changing Prices, *Statement of Financial Accounting Standards 33*

SAFS No.	Date Issued	Title
34	Oct. 1979	Capitalization of Interest Cost
35	Mar. 1980	Accounting and Reporting by Defined Benefit Pension Plans
36	May 1980	Disclosure of Pension Information (an amendment of *APB Opinion 8*)
37	July 1980	Balance Sheet Classification of Deferred Income Taxes (an amendment of *APB Opinion 11*)
38	Sept. 1980	Accounting for Preacquisition Contingencies of Purchased Enterprises (an amendment of *APB Opinion 16*)
39	Oct. 1980	Financial Reporting and Changing Prices: Specialized Assets—Mining and Oil and Gas (a supplement to *FASB Statement 33*)
40	Nov. 1980	Financial Reporting and Changing Prices: Specialized Assets—Timberlands and Growing Timber (a supplement to *FASB Statement 33*)
41	Nov. 1980	Financial Reporting and Changing Prices: Specialized Assets—Income-Producing Real Estate (a supplement to *FASB Statement 33*)
42	Nov. 1980	Determining Materiality for Capitalization of Interest Cost (an amendment for *FASB Statement 34*)
43	Nov. 1980	Accounting for Compensated Absences
44	Dec. 1980	Accounting for Intangible Assets of Motor Carriers (an amendment of Chapter 5 of *ARB 43*, and an interpretation of *APB Opinions 17 and 30*)
45	Mar. 1981	Accounting for Franchise Fee Revenue
46	Mar. 1981	Financial Reporting and Changing Prices: Motion Picture Films
47	Mar. 1981	Disclosure of Long-Term Obligations
48	June 1981	Revenue Recognition When Right of Returns Exists
49	June 1981	Accounting for Product Financing Arrangements
50	Nov. 1981	Financial Reporting in the Record and Music Industry
51	Nov. 1981	Financial Reporting by Cable Television Companies
52	Dec. 1981	Foreign Currency Translation
53	Dec. 1981	Financial Reporting by Producers and Distributors of Motion Picture Films
54	Jan. 1982	Financial Reporting and Changing Prices; Investment Companies
55	Feb. 1982	Determining Whether a Convertible Security Is a Common Stock Equivalent
56	Feb. 1982	Designation of AICPA Guide and SOP 81-1 on Contractor Accounting and SOP 81-2 on Hospital-Related Organizations as Preferable for Applying *APB Opinion 20*
57	Mar. 1982	Related Party Disclosures
58	April 1982	Capitalization of Interest Cost in Financial Statements that Include Investments Accounted for by the Equity Method
59	April 1982	Deferral of the Effective Date of Certain Accounting Requirements for Revision Plans of State and Local Government Units
60	June 1982	Accounting and Reporting by Insurance Enterprises
61	June 1982	Accounting for Title Plant
62	June 1982	Capitalization of Interest in Situations Involving Certain Tax-Exempt Borrowings and Certain Gifts and Grants
63	June 1982	Financial Reporting by Broadcasters
64	Sept. 1982	Extinguishment of Debt Made to Satisfy Sinking Fund Requirements
65	Sept. 1982	Accounting for Certain Mortgage Bank Activities
66	Oct. 1982	Accounting for Sales on Real Estate
67	Oct. 1982	Accounting for Costs and Initial Rental Operations of Real Estate Projects
68	Oct. 1982	Research and Development Arrangements
69	Nov. 1982	Disclosures about Oil and Gas Producing Activities (an amendment of *FASB Statements 19, 25, 33,* and *39*)
70	Dec. 1982	Financial Reporting and Changing Prices: Foreign Currency Translation (an amendment of *FASB Statement 33*)
71	Dec. 1982	Accounting for the Effects of Certain Types of Regulation
72	Feb. 1983	Accounting for Certain Acquisitions of Banking or Thrift Institutions (an amendment of *APB Opinion 17*, an interpretation of *APB Opinions 16 and 17,* ad an amendment of *FASB Interpretation 9*)
73	Aug. 1983	Reporting a Change in Accounting for Railroad Track Structures (an amendment of *ABP Opinion 20*)
74	Aug. 1983	Accounting for Special Termination Benefits Paid to Employees
75	Nov. 1983	Deferral of the Effective Date of Certain Accounting Requirements for Pension Plans of State and Local Governmental Units (an amendment of *FASB Statement 35*)
76	Nov. 1983	Extinguishment of Debt (an amendment of *APB Opinion 26*)
77	Dec. 1983	Reporting by Transferors for Transfers of Receivables with Recourse
78	Dec. 1983	Classification of Obligations that Are Callable by the Creditor (an amendment of *ARB 43*, Chapter 3A)
79	Feb. 1984	Elimination of Certain Disclosures for Business Combinations by Nonpublic enterprises (an amendment of *APB Opinion 16*)
80	Aug. 1984	Accounting for Futures Contracts
81	Nov. 1984	Disclosure of Postretirement Health Care and Life Insurance Benefits

INTERMEDIATE
ACCOUNTING

VOLUME II CHAPTERS 14-26

INTERMEDIATE ACCOUNTING

♦

Revised Edition

THOMAS R. DYCKMAN
Ann Whitney Olin Professor of Accounting
Cornell University

ROLAND E. DUKES
University of Washington

CHARLES J. DAVIS
California State University—Sacramento

GLENN A. WELSCH
James L. Bayless Chair for Free Enterprise Emeritus
The University of Texas at Austin

IRWIN

Homewood, IL 60430
Boston, MA 02116

Cover photo: James Frederick Housel

Material from the Examinations and Unofficial Answers, copyright © 1955, 1960, 1961, 1962, 1963, 1965, 1966, 1967, 1968, 1969, 1970, 1971, 1972, 1973, 1974, 1975, 1976, 1977, 1978, 1979, 1980, 1981, 1983, 1986, 1988, and 1989 by the American Institute of Certified Public Accountants, Inc., is adapted or reprinted with permission.

© RICHARD D. IRWIN, INC., 1992

Senior sponsoring editor: Ron M. Regis
Developmental editor: Cheryl D. Wilson
Project editor: Margaret Haywood
Production manager: Ann Cassady
Designer: Laurie Entringer
Art manager: Kim Meriwether
Compositor: Better Graphics, Inc.
Typeface: 10/12 Times Roman
Printer: Von Hoffmann Press

Library of Congress Cataloging-in-Publication Data

Intermediate accounting / Thomas R. Dyckman . . . [et al.].—Rev. ed.
    p.   cm.
   ISBN 0-256-10738-6   ISBN 0-256-11307-6 (Volume II, Chapters 14–26)
   1. Accounting.   I. Dyckman, Thomas R.
  HF5635.I529   1992b
  657′.044—dc20   91–16245

Printed in the United States of America
  3 4 5 6 7 8 9 0 VH 8 7 6 5 4 3

To our wives and families:
Ann, Daniel, James, Linda, David
Phyllis, Peter, Anna
Susan, Nicole, Michael

ABOUT THE AUTHORS

♦

Thomas R. Dyckman, Ph.D., is Ann Whitney Olin Professor of Accounting and Quantitative Analysis and Associate Dean for Academic Affairs at Cornell University's Johnson Graduate School of Management. In addition to teaching accounting and quantitative analysis, he is a program coordinator of Cornell's Executive Development Program. He earned his doctorate degree from the University of Mighigan.

A former member of the Financial Accounting Standards Board Advisory Committee, Professor Dyckman is presently a member of the Financial Accounting Foundation which oversees the FASB. He was president of the American Accounting Association in 1982 and received the association's *Outstanding Educator Award* for the year 1987. He also received the AICPA's *Notable Contributions to Accounting Literature Award* in 1966 and 1977.

Professor Dyckman has extended industrial experience that includes work with the U.S. Navy and IBM. He has conducted seminars for the University of California Management Development Program and the Credit Bureau Executives' Program, as well as for Ocean Spray, Goodyear, Morgan Guaranty, GTE, Southern New England Telephone, and Goulds Pumps.

Professor Dyckman has coauthored several books and written over 50 journal articles on topics from financial markets to the application of quantitative and behavioral theory to administrative decision making. He has been a member of the editorial boards of *The Accounting Review, The Journal of Finance and Quantitative Analysis, The Journal of Accounting and Economics* and *The Journal of Management Accounting Research.*

Roland E. (Pete) Dukes, Ph.D., is professor of accounting at the University of Washington where he teaches intermediate and advanced financial accounting at the undergraduate and graduate levels. He has served as chairman of the department of accounting since 1983. He received his doctorate from Stanford University.

A member of the American Accounting Association, Professor Dukes has chaired the Annual Meeting Technical Program Planning Committee, the Doctoral Consortium Committee, and the Notable Contribution to Accounting Literature Committee. He has also served as a Distinguished Visiting Faculty for the Doctoral Consortium, as Director of the Doctoral Consortium, and as the Puget Power Affiliate Program Professor of Accounting at the University of Washington from 1986 to 1990.

Professor Dukes has published numerous articles in accounting journals, including *The Accounting Review, Journal of Accounting Research,* and the *Journal of Accountancy.* He has served on the editorial boards of *The Accounting Review, Journal of Accounting Research,* and *Journal of Accounting Literature.* He has been a consultant to the Financial Accounting Standards Board, and authored the *FASB Research Report* which investigated the effect of *SFAS No. 8* on security return behavior. Professor Dukes also has served as a consultant to the Securities and Exchange Commission and to industry and government.

Charles J. Davis, Ph.D., C.P.A., is professor and chair of the department of accountancy at California State University, Sacramento. He received his doctorate in accounting from the University of Illinois at Urbana.

Professor Davis has taught in the areas of financial and managerial accounting and auditing at both the intermediate and advanced levels. He has also been active in CPA review programs. Professor Davis received excellence in teaching awards from both the University of Illinois at Urbana and California State University, Sacramento. In addition, he has been active in student accounting groups on campus.

Professor Davis has written journal articles in accounting and related business fields that appear in *Advances in Accounting, Issues in Accounting Education,* and *Journal of Accounting and Public Policy,* and in several health-care fiscal management journals. He serves on the editorial review board of *Advances in Accounting.* He worked as a staff auditor for Peat, Marwick, Mitchell and Company and has served as a consultant to industry and government. Professor Davis is a member of the American Accounting Association.

PREFACE

◆

PHILOSOPHY AND PURPOSE
◆

Financial reporting plays a unique role in the process of allocating resources in our economy. The subject matter of this text, *Intermediate Accounting,* Revised Edition, is the development of the principles underlying that reporting process.

This revision represents a major reorganization and rewriting effort. Our aim is to improve the text as a learning tool while continuing the comprehensiveness and technical quality of previous editions.

The text is completely current as to the date of publication, and includes discussion of the most recent FASB statements. In particular, we have incorporated FASB *Statement Nos. 102* and *104* concerning the statement of cash flows, *Statement No. 105* on financial instruments, *Statement No. 106* on postemployment benefits other than pensions, and the latest pronouncements on accounting for income taxes into the text. Every attempt has been made to assure the accuracy of this material.

Each of us has taught intermediate accounting for many years. In doing so, we have developed an awareness of the issues and applications most difficult for the student to master and have exercised special care in those areas to make the presentation as clear, understandable, and stimulating as possible.

Before embarking on this revision, we surveyed the marketplace to solicit views on topics to be included in the intermediate accounting course, chapter sequencing, desirability of real-world examples, and degree of comprehensiveness. The answers to our surveys and questionnaires were exceptionally helpful in providing overall direction for this revision. In addition, the panel of 30 reviewers were a tremendous source of information about the market and our proposed changes in pedagogy. The insights and recommendations of these reviewers helped shape the final form and substance of the text.

Objectives and Overall Approach of the Revised Edition This revised edition has several objectives. The primary objective is to provide comprehensive coverage of financial accounting topics, both application and rationale. The text emphasizes the reasons for specific accounting principles, along with clear discussions and illustrations of their applications. We believe that continual integration of theory and practice is the most efficient way to present the subject matter. When the student discovers there is a reason for a procedure, much less is relegated to pure memorization. Consequently, this text does not rely on large and complex exhibits as the sole explanation for accounting procedures.

A secondary objective is to bring the subject to life and increase the student's interest in the material. To accomplish this, we have greatly increased the text's real-world emphasis. The text has literally hundreds of examples of real-world reporting and frequent discussions of the financial reporting experiences of actual firms.

Throughout the text, we discuss the process by which specific accounting principles are developed, thus reinforcing the real-world nature of financial reporting standards. The impact of lobbying and the need for compromise by the FASB is discussed in several chapters affected by the more controversial pronouncements. One aim of this emphasis is to develop the student's ability to critically evaluate particular reporting standards. We want the student to address the question: Is a particular accounting principle successfully fulfilling the primary objective of financial statements, namely to provide information useful for decision making? A second aim is to acquaint the student with the political setting in which standard-setting takes place.

The topical sequencing of material within each chapter is designed to present the important reporting issues and the reasons financial statement users and preparers are concerned about them. This approach leads to a discussion of the current GAAP solution to the issue with appropriate rationale. In the more controversial areas, we consider other potential solutions and why these may have been rejected by the relevant rule-making body. As a result, the student is frequently reminded of the dynamic and interactive nature of the standard-setting process and the inherent difficulties facing standard setters in reaching a consensus.

We also emphasize the areas for which the accounting standards provide a choice from among several alternative methods. In related discussions, the text probes the incentives for choosing from among alternative accounting methods.

Curriculum Concerns   This revision is responsive to the concerns of the Accounting Education Change Commission. These concerns suggest a new orientation for accounting education. With this new direction, students should be encouraged "to learn how to learn." Curricula should emphasize the underlying concepts, rather than memorization of rules and regulations. The focus is on the process of inquiry in which the student learns to identify problem situations, to search for relevant information, to analyze and interpret the information, and to reach a well-reasoned conclusion.

With these goals in mind, this revised edition frequently asks questions and presents important contemporary issues in a manner that compels the student to think about the appropriate solution to a reporting problem. We believe that the discussions of the more controversial and involved issues will lead the student to his or her own position on the issues. To this end, the text often focuses on the process of inquiry, rather than encouraging memorization of the standards and procedures. What information would the user find more helpful in making decisions? What would the student do in this situation?

We view the current GAAP solutions to reporting problems as one step in the continuing evolutionary process of attempting to provide the most cost-effective and useful information possible. The text involves the student in that process. For example, many of the cases require students to identify and solve unstructured problems and to consider multiple data sources. Our computerized end-of-chapter items encourage interaction and help the student learn by doing. In addition, by weaving theory and application together throughout the text, students are encouraged to apply their knowledge to new situations.

Writing Style and Exposition   The text mixes a clear, direct, and concise writing style with an active voice to maintain the positive flow of the material and the student's attention. The text is well outlined and provides considerable structure and good transition between topics. We have clarified and simplified many of the application examples without sacrificing completeness.

The text makes generous use of outlining by using distinctive captions to provide a chronological structure for the reader. We have attempted to minimize the number of pages without any visual "break." We believe that frequent use of examples, headings and new pedagogical devices increases understandability and ease of reading, while maintaining the student's

interest. A greater use of visual aids is apparent in this edition. Furthermore, the new pedagogical features enhance the learning experience for students.

An increased use of summary tables and exhibits helps to synthesize the more complex areas, and gives the student an opportunity to evaluate progress. Many of the exhibits and illustrations were class-tested to fine tune them.

To increase the conversational tone and use of current terminology, certain terms were changed. For example, "balance sheet" replaces "statement of financial position," "income statement" replaces "statement of income," and "payment" replaces "rent" in present value discussions. *Statements of Financial Accounting Standards* are referred to as *SFAS*s. Also, in the text and the end-of-chapter material, the revised edition uses actual year designations such as 1991, rather than 19A, for increased realism.

The text assumes completion of the basic college-level introductory course in financial accounting and is intended primarily for schools covering intermediate accounting in two semesters or three quarters. For example, one logical sequencing for a two semester course is Chapters 1–14 in the first course, followed by Chapters 15–26. By quarter: Chapters 1–8, Chapters 9–16, and Chapters 17–26. This text covers material that is a foundation for a later course in advanced financial accounting and for graduate courses.

REVISION APPROACH AND ORGANIZATION
◆

Financial accounting is concerned with measurement of economic attributes and their recognition in asset, liability, owners' equity, and income statement accounts. Income determination and disclosure also are important focuses of financial reporting. The revised edition reflects a new sequencing of chapters. After considering the conceptual framework of the FASB and a review of the accounting process, the chapters in this book are grouped into modules corresponding to the major balance sheet account classifications, in natural balance sheet order. Within each is a consideration of the related income and disclosure issues. The text concludes with a series of chapters on specialized accounting topics. These chapter groupings are:

	Part	Chapters
I	Foundation and Review	1–6
II	Asset Recognition and Measurement	7–14
III	Liabilities	15–19
IV	Owners' Equity	20–22
V	Special Topics	23–26

Changes in Chapter Order   The revised edition significantly changes chapter sequencing. The major changes in chapter order are:

Chapter 2, "The FASB's Conceptual Framework of Accounting" (Chapter 6 in the previous edition) now appears earlier. We believe this is preferable because it allows the instructor to discuss theory before covering the financial statements in the review chapters. The reviewers responded to this major organizational change very favorably.

Chapter 7, "Revenue and Expense Recognition" (Chapter 13 in the previous edition) appears as the first chapter in the section of the text devoted to asset measurement. The chapter ties back to the conceptual framework (when to recognize assets), thereby linking theory with the practical issues of when to record revenues and expenses. The earlier presentation also allows the instructor to cover certain topics without first having to explain recognition criteria.

Chapter 14, "Investments: Temporary and Long Term" (Chapter 18 in the previous edition) is now sequenced as part of the asset section of the text. This grouping allows completion of revenue recognition issues (in this chapter, for intercompany investments) before taking up accounting issues related to liabilities.

Chapter 17, "Accounting for Income Taxes" (Chapter 23 in the previous edition) is now sequenced as part of the liability section of the text. In this way, the liability issues are completed before turning to owners' equity.

Chapter 22, "Earnings per Share" (part of Chapter 22 in the previous edition) is now a stand-alone special topics chapter given the overall importance and complexity of the topic.

Chapter 25, "Financial Statement Analysis and Changing Prices" (part of Chapter 22 and Chapter 25 in the previous edition) are now combined in the revised edition. Adjustments for the effect of changing prices are no longer required, yet many financial statement users continue to make such adjustments when analyzing statements. Hence, adjusting for price-level changes is treated as part of financial statement analysis.

Chapter 26, "Special Topics: Segment Reporting, Interim Reporting, and Disclosures"   is a new chapter that combines parts of chapters from the previous edition along with new material on disclosure issues from the FASB.

Flexibility in Use

In reordering the chapters, we had definite objectives in mind. The topical chapters are grouped to provide a more clear and logical transition within major parts of the text. The commonality of issues and principles within each part reinforces similar principles and enhances their understanding.

However, instructors are not bound by this order. For example, some instructors prefer to cover current liabilities immediately after current assets. This text provides the flexibility to accomplish this and virtually any other ordering desired. The chapters following Chapter 6 are topical in nature, and all rely on the first five chapters for conceptual grounding, and the "big-picture" review in Chapters 3 through 5. Given that the topical chapters are self-contained, a considerable degree of flexibility in chapter sequencing is maintained.

Also, use of appendixes increases the flexibility of topical coverage for the instructor. This additional flexibility is important given the ever-increasing scope of topics in the intermediate accounting course.

Real-World Emphasis

This text makes extensive use of financial reporting examples from actual companies when discussing specific reporting areas. We also make frequent use of the AICPA's *Accounting Trends and Techniques* for information on trends in financial reporting. In addition, many references to reporting decisions and consequences from actual businesses are taken from *The Wall Street Journal, Forbes, Financial Executive,* and many other sources. The Sherwin-Williams Company graciously permitted us to reproduce their entire 1990 financial statements and accompanying notes.

Using actual companies in examples helps show how reporting is done in practice. References to well-known corporations capture and hold the student's interest and reflect the tremendous variety of current accounting practices. The real-world examples also help to convince the student of the importance of many abstract concepts and procedures.

Ethics

A topic of continuing interest in business schools, ethical issues are treated in several chapters through an ethics case in the end-of-chapter material. Ethics cases are included in Chapters 3, 6, 8, 9, 11, 12, 16, 19, 23, and 24. Portions of the AICPA Code of Professional Conduct are reproduced in an appendix to Chapter 1. In addition, implicit references are made to the ethics of financial reporting throughout the text.

End-of-Chapter Materials

Numerous changes and revisions were made to this material. Older and more repetitive items were deleted, and many new items were added. These additions supplement the already considerable inventory of homework assignments. CPA examination questions continue to be used in this edition; many were updated.

The **questions** at the end of each chapter provide a context for in-class discussion; **exercises** are generally structured applications of specific issues in the chapter; **problems** generally are longer and less structured applications of one or more specific issues in the chapter; and **cases** often require the student to integrate several issues in the chapter and provide an opinion on a reporting problem or situation.

The cases and some problems provide an opportunity for students to practice their analytical and written communication skills. Furthermore, they frequently place the student in an unstructured setting requiring a broad view to be taken of a business reporting problem. The context in which financial reporting is used must be considered in these instances.

To help the instructor choose appropriate items, each exercise, problem, and case is titled to indicate the primary issue involved. In addition, each is keyed to one or more learning objectives to allow instructors to select those areas they wish to emphasize.

The quantity and variety of items, both in substance and level of difficulty, allows an instructor to vary the homework items from term to term. The end-of-chapter material was checked for accuracy by faculty colleagues.

NEW PEDAGOGICAL FEATURES
♦

Several new pedagogical features have been added to the revised edition. They are designed to make learning easier and, in general, to make this text more user-friendly.

Learning Objectives

Done in list form, a set of proactive learning objectives opens each chapter to provide the student with learning goals and a preview of upcoming topics.

Introductions

Immediately after the list of learning objectives are the introductions or "stage setters" that discuss events and reporting by actual companies relevant to the chapter and provide a transition to the upcoming chapter topics. These introductions are attention-grabbing and help the reader understand the significance of the area about to be studied.

Concept Reviews

Throughout the chapters, usually at the end of major sections, students are asked to respond to a brief list of questions. These questions are answerable directly from the text and help students check their understanding of the section's basic concepts or message. These questions also provide a break from the reading and reinforce the major ideas. In addition, the concept reviews give the readers an idea of how well they comprehended the material before moving ahead. The questions are analogous to a short quiz after a lecture on a particular part of a chapter. The answers to the concept review questions are provided at the end of the solutions manual for the convenience of the instructor.

Summary of Key Points

Each chapter concludes with a recap of the main ideas presented. The summaries are now done in list format rather than a paragraph style. The list format better highlights the chapter's content by making the most important ideas more easily identifiable. Each point is keyed to the relevant learning objective.

Review Problem with Solution

Immediately after the summary of key points, a review problem illustrates several of the chapter's main concepts, followed by the solution. The review problems also provide additional practice for the student and a self-test for evaluating progress.

Key Terms

Just before the end-of-chapter material, a list of the chapter's most important new terms appears. Page references indicate where the terms were defined and initially discussed. The key terms are printed in a second color for emphasis allowing the student to easily locate them, and to review their meanings in the context of the chapter.

Comprehensive Problems

In many chapters, one or more problems in the end-of-chapter material cover several of the chapter's learning objectives. Their objective is to integrate the more important ideas into a single situation. They are identified by this symbol in the margin:

COMPREHENSIVE PROBLEM
♦

Ethics Case

Many chapters include a case in the end-of-chapter material that emphasizes the ethical implications of particular actions and reporting decisions. The student often is placed in a situation requiring a decision that has ethical ramifications. These cases are identified by this symbol in the margin:

Sherwin-Williams Cases

Many chapters also include a case based on the 1990 annual statements of the Sherwin-Williams Company. This case provides an up-to-date application of the chapter material to an actual company. These problems are identified by the Sherwin-Williams logo.

Spreadsheet Applications Template Software (SPATS)

Many chapters include problems and exercises solvable on a computerized spreadsheet. Templates are provided for these problems. A spreadsheet symbol in the margin identifies these problems.

KEY CHAPTER REVISIONS
♦

The changes to the revised edition were very extensive. The following list highlights major revisions made in each chapter.

Chapter 1, "The Environment of Accounting"
* The basic accounting model has been moved to Chapter 3.
* The 1988 RJR Nabisco takeover is used to illustrate the value and limitations of financial reporting.
* Portions of the AICPA's Code of Profesional Conduct are reproduced to provide fundamental ethics coverage.

Chapter 2, "The FASB's Conceptual Framework of Accounting"
* The environment in which the FASB functions and the political nature of the standard-setting process are emphasized.
* The major parts of the *Statements of Financial Accounting Concepts,* as they reflect the development of accounting principles, are discussed in chronological order.
* The historical development of the conceptual framework highlights the nature of the standard-setting process.

Chapter 3, "Review: The Accounting Information Processing System"
* The more general systems approach to the accounting cycle is discussed in the chapter, while an appendix that includes **acetate transparencies** illustrates the worksheet.
* Greater emphasis is placed on adjusting and reversing entries.
* A new discussion comparing two methods of recording operating cash flows that precede recognition of revenue and expense helps the student to understand adjustments and reversals.

Chapter 4, "Review: The Income Statement and the Statement of Retained Earnings"
* New and detailed discussion of the measurement and reporting guidelines for discontinued operations results in comprehensive coverage of this topic.
* The coverage of intraperiod tax allocation parallels the greater emphasis on items below income from continuing operations.
* The new emphasis on the issue of current operating performance versus the all-inclusive approach to income measurement complements the discussion of comprehensive income.

Chapter 5, "Review: The Balance Sheet and the Statement of Cash Flows"
* The balance sheet and statement of cash flows of Merck and Company are used to present and illustrate many of the concepts in this chapter.
* The various valuation approaches used in the balance sheet, the usefulness of the balance sheet, and the limitations of the balance sheet are stressed.
* Both the direct and indirect forms of the statement of cash flows are discussed and illustrated.

Chapter 6, "Interest: Concepts of Future and Present Value"
* Symbols for future and present value calculations are now more user-friendly.

+ Use of summary tables and time-line exhibits simplifies the presentation.
+ The interest tables now appear in an appendix.

Chapter 7, "Revenue and Expense Recognition"
+ The earlier coverage of revenue recognition will assist the discussion of asset recognition in later chapters.
+ The fundamental concepts of revenue and revenue recognition are emphasized throughout the chapter.
+ The conceptual discussion leads to the general criteria for revenue recognition.

Chapter 8, "Cash and Receivables"
+ Three formats for bank reconciliations are covered and greater emphasis is placed on proof of cash.
+ The in-depth discussion on using receivables for financing reflects the complexities in this area.
+ New coverage of notes receivable exchanged for cash and other privileges demonstrates the variety of uses for notes and resulting accounting issues.

Chapter 9, "Inventory Measurement, Cost of Goods Sold, and DV LIFO"
+ Coverage of consignments is expanded.
+ The chapter now distinguishes between cost-flow assumptions under both the periodic and perpetual systems.
+ A new section on inventory pools emphasizes the importance of cost-benefit concerns in this area.

Chapter 10, "Alternative Inventory Valuation Methods"
+ The LCM material has been rewritten to clarify the calculation process and includes additional situations.
+ There is new coverage of the use of LCM in reporting income taxes.
+ The discussion of the gross margin and retail methods is rewritten to emphasize calculational steps.

Chapter 11, "Operational Assets: Acquisition, Disposal, and Exchange"
+ The discussion of the issue of what to capitalize includes the FASB exposure draft on donations.
+ The substantially greater emphasis on capitalization of interest includes both theory and application.
+ A generalized approach to valuing property acquired in an exchange helps to simplify this area.

Chapter 12, "Operational Assets: Depreciation and Impairment"
+ Considerably greater emphasis is placed on the nature of depreciation, incentives for choice of method, and what depreciation means to the financial statement user.
+ Depreciation policy is discussed in terms of its effect on dividend policy and cash flows.

+ A section on impairment of value considers the decade-long trend of corporations to take large write-offs of operational assets.

Chapter 13, "Intangible Assets and Natural Resources"
+ The accounting for all intangibles other than goodwill, research and development, and computer software costs is reorganized.
+ In-depth treatment of goodwill estimation emphasizes concepts and examples.
+ The oil and gas controversy complements a complete discussion of accounting for natural resources.

Chapter 14, "Investments: Temporary and Long Term"
+ Changing between the cost and equity method is discussed and illustrated.
+ Consolidations discussion is shorter and has been moved to an appendix.
+ Also moved to an appendix are special purpose funds, cash surrender value of life insurance, and future contracts.

Chapter 15, "Short-Term Liabilities"
+ New coverage of bonus payments is added.
+ The chapter now includes refinancing of short-term debt and the reporting of debt as short term.
+ The sections on taxes collected for third parties, property taxes, and conditional payments are extensively revised.

Chapter 16, "Long-Term Liabilities"
+ Greater emphasis is placed on theory discussion and the rationale for FASB positions on such controversial topics as troubled debt restructuring, debt extinguishment, and valuation of debt issued with equity securities.
+ There is new coverage of troubled debt restructure, which now appears in an appendix.
+ The FASB's financial instruments project is discussed in terms of project financing relationships, unconditional purchase obligations, zero-coupon bonds, and creative financial instruments.

Chapter 17, "Accounting for Income Taxes"
+ Accounting for operating losses precedes interperiod tax allocation.
+ The latest Exposure Draft for income taxes is incorporated in the body of the text. The more complex procedures for determining the amount of deferred tax assets are covered in the appendix.
+ The coverage in the chapter is complete and flexible so that the instructor can choose to focus on the procedures and requirements of the Exposure Draft or on those of *SFAS 96* if the Exposure Draft is not adopted.

Chapter 18, "Accounting for Leases"
- Accounting for lessor and lessee is covered in series rather than in parallel fashion; the lessee is considered first (emphasis on liabilities).
- Greater emphasis is placed on special issues including different interest rates, bargain renewal offers, and the use of guaranteed residual values to secure off-balance-sheet financing.
- An appendix covers real estate and leveraged leases.

Chapter 19, "Accounting for Pensions"
- The chapter is totally reorganized using a modularized approach to emphasize the basics and to ease into the complexities.
- New coverage of ERISA, PBGC and pension termination enhances the real-world flavor of the subject.
- Three new appendixes appear: postemployment benefits other than pensions; settlements, curtailments, and termination benefits; and accounting for the pension plan.

Chapter 20, "Corporations: Contributed Capital"
- Professional corporations and Subchapter S corporations are now discussed.
- Greater emphasis is placed on the issues underlying redeemable preferred shares.
- Examples of self-tender offers to acquire treasury stock and retirement of stock increase the comprehensive coverage of owners' equity accounting.

Chapter 21, "Corporations: Retained Earnings and Stock Options"
- Fractional share rights and stock appreciation rights receive greater emphasis.
- The discussion of quasi reorganizations is moved to an appendix.

Chapter 22, "Earnings per Share"
- EPS is given its own chapter to allow for more detailed discussion.
- Primary EPS is discussed before fully diluted EPS.
- Extensive examples are now provided.

Chapter 23, "Statement of Cash Flows"
- The spreadsheet is simplified to allow a simultaneous solution of the statement under both direct and indirect methods.
- The direct and indirect methods are discussed separately through the first complete statement example to emphasize their different characteristics; then both methods are discussed in the more complex examples because the reconciliation of net operating cash flow and net income are present in both.
- The approaches to preparing the statement are illustrated: format-free, spreadsheet, and the T-account.

Chapter 24, "Accounting Changes and Error Corrections"
- The issues affecting accounting changes and alternative views and motivations for changes are stressed.
- The direct and indirect effects of current accounting changes are now covered.
- Changing to LIFO is discussed.

Chapter 25, "Financial Statement Analysis and Changing Prices"
- The inclusion of both financial statement analysis and accounting for changing prices is a major organizational change aimed at streamlining the coverage of these two related topics now that firms no longer are required to report on changing prices.
- New ratios used in financial statement analysis are discussed.
- Discussed are four models for reporting the effects of price level changes, the advantages and disadvantages of each, and a brief example highlighting the nature of each model.

Chapter 26, "Special Topics: Segment Reporting, Interim Reporting, and Disclosures"
- The first section is an all new discussion of standards and information overload and the principle of full disclosure.
- A discussion of the conflict between the FASB and financial statement users highlights the political nature of the standard setting process.
- A more straight-forward presentation of interim and segmental disclosure is included in this chapter.

ANCILLARIES AND SUPPLEMENTARY MATERIALS
◆

FOR THE PROFESSOR:

INTERMEDIATE ACCOUNTING, Revised Edition, offers numerous teaching aids to assist the instructor.

Solutions Manual, Chapters 1–14 and 14–26—Done in two volumes, this comprehensive solutions manual provides complete solutions and explanations for all end-of-chapter questions, exercises, problems, and cases. The estimated completion time for each item is given in the assignment assistance schedule at the beginning of each chapter. Answers to the concept review questions are included at the end of the manual.

Test Bank, Chapters 1–14 and 14–26—Revised and expanded with this edition, the test bank offers approximately 4,000 questions and problems from which to choose in preparing examinations. This test bank contains true-false, short answer, problems and cases, and selected CPA examination questions. It was revised by Robert Su of California State University–Sacramento.

Solutions Transparencies—Acetate transparencies of solutions to all exercises and all problems are free to adopters. Now increased in clarity, these transparencies are especially useful when covering problems in large classroom settings.

Teaching Transparencies—Selected lecture transparencies based on text material are available for classroom use.

Instructor's Resource Manual—This manual includes overviews, learning objectives, lecture outlines, problem analysis by objective, summaries, key terms, review quizzes, and transparency masters. It was prepared by Dick D. Wasson of Central Washington University.

Computest 3—This advanced-feature test generator allows the adding and editing of questions; saves and reloads tests; creates up to 99 different versions of each test; attaches graphics to questions; imports and exports ASCII files; and permits the selection of questions based on type, level of difficulty, or keyword. Computest 3 provides password protection of saved tests and question databases and can run on a network. It is available in 5.25- and 3.5-inch versions.

Compugrade 3—More than a grading system on disk, Compugrade 3 is a complete classroom management system. This advanced software system tracks up to 100 scores per class—homework, project, bonus points, class participation, attendance, and more. A variety of reports can be printed depending on class needs, including student, class, and assignment summaries. Graphs of various statistics for individual students or the entire class may be viewed and printed.

Teletest—Through this service the instructor can create customized exams and receive masters and answer keys within 72 hours of contacting the publisher

The following item is intended for student use at the option of the instructors.

Spreadsheet Applications Template Software (SPATS)—Selected exercises and problems in each chapter, identified by a spreadsheet symbol in the margin, can be solved using SPATS. The software contains innovatively designed templates based on Lotus® 1-2-3® and includes a very effective Lotus® 1-2-3® tutorial. SPATS is available on 5.25- and 3.5-inch disks. Upon adoption, this package is available for classroom or laboratory use.

FOR THE STUDENT:

Several support materials have been designed especially for the student.

The Student Integrated Learning Systems, Chapters 1–14 (Volume I) and Chapters 14–26 (Volume II)—This option allows the student to purchase either Chapters 1–14 or Chapters 14–26 of the text with the related Study Guides and Working Papers in a three-ring binder. Students benefit by having all three course-related items in a single package at a significant cost savings.

Study Guides, Chapters 1–14 and Chapters 14–26—The study guides provide the student with a summarized look at each chapter's issues. Included are outlines, chapter overviews, key concepts, and review questions and exercises. The study guides were prepared by Rosita Chen and Sheng-Der Pan, both of California State University–Fresno.

Working Papers, Chapter 1–14 and Chapter 14–26—Two sets of working papers are available for completing assigned problems and exercises. In many instances, the working papers are partially filled in to reduce the "pencil pushing" required to solve the problems, yet not so complete as to reduce the learning impact.

Manual Practice Set—Video One, a manual practice set, can be assigned after Chapter 6 as a review of the accounting cycle.

Cases—Cases on Recognition and Measurement, prepared by Todd Johnson and Tim Lucas of the Financial Accounting Standards Board (FASB) staff contains 50 short cases that are based on the Accounting Education Change Commission (AECC) changes. The casebook includes an instructor's manual and is free to adopters of Intermediate Accounting.

Computer Supplement—Kellogg Business Systems by Leland Mansuetti and Keith Weidkamp, both of Sierra College, is a computerized simulation that can be used after Chapter 6. It is available on 5.25 and 3.5 disks.

Check Figures—A list of check figures for selected end-of-chapter material is available.

ACKNOWLEDGMENTS
◆

The text in its present form would not have been possible without the contributions of a great many people. We recognize and appreciate all of their efforts.

Our thanks and gratitude are extended to the outstanding faculty reviewers who provided criticism and constructive suggestions during the preparation of this revised edition. They spent a great deal of time with both the previous edition, letting us know of the areas needing modification, and with the first draft of the revised edition. Their comments and suggestions were instrumental in making this text more complete and understandable. They were also crucial to the text's accuracy and clarity. Each recommendation was considered, and many incorporated, to make this revised edition the most comprehensive and thorough edition to date. The reviewers were:

Myrtle Clark
University of Kentucky

Maurice Tassin
Louisiana Tech University

Joanne C. Duke
San Francisco State University

Douglas Cloud
Pepperdine University

Julie Sterner
*Southern Illinois University/
Carbondale*

Duane Baldwin
University of Nevada/Las Vegas

E. James Meddaugh
Ohio University

Mostafa M. Maksy
University of Illinois/Chicago

Abo Habib
Mankato State University

S. Thomas A. Cianciolo
Eastern Michigan University

David H. Sinason
University of North Florida

Dorian Olson
Moorehead University

Mary M. K. Fleming
California State University/Fullerton

James S. Worthington
Auburn University

Edward T. Ossman
California State University/Hayward

Gail B. Wright
University of Richmond

Charlene Abendroth
California State University/Hayward

Diane L. Adcox
University of North Florida

Joy S. Irwin
Louisiana State University

Kevin H. McBeth
Weber State College

Michael R. Lane
Bradley University

Paul H. Schwinghammer
Mankato State University

Nancy E. Smith
Western Illinois University

Walter I. Batchelder
University of Alabama

Louis F. Biagioni
Indiana University

Darrell W. David
University of Northern Iowa

Paul R. Graul
Eastern Washington University

Lola W. Dudley
Eastern Illinois University

Priscilla Slade
Florida A&M University

To the instructors who participated in our market survey go our special thanks. The information they provided was invaluable:

Lynn R. Thomas
Kansas State University

Ralph W. Newkirk, Jr.
Rutgers University

Daniel F. O'Mara
Quinnipiac College

Gary W. Heesacker
Central Washington University

Lorella J. Donlin
Black Hills State University

Kwangok Kim
University of Southern Indiana

Norman J. Gierlasinski
Central Washington University

Lynn M. Bailey
Furman University

Behrooz Amini
*California State University/
Stanislaus*

Joanne Edwards
Westbrook College

Kathleen Simons
Bryant College

Jan Gillespie
The University of Texas at Austin

Thomas Zaher
Bucks County Community College

Marilyn Young
Tulsa Junior College

Michael Trebesh
Alma College

Peter Theuri
Oakwood College

Linda H. Kistler
University of Lowell

Robert E. Hansen
Western Kentucky University

Jane B. Stockard
Georgia College

J. Richard Sealscott
Northwest Technical College

Henry Espenson
Rockford College

Barbara Parks Pooley
Mt. Mercy College

Gale Newell
Western Michigan University

Ken Macur
University of Wisconsin/Whitewater

Harold Joseph
Clayton State College

Elias E. Etinge
Paine College

G. Eddy Birrer
Gonzaga University

John E. Delaney
Southwestern University

Rebecca M. Floor
Greenville Technical College

Donald H. Minyard
Auburn University

Lloyd J. Buckwell, Jr.
Indiana University, Northwest

Ronald O. Huntsman
Texas Lutheran College

Larry A. Deppe
Brigham Young University

Richard G. Cummings
Benedictine College

LaVern E. Krueger
*University of Missouri/
Kansas City*

Christine P. Andrews
State College at Fredonia

Paul W. Parkinson
Ball State University

Donald F. Putnam
*California State Polytechnic
University/Pomona*

Barbara J. Shiarappa
Trenton State College

Glen Fackler
Northeastern Junior College

Joy Fair of the University of Washington, Ralph Robinson, Robert Donoho, and Donna Phoenix of Cornell University, and Robert Su of California State University, Sacramento, provided valuable assistance by checking the solutions to the end-of-chapter material. To numerous other colleagues and users whose constructive comments and suggestions have led to the improvements reflected in this latest edition, our thanks. We sincerely appreciate comments and suggestions from all sources. We also appreciate the permissions granted by several firms and organizations including the American Institute of Certified Public Accountants, Dow Jones & Company, The First Boston Corporation, and The Sherwin-Williams Company.

To our retired coauthor, Glenn A. Welsch, we are deeply indebted. His valuable contributions to the preceding editions of *Intermediate Accounting* established the foundation on which the present author team based its work. His tremendous energy and abilities are reflected in this and prior editions. None of us would have attempted this project without the basis of his prior efforts. We wish him well, as we do the other previous coauthors, D. Paul Newman, Thomas Harrison, and Charles T. Zlatkovich.

We are grateful to the people at Irwin for their never-ending support: Ron Regis, senior sponsoring editor; Cheryl Wilson, developmental editor; Margaret Haywood, project editor; Pat O'Hayer, copy editor; Laurie Entringer, designer; Anne Cassady, production manager; and Judy Besser, secretary—editorial. In particular, the level of involvement with Cheryl Wilson was extraordinary. She assisted in all phases of the project and kept us on track and working. She was our main source of day-to-day inspiration and we are deeply indebted to her for her work.

Finally, we wish to thank our families for giving us the encouragement and understanding needed to complete this text, and for being so patient in the process.

We welcome your ideas and comments as you use this text and look forward to hearing from you.

TO THE STUDENT

♦

Accounting has been described as the language of business. If this is so, your introductory course has given you an understanding of some fundamental building blocks: the nouns, verbs, adjectives, prepositions, and so forth. In accounting terms, these are the concepts of assets, liabilities, owner's equity, expenses, revenues, income, and so on. Intermediate acounting is designed to extend these concepts to form phrases, sentences, paragraphs, and chapters. Intermediate accounting allows us to tell the financial story of an organization. As such, intermediate accounting is essential to your education in accounting and, thereby, to your mastery of the language of business.

We believe accounting at this level is an exciting subject and have structured this text in a way that captures the excitement and realism. You will be learning about actual situations faced by companies and how accounting plays a role in the decisions. These examples are extracted from The *Wall Street Journal,* the *New York Times, Business Week,* and *Forbes,* as well as from our personal experiences. We feel they are important and illustrate the challenges that await you.

We expect that many of you will be considering a career in financial accounting either with a CPA firm or in business. Intermediate accounting is a key educational experience to have in preparing for that choice. Your instructor has selected this text from a number of alternatives because of the belief that this text will help you master the material needed in your career. Together, the instructor, the text, and your classmates provide the ingredients for a successful learning experience. Use each wisely.

We urge you to read the assigned material carefully. Sometimes two readings will be necessary. Learning is an active process. Keep paper and pencil handy. Work through each example, highlight important ideas. Actually write down answers to the concept review questions located at strategic points in the text. Work all assigned problems, particularly the comprehensive ones, and, if possible, check your answers. If the instructor permits, work with a classmate and share ideas. Remember, you are not finished until you not only have a satisfactory answer but you know why it is the best answer. Learn by doing.

It may be useful to think of an accounting issue or problem as a puzzle or mystery. Try asking what is going on and why. This will make your reading and learning more fun. In accounting, sometimes the answer depends on what is acceptable, what the rules are, or what is politically or operationally feasible.

If you find it difficult to master a chapter and to sort out what is important, try concentrating on the learning objectives given at the start of each chapter. Then, after reading the chapter, review the summary of key points and try solving the review problem located at the end of each chapter. In working the review problem, do not look at the answer until you have tried to solve the problem. When checking your answer, do not stop with noting what the authors did. Rather, ask why each step in the solution was made. Then work the problems, exercises, and cases assigned by your instructor. If you still have difficulties, talk to your instructor. The instructor wants to help you and can do so.

We think learning in general and accounting in particular can and should be both fun and exciting. We have worked many hours to achieve these goals in this text. When you finish your course, we sincerely hope you agree. We hope that you will have as much fun studying this text as we had in preparing it and the related materials, and that you find the study of accounting as interesting and challenging as we have. Our very best wishes to you in your studies and future career.

Thomas R. Dyckman
Roland E. Dukes
Charles J. Davis

CONTENTS IN BRIEF

◆

CONTENTS

♦

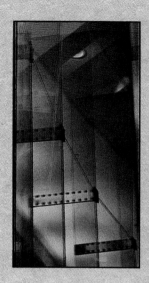

C H A P T E R
14

Investments: Temporary and Long Term

After you have studied this chapter, you will:

1. Appreciate why firms invest in debt and equity securities.

2. Understand classification criteria and the initial recording of investment securities at the date of acquisition.

3. Understand the conceptual basis for the accounting for various types of investments.

4. Be able to account for investments in short-term equity securities.

5. Be able to account for investments in short-term debt securities.

6. Understand and be able to use (*a*) the cost method, (*b*) the lower of cost or market method, (*c*) the equity method, and (*d*) the market value method in accounting for long-term investments in equity securities.

7. Be familiar with the disclosure requirements for all types of investment securities.

8. Understand how to account for stock dividends, stock splits, and stock warrants received by the investor.

9. Be familiar with the procedures for preparing consolidated financial statements. (Refer to Appendix 14A.)

10. Understand how to account for the cash surrender value of life insurance and other special purpose funds. (Refer to Appendix 14B.)

◆

INTRODUCTION
◆

I n its 1988 financial statements, Spectrum Control Inc. shows investments in marketable equity securities in the amount of $2.3 million and other investments in the amount of $.5 million, both as current assets. These total to more than 15% of current assets. There were no such investments in 1987. The note on "Investments in Marketable Equity Securities" explains that this investment was noncurrent in 1987, and management reclassified it to current in 1988 to "reflect Management's decision to make funds available for current operations." The note also explains that the marketable equity securities are carried at the lower of aggregate cost or market value, and that the other investments are carried at cost. It goes on to provide disclosures regarding "aggregate market values, gross unrealized losses, gross unrealized gains, and the recognition of a realized loss as a result of the reclassification of the marketable equity securities from noncurrent to current."

Several questions arise from the above description of Spectrum Control's financial reporting:

◆ How are investments in marketable equity securities different from investments in other securities? Why are they accounted for differently?
◆ Why is a loss recorded when an investment is reclassified from noncurrent to current? What are unrealized gains and losses? And why are they reported?
◆ Why do firms invest in the securities of other firms in the first place?
◆ In general, what types of items are included under the investments caption? How are they recorded, and how is income from investments measured?

After you have studied this chapter, you will know the answers to these questions and more. The primary objective of this chapter is developing an understanding of how to account for the investments a firm makes in the financial instruments of other firms and organizations. Investments can include many different types of financial instruments: equity securities, debt securities, stock options and warrants, municipal and state bonds and notes, U.S. Treasury bills and bonds, money market funds, commercial paper, and, in general, any contract that obligates a party to convey financial resources to the investing firm. The accounting procedures and disclosures differ according to the type of investment and whether the investments are classified as short- or long-term. Before getting into the details of accounting for each type and classification, consider first why a firm might invest in the financial instruments of another organization, and how these financial instruments are recorded at their acquisition.

◆

WHY FIRMS INVEST IN SECURITIES
◆

Sound financial management dictates that a firm maximize the profit-generating capacity of all its assets, and this includes cash. One profit-generating use of cash is to invest it in the financial instruments of other firms.[1]

More generally, firms invest in the securities of other firms for two basic reasons:

1. To earn a return on otherwise idle cash.
2. To acquire the voting stock of another firm in order to gain influence, control, or some other business advantage.

---

[1] The FASB has begun using the term *financial instrument* to describe all forms of contracts that convey ownership in firms or obligations to convey financial resources from one party to another. All the securities and other investments discussed in this chapter are financial instruments. A more detailed definition of financial instruments is found later in the chapter.

Investments made to earn a return on otherwise idle cash might be short-term (temporary), or they might be longer term. For example, a higher than necessary cash balance can arise due to seasonality of a business: the highly seasonal sales patterns generally result in greater cash needs immediately preceding the peak sales period when production and inventories are increasing. Higher cash inflows then occur at and after the peak in sales. Sound financial management requires the investment of idle funds from the peak inflow periods until they are needed during the peak outflow periods. Typically, government short-term securities and bank certificates of deposit are used for this purpose. As an example of a longer term but still profit-driven investment, a firm might accumulate the cash that will be needed within the next few years to pay off a long-term debt obligation and invest it in marketable securities prior to the maturity date of the debt. The investing firm has a long-term investment, usually in a diversified holding of government obligations or several other firms' shares, with a relatively small number of shares of each. The purpose of the investment is to earn a return.

The second reason involves establishing some form of beneficial business relationship with a second firm, generally of a long-term nature. Corning Glass Works, for example, joined with Owens-Illinois, Inc., many years ago to establish a new company, Owens Corning Fiberglas (OCF), for the purpose of entering a new market with a new product, fiberglass. Corning held its investment in OCF for nearly 50 years. A firm might invest in the securities of another corporation simply to create a desirable relationship with a supplier or customer. The 1989 annual report of IBM, for example, reports a significant ownership interest in MCI Communications Corporation. It is likely that this investment is in part to enhance the relationship between the two firms.

In this chapter, the basic topic is accounting for investments in the securities of other corporations. There are two basic classifications of securities: *equity securities* and *debt securities*. Each can be further classified according to whether management views the investment in that particular security as *short-term* (temporary), or *long-term*. Different accounting treatments are required for each type of investment, and for short- and long-term classifications. Finally, those investments which are marketable have a different accounting treatment than those that are not.

With regard to investments in debt securities, only those classified as short-term will be covered in this chapter. Accounting for long-term investments in debt securities is covered in detail in Chapter 16. Because there are important similarities in the recording of debt by the issuer and by the investor, it is useful to study the accounting for both parties at the same time.

Preliminary to the specific coverage on accounting for investments, the general characteristics of investment securities and the recording of investment securities at their acquisition are considered. Then accounting for equity securities is covered, with short-term securities considered before long-term securities. Following long-term equity securities the accounting for short-term debt securities is discussed. The chapter concludes with a discussion of some other types of investments that are not characterized as either equity or debt.

CHARACTERISTICS AND CLASSIFICATION OF INVESTMENT SECURITIES

The two broad types of investment securities are debt securities and equity securities. *Equity securities* are ownership claims on the investee firm. *Debt securities* are creditor claims, with a fixed obligation and usually some interest obligation. The distinction between ownership and debt securities is discussed in Chapter 5. Investments in either type of security can be classified as short-term or long-term.

For accounting purposes, short-term investments must satisfy the definitional requirements of a current asset. Current assets are assets that are readily marketable and are expected to be consumed or converted to cash within one year of the balance sheet date or during the normal operating cycle of the firm, if it is longer. Short-term investments must be readily marketable.[2] A security is readily marketable if it is listed on one of the stock exchanges. If an investment is not readily marketable, it does not meet the definition of a current asset and is classified as a long-term investment.

In the case of investment securities that are readily marketable, the investor's intention determines the classification as short- or long-term. Thus, short-term investments are those that meet the other criteria of current assets, and that managers of the investing firm classify as short-term. The accounting literature does not provide further guidance.

Short-term investments in equity securities often include common stock, preferred stock, warrants, options, and stock rights. Short-term debt securities include corporate and other entity bonds and notes, and other investments such as certificates of deposit, U.S. Treasury bills, commercial paper, and other types of financial instruments that have a ready market.

Long-term investments include all securities that do not meet the requirements for short-term investments. The following are examples of investments to be classified as long-term:

1. Long-term investments in the capital stock of another company. This category can include investments in common stock, preferred stock, options, warrants, and, in general, any security that represents an ownership claim on the firm.
2. Long-term investments in the bonds of another company.
3. Investments in subsidiaries, including long-term receivables from subsidiaries.
4. Funds set aside for long-term future use, such as bond sinking funds (to retire bonds payable), expansion funds, stock retirement funds, and long-term savings deposits.
5. Cash surrender value of life insurance policies carried by the company.
6. Long-term investments in tangible assets, such as land and buildings, that are not used in current operations (long-term includes operational assets that are only temporarily idle).

ACQUISITION OF INVESTMENT SECURITIES

Investment securities may be purchased directly from the issuing company, from individual investors, or indirectly from stockbrokers and dealers on the stock exchanges and the over-the-counter market. At the date of acquisition of an investment security, an appropriately designated investment account is debited for the cost of the investment in conformity with the *cost principle*. Cost includes:

1. The basic purchase price of the security.
2. Any brokerage fees and/or excise taxes.
3. Other transfer costs incurred by the purchaser.

Investments in equity securities may be by purchased for cash, on margin, or for noncash consideration. When stock is purchased on margin, only part of the purchase price is paid initially. The balance is borrowed (usually through a brokerage firm). The stock investment should be recorded at its cost, including the portion financed with borrowed funds.

When noncash consideration (property or services) is given for an investment, the cost assigned to the securities should be measured by (1) the market value of the consideration given or (2) the market values of the securities received, whichever can be more reliably determined. Inability to reliably determine either one of these market values—for example, an exchange of unlisted or closely held securities for

---

[2] *FASB Interpretation No. 16,* "Clarification of Definitions and Accounting for Marketable Securities that Become Nonmarketable" (Norwalk, Conn., February 1977), provides detailed rules pertaining to determining marketability.

property for which no established market values exists—will require the use of appraisals or estimates.

Securities frequently are purchased between regular interest or dividend dates. For such purchases, accrued interest is recorded on debt securities because interest is a legal obligation. Dividends are not accrued on equity securities because dividends are a legal liability only when declared.

The following examples illustrate applications of the preceding discussion to purchases of equity investments.

Example   On October 1, 1993, Blue Corporation purchased 5,000 shares of the common stock of Clear Inc. at $20 per share. Commissions incurred by Blue were $500. The investment is recorded as follows:

> Long-term (or short-term) investment, common shares, Clear Inc.
>   [(5,000 shares × $20) + $500] 100,500
>   Cash   100,500

Example   Assume the same facts as in Example 1 above, except Blue transferred a tract of vacant land (carried in Blue's accounts at $35,000) plus $5,500 cash as payment in full for the common stock. The common stock of Clear is currently selling at $20 per share. The disposal of the land and the purchase of the stock are recorded as follows:

> Long-term (or short-term) investment, common shares, Clear Inc.
>   [(5,000 shares × $20) + $500] 100,500
>   Land   35,000
>   Gain on disposal of land   60,000
>   Cash   5,500

Since the market value of the securities acquired is known, it is the basis for recording the investment. The gain on the disposal of the land is the difference between the market value of securities ($110,500) and the book value of the assets transferred ($40,500).

A purchase of two or more classes of securities for a single lump sum (called a *lump sum,* or *basket, purchase*) requires the allocation of portions of the total cost to each class of securities based upon available market value information. When the market value of each class is available, the *proportional method* is used to allocate the lump-sum price based on relative market values. Alternatively, if the market price(s) of all but one class of securities is known, the *incremental method* is applied. The incremental method allocates total cost first to the class(es) of securities with the known market value(s), and then assigns the remainder of the lump-sum price to the class of stock that does not have a market price.

Example   On October 3, 1993, Blue purchased 5,000 shares of common stock of Clear and 10,000 shares of preferred stock of CX Corp. for a lump sum of $170,000, and paid a commission of $1,000. At the date of the purchase, the market prices of the acquired shares were: Clear, $20 per share; CX Corp., $8 per share.

The total market value of the acquired shares is $180,000, of which 10/18 ($100,000 ÷ $180,000) is Clear, Inc. and 8/18 ($80,000 ÷ $180,000) is CX Corp. Therefore, 10/18 of the $171,000 purchase price is allocated as the cost of the investment in Clear, Inc., and 8/18 as the cost of the investment in CX Corp.:

Stock	Shares Acquired	Market Price Per Share	Market Value	Proportion of Market Value	Allocation of Purchase Price
Clear, Inc.	5,000	$20	$100,000	10/18	95,000
CX Corp.	10,000	$ 8	80,000	8/18	76,000
Totals			$180,000	18/18	171,000

The entry to record the purchase is:

Long-term (or short-term) investment, common shares, Clear, Inc.	95,000	
Long-term (or short-term) investment, preferred shares, CX Corp.	76,000	
Cash		171,000

Cost Flow Assumptions in Multiple Acquisitions and Disposals of Investment Securities   Accounting for investments is facilitated if a consistent system of security cost identification is used. A record of each individual security should be maintained. This record documents units purchased (by certificate number), dates, and unit cost. These details are important when a security is sold because its cost should be determined on a systematic basis. Otherwise, errors and possible distortions of gains and losses may occur.

Identification of securities sold is usually not difficult. However, identification can be difficult when the number of transactions is large, when blocks of securities have been transferred through an estate, or when the issuer has exchanged substitute securities for those originally purchased. When specific identification cannot be made, income tax law requires the use of the first-in, first-out method. Use of specific identification, FIFO, or average (but not LIFO) cost procedures is acceptable for financial accounting purposes. Most firms, however, use the same method for financial accounting and tax reporting purposes.

The choice of a particular cost flow assumption method may affect the gain or loss reported. To illustrate, assume 10 shares of Red Company were purchased at $150 per share, and later an additional 30 shares were purchased at $200 per share. There is a subsequent sale of 5 shares at $180 per share. If the 5 shares can be identified by certificate number as a part of the first purchase, a gain of $30 per share is recognized. Alternatively, if they are identified with the second purchase, a loss of $20 per share is recognized. The averaging procedure would report a loss of $7.50 per share computed as follows:

First purchase	10 shares × $150	$1,500
Second purchase	30 shares × $200	6,000
Total	40	$7,500
Average cost per share ($7,500/40)		$187.50
Sale price per share		180.00
Loss per share		$ 7.50

CONCEPT REVIEW

1. State two reasons why a firm might invest in securities.
2. What principle is used to determine the amount to be recorded for the acquisition of an investment security? What items are included in the recording of an investment security?
3. What methods are used to allocate the purchase cost of a group of securities for a lump sum?

ACCOUNTING FOR SHORT-TERM INVESTMENTS IN MARKETABLE EQUITY SECURITIES

Prior to the issuance of *SFAS No. 12*, accounting for short-term investments in marketable securities was characterized by a wide diversity of practice, both in initial recording and in subsequent reporting. Part of the problem was that short-term debt and equity securities have different characteristics. Because of the numerous ways that were being used to measure, record, and report investments in marketable securities, the FASB issued *SFAS No. 12*, "Accounting for Certain Marketable

Securities," in December 1975. This *Standard* improved the accounting for *equity* securities by specifying measurement and reporting rules, but did not resolve the accounting for *debt* securities. Accounting for debt securities continues to be guided by *ARB No. 43*, Chapter 3A, par. 9.

SFAS No. 12 requires that both short-term and long-term investments in marketable equity securities be valued at each balance sheet date using the **lower of aggregate cost or market (LCM) method** *(italics added):*

> The carrying amount of a marketable securities portfolio shall be the lower of its *aggregate* cost or market value, determined at the balance sheet date. The amount by which aggregate cost of the *portfolio* exceeds market value shall be accounted for as the *valuation allowance.*
>
> Marketable equity securities owned by an entity shall . . . be grouped into separate portfolios according the current or noncurrent classification of the securities for the purpose of comparing aggregate cost and market value to determine carrying amount.[3]

The LCM method of valuing the investment on the balance sheet has applicability to both short-term and long-term equity investments. In both instances, a valuation allowance is created when aggregate cost is greater than aggregate market value. The valuation allowance is a credit balance account that is contra to the investment account. The treatment of the debit side of the entry, which is the unrealized loss on the investment, differs depending on whether the investment is classified as *short-term* or *long-term.*

Aggregate versus Individual-Security Level LCM The key concept is determining aggregate market value of the total portfolio of equity securities and comparing it to the aggregate cost. An alternative that might be used is to compare the market value and cost of individual securities, and thus to have a security-by-security LCM. *SFAS No. 12* requires the portfolio approach; it does not allow individual-security level LCM for equity securities.[4]

The rationale for the portfolio level comparisons is that when management makes a decision to invest in more than one equity security, it is the overall investment that must be evaluated. To write down only those securities that declined in value while not allowing for the gains of those that increased in value would be an extremely conservative asymmetric rule. The portfolio requirement allows unrealized gains to offset unrealized losses. In addition, firms are required to disclose aggregate amounts of unrealized gains and unrealized losses. Disclosure requirements are covered in a later section. Since GAAP does not require the use of security-by-security LCM, it is not discussed further.

The following example shows the application of the LCM method to short-term equity investments. The procedure for computing the valuation allowance is also used for long-term equity investments, which are discussed in a later section.

Example of Lower of Cost or Market Assume the following transactions relate to investments by Tree Corporation:

> January 2, 1991—Tree Corporation acquires 10 shares of Pear Company common stock at a market price of $15 per share, and 20 shares of Apple Inc. common stock for $11 per share. Assume there are no brokerage fees and that these investments are classified as short-term.

---

[3] *SFAS No. 12*, par. 8 and 9. This *Statement* specifically relates only to equity securities (not to debt securities). However, it does make one exception as follows: The term *equity securities* "does not encompass preferred stock that by its terms either must be redeemed by the issuing enterprise or is redeemable at the option of the investor, nor does it include treasury stock or convertible bonds." The exception recognizes that the specified redemption requirement makes such preferred stock essentially a debt security. Also, *SFAS No. 12* is not applicable to mutual life insurance companies because of specified practices.

[4] Firms may use security-by-security level LCM for marketable debt securities. It is not expressly prohibited.

The entry to record the investment in the accounts of Tree Corporation is:

Investment in short-term marketable equity securities 370
    Cash   370

December 31, 1991—The two firms in which Tree has invested report the following results:

	Pear Company	Apple Inc.
Earnings per share for 1991	$ 2.00	$1.50
Dividends per share paid December 31	.50	.75
Market value per share at 12/31/91	$17/share	$9.50/share

The initial cost of the investment is:

Pear Company	10 shares × $ 15/share	$150
Apple Inc.	20 shares × $ 11/share	220
Total investment		$370

Investment revenue for Tree is the dividends received from the investment securities. In this example, Tree Corporation would have investment income of $20 (dividends of 50 cents per share times the 10 Pear shares owned, plus dividends of 75 cents per share times the 20 Apple shares owned).

The entry to record investment revenue is:

Cash (or dividends receivable) 20
    Investment revenue (or dividend income)   20

At the end of the year it is necessary to determine whether there is a need to write down the aggregate investment. The aggregate cost was $370. The aggregate market value at December 31 is:

Company	Market Value Computation	Market	Cost	Difference
Pear Company	10 shares × $17/share	$170	$150	+ $20
Apple Inc.	20 shares × $9.50/share	190	220	− 30
Total		$360	$370	− 10

The aggregate market value has fallen to $360, or $10 less than the aggregate original cost. The LCM method requires the investment be written down to $360 (a write-down of $10). The entry to record the write-down would be as follows:

Unrealized loss on short-term investments 10
    Allowance to reduce short-term investments to market   10

For short-term investments in equity securities, the unrealized loss on short-term investments account is an income statement account. Generally, it is netted against investment revenue. The allowance to reduce short-term investments to market account becomes a contra account to the short-term investments account on the balance sheet. These accounts are discussed in greater detail in the following section.

If the above analysis were on an individual security-by-security basis, the write-down would be $30, which is the decline in value of the investment in Apple Inc. The end-of-period market value of Pear Company is greater than its original cost ($170 market value versus $150 cost). Since market value is greater than cost for Pear, an individual-security–based LCM would not require any adjustment to the carrying amount for Pear. Apple Inc., however, has a market value of $190 and an original cost of $220—a $30 decline or loss. Individual-security–based LCM would record this decline in value of $30. This distinction between portfolio or aggregate value/cost and individual security value or cost is important. *SFAS No. 12* requires the use of portfolio level comparisons of costs and market values for marketable equity securities. As this example illustrates, the portfolio approach may result in less conservative reporting.

Realized and Unrealized Gains and Losses

SFAS No. 12 makes a careful distinction between realized and unrealized gains and losses in specifying accounting for both short- and long-term investments in equity securities. Realized gains and losses usually relate to the sale of the securities. Unrealized gains and losses relate to the application of the LCM rule to the aggregate investment portfolio (of equity securities) at the end of each annual accounting period. *SFAS No. 12* also distinguishes between an unrealized gain and an unrealized loss recovery. The following definitions are applied in accounting for investments in equity securities:

1. **Realized gain.** If at the date of sale the net amount received is more than the original cost (i.e., purchase cost) on an individual equity security basis, there is a realized gain of the amount of the difference.

2. **Realized loss.** A realized loss is recognized when:
   a. At the date of sale, there is an excess of original cost of an individual security over the net proceeds received by the investor.
   b. An individual equity security is transferred between the long- and short-term portfolios, and its market value at the date of transfer is below its original cost.
   c. An individual security is written down due to a permanent decline or impairment in its market value below its original cost.

3. **Unrealized loss.** An unrealized loss occurs when the end-of-period market value of a portfolio of investments in equity securities is less than the carrying value of the portfolio. An unrealized loss is recognized only at the end of the accounting period. If the portfolio of securities is a short-term investment, the unrealized loss is reported on the income statement. However, if the portfolio is a long-term investment, the unrealized loss is reported as a negative element of stockholders' equity (to be discussed later). In either case, the year-end adjustment is to debit an unrealized loss account (e.g., unrealized loss on equity investments) and credit an allowance account (e.g., allowance to reduce short-term equity investments to LCM). If the equity investment is classified as short term, the unrealized loss reduces current period income. The allowance account is reported on the balance sheet as a contra to the related investment account.

4. **Unrealized gain.** There is an unrealized gain when the current market value of the portfolio of investments in equity securities is above the total portfolio valued at LCM at the end of the accounting period. Unrealized gains can be recorded only to the extent that there have been previously recorded unrealized losses. The carrying value of the portfolio in the financial statements cannot exceed the original cost of the total portfolio. Thus, the only unrealized gains that are recorded are actually recoveries of previously recorded unrealized losses. In order to be clear on this point, the term *unrealized loss recovery* is used to identify an unrealized gain that is recorded because it is a recovery of a previously recorded unrealized loss. Unrealized gains in excess of the original cost cannot be recorded until they are realized.

An unrealized loss recovery requires an adjusting entry at the end of the accounting period. The debit is to the allowance account which reduces short-term equity investments to LCM. The account credited depends on whether the investment in equity securities has been carried as a short-term or long-term investment. For short-term investments the unrealized loss recovery is credited to an income statement account such as "loss recovery on short-term equity security investments." This account increases income for the period. If the equity investment is classified as long-term, the unrealized loss recovery is credited to the account established in the stockholders' equity section of the balance sheet in which the unrealized loss had previously been debited.

In sum, application of the LCM method as required by *SFAS No. 12* for marketable equity securities, is at the portfolio level, not the individual-security level. It requires the write-down of unrealized losses, and the writing back up of unrealized loss recoveries. In no case can the write-up be above the original cost of the portfolio. The sale of a short-term equity investment is recorded as a debit for the resources received, a credit to the investment account for the original cost of the equity investment, and the difference is recorded as a *realized* gain or loss.

Example of LCM for Short-Term Equity Securities   Suppose Tree Corporation's investments totaling $370 in Pear and Apple described in the previous example were short-term investments, and the market value of the portfolio at December 31, 1991, is $360 as shown in the example.

The difference between the portfolio cost ($370) and the portfolio market value ($360) is an unrealized loss of $10 as was shown before. The unrealized loss will appear as an item on the 1991 income statement (along with the investment revenue of $20), and the allowance account will be a contra to the investment in equity securities account. The balance sheet would appear as follows:

> Current assets:
> Investment in equity securities, short-term $370
> Less: Allowance to reduce to market 10 $360

When a short-term equity security is sold, amounts in the allowance account are ignored. This account is adjusted only at each year-end. To illustrate, assume Tree Corporation sold all of its short-term investments on January 30, 1992, for cash as follows: Pear common, $25 per share, and Apple common, $4 per share. The transaction would be recorded on January 30, 1992, as follows:

> Cash (10 shares × $25 + 20 shares × $4) 330
> Loss on sale of investments 40
>   Investments in short-term equity securities   370

Continuing the example, assume that on June 6, 1992, Tree purchases another short-term equity security—AB Corporation, 10 shares at $7 per share. The entry to record this transaction is:

> Investment in short-term equity securities 70
>   Cash   70

At the end of 1992, assume AB Corporation common stock is selling at $6.50. The allowance account had a credit balance of $10 at the end of 1991. At the end of 1992, the portfolio of short-term equity securities held by Tree contains only the AB Corporation stock. The portfolio cost is $70 and the portfolio market value is $65 (10 shares × $6.50). The market value is lower than cost, but the allowance account is too large at $10. It must be reduced to a balance of $5. The entry to reduce the balance at December 31, 1992 is:

> Allowance to reduce short-term investments to market   5
>   Unrealized loss recovery on short-term investments   5

As a result of the above 1992 transactions, Tree Corporation would report the following in its 1992 financial statements:

Income statement:
Loss on sale of short-term investments $40
Unrealized loss recovery on short-term investments . . . . . (5)

Net loss on short-term investments $35

Balance sheet:
Current assets:
Investment in equity securities, short-term at cost $70
Less: Allowance to reduce to market . . . . (5)
Investment (at market) $65

The effect of recording the LCM unrealized loss of $10 in 1991 was to reduce income by that amount in 1991, and to reduce the investment carrying value to its market value. In the following year (1992), when the securities are sold, the unrealized loss recorded in 1991 has the effect of reducing the amount of loss in the current period. In this example, the net impact on income in 1992 is not the total realized loss of $40, but rather the portion that occurred in 1992, $35 ($40 less the $10 that was recorded in 1991 plus the $5 that occurred on the new investment). The effect is to recognize unrealized losses in the year when they occur. This results in better compliance with the matching principle.

Disclosures Required for Investments in Short-Term Equity Investments Because all investments included in the short-term classification must be marketable, they are highly liquid. As such they are usually listed immediately after cash in the current assets section of the balance sheet. *SFAS No. 12* specifies the required disclosures for all marketable equity securities, regardless of whether they are classified as short- or long-term. The requirements listed here also apply to long-term investments in marketable equity securities.

As of each balance sheet date presented, the aggregate cost and the aggregate market value of marketable equity securities for the portfolios of short-term and of long-term investments must be disclosed, either in the body of the financial statements or in the notes. For the latest balance sheet presented, disclosures are required of (1) gross unrealized gains, and (2) gross unrealized losses.

For Tree Corporation the December 31, 1991, financial statement would include disclosures of gross unrealized gains of $20 (the unrealized gain on the Pear common) and of gross unrealized losses of $30 (the unrealized loss on the Apple common).

For each income statement presented, disclosures of (1) the net realized gain or loss included in net income, (2) the basis on which cost was determined in computing gain or loss included in net income, and (3) the change in the amount of the valuation allowance included in net income.

Examples of disclosures in accordance with *SFAS No. 12* are found in Exhibit 14–1, which presents notes to the financial statements of CSP Inc., regarding its short-term investments in addition to those in equity securities. For all the investment securities except the equity securities, cost is either less than current market value or cost approximates market value. The disclosures for these investments is simply their source and cost. CSP Inc. exceeds the disclosure requirements by disclosing gross unrealized gains and losses for both the latest balance sheet and the prior year balance sheet.

The next section covers accounting for investments in equity securities that are classified as long-term. Such investments may or may not be readily marketable. When they are readily marketable, *SFAS No. 12* applies, and the accounting is similar to the accounting for short-term equity investments. When they are not marketable, alternative accounting procedures are used.

EXHIBIT 14-1   Note disclosures by CSP Inc. of Investments in Short-Term Marketable Securities

From the Balance Sheet:	1988	1987
($ in thousands)		
Current assets:		
Cash	$2,306	$5,298
Marketable securities (Note 2)	9,047	7,952
Accounts receivable, net	2,237	2,486
Inventories	2,370	1,911
Deferred income taxes	88	153
Refundable income taxes	45	—
Prepaid expenses	76	84
Total current assets	$16,169	$17,884

Notes to Consolidated Financial Statements

Note 1. (In Part) Summary of Significant Accounting Policies: Marketable Securities:

Marketable equity securities are carried at the lower of cost or market value. Interest income is accrued as earned. Dividend income is recorded as income on the date the stock traded "ex-dividend." The cost of marketable securities sold is determined on the specific identification method and realized gains or losses are reflected in income.

Note 2. Marketable Securities:
At August 31, 1988 and 1987, marketable securities consisted of the following:

	1988	1987
($ in thousands)		
Marketable equity securities, at cost	$1,000	$1,000
Less: valuation allowance	127	137
Marketable equity securities, at market	873	863
Bonds and municipal revenue notes, at cost	2,327	2,232
Money market funds and commercial paper	3,359	4,664
Bankers' acceptance	—	193
U.S. treasury bills	2,488	—
Total	$9,047	$7,952

Net realized gains on the sale of securities included in the determination of income before taxes amounted to $13,000, and $67,000 for fiscal 1987 and 1986, respectively.

At August 31, 1988 and 1987, gross unrealized gains (losses) pertaining to marketable equity securities were as follows:

	1988	1987
($ in thousands)		
Gross unrealized loss	$ 147	$ 160
Gross unrealized gain	20	23
Net unrealized losses	$ 127	$ 137

CONCEPT REVIEW

1. How are unrealized losses computed under the LCM method? How are they treated for accounting purposes for short-term equity investments?
2. Explain the accounting entry that is made when a short-term equity investment is sold for more than its original cost. What effect will this transaction (by itself) have on any amounts in the allowance to reduce to market account when there is an unrealized loss for the portfolio recorded?
3. What entry is made when at year-end there is an increase in the aggregate market value to an amount greater than the original cost for a short-term investment portfolio that has a valuation allowance recorded?

ACCOUNTING FOR LONG-TERM INVESTMENTS IN EQUITY SECURITIES

♦

Five different methods are used to account for long-term investments, depending on the characteristics of the investment:

1. The lower of cost or market (LCM) method.
2. The cost method.
3. The equity method.
4. The market value method.
5. Consolidation.

The investor firm is not given a free choice in selecting which of these methods to apply. Based on specified conditions, only one method is appropriate for each individual investment.

For long-term investments that do not represent a *controlling interest* (to be defined), guidance on accounting procedures is found in *SFAS No. 12* and in *APB Opinion No. 18*. *APB Opinion No. 18* defines two important factors related to the investor firm's ability to control or influence the decision of the investee.

1. *Significant influence.* A firm has significant influence if it has the ability to affect, to an important degree, the operating and financial policies of another company through ownership of a sufficient portion of its voting stock. The ability to exercise significant influence also may be shown in several other ways. These include representation on the board of directors, interchange of managerial pesonnel, material intercompany transactions, and technological dependency. To attain a reasonable degree of uniformity, the APB provided an operational rule. This rule states that an investment of *20% or more* of the outstanding voting stock leads to the presumption that, in the absence of evidence to the contrary, an investor has the ability to exercise significant influence over the company.[5]

2. *Controlling interest.* A controlling interest exists when the investor company owns enough of the voting stock of the investee company to determine its operating and financing policies. Ownership of over 50% of the outstanding voting stock usually would assure control; however, in some cases, this percentage may not be sufficient. In still other cases, ownership of less than 50% of the outstanding voting stock may create a controlling interest. Factors such as the number of stockholders and the extent of stockholder participation in voting have some bearing on the point at which a controlling interest is attained. Operationally, the APB presumption is that a controlling interest is represented by over 50% of the voting stock, absent other compelling factors.

When a company owns a controlling interest in a second company, the controlling company must prepare *consolidated financial statements*. Appendix 14A is a summary discussion of preparing consolidated financial statements; the topic is covered in depth in advanced financial accounting courses. Coverage of the basic principles of consolidation is included here because a recent *Standard* issued by the FASB has increased the number of consolidated statements that are required to be prepared.

---

[5] An investor may not be able to exercise significant influence over the investee's policies, even though the investor owns more than a 20% interest, when:

Opposition by the investee, such as litigation or complaints to governmental regulatory authorities, challenges the investor's ability to exercise significant influence.

The investor and the investee sign an agreement under which the investor surrenders signficant rights as a stockholder.

Majority ownership of the investee is concentrated among a small group of stockholders who operate the company without regard to the views of the investor.

The investor tries and fails to obtain representation on the investee's board of directors.

The above list, from *FASB Interpretation No. 35*, "Criteria for Applying the Equity Method of Accounting for Investments in Common Stock" (Norwalk, Conn., May 1981), is intended to be illustrative and not all-inclusive.

Specifically, *SFAS No. 94* requires the consolidation of all majority-owned subsidiaries, including finance and other nonrelated business subsidiaries that generally were not consolidated prior to the issuance of *SFAS No. 94*.[6] *SFAS No. 94* requires that majority-owned subsidiaries not be consolidated (1) if control is likely to be temporary, or (2) if control does not rest with with the majority owner. In these situations, the cost method is used to account for the investments.

The next section of this chapter considers long-term equity investments when the investor does not have a controlling interest. In general, when the investor does not have significant influence, the LCM method is used for *marketable* equity securities. When the securities are not marketable, the cost method is used. If, however, the investor firm has significant influence, the equity method is used. Finally, the market value method is used in certain industries. The application of the LCM method is covered first.

LCM Method of Accounting for Long-Term Investments in Equity Securities

The LCM method of accounting used for short-term equity investments is, in specified conditions, also used for long-term investments in equity securities. In conformity with *SFAS No. 12*, the LCM method must be used for long-term investments in marketable equity securities except when the investor has stock holdings that confer significant influence or control. Investments in which the investor company has significant influence are accounted for by the equity method (to be discussed shortly) in compliance with *APB No. 18*. These investments are not covered by *SFAS No. 12*. Thus, the LCM method is used when the following conditions exist:

* A market value for the equity securities can be determined.
* The number of voting shares held is relatively small—defined in *APB No. 18* as less than a 20% ownership of voting stock absent other evidence that significant influence exists.

If the shares held are nonvoting, the investor does not have any control with such shares, and the LCM method is appropriate no matter what the percentage of ownership is.

The LCM method is applied to long-term investments in equity securities in the same way as for short-term investments in equity securities except for one important difference—how the unrealized loss and unrealized loss recovery are reported. In short-term investments, the unrealized loss is reported on the income statement as a current loss. In contrast, when the investment is long-term, the unrealized loss is debited to a stockholders' equity account. This account is a contra (i.e., negative) stockholders' account.

The credit to the allowance account (allowance to reduce long-term equity investments to LCM) is essentially the same as for short-term investments. This account is reported, as with short-term investments, on the balance sheet as a contra account to the related investment account.

To illustrate, consider again the Tree Corporation example presented earlier, in which the accounting for short-term equity investments was illustrated.

The entries made to account for these investments when they are classified as long-term are as follows:

To record the initial cost of the investment:

Investment in long-term equity securities	370	
Cash		370

To record investment revenue (receipt of dividends):

Cash	20	
Investment revenue		20

---

[6] See *FASB No. 94*, par. 13 and 15.

At December 31, 1991—To record unrealized loss:

Unrealized loss on long-term investments 10
    Allowance to reduce long-term investments to market   10

The unrealized loss on long-term investments account is now treated as a contra account in the stockholders' equity section. It is often labeled "Investment valuation allowance" or "Net unrealized loss on long-term marketable securities."

Continuing the example, suppose that on April 14, 1992, the market value of Apple common stock decreased to $7 per share, and that this decrease is determined to be permanent.[7] Tree must record a loss related to this permanent decline (impairment) in the value of Apple common stock:

Loss in market value of long-term investment [20 × ($11 − $7)] 80
    Long-term investments in equity securities   80

The loss decreases income by $80 for the period. The credit entry is made directly to the investment account (not to the allowance account). Since the decline in value for Apple was deemed to be permanent, the new cost basis for this investment is 20 shares × $7 per share, or $140. Even if the market value of the stock should increase above $7 per share in the future, Tree Corporation will not record the increase.

Continuing the example, suppose that in August 1992, Tree Corporation unexpectedly sells 5 shares of Pear for $24 per share cash. Since the original cost of this investment was $15 per share, Tree will record a realized gain on the transaction of $45:

Cash (5 × $24) 120
    Long-term investments in equity securities (5 × $15)   75
    Gain on sale of equity securities [5 × ($24 − $15)]   45

Finally, suppose that at December 31, 1992, the market value per share for the two investments is as follows:

Pear common stock . . . . $22 per share
Apple common stock . . . . $5 per share

Again the aggregate cost and aggregate market value of the long-term investment portfolio must be computed. The original cost was $370, but there was a permanent reduction in the value of Apple common stock of $140. Also, Tree sold 5 shares of Pear common, which had an original cost of $15 per share. These transactions have reduced the cost of the portfolio to $215:

Original aggregate cost of portfolio $370
Less: Permanent impairment writedown . . . . .   (80)
Less: Cost of securities sold . . . .   (75)
Remaining aggregate cost of portfolio $215

The aggregate market value is determined as follows:

Pear common stock   5 × $22 = $110
Apple common stock   20 × $5 =   100
    Total $210

The allowance needed to reduce the recorded cost to market for the portfolio is $215 less the market value of $210, or a total allowance of $5. Since the allowance

---

[7] Normal market fluctuations in security prices would not be considered a permanent impairment. There is little guidance in the literature in defining a permanent impairment of value. In general it must result from a significant economic event that permanently affects (decreases) the value of the investee.

was established at $10 in 1991, Tree must now reverse $5 of the allowance ($10 less the correct amount of $5) to establish the correct allowance balance:

Allowance to reduce long-term investments
 in equity securities to market 5
      Unrealized loss on long-term
       investments in equity securities   5

With this entry, a portion of the write-down that was made in 1991 is reversed. However, neither the original write-down nor the reversal has any effect on net income since neither entry affects any income statement account. The unrealized loss account for these long-term investments is a contra account to stockholders' equity.

Very few equity-decreasing and equity-increasing items are recorded directly to the stockholders' equity section rather than flowing through the income statement. Unrealized losses (and unrealized loss recoveries) on long-term marketable equity securities are one type of item that is treated this way.

The presentation of the Tree Corporation financial statements would be as follows:

	1991	1992
Income statement:		
Investment revenue:	$ 20	0
Loss in market value of long-term investments	0	($80)
Gain on sale of long-term investments	0	45

Balance sheet—December 31:	1991	1992	
Investments of equity securities, at cost	$370		$215
Less: Allowance to reduce equity			
securities to market	(10)		(5)
Investment portfolio at LCM		$360	$210
Stockholders' equity:			
Unrealized capital loss:			
Unrealized loss on long-term			
investments in equity securities		(10)	(5)

The 1988 annual report of Hecla Mining Company given in Exhibit 14–2 is an example of the disclosure that is made when there is a write-down for a long-term equity investment.

Change in Classification between Short-Term and Long-Term for Marketable Equity Securities

It is possible for management to change the classification of an investment from current to noncurrent, or visa-versa. When this happens, the security involved must be reclassified on the balance sheet. *SFAS No. 12,* par. 10, specifies that the security be transferred between the two portfolios at the lower of cost or market value at the date of transfer. If market is lower than cost, the new cost basis for the security will be the market value. The difference is accounted for as if it were a *realized loss* and included in the determination of net income.

Example   Suppose Tree Corporation in the example decides as of January 30, 1993, to reclassify its holdings of 20 shares of Apple, Inc. from long-term to short-term. Recall that Apple was originally acquired at $11 per share, but during 1992 there was a permanent impairment of value, and a loss was recognized to reduce the cost basis of the holdings to $7 per share. Assume the market price at January 30, 1993, is $6 per share.

Tree would make the following entry to record the change in classification:

Investments in short-term equity securities (20 × $6) 120
Realized loss on reclassification of equity securities 20
     Investments in long-term equity securities (20 × $7)   140

EXHIBIT 14-2   Write-Down of Long-Term Equity Investment, Hecla Mining Company

(*$ in thousands*)	1988	1987
Total current assets	$ 29,984	$ 31,459
Investments (Note 3)	15,915	13,025
Properties, plants and equipment, net	135,707	122,492
Other noncurrent assets	7,246	3,740
Total assets	$188,852	$170,716

Note 3 (In Part): Investments
Investments consist of the following components (*in thousands*):

	Carrying Value	Cost	Market Value
December 31, 1988			
Marketable equity securities	$ 6,613	$17,300	$6,613
Other investments	9,302	9,302	
Total	$15,915	$26,602	
December 31, 1987			
Marketable equity securities	$ 7,155	$15,630	$7,155
Other investments	5,870	5,870	
Total	$13,025	$21,500	

At December 31, 1988, the portfolio of marketable equity securities includes gross unrealized gains of approximately $3,000 and gross unrealized losses of approximately $10,690,000 (of which approximately $9,625,000 is attributable to the Company's ownership of Sunshine Mining Company common stock). The other investments are principally large blocks of common and preferred stock in several mining companies, and investments in various mining ventures. These securities are generally restricted as to trading or marketability, although some of the shares are frequently traded on the over-the-counter market in Spokane, Washington, and certain Canadian exchanges. At December 31, 1988 and 1987, the shares of some of these companies that were traded on these markets were quoted at values approximating or exceeding the Company's cost basis.

(*$ in thousands*)	1988	1987
Shareholders' Equity:		
Preferred stock, 25¢ par value, authorized 5,000,000 shares none issued		
Common stock, 25¢ par value, authorized 50,000,000 shares, issued 1988— 27,044,812, and 1987—27,040,832	$ 6,761	$ 6,760
Additional paid-in capital	53,326	53,286
Earnings retained in the business	94,071	80,292
Net unrealized loss on marketable equity securities (Note 3)	(10,687)	(8,475)
Less common stock required, at cost; 1988—40,999 shares, 1987—38,539 shares	(611)	(571)
Total shareholders' equity	$142,860	$131,292

No adjustment is needed to the allowance account or to the contra account in stockholders' equity relating to the long-term investment portfolio, as the appropriate adjustments will be made when the LCM method is applied to the long-term investment at year-end.

The Cost Method of Accounting for Nonmarketable, Long-Term Equity Securities

At this point it is appropriate to briefly describe how an equity security is accounted for when it is not readily marketable, and the investor does not have significant influence. When a market value is not determinable, the LCM method cannot be applied. Securities that are not readily marketable and that do not qualify for the equity method are accounted for using the **cost method.** Under the cost method, the investment is carried at the original investment amount, and investment revenue is the dividends received from the investee. Gains and losses on the investment are recorded when realized, which is when the investment is sold. There are no market values to compare with cost; thus, there are no determinations or any entries for recording unrealized losses. This is the difference between the cost method and the LCM method.

Prior to the issuance of *SFAS No. 12,* nearly all short-term equity investments and those long-term investments not qualifying for the equity method were accounted for using the cost method.

CONCEPT REVIEW

1. How are unrealized losses computed under the LCM method when a portfolio of investments is classified as long-term? How are they treated for accounting purposes for short-term equity investments?
2. Explain the accounting entries that are made when a short-term equity investment is reclassified as long-term and its current market value is less than its cost. What effect will this transaction (by itself) have on any amounts in the allowance account?
3. What is an unrealized loss recovery? How is it treated for accounting purposes when it is related to a short-term marketable equity investment? to a long-term marketable equity investment?

EQUITY METHOD FOR LONG-TERM EQUITY INVESTMENTS

The **equity method** of accounting for long-term investments is not appropriate for the investments discussed above because the investor did not own enough voting shares to be able to exercise significant influence or control. *APB No. 18* specifies that the equity method is used when the investor has significant influence or control.

Conceptual Basis of the Equity Method

For the investor, the LCM method and the equity method are different because they are based on different concepts of investment revenue and investment valuation. The conceptual difference is that under the LCM method the investor and the investee are viewed as two separate companies. In contrast, the equity method views the investor and the investee as a special type of single entity. *APB No. 18* gives the accounting guidelines for the equity method.[8]

The *single entity* concept underlying the equity method requires that the investor's investment and investment revenue be measured as follows:

1. End-of-period investment account balance equals:
   a. Beginning of period investment account balance.
   b. *Plus* proportionate share of investee's income for the period.
   c. *Minus* proportionate share of investee's dividends paid during the period.
   d. *Minus* adjustments of investee's reported income for the period.
2. Investment revenue for the period equals:
   a. Proportionate share of investee's income for the period.
   b. *Minus* adjustments of investee's reported income for the period.

It is important to distinguish between *voting* and *nonvoting* shares of equity stocks. With voting shares an investor can exercise some influence over the financial policies of the investee corporation. The proportion of voting shares owned deter-

---

[8] *APB No. 18* states that income and owners' equity amounts should be the same whether a subsidiary is consolidated or accounted for by the equity method. A discussion of the principles of consolidation is found in Appendix 14A.

mines the extent or degree of influence or control. For example, if the investor owns more than 50% of the outstanding voting shares, the investor can exercise control over the investee. With less than 50% but still a "large ownership" interest, the investor is deemed to be able to exercise "significant influence."

APB No. 18 also sets forth procedures for reporting under the equity method. The procedures include:

* The investment in common stock is shown in the balance sheet of the investor as a single amount, and the investor's share of the investee's earnings or losses is shown in the income statement of the investor as a single amount except for the items reported below income from continuing operations.
* The investor's share of the investee's extraordinary items and prior period adjustments are reported by the investor in conformity with APB No. 30 and SFAS No. 16. Specifically, the investor classifies such items in a manner similar to its own items reported below income from continuing operations and prior period adjustments.
* Gains and losses on sale of the investee's stock are accounted for as the difference between the selling price and the carrying amount of the stock sold.
* Intercompany profits and losses are eliminated.
* Any difference between the cost of an investment and the market value of the underlying net assets of an investee (i.e., goodwill) is amortized according to the requirements of APB Opinion No. 17.

Equity Method Illustrated

The application of the procedures described above can best be demonstrated with an example. On January 2, 1992, Giant Company purchased 3,600 shares of the 18,000 outstanding common shares of Small Corporation for $300,000 cash. Two Giant senior executives were voted on to the Small Corporation board of directors. Giant is deemed to be able to exercise significant influence over Small's operating and financial policies. The equity method of accounting for the investment is appropriate.

At the acquisition of the 20% interest in Small, Giant would record its investment as follows:

```
Investment in Small, at equity  . . . . . . . . . . . . . . . . . 300,000
    Cash  . . . . . . . . . . . . . . . . . . . . . . . . . . . . .      300,000
```

Suppose the balance sheet for Small at January 2, 1992, and estimated the market values of its assets and liabilities were as follows:

	Book Value	Market Value	Difference
Cash and receivables	$ 100,000	$ 100,000	$ 0
Inventory (FIFO basis)	400,000	405,000	5,000
Plant and equipment (10-year life)	500,000	700,000	200,000
Land	150,000	165,000	15,000
Total assets	$1,150,000	$1,370,000	$220,000
Liabilities	$ 150,000	$ 150,000	$ 0
Stockholders' equity	1,000,000	1,220,000	220,000
Total liabilities & equity	$1,150,000	$1,370,000	$220,000

The net book value of the claim Giant has on Small is 20% times Small's stockholders' equity ($1,000,000), or $200,000. Since Giant paid $300,000 for its interest in Small, what was acquired to justify the purchase price being $100,000 greater than book value? If items can be identified whose market value is greater than their net book value, the $100,000 premium over book value will be allocated to these items in accordance with the equity method.

The market value information presented above shows several specific assets where the market value exceeds book value. Giant acquired a portion (20%) of each of these items, including the amount by which market value exceeds book value:

	Book Value	Market Value	Difference	20% of Difference
Inventory	$400,000	$405,000	$ 5,000	$ 1,000
Plant and equipment (10-year remaining life)	500,000	700,000	200,000	40,000
Land	150,000	165,000	15,000	3,000
Excess value of assets acquired by Giant				$44,000

Thus, $44,000 of the $100,000 purchase price premium over book value that was paid by Giant is identified with the above specific assets. The remaining difference, $56,000, cannot be specifically identified with any asset. It will be termed goodwill. Recall from Chapter 13 that goodwill is the excess of the amount invested in acquiring all or a portion of another firm over the fair value of the net identifiable assets acquired. The direct computation of goodwill is as follows:

Computation of Goodwill Purchased by Giant Company

Purchase price (of 20% interest)		$300,000
Market value of identifiable assets	$1,370,000	
Less: Liabilities of Small	(150,000)	
Total market value of identifiable net assets acquired	$1,220,000	
Market value of 20% of identifiable net assets acquired: ($1,220,000 × .20)		$244,000
Purchased goodwill		$ 56,000

To summarize, Giant has acquired a 20% interest in Small at a cost of $300,000. The items acquired can be represented as follows:

20% of book value of Small	$200,000
20% of excess of market value over book value for:	
Inventory (20% × 5,000)	1,000
Plant and equipment (20% × 200,000)	40,000
Land (20% × 15,000)	3,000
Purchased goodwill	56,000
Total	$300,000

The equity method requires that Giant account for the $300,000 investment in Small as is detailed above. Thus, when Small disposes of any of the above items, either in the normal course of business or by asset sales, Giant must record the appropriate adjustments to its investment account. For example, since Small uses the FIFO method of costing its inventory, the beginning inventory will be sold during the coming year. Likewise, the plant and equipment of Small will be used and depreciated during the coming year. Since the valuation of these items from Giant's perspective is different from that recorded by Small, Giant will need to record adjustments to reflect the using up of the difference between the market value and the book value of these assets.

Thus, assuming all of Small's beginning inventory is sold during 1992, cost of goods sold for 1992 is understated by Small by $1,000 from the single entity (Giant) perspective. Also, depreciation is understated. If the plant and equipment has a remaining useful life of 10 years and Small uses straight-line depreciation, Giant will need to increase the depreciation expense for Small by $40,000 divided by 10 years, or $4,000 each year for the next 10 years. Finally, the goodwill must be amortized, as was discussed in Chapter 13, over a period of 40 years or less. Assuming Giant amortizes goodwill over the maximum period, the annual charge for goodwill amortization will be \$56,000 divided by 40, or \$1,400 each year for the next 40 years. These are the types of adjustments referred to by items 1 (*d*) and 2 (*b*) on page 708.

No adjustments need be made for the excess of market value over book value for the land. Only if Small disposes of the land would an adjustment need to be made, showing that the cost of 20% of the land from the Giant perspective is understated by \$3,000. Giant's proportionate share of any gain (loss) on disposal of the land would be decreased (increased) by \$3,000.

When Giant records investment revenue from its investment in Small, it makes adjusting entries to reflect the above analysis.

Suppose that for the fiscal year ending December 31, 1992, Small reports the following:

Income before extraordinary items	\$ 80,000
Extraordinary item	30,000
Net income	\$110,000
Cash dividends paid on December 31	\$ 50,000

At December 31, Giant would make the following entries to reflect its interest in the earnings of Small:

1. To recognize investment revenue based on Giant's proportionate share of income reported by Small:

Investment in Small, at equity (110,000 × .20)	22,000	
Investment revenue (80,000 × .20)		16,000
Extraordinary gain (30,000 × .20)		6,000

2. To record additional costs of goods sold associated with the excess of market value over book value of inventory at the acquisition of Small:

Investment revenue	1,000	
Investment in Small, at equity		1,000

3. To record depreciation on the \$40,000 of depreciable assets implicit in the purchase price paid for Small:

Investment revenue (\$40,000 ÷ 10 years)	4,000	
Investment in Small, at equity		4,000

4. To record periodic amortization of goodwill:

Investment revenue (\$56,000 ÷ 40 years)	1,400	
Investment in Small, at equity		1,400

5. To record the receipt of cash dividends paid by Small:

Cash (\$50,000 × .20)	10,000	
Investment in Small, at equity		10,000

After these entries are posted, the balance in the investment in Small account would be \$305,600:

Beginning balance (acquisition price)	\$300,000
Proportionate share of Small's net income	22,000
Additional cost of goods sold adjustment	(1,000)
Additional depreciation adjustment	(4,000)
Amortization of goodwill	(1,400)
Dividends received	(10,000)
Investment account balance, Dec. 31	\$305,600

The investment revenue for 1992, after all the adjustments, is $9,600 of ordinary income plus an extraordinary item of $6,000:

Investment revenue (ordinary):
Proportionate share of Small net income $16,000
Additional cost of goods adjustment . . . .   (1,000)
Additional depreciation adjustment . . . .   (4,000)
Amortization of goodwill . . . .   (1,400)
                                                                        $ 9,600

Extraordinary gain:
Extraordinry gain (as recorded by Small)   6,000
Total investment revenue (ordinary and extraordinary) $15,600

The total investment income Giant reports from its investment in Small is $15,600. Since Giant received $10,000 of this in the form of cash dividends, the net increase of its investment is $5,600. This increase is shown in the investment account from the beginning to the end of the year.

Summary of the Equity Method   Equity basis accounting for investments in equity securities can become complex because the investor firm must maintain records outside its own accounting records on transactions of the investee firm, and make the appropriate adjusting entries at the appropriate time. In general, six types of entries are involved in accounting for an investment under the equity method.

1. Record the proportionate share of the investee's reported income. This is a debit to the investment account, and a credit to investment revenue (also often labeled "equity in the earnings of equity-based companies"). If the investee firm reports extraordinary items, the investor firm must separately report these items. The concept being applied is that the investee and the investor firms are a single entity, at least with respect to the portion of the investee firm owned by the investor firm.

2. Record any dividends paid by the investee firm as a debit to cash and a credit to the investment account. The dividends are not income, but rather are a conversion of a portion of the investment to cash. Dividends represent a liquidation of the investment.

3. Record the proportionate share of additional expense items related to the investor's cost of the investment over the proportionate share of the book value of the investee firm. In the above example, these included the cost of goods sold and the depreciation adjustments. These entries are made to adjust the investment account and the investment revenue. These entries can be complex and are covered in considerable detail in most advanced accounting textbooks.[9]

4. Record the amortization of any purchased goodwill. Since the goodwill is associated with the investment, it is recorded as a debit to the investment revenue account and a credit to the investment account. There is no goodwill separately identified on the books of the investor firm; the purchased goodwill is included in the investment acount.

5. Record any gain or loss on the sale of portions of the investment. The gain or loss is the difference between the sale proceeds from disposing of the shares and the carrying amount of the investment. The gain or loss on disposal is separately identified in the income statement accounts of the investor firm.

6. Eliminate any intercompany gains or losses arising from transactions between the investor and investee firms. This topic is covered in more detail in Appendix 14A,

---

[9] For example, consider the complications that would arise in the example had Small been using LIFO rather than FIFO for inventory costing. In this instance, the additional cost would have been assigned to various layers of the inventory and would have been an expense adjustment only when those layers were sold.

and in more detail in advanced accounting textbooks. The basic concept being applied is the perspective that (*a*) the investor and investee are a single entity and (*b*) an entity should not earn profits in transactions with itself. Thus, when the investor firm sells an asset to the investee firm (or vice versa) at a profit, the item is carried on the books of the investee at its cost. Its cost, however, is the original cost of the item as was recorded on the books of the selling firm plus the profit that the selling firm records. The profit recorded by the selling firm (in this example, the investor) must be eliminated.

Consider a simple example. Suppose Giant sells land to Small. The land had originally cost Giant $10,000, and the sales price to Small is $15,000. Giant makes the following entry to record the disposal of land:

Cash (or Accounts receivable)	15,000	
Land		10,000
Gain on disposal		5,000

The land will be recorded by Small at a cost of 15,000, but for the single entity of Giant and Small combined, the land had an original cost of $10,000. To adjust and remove the profit recorded by Giant, the following entry is made at closing (in the year the land is sold):

Gain on disposal	5,000	
Investment in Small		5,000

With this entry, the profit that would otherwise have been reported by Giant is eliminated. The credit is to the investment account because Small has paid $5,000 more to Giant than the original cost of the land. This additional payment is analogous to a dividend, and dividends paid by the investee to the investor are credited to the investment account.

The equity basis method is a modified cost basis method. The investment account is carried at original cost plus the investor's equity in the undistributed earnings of the investee. While the notion of lower of cost or market does not appear to be applicable, nonetheless, some firms do indicate that their equity basis investments are carried at the lower of cost or market.

CONCEPT REVIEW

1. Conceptually, what are the components of the carrying amount recorded in an investments account under the equity method?
2. What are the components of investment revenue under the equity method?
3. How are dividends received by the investor firm from the investee firm recorded under the cost method? Under the equity method?

Changing between the LCM Method and the Equity Method

The ownership level or level of influence an investor company has in or over an investee company can change over time. For example, an investor company using the LCM method might acquire more shares of the investee, thereby gaining sufficient shares to have significant influence. The investor firm would then be required to account for its investment using the equity method. Alternatively, an investor accounting for an investee using the equity method might sell some of its holdings, or the investee might issue shares to parties other than the investor. The result in either case could be that the investor no longer meets the requirements of the equity method. In this case, the accounting would change from the equity method to the LCM method. In this section the accounting for changes between the LCM method and the equity method are considered.

Changing *from* **the Equity Method to the LCM Method**   When the ownership level or the level of influence an investor has over an investee currently accounted for on the equity basis falls below what is deemed necessary to continue this method, a change must be made to the LCM method. In making the change, the currently recorded carrying amount for the investment becomes the cost basis of the investment. That is, any previously recorded equity in earnings (or losses) included in the balance in the investment account remains a part of the cost of the investment when the change is made to the LCM method.

Example   Suppose Raven Corp. acquired 25% of Owl Inc. on January 2, 1991, paying $1,000,000. At the time, the net book value of the interest Raven acquired in the net assets of Owl was $800,000, and the excess of cost over book value of net assets acquired ($200,000) is accounted for as goodwill. Raven amortizes goodwill over 20 years, therefore the amortization will be $10,000 per year. Owl has earnings of $600,000 and $800,000 in 1991 and 1992, respectively, and pays no dividends. The entries Raven would make to record the investment and to record recognition of its interest in the earnings of Owl in 1991 and 1992 would be as follows:

To record the initial investment:

Investment in Owl Corp.	1,000,000	
Cash		1,000,000

To record investment revenue in 1991:

Investment in Owl Corp.	150,000	
Equity in earnings of Owl Corp. (.25 × $600,000)		150,000

To record amortization of goodwill:

Equity in earnings of Owl Corp.	10,000	
Investment in Owl Corp.		10,000

To record investment revenue in 1992:

Investment in Owl Corp.	200,000	
Equity in earnings of Owl Corp. (.25 × $800,000)		200,000

To record amortization of goodwill:

Equity in earnings of Owl Corp.	10,000	
Investment in Owl Corp.		10,000

As of January 2, 1993, the investment in Owl Corp. account has a balance of $1.33 million ($1 million initial investment, plus equity in earnings of Owl Corp. for 1991 of $150,000 and for 1992 of $200,000, less two years of amortization totaling $20,000). Assume that on January 2, 1993, Owl Corp. issues additional shares of common stock and that after the issuance, Raven Company has an ownership interest of 15%. Assuming there is no evidence to the contrary, Raven no longer is deemed to have a significant influence over Owl, and would begin accounting for its investment in Owl using the LCM method. Any dividends received from Owl would be accounted for as investment revenue. If the aggregate market value of the portfolio of long-term equity investments were less than the aggregate cost, Raven would record the unrealized loss as a reduction in the carrying amount of the investments and a reduction from stockholders' equity. The cost of Owl Corp. used for computing the aggregate cost of the portfolio would be $1.33 million. As with any LCM investment, any dividends received in subsequent periods that exceed the amount of the investor's cumulative interest in the investee's earnings is accounted for as a reduction of the carrying amount of the investment account.

Changing *to* the Equity Method from the LCM Method   At the time an investment qualifies for use of the equity method (after having been accounted for by the LCM method for one or more periods), *APB Opinion No. 18* (par. 19) requires that the investor firm adopt the equity method retroactively. That is, the investor must adjust the carrying amount, the results of operations for the current and other prior periods presented in the financial statements, and the retained earnings as if the equity method had been in effect for all previous periods.

Example   On January 2, 1991, Right Corp. purchased 10% of the outstanding common shares of Wrong Company for $1 million. On that date, the net assets acquired of Wrong Company have a net book value of $700,000. The excess of the cost of the investment over the net book value of assets acquired ($300,000) is attributed to goodwill. Right amortizes goodwill over a 10 year period. On January 3, 1993, Right Corp. purchases an additional 15% of Wrong Company's common stock for $2 million. At that date the net book value of Wrong assets acquired is $1.35 million. With a total of a 25% interest in Wrong, Right must adopt the equity method of accounting for its investment in Wrong.

The net earnings and dividends paid by Wrong during the period 1991 through 1993 are as follows:

Year	Earnings	Dividends
1991	$ 800,000	$ 300,000
1992	2,000,000	500,000
1993	2,400,000	1,000,000

During 1991 and 1992, Right accounts for its investment in Wrong using LCM method. The carrying amount of the investment is maintained at the original investment of $1 million, and investment revenue of $30,000 and $50,000 (i.e., 10% of the dividends paid by Wrong each year) is recorded as investment revenue in 1991 and 1992, respectively. To restate the investment account as of January 2, 1993, on an equity basis, a schedule of how the account would have been affected for each prior year is computed:

	1991	1992	Total
Right Corp. equity in earnings of Wrong (10% of Wrong earnings)	$80,000	$200,000	$280,000
Less: Annual goodwill amortization	(30,000)	(30,000)	(60,000)
Equity in earnings after amortization	$50,000	$170,000	$220,000
Less: Dividends received	(30,000)	(50,000)	(80,000)
Adjustment to investment account	$20,000	$120,000	$140,000

To adjust the investment account to the equity basis at January 3, 1993, the total adjustment computed above is debited to the investment account, with the credit recorded as an adjustment to retained earnings:

Investment in Wrong Corp.	140,000	
Retained earnings		140,000

With the additional investment of $2 million on January 3, 1993, reflecting the purchase of an additional 15% of Wrong, the investment account becomes $3.14 million:

Original investment	$1,000,000
Adjustment to equity basis	140,000
Additional investment	2,000,000
Total at January 3, 1993	$3,140,000

During 1993, Right receives dividends from Wrong totaling $250,000 (25% of the total dividends of $1 million). These are recorded as a reduction in the carrying amount of the investment:

Cash 250,000
    Investment in Wrong Co.   250,000

At year-end, Right must determine the amount to record as its equity in the earnings of Wrong, including the appropriate amounts of amortization for the two acquisitions:

Right Corp. equity in earnings of Wrong Co.
  before amortizations ($2,400,000 × .25) $600,000
Less: Amortization of goodwill resulting from 1991 acquisition . . . .   (30,000)
Less: Amortization of goodwill resulting from 1992 acquisition
  [($2,000,000 − $1,350,000)/10 years)] . . . . (65,000)
Equity in earnings of Wrong Co. $505,000

The entry to record equity in the earnings of Wrong for 1993 is:

Investment in Wrong Co. 505,000
    Equity in earnings of Wrong Co.   505,000

If Right Corp. includes an income statement for 1992 in its 1993 financial statements, the investment revenue it would show for its investment in Wrong would not be the $50,000 in dividends as previously reported, but rather 10% of Wrong Company earnings ($200,000) less amortization of $30,000, or $170,000. All financial statements presented by Right are restated to show the investment in Wrong on the equity basis.

Disclosures Required for Long-Term Investments in Equity Securities

SFAS No. 12 specifies the disclosures required for all investments, whether short-term or long-term, that are accounted for by the LCM method. These requirements were listed and illustrated in the section discussing short-term equity investments. Exhibit 14–1 illustrates the disclosures for investments in equity securities under the LCM requirements of *SFAS No. 12*.

Investments accounted for using the equity method have a different set of required disclosures, which are detailed in *APB Opinion No. 18:*

1. Disclose parenthetically in notes or in separate schedules:
   a. The name of each investee and percentage ownership.
   b. The accounting policies of the investor with respect to investments in common stock.
   c. The difference, if any, between the amount at which an investment is carried and the amount of underlying equity in net assets, and the accounting treatment of the difference.
2. For those investments in common stock for which a quoted market price is available, the aggregate value of each identified investment based on the quoted market price.
3. When investments accounted for under the equity method are, in the aggregate, material in relation to the financial position or results of operations of an investor, it may be necessary for summarized information regarding assets, liabilities, and results of operations of the investee to be presented.[10]

---

[10] See AICPA, *APB Opinion No. 18,* "The Equity Method of Accounting for Investments of Common Stock" (New York, May 1971), par. 20.

Investments accounted for by the equity method often are a substantial holding for the investor, and as such require the extensive disclosures outlined above. Exhibit 14–3 contains excerpts from the financial statements of The Washington Post Company relating to its investments in equity-based companies.

MARKET VALUE METHOD FOR EQUITY SECURITIES
◆

Yet another method of accounting for marketable equity securities is the **market value method.** It is an option only for those firms whose primary lines of business include investing in the securities of others. Some specialized industries, such as investment companies, stock life insurance companies, fire and casualty insurance companies, and brokers and dealers in securities, are permitted by *SFAS No. 12* to carry equity securities at market with unrealized gains and losses being classified in the equity accounts. This section discusses the accounting procedures of the market value method.

The market value method is fundamentally different from the cost or the equity methods. The market value method is based on the concept of *current value accounting*, not historical cost accounting. Under this method, each individual security investment is revalued at each financial statement date to the current market value of the securities held. The LCM concept is not applied with the market value method.

The market value is summarized as follows:

1. At date of acquisition, investments are recorded at cost in conformity with the cost principle.
2. After acquisition, each individual investment account balance is adjusted at the end of the accounting year to the current market value of the securities held. The adjusted amount then becomes the new carrying value for subsequent accounting.
3. Cash and property dividends declared and paid are recognized by the investor as investment revenue.
4. Increases or decreases in the market value of the equity securities are recognized at the end of each accounting period. One of the following approaches is used:
   a. *Current approach*—The price change during the current period is recognized as investment revenue (or loss) in the current income statement. It would be clearly labeled as the increase or decrease in market value.
   b. *Deferral approach*—The price change during the current period is recorded as a deferred item in owners' equity, labeled as unrealized market gain or loss. When a security is subsequently sold, the difference between its carrying value in the investment account and its original cost must be removed from its deferred status in the unrealized account and recognized as investment revenue or loss. Any additional difference is recognized as gain or loss on sale of investments.
5. At disposal of the investment, the difference between the carrying value at that date and its sale price is recognized as a gain or loss on disposal.

Illustration of Market Value Method for Equity Securities

Current Approach   Assume that on January 1, 1991, Intel Company purchased, as a long-term investment, 1,000 shares of common stock of Decca Corporation for $25 per share. Following the cost principle, Intel would record the investment:

Investment in Decca common stock 25,000
    Cash   25,000

At December 31, 1991, assume the market price of Decca Corporation stock is $20 per share, and Decca's reported net income is $80,000. Decca pays no dividends in 1991. Under the market value method, the carrying amount for the investment is increased (decreased) by increases (decreases) in market value of the securities.

EXHIBIT 14–3   Excerpts from Financial Statements of The Washington Post Company Relating to Investments.

Reported on the balance sheet, immediately after current assets:

	1988 (000)	1987 (000)
Investments in affiliates	$163,250	$152,636

Reported on the income statement:

Equity in earnings of affiliated companies	$19,114	$17,663

NOTES TO CONSOLIDATED FINANCIAL STATEMENTS:

Note A (In Part). Summary of Significant Accounting Policies

Investments in Affiliates. The company uses the equity method of accounting for its investments in and earnings of affiliates.

Note D (In Part). Investments in Affiliates

The company's investments in affiliates at January 1, 1989, and January 3, 1988, consists of the following (in thousands):

	1988	1987
Cowles Media Company	$ 78,399	$ 77,512
Newsprint mills	80,269	68,656
Other	4,582	6,468
Total	$163,250	$152,636

The company's investments in affiliates in 1988 include a 26 percent interest in the stock of Cowles Media Company, which owns and operates the *Minneapolis Star and Tribune* and several other smaller properties. In 1987 and 1988 the company owned a 21 percent interest.

The company's interest in newsprint mills includes a 49 percent interest in the common stock of Bowater Mersey Paper Company Limited, which owns and operates a newsprint mill in Nova Scotia; a one-third limited partnership interest in Bear Island Paper Company, which owns and operates a newsprint mill near Richmond, Virginia; and a one-third partnership interest in Bear Island Timberlands Company, which owns timberlands and supplies Bear Island Paper Company with a major portion of its wood requirements. Operating costs and expenses of the company include costs of newsprint supplied by Bowater Mersey Paper Company and Bear Island Paper Company of $71,400,000 in 1988, $63,300,000 in 1987, and $61,400,000 in 1986.

During 1983 the company acquired interests in several businesses that distribute programming, principally sports events, to pay cable and subscription television subscribers. During 1986 and a portion of 1987, the company's interests included a 33.5 percent partnership in SportsChannel Prism Associates, which operates in the metropolitan Philadelphia area; and 33.3 percent partnership interest in SportsChannel Chicago Associates, which operates in the Chicago area; and a 6.7 percent limited partnership interest in SportsChannel New England, which operates in the New England and upstate New York areas. In August 1987, the company sold its interest in each of the four sports programming businesses.

The company's other investments include a one-third common stock interest in a French corporation based in Paris that publishes the *International Herald Tribune* [the description and information disclosed continues in the same manner as in the above two paragraphs].

Summarized financial data for the affiliates' operations are as follows (in thousands):

	1988	1987	1986
Financial position:			
Working capital	$ 17,185	$100,100	$ 98,485
Property, plant, and equipment	456,160	370,761	380,518
Total assets	694,751	642,374	676,831
Long-term debt	263,773	129,651	155,033
Net equity	226,160	339,905	316,419
Results of operations			
Operating revenues	$662,691	$616,387	$640,353
Operating income	91,957	78,972	81,442
Net income	54,914	53,439	44,356

EXHIBIT 14-3 *(concluded)*

The following summarizes the status and results of the company's investments in affiliates (in thousands):

	1988	1987
Beginning investment	$152,636	$168,421
Equity in earnings	19,114	17,663
Dividends received	(1,803)	(1,638)
Additional investments	599	5,927
Sale of investments	(1,806)	(27,004)
Other	(5,490)	(10,733)
Ending investment	$163,250	$152,636

At January 1, 1989, the unamortized excess of the company's investments over its equity in the underlying net assets of its affiliates at the date of acquisition was approximately $71,000,000, which is being amortized over 40 years. Amortization included in equity in earnings of affiliates for the years ended January 1, 1989, January 3, 1988, and December 28, 1986, was $1,150,000, $1,900,000, and $2,300,000, respectively.

Under the current approach, the change in market value is included in income in the current period. Thus, the entry to be made by Intel at December 31 would record the decrease in market value for Decca:

Investment loss, market price loss on investments		
(1,000) × ($25 − $20)	5,000	
Investment in Decca		5,000

Suppose, further, that Decca pays dividends of $1 per share in October 1992. At December 31, 1992, the Decca reports net income of $65,000, and at that date the market price of Decca common stock is $22 per share. Intel must record both the receipt of dividends and the change in market value:

Cash (dividends received)	1,000	
Investment revenue (1,000 × $1)		1,000
Investment in Decca	2,000	
Investment revenue, market price gain on investments		
(1,000) × ($22 − $20)		2,000

Finally, assume Intel sells 400 shares of the Decca common in November 1993 for $26 per share. Since the investment in Decca is currently carried at $22 per share, the entry to record the sale is as follows:

Cash (400 × $26)	10,400	
Investment in Decca (400 × $22)		8,800
Gain on sale of investments		1,600

Deferral Approach If the deferral approach were used in the above analysis, only the dividends received from Decca would be recorded as investment revenue. The various market value change amounts recorded above as either investment revenue or investment loss would be recorded as unrealized gain/loss on investment, but they would *not* be closed to the income statement. Instead, they would be included in the stockholders' equity section of the balance sheet (called "unrealized market gain/loss on investments"). When the shares are sold, the amount recorded in the unrealized market gain/loss account would be recognized. Thus, when Intel sold the 400 shares in November 1993, the entry to record the sale under the deferral method would be:

```
Cash (400 × $26) . . . . . . . . . . . . . . . . . . . . . . . . . . . .  10,400
Investment loss, market value change . . . . . . . . . . . . . . . .   1,200
        Unrealized market gain/loss on investments[11] (400 × $3) . . .        1,200
        Investment in Decca (400 × $22) . . . . . . . . . . . . . . .            8,800
        Gain on sale of investments (400 × $4) . . . . . . . . . . . .            1,600
```

Both the current approach and the deferral approach result in the same carrying value for the investment. The deferral approach delays the actual recognition of any gain or loss in market value until the securities are sold. That is, the gain or loss is deferred until it is realized.

Some accountants believe that investments in all marketable equity securities, whether short-term or long-term, should be accounted for using the market value method. They contend that market value data:

1. Report the economic consequences of holding the investment.
2. Are more useful to decision makers than cost or equity data in projecting future cash flows.
3. Are objectively determinable for many stocks.
4. Avoid the LCM asymmetric treatment for market when it is above cost.
5. Prevent the opportunity to manage earnings through the sale of selected investments acquired at a low original cost with a high market value, followed later by a repurchase.[12]

Many arguments have been advanced against the valuation of marketable equity securities at market value. The principal arguments cited against the market value method are:

1. It violates the cost principle and places on the balance sheet values that may not be objectively determined and may be temporary.
2. It violates the traditional revenue principle because revenue recognition is based on market value changes rather than on a sale.
3. Because of the volatility of some stock prices, it introduces a vacillating effect on the balance sheet and on reported income.

To summarize, the market value method is not an option for firms other than those in selected specialized industries. It has conceptual appeal to many accountants, but it has been viewed as too radical a departure from the cost principle to be adopted for all marketable equity security investments.

CONCEPT REVIEW

1. How does the market value method differ from the cost method with respect to the carrying amount recorded for the investment? For the amount recorded as investment revenue?
2. Describe the difference between the current approach and the deferral approach under the market value approach.
3. What disclosures are required for long-term investments in equity securities accounted for under the equity method?

---

[11] This is the amount in the unrealized gain/loss account, which is a contra (debit balance) account in shareholders' equity, which relates to the shares sold. The amount equals the current beginning-of-period carrying amount, $22 per share, less the original cost, $25 per share, times the number of shares sold: [($22 − $25) × 400]. The amount of $1,,200 is removed from the holding account and recognized as investment loss since it is realized with the sale of the 400 shares.

[12] Variants of this view are presented by W. Morris and B. Coda, "Valuation of Equity Securities," *Journal of Accountancy,* January 1973, pp. 48-54, and by W. Beaver, "Accounting for Marketable Equity Securities," *Journal of Accountancy,* December 1973, pp. 58-64.

Disclosures of Market Values of Financial Instruments

In December 1990, the FASB issued an *Exposure Draft* that, if issued as a *Statement*, will require additional disclosures about the various investments of a firm. It does not, however, alter the accounting procedures used to account for investments. The proposed *Statement* will require all entities to disclose information about the market value of all financial instruments (with several specific exceptions) for which it is practicable to estimate market values. This proposed statement will significantly affect the disclosures of financial institutions, as these organizations invest extensively in various types of financial instruments.

Definition of Financial Instrument In addition to cash, a **financial instrument** is defined as either one of the following:

1. Includes evidence of ownership in an entity.
2. A contract that:
   a. Obligates a firm to deliver cash or another financial instrument to a second firm, or to exchange financial instruments on potentially unfavorable terms, and
   b. Conveys to the second firm the right to receive cash or another financial instrument from the first firm, or to exchange instruments on potentially favorable terms.

Evidence of ownership includes all forms of equity securities. The second part of the definition includes all forms of debt securities. Thus, the proposed *Statement* will require a firm to disclose information about the market values of all the investments it holds, assuming it is *practicable* to estimate the market value of the financial instrument. The best evidence of market value would come from quoted market prices. If quoted market prices are not available, management is to develop an estimated market price based, for example, on quoted market prices of a financial instrument with similar characteristics, or estimate the market value using valuation techniques such as those described in Chapter 6. Other possible estimation techniques include the use of option pricing models and matrix pricing models. The proposed *Statement* does state that excessive costs in developing estimates are an acceptable reason for not computing and presenting market values.

The market values of financial instruments for which it is practicable to estimate are to be disclosed either in the body of the financial statements or in the accompanying notes. The result of this proposed *Statement* will be increased disclosure for long-term investments, both in equity and debt securities, of the market values of these investments. For example, the note from The Washington Post Company annual report found in Exhibit 14–3 does not provide information on the market values of the several investments described. If the proposed *Statement* is adopted, it is likely that the firm will have to estimate the market value of these investments in future disclosures.

If enacted, the proposed *Statement* would be effective for financial statements issued for fiscal years ending after December 15, 1991, except for firms with less than $100 million in total assets at the latest balance sheet date. For these firms, the *Statement* would become effective for financial statements issued after December 15, 1992.

SPECIAL PROBLEMS IN ACCOUNTING FOR EQUITY INVESTMENTS
◆

Several special problems relating to the acquisition, holding, and sale of equity investments are discussed below under the following three headings:

1. Investment revenue—cash dividends and interest revenue.
2. Stock split of investment shares.
3. Stock rights on investment shares.

Investment Revenue

Cash dividends on short-term investments in capital stock of other companies are recognized as earned at the time of the declaration of the cash dividend. Cash dividends on capital stock held as an investment are not accrued prior to declaration. Stock dividends are not included as investment revenue.

To conserve cash and still make a distribution to stockholders, a corporation may issue a stock dividend. When a stock dividend is issued, the distributing corporation debits retained earnings and credits the appropriate capital stock accounts. The effect of a stock dividend from the issuing corporation's view is to capitalize a part of retained earnings. Significantly, a stock dividend does not decrease the assets of the issuing corporation.

From the investor's point of view, the nature of a stock dividend is suggested by the effect on the issuing corporation. The investor neither receives assets from the corporation nor owns more of the issuing corporation. The investor merely has more shares to represent the same prior proportional ownership. Thus, the receipt of a stock dividend in the same class of stock as already owned results, from the investor's viewpoint, in more shares but no increase in the cost (carrying value) of the holdings.

The investor should neither make an entry for revenue nor change the investment account other than to record a memorandum entry for the number of shares received. In case of a sale of any of the shares, a new cost per share is computed by adding the new shares to the old and dividing this sum into the carrying value.

Assume XYZ Company purchased 1,000 shares of common stock, par $5, of ABC Corporation at $90 per share. Subsequently, XYZ Company received a 50% common stock dividend. XYZ later sold 200 of the common shares at $75 per share. The entries would be:

At the acquisition date XYZ would record:

Long-term investment in equity securtities, ABC Corp.		
(1,000 × $90)	90,000	
Cash		90,000

At date of stock dividend:

Memorandum entry only—Received 50% common stock dividend of 500 shares from ABC Corporation, revised cost per share: $90,000 ÷ (1,000 + 500 = 1,500 shares) = $60.

At the date of sale of 200 common shares:

Cash (200 × $75)	15,000	
Long-term investment in equity securities, ABC Corp.		
(200 × $60)		12,000
Gain on sale of investments		3,000

(Remaining shares: 1,300 at $60 cost per share).

These procedures are followed for the cost, equity, and market value methods; the only difference in application is the total carrying value (i.e., cost, market, or equity amount). For all three methods, the appropriate total carrying value is divided by the new total number of shares owned to determine the carrying value per share after the stock dividend.

If the stock dividend is of a different class of stock than that on which the dividend is declared, such as preferred stock received as a dividend on common stock, or vice versa, three methods of accounting for the dividend are possible:

1. *Allocation method*—Record the new stock at an amount determined by allocating the carrying value of the old stock between the new stock and the old stock on the basis of the relative market values of the different classes of stock after issuance of the dividend.

EXHIBIT 14-4 Investor Accounting for a Stock Dividend in a Different Class of Stock

Case Data:

1. CD Corp. purchased 100 shares of JKL Company common stock at $75 per share (total cost, $7,500).
2. Some time later, CD Corp. received a stock dividend of 40 shares of JKL preferred stock with a market value of $2,500. At that time, the market value of the common stock was $10,000. Using the allocation method, the cost is apportioned, based on the total market value of $12,500, as follows:

$$\text{Cost allocated to common} = \$7,500 \times \frac{\$10,000}{\$12,500} = \$6,000 \text{ or } \$60 \text{ per share}$$

$$\text{Cost allocated to preferred} = \$7,500 \times \frac{\$2,500}{\$12,500} = \underline{1,500} \text{ or } \$37.50 \text{ per share}$$

Total cost allocated $7,500

Entry to Record Receipt of Stock Dividend by CD Corp.:

Investment in preferred stock of JKL Company (40 × $37.50) 1,500
    Investment in common stock of JKL Company 1,500

2. *Noncost method*—Record the new stock in terms of shares only (as a memorandum entry). When it is sold, recognize the total sale price as a gain.
3. *Market value method*—Do not change the carrying value of the old stock. Instead, record the new stock at its market value upon receipt with an offsetting credit to dividend revenue. This method is based on the assumption that stock of a different class received as a dividend is similar to a property dividend.

The *allocation method* is the most consistent with the historical cost principal. The noncost method is considered to be conservative, and the market value method is seldom used. Exhibit 14–4 shows the application of the allocation method, which assigns the original cost to the two classes of stock. This method would be followed for the cost, equity, and market value methods, with the appropriate carrying value being allocated.

Interest receivable and interest revenue on investments in debt securities (e.g., bonds) are accrued at the end of the accounting period with an adjusting entry. Bonds and similar debt securities purchased at a price above par are acquired at a premium; if acquired below par, at a discount. Premium or discount on a long-term investment is amortized. However, on a short-term investment in bonds, the discount (or premium) is not amortized because, by definition, the investment will be converted to cash in the near future.

Stock Split of Investment Shares

Although a stock split is different from a stock dividend from the point of view of the issuer, the two are virtually identical from the point of view of the investor. In both cases, the investor has more shares than before the split or dividend, but with the same total cost as before.[13] To the investor, the accounting for a stock split is the same as for a stock dividend of the same class as already owned. Only a *memorandum entry* is made to record the number of new shares received, and the cost (or carrying value) per share is recomputed.

---

[13] In a reverse split, such as a two-for-three split, the number of outstanding shares is reduced rather than increased. Reverse stock splits are rare.

Stock Rights on Investment Shares

The privilege given stockholders (investors) of purchasing additional shares of stock from the issuing corporation at a specific price (called an *option price*) and by a specified date is commonly known as a *stock right*. The certificate evidencing one or more rights is called a *stock warrant*.

The term stock right is usually interpreted as one right for each share of old stock. For example, a holder of two shares of stock who receives rights to subscribe for one new share is said to own two stock rights rather than one. There is one right per old share regardless of the entitlement of the right. In this case, each right entitles the holder to purchase one half of a share. Rights have value when the holder can buy shares through exercise of the rights at a lower price per share than on the open market. As the spread between the option price and the market price changes subsequent to issuance of the rights, the value of the rights changes.

When the intention to issue stock rights is declared, the stock with the rights sells "rights on." The market price of the share includes the value of the share and the value of a right. After the rights are issued, the shares will sell in the market "ex rights." Also, after issuance, rights usually have a separate market from that of the related stock. They will be separately quoted at a specific market price. After rights are received, the investor has shares of stock and stock rights.

To determine the gain or loss on the sale of either the stock or the rights, it is necessary to allocate the total cost of the investment between the stock and the rights. This allocation usually is based on relative market values; that is, the total cost of the old shares is allocated between the old stock and the rights in proportion to their relative market values at the time the rights are issued.

Example   Assume Garfield Company purchased 500 shares of Franklin Corporation common stock at $93 per share, a total investment of $46,500. The entry to record the investment is:

```
Investment—Franklin Corporation common stock  . . . . . . . . .  46,500
        Cash . . . . . . . . . . . . . . . . . . . . . . . . . . . . . . . .          46,500
```

Later, Garfield Company receives 500 stock rights that entitles it to acquire 100 shares of Franklin Corporation common stock at a price of $100 per share. That is, each stock right represents one fifth of a share of Franklin Corporation common stock. At the date the Franklin Corporation common stock first trades ex rights, it had a market price of $120 per share, and each stock right had a market value of $4. To determine the allocation of the cost of the investment to the stock rights and the held common shares, the relative market values are used:

```
Total market value of common shares held: (500 × $120)  . . . . .  $60,000
Total market value of stock rights held: (500 × $4)  . . . . . . . . .    2,000
Total market value of investment  . . . . . . . . . . . . . . . . . . .  $62,000
```

$$\text{Cost to be allocated to investments in stock rights} = \frac{\$2,000}{\$62,000} \times \$46,500 = \$1,500$$

$$\text{Cost to be allocated to investment in common shares} = \frac{\$60,000}{\$62,000} \times \$46,500 = \$45,000$$

The cost per share of common stock is now $45,000/500 shares, or $90 per share, and the cost of the rights is $1,500/500 rights, or $3 per right.

The entry to record the receipt of the 500 stock rights for Franklin Corporation common stock is:

```
Investment—Franklin Corporation stock rights  . . . . . . . . . . .  1,500
        Investment—Franklin Corporation common stock  . . . . . . . .          1,500
```

Suppose Garfield exercises 400 rights, acquires an additional 80 shares of Franklin at the exercises price of $100 per share, and sells the remaining 100 stock rights for $4.50 per right.

The entry to record the acquisition of these 80 shares through exercising the rights:

```
Investment—Franklin Corporation common stock  . . . . . . . . . .  9,200
     Investment—Franklin Corporation stock rights (400 × $3) . . .        1,200
     Cash . . . . . . . . . . . . . . . . . . . . . . . . . . . . . .        8,000
```

The entry to record the sale of the 100 stock rights would be:

```
Cash (100 × $4.50)                                            450
     Investment—Franklin Corporation stock rights (100 × $3) . . .        300
     Gain on sale of stock rights . . . . . . . . . . . . . . . . . . .        150
```

The 80 shares of common stock acquired by exercising the stock rights have a total cost of $9,200, or $115 per share. If Franklin Corporation common stock is sold by Garfield, the firm must determine whether the original shares with a cost of $90 per share, or these newly acquired shares with cost of $115 per share, are sold.

If stock rights are not sold or exercised, they lapse. In this situation, a loss equivalent to the allocated cost of the rights should theoretically be recognized by the investor firm. As a practical matter, however, the allocation entry is usually reversed for the portion that lapses, restoring the cost to the investment in common stock account.

ACCOUNTING FOR TEMPORARY INVESTMENTS IN MARKETABLE DEBT SECURITIES

SFAS No. 12 addresses how to account for marketable equity securities but is silent on accounting for marketable debt securities. As a result, *ARB Opinion No. 43* continues as the official guideline for accounting for short-term investments in debt securities. It specifies use of the cost method (not the lower of cost or market) for short-term investments in debt securities. Under this method, investments in debt securities are recorded and carried at acquisition cost in conformity with the cost principle. If the market value of the securities held falls below acquisition cost, there is not a write-down to market (as there is under the LCM method). *ARB Opinion No. 43* does allow for a write-down if the current market value is less than cost by a substantial amount, and if the market value decline is not due to temporary conditions. When both of these conditions exist, *ARB Opinion No. 43* requires that the short-term debt security (on a security-by-security basis) be written down to market value to recognize the permanent impairment of the asset value. There is no direct guidance on how to determine whether the decline in value is a permanent impairment. Changes in value caused by the normal changes in the market rate of interest for debt securities would probably not be viewed as causing a permanent impairment, but a decline in value resulting from a major financial difficulty for the issuer of the debt would more likely be viewed as a permanent impairment. A permanent decline is recorded as a direct credit to the investment account and a debit to a loss (realized) account, such as impairment loss on investments in marketable securities.

Since the issuance of *SFAS No. 12,* an increasing number of firms have adopted the lower of cost or market method for marketable, short-term investments in debt securities. Its application for debt securities is the same as discussed for marketable equity securities—LCM is computed on an aggregate basis, and any unrealized loss at the balance sheet date is charged to the income statement, and a valuation allowance account (a contra account) is credited. The unrealized loss can be recovered in the same manner as that for marketable equity securities. When the LCM method is used, usually a separate portfolio is set up for debt securities, and the LCM method is applied to the portfolio in exactly the same way as illustrated earlier for equity securities. In practice, then, marketable debt securities can be carried either at cost or at lower of cost or market. Since the key characteristic is the same for marketable debt and equity securities (i.e., marketability), it makes sense to account for both using the requirements of *SFAS No. 12.*

The acquisition of a debt security is recorded at cost. However, when a debt security is purchased or sold between interest dates, the accrued interest since the last interest date must be computed and recorded separately from cost. On the next interest date, the new owner of the debt security receives the full cash amount of interest for the interest period. On the transaction date, the buyer and seller agree on the price to be paid for the debt. The amount of cash to be transferred also must include an amount to pay the interest accrued since the last interest payment. This latter amount must be separately recorded in order to determine correctly the amount of interest revenue that the investor will record when interest is received at the next interest payment date.

For example, on May 1, 1992, Laurel Company purchases 100 bonds of Surber Corp. at 96 (face amount $1,000 and stated interest 12%, with interest payable semiannually on July 1 and January 1). Commissions on the purchase are $1,280. Laurel Company will have the following cash outlay:

Purchase price of bonds	$96,000
Commission	1,280
Cost of Bonds acquired	97,280
Accrued interest—January 1 to May 1	
($100,000 × 12% × 4/12)	4,000
Total cash payment	$101,280

To record the above transaction, Laurel makes the following entry:

Marketable debt securities	97,280	
Accrued interest receivable	4,000	
Cash		101,280

When the interest payment is received by Laurel on July 1, the entry to record the interest revenue is:

Cash ($100,000 × .12 × 6/12)	6,000	
Accrued interest receivable		4,000
Interest revenue		2,000

Generally, any discount or premium caused by a difference between the maturity value of the debt security and the acquisition price is not separately recorded because the holding period is short. Any discount or premium is usually not amortized. The investment is carried at cost until it is sold.

When the security is sold, the difference between the carrying amount and the selling price, less commissions and other expenses, is recorded as gain or loss. Suppose that on October 1, 1992, Laurel Company sells its holdings of Surber Corp. bonds at a price of 98 plus accrued interest, and incurs commissions and other expenses associated with the sale of the bonds of $560. The gain or loss is computed as:

Selling price of bonds	$98,000
Less: Commission and expenses	560
Net proceeds from bonds	97,440
Carrying amount of bonds	97,280
Gain on sale of bonds	$ 160

The accrued interest at the disposal date is $100,000 × .12 × 3/12, or $3,000. The entry to record the sale, including recording the receipt of interest revenue for the period July 1 to the transaction date of October 1:

Cash ($98,000 + $3,000 − $560)	100,440	
Gain on sale of bonds		160
Interest revenue ($100,000 × .12 × 3/12)		3,000
Marketable debt securities		97,280

Any gain or loss on the disposition of short-term debt securities is included in the determination of income from continuing operations. If it is determined to be unusual or infrequent, it would be separately identified, but it would not be an extraordinary item.

Accounting for Long-Term Investments in Debt Securities Long-term investments in debt securities are accounted for using the cost method. This topic is covered in Chapter 16, along with accounting for debt by the issuer. Transfers of debt securities from the short-term to long-term classification (and vice versa) are made at the carrying amount at the date of transfer.

Other Types of Investments Generally, investments in securities are the most important item included in the investments account. However, a number of other items can be included under the caption "investments and funds." Most of these investments occur infrequently and are not of a large magnitude. These include special-purpose funds, in which the company sets aside cash or other assets for a special purpose, and the cash surrender value of life insurance on key executives. Also, firms that acquire futures contracts have invested in a form of financial instrument that has the characteristics of an investment. The accounting for each of these types of investments is covered in Appendix 14B.

SUMMARY OF KEY POINTS

(L.O. 1)   1. Firms invest in the securities of other firms either to earn a return on otherwise idle cash or to gain influence, control, or some other business advantage.

(L.O. 2, 3)   2. Investment securities are recorded at acquisition using the cost principle.

(L.O. 3)   3. The four methods of accounting for investment securities are:
     a. The cost method.
     b. The lower of cost or market method (LCM).
     c. The equity method.
     d. The market value method.

(L.O. 3)   4. The LCM method records the investment at the lower of the aggregate cost or aggregate market value of a portfolio of securities. This method is required for short-term and long-term investments in marketable equity securities.

(L.O. 3, 4, 5)   5. The cost method records and maintains an investment at original cost. Only a permanent impairment of value results in a write-down of the cost. Increases in market value above cost are disregarded for accounting purposes. Dividends and interest received from the investment security are recorded as investment revenue.

(L.O. 6)   6. When the application of LCM results in a write-down of aggregate cost to aggregate market for a portfolio of short-term marketable equity securities, the write-down is closed to income during the current period. If this write-down is for a portfolio of long-term marketable equity securities, the write-down is recorded in a contra account in stockholders' equity.

(L.O. 6)   7. For LCM applied to long-term marketable equity securities, any write-down recorded in stockholders' equity can be recovered and recorded in future periods if and when market values increase. The carrying amount of the portfolio can be increased up to its original cost.

(L.O. 6)   8. The equity method must be used to account for long-term investments in voting common stock in which the investor exercises significant influence over the investee. Significant influence over the investee is presumed to exist if the investor owns over 20% or more of the investor voting stock.

(L.O. 6)   9. Conceptually, the equity method is an extension of accrual accounting to common stock investments. Increases and decreases in the net assets of the investee flow through to the investor as they occur.

(L.O. 6)   10. If the investor's initial investment in the common stock of the investee is an amount different from the net book value acquired, the difference must be accounted for as if it were recorded by the investee. Differences between book value as recorded by the investee, and fair market value at the date of acquisition is accounted for by the investor. Any difference not identifiable with specific assets or liabilities is identified as goodwill and is accounted for in accordance with *APB Opinion No. 17*.

(L.O. 6)   11. The market value method of accounting for investments is not in conformity with GAAP except for certain specialized industries. Under this method, investments are carried at market value.

(L.O. 6)   12. Under the market value method of accounting for investment in equity securities, increases or decreases in the market value of the equity securities are recorded each accounting period either currently in the determination of income (the current approach) or as a deferred item in stockholders' equity (the deferral approach). Under the deferral approach, the change in the market value of the securities is recognized as income only when the securities are sold. Dividends received from the investee are recorded as investment revenue by the investor.

(L.O. 7)   13. For each period for which an income statement is presented, an investor firm must disclose the following for its investments in marketable equity securities:
    a. Aggregate cost of the portfolios (short and long term).
    b. Aggregate market value of the portfolios.
    c. Gross unrealized gains and gross unrealized losses.
    d. Net realized gain or loss, the basis for determining the net realized gain or loss, and the change in the valuation allowance that is included in the determination of income.

(L.O. 8)   14. Stock dividends and stock splits are recorded by the investor only as a memorandum entry for the number of shares received. If the stock dividend is of a different class of stock than that on which the dividend was declared, the investor must record the dividend stock in one of three methods: (a) the allocation method, by allocating the carrying value of the old stock between the new stock and the old stock based on relative market values; (*b*) the noncost method, in which no cost is allocated to the new stock; (*c*) the market value method, in which the new stock is recorded at its market value with a credit to dividend income (no allocation of the carrying value of the old stock).

(L.O. 8)   15. When stock rights are issued by the investee, the investor must allocate the total carrying amount of the investment between the old stock and the stock rights, usually using the allocation method described for stock dividends.

(L.O. 9)   16. Consolidated financial statements are required when an investor corporation owns more than 50% of the voting stock of the investee corporation. The acquisition can be accounted for as a purchase or as a pooling of interest, depending upon the characteristcis of the acquisition.

(L.O. 9)   17. Consolidation results in reporting of the investor and the investee as if they were one firm. Minority interests in the net assets and in the earnings of the investee are recognized in the consolidated balance sheet and the consolidated income statement, respectively.

(L.O. 10)   18. The cash surrender value of life insurance is a form of investment. As insurance premiums are paid on policies that generate a cash surrender value, a portion of the premium is recorded as an investment (rather than as a period expense) such that the investment account reflects the cash surrender value of the policy.

REVIEW PROBLEM

♦

In this chapter, four different methods of accounting for investments in securities were discussed. To summarize and distinguish between them, the following designations are used:

1. *Cost method*—The investment is carried at original cost with no reference to market value even if market value is lower than original cost. Investment revenue includes dividends received from investee.

2. *Lower of cost or market (LCM)*—The investment is carried at the lower of the aggregate cost or the aggregate market value of a portfolio of securities. Investment revenue includes dividends received from investee. Unrealized losses and unrealized loss recoveries flow through the income statement for short-term investments and they are recorded in a contra account to stockholders' equity for long-term investments.

3. *Equity method*—The investment is recorded at cost plus investor's pro rata share of undistributed earnings of investee since the acquisition. Investment revenue includes the investor's pro rata share of the earnings of the investee, adjusted for amortization of goodwill and other adjustments.

4. *Market value method*—The investment is reported at current market value at the end of the reporting period. Investment revenue includes dividends received and change in market value. Use the current approach.

In this review problem, you are to apply each of these methods to an investment. That is, the purpose of this problem is to demonstrate the application of each method to a common set of data. Under GAAP, each method is not an option for the investment described below, but the problem shows how each method would be applied to the data.

Data   Assume the following transactions related to investments by Trey Corporation:

Jan. 2, 1991—Trey Corp. acquires 100 shares of Pear Company at a market price of $15 per share, and 200 shares of Apple Inc. for $11 per share. Assume there are no brokerage fees. Also, to simplify the accounting under the equity method, assume the book value of the shares acquired is exactly equal to the price paid for the shares.

Dec. 31, 1991—The two firms in which Trey has invested report the following results:

	Pear Co.	Apple Inc.
Earnings per share for 1991	$2.00	1.50
Dividends per share paid December 31	1.00	.75
Market value per share at 12/31/91	$17	$9.50

Required:

1. Compute the initial investment at cost.
2. Describe how this investment would be accounted for under each of the above four methods. For each method answer the following:
   a. What would be the carrying amount of the investment at December 31, 1991?
   b. What would be the investment revenue recognized in 1991?

SOLUTION
♦

1. Compute the initial investment at cost:

Pear Co.	100 shares × $15/share	=	$1,500
Apple Inc.	200 shares × $11/share	=	2,200
Total investment			$3,700

2. Account for this investment under each of the four methods. For each method compute the carrying amount of the investment at December 31, 1991, and determine the investment revenue to be recognized in 1991.

1. *Cost method.* Investment revenue is the dividends received from the investment securities. In this example Trey Co. would have investment revenue of $250 ($1.00 dividends per share times the 100 Pear shares owned, plus 75-cent dividends per share times the 200 Apple shares owned). The investment on the balance sheet would continue to be carried at the original cost of $3,700.

2. *Lower of cost or market.* Investment revenue includes dividends received as in (1) but it may also be decreased if there is a requirement to write down the investment. To determine whether there is a need to write down the investment, determine the aggregate cost and the aggregate market value at December 31, 1991. The aggregate cost was $3,700. The aggregate market value at December 31 is:

Pear Company	100 shares × $17/share	=	$1,700
Apple Inc.	200 shares × $9.50/share	=	1,900
Total			$3,600

The aggregate current market value has fallen to $3,600, or $100 less than the aggregate original cost. The LCM method requires that we write down the investment to $3,600; thus, investment income is reduced by the write-down of $100. There are unrealized losses of $300 and unrealized gains of $200, which net to the write-down of $100.

3. *Equity method.* The equity method is used only for certain equity investments. Under the equity method, the investing firm reports as investment revenue its pro rata share of the earnings of the investee firm and shows the investment at the original cost plus (or minus) its share of the undistributed earnings of the firm's shares it owns. Thus, the amount that Trey Co. would report as its investment in each investee would be computed as follows:

	Pear Co.	Apple Inc.
Original investment:		
Pear: 100 shares × $15/share	$1,500	
Apple: 200 shares × $11/share		$2,200
Add: Current period earnings:		
Pear: $2.00 per share × 100 shares	200	
Apple: $1.50 per share × 200 shares		300
Less: Dividends received:		
Pear: $1.00 per share × 100 shares	(100)	
Apple: $0.75 per share × 200 shares		(150)
Equity investment at 12/31/91:		
Pear	$1,600	
Apple		$2,350

The total carrying amount for the two investment securities at December 31 is $1,600 plus $2,350, or $3,950. The amount of earnings Trey will report from its investments in these two firms will be its share of each firm's earnings, or $200 from Pear and $300 from Apple.

4. *Market Method.* Under the market value method, using the current approach, investment revenue is the dividends received (or interest income received) plus the increase (or less the decrease) in market value of the investment security. The investment carrying amount is the market value of the investment security. Thus, the determination of investment revenue and carrying amounts for the above example using the market value method would be as follows:

	Pear Co.	Apple Inc.
Original investment:		
Pear: 100 shares × $15/shares	$1,500	
Apple: 200 shares × $11/share		$2,200

EXHIBIT 14-5   Four Methods of Accounting for Investments

	Cost Method	LCM Method	Equity Method	Market Method
Original investment:				
Pear	$1,500	$1,500	$1,500	$1,500
Apple	2,200	2,200	2,200	2,200
Total	$3,700	$3,700	$3,700	$3,700
Investment income for fiscal 1991:				
Pear	$ 100	$ 100	$ 200	$ 300
Apple	150		300	(150)
LCM Adjustment		(100)		
Total	$ 250	$ 150	$ 500	$ 150
Cash received from investment securities:				
Pear	$ 100	$ 100	$ 100	$ 100
Apple	150	150	150	150
Total	$ 250	$ 250	$ 250	$ 250
Change in investment carrying amount:				
Pear	$ 0	$ 0	$ 100	$ 200
Apple	0	*(0)	150	(300)
Total	$ 0	($100)	$ 250	(100)
Investment carrying amount at 12/31/91:				
Pear	$1,500	$1,500	$1,600	$1,700
Apple	2,200†	2,200	2,350†	1,900
Total	$3,700	$3,600*	$3,950	$3,600

* Under the LCM method, the write-down and decrease in carrying amount is computed for the aggregate value of the portfolio of investment securities and is not associated with any one security.

† Assume that the market value of the Apple, which is currently less than the carrying amount shown under this method, is not permanently impaired. If it were determined to be permanently impaired, there would be a write-down to market value.

Compute Investment Income

Add: Dividends received:		
Pear: $1.00 per share × 100 shares	100	
Apple: $0.75 per share × 200 shares		150
Add: Change in market value		
Pear: ($17/share − $15/share) × 100 shares	200	
Apple: ($9.50/share − $11/share) × 200 shares		(300)
Total investment income	$ 300	($150)
Investment carrying amount at 12/31/91		
Pear: $17/share × 100 shares	$1,700	
Apple: $9.50/share × 200 shares		$1,900

Thus, the total carrying amount for the investment at December 31 is $3,600. The investment income for the year totals $150, which equals the $250 in dividends received less the net reduction in market value of the two investment securities of $100.

The results of using the four different methods in this problem are summarized in Exhibit 14–5. There are considerably different results depending on which method is used and on what changes occur in the market values of the investment securities.

APPENDIX 14A: Consolidated Financial Statements

This appendix presents the fundamental concepts of **consolidated financial statements.** The complexities involved are deferred to advanced texts that develop this topic. *APB Opinion No. 16,* "Business Combinations," provides the basic accounting guidelines for consolidated financial statements. Consolidation of the financial statements of a parent company and a subsidiary is only a reporting procedure; therefore, it does not affect the accounts of either the parent company or the subsidiary. Consolidated financial statements are prepared only by the parent company, not by the subsidiary.

CONCEPT OF A CONTROLLING INTEREST

♦

When an investor company owns over 50% of the outstanding voting stock of another company, in the absence of overriding constraints, a controlling interest exists. The investor company is called the *parent* company. The second company is called a *subsidiary* company. In a parent-subsidiary relationship, both corporations continue as separate legal entities; therefore, they are separate accounting entities (refer to separate entity assumption, chapter 2). As separate entities, they have separate accounting systems and separate financial statements. However, because of the controlling ownership relationship, the parent company (but not the subsidiary) may be required to prepare consolidated financial statements. In consolidated financial statements the parent and the subsidiary (or subsidiaries) are viewed by accountants as a single economic entity. Thus, the parent company may prepare two sets of financial statements: one set as a separate entity, and another set as a consolidated entity. To prepare consolidated financial statements, the separate financial statements of the parent and subsidiary are combined each period by the parent company into one overall (i.e., consolidated) set of financial statements as if they were a single entity. The income statement, balance sheet, and statement of cash flows (SCF) are consolidated in this manner.

Consolidated financial statements are not always prepared when over 50% of the stock of another corporation is owned because certain constraints may preclude the exercise of a controlling interest. Consolidation as a single economic entity is required by *SFAS No. 94,* "Consolidation of All Majority Owned Subsidiaries" (October 1987), which defines control and exceptions:

1. *Control of voting rights*—Control is presumed to exist when more than 50% of the outstanding voting stock of another entity is owned by the investor. Nonvoting stock is excluded from consideration because control is not possible without the vote. However, there is one exception. A subsidiary that is more than 50% owned in certain circumstances and does not qualify for consolidation is called an *unconsolidated subsidiary.* In this case the investment is reported using (*a*) the equity method, if there is significant influence, and (*b*) the cost method if there is neither control nor significant influence.

2. *Exception to the general rule—SFAS No. 94* states that " a majority-owned subsidiary shall not be consolidated if control is likely to be temporary or if it does not rest with the majority owner (as, for instance, if the subsidiary is in legal reorganization or in bankruptcy or operates under foreign exchange restrictions, controls, or other governmentally imposed uncertainties so severe that they cast significant doubt on the parent's ability to control the subsidiary)." All other majority-owned subsidiaries must be consolidated.

ACQUIRING A CONTROLLING INTEREST

♦

A company accounts for the acquisition of a controlling interest in the voting stock of another company in one of two conceptually different ways:

1. *Pooling of interests*—The parent company acquires the voting stock of an existing corporation by exchanging shares of its own capital stock for shares of the subsidiary. In this case, the parent disburses relatively little cash or other assets and incurs no new liabilities in the acquisition. The owners of the acquiring firm and of the acquired firm become the owners of the combined firm. For example, the 1988 financial statements of Dun & Bradstreet Corporation included the following note (partial):

Note 3 (In Part): Acquisitions
On May 26, 1988, the Company issued shares of its common stock in exchange for all the outstanding shares of IMS common stock. This transaction was accounted for as a pooling-of-interests and, accordingly, the accompanying financial statements relating to prior periods have been restated to include the accounts of IMS.

2. *Purchase*—The parent company acquires the voting stock of an existing corporation primarily by paying cash, transferring noncash assets, or incurring debt. In this situation, the parent disburses a significant amount of resources. The owners of the acquired firm receive cash and other resources; they do not necessarily maintain an ownership interest in the combined firm. For example, the 1987 financial statements of Gerber Products Company included the following note (partial):

On July 31, 1986, the Company, through a subsidiary, Soft Care Apparel, Inc., purchased certain assets of the Baby Products Division of The Kendall Company, a subsidiary of the Colgate-Palmolive Company, for $58,403,000 in cash. The acquired assets include the manufacturing and marketing operations for infant-wear, bedding, sleepers and cloth diapers sold under the Curity label. In fiscal 1987, the Company also acquired six children's centers for cash.

All of the acquisitions have been accounted for as purchases and, accordingly, the consolidated statements of operations include the acquired businesses from their respective dates of acquisition.

ACCOUNTING AND REPORTING
◆

GAAP requires that each subsidiary prepare its own financial statements. However, the parent company is required to prepare consolidated financial statements. These statements include all subsidiaries except those designated as unconsolidated subsidiaries. The parent, not the subsidiary, prepares consolidated statements. Consolidated financial statements include an item-by-item combination (aggregation) of the parent and subsidiary statements. For example, the amount of cash shown on a consolidated statement is the sum of the amounts of cash shown on the separate statements of the parent and the subsidiaries.

While consolidated financial statements are the means by which a controlling interest is reported, the parent company records the investment in unconsolidated subsidiaries using the cost or equity method. The cost method is often used in the accounts because the parent company does not desire to formally enter into its accounts the income, dividend offset, additional depreciation, amortization of goodwill, and so on, required by the equity method.[14] Also, the accounting periods of the parent and the subsidiary may be different. Changes in percentage of ownership complicate the equity method. Frequently, when a company moves from the equity method range (i.e., 20% to 50%) to a controlling interest range (over 50%), it adjusts the accounts from the equity to the cost basis. For practical reasons, the illustrations use the cost method of accounting for the investment.

The consolidated statements are developed using a consolidation work sheet. The consolidation procedures can be adapted on the worksheet so that the results are the same whether the cost or equity method is used in the accounts of the parent company. The consolidated financial statements are prepared from these worksheets.

This section focuses on the preparation of consolidated financial statements. When preparing consolidated financial statements, the method of acquisition—pooling of interests versus purchase—has a significant impact both on the parent company and on the consolidated statements.

Before discussing the pooling of interests and purchase methods, the steps necessary to prepare the consolidation worksheet are discussed. These steps refer to worksheet entries and the resulting consolidated financial statements, not to the journals and ledgers of the separate legal entities involved. These steps are:

---

[14] The equity method is called *one-line consolidation.* Instead of a line-by-line consolidation of the individual accounts, the equity method does the equivalent in a single account labeled "equity in earnings of subsidiaries."

1. Enter the separate financial statements of the parent and each subsidiary on the worksheet, using one column for each entity. Additional column headings are provided for "eliminations" and "consolidated statements."
2. The assets and liabilities of the subsidiary are substituted for the investment account reflected on the books of the parent. This substitution is accomplished on the worksheet by eliminating the owners' equity accounts of the subsidiary against the investment account of the parent.
3. Intercompany receivables are eliminated.
4. Intercompany revenues, expenses, gains, and losses are eliminated.
5. Other intercompany items are eliminated as appropriate.
6. For purchased subsidiaries, adjustments are made on the worksheet to reflect market values that differ from the book values, such as goodwill purchased as part of the cost of the investment in the subsidiary.
7. The remaining revenues and expenses of the parent and subsidiary are combined on the worksheet to derive a consolidated income statement.
8. The assets and liabilities of the parent and subsidiary are combined to derive a consolidated balance sheet.
9. The cash inflows and outflows of the parent and subsidiary are combined on a separate worksheet to derive a consolidated statement of cash flows (SCF).

Consolidated financial statements usually are prepared at the date of acquisition of a controlling interest (balance sheet only) and for each accounting period subsequent to acquisition (income statement, balance sheet, and statement of cash flows). The consolidation worksheet and resulting financial statements are influenced by the way the consolidation is recorded, that is, whether by pooling of interests or by purchase.

Combination by Pooling of Interests

The acquisition of a controlling interest by the parent company in the stock of a subsidiary company by an exchange of shares of stock often occurs because the combination can be effected without the disbursement of cash or other resources by the parent company. The exchange of shares is viewed as the uniting of ownership interests (and not as a purchase/sale transaction) between the parent company and the stockholders of the subsidiary company. Therefore, the recorded assets, liabilities, revenues, expenses, and so forth, for both entities are combined for consolidated statement purposes at their recorded book values. The income of the parent and its subsidiaries are combined and restated as consolidated income. Because a purchase/sale transaction is not presumed when shares of stock are exchanged, market values of the assets of the subsidiary are not used in consolidation on the pooling of interests basis.

APB Opinion No. 16, "Business Combinations" (par. 47), states, "the combining of existing voting common stock interests by the exchange of stock is the essence of . . . [a] pooling of interests." The *Opinion* specifies 12 conditions (not given here) that must be met in order for the pooling of interests method to be appropriate. If they are met, the pooling of interests method *must* be used. Combinations not meeting all 12 specifications must use the purchase method. Because of these 12 conditions, not all pure stock exchanges meet the criteria for pooling of interests.

The general characteristics of the pooling of interests method of preparing consolidated statements may be summarized as follows:

1. The parent company must acquire 90% or more of the voting shares of the subsidiary.
2. The assets and liabilities of the combining companies are reported at the previously established book values of both the parent and the subsidiary. Although adjustments may be made to reflect consistent application of accounting principles, the current market values of the assets of the subsidiary at the time of the combination are not used as a substitute for their book values at that date.
3. No purchased goodwill results from the combination.
4. The retained earnings balances of the combining companies are, with minor exceptions, added to determine the retained earnings balance of the consolidated company at date of acquisition.
5. After combination, comparative financial statements that pertain to precombination periods must be restated on the combined basis as if the companies were consolidated throughout those periods.

Preparing a Consolidated Balance Sheet Immediately after Acquisition—Pooling of Interests Method
Exhibit 14A-1 shows the preparation of a consolidated balance sheet immediately after acquisition. In this case, there was an exchange of shares of a 90% voting interest that qualifies as a pooling of interests. Exhibit 14A-1 illustrates the worksheet used to prepare the consolidated balance sheet immediately after the combination.

In Exhibit 14A-1, the worksheet is begun by entering the two separate balance sheets, using *book values* for each company immediately after the acquisition entry. Notice that two account balances on the Company P balance sheet (i.e., the investment and parent common stock accounts) reflect the acquisition entry. The worksheet is designed to provide an orderly procedure for combining the two separate balance sheets into a consolidated statement (the last column). The pair of columns for eliminations is used to prevent double counting of reciprocal items; that is, transactions that are strictly between the two companies must be eliminated because there is now one entity. In this instance, two reciprocal items must be eliminated:

1. The investment account balance reflected on the balance sheet of Company P ($90,000) must be eliminated. In its place, the various assets and liabilities of Company S are added to those of the parent. Similarly, 90% of the common stock reported by Company S must be eliminated. It now is owned by the parent company. Thus, elimination entry (*a*) on the worksheet offsets the investment account balance on the balance sheet of the parent against the capital stock account reflected on the balance sheet of the subsidiary.

2. Intercompany debt—Current liabilities of Company S include a $5,000 account payable owed to Company P; therefore, accounts receivable on the balance sheet of Company P includes this amount. When the two balance sheets are combined, this intercompany debt must be eliminated because it is not a payable or receivable involving the combined entity and an outside entity. Elimination entry (*b*) on the worksheet accomplishes this offset.

After the elimination entries for all intercompany items are reflected on the worksheet, the two balance sheets are aggregated line by line. The 10% interest of the **minority stockholders** of Company S represented by their proportionate share of the stockholders' equity of the subsidiary company is set out separately (denoted by M). Minority interest is a liability for the consolidated entity. The last column of the worksheet provides the data needed to prepare a consolidated balance sheet. The book values of Company S are added to the book values of Company P. The market values do not affect the reporting for a combination by pooling of interests.

Combination by Purchase

The acquisition of a controlling interest by purchase occurs when the combination does not meet all 12 conditions specified by *APB Opinion No. 16* for a pooling of interests. Typically, an acquisition by purchase occurs when the parent company acquires a controlling interest in the subsidiary company by purchasing the voting stock from the subsidiary's stockholders primarily with cash and noncash assets. This situation is viewed as a purchase/sale transaction. Therefore, market values related to the subsidiary must be introduced into the consolidation procedures in conformity with the cost principle. *APB Opinion No. 16* (par 66) states: "Accounting for a business combination by the purchase method follows the principles normally applicable under historical cost accounting to recording acquisitions of assets and issuances of stock and to accounting for assets and liabilities after acquisition." This quote means that, at acquisition date, the parent company must debit the investment account for the market value of the shares of the subsidiary acquired. The parent company pays market value for the investment. The significant implication of this requirement is that in preparing consolidated statements, the assets of the subsidiary (including any purchased goodwill) must be valued by the parent company at their market values at date of acquisition before being aggregated with the book values of the assets of the parent company.[15]

---

[15] In a pooling of interests, book values rather than market values of the subsidiary are used in consolidation.

EXHIBIT 14A-1   Consolidated Balance Sheet, Company P (parent) and Company S (subsidiary), Pooling of Interests Method, Immediately after Acquisition of a 90% Controlling Interest by Company P

1. Company P issues 900 shares of its $100 par common stock to the stockholders of Company S for 900 of the 1,000 outstanding shares of Company S common stock, par $100. This is an exchange of shares (a continuity of the previously existing ownership). Assume that it meets the 12 conditions (specified in *APB Opinion No. 16*) for pooling of interests (including the criterion which requires at least 90% ownership). Company S will continue as a separate legal entity and as a 90% owned subsidiary of Company P. As a result of the transaction, Company P immediately makes the following acquisition entry:

Investment in Company S common stock (90% ownership)* 90,000
    Common stock (900 shares at $100 par) 90,000

* Because the acquisition under the pooling of interests concept is not viewed as a purchase/sale transaction, it is variously recorded at (*a*) par value of the stock issued, (*b*) the proportionate share acquired of the subsidiary's contributed capital, or (*c*) the proportionate book value of the subsidiary acquired. Some accountants prefer to use average contributed capital per share. This is a minor, but unsettled, issue. In any case, the elimination entry is adapted to attain the pooling of interests results.

2. Immediately after the exchange, the respective balance sheets reflect the following:

		Company S				
Assets	Company P Book Value	Book Value	Market Value	Liabilities and Owner's Equity†	Company P Book Value	Company S Book Value
Cash	$610,000	$ 20,000	$ 20,000	Current liabilities	$ 10,000	$ 20,000*
Accounts receivable (net)	10,000*	40,000	40,000	Long-term liabilities	50,000	40,000
				Common stock		
Inventories	20,000	30,000	25,000	(par $100)	690,000	100,000
Investment in Co. S	90,000			Retained earnings	200,000	50,000
Plant and equipment (net)	200,000	110,000	151,000			
Patents (net)	20,000	10,000	14,000			
	$950,000	$210,000	$250,000		$950,000	$210,000

* At date of acquisition, Company S owed Company P $5,000 accounts payable.
† S Company liabilities at book value are equal to their market value.

Worksheet to Develop Consolidated Balance Sheet

Account	Balance Sheet per Books		Eliminations		Consolidated Balance Sheet
	Company P	Company S	Debit	Credit	
Cash	610,000	20,000			630,000
Accounts receivable (net)	10,000	40,000		(*b*) 5,000	45,000
Inventories	20,000	30,000			50,000
Investment in Company S	90,000*			(*a*) 90,000	
Plant and equipment (net)	200,000	110,000			310,000
Patents (net)	20,000	10,000			30,000
	950,000	210,000			1,065,000
Current liabilities	10,000	20,000	(*b*) 5,000		25,000
Long-term liabilities	50,000	40,000			90,000
Common stock (par $100):					
Company P	690,000*				690,000
Company S		100,000	(*a*) 90,000		10,000M
Retained earnings:					
Company P	200,000				245,000
Company S		50,000			5,000M
	950,000	210,000			1,065,000

M—minority stockholders' 10% interest in Company S.

* Includes effect of acquisition entry of $90,000.

Eliminations:
  (*a*) To eliminate the investment account balance against the stockholders' equity (90%) of the subsidiary.
  (*b*) To eliminate the intercompany debt of $5,000.

Although there are numerous additional complexities in application of the *purchase method,* the general characteristics may be outlined as follows:

1. On the consolidated balance sheet, the assets and liabilities of the subsidiary are reported by the parent company at *cost* on the date of acquisition in conformity with the cost principle. Thus, the investment equals the *market value of the stock acquired.* It also is the cost of the net assets of the subsidiary purchased by the parent.
2. Individual assets of the subsidiary are reported at their individual market values as of the date of acquisition. These include all identifiable tangible and intangible assets (receivables, inventory, land, equipment, patents, etc.). Liabilities of the subsidiary are also reported at their equivalent market values.
3. At acquisition date, the difference between the total purchase cost and the market value of the identifiable tangible and intangible assets acquired (less the subsidiary's liabilities) represents an unidentifiable asset. This difference is reported as goodwill. Goodwill from the acquisition is subsequently amortized as an expense on the parent's consolidated income statement.
4. Immediately after acquisition by purchase, the retained earnings balance of the combined entity is defined as the retained earnings balance of the parent company only. Thus, the retained earnings balance of the subsidiary is eliminated and, as a consequence, is not reported on the consolidated balance sheet.
5. After combination by purchase, comparative financial statements of precombination periods must be reported on a consolidated basis.

Preparation of Consolidated Balance Sheet Immediately after Acquisition, Purchase Method Exhibit 14A–2 shows the preparation of a consolidated balance sheet on the purchase basis immediately after acquisition. Except for the method of acquisition, Exhibit 14A–2 is based upon the same data for Company P and Company S in Exhibit 14A–1.

In order to prepare the worksheet, the amount of goodwill purchased must be determined. Goodwill is computed as the difference between the purchase price paid by the parent and the market values of the identifiable net assets of the subsidiary. Also, notice that in Exhibit 14A–1, items in (2) have market values different from their book values.

The worksheet shown in Exhibit 14A–2, is started by entering the two balance sheets using amounts immediately after the acquisition entry. Two accounts (cash and investments) on Company P balance sheets reflect the acquisition entry. Also, the middle pair of columns are called "eliminations and restatements" because restatement entries must be made to change the assets of Company S from book value to market value for the proportionate part of the market value purchased by Company P. This is entry (*a*) on the worksheet. Elimination entries must also be made for intercompany items; entries (*b*) and (*c*) on the worksheet. The computations of these amounts are given in Exhibit 14A–2, items 3*a* and 3*b*. The computations indicate that inventories must be reduced by $4,500; plant and equipment increased by $36,900; patents increased by $3,600; and goodwill recorded in the amount of $40,000. The goodwill amount reflects the excess of cost over market value of each of these items acquired by Company P.[16] The net offset for these amounts is recorded in the investment account as an elimination because that account was debited at acquisition for the market value of the net assets acquired.

The worksheet is completed by extending each item horizontally, considering the eliminations and restatements. The last column gives all of the data needed to prepare a consolidated balance sheet on the purchase basis.

A comparison of Exhibit 14A–1 (pooling of interests) with Exhibit 14A–2 (purchase) reflects three underlying conceptual differences. The first difference is that in a pooling of interests, the book values of the subsidiary are added to the book values of the parent, whereas in a purchase, the proportionate share of the market values of subsidiary assets at acquisition are added to the book values of the parent. The second difference is that goodwill is not recognized in a pooling of interests; in contrast, goodwill usually is recognized in a purchase. The third difference is the treatment of retained earnings in the consolidation. In a pooling of interests, owners before the acquisition transaction continue as owners after the

---

[16] In computing goodwill (see Exhibit 14A–2, case data item 3*a*), if the total purchase cost is less than the parents' pro rata share of summed market values of the individual assets of the subsidiary less liabilities, negative goodwill occurs. Negative goodwill should be allocated to reduce the purchase cost (i.e., market estimates) of the identifiable tangible and intangible assets.

EXHIBIT 14A-2   Consolidated Balance Sheet, Company P (parent) and Company S (subsidiary), Purchase Method; Immediately after Acquisition of a 90% Controlling Interest by Company P

Case Data

1. Company P purchased, in the open market, 90% of the 1,000 shares of outstanding voting stock of Company S for $211,000 cash. Company P recorded the acquisition as follows:

Investment in Company S common stock (90% ownership) . . . 211,000
Cash   211,000

2. The balance sheet items of Company S with different book and market values given in 3.*b.* below (first 2 columns). This is the same data given in Exhibit 14A–1.
3. Analysis of the purchase:
   a. Computation of goodwill purchased by Company P:
   Purchase price for 90% interest in Company S $211,000
   Market value of 90% of the identifiable *net* assets purchased:
      Total market value of identifiable assets of Company S (Exhibit 14A–1) $250,000
      Less: total liabilities of Company S (Exhibit 14A–1) . . . .   (60,000)

      Total market value of identifiable net assets of Company S   190,000
      Proportional part purchased by Company P . . . .   × .90
      Market value of 90% of the identifiable net assets purchased   171,000

   Goodwill purchased (90%) . . . . $ 40,000

   b. Proportionate part of each asset of Company S adjusted to market value (i.e., parent's cost) as of date of combination:

	Parent's cost (Market Value)		Subsidiary's Book Value	Proportionate Part of Excess of Cost (Market) Over Book Value
Inventory	$ 25,000	–	$ 30,000	× .90 = $(4,500)*
Plant and equipment	151,000	–	110,000	× .90 = 36,900
Patents	14,000	–	10,000	× .90 = 3,600
Goodwill (per above)	40,000	–	—0—	40,000
Total (see worksheet entry [*a*] below)				$76,000

* Parent's cost (i.e., market value) is less than subsidiary's book value.

transaction. Therefore, the retained earnings of both companies are combined to derive consolidated retained earnings. In a purchase acquisition, the parent company buys the subsidiary shares, and the prior owners do not continue as owners. Therefore, the consolidated retained earnings are limited to the parent company's retained earnings. This can be observed in Exhibit 14A–1 (retained earnings, $245,000) and Exhibit 14A–2 ($200,000). These three basic differences are maintained in the consolidated financial statements of all subsequent periods.

This appendix provides an introduction to consolidated financial statements. This discussion is important for students who may not take the advanced accounting course on consolidated statements.

Consolidated statements are prepared (by the parent company) when the parent company has a controlling interest in another company (called a subsidiary). A controlling interest exists for accounting purposes when the parent company owns more than 50% of the outstanding voting stock of the subsidiary; the only exception to this basic rule is when control is likely to be temporary or if it does not rest with the majority owner.

Consolidated statements basically involve aggregation on a line-by-line basis of the assets, liabilities, equity, revenues and gains, and expenses and losses of the parent and subsidiary. The manner of acquisition—by pooling (an exchange of shares) or by purchase (using assets to acquire the subsidiary's shares)—has a significant impact on the consolidated statements. Consolidation of the financial statements of a parent company and a subsidiary is a reporting procedure only. This procedure does not affect the accounts of either the parent or the

EXHIBIT 14A–2   *(concluded)*

	Worksheet to Develop Consolidated Balance Sheet				
	Balance Sheet from Accounts		Eliminations and Restatements		Consolidated Balance Sheet
Account	Company P	Company S	Debit	Credit	
Cash	399,000*	20,000			419,000
Accounts receivable (net)	10,000	40,000		(c) 5,000	45,000
Inventories	20,000	30,000		(a) 4,500	45,500
Investment in Company S	211,000*			⎰(a) 76,000	
				⎱(b) 135,000	
Plant and equipment (net)	200,000	110,000	(a) 36,900		346,900
Patents (net)	20,000	10,000	(a) 3,600		33,600
Goodwill			(a) 40,000		40,000
	860,000	210,000			930,000
Current liabilities	10,000	20,000	(c) 5,000		25,000
Long-term liabilities	50,000	40,000			90,000
Common stock:					
Company P	600,000				600,000
Company S		100,000	(b) 90,000		10,000M
Retained earnings:					
Company P	200,000				200,000
Company S		50,000	(b) 45,000		5,000M
	860,000	210,000			930,000

M—minority stockholders' 10% interest in Company S.

* Includes effects of acquisition entry of ($610,000 − $211,000 = $399,000).

Elminations and restatements:
   (a) To record the restatement of assets to market value and to eliminate the net effect from the investment account (case data, item 3b).
   (b) To eliminate the proportionate part of the stockholders' equity of the subsidiary (90%) and to eliminate an equal amount from the investment account (which now must be zero). Entries (a) and (b) may be combined.
   (c) To eliminate the intercompany payable/receivable of $5,000.

subsidiary. Consolidated statements are prepared only by the parent company and not by the subsidiary. This appendix shows typical consolidation worksheets used to prepare the consolidated balance sheets as of the date of acquisition. Preparing consolidated financial statements subsequent to the date of acquisition is beyond the scope of this text. The effect on the income of the parent, however, is the same as that resulting from using the equity method described in the chapter.

APPENDIX 14B: *Other Unusual Investments and Funds*

Appendix 14B covers accounting for several unusual types of investments. These include special-purpose funds, cash surrender value of life insurance, and futures contracts.

SPECIAL-PURPOSE FUNDS AS LONG-TERM INVESTMENTS

Companies sometimes set aside cash and sometimes other assets, in special funds (special-purpose funds) to be used in the future for a specific, designated purpose. Although a special-purpose fund can be a current asset, it is more commonly a noncurrent asset. As such, it is not directly related to current operations. Long-term funds are reported on the balance sheet under the noncurrent classification under the caption "investments and funds."

Funds may be set aside (1) by contract, as in the case of a bond sinking fund; (2) by law, as in the case of rent deposits; or (3) voluntarily, as in the case of a plant expansion fund. The following are typical examples of long-term special-purpose funds:

1. Funds set aside to retire a specific long-term liability, such as bonds payable, mortgages payable, long-term notes payable.
2. Funds set aside to purchase preferred stock.
3. Funds set aside to purchase major assets, such as land, buildings, and plant.

Typically, special-purpose funds are deposited with an independent trustee, such as a financial institution, which agrees to pay a specified rate of interest each period on the balance in the fund. A typical fund is illustrated in Exhibit 14B–1. Special purpose funds are generally disclosed in the notes to the financial statements.

CASH SURRENDER VALUE OF LIFE INSURANCE
◆

Often a firm will insure the lives of its top executives, with the firm as the beneficiary. If the firm should lose the services of one of the insured individuals from an untimely death, it is compensated for having lost one of its valuable resources. There are three types of life insurance policies a firm might acquire on the lives of its executives: (1) ordinary or whole-life, (2) limited payment, and (3) term insurance. Whole-life and limited payment insurance policies build up value while the policy is in force and have stipulated loan values and cash surrender values. Term insurance, however, has no cash surrender value or loan value since the insurance company is not obligated to make payment except in the event of the death of the insured during the term of the policy.

The **cash surrender value (CSV)** of a policy is the amount that would be refunded should the policy be terminated at the request of the insured. It increases over time as the firm pays the insurance premium; thus, it is an asset for the firm. CSV is a form of investment and is usually accounted for on the balance sheet under investments and funds.

The cash surrender value is computed at the end of each year the policy is in force. Each policy contains a schedule that indicates the cash surrender value and the loan value for each policy year. Because a portion of the premiums paid may be returned in the form of the cash surrender value if and when a policy is canceled, only a portion of the periodic premiums are actually expensed. The firm's period life insurance expense is the excess of the premium paid over the increase in the cash surrender value for the period.

To illustrate, assume Zim Corporation took out a $100,000 whole-life policy on its top executive several years ago. In 1992, which is the fourth year the policy has been in effect, the firm pays an insurance premium in the amount of $2,200. The cash surrender value schedule for the policy shows the following:

Policy Year	Premium	Cash Surrender Value
1	$2,200	0
2	2,200	0
3	2,200	500
4	2,200	1,500
5	2,200	2,600

Based on the above information, the premium of $2,200 paid in Year 4 results in an increase in the cash surrender value of $1,000. This portion would be debited to an account called "cash surrender value of life insurance," with the remainder being recorded as expense:

Life insurance expense	1,200	
Cash surrender value of life insurance	1,000	
Cash		2,200

At the end of Year 4, the cash surrender value of the policy totals $1,500, and this is the amount that should appear in the asset account called "cash surrender value of life insurance."

EXHIBIT 14B-1   Accounting for a Special-Purpose Fund: WT Corporation

1. WT Corporation plans to build a new office building five years hence. The plans estimate the total construction cost to be $1,300,000 and a six-month construction period.
2. The company decided to make five $200,000 cash deposits to a special construction fund each July 1, starting on July 1, 1991. The fund will be administered by an independent trustee. The trustee will increase the fund each June 30 at a 10% interest rate on the fund balance at that date.
3. WT Corporation's accounting period ends December 31.
4. The office building was completed on schedule, the contractor was paid $1,300,000 on July 2, 1996, and the fund was closed.

Fund Accumulation Schedule (Annuity Due Basis)

Date	Cash Deposits	Interest revenue Earned			Fund Increases	Fund Balance
7/1/1991	$ 200,000				$ 200,000	$ 200,000
6/30/1992		$ 200,000	× 10% =	$ 20,000	20,000	220,000
7/1/1992	200,000				200,000	420,000
6/30/1993		420,000	× 10% =	42,000	42,000	462,000
7/1/1993	200,000				200,000	662,000
6/30/1994		662,000	× 10% =	66,200	66,200	728,200
7/1/1994	200,000				200,000	928,200
6/30/1995		928,200	× 10% =	92,820	92,820	1,021,020
7/1/1995	200,000				200,000	1,221,020
6/30/1996		1,221,020	× 10% =	122,102	122,102	1,343,122
	$1,000,000			$343,122	$1,343,122	

Selected Journal Entries: First Year and Final Payment

```
7/1/1991:
        Special building fund . . . . . . . . . . . . . . . . . . . . . . .   200,000
            Cash  . . . . . . . . . . . . . . . . . . . . . . . . . . . . .            200,000
12/31/1991:
        Receivable on building fund . . . . . . . . . . . . . . . . . .    10,000
            Interest revenue ($20,000 × 6/12) . . . . . . . . . . . . .             10,000
6/30/1992:
        Special building fund . . . . . . . . . . . . . . . . . . . . . .    20,000
            Receivable on building fund . . . . . . . . . . . . . . . . .            10,000
            Interest revenue . . . . . . . . . . . . . . . . . . . . . . .            10,000
7/1/1992:
        Special building fund . . . . . . . . . . . . . . . . . . . . . .   200,000
            Cash  . . . . . . . . . . . . . . . . . . . . . . . . . . . . .            200,000
7/2/1996:
        Cash  . . . . . . . . . . . . . . . . . . . . . . . . . . . . . . .    43,122
        Office building  . . . . . . . . . . . . . . . . . . . . . . . . .  1,300,000
            Special building fund . . . . . . . . . . . . . . . . . . . . .          1,343,122
```

Assume that the insured executive dies on April 1, Year 4, after the above premium has been paid and recorded. The provisions of most policies call for the refunding of any premiums paid beyond the life of the insured. Assuming that the policy anniversary date is January 1, and that the $2,200 premium paid on that date was for the entire year, the refund is $2,200 × (9/12), or $1,650. The insurance company makes payment to Zim Corporation of the face amount of the policy ($100,000) plus the refund amount ($1,650). Zim Corporation recognized insurance expense of $1,200 for the year. Since the policy is in effect only three months before the insured dies, the expense recovery is for three-fourths of the year, or $900. A portion of the $100,000 is the payment of the cash surrender value, and the remainder is a gain:

```
Cash . . . . . . . . . . . . . . . . . . . . . . . . . . . . . . . . . . . 101,650
    Life insurance expense . . . . . . . . . . . . . . . . . . . . . . .        900
    Cash surrender value of life insurance . . . . . . . . . . . .      1,500
    Gain on settlement of life insurance indemnity . . . . . . . .    99,250
```

The gain on life insurance is not usually considered to be extraordinary. The cash surrender value of life insurance policies is reported in the balance sheet as a long-term investment. Insurance premiums on which the company is the beneficiary are not deductible for tax purposes. The proceeds received from the policy payout are also not taxable income.

ACCOUNTING FOR FUTURES CONTRACTS—AN INVESTMENT

Business entities and other investors often purchase **futures contracts** as an investment or as a hedge to offset the risks of future price changes. A futures contract is a contract between a buyer and seller of a commodity or financial instrument and the clearinghouse of a futures exchange. Futures contracts vary; however, such contracts have three common characteristics:

1. They obligate the buyer (seller) to accept (make delivery of) a commodity or financial instrument at a specified time, or they provide for cash settlement periodically rather than delivery.
2. They can be effectively canceled before the specified time by entering into an offsetting contract for the same commodity or financial instrument.
3. All changes in the market value of open contracts are settled on a regular basis, usually daily.

SFAS No. 80 specifies two approaches for recording and reporting futures contracts. The two approaches are called the *market-value* approach and the *hedge-deferral* approach. The primary issue in accounting for a futures contract is whether changes in the market value of a futures contract should be recognized as a gain or loss in the reporting period when the market price changes take place, or whether the gain or loss should be deferred to a later date. *SFAS No. 80* specifies two criteria for determining the accounting approach for futures contracts:

1. The item to be hedged exposes the company to market price or interest rate risk.
2. The futures contract reduces that risk and is designated as a hedge.

The market-value approach must be used when the hedge fails to meet both of these criteria. The market-value approach requires that all gains and losses due to market price changes be recognized in the reporting period when the market price changes.

The hedge-deferral approach must be used when one or both criteria are met. The hedge-deferral approach requires that all gains or losses due to market price changes be deferred and recognized at the termination of the futures contract as an adjustment to the cost (or price) in the subsequent terminating transaction.

A simplified futures contract example is used to illustrate these approaches. Suppose the Rye Company is a producer of a grain-based product. The following events occur:

October 1991—The company determined that it needs 10,000 bushels of grain near the end of February 1992. The company expects the current price of $3 per bushel of grain to change. It does not want to assume the risk of such market price changes.

November 1, 1991—The company decides to purchase a futures contract from Chicago Clearing House Inc. to hedge (i.e., shift) the risk of market price changes of grain. The futures contract, which costs $800, provides that the company purchase the grain at the date needed at the then current market price (or pay the equivalent amount in cash if the grain is not purchased). However, between the date the futures contract is purchased (November 1, 1991) and the termination date (when the grain is purchased), Chicago Clearing House Inc. must pay the company cash for all market price increases (from the $3 beginning hedge price), and will collect cash from the company for all market price decreases (again, from the hedge price of $3). Thus, for an $800 fee, the company shifts the risk of market price changes to the clearinghouse. Changes in the market price of grain are settled daily, and each offset is payable or collectible each weekend.

December 31, 1991—At the end of the reporting period for Rye Company, the market price of grain is $2.80 per bushel.

EXHIBIT 14B–2 Illustration of Entries for Accounting for Futures Contract under the Market-Value Approach and Hedge-Deferral Approach

Market-Value Approach		Hedge-Deferral Approach	

November 1, 1991—to record the futures contract:

Prepaid expense, futures contract	800		Prepaid expense, futures contract	800	
Cash		800	Cash		800

December 31, 1991—To record cash payment to clearinghouse because of the market price decrease in grain:

Loss on futures contract	2,000		Inventory cost adjustment, futures contract	2,000	
Cash		2,000	Cash		2,000

The $2,000 is the change in price ($3.00 less the current price of $2.80) times the number of bushels, 10,000. The loss on futures contract is closed to the income statement. The inventory cost adjustment is reported as a deferred charge on the balance sheet.

February 24, 1992—To record the cash payment received from the clearing house due to the market price increase in grain:

Cash	5,000		Cash	5,000	
Gain on futures contract		5,000	Inventory cost adjustment, futures contract		5,000

The payment is computed as the price change since December 31 ($3.30 − $2.80) times the 10,000 bushels covered by the futures contract.

To record the purchase of grain:

Grain inventory	33,000		Grain inventory	30,000	
Cash		33,000	Inventory cost adjustment, futures contract	3,000	
			Cash		33,000

To record termination of the futures contract:

Expenses, futures contract	800		Expense, futures contract	800	
Prepaid expense, futures contract		800	Prepaid expense, futures contract		800

Futures contract results:

Cash inflow		$5,000	Cash inflow		$5,000
Cash outflow		2,000	Cash outflow		2,000
Net gain		$3,000	Net gain		$3,000

In sum, Rye Company has transferred the risk of price changes for grain to the clearinghouse. Under the market value approach, the gain is explicitly recognized, and the grain acquired is recorded at its current cost. Under the hedge-deferral approach, the gain is not explicitly recognized. Rather, the grain is recorded at the cost that was assured by the futures contract, $30,000. In either case the firm is $3,000 better off.

February 24, 1992—At this date (*a*) The market price of grains is $3.30, (*b*) Rye Company purchases the 10,000 bushels of grain needed for production at $3.30 per bushel, cash, and (*c*) The futures contract is terminated.

Exhibit 14B–2 presents the required entries under two cases: (1) neither criterion is met (therefore the market-value approach is used), and (2) one or both criteria are met (therefore the hedge-deferral approach is used).

KEY TERMS

Cash surrender value (740)
Consolidated financial statements (732)
Cost Method (707)
Equity Method (708)
Financial instrument (721)
Futures contracts (742)
Lower of cost or market (LCM) method (697)

Market Value method (717)
Minority stockholders (735)
Pooling of interests method (732)
Purchase method (736)
Realized gain (699)
Realized loss (699)
Unrealized gain (699)
Unrealized loss (699)

QUESTIONS

1. Distinguish between debt and equity securities; also between short-term and long-term investments.

2. What accounting principle is applied in recording the acquisition of an investment? Explain its application in cash and noncash acquisitions.

3. Briefly explain the accounting for short-term investments in equity securities.

4. An investor purchased 100 shares of PO common stock at $20 per share on March 15, 1991. At the end of the 1991 accounting period, December 31, 1991, the stock was quoted at $19 per share. On June 5, 1992, the investor sold the stock for $22 per share. Assuming a short-term investment, provide answers to the following:
   a. March 15, 1991—debit to the investment account, $____ .
   b. December 31, 1991—unrealized loss, $____ .
   c. June 5, 1992—gain or loss on sale of the investment, $____ .

5. On June 15, 1991, Baker Company purchased 500 shares of preferred stock, par $10, at $30 per share. The market value of these shares at the end of the accounting period, December 3, 1991, was $28 per share. Show how this short-term investment should be reported on the 1991 balance sheet.

6. Briefly explain the accounting for short-term investments in debt securities.

7. What is meant by an impairment loss?

8. Explain why interest revenue is accrued on investments in debt securities, but dividend revenue is not accrued on investments in equity securities.

9. Under the LCM method for investments in equity securities, no distinction is made between voting and nonvoting stock, but the distinction is important with respect to the equity method. Explain why.

10. Explain when the LCM method of accounting for equity investments is applicable.

11. Explain how the LCM concept is applied to long-term investments in equity securities. How is cost determined when an investment is reclassified from short-term to long-term or vice versa?

12. Explain the basic features of the equity method of accounting for long-term investments. When is the equity method applicable?

13. Assume Company R acquired, as a long-term investment, 30% of the outstanding voting common stock of Company S at a cash cost of $100,000. At date of acquisition, the balance sheet of Company S showed total stockholders' equity of $250,000. The market value of the assets of Company S was $20,000 greater than their book value at date of acquisition. Compute goodwill purchased, if any. What accounting method should be used in this situation? Explain why.

14. Assume the same facts as in (13), with the additional data that the net assets have a remaining estimated life of 10 years and goodwill will be amortized over 20 years (assume no residual values and straight-line depreciation). How much additional depreciation and amortization expense should be reported by the investor, Company R, each year in accounting for this long-term investment? Give the entries to record additional depreciation and amortization of goodwill.

15. The equity method of accounting for a long-term investment in equity securities usually will reflect a greater amount of investment revenue than the cost method in the same circumstances. Explain why.

16. Explain the basic features of the market value method of accounting for investments in securities. Is it a generally accepted method? Explain.

17. How would the market value method of accounting for investments in securities, in contrast to the cost method, tend to prevent "managed" earnings?

18. Basically, the investor accounts for an ordinary stock dividend and a stock split in the same way. Briefly explain the accounting that should be followed by the investor in these situations.

19. What is a convertible security? Assume an investor has a convertible security with a carrying value of $200,000, which is turned in to the issuer for conversion. The investor receives, through the conversion, common stock with a current market value of $225,000. Explain how the investor should account for the conversion of this long-term investment.

20. What is a stock right (or stock warrant)? If stock rights have a market value, how would the investor account for the receipt of stock rights?

21. Explain the characteristics of acquisition of a long-term investment accounted for by (a) the pooling of interests method and (b) the purchase method.*
22. Contrast the primary effects on the balance sheet of a pooling of interests versus a purchase. Why are the effects different?*
23. Explain why market values are used in the purchase method but not in the pooling of interests method.*
24. Explain why goodwill is recognized in a purchase but not in a pooling of interests.*

* Relates to Appendix 14A.

EXERCISES

E 14–1

Classification of Investments in Securities
(L.O. 2)

Match the different securities listed below with their usual classification as investments by entering the appropriate letter in each blank space. Usual classification as investments: A—short-term equity investment, B—short-term debt security, C—long-term equity security, D—long-term debt security, E—none of the above.

Typical Securities

_____ 1. Abbot common stock, nopar; acquired to use temporarily idle cash.
_____ 2. Land acquired for short-term speculation.
_____ 3. U.S. Treasury bills, mature in six months.
_____ 4. GE preferred stock, par $100, mandatory redemption within next 12 months.
_____ 5. Staufer common stock, par $5; acquired to attain a continuing controlling interests.
_____ 6. Frazer bonds, 9%, mature at the end of 10 years; acquired for indefinite holding period.
_____ 7. Foreign Corporation, common stock; difficulties encountered in withdrawing cash earned.
_____ 8. Certificates of deposit (CDs); mature at end of one year.
_____ 9. Savings certificate at local Savings and Loan Association.
_____10. Acorn common stock, par $1; acquired as a short-term investment, but now so profitable that management plans to hold it indefinitely.

E 14–2

Short-Term Equity Investments, LCM: Entries and Reporting.
(L.O. 4, 6)

On November 1, 1991, Decker Company acquired the following short-term investments in marketable equity securities:

Corporation X—500 shares common stock (nopar) at $60 cash per share.

Corporation Y—300 shares preferred stock (par $10, nonredeemable) at $20 cash per share.

The annual reporting period ends December 31. On December 31, 1991, the quoted market prices were Corporation X stock, $52, and Corporation Y stock, $24. Following is the data for 1992:

Mar. 2, 1992   Received cash dividends per share as follows: X stock, $1; Y stock, 50 cents.
Oct. 1, 1992   Sold 100 of the Y shares at $25 per share.
Dec. 31, 1992   Market values: X stock, $46; Y stock, $26.

Required:

1. Give the entry for Decker Company to record the purchase of the securities.
2. Give any adjusting entry needed at the end of 1991.
3. Give the items and amounts that should be reported on the 1991 income statement and balance sheet.
4. Give all of the entries for 1992.
5. Give the items and amounts that should be reported on the 1992 income statement and balance sheet.

E 14–3

Short-Term Equity Investments, LCM: Purchase, Sale, Transfer, Entries, and Reporting
(L.O. 4, 6)

At December 31, 1991, the short-term equity investments of Vista Company were as follows:

Security	Shares	Unit Cost	Unit Market Price
Preferred stock, 8%, par $10, Knight Corp.	600	$90	$88
Common stock, nopar, Dyer Corp.	200	30	31

The reporting year ends December 31. The transactions which follow relate to the above short-term equity investments and those bought and sold during 1992:

Feb. 2   Received the annual 8% cash dividend from Knight Corporation.
Mar. 1   Sold 150 shares of the Dyer stock at $34 per share.
May 1   Sold 400 shares of Knight stock at $89.50 per share.
June 1   Received a cash dividend on Dyer stock of $3.50 per share.
Aug. 1   Purchased 4,000 shares of Rote Corporation's common stock at $45 per share.
Sept. 1   Transferred all shares of Dyer common stock from the short-term portfolio to the long-term portfolio. At this date the Dyer stock was quoted at $28 per share.

At December 31, 1992, the quoted market prices were as follows: Knight preferred, $98; Dyer common, $28; and Rote common, $44.50.

Required:

1. Give the entry that Vista Company should make on December 31, 1991, to record the equity investments at LCM.
2. Give the entries for 1992 through September 1.
3. Give the entry(s) required at December 31, 1992.
4. List the items and amounts that should be reported on Vista's 1992 income statement and balance sheet.

E 14–4

Short-Term Debt Security, Cost Method: Entries and Reporting
(L.O. 5, 6)

On September 1, 1991, New Company purchased 10 bonds of Vue Corporation ($1,000, 6%) as a short-term investment at 96 (i.e., $960) plus accrued interest. The bonds pay annual interest each July 1. New paid cash, including accrued interest. New's annual reporting period ends December 31. At December 31, 1991, the Vue bonds were quoted at 95¾.

Required:

1. Give the journal entry for New Company to record the purchase of the bonds assuming the cost method will be used.
2. Give any adjusting entries required at December 31, 1991.
3. Give the items and amounts that should be reported on the 1991 income statement and balance sheet.
4. Give the required entry on July 1, 1992.
5. On August 1, 1992, New Company sold four of the bonds at 96.5 plus any accrued interest. The remaining six bonds were transferred to the long-term portfolio of debt securities. Give the required entry(s).
6. There were no additional transactions during 1992. List the short-term investment items and amounts that would be reported on the 1992 income statement and balance sheet.

E 14–5

Short-Term Debt Security, LCM Method: Entries and Reporting
(L.O. 5, 6)

On August 1, 1991, West Company purchased for cash four $10,000 bonds of Moe Corporation at 98 plus accrued interest. The bonds pay 9% interest, payable on a semiannual basis each May 1 and November 1. The bonds were purchased as a short-term investment. The annual reporting period ends December 31.

Required:

1. Give the following entries for West Company for 1991, assuming the LCM method will be used:

8/1/1991   Paid $40,100 cash for the bonds including any accrued interest.
11/1/1991   Collected interest on the bonds.
12/31/1991   Adjusting entries (if any). The bonds were quoted on the market on this date at 96.
12/31/1991   Market value, $38,400.

2. Show how the effects of this short-term investment should be reported on the 1991 income statements and balance sheet.
3. On February 1, 1992, two of the bonds were sold for $19,950 cash including any accrued interest. Give the required entry. Assume no reversing entries were made on January 1, 1992.
4. Give the entry for the collection of interest on May 1, 1992.

E 14-6
Basket Purchase of Securities: Allocation, Entry
(L.O. 2)

Voss Company purchased stock in the three different companies listed below, for a lump sum of $113,400, to be held as a long-term investment:

> N Corporation, common stock (par, $10), 300 shares.
>
> O Corporation, preferred stock (par $100), 400 shares.
>
> P Corporation common stock (nopar) 500 shares.

In addition, Voss paid transfer fees and other costs related to the acquisition amounting to $600. At the time of purchase, the stocks were quoted on the local market at the following prices per share: N common, $100; O preferred, $120; and P common, $84.

Required:

Give the entry to record the purchase of these long-term investments and payment of the transfer fees and other costs. Record each stock in a separate account and show the cost per share.

E 14-7
Long-Term Investments, LCM: Entries and Reporting
(L.O. 6)

During 1991, Shale Company purchased shares in two corporations with the intention of holding them as long-term investments. Transactions were in the following order:

a. Purchased 200 of the 10,000 shares outstanding of common stock of T Corporation at $31 per share plus a 4% brokerage fee and a transfer cost of $52.

b. Purchased 300 of 4,000 outstanding shares of preferred stock (nonvoting) of P Corporation at $78 per share plus a 3% brokerage fee and a transfer cost of $198.

c. Purchased an additional 20 shares of common stock of T Corporation at $35 per share plus a 4% brokerage fee and a transfer cost of $4.

d. Received $4 per share cash dividend on the P Corporation stock (from earnings since acquisition).

Required:

1. Give the entry in the accounts of Shale Company for each transaction, applying the LCM method.
2. The market value of the shares held at the end of 1991 were T stock, $34; P stock, $75. Give the appropriate adjusting entry for Shale Company.
3. The market values of the shares held at the end of 1992 were T stock, $36; P stock, $77. Give the appropriate adjusting entry.
4. Show how the income statement and balance sheet for Shale Company would report relevant data concerning the long-term investments for 1991 and 1992.

E 14-8
Long-Term Equity Investment, Equity Method: Compute Goodwill, Entries
(L.O. 6)

On January 1, 1991, JR Company purchased 400 of the 1,000 outstanding shares of common stock of RV Corporation for $30,000. At that date, the balance sheet of RV showed the following book values:

> Assets not subject to depreciation, $40,000.*
>
> Assets subject to depreciation (net), $26,000.†
>
> Liabilities, $6,000.*
>
> Common stock (par $50), $50,000.
>
> Retained earnings, $10,000.
>
> * Same as market value.
>
> † Market value $30,000; the assets have a 10-year remaining life (straight-line depreciation).

Required:

1. Assuming the equity method is appropriate, give the entry by JR Company to record the acquisition at a cost of $30,000. Assume a long-term investment.
2. Show the computation of goodwill purchased at acquisition.
3. Assume at December 31, 1991 (end of the accounting period), RV Corporation reported a net income of $12,000. Assume goodwill amortization over a 10-year period. Give all entries indicated on the records of JR Company.
4. In February 1992, RV Corporation declared and paid a $2 per share cash dividend. Give the necessary entry for JR Company.

E 14-9
Long-Term Equity
Investment, Equity
Method: Compute
Goodwill, Entries
(L.O. 6)

On January 1, 1991, Case Corporation purchased 3,000 of the 10,000 outstanding shares of common stock of Dow Corporation for $28,000 cash. At that date, Dow's balance sheet reflected the following book values:

Assets not subject to depreciation, $25,000.*

Assets subject to depreciation (net), $30,000.†

Liabilities, $5,000.*

Common stock (par $4), $40,000.
Retained earnings, $10,000.

* Same as market value.

† Market value $38,000; estimated remaining life of 10 years (straight-line depreciation).

Required:

1. If goodwill is relevant to this investment, show the computation of goodwill purchased at acquisition.
2. At the end of 1991, Dow reported income before extraordinary items, $20,000; extraordinary loss, $2,000; and net income, $18,000. In December 1991, Dow Corporation paid a $1 per share cash dividend. Reconstruct the following accounts (use T-account format) for Case Corporation: cash, investment in Dow Corporation stock, investment revenue—ordinary, and extraordinary loss. Apply the appropriate method of accounting for long-term investments in equity securities, and assume straight-line amortization of any goodwill is over 10 years. Date and identify all amounts entered in the accounts.

E 14-10
Long-Term Equity
Investment, LCM and
Equity Methods
Compared: Entries
(L.O. 3, 6)

On January 3, 1991, TA Company purchased 2,000 shares of the 10,000 outstanding shares of common stock of UK Corporation for $14,600 cash. At that date, the balance sheet of UK Corporation reflected the following: nondepreciable assets, $50,000 (same as market value); depreciable assets (net), $30,000 (market value, $33,000); total liabilities, $20,000; and stockholders' equity, $60,000. Assume a 10-year remaining life (straight-line depreciation) on the depreciable assets and amortization of goodwill over 10 years.

Required:

1. Give the entries, if any are required, on TA's books for each item (a) through (g) below assuming that the LCM method is appropriate.
2. Repeat 1. above assuming the equity method is appropriate.
   Entries Required and Other Information:
   a. Entry at date of acquisition.
   b. Goodwill purchased—computation only.
   c. Entry on 12/31/1991 to record $15,000 net income reported by UK.
   d. Entry on 12/31/1991 for additional depreciation expense.
   e. Entry on 12/31/1991 for amortization of goodwill.
   f. Entry on 12/31/1991 to recognize decrease in market value of UK stock, quoted market price, $7 per share. Assume this is the only long-term equity investment held.
   g. Entry on 3/31/1992 for a cash dividend of $1 per share declared and paid by UK.

E 14-11
Equity Securities, Market
Value Method: Entries
and Reporting
(L.O. 6)

On January 10, 1991, BT Company purchased as a long-term investment 15% of the 10,000 shares of the outstanding common stock of N Company (par value, $10 per share) at $50 per share. During 1991, 1992 and 1993, the following additional data were available:

	1991	1992
Reported net income N Co. at year-end	$30,000	$35,000
Cash dividends paid by N Co. at year-end	10,000	15,000
Quoted market price per share of N Co. stock at year-end	57	55

On January 2, 1993, BT Company sold 100 of N Co. shares at $56 per share.

Required:

1. Assuming the market value method is used, give all entries indicated in the accounts of BT Company, assuming the company uses the current approach.
2. Prepare a tabulation to show the investment revenue for 1991, 1992, and 1993 of BT Company and the balance in the investment account at year-end 1991, 1992, and 1993. Assume no cash dividends were paid by N Co. during 1993, and that the quoted market price of N Co. common stock was $56 per share at December 31, 1993.

E 14-12
Long-Term Equity
Investment, Stock
Dividend, Investor's
Entries
(L.O. 8)

Each of the following situations is completely independent; however, each relates to the receipt of a stock dividend by an investor.

Case A:

Doe Corporaton had 20,000 shares of $50 par value stock outstanding when the board of directors voted to issue a 25% stock dividend (i.e., one additional share for each four shares owned).

Required:

Van Company owns 2,000 shares of the Doe Corporation stock (a long-term investment) acquired at a cost of $65 per share. After receiving the stock dividend, Van Company sold 200 shares of the additional stock for $70 per share. Give the entries for Van Company to record (*a*) acquisition of the 2,000 shares, (*b*) receipt of the stock dividend, and (*c*) sale of the 200 shares. Assume the LCM method is appropriate for the investor.

Case B:

During the course of an audit, you find two accounts of the investor, May Company, as follows:

Investments in Stock of Yew Company ($100 par value):

Debits

Jan. 1   Cost of 100 shares $17,500
Feb. 1   50 shares received as a stock dividend (at par $100)   5,000

Credits

July 1   25 shares of dividend stock sold at $125 . . . . $ 3,125

Income summary

Credits

Feb. 1   Stock dividend on Yew Company stock . . . . $ 5,000
Aug. 1   Cash dividend on Yew Company stock   3,000

Required:

Assuming the LCM method is appropriate for the investor, restate these accounts on a correct basis. Give reasons for each change.

E 14-13
Long-Term Equity
Investment: Cash and
Stock Dividends, Stock
Split, Entries
(L.O. 6, 8)

PA Company purchased common stock (par value $10, 50,000 shares outstanding) of SU Corporation as a long-term investment. Transactions (which occurred in the order given) related to this investment were as follows:

a. Purchased 600 shares of SU common stock at $90 per share (designated as lot No. 1).
b. Purchased 2,000 shares of SU common stock at $96 per share (designated as lot No. 2).
c. At the end of the first year, SU Corporation reported net income of $52,000.
d. SU Corporation paid a cash dividend of $2 per share on the common stock.
e. After reporting net income of $5,000 for the second year, SU Corporation issued a stock dividend whereby each stockholder received one additional share for each two shares owned. At the time of the stock dividend, the stock was selling at $85.
f. SU Corporation revised its charter to provide for a stock split. The par value was reduced to $5. The old common stock was turned in, and the holders received in exchange two shares of the new stock for each old share turned in.

Required:

Give the entries for each transaction as they should be made in the accounts of PA Company. Show computations. Assume the LCM method is appropriate because less than 20% of SU's voting stock is held by PA.

E 14-14
Long-Term Equity
Investment: Stock Rights,
Entries
(L.O. 8)

Corporation M issued one stock right for each share of common stock owned by investors. The rights provided that for each six rights held, a share of preferred stock could be purchased for $80 (par of the preferred was $50 per share). When the rights were issued, they had a market value of $7 each, and the common stock was selling at $142 per share (ex rights). Taylor Company owned 300 shares of Corporation M common stock, acquired as a long-term investment at a cost of $22,350. Assume the LCM method is appropriate.

Required:

1. How many rights did Taylor Company receive?
2. Determine the carrying value of the stock rights received by Taylor Company and give any entry that should be made upon receipt of the rights.
3. Assume Taylor Company exercised the rights when the market value of the preferred stock of Corporation M was $130. Determine the cost of the new stock and give the entry to record the exercise of the rights.
4. Assume instead that Taylor Company sold its rights for $7.40 each. Give the entry to record the sale.

E 14–15
Long-Term Equity Investment: Stock Dividend, Stock Rights, Entries
(L.O. 8)

Give entries in the accounts of Cisco Corporation under the LCM method for the following transactions, which occurred over a period of time and in the chronological order shown:

a. Cisco Corporation purchased 100 shares of Bell Corporation common stock at $99 per share as a long-term investment.
b. Bell Corporation issued a 10% stock dividend in additional common shares.
c. Bell Corporation issued rights to current common stockholders entitling each holder of five old shares to buy one additional share of new common stock at $96. At the time, the rights sold for $4 per right and the shares outstanding sold for $116 each (ex rights). Make an allocation to the rights.
d. Cisco Corporation exercised all of its rights and bought new shares.
e. Cisco Corporation sold 120 shares of Bell stock for $100 per share, failing to identify the specific shares disposed of (use FIFO procedures). What is the status of the investment account after this sale (number of shares, cost per share, and total investment amount)?

E 14–16
Appendix 14B: Special-Purpose Fund: Accumulation Schedule, Entries
(L.O. 10)

On January 1, 1991, Koke Company decided to create a special-purpose fund to be identified as the "special contingency fund." The resources in the fund will be used to reimburse employees injured while on the job. The company desires to accumulate a $150,000 fund balance by the end of 1993 by making equal annual deposits starting on January 1, 1991. The independent trustee handling the fund will increase the fund by 9% compound interest each December 31.

Required:

1. Compute the amount of the annual deposits and prepare a fund accumulations schedule.
2. Give the entries relating to the fund that Koke Company should make each year.
3. Assume that on January 2, 1994, the trustee made the first payment from the fund in the amount of $1,000. Give the entry, if any, that Koke Company should make.

E 14–17
Appendix 14A: Pooling, 100% Ownership: Consolidation Worksheet
(L.O. 9)

On January 1, 1991, Company A acquired all of the outstanding shares of Company B common stock by exchanging, on a share-for-share basis, 4,000 shares of its own stock. The acquisition qualifies as a pooling of interests. The balance sheets reflected the following summarized data immediately before acquisition:

	Company A	Company B
Assets not subject to depreciation	$200,000	$50,000*
Assets subject to depreciation (net and 10-year remaining life)	120,000	25,000
	$320,000	$75,000
Liabilities	$ 40,000*	$ 5,000
Common stock (par $10)	200,000	40,000
Retained earnings	80,000	30,000
	$320,000	$75,000

* Includes a $5,000 debt owed by Company A to Company B.

Required:

1. Give the entry in the accounts of Company A for the acquisition of this long-term investment.
2. Prepare a consolidation worksheet immediately after acquisition.

E 14–18
Appendix 14A:
Pooling, 90% Ownership:
Consolidation Worksheet
(L.O. 9)

On January 1, 1991, Company W acquired 90% of the outstanding shares of Company X common stock by exchanging, on a share-for-share basis, 3,600 shares of its own stock. The acquisition qualifies as a pooling of interests. The balance sheet reflected the following summarized data immediately before acquisition:

	Company W	Company X
Assets not subject to depreciation	$180,000	$40,000*
Assets subject to depreciation (net and 10-year remaining life)	120,000	25,000
	$300,000	$65,000
Liabilities	$ 20,000*	$ 5,000
Common stock (par $10)	200,000	40,000
Retained earnings	80,000	20,000
	$300,000	$65,000

* Includes a $4,000 debt owed by Company W to Company X.

Required:

1. Give the entry in the accounts of Company W for the acquisition of this long-term investment.
2. Prepare a consolidation worksheet immediately after acquisition.

E 14–19
Appendix 14A:
Purchase, 100%
Ownership: Goodwill,
Worksheet
(L.O. 9)

In January 1991, Company P purchased, for $149,000 cash, all of the 10,000 outstanding voting shares of the common stock of Company S. The acquisition qualifies as a purchase. Immediately before acquisition, the following additional summarized data were available:

	Company P Book Value	Company S Book Value	Company S Market Value
Assets not subject to depreciation	$410,000	$ 80,000*	$ 85,000†
Assets subject to depreciation (net)	200,000	60,000	67,000‡
Total	$610,000	$140,000	$152,000
Liabilities	$ 40,000*	$ 10,000	
Common stock (par $10)	500,000	100,000	
Retained earnings	70,000	30,000	
Total	$610,000	$140,000	

* Includes a $12,000 debt owed by Company P to Company S.
† Entire market value excess over cost is for short-term investments.
‡ Estimated remaining life, 10 years (straight-line depreciation).

Required:

1. Give the entry in the accounts of Company P to record acquisition of this long-term investment.
2. Compute the amount of any goodwill purchased.
3. Prepare a consolidation worksheet immediately after acquisition.

PROBLEMS

P 14–1
Short-Term Equity
Investments, LCM
Method: Entries
(L.O. 4, 6)

On January 1, 1991, Joy Company acquired the following short-term investments in equity securities:

Co.	Stock	No. of Shares	Cost per Share
T	Common (nopar)	1,000	$20
U	Common (par $10)	600	15
V	Preferred (par $20, nonconvertible)	400	30

Per share data subsequent to the acquisition are as follows:

12/31/1991 Market values: T stock, $16; U stock, $15; and V stock, $34.
2/10/1992   Cash dividends received: T stock, $1.50; U stock, $1; and V stock, 50 cents.
11//1992   Sold the shares of V stock at $38.
12/31/1992 Market values: T stock, $12; U stock, $17; and V stock, $33.

Required:

1. Give all entries indicated for Joy Company for 1991 and 1992. Use the LCM basis. There was no balance in the allowance account on January 1, 1991.
2. Show how the income statement and balance sheet for Joy Company would reflect the short-term investments for 1991 and 1992.

P 14–2
Short-Term Equity Investment, LCM: Entries and Reporting
(L.O. 4, 6)

On December 31, 1991, Raven Company's portfolio of short-term investments in equity securities was as follows (purchased on September 1, 1991):

Security	Shares	Unit Cost	Unit Market
BC Corp., common stock, nopar	50	$186	$187
CD Corp., preferred stock, 6% par $40	200	40	35

Transactions relating to this portfolio during 1992 were as follows:

Jan. 25   Received a 6% dividend check on the CD shares.
Apr. 15   Sold 30 shares of BC Corporation stock at $151 per share.
July 25   Received a $45 dividend check on the BC shares.
Oct. 1   Sold the remaining shares of BC Corporation at $149.50 per share.
Dec. 1   Purchased 100 shares of EF Corporation common stock at $47 per share plus a $30 brokerage fee.
Dec. 5   Purchased 400 shares of GH Corporation common stock, par $1, at $15 per share.
Dec. 31   Transferred the CD shares to the long-term investment portfolio of equity securities.

On December 31, 1992, the following unit market prices were available: BC stock, $140; CD stock, $38; EF stock, $51; and GH stock, $14.

Required:

1. Give the entries that Raven Company should make on (*a*) September 1, 1991, and (*b*) December 31, 1991. Use the LCM method.
2. Give the short-term investment items and amounts that should be reported on the 1991 income statement and balance sheet.
3. Give the journal entries for 1992 related to the short-term investments.
4. Give the short-term investment items and amounts that should be reported on the 1992 income statement and balance sheet.

P 14–3
Short-Term Investment, Debt Securities, LCM: Entries and Reporting
(L.O. 5, 6)

On April 1, 1991, Lyn Company purchased for cash eight $1,000, 9% bonds of Star Corporation at 102 plus accrued interest. The bond interest is paid semiannually on each May 1 and November 1. Lyn Company's annual reporting period ends on December 31. Lyn Company will use the LCM basis to account for this short-term investment.

On December 1, 1991, six of these bonds were sold for cash at 101½ plus any accrued interest. At December 31, 1991, the Star Corporation bonds were quoted at 97.

Required:

1. Give the entry for Lyn Company to record the purchase of the bonds on April 1, 1991.
2. Give the entry for interest collected during 1991.
3. Give the entry on December 1, 1991.
4. Give any adjusting entry(s) required on December 31, 1991.
5. Show what items and amounts should be reported on the 1991 income statement and balance sheet.

P 14-4
Short-Term Debt
Investment, Cost Method:
Entries and Reporting
(L.O. 5)

At December 31, 1991, the portfolio of short-term investments in debt securities held by Dow Company was as follows:

			Interest		
Security	Par Value	Rate	Payable	Cash Cost*	Date Purchased
X Corp. bonds	$10,000	6%	Nov. 1	$ 9,800	Sept. 1, 1991
Y Corp. bonds	20,000	9%	Dec. 31	20,400	Dec. 31, 1991

* Excluding any accrued interest.

Dow's annual reporting period ends on December 31; the company will use the cost method in conformity with GAAP as specified in *ARB No. 43*.

Transactions relating to the portfolio of short-term investments in debt securities during 1992 were as follows:

June 1   Sold the Y Corp. bonds at 103, plus any accrued interest.
Nov. 1   Collected interest on the X Corp. bonds.
Dec. 1   Purchased $30,000 of Z Corp. bonds at 99½ plus accrued interest. These bonds pay 8% interest, semiannually each March 1 and September 1.
Dec. 31 Transferred the X Corp. bonds to the portfolio of long-term debt securities.

Required:

1. Give the 1991 entries for Dow Company to record the purchase of the debt securities, collections of interest, and all related adjusting entries.
2. Give all of the 1992 entries, including interest collections and any adjusting entries.
3. List the items and amounts that would be reported on the 1992 income statement and the current section of the balance sheet. The Z Corp. bonds were quoted at 99 on December 31, 1992.

P 14-5
Short-Term Equity
Investments, Debt
Securities, LCM: Entries
and Reporting
(L.O. 4, 5, 7)

At December 31, 1991, Piper Company held two short-term investment portfolios as follows:

Description	Quantity	Total Cost	Unit Market Prices
1. Equity securities:			
Damon common stock	50 shares	$2,300	$ 47
Martin common stock	100 shares	2,100	19
2. Debt security:			
Hydro Corp., $1,000 bonds, 9% payable annually on June 1	10 bonds	10,400	103.5

Transactions relating to short-term investments during 1992 were as follows (the annual reporting period ends December 31):

Mar. 1   Sold 30 shares of Damon common stock at $50 per share.
Apr. 1   Sold 70 shares of Martin common stock at $20 per share.
June 1   Collected interest on the Hydro bonds.
June 2   The Hydro bonds were transferred to long-term debt investments; the market price at this date was 103.
Sept. 1 Received a cash dividend of $1 per share on the Damon common stock.
Dec. 1   Purchased 300 shares of ATX common stock at $25 cash per share.

Piper Company accounts for its equity and debt securities at LCM.

Quoted market prices at December 31, 1992, were as follows: Damon common stock, $45; Martin common stock, $21; ATX common stock, $28; and Hydro Corp. bonds, $1,010 per bond (i.e., 101).

Required:

1. Show how the two investment portfolios should be reported on the 1991 balance sheet. Show computations.
2. Give the entries for the 1992 transactions through December 31, 1992.

3. Give the entry(s) to record LCM on the short-term equity securities at December 31, 1992.

4. Give the items and amounts that must be reported on the 1992 income statement and the current section of the balance sheet.

P 14–6
Long-Term Equity Investments, LCM: Entries and Reporting for Two Years
(L.O. 6, 7)

On January 1, 1991, Rae Company purchased 4,000 of the 40,000 shares outstanding of common stock (par $10) of DB Corporation for $80,000 cash, and 3,000 of the 100,000 shares outstanding of common stock (nopar) of CX Corporation for $7 per share cash as long-term investments. These are the only long-term equity investments held. The accounting periods for all the companies end on December 31.

	DB Corp.	CX Corp.
December 31, 1991:		
Income reported for 1991	$40,000	$20,000
Cash dividend per share declared and paid during 1991	1.00	None
Market price per share of stock	15	8
October 20, 1992:		
Sold 1,000 shares of CX stock at $11 per share.		
December 31, 1992:		
Income reported for 1992	50,000	26,000
Cash dividend per share declared and paid during 1992	1.00	.60
Market price per share of stock	17	6
Reclassified the CX stock as a current asset (short-term investment).		

Required:

1. Give all of the entries required for Rae Company for 1991 and 1992.

2. Show how the long-term investments in equity securities and the related investment revenue would be reported on the financial statements of Rae Company at the end of each year.

P 14–7
Long-Term Equity Investments, LCM: Entries and Reporting for Three Years
(L.O. 6, 7)

During January 1991, Poe Company purchased 5,000 of the 50,000 outstanding shares of common stock (par $1) of Styp Corporation at $15 per share cash as a long-term investment (the only long-term equity investment held). The accounting period for both companies ends December 31. During 1991, 1992, and 1993, the following additional data were available:

1. Styp Corporation:

	1991	1992
Net income reported by Styp at year-end	$15,000	$20,000
Cash dividends declared and paid by Styp during the year (total)	6,000	12,000
Market price per share (Styp stock)	6	5

2. On December 31, 1992, Poe determined that the drop in market price was permanent (not temporary) due to unusual circumstances.

3. On January 2, 1993, Poe sold 1,000 shares of the Styp stock at $5.20 per share.

4. On December 31, 1993, Styp shares were selling at $4.75.

Required:

1. Give all of the entries indicated in the accounts of Poe Company assuming the LCM method of accounting for long-term investments in equity securities is used.

2. Show how all of the related accounts and amounts would be reported on Poe's 1991, 1992, and 1993 income statement and balance sheet.

P 14–8
Long-Term Equity Investment, Goodwill: Entries and Reporting for Three Years
(L.O. 6, 7)

On January 1, 1991, Parr Company purchased 30% of the 30,000 outstanding common shares, par $10, of Stub Corporation at $17 per share as a long-term investment (the only long-term equity investment held). The following data in respect to Stub Corporation had been assembled by Parr Company:

1. At acquisition date, January 1, 1991:

	Valued at	
	Book	**Market**
Assets not subject to depreciation	$250,000	$260,000*
Assets subject to depreciation, net (10-year remaining life; straight-line)	200,000	220,000
	$450,000	
Liabilities	$ 50,000	50,000
Common stock (par $10)	300,000	
Retained earnings	100,000	
	$450,000	

* Difference due to inventory, and this inventory is sold during 1991.

2. Selected data available at December 31, 1991, and 1992:

	1991	**1992**
Cash dividends declared and paid by Stub Corporation during the year	$ 8,000	$ 5,000
Income reported by Stub:		
Income (loss) before extraordinary items	24,000	(10,000)
Extraordinary loss	(2,000)	
Quoted market price per share, Stub Corporation stock (December 31)	20	18

3. On January 2, 1993, Parr Company sold 500 of the Stub shares at $18 per share.

Required:

1. Give all of the appropriate entries for Parr Company during 1991 and 1992. Use straight-line amortization of goodwill over a 30-year period.
2. Give the entry required on January 2, 1993.
3. Show what items and amounts based on requirements 1 and 2 will be reported on the 1991, 1992, and 1993 income statements, and 1991 and 1992 balance sheets.

P 14–9
Long-Term Equity Investment, LCM: Cash and Stock Dividends, Split, Entries, and Reporting
(L.O. 6, 7, 8)

Allen Corporation completed the following transactions, in the order given, relative to the portfolio of stocks held as long-term investments:

Year 1991:

a. Purchased 200 shares of MC Corporation common stock (par value $10) at $70 per share plus a brokerage commission of 4% and transfer costs of $20.
b. Purchased, for a lump sum of $96,000, the following stocks of NP Corporation:

	Number of Shares	**Market Price at Date of Purchase**
Class A, common, par value $20	200	$ 50
Preferred, noncumulative, par value $50	300	100
Class B, nopar common stock (stated value $100)	400	150

Year 1992:

c. Purchased 300 shares of MC Corporation common stock at $80 per share plus a brokerage commission of 4% and transfer costs of $60.
d. Received a stock dividend on the MC Corporation stock; for each share held, an additional share was received.
e. Sold 100 shares of MC Corporation stock at $45 per share (from lot 1).

Year 1993:

f. Received a two-for-one stock split on the class A common stock of NP Corporation (the number of shares doubled).

g. Cash dividends declared and paid:

MC Corporation common stock—$10 per share.
NP, class A, common stock—$5 per share.
NP, preferred—6%.
NP, class B, nopar common stock—$15 per share.

	Year-End Stock Prices		
	1991	1992	1993
MC, common stock	$ 70	$ 40	$ 39.95
NP, class A, common	51	47	24
NP preferred stock	98	95	96
NP, class B, common	140	144	144

Required:

1. Give entries for Allen Corporation for the above transactions assuming the LCM method is appropriate. Show calculations and assume FIFO order when shares are sold.
2. What items and amounts would be shown on the 1991, 1992, and 1993 income statements and balance sheets by Allen Corporation in respect to the long-term investments?

P 14–10

COMPREHENSIVE PROBLEM
♦

Long-Term Equity
Investment, LCM and
Equity Methods
Compared: Entries
and Reporting
(L.O. 3, 6, 7)

On January 1, 1992, AV Company purchased 3,000 of the 15,000 outstanding shares of common stock of DC Corporation for $80,000 cash as a long-term investment (the only long-term equity investment held). At that date, the balance sheet of DC Corporation showed the following book values (summarized):

Assets not subject to depreciation	$140,000*
Assets subject to depreciation (net)	100,000†
Liabilities	40,000
Common stock (par $10)	150,000
Retained earnings	50,000

* Market value, $150,000; difference relates to short-term investments.

† Market value, $140,000, estimated remaining life, 10 years. Use straight-line depreciation with no residual value and amortization of goodwill over 20 years.

Additional subsequent data on DC Corporation:

	1992	1993
Income before extraordinary items	$25,000	$26,000
Extraordinary item—gain		5,000
Cash dividends declared and paid	10,000	12,000
Market value per share	25	26

Required:

1. For Case A, assume the LCM method is appropriate. For Case B, assume the equity method is appropriate. For each case, provide the investor's entries or give the required information for items (*a*) through (*d*) in a tabulation similar to the one below.

Entries Required and Other Information	Case A: LCM Method Is Appropriate		Case B: Equity Method Is Appropriate	
a. Entry at date of acquisition.				
b. Amount of goodwill purchased.				
c. Entries at 12/31/1992:				
(1) Investment revenue and dividends.				
(2) Additional depreciation expense.				
(3) Amortizaton of goodwill.				

Entries Required and Other Information	Case A: LCM Method Is Appropriate		Case B: Equity Method Is Appropriate	
(4) Additional expense associated with short-term investments (held by DC) for which market value (i.e., purchase price to AV) exceeded book value; these investments were sold during 1992.				
(5) Recognition of change in market value of DC stock.				
d. Entries at 12/31/1993:				
(1) Investment revenue and dividends.				
(2) Additional depreciation expense.				
(3) Amortization of goodwill.				
(4) Recognition of change in market value of DC stock.				

2. For each case, reconstruct the investment, the allowance, and the unrealized capital accounts.
3. Explain why the investment account balance is different between the LCM and equity methods.

P 14–11

Long-Term Equity Investment, Market Value Method: Current versus Deferral Approaches; Entries and Reporting (L.O. 6, 7)

On January 1, 1991, Taft Company purchased, as a long-term investment, 6% of the 50,000 (par $10) shares of the outstanding common stock of Company S at $11 per share during the years 1991, 1992, and 1993. The following additional company data were available:

End of 1991: Reported net income, $30,000; cash dividends declared and paid, $20,000; market value per share, $15.

End of 1992: reported net income, $25,000; cash dividends declared and paid, $15,000; market value per share, $14.

December 10, 1993: Taft Company sold 200 shares of Company S stock at $17.50 per share.

Required:

1. Assuming the market value method is used, give the entries for Taft Company for each transaction related to the investment, assuming:

   a. Current approach—market changes are reported on the income statement.
   b. Deferral approach—market changes are reported on the balance sheet as a separate element of owners' equity.

2. In parallel columns for each of the above assumptions, show the following at the end of 1991, 1992, and 1993:

   a. Balance of the investment account.
   b. Balance in the unrealized owners' equity each year-end.
   c. Revenue from the investment for each period.

   For this second requirement, assume there were no additional investment transactions during 1993 and the market value of Company S stock was $17.50 per share on December 31, 1993.

P 14–12

Appendix 14B: Special-Purpose Fund: Accumulation Schedule, Entries, and Reporting (L.O. 10)

On January 1, 1991, Case Corporation created a special building fund by a depositing a single sum of $100,000 with an independent trustee. The purpose of the fund is to provide resources to build an addition to the older office building during the latter part of 1995. The company anticipates a total construction cost of $500,000 and completion by January 1, 1995. The company plans to make equal annual deposits each December 31, 1991 through 1995, to accumulate the $500,000. The independent trustee will increase the fund each December 31, at an interest rate of 10%. The accounting periods of the company and the fund end on December 31.

Required:

1. Compute the amount of the equal annual deposits that will be needed and prepare a fund accumulation schedule through December 31, 1996, for Case Corporation.
2. The total cash outlay by Case will be $_____
   Total interest revenue will be $_____
   The effective interest rate will be _____ %
3. Give the entries for Case on: (*a*) January 1, 1991 and (*b*) December 31, 1991.
4. Give the entries for Case on January 3, 1996 when the addition is completed and the actual cost of $525,000 is paid in full. The trustee paid interest on the fund for two extra days at the fund rate.
5. Show what the 1992 Case income statement, balance sheet, and statement of cash flows should report in regards to the building addition program.
6. Assume the accounting period of Case Corporation ends on October 31 (instead of December 31) and the fund year-end is unchanged. Give any adjusting entry(s) that Case should make at its 1993 year-end.

P 14–13

Appendix 14A:
Pooling, 90%: Worksheet for Balance Sheet and Income Statement
(L.O. 9)

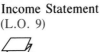

On January 1, 1991, Company C acquired 90% of the outstanding common stock of Company D by exchanging 18,000 shares of its own common stock for an equal number of shares of Company D. The acquisition qualifies as a pooling of interests.

After one year of operations, each company prepared an income statement and a balance sheet as follows (summarized):

	Reported at End of 1991	
	Company C	Company D
Income statement		
Sales revenue	$ 630,000	$180,000
Interest revenue	1,000	
Total revenues	631,000	180,000
Cost of goods sold	370,000	98,000
Depreciation expense	37,000	16,000
Other operating expenses	140,000	45,000
Interest expense	4,000	1,000
Total expenses	551,000	160,000
Net income	$ 80,000	$ 20,000
Balance sheet:		
Current assets	$ 560,000	$110,000
Investment in Company D (at cost)	180,000	
Operational assets (net)	360,000	160,000
Total assets	$1,100,000	$270,000
Current Liabilities	$ 70,000	$ 30,000
Common stock (par $10)	940,000	200,000
Retained earnings	90,000	40,000*
Total liabilities and equities	$1,100,000	$270,000

* Company D retained earnings balance at acquisition date was $20,000.

Data relating to 1991 eliminations:

a. During the year, Company C sold merchandise to Company D for $35,000 (at cost); Company D resold the merchandise during 1991.
b. During 1991, Company D paid Company C $1,000 interest on loans.
c. At the end of 1991, Company D owed Company C $20,000.

Required:

1. Prepare a worksheet at the end of 1991 to develop a consolidated income statement and balance sheet.
2. Prepare a consolidated income statement and balance sheet clearly identifying the minority interest.

CASES

C 14–1
Appendix 14A:
Analytical, Challenging:
Should the Acquisition Be
Purchase or Pooling?
(L.O. 10)

Lee Corporation is currently negotiating to acquire Rudd Corporation, a successful enterprise that would complement the operations of Lee. An important factor in the negotiations has been the potential effects of the acquisition on Lee's financial statements. Accordingly, Lee's management has requested that you prepare pro forma (i.e., "as if") balance sheets for the year just ended, under two assumptions—(1) pooling of interests and (2) purchase.

The balance sheets and income statements for the two corporations for the year just ended (prior to acquisition) are as follows:

	Lee Corp.	Rudd Corp. Book Value	Rudd Corp. Appraised
Balance sheet:			
Cash	$ 485,000	$ 15,000	$ 15,000
Receivables (net)	30,000	65,000	50,000
Inventories	85,000	70,000	70,000
Land	50,000		
Plant (net)	600,000	100,000	230,000
Patents (net)	10,000	30,000	40,000
	$1,260,000	$ 280,000	
Current liabilities	$ 40,000	$ 15,000	15,000
Long-term liabilities	110,000	25,000	25,000
Common stock (par $10)	1,000,000	200,000	
Retained earnings	110,000	40,000	
	$1,260,000	$ 280,000	
Income statement:			
Sales revenue	$6,000,000	$1,000,000	
Costs and expenses (excluding depreciation and amortization)	$5,754,000	$ 967,000	
Depreciation	65,000	10,000	
Amortization of patents	1,000	3,000	
Net income	$ 180,000	$ 20,000	
Market price per share (average shares sold per trading day, 650)	$24.00	Not quoted	

At year-end, Rudd Corporation owed a $10,000 current liability to Lee Corporation. For case purposes, assume that all depreciable assets and intangible assets have a remaining useful life of 10 years from date of acquisition (and straight-line).

Required:

1. Assumption No. 1—At the start of the new year, Lee will acquire all outstanding shares of Rudd by exchanging stock on a share-for-share basis so that the acquisition would qualify as a pooling of interests.
   a. Give the pro forma entry that Lee would make to record the investment.
   b. Prepare a pro forma consolidation worksheet immediately after acquisition.
2. Assumption No. 2—At the start of the new year, Lee will purchase all of the outstanding stock of Rudd for $460,000 cash so that the acquisition would qualify as a purchase.
   a. Give the pro forma entry that Lee would make to record the investment.
   b. Prepare a pro forma consolidation worksheet immediately after acquisition.
3. Which course of action would you recommend to Lee's management? Discuss the primary advantages and disadvantages of your recommendation. Use appropriate data developed for the two assumptions.

C 14–2
Market Value Method: A
Decision—Current versus
Deferral
(L.O. 6)

ACE Investors Company buys and sells various equity securities. These securities are approximately 90% of their total assets. Because ACE operates in one of the specialized industries permitted to use the market value method, ACE accounts for, and reports, its long-term investments on that basis. Currently, ACE uses the deferral approach to account for, and report, the market value changes in this investment portfolio. The company has decided to reconsider its use of the deferral approach because some major competitors use the current approach. Some of ACE's executives are opposed to changing because they are concerned about its effects on their retirement pay. You have been asked to consult with ACE on this proposed change. Accordingly, you have assembled the following data taken from their records:

a. January 1, 1991—purchased long-term equity securities, cost $50 million.
b. December 31—market value (millions of dollars):

1991, $56.0; 1992, $52.0; 1993, $49.5.

c. Cash dividends received (millions of dollars):

1991, $4.0; 1992, $4.2; 1993, $4.1.

d. December 1, 1993—sold for $6.0 million, 10% of the securities from the portfolio that originally cost $5.0 million; carrying value, $5.2 million.

ACE's accounting period ends December 31.

Required:

1. Briefly explain the difference between the two approaches under consideration by ACE.
2. Give possible reasons why some of the ACE executives are concerned about their retirement pay.
3. (*a*) Which approach would you recommend for ACE? To support your recommendations, you have been requested to provide comparative accounting entries under each approach and to complete the schedule given below.
   (*b*) After completing the schedule, what general conclusions can you draw from it in regard to financial statement effects?
4. What is the fundamental distinction between the two approaches?

Schedule of Comparative Effects on the Balance Sheet and Income Statement

Items	1991		1992		1993	
	Current	**Deferral**	**Current**	**Deferral**	**Current**	**Deferral**
Balance sheet:						
Assets						
Liabilities						
Stockholders' equity						
Income statement:						
Revenues						
Expenses						
Income						

5. Do you see any ethic issues involved in the assignment you have been asked to undertake?

C 14–3
Sherwin-Williams:
Analysis of Financial
Statements
(L.O. 9)

Note 15 to the Sherwin-Williams financial statements provides information on the Sherwin-Williams Development Corporation (SWDC), a wholly owned subsidiary that is consolidated in the financial statements. Summarized data are presented on SWDC.

Required:

1. Suggest some reasons why the FASB would require firms to consolidate nonhomogeneous businesses such as a manufacturer and its finance subsidiary.
2. For the December 31, 1990, financial statements of Sherwin-Williams, by what amount would the following account balances change if SWDC were not consolidated, but rather accounted for as an investment using the equity method?
   a. Total assets
   b. Property, plant and equipment
   c. Long-term debt
   d. Total revenue

e. Interest expense

f. Net income

3. How did Sherwin-Williams account for the two firms it acquired in 1990? See Note 4. What was the total purchase price for these two acquisitions? Can you determine approximately what portion of this purchase price was for tangible assets acquired, and what portion was for goodwill? Discuss, using observations of account balances in the financial statements.

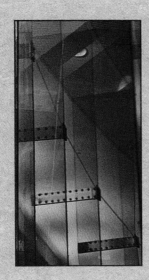

P A R T

III

LIABILITIES

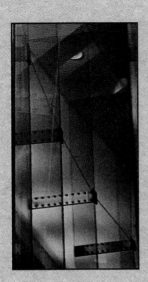

15

Short-Term Liabilities

LEARNING OBJECTIVES

◆

After you have studied this chapter, you will:

1. Be able to define a liability and specify its characteristics.

2. Know how to distinguish short-term (current) from long-term liabilities.

3. Know when it is appropriate to recognize a liability in a firm's accounts and how to measure the amount attached to the liability.

4. Understand the accounting for interest-bearing and noninterest-bearing current liabilities as well as how to treat notes with unrealistic interest rates.

5. Be able to explain why cash collected in advance of delivery of a good or service creates a liability for the firm.

6. Be able to properly account for the incurrence and payment of short-term liabilities.

7. Know what contingent and estimated liabilities are and the accounting appropriate to such liabilities.

INTRODUCTION
◆

On Thursday, August 26, 1982, Manville Corporation, a supplier of asbestos insulation, and its principal U.S. and Canadian affiliates filed for reorganization under Chapter 11 of the bankruptcy laws in New York. In an interview published as an advertisement August 27 in *The Wall Street Journal,* John A. McKinney, Manville's chief executive officer, answered questions about this action:

Question: Why did you file [for reorganization under the bankruptcy laws] now?

McKinney: We're a public company. We are required to comply with certain accounting requirements. Under these rules we're supposed to estimate the costs of current and probable litigation wherever possible and create a reserve for the liability in an amount equal to the estimate. When the asbestos cases began to proliferate, we couldn't estimate their probable number or cost, and our auditors qualified their opinion about our financial statements. . . . We hired epidemeologists and other professionals to develop an estimate of probable future disease cases. On the basis of their work so far, we forecast that we could get at least 32,000 more lawsuits on top of the 20,000 already asserted.

Question: A total of 52,000 lawsuits at a cost of $40,000 apiece could mean a total cost of $2 billion. . . . Could Manville afford it?

McKinney: Not on our own. . . . The booking of a large reserve [liability] now for current and future asbestos health liabilities would wipe out most of our net worth. Without showing a good sized net worth on our balance sheet, affordable credit would have dried up, and we simply could not have operated. So, when our board of directors learned this morning of the probable need for a large reserve, it considered the options and concluded we had to file for relief under Chapter 11.[1]

In the interview, McKinney further asserts that Manville's "businesses are in good shape," it "will not go out of business," not "a single employee will lose a job, pay or benefits," there is "no significant problem in making full, timely payment [to suppliers]," and that there will be no effect on customers. Yet, Manville filed for reorganization under Chapter 11. Moreover, not to have done so, in McKinney's words, "would have strangled the Company slowly, by deferring maintenance and postponing capital expenditures, and would also have led to cannibalizing good businesses just to keep going." And all of this would not have happened, at least not on August 26, 1982, if it hadn't been for an accounting standard, namely, *SFAS No. 5,* "Accounting for Contingencies." This standard is considered in detail in the current chapter.

◆

WHAT IS A LIABILITY?
◆

On the surface the answer may seem rather simple. A *liability* is something a company owes and must pay to someone else. Generally, this description will do quite well, but it is not sufficient for certain difficult situations. A good example is provided by the interview with Manville's McKinney. Should a liability be recorded

---

[1] The impact on net worth alluded to by Mr. McKinney in the quote is caused by the following entry needed to establish the expected liability under future litigation of the alleged injuries caused by asbestos (the reserve mentioned in the quote):

Loss due to litigation of asbestos-related claims XXX
    Liability under litigation XXX

The loss reduces the company's retained earnings and net worth.

for potential health claims, arising from potential lawsuits that have not even been submitted to the firm or to the courts for consideration?

Manville's case is not unique. A. H. Robins experienced a similar situation regarding the sale of the company's Dalkon Shield. Problems with this intrauterine device surfaced by the mid-1970s; yet a liability was not recorded until 1984, and this liability was only about 25% of the final amount required.

For other situations where accountants wrestle with whether a liability exists and, if so, in what amount, consider these issues:

* Coupons that have not been presented for redemption.
* Frequent flier miles earned by airline travelers.
* Potential requirements to clean up toxic waste dumps.
* Preferred stock with cumulative dividends, nonparticipating as to voting, and callable by the issuer or redeemable by the holder on demand.[2]

The FASB found it necessary to try to bring some order to the chaos of defining just what is and what is not a liability. In *SFAC No. 6*, the Board defines liabilities as "probable future sacrifices of economic benefits arising from present obligations of a particular entity to transfer assets or provide services to other entities in the future as a result of past transactions or events." Thus, a liability possesses three essential characteristics:

* An obligation exists that can be satisfied only by the transfer of an asset or a service to another entity.
* The event that gave rise to the obligation has occurred.
* The obligation must be probable.

When a liability is incurred in conformity with the definition given above, it should be immediately recognized and recorded. The FASB definition of a liability is important because it is specific about the essential distinctions defining a debt. Prior to *SFAC No. 6*, the accounting definition of a debt was vague. Conceptually, the amount of a liability should be measured at the present value of all future cash payments (or the cash equivalent of noncash assets and services received), discounted at the interest rate consistent with the risks involved. A liability involves a principal amount that is subject to interest that is incurred as time passes.

Accounting recognition of a liability should take place on the date the liability is incurred. The transaction that creates a liability usually identifies the date when the obligation comes into existence. However, the recognition date of a liability is not always clear-cut, such as in the case of an injury to an employee, or outsider, when the final determination of liability depends on the decision of a court of law.[3]

Furthermore, current liabilities can influence operations in a way that long-term liabilities generally do not because current liabilities represent a claim on current resources that are thereby otherwise unavailable for day-to-day operations. These claims differ from those, such as bonds, that mature years into the future. The distinction is critical to the classification of liabilities as either current or long-term.

Measurement of the amount of a liability sometimes is difficult. The transaction that creates a liability usually provides the basis for measuring its amount. Transactions lead to one or more debits that balance the liability credit. Examing the reason for the debit provides the clue to measuring the related liability. For example:

---

[2] The IRS has been known to allow preferred dividends to be counted as interest expense for tax purposes.

[3] From an auditing standpoint, identification of existing liabilities is a critical problem because many liabilities are easy to hide or overlook. This issue—determining the existence of liability—is precisely the one faced by Manville in deciding whether to record the liability for asbestos-related health claims.

Type of Account Debited	Cause of liability
An asset.	Inventory purchased on account.
Another liability.	A note signed for an account due and indicated on the balance sheet as an account payable.
Retained earnings.	Cash dividends declared.
An expense.	Repair services received.
A loss.	A litigation award against the company.
Cash collected in advance of service rendered.	Cash collected for magazine subscriptions to be delivered over the coming year.

For example, when an asset is acquired on credit, the asset and related liability are recognized at cost under the *cost principle*. The cost of the asset received measures the amount of the liability. Sometimes, the relationship between the cost of the asset and the valuation of the liability is not clear-cut. Assume a company acquired a machine and promised to pay the quoted price (a single amount) of $10,000 at the end of one year from date of purchase, with no separate interest payments specified. The amount of the liability and the cost of the machine are not $10,000. The liability, and the cost of the asset, should be measured as the present value of the future cash payment. If the market interest rate for transactions involving this level of risk is 15%, the present value is:

$$\$10,000 \ (PV1, \ 15\%, \ 1) = \$10,000(.86957) = \$8,696(\text{rounded})$$

The appropriate journal entries are (note recorded net):

Purchase date:

Machine	8,696	
Note payable, 15% (face, $10,000)		8,696

Payment date:

Note payable ($10,000 − $1,304)	8,696	
Interest expense ($8,696) (.15)	1,304	
Cash		10,000

Implicit interest on short-term liabilities (particularly those involving accrued liabilities and accounts payable of one to three months), need not be separately recognized in accounting. This is in conformity with *APB No. 21* (par. 3a), which states that the requirement to account separately for interest does not apply to "receivables and payables arising from transactions with customers or suppliers in the normal course of business which are due in customary trade terms not exceeding approximately one year." This is an application of the *materiality and cost-benefit constraints* discussed in Chapter 2.

Companies usually measure, record, and report short-term liabilities at their maturity amount because the cost of the asset received and the maturity amount of the liability coincide. When the stated and effective rates are the same, the maturity amount and the present value of the liability are the same.

Aside from cases covered by the *materiality and cost-benefit constraints,* short-term liabilities should be recorded and reported at their present value when they are acquired.

Although exchange transactions usually establish the amount and maturity date of a liability, in some situations a definite liability is known to exist, or it is probable that one exists, but either the amount or the maturity date is not known precisely. One section of this chapter is devoted to this problem and discusses the recording and reporting of what are called *estimated liabilities* and *loss contingencies*.

> ### CONCEPT REVIEW
>
> 1. What are the three essential characteristics of a liability?
> 2. When should a liability be recognized?
> 3. Most accountants would agree that the amount of a liability incurred is the present value of all future payments. Why, then, is the gross amount to be paid at the future date typically recorded for short-term liabilities?

WHAT IS A CURRENT LIABILITY?

Current (short-term) liabilities are defined as "obligations whose liquidation is reasonably expected to require the use of existing resources properly classifiable as current assets, or the creation of other current liabilities."[4] Current assets are those assets that are expected to be converted to cash or used in normal operations during the operating cycle of the business,[5] or one year from the balance date, whichever is longer. Because of the association between current assets and current liabilities, the time dimension that applies to current assets also generally applies to current liabilities. Liabilities that do not conform to this definition are called *long-term,* or *noncurrent, liabilities.* Long-term liabilities are discussed in the next chapter.

Common current liabilities are:

* Accounts payable.
* Short-term notes payable.
* Cash and property dividends payable.
* Accrued liabilities related to expenses.
* Advances and returnable deposits.
* Unearned revenues collected in advance (e.g., cash collected before rendering service, such as prepaid rent).
* Taxes (income, sales, property, and payroll).
* Conditional payments.
* Compensated-absence liabilities.
* Current maturities of long-term debt.
* Obligations callable on demand by the creditor.

Special accounting problems related to these current liabilities are discussed in the following sections.

Accounts Payable

Accounts payable—more descriptively, *trade accounts payable*—is a designation reserved for recurring trade obligations. These obligations arise from the firm's ongoing operations including the acquisition of merchandise, materials, supplies, and services used in the production and sale of goods or services.[6] Other current

---

[4] AICPA, *Accounting Research Bulletin 43*, "Restatement and Revision of Accounting Research Bulletins" (New York, 1961), Chapter 3, par. 7

[5] The normal operating cycle of a business is the average period of time between the expenditure of cash for goods and services and the time that those goods and services are converted back to cash. This cash-to-cash cycle is illustrated by the following sequence: cash expenditure to buy inventory, inventory fabricated to finished product, product sold on account, account collected in cash.

[6] In determining the amount of the liability, the accountant must adjust for purchase discounts, allowances, and returns. (See Chapter 9 for a discussion of these topics.)

payables that do not conform to the definition of trade accounts (such as income taxes and the current portion of long-term debt) should be reported separately from accounts payable.

Short-Term Notes Payable

A short-term note might be a trade note payable that arises from the same source as an account payable, a nontrade note payable that arises from some other source, or the current maturity of a long-term liability, which arises when the next debt payment will be made from current assets. A short-term note is either secured by a mortgage or another type of lien that specifies particular assets pledged as security or it is unsecured, if repayment is based only on the general creditworthiness of the debtor. Disclosure for a secured note payable should include an explanation of the primary terms of the debt agreement, including the identity of any pledged assets.

A note payable may be designated as either interest-bearing or noninterest-bearing. An interest-bearing note explicitly states a rate of interest. This rate is called the **stated rate of interest.** Notes designated as noninterest-bearing do not bear an explicit interest rate but, instead, implicitly reflect a rate of interest called the *effective rate,* or *yield.* In other words, regardless of designation, all commercial debt instruments implicitly or explicitly require the debtor to pay interest. This is because the cost of using money over time cannot be avoided. The stated rate determines the amount of cash interest that will be paid on the principal amount of the debt. In contrast, the **effective rate of interest (yield)** on a debt is the market interest rate based on the actual cash, or cash-equivalent, amount that was borrowed. The effective rate is used to discount the future cash payments on a debt to the cash equivalent borrowed. The cash or cash equivalent amount received by the debtor is the amount that is subject to the effective interest rate. The maturity amount of a debt is the amount to be paid on the maturity date, excluding any separate interest payments due on that date. These two types of notes are discussed in more detail next.

Interest-bearing Notes   Interest-bearing notes specify a stated rate of interest on the face of the note. For an interest-bearing note, the debtor receives cash, other assets, or services and pays back the face amount of the note plus interest at the stated rate on one or more interest dates. When the stated rate appropriately reflects the note's risk, the stated and effective interest rates are the same. This is the usual case.

To illustrate an interest-bearing note, assume that on October 1, 1991, Biloxi Company borrowed $10,000 cash on a one-year note with 12% interest payable at the maturity date. Biloxi Company received cash equal to the face amount of the note, $10,000.[7] The accounting year ends December 31, and the maturity date of the note is September 30, 1992. This transaction requires the following accounting and reporting:

Entries during 1991:

October 1, 1991—To record the interest-bearing note at its present value:

```
Cash  . . . . . . . . . . . . . . . . . . . . . . . . . . . . . . . . . . 10,000
        Note payable, short term  . . . . . . . . . . . . . . . . . . . .         10,000
```

---

[7] It may be useful to demonstrate that under the conditions specified, the present value of the two cash flows of this interest-bearing note is equal to the cash borrowed:

$$\text{Maturity amount: } \$10,000 \ (PV1, 12\%, 1) = \$10,000(.89286) = \ \$ 8,929$$
$$\text{Interest: } \$1,200 \ (PVA, 12\%, 1) = \$1,200(.89286) = \ \underline{\hspace{0.3cm} 1,071}$$
$$\text{Total present value (cash borrowed)} \ldots \ldots \ldots \ldots \ \underline{\underline{\$10,000}}$$

December 31, 1991—Adjusting entry for accrued interest:

Interst expense ($10,000) (.12)(³⁄₁₂)   300
    Interest payable   300

Reporting at December 31, 1991—Interest-bearing note payable:

Income statement:
    Interest expense . . . . $ 300
Balance sheet:
    Current liabilities:
        Note payable, short term $10,000
        Interest payable   300

Entry at maturity date:

September 30, 1992—Payment of face amount plus interest at maturity:[8]

Interest payable   300
Interest expense ($10,000)(.12)(⁹⁄₁₂)   900
Note payable, short term 10,000
    Cash   11,200

Noninterest-bearing Notes   Noninterest-bearing is not a good descriptive designation for this type of note because such notes do, in fact, bear interest. The face amount of this type of note includes both the amount borrowed and interest as a single amount to be paid back at the maturity date. The borrower does not receive cash or other resources equal to the face amount of the note; rather, the borrower receives the difference between the face amount and the interest on the note. The cash to be received is the discounted value of the face amount using the effective interest rate. The difference between the discounted cash value and the face amount of the note, is the interest. The effective interest rate is determined by reference to market rates for instruments of similar risk. The effective rate is not specified on the note. However, the effective rate for a short-term noninterest-bearing note with a specified term can be determined.[9]

Consider an example. Brite Lite Company signed an $11,200, one-year, noninterest-bearing note but received only $10,000 cash. Since Brite Lite Company received only $10,000 cash, the effective rate of interest is 12% ($1,200 ÷ $10,000). The present value of this note is $10,000; that is:

$$\$11,200(PV1, 12\%, 1) = \$11,200(.89286) = \$10,000$$

This debt should be recorded at its present value, which can be done by recording the note on a net basis, or by recording it on a gross basis at its face value and offsetting this account with a discount account. Both approaches are illustrated next.

---

[8] The entry given in the text assumes no reversing entry on January 1, 1982. If a reversing entry were made on January 1, 1982, the entry would be:

Interest payable   300
    Interest expense   300

Then on September 30, 1992, the required entry is:

Interest expense   1,200
Note payable, short term 10,000
    Cash   11,200

Reversing entries simplify the process of recognizing interest expense in the next period particularly in computerized accounting systems.

[9] A noninterest-bearing note is also called a *discounted note* because the cash received is less than the face amount of the note.

Accounting Entries and Reporting, (Net Basis)

Entries during 1991:

October 1, 1991—To record the noninterest-bearing note payable at its net present value amount:

```
Cash . . . . . . . . . . . . . . . . . . . . . . . . . . . . . . . . . . 10,000
    Note payable, short term* . . . . . . . . . . . . . . . . . .          10,000
```

* The note was recorded at its present value (i.e., principal amount) rather than at its face amount of $11,200. The interest entries will increase the $10,000 initially recorded to $11,200, which is the payment required at maturity.

December 31, 1991—Adjusting entry to record accrued interest:

```
Interest expense ($10,000)(.12)(3/12) . . . . . . . . . . . . . . . .     300
    Note payable, short term* . . . . . . . . . . . . . . . . . .              300
```

* The carrying value of the note after this entry is $10,300 ($10,000 + $300). An alternative would be to credit interest payable.

Reporting at December 31, 1991:

```
Income statement:
    Interest expense . . . . . . . . . . . . . . . . . . . . . . $   300
Balance sheet:
  Current liabilities:
    Note payable, short term ($10,000 + $300) . . . . . $10,300
```

Entries at maturity date:

September 30, 1992—To record accrued interest to date and payment of the face amount of the note at maturity:

```
Interest expense ($10,000)(.12)(9/12) . . . . . . . . . . . . . . . .     900
    Note payable, short term . . . . . . . . . . . . . . . . . . . .           900
Note payable, short term ($10,000 + $300 + $900) . . . . . . . . . 11,200
    Cash . . . . . . . . . . . . . . . . . . . . . . . . . . . . . . .        11,200
```

Accounting Entries and Reporting: (Gross Basis):

Entries during 1991:

October 1, 1991—To record a noninterest-bearing note payable at its gross (face) amount:[10]

```
Cash . . . . . . . . . . . . . . . . . . . . . . . . . . . . . . . . . . 10,000
Discount on note payable, short-term . . . . . . . . . . . . . . .  1,200
    Note payable, short-term . . . . . . . . . . . . . . . . . . . . .       11,200
```

December 31, 1991—Adjusting entry for accrued interest:

```
Interest expense ($1,200)(3/12) . . . . . . . . . . . . . . . . . . . .     300
    Discount on note payable, short-term . . . . . . . . . . . . .           300
```

Reporting at December 31, 1991—Noninterest-bearing note payable:

```
Income statement:
    Interest expense . . . . . . . . . . . . .         $   300
Balance sheet:
  Current liabilities:
    Note payable . . . . . . . . . . . . . . $11,200
    Less: Unamortized discount . . . . .         900    $10,300
```

---

[10] The amount of interest expense and the net liability balances are the same regardless of whether the note is recorded at net or gross.

Entries at maturity date:

September 30, 1992—Payment of the face amount of the note:

```
Interest expense ($1,200)(9/12) . . . . . . . . . . . . . . . . . . . . . .    900
Note payable, short-term . . . . . . . . . . . . . . . . . . . . . . . . . 11,200
    Discount on note payable, short-term . . . . . . . . . . . . .          900
    Cash . . . . . . . . . . . . . . . . . . . . . . . . . . . . . . . .       11,200
```

Accounting for Short-Term Notes Payable with Unrealistic Interest Rates   Sometimes a noncash asset is acquired and a note is given with a stated rate of interest that is less than the current market rate (the effective rate) of interest for the level of risk involved. When this happens, the cost of the asset is the present value of the future cash payments discounted at the current market rate of interest rather than at the stated interest rate. Assume, for example, that a machine is purchased on January 1, 1991 with a one-year, $1,000, 6% interest-bearing note. The current market rate of interest for obligations with this level of risk is 12%.

1. Cost of the machine:

$$(\$1,000 + \$60)(PV1, 12\%, 1) = (\$1,060)(.89286) = \$946.43$$

2. Entries (net method):

   January 1, 1991—Acquisition date:

```
Machine . . . . . . . . . . . . . . . . . . . . . . . . . . . . . . . 946.43
    Note payable, short term . . . . . . . . . . . . . . . . . . .          946.43
```

   December 31, 1991—Payment date:

```
Note payable, short term . . . . . . . . . . . . . . . . . . . . . . 946.43
Interest expense ($946.43)(.12) . . . . . . . . . . . . . . . . . . 113.57
    Cash ($1,000 + $60) . . . . . . . . . . . . . . . . . . . . . .        1,060.00
```

This example uses the current market interest rate for similar notes with the same risk for the effective rate. This rate may be difficult to estimate reliably. Alternatively, if the competitive cash price of the noncash asset received is known, it should be used to establish the effective rate of interest.

Cash and Property Dividends Payable

After declaration by the board of directors, cash dividends payable should be reported as a current liability if they are to be paid within the coming year or operating cycle, whichever is longer. Cash and property dividends payable are reported as a liability between the date of declaration and payment on the legal basis that declaration gives rise to an enforceable contract.[11]

Liabilities are not recognized for undeclared dividends in arrears on preferred stock or for any other dividends not formally declared by the board of directors. Dividends in arrears on cumulative preferred stock should be disclosed in the notes to the financial statements. Scrip dividends payable are reported as a current liability unless there is no intention to make payment in the next fiscal year.[12]

---

[11] Technically, it can be argued that dividends payable are not current liabilities since they are distributions to owners. Stock dividends payable are not liabilities but rather merely a division of the assets into more ownership shares.

[12] A dividend payable in scrip is a promise by the corporation to pay the dividend at a later date. Scrip dividends are declared when the corporation wishes to keep its record of continuous dividend payments uninterrupted, has the necessary retained earnings to legally declare the dividend, but is currently short of cash.

Accrued Liabilities

Accrued liabilities include wages earned by employees and interest earned by creditors but not as yet paid. Accrued liabilities are recorded in the accounts by making adjusting entries at the end of the accounting period. For example, any wages that have not yet been recorded or paid at the end of the accounting period must be recorded by debiting wage expense and crediting wages payable. Recognition of accrued liabilities is consistent with the definition of a liability and the *matching principle*.

Advances and Returnable Deposits

A special liability arises when a company receives cash deposits from customers and employees. Deposits may also be received from customers as guarantees for payment of obligations that may be incurred in the future or to guarantee peformance of a contract or service. For example, when an order is taken, a company may require an advance payment to cover losses that would be incurred if the order is canceled. Such advances create liabilities for the company receiving the cash until the underlying transaction is completed. Advances are recorded by debiting cash and crediting a liability account such as customer deposits.

Deposits frequently are received from customers as guarantees in case of noncollection or for possible damage to property left with the customer. For example, deposits required from customers by gas, water, light, and other public utilities are liabilities of such companies to their customers. Also, employees may make returnable deposits to ensure the return of keys and other company property, for locker privileges, and for club memberships. Deposits should be reported as current or long-term liabilities depending on the time involved between date of deposit and expected termination of the relationship. If the advances or deposits are interest-bearing, an adjusting entry is required to accrue interest expense and to increase the related liability.[13]

Unearned Revenues (Revenues Collected in Advance)

Cash collected in advance of the delivery of a good or service creates a liability. The transaction does not yet qualify for recognition as revenue in conformity with the *revenue principle*. Examples of revenues collected in advance include gift certificates, college tuition, rent, ticket sales, and magazine subscriptions. Such transactions are recorded as a debit to cash and a credit to an appropriately designated current liability account. This account is often titled unearned revenues and may be given a modifying adjective, for example, unearned subscription revenues in the case of subscriptions. Other titles for this account include prepaid subscription revenue and subscription revenue collected in advance. The phrase *deferred revenues* is also occasionally encountered in this type of account title. This title is not the preferred description of the account.

Subsequently, when the product or service is delivered and the revenue is earned, the liability account is decreased and the appropriate revenue account is credited. This latter entry often is one of the year-end adjusting entries (see Chapter 3 on adjusting entries).

---

[13] Employees also have portions of their wages withheld for saving bond purchase programs, stock purchase plans, medical insurance premiums, and retirement programs. These withholdings constitute liabilities until the amounts are either delivered to a trustee or the service (delivery of the savings bond, for example) is completed.

To illustrate, on November 1, 1991, Zorex Company collected rent of $6,000 for the next six months. The accounting period ends December 31. The entries are:

November 1, 1991–Rent collected in advance:

```
Cash . . . . . . . . . . . . . . . . . . . . . . . . . . . . . . . . . 6,000
    Rent revenue collected in advance [or unearned
        rent revenue]  . . . . . . . . . . . . . . . . . . . . . . . . . .     6,000
```

December 31, 1991—Adjusting entry for the portion earned:

```
Rent revenue collected in advance [or unearned
    rent revenue]  . . . . . . . . . . . . . . . . . . . . . . . . . . 2,000
    Rent revenue ($6,000)(⅔) . . . . . . . . . . . . . . . . . . . .     2,000
```

The remaining prepaid rent revenue of $4,000 is reported as a current liability because Zorex has an obligation to render future occupancy services during the following four months.

Another example of an obligation to render future service is newspaper and magazine subscriptions for which the cash has been collected prior to delivery. This liability is illustrated by the 1988 financial statements of the New York Times Company. In their Summary of Significant Accounting Policies **(Note 1),** the company states:

> *Subscription Revenues.* Proceeds from subscriptions are deferred at the time of sale as unexpired subscriptions and are included in revenues on a pro rata basis over the terms of the subscriptions.

The company titles the current liability unexpired subscriptions.

Taxes

State and federal laws require businesses to collect certain taxes from customers and employees for remittance to designated governmental agencies. These taxes include sales taxes, income taxes withheld from employee paychecks, property taxes, and payroll taxes. Similar collections also are made on behalf of unions, insurance companies, and employee-sponsored activities. When collections are made for third parties, cash and current liabilities both increase. The collections represent liabilities that are settled when the funds are remitted to the designated parties. Three typical situations are illustrated. They involve:

* Sales taxes.
* Payroll taxes.
* Property taxes.

Sales Taxes   In most states, retail businesses are required to collect a sales tax at the time of sale and to remit the tax to the taxing authority. Typical entries, assuming a 6% sales tax and $500,000 of sales, are:

1. At date the tax is assessed (point of sale):

```
Cash and accounts receivable . . . . . . . . . . . . . . . . . . . 530,000
    Sales revenue  . . . . . . . . . . . . . . . . . . . . . . .     500,000
    Sales tax payable ($500,000) (.06) . . . . . . . . . . . . . .      30,000
```

2. At date of remittance to taxing authority:

```
Sales tax payable . . . . . . . . . . . . . . . . . . . . . . . . 30,000
    Cash  . . . . . . . . . . . . . . . . . . . . . . . . . . . .      30,000
```

The entry above assumes the sales tax is separately recognized at the point of sale. Some companies simply include the sales tax in sales revenue. In this case, an adjusting entry is required at the end of the accounting period debiting sales revenue and crediting sales tax payable (or cash).

Payroll Taxes   Companies must pay various payroll taxes in addition to the wages and salaries paid to employees. Also, companies must deduct amounts from their employees' pay for employees' federal income taxes, social security taxes, union dues, insurance premiums, and the like. The primary federal payroll taxes are the FICA and FUTA taxes.

FICA payroll tax is authorized by the social security laws. The employer must deduct tax from the pay of each employee under specified conditions. In addition to the tax paid by the employee, the employer usually must match the contribution of the employee and remit both amounts to the U.S. Treasury. FICA taxes, so called because the enabling legislation is the Federal Insurance Contribution Act (also known as the Federal Old-Age Survivor and Disability Insurance, or O.A.S.D.I.), include the Federal Hospital Insurance tax. Together these two taxes are commonly referred to as the social security tax. The rate for these two taxes is changed from time to time by acts of Congress. For example, for 1991, employers and employees each pay a tax of 7.65% on the first $53,400 earned by the employee. The purpose of the social security taxes is to provide retirement pay and medicare for retirees and death benefits for the retiree's survivors.

FUTA payroll tax, also authorized by federal law, is used to finance the cost associated with the federal-state unemployment and compensation program. In most but not all states, this payroll tax is paid only by the employer (of one or more persons). The federal portion of this payroll tax is known as the FUTA tax because the enabling legislation is the Federal Unemployment Tax Act. The state portion of this tax is commonly referred to as SUTA. Assume for 1991 the FUTA rate is 6.2% on the first $7,000 in wages paid to each employee, with 5.4% the maximum payable to the state of employment, and the remaining 0.8% payable to the U.S. Treasury.

Illustration of Payroll Taxes   Assume Thor Company paid January 1991 salaries of $100,000. Income tax withholding was $20,000, and the FICA and FUTA rates applied to all salaries paid (1991 rates are used in the illustration):

a. To record salaries and employee deductions:

Salary expense	100,000	
Federal income tax payable (from a tax table)		20,000
FICA tax payable, employees ($100,000)(.0765)		7,650
Cash		72,350

b. To record payroll taxes payable by the employer:

Expense, payroll taxes	13,850	
FICA tax payable, employer ($100,000)(.0765)		7,650
FUTA tax payable, ($100,000)(.008)		800
SUTA tax payable, ($100,000)(.054)		5,400

c. To record remittance of payroll taxes:

Federal income tax payable	20,000	
FICA tax payable, employees*	7,650	
FICA tax payable, employer*	7,650	
FUTA tax payable†	800	
SUTA tax payable	5,400	
Cash		41,500

* These taxes are usually recorded in one account, FICA tax payable, with no distinction between the employee and employer contributions. The taxes are paid as frequently as within three working days after release of the employee paychecks but no less frequently than once a quarter.

† Usually paid quarterly.

Property Taxes Property taxes are paid directly by the company to the taxing authority. These taxes are based on the assessed value of real and personal property and are levied at the local governing level to support school, city, county, and other designated activities. Unpaid taxes constitute a lien on the assessed property.

Property taxes for the current year usually are assessed near the end of the year and billed at the end of the year. In this situation, the accounting period during which these taxes should be recognized precedes the period in which the taxes are paid. Correct matching of the property tax expense with the period benefited means that the expense must be accrued before the actual amount of the tax is known. Therefore, estimates often must be used. The typical sequence of assessing property taxes is as follows: by midyear, tentative taxable valuations are developed along with estimated tax rates; by year-end, each property owner receives the actual taxable valuation, tax rate, and the resulting property tax; and during the early part of the following year, payment is made to the taxing authority. Therefore, 1991 property taxes typically would be assessed late in 1991 and paid in 1992. Most businesses accrue property tax expense each month based on best estimates and handle revisions as changes in estimates (i.e., prospectively). At year-end, the estimated amounts that have been recorded in the related expense and liability accounts are adjusted to agree with the actual amount assessed, which must be used for annual accounting and reporting purposes.

To illustrate accounting for property taxes, consider a situation that involves quarterly recognition of property taxes during 1991. The following sequence of events and their accounting treatment are appropriate:

1. January 1991—*Estimate* of 1991 property tax based on an expected 20% increase over the 1990 actual tax ($2,061):

   ($2,061 × 1.20) ÷ 4 = $618. (Use $600 per quarter as the estimate)

   March 31, 1991—Accrued tax for first quarter:

Property tax expense 600	}	Entry made March and
Property tax payable . . .	600	June; total $1,200.

2. July 1991—Received the following from taxing authority:

   Tentative 1991 taxable valuation, $190,076 × Estimated 1991 tax rate per $100 valuation, $1.4470 = Estimated 1991 property tax, $2,750

   September 30, 1991 (change in estimate) = ($2,750 − $1,200) ÷ 2 quarters remaining = $775 (use $780 per quarter as the estimate.)

Property tax expense 780	}	Entry made
Property tax payable . . .	780	September

3. December 29, 1991—Received actual 1991 tax assessment:

   1991 taxable valuation $197,076 × 1991 tax rate per $100 valuation, $1.45 = $2,858

   December 31, 1991:

Property tax expense ($2,858 − $1,200 − $780) 878		
Property tax payable		878

4. January 1992—Payment of 1991 property tax:

Property tax payable 2,858		
Cash		2,858

The December 31, 1991 financial statements would show:

Income statement:
Property tax expense $2,858

Balance sheet:
Current liabilities:
Property tax payable $2,858

Regardless of the respective tax and accounting fiscal periods, the accounting approach can be adapted to conform to GAAP.[14]

Conditional Payments

Some liabilities are established on the basis of a firm's periodic income. Two primary examples are certain bonuses or profit-sharing plan payments to employees and income taxes based on taxable income. These items can be established at year's end, but the liability must be estimated quarterly. Until paid, they represent current liabilities of the organization.[15]

Income Taxes Payable   Federal and state income taxes are based on federal and state legislation. There will inevitably be differences between taxable income computed for financial reporting purposes and taxable income used in the determination of state and federal tax liabilities. Indeed, these differences have increased in recent years. Since the interpretation of the tax code often depends on the courts and since quarterly reports require a provision for the tax liability, estimates are required. The estimated liability should be reported as a current liability based on the firm's best estimates. Periodic payments, which will change through the year as the estimated tax changes, are required.

Bonuses   Many companies pay cash bonuses to selected employees based on earnings. Accountants should insist that any agreement be specific. For example, if earnings are involved, it should be clear whether the earnings are before or after taxes. Further, when earnings are involved, the adjusting entry to recognize the bonus cannot be established until all other adjusting entries have been made.

Bonus payments to employees should be considered additional wages in the year earned. As such, bonuses increase the period's wage expense and establish a concurrent liability. The liability is usually payable within a short period of time and, hence, is properly considered a current liability.

Computation of the bonus and the accompanying entries is complex because the bonus is an expense and hence deductible from income. In addition, the bonus affects the computation of the company's tax expense and, thereby, also income. Consider an example.

Suppose Aldar Corporation has pretax income of $500,000 in 1991 before establishing the year's bonus. Suppose, further, that the bonus agreement specifies the employees are to be paid 10% of income as this year's bonus. Now if the bonus were not a taxable expense, the bonus amount would be ($500,000)(.10), or $50,000. However, the bonus is an expense and must be deducted in determining the income on which the bonus is to be paid. To properly establish the bonus, assume for the moment there is no tax effect. Then the bonus is 10% of income, with income first reduced by the bonus.

In symbols:

$$\text{Bonus} = .10(\$500,000 - \text{Bonus})$$

and solving:

$$\text{Bonus} = \$50,000 - .1(\text{Bonus})$$

---

[14] In a situation where property taxes are levied in advance of the taxing jurisdiction's fiscal year, the appropriate accounting would use the deferral method. Cash (or a liability) is credited, and deferred (or prepaid) property tax expense is debited. The prepayment is written off to expense over the period covered by the assessment.

[15] Royalty agreements are another example of a conditional payment based on a percentage of income and create a current liability.

$$1.1(\text{Bonus}) = \$50,000$$
$$\text{Bonus} = \$45,455$$

Unfortunately, this is only a partial solution since the effect of the bonus on the company's tax expense has, so far, been ignored. Fortunately, a similar argument will resolve the problem. The argument proceeds as follows, assuming a 40 percent tax rate. If the bonus were known, the tax expense would be:

$$\text{Tax} = .40(\$500,000 - \text{Bonus})$$

And if the tax were known, the bonus would be:

$$\text{Bonus} = .10(\$500,000 - \text{Tax} - \text{Bonus})$$

These two equations, involving two unknowns, can be solved simultaneously to yield both the bonus and the tax expense. Simplifying these two equations:

$$\text{Tax} = \$200,000 - .4(\text{Bonus})$$
$$\text{Bonus} = \$\ 50,000 - .1(\text{Tax}) - .1(\text{Bonus})$$

Now substituting this expression for tax into the simplified expression for the bonus gives:

$$\text{Bonus} = \$50,000 - .1[\$200,000 - .4(\text{Bonus})] - .1(\text{Bonus})$$

or:

$$\text{Bonus} = \$50,000 - \$20,000 + .04(\text{Bonus}) - .1(\text{Bonus})$$
$$\text{Bonus} = \$50,000 - \$20,000 - .06(\text{Bonus})$$
$$1.06\ \text{Bonus} = \$30,000$$

giving:

$$\text{Bonus} = \$28,302$$

Using this figure for the bonus:

$$\text{Tax} = \$200,000 - .4(\$28,302)$$
$$\text{Tax} = \$188,679$$

The calculation of the bonus and the tax require that all other adjusting entries be completed first. Once this has been done, the bonus can be figured as illustrated and entered into the accounts.

Wage expense (employee bonus)	28,302	
Bonus payable		28,302

Compensated-Absence Liabilities

Companies often grant employees specified periods such as vacations and holidays away from work. During this time, the regular salary or wage is continued. When salaries and wages are paid during these absences from work, the expense is recognized in the current year. However, when the employees can retain and carry over unused time for these events to future years, the question arises as to when the expense for this unused time should be recognized: in the prior year in which it was earned or the later year(s) in which it is taken? Because both approaches were prevalent,. the FASB issued *SFAS No. 43,* "Accounting for Compensated Absences." *SFAS No. 43* requires that any expense that is due to compensated absences must be recognized (accrued) in the year in which it is earned, provided:

♦ The absence from work relates to services already rendered.
♦ The carryover accumulates (or vests).
♦ The payment is probable (the absence will occur).
♦ The amount (i.e., cost) can be reliably estimated.[16]

---

[16] In the case of accumulated rights to receive nonvesting (employees are not entitled to nonvesting benefits if employment ceases) sick pay benefits, accrual is not required but is permitted. A strong case can be made that the illness (when it occurs) is the major event rather than the employee's previous service.

Implementing *SFAS No. 43* involves an adjusting entry at the end of each fiscal year to accrue all of the compensation cost for the vacation and holiday time that is to be carried over. This is done by recognizing an expense and a current liability. When the vacation or holiday time is taken, the liability account is debited at the time the employee is paid. These entries recognize the cost of the compensated absences as an expense in the period earned rather than when taken.

For example, consider a situation that involves the carryover of vacation time. Conway Company has 500 employees. Each employee is granted three weeks vacation time each year with full pay. Vacation time, up to a maximum accumulation of four weeks, may be carried over to subsequent years prior to termination of employment. At the end of 1991, the end of the annual accounting period, personnel records revealed the following information concerning carryover vacation times and amounts.

Number of Employees	Weeks per Employee	Carryovers from 1991*	
		Total Weeks	Total Salaries
10	2	20	$30,000
3	1	3	6,000

* These are carryovers from 1991 to future years.

Disregarding payroll taxes, the indicated entries are as follows:

December 31, 1991—Adjusting entry to accrue vacation salaries not yet taken or paid:

Salary expense	36,000	
Liability for compensated absences		36,000

During 1992—Vacation time carryover is taken and the salaries paid (one person did not take two weeks of carryover, $3,000):

Liability for compensated absences	33,000	
Cash ($36,000 − $3,000)		33,000

The balance remaining in the liability account is $3,000.

This illustration assumed that there was no change in the rate of pay from 1991 to 1992 (when the carryover was used) for those employees who had the carryover. If there were rate changes, the pay difference would be debited (if an increase) or credited (if a decrease) to wage expense during 1992. The change is considered a change in estimate.[17] For example, if the 1992 wages relating to the employees who used their carryovers during 1992 increased by $1,000, the 1992 entry would have been:

Liability for compensated absences	33,000	
Wage expense (1992)	1,000	
Cash ($36,000 + $1,000 − $3,000)		34,000

The balance remaining in the liability account remains $3,000.

Current Maturities of Long-Term Debt

How should a debt that is part current and part noncurrent be reported? The problem arises when periodic payments are made on a debt. A payment is due in the next accounting period while additional payments will be made in later accounting periods. If the next payment is to be made from current assets, that portion of the debt should be reported as a current liability on the balance sheet. For example:

---

[17] In practice, many firms would simply recalculate the liability at the next year-end and adjust it through salary expense.

Current liabilities:
   Current payment on bond issue $100,000

Long-term liabilities:
   Bonds payable (less current portion: $100,000) $400,000

The current payment is often combined with another current liability rather than reported separately.

Obligations Callable on Demand by the Creditor

SFAS No. 78, "Classification of Obligations That Are Callable by the Creditor," amends *ARB No. 43,* Chapter 3A, to specify that the kinds of debt illustrated in the following cases must be included in the current liability classification:

Case 1—obligations that are payable on demand (i.e., callable) or will be due on demand within one year from the balance sheet date, or the operating cycle, if longer, even though liquidation within that period is not expected.

Case 2—long-term obligations that are or will be callable by the creditor either because of a violation of the terms of the debt at the date of the balance sheet or because the violation, if not cured within a specified grace period, will make the debt callable.

The concept that supports these current liability classifications is that the debtor of a long-term obligation or a callable note meeting the above specifications cannot control the payment date.

CONCEPT REVIEW

1. What are the different categories of current liabilities?
2. What is the difference between the stated and the effective rates of interest?
3. How is the liability for a bonus based on income calculated?

SHORT-TERM OBLIGATIONS EXPECTED TO BE REFINANCED
♦

A company may be motivated to reclassify liabilities from current to long term to improve its reported working capital position. One reason given for such reclassifications is that because the company intends to refinance the liability, it does not expect to be making any payments on it from current assets. *SFAS No. 6,* "Classification of Short-Term Obligations Expected to Be Refinanced," was issued to establish guidelines and to prevent abuses. *SFAS No. 6* provides that current liabilities expected to be refinanced can be reclassified as long-term liabilities only if the debtor fully intends to refinance the specific short-term liability and shows an ability to do so by actually refinancing it on a long-term basis before the financial statements are issued, or by entering in good faith into a long-term, noncancelable refinancing agreement that is supported by a viable lender. The maximum amount that may be classified as long term cannot exceed the amount irrevocably refinanced less the effect of all refinancing restrictions.

Firms, for example, often finance new plant and equipment with short-term commercial paper, expecting to finance it later on a long-term basis. They then report the debt as long term. Penn Central had extensive debt classified as long term because the railroad felt it was covered by refinancing commitments from lenders. When the commitments did not materialize, Penn Central went bankrupt.

When a financing agreement is relied upon to support classification of short-term obligations as long-term debt, it must meet the following criteria under *SFAS No. 6:*

1. The agreement must be noncancelable by all parties (except for violations by the debtor) and extend beyond one year from the balance sheet date or from the start of the operating cycle, whichever is longer.
2. At the balance sheet date and the issue date, the company must not be in violation of the agreement (unless a waiver is obtained).
3. The lender must be financially capable of honoring the agreement.

The amount of the short-term debt that can be classified as long term cannot exceed the amount available under the agreement, must be adjusted for any limitations in the agreement, and cannot exceed a reasonable estimate of the minimum amount expected to be available (if the amount available for refinancing will fluctuate). If any of these three amounts cannot be estimated, the entire amount of the short-term debt must remain a current liability. Short-term obligations liquidated after the balance sheet date but before the statement issue date must be reported as short-term obligations if the funds used in refinancing were short-term. This is the case even if long-term financing is ultimately obtained before the financial statement issue date.

Replacement of one short-term obligation with another is no longer sufficient to avoid classification as a current liability. A revolving credit agreement cancelable at any time by the creditor, for example, does not fulfill the requirements of *SFAS No. 6*.

Furthermore, short-term obligations that are extinguished with current assets that were replenished with long-term financing before the balance sheet issue date, are classified as current liabilities. For example, Rell Company liquidates a $30,000 short-term note by paying cash in February 1991, before the 1990 financial statements are published. Even if Rell replaces the $30,000 cash used to pay the note with long-term debt before the issue date, the short-term debt is not classified as long-term in the 1990 balance sheet. In so ruling, *FASB Interpretation No. 8* reaffirmed the concept that short-term obligations requiring the use of current assets for payment are current liabilities.

SFAS No. 6 also precludes classification of a short-term obligation as long term if the creditor is able to cancel the underlying financing agreement. However, some long-term debt agreements contain a subjective clause permitting the creditor to accelerate the due date. Are these liabilities classified as current? *FASB Technical Bulletin 79-3* states that if the likelihood of acceleration is remote, the debt is not reclassified as current. However, if the debtor is experiencing financial difficulties and if a reasonable probability exists that the due date may be accelerated to within a year of the balance sheet date, reclassification is warranted.

The following information must be disclosed under *SFAS No. 6:* total current liabilities and a general description of the financing arrangements of short-term obligations excluded from current liabilities. If debt or equity securities are issued to replace the short-term obligation, the terms of the new issues are disclosed.

The footnotes to the 1988 annual report of American Greetings Corporation provide an example of short-term obligations refinanced with long-term debt before the balance sheet was issued:

> In March 1988, the Company issued $100,000 of 8.375% five-year notes to refinance short-term obligations. Accordingly, $82,795 of commercial paper and the $11,126 note due to a bank in December 1988 have been classified as long-term debt at February 29, 1988.

If a short-term obligation is to be excluded from current liabilities under a financing agreement, footnote disclosure is required and should include:

1. A general description of the financing agreement.
2. The terms of any new obligation to be incurred.
3. The terms of any equity security to be issued.

In certain specialized industries (including broker-dealers, real estate, and stock life insurance companies) the current-noncurrent distinction is not useful. These firms prepare unclassified balance sheets and are thus not covered by *SFAS No. 6*. Short-term obligations that satisfy the requirements to be shown as long-term can be given a specific and distinct caption if desired, such as "short-term debt expected to be refinanced."

CONCEPT REVIEW

1. Why might a company be motivated to reclassify a liability from short to long term?
2. Under what conditions can a short-term liability be reclassified as a long-term liability?
3. When a short-term obligation is excluded from current liabilities under a financing agreement, what footnote disclosure is required?

CONTINGENCIES AND ESTIMATED LIABILITIES

The central issue here is the definition of a debt when one or more specific events have not occurred. Liabilities often must be estimated because a known liability exists but the ultimate amount is uncertain or because a loss contingency exists. A **contingency** is defined in *SFAS No. 5*, "Accounting for Contingencies," as

> an existing condition, situation, or set of circumstances involving uncertainty as to possible gain (hereinafter, 'gain contingency') or a loss (hereinafter, 'loss contingency') to an enterprise that ultimately will be resolved when one or more future events occur or fail to occur. Resolution of the uncertainty may confirm the acquisition of an asset or the reduction of a liability or the loss or impairment of an asset or the incurrence of a liability.

SFAS No. 5 is the basic pronouncement on contingencies and estimated liabilities and is the basis for the discussion. This section is divided into three parts:
- Contingent liabilities (loss contingencies) that must be accrued and reported at estimated dollar amounts in the body of the financial statements.
- Contingent liabilities that are reported only in the notes to the financial statements.
- Gain contingencies.

SFAS No. 5 delineates contingencies and specifies particular accounting treatments on the basis of whether the contingency is:

1. *Probable*—The future event (or events) is likely to occur.
2. *Reasonably possible*—The chance of occurrence of the future event (or events) is more than remote but less than likely.
3. *Remote*—The chance of occurrence of the future event (or events) is slight.

The provisions on *SFAS No. 5* relating to contingencies are summarized in Exhibit 15–1. In 1989, 63% of the firms surveyed in *Accounting Trends & Techniques* reported loss contingencies due to litigation alone.

Loss Contingencies that Must Be Accrued and a Liability Recognized

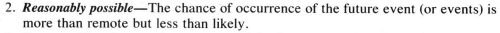

SFAS No. 5 requires that a loss contingency must be accrued if *both* of the following conditions are met:

1. Information received prior to the issuance of the financial statements indicates that it is *probable* that an asset has been impaired or a liability has been incurred

EXHIBIT 15-1   Summary of Accounting for Contingencies

Probablistic Nature of the Occurrence of the Contingent Event	Amount Can Be Reasonably Estimated	Amount Cannot Be Reasonably Estimated
	Loss Contingency	
Probable	1. Accrue *both* a loss and a liability, and report them in the body of the statements.	2. Do not accrue; report as a *note* in the financial statements.
Reasonably possible	3. Do not accrue; report as a *note* in the financial statements.	4. Do not accrue; report as a *note* in the financial statements.
Remote	5. No accrual or *note* required; however, a note is permitted.	6. No accrual or *note* required; however, a note is permitted.

Probablistic Nature	Amount Can Be Reasonably Estimated	Amount Cannot Be Reasonably Estimated
	Gain Contingency	
Probable	7. No accrual except in unusual circumstances. *Note* disclosure required.	8. *Note* disclosure required; exercise care to avoid misleading inferences.
Reasonably possible	9. *Note* disclosure required; exercise care to avoid misleading inferences.	10. *Note* disclosure required; exercise care to avoid misleading inferences.
Remote	11. Disclosure not recommended.	

at the date of the financial statements. It must be *probable* that one or more future events will or will not occur confirming the fact of the loss.

2. The amount of the loss can be reasonably estimated.[18]

This situation corresponds to statement 1 in Exhibit 15–1.

A loss contingency that meets both of the previously noted criteria, in addition to being accrued in the accounts, must be reported on the balance sheet as a liability and on the income statement as an expense or loss in the period in which the two criteria are first met.

SFAS No. 5 identified a number of loss contingencies that must be considered for appropriate disclosure. These contingencies include estimated losses on receivables (allowance for doubtful accounts); estimated warranty obligations; litigations, claims, and assessments; and anticipated losses on the disposal of a segment of the business. Three examples illustrate the accrual of a loss contingency and recognition of a liability.

Case A—Product Warranty Liability   Rollex Company sold merchandise for $200,000 cash during the current period. Experience has indicated that warranty and guarantee costs will approximate .5% of sales. The indicated entries are:

1. In year of sale:

Cash	200,000	
Sales revenue		200,000
Warranty expense	1,000	
Estimated warranty liability ($200,000)(.005)		1,000

---

[18] If the two conditions mentioned are met but the information available indicates only that the loss is within a range (no single amount in the range being a better estimate than any other amount), the minimum amount is accrued. The exposure to an additional amount (up to the maximum in the range) should be disclosed in the notes.

2. Subsequently, actual warranty expenditures of $987 were made during the warranty period:

Warranty liability	987	
Cash (and other resources used)		987

3. Instead, if the actual expenditure was $1,100, the entry would be:

Warranty liability	1,000	
Warranty expense	100	
Cash (and other resources used)		1,100

Under the entry in (2) $13 remains in the liability account. This means the warranty expense, recognized in previous periods, was overstated by $13. No attempt is made to correct prior years' accounts. The situation is treated as a change in estimate. The current year's warranty expense, based on current year's sales, would simply be reduced by $13.

For an example of the type of disclosure provided, Mountain Medical Equipment's 1988 financial statements include the following note related to warranties.

> *Estimated Liability for Future Warranty Claims*
> The Company provides customers with warranties ranging from one to three years primarily covering the cost of parts. The liability for future warranty claims reflects the estimated cost of warranty repairs on products previously sold.

Case B—Liability from Premiums, Coupons, and Trading Stamps As a promotional device, many companies offer premiums to customers who turn in coupons, proof of purchase and so on. At the end of each accounting period, a portion of these will be unredeemed by the customers, some of which ultimately will be turned in for redemption. These outstanding claims for premiums represent an expense and an estimated liability that must be recognized in the period of sale of the merchandise.

The amounts involved can be substantial. For example, in 1980, Sperry and Hutchinson (licensor of S&H Green Stamps) reported a liability for $308 million to match the prior recognized expense for green stamps issued, representing unredeemed stamps. Before 1979, Sperry estimated that 95 percent of the stamps it issued would ultimately be redeemed. After 1979, new information suggested a lower redemption rate. Sperry altered its estimated redemption rate to 90%, reducing expenses by some $10 million per year.[19]

To illustrate the accounting, Baker Coffee Company offered its customers a premium—a special coffee cup free of charge (cost to Baker, 75 cents each) with the return of 20 coupons. One coupon is placed in each can of coffee when packed. The company estimated, on the basis of past experience, that only 70% of the coupons would be redeemed. The following additional data for two years are available:

	First Year	Second Year
Number of coffee cups purchased at $.75	6,000	4,000
Number of cans of coffee sold	100,000	200,000
Number of coupons redeemed	40,000	120,000

The indicated entries are as follows:

1. To record purchase of cups:

	First Year	Second Year
Premium inventory	4,500	3,000
Cash	4,500	3,000

---

[19] "This Year, Next Year . . . ," *Forbes*, October 12, 1981, pp. 73–74.

2. To record the estimated liability and premium expense based on sales:

Premium expense* 2,625		5,250
Premium claims payable	2,625	5,250

* Computations:
Year 1: (100,000 ÷ 20) ($.75 × .70) = $2,625.
Year 2: (200,000 ÷ 20) ($.75 × .70) = $5,250.

3. To record redemption of coupons:

Premium claims payable* 1,500		4,500
Premium inventory	1,500	4,500

* Computations:
Year 1: (40,000 ÷ 20) ($.75) = $1,500.
Year 2: (120,000 ÷ 20) ($.75) = $4,500.

Case C—Liability from Litigation   Solon Company was sued during the last quarter of the current year because of an accident involving a vehicle owned and operated by the company. The plaintiff is seeking $100,000 damages. If, in the opinion of management and company counsel, it is probable that damages will be assessed and a reasonable estimate is $50,000,[20] the indicated entry is:

Estimated loss from pending lawsuit 50,000	
Estimated liability from pending lawsuit	50,000

Estimated liabilities, such as the one illustrated, may ultimately require expenditures that differ from the amount estimated to satisfy the actual liability. When the estimated liability varies from the actual, the difference is accounted for as a change in estimate under the provisions of *APB No. 20.* The expense is increased or decreased when the amount becomes known.

Loss Contingencies that Are Disclosed Only in Notes

Potential loss contingencies, such as guarantees of indebtedness, accommodation endorsements, threat of expropriation of assets, standby letters of credit (guarantees of the credit of a third party), and risks due to fire, flood, and other hazards, also must be assessed and accounted for in conformity with *SFAS No. 5.* For example, Briggs and Stratton, Inc., reported in a note to their 1988 financial statements:

Note 7:
The Company is a 50% guarantor on bank loans of an unconsolidated Japanese joint venture for the manufacture of engines which has not yet begun operations. These bank loans totaled approximately $15,400,000 at June 30, 1988.

In Exhibit 15–1, statement 1, a loss contingency and the related liability are accrued and reported only when the loss is probable and the amount can be reasonably estimated. In contrast, Exhibit 15–1 identifies three situations involving loss contingencies for which disclosures in the notes are required (accrual is not permitted):
+ Statement 2, the loss is probable but cannot be reasonably estimated.
+ Statement 3, the loss is reasonably possible and can be reasonably estimated.
+ Statement 4, the loss is reasonably possible but cannot be reasonably estimated.

---

[20] It is unlikely that legal counsel and management would disclose a belief that a contingent loss is probable and can be reliably estimated. This situation would suggest that it may be advisable to settle out of court. To disclose a tacit expectation of loss in advance may prejudice the outcome of the trial. For this reason, lawyers vehemently object to such disclosures. The information will appear, if at all, in the notes to the financial statements. Even then, it is extremely unusual for a firm to mention specific amounts unless court judgments have already been rendered.

The note must describe the nature of the contingency and disclose any amount of loss than can be estimated and that is at least reasonably possible.[21] For example, the 1988 financial statements of Kmart, Inc., included the following note:

(Note C):
In a lawsuit resulting from a dispute with Fashion House, Inc., a judgment was rendered against Kmart Corporation in the amount of $59 million plus interest, a total of $79 million at January 25, 1989. The dispute involved Fashion House acting as a buying agent with respect to acquiring certain types of apparel merchandise for Kmart. Kmart plans to appeal the judgment. While management and legal council are presently unable to predict the outcome or to estimate the amount of any liability the company may have with respect to this lawsuit, it is not expected that this matter will have a material adverse effect on the company.

The conclusion is certainly different from the one the Manville Corporation arrived at when, as was described in the introduction to this chapter, the corporation declared bankruptcy when forced to disclose its loss contingency.

Another example of such disclosure is given by Apple in its 1988 statements.

NOTES TO CONSOLIDATED FINANCIAL STATEMENTS
Litigation (in part)
In May 1987, an action was commenced against Apple and certain of its current and former directors and officers, alleging that in 1985 Apple entered into and breached an alleged oral and written agreement to acquire the business of Woodside Design Associates, Inc. The complaint seeks up to $25 million in compensatory damages and up to $1 billion in punitive damages from Apple. Although discovery has only recently commenced in this action, Apple believes that the suit is without merit, and Apple intends to litigate vigorously the asserted claims, and, in the opinion of management, this litigation will not have a material effect on results of operations or financial condition.

Gain Contingencies

For a gain contingency to arise, the characteristics of a contingency must be present: an increase in assets or a decrease in liabilities, depending upon the occurrence of future events.

Contingent gains are rarely accrued. However, they are accorded note disclosure, provided the note does not give misleading implications. The different treatment accorded gain contingencies, compared with loss contingencies, is justified by the *conservatism constraint. Accounting Trends & Techniques* reports that 47% of the surveyed firms reported contingent gains in 1989.

An example of a contingent gain is provided by Rorer Group, Inc., in a note to its 1988 financial statements:

Note 16:
In accordance with the terms of a merger agreement with A. H. Robins Company, Incorporated (Robins), the company is entitled to termination fees and expense reimbursement as a result of the acceptance by Robins of a merger proposal with American Home Products Corporation (AHP). The bankruptcy court has ordered Robins to pay $29.9 million to Rorer immediately upon consummation of the proposed merger with AHP. If completed, this will result in approximately a $20 million pretax gain.

---

[21] *FASB Interpretation No. 14* to *SFAS No. 5*, Par. 5.

Executory Contracts

Executory contracts or agreements occur when two parties agree to transfer resources or services, but neither party has yet peformed. For example, a purchase agreement has been made, but no assets have been received and no payments have been made. Other examples include lines of credit, pensions, leases, and promises of future compensation prior to any transfer of resources. When a transfer of resources occurs, the contract or agreement is no longer executory. Executory contracts usually are not recorded because a transfer of assets or liabilities has not yet occurred. However, if the anticipated considerations are material, full disclosure should be made.

CONCEPT REVIEW

1. When must a loss contingency be accrued?
2. When is it necessary to report a loss contingency in the notes? What value, if any, should be reported?
3. How are executory contracts treated in the accounting records?

SUMMARY OF KEY POINTS

(L.O. 1)   1. A liability possesses three essential characteristics:
   a. Existence of an obligation that can only be satisfied by the transfer of an asset or a service to another entity.
   b. The event that gave rise to the obligation has occurred.
   c. The obligation is highly probable.

(L.O. 2)   2. Current liabilities are those whose liquidation is reasonably expected to require the use of existing resources properly classified as current assets, or the creation of other current liabilities.

(L.O. 3)   3. A liability is measured as the present value of all future cash payments discounted at the interest rate consistent with the risks involved. However, APB No. 21 specifically excludes the requirement to account separately for interest on liabilties to be paid within one year.

(L.O. 3)   4. All obligations with terms beyond normal trade terms, explicitly or implicitly involve interest.

(L.O. 4)   5. Cash or other assets received in advance of the delivery of goods or services create liabilities for the receiving firm.

(L.O. 3, 6)   6. Short-term obligations expected to be refinanced on a long-term basis can be classified as long-term only if the debtor (a) fully intends to refinance and (b) shows an ability to refinance by so doing or by entering into a noncancelable refinancing agreement supported by a viable lender.

(L.O. 7)   7. A loss contingency must be accrued if (a) prior to issuance of the financial statements, information suggests that it is probable that an asset has been impaired or a liability incurred as of the balance sheet date, and (b) the amount of the loss can be reasonably estimated.

(L.O. 7)   8. Loss contingencies for guarantees of indebtedness, stand-by letters of credit, and related events are reported in the notes either if they are probable but cannot be reasonably estimated or if they are reasonably possible.

(L.O. 7)   9. Gain contingencies are usually not accrued but rather reported in the notes if probable or reasonably possible.

**REVIEW
PROBLEM**

◆

In the introduction to this chapter, the situation faced by the Manville Company in 1982 was described. How do you feel about the following issues?

1. Does Manville face a contingent liability?
2. If so, must it be accrued?
3. If not, is footnote disclosure appropriate?
4. If accrual or footnote disclosure is appropriate, what amount should be shown?
5. Would you have filed for reorganization under Chapter 11? What do you think about the impact of accounting rules on Manville's action?

SOLUTION

◆

Your authors believe that a loss is probable and that an amount can be reasonably estimated. The minimum, which would appear from the limited published data to be at least $2 billion, should be accrued. Further, an estimate of the upper end of the possible loss range should be disclosed in a footnote.

We believe Manville was probably justified in filing for bankruptcy under Chapter 11. However, the contingent loss is there whether an accounting rule (*SFAS No. 5*) requires reporting it or not. Manville should not hide behind accounting rules. The rule is simply there to guarantee disclosure of the facts to those relying on the reports of Manville's management.

KEY TERMS

Contingency (783)
Current (short-term) liabilities (769)
Effective rate of interest (yield) (770)

Liabilities (767)
Stated rate of interest (770)

QUESTIONS

1. Give a conceptual definition of a liability.
2. Conceptually, how should a liability be measured?
3. Relate the measurement of a liability to its cause.
4. Why are most liabilities recognized at maturity value at the beginning of the term?
5. Compute the present value of a $10,000, one-year note payable that specifies no interest, although 10% would be a realistic rate. What is the amount of the principal and the interest?
6. In evaluating a balance sheet, some bankers say the liability section is one of the most important parts. What are the reasons justifying this position?
7. Some liabilities are reported at their maturity amount. In general, when should liabilities, prior to maturity date, be reported at less than their maturity amount?
8. How is the cost principle involved in accounting for current liabilties?
9. Define a current liability.
10. Differentiate between secured and unsecured liabilities. Explain the reporting procedures for each.
11. Distinguish between the stated rate of interest and the effective rate of interest (yield) on a debt.
12. Briefly define the following terms related to a note payable: principal, face, and maturity amounts.
13. Distinguish between an interest-bearing note and a noninterest-bearing note.
14. Assume $4,000 cash is borrowed on a $4,000, 10%, one-year note payable that is interest-bearing and that another $4,000 cash is borrowed on a $4,400 one-year note that is noninterest bearing. For each note give the following:
    a. Face amount of the note.
    b. Principal amount.
    c. Maturity amount.
    d. Total interest paid.
15. Are all declared dividends a liability between declaration and payment dates? Explain.
16. Why is an unearned revenue classified as a liability?

17. What is a compensated absence? When should the expense related to compensated absences be recognized?
18. What is the accounting definition of a contingency? What are the three characteristics of a contingency? Why is the concept important?
19. How does the accountant measure the likelihood of the outcome of a contingency? In general, how does this affect the accounting for and reporting of contingencies?
20. Briefly explain the accounting and reporting for loss contingencies.

EXERCISES

E15–1
Characteristics of Liabilities
(L.O. 1)

Listed below are five characteristics that may be associated with any liability:

a. The transfer of an asset or the obligation to provide a service is assured.
b. The magnitude of the obligation must be of material size relative to the firm's assets.
c. The obligation to transfer assets or provide services must be unavoidable if the existence of the obligation is at least probable.
d. The obligation arises from a past event.
e. An explicit interest rate must be stated as attaching to the obligation.

Required:
Indicate which of the above are necessary characteristics for the item to be a liability. Explain.

E 15–2
Identifying Liabilities and Current Liabilities
(L.O. 1, 2)

Five items, noted in the chapter, are repeated here:

a. Coupons that may be redeemed for merchandise or service.
b. Frequent flier miles earned by airline passengers.
c. Probable requirements to clean up toxic wastes.
d. Company contract promises to pay postretirement health benefits.
e. Preferred stock that is cumulative as to dividends, nonparticipating as to voting, and callable by issuer or redeemable by holder on demand.

Required:
Which of these items, if any, should be considered liabilities and recognized on the balance sheet? Should any of them or portions thereof be recognized as current liabilities? Explain.

E 15–3
Identifying Current Liabilities
(L.O. 2)

Listed below are six items:

a. Bank overdraft.
b. Retained earnings.
c. Long-term debt.
d. Dividends declared but not paid.
e. Customer payments for magazine subscriptions not yet delivered.
f. Income taxes payable.

Required:
Identify the current liabilities among these six items.

E 15–4
Identifying a Current Liability
(L.O. 2)

Suppose a firm has an obligation that requires it to pay another organization $500,000 two years from today.

Required:
Normally such a liability would be considered long-term and not current. Is there any situation in which this obligation could be considered a current liability? Explain.

E 15–5
Interest-Bearing and Noninterest-Bearing Notes Compared
(L.O. 4)

a. On January 1, 1991, a heavy-duty truck was purchased with a list price of $33,500. Payment included cash, $8,500, and a two-year, noninterest-bearing note of $25,000 (maturity date, December 31, 1992). A realistic interest rate for this level of risk was 12%. The accounting period ends December 31. Assume that this note is a current liability in this company.
b. On January 1, 1991, a small truck was purchased and payment was made as follows: cash, $5,000, and a one-year, 6%, interest-bearing note of $10,000, maturity date December 31,

1991 (which also is the end of the accounting period). A realistic interest rate for this level of risk is 12%.

Required:

Give all entries for each case from purchase date through maturity date of each note. Disregard depreciation. Round to the nearest dollar.

E 15–6
Interest-Bearing Note:
Entries and Reporting
(L.O. 4)

On May 1, 1991, Murray Meters borrowed $100,000 cash and signed a one-year, 12% interest-bearing note for that amount. Murray's accounting period ends December 31.

Required:

1. Give all of the required entries from May 1, 1991, through the maturity date of the note. Disregard reversing and closing entries.
2. Show how all amounts related to the note should be reported on the debtor's balance sheet at December 31, 1991, and the 1991 income statement.

E 15–7
Analysis of Two
Noninterest-Bearing
Notes—One Has an
Unrealistic Rate
(L.O. 4)

On March 1, 1991, Lasorda Lumber borrowed $60,000 cash from SP Bank and signed a one-year note for $70,650 (designated Note A); no interest was specified in the note. On June 1, 1991, Lasorda borrowed additional cash and signed a one-year note, face amount, $17,775 (designated Note B). No interest was specified in the note; however, the going rate of interest for this level of risk was 18.5%. The accounting period ends December 31.

Required:

	Note A	Note B
1. How much cash was received? . . . . $_____	$_____
2. What was the face amount of the note? . . . . $_____	$_____
3. What was the principal of the note? . . . . $_____	$_____
4. How much interest expense should be reported in:		
1991 . . . . $_____	$_____
1992 . . . . $_____	$_____
5. What was the stated interest rate? . . . . _____%	_____%
6. What was the yield or effective interest rate? . . . . _____%	_____%

E 15–8
Analysis and Comparison
of Interest-Bearing and
Noninterest-Bearing
Notes
(L.O. 4)

On September 1, 1991, Dyer Company borrowed cash on a $10,000 note payable due in one year. Assume the going rate of interest was 12% per year for this particular level of risk. The accounting period ends December 31.

Required:

Complete the following tabulation; round to the nearest dollar.

	Assuming the note was—	
	Interest-bearing	Noninterest-bearing
1. Cash received . . . . $_____	$_____
2. Cash paid at maturity date . . . . $_____	$_____
3. Total interest paid (cash) . . . . $_____	$_____
4. Interest expense in 1991 . . . . $_____	$_____
5. Interest expense in 1992 . . . . $_____	$_____
6. Amount of liabilities reported on 1991 balance sheet:		
Note payable (net) . . . . $_____	$_____
Interest payable . . . . $_____	$_____
7. Principal amount . . . . $_____	$_____
8. Face amount . . . . $_____	$_____
9. Maturity value . . . . $_____	$_____
10. Stated interest rate . . . . _____%	_____%
11. Yield or effective interest rate . . . . _____%	_____%

E 15–9
Noninterest-Bearing Note:
Entries and Reporting
(L.O. 4)

On April 1, 1991, Martin Manufacturing purchased a heavy machine for use in operations by paying $10,000 cash and signing a $40,000 (face amount) noninterest-bearing note due in one year (on March 31, 1992). The going rate of interest for this type of note was 14% per year. The company uses straight-line depreciation. The accounting period ends on December 31. Assume a five-year life for the machine and 10% residual value.

Required:

1. Give all entries from April 1, 1991, through March 31, 1992 (round amounts to the nearest dollar).
2. Show how all of the related items would be reported on the 1991 income statement and balance sheet.

E 15–10
Current Liabilities:
Original and Adjusting
Entries
(L.O. 4, 5, 6)

Voss Company, a large retail outlet, completed the following selected transactions during 1991 and 1992.

a. At the end of 1991, accrued wages that have not yet been recorded amounted to $34,000. These accrued wages were paid in the January 15, 1992, payroll, which amounted to $173,000 (disregard payroll taxes).
b. On November 1, 1991, rent revenue for the following six months was collected, $8,400.
c. On October 1, 1991, Voss received $800 as a deposit from a customer for some special containers that are to be returned on or about March 31, 1992. Voss agreed to "give the customer credit at an annual rate of 6% interest on the deposit." The containers were returned on April 1, 1992.

Required:

Give all of the required entries (omit closing and reversing entries) during 1991 and 1992 for each of the above transactions. The accounting period of Voss ends on December 31.

E 15–11
Reporting Liabilities:
Dividends and Secured
Notes
(L.O. 4, 6)

The records of the Fisk Corporation provided the following information at December 31, 1991.

a. Notes payable (trade), short-term (includes a $4,000 note given on
purchase of equipment that cost $20,000; assets were mortgaged
in connection with purchase) . . . . $ 30,000
b. Bonds payable ($30,000 due each April 1) 120,000
c. Accounts payable (including $3,000 owed to president of the company) 50,000
d. Accrued property taxes (estimated) 1,000
e. Stock dividends issuable on 3/1/1992 (at par value) 26,000
f. Cash dividends declared, payable 3/1/1992 20,000
g. Long-term note payable, maturity amount (unamortized amount, $14,500) 16,000
h. Accrued interest on all bonds and notes 13,500

Required:

Assuming the fiscal year ends December 31, show how each of the above items should be reported on the balance sheet at December 31, 1991.

E 15–12
Entries to Record Payroll
and Related Deductions
(L.O. 6)

Ryan Company paid salaries for the month amounting to $120,000. Of this amount, $30,000 was received by employees who had already been paid the $53,400 maximum amount of annual earnings taxable in one year under FICA laws (FICA rate, 7.65%).

Of the $120,000, $14,000 was paid to employees who had already been paid the $7,000 maximum (SUTA rates: 5.4% state and .8% federal). Withholding taxes amounted to $36,000, and $1,450 was withheld from the $120,000 for investment in company stock per an agreement with certain employees.

Required:

Give entries to record (*a*) salary payment and the liabilities for the deductions, (*b*) employer payroll expenses, and (*c*) remittance of the taxes.

E 15–13
Recording Payroll and
Related Deductions
(L.O. 6)

Smiley Corporation paid salaries and wages of $143,800. Of this amount, $3,800 was paid to employees who had already exceeded the FICA maximum. Also, $43,800 was paid to employees who had already been paid the SUTA maximum. Use the FICA and FUTA rates given in the chapter. Income tax withholding was $35,000. Deductions: union dues (in conformity with the union agreement), $3,000, and insurance premiums, $12,000.

Required:

Give the entries to record liabilities for payroll deductions, payroll expenses, and remittance of the deductions.

E 15-14
Compensated Absences:
Entries and Reporting
(L.O. 6)

Langston Mowers allows each employee to earn 15 paid vacation days each year with full pay while on vacation. Unused vacation time can be carried over to the next year; if not taken during the next year it is lost. By the end of 1991, all but 3 of the 30 employees had taken their earned vacation time; these three carried over to 1992 a total of 20 vacation days, which represented 1991 salary of $5,000. During 1992, each of these three used their 1991 vacation carryover; none of them had received a pay change from 1991 to the time they used their carryover. Total cash wages paid 1991, $700,000; 1992, $740,000.

Required:

1. Give all of the entries for Langston related to vacations during 1991 and 1992. Disregard payroll taxes.
2. Compute the total amount of wage expense for 1991 and 1992. How would the vacation time carried over from 1991 affect the 1991 balance sheet?

E 15-15
Estimated Warranty
Expense: Recording and
Reporting
(L.O. 7)

Franco Furniture sells a line of products that carry a three-year warranty against defects. Based on industry experience, the estimated warranty costs related to dollar sales are the following: first year after sale, 1% of sales; second year after sale, 3% of sales; and third year after sale, 5%. Sales and actual warranty expenditures for the first three-year period were as follows:

	Cash Sales	Actual Warranty Expenditures
1991	$ 80,000	$ 900
1992	110,000	4,100
1993	130,000	9,800

Required:

1. Give entries for the three years for the (*a*) sales, (*b*) estimated warranty expense, and (*c*) the actual expenditures.
2. What amount should be reported as a liability on the balance sheet at the end of each year?

E 15-16
Liability for Premiums:
Entries and Reporting
(L.O. 7)

Van Slyke Stereos has initiated a promotion program whereby customers are given coupons redeemable in $25 special savings certificates. Each certificate can be turned in to the savings company for its face amount at the end of the third year from its issuance to the customer. One coupon is issued for each dollar of sales. On the surrender of 500 coupons, one $25 savings certificate (cost $20) is given. It is estimated that 25% of the coupons issued will never be presented for redemption. Sales for the first period were $400,000, and the number of coupons redeemed totaled 210,000. Sales for the second period were $440,000, and the number of coupons redeemed totaled 300,000. The savings certificates are acquired as needed.

Required:

Prepare journal entries (including closing entries) relative to the premium plan for the two periods. Show amounts that should be reported in the balance sheet and income statement for the two periods. *Hint:* Use the following accounts: cash, premium expense; estimated premium claims payable; and income summary.

E 15-17
Loss Contingency—
Three Cases: Entries
and Explanation
(L.O. 7)

Canseco Company is preparing the annual financial statements at December 31, 1992. During 1992, a customer fell while riding on the escalator and has filed a lawsuit for $40,000 because of a claimed back injury. The lawyer employed by the company has carefully assessed all of the implications. If the suit is lost, the lawyer's reasonable estimate is that the $40,000 will be assessed by the court.

Required:

How should the contingency be handled during 1992 in each of the following cases? Give all necessary entries and/or any notes:

1. Assume that the lawyer and the management concluded that it is reasonably possible that the company will be liable, and it is reasonably estimated that the amount will be $40,000.
2. Assume, instead, that the lawyer, the independent accountant, and management have reluctantly concluded that it is probable that the suit will be successful.

3. Assume that the conclusion of the legal counsel and management is that it is remote that there will be a contingency loss. They believe the suit is without merit.

E 15–18
Property Taxes:
Recording
(L.O. 7)

Tudor Company is located in a relatively small town that has recently restructured its property tax procedures. During the past year (1991) the company experienced a significant increase in the property appraisal for taxes. The company paid property taxes of $120,000. However, it expects the tax for the current year, 1992, to decrease some because of citizen complaints. Both the city tax year and Tudor's accounting year end on December 31. The following events occurred during 1992:

January 20—paid the 1991 property taxes.

January 30—estimated a 10% decrease in property taxes for 1992. The company accrues propety taxes each month.

July 10—received a tentative tax notice assessment for taxes, $2,280,000, preliminary tax rate per $100 valuation, $5.00. The company will revise its estimate to these assessments.

December 28—received final tax notice, 1991 tax assessed, $111,000, payable by January 15, 1993.

January 24, 1993—paid the 1992 property tax.

Required:

Give the journal entries related to property taxes from January 1, 1992, through January 1993.

PROBLEMS

P 15–1
Interest-Bearing and
Noninterest-Bearing
Notes Compared: Entries
and Reporting
(L.O. 4)

Herzog Company borrowed cash on August 1, 1991, and signed a $15,000 (face amount), one-year note payable, due on July 31, 1992. The accounting period ends December 31. Assume a going rate of interest of 11% for this company for this level of risk.

Required:
Round amounts to nearest dollar.
1. How much cash should Herzog receive on the note, assuming two cases: Case A, an interest-bearing note; and Case B, a noninterest-bearing note?
2. Give the following entries for each case:
   a. August 1, 1991, date of the loan.
   b. December 31, 1991, adjusting entry.
   c. July 31, 1992, payment of the note, assuming no reversing entry was made.
3. What liability amounts should be shown in each case on the December 31, 1991, balance sheet?

P 15–2
Interest-Bearing and
Noninterest-Bearing
Notes Compared: Entries
(L.O. 4)

On October 1, 1991, Uribe Company borrowed $30,000 cash and signed a one-year note payable, due on September 30, 1992. The going rate of interest for this level of risk was 16%. The accounting period ends on December 31.

Required:
1. Compute the face amount of the note assuming:
   a. Case A—An interest-bearing note.
   b. Case B—A noninterest-bearing note.
2. Complete a tabulation as follows:

	Case A: Interest-bearing	Case B: Noninterest-bearing
a. Total cash received	$30,000	$30,000
b. Face amount of note	$_____	$_____
c. Total cash paid	$_____	$_____
d. Total interest	$_____	$_____
e. Interest expense, 1991	$_____	$_____
f. Interest expense, 1992	$_____	$_____

	Case A: Interest- bearing	Case B: Noninterest- bearing
g. Amount of liabilities reported on the 1991 balance sheet:		
Note payable . . . . $_____		$_____
Interest payable . . . . $_____		$_____
h. Principal amount . . . . $_____		$_____
i. Stated interest rate . . . . _____%		_____%
j. Yield or effective interest rate . . . . _____%		_____%
k. Time to maturity:		
October 1, 1991 . . . . Months_____		Months_____
December 31, 1991 . . . . Months_____		Months_____

3. Give entries for each case from October 1, 1991, through maturity date (assume reversing entries were not made).

4. Show how the liability and expense amounts should be reflected for each case on the December 31, 1991, balance sheet and the 1991 income statement.

P 15–3
Noninterest-Bearing Note, Two-Year: Entries and Reporting
(L.O. 4)

On January 1, 1991, Gagne Company acquired a machine (an operational asset) that had a list price of $35,000. Because of a serious cash problem, Gagne paid $5,000 cash and signed a two-year note with a maturity amount of $30,000 due on December 31, 1992. The note did not specify interest. Assume the going rate of interest for this company for this level of risk was 15%. The accounting period ends December 31.

Required:

Round amounts to the nearest dollar.

1. Give the entry to record the purchase of the machine.
2. Complete the following tabulation related to the note:

    a. Cash equivalent received . . . . $_____
    b. Face amount . . . . $_____
    c. Total interest to be paid . . . . $_____
    d. Interest expense:
        1991 . . . . $_____
        1992 . . . . $_____
    e. Liability on the 1991 balance sheet . . . . $_____
    f. Depreciation expense (on cost) (10-year estimated life;
        no residual value; straight-line) . . . . $_____
    g. Effective interest rate . . . . _____%
    h. Stated interest rate . . . . _____%

3. Give all entries (exclude closing and reversing entries) from January 1, 1991, through the end of 1992.

4. Show how the liabilities and expenses would be reported on the 1991 and 1992 financial statements (assume the company has a two-year operating cycle).

P 15–4
Noninterest-Bearing Note, Two-Year: Entries and Reporting
(L.O. 4)

On January 1, 1991, Lyle Company purchased a large used machine for operations; the asking price was $46,000. Payment was $6,000 cash and a $40,000 (maturity value), two-year, noninterest-bearing note payable due on December 31, 1992. The note did not specify interest; however, for Lyle, the rate for this level of risk was 15%. Assume straight-line depreciation, a five-year life, and no residual value. The accounting period ends on December 31.

Required:

Round amounts to nearest dollar.

1. Give the entry to record the purchase of the machine.
2. Complete the following tabulation related to the note:

    a. Cash equivalent received . . . . . . $_____
    b. Face amount of note . . . . $_____
    c. Cash to be paid at maturity . . . . . $_____

  d. Total interest expense . . . . $_____

  e. Interest expense:

    1991 . . . . $_____

    1992 . . . . $_____

  f. Depreciation expense . . . . $_____

  g. Effective interest rate . . . . _____%

  h. Stated interest rate . . . . _____%

3. Prepare a debt amortization schedule for this note. Use the following column headings: date, interest expense, and carrying value of the liability.
4. Give all entries (except closing and reversing entries) from January 1, 1991, through the end of 1992.
5. Show how the liabilities and expenses should be reported on the 1991 and 1992 financial statements (assume the company's operating cycle is two years).

P 15–5
Property Tax and Sales Tax: Recording and Reporting
(L.O. 6)

Santago Department Store has asked you to assist in improving its accounting for taxes. The following selected transactions that were completed during 1992 have been presented to you for analysis; the accounting period ends on December 31.

a. Property taxes—Property taxes for 1991 amounted to $24,000. During January 1992, Santago estimated that the property tax would increase approximately 10% for 1992. During June 1992, the company received a tentative property tax appraisal that indicated a property valuation of $2,100,000 and an estimated 1992 tax rate per $1,000 of $13.10. The final tax assessment notice was received December 9, 1992 and specified a 1992 property tax of $30,000. The 1992 property taxes were paid in full on January 17, 1993.

b. Sales revenue for 1992 amounted to $8 million; the sales tax rate is 6%, and 98% of all sales were subject to tax. Unremitted sales tax at the end of 1992 amounted to $18,000.

Required:

Round to the nearest dollar.

1. Give all entries indicated for (*a*) the accrual of property tax (during 1992 on a monthly basis) and the payment on January 17, 1993 and (*b*) the sales tax (for 1992) transactions.
2. Show how the effects of the above tax transactions should be reported on the 1992 financial statements.

P 15–6
Compensated Absences: Entries and Reporting
(L.O. 6)

Alomar Company has a personnel policy that allows each employee with at least one year's employment 20 days' vacation time and 2 holidays with regular pay. Unused days are carried over to the next year. If not taken during the next year, the vacation and holiday times are lost. Alomar's accounting period ends December 31.

At the end of 1992, the personnel records showed the following:

Vacations Carried over to 1993		Holidays Carried over to 1993	
Total Days	**Total Salaries**	**Total Days**	**Total Salaries**
70	$8,400	10	$1,280

During 1993, all of the 1992 vacation time, and eight days of the holiday time, which were carried over, were taken. Salary increases in 1993 for these employees relating to the days carried over amounted to $800. Total cash wages paid: 1992, $890,000; 1993, $920,000.

Required:

1. Give all of the entries for Alomar Company related to vacations and holidays during 1992 and 1993. Disregard payroll taxes.
2. Show how the effects of the above transactions should be reported on the 1992 and 1993 financial statements of Alomar.

P 15–7
Contingency Losses, Five Events: Explanations, Entries, Reporting
(L.O. 7)

Davis Corporation is preparing its first set of financial statements at December 31, 1991, along with the appropriate adjusting entries. Among the contingent losses under consideration are the following transactions and events:

a. Sales revenue for 1991 was $960,000. Unpaid credit sales at year-end amounted to $22,000, and it is probable that $1,000 of that amount will result in a loss.

b. Two of the major product lines sold during the year carry a two-year warranty for defects (both labor and parts cost). Sales of these items amounted to $40,000. On the average, warranty expenditures approximate 4% of sales price.

c. During 1991, Davis issued 5,000 "DC orange coupons." Each 10 coupons held can be turned in, within one year from the date on the coupon, for a $15 credit on any item sold by Davis that costs more than $50. Davis estimates that 25% of the coupons will be redeemed.

d. Davis was sued by a shopper for $50,000 damages due to an accident in the retail store. The shopper asserts a permanent back injury, characterized primarily by pain and stiffness. Legal counsel is of the opinion that it is probable that the plaintiff will prevail in court and that Davis will have to pay 10% of the claim; it is anticipated that the insurance company will pay the balance. The suit is expected to be resolved in mid-1992.

e. Davis Corporation endorsed and guaranteed a $25,000, 15%, one-year mortgage note given by a local supplier (of merchandise) to Davis. The bank required a guarantor. The bank indicated that the probability of default by the supplier was reasonably possible.

f. The comprehensive liability insurance policy carried by Davis Corporaton covers all claims for damages to individuals or groups due to accident, negligence, and other injuries relating to the legitimate operations of the company. However, the insurance policy carries an escape clause that states: "When the insured is willfully negligent, as determined by an independent third party, 10% of the loss must be paid by the insured."

Required:

1. Evaluate each of the above transctions and events and recommend appropriate accounting and reporting actions. Give any entry or note required for each item.

2. Identify each liability and the amount that should be reported on the 1991 balance sheet.

P 15–8

Redeemable Coupons: Accounting and Reporting (L.O. 7)

For the purpose of stimulating sales, Carter Cereal Company places a coupon in each box of cereal sold; the coupons are redeemable in chinaware. Each premium costs the company 90 cents (the cost of printing the coupons is negligible). Ten coupons must be presented by the customers to receive one premium. The following data are available:

Month	Boxes of Cereal Sold	Premiums Purchased	Coupons Redeemed
January	650,000	25,000	220,000
February	500,000	40,000	410,000
March	560,000	35,000	300,000

It is estimated that only 50% of the coupons will be presented for redemption.

Required:

1. Prepare entries for each event listed below for each of the three months:
   a. Premiums purchased.
   b. Premium expense and related liability.
   c. Coupons redeemed.

2. Complete the following schedule for each month:

Accounts	Ending Account Balances		
	January	February	March
Premiums—Chinaware			
Estimated premium claims payable			
Premium expense (monthly)			

P 15–9

Estimated Warranty Costs: Entries and Reporting (L.O. 7)

Habek Hardware, Inc., provides a product warranty for defects on two major lines of items sold since the beginning of 1991. Line A carries a two-year warranty for all labor and service (but not parts). The company contracts with a local service establishment to service the warranty (both parts and labor). The local service establishment charges a flat fee of $60 per unit payable at date of sale.

Line B carries a three-year warranty for parts and labor on service. Habek purchases the parts needed under the warranty and has service personnel who perform the work and are paid by the job. On the basis of experience, it is estimated that for Line B, the three-year warranty costs are 3% of dollar sales for parts and 7% for labor and overhead. Additional data available are as follows:

	Year		
	1991	**1992**	**1993**
Sales in units, Line A	700	1,000	
Sales price per unit, Line A	$ 610	$ 660	
Sales in units, Line B	600	800	
Sales price per unit, Line B	$ 700	$ 750	
Actual warranty outlays, Line B			
Parts	$3,000	$ 9,600	$12,000
Labor and overhead	$7,000	$22,000	$30,000

Required:

1. Give entries for annual sales and expenses for Years 1991 and 1992 separately by product line. Assume all sales were for cash.
2. Complete a tabulation as follows:

	Year-end Amounts		
Accounts	**Year 1991**	**Year 1992**	**Year 1993**
a. Warranty expense (on income statement)	$_____	$_____	
b. Estimated warranty liability (on balance sheet)	$_____	$_____	$_____

P 15–10
Recording and Reporting Liabilities, Including Payroll Deductions
(L.O. 6)

The following selected transactions of Mattingly Company were completed during the accounting year just ended, December 31, 1991.

a. Merchandise was purchased on account; a $10,000, one-year, 16% interest-bearing note, dated April 1, 1991, was given to the creditor. Assume a perpetual inventory system.
b. Cosigned an $8,000 note payable for another party (no entry required).
c. On July 1, the company borrowed cash; a one-year, noninterest-bearing note with a face amount of $28,750 was signed. Assume a going rate of interest of 15%.
d. Payroll records showed the following (assume amounts given are correct):

	Employee			Employer		
Gross Wages	**Withholding**	**FICA**	**Union Dues**	**FICA**	**SUTA (State)**	**FUTA (Federal)**
$50,000	$15,000	$3,100	$500	$3,100	$1,350	$350

Remittances: withholding taxes, $13,000; FICA, $6,000; SUTA, state, $1,200; FUTA, federal, $340; and union dues, $280.
e. The company was sued for $150,000 in damages. It appears a court judgment against the company that is reasonably estimated to be $125,000 is probable. For problem purposes, assume this is an extraordinary item.
f. On November 1, 1991, the company rented some office space in its building to Zorn Company and collected rent in advance for six months; total $2,400.
g. Cash dividends declared but not yet paid, $14,000.
h. Accrued interest on the notes at December 31.

Required:

1. Give the entry or entries for each of the above transactions and events.
2. Prepare a list (title and amount) of the disclosures related to the liabilities at December 31, 1991.

P 15–11
Contingencies and Warranty Costs
(L.O. 7)

Cope Company is a manufacturer of household appliances. During the year, the following information became available:

a. Probable warranty costs on its household appliances are estimated to be 1% of sales.
b. One of its manufacturing plants is located in a foreign country. There is a threat of

expropriation of this plant. The threat of expropriation is deemed to be reasonably possible. Any compensation from the foreign government would be less than the carrying amount of the plant.

c. It is probable that damages will be received by Cope next year as a result of a lawsuit filed this year against another household appliances manufacturer.

Required:

In answering the following, do not discuss deferred income tax implications.

1. How should Cope report the probable warranty costs? Why?
2. How should Cope report the threat of expropriation of assets? Why?
3. How should Cope report this year the probable damages that may be received next year? Why?

(AICAP adapted)

P 15–12 Contingencies and Warranty Costs (L.O. 7)	Spackenkill Company is a manufacturer of household appliances. During the year, the following information became available: a. Potential costs due to the discovery of a safety hazard related to one of its products. These costs are probable and can be reasonably estimated. b. Potential costs of new product warranty costs. These costs are probable but cannot be reasonably estimated. c. Potential costs due to the discovery of a possible product defect related to one of its products. These costs are reasonably possible and can be reasonably estimated. *Required:* 1. How should Spackenkill report the potential costs due to the discovery of a safety hazard? Why? 2. How should Spackenkill report the potential costs of warranty costs? Why? 3. How should Spackenkill report the potential costs due to the discovery of a possible product defect? Why? (AICPA adapted)
P 15–13 Compensated Absences (L.O. 6)	Carol Company has many long-time employees who have built up substantial employee benefits. These employee benefits include compensation for future vacations. *Required:* What conditions must be met for Carol to accrue compensation for future vacations? Include in your answer the theoretical rationale for accruing compensation for future vacations. (AICPA adapted)
P 15–14 **COMPREHENSIVE PROBLEM** ♦ Overview: Liabilities, Contingency Losses, Recording, and Reporting (L.O. 4, 6, 7)	The following selected transactions of Gaetti Company were completed during the current accounting year ended December 31, 1991. a. March 1, 1991, borrowed $20,000 on a two-year, 12%, interest-bearing note. b. April 1, 1991, borrowed cash and signed an $18,838, two-year, noninterest-bearing note (no interest was specified). The market rate of interest for this level of risk was 16%. c. June 1, 1991, purchased a special truck with a list price of $29,000. Paid $9,000 cash and signed a $20,000, one-year, noninterest-bearing note (no interest was specified). The market rate of interest for this level of risk was 16%. d. During 1991, sold merchandise for $40,000 cash that carried a two-year warranty for parts and labor. A reasonable estimate of the cost of the warranty is 1.5% of sales revenue. By December 31, 1991, actual warranty costs amounted to $250. e. June 1, 1991, Gaetti cosigned and guaranteed payment of a $60,000, 14%, one-year note owed by a local supplier to City Bank. The bank required a cosignature; however, they believe that default by the debtor is only reasonably possible. f. October–November 1991, in order to promote sales during these two months, Gaetti gave its customers 10,000 premium certificates based on cash sales. Each certificate turned in during December 1991 and January 1992 will reduce the price by 50 cents on all single items that sell above $20. A reasonable estimate is that 75% of the certificates will be redeemed. By December 31, 1991, 60% of those issued had been redeemed. g. Year 1991 property taxes to be recorded monthly: (1) Prior year property taxes, $2,087; expected to increase by 15% during 1991.

(2) December 10, 1991—Final tax assessment received, $2,500; paid on February 1, 1992, the latest payment date without penalty.

h. December 1991, dividends declared (not yet paid or issued):

(1) Cash, $18,000 (use payable account).

(2) Stock, $12,000 (use issuable account).

i. December 1991—Sales revenue (excluding sales taxes collected) for the month, $300,000. Sales tax 5%, applicable to 98% of the sales. No unpaid sales tax carried over from November 1991.

j. December 31, 1991, accrual of interest payable.

Required:

Round to the nearest dollar.

1. For each of the 10 transactions, give all entries that Gaetti should make in 1991 based on the data given.

2. List each current liability (account title and the amount) that should be reported on the 1991 balance sheet of Gaetti Company.

CASES

C 15-1
Evaluation of a Liability: Recommendations
(L.O. 7)

Evans Equipment Company sells new and used earth-moving equipment. It uses a perpetual inventory system, and its accounting period ends December 31. On December 28, 1990, Evans purchased a used backhoe for resale, at an agreed price of $40,000. Terms of the purchase: cash down payment, $10,000, plus a note payable, face amount, $30,000, maturity date, December 28, 1992. The company bookkeeper entered the equipment in the perpetual inventory account at $40,000 and reported no interest expense for 1990 because the note did not specify that any interest would be paid. In answer to a question by the newly engaged independent auditor, the bookkeeper said that the entry on maturity date of the note would be a debit to notes payable and a credit to cash of $30,000. The transaction was recorded on January 5, 1991, because it was on that date that Evans received the equipment and the check was drawn.

Required:

1. Evaluate the accounting treatment of the purchase of the equipment. Consider both theoretical and GAAP issues. State any assumptions that you make.

2. If the company's accounting seems in error, give recommendations for what should be done, including reasons. Also provide the necessary journal entries. State any factual assumptions made.

C 15-2
Contingencies: Four Situations
(L.O. 7)

Unlucky Company is preparing its annual financial statements at December 31, 1991, and is concerned about application of *SFAS No. 5*, "Accounting for Contingencies." Four unrelated situations are under consideration:

a. During 1992, a shopper sued the company for $500,000 for a claimed injury that occurred on the premises owned by Unlucky. No date for the trial has been set; however, the lawyer employed by Unlucky has completed a thorough investigation. Because it can be proven that the customer did fall on the premises, the legal counsel believes it will not be difficult for the plaintiff to prove injury. There is some evidence that it was due, at least partially, to negligence by the plaintiff. The attorney believes that it is not probable, but is reasonably possible, that the suit will be successful (for the plaintiff), but for a signifcantly smaller amount that cannot be reasonably estimated at this time.

b. The company held a $10,000, 8%, one-year note receivable from a customer. Unlucky discounted the note, with recourse, at the bank to obtain cash before its due date (due on June 1, 1992). If the maker does not pay the bank by the due date, Unlucky will have to pay it. The customer has an excellent credit rating (having never defaulted on a debt).

c. An outside party has filed a suit against Unlucky for $25,000 claiming that certain actions by Unlucky caused the party to lose a contract on which the estimated profit was this amount. In the opinion of the legal counsel engaged by Unlucky, the probability of the claim being successful is remote. Counsel does not believe it will ever be brought to trial. If necessary, Unlucky will defend itself in court.

d. The company owns a small plant in a foreign country that has a book value of $3 million and an estimated market value of $4 million. The foreign government has indicated its unalterable intention to expropriate the plant during the coming year and to reimburse Unlucky for 50% of the estimated market value.

Required:

For each situation, respond to the following:
1. What accounting recognition if any, should be accorded each situation at the end of 1991? Explain why and give journal entries.
2. Indicate how each situation should be reported on the balance sheet.

C 15-3
Sherwin-Williams:
Analysis of Actual
Financial Statements
(L.O. 2)

This case relates to the Sherwin-Williams financial statements located at the end of the book.

Required:

1. What current liabilities does Sherwin-Williams list on its balance sheet? Indicate the type of liability using the list under the text title "What Is a Current Liability?"
2. Does Sherwin-Williams discuss any of its current liabilities in the notes to its financial statements? If so, describe.

16

Long-Term Liabilities

LEARNING OBJECTIVES

◆

After you have studied this chapter, you will:

1. Be familiar with long-term liabilities and how to value them for financial reporting purposes.

2. Understand the nature of bonds and how to compute the price of a bond at issuance.

3. Know how to account for basic and more complex bond situations from the viewpoint of both the issuer and investor.

4. Appreciate the accounting issues surrounding long-term debt instruments issued with equity rights.

5. Be familiar with the different ways long-term debt is extinguished.

6. Be able to value long-term notes and measure periodic interest.

7. Know how to account for serial bonds. (Refer to Appendix 16A.)

8. Understand the issues underlying accounting for troubled debt restructuring. (Refer to Appendix 16B.)

◆
_____

INTRODUCTION
◆

I n 1989, Motorola issued $1.32 billion of long-term notes due in 2009. Yet the firm's long-term liability section disclosed only $413 million in notes. If Motorola promised to pay $1.32 billion in 20 years, does the company owe only $413 million at the end of 1989?

In 1985, U.S. Steel placed funds into a trust for the eventual retirement of $399 million of long-term debt. In so doing, the firm recognized a $51 million gain (13% of total income). The creditors were not actually paid, but the debt was removed from the balance sheet. Although the funds could not be used for general purposes and did not appear in the balance sheet, is U.S. Steel legally or economically free of the obligation? And what is the meaning of the gain?

These and many other issues related to long-term debt are of great interest to financial statement users. Long-term debt is a major source of capital for most firms. For example, in 1989, total corporate debt amounted to 40% of GNP, up from 30% in 1979. Interest payments by nonfinancial corporations consumed almost 50% of corporate income in 1989.[1]

The following outline highlights this chapter's major topics in accounting for long-term debt:
- Characteristics and valuation of long-term liabilities.
- Bonds payable: characteristics, valuation, accounting principles for issuer and investor, and bonds issued with equity rights.
- Debt extinguishment: by open-market purchase, by call, by refunding, and by in-substance defeasance.
- Long-term notes and mortgages.
- Additional issues and disclosures.
- Accounting for serial bonds (Appendix 16A).
- Troubled debt restructure (Appendix 16B).

Income taxes, pensions, and leases are topics that also involve long-term liabilities; they are discussed in later chapters.

_____

◆

CHARACTERISTICS AND VALUATION OF LONG-TERM LIABILITIES
◆

A long-term liability is an obligation that extends beyond one year from the current balance sheet date or the operating cycle of the debtor (borrower), whichever is longer.

Debt capital is an attractive means of financing for the debtor. Creditors do not acquire voting privileges in the debtor company. Debt capital is obtained more easily than equity capital by many new and risky firms. In some cases, the overall cost of debt financing is lower than equity financing. Interest expense, unlike dividends, is tax deductible. Furthermore, a successfully *leveraged* firm earns a return on borrowed funds that exceeds the rate it must pay in interest.

Debt financing often supplies the capital for expansion and takeover activities when issuance of new stock is difficult. The potential increase in profits from expansion can be sufficiently attractive to induce firms that traditionally avoid debt to increase liability levels. For example, Adolph Coors Company planned the first

_____
[1] "Corporate Debt Rises Despite Worries," *The Wall Street Journal*, June 26, 1989, p. A1.

tax deductible. Furthermore, a successfully *leveraged* firm earns a return on borrowed funds that exceeds the rate it must pay in interest.

However, leverage is dangerous if sales or earnings decline. Under these circumstances, interest expense becomes an increasing percentage of earnings. Business failures frequently are caused by incurring too much debt on unfulfilled expectations of high sales and profits. For example, Petrolane Gas Service is a highly leveraged firm that sells propane for residential heating. After two consecutive warm winters and rising wholesale propane prices, the firm barely had enough money to pay its interest bill.[3]

In addition, debt agreements often restrict the operations and financial structure of the debtor company. The purpose of restrictions is to reduce the risk of default. Restrictions include ceilings on dividends and future debt, requirements that specific income and liquidity levels be maintained, and the creation of sinking funds to ensure that adequate funds will be available to extinguish the debt. A **sinking fund** is a cash fund restricted for a specific purpose and is classified as an investment. Violation of restrictions places the debtor in technical default, meaning that the debt is due at the creditor's discretion.

Debt also is an attractive investment for creditors who enjoy the increased security of legally enforceable debt payments, eventual return of principal, and prior claim to assets upon corporate liquidation. Although debt investments provide, on average, a lower overall return to investors than equity investments, they are generally less risky. Debt securities with claims on specific assets further reduce the risk.

Three General Valuation and Measurement Principles   The measurement and valuation of long-term liabilities coincides with that of long-term notes receivable, discussed in Chapter 8. Three general principles are emphasized.
* First, long-term liabilities are recorded at the fair value of the goods or services obtained by incurring debt. The market rate of interest is the rate implicit in the transaction and equates the present value of the required future cash payments to the fair value of goods and services.[4]
* Second, periodic interest expense is based on the market interest rate on the date of debt issuance, and the liability balance at the *beginning* of the reporting period.
* Third, the book value of long-term debt at a balance sheet date is the present value of all remaining cash payments required, discounted at the market interest rate at issuance. The rate of interest used for this purpose is not changed during the term of the debt.

These three principles are the foundation for measuring and recording most long-term liabilities and interest expense.

BONS PAYABLE
♦

A **bond** is a debt security issued by companies and government units to secure large amounts of capital on a long-term basis. Bonds are legal documents representing a formal promise by the issuing firm to pay principal and interest in return for the capital invested by the bondholders (investors).

A formal bond agreement, or **bond indenture,** specifies the terms of the bonds and the rights and duties of issuer and bondholder. The indenture specifies any restrictions on the issuing company, the dollar amount authorized for issuance, the interest rate and payment dates, the maturity date, conversion and call privileges,

---

[2] "Adolph Coors Might Offer Millions in Debt, *The Wall Street Journal*, March 16, 1990, p. C21.

[3] "Warm Spell Melts Dreams of Petrolane," *The Wall Street Journal*, January 10, 1991, p. C1.

[4] If the fair value of goods and services cannot be determined, the liability is recorded at the present value of required future cash payments discounted at the market interest rate for similar debt instruments.

and the responsibilities of an *independent trustee* appointed to protect the interests of both the issuer and the investors. The trustee, usually a financial institution, maintains the necessary records and disburses interest and principal. The investors receive *bond certificates,* which represent the contractual obligations of the issuer to the investors.

Bonds normally are issued in small denominations such as $1,000 and $10,000. The small denominations increase the affordability of the bonds and allow investors greater diversification in their portfolios which in turn reduces overall investment risk.

Bonds are marketed in several ways. Typically, an entire bond issue is sold to investment bankers. Investment bankers *underwrite* (assist in selling and assume all or part of the risk) the bond issue at a specified price and then market the bonds at a higher price to individual investors, thus realizing underwriter's compensation. Alternatively, the underwriting firm may agree to buy any unsold portion of the issue at a specified price. Private direct placement with financial institutions and individual investors is an alternative to underwriting.

Many bond issues are offered through a prospectus. A **prospectus** is a document that includes audited financial statements of the issuer, states the offering price, and describes the securities offered, the issuing company's business, and the conditions under which the securities will be sold. A "tombstone" advertisement announcing the issue and listing the underwriters is placed in the financial press to generate interest in the securities. An example of such an advertisement appears in Exhibit 16–1.

Many bond issues are actively listed and traded on a daily basis on bond exchanges. Trades between investors are not recorded by the issuing company. *The Wall Street Journal* publishes daily information about listed bonds.

Information about the risk of bond issues is available from Standard & Poor's Corporation, Moody's Investor Services, and other rating services. These services use the following quality designations and rating symbols:

	Rating Symbols	
Quality Designation	**Standard & Poor's**	**Moody's**
Prime	AAA	Aaa
Excellent	AA	Aa
Upper Medium	A	A
Lower Medium	BBB	Baa
Marginally speculative	BB	Ba
Very speculative	B	B, Caa
Default	D	Ca, C

The bond rating reflects the perceived ability of the issuing company to pay principal and interest and is affected by the firm's recent financial statements. For example, the long-term debt ratings of Sears, Roebuck & Co. were downgraded in 1989 to reflect the increased potential for risk and earnings volatility from a plan to restructure its retailing operations.[5] A firm's bond rating affects the bond price and the ability of the company to raise additional debt capital.[6] The value of one RJR Nabisco bond issue dropped $200 per $1,000 bond after being downgraded by Moody's.

---

[5] "Duff & Phelps Cuts Ratings on Sears Debt," *The Wall Street Journal,* December 28, 1989, p. A2.

[6] Some argue that bond ratings are too slow to react to changes in risk. For example, Moody's did not reduce the rating of the bonds of Integrated Resources until their value declined 50% in market value. See "Guess Who's Talking Tough on Junk? Staid Moody's," *The Wall Street Journal,* February 23, 1990, p. C1.

EXHIBIT 16-1   Example of a Tombstone Advertisement for a New Bond Issue

This announcement is neither an offer to sell nor a solicitation of offers to buy any of these securities. The offering is made only by the Prospectus.

NEW ISSUE   February 13, 1990

$50,000,000

Presidio Oil Company

9% Convertible Subordinated Debentures Due 2015

The 9% Convertible Subordinated Debentures Due 2015 of Presidio Oil Company (the "Company") are convertible into shares of the Company's Class A Common Stock, $.10 par value per share, at any time at or before maturity, unless previously redeemed, at a Conversion Price of $9.38 per share, subject to adjustment in certain events.

Price 100%
plus accrued interest, if any, from February 14, 1990

Copies of the Prospectus may be obtained in any State in which this announcement is circulated only from such of the undersigned as may legally offer these securities in such State.

The First Boston Corporation   Drexel Burnham Lambert
                                                    INCORPORATED

Source: *The Wall Street Journal,* February 23, 1990, p. C21. Reproduced with permission of The First Boston Corporation.

Classification of Bonds

Investors have a wide variety of investment goals, preferences, and policies. As a result, many different types of bonds are issued. The following classification of bonds reflects this diversity.

Classification by:
1. Issuing entity.
    a. *Industrial* bonds: issued by private companies.
    b. *Municipal* bonds: issued by public entities.

2. Collateral.
   a. *Secured* bonds: supported by a lien on specific assets; bondholders have first claim on the proceeds from sale of secured assets
   b. *Debenture* bonds: unsecured; backed only by issuer's credit; upon bankruptcy of issuer, bondholders become general creditors for distribution of issuer's assets.[7]
3. Purpose of issue.
   a. *Purchase money* bonds: issued in full or part payment for property.
   b. *Refunding* bonds: issued to retire existing bonds.
   c. *Consolidated* bonds: issued to replace several existing issues.
4. Payment of interest.
   a. *Ordinary (term)* bonds: provide cash interest at a stated rate.
   b. *Income* bonds: interest is dependent on issuer's income.
   c. *Registered* bonds: pay interest only to the person in whose name the bond is recorded or registered.
   d. *Bearer* bonds: not registered; interest and principal is paid to the holder; transfers require no endorsement.
   e. *Coupon* bonds: pay interest upon receipt of coupons detached from bonds.
5. Maturity.
   a. *Ordinary (term)* bonds: mature on a single specified date.
   b. *Serial* bonds: mature on several installment dates.
   c. *Callable* bonds: issuer can retire bonds before maturity date.
   d. *Redeemable* bonds: bondholder can compel early redemption.
   e. *Convertible* bonds: bondholder can convert bonds to equity securities of the issuer.

Valuation of Bonds Payable

Several bond features affect the valuation and accounting for bonds. To illustrate, assume that late in 1990, Randolph Company plans to issue $100,000 of 10% debentures dated January 1, 1991.[8] Each bond has a $1,000 face value. The bonds mature December 31, 2000, and pay interest on June 30 and December 31. Five features are generally noted in the bond indenture, appear on the bond, and do not change:

1. The *face* (*maturity, principal, or par*) value of a bond is the amount payable when the bond is due ($1,000 for Randolph).
2. The *maturity* date is the end of the bond term and the due date for the face value (December 31, 2000 for Randolph). The length of the bond term reflects the issuer's long-term cash needs, the purpose for which the funds will be used, and the issuer's expected ability to pay principal and interest.
3. The *stated* (*coupon, nominal, contractual*) *interest rate* is the rate applied to face value to determine periodic interest payments (10% for Randolph). This rate is normally set to approximate the rate of interest on bonds of a similar risk class.
4. The *interest payment dates* are the dates the periodic interest payments are due (June 30 and December 31 for Randolph). Semiannual interest payments are common.[9] Randolph pays $50 interest on these dates for each bond (.10 × $1,000 × 1/2), regardless of the issue price or market rate of interest at date of issue.
5. The *bond* (*authorization*) *date* is the earliest date the bond can be issued and represents the planned issuance date of the bond issue (January 1, 1991 for Randolph).

---

[7] A *junk* bond is a high-interest rate, high-risk, unsecured bond. They were used extensively in the 1980s to finance leveraged-buyouts.

[8] Debenture bonds are used for the examples, but the general valuation principles apply to most bond issues.

[9] The decision to pay interest twice per year represents a trade-off between investors' desire for more frequent cash payments and the issuing company's desire to reduce clerical costs.

Two other features that are necessary for valuation, do not appear on the bond, and are dependent on market factors are:

6. The *market* (*effective, yield*) *interest rate* is the true compounded rate that equates the price of the bond issue to the present value of the interest payments and face value. This rate is not necessarily the same as the stated rate. (Assume this rate is 12% for the Randolph issue.)
7. The bond *issue date* is the date the bonds are actually sold to investors. Bonds often are issued after the bond date. (Assume the issue date is July 1, 1991, for the Randolph issue.)

The process of issuing bonds often requires more time than expected, causing the bonds to be issued after the *bond date*. The process includes registration with the SEC, negotiations with underwriters, printing, and other clerical tasks. Changes in the firm and in the economy can increase unexpectedly the difficulty of marketing the bonds. The issuing company also may delay issuance to take advantage of declining interest rates.

The *market interest rate* depends on several interrelated factors, including the general rate of interest in the economy, the perceived risk of the bond issue, yields on bonds of similar risk, inflation expectations, the overall supply of and demand for bonds, and the bond term.

Bond Prices If the market and stated interest rates are equal, bonds sell at face value. In this case, the interest payments yield a return equal to the market rate for bonds of similar duration and risk. However, the stated and market rates are frequently not the same. Changes in the market rate and issue price are *inversely* related. If the market rate (12%) exceeds the stated rate (10%), the issue price of the Randolph bonds must decline below the face value to give the investor a return equal to the market rate. Investors are not willing to pay the $1,000 face value per bond (a price that yields 10%) because competing debt securities yield 12%.

When the market interest rate exceeds the stated rate, bonds sell at a **discount** (below face value). The Randolph bonds sold at a discount. When the stated rate exceeds the market rate, the reverse is true and the bonds sell at a **premium** (above face value). In this case, the bonds offer a stated rate above the market rate, making them more attractive. The price of the bonds increases until the yield decreases to the market rate. The terms *discount* and *premium* do not imply negative or positive qualities of the bond issue. They are the result of adjustments to the selling price to bring the yield rate in line with the market rate on similar bonds.

The investor buys two different types of cash flows when purchasing a bond: principal and interest. The *price* of a bond issue (and *valuation* at issuance) equals the present value of these payments discounted at the market rate of interest:

Randolph bonds:
Present value of principal
  [$100,000(PV1, 6%*, 19†) = $100,000(.33051)] $33,051
Present value of interest payments
  [$100,000(.10)(½)(PVA, 6%, 19)
  = $5,000(11.15812)] 55,791
Price of Randolph bonds, July 1, 1991 . . . . $88,842
Discount on bonds ($100,000–$88,842) $11,158

* Market rate of interest: 12% (6% per semiannual period).

† Bond term: July 1, 1991 through December 31, 2000 (19 semiannual periods)

Investors who purchase the Randolph bonds (at a discount) and hold them for the entire term earn 6% compounded semiannually on their original investment of $88,842.

Although issuers usually attempt to set the stated rate close to the expected market rate at issuance (which minimizes the discount or premium), *deep discount* bonds and *zero coupon* bonds are exceptions. Deep discount bonds sell for a small fraction of the face value because the stated interest rate is much lower than the market rate. Zero coupon bonds pay *no* interest whatsoever. The investor receives only one payment: face value at maturity. For example, if the Randolph bonds were zero coupon bonds and were sold to yield 12%, the issue price would be $33,051.

Deep discount bonds and zeros are issued for a variety of reasons.[10] The issue price is small relative to face value, which attracts investors. Zeros, and all bonds issued at a discount, generally increase in value each year as they approach maturity. Although the annual increase in value of a zero is taxable, some investors can structure their investment to defer taxes until maturity (e.g., through an individual retirement account). When so structured, zeros are a popular investment for parents wishing to save for their children's college education. Issuing companies find the reduced or nonexistent interest payments attractive. Pension funds, which do not pay taxes, also find these investments attractive.

After issuance, bond prices and interest rate changes are inversely related. Firm-specific factors such as changes in income, financial position and risk also affect bond prices. For example, when Burlington Holdings Inc. released a disappointing income statement, its 14¼% subordinated bonds dropped $110 for each $1,000 of face value.[11]

Bond prices are quoted as a percentage of face value to accommodate all denominations. For example, a $1,000 bond quoted at 97 sells for $970 (.97 × $1,000). Exhibit 16–2 is an excerpt from a table of bond prices in *The Wall Street Journal*.

The 5⅝% ATT bonds in Exhibit 16–2 sold below face value on January 29, 1991, because the market rate (6.1%) exceeded the stated rate (5⅝%).

Bond prices *exclude* accrued interest. Total *proceeds* on bonds sold between interest dates include accrued interest at the stated rate since the last interest date. If the Randolph bonds sell on August 1, 1991, at 90, for example, total proceeds are computed as follows:

Price .90($100,000)	$90,000
Accrued interest from July 1, 1991	
$100,000 (.10)(1/12)	833
Proceeds	$90,833

An investor who purchases the bonds on August 1 and holds the bonds five months to December 31 earns only *five* months' worth of interest. Yet the investor receives *six* months' worth of interest on December 31. Therefore, the investor must pay *one* month of interest at purchase. This system facilitates the trading of bonds.

Fundamental Bond Accounting Principles for Issuer and Investor

Although the primary focus of this chapter is on accounting for the debtor company, accounting for the bondholder (investor) is also illustrated. The accounting concepts and procedures are essentially the same for both. A long-term liability for the debtor is usually a long-term investment (or receivable) for the creditor. At issuance, both

---

[10] Zero coupon bonds were first conceived in 1973 during the Arab oil embargo. Investment bankers worried that interest-bearing bonds would be difficult to market in the Middle East because the Koran prohibits interest. See "A Strange Breed of Bond," *Forbes*, May 25, 1981, p. 142.

[11] *The Wall Street Journal*, February 20, 1990, p. C1.

EXHIBIT 16-2 Bond Table Excerpt from *The Wall Street Journal*

C14 THE WALL STREET JOURNAL WEDNESDAY, JANUARY 30, 1991

NEW YORK EXCHANGE BONDS

Quotations as of 4 p.m. Eastern Time
Tuesday, January 29, 1991

Explanation: The first listed bond issue of American Telephone and Telegraph Company (ATT) has a 5⅝% stated interest rate, matures in 1995, has a current yield (*Cur Yld*) or effective interest rate of 6.1% if purchased at the close of business, January 29, 1991, at the 91½ closing price (.9150 × face value). The *Vol* column indicates the dollar amount of bonds that changed hands, in thousands. $83,000 worth of the 5⅝% ATT bonds were traded on this day. (The "s" shown for several companies is a separator and has no further meaning.)

Note: The current yield as listed is a one-year approximation to the true compounded rate and equals the quotient of the stated rate and closing price stated in percent of face value. For the 5⅝ ATT bonds, 6.1% = (5⅝%)/91.5%.

Source: "New York Exchange Bonds," *The Wall Street Journal*, January 30, 1991, p. C14. Reprinted by permission of *The Wall Street Journal*, © 1991 Dow Jones & Company, Inc. All Rights Reserved Worldwide.

parties record the same amounts and use the same interest rate.[12] Chapter 14 discussed accounting for investments in short-term debt securities.

To demonstrate accounting for bonds, several case examples are used to illustrate different reporting situations. In Case 1, bonds are issued on the bond date and at the beginning of the fiscal year. Three different effective market interest rates are illustrated.

Case 1: Common Information: bonds issued on bond date, the beginning of fiscal year

On January 1, 1991, Gresham Company issues $100,000 of 7% debentures dated January 1, 1991, which pay interest each December 31. The bonds mature on December 31, 1995. Elmhurst Company purchased the entire bond issue. Both companies have calendar fiscal years.

Part A: effective interest rate = 7%.

Part B: effective interest rate = 6%.

Part C: effective interest rate = 8%.

---

[12] However, transaction costs can cause the rate used by the investor and issuer to differ.

Case 1, Part A: Bonds sell at face value, effective and stated rate = 7%

$$\text{Price} = \$100,000(PV1, 7\%, 5) + \$100,000(.07)(PVA, 7\%, 5)$$
$$\$100,000(.71299) + \$7,000(4.10020) = \$100,000$$

When a bond is issued, the *issuer* records the maturity value of the bond in bonds payable, a long-term liability account. The *investor* records the cash equivalent paid for the bond in an investment account. In this case, the maturity value equals the amount paid. The following entries are made during the bond term, assuming Elmhurst holds the bonds to maturity.

Gresham Company (Issuer)			Elmhurst Company (Investor)		
January 1, 1991—Issue bonds:					
Cash	100,000		Bond investment	100,000	
Bonds payable		100,000	Cash		100,000
December 31, 1991–1995—Interest payment:					
Interest expense	7,000		Cash	7,000	
Cash ($100,000 × .07) .		7,000	Interest revenue		7,000
December 31, 1995—Bond maturity:					
Bonds payable	100,000		Cash	100,000	
Cash		100,000	Bond investment		100,000

Interest expense for bonds issued at face value equals the amount of the interest payment. The book value of the bonds remains $100,000 to maturity for both firms. Subsequent changes in the market rate of interest are ignored for journal entry purposes.[13] At maturity, bonds payable and the investment account are closed as shown in the last entry above. Matured bonds are canceled to prevent reissuance.

Case 1, Part B: Bonds sell at a premium, effective rate = 6%

$$\text{Price} = \$100,000(PV1, 6\%, 5) + \$100,000)(.07)(PVA, 6\%, 5)$$
$$\$100,000(.74726) + \$7,000(4.21236) = \$104,213$$

The bonds sell at a premium because they pay a stated rate that exceeds the yield rate on similar bonds. The initial $4,213 premium is recorded in premium on bonds payable, an *adjunct* valuation account. The premium *increases* the net bond liability. The present value (which equals book value) at issue date ($104,213) is the amount that, if invested by the issuing company at the effective interest rate, satisfies all payments required on the bond issue, including the face value. The following entry is made to record the issue.

Gresham Company (Issuer)			Elmhurst Company (Investor)		
January 1, 1991—Issue bonds:					
Cash	104,213		Bond investment	104,213	
Bonds payable		100,000	Cash		104,213
Premium on bonds					
payable		4,213			

Investors typically use the net method (no premium or discount) to account for long-term investments in bonds. In contrast, issuers tend to use the gross method as

---

[13] It may be argued that the current market interest rate should be incorporated into accounting for bonds. Otherwise, the book value of the debt does not equal its market value. However, it is assumed that the bond will be carried to maturity, in which case the market rate at issuance reflects the true interest rate over the bond term.

illustrated. If the investor does not intend to hold bonds for a long period, separate disclosure of the premium or discount has little value.[14]

Total interest expense over the term of a bond issue equals total cash payments required by the bond (face value and interest) less the aggregate issue price. Total interest expense is not equal to total cash interest over the term for a bond sold at a premium or discount, as shown for Gresham Company:

Face value	$100,000
Total cash interest .07($100,000)(5 years)	35,000
Total cash payments required by bond	135,000
Issue price	104,213
Total interest expense for bond term	$ 30,787

Gresham received $4,213 more than face value but will pay only face value at maturity, and the effective rate is less than the stated rate. Therefore, total interest expense for Gresham over the bond term is less than total interest paid.

Subsequent to issue, the premium or discount is amortized over the bond term. Amortized premium reduces periodic interest expense relative to interest paid, and amortized discount increases interest expense. The net bond liability equals face value plus the remaining *unamortized* bond premium or less the remaining *unamortized* bond discount. The discount or premium is completely amortized at the end of the bond term. Therefore, net book value equals face value at maturity. The same generalizations apply to the investor.

Interest Method Two amortization methods are in use: the *interest* method and the *straight-line* method. The interest method is preferable because it applies the correct yield rate to the liability balance at the beginning of each period. That liability balance represents the true present value of the obligation at that date. The straight-line method amortizes an equal amount of premium or discount per month. In certain situations (discussed later), the straight-line method cannot be used. The interest method is illustrated first, using the entries for the first two years:

Interest Method

Gresham Company (Issuer)			Elmhurst Company (Investor)	
December 31, 1991—Interest payment:				
Interest expense 6,253*			Cash 7,000	
Premium on bonds payable 747			Bond investment	747
Cash ($100,000 × .07)	7,000		Interest revenue	6,253
* $6,253 = $104,213(.06).				
December 31, 1992—Interest payment:				
Interest expense 6,208*			Cash 7,000	
Premium on bonds payable 792			Bond investment	792
Cash ($100,000 × .07)	7,000		Interest revenue	6,208
* $6,208 = ($104,213 − $747)(.06).				

After two years, Gresham's balance sheet would report:

---

[14] Under the gross method, Elmhurst would record:

Bond investment	100,000	
Premium on bond investment	4,213	
Cash		104,213

The premium increases the investment account.

GRESHAM COMPANY
Portion of Long-Term Liability Section of Balance Sheet
December 31, 1992

Bonds payable $100,000
Unamortized premium on bonds payable ($4,213 − $747 − $792)   2,674
Net book value of bonds payable $102,674

Interest expense under the interest method is the product of the effective interest rate (6%) and net liability balance at the *beginning* of the period. Interest expense is therefore a constant percentage of beginning book value. The investor receives part of the original investment back with each interest payment.[15] In 1991, this amount is $747, which reduces the net investment and net bond liability at the beginning of 1992. Consequently, 1992 interest expense is less than that for 1991. The book value of the bonds at December 31, 1992, is the present value of *remaining* cash flows:

$$\$102,674 = \$100,000(PV1, 6\%, 3) + \$100,000(.07)(PVA, 6\%, 3)$$
$$= \$100,000(.83962) + \$7,000(2.67301)(\text{rounded})$$

In practice, most firms do not separately disclose the unamortized premium or discount as a separate line item in the balance sheet. The unamortized discount or premium typically is disclosed in a footnote or parenthetically in the balance sheet, as illustrated in the following disclosure from the 1989 balance sheet of Stone Container Corporation:

	1989	1988
Long-Term Liabilities:		
(*In millions of dollars*)		
12.125% debentures with annual sinking fund payments of $14 commencing on September 15, 1996, and maturing in the year 2001 with a lump sum payment of $70 (including unamortized debt premium of $3.2 and $3.7)	$93.2	$98.7

An **amortization table** often is prepared by the issuer to support bond journal entries. The table gives all the data necessary to make the journal entries over the term of the bond, and each year's ending net liability balance. An amortization table for Gresham is shown in Exhibit 16–3. This table repeats the information recorded in the 1991 and 1992 entries above.

Straight-Line Method   This popular alternative to the interest method directly determines the amortization of premium or discount. An equal amount of discount or premium is amortized each interest period. Interest expense equals the cash interest paid less premium amortized or plus the discount amortized. This method produces a stable dollar *amount* of interest expense each period rather than a constant rate of interest each period. The following entry is recorded each period by Gresham (premium example) under this method:

Straight-Line Method

Gresham Company (Issuer)			**Elmhurst Company** (Investor)		
December 31, 1991–1995—Interest payment:					
Interest expense 6,157			Cash 7,000		
Premium on bonds payable 843*			Bond investment		843
Cash ($100,000 × .07)		7,000	Interest revenue		6,157

* $843 = $4,213/5 years

---

[15] The amortization period for the *issuer* runs from date of sale to maturity date (the bond term); for the *investor*, it runs from the purchase date to maturity date. The example assumes Elmhurst holds the bonds to maturity.

EXHIBIT 16-3   Amortization Table for Gresham Company Bonds Sold at Premium—Interest Method

Date	Interest Payment	Interest Expense*	Premium Amortization†	Unamortized Premium‡	Net Bond Liability§
1/1/91				$4,213	$104,213
12/31/91	$ 7,000	$ 6,253	$ 747	3,466	103,466
12/31/92	7,000	6,208	792	2,674	102,674
12/31/93	7,000	6,160	840	1,834	101,834
12/31/94	7,000	6,110	890	944	100,944
12/31/95	7,000	6,056	944	0	100,000
	$35,000	$30,787	$4,213		

* (Previous net liability balance)(.06)
  $6,253 = $104,213(.06)

† (Interest payment) − (Interest expense)
  $747 = $7,000 − $6,253

‡ (Previous unamortized premium) − (Current period amortization)
  $3,466 = $4,213 − $747

§ $100,000 + (Current unamortized premium)
  $103,466 = $100,000 + $3,466

The straight line method recognizes the *average* amount of interest each year ($6,157 = $30,787/5), while the interest method reflects the changing debt balance. The straight-line method is allowed only when interest expense is not materially different under the two methods (*APB Opinion No. 21*, par. 15).

The use of the straight-line method is questionable when the discount or premium is material, or when the bond term is exceptionally long. For example, the method seriously misstates interest expense early in the term of a zero coupon bond. Similarly, very long bond terms magnify the differences between the two methods because the initial net liability can be considerably smaller or larger than face value.[16]

Case 1, Part C: Bonds sell at a discount, effective rate = 8%

$$\text{Price} = \$100,000(PV1, 8\%, 5) + \$100,000(.07)(PVA, 8\%, 5)$$
$$= \$100,000(.68058) + \$7,000(3.99271) = 96,007$$

The Gresham bonds sell at a discount because the stated rate is less than the yield rate on similar bonds. The discount is recorded in the discount on bonds payable account. This account is a contra liability valuation account, which is subtracted from bonds payable to yield the net liability at present value. The entries for the first two years follow, along with an amortization table for the entire bond term (see Exhibit 16–4) and the relevant portion of the balance sheet after two years.

	Gresham Company (Issuer)		**Elmhurst Company (Investor)**	
January 1, 1991—Issue bonds:				
Cash	96,007		Bond investment	96,007
Discount on bonds payable	3,993		Cash	96,007
Bonds payable		100,000		

---

[16] For example, under the interest method, the issuer of 15%, $1,000, 25-year bonds yielding 10% ($1,454 issue price) recognizes $145 of interest expense in the first year per bond, 10% more than the $132 under the straight-line method.

EXHIBIT 16–4   Amortization Table for Gresham Company Bonds Sold at Discount—Interest Method

Date	Interest Payment	Interest Expense*	Discount Amortization†	Unamortized Premium‡	Net Bond Liability§
1/1/91				$3,993	$ 96,007
12/31/91	$ 7,000	$ 7,681	$ 681	3,312	96,688
12/31/92	7,000	7,735	735	2,577	97,423
12/31/93	7,000	7,794	794	1,783	98,217
12/31/94	7,000	7,857	857	926	99,074
12/31/95	7,000	7,926	926	0	100,000
	$35,000	$38,993	$3,993		

* (Previous net liability balance).08
  $7,681 = $96,007(.08)

† (Interest expense) − (Interest payment)
  $681 = $7,681 − $7,000

‡ (Previous unamortized discount) − (Current period amortization)
  $3,312 = $3,993 − $681

§ $100,000 − (Current unamortized discount)
  $96,688 = $100,000 − $3,312

Interest Method

December 31, 1991—Interest expense:

Interest expense 7,681*			Cash 7,000		
Discount on bonds			Bond investment 681		
payable	681		Interest revenue . . .		7,681
Cash ($100,000 × .07)	7,000				

* $7,681 = $96,007(.08)

December 31, 1992—Interest expense:

Interest expense 7,735*			Cash 7,000		
Discount on bonds			Bond investment 735		
payable	735		Interest revenue . . .		7,735
Cash ($100,000 × .07)	7,000				

* $7,735 = ($96,007 + $681)(.08)

GRESHAM COMPANY
Portion of Long-Term Liability Section of Balance Sheet
December 31, 1992

Bonds payable	$100,000
Unamortized discount on bonds payable ($3,993 − $681 − $735)	(2,577)
Net book value of bonds payable	$ 97,423

The initial $3,993 discount is the amount in excess of the total bond price that the issuer must pay the investor at maturity. Therefore, the discount represents interest, in addition to the cash interest payments required over the bond term. A portion of the discount is recognized (amortized) each period, causing both interest expense and the net bond liability to increase. When completely amortized, the net bond liability has increased to $100,000, the maturity amount. Total interest expense over the bond term is $38,993, the sum of cash interest payments ($35,000) and the bond discount ($3,993).

EXHIBIT 16-5   Summary Table: Accounting for Bonds—Assume *Semiannual* Interest Payments

Price of
bond issue = Present value of principal and interest payments
           = (Face value)($PV1, e, n$) + (Face value)(s)(PVA, e, n)

where e = effective interest rate per six-month period.
       s = stated interest rate per six-month period.
       n = number of semiannual periods in bond term.

Initial discount = Face value − Price of bond issue
                  (effective rate exceeds stated rate)

Or:
Initial premium = Price of bond issue − Face value
                 (stated rate exceeds effective rate)

Net book value of bonds = Face value + Unamortized premium

Or: = Face value − Unamortized discount

	Premium	**Discount**
As maturity approaches:		
Unamortized amount	declines	declines
Net book value	declines	increases
Annual interest expense*	declines	increases

* under interest method

Two Methods of Amortizing Premium and Discount

	Straight-line Method	**Interest Method**
Annual interest expense	Constant over term	Changes each year
Annual interest expense as a percentage of beginning book value	Changes each year	Constant over term

Exhibit 16–5 summarizes several aspects of bond accounting. The exhibit is designed for semiannual interest payments, the usual situation.

CONCEPT REVIEW

1. How does a premium on bonds payable occur? What does it represent?
2. Why is interest expense increased by the amount of discount amortized?
3. Why is the straight-line method of amortization not appropriate for deep-discount bonds?

ADDITIONAL ISSUES IN ACCOUNTING FOR BONDS
◆

Accounting for bonds becomes somewhat more complex when the issue date or bond date does not coincide with the first day of the fiscal year or with an interest payment date. However, the basic principles already discussed are applicable. In Case 2, assume the Gresham Company bonds are issued during the fiscal year, on an interest payment date. Also assume now that interest is paid semiannually.

Case 2: Interest payment date does not coincide with fiscal-year-end, bonds issued on interest payment date

Information for Gresham bond issue:

1. The bond date is March 31, 1991, and the maturity date is March 31, 1996.
2. The issue date is September 30, 1991.
3. The bonds pay interest on a semiannual basis: September 30 and March 31.
4. The stated interest rate is 8% (4% per semiannual period), and the effective interest rate is 6% (3% per semiannual period).
5. Face value: $100,000.
6. Both Gresham and Elmhurst have calendar fiscal years.
   Therefore:

$$\text{Bond term is } 4\frac{1}{2} \text{ years, or 9 semiannual periods.}$$
$$\text{Price} = \$100,000(PV1, 3\%, 9) + \$100,000(.04)(PVA, 3\%, 9)$$
$$\$100,000(.76642) + \$4,000(7.78611) = \$107,786$$

Typically, the end of the accounting period does not coincide with an interest date. In this situation, the issuer and investor *accrue* interest on the bond issue from the last interest date in the accounting period to the end of the accounting period. The issuance entry, the adjusting entry, and the first two interest payment entries for Gresham and Elmhurst are recorded as follows under the interest method:

Gresham Company (Issuer)			Elmhurst Company (Investor)		
September 30, 1991–Issue bonds:					
Cash	107,786		Bond investment	107,786	
Premium on bonds payable		7,786	Cash		107,786
Bonds payable		100,000			

Interest method

December 31, 1991—Recognize interest expense:					
Interest expense	1,617*		Interest receivable	2,000	
Premium on bonds payable	383		Bond investment		383
Interest payable		2,000**	Interest revenue		1,617

* $1,617 = \$107,786(.06)(\frac{3}{12})$

** $2,000 = \$100,000(.08)(\frac{3}{12})$

GRESHAM COMPANY
Portion of Liability Section of Balance Sheet
December 31, 1991

Current liabilities:		
Interest payable		$ 2,000
Long-term liabilities:		
Bonds payable	$100,000	
Unamortized premium on bonds payable	7,403*	
Net book value of bonds payable		$107,403

* $7,403 = \$7,786 - \$383$

Under the interest method, when fiscal and interest periods do not coincide, interest expense is allocated on a proportional basis *within* interest periods. For example, the December 31, 1991, entry recognizes one half of the first semiannual interest expense amount.[17]

---

[17] If Gresham used the straight-line method, $433 of premium ($7,786 × $\frac{1}{9}$ × $\frac{1}{2}$) is amortized, and $1,567 of interest expense ($2,000 − $433) is recognized on December 31.

The March 31 entry, shown below, settles the interest payable from the previous year and recognizes the last half of the first semiannual interest expense amount. Assume reversing entries are not recorded.

Interest Method

Gresham Company (Issuer)		Elmhurst Company (Investor)	

March 31, 1992—Interest payment:

Interest expense 1,617*		Cash 4,000	
Premium on bonds payable 383		Bond investment	383
Interest payable 2,000		Interest revenue	1,617
Cash ($100,000 × .08/2) . . .	4,000	Interest receivable	2,000

* $1,617 = $107,786(.06) (3/12)

Only one quarter of a year's interest expense is recognized on this date. The $4,000 cash payment is composed of the interest receivable from 1991, three months' interest in 1992, and a return of the original investment (premium amortization). For completeness, the September 30, 1992, entry is shown:

Interest Method

Gresham Company (Issuer)		Elmhurst Company (Investor)	

September 30, 1992—Interest payment:

Interest expense 3,211*		Cash 4,000	
Premium on bonds payable 789		Bond investment	789
Cash ($100,000 × .08/2) . . .	4,000	Interest revenue	3,211

* 3,211 = ($107,786 − $383 − $383) (.06) (9/12)

Amortization tables in this situation are based on interest periods rather than reporting periods. The information to compute the amounts in the preceding entries is found in the partial amortization table below for the interest method:

Date	Interest Payment	Interest Expense	Premium Amortization	Unamortized Premium	Net Bond Liability
9/30/91				$7,786	$107,786
3/31/92	$4,000	$3,234	$766	7,020	107,020
9/30/92	4,000	3,211	789	6,231	106,231

For example, the $383 of premium amortized on December 31, 1991, is one half the $766 amount shown in the amortization column for 3/31/92.

Bond Issue Costs

Several costs are incurred in preparing and selling a bond issue. **Bond issue costs** include legal, accounting, underwriting, commission, engraving, printing, registration, and promotion costs. These costs are paid by the issuer and reduce the net proceeds from the bond issue, thus raising the effective interest rate for the issuer.

Bond issue costs are classified as a *deferred charge* (long-term asset) rather than as a reduction of the premium or increase in the discount (*APB Opinion No. 21,* par. 16). Bond issue costs contribute to the financing of operations that produce revenue. Under the matching principle, bond issue costs are expensed against revenues during the bond term. For materiality reasons, the straight-line method of amortization generally is used.

Waxman Industries disclosed the following information in its 1988 annual report related to debt issue costs:

	1988 ($000)	1987 ($000)
Other assets: Unamortized debt issuance costs	$1,122	$1,511

Note 1 (in part): *Summary of Significant Accounting Policies*
Unamortized Debt Issuance Cost:
   Debt issuance costs are being amortized on a straight-line basis over the term
   of the related debt.

To illustrate accounting for bond issue costs, assume $3,600 of bond issue costs are incurred to issue the bonds in Case 2 (four-and-one-half-year bond term). The bond issue costs are amortized at the rate of $400 per semiannual period ($3,600/9 semiannual periods). Gresham makes the following entries *in addition* to those recorded for Case 2.

Gresham Company
(Issuer)

September 30, 1991—Record bond issue cost:

| Bond issue cost . . . . | 3,600 | |
| Cash . . . . | | 3,600 |

December 31, 1991—Amortize bond issue cost:

| Bond issue expense ($3,600 × 1/9 × 1/2) . . . . | 200 | |
| Bond issue cost . . . . | | 200 |

Effects on Gresham Company's 1991:
   Income statement: bond issue expense $200

   Balance sheet: long-term deferred charge balance $3,400

March 31, 1992—Amortize bond issue cost:

| Bond issue expense . . . . | 200 | |
| Bond issue cost . . . . | | 200 |

Bond issue costs are not assets, however, according to *SFAC No. 6* (par. 237) because they produce no future benefit. Rather, they reduce the funds derived from the bond issue. Treatment as an adjustment to the premium or discount, or as an expense in the borrowing period is suggested by this view. Although an SFAC does not constitute GAAP, the FASB is expected to develop new guidelines for reporting these and other deferred charges.[18]

Bonds Issued between Interest Dates

In the previous two cases, bonds were issued on an interest date. The objective of these cases is to emphasize the principles underlying bond accounting. However, bonds typically are not issued on an interest date for the same reasons that the issue date is usually not the bond date. Two new problems arise: accounting for accrued interest from the most recent interest payment date, and computing the issue price.

Case 3: Bonds issued between interest payment dates

Information for Gresham bond issue:

1. The bond date is March 31, 1991, and the maturity date is March 31, 1996.
2. The issue date is June 1, 1991 (between interest dates).

---

[18] If the method of amortizing premium or discount and bond issue costs are the same, deferral and amortization of bond issue costs yields the same periodic income as does treating bond issue costs as a reduction of the proceeds. Only the classification of expense is different (interest expense versus bond issue expense). However, deferral and amortizaton (present GAAP) causes an asset to be recorded at issuance rather than a liability to be reduced.

3. The bonds pay interest each September 30 and March 31.
4. The stated rate is 8%, and the effective interest rate is 10%.
5. Face value: $100,000.
6. Both Gresham and Elmhurst have calendar fiscal years.

The calculation of the price of a bond issued between interest payment dates is shown below:

Price of bond at immediately preceding interest date (3/31/91):
    Face value [$100,000(PV1, 5%, 10) = $100,000(.61391)] $61,391
    Interest [$100,000(.08/2) (PVA, 5%, 10) = $4,000(7.72173)]   30,887

    Total present value $92,278
Growth in bond value at yield rate, from
    3/31/91 to 6/1/91 [$92,278(.10) ($\frac{2}{12}$)]   1,538
Cash interest at stated rate from
    3/31/91 to 6/1/91 [$100,000(.08) ($\frac{2}{12}$)] . . . .   (1,333)
Price of bond at 6/1/91 . . . . $92,483

The $1,538 growth component is the normal interest return on the bond from March 31 to June 1 and is added for bonds issued at either a discount or premium. The cash interest is the portion of that return due September 30 as a separate payment but not earned by the holder for the two months the bond was not outstanding. Therefore, it is deducted from the bond price.

Interpolation, using the bond prices at the two interest payment dates *bordering* the issue date, also can be used to determine the issue price:

Price at 3/31/91 (from previous calculation) $92,278
Price at 9/30/91:
    Face value [$100,000(PV1, 5%, 9) = $100,000(.64461)] $64,461
    Interest [$100,000(.08/2) (PVA, 5%, 9) = $4,000(7.10782)]   28,431
    Total present value $92,892
Interpolated price at 6/1/91:

$$\$92,278 - 2/6(\$92,278 - \$92,892) = \$92,483$$

Or:

$$\$92,892 + 4/6(\$92,278 - \$92,892) = \$92,483$$

The bond issue date (June 1) is two months, that is $\frac{2}{6}$ of a semiannual period after March 31. Therefore, $\frac{2}{6}$ of the difference between the March 31 and September 30 prices is subtracted from the March 31 price in the first interpolation. In the second interpolation, $\frac{4}{6}$ of the difference is added to the September 30 price to account for the additional four months the bond is outstanding. This approach is followed independently of whether the bond is issued at a premium or discount.[19]

Accrued interest at the stated rate from March 31 to June 1 is collected from the investor. The accrued interest amounts to an interest-free loan to the issuer. The initial discount or premium amount is independent of accrued interest and equals face value less the bond price, as usual. The following entry records the bond issuance:

---

[19] The two methods of computing the price of a bond issued between interest dates are equivalent because the difference in bond prices at adjacent interest dates equals the growth in bond value at the yield rate less the cash interest for an interest period. The first method applies the appropriate fraction of the partial interest period to the growth at the yield rate and subtracts the stated interest. The second method (interpolation) focuses only on the prices exclusive of accrued interest; therefore, no subtraction of accrued interest is necessary.

| **Gresham Company**
(Issuer) | **Elmhurst Company**
(Investor) |

June 1, 1991—Issue bonds:

Cash 93,816*		Bond investment 92,483	
Discount on bonds		Interest receivable 1,333	
payable . . . . 7,517†		Cash	93,816
Interest payable	1,333‡		
Bonds payable	100,000		

* $92,483 + $100,000(.08)\frac{2}{12}$

† $100,000 − $92,483

‡ $100,000(.08)\frac{2}{12}$; two months' accrued interest from the bond date to the issue date is collected from the investor and then is reimbursed on the first interest payment date.

The entry to record the first interest payment after issuance (September 30) takes into account the partial interest period. The amortization table constructed for the same bond but assuming issuance on *March 31, 1991,* the interest date immediately preceding the actual issue date, is used as the basis for this entry under the interest method. Part of this table, as well as the September 30, 1991, interest entry, is illustrated below:

Partial Amortization Table for Gresham Company Bonds
Sold at Discount on June 1, 1991—Interest Method—
under the Assumption of Issuance on March 31, 1991

Date	Interest Payment	Interest Expense	Discount Amortization	Unamortized Discount	Net Bond Liability
3/31/91				$7,722	$92,278*
9/30/91	$4,000†	$4,614‡	$614§	7,108‖	92,892#
3/31/92	4,000	4,645	645	6,463	93,537

* Price if sold on 3/31/91 to yield 10% (see text discussion).

† $100,000(.08)\frac{1}{2}$

‡ $92,278(.10)\frac{1}{2}$

§ $4,614 − $4,000

‖ $7,722 − $614

$92,278 + $614, or $100,000 − $7,108

Interest Method

| **Gresham Company**
(Issuer) | **Elmhurst Company**
(Investor) |

September 30, 1991—Interest payment:

Interest payable 1,333		Cash 4,000	
Interest expense 3,076*		Bond investment 409	
Discount on bonds		Interest receivable	1,333
payable	409†	Interest revenue	3,076
Cash ($100,000 × .08/2)	4,000		

* The interest for four months based on the March 31 issue price: $3,076 = $92,278(.10)(\frac{4}{12})$. Also, $3,076 = $4,614(\frac{4}{6})$.

† The amortization for four months based on the March 31 issue price: $409 = $614(\frac{4}{6})$. Also, the growth in bond value from June 1 to September 30: $409 = $92,892 − $92,483.

After the first interest payment entry, the amortization table above (based on issuance at March 31) is used for the remaining entries during the bond term.

Under the straight-line method of amortization, the bond discount is amortized over the 58-month bond term at $129.60 per month ($7,517/58). The September 30 entry under the straight-line method follows:

Straight-line Method

Gresham Company (Issuer)			Elmhurst Company (Investor)		

September 30, 1991—Interest payment:

Interest payable	1,333		Cash	4,000	
Interest expense	3,185		Bond investment	518	
Discount on bonds			Interest receivable		1,333
payable		518*	Interest revenue		3,185
Cash ($100,000 × .08/2)		4,000			

* ($7,517/58-month bond term) (4 months)

CONCEPT REVIEW

1. What new accounting issues arise when bonds are issued between interest dates.
2. If bonds issued May 1, 1991, pay interest on June 30 and December 31, how many months of accrued interest does the issuer receive from the investor? What interest rate is used to compute the accrued interest?
3. Are bond issue costs an asset or a reduction of a liability? Defend both points of view.

DEBT SECURITIES WITH EQUITY RIGHTS

Firms issue debt securities that include rights to acquire capital stock. Rights to acquire equity securities enhance marketability and improve the terms to the issuer. The investor receives a potential right to become a shareholder and participate in stock price appreciation in addition to principal and interest payments. Two common examples of this type of hybrid security are nonconvertible bonds with detachable stock warrants and bonds convertible into capital stock.

Nonconvertible Bonds with Detachable Stock Purchase Warrants A *stock warrant* conveys the option to purchase from the issuer a specified number of shares of common stock at a designated price per share, within a stated time period (the exercise period). The warrant is valuable because it enables the holder to buy stock for less than market value if the market value rises above the designated price. Warrants generally increase the bond price on the expectation that the common stock price will increase and create a market for the warrants.[20]

For example, BMC Industries, Inc., disclosed the following information related to detachable warrants in its 1989 annual report:

> Additionally, detachable warrants to purchase 960,000 shares of the Company's common stock at $7.00 per share were issued to the purchasers of the subordinated notes. . . . $1,526,000 of the proceeds of the subordinated notes was allocated to the detachable warrants and included in common stock. . .

APB Opinion No. 14 requires that a portion of the bond price be allocated to the warrants if detachable. The warrant market value is sufficiently objective to justify

---

[20] Warrants are detachable or nondetachable. If detachable, the warrants are traded as separate securities. If nondetachable, the debt security must be surrendered to obtain the stock.

the separate valuation for warrants. The allocation is credited to a contributed capital (owners' equity) account and is based on the market values of the two securities on the date of issuance (the *proportional* method). If only the warrants, for example, have a readily determinable market value, the bonds are valued at the difference between the total bond price and the market value of the warrants (the *incremental* method).

In contrast, if the stock purchase warrants are *not detachable,* no separate market for them exists. *APB Opinion No. 14* therefore stipulates that the entire bond price be allocated to the bonds.

After the issue price is allocated to the bonds and detachable warrants, bond accounting is not affected by the warrants. Therefore, the following example of accounting for nonconvertible bonds with detachable stock purchase warrants does not illustrate interest recognition.

> Embassy Corporation issues $100,000 of 8%, 10-year, nonconvertible bonds with detachable stock purchase warrants to Nuvolari Corporation.
>
> Each $1,000 bond carries 10 warrants. Each warrant entitles Nuvolari to purchase one share of $10 par[21] common stock for $15. The bond issue therefore includes 1,000 warrants (100 bonds × 10 warrants per bond).
>
> The bond issue sells for 105 exclusive of accrued interest. Shortly after issuance, the warrants trade for $4 each.

1. *Incremental method* (only one security has a market value; no market value is determined for the bonds as separate securities).

Embassy Corporation (Issuer)			Nuvolari Corporation (Investor)		
Issuance entry:					
Cash	105,000		Investment in		
Bonds payable		100,000	bonds	101,000	
Detachable stock			Investment in		
warrants		4,000*	detachable stock		
Premium on bonds			warrants	4,000	
payable		1,000†	Cash		105,000

* (1,000 warrants) ($4); detachable stock warrants is a contributed capital account (owners' equity).

† Value allocated to bonds − face value of bonds, or ($105,000 − $4,000) − $100,000.

The warrants are credited at market value. The remaining, or *incremental,* portion of the proceeds ($101,000) is allocated to the bonds. The amount of premium recorded is consistent with the previous discussion and equals the difference between the amount allocated to the bonds and face value. Nuvolari classifies its two investment accounts as current or long-term depending on the intended holding period.

2. *Proportional method* (both securities have market values)—Shortly after issuance the bonds were quoted at 103 ex-warrants (without warrants attached).

Market value of bonds ($100,000 × 1.03)	$103,000
Market value of warrants: ($4 × 1,000)	4,000
Total market value of bonds and warrants	$107,000
Allocation of proceeds to bonds	
[$105,000 × ($103,000 ÷ $107,000)]	$101,075
Allocation of proceeds to warrants	
[$105,000 × ($4,000 ÷ $107,000)]	$ 3,925
Total proceeds allocated	$105,000

---

[21] *Par* value for common stock is the minimum stock issue price, appears on the stock certificate, is used in certain dividend calculations, and constitutes the minimum capital per share to be retained. Common stock is credited with par value; contributed capital in excess of par is credited with proceeds in excess of par value.

Embassy Corporation (Issuer)			Nuvolari Corporation (Investor)		
Issuance entry:					
Cash 105,000			Investment in		
Bonds payable . . .	100,000		bonds 101,075		
Detachable stock			Investment in		
warrants	3,925		detachable stock		
Premium on bonds			warrants	3,925	
payable	1,075*		Cash		105,000

* $101,075 − $100,000

The entries to account for *exercise* and *expiration* using the incremental method example follow:

Warrant Exercise and Expiration: Data from Incremental Method Example

Embassy Corporation (Issuer)			Nuvolari Corporation (Investor)		
Entry to account for exercise of 900 warrants:					
Cash (900 × $15) 13,500			Investment in		
Detachable stock			common stock 17,100		
warrants 3,600*			Investment in		
Common stock			detachable stock		
(900 × $10)	9,000		warrants		3,600
Contributed capital in			Cash		13,500
excess of par	8,100				

* $4(900 warrants)

Entry to account for expiration of remaining 100 warrants:					
Detachable stock			Loss on investment	400	
warrants 400*			Investment in		
Contributed capital			detachable stock		
from expiration of			warrants		400
detachable stock					
warrants	400				

* $4(100 warrants).

The entry to record the stock issued upon exercise is not affected by the market price at issuance. The warrant conveys the right to purchase stock for $15 per share regardless of the current market price. Detachable stock warrants is reduced by the original amount allocated to it ($4 per warrant). $3,600 of the resources allocated to warrants is allocated to other owners' equity accounts. Under the facts of the proportional method example, the debit to detachable stock warrants is $3,532.50 ($3,925 × 900/1,000) with a corresponding adjustment to contributed capital in excess of par.

The *expiration* entry is recorded at the end of the exercise period for any warrants that remain outstanding. Warrants are not exercised by the end of the expiration period through oversight or because of an unfavorable stock price. The issuing company retains the portion of the bond price originally allocated to the expired warrants. Firms may choose to credit premium on bonds payable instead of contributed capital from expiration of detachable stock warrants if the bonds are outstanding.

Convertible Bonds   A **convertible bond** is exchanged for capital stock (usually common stock) of the issuer at the *option of the investor*. Typically, convertible bonds also are *callable* at a specified redemption, or call price at the *option of the issuer*. If the bonds are called, the holders either convert the bonds or accept the call price. Convertible bonds often are marketable at lower interest rates than conventional bonds because investors assign a value to the conversion privilege. Convertible bonds typically are not issued with stock warrants.

The bond indenture of convertible bonds specifies a *conversion ratio* or *conversion price*. The conversion ratio is the number of shares of common stock issued upon conversion of one bond. The conversion price is the quotient of bond face value and conversion ratio.

For example, assume American Corporation issues 5,000 bonds, each convertible into 10 shares of American common stock and callable at $1,020. Face value is $1,000. Conversion can occur at the option of the holder on any date two years after issuance. The conversion ratio is 10 and the conversion price is $100 ($1,000 face value/10). The conversion price is the dollar amount of face value exchanged for each share of stock. The conversion price approximates the cost per share, and typically is set 10% to 20% above the stock price at issuance.[22]

The footnotes to the Durr-Fillauer Medical Company 1989 balance sheet include this example of a convertible bond:

> The Company's 8½% Convertible Subordinated Debentures due 2010 converted into common stock. The debentures were convertible into 72.5 shares of common stock for each $1,000 principal amount of debenture.

Convertible bonds offer certain advantages to the issuer. The bonds often sell at a lower interest rate (or a higher price) and with fewer restrictions than nonconvertible bonds. The convertibility feature improves the prospects for raising debt capital. Companies also use convertibles as a means of securing equity financing at a lower cost. By setting the conversion price above the prevailing stock price, fewer shares must be issued to obtain the same amount of capital. Furthermore, if the bonds are converted, the bond face value is never paid.

The call option protects the issuer from being forced to issue stock with an aggregate value greatly in excess of the call price. In the American example, if the stock price is $104 and rising a year after issuing the convertible bonds, American can call the bonds at $1,020 before the stock price rises much higher. In this case, the investors can choose to convert and receive stock worth $1,040 per bond (10 × $104) rather than accept the call price.[23]

Convertible bonds are not without disadvantages, however. If the stock price does not rise, the firm must service the debt. Stable to declining stock prices indicate financial problems that can be compounded by interest on the convertible debt. In the opposite case, if the issuing company is very successful and its stock price increases significantly after issuing convertible bonds, the company incurs the opportunity cost of foregoing the sale of converted shares at a higher price.

The primary advantage of convertible bonds to the investor is the potential for increased wealth if the stock appreciates. If not, the investor continues to receive interest (although most likely at a lower rate than on nonconvertible bonds) and the face value at maturity.

Accounting for the issuance of convertible bonds poses a conceptual problem. A popular view holds that the economic value of the conversion feature, reflected in the bond price, should be recorded as stockholders' equity. However, *APB Opinion No. 14* specifies that convertible bonds be recorded as *debt only,* with no value assigned to the conversion privilege. The APB reasoned that the debt and equity features of a convertible bond are inseparable and do not exist independently of each other.

---

[22] Otherwise the bonds would be converted immediately, if allowed by the indenture, to the detriment of the issuing corporation.

[23] Investors often do not convert at the earliest date on which the market value of stock to be received upon conversion exceeds the market value of the bonds. Expectations of further stock price increases may convince them to wait longer.

A separate market does not exist for either the bond standing alone or the conversion privilege. There is no objective basis (e.g., a market or an exchange transaction) for allocating the bond price to the bond and the conversion feature. The value of the conversion feature is contingent on a future stock price, which cannot be predicted.

Accounting for interest expense and amortization of premium or discount is not affected by convertibility. The bond term is used for amortization because the date of conversion cannot be anticipated. Accounting for interest is omitted in the example to follow.

> Assume Tollen Corporation sells $100,000 of 8% convertible bonds for $106,000 to Menton Corporation.

> At the option of the investor, each $1,000 bond is convertible to 10 shares of Tollen Corporation $10 par common stock on any interest date after the end of the second year from date of issuance. (In practice, conversion generally is possible on any date within the conversion period. The restriction on conversion is used only to facilitate the example.)

Tollen Corporation (Issuer)			**Menton Corporation** (Investor)		

Issuance entry:

Cash	106,000		Bond investment	106,000	
Premium on bonds			Cash		106,000
payable		6,000			
Bonds payable		100,000			

When the bonds are converted, the issuer (and investor) update interest expense (revenue) and amortization of premium or discount to the date of conversion. Then, bonds payable and bond investment are closed. Two methods are acceptable for valuing the stock issued upon conversion:

1. *Book value method:* record the stock at the book value of the convertible bonds; recognize neither gain nor loss.
2. *Market value method:* record the stock at the market value of stock or debt, whichever is more reliable. A gain or loss equal to the difference between the market value and the book value of debt is recognized.

The following entries illustrate both methods:

> Menton converts the bonds on an interest date. Both firms record interest in the usual way.

> The stock price is $110 per share, and $3,000 of premium remains unamortized for both firms after updating the premium account.

Tollen Corporation (Issuer)	**Book Value** Method	**Market Value** Method
Entry for conversion of bonds:		
Bonds payable 100,000	100,000	
Premium on bonds payable 3,000	3,000	
Loss on conversion of bonds	7,000‡	
Common stock	10,000*	10,000
Contributed capital in excess of par	93,000†	100,000§

* (100 bonds) (10 shares per bond) ($10 par).

† Book value of bonds is $103,000; $103,000 − $10,000 = $93,000

‡ Market value of stock issued ($1,000 shares × $110 = $110,000) less book value of bonds (103,000) equals loss of $7,000.

§ $110,000 (market value of shares issued) less $10,000 (par value of shares issued)

Menton Corporation (Investor)	Book Value Method	Market Value Method
Entry for conversion of bonds:		
Investment in stock 103,000		110,000
Bond investment	103,000	103,000
Gain on conversion of bonds		7,000

Under the book value method, the owners' equity accounts replace the bond accounts for the issuer. Under the market value method, the owners' equity accounts are credited at full market value, as if the issued stock were sold on the date of conversion. The gain or loss on conversion is not classified as extraordinary because the investor initiated the conversion. Tollen's $7,000 loss is the cash forgone by issuing shares on bond conversion. However, the loss is not necessarily equal to the economic loss (or gain) because the market value of the bonds is not considered in the accounting.

If the book value of the bonds is less than the par value of stock issued on conversion, retained earnings is debited for the difference. For example, if the total par of Tollen stock issued is $110,000 (assume $110 par), retained earnings is debited for $7,000 under the book value method.

The book value method appears to be more popular. Many accountants view the conversion as the culmination of a single transaction that started when the convertible bonds were issued. The valuation of issued stock is restricted to the actual resources received on the bond issue, adjusted for amortization to date of conversion. Furthermore, this view holds that the gain (loss) under the market value method is not supported by the value of resources originally received on the bond issue. Others prefer the market value method because it uses current value to measure the investment. The valuation of the stock issued is based on the value received if the shares were sold.

Induced Conversion of Convertible Debt   Issuers of convertible debt sometimes change the conversion provisions after the issuance date to induce prompt conversion. The inducement is an incentive over and above the original shares to be issued on conversion. Common inducements include an increase in the conversion ratio, issuance of stock rights, and payment of cash or other consideration. Decreasing interest rates and a preference for lower debt levels can prompt an induced conversion.

SFAS No. 84, "Induced Conversions of Convertible Debt," requires that in an induced conversion, the issuer recognize an expense equal to the fair value of consideration transferred in excess of the fair value of the securities issuable under the *original* conversion terms. The expense is not classified as an extraordinary item because the original debt agreement remains in effect during the inducement period, and the debt is extinguished at the bondholder's option rather than the issuer's. *SFAS No. 84* applies only to changes in conversion provisions exercisable for a limited time. Therefore, only changes made to induce prompt conversion are covered under the statement.

The expense is recognized only for bonds converted during the limited time period. The market value of consideration transferred is measured at the date the inducement is accepted. The following is an example of induced conversion:

Cologne Corporation holds 500, 6% convertible bonds payable issued at face value ($1,000) by Berlin Corporation. Each bond is convertible into 10 shares of $20 par common stock.

Berlin offers two additional shares of common stock for each bond as an inducement to convert. The offer is open for a two-month period.

The bondholders accept the inducement within the required period. The market price of the common stock on the acceptance date (also an interest date) is $110.

| | Berlin Corporation
(Issuer) | | Cologne Corporation
(Investor) | |

Book Value Method

Conversion entry:

Bonds payable	500,000		Investment in stock . . .	500,000	
Debt conversion			Bond investment . .		500,000
expense	110,000*				
Common stock . . .		120,000†			
Contributed capital in					
excess of par . . .		490,000			

* (12 − 10)(500)($110)—The market value of 2 additional shares per bond.

† 12(500) $20.

Market Value Method

Conversion entry:

Bonds payable	500,000		Investment in stock . . .	660,000‡	
Debt conversion			Bond investment . .		500,000
expense	110,000		Gain on		
Loss on conversion . . .	50,000*		conversion		160,000
Common stock . . .		120,000			
Contributed capital in					
excess of par . . .		540,000†			

* Difference between market value of stock issued ($660,000) and book value of bonds converted ($500,000), less the cost of the inducement ($110,000)

† $660,000 − $120,000.

‡ Market value of stock issued: $110(12) (500) = $660,000.

The issuer recognizes the market value of the two additional inducement shares per bond as an expense under both methods. Under the book value method, the expense effectively is capitalized as an increase in owners' equity reflecting the issuance of additional common shares without proceeds.[24] Under the market value method, part of the total loss on conversion is reclassified as debt conversion expense. The increase to owners' equity is measured at the total market value of shares issued. Under either method, if cash is the inducement, the debt conversion expense equals the amount of cash paid and credited.

One view of induced conversions holds that expense recognition is inappropriate for transactions involving a firm and its equity investors. Others believe the inducement is an extinguishment, implying that market values should be recorded. Another view holds that the cost of the inducement should be treated as a reduction of the equity capital provided. However, in *SFAS No. 84,* the FASB reasoned that a firm incurs a cost not expected under the original agreement when inducing conversion (par. 27):

> In exchange for the assets or securities given up in excess of those it was already committed to pay or issue, the enterprise receives performance. In the absence of such consideration, the conversion would not have occurred at that time. The Board believes that this type of an exchange of consideration for performance is a transaction that should be recognized as a cost of obtaining that performance.

---

[24] The additional shares issued are similar to a stock dividend. A stock dividend is the issuance of shares to existing shareholders without proceeds to the issuing firm. Stock dividends reduce retained earnings. In the Berlin example, debt conversion expense also reduces retained earnings.

CONCEPT REVIEW

1. Why is a value recorded for detachable warrants, but not for the conversion feature of convertible bonds?
2. How is the premium (discount) computed for bonds issued with detachable warrants?
3. What is the rationale for the market value method of accounting for conversion of convertible bonds? And what does the gain or loss on conversion represent?

DEBT EXTINGUISHMENT

Firms typically use the proceeds of most bond issues and other long-term debt instruments for the entire debt term. At the maturity date all discount or premium is fully amortized; gains and losses are not recognized on normal retirement. However, it is not uncommon for firms to retire debt before or after maturity. Early retirement of debt decreases the debt-equity ratio and can facilitate future debt issuances.

Another major incentive to retiring bonds before maturity occurs when interest rates *increase* enough to cause bond prices to decrease significantly below book value. The decline in prices enables the issuer to retire bonds at a gain. When interest rates *decrease,* firms use the opportunity to retire more expensive bonds and issue bonds with lower interest rates. However, a loss occurs in this case because bond prices increase above book value.

Accounting for debt retirement is affected by several pronouncements. The main reporting issues are determining when a debt extinguishment occurs and classifying the gain or loss on extinguishment. The gain or loss is the difference between the book value and market value of the debt on the date of extinguishment. The relevant pronouncements are summarized below:

1. *APB Opinion No. 26,* "Early Extinguishment of Debt," (1972), defines early extinguishment of debt as any retirement of debt before scheduled maturity (except through conversion by holder) and required recognition of the difference between the market value and book value of debt retired as an ordinary gain or loss in the year of extinguishment.
2. *SFAS No. 4,* "Reporting Gains and Losses from Extinguishment of Debt," (1975), amended *APB Opinion No. 26* by requiring that gains and losses from extinguishment of debt (whether early, at maturity, or after maturity) be classified as extraordinary and disclosed net of tax effect. Gains and losses from cash purchases of debt made to satisfy sinking-fund requirements were exempt from classification as extraordinary.
3. *SFAS No. 64,* "Extinguishments of Debt Made to Satisfy Sinking-Fund Requirements," (1982), amends *SFAS No. 4* by restricting the exemption from extraordinary classification to those gains and losses from extinguishments made to satisfy sinking fund requirements that must be met within one year of the date of the extinguishment. Also, such classification is determined without regard to the means used to retire the debt.
4. *SFAS No. 76,* "Extinguishment of Debt," (1983), amends *APB Opinion No. 26* by redefining debt extinguishment for financial reporting purposes to include only the following three circumstances (par. 3):
   a. The debtor is relieved of all obligations associated with the debt through direct payment or purchase of its own debt securities on the market, replacement (refunding) of debt with another issue, or by calling debt.

> *b.* The debtor is legally released from the debt judicially or by the creditor, and it is probable (as defined in *SFAS No. 5,* "Accounting for Contingencies") that the debtor will not be required to make future payments on the debt. This occurs, for example, when mortgage debt secured by an asset is assumed by another firm purchasing that asset.
>
> *c.* The debtor irrevocably places cash or other assets in trust solely to satisfy the scheduled payments under the debt, and the possibility that the debtor will be required to make future payments on the debt is remote. This is called **in-substance defeasance** of debt. However, the debtor remains legally liable for the debt.

Gains and losses on debt extinguishment are now classified as extraordinary items even though they might be frequent occurrences. In many instances, extinguishment gains were significant in relation to operating income.[25] Classification as extraordinary brings the gains into the open. Firms no longer are able to report a large extinguishment gain as a component of ordinary income.

Extinguishment of debt is now broadly defined and is not restricted to early retirement or to cash reacquisitions of debt.[26] Normal conversion and induced conversion of convertible bonds are not debt extinguishments for purposes of classifying the gain or loss because retirement occurs at the option of the investor. However, retirement of debt accomplished through issuance of equity securities is a debt extinguishment for purposes of applying *SFAS No. 76.*[27]

Accounting for debt extinguishment involves:

* Updating interest expense, discount or premium, and related issue costs to the retirement date.
* Removing the liability accounts.
* Recording the transfer of cash, other resources, or debt securities.
* Recording an extraordinary gain or loss.

Required disclosures for extraordinary gains and losses from extinguishment include (*SFAS No. 4,* par. 9):

* A description of the transaction, including the means used for extinguishment.
* The income tax effect of the gain or loss.
* The per share amount of the aggregate gain or loss net of related tax effect.

The following examples use bonds to illustrate debt extinguishment.

Extinguishment of Bonds by Open-Market Purchase

In an open-market purchase of bonds, the issuer pays the current market price as would any investor purchasing the bonds. As a basis for an example, Exhibit 16–6 repeats a portion of the amortization table for the Gresham bonds.

Assume that interest rates have increased since these bonds were issued and on March 1, 1992, Gresham purchases 20% ($20,000 face value) of the bonds on the open market at 90. The price decline reflects the increased interest rates.[28] The entries to record the extinguishment under effective interest and straight-line methods follow:

---

[25] For example, in 1973, United Brands refunded $125 million (book value) of 5½% bonds by issuing $75 million of 9⅛% bonds and paying $12.5 million cash. United Brands recognized a $37.5 million *ordinary* gain. The market value of the old bonds had fallen $37.5 million because of the rise in interest rates. The company had averaged only $6.6 million in earnings during the preceding five years!

[26] Some troubled debt restructures, discussed in Appendix 16B, result in debt retirement but are not considered debt retirements for purposes of classifying gains and losses.

[27] *FASB Technical Bulletin No. 80–1.*

[28] The price equals the present value of all remaining payments at the current market rate. For simplicity, the market price is given, but could be computed as in Case 3, for bonds issued between interest dates.

EXHIBIT 16-6   Data for Open-Market Extinguishment: Gresham Company Bonds, Case 1, Part B (Premium)

Issue date: January 1, 1991
Stated interest rate: 7%
Interest payment date: December 31
Maturity date: December 31, 1995

Total face value: $100,000
Bond date: January 1, 1991
Yield rate at issuance: 6%
Bond issue costs: $3,600*

**Amortization Table for Gresham Company Bonds
Sold at Premium—Interest Method**

Date	Interest Payment	Interest Expense	Premium Amortization	Unamortized Premium	Net Bond Liability
1/1/91				$4,213	$104,213
12/31/91	$7,000	$6,253	$747	3,466	103,466
12/31/92	7,000	6,208	792	2,674	102,674

* New information.

	Interest Method	Straight-Line Method
March 1, 1992—Update interest and premium amortization on portion retired:		
Interest expense	207*	205
Premium on bonds payable	26	28†
Interest payable	233‡	233

* .06($103,466)(²⁄₁₂)(.20)
(Market rate at issue) (Book value on 1/1/92) (²⁄₁₂ year) (Portion of bond issue retired)

† $4,213(2/60) (.20)
(Original premium) (2 months/60 months bond term) (Portion of bond issue retired)

‡ $20,000(.07) (2/12)
(Accrued interest from January 1, 1992)

March 1, 1992—Update bond issue expense:		
Bond issue expense	24*	24
Bond issue cost	24	24

* $3,600(²⁄₆₀)(.20)
(Total issue cost) (2 months/60 month bond term)(Portion of bond issue retired)

March 1, 1992—Remove relevant accounts and recognize gain:		
Bonds payable	20,000	20,000
Premium on bonds payable	667*	646†
Interest payable	233	233
Cash	18,233‡	18,233
Bond issue cost	552§	552
Extraordinary gain, bond extinguishment	2,115‖	2,094#

* $3,466(.20) − $26
(Unamortized premium 1/1/92) (Portion of bond issue retired) − (Amount of premium amortized through 3/1/92)

† $4,213(⁴⁶⁄₆₀)(.20)
(Original premium) (46 months remaining/60 month bond term) (Portion of bond issue retired)

‡ $20,000(.90) + 233 interest payable

§ $3,600(⁴⁶⁄₆₀) (.20)
(Total issue cost) (46 months remaining/60 month bond term) (Portion of bond issue retired)

‖ Book value of bonds retired ($20,000 + $667 = $20,667) less price of bonds ($18,000) less unexpired bond issue cost on bonds retired ($552) equals the extraordinary gain of $2,115.

Calculation is similar to interest method.

Extinguishment does not affect the accounting for the remaining 80% of the bond issue; 80% of the values in the amortization table would be used for the remaining bond term, as well as 80% of the bond issue costs.

The first entry under the interest method employs the most recent book value for the entire bond issue as the basis for computing interest expense for the two-month period ending March 1, 1992 ($103,466), for 20% of the bond issue. Amortization of premium and bond issue cost is recorded as usual, but only for 20% of the bond issue.

Under the interest method, on January 1, 1992, $693 ($3,466 × .20) of unamortized premium remains on the portion of the issue retired. $26 of that amount is amortized on March 1. Therefore, the remaining $667 ($693 − $26) is removed from the accounts.

Under the straight-line method, the fraction of the bond term remaining on March 1, 1992, is ⁴⁶⁄₆₀, which is used to determine the amount of bond issue cost and premium to remove. Only 20% of the total remaining on March 1, 1992, is removed from the two accounts.

The Nature of the Extraordinary Gain   The extraordinary gain is the difference between the total market price, and book value of the bonds decreased by the unexpired portion of the bond issue costs relating to the retired bonds. The remaining bond issue costs generate no future benefit. Brokerage fees and other costs of retiring the bonds also decrease the gain (increase the loss).

The extraordinary gain occurs because the market value of the bonds decreased below book value. GAAP requires the use of the market rate at issuance for measuring the book value of the bond. However, the gain fails to reflect economic reality.[29] For example, it can be argued that the bond extinguishment did not alter Gresham's economic position because the debt was retired at market value. A more profitable alternative might be to apply the $18,000 to a higher-yield investment. Retiring low-cost debt when interest rates rise is questionable, particularly if additional debt issuances are contemplated.

Sinking-Fund Retirements: Ordinary Gain and Loss Classification   Early retirement of bonds fulfills the sinking-fund requirements of some bond issues. Under *SFAS No. 64,* gains and losses from such extinguishments made to satisfy requirements that must be met within one year of the extinguishment are treated as ordinary income items, without regard to the means used to retire the debt.

For example, if Gresham is *required* by the bond indenture to purchase the $20,000 of bonds it retired on March 1, 1992, within one year of that date to satisfy a sinking-fund requirement, the gain is reported as ordinary income. In contrast, if the sinking-fund retirement deadline is May 1, 1993, the gain is classified as extraordinary because retirement did not occur within one year of the required date.

This exemption recognizes the difference between required and discretionary extinguishments and allows one year to complete the necessary arrangements for bond retirement. If an issuer *must* retire bonds under the indenture and does so within a year of the deadline, it is difficult to argue that the purpose of the retirement is to manipulate income. However, if bonds are retired two years ahead of schedule, the issuer could have motivations other than meeting a distant deadline.[30]

Treasury Bonds   Regardless of the form extinguishment takes, if the issuer does not cancel its bonds after reacquisition but contemplates reissue at a later date, treasury bonds is debited in lieu of bonds payable. Treasury bonds is a contra bond payable account. When the bonds are reissued, treasury bonds is credited rather than bonds

---

[29] Financial statement and footnote disclosures often do not provide sufficient information to completely analyze the economic effect of a bond retirement on the company. The economic gain or loss depends on the discount rate chosen. Only coincidentally will the reported gain equal the computed economic gain. See J. Dietrich and J. Deitrick, ''Bond Exchanges in the Airline Industry: Analyzing Public Disclosures,'' *The Accounting Review,* January 1985, pp. 109–26.

[30] Some bond indentures specify serial retirement of bonds. These scheduled maturities are preplanned and do not qualify for the exemption from extraordinary classification under *SFAS No. 64.*

payable, and a new discount or premium is recorded. If canceled, treasury bonds is credited and bonds payable is debited. Like bonds payable, treasury bonds is debited or credited only with face value.

Retirement of Convertible Debt   When convertible bonds are converted, the gain or loss under the market value method is classified as ordinary. Occasionally, firms retire convertible bonds through open-market purchase or other methods. Gains and losses on these retirements are classified as extraordinary, consistent with the intent of *SFAS No. 4.*

Extinguishment by Exercise of Call Privilege by Issuer

If bonds carry a *call privilege,* the issuer may retire the debt by paying the call price during a specified period. The call price places a ceiling on the market price. Investors who purchase callable bonds are thus placed at a disadvantage if interest rates decline because they may have to surrender bonds that pay higher interest than noncallable bonds. For this reason, callable bonds are often issued with higher interest rates than noncallable bonds. In addition, the call price typically exceeds face value by the *call premium,* which can decline each year of the bond term.

Issuers account for callable and noncallable bonds in the same way because exercise of the call privilege is not a certainty. The full bond term is used for amortization and interest recognition. When bonds are called, the usual procedures for recording debt extinguishment are followed. A loss is more likely than a gain because callable bonds are normally issued below the call price.

To illustrate the exercise of a call privilege, assume that Pana Company calls all $100,000 of its 5-year, 10%, bonds callable at 101 on June 30, 1991, an interest payment date. After the entry to record the interest payment, interest expense and amortization of discount, $1,200 of discount remains unamortized. The remaining bond term is three and a half years. Pana spent $2,000 to issue the bonds, and $600 to call them. The following entry records the extinguishment:

Entry to exercise call privilege:

Bonds payable	100,000	
Extraordinary loss, bond extinguishment	4,200	
Discount on bonds payable		1,200
Cash (1.01 × $100,000) + $600		101,600
Bond issue cost ($2,000 × 3.5/5)		1,400

Extinguishment of Bonds by Refunding

When a **refunding** takes place, a bond issue is replaced with another bond issue. One way of refunding is to issue new bonds in exchange for the old bonds. Cash is involved if the bond issues have different market values. More frequently, however, the proceeds from a new bond issue are used to retire the old issue because the holders of the old issue do not necessarily wish to become the new creditors. In both cases, the accounting for refunding is similar to all other forms of debt extinguishment. The following information is used to illustrate the two situations involving refunding:

1. *Refunding—by direct exchange of debt securities:* On January 1, 1991, WestCal Corporation issues $100,000 of 10-year, 5% bonds at face value with interest payable each June 30 and December 31. On January 1, 1995, the bondholders agreed to accept $90,000 of 20-year, 8% bonds with the same interest dates as the 5% bonds. The market rate of interest on similar bonds is 8%.

Analysis:

    a. The bondholders receive 10% less principal but a 60% increase in the interest rate.

    b. PV (market value) of new bonds $90,000

        PV (market value) of old bonds (12 semiannual

          periods remain in the old issue):

          Principal [$100,000 (*PV*1, 4%, 12) = $100,000(.62460)] $62,460

          Interest: [$2,500 (*PVA*, 4%, 12) = $2,500(9.38507)] 23,463   85,923

        Difference: economic loss to WestCal . . . . $ 4,077

January 1, 1995—Refunding entry:

Bonds payable, 5%	100,000	
Bonds payable, 8%		90,000
Extraordinary gain, bond extinguishment		10,000

WestCal accepts the economic loss to extend the maturity 20 years and to avoid the costs of issuing the new bonds for cash. The creditors receive $2,200 more in interest each year ($7,200 − $5,000). WestCal records a $10,000 *accounting gain* yet sustains an *economic loss* of $4,077 because increases in interest rates allow new bonds with a lower face value but higher present value to replace the old bonds. By refunding the old bonds, WestCal has committed to a new stream of future cash payments with an increased present value.

This is yet another example of the problems that arise from using the market rate at issuance to measure the book value of bonds. WestCal could invest $85,923 at 8% and satisfy the remaining payments on the 5% bonds. Many accountants view this value as a more appropriate valuation of the 5% bonds, particularly if WestCal intends to extinguish the bonds early.

2. *Refunding—by issuing new debt and purchasing old debt:* On January 1, 1991, WestCal Corporation issues $100,000 of 10-year, 5% bonds at face value with interest payable each June 30 and December 31. On January 1, 1995, WestCal issues at face value $86,000 of 20-year, 8% bonds with the same interest dates as the 5% bonds. The market price of the old bonds is 86. The old bonds are retired.

January 1, 1995–Issue 8% bonds:

Cash	86,000	
Bonds payable		86,000

January 1, 1995–Retire 5% bonds:

Bonds payable	100,000	
Cash		86,000
Extraordinary gain, bond extinguishment		14,000

The *accounting gain* is $14,000, but *no economic gain or loss* occurs because the 5% bonds were extinguished at market value.

Extinguishment by In-Substance Defeasance

SFAS No. 76 expands the concept of debt extinguishment to include in-substance defeasance: the irrevocable placement of assets into a trust for the sole purpose of paying interest and principal on the debt. The debtor does not actually pay the creditor but, instead, surrenders assets sufficient to cover all future debt payments. The FASB reasoned that the economic position of the debtor under in-substance defeasance is equivalent to immediate retirement of the debt. Both the liability and assets placed in trust are removed from the accounts.

Firms extinguish debt by in-substance defeasance for several reasons. Recognition of a gain is one incentive. The gain on extinguishment may be larger if recognized earlier (through in-substance defeasance), depending on interest rate changes.

The debt rating of the extinguished debt may be improved, and the general perception of the riskiness of the debtor consequently reduced. Debt-to-equity and other ratios are improved. Prepayment penalties from direct payments to creditors are avoided. The call premium on callable bonds is also avoided by in-substance defeasance.

Certain requirements must be met to fulfill in-substance defeasance (*SFAS No. 76*, par. 4):

1. Qualifying assets include only monetary assets that are essentially risk-free as to the amount and timing of interest and principal collection. The assets must be denominated in the currency in which the debt is payable. Examples of qualifying assets for debt payable in U.S. dollars are direct obligations of the U.S. government and obligations guaranteed by the U.S. government.
2. The assets placed in trust must provide cash flows (interest and principal) that approximately coincide, as to timing and amount, with payments required on the debt.
3. The probability that the debtor will be required to make future payments on the debt is remote.
4. Assets placed in trust to be used for trustee fees and other associated costs do not qualify as assets to be used to satisfy the debt payments.
5. Footnote disclosure of the extinguishment arrangements and the amount of the debt extinguished is required until the debt is legally retired.[31]

The intent of the in-substance defeasance requirements is to eliminate essentially all risk that funds will be unavailable to meet the required debt payments. Only those basically risk-free assets that yield scheduled cash flows can supply the assurance that all debt payments will be satisfied. Investments in equity securities do not qualify for this reason. There can be no other provisions in the debt agreement calling for a future payment by the debtor that could not be fulfilled by the assets placed in trust.

SFAS No. 76 applies only to debt with specified maturities and fixed payment schedules. In-substance defeasance extinguishment is not available to variable interest rate debt. The second and third requirements listed above could not be fulfilled for such debt. For example, the trust assets would be insufficient to cover all debt payments if interest rates increased.

The following example illustrates in-substance defeasance.

Example   On January 1, 1989, the Eugene Company issues 100, 7% $1,000 debenture bonds dated January 1, 1989, to yield 6%. The bonds pay interest each January 1 and mature January 1, 1994.

On January 1, 1991, Eugene purchases $100,000 (face value) of 7% U.S. treasury bonds maturing in three years for $97,400 to yield approximately 8%. Eugene irrevocably transfers these bonds to a trust for the sole purpose of satisfying the remaining interest and principal payments on its 7% bonds.

The market rate of interest on the 7% debenture bonds is 9% on January 1, 1991. The book value of the bonds is $102,673 [$100,000(*PV*1, 6%, 3) + $7,000(*PVA*, 6%, 3)]. The current price of the bonds is $94,937 [$100,000(*PV*1, 9%, 3) + $7,000(*PVA*, 9%, 3)].

After purchasing the treasury bonds and recording the January 1, 1991, interest payment, Eugene records the following entry to extinguish the bonds:

---

[31] Some respondents to the exposure draft preceding *SFAS No. 76* considered this disclosure requirement to contradict the substance of the statement and to cast doubt on the extinguishment. They reasoned that if debt is "in-substance" extinguished, further disclosure serves no purpose.

January 1, 1991—In-substance defeasance:

Bonds payable	100,000	
Premium on bonds payable	2,673	
Investment in U.S. treasury bonds		97,400
Extraordinary gain, bond extinguishment		5,273

The Eugene extinguishment fulfills the requirements of in-substance defeasance. The treasury bonds are essentially risk-free, and their scheduled principal and interest payments closely coincide with those of the Eugene bonds.

The extraordinary gain equals the difference between the book value of the bonds and the market value of the consideration paid. The yields are not the same for the treasury bonds and the Eugene bonds; therefore, the market values are somewhat different. If Eugene purchased the treasury bonds before January 1, 1991, the market value may be different from book value. In this case, a gain or loss equal to the difference between these two values is recognized on disposal of the investment. This gain or loss does not affect the extraordinary gain on extinguishment.

The Eugene example illustrates the importance of coinciding schedules of interest and principal payments. If the treasury bonds pay significantly less (or more) interest than the Eugene bonds or if the timing of cash flows is significantly different, the trust experiences periods of cash deficiency (or surplus). Cash deficiencies contradict the intent of in-substance defeasance, and surpluses require an assumption about reinvestment. *SFAS No. 76* contains no provision for assumptions about reinvestment of surplus assets. After the assets are placed into the trust, interest rate changes in the market are irrelevant. Only the schedule of cash flows is meaningful.

Partial in-substance defeasance also is allowed under *SFAS No. 76* (par. 36). A pro rata portion of all remaining principal and interest payments on a debt instrument with a specified maturity can be extinguished in this manner. A firm cannot partially extinguish only interest or only principal.

SFAS No. 76 prompted some firms to instantaneously retire debt by investing in essentially risk free securities yielding a higher rate than newly issued debt and then placing the securities into irrevocable trusts. Immediate gains were recognized because of the lower present value of the securities. *FASB Technical Bulletin No. 84-4* ruled that such transactions are counter to the intent of in-substance defeasance. The FASB did not wish to create an incentive for income manipulation. Consequently, in-substance defeasance applies only to existing debt, not to newly issued debt.

The Debate over In-Substance Defeasance   The four-to-three vote with which *SFAS No. 76* was adopted reveals the controversial nature of in-substance defeasance. Those in opposition to the statement maintain that unless the debtor is legally released from debt, the liability should remain on the books. They argue that the resulting gains erode the quality of earnings and benefit managers with compensation contracts tied to reported income.

The issue of violation of a debt agreement remains to be addressed. Debt previously extinguished through in-substance defeasance becomes immediately payable if the indenture agreement is violated. For example, the ending current ratio for a reporting period may fall below the required level. In this case, should the debt be reinstated and trust assets placed on the books? The trust assets also may be insufficient to cover the debt because not enough interest has been earned on the fund.

Another potential problem is default by the trustee for the government securities. Defaults have involved trustees and firms dealing in government securities, including

EXHIBIT 16–7   Summary of Gain and Loss Classification on Debt Extinguishments and Retirements

Method of Retirement or Extinguishment	Classification of Gain or Loss
1. Conversion of convertible bonds	Ordinary
2. Induced conversion of convertible bonds (gain, loss, and conversion expense)	Ordinary
3. Direct payment to creditors	Extraordinary
4. Sinking-fund purchases made to satisfy sinking fund requirements that must be met within one year of the purchase	Ordinary
5. Issuance of equity securities	Extraordinary
6. Retirement of convertible debt	Extraordinary
7. Call	Extraordinary
8. Refunding	Extraordinary
9. Legal release from obligation	Extraordinary
10. In-substance defeasance	Extraordinary

Drysdale Government Securities, Lombard-Wall, and Lion Capital Associates.[32] In addition, if the debtor declares bankruptcy, is the trust fund a secured asset, or is it available to all creditors?

Summary of Gain and Loss Classification

Exhibit 16–7 provides a summary of gain and loss classification for debt extinguishments and retirements.

CONCEPT REVIEW

1. If gains and losses on debt extinguishment are not particularly unusual, why are they classified as extraordinary?
2. Why is the gain or loss on a debt retirement made June 30, 1991, to fulfill sinking fund requirements that must be met by January 1, 1992, classified as ordinary?
3. What is the main justification for treating in-substance defeasance as a debt extinguishment when the debt is not legally discharged?

LONG-TERM NOTES AND MORTGAGES

A long-term note is a formal document that specifies the terms of a debt. Notes often are used for specific asset acquisitions or loans for particular purposes. In contrast, bonds are used to raise large amounts of capital for several purposes. Notes generally have shorter maturities than bonds and typically are not traded in organized exchanges or markets.

Chapter 8 discussed notes at length, and their accounting from the creditor perspective. The accounting for the debtor applies the three general valuation and measurement principles cited at the beginning of this chapter. Present value tech-

---

[32] B. Gaumnitz and J. Thompson, "In-substance Defeasance: Costs, Yes; Benefits, No," *Journal of Accountancy,* March 1987, p. 105.

niques are used for valuation and interest recognition for all notes except the following (*APB Opinion No. 21*):

1. Payables from ordinary business transactions due in one year or less.
2. Payables arising from advances and deposits not requiring repayment but that will be applied to the price of goods and services in the future.
3. Payables arising from security deposits.
4. Payables arising from cash lending and demand or savings deposits of financial institutions.
5. Payables whose interest rates are affected by the tax attributes or legal restrictions prescribed by government.
6. Payables between parent company and subsidiary, or between subsidiaries of a common parent company.

The following examples illustrate accounting for notes by the debtor firm.

Example 1: Long-Term Note, Stated Rate = Market Rate On April 1, 1991, Baylor Company borrowed $12,000 from Lionel Company and issued a three-year, 10% note. Interest is payable each March 31, and the principal is payable at the end of the third year. The stated and market interest rates are equal. The entries for Baylor, a calendar fiscal year company, follow:

April 1, 1991–Issue note:

Cash	12,000	
Long-term note payable		12,000

December 31, 1991, 1992, 1993—Adjusting entries:

Interest expense ($12,000 × .10 × 9/12)	900	
Interest payable		900

March 31, 1992, 1993—Interest payment:

Interest expense ($12,000 × .10 × 3/12)	300	
Interest payable	900	
Cash ($12,000 × .10)		1,200

March 31, 1994—Note maturity:

Interest expense	300	
Interest payable	900	
Long-term note payable	12,000	
Cash		13,200

This example poses no significant measurement issues because the market and stated interest rates are the same and cash is received in exchange for the note.

Example 2: Long-Term Note, Stated and Market Rates Different Fema Company purchased goods on January 1, 1991, and issued a two-year, $10,000 note with a 3% stated interest rate. Interest is payable each December 31, and the entire principal is payable December 31, 1992. The merchandise does not have a ready market value. The market rate of interest appropriate for this note is 8%. The present value of the note and its recorded value are computed as follows:

Present value of maturity amount
$10,000(PV1, 8%, 2) = $10,000(.85734) = ... $8,573
Present value of the nominal interest payments
$10,000(.03)(PVA, 8%, 2) = $300(1.78326) = ... 535
Present value of the note at 10% $9,108

The present value of the note is less than its face value because the note pays less interest than is available elsewhere in the market. For that reason, a higher face value must be paid to compensate the seller for the lower interest rate. The difference between face value and present value is the discount on the note. The $892 discount ($10,000 − $9,108) represents interest beyond the 3% cash payments. The following entry records the note and purchase (assuming a perpetual inventory system) and reflects the gross method of recording:

January 1, 1991—Issue note

Inventory	9,108	
Discount on long-term notes payable	892	
Long-term notes payable		10,000

The January 1, 1991, long-term liability section of Fema Company includes the following:

Long-term notes payable	$10,000
Discount on long-term notes payable	(892)
Net long-term notes payable	$ 9,108*

*Under the net method, $9,108 is recorded in the notes payable account; a discount account is not used.

December 31, 1991—Interest payment

Interest expense ($9,108 × .08)	729	
Discount on long-term notes payable		429
Cash		300

Interest expense exceeds the cash payment reflecting recognition of part of the discount as interest expense. The amortization of the discount account increases the net long-term note payable as the following balance sheet disclosure reveals:

Long-term Liability Section of Balance Sheet at January 1, 1992

Long-term notes payable	$10,000
Discount on long-term notes payable	(463)*
Net long-term notes payable	$ 9,537

* $892 − $429

The straight-line method is acceptable if it yields results not materially different from the interest method. Under the straight-line method, Fema amortizes $446 ($892/2) of the discount and recognizes $746 of interest expense ($300 + $446) each period. The remaining entries for Fema are:

December 31, 1992—Interest payment

Interest expense ($9,537 × .08)	763	
Discount on long-term notes payable		463
Cash		300

December 31, 1992—Note maturity

Long-term notes payable	10,000	
Cash		10,000

Example 3: Long-Term Note Issued for Noncash Consideration, Payments Include Interest and Principal On January 2, 1991, Bellow Company purchased equipment by paying $5,000 down and issuing a $10,000, 4% note payable in four equal annual installments starting December 31, 1991. The current market rate on notes of a similar nature and risk is 10%. The market value of the equipment is not readily determinable.

The payment (*P*) and present value of the note are determined as follows:

$$\$10,000 = P(PVA, 4\%, 4) = P(3.62990)$$
$$\$10,000/3.62990 = \$2,755$$

Present value of note:

$$\$2,755(PVA, 10\%, 4) = \$2,755(3.16987) = \$8,733$$

January 2, 1991—Issue note (net method):

Equipment ($5,000 + $8,733)	13,733	
Cash		5,000
Long-term notes payable		8,733

December 31, 1991—Interest expense:

Interest expense ($8,733 × .10)	873	
Long-term notes payable	1,882	
Cash		2,755

The entries for the remaining term of the note parallel Example 2. The main difference between Examples 2 and 3 is the payment structure.

In response to high and unstable interest rates, innovative debt arrangements were developed to supplement notes with traditional terms. These notes include point-system mortgages, shared-appreciation mortgages, and adjustable-rate mortgages.

Point-System Mortgages A point is 1% of the face value of a point-system mortgage note. Proceeds are reduced (held back) on the note by the product of points and face value. Consequently, the effective interest rate exceeds the stated rate on the note.

For example, assume that First Sacramento Savings assesses Elkhorn Company five points on a $100,000, 12%, five-year mortgage note used to purchase a building. The note requires (for simplicity) annual mortgage payments, which include interest and principal. Proceeds equal $95,000 ($100,000 × .95). However, the debtor agreed to pay five mortgage payments which reflect 12% on a $100,000 face value. The mortgage payment and effective rate are computed as follows:

$$\$100,000 = (PVA, 12\%, 5) \text{ (Mortgage payment)}$$
$$\$100,000/3.60478 = \$27,741 = \text{Mortgage payment}$$

Let *i* be the effective rate for the mortgage agreement, then:

$$\$95,000 = \$27,741(PVA, i, 5)$$
$$\$95,000/\$27,741 = 3.42453$$

From Table 6A–4, the rate is between 14% and 15% and can be approximated by interpolation:

$$i = 14\% + \frac{3.43308 - 3.42453}{3.43308 - 3.35216} (15\% - 14\%) = 14.1\%$$

The effective rate of interest exceeds the 12% stated rate specified on the note payable and reflects the effective interest rate paid by Elkhorn over the term of the mortgage. Elkhorn records the note for $95,000, the amount received. The $5,000 excess of face value over proceeds represents interest recognized over the note term (a discount).

The complete amortization table for the Elkhorn point-system mortgage appears below:

Date	Payment	Interest Expense*	Principal Reduction†	Principal Balance‡
1/1/91				$95,000
12/31/91	$ 27,741	$13,395	$14,346	80,654
12/31/92	27,741	11,372	16,369	64,285
12/31/93	27,741	9,064	18,677	45,608
12/31/94	27,741	6,431	21,310	24,298
12/31/95	27,741	3,443§	24,298	0
	$138,705	$43,705	$95,000	

* (Previous principal balance)(.141)
$$\$13,395 = \$95,000(.141)$$

† Payment − Interest expense
$$\$14,346 = \$27,741 - \$13,395$$

‡ Previous principal balance − Principal reduction
$$\$80,654 = \$95,000 - \$14,346$$

§ Rounded up $17 to compensate for rounding the effective interest rate.

Shared-Appreciation Mortgages (SAMs)   Under the terms of this type of note, the lender charges a lower stated interest rate in return for a share of market value appreciation on property financed with the note. Decreases in market value are not shared. Appreciation also can include a share of the earnings in an investment project financed by the mortgage note.

The effective interest rate on shared-appreciation mortgages equates the net proceeds with the future cash payments on the note. The forecasted amount of property appreciation accruing to the lender reduces the loan proceeds for this purpose. However, the borrower receives the full amount of the loan initially and pays the appreciation on sale of the property. Modifying the Elkhorn example above, assume a lower rate of 8% on the $100,000 loan. Elkhorn receives the entire $100,000 and agrees to the annual payment implied by these terms. In return for the lower interest rate, First Sacramento expects to receive approximately $10,000 of appreciation (at present value) on the property. The payments and effective rate are computed as follows:

$$\$100,000 = (PVA,\ 8\%,\ 5)\ \text{Mortgage payment}$$
$$\$100,000/3.99271 = \$25,046 = \text{Mortgage payment}$$

Let i be the effective rate for the mortgage agreement:

$$\$100,000 - \$10,000 = \$25,046(PVA,\ i,\ 5)$$
$$\$90,000/\$25,046 = 3.59339 = (PVA,\ i,\ 5)$$

The value for i falls between 12% and 14%. A closer approximation to the effective rate (12.13%) is found by applying a business calculator to the problem. Interpolation also can be used.

Adjustable-Rate Mortgages (ARMs)   The stated rate of interest on ARMs (also called *floating-rate,* or *variable-rate,* mortgages) changes periodically as the market rate changes. ARMs shift the risk of changing interest rates from the lender to the borrower. The interest rate on long-term notes usually is changed quarterly, semiannually, or annually, although three-year intervals are not uncommon. In contrast, the floating rate charged on short-term notes often is changed when the *prime* interest rate changes. The prime rate is the rate charged by commercial banks to preferred corporate customers.

When interest rates are adjusted, a new payment is computed which equates the note's principal balance to the present value of all remaining payments using the new interest rate. The new rate is used until the rate changes again.

ADDITIONAL ISSUES AND DISCLOSURES FOR LONG-TERM LIABILITIES
◆

Unconditional Purchase Obligations, Project Financing Arrangements, and R&D Arrangements

Do long-term unconditional purchase obligations and project financing arrangements constitute a reportable liability? An **unconditional purchase obligation** is a future obligation to transfer funds for fixed or minimum quantities of goods and services (*SFAS No. 47,* par 6). [33] Firms often contract with suppliers to guarantee a long-term source of goods and services. Generally, until goods and services are received by the buyer, no liability exists. However, information about unconditional long-term purchase commitments and other project financing relationships is relevant to financial statement users attempting to assess the future obligations and cash flows of the business. In *SFAS No. 47,* the FASB decided to postpone answering the question of whether a liability should be reported, but increased the disclosure requirements for these relationships.

The unconditional obligations covered by *SFAS No. 47* are those that (par. 6a):

1. Are noncancelable or cancelable if a remote contingency occurs or with permission of the seller.
2. Have a remaining term exceeding one year.

If the firm does not record the obligations in the balance sheet (firms are not required to do so), the nature and term of the obligation, as well as the amount as of the balance sheet date and for the succeeding five annual balance sheet dates, must be disclosed in the notes. Disclosure of the amount of imputed interest necessary to reduce the obligations to present value is encouraged. The discount rate is the effective initial rate of borrowing used to finance the obligation, if known, or the incremental borrowing rate of the purchaser.

If the obligation is recorded in the balance sheet as a liability, only the relevant amounts for the succeeding five annual balance sheet dates also must be reported. The FASB did not specify criteria for deciding whether the substance of the arrangement is an acquisition of an asset and the incurrence of a liability.

In its 1989 annual report, Tenneco Inc. disclosed the following note related to unconditional purchase obligations:

> In connection with the financing commitments of certain joint ventures, Tenneco has entered into unconditional purchase obligations of $283 million ($165 million on a present value basis). Tenneco's annual obligations under these agreements are $27 million for each of the years 1990, 1991, and 1992, and $26 million for each of the years 1993 and 1994.

SFAS No. 68, "Research and Development Arrangements," addresses a similar issue. For example, in December 1985, Electro-Nucleonics agreed to a limited partnership with Pru-Tech. The agreement specified that Pru-Tech would advance $6,919,000 to Electro for rights to royalties from the sales of products developed by Electro. Pru-Tech was able to raise its own funds, which it advanced to Electro. The impetus for Electro to enter into this arrangement was to avoid expensing R&D and to avoid recognizing a liability for funding the activities.

Under *SFAS No. 68,* Electro records a liability if it is obligated to repay any of the funds advanced (in any form) regardless of the outcome of the activity. If this is the case, Electro has not transferred the risk of the venture to Pru-Tech. In addition, Electro recognizes R&D expense as incurred. In contrast, if the financial risk of the project is transferred because repayment of funds provided by the other party depends *solely* on the project results, then Electro accounts for the arrangement as a contract to perform R&D services and does not record a liability.

---

[33] A project financing arrangement is an agreement through which a firm finances a capital project with cash flows from the project. The firm incurs debt that is serviced by those cash flows.

The importance of long-term liability measurement and disclosure as a measure of the risk and financial strength of companies is unquestioned. However, as the discussion of unconditional purchase obligations and other arrangements implies, the criteria for recognizing liabilities are imprecise. The *SFAC No. 6* definition of a liability allows substantial latitude in interpretation. As discussed in the next section, creative financial instruments are increasing the complexity of liability recognition and measurement. Creative financial instruments increase the opportunity for off-balance-sheet financing. Through **off-balance-sheet financing,** firms raise debt capital without reporting liabilities. The FASB initiated a project on financial instruments, part of which considers this issue.

The FASB Financial Instruments Project

The 1980s ushered in an enormous number of new and creative financial instruments.

> A Rip Van Winkle who fell asleep in 1979 and just woke up would hardly recognize today's financial landscape. . . . Arthur Andersen & Company has kept a list of new financial products since 1986; it now . . . totals more than 600.[34]

An *exchangeable debenture* is an example of an innovative debt instrument. For example, InterNorth Company issued 10.5% callable debentures, due 2008, exchangeable for shares of Mobil Corporation owned by InterNorth. The exchange provision lowered the interest rate for InterNorth. Until the exchange, InterNorth receives Mobil dividends. The bondholders stand to benefit from Mobile stock price appreciation. Several accounting issues arise. Is this one financial instrument or two? Does exchangeability affect the reporting of InterNorth's investment in Mobil stock? How is the income statement affected?

Another example is an *interest rate swap,* an arrangement between two companies agreeing to trade interest payments. For example, one company has variable-rate debt outstanding but prefers more stable fixed-rate financing. However, this company is prohibited from issuing fixed-rate debt because of its poor credit rating. Another company with fixed-rate debt is willing to risk interest rate fluctuation and exchanges its fixed interest payments for the variable payments of the first company.

Internationalization, deregulation, increased competition, inflation, changes in the financial services industry, tax law changes, and interest rate volatility contributed to this explosion of financial instruments. Many financial instruments were developed to reduce exposure to loss from changes in interest rates and foreign exchange rates.

Voluntary disclosure of information about financial instruments varies across firms. Several pronouncements already address specific instruments and issues on an ad hoc basis. The SEC and others asked the FASB to develop pronouncements to fill a void in accounting for financial instruments. In response, the FASB began a long-term project on financial instruments and off-balance-sheet risk in 1986.

The project is expected to yield several SFASs and has several parts. The first part addresses the disclosure of off-balance-sheet risk, significant concentrations of credit risk, and the market value of financial instruments. Other parts of the project will address recognition and measurement issues. Prominent among the issues addressed by the project are the following:

♦ Whether financial assets are considered sold if the seller is subject to recourse, and whether liabilities are settled if the debtor dedicates assets to them.

♦ How to account for transactions that transfer market and credit risk.

---

[34] "Is Financial Product Explosion Perilous for Investors?" *The Wall Street Journal,* December 21, 1989, p. C1.

- How financial instruments are measured.
- How to distinguish between debt and equity instruments.[35]

Off-Balance-Sheet Risk The risk of loss from many financial instruments exceeds the amount recorded in the accounts for the instrument. For example, if a firm transfers receivables with recourse, the transferee can seek payment from the transferor if the original maker of the receivable defaults. If the transferor records the transfer as a sale, no liability for this contingency is recognized. Yet the potential for loss is of interest to users of the transferor's financial statements.

If the potential accounting loss for a financial asset exceeds the amount recognized as an asset, or if the potential obligation for a liability exceeds the amount recognized as a liability, the financial instrument has *off-balance-sheet* risk of accounting loss. An obligation for receivables transferred with recourse is an example.

Off-balance-sheet risk arises from *credit risk, market risk,* or *physical risk.* Credit risk is the possibility of loss from failure of a party to perform according to the agreement underlying the financial instrument. The transferor of receivables with recourse has credit risk. Market risk is the possibility that market price changes will make a financial asset less valuable or a financial liability more costly to extinguish. Physical risk involves potential theft or damage.

SFAS No. 105, "Disclosure of Information about Financial Instruments with Off-Balance-Sheet Risk and Financial Instruments with Concentrations of Credit Risk," is the result of the first phase of the disclosure part of the FASB project. The statement, which applies to all entities, including not-for-profit organizations, bridges the information gap between amounts disclosed in the balance sheet, if any, and the potential off-balance-sheet risk of financial instruments.

Financial Instrument Defined *SFAS No. 105* defines a financial instrument thus: cash, evidence of an ownership interest in an entity, or a contract that both:

1. Imposes on one entity a contractual obligation (*a*) to deliver cash or another financial instrument to a second entity or (*b*) to exchange financial instruments on potentially unfavorable terms with the second entity.
2. Conveys to that second entity a contractual right (*a*) to receive cash or another financial instrument from the first entity or (*b*) to exchange other financial instruments on potentially favorable terms with the first entity. (par. 6)

Accounts receivable and bonds payable are examples of financial instruments for which the balance sheet amount equals the total possible risk associated with the instrument. The holder of a $10,000 accounts receivable can lose at most $10,000 if the customer does not pay the debt.

Other financial instruments have off-balance-sheet risk including recourse obligations on receivables sold, financial guarantees, options, interest rate caps and floors, and futures contracts. An option to buy a U.S. Treasury note at a fixed price four months in the future is another example. The holder of the option (the potential buyer) has the right to exchange cash for the note on potentially favorable terms. If interest rates change and the value of the note exceeds the fixed price in four months, the holder will exercise the option. The writer of the option has a contractual obligation to exchange the note for cash on potentially unfavorable terms.

---

[35] An *FASB Discussion Memorandum,* "Distinguishing between Liability and Equity Instruments and Accounting for Instruments with Characteristics of Both" (August 1990), is devoted exclusively to this issue. It discusses several issues covered in this chapter, including induced conversions of convertible debt, and convertible bonds.

A financial guarantee is another example of a financial instrument with off-balance-sheet risk. A borrower pays a fee to a guarantor. In return, the guarantor agrees to pay the lender if the borrower defaults. The guarantor has a financial instrument: a contractual obligation to pay the lender if the borrower defaults. The lender also has a financial instrument: the right to receive cash from the guarantor if the borrower defaults. The fact that the contingency is remote has no bearing on whether the item is a financial instrument.[36]

The footnotes to the 1989 annual report of United Foods disclosed the following information about a guarantee of indebtedness:

> In February 1988 a bank made a $1,000,000, five-year term loan to the Chairman of the Company. The Company has guaranteed the indebtedness in the event the Chairman defaults under the terms of the loan agreement and the guarantee is collateralized by 725,000 shares of United Foods, Inc.

Disclosure Requirements of *SFAS No. 105*   Entities must disclose the following information for financial instruments with off-balance-sheet risk:

+ The face, contract, or notional[37] principal amount.
+ The nature and terms of the instrument.
+ A discussion of credit and market risk, any cash requirements, and accounting policies related to the instruments

For those instruments with credit risk, firms must disclose the amount of accounting loss incurred by the holder if any party to the instrument fails to perform.

The required information about financial instruments with off-balance-sheet risk describes characteristics not disclosed in the balance sheet and helps investors and creditors assess risk.

Disclosures about Market Value   The FASB issued the exposure draft "Disclosure about Market Values of Financial Instruments" in December 1990 as the second phase of the disclosure part of the project. It proposes a requirement that all entities disclose the market value of all financial instruments, both asset and liability, to help users comprehensively assess the entity's management of market risk.

For example, a firm would disclose the market value of its bonds payable outstanding under this requirement. This information would help users identify the effects of interest rate changes on debt, and whether unrealized gains or losses occurred.

General Disclosure Requirements for Long-Term Liabilities

Disclosure requirements relating to specific long-term debt topics were mentioned in previous sections of this chapter. In general, footnotes supply information not conveniently disclosed in the balance sheet. For example, interest rates, maturity dates, debt restrictions, call provisions and conversion privileges usually are disclosed in the footnotes. Any assets pledged as collateral for debt also are disclosed in the footnotes.

In addition, *SFAS No. 47,* "Disclosure of Long-Term Obligations," requires disclosure of the aggregate amount of maturities and sinking fund requirements for all long-term debt for each of the five years following the balance sheet date (par.

---

[36] Financial guarantees often are not recognized as a liability in the balance sheet. However they are required to be disclosed under *SFAS No. 5* and FASB *Interpretation No. 34,* "Disclosure of Indirect Guarantees of Indebtedness of Others." *SFAS No. 105* increases the disclosure requirements.

[37] The fictional amount upon which interest payments are computed by both parties, for example, in interest rate swaps.

10*b*). For example, Bausch & Lomb included the following disclosure in the foot-notes to its 1989 financial statements:

> Long-term borrowing maturities during the next five years are $7,218,000 in 1990, $8,406,000 in 1991, $7,135,000 in 1992, $6,495,000 in 1993, and $5,788,000 in 1994.

SUMMARY OF KEY POINTS

(L.O. 1)   1. Long-term liabilities are those fulfilling the *SFAC No. 6* definition of a liability and having a term extending more than one year from the balance sheet date or the operating cycle, whichever is longer.

(L.O. 1)   2. Three basic principles are used for valuing long-term liabilities. The recorded value at issuance is the present value of all future cash flows discounted at the current market rate of interest for debt securities of equivalent risk. Interest expense is the product of the market rate at issuance and the balance in the liability at the beginning of the reporting period. And the book value of long-term debt at a balance sheet date is the present value of all remaining cash payments required, using the market rate at issuance.

(L.O. 2)   3. Bonds are long-term debt instruments that specify the face value paid at maturity and the stated interest rate payable according to a fixed schedule. Bonds are a significant source of capital for many firms; many different types of bonds are issued to appeal to investor preferences.

(L.O. 2)   4. The price of a bond at issuance, which excludes accrued interest at the stated rate, is the present value of all future cash flows discounted at the current market rate of interest for bonds of a similar risk class.

(L.O. 3)   5. Bonds are sold at a premium if the stated rate exceeds the market rate, and vice versa for bonds sold at a discount. The premium or discount is amortized over the remaining life of the security. Bond premiums and discounts are amortized under the straight-line method (acceptability depends on the materiality constraint) or the interest method (conceptually preferable because it is based on present value concepts).

(L.O. 3)   6. Accounting for bonds depends on the features inherent in the particular bond issue. Bonds issued between interest dates require payment of accrued interest by the investor, and calculation of the bond price using present value techniques.

(L.O. 4)   7. Certain long-term debt instruments are issued with equity rights, including bonds issued with detachable stock warrants and convertible bonds. The equity feature is recorded by the issuer only if a separate market exists for the equity feature. Accounting for convertible bonds is the same as for nonconvertible bonds until they are converted because the value of the conversion feature cannot be estimated reliably.

(L.O. 5)   8. Extinguishment of debt can occur before, at, or after the maturity date. Extinguishment is accomplished by direct payment or replacement with another debt instrument, by obtaining a release from the creditor, or by placing assets in an irrevocable trust to pay the debt.

(L.O. 5)   9. The gain or loss from extinguishment, which is the difference between the market value of consideration used for extinguishment and book value of debt extinguished, is classified as extraordinary.

(L.O. 6)   10. Long-term note valuation follows the three general principles for valuing long-term liabilities. Notes are formal promises by a debtor to pay principal and interest.

(L.O. 7)   11. Serial bonds mature according to a schedule rather than at one date. Accounting for serial bonds parallels regular bonds, although certain computational complexities arise. The bonds outstanding method simplifies the accounting for interest and amortization of premium and discount.

(L.O. 8)   12. A troubled debt restructure (TDR) occurs when the debtor cannot meet the required debt payments and the creditor makes a concession to the debtor such as reducing or deferring interest or principal payments. TDRs are settlements or modifications of debt terms.

(L.O. 8)   13. Restructured debt is recorded at the lower of the sum of restructured flows and the book value of the old debt. Gains recognized by the debtor on restructure are classified as extraordinary.

REVIEW PROBLEM

◆

On August 1, 1992, Pismo Corporation, a calendar year corporation that records adjusting entries only once per year, issued bonds with the following characteristics:

1. $50,000 total face value.
2. 12% stated rate.
3. 16% yield rate.
4. Interest dates are February 1, May 1, August 1 and November 1.
5. Bond date is October 31, 1991.
6. Maturity date is November 1, 1996.
7. $1,000 of bond issue costs were incurred.

Required:

1. Provide all entries required for the bond issue through February 1, 1993, for Pismo assuming the interest method.
2. On June 1, 1994, Pismo retired $20,000 of bonds at 98 through open market purchase. Provide the entries to update the bond accounts for this portion of the bond issue, and to retire the bonds assuming the interest method.
3. Provide the entry required on August 1, 1994 under the:
   a. Interest method
   b. Straight-line method

SOLUTION

◆

1.

August 1, 1992—Issue bonds and incur issue costs:

Bond issue cost	1,000	
Cash		1,000
Cash	43,917*	
Discount on bonds payable	6,083	
Bonds payable		50,000

* Four and one-quarter years, or 17 quarters, remain in the bond term.
$$\$43,917 = \$50,000(PV1, 4\%, 17) + .03(\$50,000)(PVA, 4\%, 17)$$
$$= \$50,000(.51337) + \$1,500(12.16567)$$

November 1, 1992—Interest payment date

Interest expense	1,757*	
Discount on bonds payable		257
Cash		1,500†
Bond issue expense	59‡	
Bond issue cost		59

* $1,757 = $43,917(.04)

† $1,500 = $50,000(.03)

‡ $59 = $1,000/17

December 31, 1992—Adjusting entry:

Interest expense	1,178*	
Discount on bonds payable		178
Interest payable		1,000†
Bond issue expense	39‡	
Bond issue cost		39

* $1,178 = ($43,917 + 257)(.04)(⅔ of quarter)

† $1,000 = $1,500(⅔)

‡ $39 = $59(⅔)

February 1, 1993—Interest payment date:

Interest expense	589*	
Interest payable	1,000	
Discount on bonds payable		89
Cash		1,500
Bonds issue expense	20†	
Bond issue cost		20

* $589 = ($43,917 + 257)(.04)(⅓ of quarter)

† $20 = $59(⅓)

2. On May 1, 1994, the remaining term of the bonds is two and one-half years, or 10 quarters, and the $20,000 of bonds to be retired have the following book value:

$$\$18,378 = \$20,000(PV1, 4\%, 10) + \$20,000(.03)\ (PVA, 4\%, 10)$$
$$= \$20,000(.67556) + \$600(8.11090)$$

On May 1, 1994, the remaining discount on the portion of bonds to be retired is therefore $1,622 ($20,000 − $18,378).

June 1, 1994—Update relevant bond accounts before retirement:

Interest expense	245*	
Discount on bonds payable		45
Cash		200†
Bond issue expense	8‡	
Bond issue cost		8

June 1, 1994—Remove relevant bond accounts:

Bonds payable	20,000	
Extraordinary loss, bond extinguishment	1,404	
Discount on bonds payable		1,577§
Bond issue cost		227‖
Cash (.98 × $20,000)		19,600

* $245 = $18,378(.04)(⅓ of quarter)

† $200 = $20,000(.03)(⅓)

‡ $8 = $1,000(1/17)(⅓)(.40 of issue retired)

§ $1,577 = $1,622 − $45

‖ At June 1, 1994, nine and two-thirds quarters remain in bond term: $227 = $1,000(.40)(9⅔)/17

3. On May 1, 1994, the remaining term of the bonds is two and one-half years, or 10 quarters, and the remaining $30,000 of bonds have the following book value:

$$\$27,567 = \$30,000(PV1, 4\%, 10) + \$30,000(.03)\ (PVA, 4\%, 10)$$
$$= \$30,000(.67556) + \$900(8.11090)$$

On May 1, 1994, the remaining discount is therefore $2,433 ($30,000 − $27,567).

a. August 1, 1994—Interest payment date:

Interest expense		1,103*
Discount on bonds payable	203	
Cash		900†
Bond issue expense	35	
Bond issue cost		35‡

* $1,103 = $27,567(.04)

† $900 = $30,000(.03)

‡ $35 = (.60 of issue remaining)($1,000)/17

b. Under the SL method, the discount is amortized $358 ($6,083/17) per quarter on the entire bond issue.

August 1, 1994—Interest payment date:

Interest expense		1,115
Discount on bonds payable	215*	
Cash		900
Bond issue expense	35	
Bond issue cost		35

* $215 = $358(.60)

APPENDIX 16A *Accounting for Serial Bonds*

A **serial bond** issue matures in a series of *installments* rather than in one maturity amount. The advantages of serial bonds to the issuer include:

* Less need for a sinking-fund.
* Lower perceived risk of the issue.
* Improved marketability.
* Less burdensome debt retirement schedule.

Price of Serial Bonds, Accounting Considerations

Serial bonds are sold either as separate issues or as one aggregate issue. If the bonds are sold separately, it is possible to identify the yield rate on each, which normally increases with the length of the term to compensate for increased risk. If sold in the aggregate, the entire bond issue carries a single average yield rate. Either way, the price of serial bonds is the sum of the present values of each issue using the appropriate yield rate. Serial bond valuation is consistent with ordinary bond issues.

Three methods of accounting for serial bonds are available:

Interest method: If the yield rate on each issue is known, each issue is treated as an individual bond issue. If not, the entire issue is treated as one bond issue, and the average yield rate is used to recognize interest. The book value of serial bonds payable is reduced by the face amount of serial bonds retired at each maturity date. Otherwise, procedures for amortizing discount and premium are identical to ordinary bonds.

Straight-line method: An equal amount of premium or discount is allocated to each reporting period for each separate issue. Then the amounts for each issue are totaled by reporting period. Total amortization for a reporting period reflects each separate issue outstanding that period. This method is permitted only if it produces results not materially different from the interest method.

Bonds outstanding method: The discount or premium for each separate issue need not be identified under this method. A constant rate of discount or premium per dollar of bond outstanding per period is used for amortization. This is a modified straight-line method, and it is permitted only if it produces results not materially different from the interest method.

All three methods relate the premium or discount to the total face value of bonds *outstanding* during the period. This amount decreases by the face value of each maturing issue. Consequently, relative to an ordinary bond, discounts and premiums are amortized more quickly.

Serial Bond Amortization, Early Retirement, and Maturity

The following examples illustrate accounting for serial bonds and early retirement. An unrealistically short bond term simplifies the presentation.

Example   Michael Corporation issues $100,000 of 8% serial bonds on January 1, 1991. The bonds are sold as one issue to yield 10%. The bonds pay interest each December 31 and mature according to the following schedule:

Maturity Date	Maturity Amount
January 1, 1992	$ 20,000
January 1, 1993	50,000
January 1, 1994	30,000
	$100,000

On January 1, 1992, Michael retired $10,000 of the issue scheduled to mature January 1, 1994 on the open market at 99.

Issue Price of Serial Bonds

		Serial Bond Price	Discount*
Bonds due 1/1/92:			
Face value [$20,000(*PV*1, 10%, 1) = $20,000(.90909)]	$18,182		
Interest [$1,600(*PVA*, 10%, 1) = $1,600(.90909)]	1,455		
		$19,637	$ 363
Bonds due 1/1/93 (similar computations)		48,265	1,735
Bonds due 1/1/94 (similar computations)		28,508	1,492
Total serial bond price		$96,410	
Total serial bond discount			$3,590

* Face value minus price of individual issue.

January 1, 1991—Issue serial bonds:

```
Cash . . . . . . . . . . . . . . . . . . . . . . . . . . . . . . . . . . . . 96,410
  Discount on serial bonds  . . . . . . . . . . . . . . . . . . . . . . .  3,590
  Serial bonds payable  . . . . . . . . . . . . . . . . . . . . . . .               100,000
```

Interest method   Selected entries under the interest method follow.

December 31, 1991—Interest payment:

```
Interest expense (.10 × $96,410) . . . . . . . . . . . . . . . . . 9,641
  Discount on serial bonds . . . . . . . . . . . . . . . . . . . . .            1,641
  Cash (.08 × $100,000)  . . . . . . . . . . . . . . . . . . . . . .            8,000
```

January 1, 1992—Retire bonds due 1/1/92:

```
Serial bonds payable . . . . . . . . . . . . . . . . . . . . . . . . . . 20,000
  Cash  . . . . . . . . . . . . . . . . . . . . . . . . . . . . . . . . . .           20,000
```

January 1, 1992—Retire $10,000 of the $30,000 of bonds due 1/1/94 at 99:

```
Serial bonds payable . . . . . . . . . . . . . . . . . . . . . . . . . 10,000
Extraordinary loss, bond extinguishment  . . . . . . . . . . . . .   247
  Discount on bonds payable . . . . . . . . . . . . . . . . . . . .             347*
  Cash (.99 × $10,000) . . . . . . . . . . . . . . . . . . . . . . . .          9,900
```

* $10,000 less the book value of retired bonds (2 years before schedule):
$10,000 − [$10,000(*PV*1, 10%, 2) + $800(*PVA*, 10%, 2)] =
$10,000 − [$10,000(.82645) + $800(1.73554)] = $347

After the early retirement, the book value of the remaining serial bonds equals:

```
Book value of serial bonds 1/1/91 . . . . . . . . . . . $96,410
Amortization of discount on 12/31/91 . . . . . . . . . .   1,641
Book value of bonds maturing 1/1/92 . . . . . . . . . .  (20,000)
Book value of bonds retired early on 1/1/92 . . . . . . .  (9,653)
Book value of $70,000 remaining bonds 1/1/92 . . . . . $68,398*
```

* This value is also the present value of remaining cash flows.

December 31, 1992—Interest payment:

```
Interest expense (.10 × $68,398) . . . . . . . . . . . . . . . . . . . .  6,840
    Discount on serial bonds . . . . . . . . . . . . . . . . . . . . . .        1,240
    Cash (.08 × $70,000) . . . . . . . . . . . . . . . . . . . . . . . .        5,600
```

The remaining entries under the interest method are consistent with the previous ones and follow the same principles. These entries are the maturity of bonds on January 1, 1993, and January 1, 1994, at face value, and the interest payment on December 31, 1993.

Straight-Line Method   The following table illustrates this method for the Michael issue:

Amortization Table—Straight-Line Method

Bond maturity January 1	Discount on Issue	Bond Term (Years)	Amortization per Period	Amortization Recognized in		
				1991	1992	1993
1992	$ 363	1	$363	$ 363		
1993	1,735	2	868	868	$ 868	
1994	1,492	3	497	497	497	$497
	$3,590			$1,728	$1,365	$497

When bonds are retired early, the amount of discount remaining on those bonds can be computed directly from the above table.

December 31, 1991—Interest payment:

```
Interest expense . . . . . . . . . . . . . . . . . . . . . . . . . . . .  9,728
    Discount on serial bonds . . . . . . . . . . . . . . . . . . . . .        1,728
    Cash (.08 × $100,000) . . . . . . . . . . . . . . . . . . . . . .        8,000
```

January 1, 1992—Retire bonds due 1/1/92:

```
Serial bonds payable . . . . . . . . . . . . . . . . . . . . . . . .  20,000
    Cash . . . . . . . . . . . . . . . . . . . . . . . . . . . . . . . . .       20,000
```

January 1, 1992—Retire $10,000 of the $30,000 of bonds due 1/1/94 at 99:

```
Serial bonds payable . . . . . . . . . . . . . . . . . . . . . . . .  10,000
Extraordinary loss, bond extinguishment . . . . . . . . . . . . .     231
    Discount on bonds payable . . . . . . . . . . . . . . . . . . .         331*
    Cash (.99 × $10,000) . . . . . . . . . . . . . . . . . . . . . .        9,900
```

* ($497 + $497)($10,000/$30,000) = $331

(Discount remaining at 1/1/92 on the 1/1/94 issue)(Fraction retired)

December 31, 1992—Interest payment:

```
Interest expense . . . . . . . . . . . . . . . . . . . . . . . . . . . .  6,799
    Discount on serial bonds . . . . . . . . . . . . . . . . . . . . .        1,199*
    Cash (.08 × $70,000) . . . . . . . . . . . . . . . . . . . . . . .        5,600
```

* $868 + ($497)($20,000/$30,000)

Bonds Outstanding Method   Under the **bonds outstanding method,** the amount of premium or discount allocated to each reporting period is the product of three amounts:

1. A constant *rate* of amortization per dollar of bond per period.
2. The dollar amount of *bonds outstanding* (at face value) *during* the period.
3. The length of the period.

The following table develops the *rate* of amortization:

Bonds Outstanding Method
Computation of Amortization Rate

Face Value of Bonds Outstanding *during*		Rate of Discount Amortization per Dollar of Face Value per Year
1991	$100,000	
1992	80,000*	$\dfrac{\text{Initial discount}}{\text{Sum of bonds outstanding}} = \dfrac{\$3,590}{\$210,000} = \$.0171$
1993	30,000	
Sum	$210,000	

* On January 1, 1992, $20,000 of bonds mature; therefore $80,000 of bonds are outstanding *during* 1992.

The amortization rate indicates that $.0171 of discount is associated with each dollar of bond face value per year. The following entries complete the example.

December 31, 1991—Interest payment:

Interest expense	9,710	
Discount on serial bonds (.0171 × $100,000 × 1 year) . . .		1,710
Cash (.08 × $100,000)		8,000

January 1, 1992—Retire bonds due 1/1/92:

Serial bonds payable	20,000	
Cash		20,000

January 1, 1992—Retire $10,000 of the $30,000 of bonds due 1/1/94 at 99:

Serial bonds payable	10,000	
Extraordinary loss, bond extinguishment	242	
Discount on bonds payable		342*
Cash (.99 × $10,000)		9,900

* (.0171 × $10,000 × 2 years remaining in bond term) = $342

December 31, 1992—Interest payment:

Interest expense	6,797	
Discount on serial bonds (.0171 × $70,000 × 1 year)		1,197
Cash (.08 × $70,000)		5,600

The amortization rate is applied to any amount of face value or any period length without further complication. For example, if the bonds scheduled to mature January 1, 1994, are retired March 1, 1992, rather than on January 1, 1992, the amount of discount to be removed from the accounts is $314 (.0171 × $10,000 × 1¹⁰/₁₂ years).

The complications arising when serial bonds are issued during a fiscal year are minimized by the bonds outstanding method. For example, assume that $100,000 of serial bonds are issued March 31, 1991, at a premium and that the amortization rate is $.02. If $25,000 of bonds mature on March 31, 1992, the total amount of premium amortized during 1992 is $1,625:

$$(.02 \times \$100,000 \times \text{\small 3/12}) + (.02 \times \$75,000 \times \text{\small 9/12}) = \$1,625$$

APPENDIX 16B *Troubled Debt Restructure*

With increasing frequency during the 1980s, debtor firms (and many nations) were unable to make interest and principal payments on long-term debt. Others experienced a related problem: violation of debt indentures. Rising interest rates, nonperforming loans, poor management, unsatisfactory returns on investments, and lack of demand for the products and services provided by firms contributed to troubled debt.

Faced with nonperforming investments in debt securities or receivables, creditors frequently agree to a debt restructure allowing the debtor to remain in operation. The following terms are typical of restructure agreements:

- Elimination of some interest and principal payments.
- Reduction of interest rates and principal amounts.
- Extension of debt terms.
- Settlement of debt through cash payment or transfer of equity securities.

Creditors agree to such provisions in the hope that the debtor can resolve its financial difficulties. Creditors frequently receive more on restructured debt than through bankruptcy by the debtor.[38]

SFAS No. 15, "Accounting by Debtors and Creditors for Troubled Debt Restructuring," defines a **troubled debt restructure** (TDR) as follows (par. 2):

> A restructuring of a debt constitutes a *troubled debt restructuring* . . . if the creditor for economic or legal reasons related to the debtor's financial difficulties grants a concession to the debtor that it would not otherwise consider.

For a debt restructure to be troubled, the creditor must accept new debt or assets with an *economic value less* than the *book value* of the *original* debt. An example of a TDR is the acceptance by a creditor of $10,000 in full payment of a $15,000 receivable. The creditor must make a *concession,* which can arise from an agreement between the creditor and the debtor or can be imposed by a law or court.

A creditor normally makes no concession in an ordinary refinancing of debt; therefore, most refinancings are not TDRs.[39] Although debt is settled in some TDRs, the provisions of *SFAS No. 76,* "Extinguishment of Debt," do not apply.

The accounting issues arising from the creditor's concession include the measurement of the new liability and receivable (or consideration transferred in settlement), and the reporting of any gain or loss on restructure.

Types of TDRs

TDRs are accomplished in two fundamentally different ways:

1. *Settlement* of debt by *transfer of assets* or *equity interest* of the debtor to the creditor. The market value of the assets or equity securities must be *less* than the book value (including accrued interest) of the debt or receivable.[40]
2. *Continuation* of debt with *modification of debt terms.* TDRs effected by modifying terms fall into two categories:
   a. Total restructured payments are less than or equal to the *book value* (including accrued interest) of the debt or receivable.
   b. Total restructured payments exceed the *book value* (including accrued interest) of the debt or receivable.

Accounting Provisions of *SFAS No. 15* and Examples

Accounting for Settlements   The main provisions of SFAS No. 15 relating to settlements follow:

Debtor:

1. The *debtor* recognizes an *extraordinary* gain equal to the difference between debt book value and market value of consideration paid.

---

[38] Some debtors intentionally default on debt to force a consideration of restructure. Campeau, a Toronto retailer, deliberately defaulted on $705 million of its loans to two major secured creditors in 1990 in an attempt to obtain favorable restructuring terms. See "Campeau Wins Pact to Defer Late Payments," *The Wall Street Journal,* March 6, 1990, p. A8.

[39] Nor does a TDR occur if the creditor reduces the effective interest rate on debt to match a decrease in market rates in order to maintain a relationship with a debtor that can readily obtain debt financing from other sources at the market rate.

[40] A transfer of equity securities pursuant to the existing terms of convertible debt does not qualify as a TDR.

2. The accounts related to the debt are removed.
3. A gain or loss on disposal is recognized equalling the difference between the market value and book value of consideration transferred (no gain or loss is recognized if the debtor issues stock) and is classified in conformity with *APB Opinion No. 30*.

Creditor:

1. The *creditor* records the consideration received at market value and recognizes an ordinary, unusual or infrequent, or extraordinary loss in conformity with *APB Opinion No. 30*. The loss equals the difference between the recorded value of the investment or receivable less the market value of consideration received.
2. The accounts related to the investment or receivable are removed.

Example 1: Settlement by Transfer of Assets Data for example 1:

1. Debb Company issues a 10%, 2-year, $500,000 note on January 1, 1991, to Credex Company in exchange for merchandise. The note pays simple interest each January 1.
2. Debb experiences financial difficulties and is unable to meet the $50,000 interest payment on January 1, 1992. Both companies accrue interest on December 31, 1991.
3. On January 1, 1992, Debb agrees to transfer a factory building and land to Credex in full settlement of the note. The following information relates to the land and building:

	Land	Building
Market value, January 1, 1992	$100,000	$250,000
Original cost to Debb	75,000	300,000
Accumulated depreciation through January 1, 1992		100,000
Book value, January 1, 1992	75,000	200,000

This restructuring is a settlement TDR because the market value of the consideration transferred to the creditor ($350,000) is less than the $550,000 book value of the debt ($500,000 face value + $50,000 accrued interest). The entries to record the TDR for both companies follow:

Debb **(Debtor)**			**Credex** **(Creditor)**		

January 1, 1992:

Land	25,000				
Building	50,000				
Gain on disposal					
of land and					
building		75,000			
Note payable	500,000		Land	100,000	
Interest payable	50,000		Building	250,000	
Accumulated			Loss on debt		
depreciation,			restructure	200,000	
building	100,000		Interest		
Land		100,000	receivable		50,000
Building		350,000	Note receivable . . .		500,000
Extraordinary gain,					
debt restructure . .		200,000			

Extraordinary gain:	
Book value of debt:	
Face value	$500,000
Accrued interest	50,000
Total book value	550,000
Revised book value (and market value) of land and building	
($100,000 + $250,000)	$350,000
Extraordinary gain	$200,000

The debtor recognizes a gain from the increased market value of land and building. Transfer of assets in a TDR is a disposal requiring the same gain or loss recognition as a cash sale. The extraordinary gain reflects the amount of liability excused and the improvement in economic position of the debtor. The FASB concluded that the debtor's gain on the TDR is indistinguishable from gains and losses on other debt extinguishments. The extraordinary classification serves to emphasize the unusual and infrequent nature of the gain.

The creditor removes the accounts related to the receivable, records the assets received at market value, and recognizes a loss equal to the difference between the book value of the receivable and the market value of the assets. Losses on unsuccessful investments and receivables are not generally considered extraordinary.[41] Subsequent accounting for the assets (or equity interest in debtor) received is not affected by the TDR.

Example 2: Settlement by Transfer of Equity Interest in Debtor   Data for Example 2:

1. Debb Company issues a 10%, 2-year, $500,000 note on January 1, 1991, to Credex Company in exchange for merchandise. The note pays simple interest each January 1.
2. Debb experiences financial difficulties and is unable to meet the $50,000 interest payment on January 1, 1992. Both companies accrue interest on December 31, 1991.
3. On January 1, 1992, Debb agrees to issue 2,500 shares of its $10 par common stock in full settlement of the note. The market price per share is $60 on January 1, 1992, and the increase in outstanding shares is not expected to affect the stock price appreciably.

The accounting for transfer of equity interest is essentially the same as for a transfer of assets except that the debtor recognizes no gain or loss on disposal. The debtor applies the *total market value* of the issued stock to the appropriate contributed capital accounts.[42] The creditor records the stock received as an investment at current market value.[43] The gain and loss on the TDR is computed as in the transfer of assets example.

Debb (Debtor)			**Credex** (Creditor)		
January 1, 1992:					
Note payable	500,000		Investment in		
Interest payable	50,000		common stock	150,000	
Common stock		25,000*	Loss on debt		
Contributed capital			restructure	400,000	
in excess of par		125,000†	Interest		
Extraordinary gain,			receivable		50,000
debt restructure		400,000‡	Note receivable		500,000

* (2,500 shares × $10 par)
† 2,500($60 − $10)
‡ $550,000 book value of debt − $150,000 market value of stock

Accounting for Modification of Debt Terms   This type of restructure does not terminate the creditor's claim on the assets of the debtor and more closely fulfills the general notion of a debt restructure.

Total restructured payments are less than the book value of the debt or receivable

Debtor:

1. The *debtor* recognizes an *extraordinary* gain equal to the difference between debt book value and the *sum* of restructured cash flows.
2. The liability is reduced to the sum of the restructured cash flows.
3. All postrestructure payments reduce the restructured debt; no further interest expense is recognized.

[41] If the receivable was considered when bad debts were estimated, the allowance for doubtful accounts, rather than a loss, is debited. If the allowance is insufficient, a loss is debited for any excess.

[42] Rationale: if the shares were sold before transfer to the creditor, the total market value would be available for use in the settlement.

[43] If no basis exists for valuing the stock received by the creditor, the market value of the debt may be used to value the stock (*SFAS No. 15*, footnote 5).

Creditor:

1. The *creditor* recognizes an ordinary, unusual or infrequent, or extraordinary loss in conformity with *APB Opinion No. 30*. The loss equals the difference between investment or receivable book value and the *sum* of restructured cash flows.
2. The investment in receivable is reduced to the sum of the restructured cash flows.
3. All postrestructure receipts reduce the restructured investment; no further interest revenue is recognized.

Example 3: Modification of Terms—Total Restructured Payments Are Less than Debt Book Value
Data for Example 3:

1. Debb Company issues a 10%, 2-year, $500,000 note on January 1, 1991, to Credex Company in exchange for merchandise. The note pays simple interest each January 1.
2. Debb experiences financial difficulties and is unable to meet the $50,000 interest payment on January 1, 1992. Both companies accrue interest on December 31, 1991.
3. On January 1, 1992, Debb and Credex agree to a debt restructure agreement with the following provisions:
   a. Face value of the note is reduced to $400,000.
   b. Accrued interest for 1991 is forgiven.
   c. Maturity is extended to January 1, 1994 (a one-year extension).
   d. The interest rate is reduced to 5%; interest payments are due December 31, 1993 and 1994.

Book value of debt, January 1, 1992		$550,000
Sum of restructured cash flows:		
Face value payable January 1, 1994	$400,000	
January 1, 1993 interest payment (.05 × $400,000)	20,000	
January 1, 1994 interest payment	20,000	440,000
Loss (creditor) and gain (debtor) on restructure		$110,000

This is a modification-of-terms TDR with total restructured flows less than the book value of the debt. *SFAS No. 15* does not allow discounting of the restructured cash flows in determining the gain and loss. Although the interest rate is reduced to 5%, the two $20,000 "interest" payments are in fact principal payments because the original principal and missed interest payment are not fully recovered by the creditor. To increase the clarity of the entries, the old liability and receivable accounts are replaced with completely new accounts.[44]

Debb (Debtor)			Credex (Creditor)		
January 1, 1992:					
Note payable	500,000		Note receivable	440,000	
Interest payable	50,000		Loss on debt		
Note payable		440,000	restructure	110,000	
Extraordinary			Interest		
gain, debt			receivable		50,000
restructure		110,000	Note receivable . . .		500,000
January 1, 1993:					
Note payable	20,000		Cash	20,000	
Cash		20,000	Note receivable . . .		20,000
January 1, 1994:					
Note payable	420,000*		Cash	420,000	
Cash		420,000	Note receivable . . .		420,000

* $420,000 = $400,000 new "principal" + $20,000 "interest."

---

[44] An alternative accounting decreases the liability and receivable accounts by the amount of the gain and loss, respectively. However, reclassification of the liability may be required, depending on the terms of the original and restructured debt.

When total restructured flows *equal* the book value of debt, the accounting is the same as in the above example except that no gain (debtor) or loss (creditor) is recognized.

Total restructured payments exceed the book value of the debt or receivable

1. For both *debtor* and *creditor,* no entry is required at restructure date and no gain or loss is recognized. However, a reclassification entry is typically recorded.
2. No change is made to the book value of the old debt (receivable).
3. The rate of interest equating the old book value and present value of restructured cash flows is used to measure interest expense (revenue). This interest rate must be less than the prerestructure effective rate (the creditor's concession).
4. Every restructured flow includes principal and interest except for those which immediately follow the restructure. The excess of restructured flows over the old book value represents interest recognized over the term of the restructured debt.

Example 4: Modification of Terms—Total Restructured Payments Exceed Debt Book Value   Data for Example 4:

1. Debb Company issues a 10%, two-year, $500,000 note on January 1, 1991, to Credex Company in exchange for merchandise. The note pays simple interest each January 1.
2. Debb experiences financial difficulties and is unable to meet the $50,000 interest payment on January 1, 1992. Both companies accrue interest on December 31, 1991.
3. On January 1, 1992, Debb and Credex agree to a debt restructure agreement with the following provisions:
   a. Accrued interest for 1991 is forgiven.
   b. Maturity is extended to January 1, 1994 (a one-year extension), and regular interest payments are required January 1, 1993 and 1994.

Sum of restructured cash flows		
Face value payable January 1, 1994	$500,000	
January 1, 1993, interest payment (.10 × $500,000)	50,000	
January 1, 1994, interest payment	50,000	$600,000
Book value of debt, January 1, 1992		550,000
Excess of restructured cash flows over debt book value		$ 50,000

This is a modification-of-terms TDR with total new cash flows exceeding the book value of debt. Although the restructured cash flows equal the original expected cash flows, the entire cash flow schedule is shifted ahead one year. Thus, the effective rate is reduced. However, the new cash flows are sufficient to pay all the original principal and missed interest, and $50,000 more. Therefore, neither party records a gain or loss, but each must determine the new effective interest rate. This rate is applied to the beginning balance in restructured debt or receivable (the interest method is required) in each period following the restructure to determine interest expense or revenue.

Computer programs, financial calculators, and interpolation can be used to determine the effective rate. Interpolation is illustrated:

New effective rate (i) equates the current book value and the present value of restructured cash flows. The restructured term is two years:

$$\text{Current book value} = \text{Present value of restructured cash flows}$$
$$\$550,000 = \$500,000(PV1, i, 2) + \$50,000(PVA, i, 2)$$

The new effective rate, $i,$ is less than 10% (the original interest rate). If $i = 8\%$ in the above equation, the present value is less than $550,000, indicating that i is less than 8%. As i is reduced further, the present value increases. When $i = 4\%$, the present value finally exceeds $550,000. Therefore, i falls between 4% and 5%:

$$i = 5\%: \$500,000(PV1,5\%,2) + \$50,000(PVA,5\%,2) = \$546,486$$
$$i = 4\%: \$500,000(PV1,4\%,2) + \$50,000(PVA,4\%,2) = \$556,585$$

$$i = 5\% - \frac{\$550,000 - \$546,486}{\$556,585 - \$546,486} \times (.05 - .04) = 4.652\%$$

When a computer program was applied to the problem, i was computed more precisely as 4.64875%. The iterative approach is illustrated only to reinforce the nature of the calculation. However, in this case the results are virtually indistinguishable from those of a computer program.

The new effective rate is the true rate of interest earned by the creditor on the original book value ($550,000) if the terms of the restructure agreement are met. Using 4.64875%, the following entries record the restructure and future cash flows.

	Debb **(Debtor)**			**Credex** **(Creditor)**		
January 1, 1992:						
Note payable	500,000			Note receivable	550,000	
Interest payable . . .	50,000			Interest receivable . .		50,000
Note payable		550,000		Note receivable		500,000
January 1, 1993:						
Note payable	24,432			Cash	50,000	
Interest expense	25,568*			Interest revenue . . .		25,568
Cash		50,000		Note receivable		24,432
January 1, 1994:						
Note payable	25,568			Cash	50,000	
Interest expense	24,432†			Interest revenue . . .		24,432
Cash		50,000		Note receivable		25,568

* $550,000(.0464875)
† ($550,000 − $24,432) (.0464875)

	January 1, 1994:					
Note payable	500,000			Cash	500,000	
Cash		500,000		Note receivable		500,000

In this example, Credex recognizes no loss but does incur an opportunity loss because the cash flows were postponed.

Combination of Settlement and Modification of Terms   When only a *portion* of a debt is settled, the terms of the remaining portion may be modified. The amount of original debt settled is treated as a settlement, at the market value of consideration transferred. No gain or loss is recognized on the settlement, and the remaining portion is treated as a modificaton of terms TDR, if necessary.

For example, assume that a $100,000 debt is restructured by transferring assets with a market value of $30,000. The terms of the remaining debt are modified, and the debt (receivable) is reduced by $30,000. The accounting for the $70,000 portion follows the modification provisions. To determine which modification case applies, $70,000 is compared to the sum of restructured flows.

Exhibit 16B–1 summarizes accounting for TDRs.

Accounting for TDRs: Conceptual Problems

The requirement that the *sum*, rather than the *present value* of restructured cash flows, be used to value the restructured debt and receivable is not consistent with the basic principles of long-term debt accounting. One view, alternative to the provisions of *SFAS No. 15*, maintains that discounting the restructured flows at the current market rate would result in restructured debt and receivables that more closely reflect their economic value.

Applying this present value approach to Example 3 above, and assuming that the current market rate applicable to the debtor and creditor is 10%, the restructured debt is recorded at $365,291 [$400,000(PV1,10%,2) + $20,000(PVA,10%,2)]. This is the present value of the future cash flows to the creditor as computed for any investment with this stream of expected cash flows. This value is considerably less than the $440,000 value reported under GAAP.

Furthermore, the debtor (creditor) recognizes a much larger gain (loss) of $184,709 ($550,000 − $365,291) compared to the $110,000 reported gain (loss). Many financial state-

EXHIBIT 16B-1   Summary Table: Troubled Debt Restructures

		Modification of Terms, Restructured Cash Flows Are:	
		---	---
	Settlement	Less than Current Book Value*	Greater than Current Book Value*
New debtor liability	n.a.†	Sum of new flows	Current book value
New creditor receivable	n.a.	Sum of new flows	Current book value
Debtor gain on restructure	Extraordinary	Extraordinary	None recognized
Debtor gain, loss on transfer of assets	Classify according to APB Opinion No. 30	n.a.	n.a.
Creditor loss on restructure	Classify according to APB Opinion No. 30	Classify according to APB Opinion No. 30	None recognized
Future interest	n.a.	None; all cash flows are returns of principal	Based on rate equating current book value and new cash flows

* Includes accrued interest.

† n.a. = Not applicable.

ment users ask, how much is the new receivable really worth? Many argue that it *must* be worth less than the nominal sum ($440,000) because it is not received immediately.

In general, the approach prescribed by the FASB for modification-of-terms TDRs has the following effects relative to the usual present value approach using current market interest rates:

1. Overstates the restructured liability and receivable.
2. Understates the gain (debtor) and loss (creditor) on restructure.[45]

Major creditors, including banks and other financial institutions, had an incentive to exert pressure on the FASB to develop *SFAS No. 15* as written. Under the present value approach, creditors would recognize much larger losses. Their concerns included the negative impact on their financial statements as well as the potential for reduced public confidence in the banking system. The owners' equity of many banks and other financial institutions was threatened by the traditional present value approach to valuation of receivables (loans).

When total restructured cash flows *exceed* the book value of debt, the FASB reasoned that none of the original principal is lost. Rather, the investment return has merely declined. Introducing a current market rate of interest is inappropriate because the old agreement is still in place. Furthermore, the FASB maintained that the new agreement is not negotiated based on current market rates. The current market rates do not reflect the effective cost to the debtor or the effective return to the creditor because the creditor agreed to a lower rate.

Additional Measurement and Disclosure Requirements for TDRs

Each party to a TDR applies the provisions of *SFAS No. 15* separately. *FASB Technical Bulletin 80-2* clarified the nature of a troubled debt restructure by confirming that it is possible for only one party to have a TDR. This can occur if the book value of debt and receivable differ.

For example, Debtor Company owes $25,000 to Creditor-A Company. Debtor Company experiences financial difficulties and Creditor-A Company sells its receivable to Creditor-B

---

[45] To compound the problem, banks (creditors) usually charge a fee for restructuring that is recognized in income immediately. In addition, the market price of the creditor's stock often decreases as news of its troubled receivables becomes known.

Company for $15,000 on a nonrecourse basis. Subsequently, Debtor Company transfers $18,000 to Creditor-B Company in settlement of the debt. Debtor Company records a troubled debt restructure because $18,000 is less than the book value of its liability. However, Creditor-B Company does not because it receives more than the book value of its $15,000 investment.

Other sources of asymmetry between the debtor and creditor include estimation of the market value of assets transferred and classification of gains and losses (the debtor's gain on reduction of debt is always extraordinary but the creditor's loss may not be).

Legal and other direct costs incurred by the debtor to restructure debt reduce the extraordinary gain unless an equity interest is transferred, in which case the equity interest is reduced by the amount of those costs. If no gain on restructure is recognized, the costs are recognized as expense in the period of restructure. Legal and other direct costs of restructuring borne by the creditor are expensed when incurred.

After the restructure, should allowance be made for uncollectibility of receivables remaining after restructure? *FASB Technical Bulletin 79–6* reaffirms the need for creditor firms to assess the collectibility of assets after restructure. The investment in receivables is subject to recognition of anticipated losses if probable and estimable under *SFAS No. 5.*

In some cases, creditors receive more cash than expected under the terms of the restructuring agreement. Before the restructure, the creditor may have recognized a direct write-down of the receivable. Although the cash received after the restructure is in part a receipt of a portion of the account previously written down, the excess of cash received over the recorded investment is recorded as interest revenue. The previous direct write-down is not reversed (*FASB Technical Bulletin 79–7*).

SFAS No. 15 does not apply to debtors involved in restructurings that require general restatement of liabilities, such as bankruptcy proceedings and quasi-reorganization restructurings. For example, the debtor may be able to pay only 40% of the dollar amount of all liabilities. Because all liabilities are restated, *SFAS No. 15* does not apply. However, if a restructuring does not involve general restatement of all liabilities, the statement applies to isolated troubled debt restructurings that occur simultaneously with the restructure proceedings (*FASB Technical Bulletin 81–6*).

SFAS No. 15 requires extensive footnote disclosures for TDRs to supplement the financial statements of both debtors and creditors. These include a description of the restructure, amount of gain and loss and any tax effects, amounts contingently payable under the agreement, and commitments to lend additional funds to debtors owing receivables whose terms were modified in TDRs.

KEY TERMS

Amortization table (814)	Off-balance-sheet financing (844)
Bond (805)	Premium (809)
Bond indenture (805)	Prospectus (806)
Bond issue costs (819)	Refunding (834)
Bonds outstanding method (852)	Serial bonds (850)
Convertible bond (825)	Sinking fund (805)
Discount (809)	Troubled debt restructure (854)
In-substance defeasance (831)	Unconditional purchase obligations (843)

QUESTIONS

1. List and briefly explain the primary characteristics of long-term debt securities.
2. What are the primary distinctions between a debt security and an equity security?
3. Explain the difference between the stated rate of interest and the effective rate on a long-term debt security.
4. Briefly explain point-system mortgages, SAMs, and variable-rate mortgages.
5. Briefly explain the effects on interest recognized when the stated and effective rates of interest are different.
6. What are the primary characteristics of a bond? What distinguishes it from capital stock?
7. Contrast the following classes of bonds: (*a*) industrial versus municipal, (*b*) secured versus debenture, (*c*) ordinary versus income, (*d*) ordinary versus serial, (*e*) callable versus convertible, and (*f*) registered versus coupon.
8. What are the principal advantages and disadvantages of bonds versus common stock for (*a*) the issuer and (*b*) the investor?

9. Distinguish between the par amount and the price of a bond. When are they the same? When different? Explain.

10. Explain the significance of bond discount and bond premium to (a) the issuer and (b) the investor.

11. Assume a $1,000, 8% (payable semiannually), 10-year bond is sold at an effective rate of 6%. Explain how to compute the price of this bond.

12. Explain why and how bond discount and bond premium affect (a) the balance sheet and (b) the income statement of the investor.

13. What is the primary conceptual difference between the straight-line and interest methods of amortizing bond discount and premium?

14. Under GAAP, when is it appropriate to use the (a) straight-line and (b) interest method of amortization for bond discount or premium?

15. When the end of the accounting period of the issuer is not on a bond interest date, adjusting entries must be made for (a) accrued interest and (b) discount or premium amortization. Explain in general terms what each adjustment amount represents.

16. When bonds are sold (or purchased) between interest dates, accrued interest must be recognized. Explain why.

17. What are convertible bonds? What are the primary reasons for their use?

18. Why is the accounting different for nonconvertible bonds with detachable stock purchase warrants and nonconvertible bonds with nondetachable stock purchase warrants?

19. Define extinguishment of debt.

20. When may extinguishment of debt occur? List the various ways that extinguishment of debt occurs.

21. Explain how an accounting gain or loss to the debtor may occur when a call privilege is exercised.

22. When the issuer purchases its own debt securities in the open market to extinguish the debt, two entries usually must be made. Explain.

23. What is meant by refunding?

24. What is meant by in-substance defeasance?

25. What effect does in-substance defeasance have on the balance sheet?

26. What is meant by troubled debt restructuring? What are some of the features of typical restructuring arrangements?

27. Explain the classification of gains and losses from troubled debt restructuring.

28. Differentiate between a debt restructure in which debt is settled and one in which it continues after the restructure.

EXERCISES

E 16–1
Bonds—Issue above, at, and below par: Effective Rates and Interest Expense
(L.O. 2, 3)

Rowe Corporation authorized $600,000, 8% (interest payable semiannually), 10-year bonds payable. The bonds were dated January 1, 1991; interest dates are June 30 and December 31.

Assume four different cases with respect to the sale of the bonds: *Case A*—Sold on January 1, 1991, at par; *Case B*—Sold on January 1, 1991, at 102; *Case C*—Sold on January 1, 1991, at 98; *Case D*—Sold on March 1, 1991, at par.

Required:

1. For each case, what amount of cash interest will be paid on the first interest date, June 30, 1991?

2. In what cases will the effective rate of interest be (a) the same, (b) higher, or (c) lower than the stated rate?

3. After sale of the bonds, and prior to maturity date, in what cases will the carrying or book value of the bonds (as reported on the balance sheet) be (a) the same, (b) higher, or (c) lower than the maturity or face amount?

4. After the sale of the bonds, in Cases A, B, and C, which case will report interest expense (a) the same, (b) higher, or (c) lower than the amount of cash interest paid each period?

E 16–2
Bonds: Compute Four Bond Prices
(L.O. 2)

Compute the bond price for each of the following situations (show computations and round to nearest dollar):

a. A 10-year, $1,000 bond with annual interest at 7% (payable 3½% semiannually) purchased to yield 6% interest.

b. An eight-year, $1,000 bond with annual interest at 6% (payable annually) purchased to yield 7% interest.

c. A 10-year, $1,000 bond with annual interest at 6% (payable semiannually) purchased to yield 8% interest.

d. An eight-year, $1,000 bond with annual interest at 6% (payable annually) purchased to yield 6% interest.

E 16–3
Issue above, at, below Par, Straight-Line: Issuer and Investor Entries
(L.O. 2, 3)

Yale Corporation issued to Zepher Corporation a $30,000, 8% (interest payable semiannually on June 30 and December 31), 10-year bond dated and sold on January 1, 1991. Assumptions: *Case A*—Sold at par; *Case B*—Sold at 103; and *Case C*—Sold at 97.

Required:

In parallel columns for the issuer and the investor (assume a long-term investment), give the appropriate journal entries for each case on (1) January 1, 1991, and (2) June 30, 1991 (use the gross method). Assume the difference between the interest method and the straight-line method of amortization is not material; therefore, use straight-line amortization.

E 16–4
Compute Bond Price, Interest Method, Straight-Line, Issuer and Investor Entries
(L.O. 2, 3)

New Corporation sold and issued to Old Corporation a $10,000, 9% (interest payable semiannually on June 30 and December 31), 10-year bond, dated and sold on January 1, 1991. The bond was sold at an 8% effective rate (4% semiannually).

Required:

1. Compute the price of the bond.
2. In parallel columns for the issuer and the investor (assume a long-term investment), give the appropriate journal entries on (*a*) January 1, 1991, and (*b*) June 30, 1991 (use the gross method). Assume the difference between the interest method and the straight-line method of amortization is material; therefore, use the interest method.

E 16–5
Bonds at a Premium, Accrued Interest: Straight-Line, Gross, and Net Methods
(L.O. 3)

On September 1, 1991, Golf Company sold and issued to Youngblood Company $60,000, five-year, 9% (payable semiannually) bonds for $64,640 plus accrued interest. The bonds were dated July 1, 1991, and interest is payable each June 30 and December 31. The accounting period for each company ends on December 31.

Required:

In parallel columns, give entries, using the gross method for the issuer and the net method for the investor (assume a long-term investment) for the following dates: September 1, 1991; December 31, 1991; January 1, 1992; and June 30, 1992. Assume the difference between the interest method and straight-line method amortization amounts is not material; therefore, use straight-line amortization.

E 16–6
Bonds, Accrued Interest, Issuer Entries: Straight-Line, Gross
(L.O. 3)

Ryan Corporation sold and issued $300,000, three-year, 8% (payable semiannually) bonds payable for $312,800 plus accrued interest. Interest is payable each February 28 and August 31. The bonds were dated March 1, 1991, and were sold on July 1, 1991. The accounting period ends on December 31.

Required:

1. How much accrued interest should be recognized at date of sale?
2. How long is the amortization period?
3. Give entries for Ryan Corporation through February 1992 (including reversing entries). Use straight-line amortization and the gross method.
4. Would the above amounts also be recorded by the investor? Explain.

E 16–7
Compute Bond Price: Amortization Schedule, Interest Method, Entries, Issuer Gross, Investment
(L.O. 2, 3)

Radian Company issued to Seivers Company $30,000, four-year, 8% bonds dated June 1, 1991. Interest is payable semiannually on May 31 and November 30. The bonds were issued on March 1, 1992, for $28,371 plus accrued interest. The bonds would have sold at the effective rate on the next interest date for $28,478. The accounting period ends December 31 for both companies. The effective interest rate was 10%.

Required:

Round to the nearest dollar.

1. Verify the bond price. Use straight-line interpolation between interest dates.

2. Prepare a bond amortization schedule. Use interest method amortization.
3. In parallel columns, give entries for the issuer and the investor (as a long-term investment) for the following dates: March 1, 1992, and May 31, 1992. Use interest method amortization, and the gross method for issuer and the net method for the investor.

E 16-8
Nonconvertible Bonds with Detachable Warrants: Entries, Issuer and Investor
(L.O. 4)

Hardware Corporation issued $150,000, 6%, 10-year, nonconvertible bonds with detachable stock purchase warrants. Each $1,000 bond carried 20 detachable warrants, each of which was for one share of Hardware common stock, par $20, with a specified option price of $60. The bonds sold at 102 including the warrants (no bond price ex-warrants were available), and, immediately after date of issuance, the detachable stock purchase warrants were selling at $4 each. The entire issue was acquired by Software Company as a long-term investment.

Required:

1. Give entries for both the issuer and the investor at date of acquisition of the bonds. Use the gross method.
2. Give the entry for the investor assuming a subsequent sale of all of the warrants to another investor at $5.50 each.
3. Disregard (2). Give the entries for the issuer and the investor assuming subsequent tender of all of the warrants by the investor for exercise at the specified option price. At this date, the stock was selling at $75 per share.

E 16-9
Convertible Bonds: Entries, Issuer and Investor, Conversion
(L.O. 4)

Stonewall Corporation issued $40,000, 5%, 10-year convertible bonds. Each $1,000 bond was convertible to 10 shares of common stock (par $50) of Stonewall Corporation at any interest date after three years from issuance. The bonds were sold at 105 to Mason Corporation as a long-term investment.

Required:

1. Give the entry for both the issuer and the investor at the date of issuance. Use the gross method.
2. Give entries under both the book value and market value methods for both the issuer and the investor assuming that the conversion privilege is subsequently exercised by Mason Corporation immediately after the end of the third year. Assume that 30% of any premium or discount has been amortized and that, at date of conversion, the common stock was selling at $125 per share.

E 16-10
Debt Issuance and Early Retirement
(L.O. 3, 5)

On January 1, 1991, Quaid Company issued $100,000 of 10% debentures. The following information relates to these bonds:

Bond date: January 1, 1991.
Yield rate: 8%.
Maturity date: January 1, 1996.
Interest payment date: December 31.
Bond issue costs incurred: $2,000.

On March 1, 1992, Quaid retires $10,000 (face value) of the bonds when the market price is 110.

Required:

Provide entries for Quaid on the following dates under both the interest and straight-line methods of amortization.

1. January 1, 1991, bond issuance.
2. December 31, 1991, first interest payment.
3. March 1, 1992, entries to update the portion of the bond issue retired and to extinguish the bonds.

E 16-11
Bond Issuance, Interest, and Early Retirement
(L.O. 2, 3, 5)

This exercise has three independent situations:

a. On April 1, 1991, Felly Company issued 400 of its 10%, $1,000 bonds at 97 plus accrued interest. The bonds are dated January 1, 1991, and mature on January 1, 2001. Interest is payable semiannually on January 1 and July 1.
b. On July 1, 1991, Center Company issued 9% bonds in the face amount of $1,000,000, which

mature on July 1, 2001. The bonds were issued for $939,000 to yield 10%, resulting in a bond discount of $61,000. Center uses the interest method of amortizing bond discount. Interest is payable annually on June 30.

c. On July 1, 1992, Fondue Company issued 2,000 of its 9%, $1,000 callable bonds for $1,920,000. The bonds are dated July 1, 1992, and mature on July 1, 2002. Interest is payable semiannually on January 1 and July 1. Fondue uses the straight-line method of amortizing bond discount. The bonds can be called by the issuer at 101 at any time after June 30, 1997. On July 1, 1998, Fondue called in all the bonds and retired them.

Required:
1. Compute the proceeds on the Felly bond issue.
2. Compute the unamortized discount on the Center bond issue on July 1, 1993.
3. Give the entry to record the extinguishment of the Fondue bond issue.

(AICPA Adapted)

E 16–12
Extinguishment by Call: Issuance and Extinguishment Entries (L.O. 5)

On January 1, 1991, Radar Company issued $100,000 bonds payable with a stated interest rate of 12%, payable annually each December 31. The bonds mature in 20 years and have a call price of 103, exercisable by Radar Company after the fifth year. The bonds originally sold at 105.

On December 31, 2002, the company called the bonds. At that time, the bonds were quoted on the market at a price to yield 10%. Radar Company uses straight-line amortization; its accounting period ends December 31.

Required:
1. Give the issuance entry for Radar Company required on January 1, 1991. Use the gross method.
2. Give the entry for extinguishment of the debt.

E 16–13
Extinguishment by Call: Update, Issuance, and Extinguishment Entries (L.O. 5)

On January 1, 1991, Sty Company issued $200,000 bonds payable with a stated interest rate of 5%, payable annually each December 31. The bonds mature in 10 years and are callable after the 4th year at 101. The bonds originally sold on January 1, 1991, at 104.

On June 30, 1996, the bonds were called. The company uses straight-line amortization, and the accounting period ends December 31.

Required:
1. Give the issuance entry on January 1, 1991. Use the gross method.
2. Give any entries on the extinguishment (i.e., call) date.

E 16–14
Extinguishment by Refunding: Issuance and Extinguishment Entries (L.O. 5)

On January 1, 1991, Rocket Corporation issued $500,000, 6%, 20-year bonds at 98. The interest is payable each December 31. Rocket uses straight-line amortization and the gross method. Its accounting period ends December 31.

On January 1, 2002, Rocket issued $500,000, 9%, 20-year, refunding bonds at par. On this date, the old 6% bonds could be purchased in the open market at their present value based on the current effective rate of 9%. Rocket immediately purchased all of the 6% debt.

Required:
Round to the nearest dollar.
1. Give the entry for issuance of the 6% bonds.
2. Give the entry for issuance of the 9% bonds.
3. Give the entry to record the extinguishment of the old debt by refunding.

E 16–15
Extinguishment by Purchase in the Open Market: Entries (L.O. 5)

On January 1, 1991, Nue Corporation issued $100,000, 10%, 10-year bonds at 98. Interest is paid each December 31, which also is the end of the accounting period. The company uses straight-line amortization and the gross method. On July 1, 1996, the company purchased all of the bonds at 101 plus accrued interest.

Required:
1. Give the issuance entry.
2. Give the interest entry on December 31, 1991.
3. Give the related entries on July 1, 1996.

E 16–16
Extinguishment by
In-Substance Defeasance
(L.O. 5)

On January 1, 1991, Slick Corporation borrowed cash on a $900,000, 10%, seven-year, note payable. Interest is payable semiannually on each June 30 and December 31. On January 1, 1995, the company entered into an agreement with the creditors to irrevocably transfer the note to an independent trustee to administer the payment of 10% interest each interest period and the principal at maturity. Slick transmitted to the trustee cash equal to the present value of the note so that the trustee can pay each of the six remaining interest payments and the note principal on maturity date. Cash in the amount of $855,743 was paid to the trustee to invest so that there will be sufficient cash to make the payments. Slick's accounting period ends December 31.

Required:

1. Give the entry for Slick Corporation on January 1, 1991.
2. Give the related entries on June 30 and December 31, 1991.
3. Give the extinguishment entry on January 1, 1995.
4. Show how the $855,743 was computed, assuming an expected net earning rate by the trust of 12%, compounded semiannually.
5. What conditions must be met to qualify the transaction, on January 1, 1995, as an extinguishment of the $900,000 debt?

E 16–17
LT Noninterest-Bearing
Note
(L.O. 6)

Fox purchases goods on January 1, 1991, and issues a $10,000 noninterest-bearing note requiring $5,000 to be paid on December 31 of 1991 and 1992. Each payment includes principal and interest. The market rate of interest is 10%.

Required:

1. Compute the amount to be recorded in purchases.
2. The entry to record the purchase.
3. The entry to record the 1991 payment on the note.
4. The entry to record the 1992 payment on the note.

E 16–18
Long-Term (LT) Note;
Borrower and Lender,
Entries and Reporting
(L.O. 6)

On May 1, 1991, Watt Company borrowed $24,000 cash from Tandy Bank on a $24,000, 10%, three-year note. Interest is payable each April 30, and the principal is payable on April 30, 1994. The accounting period ends on December 31 for each party.

Required:

1. Give all current and adjusting entries through April 30, 1992, for both the borrower and the lender.
2. Show how this note and the related items would be shown on the 1991 financial statements of each party.

E 16–19
LT Note: Borrower and
Lender, Effective Rate,
Amortization Schedule,
Entries
(L.O. 6)

On January 1, 1991, Derek Company borrowed cash from Patricia Finance Company on a $30,000, 12%, two-year note. The note will be paid off in two equal installments each December 31. Patricia assessed Derek two points. The accounting period for each company ends December 31.

Required:

1. Compute the amount of each annual payment.
2. The effective rate was computed to be 13.55%. Show how this rate was computed.
3. Prepare a debt amortization schedule for the two parties.
4. Give all entries for each party from January 1, 1991, through the maturity date.

E 16–20
LT Note: Borrower and
Lender, Amortization
Schedule, Entries
(L.O. 6)

The following data are available: on January 1, 1991, a borrower signed a long-term note, face amount, $100,000; time to maturity, three years; stated rate of interest, 8%. The effective rate of interest of 10% determined the cash received by the borrower. The note will be paid in three equal annual installments on each December 31 (also, this is the end of the accounting period for both parties.)

Required:

1. Compute the cash received by the borrower and prepare a debt amortization schedule.
2. Give the required entries for both the borrower and lender for each of the three years.

E 16–21

LT Note: Borrower and Lender Entries, Effective Rate, Amortization Schedule

(L.O. 6)

The following information is known: on January 1, 1991, a borrower signed a long-term note, face amount $100,000; time to maturity, three years; stated interest rate, 12%; and cash proceeds from the loan, $96,661. The note will be paid in equal annual installments on each December 31 (also, this is the end of the accounting period for both parties).

Required:

1. Prepare a debt amortization schedule.
2. Give the required entries for both the borrower and lender for each of the three years.

E 16–22

LT Note: Unrealistic Rate, Amortization Schedule, Entries for Debtor and Creditor

(L.O. 6)

Cathy Company purchased a machine at the beginning of 1991 with a three-year, $2,000, 5% note, payable in three equal annual payments of $734 (including principal and interest) at each year-end. The current market rate of interest for this level of risk was 12%.

Required:

1. What was the cost of the machine to Cathy Company?
2. Give the entry by Cathy to record the purchase. Use the net approach.
3. Prepare the amortization schedule for the note.
4. Give the entries for both the debtor and the creditor at the end of each year (assuming the accounting year-end for the debtor and creditor coincides with the note's year-end).

E 16–23

Appendix 16B: Restructure, Transfer of Noncash Asset, Entries by Each Party

(L.O. 3)

Down Company owed Super Bank a $50,000, three-year, 10% (payable each December 31) note dated January 1, 1991. During 1993, Down Company experienced unusual financial difficulties and was unable to pay the note, and interest for 1993 that had been accrued. On January 1, 1994, the bank agreed to settle the debt and interest (for 1993) for $2,000 cash plus some land that had a current market value of $30,000. At December 31, 1993, the records of Down Company showed the acquisition cost of the land to be $20,000.

Required:

Give all entries required on January 1, 1994, to record this debt restructure (*a*) for Down Company and (*b*) for Super Bank.

E 16–24

Appendix 16B: Restructure, Transfer Cash and Noncash Assets, Entries by Each Party

(L.O. 8)

Slow Company owed Quick Finance Company a three-year, $100,000, 10% (payable annually each December 31), note dated January 1, 1991. At December 31, 1993, Slow was experiencing serious financial problems and could not pay the principal and interest for 1993 that had been accrued. Quick agreed to settle the debt and interest in full for $12,000 cash plus a tract of land (Slow's acquisition cost was $7,000) plus 1,000 shares of Slow common stock, par $10, that had a current market price of $35 per share. The current market value of the land on January 1, 1994, was $20,000. The agreement was accepted by both parties, and settlement was effected on January 1, 1994.

Required:

Give all entries required to record the debt restructure for (*a*) Slow Company and (*b*) Quick Finance Company.

E 16–25

Appendix 16B: Restructure, Modification of Terms, Compute New Interest Rate, Entries for Both Parties

(L.O. 8)

Brown Company owed City Bank a $50,000, 10% (payable each December 31), four-year note dated January 1, 1991. Early in 1992, it became clear that Brown Company was experiencing difficulty in making the annual interest payment, although the company did manage to make the 1991 payment. Due to expected continuing difficulties, it appeared that there was a good chance the company would default on the note (as well as on other obligations). On January 2, 1993, the two parties agreed to restructure the debt by (*a*) reducing the remaining annual interest payments to $2,240 each and (*b*) reducing the principal amount (maturity amount) to $48,000. Brown paid the interest for 1992.

Required:

1. Compute the new yield or effective rate of interest.
2. Give all entries required on date of restructure (January 2, 1993) for each company. If no entry is required, explain the reason.
3. Give all entries required at December 31, 1993, and 1994, for each company.

E 16–26
Appendix 16B:
Restructure, Modification
of Terms, Entries by Both
Parties
(L.O. 8)

Orange Company owed National Bank a $60,000, 10% (payable each December 31), four-year note dated January 1, 1991. Orange Company has experienced severe financial difficulties and is likely to default on the note and interest during 1993 unless some concessions are made by the bank. Consequently, on January 2, 1993, the parties agreed to restructure the debt as follows: (*a*) interest payments each year to be reduced to $1,000 per year for 1993 and 1994, and (*b*) reduce the principal amount to $30,000. On December 31, 1992, Orange paid $6,000 interest for 1992.

Required:

1. Does this restructure change the yield or effective interest rate? Explain. Is a new effective rate of interest needed for accounting purposes in this situation? Explain.
2. Give all entries required for each party on the date of restructure, January 2, 1993.
3. Give all entries required for each party on December 31, 1993 and 1994.

PROBLEMS

P 16–1
Bonds: Price
Computation,
Amortization Schedule,
Gross, Interest Method,
Entries, Reporting
(L.O. 2, 3)

Alpha Corporation sold and issued to Beta Corporation $400,000, 8% (payable semiannually on June 30 and December 31), three-year bonds. The bonds were dated and sold on January 1, 1991, at an effective interest rate of 10%. The accounting period for each company ends on December 31.

Required:

1. Compute the price of the bonds.
2. Prepare a debt amortization schedule for the life of the bonds (use the interest method and round to the nearest dollar).
3. In parallel columns prepare entries for the issuer and the investor (as a long-term investment) through December 31, 1991. Use the gross method.
4. Show how the issuer and the investor would report the bonds on their respective balance sheet at December 31, 1991.
5. What would be reported on the income statement for each party for the year ended December 31, 1991?

P 16–2
Bonds: Accrued Interest,
Straight-Line, Gross,
Entries, Reporting
(L.O. 3)

Foyt Corporation sold and issued to Mears Corporation $50,000 of bonds on June 1, 1991, for $51,320 plus accrued interest. The bond indenture provided the following information:

Maturity amount	$50,000
Date of bonds	April 1, 1991
Maturity date	March 31, 1993 (2 years)
Stated interest rate	6½%, payable semiannually
Interest payments	March 31 and September 30

Required:

1. In parallel columns, give entries for the issuer and investor (as a long-term investment) from date of sale to maturity. Assume the difference between the amortization amounts is not material; therefore, use straight-line amortization. Also assume the accounting period for each company ends on December 31. Use the gross method.
2. Show how the bonds would be reported on the balance sheet of each company at December 31, 1991.
3. What would be reported on the income statement for each company for the year ended December 31, 1991?

P 16–3
Bonds: Interest Method,
Adjusting Entries
(L.O. 3)

Jones Corporation issued bonds, face amount $100,000, three-year, 8% (payable semiannually on June 30 and December 31). The bonds were dated January 1, 1991, and were sold on November 1, 1991, for $100,739 (including interest of $2,667 and a bond price of $98,072) at an effective interest rate of 9%. The bonds would have sold at the effective rate on December 31, 1991, for $98,206. The bonds mature on December 31, 1993. The bonds were purchased as a long-term investment by Smith Corporation.

Required:

1. Construct a time scale that depicts the important dates for this bond issue.
2. In parallel columns, give the entries at November 1, 1991, for the issuer and the investor.
3. Prepare a bond amortization schedule using the interest method.

4. In parallel columns, give the entries for both the issuer and investor for interest and amortization at the interest date, December 31, 1991. Use the interest method of amortization.
5. Compute and verify the balance in the interest accounts of the two parties to the transaction immediately after (4) above.
6. Assume the accounting period for each party ends on February 28. In parallel columns, give the adjusting entries for each party on February 28, 1992. Assume the interest method of amortization.
7. Compute the amount of amortization per month for each party, assuming straight-line amortization is used (i.e., the difference between the amortization amounts is not material).

P 16–4

Bonds: Price Computation, Interest Method, Entries for Both Parties

(L.O. 2, 3)

Randy Corporation issued $200,000, 8% (payable each February 28 and August 31), four-year bonds. The bonds were dated March 1, 1991, and mature on February 28, 1995. The bonds were sold on August 1, 1991, to yield 8½% interest. The bonds were purchased by Voss Corporation as a long-term investment. The accounting period for each company ends on December 31. The bonds were sold for $196,967 plus accrued interest of $6,667. They would have sold on August 31, 1991 for $197,027.

Required:

1. Diagram a time scale depicting the important dates for this bond issue.
2. Prepare an amortization schedule using the interest method of amortization.
3. In parallel columns, give entries for the issuer and the investor from date of sale through February 28, 1992. Base amortization on (2) above.
4. Compute the amount of amortization per month for each party, assuming the straight-line method is used (because the difference between the amortization amounts is not material).

P 16–5

Bonds: Bond Price, Computation, Straight-Line, Entries for Issuer (Gross) and Investor (Net)

(L.O. 2, 3)

Koy Corporation sold and issued to Lott Corporation (as a long-term investment) $100,000 four-year, 11% bonds on September 1, 1991. Interest is payable semiannually on February 28 and August 31. The bonds mature on August 31, 1995, and were sold to yield 10% interest. The accounting period for both companies ends on December 31. Use the gross method for the issuer and the net method for the investor.

Required:

1. Compute the price of the bonds (show computations and round to nearest dollar).
2. In parallel columns, give all entries required through February 1992 (including reversing entries) in the accounts of the issuer and the investor. Assume the difference between the interest method and the straight-line method of amortization is not material; therefore, use straight-line amortization.

P 16–6

Case A, Entries for Convertible Bonds; Case B, Detachable Stock Warrants

(L.O. 4)

This problem involves two independent cases:

Case A

On January 1, 1991, when its $30 par value common stock was selling for $80 per share, Ancil Corporation issued $5,000,000 of 4% convertible debentures (i.e., bonds) due in 10 years. The conversion option allowed the holder of each $1,000 bond to convert the bond into five shares of the corporation's $30 par value common stock. The debentures were issued for $5,500,000. The present value of the bond payments at the time of issuance was $4,250,000, and the corporation believes the difference between the present value and the amount paid is attributable to the conversion feature. On January 1, 1992, the corporation's $30 par value common stock was split 3 for 1. On January 1, 1993, when the corporation's $10 par value common stock was selling for $90 per share, holders of 40% of the convertible debentures exercised their conversion options. For convenience, assume the corporation uses the straight-line method for amortizing any bond discount or premium.

Required:

1. Give the entry to record the original issuance of the convertible debentures.
2. Give the entry to record the exercise of the conversion option, using the book value method. Show supporting computations.

Case B

On July 1, 1993, Salem Corporation issued $1,000,000 of 7% bonds payable in 10 years. The bonds pay interest semiannually. Each $1,000 bond includes a detachable stock purchase right. Each right gives the bondholder the option to purchase for $30, one share of $1 par value common stock at any time during the next 10 years. The bonds were sold for $1,000,000. The value of the stock purchase rights at the time of issuance was $50,000.

Required:

Prepare the entry to record the issuance of the bonds.

(AICPA adapted)

P 16–7
Bonds: Detachable Stock Warrants, Entries for Issuer and Investor
(L.O. 4)

Friendly Corporation issued $1,000,000, 6%, nonconvertible bonds with detachable stock purchase warrants. Each $1,000 bond carried 20 detachable stock purchase warrants, each of which called for one share of Friendly common stock, par $50, at the specified option price of $60 per share. The bonds sold at 106, and the detachable stock purchase warrants were immediately quoted at $1 each on the market.

Goode Company purchased the entire issue as a long-term investment.

Required:

1. Give the following entries for Friendly Corporation (the issuer):
   a. To record the issuance of the bonds.
   b. To record the subsequent exercise by Goode of the 20,000 stock purchase warrants.
2. Assuming Goode did not exercise all 20,000 stock purchase warrants in requirement (1) above, give the following entries for Goode Company (the investor):
   a. Acquisition of the bonds (including the stock purchase warrants).
   b. Subsequent sale to another investor of half of the stock purchase warrants at $1.50 each.
   c. Subsequent exercise of the remaining half of the stock purchase warrants (by tendering them to Friendly Corporation). The market value of the stock was $62 per share.

P 16–8
Induced Conversion of Convertible Bonds
(L.O. 4)

Convee Company issued $75,000 of 12% convertible bonds at face value on an interest payment date several years ago. The face value of each bond is $1,000, and each bond is convertible into 15 shares of $5 par common stock of Convee. Convee has embarked on a program of debt reduction; U.S. interest rates have declined during the term of the convertible bonds. Consequently, Convee offers the convertible bondholders $50 cash per bond as an inducement to convert. The market price of Convee stock is currently $70 per share. The bonds must be converted within a three-month period to receive the cash inducement. The bondholders accept the inducement and convert within the required period.

Required:

1. Why did the bondholders convert?
2. Record the conversion; assume that Convee uses the book value method to record conversions of convertible bonds.
3. Record the conversion, but assume that Convee uses the market value method to record conversions of convertible bonds.
4. Explain why induced conversion is not treated as debt extinguishment for purposes of classifying the inducement cost.

P 16–9
Extinguishment by Using In-Substance Defeasance
(L.O. 5)

Dusty Corporation borrowed $2 million cash on a 6% note on January 1, 1991. This five-year note is payable in five equal annual installments of $474,793 starting on December 31, 1991. On January 1, 1993, the company entered into an agreement with the three creditors to irrevocably transfer the government securities (held by Dusty as a long-term investment) to a trustee. The trustee will make the three remaining equal interest payments on each payment date and will pay the principal on December 31, 1995. The government securities cost Dusty $1,100,000, and they will be valued at their current market value based on a 9% effective rate.

Required:

1. Give the entry that Dusty Corporation made on January 1, 1991.
2. Give the entries that Dusty Corporation made on December 31 of 1991 and 1992.
3. Give the extinguishment entry on January 1, 1993.
4. What conditions must be met by Dusty Company to qualify the transaction on January 1, 1993, as an extinguishment of the debt?

P 16–10

Extinguishment: Debtor
Entries, Purchase in the
Open Market
(L.O. 5)

On July 1, 1991, Coputer Corporation issued $600,000, 5% (payable each June 30 and December 31), 10-year bonds payable. The bonds were issued at 97, and issue costs of $2,000 were paid from the proceeds. Assume straight-line amortization of discount and bond issue costs.

Due to an increase in interest rates, these bonds were selling in the market at the end of June 1994 at an effective rate of 8%. Because the company had available cash, $200,000 (face amount) of the bonds were purchased in the market and retired on July 1, 1994.

Required:

1. Give the entry by Coputer Corporation to record issuance of the bonds on July 1, 1991.
2. Give the entry by Coputer Corporation to record the extinguishment of part of the debt on July 1, 1994. How should the gain or loss be reported on the 1994 financial statements of Coputer Corporation?
3. Was the extinguishment economically favorable to the issuer, investor, or neither?

P 16–11

Extinguishment by
Refunding: Debtor Entries
(L.O. 5)

Davis Corporation issued $200,000, 4½% (payable each December 31), 10-year bonds on January 1, 1991. The issuer may call them at any time after 1994 at 104. The bonds sold on January 1, 1991, at 98. Straight-line amortization is used.

Due to a large increase in interest rates, the bonds were being sold in the market at the end of 1995 at 86 (i.e., at an effective rate of 8%). In view of this situation, Davis decided to issue a new series of bonds (a refunding issue) in the amount of $150,000 (8% payable annually, five-year term) on January 1, 1996. Davis had cash on hand sufficient to retire the old bonds.

Required:

1. Give the entry for Davis Corporation to record issuance of the bonds at 98 on January 1, 1991.
2. Assume that the $150,000 refunding issue was sold at par; give the required entry for Davis.
3. Assume all of the old bonds were immediately purchased in the open market at 86 on January 2, 1996. Give the required entry for Davis. How should the gain or loss be reported on the financial statements?
4. What was the economic gain or loss to the issuer and the investor?

P 16–12

Extinguishment with
Equity Securities; Call,
Refunding, Entries
(L.O. 5)

On January 1, 1991, Grand Corporation issued $100,000, 9% (payable each June 30 and December 31), 10-year bonds payable (convertible and callable) at a 10% effective rate of interest. Each $1,000 bond is convertible, at the option of the holder, into Grand common stock (par $10) as follows: first five years—25 shares for each bond tendered; second five years—20 shares for each bond. The bonds can be called, at the option of Grand, after the fifth year at 101.

On July 1, 1997, the market interest rate on comparable bonds is 8%, and the common stock is quoted on the market at $52 per share.

Required

1. Give the entry to record the issuance of bonds on January 1, 1991. Show computation of the bond issue price. Use the gross method.
2. Give the entry to record payment of bond interest and the amortization of bond premium or discount on June 30, 1991. Use the interest method.
3. Prepare the journal entries at July 1, 1997, to record each of the following separate assumptions (use straight-line amortization):

   Assumption A—All of the bondholders converted their bonds to common stock. Use the market value method to record the conversion.

   Assumption B—Grand called all of the bonds at the stipulated call price.

   Assumption C—Grand refunded all of the outstanding 9% bonds by purchasing them in the open market at the current yield rate of interest. Cash for the refunding was obtained by issuing new 8% bonds (interest payable semiannually) at par; cash proceeds were $103,000 (face amount of bonds sold).

4. Which of the three above alternative means of retiring the old 9% bonds is most likely to occur? Why?

P 16–13

Three Transactions:
Bonds, Detachable
Warrants,
Extinguishment—Entries
(L.O. 3, 4, 5)

This problem involves three independent situations.

a. On January 1, 1995, Hopewell Company issued its 8% bonds that had a par value of $1,000,000. Interest is payable at December 31 each year. The bonds mature on December 31, 2004. The bonds were sold to yield a rate of 10%.

b. On September 1, 1991, Junction Company issued at 104 (plus accrued interest) 4,000 of its 9%, 10-year, $1,000 par value, nonconvertible bonds with detachable stock purchase warrants. Each bond carried two detachable warrants; each warrant was for one share of common stock, at a specified option price of $15 per share. Shortly after issuance, the warrants were quoted on the market for $3 each. No market value can be determined for the bonds above. Interest is payable in December 1 and June 1. Bond issue costs of $40,000 were incurred and were deducted from the proceeds.

c. On December 1, 1991, Cone Company issued its 7%, $2,000,000 par value bonds for $2,200,000 plus accrued interest. Interest is payable on May 1 and November 1. On July 1, 1994, Cone purchased and retired the bonds at 98 plus accrued interest. Cone uses the straight-line method for the amortization of bond premium because the results do not materially differ from the interest method; the total amortization period at the date of issuance was 50 months.

Required:

1. Give the entry to record the issuance of the bonds by Hopewell Company. Show supporting computations.
2. Give the entry to record the issuance of the bonds by Junction Company. Show computations.
3. Give the entries required by Cone Company:
   a. At issue date.
   b. At reacquisition date.

(AICPA adapted)

P 16–14

LT Note: Borrower
and Lender Entries,
Amortization Schedule,
Adjusting Entry
(L.O. 6)

On January 1, 1991, Baker Company borrowed cash from Alter Finance Company and signed a three-year, $30,000 note. Interest is payable each December 31 at a stated interest rate of "floating prime at January 1 of each year plus 2%" The principal is due on December 31, 1993. The following actual prime rates were used by Alter: January 1, 1991, 13%; January 1, 1992, 12%; and January 1, 1993, 15%. The accounting period for each company ends on December 31.

Required

1. Compute the total amount of interest paid, by year.
2. What was the difference between the stated and effective rates? Explain.
3. Give all entries for each company through maturity date.
4. Give the 1991 adjusting entry that would have been necessary had the accounting periods for each company ended on August 31 instead of December 31.

P 16–15

Note with Share
Appreciation:
Amortization Schedule,
Entries and Reporting for
Borrower and Lender
(L.O. 6)

On January 1, 1991, Cantral Company borrowed cash from Tenor Financing Company on a $60,000, 14% three-year note. Interest is payable each December 31, and the principal is payable December 31, 1993. This note is designated as *Note A.*

On the same date, Cantral Company also borrowed cash from Tulare Commercial Loan Company on a $200,000, 9%, five-year note. This note, designated as *Note B,* will be paid with five equal annual payments each December 31. Tulare granted a low 9% stated rate in exchange for a 10% share appreciation in an office building under construction. The current best estimate of the present value of the share appreciation at January 1, 1991, was $52,754. The accounting period for each company ends on December 31.

Required:

1. What is the amount of each annual payment on Note B?
2. For each note, what is (*a*) the stated interest rate and (*b*) the effective interest rate?
3. Prepare a debt amortization schedule for Note B.
4. For each note separately, give all entries for both the borrower and the lenders through December 31, 1991.
5. Show the items and amounts that would be reported on the December 31, 1991, financial statements, by each company under the captions: revenues, expenses, assets, liabilities, and stockholders' equity (current and noncurrent classifications are not required.)

P 16–16
Note with Unrealistic
Interest Rate: Entries and
Reporting for Both
Parties, Gross Method
(L.O. 6)

Sable Company purchased merchandise for resale on January 1, 1991, for $5,000 cash plus a $20,000, two-year note payable. The principal is due on December 31, 1992; the note specified 8% interest payable each December 31.

Assume Sable's going rate of interest for this type of debt was 15%. The accounting period ends December 31.

Required:

1. Give the entry to record the purchase on January 1, 1991. Show computations (round to the nearest dollar).
2. Complete a tabulation as follows:

   a. Amount of cash interest payable each December 31 . . . . $_____
   b. Total interest expense for the two-year period . . . . $_____
   c. Amount of interest reported on income statement for 1991 . . . . $_____
   d. Amount of liability reported on the balance sheet at
   12/31/1991 (excluding any accrued interest) . . . . $_____

3. Give the entries at each year-end for the debtor.
4. Give the entries at each year-end for the creditor.
5. Show how the debtor and creditor should report or disclose the data related to the note on the income statement and balance sheet at each year-end.

P 16–17
Appendix 16A:
Serial Bonds
(L.O. 7)

A $700,000 issue of serial bonds dated April 1, 1991, was sold on that date for $707,600. The interest rate is 8%, payable semiannually on March 31 and September 30. Scheduled maturities are as follows:

Serial	Date Due	Amount
B	March 31, 1992	$100,000
C	March 31, 1993	200,000
D	March 31, 1994	200,000
E	March 31, 1995	200,000

Required

1. Prepare an amortization schedule for the issuer; use the bonds outstanding method.
2. Give all entries for the issuer relating to the bonds, including reversing entries, through March 31, 1992. The issuing company adjusts and closes its books each December 31.

P 16–18
Appendix 16A:
Serial Bonds
(L.O. 7)

On January 1, 1991, Tobin Corporation sold serial bonds (dated January 1, 1991) due as follows: Serial A, $10,000, December 31, 1995; Serial B, $15,000, December 31, 1996; and Serial C, $25,000, December 31, 1997. The bonds carried a 3% coupon (stated) interest rate per semiannual period (each June 30 and December 31) and were sold to yield 4% interest per semiannual period.

Required:

Round to the nearest dollar

1. Compute the selling price of the bond issue.
2. Prepare an amortization schedule for Tobin for the life of the bond issue, assuming the interest method is used. (Hint: Discount amortization—6/30/91, $306; 6/30/96, $352.)
3. Give Tobin's entry to record retirement of half of Serial C at 99½ on June 30, 1997. Assume the accounting period ends December 31.

P 16–19
Appendix 16B:
Restructure Entries,
Assets, New Debt and
Equity Securities
(L.O. 8)

DEM Company owed RUB Finance Company a $300,000, five-year, 18% (payable each year-end) mortgage note, dated January 1, 1991. DEM has experienced serious financial problems, and as a consequence, has not paid the interest at December 31, 1993. However, each company included its accrual in the adjusting entries at that date. On January 2, 1994, a debt restructure was agreed upon that provided that the principal and interest accrued will be paid in full as follows:

Cash, $10,000.

Transfer of land—original cost to DEM, $45,000, and appraised value, $137,000.

Transfer of 20,000 shares of DEM common stock, par $1; estimated current market value, $3.00 per share.

Transfer of $30,000 of accounts receivable; the related allowance for doubtful accounts on DEM's books is $4,000 (this appears to be realistic).

Transfer of 5,000 shares of WIT Corporation stock held by DEM as a long-term investment; cost to DEM, $2 per share, and current market value, $10 per share.

Required:
Give all entries to record the debt restructure for each company.

P 16–20

Appendix 16B: Restructure by Modification of Terms, Entries by Both Parties (L.O. 8)

Baker Company owed Cox Company a $20,000, 10% (annual interest payable each December 31), four-year note, dated January 1, 1991. Baker Company faced extreme financial difficulties. Both companies had accrued interest for the year 1992. On January 2, 1993, the parties agreed that the principal would be paid in full on maturity date and that the interest for 1992, 1993, and 1994 would be settled by payment of $3,340 cash on December 31, 1994 (maturity date).

Required:
1. Compute the new effective rate of interest.
2. Give all entries required on date of restructure (January 2, 1993) for each company.
3. Give all entries required on December 31, 1993, and 1994, for each company.

P 16–21

Appendix 16B: Restructure with Modification of Terms, Entries by Both Parties (L.O. 8)

On January 1, 1996, Day Corporation owed a $65,000 note payable to Cox Corporation that required the payment of 10% interest on each December 31; the note was due on December 31, 1996. Because of continuing serious financial difficulties, Day informed Cox that default (and discontinuance of the business) was probable unless a concession on terms could be negotiated. Day has paid interest through December 31, 1995. On January 1, 1996, Cox agreed to the following restructure of the debt:

a. Day will immediately transfer $15,000 of its accounts receivable to the creditor in settlement of $14,000 of the debt. The accounts of Day reflected $1,000 in the allowance for doubtful accounts that related to these receivables; thus, the current net realizable value of the receivables was reasonably stated at $14,000.
b. Day will immediately transfer its long-term investment in 800 shares of common stock (par $10) of Tye Corporation in partial settlement of the debt. Day accounts reflected a carrying value of $30,000 for the Tye stock, and its current market value was $32,000.
c. Day will pay $10,000 cash at the end of the fifth year from January 1, 1996 (date of restructure), to settle the remaining $19,000 of the principal. Therefore, the restructured maturity date is December 31, 2000.
d. Day will pay $5,000 total interest over the five-year period from January 1, 1996, to December 31, 2000 (i.e., $1,000 cash interest per year at December 31).

Required:
1. Give any required entry of the debtor and the creditor on date of restructure, January 1, 1996. Explain how you made the decision as to (*a*) whether entries are required and (*b*) the basis for the values used. How would values other than market value but agreed upon by debtor and creditor produce a biased measure of restructure gain or loss?
2. Give the required entries for the debtor and the creditor on the next interest date, December 31, 1996, and on the restructured maturity date, December 31, 2000.

P 16–22

Appendix 16B: Restructure by Modification of Terms, Entries for Both Parties (L.O. 8)

On January 1, 1991, Overdue Corporation sold and issued to Liquid Corporation $100,000, 7% (payable annually on December 31), 10-year bonds payable to yield 8% interest. After paying interest for 1991 and 1992, Overdue Corporation encountered severe financial difficulties, which made it apparent that Liquid Corporation would have to make concessions as to debt terms. Therefore, a debt restructure was agreed to on January 1, 1993, that provided (*a*) the remaining term to maturity would be 20 years from January 1, 1993, and (*b*) interest would be reduced so that the same total dollar amount of interest would be paid over the new term to maturity (20 years) as would have been paid over the old term to the old maturity date (8 years).

Required:
1. Give the entry by each party to record issuance of the bonds payable on January 1, 1991. Show computations of the original bond issuance price. Use the gross method.

2. Compute the carrying amount of the bonds for the debtor and creditor on January 1, 1993. Assume straight-line amortization.
3. Compute the new effective rate of interest (round to the nearest percent; then use straight-line interpolation to compute the approximate interest rate to two decimal places.)
4. Give all entries for both the debtor and the creditor on the date of restructure, January 1, 1993. If no entry is required, explain why. Use the approximate interpolated interest rate computed in (3) above and then round to the nearest dollar.
5. Give all entries for both the debtor and the creditor on the two interest dates, December 31, 1993, and December 31, 1994.

P 16–23
Appendix 16B:
Combination Restructure
(L.O. 8)

Janco Inc. issued a five-year, 10%, $500,000 note on January 2, 1991, for a merchandise purchase. The stated interest rate reflects the market rate on similar notes. The note requires equal annual payments each December 31 beginning 1991. Each payment includes principal and interest.

Subsequently, Janco experienced financial difficulties and on January 1, 1994, reached an agreement with the creditor to restructure the loan. Janco did not make the payment due December 31, 1993. According to the restructure agreement, the remaining payments under the original loan agreement are replaced by the following:

An immediate payment of $200,000.

$200,000 due January 2, 1998, the revised maturity date.

Required:

Use interpolation if a new effective interest rate is required and record the following entries for Janco:

1. Interest accrual on December 31, 1993, using interest payable.
2. Entry to record the troubled debt restructure on January 1, 1994, and to reclassify the remaining liability accounts.
3. Entry to record interest on December 31, 1994.
4. Entry to record the final payment on January 2, 1998.

P 16–24

COMPREHENSIVE PROBLEM
♦

Bond Issuance,
Retirement, Restructure
(Appendix 16B)
(L.O. 2, 3, 5, 8)

Westlawn Company issues $200,000 of 10% bonds on March 1, 1991. Additional information on the bond issue is as follows:

Bond date: January 1, 1991.

Maturity date: January 1, 2001.

Yield rate: 12%.

Interest payment dates: June 30, December 31.

Required:

1. Record the bond issue and the first interest payment for Westlawn under the interest method.
2. On August 1, 1996, Westlawn purchased 30% of the bonds on the open market for 103. Record the necessary entries to update the portion of the bond issue retired and to record the extinguishment.
3. Have interest rates risen or fallen between the issuance of the bonds and the early extinguishment? (Assume no significant change in Westlawn's risk.)
4. Discuss the nature of the extraordinary item you recorded in (2). In explaining this item to a financial statement user, what cautions would you include in your discussion?
5. Westlawn's going-concern status suddenly becomes questionable. The company is unable to make the December 31, 1996, payment. Record the entry to accrue interest expense on that date, using interest payable.
6. Westlawn and the bondholders agree to a restructuring plan on January 1, 1997, with the following stipulations: (omit unless you have been assigned Appendix 16B)
   a. Postpone interest payments until June 30, 1999, at which time interest payments resume at 8% (annual rate) applied to the revised principle. See (d) below.
   b. Forgive the December 31, 1996, interest payment.
   c. The maturity date remains unchanged.
   d. The face amount is halved.

Provide the entry to record the restructure on January 1, 1997 (reclassify the liability accounts), and the entry to record the first payment under the restructure plan, on June 30, 1999.

CASES

C 16-1
Convertible Bonds versus Detachable Stock Warrants
(L.O. 4)

Seton Corporation is considering the issuance of $100,000, five-year bonds. Two alternatives are under consideration as follows:

Alternative A—At the beginning of 1991, issue convertible bonds that would specify that each $1,000 bond can be tendered for conversion to 15 shares of Seton's common stock, par $10, at any time after the second year from the issue date of the convertible bonds. Seton's best estimate is that the convertible bonds can be sold to Investor X for $108,000 cash at the beginning of 1991 if the common stock is selling at that time for not less than $65 per share.

Alternative B—At the beginning of 1991, issue 100 nonconvertible $1,000 bonds with 15 detachable stock purchase warrants per bond. Each warrant can be tendered at any time after 1992 for one share of Seton's common stock, par $10, at an option price of $60 per share. Seton's best estimate is that the nonconvertible bonds can be sold to Investor XX for $108,000 cash at the beginning of 1991 if the common stock is selling at that time for not less than $65 per share. The warrants are expected to have a market value of $2 each immediately after issuance of the bonds; the bonds do not have a listed market price.

Seton's management is considering which alternative to select. The management is concerned about several issues that may influence the decision. One such issue is the comparative impact of the two alternatives on the financial statements. Your assistance in selecting an alternative has been requested.

Required:

1. Using Seton's best estimate, give the journal entries for each alternative that each party would make at the beginning of 1991. Use the gross method. Explain any differences in accounting values between the two alternatives.
2. Give the entries for each alternative that each party would make at the beginning of 1994, assuming all of the bonds in Alternative A are tendered for conversion and all of the warrants are turned in for shares in Alternative B. Seton's common stock is selling for $75 per share. Use the market value method for Alternative A. Assume straight-line amortization.
3. Complete the schedule given below, assuming the transactions in (1) and (2) have taken place.
4. Outline your response to management's request for assistance in choosing between the two alternatives. Consider the results of requirement 2.

	A—Convertible Bonds		B—Detachable Warrants	
Items	Issuer	Investor	Issuer	Investor
Gain (loss) conversion				
Investments:				
Bonds				
Common stock				
Liabilities				
Bonds payable				
Stockholders' equity:				
Common stock				
Contributed capital in				
excess of par				
Cash:				
Inflow				
Outflow				

C 16-2
Zero Coupon Bonds and Amortization Methods
(L.O. 3)

The Shelby Company issues $10 million of bonds maturing 25 years after issuance. The bonds yield 16% but pay no interest.

Required:
1. Why would Shelby issue bonds paying no interest?
2. Why would investors buy them?
3. Compute the issue price (assume annual compounding periods and that issue date and bond date are the same).
4. Compute interest expense for the 1st, 16th, and 25th year under the interest method.
5. Compute interest expense for the 1st, 16th, and 25th year under the straight-line method.
6. Comment on your findings in (4) and (5). Why is the straight-line method inappropriate for the Shelby bonds?

C 16-3
Ethical Considerations: Reporting Liabilities
(L.O. 1, 3)

Discuss the following two situations from an ethical and financial reporting viewpoint. (Note: (*b*) requires knowledge of material from Chapter 15.)

a. "Accounting for an Albatross," *Forbes*, June 13, 1988, p. 62, states that American Airlines has accumulated a liability of 4 billion miles due to its frequent-flier program. Its estimated liability for free flights amounts to $270 million but could be $40 million higher if the opportunity cost of lost revenue from displaced passengers is considered.

The airlines argue that the actual cost of each free flight is only approximately $8—for food, insurance, and other miscellaneous costs. That is the cost of filling an otherwise empty seat. Furthermore, flyers with free tickets often bring along a paying customer, which more than offsets the negligible cost. Consequently, the average liability disclosed is only a fraction of the amount industry analysts insist exists.

b. In December, Mr. Wilson, the controller of Fargo Company, a calendar-fiscal-year company, is faced with a tough situation. The bond indenture of a major issue of Fargo bonds requires maintaining a 3 to 1 current ratio as measured at each balance sheet date. Fargo has recently experienced cash shortages caused by a downturn in the general economy and demand for Fargo's products. However, leading economic indicators suggest that an upturn is expected.

A substantial account payable is due in January. Fargo does not have the cash to pay the debt. Furthermore, the January cash budget based on a realistic estimate of sales and collections from accounts receivable indicates a cash shortage requiring short-term financing. The payable due in January is large enough to cause the current ratio at December 31 to fall below 3.0. The controller begins the search for a financial institution willing to refinance the payable on a long-term basis. If successful, the payable would be reclassified as long-term, allowing Fargo to comply with the bond indenture. Several financial institutions are willing to refinance the payable, but none agree to do so on a noncancelable basis.

The controller is quite stressed by the situation. Noncompliance with the bond indenture may lead to technical default. If the bondholders exercise their right and call the bonds, Fargo may be forced into bankruptcy. The controller is confident that Fargo will rebound in the coming year and reasons that more harm will come to the company, its employees, and shareholders if he does not take action that will result in compliance with the bond indenture. Mr. Wilson therefore decides to refinance the payable on a long-term basis, and include in the footnotes a statement that the refinancing agreement complies with *SFAS No. 6*, "Classification of Short-Term Obligations Expected to Be Refinanced."

C 16-4
Sherwin-Williams: Analysis of Actual Financial Statements
(L.O. 1)

Refer to the 1990 financial statements of Sherwin-Williams that appear at the end of this text. Respond to the following questions.

1. What was total interest expense for 1990?
2. What percent of total interest in 1990 is related to long-term debt?
3. If your answer to question 2 is less than 100%, what other debt could have given rise to interest charges?
4. What was the amount of interest paid in 1990?
5. For 1990, what percent of income before income taxes is total interest expense?
6. At the end of 1990, what is the ratio of total debt to total assets?
7. From your answers to questions 5 and 6, how would you characterize the market's perceived riskiness of this company? Are there any indications within the annual report that outside parties share your view?

C H A P T E R
17

Accounting for Income Taxes

After you have studied this chapter, you will:

1. Be able to account for and provide required disclosures of tax loss carrybacks and carry-forwards.

2. Understand the major problems in accounting for income taxes.

3. Be familiar with the conceptual differences underlying the basic alternative methods for accounting for income taxes.

4. Understand the theory and application of the asset/liability method of accounting for income taxes as it is presented in *SFAS No. 96* and proposed *SFAS No. 109*. (*SFAS No. 109* is expected to supersede *SFAS No. 96* in 1992.)

5. Understand the theory and application of the deferral method of accounting for income taxes as presented in *APB Opinion No. 11*.

6. Be familiar with the disclosure requirements as they relate to accounting for income taxes.

7. Understand the accounting treatment alternatives in accounting for the investment tax credit.

8. Be able to determine the limitation on recognizing a deferred tax asset specified in *SFAS No. 96*. (Refer to the appendix at the end of the chapter.)

◆

INTRODUCTION
◆

U nion Pacific Corporation is a major transportation company with large investments in capital equipment such as locomotives, railroad cars, trucks, and trailers. In 1990, the company reported income before federal income taxes of $952 million and federal income tax expense of $334 million. However, like many large corporations, the amount of income taxes the company actually had to pay in 1990 was far less—the current portion of the $334 million is reported in the notes to the financial statements to be only $173 million. The remaining $161 million is identified as "deferred." Moreover, the second largest account amount on the liabilities side of the balance sheet, in the amount of $2,257 million, is deferred federal income taxes. Since the total stockholders' equity for Union Pacific is $4,277 million, these deferred taxes equal 57% of the net worth of the company.

Several questions are suggested by the Union Pacific situation. But before their consideration, it is important to point out that Union Pacific, and indeed virtually any business, may report a current obligation to pay income taxes arising from current period operations that is much different from the amount the company reports as income tax expense for the current period. As we will see, the rules for determining *taxable* income often are very different from the rules for determining accounting income under GAAP. Thus, the fact that Union Pacific actually paid less in income tax than the amount reported as income tax expense is not unusual. What is difficult to understand, however, is exactly what the $2.2 billion amount reported on the balance sheet as deferred federal income taxes means. Is it a liability in the same sense as accounts payable or long-term debt? Will it ever have to be paid? How did it get to be so large? Why don't companies simply report as income tax expense the currently payable amount as determined in the tax return? If this were done for Union Pacific, the $2.257 billion would appear on the balance sheet as stockholders' equity!

Income taxes are a fact of life for everyone, including corporations. Unfortunately, accounting for them is rather complicated, in large part because the rules for measuring taxable income often differ from the rules for measuring income for financial reporting. A large portion of this chapter will focus on developing an understanding of how to account for income taxes when taxable income and financial reporting income differ. Accounting for income taxes is a controversial subject, and one that is not fully resolved.

This chapter is based on the latest pronouncement on the topic, which is an *Exposure Draft* entitled "Accounting for Income Taxes," issued in June 1991. All indications are that this *Exposure Draft* will supersede the current *Standard* on this topic, *SFAS No. 96,* as early as the first quarter of 1992. Your authors are confident that the key changes in the *Exposure Draft* will be implemented. Much of the *Exposure Draft* is the same as *SFAS No. 96,* with the important exception that the *Exposure Draft* eases the computational complexity of accounting for income taxes. We will refer to the *Exposure Draft* as proposed *SFAS No. 109.* We are confident it will be issued as *SFAS No. 109.* The more difficult computations relating to deferred tax asset limitations of *SFAS No. 96* are discussed in the appendix to this chapter. Assuming the *Exposure Draft* is issued as a *Standard,* the material in the appendix would be less important. If the *Exposure Draft* is not issued as a *Standard* and *SFAS No. 96* continues as the required procedures for accounting for income taxes, reading and understanding the appendix will be essential.

Before considering the complex and controversial topic of accounting for income taxes when taxable income and financial income differ, it is necessary to consider one important aspect of income tax law that will affect our understanding of the accounting rules in this area. Because it will affect our approach to analyzing and determining income tax expense, it is necessary to understand how to account for income taxes when a company incurs a loss for tax purposes. Thus, the first topic covered is accounting for income taxes when a firm experiences a net operating loss.

◆

NET OPERATING TAX LOSS CARRYBACKS AND CARRYFORWARDS

In this section of the chapter, it is assumed that there are no differences between taxable income on the tax return and what is reported as taxable income in the financial statements. The focus is on understanding the tax law provisions dealing with choices the firm has when it experiences a loss for tax purposes, and how this is reported in the financial statements.

For-profit organizations undertake various activities with the objective of earning a profit. If and when they are successful, they are subject to income taxes. However, from time to time, some organizations do not achieve this objective and, instead, incur net losses for tax purposes. Current tax laws allow this loss, often called a **net operating loss (NOL),** to be carried back or carried forward for income tax purposes. These companies receive either a cash refund of prior years' taxes paid or a tax reduction in subsequent years. The application of current period operating losses to prior or future year operating profits is called *operating loss carrybacks* and *carryforwards*. The first objective is understanding current tax law treatment of net operating losses.

Under current tax laws, the company with an NOL must, at the end of the year of the NOL, make an irrevocable choice of one of two options:

1. **Carryback-carryforward option.** A carryback of three years (in order of years, starting with the oldest year) of such losses is permitted in order to secure a refund of prior years' taxes on income of an equivalent amount. If the loss is so large that the carryback provision does not fully absorb it, the remaining loss may be carried forward until it is fully absorbed, with a limit of 15 years. With the selection of this option, a total of 18 years is available to absorb the NOL. The carryforward results in a reduction of tax payable for each year to which it extends.
2. **Carryforward-only option.** A carryforward only is permitted for up to 15 years (in order of year) in order to reduce future income tax payments.

The tax provision options can be diagrammed as follows:

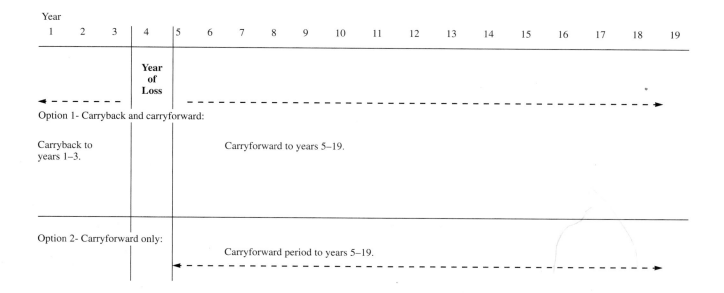

The accounting issue posed by income tax loss carrybacks and carryforwards is the extent to which any carryback tax refunds and potential carryforward tax benefits should be matched in the year of loss against the pretax accounting loss of the period. To illustrate the accounting for tax loss carrybacks and carryforwards, the following data for Drucker Corporation are used:

Year	Taxable Income (Loss)	Marginal Tax Rate	Taxes Paid
1991	$5,000	20%	$1,000
1992	$9,000	20	1,800
1993	$11,000	20	2,200
1994	*(35,000)*	*20*	
1995	Est. 10,000	20	
1996	Est. 5,000	20	
1997	Est. 50,000	40	
1998	Est. 55,000	40	
1999	Est. 60,000	40	
2000	Est. 75,000	40	

Assume the data for Drucker Corporation are actual results up to the end of 1994, the year of the NOL, and estimates for future periods.

Based on the data presented, would Option 1 (carryback first, then carryforward) or Option 2 (carryforward only) be in the best interests of Drucker Corporation? The choice must be made at the end of 1994, the year of the loss, and the choice is critical because the two different options result in different cash flows for the firm. Management must weigh the benefit of a certain cash refund from the carryback against the likelihood of future profitability and increases in future tax rates. Tax rate increases may make the carryforward-only option attractive because of the greater tax savings. The carryforward-only option should be selected only if the corporation expects to earn sufficient taxable income in future years to absorb the loss and is able to do so quickly enough to offset the present value advantage of the carryback option. The choice between the two options, then, involves a projection of future tax rates and of future income amounts.

The Drucker Corporation situation and options can be illustrated graphically as follows:

	Actuals				Estimated				
Year	91	92	93	94	95	96	97	98	99
Taxable income (loss) (in 000s)	$5	$9	$11	$(35)	$10	$5	$50	$55	$60
Tax rate (%)	20	20	20	20	20	20	40	40	40
Taxes paid (in 000s)	$1	$1.8	$2.2						
Carryback and carryforward option: Tax refund and savings (in 000s) $1		$1.8	$2.2		$2*			Total benefit = $ 7	
Carryforward only option: Tax savings (in 000s)					$2	$1	$8†	Total benefit = $11	

* Remaining NOL ($10,000) × .20 = $2,000

† Remaining NOL ($20,000) × .40 = $8,000

In the Drucker Corporation example, the carryforward-only option may be preferable because the cash saved (income tax benefit of the loss) totals $11,000, compared to $7,000 under the carryback-carryforward option. The difference is caused by the increase in the tax rate. The final $20,000 of NOL is used to offset income that would be taxed at 40% rather than 20%; the difference in the tax rate of 20% times the amount affected ($20,000) gives the $4,000 net benefit of using the carryforward-only option. This benefit must be tempered with the uncertainty implicit in Option 2. That is, the results will differ substantially if the actual incomes in future years differ from the above estimates. Additionally, since the cash flows for the two options occur at different times, the future projections of tax savings should be discounted to present value to fully evaluate the benefit.

The Economic Recovery Act of 1981 lengthened the carryforward period to 15 years. The Tax Reform Act of 1986 did not change the carryback or carryforward provisions, thus they remain as 3 years back and 15 years forward.

Accounting for the Carryback-Carryforward Option

When an operating loss follows a three-year period of sufficient taxable income to offset the loss, the resultant loss carryback will produce a refund (or tax payable offset) of all or a portion of the taxes paid during that three-year period. Because the offset or refund is certain, the tax effect is recorded in the accounts and reflected in the financial statements for the period of the loss as a reduction of the loss and a tax refund receivable.

To illustrate the accounting for the carryback-carryforward option, the data presented above for Drucker Corporation will be used under the assumption that the company selects Option 1—the carryback-carryforward option. The carryback of the NOL absorbs $25,000 of the $35,000 NOL and will result in a refund receivable of taxes previously paid of $5,000:

Year	Amount Carried Back	Taxes to Be Refunded
1991	$ 5,000	$1,000
1992	9,000	1,800
1993	11,000	2,200
Totals	$25,000	$5,000

The entry Drucker would make to record the carryback of the NOL would be:

Receivable for income tax refund (loss carryback) 5,000
    Gain, income tax refund (close to income tax expense)   5,000

After the carryback, there remains $10,000 of NOL that can be carried forward to reduce future income taxes. Proposed *SFAS No. 109* requires that the tax benefit of the carryforward be recorded in 1994 as a reduction of the loss:

Deferred tax asset ($10,000 × .20) 2,000
    Income tax expense   2,000

Under Proposed *SFAS No. 109*, future tax benefits of NOL carryforwards are recognized in the year of the loss. If it is more likely than not that the benefit of the tax loss carryforward will not be realized, the *Standard* requires that a valuation allowance (a contra account to the deferred tax asset) be established to reduce the net value of the deferred tax asset to the amount with a greater than 50% probability of being realized. The establishment of a valuation allowance is covered in more detail in a later section.

The two credit entry accounts above are reported on the income statement as adjustments to income tax expense. The effect of the above entries is to report a tax refund receivable of $5,000, a deferred tax asset of $2,000, and a reduction of the net loss from $35,000 to $28,000 in 1994.

Assuming Drucker Company does have taxable income of $10,000 in 1995 and had recorded a deferred tax asset, the effect of the tax reduction would be recorded as:

Income taxes payable 2,000
    Deferred tax asset   2,000

It is assumed an entry to record income taxes payable and income tax expense has already been made in 1995:

Income tax expense 2,000
    Income tax payable   2,000

The previous standard, *APB Opinion No. 11*, required "assurance beyond a reasonable doubt" that the benefit would be realized before it could be recorded. Also, under *SFAS No. 96* and Proposed *SFAS No. 109*, the gain accounts above are reported on the income statement as a reduction of income tax expense. Under *APB Opinion No. 11*, they were reported as extraordinary items.

Accounting for the Carryforward-Only Option

If Drucker expects higher income tax rates in future years and is reasonably certain to have taxable income sufficient to use the NOL, management may elect the carryforward-only option. The accounting is similar to that presented above, except that there is a greater likelihood that a valuation allowance would be required. To illustrate, assume Drucker Corporation elects the carryforward-only option and that estimates of future taxable income are realized. Under proposed *SFAS No. 109,* the accounting is as follows.

In 1994 (the year of the loss), Drucker would recognize the tax benefit of the tax loss carryforward as a reduction of the current year loss and as a deferred tax asset:

Deferred tax asset	11,000	
Income tax expense		11,000

The $11,000 amount is based on management's estimates of future taxable income and the future tax rates, as was illustrated earlier. As was discussed above, it may be necessary to establish a valuation allowance to the deferred tax asset, with the debit to income tax expense, if it is more likely than not that some or all of the tax benefit will not be realized. Assuming no valuation allowance is needed, and actual taxable income is equal to that estimated, the entries in 1995, 1996 and 1997 to record the benefit of the tax loss carryforward are:

To record income tax expense and income taxes payable (before effects of NOL carryforward):

Year	1995	1996	1997
Income tax expense	2,000	1,000	20,000
Income taxes payable . . .	2,000	1,000	20,000

To record the effects of the NOL carryforward on income taxes payable:

	1995	1996	1997
Income taxes payable	2,000	1,000	8,000
Deferred tax asset	2,000	1,000	8,000

The NOL carryforward amount remaining to carryforward to 1997 is $20,000 ($35,000 loss in 1994, less the $10,000 used in 1995 and the $5,000 used in 1996). In 1997, the tax rate is 40%. Thus the tax savings are $20,000 times .40, or $8,000.

The effect of the above accounting procedures is to recognize the expected tax benefit of the NOL carryforward in the year of the loss (1994), thus reducing the net amount of reported loss in that year by $11,000. As the benefits are realized in future years, the deferred tax asset is reduced. There is no effect on income in the years when the benefits are being realized. This accounting treatment is quite different from that which was required under *APB Opinion No. 11.* Under the accounting guidelines in that *Opinion,* a firm could not recognize the tax benefit of an NOL carryforward except when the benefit was "assured beyond a reasonable doubt" of being realized. Given this stringent requirement for recognition, very few firms ever recognized the carryforward benefit of the NOL in the year of the loss. This treatment results in the loss not being reduced in the year of the loss. The benefits of the NOL carryforward are recognized only when realized in future years. Moreover, when the benefits of NOL carryforwards are realized under *APB Opinion No. 11,* they were reported as extraordinary gains.

CONCEPT REVIEW

1. Over what period can a net operating loss for tax purposes be carried back? Over what period can a net operating loss for tax purposes be carried forward?
2. Why would a firm ever choose option 2?
3. Why might an NOL carryforward that is recognized in the period of loss not reduce the net reported loss?

ACCOUNTING FOR DIFFERENCES BETWEEN GAAP AND TAX LAWS

♦

Over the past several decades, tax laws have provided increasing opportunities for taxable income to differ from pretax accounting income. This creates the accounting problem of how to measure income tax expense when what is measured as income differs significantly between tax and financial reporting. In 1967, *APB Opinion No. 11* was issued to deal with this issue. It required interperiod tax allocation using a conceptual approach known as the *deferral method*. Over the following two decades, *APB Opinion No. 11* was the frequent subject of criticism. The meaningfulness of the results was questioned, and the complexity of the accounting requirements was criticized. In 1982 the FASB added accounting for income taxes to its agenda. In December 1987, *SFAS No. 96* was issued to supersede *APB Opinion No. 11*. *SFAS No. 96* required a different conceptual approach, known as the *asset/ liability method,* to be used in accounting for income taxes. It was to become effective for fiscal years beginning after December 15, 1988, but *SFAS No. 100* and later *SFAS No. 103* delayed the effective date of *SFAS No. 96* to fiscal years beginning after December 15, 1991. These delays were in part because of dissatisfaction with the *Standard.*

In June 1991 the FASB issued an *Exposure Draft* entitled "Accounting for Income Taxes" that will, if issued, most likely be *SFAS No. 109* and will supersede *SFAS No. 96.* The proposed *SFAS No. 109* also requires the use of the *asset/liability method,* but its procedures for implementation are simpler and, to many accountants, better than those found in *SFAS No. 96.* Proposed *SFAS No. 109* is to be effective for fiscal years beginning after December 15, 1992.

Proposed *SFAS No. 109* has been well received by the accounting and business community as a substantial improvement over *SFAS No. 96.* Proposed *SFAS No. 109* very likely will be approved and issued as a *Standard* by the FASB, probably early in 1992. Thus, it is likely that *SFAS No. 96* will never be the *required* method of accounting for income taxes.[1]

Given the high likelihood that proposed *SFAS No. 109* will be adopted, and that it is essentially a modification of the implementation procedures of *SFAS No. 96,* this chapter is written based on the accounting procedures prescribed in proposed *SFAS No. 109.* If proposed *SFAS No. 109* is not adopted and *SFAS No. 96* continues to be the applicable *Standard,* the procedures in the body of the text still apply except for the determination of whether a deferred tax asset can be recorded. The procedures for determining whether a deferred tax asset can be recorded, under certain conditions for proposed *SFAS No. 109,* and for *SFAS No. 96,* are found in the appendix to this chapter.

A key objective of this chapter is to provide an understanding of the conceptual issues and alternative approaches available to account for income taxes. The discussion continues with an overview of why this is a problem area, and an outline of the accounting alternatives.

Taxable Income and Pretax Accounting Income

Nearly all corporations organized to earn a profit must pay a tax on their income. The tax on income is calculated by determining the amount of taxable income in accordance with the Internal Revenue Code and other Internal Revenue Service

---

[1] If the *Exposure Draft* were to be quickly approved as a *Standard,* there would be three choices of accounting for income taxes in 1991:

♦ Use the deferral method as specified in *APB Opinion No. 11.*

♦ Use the asset/liability method as specified and implemented in *SFAS No. 96.*

♦ Use the asset/liability method as specified and implemented in Proposed *SFAS No. 109.*

These same three choices will be options for fiscal years ending on or before Decembr 14, 1993. However, it is likely that firms using *SFAS No. 96* will quickly adopt the *Exposure Draft,* as the same basic procedures are involved, and the *Exposure Draft* will allow firms to record deferred tax assets that are not allowed by *SFAS No. 96.*

(IRS) regulations and pronouncements, and then applying the appropriate tax rates to determine the income tax liability. A similar procedure is followed if the company operates in a state that levies a state income tax on corporations.

Taxable income, as defined by the IRS, is determined by applying the various measurement rules contained in IRS publications and regulations. These measurement rules are established by the federal (and, where appropriate, state) government. The most important purpose of taxing income is to generate resources for government operations. A secondary purpose, which sometimes influences the measurement rules for taxable income, is to shift the tax burden in desired ways to encourage or discourage certain types of economic activities. For example, the IRS Code allows oil and gas firms to deduct a statutory depletion allowance which can be in excess of their costs. This beneficial tax treatment effectively constitutes a tax-free profit intended to encourage the exploration for oil and gas, which is deemed in the national interest by the government.

On the other hand, the purpose of measuring income before tax for financial reporting purposes, on what is called **pretax accounting income,** is to provide users of financial statements with information for decision making. Income for financial reporting purposes is measured using generally accepted accounting principles. One important concept under GAAP that influences financial accounting income measurement but not the determination of taxable income is the *matching* of revenues and expenses. The conceptual differences between taxable income and pretax accounting income are illustrated as follows:

Basis of Difference	Taxable Income	Pretax Accounting Income
Basic purpose—why it is required	To raise resources for government and encourage or discourage various activities by tax paying entities	Provide users of financial statements with information useful for decision making
Guidance in computing	Revenue Code and IRS regulations	GAAP
Purpose for computing	Determine taxes currently payable	Provide users of financial statements with information on results of operations
Management objectives when computing	Minimize the impact of the income tax obligation within the choices provided in Code	Present financial information in form relevant to outside decision makers

Given the differences in purpose, sources of guidance in computing, and objectives management may wish to pursue when computing taxable income and pretax accounting income, it should not come as a surprise that these amounts often will differ.

Exhibit 17–1 shows only a few of the situations in which a difference occurs in calculating taxable income and pretax accounting income as prepared for the financial statements of the company.

CONCEPTUAL ISSUES
♦

Most transactions that give rise to a revenue, expense, gain, or loss for financial reporting also give rise to either a revenue or deduction for tax purposes. However, because of the different procedures required under IRS regulations and under GAAP, differences will exist between the recognition and measurement of taxable income and pretax accounting income. These differences will, in turn, create differences in the related assets and liabilities for financial reporting and tax purposes. The two basic types of differences are permanent differences and temporary differences.

EXHIBIT 17-1   Examples of Transactions and Activities that Give Rise to Differences between Taxable Income and Pretax Accounting Income

Permanent differences:

1. **Tax-free interest income.** State and local government obligations usually pay interest that is not taxable. In these situations, the holders of the government obligations have pretax accounting income that is not included in taxable income. The purpose of this tax exclusion is to assist local and state governments raise capital for their activities at the lowest possible cost.
2. **Investment tax credit (ITC).** The federal tax laws from time to time have included a provision to reduce the taxes payable for a tax-paying entity if that organization purchases certain types of capital equipment during the period. The purpose of this provision in the tax law has been to encourage the purchase of capital equipment.
3. **Corporate dividend exclusion.** When one corporation acquires preferred or common shares of a second corporation, and the second corporation pays dividends to the first, a portion of the dividend income received is excluded from taxable income because the second corporation has already paid income taxes on the income. This has the effect of providing the first corporation with accounting income but not taxable income.
4. **Amortization of goodwill.** Goodwill arises in an acquisition or merger. Often the transaction results in the purchase price being greater than the fair value of the net assets acquired. The excess, labeled *goodwill,* is expensed over time for financial reporting, but it is not tax deductible.

Temporary differences:

5. **Accelerated depreciation.** For tax purposes, companies often use a modified accelerated cost recovery system (MACRS) for depreciation. Under MACRS, capital expenditures can be deducted for tax purposes over periods generally shorter than their estimated useful lives. For example, under MACRS, trucks and automobiles may be depreciated for tax purposes over a five-year recovery period using an accelerated depreciation schedule (see Chapter 12). For financial accounting purposes, the equipment would be depreciated over its estimated useful life, often using a straight-line method of depreciation.
6. **Installment sales.** When a firm has a sale that the purchaser will pay for over time (an installment sale), income usually is recognized at the sale (the delivery method) for financial reporting purposes, but often is recognized on a cash basis for tax purposes. In this case, accounting income is recognized in the period in which the sale occurs, but taxable income occurs in later periods when the cash is collected.
7. **Warranty expense.** Warranty obligations are recognized as expenses in the period incurred (that is, the period in which the sale is recognized and the warranty obligation is incurred), but are recognized for tax purposes only when paid. This gives rise to pretax accounting income being less than taxable income in the period of sale (the warranty obligation is expensed for financial reporting but cannot be for tax purposes), and in later periods will give rise to taxable income being less than pretax accounting income (when the warranty costs are paid and deducted for tax purposes).
8. **Prepaid expenses.** A company can prepay various operating expenses (such as insurance or rent) and can usually deduct the outlay in the current period for tax purposes, but for financial reporting the outlay is accrued as an asset (prepaids) and expensed in the period the service is used. This gives rise to pretax accounting income in excess of taxable income in the period the outlay occurs, and vice versa in the period or periods in which the service is used.

Permanent Differences

Permanent difference arises from transactions included in computing either pretax accounting income or taxable income, but not both. The first four items in Exhibit 17–1 are examples of permanent differences. For example, interest received from tax-free municipal bonds is included in pretax accounting income, but is not ever included in taxable income. Permanent differences are easily dealt with in financial reporting; the income tax expense effect of these items is equal to the effect they have on income taxes payable. Thus, if a permanent difference is the only item creating a difference between taxable income and pretax accounting income, income tax expense for financial reporting is equal to the amount computed as taxes payable on the tax return for the period.

Assume that Piper Co. has taxable revenues of $100,000 and tax deductible expenses of $60,000. In addition, Piper Co. receives interest from state bonds in the amount of $10,000 which is not subject to income taxation. All the above revenues and expenses are included in pretax accounting income for the period. The tax rate is 40%. The computation of income taxes payable is:

Taxable revenues	$100,000
Tax deductible expenses	60,000
Taxable income	$ 40,000
Tax rate	× .40
Income taxes payable	$ 16,000

For financial reporting Piper includes the tax-free interest as revenue. Assuming there are no temporary differences (which will be covered in detail in the remainder of this chapter), income tax expense will equal income taxes payable. The income statement for financial reporting purposes will show the following:

Revenues (includes tax-free interest income)	$110,000
Expenses	60,000
Pretax accounting income	$ 50,000
Income tax expense	16,000
Net income	$ 34,000

The *effective tax rate,* or apparent tax rate, that the company appears to be paying is computed by dividing pretax accounting income into the income tax expense. When a company has nontaxable revenue (e.g., interest revenue from municipal bonds) or has deductions for tax purposes not reportable in the financial statements (e.g., statutory depletion in excess of cost depletion on certain wasting assets such as mineral deposits and oil and gas), the apparent tax rate for the company will be reduced. Dividing income tax expense by the pretax accounting income, the apparent, or effective, tax rate for Piper Co. is:

$$\text{Effective tax rate} = \frac{\$16,000 \text{ income tax expense}}{\$50,000 \text{ pretax accounting income}} = 32\%$$

Piper Co. has an effective tax rate lower than the statutory rate of 40% because its pretax accounting income is increased by a nontaxable revenue item. To explain this difference, the following reconciliation would often be disclosed in a footnote:

Statutory tax rate	.40
Effect of municipal bond interest	(.08)
Effective tax rate	.32

Temporary Differences

A **temporary difference,** called a *timing difference* in *APB Opinion No. 11,* arises because accounting standards (GAAP) and tax laws differ as to when they recognize assets, liabilities, owners' equity, gains, losses, revenues, and expenses. Temporary differences usually originate in one or more accounting periods, and turn around, or reverse, in one or more subsequent accounting periods. Items 5 through 8 in Exhibit 17–1 are examples of temporary differences. Thus, when a firm prepays its rent a year in advance, tax laws usually allow the firm to deduct the payment on its tax return in the year of payment. Financial accounting, however, requires that the payment be accrued as an asset (prepaid rent) and expensed over the term covered by the payment. Thus, a temporary difference results. The deduction for tax purposes results in taxable income being less than pretax accounting income in the payment period. When the prepaid rent is expensed in one or more subsequent periods, a reversal of the temporary difference occurs. In those periods, the expenses for financial reporting are greater than those for tax purposes, thus, taxable income is greater than pretax accounting income.

Temporary differences give rise to two effects:

1. The amount of taxable income (as reported in the tax return) is different from the pretax accounting income (in the income statement) in one direction in one or more periods, and this effect is reversed in one or more subsequent periods.
2. Assets or liabilities have a tax basis different from their reported amounts in the financial statements. A tax basis is the value an item has for tax purposes. If a firm takes a tax deduction for rent paid in advance but records it as a prepaid expense for financial reporting, the tax basis of the prepaid rent is zero because it has already been deducted for tax purposes.

To illustrate a temporary difference, assume Slim Inc. (in 1991 and 1992, its first two years of operation) has revenue of $100,000 for both book (financial reporting) and tax purposes. In 1991, however, it has expenses of $60,000 for financial reporting purposes, and $72,000 for tax purposes. Assume that the difference arises because in 1991 Slim Inc. prepaid rent for 1992 in the amount of $12,000, and that this outlay is tax deductible in 1991. For financial reporting, rent payments are an expense as the rental period expires. Thus, in 1992 the prepaid rent becomes an expense for financial reporting and is included in the $60,000 of expenses for 1992. Assume a corporate income tax rate of 30% in 1991 and 35% in 1992. (A flat income tax rate is assumed in this and all examples. A graduated rate could be used, but the results do not change and the computations are unnecessarily complex.) Assume Slim Inc. does not prepay its 1993 rent in 1992. With the above information, Slim Inc. would calculate pretax accounting income and taxable income for each of the two years as follows:

	Financial Statements		Tax Returns	
	1991	1992	1991	1992
Revenues	$100,000	$100,000	$100,000	$100,000
Expenses	60,000	60,000	72,000	48,000
Pretax accounting income	40,000	40,000		
Taxable income			28,000	52,000

The calculation of income taxes payable for each of the two years is straightforward:

	1991	1992
Taxable income	$ 28,000	$ 52,000
Tax rate	× .30	× .35
Income taxes payable	$ 8,400	$ 18,200

On the balance sheet dated December 31, 1991, Slim would report an asset, prepaid rent, in the amount of $12,000. However, the tax basis (the amount yet to be deducted for tax purposes) is zero since the $12,000 was deducted in computing taxable income in 1991. The 1992 financial statements will treat the $12,000 as an expense, but the 1992 tax return cannot include it as a deduction because it was deducted in 1991. The prepaid rent transaction gives rise to $12,000 less of taxable income in 1991 (compared to pretax accounting income), and to $12,000 of additional taxable income in 1992. In 1991, there is an originating temporary difference of $12,000. In 1992, there is a reversal of the temporary difference.

The question with which the accounting profession has wrestled for several decades is how, if at all, should the tax consequences of temporary differences arising in a given period be recognized in the financial statements. More specific to our example, should the potential increased tax obligation in 1992, which occurs because of the temporary difference arising in 1991 and reversing in 1992, be included in income tax expense for financial reporting for 1991? If so, in what amount? If it is recorded as an expense, how should it be recorded on the balance sheet at the end of 1991? The two possible approaches to the first question: either no allocation of income tax expense between periods, or allocate income tax between periods.

CONCEPT REVIEW

1. Why are there differences between taxable income and pretax accounting income? What are two basic types of differences?
2. How are permanent differences handled in determining income tax expense for financial reporting? What are some examples of permanent differences?
3. What is a temporary difference? Give two examples of a temporary difference.

No Interperiod Allocation of Income Tax

One approach is to ignore temporary differences and *recognize income taxes payable for the period as calculated on the tax return as the income tax expense for the period*. This approach is also known as the cash method or the no-allocation method. Several arguments for this approach include:

* Income taxes are incurred only because there is taxable income. Any tax payments in future years will be solely the result of the firm generating taxable income in those years.
* Matching is not relevant. While most expenses are incurred in order to generate revenues, income taxes arise only because there is taxable income.
* Income taxes are the result of total taxable income, not the individual items that give rise to it. There is no definite tax effect related to these individual items.
* Using taxes payable in a period as the tax expense results in better predictions of future cash flows, especially since in many instances the deferred taxes will never be paid.
* The tax return determines the only legal liability for income taxes; this is all that should be recognized for financial reporting. Taxes are an expense only when levied.

In the Slim Inc. example, a simplified income statement would appear as follows under the no-allocation approach:

No Allocation: Tax Expense Equals Taxes Payable

	1991	1992
Revenues	$100,000	$100,000
Expenses	60,000	60,000
Income before income taxes	40,000	40,000
Income tax expense:		
Current period taxes payable	8,400	18,200
Net income	$ 31,600	$ 21,800

Prior to issuance of *APB Opinion No. 11* in 1967, most companies reported using the no-allocation approach. The amount of income tax payable shown on the income tax return was reported as the amount of income tax expense on the income statement. Many accountants and others criticized this method of determining income tax expense, arguing that it did not properly match income tax expense with the items that caused the tax. In the above example, income tax expense has increased 67% from 1991 to 1992, even though the tax rate increased only 5%. While it is true that the tax expense as shown provides an estimate of the cash payment of income taxes for the current period, many accountants believe that this result is not useful in predicting future tax payments. Also, the amount recorded as income tax expense bears little relation to income before taxes. If more temporary differences were included in the example, the affect would become even larger.

The no-allocation method is not acceptable under GAAP. Alternatives to the no-allocation approach are considered next.

Interperiod Allocation of Income Taxes

A second approach, generally called **interperiod tax allocation,** involves recognizing the tax consequences of period transactions by including the tax effects of the temporary differences as a component of income tax expense, and recognizing the effects on the balance sheet. Income tax expense relates to all tax consequences associated with items included in pretax accounting income, thus a better matching is achieved.

The conceptual framework presented in Chapter 2 provides the rationale supporting this approach. Briefly, accrual accounting attempts to capture transactions and events that have present and future cash flow consequences. Accrual accounting does not focus only on present period cash receipts and disbursements. Assets are probable future economic benefits resulting from past transactions or events; liabilities are probable future economic outlays or sacrifices due to obligations of the firm as a result of past transactions or events. Arguments in support of the allocation of income taxes across periods are extensive and generally consistent with the conceptual framework presented in Chapter 2.

Once allocation is accepted as the appropriate approach, there remains the question of how to implement it. As this text goes to press, two conceptually different methods of allocating income taxes among periods are acceptable under GAAP:

1. The *deferral method,* while required by *APB Opinion No. 11,* will be superseded by proposed *SFAS No. 109.*
2. The *asset/liability method* as defined in *SFAS No. 96,* which was to supersede *APB No. 11.* Although a number of firms have already adopted the measurement procedures of *SFAS No. 96,* the FASB has not yet required the use of only this method. This chapter will focus on proposed *SFAS No. 109* since it is expected to supersede *SFAS No. 96* in 1992.

Deferral Method

In response to concerns about the no-allocation method, *APB Opinion No. 11* was issued in 1967. It had as its conceptual focus the matching of expenses of a period with all the revenues of that period. It did not focus on measuring the asset or liability amount related to the timing difference. As such, it employed an approach for determining income tax expense that is identified as the **deferral method.** Under the deferral method:

* Income tax expense is determined as the amount of income taxes that would be payable currently if all revenues and expenses reported in the income statement (except for permanent differences) were also included in taxable income in the current period.
* In determining the amount of income tax expense, the current tax rate is used. Future tax rates or known changes in future tax rates are not used under the

deferral method because the focus of the deferral method is on matching expenses and revenues for the current period.

• The resulting deferred credit (debit) to be recorded on the balance sheet is not viewed as a liability (asset) under the deferral method. Instead, it is identified as a deferred debit or deferred credit. As such, it represents the cumulative result of application of the deferral method over time. Under this approach, the valuation of the deferred tax balance is not considered important. The deferred tax balance is not an asset or liability, but simply an amount recorded on the balance sheet until it is carried forward to the income statement.

The deferral method focuses on the income statement and on matching in the current period. As such, it may not accurately measure the future cash flow consequences of the timing differences that underlie the deferral. For example, if there are any changes in future tax rates, the eventual reversal of timing differences will have tax consequences measured by future rates, not current rates.

The approach to measuring income tax expense under the deferral method begins with determination of the income taxes payable in the current period. Then income tax expense to be reported on the income statement is computed, essentially, as pretax accounting income (adjusted for permanent differences) times the current income tax rate. The difference between these amounts is recorded as a deferred income tax credit (or debit) as needed to balance the journal entry. The deferral is equal to the net amount of temporary difference between taxable income and pretax accounting income, multiplied by the current period tax rate.

Application of the deferral method to the Slim Inc. example would proceed as follows. Pretax accounting income is determined in each year, which in the example is $40,000 in 1991 and 1992. The current year income tax rate would be applied to determine the amount of income tax expense for the period. Thus, in this example, the amounts for income tax expense are:

$$\text{Income tax expense, } 1991 = \$40,000(.30) = \$12,000$$
$$\text{Income tax expense, } 1992 = \$40,000(.35) = \$14,000$$

The difference between each amount and the income taxes payable for the period is the amount of deferred income taxes for the period. The deferred tax amount is reported on the balance sheet as a deferred credit or deferred debit, as appropriate.

Ignoring for the moment the change in the tax rate and the fact that the item giving rise to the deferred tax account balance fully reverses itself in 1992, the journal entries to record income tax expense and taxes payable in each year 1991 and 1992 would be as follows:

1991:

Income tax expense (40,000 × .30)	12,000	
Income taxes payable (from tax return)		8,400
Deferred income taxes (residual amount)		3,600

1992:

Income tax expense (40,000 × .35)	14,000	
Deferred income taxes (residual amount)	4,200	
Income taxes payable (from tax return)		18,200

A simplified income statement prepared under the deferral method would appear as follows[2]:

---

[2] There is a complication for the deferred method as applied above because of the change in the income tax rate between 1991 and 1992. If the above entries were made, the company would have a debit balance of $600 in the deferred tax account on the balance sheet at December 31, 1992. There are no future reversals of a prior temporary difference that will remove the deferred tax balance. Since the item giving rise to the temporary difference is completely reversed in 1992, the deferred tax amount on the balance sheet should also be removed (i.e., made to have a zero balance). Usually the journal entry that would be made in 1992 would debit the deferred tax balance to zero, and adjust the amount recorded as income tax expense.

Interperiod Tax Allocation: The Deferral Method

	1991	1992
Revenues	$100,000	$100,000
Expenses	60,000	60,000
Income before income taxes	40,000	40,000
Income tax expense:		
Current	8,400	18,200
Deferred	3,600	(4,200)
Total income tax expense	12,000	14,000
Net income	$ 28,000	$ 26,000

Under the deferral method, changes in the future tax rates, even when known, are not taken into account in the originating period. The prepaid rent that is deducted for tax purposes in 1991, when the tax rate is 30%, results in less tax savings than if it had been deducted in 1992, when the tax rate is 35%. Alternatively, the taxes payable in 1992 are greater by more than the amount provided for in the deferred tax account ($3,600) by $600:

$$\begin{array}{l}\text{Increase in taxes payable in 1992 due} \\ \quad \text{to tax rate increase and reversal} \\ \quad \text{of temporary difference beyond} \\ \quad \text{amount provided in deferral taxes}\end{array} = (.35 - .30)\$12,000 = \$600$$

The income tax consequences as they are accounted for under the deferral method will be compared with the consequences under the second method, called the *asset/liability method*.

Asset/Liability Method

Under the asset/liability method, all current period tax consequences are included either in the income taxes payable in the current period, or recorded as a (deferred) tax asset or liability. Recording the tax consequences as an asset or liability implies that the future cash flows related to the tax consequences are taken into account. Deferred tax amounts are determined by answering the question: What is the future obligation or benefit that will result from this temporary difference? More specifically, if future tax rates are known to be different from current tax rates, the future tax rates are used in determining the amount of the asset or liability.

Illustration of Asset/Liability Method   Under the asset/liability method, the income taxes payable for Slim Inc. are computed as before to be $8,400 in 1991 and $18,200 in 1992. The tax consequences of all the individual temporary differences are then analyzed. In what period or periods will the tax consequences of the temporary difference be reversed? And what will be the income tax rate in those periods? Knowing these, the income tax benefit or obligation can be determined. In the Slim Inc. example, the answer is 1992, and the tax rate will be 35% in that period. Therefore, the cash flow implications are that not having the $12,000 in prepaid rent available as a tax deduction in 1992 will cause 1992 taxable income to increase by this amount. The result of increasing 1992 taxable income by $12,000 will cause taxes payable to increase by this amount times the 1992 tax rate, or:

$$\begin{array}{l}\text{Deferred tax liability} \\ \quad \text{arising in 1991}\end{array} = \text{Income tax rate} \times \$12,000 = (.35)\$12,000 \\ \qquad\qquad\qquad\quad = \$4,200$$

Having determined the future tax liability to be $4,200, all of which arises from temporary differences arising in 1991, the computation of 1991 income tax expense is computed as the sum of the income taxes payable and the increase in the deferred income tax liability:

Income taxes payable	$ 8,400
Increase in deferred tax liability	4,200
Income tax expense	$12,600

The journal entries to record the taxes using the asset/liability method for 1991 and 1992 are as follows:

1991:

Income tax expense.	12,600	
Income tax payable		8,400
Deferred income tax liability		4,200

1992:

Income tax expense.	14,000	
Deferred income tax liability.	4,200	
Income tax payable		18,200

A simplified income statement prepared under the asset/liability method would appear as follows:

Interperiod Tax Allocation: The Asset/Liability Method

	1991	1992
Revenues	$100,000	$100,000
Expenses	60,000	60,000
Incone before income taxes	40,000	40,000
Income tax expense:		
Current	8,400	18,200
Deferred	4,200	(4,200)
Total income tax expense	12,600	14,000
Net income	$ 27,400	$ 26,000

The asset/liability method takes into account the expected change in tax rate, while the deferral method does not. Had there not been a change in the expected future tax rate in this example, the two methods would have resulted in the same entries. A change in rates, however, is not the only aspect that causes the two methods to differ. The asset/liability method also requires determining whether a potential tax asset or liability will be realized. As such it sometimes places limitations on the recognition of deferred tax assets. The deferral method, as required under *APB No. 11,* placed no such limits on the recognition of deferred debits. There are, however, different approaches for determining just how much can be recognized as a deferred tax asset. The primary difference between *SFAS No. 96* and proposed *SFAS No. 109* relates to how the limit on recording deferred tax assets is determined. Before expanding on this issue, two additional conceptual issues are covered.

Additional Conceptual Issues in Interperiod Tax Allocation

Both additional issues relate to how interperiod tax allocation might be accomplished and can apply to either the deferral method or the asset/liability method.

Comprehensive or Partial Allocation   Suppose that in the Slim Inc. example, the company must always pay its rent one year in advance. Thus, in 1992, when there is a reversal of the $12,000 temporary difference that arose in 1991, there is instead a new and equal temporary difference arising in 1992 that exactly offsets the reversal. In cases such as this, an argument could be made for not allocating income taxes. The recurring nature of the activity results in a deferred tax amount being recorded on the balance sheet that is never removed. Under **partial allocation,** temporary differences that are not expected to reverse in the foreseeable future are not allocated. The logic is when regular, similar, and recurring transactions occur that continually create temporary differences that offset subsequent reversals of the temporary differences and indefinitely postpone the tax payments, no allocation is needed.

Many transactions might be considered in this category, such as depreciation for manufacturing companies that are continually making investments in capital equipment, or merchandising companies that have continuous installment sales. Taking the continuous investment in capital goods as an example, the firm can, under current tax law, depreciate those assets over a period considerably shorter than their estimated useful lives. This gives rise to a temporary difference. However, as the firm replaces worn-out assets (especially if it increases its level of investment in the assets and the assets are viewed as a group), the deferred taxes arising from the new assets offsets the reversing deferred taxes arising from earlier period assets. The example of Union Pacific cited at the introduction of this chapter, with its large and increasing deferred tax account, is an example for which partial allocation might be advocated. If partial allocation were used for the Slim Inc. example (assuming the prepaid rent recurs in 1992 and years thereafter), the income statements and tax returns would be as follows (1992 and thereafter includes prepayment of rent):

	Financial Statements		Tax Returns	
	1991	1992 (and thereafter)	1991	1992 (and thereafter)
Revenues	$100,000	$100,000	$100,000	$100,000
Expenses	60,000	60,000	72,000	60,000
Pretax accounting income	40,000	40,000		
Taxable income			28,000	40,000
Tax rate			× .30	× .35
Income taxes payable			$ 8,400	$ 14,000

In 1992 and thereafter as long as Slim prepaid rent for the following year, pretax accounting income would equal taxable income. That is, the originating temporary differences in a year would be offset by a reversing difference arising from the prior year. With partial allocation resulting in no allocation for the prepaid rent and no other items creating a deferral, the income statements for Slim Inc. would appear as follows:

Interperiod Tax with Partial Allocation

	1991	1992 (and thereafter)
Revenues	$100,000	$100,000
Expenses	60,000	60,000
Income before income taxes	40,000	40,000
Income tax expense:		
Current	8,400	14,000
Deferred (for selected items)	0	0
Total income tax expense	8,400	14,000
Net income	$ 31,600	$ 26,000

The alternative to partial allocation is **comprehensive allocation.** Under comprehensive allocation, all the temporary differences entering into the determination of pretax accounting income are considered in the computation of deferred taxes and income tax expense. All temporary differences are considered, regardless of their size or recurrent nature. All such transactions are viewed as affecting cash flows in both the period in which they originate and the period in which they reverse. The earlier allocation examples of the deferral and asset/liability methods of Slim Inc. were done using comprehensive allocation.

Arguments in favor of partial interperiod tax allocation include:

* Income tax temporary differences are not like other accounting items, such as accounts payable. Accounts payable "roll over" with actual payment transactions, whereas recurring deferred tax items do not result in tax payments.
* Comprehensive allocation is not a good representation of tax assets and liabilities. The tax regulations creating temporary differences are expected to continue indefinitely; thus, future originating differences are likely to continue to offset reversing temporary differences.
* Using partial allocation improves our ability to predict future cash flows for the firm because future tax payments are more closely related to these amounts than to comprehensive tax allocation amounts.
* Accounting results should not be distorted by using a rigid, mechanical method for computing deferred income taxes.

All GAAP pronouncements to date, however, have required comprehensive interperiod tax allocation. The primary arguments for this point of view are:

* All individual temporary differences do eventually reverse. They are not permanent. Financial statements should not be prepared under the assumption that reversal will not take place. (The manufacturing firm may wish to decrease its investment in capital equipment, which will cause a reversal.) The focus is on the individual items giving rise to temporary differences, not on the group.
* Partial allocation violates the matching concept. It is not proper to offset the income tax effects of current transactions with possible future transactions.
* Matching requires that the effects of transactions, including temporary differences, be reported in the period in which they arose.

Current GAAP, including *SFAS No. 96* and proposed *SFAS No. 109*, requires comprehensive allocation. There is currently not much support in the accounting and business communities for moving to partial allocation.

Discounting   A second conceptual issue is the possibility of discounting the deferred tax amount on the balance sheet to reflect its present value. This concept would seem to be consistent with the framework and rationale that underlie the asset/liability method, although it has been proposed for use with the deferral method as well. The discounting concept takes into account the expected time of payment of the deferred tax, and records the deferred tax amount at its present value. If temporary differences do not reverse until many years in the future, the deferred tax balance would reflect the present value of the expected future cash flows. Proponents of discounting argue that discounting is consistent with the accounting principles used in accounting for long-term notes receivable and payable, and for pensions and leases. Others argue that discounting results in a mismatching of the full tax effects of taxable transactions with the transactions themselves. The basic transaction giving rise to taxes occurs in one period, and the related tax effects are recorded over subsequent periods as the "interest" on the deferred tax balance is recorded. Opponents of discounting also argue that discounting would tend to hide the true tax consequences of transactions because they become buried in the subsequent interest expense. Finally, opponents argue that deferred taxes are essentially an interest-free loan from the government; hence, the appropriate interest rate to use in discounting is zero—and a zero interest rate results in no discounting.

Current GAAP does not allow for discounting of deferred taxes. It is not likely to be accepted in the near future. None of the examples in this chapter will be discounted. The computational complexities are also formidable.

Summary   The discussion to this point has been an overview of the general issues of interperiod tax allocation. Accounting for income taxes currently requires comprehensive interperiod tax allocation without discounting. Of the two tax allocation methods currently found in GAAP (the deferral method and the asset/liability method), only the asset/liability method will be acceptable in the future. The asset/liability method as defined in the proposed *SFAS No. 109,* will be the basis for the remainder of the presentation in this chapter. Issues where the *Exposure Draft* differs from *SFAS No. 96* are covered in the Appendix.

CONCEPT REVIEW

1. How is income tax expense determined if there is to be no interperiod allocation in determining income tax expense?
2. What is the guiding principle underlying the deferral method of interperiod tax allocation? What is the guiding principle underlying the asset/liability method of interperiod tax allocation?
3. What is the difference between partial allocation and comprehensive allocation? Which is required under GAAP?

OVERVIEW OF CURRENT ACCOUNTING STANDARDS

◆

The criticisms of *APB Opinion No. 11* which led to the issuance of *SFAS No. 96* and then to proposed *SFAS No. 109* include:
* The deferred method is deficient.
* The provisions of *APB No. 11* are too vague.
* The implementation of *APB No. 11* requires too much time.
* The deferred tax amounts reported on the balance sheet are excessive, confusing, and meaningless. They are not assets and liabilities.

The last point is perhaps the most persuasive. Many firms, as a result of applying *APB No. 11* for several years to a continually growing firm with recurring temporary differences, were showing very large deferred income tax credit balances on the balance sheet. Some balances were nearly as large as the total stockholders' equity. The information presented for Union Pacific at the introduction of this chapter is typical. Some users of financial statements are uncertain about whether these large balances represent a liability, or should be viewed as equity. When asked, many in the accounting profession responded by quoting *APB No. 11* and identifying the deferred taxes as deferred credits (or deferred debits), not liabilities (or assets) nor as equity. Many financial analysts often simply add the deferred tax amounts to equity. There is little or no guidance on exactly how deferred credits should be viewed as items on the balance sheet. The proposed *SFAS No. 109* attempts to deal with this problem.

Both *SFAS No. 96* and proposed *SFAS No. 109* require the use of the asset/liability method, but with different procedures for implementation. The basic differences between *APB No. 11, SFAS No. 96,* and proposed *SFAS No. 109* are summarized in Exhibit 17–2. Some terminology and definitions of *SFAS No. 109* are introduced before covering its objectives and procedures.

Some Income Tax Terminology and Definitions

Temporary differences were introduced earlier. They occur because accounting standards and income tax laws differ as to when assets, liabilities, owners' equity, revenues, gains, expenses, and losses are recognized. All temporary differences *originate* in one or more periods (an **originating difference**), and *reverse,* or turn around, in one or more subsequent periods, (a **reversing difference**). Proposed *SFAS No. 109* identifies two sources of temporary differences:

EXHIBIT 17-2   Comparison of *APB No. 11*, *SFAS No. 96*, and Proposed *SFAS No. 109*.

	APB No. 11	**SFAS No. 96**	**Proposed SFAS No. 109**
Basic conceptual approach	Deferral method	Asset/liability method	Same as *SFAS No. 96*
How differences are determined	Timing differences between pretax accounting income and taxable income occurring during the year	Temporary differences between book and tax bases of assets and liabilities	Same as *SFAS No. 96*
Method for computing income tax expense	Essentially equals income taxes payable plus the amount that would be payable if all timing differences had tax effects in the current period	Essentially equals income taxes payable plus increase in net deferred tax liability, less increase in net deferred tax asset	Same as *SFAS No. 96*
Limitation of deferred tax asset (debit)	None specified in the *Opinion*	Limited to the amount assured of being realized using carryback, carryforward procedures to offset other taxable amounts	Limited to the amount more likely than not to be realized
Effect of changes in enacted marginal tax rates	No adjustment of deferred balance sheet amounts when new rate enacted	Adjust deferred tax assets and liabilities when rate is changed	Same as *SFAS No. 96*
Balance sheet classification of deferred tax assets and liabilities	Based primarily on classification of related assets and liabilities giving rise to temporary differences	Based on timing of expected reversals	Based primarily on classification of related assets and liabilities giving rise to temporary differences
Sources of future taxable income to consider in determining limit on deferred tax asset	Not applicable because there is no limit	Tax benefits realizable from taxable temporary difference reversals and carryback, carryforward procedures for NOLs and future taxable amounts	All of those available for *SFAS No. 96*, and also estimated future taxable income from operations
Benefits of loss carryforwards that are not offset by taxable temporary differences	Record in the year of the loss only if assured beyond a reasonable doubt	Not recognized	Record as deferred tax asset, and establish a valuation allowance if benefits are not likely to be realized

1. The amount of taxable income (in the tax return) is different from the pretax accounting income (on the income statement) for a year.
2. Assets or liabilities have a different tax basis than their reported amounts in the financial statements.

Most transactions and events do not cause temporary differences because they are recognized in the financial statements and the income tax return in the same period. However, when they occur, temporary differences are recorded in one area (tax or financial reporting) before the other, and then later in the second area. Temporary differences are classified into two basic categories—**future taxable amounts** and **future deductible amounts**. Each arises from basic sources:

A. *Future taxable amounts* (resulting in deferred tax liabilities) arise from three sources:

1. Revenues and gains that are included in the tax return *after* they are included in pretax accounting income. Example: Sales on account, recorded for accounting purposes at delivery and for tax purposes when payment is received.
2. Expenses and losses that are included in the tax return *before* they are included in pretax accounting income. Example: Depreciation taken using straight line for accounting and some accelerated basis for tax.

3. Reductions in the tax basis of assets, usually because of tax credits, which do not have this effect in financial reporting. Example: A tax law change in 1982 allowed taxpayers with the choice of (*a*) taking the full amount depreciation deductions and a partial tax credit, or (*b*) the full amount of a tax credit and a reduced tax basis (amount deductible for tax purposes). Firms choosing option (*b*) will have a depreciable asset with a reduced tax basis.

These sources cause a deferred tax liability to be recorded in the current period because there is a *taxable amount* that will give rise to income taxes payable in future years.

B. *Future deductible amounts* (resulting in deferred tax assets) arise from four sources:

1. Revenues and gains that are included in the tax return *before* they are included in pretax accounting income. Example: Rent revenue received in advance, taxable in the period received but recorded for accounting purposes when earned.
2. Expenses and losses that are included in the tax return *after* they are included in pretax accounting income. Example: Warranty costs, recorded for accounting purposes at the sale of the warranted product but tax deductible only when incurred.
3. Increases in the tax basis of assets but not for financial reporting. Example: In some tax jurisdictions, the tax basis of assets might be required to be adjusted for the effects of inflation. The inflation-adjusted cost of the asset is used for tax purposes, but GAAP requires historical cost to be used for financial reporting.
4. Intercompany sales of inventory or assets at a profit when a firm is not preparing a consolidated tax return. Example: Intercompany profits are eliminated for affiliated companies in which consolidated financial statements (or the equity method) is used for financial reporting. The profits would not be eliminated if the affiliated firms are preparing separate tax returns.

These situations cause taxable income to be greater than pretax accounting income in originating periods. Thus a deferred tax asset will be recorded (subject to realizability limitations to be discussed shortly) because they will cause pretax accounting to exceed taxable income in future years.

To summarize, temporary differences:

1. Relate to items that are recognized in both the income statement and the income tax return in different years, or for assets and liabilities which have a tax basis different than their financial reporting basis.
2. Result in a deferred tax liability (a credit) or a deferred tax asset (a debit).
3. Are generally expected to reverse (i.e., turn around) in one or more future years.

Deferred Income Tax Liabilities and Assets

In accounting for deferred income taxes, a distinction must be made between a temporary difference and the deferred income tax liability or asset to which it gives rise. Temporary differences are *pretax* amounts that give rise to either *taxable amounts* in future periods, or to *deductible amounts* in future periods. Future taxable amounts give rise to a **deferred tax liability;** future deductible amounts give rise to a **deferred tax asset.** However, other factors such as net operating losses and tax credits can also affect the computation of deferred tax amounts.

A deferred income tax liability (or asset) is the result of multiplying a temporary difference by the appropriate enacted future marginal income tax rate(s). A taxable amount is multiplied by the appropriate income tax rate to determine a deferred tax liability, and a deductible amount is multiplied by the appropriate income tax rate to determine a deferred tax asset.

There is a practical problem in implementing these definitions and procedures. Taxable income comes from the income tax return, which is often prepared after the end of the accounting period. In reality, management often must prepare financial statements before the final income tax return is completed; thus, an estimate of taxable income is often developed by adjusting pretax accounting income for current period temporary differences.

Basic Objectives and Principles

Under proposed *SFAS No. 109,* the objective in accounting for income taxes on an accrual basis is to recognize the amount of current and deferred taxes payable or refundable at the date of the financial statements (1) as a result of all events that have been recognized in the financial statements, and (2) as measured by the provisions of enacted tax laws. To implement this objective, all of the following basic principles are applied in accounting for income taxes at the date of the financial statements:

1. A current or deferred tax liability or asset is determined for the current or deferred tax consequences of all events that have been recognized in the financial statements.
2. The current or deferred tax consequences of an event are measured by applying the provisions of enacted tax laws to determine the amount of taxes payable or refundable currently or in future years.
3. Deferred tax assets are reduced by a valuation allowance (to be defined shortly) if it is *more likely than not* that some portion of the deferred tax asset will not be realized.

All temporary differences must be considered in determining current or future tax consequences. This is consistent with the requirements of *APB Opinion No. 11.* A significant difference is the second principle. *APB Opinion No. 11* required the measurement of tax consequences applying only current tax rates, and proposed *SFAS No. 109* requires the measurement of tax consequences using enacted laws and rates. Known enacted rates for future years may be different than current period rates. The third implementation principle stated above is the key difference between *SFAS No. 96* and proposed *SFAS No. 109. SFAS No. 96* strictly limits the amount of deferred tax asset to that which is assured of being realized by offsetting future taxable amounts, or by loss carryback from the future year to reduce taxes paid in the current or a prior year. *SFAS No. 96* prohibits assuming the firm would generate taxable income in future periods. Under proposed *SFAS No. 109,* the deferred tax asset is not limited so long as management determines that it is more likely than not that there will be sufficient taxable income in future periods to realize the tax benefit.

Proposed *SFAS No. 109* is procedurally implemented each accounting period as follows:

1. Compute income tax payable on the income tax return in conformity with income tax laws and regulations. This liability, less any payments made, is reported on the balance sheet as income taxes payable.
2. Compute the total deferred income tax obligation and the total deferred tax benefit at year-end based on temporary differences existing at year-end. The marginal tax rate, defined as the enacted tax rate expected to apply to the last dollar of taxable income in the periods in which the deferred tax liability or asset is expected to be settled or realized, is used to compute the deferred tax amounts. This computation may involve both a deferred tax liability for future taxable amounts and a deferred tax asset for future deductible amounts. Future deductible and taxable amounts are not netted to determine a net deferred tax asset or

liability. The liability and asset amounts are reported on the balance sheet.[3] Once the end-of-period obligation is computed, the change in the obligation from the beginning to the end of the period is the amount of deferred taxes arising during the period that is included in income tax expense.

3. Reduce deferred tax assets by a **valuation allowance** if, based on the weight of available evidence, it is more likely than not that some portion or all of the deferred tax assets will not be realized. The valuation allowance should be sufficient to reduce the deferred tax asset to the amount that is more likely than not to be realized.

4. Compute income tax expense as the net sum of the income tax payable and the change in the deferred income tax accounts for the period, including the change in the valuation allowance. This expense is reported on the income statement. Income tax is indirectly derived rather than computed directly. It is a residual amount resulting from the computation of income taxes payable and deferred tax amounts.[4]

Example Consider Slim Inc. one more time. Pretax accounting income for 1991 is $40,000, and taxable income is only $28,000 because of the prepaid rent of $12,000. Slim makes the entries shown earlier using the asset/liability method. The company has a deferred tax liability at December 31, 1991, in the amount of $4,200.

Assume the following new data in 1992 for financial reporting:

Revenues	$120,000
Expenses	72,000
Pretax accounting income	$ 48,000

In addition, suppose taxable income for 1992 differs from pretax accounting income as follows:

Pretax accounting income (from above)	$48,000
Add: Rent expense (deducted for tax in 1991)	12,000
Deduct: $8,000 in installment sales (included in pretax accounting income, but taxable when collected, expected to be in 1994)	(8,000)
Deduct: $12,000 rent prepaid (tax deductible in 1992 but will be an expense in 1993)	(12,000)
Taxable income	$40,000

Assume the enacted and known marginal tax rate is 35% for 1992 and 1993, 40% for 1994 and thereafter. The determination of income tax expense proceeds as follows:

1. Compute the amount of income taxes payable for 1992:

$$\text{Income taxes payable} = \text{Taxable income} \times \text{Tax rate}$$
$$= \$40,000 \times .35 = \$14,000$$

2. Compute the deferred tax liability or asset at December 31, 1992. Installment sales that will be collected and thus taxable in 1994 equal $8,000 and the tax rate when this amount is expected to be taxable will be 40%. This gives rise to a deferred tax liability:

$$\begin{bmatrix} \text{Deferred tax liability} \\ \text{related to installment} \\ \text{sale collectible in 1994} \end{bmatrix} = \$8,000 \times .40 = \$3,200$$

---

[3] However, the current deferred tax asset and liability are netted and a current asset or liability reported. The same netting is done for the noncurrent deferred tax asset and liability.

[4] Under proposed *SFAS No. 109*, the form of the equation to determine income tax expense is:

Income tax payable + (or −) Deferred tax amount = Income tax expense

Under *APB No. 11*, the form reflects that the deferred tax amount is the derived amount:

Income tax payable − (or +) Income tax expense = Deferred tax amount

There is $12,000 of prepaid rent that will not be deductible in 1993 (therefore it is a taxable amount in 1993). That is, this amount increases the deferred tax liability because it will increase taxable income relative to pretax accounting income in 1993. This also gives rise to a deferred tax liability:

$$\begin{bmatrix} \text{Deferred tax liability} \\ \text{related to prepaid rent} \\ \text{deducted for tax in 1992} \\ \text{and taxable in 1993} \end{bmatrix} = \$12,000 \times .35 = \$4,200$$

Thus, the total deferred tax liability at December 31, 1992, is $3,200 plus $4,200, or $7,400.

3. Compute the change in the deferred tax liability from the beginning to the end of 1992:

Deferred tax liability at December 31, 1991		$4,200
Deferred tax liability at December 31, 1992:		
Deferred tax related to installment sale	$3,200	
Deferred tax related to prepaid rent	4,200	7,400
Increase in deferred tax liability		$3,200

4. The amount to recognize as income tax expense is the income tax payable arising in the period, plus the net change in the deferred tax account:

Income tax expense:	
Income taxes payable	$14,000
Increase in deferred tax liability	3,200
Income tax expense	$17,200

The journal entry to record income taxes in 1992:

Income tax expense	17,200	
Income taxes payable		14,000
Deferred income taxes		3,200

With this entry, the end-of-period deferred tax balance reported as a liability on the balance sheet will be $7,400 ($4,200 beginning balance plus the $3,200 credited to the account by the above entry).

We now consider the actual application of proposed *SFAS No. 109* in a number of illustrative examples.

COMPUTATION OF INCOME TAXES
♦

The discussion to this point has emphasized the objectives and principles of income tax accounting as required by proposed *SFAS No. 109*. The following discussion gives an approach that can be used in to compute the deferred tax amounts each year, and to provide the journal entry to record income taxes. This approach involves the following five steps:

Step 1: Collect the essential accounting and income tax data for the year. Identify the types and amounts of all temporary differences, the amounts and types of any tax loss carryforwards, and the amounts of any tax credit carryforwards (including the remaining length of the carryforward period).

Step 2: Compute the amount of income taxes payable for the year. It is also useful to reconcile pretax accounting income to taxable income.

Step 3: Compute the total deferred tax liability, based on future taxable amounts at the end of the year and on future enacted tax rates. Compute the total deferred tax asset, based on future deductible amounts at the end of the year and future enacted tax rates. If the tax rate is constant for future periods, scheduling of reversals occur may not be necessary. If there are known, enacted rates for future periods that differ from period to period, it will be necessary to schedule the amounts and periods of future reversals in order to correctly compute the deferred tax asset and liability amounts.

Step 4: Reduce the deferred tax asset by a valuation allowance, if based on the available evidence, there is a greater than 50% probability that some portion of the deferred tax asset will not be realized. ("More likely than not" is operationally interpreted as a greater than 50% probability.)

Step 5: Prepare the journal entry to record income tax payable, changes in the deferred tax asset, liability and valuation allowance amounts, and income tax expense. Income taxes payable is computed on the tax return as taxable income multiplied by the appropriate income tax rate. The remaining amounts can be determined with the following schedule:

	Deferred Tax Asset	Deferred Tax Liability	Valuation Allowance
Ending balance (computed in steps 3 and 4 above)	\$XXX,XXX	(\$XXX,XXX)	(\$XXX,XXX)
Less: Beginning balance (taken from opening balances)	XXX,XXX	(XXX,XXX)	(XXX,XXX)
Adjustment amount	XXX,XXX	XXX,XXX	XXX,XXX

Each account is debited or credited as needed by the adjustment amount, with the other side of the entry made to income tax expense.

The application of these five steps is illustrated in a series of examples. In order to clearly show the use of current and future known enacted tax rates, the following tax rate schedule is assumed for all the following examples:

Year	1992	1993 and Thereafter
Enacted marginal tax rate	30%	40%

Example 1: A Deferred Tax Liability Max Company sells merchandise on credit. In 1992, its first year of operations, pretax accounting income totals \$130,000. This amount includes \$90,000 related to credit sales that have not yet been collected and will not be included in taxable income for the period. Credit sales are the only item giving rise to temporary differences.

Step 1. Collect the essential accounting and income tax data for the year. Identify the types and amounts of all temporary differences, the amounts and types of any tax loss carryforwards, and the amounts of any tax credit carryforwards (including the remaining length of the carryforward period).

Pretax accounting income			\$130,000	
Sources and types of temporary differences:				

	Beginning Balance	Ending Balance	Increase (Decrease)	Type of Difference
Accounts receivable	\$0	\$90,000	\$90,000	Taxable

This schedule provides data on the temporary difference, including the amount affecting the current year difference between pretax accounting and taxable income (the increase or decrease amount) and the total amount that will affect future periods (the ending balance amount). For Max Company with a zero beginning balance, these two amounts are the same.

Step 2: Compute the amount of income taxes payable for the year.

Step 3: Compute the total deferred tax liability, based on future taxable amounts at the end of the year and future enacted tax rates. Compute the total deferred tax asset, based on future deductible amounts at the end of the year and future enacted tax rates.

Steps 2 and 3 can be performed together on one schedule:

Schedule: Temporary Differences, Taxes Payable, and Deferred Tax Balances

	Current Year 1992	Future Years	Effect on Future Years' Income	
			1993 and Thereafter: Deductible	1993 and Thereafter: Taxable
Pretax accounting income (loss)	$130,000			
Temporary differences:				
Credit sales	($90,000)	$90,000	$0	$90,000
Net taxable income	$40,000			
Total temporary differences		$90,000	$0	$90,000
Marginal tax rate	0.30		0.40	0.40
Taxes currently payable	$ 12,000			
Deferred tax asset balance, December 31, 1992			$0	
Deferred tax liability balance, December 31, 1992				$36,000

Step 4: Reduce the deferred tax asset by a valuation allowance if, based on the available evidence, there is a greater than 50% probability that some portion of the deferred tax asset will not be realized.

There is no deferred tax asset in this example, thus no valuation allowance is needed.

Step 5: Prepare the journal entry to record income tax payable, changes in the deferred tax asset, liability, and valuation allowance amounts, and income tax expense.

A schedule such as the following is useful for computing the change amounts for the three accounts:

	Deferred Tax Asset*	Deferred Tax Liability*	Valuation Allowance*
Ending balance (computed in steps 3 and 4 above)	$0	($36,000)	($0)
Less: Beginning balance (taken from opening balances)	0	(0)	(0)
Adjustment amount	$0	($36,000)	$0

* Debit (credit)

With this information and the income tax payable amount of $12,000 computed in the above schedule, the journal entry to record income taxes is:

Income tax expense 48,000		
Deferred income tax liability	36,000	
Income tax payable	12,000	

The deferred tax liability is computed using the marginal tax rate enacted for the future period when the liability will be realized, not the current rate. Also, the income tax expense is a residual amount, composed of the amount of income tax payable for the period, plus the change in the deferred tax amounts.

Example 2: A Deferred Tax Asset and a Deferred Tax Liability Suppose the Max Company of Example 1 has the same credit sales as shown in that problem for its first year of operations, but that it also records as an expense a provision for warranty costs of $30,000. This amount is expensed for financial reporting in 1992 but is not deductible for tax purposes until incurred. However, $10,000 of warranty costs are incurred in 1992. Pretax accounting income is $100,000.

Step 1. Collect the essential accounting and income tax data for the year.

Pretax accounting income $100,000
Temporary differences:

Account	Beginning Balance	Ending Balance	Increase (Decrease)	Type of Difference
Accounts receivable	$0	$90,000	$90,000	Taxable
Provison for warranty costs	0	(20,000)	20,000	Deductible

Warranty costs of $30,000 were expensed for financial reporting, and incurred in the amount of $10,000. The $10,000 amount is deductible for tax purposes in 1992, but the remaining $20,000 is a future deductible amount.

Step 2: Compute the amount of income taxes payable for the year.

Step 3: Compute the total deferred tax liability, based on future taxable amounts at the end of the year and future enacted tax rates. Compute the total deferred tax asset, based on future deductible amounts at the end of the year and future enacted tax rates.

Schedule: Temporary Differences, Taxes Payable, and Deferred Tax Balances

	Current Year 1992	Future Years	Effect on Future Years' Income	
			1993 and Thereafter: Deductible	1993 and Thereafter: Taxable
Pretax accounting income (loss)	$100,000			
Temporary differences:				
Credit sales	($90,000)	$90,000	$0	$90,000
Warranty costs	$20,000	($20,000)	$20,000	
Net taxable income	$30,000			
Total temporary differences		$70,000	$20,000	$90,000
Marginal tax rate	0.30		0.40	0.40
Taxes currently payable	$9,000			
Deferred tax asset balance, December 31, 1992			$ 8,000	
Deferred tax liability balance, December 31, 1992				$36,000

Future deductible amounts are not netted against the taxable amounts to determine a net deductible or taxable amount. At this point it is not necessary to schedule when the reversals occur. This is the case so long as the firm expects to realize the benefit of the deferred tax asset through the generation of taxable income in the future. If the firm is not likely to have taxable income in the future other than that resulting from future taxable amounts, then a scheduling of the reversals of the deductible and taxable amounts would be completed. This is in fact the procedures used in *SFAS No. 96.* This issue is covered in the appendix.

Step 4: Reduce the deferred tax asset by a valuation allowance if, based on the available evidence, there is a greater than 50% probability that some portion of the deferred tax asset will not be realized.

The issue is whether the deferred tax asset of $8,000 is likely to be realized as a future benefit of the firm. In a later section, the procedure is presented for determining whether a valuation allowance is needed. For the moment it is assumed that the deferred tax asset is expected to be realized, hence no valuation allowance is needed.

Step 5: Prepare the journal entry to record income tax payable, changes in the deferred tax asset, liability, and valuation allowance amounts, and income tax expense.

	Deferred Tax Asset*	Deferred Tax Liability*	Valuation Allowance*
Ending balance (computed in steps 3 and 4 above)	$8,000	($36,000)	($0)
Less: Beginning balance (taken from operating balances)	0	(0)	(0)
Adjustment amount	$8,000	($36,000)	$0

* Debit (credit)

With this information and the income tax payable amount of $9,000 computed in the above schedule, the journal entry to record income taxes is:

Income tax expense	37,000	
Deferred tax asset	8,000	
Deferred income tax liability		36,000
Income tax payable		9,000

Example 3: Max Company, Year 2 Suppose Max Company has a year of operations as described above in Example 2. The Company makes the above entry to record income taxes in 1992. In 1993, the company continues to sell on credit, and to warranty its products. Credit sales in 1993 total $120,000 and warranty expense is $40,000. Collections on credit sales in 1993 total $50,000, and actual warranty costs incurred total $15,000. Pretax accounting income totals $80,000 for 1993.

Step 1: Collect the essential accounting and income tax data for the year.

Pretax accounting income $80,000
Temporary differences:

	Beginning Balance	Ending Balance	Increase (Decrease)	Type of Difference
Accounts receivable	$90,000	$160,000*	$70,000	Taxable
Provision for warranty costs	(20,000)	(45,000)†	25,000	Deductible

* $90,000 + $120,000 − $50,000
† $20,000 + $40,000 − $15,000

The increase(decrease) column amounts are useful in reconciling pretax accounting income to taxable income in the current year. For example, pretax accounting income is $70,000 greater than taxable income in 1992 because of the increase in the accounts receivable. At the end of 1992, however, there is a total of $160,000 in future taxable amounts related to the accounts receivable. This latter amount is used to compute the amount of the deferred tax liability at the end of the 1992.

Step 2: Compute the amount of income taxes payable for the year.
Step 3: Compute the total deferred tax liability, based on future taxable amounts at the end of the year and future enacted tax rates. Compute the total deferred tax asset, based on future deductible amounts at the end of the year and future enacted tax rates.

Schedule: Temporary Differences, Taxes Payable, and Deferred Tax Balances

	Current Year 1993	Future Years	Effect on Future Years' Income 1994 and Thereafter: Deductible	1994 and Thereafter: Taxable
Pretax accounting income (loss)	$80,000			
Temporary differences:				
Credit sales	($70,000)	$160,000	$0	$160,000
Warranty costs	$25,000	($45,000)	$45,000	
Net taxable income	$35,000			
Total temporary differences		$115,000	$45,000	$160,000
Marginal tax rate	0.40		0.40	0.40
Taxes currently payable	$14,000			
Deferred tax asset balance, December 31, 1993			$18,000	
Deferred tax liability balance, December 31, 1993				$ 64,000

Step 4: Reduce the deferred tax asset by a valuation allowance if, based on the available evidence, there is a greater than 50% probability that some portion of the deferred tax asset will not be realized.

The issue is whether the deferred tax asset of $18,000 is likely to be realized as a future benefit of the firm. Without getting into the details of how the valuation allowance is determined, assume it is determined that $6,000 of the deferred tax is "more likely than not" to expire and not be realized. A valuation allowance of $6,000 must be recorded.

Step 5: Prepare the journal entry to record income tax payable, changes in the deferred tax asset, liability, and valuation allowance amounts, and income tax expense.

	Deferred Tax Asset*	Deferred Tax Liability*	Valuation Allowance*
Ending balance (computed in steps 3 and 4 above)	$18,000	($64,000)	($6,000)
Less: Beginning balance (taken from operating balances)	$ 8,000	(36,000)	(0)
Adjustment amount	$10,000	($28,000)	($6,000)

* Debit (credit)

With this information and the income tax payable amount of $14,000 computed in the above schedule, the journal entry to record income taxes is:

Income tax expense	38,000	
Deferred tax asset	10,000	
Valuation allowance		6,000
Deferred income tax liability		28,000
Income tax payable		14,000

The above three examples illustrate the basic procedures for computing income tax expense. The procedures also demonstrate how income tax expense for a period is determined indirectly. It is the sum of taxes payable and the change in deferred tax asset, deferred tax liability, and valuation allowance amounts for the period. Each of these items is computed directly.

CONCEPT REVIEW

1. What is a future taxable amount? What is a future deductible amount? Why are they important in determining income tax expense?
2. How are deferred tax assets and liabilities determined?
3. If the likelihood of a deferred tax asset being realized is less than 50%, what entry must be made?

A Limitation on Deferred Tax Assets

In order to realize the benefit of a deferred tax asset, either there must be future taxable income against which taxes payable can be offset by the deferred tax asset or it must be possible to obtain a refund of previously paid taxes. Given this requirement, *SFAS No. 96* specified a rigid limit on the amount of deferred tax asset that could be recorded. Only the amount that was certain to be realized could be recorded. The firm could not assume it would have taxable income in the future other than that from future reversals of taxable temporary differences. The benefit of the deferred tax asset would be realized from the use of tax loss carrybacks and carryforwards to offset income taxes on the future taxable amounts. The determination of whether the deferred tax asset will be realized involves extensive analysis of when reversals would occur and how they could be carried back or forward to realize the benefit of the deferred tax asset. The appendix to this chapter covers this form of analysis. There are times such analysis will be needed under proposed *SFAS No. 109*, but the frequency of such analysis is expected to be greatly reduced under the proposed *Statement*.

The proposed *SFAS No. 109* also provides for possible limitations on the net amount of deferred tax asset that is recorded. However, the procedure for determining whether a deferred tax asset is to be reduced is much different than that under *SFAS No. 96*. What follows is an explanation of the limitation as it is determined under proposed *SFAS No. 109*.

Paragraph 21 of proposed *SFAS No. 109* states:

Future realization of the tax benefit of an existing deductible temporary difference or carryforward ultimately depends on the existence of sufficient taxable income of the appropriate character (for example, ordinary income or capital gain) within the carryback, carryforward period available under the tax law. The following sources of taxable income may be available under the tax law to realize a tax benefit for deductible temporary differences and carryforwards:

a. Future reversals of existing taxable temporary differences
b. Future taxable income exclusive of reversing temporary differences and carryforwards
c. Taxable income in prior carryback year(s) if carryback is permitted under the tax law
d. Tax-planning strategies that would, if necessary, be implemented to, for example:
  (1) Accelerate taxable amounts to utilize expiring carryforwards
  (2) Change the character of taxable or deductible amounts from ordinary income or loss to capital gain or loss
  (3) Switch from tax-exempt to taxable investments.

Essentially, *SFAS No. 96* allowed the recording of a deferred tax asset only when sources *a, c,* and *d* explicitly demonstrated that the benefit of the deferred tax asset will be realized. Proposed *SFAS No. 109* introduces item *b*, which allows the firm to consider expected future taxable income from its operations and other sources (for example, capital gains) in determining whether the benefit of a deferred tax asset is likely to be realized.

Ignoring for the moment the use of tax-planning strategies, there are three sources of future taxable income that can be considered in determining whether a deferred tax asset is likely to be realized. Each source is considered in an abstract setting before getting into the details.

For simplicity in this illustration, assume the tax laws allow a three-year carry-back and a six-year carryforward of NOLs. Suppose that the current year is year 3, and a firm's past and expected future taxable income amounts, and reversals of deductible or taxable temporary differences in future years are as shown:

| | | | | | Year | | | | |
| | | | Current Year | | | | | | |
Item	1	2	3	4	5	6	7	8	9
Taxable income exclusive of reversals and carryforwards	T1	T2	T3	ET4	ET5	ET6	ET7	ET8	ET9
Deductible temporary diff.				D4	D5	D6		D8	
Taxable temporary diff.				T4	T5		T7		T9

T1, T2, and T3 are actual taxable income amounts on which taxes have been paid, and ET4, ET5, etc., are estimates of future taxable income amounts exclusive of any reversals of temporary differences or carryforwards. The D4, D5, etc., and T4, T5, etc. amounts are deductible or taxable amounts expected to reverse in the year given. In this illustration there are deductible temporary differences expected to reverse in years 4, 5, 6 and 8, and taxable temporary differences expected to reverse in years 4, 5, 7 and 9. The deductible temporary differences give rise to a deferred tax asset, and the taxable temporary differences give rise to a deferred tax liability.

Paragraph 17 of the proposed *SFAS No. 109* requires that realization of the benefit of the deferred tax asset be more likely than not, using the sources of income identified in paragraph 21 (quoted above), to determine whether sufficient taxable income will be available to realize the benefit of the deferred tax asset. If the realization of the benefit is not more likely than not, a valuation allowance must be established to reduce the net amount of the deferred tax asset to the amount that is more likely than not to be realized. Consider the three sources of taxable income listed above.

Source 1: Future reversals of existing taxable temporary differences—items T4, T5, T7 and T9. In order for this source (by itself) to meet the criteria for not requiring a valuation allowance to be recorded, the sum of T4, T5, T7 and T9 would have to be greater the sum of the future deductible amounts, D4, D5, D6 and D8. If this is the case, and the various deductible amounts could be carried back or forward to the years the taxable temporary differences reverse and generate taxable income, then the tax benefit of the deductible amounts will be realized. The deductible amounts would offset an equal taxable amount, thereby realizing the benefit of the deferred tax asset. If the sum of the taxable amounts is less than deductible amounts (or the taxable amount reversals occur so far in the future that the deductible amounts cannot be carried forward to them), then other sources of taxable income would be needed to realize the benefit of the deferred tax asset.

Source 2: Future taxable income exclusive of reversing temporary differences and carryforwards—items ET4 through ET9. The firm has an expectation of future taxable income exclusive of the temporary differences and any carryforwards as shown by ET4 through ET9. Assume these are the sources of future taxable income. The expectations for these amounts must total to greater than the sum of the future deductible amounts in order to assure the realizability of the deferred tax asset. When such estimates are made, they can provide the basis for expecting that the deferred tax asset will be realized. *SFAS No. 96* did not allow estimates of future taxable income to support the recording of deferred tax assets. Proposed *SFAS No.*

109 explicitly requires estimates of future taxable income be considered. This is a major difference between *SFAS No. 96* and proposed *SFAS No. 109*.

Source 3: Taxable income in prior carryback year(s) if carryback is permitted under the tax law—items T1 through T3. Assume that carryback is permitted for three years. For the moment disregard future taxable income and reversals of taxable temporary differences. The future deductible amounts in periods D4, D5, and D6, can be carried back to the current and earlier periods (subject to the provisions of the carryback laws) in order to realize the benefit of the deferred tax asset. Suppose, for example, the sum of D4, D5, and D6 is less than the current period taxable income, T3. Then the benefit is reasonably assured for these three periods since the carryback feature for NOLs can be used if the future deductible amounts are the only tax item in the three future periods. If these deductible amounts are the only item in taxable income in the future periods, they become NOLs. However, the D8 amount cannot be carried back because it occurs five periods in the future, and the carryback limit is three periods. If there are no other sources of taxable income (estimates of future taxable income are zero in all periods and T7 and T9 are also zero), then a valuation allowance would be needed for the deferred tax asset arising from D8.

Tax-planning strategies provide an additional procedure that can be implemented in order to realize the benefit of a deferred tax asset. This topic is covered in a later section of this chapter. First the above sources of taxable income are illustrated as ways to determine whether the deferred tax asset is "more likely than not" to be realized.

Example 4 The Lake Company has the following results of operations at December 31, 1991:

1. Pretax accounting income in 1991, its first year of operations, totals $100,000. Taxable income is $90,000.
2. Lake Company has credit sales included in pretax accounting income totaling $60,000, none of which is included in taxable income. This amount will be included in taxable income in future years.
3. The firm expensed in its financial statements $50,000 as a provision for future warranty costs in 1991. This amount was not deductible for tax purposes in 1991; but will be deductible in future years.
4. The enacted marginal tax rate for 1991 and all future years is 30%.

The determination of deferred tax assets and liabilities proceeds using the five steps outlined earlier.

Step 1: Identify and collect the essential accounting and income tax data for the year. A format like the following can be used to schedule the various information items:

	1991	Future Years	Effect on Future Taxable Income: Deductible	Taxable
Pretax accounting income	$100,000			
Temporary differences:				
Credit sales	(60,000)	$60,000		$60,000
Warranties	50,000	(50,000)	$50,000	
Taxable income	$ 90,000			

The first column labeled 1991 is used to identify temporary differences occurring in the current year that cause pretax accounting income to differ from taxable income. It is useful to reconcile pretax accounting income to taxable income, and then to compute taxes currently payable. The Future Years column identifies the full amount of all existing temporary differences. These amounts are carried forward to the appropriate "taxable" or "deductible" column. These last two columns are summed to determine the total future taxable and deductible amounts.

Steps 2 and 3: Compute the amount of income taxes payable for the year. Compute the end-of-period deferred tax asset and deferred tax liability amounts.

The amounts under the Deductible and the Taxable columns are the total amounts of temporary differences existing at the end of the period. The deductible column gives rise to an end-of-period deferred tax asset amount, and the taxable column gives rise to an end-of-period deferred tax liability amount:

	1991	Future Years	Effect on Future Taxable Income: Deductible	Taxable
Pretax accounting income	$100,000			
Temporary differences:				
Credit sales	(60,000)	60,000		$60,000
Warranties	50,000	(50,000)	$50,000	
Taxable income	$ 90,000			
Total deductible			$50,000	
Total taxable				$60,000
Times: Marginal tax rate	× .30		× .30	× .30
Taxes payable	$ 27,000			
Deferred tax asset, 12/31/91			$15,000	
Deferred tax liability, 12/31/91				$18,000

The income taxes payable are computed as $27,000, and the gross amounts of deferred tax assets and deferred tax liabilities are $15,000 and $18,000, respectively.

Step 4: Reduce the deferred tax assets by a valuation allowance, if necessary.

At this point the analysis considers whether the benefit of the deferred tax asset is "more likely than not" to be realized. It would appear that any of the three possible sources of taxable income may well be available to make the likelihood greater than 50–50 that the benefit will be realized. For the moment assume future taxable income exclusive of temporary differences is expected to be greater than $50,000 for the foreseeable future. If this is the case the future taxable income exceeds the future deductible amount and the benefit is likely to be realized.

Step 5: Prepare the journal entry to record income taxes payable, deferred tax asset and liability amounts, valuation allowance (if necessary), and income tax expense.

First, the change in the deferred tax asset and liability accounts must be determined, since the above computation determines the end-of-period amounts. Because this is the first year of operations for Lake Company, the beginning-of-period balances are zero:

	Deferred Tax Asset	Deferred Tax Liability
End-of-period balance (computed above)	$15,000	$(18,000)
Less: Beginning-of-period balance, (taken from beginning-of-period balance sheet)	0	0
Debit (credit) to be made to account:	$15,000	$(18,000)

Finally, the amount to be recorded as income tax is the sum of the income taxes payable, plus the increase in the deferred tax liability, less the increase in the deferred tax asset:

Computation of income tax expense:
Income taxes payable	$27,000
Increase (decrease) in deferred tax liability	18,000
(Increase) decrease in deferred tax asset	(15,000)
Income tax expense in 1991	$30,000

The journal entry to record income taxes for Lake Company in 1991 is:

Income tax expense	30,000	
Deferred tax asset	15,000	
Income taxes payable		27,000
Deferred tax liability		18,000

Example 5 The Lake Company described in Example 4 continues operations in 1992, with the following activities and results:

1. Pretax accounting income in 1992 totals $180,000. This includes $100,000 of installment sales that are not included in taxable income. Collections during 1992 of prior years installment sales totals $30,000.
2. Included in expenses for financial reporting are estimated warranty costs of $120,000. Warranty costs actually incurred during 1992 total $10,000.
3. On January 1, 1992, Lake Company purchases machinery at a cost of $100,000. The machinery has a five year estimated useful life with zero salvage value. Straight line depreciation will be used for financial reporting. For tax reporting, the machinery will be depreciated in the amounts of $45,000, $35,000 and $20,000 in 1992, 1993, and 1994, respectively.
4. Lake Company sublets a portion of its warehouse to another company and requires rent to be paid in advance. Lake has received an advanced rent payment of $20,000. This amount is included in taxable income in 1992, but will be included in pretax accounting income in 1993.
5. During 1992 a new tax law is enacted, raising the marginal tax rate to 35% beginning January 1, 1993.

This example has several complications over Example 4. The analysis that is needed, however, is the same as before. The five steps presented earlier provide the structure for the analysis.

Step 1: Identify and collect the essential accounting and income tax data for the year.

Consider the credit sales activity of Lake Company. Lake began the year with a taxable temporary difference of $60,000 (this is the amount in the credit sales receivable account). This amount is increased by credit sales of $100,000 during the period, and is decreased by collections of $30,000. The difference between the amount included in pretax accounting income ($100,000) and the amount collected ($30,000) is the amount ($70,000) which must be deducted from pretax accounting income to determine taxable income (ignoring for the moment other temporary differences). The ending balance in the credit sales receivable account is $60,000 plus $100,000, less collections of $30,000, or $130,000. This is the amount of temporary difference that will reverse in future years. A schedule computing the current period effect and the total effect of the temporary difference arising from the installment sales activities of Lake Company is:

Installment sales receivables:		Debit (Credit)
Balance, January 1, 1992		$ 60,000
Add: Installment sales in 1992	100,000	
Deduct: Collections of receivables in 1992	(30,000)	
Amount pretax accounting income is greater than (less than) taxable income in 1992		$ 70,000
Balance, December 31, 1992 (a temporary difference)		$130,000

The $130,000 has been included in pretax accounting in the current and past periods but not in taxable income. It will be taxable income in future years.

The change in the provision for warranty costs liability account can be similarly analyzed:

Estimated warranty liability:		Debit (Credit)
Balance, January 1, 1992		$(50,000)
Add: Warranty expenses in 1992	(120,000)	
Deduct: Warranty costs incurred in 1992	10,000	
Amount pretax accounting income is greater than (less than) taxable income in 1992		(110,000)
Balance, December 31, 1992 (a temporary difference)		$(160,000)

The balance in the provision for warranties account at December 31, 1992, is a future deductible amount. This balance has been deducted from pretax accounting income in the current and prior years, and will be deducted from taxable income in future years.

The information from the above two schedules can be entered into the schedule used to determine taxable income and various future deductible and taxable temporary differences:

	1992	Future Years	Effect on Future Taxable Income:	
			Deductible	Taxable
Pretax accounting income	$180,000			
Temporary differences:				
Credit sales	(70,000)	130,000		130,000
Warranties	110,000	(160,000)	160,000	

The current year column (1992) shows the temporary differences arising in the current year, and the future years column shows the reversal effects of all temporary differences that exist at December 31, 1992.

The depreciation differences between book and tax reporting in 1992 totals $25,000 ($45,000 of depreciation for tax, less $20,000 of depreciation for book). However, the depreciation schedules for book and tax show that tax depreciation for 1993 also will exceed book depreciation ($35,000 for tax and $20,000 for book). This item by itself will cause taxable income in 1993 to be $15,000 less than pretax accounting income. That is, it is like a future deductible amount—it will reduce taxable income relative to pretax accounting income in 1993. In 1994, tax and book depreciation are the same ($20,000). In 1995 and 1996 reversal occurs, creating a taxable amount of $20,000 in each year.

At this point the schedule reconciling pretax accounting income and taxable income, and identifying deductible and taxable amounts is as follows:

	1992	Future Years	Effect on Future Taxable Income:	
			Deductible	Taxable
Pretax accounting income	$180,000			
Temporary differences:				
Credit sales	(70,000)	130,000		130,000
Warranties	110,000	(160,000)	160,000	
Depreciation	(25,000)	25,000	15,000	40,000*

* $20,000 each in 1995 and 1996.

The final item to be considered is the advanced rent payment which Lake received in the amount of $20,000. This amount is included in taxable income in 1992, but not included in pretax accounting income until 1993. This item creates a deductible difference because it causes pretax accounting income to be greater than taxable income in the future.

A procedure or guideline is useful for determining whether temporary difference items give rise to future deductible or taxable amounts. The combinations of possible answers to the following two questions provide a guide as to the future tax consequences of the item:

Example	Question One: How will this item affect pretax accounting income in future years?	Question Two: How will this item affect taxable income in future years?	Future Tax Consequence
Credit sales	a. No effect	Increase	Taxable
Warranty cost	b. No effect	Decrease	Deductible
Advances from customers	c. Increase	No effect	Deductible
Prepaid expenses	d. Decrease	No effect	Taxable

The term *deductible* normally implies that an item will be deductible for tax purposes in future years, causing taxable income to be reduced relative to pretax accounting income. However, the same result occurs when an item is added to pretax accounting income but not taxable income in future years (such as an advance from customers that is included in financial reporting revenue in future years). This is the more general meaning that will be attached to the term deductible in the analysis of future income tax effects.

A more general form of the above guideline is:

If a temporary difference causes future taxable income to be:

a. *Greater* than future pretax accounting income, then it is a *taxable* temporary difference.

b. *Less* than future pretax accounting income, then it is a *deductible* temporary difference.

The schedule reconciling pretax accounting income with taxable income and identifying all the various deductible and taxable amounts at the end of 1992 is as follows:

	1992	Future Years	Effect on Future Taxable Income: Deductible	Effect on Future Taxable Income: Taxable
Pretax accounting income	$180,000			
Temporary differences:				
Credit sales	(70,000)	130,000		$130,000
Warranties	110,000	(160,000)	$160,000	
Depreciation	(25,000)	25,000	15,000	40,000
Rent received in advance	20,000	(20,000)	20,000	
Taxable income	$215,000			
Total deductible amounts			$195,000	
Total taxable amounts				$170,000

Steps 2 and 3: Compute the amount of income taxes payable for the year. Compute the end-of-period deferred tax asset and deferred tax liability amounts.

The computation of income taxes payable and of deferred tax asset and deferred tax liability ending balance amounts is straight forward once the above schedule is completed. Remember to use the enacted marginal tax rate for the relevant periods. In this example, the rate is 30% for 1992 and 35% for all subsequent years.

	1992	Future Years	Effect on Future Taxable Income: Deductible	Effect on Future Taxable Income: Taxable
Pretax accounting income	$180,000			
Temporary differences				
Credit sales	(70,000)	130,000		$130,000
Warranties	110,000	(160,000)	$160,000	
Depreciation	(25,000)	25,000	15,000	40,000
Rent received in advance	20,000	(20,000)	20,000	
Taxable income	$215,000			
Total deductible amounts			$195,000	
Total taxable amounts				$170,000
Marginal tax rate	× .30		× .35	× .35
Taxes payable	$ 64,500			
Deferred tax asset, 12/31/92			$ 68,250	
Deferred tax liability, 12/31/92				$ 59,500

Step 4: Reduce the deferred tax assets by a valuation allowance, if necessary.

Suppose Lake Company management is not confident it will be able to generate taxable income from sources exclusive of the reversals of taxable temporary differences. That is, suppose Lake estimates future taxable income for all periods is zero. Further assume that the reversals of the future deductible amounts occur more than three periods in the future (thus carryback procedures to the current period cannot be used to obtain the benefit of the deferred tax asset). However, assume that the future reversals of taxable amounts can be used to realize at least that amount of the deferred tax asset benefit. The excess of the deferred tax asset over the deferred tax liability, however, has a less than .5 probability of being realized. If this is the case, then Lake Company must recognize a valuation allowance for the difference:

Deferred tax asset ending balance, gross	$68,250
Amount more likely than not to be realized	59,500
Amount of valuation allowance required at December 31, 1992	$ 8,750
Less: Amount of valuation allowance at January 1, 1992	0
Increase (decrease) in valuation allowance for the period	$ 8,750

Had there been a beginning balance in the valuation allowance account, the change in the amount for the period is the amount to be included in the income tax expense computation. If the amount at the beginning of the period is greater than determined to be needed at the end of the period, income tax expense will be reduced by the difference.

Step 5: Prepare the journal entry to record income taxes payable, deferred tax asset and liability amounts, valuation allowance (if necessary), and income tax expense.

The change in the deferred tax asset and liability accounts must be determined:

	Deferred Tax Asset	Deferred Tax Liability
End-of-period (computed above)	$68,250	$(59,500)
Less: Beginning-of-period balance, (taken from beginning-of-period balance sheet)	15,000	(18,000)
Debit (credit) change in account balance	$53,250	$(41,500)

The amount to be recorded as income tax expense is the sum of the income taxes payable, plus the increase in the deferred tax liability, less the increase in the deferred tax asset, plus the increase in the valuation allowance:

```
Computation of income tax expense:
  Income taxes payable  . . . . . . . . . . . . . . . . . . $64,500
  Increase (decrease) in deferred tax liability  . . . . . .  41,500
  (Increase) decrease in deferred tax asset . . . . . . . . (53,250)
  Increase (decrease) in the valuation allowance  . . . . .   8,750
  Income tax expense in 1992 . . . . . . . . . . . . . . . $61,500
```

The journal entry to record income taxes for Lake Company in 1992 is:

```
Income tax expense . . . . . . . . . . . . . . . . . . . . . . . . 61,500
Deferred tax asset . . . . . . . . . . . . . . . . . . . . . . . . 53,250
  Income taxes payable . . . . . . . . . . . . . . . . . . .         64,500
  Deferred tax liability . . . . . . . . . . . . . . . . . . .        41,500
  Valuation allowance . . . . . . . . . . . . . . . . . . . .          8,750
```

Determination Whether a Valuation Allowance Is Needed

A valuation allowance is required when, based on available evidence, it is *more likely than not* that some portion (or all) of the deferred tax asset will not be realized. A firm must consider all available evidence, both positive and negative, to make the determination. Such evidence includes:
* Information about a firm's current financial position.
* Information about a firm's results of operations for the current and preceding years.
* Information about a firm's future operations.

If a firm has a recent history of several years of losses, this is strong tangible evidence that will make it difficult to conclude that a valuation allowance is not needed. Other negative evidence includes, but is not limited to, the following:
* A history of operating loss carryforwards that expire unused.
* Losses expected in future years.
* Circumstances that if unfavorably resolved, would adversely affect future operations.
* A remaining carryback or carryforward period that is so short as to be of limited use in realizing tax benefits if a large deductible temporary difference is expected to reverse in a single year, or if the firm operates in a highly cyclical business.

Positive evidence that a valuation allowance is not needed includes the following:
* A history of profitability with positive taxable income.
* Existing contracts or firm sales backlog that will produce more than enough taxable income to realize the deferred tax asset.
* An excess of appreciated asset value over the tax basis of the assets sufficiently large to realize the deferred tax asset.

Each of the above items provides information useful for estimating future taxable income. If the amount expected for future taxable income is sufficiently large to realize the deferred tax asset, no valuation allowance is needed. If it is not, it is still possible that a valuation allowance will not be required. If the deductible temporary difference that is creating the deferred tax asset is to reverse soon enough such that it can be carried to the current and prior years to realize the benefit, then no valuation allowance is required. Also, if the future reversals of taxable temporary differences occur such that they can offset deductible temporary differences by carryback and carryforward procedures, and the taxable temporary differences are large enough to cause the deferred tax assets to be realized, then no valuation allowance is needed. Finally, if there are prudent and feasible tax-planning strategies which a firm could implement to prevent an operating loss or tax credit carryforward from expiring, or which in general would result in the realization of the deferred tax asset, then again a valuation allowance is not needed.

Strong positive evidence from any one of the possible sources is sufficient to support a conclusion that a valuation allowance is not necessary. If such evidence is available from one source, other sources need not be considered. Thus, a firm with a history of strong profitability need not consider the other three sources of evidence, assuming it is more likely than not that it will generate sufficient taxable income from sources exclusive of the temporary differences to realize the benefits of the deferred tax assets.

An important aspect of *SFAS No. 109* is that conclusive evidence of realizability is not required as was true of prior GAAP standards. *SFAS No. 109* uses the phrase "more likely than not" in referring to the strength of evidence required. Thus, the requirement is that a firm must conclude there is a better than 50–50 chance that the benefit will be realized in order to avoid recording a valuation allowance. Alternatively, if there is a 50–50 or less chance that the deferred tax asset will be realized, then a valuation allowance must be recorded.

Tax-Planning Strategies

In the normal course of business, a firm's management undertakes many actions, pursues strategies, and makes elections that are designed to minimize the firm's long-run tax obligation. For example, a firm might structure its credit sales activities such that they qualify as installment sales for tax purposes, allowing the deferral of a taxable revenue until cash is received. While this is a kind of tax-planning strategy in the normal or traditional sense, it is not the meaning of the term as intended by *SFAS No. 109.* For purposes of *SFAS No. 109,* a **tax-planning strategy** is an action:

+ That would result in the realization of deferred tax assets.
+ The firm might not take in the ordinary course of business, but would be expected to take to prevent an operating loss or tax credit carryforward from expiring unused.
+ That is prudent and feasible. That is, management must have the ability to implement the strategy and be expected to do so unless the need to do is eliminated.

Tax planning strategies can assist in the realization of deferred tax assets in a number of different ways. For example, a tax-planning strategy might shift future taxable income between future years. A firm facing a need for taxable income to realize the benefit of deferred tax assets might structure its sales contracts such that they can be included in taxable income in the current period rather than being deferred. Other actions of this nature include changing depreciation schedules and procedures for tax purposes, thereby increasing taxable income in the current year. A firm might even change from the LIFO to FIFO inventory method in order to shift taxable income from one period to another.

Alternatively, tax-planning strategies might shift the pattern and timing of future reversal of temporary differences in ways that result in the deferred tax assets being realized. Factoring or selling installment sales receivables accelerates the future reversal of a taxable temporary difference to the period of the sale. Accelerating the reversal of future deductible temporary differences might be an appropriate action in some circumstances. For example, disposing of obsolete inventory that is reported at net realizable value for book purposes (and at historical cost for tax purposes) would accelerate a tax deduction for the amount of the difference.

A firm might incur a significant expense or incur a significant loss as a result of implementing a tax-planning strategy. The expense or loss reduces the net benefit realized from the tax-planning strategy. The actual amount of the expense or loss is not important so long as the criteria listed above are met. The amount of benefit from the deferred tax asset must be greater than the expense or loss, otherwise the tax-planning strategy would not be prudent.

Example Suppose the Tasha Company has an operating tax loss carryforward of $10,000 that will expire on December 31, 1992. The current date is December 31, 1991. The enacted marginal tax rate is 30%, thus the tax loss carryforward results in a deferred tax asset of $3,000 if its realization is more likely than not. Assume the following additional information:

* Management expects taxable income in 1992, exclusive of the operating tax loss carryforward and any reversal of existing temporary differences to be $2,000.
* At December 31, 1991, a taxable temporary difference totaling $9,000 exists from an installment sale. It is expected to reverse in equal amounts for the next three years.
* Tasha could sell the installment accounts receivable to a financing company for cash and accelerate the reversal of the taxable temporary difference. Tasha would incur legal and other expenses of approximately $1,000 in order to implement this tax-planning strategy.

Without implementing the tax-planning stragegy, Tasha will have taxable income in 1992 of only $5,000 (a reversal of taxable temporary difference of $3,000 resulting from collection of a portion of the installment sale, and the $2,000 of taxable income expected from operations). If this were the case, half of the tax loss carryforward would be used to offset taxes payable, but the remaining $5,000 of tax loss carryforward will expire unused. If there were no tax-planning strategy available, Tasha would have to record a valuation allowance of $5,000 times 30%, or $1,500 to reflect the amount of the deferred tax asset not expected to be realized.

However, if Tasha could implement the tax-planning strategy described above, enough taxable income would be generated in 1992 to fully use the tax loss carryforward. The full amount of the installment sale ($9,000) plus the regularly expected taxable income ($2,000) is more than enough to offset the tax loss carryforward. However, the cost of implementing the tax-planning strategy is $1,000, which on an after-tax basis is a cost of $700. Given the tax-planning strategy meets all the criteria listed above, it can be used as a plan to realize the deferred tax asset benefit. However, its after-tax cost of $700 must be recorded as a valuation allowance, since it will have to be incurred if the tax-planning strategy is implemented. The net gain from the tax-planning strategy is $800, which is the difference between the valuation allowance without the strategy ($1,500) and with the strategy ($700). Assuming the tax-planning strategy is used in planning for the realization of the deferred tax asset, Tasha would report the following in its December 31, 1991 financial statements:

* A deferred tax liability of $2,700—relating to the taxable temporary difference of $9,000.
* A deferred tax asset of $3,000—relating to the tax loss carryforward.
* A valuation allowance of $700—relating to the after-tax expense that would be incurred to implement the tax-planning strategy.
* Income tax expense for 1991 would include the $700 amount that was recorded as a valuation allowance.

CONCEPT REVIEW

1. What is a valuation allowance? When is one required?
2. Do taxable temporary differences give rise to deferred tax assets or deferred tax liabilities? What about deductible temporary differences?
3. What is a tax-planning strategy? When is one considered?

INVESTMENT TAX CREDIT (ITC)

The **investment tax credit (ITC)** is an income tax provision implemented from time to time by the Federal government to encourage investments in new productive assets such as plant and equipment. First enacted as part of the federal tax regulations in

1962, it has been repealed and restored seven times in the past 30 years. Prior to its repeal in the Tax Reform Act of 1986, the law provided that taxpayers could receive a 10% tax credit as a direct offset to income tax payable. The tax credit was important because it reduced income tax payable in the year of purchase of qualified assets by 10% of the cost. Also, the ITC did not reduce the tax basis of the asset to which it applied. A tax credit, as opposed to a tax deduction, results in a direct dollar-for-dollar tax saving. A tax deduction decreases income tax only by the deduction amount multiplied by the income tax rate.

The first investment tax credit was provided by the Revenue Act of 1962. Its provisions were revised by the 1964 act, suspended in 1966, and restored in 1967. The Revenue Act of 1978 set the credit permanently at 10% of the cost of qualifying property; however, the Tax Reform Act of 1986 again suspended the ITC. Accounting rules for the ITC have been issued and are still in effect. Because the financial statements of many companies still report deferred investment tax credits, and it is reasonable to expect the ITC to be restored at some future time, the accounting standards applicable to the ITC are briefly discussed next.

Two alternative methods are acceptable under GAAP for recording and reporting the ITC:

1. *Flow-through (or current reduction) method.* Under the **flow-through method for ITC,** the full amount of the ITC is recorded and reported as a direct reduction of income tax expense in the period in which the related asset is acquired. Income taxes payable is debited and income tax expense is credited for the amount of the ITC. The full amount of the ITC "flows through" the current period income statement. As a result, it increases the reported income in the period of acquisition on a dollar-for-dollar basis. This method relates the ITC to the purchase, rather than to the use, of the asset.

2. *Deferral (or allocated reduction) method.* Under the **deferral method for ITC,** the total amount of the ITC is recorded (credited) to an account labeled deferred investment tax credit. This account may appear among the liabilities on the balance sheet, or less frequently, as a contra account to the related asset account. The ITC is allocated to each period over the life of the asset as a direct reduction of periodic income tax expense. The ITC amount decreases reported income tax expense over the estimated useful life of the asset which caused it. This method relates the ITC to the use, rather than to the purchase, of the asset.

Example Suppose in 1985 Trans National Airways (TNA) purchased 10 Boeing 747 airplanes for a total purchase price of $400 million, and the purchase qualified for a 10% investment tax credit (ITC). The airplanes have an estimated useful life of 20 years. TNA had taxable income of $200 million in the year of the purchase. The income tax rate was 30%. TNA has no other permanent or temporary differences.

The income tax payable in 1985 by TNA is computed as follows:

Taxable income		$200 million
Tax rate		× .30
Income taxes payable before investment tax credit		$60 million
Less: Investment tax credit:		
Qualified assets acquired	$400 million	
ITC rate	× .10	40 million
Taxes payable (after ITC)		$20 million

There are two alternative methods of accounting for the $40 million of ITC.

A. Flow-through method

1. To record income taxes payable and income tax expense before consideration of the ITC:

```
Income tax expense . . . . . . . . . . . . . . . . . . . . . . 60 million
      Income taxes payable . . . . . . . . . . . . . . . . .              60 million
```

2. To record the ITC:

```
Incomes taxes payable . . . . . . . . . . . . . . . . . . . 40 million
      Income tax expense . . . . . . . . . . . . . . . . . .              40 million
```

The entire amount of the ITC is "flowed through" to reduce income tax expense in the current period.

B. Deferral method

1. To record income taxes payable and income tax expense before consideration of the ITC:

```
Income tax expense . . . . . . . . . . . . . . . . . . . . . . 60 million
      Income taxes payable . . . . . . . . . . . . . . . . .              60 million
```

2. To record the ITC:

```
Income tax payable . . . . . . . . . . . . . . . . . . . . . . 40 million
      Deferred investment tax credit . . . . . . . . . . . .              40 million
```

3. To record the first year of amortization of the deferred ITC:

```
Deferred investment tax credit . . . . . . . . . . . . . . . 2 million
      Income tax expense . . . . . . . . . . . . . . . . . .              2 million
```

For the flow-through method, the entire $40 million is recognized as a reduction of income tax expense in the year in which the ITC arises, thus increasing net income by this amount in the year of the acquisition. Under the deferral method, the ITC is deferred and recognized as a reduction of income tax expense in the amount of $2 million for each year during the airplanes' useful lives.

Accountants generally believe the deferral method to be conceptually preferable. They view the benefit of the ITC (immediate reduction of taxes payable) as attaching to the assets that gave rise to it, not to the period in which the IRS allows the tax reduction. The tax code has generally provided for "recapture" of the ITC if the firm sells the assets which generated the ITC in the immediate (generally within five years) future. Nonetheless, the majority of firms use the flow-through method to account for investment tax credits because it provides an immediate boost to reported earnings.

Even though the ITC is not a part of current tax law, it has been in the recent past and may again be instituted in the future. The recession in the last half of 1991 has several members of Congress considering restoring the ITC.[5] Companies that choose the deferral method for assets with lives extending to the current year will be allocating the ITC to current periods in accordance with the procedures outlined above under the deferral method.

CONCEPT REVIEW

1. How are deferred tax assets and liabilities classified on the balance sheet?
2. What is an investment tax credit and how does it work?
3. What are two methods for accounting for an investment tax credit, and which is the more conservative?

---

[5] *Business Week*, December 16, 1991, p. 31.

FINANCIAL STATEMENT PRESENTATION AND DISCLOSURES

◆

Financial Statement Presentation

Proposed *SFAS No. 109* requires a specific presentation of items related to income taxes. The requirements of *SFAS No. 96* are similar.

Income taxes payable (or income tax refund receivable) are reported as a current liability (current asset) on a classified balance sheet. Deferred tax assets and deferred tax liabilities are separated into a net current amount and a net noncurrent amount for reporting on a classified balance sheet. The components of deferred tax assets or liabilities are classified as current or noncurrent based on the classification of the related asset or liability. For example, a source of temporary differences is installment receivables arising from installment sales. Suppose the only temporary difference a firm reports arises from an installment receivable, $100,000 of which is classified as a current asset, and $300,000 of which is classified as a noncurrent receivable. Assuming a marginal tax rate of 30% and a total deferred tax liability of $120,000, the firm would have a current deferred tax liability of $30,000, and a noncurrent deferred tax liability of $90,000.

If a deferred tax asset or liability is not related to an asset or liability, including such items as a deferred tax asset related to loss carryforwards, the classification as current or noncurrent depends on the expected period of reversal. Thus a deferred tax asset arising from a tax loss carryforward will be classified as current if management expected the tax benefit to be realized in the following year (assuming an operating cycle of one year or less). If the expectation is that the realization of the benefit will occur in later years it will be classified as noncurrent.

Consider the classification that Lake Company (Example 5) would make regarding its deferred tax assets and liabilities at December 31, 1992. The schedule used to determine the income taxes payable and the deferred tax amounts was:

LAKE COMPANY
Schedule of Deductible and Taxable Amounts

	1992	Future Years	Effect on Future Taxable Income: Deductible	Taxable
Pretax accounting income	$180,000			
Temporary differences:				
Credit sales	(70,000)	130,000		$130,000
Warranties	110,000	(160,000)	$160,000	
Depreciation	(25,000)	25,000	15,000	40,000
Rent received in advance	20,000	(20,000)	20,000	
Taxable income	$215,000			
Total deductible amounts			$195,000	
Total taxable amounts				$170,000
Marginal tax rate	× .30		× .35	× .35
Taxes payable	$ 64,500			
Deferred tax asset			$ 68,250	
Deferred tax liability				$ 59,500

The proposed *SFAS No. 109* requires that, within a particular tax jurisdiction (such as federal, or a particular state or foreign country), all *current* deferred tax assets and liabilities are to be offset so as to report one net amount, and likewise for *noncurrent* deferred tax asset and liability amounts. Assume that $50,000 of the receivables related to the credit sales are classified as current and that the rent received in advance are classified as current. All other items are classified as noncurrent. The amounts of current and noncurrent deferred tax liability are calculated as follows:

	Current Portion	Noncurrent Portion
Credit sales receivables	$50,000	$ 80,000
Depreciation		$ 40,000
Total	$50,000	$120,000
Marginal tax rate	× .35	× .35
Deferred tax liability	$17,500	$ 42,000

The amounts of current and noncurrent deferred tax asset are determined, and the net current and noncurrent asset or liability amounts computed:

	Current Portion	Noncurrent Portion
Rent received in advance	$ 20,000	0
Warranties	0	$160,000
Depreciation	0	15,000
Total	$ 20,000	$175,000
Marginal tax rate	× .35	× .35
Deferred tax asset	$ 7,000	$ 61,250
Deferred tax liability (from above)	(17,500)	(42,000)
Net deferred tax asset (liability)	$(10,500)	$ 19,250

For Lake Company, a net current deferred tax liability of $10,500 would be reported on the balance sheet. Similarly, a net noncurrent deferred tax asset of $19,250 would be reported. The valuation allowance of $8,750 would be deducted from the deferred tax asset.[6]

In addition to the above, footnotes to the financial statements should provide the following supplemental disclosures regarding deferred tax assets and liabilities:
* The total of all deferred tax liabilities ($59,500)
* The total of all deferred tax assets ($68,250)
* The total valuation allowance ($8,750)

For the above Lake Company example, the following presentations and disclosures would be made:

On the balance sheet:

Noncurrent assets:		
Deferred tax assets	$19,250	
Less: Valuation allowance	(8,750)	
Net deferred tax assets		$10,500
Current liabilities:		
Deferred tax liabilities		$10,500

In the disclosure notes:

Total deferred tax assets are $68,250, and total deferred tax liabilities are $59,500. There is a valuation allowance of $8,750 because it is more likely than not that the full amount of the deferred tax assets will not be realized.

---

[6] The *Exposure Draft* is silent on how valuation allowances are to be classified. It is likely that the valuation allowance classification will be linked to the timing of when the opportunity to utilize the deferred tax asset would expire. For example, a valuation allowance established because a tax loss carryforward that will expire in the coming year is not likely to be realized, would be classified as current.

Intraperiod Tax Allocation

Proposed *SFAS No. 109* requires intraperiod tax allocation for items such as continuing operations, discontinued operations, extraordinary items, accounting changes and other items charged or credited directly to shareholders' equity (for example, prior period adjustments). The amount allocated to continuing operations includes the tax effect of the pretax income or loss from continuing operations for the year, plus or minus the income tax effect of:

* Changes in tax laws or rates.
* Changes in tax status.
* Changes in estimates about the realization of deferred tax assets.
* Tax-deductible dividends paid to shareholders.

If there is only one item remaining after the above allocation to continuing operations, the remainder of the unallocated income tax expense is allocated to it. If there is more than one additional item, the tax effect of each item is determined and the remaining unallocated income tax expense is allocated ratably to each item.

Example Seeley Corporation reports pretax accounting income of $6,000, resulting from a loss of 3,000 from continuing operations and an extraordinary gain (taxable at capital gain rates) of $9,000. Taxable income is $4,000. The difference is a future taxable temporary difference, and it gives rise to a deferred tax liability of $800. The tax rate is 40% on ordinary income, and 30% on capital gains. The capital gain is used to offset the operating loss, hence income taxes payable are $4,000 times the capital gains tax rate of 30%, or $1,200. Income tax expense totals $2,000.

The allocation of income tax expense begins with the loss from continuing operations of $3,000. The normal tax rate would be 40%, but in this instance the tax benefit from the loss has been to offset a capital gain. Therefore, the tax rate used to determine the allocation to continuing operations is the capital gains rate:

```
Total income tax expense . . . . . . . . . . . . . . . . . . . . . $2,000
Tax benefit allocated to continuing operations:
    $3,000 × .30 . . . . . . . . . . . . . . . . . . . . . . . . . . . (900)
Incremental tax expense allocated to extraordinary gain  . . . . . $2,900
```

Further discussion of intraperiod tax allocation is found in Chapter 4.

Additional Disclosures

The following significant components of income tax expense attributable to continuing operations must be disclosed, either in the financial statements or in disclosure notes:

* The current income tax expense or benefit.
* The deferred tax expense or benefit.
* Any investment tax credits.
* Government grants to the extent they are used as reductions of income tax expense.
* The benefits of operating loss carryforwards.
* Adjustments of deferred tax assets or liabilities as a result of enacted tax law or rate changes, or changes in the tax status of the firm.

If income tax expense or benefit is allocated to items in addition to continuing operations, the amounts allocated separately to these additional items must be disclosed for each year for which those items are presented.

Final Comments

Proposed *SFAS No. 109* is expected to be approved and to become effective for fiscal years beginning after December 15, 1992. However, it is likely that many firms will adopt this new *Statement* early, especially those currently using *SFAS No. 96,* because it is much simpler to apply. However, the procedures of *APB No. 11* and of *SFAS No. 96* will continue to be acceptable methods of accounting for income taxes until the mandated effective date of *SFAS No. 109.*

SUMMARY OF KEY POINTS

♦

(L.O. 1)   1. A tax benefit related to a taxable loss can be realized by carrying back the loss to three immediately prior periods, oldest period first, to request a refund of taxes paid on amounts of taxable income equal to the amount of the net operating loss. Benefits can also be realized in the future by carrying the loss forward up to 15 years to offset taxable income in future periods.

(L.O. 1)   2. At the time a net operating loss occurs, a firm can elect to carryback the loss (and also use the carryforward provision for any amounts of the loss not recovered by the carryback provision), or the firm can elect to only carry forward the net operating loss to offset future taxable income. The choice must be made in the period of the loss, and it is irrevocable.

(L.O. 3)   3. Income measurement for financial reporting is governed by generally accepted accounting principles. Income measurement for purposes of determining income taxes payable is governed by the tax laws and their interpretation by the Internal Revenue Service and state income tax authorities. Taxable income and pretax accounting income may differ.

(L.O. 2, 3)   4. There are two types of differences between pretax accounting income and taxable income. The first is permanent differences, in which a revenue or expense item is included in the determination of either pretax accounting income or taxable income, but it does not, nor will it ever, appear in the computation of the other. Permanent differences do not require the recognition of deferred tax assets or deferred tax liabilities because they have no future tax consequences.

(L.O. 2, 3)   5. The second type of differences are called temporary differences. Temporary differences are items which are included in the current or past period determination of either pretax accounting income or taxable income, but not both, and which are expected to be included in the other at a later date.

(L.O. 3)   6. Under GAAP, the tax consequences of temporary differences are measured and included in the computation of income tax expense. This approach is generally referred to as the interperiod tax allocation approach.

(L.O. 4)   7. Under GAAP using the asset/liability method, the tax consequences of temporary differences are analyzed to determine what the tax effects will be in the future periods in which the temporary differences reverse. The enacted tax rates for those future periods are applied to the temporary differences to determine the future (deferred) tax asset and liability. The income tax expense for the period is income taxes payable plus the net amount of these deferred tax asset or liability amounts arising in the period.

(L.O. 5)   8. Under the deferral method, the income tax expense for the current period is determined as if pretax accounting income, including temporary differences, were all taxable in the current period. The current tax rate is applied to pretax accounting income to determine income tax expense. Any difference between taxes payable and income tax expense computed as above is recorded as a deferred tax credit or deferred tax debit. It is not identified as an asset or liability as such, but it does appear on the balance sheet in either the asset or liability sections. This method was required by *APB Opinion No. 11*, and will continue to be acceptable until proposed *SFAS No. 109* is mandated.

(L.O. 5)   9. Proposed *SFAS No. 109* imposes a limitation on the net amount of deferred tax asset that can be reported. After the deferred tax is recorded, a determination is made regarding the likelihood that the benefit of the deferred tax asset will be realized. If it is determined that it is more likely than not that some portion of the deferred tax asset will not be realized as a benefit, a valuation allowance is established as a contra account to the deferred tax asset.

(L.O. 5)   10. The limitation on the recording of deferred tax assets under *SFAS No. 96* assumed that the only sources of future taxable income (or net operating loss in future periods) are temporary differences that have arisen in the current and prior periods. Proposed *SFAS No. 109* relaxes that assumption such that a deferred tax asset is to be recorded as long as taxable income is more likely than not in future periods, including taxable income expected to be generated from operations.

(L.O. 6)   11. Deferred tax assets and liabilities are classified as either current or noncurrent, depending on the classification of the asset or liability giving rise to the deferred tax item. Current deferred tax assets and current deferred tax liabilities are offset and a net current deferred tax asset or liability is reported. The same type of offset is applied to noncurrent deferred tax assets and liabilities.

(L.O. 7)   12. The ITC is accounted for either by taking the entire tax saving as a reduction of income tax expense in the current year, or deferring and allocating it to reduce income tax expense over the life of the asset to which it applies.

REVIEW PROBLEM
◆

The Duesing Company began operations in 1986, engaging in a number of business activities ranging from manufacturing and marketing durable goods to writing technical business textbooks on which the firm collected royalty income. The accounting for these many activities resulted in a number of differences between reporting for book and tax purposes. For financial reporting purposes, the company accrued estimated warranty costs when it sold products under warranty, deferred advanced royalty payments it received, and prepaid many operating expenses. For tax purposes, it recognized warranty costs when paid, royalty income when cash was received, and operating expenses when cash was paid. The opening and closing balances in these accounts for 1991 were as follows:

Balance: Debit (credit)	January 1	December 31	Change during Year
Accrued warranty costs	$(50,000)	$(40,000)	$ 10,000
Deferred royalty income	$(10,000)	$(40,000)	$(30,000)
Prepaid expenses	$ 33,000	$ 25,000	$ (8,000)

All three accounts are classified as current items on the balance sheet. The company depreciates its manufacturing equipment using an accelerated method for tax purposes and straight line for financial reporting. The schedule of book and tax depreciation for 1991 and all remaining years for the company's existing equipment is:

Year	Book Depreciation	Tax Depreciation
1991 (current year)	$ 9,000	$14,000
Future years:		
1992	9,000	9,000
1993	9,000	6,000
1994	9,000	3,000
Totals	$27,000	$18,000

The company's 1991 pretax accounting income was $8,000. This includes $2,000 of interest income on municipal bonds that is not taxable. The history of taxable income reported by the company since it began operations is as follows:

Year	Taxable Income (loss)
1986	$ 2,000
1987	17,000
1988	(78,000)
1989	24,000
1990	9,000

The company elected to carryback the maximum amount of the 1988 loss.

EXHIBIT 17-3   Worksheet to Compute Deferred Tax Asset and Liability for Duesing Company under Proposed *SFAS No. 109*

	1986	1987	1988	1989	1990	1991	1992 Deductible	1992 Taxable	1993 and Thereafter: Deductible	1993 and Thereafter: Taxable
								Effect on Future Years' Income		
Pretax accounting income (loss)						$8,000				
Less: Nontaxable income						(2,000)				
Temporary differences:										
Warranty costs						(10,000)	$40,000			
Royalty income						30,000	$40,000			
Prepaid expenses . . .						8,000		$25,000		
Depreciation						(5,000)				$9,000
Net taxable income before carryback and carryforward	$2,000	$17,000	($78,000)	$24,000	$9,000	$29,000				
Total temporary differences							$80,000	$25,000	$0	$9,000
Net operating loss carrybacks and carryforwards	($2,000)	($17,000)	$78,000	($24,000)	($9,000)	(26,000)				
Total taxable income . .						$3,000				
Total future taxable and deductible amounts							$80,000	$25,000	$0	$9,000
Marginal tax rate						0.34	0.34	0.34	0.40	0.40
Taxes currently payable						$1,020				
Gross deferred tax asset at December 31, 1991							$27,200		$0	
Gross deferred tax liability at December 31, 1991								$ 8,500		$3,600

The marginal tax rate the company expected to be effective on its last dollar of income in 1991 and 1992 (and for all prior years) is 34%. However, during 1991 a tax law was enacted which will change the tax rate to 40% for 1993 and subsequent years.

There are no prior taxes currently payable, nor any prior tax refunds currently receivable. At January 1, 1991, there are opening balances in the deferred tax asset account of $29,240, the valuation allowance of $5,100, and the deferred tax liability account of $15,980.

Required:

1. Determine the 1991 income tax expense assuming three different possible cases regarding estimates of future taxable income:
   a. The company expected taxable income exclusive of temporary differences of $20,000 in 1992, but cannot support a forecast of taxable income for subsequent years.
   b. The company cannot support a forecast of taxable income in any future year. (This is essentially the assumption that is made under *SFAS No. 96*.)
   c. The company can support a forecast of $30,000 per year for the next three years.
2. In each of the 3 cases above, prepare the journal entry to record the company's income tax expense for 1991, and determine the net current and noncurrent deferred tax asset and deferred tax liability to be reported in the balance sheet.

SOLUTION
◆

The solution to this problem begins with the worksheet computation of income taxes payable and the ending deferred tax asset and liability balances as presented in

Exhibit 17–3. Because of the NOL in 1988 of $78,000, there are tax loss carrybacks and carryforwards that must be considered in addition to the temporary differences.

The temporary differences are identified and categorized on the top portion of the worksheet under the 1991, 1992, and 1993 and thereafter columns. The 1991 column computes taxable income starting from pretax accounting income. The adjustments begin with subtraction of the nontaxable permanent difference (municipal interest income of $2,000). The next four items in the 1991 column are the current year effects of either originating or reversing temporary differences. After these adjustments are made, taxable income for 1991 is $29,000. Carryforward of the remaining $26,000 of the 1988 NOL reduces the taxable income to $3,000.

The 1992 and 1993 and thereafter columns are further divided into deductible and taxable columns in order to determine the deferred tax asset and deferred tax liability amounts. The two different future period columns are needed because there is a known, enacted change in the tax rate for 1993 and thereafter. The new tax rate must be used for temporary differences reversing in 1993 and thereafter in determining the deferred tax asset or liability.

Once the taxable income and temporary differences are determined, the worksheet proceeds to compute taxes payable in 1991 of $1,020, and gross amounts of deferred tax assets and liabilities at December 31, 1991, of $27,200 and $12,100, respectively. This worksheet is the same for all three assumptions that are made regarding estimates of future taxable income.

Assumption (a): Estimated taxable income exclusive of temporary differences, $20,000 in 1992 and zero thereafter.

The top portion of Exhibit 17–4 computes the amount of the valuation allowance under the above assumption. On the valuation allowance worksheet, the gross amounts of future deductible temporary differences are entered, then sources of income considered. Three sources are used in part (a) of this problem:

1. Future reversing taxable temporary differences—$25,000 in 1992, and $9,000 in 1993 and thereafter.
2. Estimated taxable income in 1992 ($20,000) and thereafter ($0).
3. A tax loss carryback of $3,000 to 1991, recovering taxes paid in 1991 of $1,020. The worksheet shows that $23,000 of the deductible temporary difference is not expected to be realized, thus a valuation allowance balance of $7,820 is required at December 31, 1991.

The worksheet in the second portion of Exhibit 17–4 presents the computation of the amounts to be recorded in the deferred tax asset and liability accounts, and in the valuation allowance account to adjust these accounts to their correct ending balances. In each case, the other side of the entry is to income tax expense. The worksheet also determines the classification of current and noncurrent amounts of deferred tax assets and liabilities, and presents the journal entry to record the income tax expense, taxes payable, changes in the deferred tax asset and liability accounts, and the change in the valuation allowance. The income tax expense for the period can be computed directly:

Computation of Income Tax Expense

Income taxes payable (from Exhibit 17–3)	$1,020
Less: Decrease in deferred tax liability (from Exhibit 17–4)	(3,880)
Add: Decrease in deferred tax asset (from Exhibit 17–4)	2,040
Add: Increase in valuation allowance (from Exhibit 17–4)	$2,720
Income tax expense	$1,900

Finally, the classification of the deferred tax asset and liability amounts as current and noncurrent is determined by the classification of the related balance sheet items giving rise to them. After these amounts are determined and the ending valuation allowance determined, the current asset and liability amounts are netted for presentation on the balance sheet as a net current deferred tax asset of $10,880. The same

EXHIBIT 17-4 Valuation Allowance and Balance Sheet Classification Worksheet under Proposed *SFAS No. 109.* Assumption: Expect Taxable Income of $20,000 in 1992, and Zero in 1993 and Thereafter

Valuation Allowance Worksheet

		1992	1993 and Thereafter
Gross deductible temporary difference		$80,000	$0
Less:			
Gross taxable temporary difference	$25,000	$9,000	
Estimated taxable income before temporary differences	20,000	$45,000	0 9,000
Excess deductible (taxable)		$35,000	($9,000)
Carryforward of future deductible amounts to offset future taxable amounts		(9,000)	9,000
Carryback of future deductible amounts to offset prior years' taxable income		(3,000)	
Excess deductible amounts not expected to be realized		$23,000	
Marginal tax rate		0.34	
Valuation allowance		$ 7,820	

Adjustments and Balance Sheet Classification—Debit (Credit)

Debit (credit)	Gross Amount	Current	Noncurrent
Deferred tax asset, December 31, 1991	$27,200	$27,200	$0
Deferred tax asset, January 1, 1991	29,240		
Adjustment (include in income tax expense)	($2,040)		
Valuation allowance, December 31, 1991	($7,820)	(7,820)	
Valuation allowance, January 1, 1991	(5,100)		
Adjustment (include in income tax expense)	($2,720)		
Net deferred tax asset after valuation allowance		$19,380	$0
Deferred tax liability, December 31, 1991 ($8,500 plus $3,600)	($12,100)	(8,500)	(3,600)
Deferred tax liability, January 1, 1991	(15,980)		
Adjustment (include in income tax expense)	$3,880		
Net deferred tax asset (liability) reported on balance sheet		$10,880	($3,600)

Journal entry:

	Gross Amount	Current
Deferred tax liability	3,880	
Income tax expense	1,900	
Income taxes payable		1,020
Deferred tax asset		2,040
Valuation allowance		2,720

netting concept applies to noncurrent asset and liability amounts, resulting in a noncurrent liability of $3,600 for Duesing Company.

Assumption (*b*): Estimated taxable income of zero in all future years.

Exhibit 17–5 presents the same analysis as Exhibit 17–4, except the expectation is that the firm expects zero taxable income exclusive of temporary differences in future years. The result is a larger ending valuation allowance ($14,620), and thus an increase in income tax expense of $6,800. This $6,800 is equal to the amount of estimated taxable income expected in case (*a*) ($20,000) but not expected in case (*b*),

EXHIBIT 17-5 Valuation Allowance and Balance Sheet Classification Worksheet under Proposed *SFAS No. 109*. Assumption: Expect Taxable Income of Zero in 1992 and Thereafter

Valuation Allowance Worksheet

		1992		1993 and Thereafter
Gross deductible temporary difference		$80,000		$0
Less:				
Gross taxable temporary difference	$25,000		$9,000	
Estimated taxable income before temporary differences	0	25,000	$0	9,000
Excess deductible (taxable)		$55,000		($9,000)
Carryforward of future deductible amounts to offset future taxable amounts		(9,000)		9,000
Carryback of future deductible amounts to offset prior years' taxable income		(3,000)		
Excess deductible amounts not expected to be realized		$43,000		
Marginal tax rate		0.34		
Valuation allowance		**$14,620**		

Adjustments and Balance Sheet Classification—Debit (Credit)

Debit (credit)	Gross Amount	Current	Noncurrent
Deferred tax asset, December 31, 1991	$27,200	$27,200	$0
Deferred tax asset, January 1, 1991	$29,240		
Adjustment (include in income tax expense)	**($2,040)**		
Valuation allowance, December 31, 1991	($14,620)	($14,620)	
Valuation allowance, January 1, 1991	($5,100)		
Adjustment (include in income tax expense)	**($9,520)**		
Net deferred tax asset after valuation allowance		$12,580	$0
Deferred tax liability, December 31, 1991 ($8,500 plus $3,600)	($12,100)	(8,500)	(3,600)
Deferred tax liability, January 1, 1991	($15,980)		
Adjustment (reduction of income tax expense)	**$3,880**		
Net deferred tax asset (liability) reported on balance sheet		$ 4,080	($3,600)

Journal entry:

Deferred tax liability	3,880	
Income tax expense	8,700	
Income taxes payable		1,020
Deferred tax asset		2,040
Valuation allowance		9,520

multiplied by the marginal tax rate of 34%. This shows the effect of expectations regarding future taxable income on current period income tax expense.

Assumption (*c*): Estimated taxable income of $30,000 in 1992 and 1993.

Exhibit 17–6 presents the results when there is evidence to support an expectation that Duesing will generate taxable income of $30,000 in 1992 and 1993. Under this expectation, the full amount of the deferred tax asset is expected to be realized, hence no valuation allowance is needed. In this scenario, the income tax expense

EXHIBIT 17-6   Valuation Allowance and Balance Sheet Classification Worksheet under Proposed *SFAS No. 109*. Assumption: Expect Taxable Income of $30,000 in 1992 and Thereafter

Valuation Allowance Worksheet

		1992		1993 and Thereafter
Gross deductible temporary difference		$80,000		$0
Less:				
Gross taxable temporary difference	$25,000		$ 9,000	
Estimated taxable income before				
temporary differences	30,000	55,000	30,000	$39,000
Excess deductible (taxable)		$25,000		($39,000)
Carryforward of future deductible amounts to offset future taxable amounts		(22,000)		22,000
Carryback of future deductible amounts to offset prior years' taxable income		(3,000)		
Excess deductible amounts not expected to be realized		$0		
Marginal tax rate		0.34		
Valuation allowance		$0		

Adjustments and Balance Sheet Classification—Debit (Credit)

Debit (credit)	Gross Amount	Current	Noncurrent
Deferred tax asset, December 31, 1991	$27,200	$27,200	$0
Deferred tax asset, January 1, 1991	29,240		
Adjustment (include in income tax expense)	($2,040)		
Valuation allowance, December 31, 1991	$0	0	
Valuation allowance, January 1, 1991	(5,100)		
Adjustment (include in income tax expense)	(5,100)		
Net deferred tax asset after valuation allowance		$27,200	$0
Deferred tax liability, December 31, 1991 ($8,500 plus $3,600)	($12,100)	(8,500)	(3,600)
Deferred tax liability, January 1, 1991	(15,980)		
Adjustment (include in income tax expense)	$3,880		
Net deferred tax asset (liability) reported on balance sheet		$18,700	($3,600)

Journal entry:

Deferred tax liability	3,880	
Valuation allowance	5,100	
Income tax expense		5,920
Income taxes payable		1,020
Deferred tax asset		2,040

becomes a credit balance of $5,920. Thus, net income will be the pretax accounting income of $8,000 given in the problem, plus the credit amount in the income tax expense account of $5,920, or a total of $13,920.

The three different assumptions regarding the likelihood of future taxable income presented in Exhibits 17–4 through 17–6 demonstrate the importance of the estimation of future taxable income to the determination of income tax expense under proposed *SFAS No. 109*. The different amounts that result from the different assumptions are summarized as follows:

	Assumption (a): Taxable income of $20,000 in 1992, zero thereafter.	Assumption (b): Zero taxable income in all future years.	Assumption (c): Taxable income of $30,000 in 1992 and 1993.
Pretax accounting income	$ 8,000	$8,000	$ 8,000
Income tax expense (credit)	1,900	8,700	(5,920)
Income (loss) after taxes	$ 6,100	$ (700)	$13,920
Balance sheet amounts:			
Current assets:			
Deferred tax assets	$10,880	$4,080	$18,700
Noncurrent liabilities:			
Deferred tax liability	3,600	3,600	3,600

APPENDIX   Accounting for Deferred Taxes under SFAS No. 96

The text of this chapter describes accounting for income taxes under the provisions of the proposed *SFAS No. 109*. A key difference between the proposed *Standard* and *SFAS No. 96* is the computation and recording of deferred tax assets. Briefly, the proposed *SFAS No. 109* determines the full or gross amount of deferred tax assets that are the result of deductible temporary differences, tax loss carryforwards, and carryforwards of unused tax credits. Then a determination is made as to whether the amount recorded as a deferred tax asset is not likely to be realized. If this the case, a valuation allowance is recorded to reduce the gross deferred tax asset to the amount expected to be realized.

SFAS No. 96 records only the net amount of deferred tax asset to be realized. More importantly, *SFAS No. 96* allows only the amount that is assured of being realized by either carryback of future deductible amounts to the current and appropriate prior periods as is allowed under the tax laws, or by offsetting future deductible amounts against future taxable amounts using carryforward and carryback procedures. *SFAS No. 96* does not allow the firm to use an estimate of future taxable income exclusive of future taxable temporary differences. Essentially, *SFAS No. 96* requires the estimate of future taxable income exclusive of future taxable temporary differences to be zero.

In this appendix, the limitation on deferred tax assets under *SFAS No. 96* is demonstrated. The analysis that is required under *SFAS No. 96* can be useful in proposed *SFAS No. 109* when the only source of future taxable income is future reversals of taxable temporary differences.

Application of Carryback and Carryforward Procedures to Future Deductible Amounts

A complex aspect of computing income tax expense under *SFAS No. 96* is applying a carryback (CB) and carryforward (CF) procedure to future deductible amounts and determining whether the company can record a deferred tax asset. The carryback/carryforward procedure is used in the *analysis* of both taxable amounts and deductible amounts to determine whether the firm can record a deferred tax asset. The procedure is independent of any actual net operating loss carryback and carryforward. However, it uses the same rules and conforms to the 3-year carryback and 15-year carryforward time limits. *SFAS No. 96* uses the carryback/carryforward procedure as follows:

1. Determine the net taxable amounts for future years. Deductible and taxable amounts in a given year are offset to yield a net taxable or deductible amount for that given year.
2. Determine the net deductible amounts for future years and, thus, determine the potential deferred tax asset amounts.
3. Deferred tax asset amounts recognized are limited to the current income tax payable plus any tax refundable for the two years prior as permitted under the three-year carryback rule.
4. In analyzing temporary differences, apply the carryback/carryforward procedure to deductible amounts in order to offset future taxable amounts and current income taxes payable. The carryback of deductible amounts cannot exceed 3 consecutive years, and the carryforward amounts cannot exceed the taxable amounts (and cannot be more than 15 years forward). Deferred tax asset and liability amounts are determined after the carryback and carryforward procedures have been applied.

Example Using Carryforward and Carryback Procedures   MFG Company, in 1992, its first year of operations, has income of $2,000 before depreciation and income taxes. Its plant has an original cost of $4,500 and an estimated useful life of five years. It will be depreciated on a straight-line basis, with no residual value. For tax purposes, assume the plant is to be depreciated using the straight-line method over three years. The enacted tax rates for future periods, which are known in 1992, are:

	1992	1993
Enacted tax rates	30%	40%

Step 1. Gather data and identify temporary differences. The one temporary difference is the different depreciation amounts to be deducted for tax and book purposes. The tax depreciation will be $4,500 divided by three years, or $1,500 per year for each of three years. The book depreciation is $900 per year for five years ($4,500/5 years).

Temporary difference at December 31, 1992:
Book value of depreciable asset	$3,600
Tax basis (value) of depreciable asset	3,000
Temporary difference	$ 600

Step 2. Computation of income tax payable:

	1991
Accounting income before depreciation and taxes	$2,000
Depreciation for reporting purposes	900
Pretax accounting income	$1,100
Temporary differences:	
Excess of tax over book depreciation	600
Taxable income	$ 500
Multiply by the enacted tax rate	× .30
Income taxes payable (shown on tax return)	$ 150

Step 3. Schedule of temporary differences between pretax accounting income and taxable income and compute the balance in the deferred tax account.

		(Deductible) Taxable			
	1992	1993	1994	1995	1996
Pretax accounting income	$1,100				
Reconcile to taxable income:					
Temporary difference: Depreciation	(600)				
Taxable income	$ 500				
Temporary difference: Depreciation		($600)	($600)	$900	$900
Subtotal		($600)	($600)	$900	$900
Carryback	(500)	500			
Carryforward		100	600	(700)	
Subtotal	($500)	$0	$0	$200	$900
Tax rate	30%	40%	40%	40%	40%
Deferred tax asset	$ 150				
Deferred tax liability		$ 0	$ 0	$ 80	$360

The deferred tax asset totals $150, and the deferred tax liability is $440.

Step 4. Develop the journal entry to record the income taxes payable, deferred income taxes, and income tax expense for the period.

Income tax payable for the period (per tax return)	$150
Deferred tax liability	440
Deferred tax asset	(150)
Income tax expense	$440

Therefore the journal entry to record income taxes for 1992 is:

Income tax expense 440		
Deferred tax asset 150		
Income taxes payable	150	
Deferred tax liability	440	

The computations in Step 3 are significantly different than those used under proposed *SFAS No. 109*. First, the complete depreciation schedule for all future years for the depreciable asset is presented. It gives rise to future deductible amounts for 1993 and 1994 ($600 in each year). Then reversal begins, and there are future taxable amounts in 1995 and 1996 ($900 in each year). The net of these future effects is a future taxable amount of $600 ($1,800 in future taxable amounts, less $1,200 of future deductible amounts). This is exactly equal to the difference in book and tax basis of the asset at December 31, 1992.

The future deductible amounts in 1993 and 1994 give rise to a possible deferred tax asset, but *SFAS No. 96* specifies that it can be recorded only if the deductible amounts can be carried back to offset current taxes payable, or carried forward to offset future taxable amounts. The *Standard* also requires that Option 1 (carryback and carryforward) be used in the analysis. Thus, the analysis begins with a carryback to 1992 (the first year of operations), of $500 of the $600 deductible amount of 1993. Only $500 can be carried back because taxable income in 1992 is $500. The remaining $100 in 1993, and the entire $600 of deductible amount arising in 1994, are carried forward to absorb $700 of the $900 of taxable amount in 1995.

After determining the net deductible and taxable amounts, complete the computation of deferred tax asset resulting from the carryback and the liabilities for each future period, using the enacted tax rate for the period. The deferred tax asset is computed using the current period tax rate because it is carried back to the current period in the analysis. If in fact the future deductible amount were to be the only income tax return amount for 1993, it would result in an actual carryback to 1992 for a tax refund based on taxes paid in 1992. The liability amounts are summed to determine a total deferred tax liability.

In view of the complexities and some of the misconceptions of deferred tax liabilities and assets, the following direct quotations from *SFAS No. 96* are provided (emphasis supplied):

Annual Computation of a Deferred Tax Liability or Asset

17. In concept, this Statement requires determination of the amount of taxes payable or refundable in each future year *as if a tax return were prepared* for the net amount of temporary differences that will result in taxable or deductible amounts in each of those years. That concept is illustrated by the following procedures:
    a. Estimate the particular future years in which temporary differences will result in taxable or deductible amounts.
    b. Determine the *net* taxable or deductible amount in each future year.
    c. Deduct *actual operating loss carryforwards for tax purposes* (as permitted or required by tax law) from net taxable amounts that are scheduled to occur in the future years included in the loss carryforward period.
    d. Carry back or carry forward (as permitted or required by tax law) net deductible amounts occurring in particular years to offset net taxable amounts that are scheduled to occur in prior or subsequent years.

Deferred Tax Assets

    e. Recognize a deferred tax asset for the tax benefit of *net deductible amounts* that could be realized by loss carryback from future years (1) to reduce a current deferred tax liability and (2) to reduce taxes paid in the current or a prior year.

Deferred Tax Liabilities

    f. Calculate the amount of tax for the remaining net taxable amounts that are scheduled to occur in each of those years by applying presently enacted tax rates and laws for each of those years to the type and amount of net taxable amounts scheduled for those years.
    g. Deduct *tax credit carryforwards for tax purposes (as permitted or required by tax law)* from the amount of tax (calculated above) for future years that are included in the carryforward periods. (No asset is recognized for any additional amount of tax credit carryforward.)
    h. Recognize a deferred tax liability for the remaining amount of taxes payable for each future year.

In (e), "prior year" refers to any taxes refundable for the two prior years under the three-year carryback rule. The key procedure outlined above is estimating income tax consequences for future periods for the temporary differences *as if* they were the only source of taxable income (if the net reversing temporary difference is a taxable amount) or of operating loss (if the net reversing temporary difference is a deductible amount) in that particular year. The current tax law for tax loss carryback and carryforward is applied in the analysis to offset net deductible amounts against net taxable amounts, or else the NOL is carried back to the current or earlier periods to effect a deferred tax asset. When this has been completed for net deductible amounts, a final series of future net taxable or deductible amounts is determined. Finally, the limitation on the recording of deferred tax assets is such that any net deductible amounts (after application of carryback and carryforward) three years or more in the future will not be recognized under *SFAS No. 96*.

These procedures are illustrated in a series of examples, beginning with the relatively straightforward and proceeding to the more complex. In all the examples which follow, the tax rates for the current and future years are as follows:

	1991	1992	1993 and Thereafter
Enacted tax rates	30%	40%	40%

Application of the Carryback and Carryforward Procedures with No Loss of Future Deductible Amounts. This example is summarized in Exhibit 17A–1. Sales Company is assumed to have begun operations in 1991. During 1991, two sources of temporary differences arise. The first is an installment sale that generates $15,000 of revenues for financial reporting purposes that will become taxable in future years when the receivable is collected. The second source of temporary differences is an accrued estimated future warranty expense in the amount of $13,000. This item is an expense in the 1991 income statement, but it will not be deductible for tax purposes until it is paid. Management expects the entire amount of the warranty to be paid in 1995. Pretax accounting income for Sales Company in 1991 is $11,000.

Exhibit 17A–1 shows the reconciliation of pretax accounting income to taxable income for 1991. The net temporary difference is a taxable amount of $2,000 (the $15,000 future taxable amount arising from the receivable, less the $13,000 future deductible amount arising from the future deducibility of the warranty costs). With a taxable income of $9,000 and a current tax rate of 30%, the income tax payable in 1991 is computed to be $2,700. This amount is the first component of the income tax expense journal entry to be made.

Second, Exhibit 17A–1 shows the estimated or expected reversing periods and amounts for the temporary differences. The receivable is expected to be collected in $3,000 amounts in each of the next five years, and the warranty is expected to be paid in 1995. With this information spread over the next five years, amounts are summed algebraically to determine net taxable or deductible amounts for future years.

When the net deductible amount of $10,000 is computed for 1995, the carryback and carryforward procedures of *SFAS No. 96* must be applied to determine whether the full amount of the future deductible amount can be used to offset future taxable amounts. Since these are future taxable amounts of $3,000 in each of the three years preceding 1995, the analysis shows the carryback of this amount to each of the years 1992, 1993, and 1994. There is still a net deductible amount of $1,000 remaining for 1995. This amount can be carried forward to 1996 since there is a net taxable amount of $3,000 expected in that year. Thus, by using the tax loss carryback and carryforward procedures the entire amount of the future net deductible amount can be absorbed by future taxable amounts.

After the above analysis using the carryback and carryforward procedures, a final net future taxable or deductible amount is determined for each future year. The enacted future tax rates are applied to determine the amount of the deferred tax liability. In this example, the only amount is a future taxable amount of $2,000 in 1996, and the enacted tax rate for that period is 40%. Thus, the deferred tax liability is $800.

Income tax expense for the period is calculated as the sum of the income tax payable plus any increase in deferred tax liability, less any increase deferred tax asset amount. The computation at the bottom of Exhibit 17A–1 shows income tax expense for 1991 to be $3,500. The journal entry to record income tax expense for the period is shown at the bottom of Exhibit 17A–1.

In sum, this example shows the application of the carryback and carryforward procedures to offset future taxable amounts by future deductible amounts. The full amount of the future deductible amount can be offset against future taxable amounts.

EXHIBIT 17A-1   Illustration of Carryback and Carryforward with No Loss of Future Deductible Amounts

Information:

1. Sales Company has an installment receivable of $15,000 to be received in five equal installments over the next five years. The entire amount of the receivable is included in pretax accounting income for 1991, but will not be included in taxable income until it is received in cash.

2. All expenses except warranty expenses have been paid and included in both pretax accounting income and taxable income. Warranty expense in the amount of $13,000 has been estimated and included in the determination of pretax accounting income but not taxable income. The Company expects that all warranty costs will be paid in 1995.

Reconciliation of Pretax Accounting Income and Taxable Income

Pretax accounting income (assumed)	$11,000
Temporary differences:	
Future taxable amounts:	
Accounts receivable . . . . ($15,000)	
Future deductible amounts:	
Warranty costs $13,000	
Net (taxable) deductible amount	($2,000)
Taxable income	$9,000
Current period tax rate	× 0.30
Current period income tax payable	$2,700

Analysis of Reversals of Temporary Differences   **(Deductible) Taxable**

Year	1992	1993	1994	1995	1996
Future taxable amounts from future collection of receivable of $15,000	$3,000	$3,000	$3,000	$3,000	$3,000
Future (deductible) amounts from payment of warranty costs of $13,000				(13,000)	
Net taxable (deductible) amounts	$3,000	$3,000	$3,000	($10,000)	$3,000
Three-year carryback of net deductible amount	(3,000)	(3,000)	(3,000)	9,000	
Carryforward of remaining net deductible amount to offset future taxable amounts				1,000	(1,000)
Net taxable (deductible) amounts after carryback and carryforward	$ 0	$ 0	$ 0	$ 0	$2,000
Multiply by enacted future tax rates	× 0.4	× 0.4	× 0.4	× 0.4	× 0.4
Deferred tax liability (asset)	$ 0	$ 0	$ 0	$ 0	$ 800

Computation of Income Tax Expense

Income tax payable (see above)	$2,700
Future tax liability (asset)	800
Income tax expense	$3,500

Income Tax Journal Entry for 1991

Income tax expense	3,500	
Income taxes payable		2,700
Deferred tax liability		800

Application of the Carryback and Carryforward Procedures with Loss of Future Deductible Amounts
Exhibit 17A–2 extends the previous illustration such that there are not enough future taxable amounts to offset the future deductible amount. The example is modified on only one dimension: instead of a receivable of $15,000 arising from the installment sale, in this example the receivable is only $9,000, collectable in equal amounts of $3,000 in each of the next three years. Pretax accounting income is reduced from $11,000 to $5,000. There is no change in the warranty cost amounts or expected period of reversal.

As before, Exhibit 17A–2 begins with a reconciliation of pretax accounting income and taxable income, identifying the various sources of temporary differences. Note that in this example there is a net deductible amount originating in 1991 of $4,000. The taxable income is again $9,000. The tax rate is 30%. Thus, as before, the income tax payable is $2,700.

EXHIBIT 17A-2   Illustration of Carryback and Carryforward with Loss of Future Deductible Amounts

Information:

1. Sales Company has an installment receivable of $9,000 to be received in three equal installments over the next three years. The entire amount of the receivable is included in pretax accounting income for 1991, but will not be included in taxable income until it is received in cash.

2. All expenses except warranty expenses have been paid and included in both pretax accounting income and taxable income. Warranty expense in the amount of $13,000 has been estimated and included in the determination of pretax accounting income but not taxable income. It is expected that all warranty costs will be paid in 1995.

Reconciliation of Pretax Accounting Income and Taxable Income

Pretax accounting income		$5,000
Temporary differences:		
Future taxable amounts:		
Accounts receivable	($9,000)	
Future deductible amounts:		
Warranty costs	$13,000	
Net (taxable) deductible amount		$4,000
Taxable income		$9,000
Current period tax rate		× 0.30
Current period income tax payable		$2,700

Analysis of Reversals of Temporary Differences

	1992	1993	1994	1995
		(Deductible) Taxable		
Future taxable amount from future collection of receivable of $9,000	$3,000	$3,000	$3,000	
Future deductible amounts from payment of warranty costs of $13,000				($13,000)
Net taxable (deductible) amounts	$3,000	$3,000	$3,000	($13,000)
Three-year carryback of net deductible amount	(3,000)	(3,000)	(3,000)	9,000
Carryforward of remaining net deductible amount to offset future taxable amounts				
Net taxable (deductible) amounts	$ 0	$ 0	$ 0	($ 4,000)
Multiply by enacted future tax rates	× 0.4	× 0.4	× 0.4	× 0.4
Deferred tax liability (potential asset)	$ 0	$ 0	$ 0	($ 1,600)

Computation of Income Tax Expense

Income tax payable (see above)	$2,700	
Deferred tax liability (asset)	0	
Income tax expense	$2,700	

Income Tax Journal Entry for 1991

Income tax expense	2,700	
Deferred tax asset	0	
Income taxes payable		2,700
Deferred tax liability		0

Second, the temporary differences are spread over the years in the future in which they are expected to reverse, and net temporary differences for each year are computed. The result at this point shows net taxable amounts of $3,000 in each of the years 1992, 1993, and 1994, and a net deductible amount of $13,000 in 1995. Following the carryback procedure for three years to offset the taxable amounts in 1992, 1993, and 1994, the deductible amount is reduced to

$4,000. However, at this point there are no more taxable amounts against which the remaining deductible amount can be offset. In Exhibit 17A–1, there was a taxable amount arising in 1996 against which the deductible amount was carried forward; there are no such taxable amounts in this example. Therefore, *SFAS No. 96* does not allow Sales Company to record a deferred tax asset. The computation of income tax expense and the entry to record it are shown at the bottom of Exhibit 17A–2. It is useful again to point out that the computation in Exhibits 17A–1 and 17A–2 for deferred tax asset and liability amounts are for the end-of-period amounts. In the examples to this point, the beginning balances are always zero; thus, the computations give the amount to be recognized in the current period. If there were beginning balances in the deferred tax asset or liability accounts, the amount to be recorded as part of income tax expense this period would be the difference between the beginning and ending balances.

Carryback of Net Deductible Amounts to the Current Period   Consider what the entries would have been if, in the above example, the warranty costs were expected to reverse in 1994 instead of 1995. This modification to Exhibit 17A–2 is presented in Exhibit 17A–3. The net deductible amount in 1994 is $10,000 (a taxable amount of $3,000 less a deductible amount of $13,000). This amount can be carried back three years to 1991, the current year, to offset taxable income. Thus, the carryback to 1991 of $9,000 (the amount of taxable income in 1991) is used to generate a $2,700 deferred tax asset ($9,000 × .30). The remaining net deductible amount of $1,000 is carried back to offset taxable amounts in 1992, leaving $2,000 of net taxable amount in that year which gives rise to a deferred tax liability of $800. The net taxable amount of 1993 is still $3,000, giving rise to a deferred tax liability of $1,200. The computation of income tax expense is as follows:

Income tax payable		$2,700
Add: Increase in deferred tax liability:		
Amount for 1992	$ 800	
Amount for 1993	1,200	
		$2,000
Less: Increase in deferred tax asset:		
Amount for carryback to 1991		($2,700)
Income tax expense		$2,000

Changing the expected year of deductibility of the warranty cost from 1995 to 1994 produced a significant change in the recognition of a deferred tax asset and, hence, in the recognition of income tax expense. Since income tax expense is $700 less in 1991 when the reversal of the future deductible amount (the warranty costs) is changed from 1995 to 1994, management may desire this change. This change may be possible using a tax-planning strategy.

Computations in the Following Year (1992)   Suppose that Sales Company records the entry shown in Exhibit 17A–3 above for income tax expense in 1991. Further, assume that in 1992 the company has pretax accounting income of $8,000. Also assume that no originating temporary differences arise in 1992. The only temporary difference is the collection of $3,000 of the installment receivable, which is taxable but has previously been included in pretax accounting income.

Exhibit 17A–4 presents the analysis for 1992. The reconciliation of pretax accounting income with taxable income shows the additional taxable amount of $3,000 increasing taxable income to $11,000. With a current period tax rate of 40%, the income tax payable is $4,400.

The analysis of future reversals of temporary differences again results in a net deductible amount of $10,000 in 1994. Of this amount, $9,000 is again carried back to 1991, and the remaining $1,000 is carried back to 1992. Recall that the carryback procedure requires that the carryback be to the earliest possible year first. The remaining net taxable amount in 1993 results in a deferred tax liability amount of $1,200.

The above computations result in ending-balance amounts. To compute the amount to be recognized in the current year, find the difference between amounts currently recorded as deferred tax assets and deferred tax liabilities and the newly determined ending-balance amounts. The ending balance in the deferred tax asset account at the end of 1991 was $2,700. The ending balance at the end of 1992 is to total $3,100 ($2,700 carried back to 1991 and $400

EXHIBIT 17A-3   Illustration of Carryback and Carryforward with No Loss of Future Deductible Amounts

Information:

1. Sales Company has an installment receivable of $9,000 to be received in three equal installments over the next three years. The entire amount of the receivable is included in pretax accounting income for 1991, but will not be included in taxable income until it is received in cash.
2. All expenses except warranty expenses have been paid and included in both pretax accounting income and taxable income. Warranty expense in the amount of $13,000 has been estimated and included in the determination of pretax accounting income but not taxable income. It is expected that all warranty costs will be paid in 1994.

Reconciliation of Pretax Accounting Income and Taxable Income

Pretax accounting income (assumed) $5,000

Temporary differences:
  Future taxable amounts:
    Accounts Receivable . . . . ($9,000)
  Future deductible amounts:
    Warranty costs 13,000

Net (taxable) deductible amount 4,000

Taxable income $9,000
Current period tax rate . . . . × 0.30

Current period income tax payable $2,700

Analysis of Reversals of Temporary Differences

	1991	1992	1993	1994	1995
Future taxables amounts from future collection of receivable of $9,000		$3,000	$3,000	$3,000	
Future deductible amounts from payment of warranty costs of $13,000				(13,000)	0
Net taxable (deductible) amounts		$3,000	$3,000	($10,000)	$0
Three-year carryback of net deductible amount	(9,000)	(1,000)		10,000	0
Carryforward of remaining net deductible amount to offset future taxable amounts					$ 0
Net taxable (deductible) amounts	($9,000)	$2,000	$3,000	$ 0	$ 0
Multiply by enacted future tax rates	× 0.3	× 0.4	× 0.4	× 0.4	× 0.4
Deferred tax liability (asset)	($2,700)	$ 800	$1,200	$ 0	$ 0

Computation of Income Tax Expense

Income tax payable (see above) $2,700
Net deferred tax liability (asset) recognizable . . (700)

Income tax expense $2,000

Income Tax Journal Entry for 1991

Income tax expense 2,000
Deferred tax asset 2,700
    Income taxes payable 2,700
    Deferred tax liability 2,000

carried back to 1992); hence, the amount to be debited to the deferred tax asset account is $400. Similarly, the decrease (requiring a debit entry) to the deferred tax liability account is $800 (the ending balance of $1,200 less the beginning balance of $2,000). The entry to record income tax for 1992 is shown at the bottom of Exhibit 17A-4.

Exhibits 17A-1 through 17A-4 demonstrate the application of the carryback and carryforward procedures required by *SFAS No. 96* in the computation of income tax expense and the related deferred tax asset and liability amounts.

EXHIBIT 17A-4   Illustration of Carryback and Carryforward with No Loss of Future Deductible Amounts

---

Information (Continuation of Exhibit 17A-3 Illustration):

1. Sales Company collects $3,000 on the installment receivable in 1992, leaving two $3,000 installments to be received over the next two years. The $13,000 in warranty costs are expected to be paid in 1994. There are no additional temporary differences. Pretax accounting income is $8,000 in 1992.

Reconciliation of Pretax Accounting Income and Taxable Income

Year	1991	1992
Pretax accounting income (assumed)	$5,000	$8,000
Temporary differences:		
Future taxable amounts:		
Accounts Receivable	($9,000)	$3,000
Future deductible amounts:		
Warranty costs	$13,000	0
Net (taxable) deductible amount	*4,000*	*3,000*
Taxable income	$9,000	$11,000
Current period tax rate	× 0.30	× 0.4
Current period income tax payable	*$2,700*	*$4,400*

Analysis of Reversals of Temporary Differences

Year	1991	1992	1993	1994	1995
Future taxables amounts from future collection of receivable of $6,000			$3,000	$3,000	
Future deductible amounts from payment of warranty costs of $13,000				($13,000)	$ 0
Net taxable (deductible) amounts			$3,000	($10,000)	$ 0
Three-year carryback of net deductible amount	($9,000)	($1,000)	0	10,000	0
Net Taxable (deductible) amounts	($9,000)	$1,000	$3,000	$ 0	$ 0
Multiply by enacted tax rates	× 0.30	×0.40	×0.40	× 0.40	× 0.40
Deferred tax liability (asset)	*($2,700)*	*($400)*	*$1,200*	*$ 0*	*$ 0*

Computation of Income Tax Expense in 1992:

Income tax payable		$4,400
Deferred tax asset:		
Beginning balance	$2,700	
Ending balance ($2,700 plus $400)	$3,100	
Adjustment: Increase in deferred tax asset		($400)
Deferred tax liability:		
Beginning balance	$2,000	
Ending balance	$1,200	
Adjustment: Decrease in deferred tax liability		($800)
Income tax expense in 1992		$3,200

Journal Entry:

Income tax expense	3,200	
Deferred tax asset	400	
Deferred tax liability	800	
Income taxes payable		4,400

KEY TERMS

Asset/liability method (893)
Carryback-carryforward option (881)
Carryforward-only option (881)
Comprehensive allocation (895)
Deferral method (891)
Deferral method for ITC (919)
Deferred tax asset (899)
Deferred tax liability (899)
Flow-through method for ITC (919)
Future deductible amount (also deductible amount) (898)
Future taxable amount (also taxable amount) (898)

Interperiod tax allocation (891)
Intraperiod tax allocation (923)
Investment tax credit (ITC) (918)
Net operating loss (NOL) (881)
Originating difference (897)
Partial allocation (895)
Permanent difference (887)
Pretax accounting income (886)
Reversing difference (897)
Taxable income (886)
Tax-planning strategy (917)
Temporary difference (888)
Valuation allowance (901)

QUESTIONS

1. Briefly distinguish between interperiod tax allocation and intraperiod tax allocation.
2. Relate the matching principle to interperiod income tax allocation.
3. Explain when deferred income tax can be either an asset or a liability.
4. Briefly define pretax accounting income and taxable income.
5. Define an income tax difference. Identify and briefly define the two types of differences.
6. XTE Corporation (a) uses straight-line depreciation in its accounting and uses accelerated depreciation on its income tax return, and (b) holds a $50,000 investment in tax-free municipal bonds. What kind of tax difference is caused by each of these items? Explain.
7. Does the "deferred" caption in deferred income taxes mean that deferred income tax is always a long-term (noncurrent) item? Explain.
8. ATW Corporation has completed an analysis of its accounting income, taxable income, and the temporary differences. Taxable income is $100,000, and there are several temporary differences which result in: (a) a deferred tax asset of $15,000 and (b) a deferred tax liability of $20,000. The income tax rate for the current and all future periods is 32%. There were no deferred tax assets or deferred tax liabilities as of the beginning of the current year. Give the entry to record income taxes and indicate how the amounts were determined.
9. Explain the difference between a deferred tax liability and a deferred tax asset.
10. Define partial allocation. Summarize the argument for partial allocation.
11. Define comprehensive allocation. Summarize the arguments for comprehensive allocation.
12. Explain the difference between a taxable amount and a tax deductible amount.
13. Define income tax net operating loss (NOLs), carrybacks and carryforwards. Briefly explain the two options available to taxpayers.
14. In respect to NOL carrybacks and carryforwards, which one involves greater certainty of realization? How does this difference in certainty affect the accounting treatment for loss carrybacks and carryforwards?
15. Define an investment tax credit. How does it differ from a tax deduction?
16. Explain the limitation on reporting deferred income tax asset in interperiod income tax allocation under proposed SFAS No. 109.
17. RVA Corporation's accounting and income tax records provided the following data at the end of 1991: Pretax accounting income, $60,000; deductible temporary differences, $14,000; taxable income, $50,000; and taxable temporary differences, $23,000. Prepare a reconciliation of pretax accounting income and taxable income.
18. Bye Corporation is preparing its 1991 financial statements. The following are its pretax amounts: income before extraordinary items, $300,000; extraordinary gain, $20,000; and prior period adjustment, $16,000 (a loss). Interperiod income tax computations showed income tax expense (including the prior period adjustment) of $104,880. How much income tax should be allocated to each of the three intraperiod amounts under proposed SFAS No. 109?

EXERCISES

E 17–1
Analysis of Interperiod
Income Tax Deferrals
(L.O. 3)

Listed below are six independent situations that require interperiod income tax allocation. For each item indicate with a check (√) whether the deferred income tax account would be an asset or a liability.

Item	The Deferred Income Tax Account Would Be	
	Asset	Liability
a. Construction contracts: percentage of completion for accounting and completed contract for income tax	_____	_____
b. Estimated warranty costs: accrual basis for accounting and future cash basis for income tax	_____	_____
c. Straight-line depreciation for accounting and accelerated depreciation for income tax	_____	_____
d. Unrealized gain (i.e., loss recovery): LCM recognized for accounting; and gain recognized only on later disposal of the asset for income tax	_____	_____
e. Rent revenue collected in advance: accrual basis for accounting, cash basis for income tax	_____	_____
f. Unrealized loss: LCM recognized for accounting and loss recognized only on later disposal of the asset for income tax	_____	_____

E 17–2
Terminology Overview
(L.O. 3)

Listed below to the left are some terms frequently used in *SFAS No. 96* and proposed *SFAS No. 109*. Brief definitions are listed to the right. Match the definitions with the terms by entering the appropriate letters in the blanks.

Term	Brief Definition
_____ 1. Deferred tax asset.	A. Income tax payable plus net changes in the deferred tax liability, deferred tax asset, and valuation allowance accounts.
_____ 2. Taxable amount.	B. An amount used to compute income tax payable
_____ 3. Permanent difference.	C. The difference between a current deferred asset and a current deferred liability when the latter is higher.
_____ 4. Valuation allowance	D. May result in a cash refund or a reduction of income tax payable in future periods.
_____ 5. Temporary difference.	E. An amount used to compute deferred tax assets and liabilities, and a portion of income tax expense
_____ 6. Taxable income.	F. A deferred tax that has a net debit reported as an _____ .
_____ 7. Net current deferred tax liability.	G. A deferred tax amount that has a debit balance.
_____ 8. Income tax expense	H. A tax difference that does not reverse, or turn around.
_____ 9. Asset.	I. An allocation of tax among the components in the financial statements.
_____ 10. NOL carryback.	J. A contra account used to reduce deferred tax assets to the portion more likely than not to be realized.
_____ 11. Intraperiod income tax allocation.	K. An amount that represents a difference between financial accounting and tax accounting that will increase taxable income in future periods.
_____ 12. Investment tax credit.	L. An income tax provision intended to encourage investments in qualifying assets.

E 17–3
Reporting Deferred
Income Tax on the
Balance Sheet
(L.O. 4)

At the end of 1995, Raleigh Corporation had a $90,000 credit balance in its deferred tax liability account. The income tax rate was 30%. This credit balance was due only to the following temporary differences:

a. Depreciation for accounting purposes, $200,000; for income tax purposes, $300,000. The related asset has a five-year remaining life.

b. Installment sale revenue: for accounting purposes, $600,000; for income tax purposes, $400,000. The collection period for the $200,000 receivable is the following four years with equal amounts each year.

Required:

Show how the deferred tax amounts would be reported on the 1995 balance. Show computations.

E 17-4

Recording and Reporting Income Tax Consequences for a Two-Year Period

(L.O. 4)

The records of Star Corporation provided the following data related to accounting and taxable income:

	1991	1992
Pretax accounting income	$200,000	$220,000
Taxable income (tax return)	220,000	200,000
Income tax rate	34%	34%

There are no existing temporary differences other than those reflected in this data.

Required:

1. Give the journal entry to record the income tax consequences for each year.
2. Show how income tax expense, income tax payable, and deferred income tax should be reported on the financial statements each year.

E 17-5

Interperiod Tax Allocation, a Revenue and an Expense

(L.O. 4)

The records of TNA Corporation, at the end of 1991, provided the following data related to income taxes:
a. Gain on disposal of an asset, $50,000; recorded for accounting purposes at the end of 1991; reported for income tax purposes at the end of 1993.
b. Estimated expense, $30,000; accrued for accounting purposes at the end of 1991; reported for income tax purposes when paid at the end of 1992.
c. Taxable income (from the tax return) at the end of 1991, $100,000; the enacted income tax rate is 34%. There were no deferred tax amounts as of the beginning of 1991.

Required:

1. Did the gain and expense cause temporary differences? Explain why. Classify each item as deductible or taxable and explain why.
2. Prepare the following for 1991: (*a*) reconciliation of taxable income with pretax accounting income and compute income taxes payable, (*b*) schedule of temporary differences, and (*c*) entry to record income taxes at the end of the year.
3. Show the amounts that will be reported on the (*a*) balance sheet statement and (*b*) and income statement for 1991.

E 17-6

Analyze a Tax Difference, Deferred Asset: Entries and Reporting

(L.O. 5)

Voss Corporation reported accounting income before taxes and rent revenue collected in advance as follows: 1991, $75,000; 1992, $88,000. Taxable income for each year would have been the same as pretax accounting income except for the tax effects rising for the first time in 1991 of $300 per month rent revenue collected in advance on October 1, 1991, for the six months ending March 31, 1992. Rent revenue is taxable in the year collected. The tax rate for 1991 and 1992 is 30%, and the year-end for both accounting and tax purposes is December 31. The rent revenue collected in advance is the only difference and, it is repeated in October 1992.

Required:

1. Is this a temporary difference? Why or why not?
2. Reconcile accounting income with taxable income, calculate income tax payable, prepare a schedule of temporary differences, compute the balance in the deferred tax asset account, and prepare journal entries for each year-end.
3. Prepare a partial income statement for each year starting with pretax accounting income.
4. What amount of deferred income tax asset or liability would be reported on the 1991 and 1992 balance sheet?

E 17-7

Analyze a Tax Liability: Entries and Reporting

(L.O. 4)

Stacy Corporation would have had identical income before taxes on both its income tax returns and income statements for the years 1991 through 1994 except for an operational asset that cost $120,000. The asset was depreciated for income tax purposes using the following amounts: 1991, $48,000; 1992, $36,000; 1993, $24,000; and 1994, $12,000. However, for accounting purposes, the straight-line method was used (i.e., $30,000 per year). Both the accounting and tax periods end December 31. The operational asset has a four-year estimated life and no residual value. Income amounts before depreciation expense and income taxes for each of the four years were as follows (this is the only temporary difference):

	1991	1992	1993	1994
Accounting income before taxes and depreciation	$60,000	$80,000	$70,000	$70,000

Assume the average and marginal income tax rate for each year was 30%.

Required:

1. Is this a temporary difference? Explain why.
2. Using the steps suggested in the text, reconcile accounting and taxable income, calculate income tax payable, compute the balance in the deferred tax liability account, and prepare journal entries for each year-end.
3. For each year show the deferred income tax amount that would be reported on the balance sheet.

E 17–8
Operating Carryback-Carryforward (NOL) Options: Entries and Reporting
(L.O. 1, 2)

Tyson Corporation reported pretax income from operations in 1991 of $80,000 (the first year of operations). In 1992, the corporation experienced a $40,000 pretax loss from operations (NOL). Assume an average income tax rate of 45%.

Required:

1. Assess Tyson's income tax situation for 1991 and 1992 separately. How should Tyson elect to handle the loss in 1992?
2. Based on your assessments in (1), give the 1991 and 1992 income tax entries that Tyson should make.
3. Show how all tax-related items would be reported on the 1991 and 1992 income statement and balance sheet.

E 17–9
Operating Carryback-Carryforward (NOL) Options: Choice Required, Entries
(L.O. 1, 2)

Toner Corporation reported the following taxable income and loss: 1991, income, $10,000 (tax rate 20%), and 1992, $40,000 loss (tax rate 20%). At the end of 1992, Toner made the following estimates: 1993 income, $4,000 (tax rate 20%); 1994 income, $11,000 (tax rate 20%); and 1995 income, $50,000 (tax rate 30%). On the basis of these estimates, which the company considered to be conservative, Toner elected the carryforward-only option and believes the full amount of tax loss carryforward benefit is more likely than not to be realized. There are no other temporary differences, and assume no valuation allowance is needed.

Required:

1. Give the income tax entry for 1991.
2. Give the income tax entry for 1992. Explain the basis for your response.
3. Give the income tax entry for 1993, assuming the actual income was $6,000 (tax rate, 20%).
4. Give the income tax entry for 1994, assuming the actual income was $13,000 (tax rate, 20%).
5. Give the entry for 1995, assuming the actual income was $45,000 (tax rate 35%).
6. Did Toner make a wise choice? Explain.

E 17–10
Comparison of Deferral Method and Asset/Liability Method
(L.O. 3, 4, 5)

Fluery Company reports pretax accounting income in 1991, its first year of operations, at $100,000. Taxable income is $70,000, with temporary differences arising in 1991 from the following sources:

a. Prepayment of 1992 rent in the amount of $12,000 in 1991.
b. An installment sale in the amount of $18,000, with cash collections expected in two equal amounts in 1993 and 1994.

The enacted tax rates are: 1991, 30%; 1992, 30%; and 1993 and thereafter, 40%.

Required:

1. Prepare the journal entry to record income taxes under the deferral method.
2. Prepare the journal entry to record income taxes under the asset/liability method as required under *SFAS No. 109.*

E 17–11
Comparison of
Deferral Method and
Asset/Liability Method
(L.O. 3, 4, 5)

Assume the Chicago Company has a deferred tax liability in the amount of $6,000 at December 31, 1991, relating to a $20,000 installment sale receivable expected to be collected in 1992. The tax rate in 1992 is 30%. However, the rate for 1993 and thereafter is changed during 1992 to 40%. Warranty expense in 1992 included in the determination of pretax accounting income is $50,000, with these amounts expected to be incurred and deductible for tax purposes in 1993. Taxable income is $200,000 in 1992.

Required:

1. Prepare the journal entry to record income taxes in 1992 under the deferral method.
2. Prepare the journal entry to record income taxes in 1992 under the asset/liability method under *SFAS No. 109*.

PROBLEMS

P 17–1
Operating Carryback-
Carryforward (NOL)
Options: Entries
(L.O. 1, 2)

The financial statements of Bayshore Corporation for the first four years of operations reflected the following pretax amounts:

	1991	1992	1993	1994
Income statement (summarized):				
Revenue	$125,000	$155,000	$180,000	$230,000
Expenses	120,000	195,000	160,000	200,000
Pretax income (loss)	$ 5,000	($40,000)	$ 20,000	$ 30,000

Assume an average income tax rate of 30% during 1991 and 1992 and 40% in 1993 and 1994. Assume that future incomes are uncertain at the end of each year, thus a valuation allowance is needed for any deferred tax asset. Management of Bayshore Corporation elects the carryback-carryforward option in order to lock in the immediate cash refund on the NOL carryback. There are no temporary differences.

Required:

1. Recast the above statements to incorporate the income tax effects as required by *SFAS No. 109*. Show computations.
2. Give entries to record the NOL income tax effects for each year.
3. Explain the alternative option that Bayshore might have considered. What are the primary considerations that Bayshore should assess in making its choice?

P 17–2
Operating Carryforward-
Carryback (NOL)
Options: Entries and
Reporting
(L.O. 1, 2)

The pretax financial statements of Gibson Corporation for the first two years of operation reflected the following amounts:

	1991	1992
Revenues	$295,000	$330,000
Expenses	320,000	315,000
Pretax income (loss)	($25,000)	$ 15,000

Assume an average tax rate of 20% for 1991 and 1992.

Required:

Gibson will have to apply the NOL carryforward-only option because there are no prior earnings. Estimates of future earnings are uncertain.

1. Restate the above financial statements incorporating the income tax effects. There are no temporary differences.
2. Give entries to record the NOL income tax effects for 1991 and 1992 as required under *SFAS No. 109*. Explain the basis for your entries.

P 17–3
Income Tax Allocation:
Depreciation
(L.O. 2, 3, 4)

The financial statements of Dakar Corporation for a four-year period reflected the following pretax amounts:

	1991	1992	1993	1994
Income statement (summarized):				
Revenues	$110,000	$124,000	$144,000	$164,000
Expenses	(80,000)	(92,000)	(95,000)	(128,000)
Depreciation expense (straight-line)	(10,000)	(10,000)	(10,000)	(10,000)
Balance sheet (partial):				
Machine (four-year life, no				
residual value), at cost	$ 40,000	$ 40,000	$ 40,000	$ 40,000

Dakar has an average and marginal tax rate of 40% each year and uses accelerated depreciation for income tax purposes as follows: 1991, $16,000; 1992, $12,000; 1993, $8,000; and 1994, $4,000. There are no recorded deferred tax assets or liabilities at January 1, 1991.

Required:

1. Is this a temporary difference? Explain your answer.
2. Prepare the following for each year: (*a*) schedule to reconcile accounting and taxable incomes, (*b*) schedule to compute income tax payable, (*c*) schedule to compute deferred income tax, and (*d*) journal entry at each year-end to record income taxes.
3. For each year show the deferred income tax amount that should be reported on the balance sheet.

P 17–4
Analyze Three Income Tax Items: Entries and Reporting
(L.O. 2, 3, 4)

The income statements for Victor Corporation for two years (summarized) were as follows:

	1991	1992
Revenues	$180,000	$200,000
Expenses	142,000	181,000
Accounting income before permanent and temporary differences	$ 38,000	$ 19,000
Taxable income (per tax return)	$ 56,000	$ 11,000

Income tax rate, 40%.

For tax purposes, the following income tax differences existed:

a. Expenses (given above) on the 1992 income statement include goodwill amortization of $10,000, which will never be deductible for income tax purposes.
b. Revenues (given above) on the 1992 income include $10,000 rent revenue, which was taxable in 1991 but was unearned at the end of 1991.
c. Expenses (given above) on the 1991 income statement include $8,000 of estimated warranty costs, which are not deductible for income tax purposes until 1992.

There were no other differences. Assume *SFAS No. 109* applies.

Required:

1. Explain why each one of the three income tax consequences given above is or is not a permanent or temporary difference?
2. Prepare the following for each year: (*a*) schedule to reconcile accounting and taxable incomes, (*b*) schedule to compute income tax payable, (*c*) schedule to compute deferred income tax, and (*d*) journal entry at each year-end to record income taxes.
3. Show how the deferred income tax asset and/or liability would be reported on the income statements and balance sheet for 1991 and 1992.

P 17–5
Recording and Reporting the Income Tax Consequences of a Deferred Asset and a Deferred Liability
(L.O. 4, 6)

The records of Lollie Corporation provided the following income tax–related information.

	1991	1992	1993	1994
Pretax accounting income	$90,000	92,000	95,000	98,000
Taxable income (tax return)	63,000	101,000	104,000	107,000

Income tax rate, 30%.

The above amounts include only two temporary differences as follows:

a. Installment sales—for accounting purposes in 1991, $30,000; included in the tax return, $10,000 each year, 1992 through 1994.

b. Cost of warranties—for accounting purposes, $4,000 in 1991; deducted for income tax $1,000 each year,1991 through 1994.

Required:

1. Assuming *SFAS No. 109* applies, prepare the following for each year: (*a*) schedule to reconcile accounting and taxable income and to compute taxes payable, (*b*) schedule of temporary differences, (*c*) schedule to compute deferred income taxes, and (*d*) journal entry at the end of each year to record income taxes.
2. Show how income tax expense, deferred income tax asset and/or liability, and income taxes payable should be reported on the financial statements for each year.

P 17–6

Interperiod Tax Allocation: Comparison of Asset/Liability Method and Deferral Method

(L.O. 4, 5)

Fox Corporation purchased a machine on January 1, Year 1, that cost $40,000. The machine had an estimated service life of five years and no residual value. Fox uses straight-line depreciation for accounting purposes and accelerated depreciation for the income tax return as follows: Year 1, 30%, Year 2, 25%, Year 3, 20%, Year 4, 15%, and Year 5, 10%. Taxable income on the tax return for Year 1 was $150,000. The Year 1 income statement showed a $15,000 deduction for amortization of goodwill; income tax regulations do not permit the amortization of goodwill for income tax purposes. There were no other factors to complicate the company's income tax computations during Year 1. The income tax rate is 20% in Year 1 and 40% in all subsequent years.

Required:

1. Identify any temporary difference and explain the basis for your decisions. Also, identify any taxable amounts and deductible amounts and explain their effects on the analysis of the income tax differences.
2. In accordance with the requirements of proposed *SFAS No. 109,* prepare the following at the end of Year 1: (*a*) schedule to reconcile accounting income and taxable income and to compute income tax payable, (*b*) schedule of temporary differences, (*c*) schedule to compute deferred income taxes, and (*d*) journal entry to record income taxes at year-end.
3. Repeat (2) using the deferred method.

P 17–7

Recording and Reporting Income Tax Consequences for Temporary Differences

(L.O. 2, 4)

The records of Hicks Corporation provided the following information: taxable income based on tax return, 1991, $47,600; income tax rate, 30%. There were two temporary differences as follows:

a. December 1, 1991, collected $2,400 rent in advance for 1992. The $2,400 must be included on the 1991 tax return.

b. On December 1, 1991, the company recorded a $10,000 estimated expense that will be paid in 1992 and included in the 1992 income tax return.

Assume *SFAS No. 109* applies.

Required:

1. Prepare a reconciliation of taxable income with pretax accounting income for 1991.
2. Prepare a schedule of temporary differences for 1991.
3. Give the entry to record income taxes at the end of 1991. Show computations for each amount.
4. Show how the income tax consequences should be reported on the three required financial statements for 1991 assuming 75% of the income tax payable was paid by the end of 1991.

P 17–8

COMPREHENSIVE PROBLEM
♦

Recording and Reporting a Deferred Tax Liability and Change in Tax Rate

(L.O. 2, 3, 4, 6)

The records of Morgan Corporation provided the following data at the end of Years 1 through 4 relating to income tax allocation:

	Year 1	Year 2	Year 3	Year 4
Pretax accounting income	$58,000	$70,000	$80,000	$88,000
Taxable income (tax return)	28,000	80,000	90,000	98,000

The above amounts include only one temporary difference; no other changes occurred. At the end of Year 1, the company prepaid an expense of $30,000, which will be amortized for accounting purposes over the next three years (straight-line). The full amount is included in

Year 1 for income tax purposes. At the end of Year 1, the enacted tax rate was 35%. At the end of Year 2, the enacted tax rate was changed to 30% to remain in effect through Year 4.

Required:

1. Prepare a schedule of temporary differences at the end of Year 1.
2. Give the entry to record income taxes at the end of Year 1.
3. Give any entry that should be made in Year 2 to reflect the change in the enacted income tax rate. If none is required, explain why.
4. Give the entry at the end of each year for Years 2 through 4 assuming the new enacted tax rate is not changed.
5. Complete the following tabulation:

	Year 1	Year 2	Year 3	Year 4
Income statement:				
Income tax expense				
Balance sheet:				
Liabilities:				
Income tax payable				
Deferred tax liability				

P 17–9

Recording and Reporting Income Tax Consequences for a Four-Year Period

(L.O. 2, 4, 6)

The records of Aris Corporation provided the following income tax allocation data:

	1991	1992*	1993*	1994*
Taxable income (tax return)	$60,000	$80,000	$85,000	$ 75,000
Pretax accounting income	40,000	70,000	90,000	100,000
Income tax rate, 30%.				

* Estimated amounts

The deferred tax account reflected a zero balance at the start of 1991. There was only one temporary difference, an estimated expense, which was recorded (i.e., accrued) for accounting purposes in 1991 and 1992 but was deductible for tax purposes in 1993 and 1994.

Required:

1. Prepare a schedule to reconcile taxable and accounting income and to compute the temporary difference for each year.
2. Prepare a schedule of temporary differences at the end of 1991.
3. Give the entry to record income taxes at the end of 1991.
4. Give the entry at the end of each year for years 1992 through 1994 assuming the enacted tax rate is not changed.
5. Complete the following tabulation:

	Estimated		
1991	1992	1993	1994
Income statement:			
Income tax expense			
Balance sheet:			
Deferred tax liability			

P 17–10

Overview of the Concept of Interperiod Income Tax Allocation: Depreciation

(L.O. 4, 5)

On January 1, 1991, Keefe Corporation purchased a machine that cost $60,000. The machine has an estimated five-year life and no residual value. The company uses the straight-line method for accounting purposes and accelerated depreciation for tax purposes as follows: 1991, $20,000; 1992, $16,000; 1993, $12,000; 1994, $8,000; and 1995, $4,000. The enacted income tax rates are 1991 through 1994, 30%; and 1995, 35%. These rates are known as of January 1, 1991. Taxable income (from the tax return): 1991, $80,000; 1992, $84,000; 1993, $88,000; 1994, $92,000; and 1995, $96,000. Depreciation on the machine is the only temporary difference. *SFAS No. 109* is assumed to apply.

Required:

1. Complete the following schedules:

| | | Estimated | | | |
	1991	1992	1993	1994	1995
a. Temporary differences:					
Taxable income (tax return)					
Temporary differences:					
Depreciation, accounting					
Depreciation, income tax return					
Temporary difference					
b. Income tax payable					
c. Deferred tax liability					

2. Use the format shown for the summary review problem to give the journal entry at each year-end for income taxes:

P 17–11
Reporting a Deferred Tax Asset
(L.O. 3, 4, 6)

Ajax Corporation began operations on January 1, 1991. At the end of 1991, the company had two temporary differences, and the reversing period ends in 1995. The two differences relate to (1) litigation loss and (2) depreciation. The company's records at the end of 1991 showed pretax accounting income of $100 million, and the 1991 income tax return shows taxable income of $95 million. An analysis of these two sources provided the following data about the two temporary differences at the end of 1991 (in millions):

a. Depreciation of machinery acquired at start of 1991 that cost $90. For accounting purposes, depreciate using the straight-line basis over years 1991 through 1995 ($18 per year).
For income tax purposes the accelerated depreciation was as follows: 1991, $30; 1992, $24; 1993, $18; 1994, $12, and 1995, $6 (total, $90).

b. Litigation loss accrual, recorded at the end of 1991, $7. Accounting—the company was sued and an expected loss of $7 was recorded at the end of 1991, and it is expected to be finally settled in 1993 at which time it will be reported on the tax return; that is, the loss is deductible when the liability is paid.

Accounting for income taxes is to be completed under the requirements of *SFAS No. 109*. At the end of 1991 a reconciliation of pretax accounting income and taxable income (from the 1991 tax return) was as follows:

	1991
Taxable income (from the tax return)	$ 95
Temporary differences:	
a. Depreciation	12
b. Litigation loss	(7)
Pretax accounting income	$100

The average and marginal tax rate for all periods is 30%.

Required:
1. Prepare a schedule of temporary differences at the end of 1991.
2. Give the 1991 journal entry to record income taxes.
3. Show how the 1991 tax-related items should be reported in the 1991 financial statements.

P 17–12
Analysis of Three Temporary Differences
(L.O. 4)

Triple Corporation started operations on January 1, 1992. At the end of 1992, the following income tax–related data were available:

	1992	1993	1994
Taxable income (tax return)	$116,500	$	$
a. Gross margin on installment sales:			
Accounting	175,000		
Tax return	65,000	70,000	40,000
b. Rent revenue collected in advance:			
Accounting	6,000		
Tax return	4,000	2,000	
c. Estimated warranty expense:			
Accounting (accrued)	15,000	16,000	
Tax return	12,000	16,500	2,500
Income tax rate	30%	30%	30%

Required:
1. What kind of tax difference is represented by each one of the three income tax consequences given above? Explain. Also identify the taxable and deductible amounts.
2. Prepare the following schedules related to income tax allocation for 1992:
    a. Schedule to reconcile taxable accounting and taxable income.
    b. Schedule of temporary differences.
3. Give the entry at the end of 1992 to record income taxes as required by *SFAS No. 109.* Show computations. Assume no valuation allowance is needed.
4. Show the items that should be reported on the 1992 financial statements assuming 75% of taxes payable were paid.

P 17–13
Analysis of Two Temporary Differences
(L.O. 4, 5)

Cruse Corporation started operations on January 1, 1991. At the end of 1991 the data related to income taxes were as follows (in $000s):

Taxable income from the tax return $2,850

Income tax consequences:

a. Gain on installment sale, $330—in 1991, recognized for accounting purposes and will be included on tax return equally over 1992, 1993, and 1994 . . . . ($330)
b. Litigation loss, $270—in 1991, accrued as expense for accounting purposes and will be included in the tax return in 1994 . . . . $270
Income tax rate, 30%. *SFAS No. 109* applies.

Required:
1. Analyze each of the income tax consequences given above to determine whether each one is a temporary difference, a taxable or deductible amount, and a deferred tax liability or asset. Explain each determination.
2. Prepare the following schedules for 1991: (*a*) reconciliation of taxable income and pretax accounting income and (*b*) temporary differences.
3. Give the entry to record income taxes at the end of 1991. Show computations.
4. Show the amounts that should be reported on the three required financial statements at the end of 1991. Assume that none of the 1991 income tax liability is paid before the end of 1991.

P 17–14

COMPREHENSIVE PROBLEM
♦

Accounting for Deferred Taxes, Changes in Tax Rate
(L.O. 1, 2, 4, 6)

The first year of operations for Blair Corporation is 1991. The accounting and income tax periods end on December 31. The records of the company provided the following income tax-related data at the end of 1991 (In $000s):

Marginal income tax rate is 40% for 1991–1993, and becomes 30% in 1994. This is known in 1991.
Taxable income $150

Temporary differences:

a. A $300 estimated expense was accrued (i.e., recognized) at the end of 1991 for accounting purposes; expected settlement date, year end 1994 for income tax purposes.
b. A $200 gain on a special installment sale, recognized for accounting purposes at the end of 1991; included in income tax return as collected in equal amounts for 1992 through 1995.
c. A depreciable asset that cost $200 (estimated useful life five years and no residual value) is depreciated as follows:

	1991	1992	1993	1994	1995
Accounting purposes	$40	$40	$40	$40	$40
Income tax purposes	66	54	40	26	14
Differences	($26)	($14)	$ 0	$14	$26

d. Rent revenue collected in advance at the end of 1991, $40; recognized for accounting purposes in 1992 and 1993. The full amount must be included in the 1991 income tax return.

Required:
1. Analyze each of the four income tax consequences given above to determine whether each one is a taxable or deductible temporary difference.

2. Use the procedures shown in the Summary Review Problem to determine the entry for income taxes in 1991.
3. Give the entry to record income taxes at the end of 1991. Show computations.
4. Show the amounts that should be reported on the financial statements at the end of 1991. Assume that 75% of the 1991 income tax liability was paid before the end of 1991.

P 17–15
Operating Carryback-
Carryforward (NOL)
Options: Entries and
Reporting
(L.O. 1, 2, 4)

Decker Corporation experienced a loss year in 1994. The company reported taxable income (loss) for 1991 to 1994, and had average tax rates as follows:

	1991	1992	1993	1994
Taxable income (loss)	$8,000	$32,000	$15,000	$(65,000)
Income tax rate	30%	30%	35%	40%

There were no temporary differences from 1991 to 1994.

Required:

1. Record income taxes for 1994 and 1995 assuming Decker elects the carryback-carryforward option. Also assume:
   a. For 1994, any tax refund receivable was collected early in 1995.
   b. For 1995, the company reported taxable income of $45,000 and pretax accounting income of $50,000 (a $5,000 credit timing difference). The income tax rate for 1995 was 45%.
2. List the accounts and amounts that should be reported on the income statements and balance sheet for each of the above requirements.
3. Repeat the requirements of 1 and 2, assuming Decker elects the carryforward only option, and no valuation allowance is deemed necessary.

P 17–16

COMPREHENSIVE PROBLEM
◆

Taxable and Deductible
Amounts with NOL
Carryback and
Carryfoward, Valuation
Allowance
(L.O. 1, 2, 4, 6, 7)

Nary Company started operations on January 1, 1991. The accounting period ends December 31. This problem encompasses a four-year period, 1991 through 1994. During this period, the Company has several temporary differences and incurs an operating loss in 1992. The enacted tax rate for all periods is 40%, and all amounts are given in thousand of dollars.

Case Data	1991	1992	1993	1994
a. Pretax accounting income (loss)	$400	($700)	100	200
b. Temporary differences:				
Gross margin on installment sales				
Accounting basis (when sold)	200	50	150	100
Tax basis (when collected)	0	125	75	125
Deferred gross margin, December 31	200	125	200	175
Accrued estimated warranty costs:				
Accounting basis	100	100	180	160
Tax basis	0	80	110	130
Accrued warranty costs, December 31	100	120	190	220

Assume that one-half of the end-of-product deferred gross margin is classified as a current asset in each year, and that 25% of the ending accrued provision for warranty costs is classified as a current liability. Also assume Nary elects the carryback and carryforward option for any NOL that occurs and that management cannot expect positive taxable income exclusive of reversals of temporary differences in any year. That is, in determining whether a valuation allowance is needed, assume future taxable income exclusive of temporary differences is zero. Assume it is possible to utilize future taxable amounts to realize the tax benefit of an equal amount of any future deductible amounts. Also assume it is possible to use the carryback option to realize the tax benefit of any future deductible amount up to the amount of the current period taxes paid.

Required:

1. Compete the appropriate schedules and prepare the journal entry to record income taxes for each year under the provisions of *SFAS No. 109*.
2. For each year, show how the income tax information would be reported on the income statement and balance sheet, including the current and noncurrent classifications.

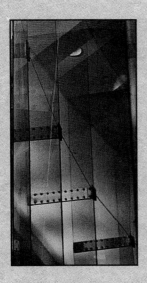

C H A P T E R

18

Accounting for Leases

◆

INTRODUCTION
◆

Well over $100 billion in business assets will be leased this year by large and small companies alike. Assets such as construction equipment, computer mainframes, delivery vehicles, office furnishings, real estate, commercial aircraft, communications systems—even entire manufacturing plants, equipment included—will be leased at some point during the year. Although leasing, rather than buying, business assets has always been fairly common, in the late 1960s, many companies discovered leasing in a big way, changing the face of asset leasing forever.

From the relatively simple idea of renting space or equipment, the concept of leasing has expanded and become a complex proposition in which leasing is used to finance asset acquisitions, usually involving both economic and tax benefits. To understand this new face of leasing, consider the following situations.

Gino's Inc., a major fast-food pizza chain, had to revise the debt it was reporting on its balance sheet from $30 million to $156 million.[1] That's a 420% increase in debt! The chain had been growing by leaps and bounds, seemingly without having to borrow money to finance its growth, which mystified a number of people. But it was no mystery to astute investors and accountants who knew what was going on. Gino's was using leases to finance it growth. Everything was leased—stores, baking ovens, restaurant seating, delivery trucks, everything! The problem was that none of the liabilities incurred in conjunction with these leases was being reported on Gino's balance sheet. But then the accounting rules were changed, forcing Gino's to change too. Before the change, Gino's total stockholder's equity was only $46 million, and with $30 million in debt, the debt-to-equity ratio was about two to three (65%), which many analysts would consider less than satisfactory debt coverage. With debt now reported at $156 million, the ratio reversed to three to one (339%) (3:1), a rather frightening ratio by anyone's standards.

Kmart Stores had a similar experience. After the change in accounting rules became effective, the retailer's reported balance sheet debt grew from a rather modest $211 million to a towering $1.7 billion. Again, the increase reflected leases.

On another front, it is not widely known that many banks and Wall Street investment firms have been active in the lease investment market for the past two decades. Rather than investing in stocks or bonds, some investors prefer something a little more exotic—like a $250,000 pooled participation investment in a Boeing 767, leased and operated by American Airlines, but owned jointly by 25 or more private investor-lessors. Instead of a jet airliner, the lease might involve a string of railroad freight cars or a 3-million-gallon liquid storage tank. Investment firms can arrange lease investments in all types of assets.

In addition to investor lease services, brokerage houses and others also work with noninvestor lessees and lessors. For example, a major rail shipper, or even a railroad itself, may need freight cars. If so, investment firms will, for a fee, put shippers in touch with investors who lease out freight cars as a business.

Assume an investor has $1 million and is looking for an investment opportunity. Suppose an investment firm knows of a food products company that wants to build a liquid storage tank for holding soybean oil and other food ingredients. But the company, for a number of reasons, doesn't want to take on the $1 million in debt it would take to build the facility. The investment firm arranges to use the investor's money to build the storage tank and lease it to the food products company for 25 years. Further, the firm will help structure the lease so that the lessee company won't have to include the $1 million leasing debt obligation as a line item on its balance sheet (although the lease will have to be disclosed in the notes to financial statements).

The rent-a-car industry could not have achieved its present stature were it not for leasing (meaning the rent-a-car companies' leasing of cars from the automakers, not

---

[1] See S. Pulliam, "Beating FAS-13," *Corporate Finance*, December 1988, p. 31.

their renting of them to customers). If Hertz and the other rent-a-car companies had had to buy all the cars in their inventories, they probably couldn't have done so because it would have taken enormous amounts of capital. Instead, they leased major portions of their car fleets from the automakers, usually for relatively short lease terms such as 11 or 14 months. This, incidentally, is how the rental companies were able to advertise "brand-new, low-mileage" Fords, Chevrolets, or whatever make of auto they were featuring.

◆

BASIC LEASE ACCOUNTING ISSUES
◆

SFAS No. 13, "Accounting for Leases," par 1, defines a **lease** as "an agreement conveying the right to use property, plant, or equipment (land and/or depreciable assets), usually for a stated period of time."[2] In the commonly used sense of the term, a lease is a fee-for-usage contract between an owner of property and a renter. The owner of the property is referred to as the **lessor** and the renter is the **lessee.** The lease specifies the terms under which the lessee shall have the right to use the owner's property and the compensation to be paid to the lessor in exchange. The lessee is obligated to make periodic rent payments to the lessor in accordance with a schedule of lease payments normally included as a provision of the lease.

In a leasing context, property includes both real and personal assets. Personal property includes both tangible assets (such as machinery, equipment, or transportation vehicles), and intangibles (such as patents).

Accounting for leases in the commonly used sense of the term is not complicated. The lessee makes periodic rent payments to the lessor, which are accounted for as normal expense items. Meanwhile, the lessor collects the rent payments, crediting an income account such as leasing revenue (or "other income" if leasing is not one of the company's mainstream business activities). For example, assume a lessee rents space for $1,000 a month.

Lessee's books—Entry to record payment of monthly rent expense:

Rent expense 1,000
    Cash   1,000

Lessor's books—Entry to record receipt of monthly rent payment as income:

Cash 1,000
    Leasing revenue   1,000

The Lease from the Lessee's Viewpoint

Leasing evolved from being a relatively simple business activity to a complex one with financing issues and multiple business motives. As the popularity of leasing grew, lessee companies were pleasantly surprised to find that leasing could afford them special economic and tax advantages if the lease were structured properly.[3] Specifically, lessees were quick to discern the key distinction between a capital lease and an operating lease.

---

[2] This definition does not include "(*a*) agreements that are contracts for services that do not transfer the right to use property, plant, or equipment from one contracting party to the other . . . , (*b*) lease agreements concerning the rights to explore for or to exploit natural resources such as oil, gas, minerals, and timber . . . , (*c*) licensing agreements for items such as motion picture films, plays, manuscripts, patents, and copyrights."

[3] Leasing activity can also change rapidly due to business conditions and to changes in the tax law. For example, the legislation that allowed and later rescinded the investment tax credit had immediate effects on the amount of leasing activity in the United States.

Capital lease   SFAS No. 13 defines a **capital lease** as one in which substantially all the risks and benefits of ownership in the leased asset are transferred from the lessor to the lessee. The lessee records the leased property on the balance sheet. The fair market value of the property involved is capitalized and reported as a balance sheet asset, and the debt obligation incurred in signing the lease is recorded as a liability on the balance sheet. From an accounting standpoint, this is much the same as if the property were purchased, with the acquisition being made possible by 100% debt financing. The lessee (owner) even takes depreciation expense on the leased asset.

Operating lease   All leases that do not transfer substantially all the risks and benefits of ownership from the lessor to the lessee are **operating leases.** The lessee does not report the property on the balance sheet. The lessee rents the property, and the rent payments are charged to expense as they come due.

The specific provisions of the lease contract, rather than the characteristics of the leased asset, determine whether the lease is a capital lease or an operating lease. An example of a lease provision that indicates a capital lease is the transfer of title to the leased asset from the lessor to the lessee at the conclusion of the lease term. Ownership *risk* involves the responsibility for casualty loss, wear and tear, obsolescence, and maintenance. Ownership *rewards* involve benefits such as the right of use, increases in the value of the leased asset, and ultimate transfer of title. *SFAS No. 13* provides specific criteria (discussed shortly) for identifying a capital lease. All leases failing to meet these criteria are considered operating leases. Distinctions between capital and operating leases and the basic accounting treatments for both lease classifications are summarized in Exhibit 18–1 (numbers assumed).[4]

Before *SFAS No. 13,* the criteria for determining whether a lease transaction should be accounted for as a capital or operating lease were rather ambiguous. However, the central issue then and now remains management's intent when the asset is leased. Consider two situations:

Leasing situation No. 1: In conjunction with a one-time-only major building project, a construction company leases bulldozers for a period of two years to supplement its own equipment. Following this two-year period the company intends to return the equipment to the lessor. This lease should be accounted for as an operating lease.

Leasing situation No. 2: Working in close contact with a lending institution, a group of physicians arrange to have a medical clinic custom-designed and constructed for their medical practice use. Their intention is to lease the property from the lending institution holding title to the property using a lease contract for a period of 30 years. This lease should be accounted for as a capital lease.

Off-Balance-Sheet Financing   By structuring leasing transactions as operating leases rather than capital leases (in situations where management's intent points to capital lease accounting treatment), lessees are able to take possession and make full use of assets without capitalizing them or reporting the attending lease payment obligations as balance sheet debt. This accounting treatment is referred to as **off-balance-sheet financing.** Since most companies routinely take on debt in conjunction with asset acquisitions, off-balance-sheet financing is attractive to lessee companies for two primary reasons:

* *Debt-equity ratio.* Adding more debt to a company's capital structure causes the debt part of the ratio to increase, which is an adverse development if the debt-equity ratio is already considered high. As a result, stockholders might sell their

---

[4] Exhibit 18–1 suggests symmetry in the lessor and lessee entries. This symmetry is prevalent in other transactions such as credit sales between a seller and buyer. But such symmetry is not always present in leasing. In some cases, a lease may be classified differently by the lessor and the lessee. Later in this chapter, cases are discussed in which the lessor records a capital lease while the lessee records the same lease as an operating lease.

EXHIBIT 18-1   Summary of Lease Accounting Basic Issues for Lessees and Lessors

Lessee	Lessor
Operating lease:	**Operating lease:**
• Lessee is considered to be renting (not owning) the asset from the lessor.	• Lessor continues to own the asset that is leased to the lessee.
• Lessee makes periodic rent payments to the lessor which are accounted for as current operating expenses:	• Lessor collects periodic rent payments that are accounted for as current operating revenue:

Rent expense 100
      Cash   100
	Cash 100
	      Leasing revenue . . . 100

• At end of lease term, the asset is returned to the lessor.	• At end of lease term, the asset is returned to the lessor.
• Lessee does not record depreciation expense.	• Lessor records depreciation on the asset.
Capital lease:	**Direct financing lease:**
• Lessee is considered to own the asset for accounting purposes.	• Asset is considered to be sold to the lessee at the inception of the lease.
• Lease is capitalized on lessee's books:	• Asset is removed from the lessor's books and replaced by receivable:*

Leased asset 1,000
      Lease liability . .   1,000
	Lease receivable . . . 1,000
	      Asset 1,000

• Lessee recognizes periodic payment as part interest and part reduction of principal:	• Lessor recognizes periodic collection of rent as part interest and part as reduction of principal:

Interest expense 10
    Lease liability 90
      Cash   100
	Cash 100
	      Interest revenue 10
	      Lease receivable . . . 90

• At the end of the lease term, the asset generally is retained by the lessee.	• At the end of the lease period, the asset is generally retained by the lessee.
• Depreciation expense is recorded on the asset.	• No depreciation expense is taken during the time the asset is on lease.

* If an immediate recognition of profit is involved, the lease is called a sales-type lease and the accounting entry is:

    Lease receivable 1,000
    Cost of goods sold 800
      Sales revenue 1,000
      Asset 800

shares, causing the stock price to decline, or creditors may refuse to extend credit (or call in loans).[5]

• *Existing debt convenants.* If there are bondholders, the bond indenture agreement may include restrictive covenants that are designed to protect the bondholders' investments. One such convenant prohibits a company from taking on additional debt without the consent of the present bondholders. Bank loans frequently carry similar debt restrictions. Thus, a company may be prohibited from leasing if the lease had to be capitalized.

The accounting profession has had concerns over the accounting for leases dating back at least to 1949, when *ARB No. 38* was issued. But *ARB No. 38* only loosely set forth defined standards on how to account for leased assets. As a result, lease

---

[5] The appearance of more debt on the balance sheet can create the perception to the statement reader that the firm faces larger periodic interest charges and, hence, greater risk when business conditions deteriorate. The perception may hold even though there would be no change in the firm's interest payments if it had borrowed the money from a bank rather than financing the acquisition under a lease.

accounting continued to be a matter of private interpretation using a case-by-case approach to the application of the rules then in existence.

The accounting profession's most current efforts to set standards for lease accounting are embodied in four pronouncements:

- *SFAS No. 13,* "Accounting for Leases," November 1976.
- *SFAS No. 23,* "Inception of the Lease," August 1978.
- *SFAS No. 91,* "Accounting for Nonrefundable Fees and Costs Associated with Originating or Acquiring Loans and Initial Direct Costs of Leases," December 1986, as amended.
- *SFAS No. 98,* "Accounting for Leases: Sale-Leaseback Transactions Involving Real Estate, Sales-Type Leases of Real Estate, Definition of the Lease Term, and Initial Direct Costs of Direct Financing Leases," May 1988.

Scanning this list provides an idea of the scope of subject matter covered in lease accounting. The subject is both detailed and complex. This chapter concentrates on the more pervasive and significant issues.

SFAS No. 13, No. 23, and *No. 91* are the foundation for this chapter. The essence of these pronouncements is a set of tightly defined criteria for determining when and how a lessee must account for a leasing transaction as either an operating lease or a capital lease. These same pronouncements also set forth specific criteria for lessor accounting.

The Lease from the Lessor's Viewpoint

The widespread popularity of business leasing is evident in a survey of 600 companies conducted by the AICPA in 1989 which disclosed that 530 of these companies (88%) engaged in leasing activities in one form or another.[6] On the lessor side, the largest share of the market is represented by banks, other lending institutions, and commercial leasing companies.[7] The other major portion of the lessor market is made up of manufacturers and dealer/distributors of industrial products that offer business buyers a choice of either buying their products outright or leasing them.[8]

Financial institutions and commercial leasing companies generally engage in lease transactions structured as either operating leases or direct-financing leases. Direct-financing leases account for the majority of these leasing transactions.

Direct Financing Capital Lease In a **direct financing lease,** the lessor purchases an asset (only to accommodate the leasing transaction) and immediately leases it to the lessee. The purchased asset resides on the lessor's books only momentarily. The lease transaction removes the asset from the books, replacing it with a receivable. Conceptually, accounting for a direct-financing lease is identical to accounting for a sale on credit. But rather than reporting an account receivable, the lessor reports a lease receivable on the balance sheet. Since the asset itself is considered sold, no asset depreciation is taken by the lessor. The lessor's profit comes entirely from interest.

Sales-Type Capital Lease **Sales-type leases,** used by manufacturers and dealer/distributors, are first cousins to direct-financing leases. Unlike a direct financing lease, in which the asset is purchased and immediately leased, a sales-type lease does not involve a prior purchase. The manufacturer leases the asset directly out of finished goods inventory, or a dealer/distributor leases the asset out of its inventory account. The key distinction to this type of lease is the way the lessor accounts for the transaction. As shown at the end of Exhibit 18–1, a lease receivable account is opened with entries made to cost of goods sold, sales revenue, and the asset. The

---

[6] AICPA, *Accounting Trends & Techniques—1990* (New York, 1990), Table 2–28.

[7] Some of these nonbank commercial lessors are tiny one-person shops, while others are giant organizations such as Walter E. Heller & Co. and Commercial Credit Corporation.

[8] Manufacturers often set up subsidiary companies to handle leasing and other product financing arrangements. GMAC (General Motors Acceptance Corporation) and General Electric Capital Corporation are two such finance subsidiaries.

lessor recognizes sales revenue and cost of sales as if the asset were sold. The lessor's profit comes partly through selling the asset above cost and partly through interest.

Operating Lease In an **operating lease,** the lessor acquires an asset and leases it to a lessee in two separate transactions. The asset stays on the lessor's books throughout the term of the lease and is accounted for in the same way that other revenue-producing assets are accounted for on the balance sheet. When the asset is leased (which may or may not coincide with its acquisition), the lessor sets up a lease revenue (income account) to record and account for rent receipts from the lessee. No lease receivable (asset account) is used. The lessor depreciates the asset in the normal manner.

In summary, the types of leases considered so far are:

For the lessee:
1. Capital lease.
2. Operating lease.

For the lessor:
1. Capital lease.
   a. Direct financing.
   b. Sales type.
2. Operating lease.

Advantages of Leasing

In general, leasing affords the following primary advantages for lessees, which contribute to the demand for leasing transactions:

* Leasing may resolve cash problems by making financing available for up to 100% of the leased asset value. Bank loans typically are limited to 80% of the asset's value.[9] Also, interest rates on leases may be negotiated at fixed rates, while some bank loans feature variable rates.
* Leasing transactions can be structured as operating leases, allowing the lessee to achieve off-balance-sheet financing when debt restrictions or limitations exist based on balance sheet values.
* In the case of industrial equipment that frequently must be built to order and can require lengthy asset-implementation delays, leasing ready-to-use equipment can be attractive.
* If assets are needed only temporarily, seasonally, or sporadically, leasing may avoid the problem of owning assets that cannot be kept in full-time productive use.
* Leasing assets for relatively short lease periods rather than owning them affords the lessee protection from equipment obsolescence.
* Leasing can provide income tax advantages derived from accelerated depreciation and interest expense.[10]
* In general, lease payment schedules can be tailored to dovetail with the lessee's expected cash inflows from operations.

On the lessor side of the market, manufacturers and dealers/distributors of industrial equipment use leasing to facilitate sales.[11] For lending institutions and commercial lessors, leasing is simply another addition to their financial services product line.

Disadvantages of Leasing

Leasing has disadvantages as well as advantages; the following is a list of drawbacks, loosely tracking the above stated advantages of leasing:

---

[9] An important issue to the lessee is the determination of whether to lease or buy the needed asset using bank financing. Finance texts consider this issue in detail.

[10] Lease agreements are sometimes drawn up to shift tax advantages to the party (lessee or lessor) in the higher tax bracket. In exchange, the benefiting party compensates the forfeiting party in the form of either higher lease payments to the lessor (if the lessee gains the tax benefits) or lower payments (if the lessor gains the benefits).

[11] Due to the high cost of such equipment, purchase financing is often a virtual necessity. To ensure sales, many manufacturers offer product financing options, including leasing programs, in what has come to be known as full-service selling strategies. Today, this approach is becoming a common means, for example, of selling new automobiles.

- The 100% financing of leased assets also means higher interest in terms of the total dollar outlay for interest.
- Off-balance-sheet financing merely masks the fact that new layers of debt are being assumed.
- Leasing ready-to-use equipment (as opposed to custom built) may result in lower quality product and ultimately lost sales to the lessee.
- With seasonal leasing, there is no guarantee that equipment will be available when needed. Also, leasing interest rates may be based on what the traffic will bear.
- Short-term leases may avoid protection from product obsolescence, but short-term leasing rates are normally set a premium over longer term rates (to compensate the lessor for assuming the obsolescence risk).
- Tax benefits may be temporary. A new tax code can be enacted at any time, counteracting the provisions of the old code. This is a danger with all long-term leases featuring tax benefits.
- Long-term leases at fixed rates expose the lessor-lender to the risk of opportunity losses if interest rates advance.[12]

CONCEPT REVIEW

1. What is the basic difference between a capital lease and an operating lease to the lessee?
2. What is the basic difference between a direct financing capital lease and a sales-type capital lease to the lessor?
3. List three advantages and three disadvantages of leasing.

ACCOUNTING FOR OPERATING LEASES

The following example illustrates the characteristics of an operating lease. Assume Grafixs Inc. (lessee) leases a computer from Comfast Inc. (lessor) for two years beginning March 1, 1991. Grafixs agrees to pay Comfast $4,800 a year, payable in advance on March 1 of each year. Comfast is responsible for ownership (executory) costs, such as maintenance, property taxes, and insurance. In this lease, the lessee incurs only one risk, payment of the rentals, and obtains only one benefit, temporary use of the asset. Since the risks and benefits of ownership are not transferred, this is an operating lease.

Assume both firms' accounting periods end on December 31. Entries for the lessor (Comfast) to recognize receipt of the lease payments for 1991 are as follows:

March 1, 1991—To record receipt of initial rent payment:

Cash	4,800	
Unearned rent revenue		4,800

December 31, 1991—To recognize revenue earned and depreciation of the asset:

Unearned rent revenue	4,000	
Rent revenue ($4,800 × $^{10}/_{12}$)		4,000
Depreciation expense*	500	
Accumulated depreciation		500

* Amount based on an assumed cost of $5,000, a life of 10 years, and straight-line depreciation with no salvage.

---

[12] This risk applies to financial institutions and commercial lessors that participate in direct financing leases and to manufacturers and dealer/distributors that engage in sale-type leases. The latter are susceptible to rising interest rates because most use bank borrowings or issue commercial paper (both sensitive to interest rates) to finance lease-sales.

Unearned rent revenue is a liability of the lessor and reflects the lessor's obligation to make the computer available in the future.

Entries for the lessee (Grafixs) are:

March 1, 1991—To record payment of initial rent prepayment:

```
Prepaid rent  . . . . . . . . . . . . . . . . . . . . . . . . . . . . 4,800
     Cash  . . . . . . . . . . . . . . . . . . . . . . . . . . . . .        4,800
```

December 31, 1991—To recognize rent expense for 10 months:

```
Rent expense . . . . . . . . . . . . . . . . . . . . . . . . . . . 4,000
     Prepaid rent . . . . . . . . . . . . . . . . . . . . . . . . .         4,000
```

The prepaid rent of $4,800 initially represents an asset to the lessee.

In some cases, an operating lease provides that, in addition to the periodic rent, a nonrefundable down payment is made at the inception of the lease agreement. In this case, the lessor debits cash and credits unearned rent revenue when the down payment is received. The lessee debits an asset account called "leasehold" (or "prepaid rent") and credits cash. Each party then amortizes the prepayment over the life of the lease on a systematic and rational basis.

For example, suppose Grafixs also makes a nonrefundable down payment March 1, 1991, of $720 to Comfast to cover both years. The lessor's additional entries would be:

March 1, 1991—To record receipt of nonrefundable payment:

```
Cash . . . . . . . . . . . . . . . . . . . . . . . . . . . . . . . . . 720
     Unearned rent revenue . . . . . . . . . . . . . . . . . . . . . .        720
```

December 31, 1991—To recognize rent revenue:

```
Unearned rent revenue  . . . . . . . . . . . . . . . . . . . . . . 300
     Rent revenue ($720 × $^{10}/_{24}$)                                    300
```

The nonrefundable payment is recognized as additional rent when earned. The straight-line method is used here to recognize revenue as time passes. While an interest method is theoretically justified, it is unlikely to be employed in practice. Simplicity and materiality would prevail.

The lessee's additional entries would be:

March 1, 1991—To record payment of nonrefundable rent:

```
Prepaid rent  . . . . . . . . . . . . . . . . . . . . . . . . . . . . 720
     Cash  . . . . . . . . . . . . . . . . . . . . . . . . . . . . .        720
```

December 31, 1991—To recognize rent expense:

```
Rent expense . . . . . . . . . . . . . . . . . . . . . . . . . . . 300
     Prepaid rent . . . . . . . . . . . . . . . . . . . . . . . . .         300
```

ACCOUNTING FOR CAPITAL LEASES

♦

Prior to the issuance of *SFAS No. 13,* most lessees accounted for leases as operating leases. Proponents of lease capitalization contended that in many cases the operating lease approach was improper because it resulted in off-balance-sheet financing; that is, obtaining financing without recording the contractual debt. In their view, a lease that transfers a material economic interest in the leased property creates an asset for the leesee that is more than a temporary right to use the leased property. Hence, they argued that the lessee should recognize this material interest by capitalizing as an asset the present value of the future lease rentals. Further, they reasoned that such a lease creates a liability equal to the present value of the future rents, which also should be recognized by the lessee. Similar reasoning led to the conclusion that, where a material economic interest in the property is transferred, the lessor should recognize a transfer of the asset. Thus, the lessor would both record a receivable and remove the cost of the asset from its records. Thereafter, the asset should be depreciated by the lessee rather than by the lessor. Moreover, the lease rental payments should be accounted for by both parties in the same manner as periodic payments on a long-term liability for which each rental payment is a combination of interest and debt reduction.

The proponents of lease capitalization also pointed out that recognition of an asset and a liability on the lessee's financial statements would make their statements comparable with those of firms that purchased assets and financed the purchase with long-term debt. They argued that a lessee company that leased properties under long-term leases and a company that owned similar properties financed by long-term debt were in the same economic position. Both companies were committed to a series of regular payments over a long term; lessees paid rents, while owners paid interest and principal on the debt. Both had exclusive rights to use similar assets over most or all of the useful lives of the assets. Also, in many long-term lease contracts, the lessee is committed to pay repairs and maintenance, property taxes and insurance, and similar **executory costs** associated with assets over their useful lives. If lessees could avoid recognition of assets and liabilities while owners could not, their financial statements would not be comparable even though they were in similar economic and, to some extent, similar legal positions.

Opposition to the capitalization of lease rentals arose because lessees were reluctant to recognize a lease-related liability. They pointed out that various other long-term contracts were not recognized under GAAP, and that lease contracts should not be singled out for different treatment.[13] Lessees argued that sudden recognition of large, previously unrecorded long-term lease liabilities could cause some lessees to be in technical default on other long-term debt convenants, which limited their indebtedness to a certain amount or required a specified debt-equity ratio. These loan covenants based on financial ratios often did not consider the possible recognition of liabilities related to lease contracts because at the time the loan was negotiated, GAAP did not require such recognition. (In fact, altering accounting rules for leases caused some companies to change existing debt agreements.) The FASB moved ahead because it did not accept the opposition's arguements as persuasive.

Accounting for Capital Leases: Lessee

Because of the significant differences between accounting for operating and capital leases and the difficulty in determining when substantially all the risks and benefits of ownership have been transferred, *SFAS No. 13* specifies detailed criteria that qualify a lease contract as a capital lease. These criteria are outlined in Exhibit 18–2 for lessees. Four criteria apply to lessees; if *any one* of these four criteria is met by the lessee, the lease qualifies as a capital lease for the lessee.

Transfer of Ownership (Criterion No. 1)   If a lease explicitly states that ownership of the asset transfers to the lessee at the end of the lease term, without payment of additional compensation to the lessor, the lease is just a purchase financing arrangement, similar to an installment purchase.

Bargain Purchase Option (Criterion No. 2)   A **bargain purchase option (BPO)** is an inducement designed to ensure that the lessee buys the asset being leased at the end of the lease term. BPOs are often found in leases that contain no explicit transfer of

---

[13] Employment contracts whereby employers agree to pay certain salaries for future services, purchase commitments that do not involve probable losses, and most postemployment benefits including pensions were but a few of the types of executory contracts for which an asset and corresponding liability were not recognized under GAAP at this time.

EXHIBIT 18-2   Criteria for Identifying a Capital Lease for the Lessee

---

If the lease meets *any one* of the following four criteria, the lease is a capital lease to the lessee.*

1. The lease transfers ownership of the leased asset to the lessee by the end of the lease term.
2. The lease contains a bargain purchase option.
3. The lease term is equal to 75% or more of the remaining estimated economic life of the leased asset at the lease inception.
4. The present value of the minimum lease payments at the inception of the lease is at least 90% of the market value of the leased asset at that time.†

* Criteria 3 and 4 do not apply if the beginning of the lease term falls within the last 25% of the total economic life of the leased asset, land is the only asset leased, or the lease involves both land and building(s).

† The term *miminum lease payments* is defined later in the chapter.

ownership provision. Essentially, the BPO serves the same purpose. A BPO requires comparing the option's purchase price to the leased asset's residual value at the end of the lease term. If an asset's residual value is expected to be $10,000, for example, the BPO price might be $5,000 or even less. The lessee is not expected to pass up these savings, and the probability is high that the lessee will buy the asset at the BPO date.

Lease Term Equals 75% of Asset's Remaining Useful Service Life (Criterion No. 3)   If the remaining estimated useful economic life of an asset is 30 years at the lease's inception, for example, and the term of the lease is 25 years, this means the lessee will have possession and unrestricted use of the asset for five sixths (83%) of its remaining life. This control is considered equivalent to ownership. A **bargain renewal option (BRO),** which allows the lessee to renew the lease for a rental below the expected fair market rental at the time the BRO is exercisable, lengthens the lease life used in the comparison.

Minimum Lease Payments (at Present Value) at Least 90% of the Asset's Fair Value (Criterion No. 4) **Minimum lease payments** is a technical term for the total dollars the lessee is obligated to pay the lessor over the course of the lease—including the BPO, if any. The bulk of the minimum lease payments take the form of periodic rental payments, meaning the amount to be paid each year for the use of the asset. For a complete definition of minimum lease payments and its components refer to Exhibit 18–3.

To illustrate the application of this criterion assume that an asset is being leased for five years at a periodic rental payment of $25,000 each year paid in advance. Assume the appropriate interest rate on the lease is 10%. (Determination of the appropriate interest rate is discussed in the next subsection.) The present value of $25,000 annual payments at 10% for five years is $104,247 = $25,000(*PVAD*, 10%, 5) = $25,000(4.16987). Next assume that the fair market value of the leased asset is $110,000. In this case the present value of the $104,247 minimum lease payments equals 94.8% of the asset's fair market value ($104,247 ÷ $110,000), meeting criterion No. 4 and requiring capital lease accounting treatment. Meeting criterion 4 implies a commitment by the lessee to a schedule of payments essentially equivalent to the asset's purchase price.

---

[14] *SFAS No. 13*, par. 5(k), requires that the recorded value of the leased asset not exceed its fair market value; that is, if the present value of the lease payments is greater than the market value of the leased asset at the lease inception date, both the asset and liability must be recorded at the market value of the leased asset. In this case, the implied interest rate would have to be computed. For example, if the market value of the leased asset in the example were $96,375 instead of $110,000, the implicit interest rate would be computed as follows: $96,375 ÷ $25,000 = 3.855; reference to Table 6A–6, for $n = 5$, shows that the implicit interest rate is almost exactly 15%. The entries for the lessee would reflect the 15% rate based on the $96,375 value.

EXHIBIT 18-3   Miminum Lease Payment Components

Minimum Lease Payments*

Minimum lease payments are defined in *SFAS No. 13* to mean "the payments that the lessee is obligated to make or can be required to make in connection with the leased property." The *Statement* goes on to explain the components that make up minimum lease payments:

♦ **Periodic rental payments (minimum rental payments):** The periodic rental payments are the base component. They are the total amount paid to the lessor for use of a leased asset. In business leasing situations, periodic rental payments are ordinarily made annually, with the first payment at the inception of the lease, and subsequent payments on the lease anniversary date. *When lease payments are made at the front end of each lease period, present value annuity due (PVAD) table are used rather than ordinary annuity tables to compute the present values of such payments.*

♦ **Bargain purchase option (BPO):** A BPO is an inducement offered to ensure that the lessee buys the leased asset at the end of the lease period. If a bargain purchase option is offered, the dollar amount is included in the minimum lease payments computation. *Because a BPO is a one-time-only payment at the end of the lease term, its present value is computed using present value of 1 (PV1) table.*

Leases that do not feature BPOs (and which do not provide for transfer of ownership as a provision of the lease) may contain one or the other of the following two lease provisions—both of which are intended to protect the lessor's investment in the asset's residual value.

♦ **Guaranteed residual value:** The lessee may be required to guarantee to the lessor the leased asset's residual value at the end of the lease term. If so, the present value of the guaranteed amount is included in the minimum lease payments.

♦ **Failure to renew penalty:** Some leases feature a base lease term plus term extensions. At the end of the base term, the lessee has the option to renew or terminate the lease. In certain instances, failure to renew the lease may impose a penalty on the lessee, which compensates the lessor for the loss of leasing income and any decline in the asset's residual value. If a penalty clause is present in the lease, the penalty is included in the minimum lease payments if it is expected that the renewal option will be rejected by the lessee.

---

* **Executory costs:** Insurance, routine maintenance, and property taxes due on the leased asset are the main items that make up executory costs. Lease contracts may require the lessee to pay these costs to the lessor in conjunction with the periodic rental payments. For lease computation purposes, any executory costs paid to the lessor are deducted from periodic rental payments since these payments merely maintain the asset. *Unless otherwise noted, periodic rental payment amounts included in all examples and illustrations in this text are assumed to be net of executory costs.*

If any one of the above four criteria is met, the leased asset is considered to be purchased from the lessor at the inception of the lease; therefore, the asset must be capitalized on the lessee's books (capital lease). If none of the criteria is met, the transaction is accounted for as an operating lease.

The lessee records a capital lease, at the date of inception of the lease at the lower of the asset's fair market value or the present value of the rental payments.[14] The lessee records the lease by a debit to an asset account, with a title such as "leased property," and a credit to lease liability for the present value of all future payments required in the lease agreement. Thus, the lessee's basic approach to lease valuation can be expressed as:

$$\begin{pmatrix} \text{Valuation of leased} \\ \text{asset and related} \\ \text{liability at lease inception} \end{pmatrix} = \begin{pmatrix} \text{Periodic lease} \\ \text{payment} \end{pmatrix} \begin{pmatrix} \text{Present value of} \\ \text{annuity of } n \text{ payments} \\ \text{at } i \text{ rate of interest} \end{pmatrix}$$

Consider the following example:

1. On January 1, 1991, Lessor Company and Lessee Company sign a three-year lease for an asset with an estimated economic life of three years.
2. The agreement involves no collection uncertainties, and the lessor's performance is complete.
3. The three rental payments are $36,556 each, payable January 1, 1991, 1992, and 1993.

4. The fair market value of the asset at the inception of the lease is $100,000, which is also the carrying value (cost) on the lessor's books.
5. The lease contains no renewal or bargain purchase option and the asset reverts to the lessor at the end of the three-year period.
6. The lessee's incremental borrowing rate is 10%.
7. Lessee Company and Lessor Company depreciate the asset using the straight-line method for book purposes. The asset's residual value is estimated to be $0.
8. The accounting year ends December 31 for each party.
9. The lessor's **implicit interest rate** (target rate of return), the rate which equates the present value of the payments to the asset's market value, is 10%.

Because of (1), the lease described in the example meets criterion 3 of Exhibit 18–2, and that is sufficient to classify it as a capital lease. (The lease also meets criterion 4, as is shown below. Criteria 1 and 2 are not met since there is neither a provision for transfer of ownership nor a bargain purchase offer, but the lease is still a capital lease to the lessee since only one of the four criteria needs to be met.

Using the lessee's incremental borrowing rate, (6) in the example, the lessee's computation of the valuation of the leased asset and the related lease liability is[15]

$$\$36,556(PVAD,\ 10\%,\ 3) = \$36,556(2.73554) = \$100,000$$

The lessee's journal entries for the first year based on the rentals specified are:

January 1, 1991—To record the lease

Leased asset	100,000	
Lease liability		100,000
Lease liability	36,556	
Cash		36,556

December 31, 1991—To recognize interest and depreciation expense

Interest expense (see Exhibit 18–4)	6,344	
Lease liability		6,344
Depreciation expense $100,000(⅓)	33,333	
Accumulated depreciation		33,333

The amortization schedule for the lease is shown in Exhibit 18–4.

Only the entries for 1991 are shown. The entries for each of the next two years are identical except for the accrual of interest expense. Interest expense for 1992 is $3,324 as shown in column 3 of the lease amortization schedule in Exhibit 18–4.

Lessee's Interest Rate   Determining the appropriate interest rate to use in the present value discounting by the lessee is important. The rate directly affects the valuation of the leased asset and the related lease liability recorded at the inception of the lease. The higher the interest rate, the lower the amount capitalized for the asset and recorded for the liability, and vice versa.

The lessee must compute the valuation of the asset leased and the lease liability by discounting the lease payments using *the lower* of the lessee's incremental borrowing rate or the discount rate used by the lessor (also called the lessor's implicit interest rate) *if known or determinable by the lessee.*[16] If the lessor's implicit interest rate is not known, or cannot be reliably estimated, the lessee's incremental borrowing rate must be used. The lessee's incremental borrowing rate is, according to *SFAS No. 13* "the rate that, at lease inception date, the lessee would have incurred to borrow (over a similar term) the funds necessary to purchase the leased asset." The choice

---

[15] Throughout this section, lease payments are assumed to be made on the first day of each period; thus, the present value of an annuity due is used. If the payments are not in the form of an annuity, each payment would need to be discounted separately.

[16] The problem of whose rate to use is, typically, resolved by the limitation of market value. Only in the case of an unguaranteed residual value (discussed later) does a substantive recording issue emerge.

EXHIBIT 18-4   Lease Amortization Schedule (Annuity Due Basis)

Date	Annual Lease Payments	Annual Interest at 10%	Decrease (Increase) in Lease Liability	Lease Liability Balance
1/1/91				$100,000
1/1/91	$ 36,556	—	$ 36,556	63,444
12/31/91	—	$6,344	(6,344)	69,788
1/1/92	36,556	—	36,556	33,232
12/31/92	—	3,324	(3,324)	36,556
1/1/93	36,556	—	36,556	–0–
	$109,668	$9,668	$100,000	

of a specific interest rate by the lessee does not affect total expenses (interest expense plus depreciation expense) over the life of the lease. However, the timing of the recognition of each of these two expenses is affected.

Lessee's Depreciation   Under *SFAS No. 13* the lessee depreciates this asset over the lease life (also here the economic life) of three years.[17] The residual value, any bargain purchase options, and any guaranteed residual value may affect depreciation by the lessee. These topics are discussed later in this chapter.

The lessee's entries parallel those that would be recorded for an actual purchase on a credit basis involving periodic payments that are part principal and part interest. For the current example, on December 31, 1991, the lessee reports:

1. Leased property at cost of $100,000 with accumulated depreciation of $33,333 with property, plant, and equipment.
2. A lease liability of $69,788 ($100,000 − $36,556) plus accrued interest payable of $6,344. A portion is reported as current, the rest long-term.
3. Interest expense of $6,344.
4. Depreciation expense of $33,333.

CONCEPT REVIEW

1. What entries does a lessee make for an operating lease?
2. What four criteria are used to determine whether a lease must be recognized on the balance sheet of a lessee?
3. What is the most important difference between the accounting for an operating lease and a capital lease?

Accounting for Capital Leases: Lessor

The criteria for determining whether the lessor must capitalize a lease include the criteria given in Exhibit 18-2. If the lease meets *any one* of the four criteria in Exhibit 18-2 *and both* of the criteria given next, the lease must be capitalized by the lessor:

---

[17] If the lease is capitalized because of either criterion one (title transfer) or 2 (BPO), the asset is depreciated consistent with the lessee's normal depreciation policy. Otherwise, the leased asset is depreciated over the life of the lease.

a. Collectiblity of the minimum lease payments is reasonably assured.

b. No important uncertainties surround the amount of unreimbursable costs yet to be incurred by the lessor under the lease.[18] (If uncertainties exist, they call into question whether the payments will be made and thereby the capitalizable amount.)

These two additional criteria provide for risks that might make the first four criteria inoperative for the lessor.

In addition to making a careful distinction between operating and capital leases, *SFAS No. 13* further defines capital leases for the lessor as either direct financing leases or sales-type leases. In the most simple terms, a sales-type lease involves a profit to the lessor, a direct-financing lease does not.[18] There is no distinction between a direct-financing lease and a sales-type lease for the lessee.

The lessor classifies a lease as a direct-financing lease if there is no "manufacturer's or dealer's profit or loss." In this situation, the lessor's cost (or carrying amount, if different) of the leased asset equals its market value at the inception date; therefore, this value is used by the lessor to compute the lease rentals. Typically, leasing companies (as opposed to manufacturers and dealers) have direct financing leases, rather than sales-type leases, because they purchase property for lease and not for resale. The lessor's profit objective is to set the periodic lease rentals at a level sufficiently high to yield the target (implicit) rate of return on the lessor's investment in the leased asset. The lessor's basic approach is to compute the amount of the periodic lease rentals so that:

$$\text{Investment} = \text{Periodic lease rental } (PVAD, i, n)$$

Direct-Financing Leases   The lease in the previous example is a capital lease to the lessor because it meets criterion 3 from Exhibit 18–2 (see Item 1 of the example) and satisfies both criteria *a* and *b* above (see Item 2 of the example). It is a direct-financing lease since (under Item 4 in the example) the fair market value is equal to the cost on the lessor's books implying there is no dealer profit. The lessor's profit arises from the interest revenue earned in financing the transaction. The lessor's implicit interest rate is 10%, see Item 9. Therefore, the lessor's computation of the periodic lease rental is:

$$\text{Rent} = \$100,000 \div (PVAD, 10\%, 3) = \$100,000 \div (2.73554)$$
$$= \$ 36,556$$

The lessor's entries for this annuity-due payment lease are:

January 1, 1991—To record the lease:

Lease receivable	100,000	
Asset		100,000

January 1, 1991—First rental:

Cash	$36,556	
Lease receivable		36,556

December 31, 1991—To recognize interest earned:

Lease receivable: ($100,000 − $36,556).10	6,344	
Interest revenue		6,344

---

[18] Important uncertainties might include commitments by the lessor to guarantee performance of the leased asset in a manner more extensive than the typical product warranty or to protect the lessee from obsolescence of the leased asset. However, the necessity of estimating executory costs, such as insurance, maintenance, and taxes to be paid by the lessor, does not by itself constitute an important uncertainty under this provision.

Sales-Type Leases   The basic distinction between direct-financing leases and sales-type leases is that in a sales-type lease, a manufacturer's or dealer's profit or loss is recognized by the lessor at the inception of the lease. This means that in a sales-type lease, the market value of the leased asset at the inception of the lease is greater or less that the lessor's cost (or carrying amount, if different).

Sales-type leases typically arise when a manufacturer or dealer uses a leasing arrangement as a secondary means of marketing its products. The objectives of a company that either sells or leases its products are to earn a profit on the sale of the leased asset and also to earn interest on the related lease receivable. Thus, for a sales-type lease, two different profits are recognized during the lease term:

1. Manufacturer's or dealer's profit (gross margin or gross profit) is recognized in full at date of inception of the lease. Profit is computed as follows:

$$\begin{pmatrix} \text{Normal sales price} \\ \text{(market value)} \\ \text{of the leased asset} \end{pmatrix} - \begin{pmatrix} \text{Cost (or carrying} \\ \text{amount, if different)} \\ \text{of the leased asset} \end{pmatrix} = \begin{pmatrix} \text{Manufacturer's or} \\ \text{dealer's profit or} \\ \text{loss} \end{pmatrix}$$

2. Interest revenue on the lease receivable is recognized over the term of the lease. The total amount of interest is computed as follows:

$$\begin{pmatrix} \text{Gross lease} \\ \text{receivable (includes} \\ \text{the interest charge)} \end{pmatrix} - \begin{pmatrix} \text{Normal sales price} \\ \text{(market value)} \\ \text{of the leased asset} \end{pmatrix} = \begin{pmatrix} \text{Total interest} \\ \text{revenue over} \\ \text{the lease life} \end{pmatrix}$$

The example to this point has involved a direct-financing lease. To illustrate the accounting for a sales-type lease, item 4 on page 963 is changed to read:

4. The fair market value of the asset at the inception of the lease is $100,000, while the carrying value (cost) on the lessor's books is $80,000.

With this one change, a dealer's profit of $20,000 is introduced. The periodic rental payment remains at $36,556 because it is based on the asset's market value.

The accounting entries for the lessor in 1991 are:

January 1, 1991—Inception of lease:

Lease receivable	100,000	
Cost of goods sold	80,000	
Sales revenue		100,000
Asset		80,000

January 1, 1991—First rental:

Cash	36,556	
Lease receivable		36,556

December 31, 1991—Accrual of 1991 interest:

Lease receivable ($100,000 − $36,556).10	6,344	
Interest revenue		6,344

There is no depreciation expense for one year since the asset was sold.

The related amortization schedule from which the entries for future years can be obtained is given in Exhibit 18–4.

In the December 31, 1991, financial statements, the lessor reports:

1. A lease receivable of $69,788.
2. Sales revenue of $100,000, cost of sales of $80,000, and interest revenue of $6,344.

The lessor's entry at the date of inception of a sales-type lease is similar to the entry that would be made if the leased asset had been sold outright on credit. That is, the lessor debits lease receivable and credits sales revenue for the sale price of the

EXHIBIT 18-5   Lease Classification: Lessor

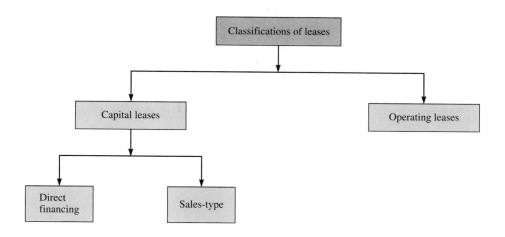

EXHIBIT 18-6   Lease Classification by Lessors and Lessees

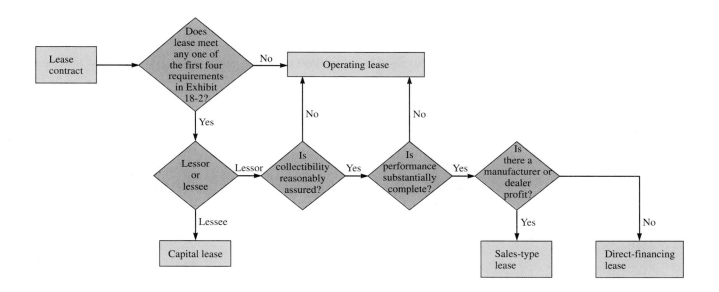

leased asset ($100,000). This amount is the same as the present value of the payments to be received. At the same time, the lessor debits cost of goods sold and credits the leased asset for its cost or carrying amount (in inventory), $80,000. The difference of $20,000 ($100,000 − $80,000) measures the lessor's manufacturer's or dealer's profit on the sale. The subsequent entries by the lessor to record collections of periodic rent, interest revenue, and reduction of the lease receivable are the same as the lessor's entries under a direct financing lease.

The classification of leases by the lessor is diagramed in Exhibit 18–5. A flowchart for classifying leases for both the lessee and the lessor is provided in Exhibit 18–6. (Exhibit 18–6 does not cover leases involving real estate. See Appendix 18A.)

Termination of Lease Agreements

A capital lease agreement may terminate due to a change of provisions in the lease, renewal or extension of the original lease, or expiration of the lease term. *SFAS No. 13* specifies the accounting for termination by the lessee and lessor as follows:

> *By lessor:* On termination, the net carrying value of the lease receivable is removed from the accounts, and the leased asset is recorded at its current market value. Any difference is recognized as gain or loss in the period of termination.

> *By lessee:* On termination, both the net carrying value of the leased asset and the lease liability are removed from the accounts. A gain or loss is recognized in the period of termination for any difference.

For example, suppose the lease situation described in Exhibit 18–4 is terminated on January 1, 1992. The January 1 payment is not made. Assume the fair market value of the leased asset on this date is $61,000. The entries are:

Lessor			Lessee		
Asset	61,000		Lease liability	69,788	
Loss on lease			Accumulated		
termination	8,788		depreciation	33,333	
Lease receivable		69,788	Leased asset		100,000
			Gain on lease		
			termination		3,121

Lease Entries under an Ordinary Annuity

While it is common for the lease payments to be in the form of an annuity due as is true in the examples used so far in this chapter, the payments can also be in the form of an ordinary annuity. This would be true in the previous example if the payments were due December 31, 1991, 1992, and 1993. In this case, the payments would become $40,212 = $100,000 \div (PVA, 10\%, 3) = $100,000 \div 2.48685$.

If the lease had involved an ordinary annuity, the lessor's entries for 1991 would have been:

January 1, 1991—Inception of lease:

Lease receivable	100,000	
Asset		100,000

December 31, 1991—Accrual of interest:

Lease receivable: ($100,000).10	10,000	
Interest revenue		10,000

December 31, 1991—First rental receipt:

Cash	40,212	
Lease receivable		40,212

The lessor does not record depreciation since the asset is considered transferred. The entries for the following years are identical to those for 1991 except for the interest revenue, which declines each year. On December 31, 1991, the lessor would report:

1. A lease receivable of $69,788: ($100,000 + $10,000 − $40,212)
2. Interest revenue of $10,000.

The entries for 1991 on the lessee's books would be:

January 1, 1991—Inception of lease:

Leased asset	100,000	
Lease liability		100,000

December 31, 1991—Accrual of interest:

Interest expense: $90,909(.10)	10,000	
Lease liability		10,000

December 31, 1991—First rental payment:

Lease liability	40,212	
Cash		40,212

December 31, 1991—Record depreciation:

Depreciation expense $90,909(1/3)	33,333	
Accumulated depreciation		33,333

For realism, annuities due are used throughout the rest of this chapter.

CONCEPT REVIEW

1. What two additional criteria must be met before a lease is capitalized by a lessor?
2. What type of annuity is most common for lease payments.
3. Does the lessor recognize depreciation on a sales-type lease or a direct-financing lease?

SPECIAL ISSUES IN ACCOUNTING FOR CAPITAL LEASES

◆

Up to this point, the discussion has illustrated the fundamentals of accounting and reporting for leases by lessees and lessors. The following additional issues in accounting for leases that make the accounting more complex are considered in this section:

1. Bargain purchase options.
2. Bargain renewal options.
3. Residual values.
4. Different interest rates.
5. Depreciation of a leased asset by the lessee.
6. Executory and initial direct costs.
7. Sale-leaseback arrangements.
8. Classification of lease receivables and payables.
9. Lease disclosure requirements.

Exhibit 18–7 presents a list of technical lease terms and their definitions as set forth in *SFAS No. 13*. These terms are used extensively in the remainder of this chapter.

EXHIBIT 18-7   Technical Lease Definitions

Bargain purchase option (BPO)—An option allowing the lessee to purchase the leased property for a price that is sufficiently lower than the expected market value of the property at the exercise date of the option, that exercise appears (at the lease inception date) to be reasonably assured.

Bargain renewal option—An option allowing the lessee to renew the lease for a rental that is sufficiently lower than the expected market rental of the property at the exercise date of the option. Exercise of the option appears (at the lease inception date) to be reasonably assured.

Estimated residual value of the leased asset—The estimated market value of the leased asset at the end of the lease term.

Executory costs—Costs of insurance, maintenance, and taxes. These are costs of ownership and use regardless of who pays them and are neither capitalized nor considered in the 90% test (Criterion 4 in Exhibit 18-2).

Initial indirect costs—Costs incurred by the lessor in negotiating and consummating a lease agreement, including legal fees, cost of credit investigations, commissions, compensation, and clerical costs directly related to initiating the lease.

Interest rate implicit in the lease—The interest rate that, at the lease inception date, causes the present value of (1) the minimum lease payments (excluding any executory costs to be paid by the lessor or lessee) and (2) the unguaranteed residual value to be equal to the market value of the leased property (less any investment tax credit retained by the lessor).

Lease term—The fixed noncancelable term of the lease plus periods covered by bargain renewal options and plus all periods covered by renewal options during which the lessee guarantees debt of the lessor, before the exercise date of a bargain purchase option. However, the lease term cannot extend beyond the exercise date of a bargain purchase option. In other words, the lease term is the period during which the lessee can resonably be expected to continue leasing (due, in some cases, to a bargain renewal option or a bargain purchase option)*.

Lessee's incremental borrowing rate—The rate that, at lease inception date, the lessee would have incurred to borrow (over a similar term) the funds necessary to purchase the leased asset.

Minimum lease payments—lessee—The rental payments that the lessee is obligated (or can be required) to make in connection with the leased property, excluding executory costs (insurance, maintenance, and taxes) that the lessee is required to pay. If the lease contains a BPO, only the minimum rental payments over the lease term and the BPO payment are included in the minimum lease payments. If the lease does not contain a BPO, minimum lease payments include (1) the minimum rental payments called for by the lease over the lease term, (2) any residual value guarantee by the lessee at the expiration of the lease term, and (3) any penalty payment the lessee can be required to make if the lease is not renewed or extended at the expiration of the lease term.

Minimum lease payments—lessor—Same as the payments described for the lessee plus any residual value guarantee by a third party unrelated to either the lessee or the lessor. (When there is a BPO, residual value is of no further concern to the lessor because the leased asset will be retained by the lessee at the end of the lease term.)

Unguaranteed residual value—The estimated residual value less any portion guaranteed by the lessee or by a third-party guarantor.

* As amended by *SFAS No. 98*, par. 22, May 1988.

Bargain Purchase Options

A bargain purchase option (BPO) permits a lessee to purchase the leased property, during a specified period of the lease term, at a price below the expected market value at that time. This price is sufficiently low to assure that the lessee will take advantage of the bargain. In effect, a BPO is viewed as a pending sale and transfer of ownership of the leased asset to the lessee at the specified bargain price. The definition of minimum lease payments in Exhibit 18-7 states (italics added): "If the lease contains a BPO, *only the rental payments* over the lease term and *the BPO payment* are included in the minimum lease payments.'' This means that when there is a BPO, any residual values are disregarded when computing the lease rent amount. In this case, the residual value is used only to determine whether the purchase option is a bargain.

Including a BPO in a capital lease contract means that there are two sources of cash flows to the lessor from the lessee: one is from the periodic rentals and the other is from the BPO price. Thus, a BPO affects the amount of the annual rentals required to meet the lessor's target rate of return and the lessee's capitalizable cost of the leased asset. Compared with a situation in which a leased asset has no BPO, the annual rental in a lease with a BPO is less than in a lease without a BPO. This occurs because the lessor recovers part of the investments in the leased asset through the BPO price. The recovery reduces the amount that must be received from the periodic rentals. Therefore, the lessor includes the BPO price when computing the amount of each annual rental. The lessee includes the present value of the BPO price in computing the cost of the leased asset to be capitalized.

The original and continuing example is adapted to a BPO situation by changing Items 1, 5, and 7 as follows:

1. The estimated life of the asset is four years.
5. There is a BPO of $10,000 exercisable at the end of the three-year lease term.
7. The estimated residual value of the leased asset is $15,000 at the BPO exercise date. The asset's residual value at the end of the fourth year is $0.

The lease continues to be a *direct-financing lease* to the *lessor* and a *capital lease* to the *lessee*. The annual lease payment, *P*, is calculated to be:

$$\$100,000 = P(PVAD, 10\%, 3) + BPO(PV1, 10\%, 3)$$
$$\$100,000 = P(2.73554) + \$10,000(.75131)$$

$$P = (\$100,000 - \$7,513) \div 2.73554$$
$$P = \$33,809$$

Exhibit 18–8 illustrates lessor and lessee accounting for this BPO.

If the lessee knows the market value of the asset, the lessee can determine the lessor's implicit interest rate on the lease. Alternatively, the lessor may inform the lessee of the rate.[19] With these data, the lessee can compute the capitalizable cost of the leased asset:

$$\$33,809(PVAD, 10\%, 3) + \$10,000(PV1, 10\%, 3) =$$
$$\$33,809(2.73554) + \$10,000(.75131) = \$100,000$$

Only the lessee records depreciation expense on the leased asset because under a capital lease a purchase of the leased asset by the lessee is implied. When there is a BPO, the lessee depreciates the leased asset over its total expected useful life (less any estimated residual value at the end of that time) rather than the lease term of three years. It always is assumed that the BPO will be exercised which further implies that the lessee will receive title and permanent ownership of the leased asset.

If, on December 31, 1993 (the BPO date), the lessee lets the bargain purchase option lapse, the lessor and the lessee would remove from their respective accounts all remaining balances related to the lease contract and recognize a loss. The following entries on December 31, 1993, would replace those in Exhibit 18–8 assuming:[20]

---

[19] Assumed here also to be equal to the incremental borrowing rate of the lessee.

[20] The lessor has a loss of $2,000 because the estimated $8,000 residual value on the BPO date, December 31, 1993, is less than the balance in the lease receivable account of $10,000. If there were no change in the original estimate of residual value of $15,000, the lessor would record a gain of $5,000.

EXHIBIT 18-8   Accounting for a Direct-Financing Lease with a Bargain Purchase Option

Lessor			Lessee		
January 1, 1991—Inception of lease					
Cash	33,809		Leased asset	100,000	
Lease receivable	66,191		Lease liability		66,191
Asset		100,000	Cash		33,809
December 31, 1991–Adjusting entries:					
Lease receivable	6,619		Interest expense**	6,619	
Interest revenue*		6,619	Lease liability		6,619
			Depreciation expense	25,000	
* Computations: See schedule below.			Accumulated depreciation		25,000
			($100,000 × ¼ = $25,000)		
December 31, 1993—Exercise of BPO:					
Cash	10,000		Lease liability	10,000	
Lease receivable		10,000	Cash		10,000

Lease Amortization Schedule with Bargain Purchase Option (Annuity Due Basis)

Date	Annual Lease Payments	Annual Interest at 10%	Decrease (Increase) in Lease Receivable/Liability	Lease Receivable/Liability Balance
1/1/91	Initial value			$100,000
1/1/91	$ 33,809	—	$ 33,809	66,191
12/31/91	—	$ 6,619	(6,619)	72,810
1/1/92	33,809	—	33,809	39,001
12/31/92	—	3,900	(3,900)	42,901
1/1/93	33,809	—	33,809	9,092
12/31/93	—	909	(909)	10,000 (rounded)
12/31/93	10,000	—	10,000	–0–
	$111,427	$11,428	$100,000 (rounded)	

1. A new estimated residual value of $8,000 instead of the original $15,000 estimate.
2. The lease was not renewed.

Lessor:

Asset (new residual value)	8,000	
Loss on lapse of lease purchase option	2,000	
Lease receivable		10,000

Lessee:

Lease liability	10,000	
Loss on lapse of lease purchase option	15,000	
Accumulated depreciation ($25,000 × 3)	75,000	
Leased property		100,000

Bargain Renewal Option

Criterion 3 in Exhibit 18–2 requires that a lease be a capital lease if the lease term is at least 75% of the remaining estimated economic life of the leased asset. Determining an asset's **lease term** is not a simple matter.[21] For example, the lease term is generally fixed. However, this period can be extended by a bargain renewal option

---

[21] Determining the economic life is also not simple, particularly for specialized assets. This issue is covered in Chapter 12.

(BRO). A BRO allows the lessee to renew the lease for a rental that is less than the expected fair market rental at the time the option is exercisable.

If it can be established at the inception of the lease that the difference between the rent under the renewal option is sufficiently less than the expected fair market rental amount at the option's exercise date implies acceptance of the option, the lease term is extended to cover the additional period. Under similar reasoning *SFAS No. 98,* par. 22, specifies that the lease life would also be extended if substantial penalties were incurred by the lessee for failure to renew or extend the lease for renewal periods preceding a BPO, for renewal periods during which the lessee is a guarantor of the lessor's debt, and for periods representing renewals or extensions of the lease at the lessor's option. The lease term never extends beyond the date when a BPO becomes exercisable.

Residual Values

Residual values can affect the accounting of the lessor and lessee in several ways, including the computation of the minimum lease payments, the amount to be capitalized by the lessee, and the periodic depreciation expense. Furthermore, when the lease term is less than the estimated useful economic life of the leased property, two different calculations of **estimated residual value** need to be considered: the value at the end of the lease term and the value at the end of the property's estimated useful life. For example, in the example depicted in Exhibit 18–8, the estimated residual value at the end of the three-year lease term is $15,000, while the estimated residual value at the end of the asset's four-year life is $0.

The accounting impact of an estimated residual value at the end of the lease term in a capital lease depends on whether the residual value is retained by the lessor or transferred to the lessee.

The lessee receives the residual value in one of two ways:
* If the lease provides for transfer of title to the lessee, the leased property and its residual value at the end of the lease term belong to the lessee at no additional cost (above the annual lease rentals). In this situation, the residual value does not affect the *lessor's* computation of the periodic lease payments or the lessor's accounting, or the *lessee's* cost to be capitalized. However, the lessee should depreciate the asset over its total economic life, less any estimated residual value at the end of that total life.
* If the lease includes a BPO, the estimated residual value at the end of the lease term is transferred to the lessee. The residual value is ignored by the lessee if the BPO is not exercised.

If only criterion 3 or 4 is met, the lessor retains the residual value:
* When the lessor retains the residual value by getting the leased assets back at the end of the lease term, there is a risk that the lessee will not properly maintain the leased asset, in which case the residual value would be reduced. To minimize this risk, the lease agreement may require the lessee to guarantee all or part of the estimated residual value. Thus, the estimated residual value retained by the lessor at the end of the lease term may be:
* *Unguaranteed* by the lessee.
* *Guaranteed in full* by the lessee.
* *Guaranteed in part* by the lessee.
* *Guaranteed by a third party* for a fee depending upon the provisions of the lease agreement. These four cases are discussed next.

Unguaranteed Residual Value Retained by Lessor   When the lease agreement provides that the lessor retains the leased asset at the end of the lease term, any residual value is also retained by the lessor. When that residual value is unguaranteed by the lessee, the

EXHIBIT 18-9   Accounting for a Direct-Financing Lease with Unguaranteed Residual Value

Lessor	Lessee
January 1, 1991—Inception of lease:	
Lease receivable 100,000*	Leased asset . . . . 92,487†
Asset 100,000	Lease liability 92,487
* This entry includes the present value of the $10,000 residual value in the lease receivable account.	† Lessee's computation of cost of leased asset (the unguaranteed residual value is not capitalized by the lessee): $33,809 (*PVAD*, 10%, 3) = $33,809(2.73554).
January 1, 1991—First rental:	
Cash 33,809	Lease liability 33,809
Lease receivable 33,809	Cash 33,809
December 31, 1991—Adjusting entries:	
Lease receivable 6,619	Interest expense 5,868
Interest revenue 6,619	Lease liability 5,868
See lessor's amortization schedule below.	See lessee's amortization schedule below.
	Depreciation expense 30,829
	Accumulated depreciation 30,829
	($92,487 × ⅓ = $30,829)
December 31, 1993—End of lease term: to remove the residual value from the lease receivable account:	(to remove the asset from the accounts:)
Asset 10,000	Accumulated depreciation 92,487
Lease receivable 10,000	Leased asset 92,487

Lease Amortization Schedule (Annuity Due Basis)

		Lessor			Lessee		
Date	Lease Payments	Interest at 10%	Receivable Decrease (Increase)	Receivable Balance	Interest at 10%	Liability Decrease (Increase)	Liability Balance
1/1/91	Initial value			$100,000			$92,486
1/1/91	$ 33,809	—	$33,809	66,191	—	$33,809	58,678
12/31/91	—	$ 6,619	(6,619)	72,810	$5,868	(5,868)	64,546
1/1/92	33,809	—	33,809	39,001	—	33,809	30,737
12/31/92	—	3,900	(3,900)	42,901	3,074	(3,074)	33,811
1/1/93	33,809	—	33,809	9,092	—	33,809	-0-*
12/31/93	—	909	(909)	10,000*			
	$101,427	$11,427 *	$90,000 *		$8,942	$92,487 *	

* Rounded

lessor computes the periodic rentals by deducting the present value of the estimated residual value from the total amount to be recovered under the lease agreement. The lessee capitalizes only the lease payments, excluding any amount for residual value because the lessee does not guarantee the residual value. (This creates a situation in which the entries by lessee and lessor are not symmetrical).

Exhibit 18–9 illustrates a direct financing lease with a $10,000 **unguaranteed residual value** at the end of the lease term. The residual value replaces the BPO in the previous example. Otherwise the data is unchanged. The lessor's computation of the annual rentals in which the present value of the unguaranteed residual value is deducted yields $33,809, the same amount as was calculated for the lease when a $10,000 BPO was involved. However, since the $10,000 residual value is not guaranteed by the lessee, the lessee capitalizes only the net asset cost of $92,487 =

$33,809(*PVAD*, 10%, 3). Exhibit 18–9 gives selected entries for the lessor and lessee and the lessee's computation of the cost of the leased asset. The entries (and the amortization schedules) of the lessor and lessee differ (even though they use the same implicit interest rate) because the estimated unguaranteed residual value is retained in the lessor's accounts but is not capitalized in the lessee's accounts. The lessor's entry on January 1, 1991, the date of inception of the lease, removes the cost of the leased asset and records the receivable, which includes the $10,000 residual value. The last entry, made at the termination of the lease by the lessor, removes the residual value ($10,000) from the receivable account and returns it to its original asset account.[22]

The lessor's amortization schedule, shown in Exhibit 18–9, leaves an ending asset balance of $10,000 (the residual value) in the lessor's lease receivable account. The initial value in the lease receivable account for the lessor is the lessor's cost of the leased asset, $100,000, because the lessor plans to recover the total cost from the lessee's payments and the asset's residual value. In contrast, the lessee's amortization schedule starts with the lease liability amount ($92,487), which excludes the present value of the residual value and ends with a zero balance. Because there is no transfer of title or BPO, the lessee depreciates the leased asset over the lease term, disregarding the unguaranteed residual value.

For a sales-type lease with an unguaranteed residual value, SFAS No. 13 requires that the lessor deduct the present value of the unguaranteed residual value from both sales revenue and cost of goods sold. The main purpose of this requirement is to avoid overstating sales revenue. This does not affect the manufacturer's or dealer's profit, the lease receivable, or annual interest revenue. Exhibit 18–10 shows the case of the sales-type lease used earlier but now with an unguaranteed residual value of $10,000. Both sales revenue ($92,487) and cost of goods sold ($72,487) are computed by deducting the present value of the unguaranteed residual value [$10,000 (*PV1*, 10%, 3) = $10,000(0.75131) = $7,513] from the cash equivalent price ($100,000) and carrying value ($80,000), respectively. This approach results in the same manufacturer's or dealer's profit as when the residual value is guaranteed. However, both sales revenue and cost of goods sold are reduced because the residual value reverts to the lessor.

Residual Value Guaranteed by Lessee and Retained by Lessor When the lessor retains the residual value of the leased asset, the lease agreement may require the lessee to guarantee all or part of the estimated residual value at the end of the lease term. Such guarantees are made to motivate the lessee to take better care of the leased asset.

Residual Value Fully Guaranteed by the Lessee In this case, the residual value estimated at the inception of the lease is fully guaranteed by the lessee, which means that the lessee must pay the cash equivalent to make up any residual value deficiency. The deficiency is based on an appraisal (usually by an independent party) at the end of the lease term. To continue the extended example used in Exhibit 18–9, assume the actual residual value at the end of the lease term determined in accordance with the lease contract is $9,000, rather than the previously estimated $10,000. Assuming a fully guaranteed residual value, the lessee must pay the lessor $1,000 cash.

---

[22] Some accountants prefer to leave the present value of the residual value in its original asset account for amortization during the lease term because it will not be "collected for" during that term. Both approaches produce the same end results. *SFAS No. 13*, par. 18a, states that "the unguaranteed residual value accruing to the benefit of the lessor" should be "recorded as [included in] the gross investment in the lease." This specification relates more fundamentally to computation of the lease payments by the lessor and not to the details of a specific journal entry.

EXHIBIT 18-10 Accounting for a Sales-Type Lease with Unguaranteed Residual Value

Lessor			**Lessee**		

January 1, 1991–Inception of lease:

Lease receivable	100,000		Leased asset	92,487†	
Cost of goods sold	72,487*		Lease liability		92,487
Sales revenue		92,487**			
Asset		80,000			

* Lessor's cost of goods sold is the carrying value of the asset ($80,000) less the present value of the unguaranteed residual value $10,000(PV1, 10%, 3) = $7,513. Thus, ($80,000 − $7,513) = $72,487.
** Lessor's sales revenue: $100,000 − $7,513 = $92,487.

† Lessee's computation of leased asset cost excluding the unguaranteed residual value is $33,809 × (PVAD, 10%, 3) = $33,809(2.73554) = $92,487.

January 1, 1991—First rental:

Cash	33,809		Lease liability	33,809	
Lease receivable		33,809	Cash		33,809

December 31, 1991—Adjusting entries:

Lease receivable	6,619		Interest expense	5,868	
Interest revenue		6,619	Lease liability		5,868

See lessor's amortization schedule in Exhibit 18-9.

See lessee's amortization schedule Exhibit 18-9.

			Depreciation expense	30,829	
			Accumulated depreciation		30,829
			($92,487 × 1/3 = $30,829)		

December 31, 1993—End of Lease term:
to remove the residual value from the lease receivable account:

(to remove the asset from the accounts:)

Asset	10,000		Accumulated depreciation	92,487	
Lease receivable		10,000	Leased asset		92,487

Lease Amortization Schedule (Annuity Due Basis)—Same as in Exhibit 18-9

To compute the periodic lease payments when the residual value is fully guaranteed, the lessor deducts the present value of the total residual value from the total amount to be recovered under the lease agreement because at the inception of the lease, the lessor expects to realize the full amount of the residual value at the end of the lease term. This situation is the same as with an unguaranteed residual value.

A capital lease with a residual value fully guaranteed by the lessee is illustrated in Exhibit 18-11, using the same data as in the prior example. The lessor deducts the present value of the guaranteed residual value to compute the periodic rentals. The lessee capitalizes $100,000 (the same amount recognized by the lessor), which is the present value of the payments committed to by the lessee as well as the asset's market value. The lessee capitalizes the sum of these two amounts because the lease liability is the total present value guaranteed to be transferred from the lessee to the lessor. The guaranteed residual value is added by the lessee; in contrast, an unguaranteed residual value is excluded from the capitalized lease value.

At termination of the lease on December 31, 1993, the actual residual value is determined (independently, as specified in the lease agreement). This residual value then is compared with the guaranteed residual value to determine whether the lessee owes the lessor additional consideration. If, as is assumed here, the actual residual value at the end of 1993 is determined independently to be $9,000, then the lessee is obligated to pay the lessor $1,000 cash ($10,000 − $9,000). If the guaranteed value had been less than the actual value, the lessor would have no obligation to make a refund to the lessee.

EXHIBIT 18-11   Accounting for a Direct-Financing Lease with a $10,000 Residual Value Guaranteed by the Lessee

Lessor		Lessee	
January 1, 1991—Inception of lease:			
Lease receivable 100,000*		Leased asset 100,000*	
Asset	100,000	Lease liability	100,000
January 1, 1991—First rental:			
Cash 33,809		Lease liability 33,809	
Lease receivable	33,809	Cash	33,809
December 31, 1991—Adjusting entries:			
Lease receivable .... 6,619†		Interest expense .... 6,619†	
Interest revenue	6,619	Lease liability	6,619
		Depreciation expense 30,000	
		Accumulated depreciation	30,000
		($100,000 − $10,000) × ⅓ = $30,000	

December 31, 1993—Lease termination assuming an actual residual value of $9,000:

Lessor		Lessee	
Asset (market value) 9,000		Accumulated depreciation 90,000	
Cash ($10,000 − $9,000) 1,000		Lease liability 10,000	
Lease receivable	10,000‡	Loss on lease contract 1,000	
		Leased asset	100,000
		Cash	1,000

* $33,809 (*PVAD*, 10%, 3) + $10,000 (*PVI*, 10%, 3) =
$33,809(2.73554) + $10,000(0.75131).
† See amortization schedule below.
‡ Guaranteed residual value.

Lease Amortization Schedule (Annuity Due Basis)

Date	Lease Payments	Interest at 10%	Decrease (Increase) in Receivable/Liability	Lease Receivable/Liability Balance
1/1/91 .... Initial value				$100,000
1/1/91	$ 33,809	—	$33,809	66,191
12/31/91	—	$ 6,619	(6,619)	72,810
1/1/92	33,809	—	33,809	39,001
12/31/92	—	3,900	(3,900)	42,901
1/1/93	33,809	—	33,809	9,092
12/31/93	—	908	(908)	10,000 (guaranteed
	$101,427	$11,427	$90,000	residual value)

The estimated residual value on an asset under a capital lease must be reviewed annually to determine whether it is realistic (*SFAS No. 13,* par. 17 *d*). If the estimate is revised by a material amount, a change in estimate should be recognized and the subsequent lease entries (and schedules) revised accordingly. A fully guaranteed residual value is accounted for in the same way for both direct and sale-type leases. Finally, since there is neither a transfer of title at the end of the lease nor a BPO (neither condition 1 or 2 of Exhibit 18–2 is met), depreciation is again based on the life of the lease, three years.

Residual Value Partially Guaranteed by the Lessee   When the lessee guarantees only a part of the estimated residual value of the leased asset, the lessor bases the computation of the periodic lease payments (and the related amortization schedule) on the total estimated residual value. In contrast, to compute the amount to be capitalized, the lessee adds the present value of only the partially guaranteed amount to the present value of the lessor's lease payments. Therefore, the amounts recorded by the lessor and lessee would not be the same. This procedure is the same for direct financing and sales-type leases.

Residual Value Guaranteed by Third Party and Retained by Lessor   The residual value of a leased asset may be guaranteed in full or in part by a third party guarantor, usually retained by the lessor for a fee. In this case, the lessor would deduct the amount of the guarantee to compute the lease payments because the cash for any residual value deficiency will come from a different source. The lease receivable includes both sources, the present value of both the rental payments and the guaranteed residual value. The lessee does not include the present value of the guaranteed residual value in the cost of the leased asset because the residual value is guaranteed by a third party (not the lessee). This again results in asymmetrical entries between the lessor and lessee. To illustrate this case, assume now that the $10,000 residual value is guaranteed by a third party. The entries are the same as those shown in Exhibit 18–9. The procedure is the same for direct-financing and sales-type leases. The calculations once again lead to rental payments of $33,809 by the lessee since the lessor is assured of the $10,000 from a third party.

The lessor includes the present value of the residual value as part of the lease payments, resulting in a lease receivable of $92,487 + $7,513 = $100,000. This amount is greater than 90% of the leased asset's market value, $100,000(.90) = $90,000, at the inception of the lease. Therefore, for the lessor, the lease satisfies criterion 4 in Exhibit 18–2 for a capital lease in this case. Since the present value of the lease payments, excluding the residual value, is $92,487, which also exceeds 90% of the leased asset's market value of $100,000, the lessee also treats the lease as a capital lease.

An interesting result occurs if the lessor has a third-party guarantee $20,000 for the residual value. (Suppose, also, that the asset's economic life is now five years.) In this situation, the lessor reduces the rentals to $31,063 in recognition of the larger receivable guaranteed for the residual value:

$$[\$100,000 - \$20,000(PV1, 10\%, 3)] \div (PVAD, 10\%, 3) =$$
$$[\$100,000 - \$20,000(.75131)] \div (2.73554) = \$31,063$$

The lessor capitalizes the value of the lease payments plus the present value of the residual value to obtain $100,000: $31,063(2.73554) + $20,000(.75131). This amount exceeds 90% of the leased asset's fair market value (.9 × $100,000 = $90,000), and hence the lease satisfies criterion 4 in Exhibit 18–2 for a capital lease. However, the guaranteed residual value by a third party is excluded from the minimum lease payments for the lessee. The lessee computes only the present value of the $31,063 payments obtaining $84,974 = $31,063(PVAD, 10%, 3) = $31,063(2.73554). This amount is less than 90% of the market value of the asset at lease inception (.90 × $100,000 = $90,000). Because of this result, and the fact that no other requirement for a capital lease is met in this case (no transfer of ownership at the end of the lease term, no bargain purchase option, and a lease term here that is less than 75% of the leased asset's life), the lessee treats the lease as an operating lease. The entries for this special case are given in Exhibit 18–12.

Thus, by using a third-party guarantor, a lessor may be able to record a lease as a capital lease, while the lessee may be able to record the lease as an operating lease, thereby circumventing the FASB's attempt to ensure accounting symmetry between lessor and lessee (equivalent accounting treatment of a lease contract between contracting parties). Unwittingly, the FASB, in publishing *SFAS No. 13,* must take credit for spawning a new submarket of third-party guarantor companies whose sole function is, for a fee, to guarantee the residual values of business leases.

EXHIBIT 18-12 Accounting for a Direct-Financing Lease with a $20,000 Residual Value Guaranteed by a Third Party

Lessor (Direct-Financing Lease)		Lessee (Operating Lease)	
January 1, 1991—Inception of lease:			
Lease receivable	100,000	No entry.	
Asset	100,000		
January 1, 1991—First rental:			
Cash	31,063	Rent expense	31,063
Lease receivable	31,063	Cash	31,063
December 31, 1991—Adjusting entries:			
Lease receivable	6,894	No entry.	
Interest revenue	6,894		
See lessor amortization schedule below.			

Lessor's Lease Amortization Schedule (Annuity Due Basis)

Date	Lease Payments	Interest at 10%	Decrease (Increase) in Receivable	Lease Receivable Balance
1/1/91	Initial value			$100,000
1/1/91	$31,063	—	$31,063	69,937
12/31/91	—	$ 6,894	(6,894)	75,831
1/1/92	31,063	—	31,063	44,768
12/31/92	—	4,477	(4,477)	49,245
1/1/93	31,063	—	31,063	18,182
12/31/93	—	1,818	(1,818)	20,000 (guaranteed residual value)
	$93,189	$13,189	$80,000	

The introduction to this chapter indicated that many investment banking and securities firms are in the leasing service business. One of the leasing services they provide is professional assistance in structuring leases so that lessees are able to keep leases off their balance sheets, while lessors account for them as direct-financing leases. The use of a third-party guarantor is one of the means used to accomplish this result. Investment banking firms generally engage in this business as commission brokers and underwriters rather than as long-term principals to the leases themselves. Furthermore, not all leases handled by investment banking firms are split operating/direct-financing deals. A typical lease deal might entail a $50 million equipment lease, with a Fortune 500 company as the lessee and a syndicate of institutional investors (insurance companies and pension plan managers, primarily) as the lessors. The investment banking firm earns a fee for putting the deal together and finding the lender-lessors. Exhibit 18–13 summarizes the accounting under different residual value situations.

Different Interest Rates

To this point in this chapter, all leasing examples and illustrations have been based on the assumption that the lessor's implicit interest rate and the lessee's incremental borrowing rate were equal. For convenience and math ease, a 10% rate was used in most of the illustrations. Suppose, instead, that the lessor's implicit interest rate was 9% while the lessee's incremental borrowing rate remained at 10%. If so, which rate should be used?

The question of which rate to use applies only to the lessee. The lessor knows the asset's cost and the amount and number of payments, and thus can determine the interest rate implicit in the lease. The rate used by the lessee is of concern to the

EXHIBIT 18-13   Summary of Residual Value Accounting (Assuming the Lessor and Lessee Use the Same Interest Rate)

Situation	Symmetrical Entries and Schedules?	Reason
1. No residual value	Yes	No residual value effect on either party.
2. Unguaranteed residual value (Exhibits 18-9 and 18-10)	No	Lessor includes the present value of the residual value in the capitalized lease asset. Lessee excludes the present value of the residual from the leased asset.
3. Residual value fully guaranteed by lessee (Exhibit 18-11)	Yes	Lessor includes total residual value in the capitalized lease asset. Lessee includes the present value of the fully guaranteed residual in the leased asset.
4. Residual value partially guaranteed by lessee (not illustrated)	No	Lessor includes total residual value in the capitalized lease asset. Lessee includes the present value of the guaranteed portion of residual value in the leased asset.
5. Full or part residual value guarantee by third party (Exhibit 18-9 if capital lease to lessee and Exhibit 18-12 if operating lease to lessee.)	No.	Lessor includes residual value guarantee in the capitalized lease asset. Lessee excludes the present value of the residual value from the leased asset.

FASB. *SFAS No. 13* instructs lessees to use their incremental borrowing rate unless the lessor's implicit interest rate is known to the lessee and that rate is lower than the lessee's own borrowing rate.

The phrasing "if it is known" as used in *SFAS No. 13* may conjure up images of the lessor playing cat and mouse games, keeping the lessee in the dark about the interest rate being charged. In truth, most leasing transactions are conducted completely in the open. Although the lessor's interest rate is not explicitly stated in the lease contract, it usually is communicated orally and also may be found in business documents accompanying the lease. In fact, the rate charged by the lessor is frequently subject to negotiation. Thus, in most cases, the lessee simply uses the lower of the incremental borrowing rate or the lessor's implicit interest rate.

In some cases, however, even though the implicit interest rate may be known to the business executive who negotiated the lease, the company's accounting staff (or external accountants) may not be fully briefed on the terms of the lease transaction and, therefore, must rely on the lease itself for accounting detail information. Also, in many instances, lessee companies use independent business brokers to negotiate leases, subject to review and approval by legal counsel. These outside representatives may be unavailable for detail information gathering or not attuned to the information needs of accountants.

The true target audience for *SFAS No. 13* is those lessees who persist in treating lease transactions as operating leases rather than capital leases. Here's how interest rates fit into their plans: The higher the interest rate assigned to a leasing transaction, the lower the dollar amount capitalized as a leased asset. This is because, from the lessee's point of view, the total dollar amounts of the minimum lease payments are fixed. Now, if the capitalized portion can be kept below 90% of the leased asset's cost (and none of the other criteria for capitalization is met), the lessee can treat the transaction as an operating lease, substituting rental expense for capital expenditures.

To illustrate, assume that a lessee—for whatever reason—wishes to account for a leasing transaction as an operating lease rather than a capital lease. The same $100,000 example asset used throughout this chapter will also be used here. Again, the lease term is three years, and the asset is assumed to have a $10,000 residual value at the lease's end point. The minimum lease payments are $33,809 for three years, which everyone but the lessee knows is based on the lessor's implicit interest rate of 10%.[23]

The lessee knows only two facts: The market value of the asset being rented is $100,000 and the annual rental payments will be $33,809. The residual value is unknown to the lessee. Suppose the lessee claims that its incremental borrowing rate is 14%. The lessee will then compute the present value to be:

$$\$33,809 \ (PVAD, 14\%, 3) = \$33,809(2.64666) = \$89,481$$

The calculations for both interest rates are:

Rate	Minimum Lease Payments	Present Value Annuity Due Factor	Present Value of Lease Payments	Percent of Asset's Market Value
10%	$33,809 ×	2.73554 =	92,487	92.487%
14%	$33,809 ×	2.64666 =	89,481	89.481%

If left unchallenged, the lessee would account for the transaction as an operating lease, and the lessor would account for it as a direct-financing lease.

Lessees are normally well aware of the fair market cost of the assets they lease, and they know the minimum lease payments and term of the lease. But they may not know the leased asset's residual value as of the end of the lease term (a value whose future amount is discounted by lessors), since lessees are not interested in buying this portion of the asset's value. If the residual value is not known, it can be further argued that the implicit interest rate used by the lessor may be impossible for the lessee to determine, in which case lessees use their incremental borrowing rate as described above.

The illustration here allowed the lessee to use a higher discount rate than the lessor's rate. If the lower (lessor) rate were known to the lessee, *SFAS No. 13* requires the lessee to use the lower rate. Not only does this make it more likely the lessee will capitalize the lease, but it also prevents the lessee from understating the liability in the accounts if capitalization is required.

---

[23] This example also assumes that the lease contains neither a transfer of ownership provision nor a bargain purchase option, and that the lease term is less than 75% of the asset's total useful economic life.

Depreciation of a Leased Asset by the Lessee

The depreciable life and estimated residual value used by the lessee in computing periodic depreciation expense on a leased asset in a capital lease arrangement depend on the terms of the lease contract. If the lease does not provide for a transfer of ownership to the lessee at the end of the lease term or a BPO (criteria 1 and 2 in Exhibit 18–2), the period of depreciation must be the lease term rather than the life of the leased property. In this case, any unguaranteed residual value is ignored by the lessee when computing the depreciation expense.

If ownership of the leased asset is transferred from the lessor to the lessee at the end of the lease term or the lease contains a BPO, the lessee depreciates the capitalized cost over the total economic life of the leased asset to the lessee (rather than over the term of the lease). In this case, the lessee uses the estimated residual value as of the end of the asset's useful life (rather than as of the end of the lease term). The longer economic life and lower residual value are used in such cases because the parties assume that the lessee will retain the asset after the end of the lease term.

Executory and Initial Direct Costs

Two kinds of lease costs incurred by the lessor are given special accounting treatment. They are executory costs and initial direct costs.

Executory costs are expenses of ownership and use that include insurance, property taxes, and maintenance. In the case of an operating lease, the executory costs, typically, are paid by the lessor and are recovered by the lessor in the periodic lease rentals. In the case of a capital lease, a major part, if not all, of the executory costs usually are shifted by the lease contract for direct payment by the lessee. Therefore, they are not included in the periodic rentals. However, to the extent that the executory costs are incurred by the lessor and then added each year to the current lease payment, they should be excluded by both parties in computing the present value of the periodic rentals for capitalization purposes. Instead, they should be reported as an expense when incurred. If such executory costs are not known by the lessee at the time the current lease payment is made, they should be estimated.

Assume that the *lessor* in the example illustrated by Exhibit 18-4, agreed to insure the leased asset at a cost of $1,000 per year and then to bill the lessee. The current lease payment would then be $37,556. This amount is equal to the minimum lease rentals required to yield a 10% rate of return to the lessor ($36,556) plus the annual executory costs ($1,000). The executory costs are excluded by the lessee in computing the amount capitalized. The interest revenue accruing to the lessor and the interest expense of the lessee are unaffected by the inclusion of executory costs since the $1,000 is paid directly to the insurer; thus, discounting would be inappropriate. Journal entries to reflect the annual executory costs incurred by the lessor on the date of the first rental are as follows:

January 1, 1991—First rental payment:

Lessor:

Cash	37,556	
Lease receivable		36,556
Insurance payable (or prepaid insurance if already paid)		1,000

Lessee:

Lease liability	36,556	
Insurance expense (or prepaid insurance)	1,000	
Cash		37,556

Initial direct costs are incremental costs incurred by the lessor in negotiating and consummating a lease agreement. They include legal fees, cost of credit and other investigations, commissions and employees' compensation directly related to initiating the lease, and clerical costs of preparing and processing the lease documents. These costs have no effect on the lessee's accounting but do affect the lessor's accounting.

In the case of an operating lease, the initial direct costs should be expensed by the lessor over the lease term on a reasonable basis (usually straight-line) in order to match them with revenues that they helped earn. In the case of a direct-financing lease, initial direct costs must be included in the lessor's gross investment in the lease. This means that these costs must be added to the cost of the leased asset to compute the annual rentals. On this point *SFAS No. 91*, par. 23, states that "lessors shall account for initial direct costs as part of the investment in a direct financing lease. The practice of recognizing a portion of the unearned income at inception of the lease to offset initial direct costs shall no longer be acceptable." The effect of this Statement is to spread the indirect costs over the term of the lease and thereby match the expenditures with the related interest revenue. For example, suppose the lease in the continuing example (see Exhibit 18–4) involved initial direct costs of $6,000. The lease is a direct financing lease to the lessor. The investment to be recovered is now $100,000 plus $6,000, or $106,000. The lessor's entries for the first year would be:

January 1, 1991—To record the lease:

Lease receivable	100,000	
Deferred expenses	6,000	
Asset		100,000
Cash		6,000

January 1, 1991—First rental:

Cash	36,556	
Lease receivable		36,556

December 3, 1991—To recognize interest earned and amortization of initial indirect expenses using the straight-line method:

Lease receivable	6,344	
Indirect lease expense ($6,000 ÷ 3)	2,000	
Interest revenue		6,344
Deferred expenses		2,000

In the case of a sales-type lease, the initial direct costs should be expensed by the lessor in the year in which the lease is initiated (as an offset to the manufacturer's or dealer's profit) because these costs are considered to be a selling expense in the year of sale.

CONCEPT REVIEW

1. Explain why for a lessee, the present value of the guaranteed residual value by the lessee is included in the recorded lease obligation but is excluded if the guarantee is by a third party.
2. Under what conditions must the lessee use the lessor's implicit interest rate? Why does this requirement exist?
3. What are executory costs and why does the lessee exclude them from the present value calculation of the lease liability?

Sale-Leaseback Arrangements

As its name indicates, in a **sale-leaseback (SLB)** arrangement, the owner of an asset sells it to a leasing company or other party and immediately leases it back.[24] The asset itself never leaves the seller-lessee's possession and continues in operation without interruption.

Like leasing in general, from the lessee's perspective, sale-leaseback transactions are essentially financing transactions and, in some cases, off-balance-sheet financing devices. Some of the major aspects that should be considered regarding sale-lease-back transactions include the following:

+ *Fact:* Fully depreciated assets afford no tax savings beyond maintenance and insurance expenses. *Action:* Sell the asset and lease it back. The lease payments will be tax deductible.
+ *Fact:* In the majority of sale-leaseback transactions, the sale of assets generates immediate cash inflow. *Action:* If liquidity is a problem or if business expansion capital is needed, the sale-leaseback of assets (without giving up operating possession) provides an immediate inflow of needed cash equal to 100% of the asset's current market value. In contrast, asset-secured bank loans are typically limited to 75% or 80% of the asset's market value.
+ *Fact:* A sale-leaseback often entails a gain on the sale of the asset, which normally must be deferred and amortized over the life of the accompanying leasing arrangement. However, if the total value of the leaseback (minimum lease payments at present value) is less than "substantially all" of the asset's total market value, a sizable portion of the gain may be recognized as a current income.[25] *Action:* Buildings and other tangible assets that are owned, but only partially occupied or utilized for business purposes, can be sold for a profit; only a portion of the building's space, or only a portion of a tangible asset's utility value, would be leased back to the seller. Thus, a portion of the profits on the sale most likely would be reported as current income.[26]
+ *Fact:* Sale-leaseback can be used as refinancing tools to save current interest expense. *Action:* If past asset acquisitions are being financed at high interest rates in effect at the time of purchase, and interest rates have since declined, sale-leaseback is an effective means for refinancing at lower interest rates.
+ *Fact:* The tax liability due to alternative minimum tax requirements (and burdensome personal property taxes in some states) can result in serious drains of cash resources. *Action:* Sale-leaseback can alleviate the tax burden.

From the lessor's standpoint, sale-leaseback represents no special advantages or disadvantages; it's simply business as usual for lessors. The characteristics of a typical sale-leaseback arrangement may be diagramed for the seller-lessee and buyer-lessor as follows:

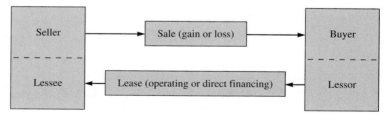

---

[24] Sale-leaseback transactions are subject to the provisions of *SFAS No. 13*, par. 32–34, as amended by *SFAS No. 28*.

[25] The phrase "substantially all" is generally interpreted to mean 90% of the asset's fair market value at the inception of the lease. *SFAS No. 28* calls for profits on the sale of assets included in a sale-leaseback transaction to be deferred and amortized up to the extent of the total minimum lease payments, computed at present value. Profits in excess of the minimum lease payments should be recognized and reported at the time of the sale-leaseback.

[26] Perhaps the best example of this application concerns large corporations that own major office buildings as corporate headquarters. In many of these office towers, the owner-tenant may occupy only 30% or 40% of the total space, renting out the remaining space to other businesses. Rather than keeping its capital tied up in owning real estate, the owner-tenant may find it advantageous to sell the property (usually at a sizable profit over the building book value) and lease back only the space actually occupied. In many such instances, the sale profits will exceed the total minimum lease payments, with excess profits reported as additions to income for the year in which the sale takes place.

Accounting for Sale-Leaseback Transactions   Sale-leaseback, like regular leases, are accounted for by lessees as either capital or operating leases based on the criteria listed earlier in the text. If the lease provisions meet any of the four criteria in Exhibit 18–2, the lessee must account for the transaction as a capital lease; if none of the criteria is met, the transaction is accounted for as a operating lease.

The same criteria apply to the lessor, plus the two additional criteria (*a* and *b*) relating to lessors. Lessors account for sale-leaseback transactions as direct-financing or operating leases. Sales-type leases are not permitted (as they would result in overstatements of sales revenue and gross margins). Accounting entries for lessors engaged in sale-leaseback are identical to those used to record regular leases.

For lessees, however, accounting entries for sale-leaseback transactions in most instances have extra considerations, summarized as follows:[27]

* If a capital lease is involved, the gain or loss on the sale of the asset must be deferred and amortized over the term of the lease and in the same proportion as the leased asset itself is amortized.
* If an operating lease is involved, essentially the same gain or loss deferral and amortization process applies, but the terminology and accounts change. The deferred gain or loss is amortized over the term of the lease in proportion to each year's gross rental expense.
* In amortizing deferred gains over the term of the lease, the credit side of the entry is normally to depreciation expense if a capital lease is involved, while rent expense is credited if it is an operating lease. In both cases, the effect is to reduce current expenses. When deferred losses are amortized, the opposite holds true.
* In instances where the book value of the asset being sold is more than the asset's fair market value but exceeds the sales price, a portion of the loss is taken immediately and is not deferred. Consider the following two sale-leaseback situations involving a sale price of $500,000:

	Situation No. 1	Situation No. 2
Asset at book carrying value	$1,000,000	$1,000,000
Less: Accumulated depreciation	200,000	200,000
Net undepreciated cost of asset	$ 800,000	$ 800,000
Fair market value of asset at time of sale-leaseback	$ 900,000	$ 300,000
Loss on sale of asset ($800,000 − $500,000)	$ 300,000	$ 300,000

In situation no. 1, the asset's $900,000 fair market value at the time of the transaction is greater than the $800,000 undepreciated cost. The loss is considered artificial. The loss is more logically treated as prepaid rent and is deferred and amortized over the term of the lease. In situation no. 2, however, the asset's $300,000 fair market value is less than the asset's undepreciated cost of $800,000. The $300,000 loss is accounted for as an immediate loss.

Sell-Leaseback Example Accounting Entries   To illustrate how sale-leaseback transactions are accounted for, consider the following case background information:

* On January 1, 1991, a seller-lessee sells a warehouse to a buyer-lessor for $95,000. The warehouse was carried on the seller-lesseee's books at $80,000 and had an estimated remaining useful economic life of ten years, with no residual value. The fair market value of the warehouse is $110,000. There is no transfer of title or BPO.

---

[27] Under the provisions of *SFS No. 13* and *No. 28*, asset sales and leaseback transactions are treated as single financing transactions, similar to a loan, rather than as two independent transactions. The purpose of this single-transaction ruling is to prevent abusive and manipulative dealings between borrowers and lenders. Without constraints, the seller-lessee could conceivably sell an asset to a buyer-lessor for an unrealistically high (or low) price purposely to report a gain (or loss) on the sale. The seller-lessee could then lease the asset back under an agreement with a present value equal to the sale price of the asset. Upon completion of both "independent" transactions, the seller-lessee would be in the same economic position that would have prevailed if neither the sale nor the leaseback had occurred. However, a phantom gain or loss on the sale would be reported.

+ In conjunction with the sale of the warehouse, the seller-lessee and the buyer-lessor enter into a five-year lease. The buyer-lessor's implicit interest rate is 12%, which is the same as the seller-lessee's incremental borrowing cost.
+ The sale of the warehouse produced a gain of $15,000 ($95,000 selling price less $80,000 carying value). This gain is deferred and will be amortized over the five-year lease term.
+ Annual lease payments, starting January 1, 1991, are $23,530, computed as $95,000 ÷ ($PVAD$, 12%, 5) = $95,000 ÷ 4.03735 = $23,530.
+ Depreciation expense applicable to the leaseback portion of this transaction is computed using the straight-line method over five years, with no residual value.

Exhibit 8-14 shows the basic entries used by both the seller-lessee and buyer-lessor to account for the above described sale-leaseback transaction over the first year of the lease. Since none of the criteria in Exhibit 18-2 is met, the lease is an operating lease for both parties. Suppose, to change the example, the economic life of the warehouse is only five years. Criterion 3 now is met and the lease is a capital lease for both parties. Exhibit 18-15 gives the accounting for the same sale-leaseback transaction, this time accounted for as a capital lease by the seller-lessee and as a direct-financing lease by the buyer-lessor.

Classification of Lease Receivables and Payables

When a lessor has lease receivables (and the lessee has lease payables) extending beyond one year (or the operating cycle of the business, if longer), the amount of the lease to be reported as a current asset by the lessor and as a current liability by the lessee must be determined. The lessor's total lease receivable, as well as the lessee's payable, should be reported at their present values using the interest rate applied to the lease. The problem is to separate the current and long-term portion. There are two approaches. The first approach recognizes the present value of the next year's payment as the current portion. The second approach records the coming year's decline in the total lease receivable (payable) as the current portion. To illustrate the classification of lease receivables (payables) for reporting purposes involving an annuity due, refer to the amortization schedule in Exhibit 18-4.

The first approach would report on December 31, 1991, the next payment of $36,556, which is due January 1, 1992, as the current portion of the lease and $33,232 ($69,788 − $36,556) as the long-term portion. The second approach reports the decline in the lease during 1992, namely, $33,232 ($69,788 − $36,556), as the current portion. The latter method is more common, but the former is not proscribed under GAAP and may be found in financial reports.[28]

Both approaches can be defended. The next payment represents the sacrifice that must be made by the lessee and the payment to be received by the lessor. The present value in the current value of this amount. Alternatively, the coming year's decline in the lease is also a relevant measure of the currently recorded value. In practice, the prevailing approach is to show the coming year's decline in the lease as the current amount.

Lease Disclosure Requirements

SFAS No. 13 requires disclosure of many details concerning leasing arrangements in the financial statements or the accompanying notes. The primary lease disclosures are:

---

[28] For a discussion of these issues, see R. Swieringa, "When Current Is Noncurrent and Vice Versa!" *The Accounting Review*, January 1984, pp. 123–30, and A. Richardson, "The Measurement of the Current Portion of Long-Term Lease Obligations—Some Evidence from Practice," *The Accounting Review*, October 1985, pp. 744–52.

EXHIBIT 18-14 Accounting for Sale-Leaseback: Operating Lease

Seller-Lessee			Buyer-Lessor		
Jan. 1, 1991—Sale of warehouse:			**Jan. 1, 1991—Purchase of warehouse:**		
Cash	95,000		Warehouse	95,000	
Warehouse (net)		80,000	Cash		95,000
Unearned gain on SLB sale		15,000			
Jan. 1, 1991—To record first lease payment:			**Jan. 1, 1991—To record the first lease receipt:**		
Rent expense	23,530		Cash	23,530	
Cash		23,530	Rent revenue		23,530
Dec. 31, 1991—To record amortization of unrecognized gain:*					
Unearned gain on SLB sale	3,000		Depreciation expense†	9,500	
Rent expense		3,000	Accumulated depreciation		9,500
($15,000 × ⅕ = $3,000)			($95,000 × 1/10 = $9,500)		

* Straight-line method is used (over the lease life) because equal payments are made each year.

† Based on a 10-year economic life.

EXHIBIT 18-15 Accounting for Sale-Leaseback: Direct-Financing Lease for the Lessor and a Capital Lease for the Lessee

Seller-Lessee			Buyer-Lessor		
Jan. 1, 1991—Sale of warehouse:			**Jan. 1, 1991—Purchase of warehouse:**		
Cash	95,000		Warehouse	95,000	
Warehouse		80,000	Cash		95,000
Unearned gain on SLB sale		15,000			
Jan. 1, 1991—To record capital lease:			**Jan. 1, 1991—To record direct financing lease:**		
Leased asset	95,000		Lease receivable	95,000	
Lease liability		95,000	Warehouse (on lease)		95,000
Jan. 1, 1991—Payment of first lease payment (see amortization schedule below):			**Jan. 1, 1991—Receipt of first lease payment:**		
Lease liability	23,530		Cash	23,530	
Cash		23,530	Lease receivable		23,530
Dec. 31, 1991—Adjusting entries:					
To record depreciation expense:					
Depreciation expense	19,000				
Accumulated depreciation					
($95,000 × ⅕)		19,000			
To record amortization of unrecognized gain:					
Unearned gain on SLB sale	3,000				
Depreciation expense		3,000			
($15,000 × ⅕ = $3,000)					
To record accrued interest on lease receivable liability (see amortization schedule below):			**Dec. 31, 1991—To record accrued interest on lease receivable:**		
Interest expense	8,576		Lease receivable	8,576	
Lease liability		8,576	Interest revenue		8,576

Lease Amortization Schedule (Annuity Due Basis)

Date	Annual Lease Payment	Annual Interest at 12%	Lease Receivable/Liability Decrease (Increase)	Receivable/Liability Balance
1/1/1991				$95,000
1/1/1991	$ 23,530		$23,530	71,470
12/31/1991		$ 8,576	(8,576)	80,046
1/1/1992	23,530		23,530	56,516
12/31/1992		6,782	(6,782)	63,298
1/1/1993	23,530		23,530	39,768
12/31/1993		4,772	(4,772)	44,540
1/1/1994	23,530		23,530	21,010
12/31/1994		2,520	(2,520)	23,530
1/1/1995	23,530		23,530	—0—
	$117,650	$22,650	$95,000	

Lessee disclosures:

1. For capital leases, disclose:
   a. The gross amount of assets recorded under capital leases presented by major classes according to nature or function.
   b. Future minimum lease payments in the aggregate and for each of the five succeeding fiscal years, with separate deductions from the total for executory costs (including any profit thereon) included in the minimum lease payments and the amount of the imputed interest necessary to reduce the net minimum lease payments to present value.
   c. The total of minimum sublease rentals to be received in the future under noncancelable subleases.
   d. Total contingent rentals (these amounts are dependent on some factor other than the passage of time)
2. For operating leases having initial or remaining noncancelable lease terms in excess of one year, disclose:
   a. Future minimum rental payments required in the aggregate and for each of the five succeeding fiscal years.
   b. The total of minimum rentals to be received in the future under noncancelable subleases.
3. For all operating leases, disclose rental expense, with separate amounts for minimum rentals, contingent rentals, and sublease rentals.
4. Provide a general description of the lessee's leasing arrangements including, but not limited to, the following:
   a. The basis on which contingent rental payments are determined.
   b. The existence and terms of renewal or purchase options and escalation clauses.
   c. Restrictions imposed by lease agreements, such as those concerning dividends, additional debt, and further leasing.

Lessor disclosures:

1. For sales-type and direct-financing leases, disclose:
   a. The components of the net investment in sales-type and direct-financing leases:
      (1) Future minimum lease payments to be received, with separate deductions for amounts representing executory costs (including any profit thereon) included in the minimum lease payments and the accumulated allowance for uncollectible minimum lease payments receivable.
      (2) The unguaranteed residual values accruing to the benefit of the lessor.
      (3) Unearned interest revenue.
   b. Future minimum lease payments to be received for each of the five succeeding fiscal years.
   c. Total contingent rentals included in income.
2. For operating leases, disclose:
   a. The cost and carrying amount, if different, of property on lease or held for leasing by major classes of property according to nature or function, and the amount of accumulated depreciation in total.
   b. Minimum future rentals on noncancelable leases in the aggregate and for each of the five succeeding fiscal years.
   c. Total contingent rentals included in income.
3. Provide a general description of the lessor's leasing arrangements.

Firms usually provide information on their leases in the notes to financial-statements section. The information differs according to the extent of leasing activity in which the firm engages and the extent of disclosure the firm elects to provide. Two examples are provided by Note 3 to Boise Cascade's 1989 annual report and an unnumbered note to Ameritech's 1990 annual report:

Notes to Financial Statements
Boise Cascade Corporation and Subsidiaries
3. Leases

Lease obligations for which the Company assumes substantially all property rights and risks of ownership are capitalized. All other leases are treated as operating leases. Rental expenses for operating leases, net of sublease rentals, were $24,903,000 in 1989, $26,823,000 in 1988, and $26,488,000 in 1987.

The Company has various operating leases with remaining terms of more than one year. These leases have minimum lease payment requirements, net of sublease rentals, of $12,003,000 for 1990, $9,257,000 for 1991, $5,963,000 for 1992, $4,627,000 for 1993, and $4,202,000 for 1994, with total payments thereafter of $96,567,000.

Substantially all lease agreements have fixed payment terms based upon the lapse of time. Certain lease agreements provide the Company with the option to purchase the leased property. Additionally, certain lease agreements contain renewal options ranging up to 20 years, with fixed payment terms similar to those in the original lease agreements.

Notes to Consolidated Financial Statements
American Information Technologies Corporation and Subsidiaries

Lease Commitments

The Company leases certain facilities and equipment used in its operations under both capital and operating leases. Rental expense under operating leases was $209.8, $172.2, and $182.8 million for 1990, 1989, and 1988, respectively. At December 31, 1990, the aggregate minimum rental commitments under non-cancelable leases were approximately as follows (millions):

Years	Operating	Capital
1991	$ 84.6	$13.4
1992	72.4	10.1
1993	56.8	7.2
1994	43.0	6.3
1995	35.3	5.3
Thereafter	206.5	15.4
Total minimum rental commitments	$498.6	57.7
Less: Executory costs		5.8
		15.0
Present value of minimum lease payments		$36.9

A Continuing Issue Many financial institutions have entered the business of structuring leases so that the *lessor* can treat the transaction as a sale or financing lease while the lessee treats the lease as an operating lease, thereby keeping the debt off the balance sheet.[29] The effect on lessee debt-equity ratios can be substantial as indicated at the start of this chapter. Avoiding capitalization also decreases expenses initially since book depreciation plus interest will exceed the operating lease payment in the early years of the lease, generally without any mitigating tax benefit.

---

[29] Banks and other financial institutions, when acting as lessors, normally prefer (if not insist) that leases be structured as direct-financing leases, not operating leases. The logic behind this preference is the fact that banks are in the business of financing the acquisition of business assets (direct-financing lease) and not owning assets rented out to businesses (operating leases). Also, direct-financing leases tend to be more profitable for banks and other lenders than operating leases. This is due primarily to the simpler, cleaner nature of the lease-servicing work involved in a direct-financing lease.

Just how this works was covered in the discussion of residual values and interest rates. First it is relatively easy to avoid transferring asset ownership, criterion 1, and to avoid selling the property at a bargain price, criterion 2. To ensure that the asset fails the 75% of economic life test, criterion 3, the lessee usually signs a short-term lease.

The more difficult criterion to overcome is criterion 4, which requires that the present value of the lease payments exceed 90% of the asset's fair value. It is this criterion that requires ingenuity to defeat. Use of a guaranteed residual value put up by a third party, and assuring the use of the lessee's incremental borrowing rate by keeping the lessor's interest rate unknown to the lessee are the two primary means of keeping the lease payments under the 90% level and hence, keeping the lease off the lessee's books.[30] Third-party guarantees of residual values are included in the payment calculations by the lessor (but are excluded by the lessee) and thereby lower the lease payment. Furthermore, if the guaranteed residual value by the third party is unknown to the lessee, the lessee will not be able to calculate the lessor's implicit rate. A higher discount rate for the lessee lowers the present value of the rental payments, thus allowing the 90% test to be circumvented.

Whenever very specific reporting requirements have been set down by accounting policymakers leading to undesired disclosures, some firms are able to alter transactions so as to avoid those requirements. Lease reporting is only one example.[31] Many accountants believe that most, if not all, leases should be capitalized. In general, they do not agree with the current situation.

CONCEPT REVIEW

1. Why would the owner of an asset be interested in selling the asset and then leasing it back?
2. Is the discounted value of the next year's payment, typically, shown as the current portion of a lessee's liability? If not, what is shown?
3. What are the primary disclosure requirements for capital and operating leases?

SUMMARY OF KEY POINTS

◆

(L.O. 1)   1. A lease is an agreement that conveys the right from the lessor to a lessee to use property, plant, or equipment, usually for a stated period of time.

(L.O. 1)   2. Leasing is popular because it can conserve cash, protect against obsolescence and interest rate changes, and provide a means of avoiding the recognition of liabilities.

(L.O. 1)   3. Lessees generally prefer to keep leases off their balance sheets to reduce their reported liabilities. Doing so causes their debt ratios (such as debt to equity) to

---

[30] Third-party guarantors, in effect, insure the market value of a leased asset. For a fee, they assume the risk that, for whatever reason, the asset's residual value at the end of the lease term will fall short of the original estimate made at the outset of the lease. Insurance losses for third-party guarantors can be substantial, as Lloyd's of London (a consortium of insurance companies) found out with its guarantee business in the computer-leasing field.

[31] See R. Abdel-khalik, "The Economic Effects on Lessees of *FASB Statement 13*, 'Accounting for Leases,'" Research Report (Norwalk, Conn: FASB, 1981).

appear smaller. Lessors, on the other hand, prefer to treat leases as sale or financing capital leases. In other words, lessees prefer to account for leases as operating leases, while lessors prefer to account for leases as capital leases. This preference for a lack of accounting symmetry was what the FASB wished to avoid. However, clever structuring of leases can lead to this asymmetric reporting result.

(L.O. 2) 4. For accounting purposes, a lease agreement is considered to be either an operating lease or a capital lease.

(L.O. 3) 5. An operating lease is equivalent to a rental agreement. The lessee pays a periodic fee for use of the asset. This fee is revenue to the lessor. The asset remains the property of the lessor, who depreciates the asset's cost.

(L.O. 3) 6. The lessee treats a lease as a capital lease if it meets any one of the following four criteria: (1) the lease transfers ownership, (2) the lease contains a bargain purchase offer, (3) the lease term equals or exceeds 75% of the estimated economic life of the asset, and (4) the present value of the minimum lease payments equals or exceeds 90% of the fair market value of the leased asset.

(L.O. 3) 7. The lessor treats the lease as a capital lease if in addition to satisfying any one of the criteria for lessees (see Key Point 6 above), it meets two additional criteria: (1) collectibility of all rentals is reasonably predictable, and (2) future costs are reasonably predictable or the lessor's peformance is substantially complete.

(L.O. 3) 8. The lessor treats a capital lease as a sale if a dealer profit (loss) accrues (the present value of the receivable obtained exceeds (is less than) the carrying value of the transferred asset). Otherwise, the lease is accounted for as a direct-financing lease, and the lessor recognizes only interest revenue.

(L.O. 4) 9. A capital lease to the lessee is a means of financing an asset acquisition. The asset is entered on the books of the lessee. The lessee also recognizes a liability for the contract lease payments and recognizes depreciation on the asset. The periodic payment by the lessee represents payment of principal and interest on the loan to the lessor. Present values are used.

(L.O. 5) 10. A direct-financing lease to the lessor results in removing the asset from lessor's books. Interest revenue is earned through time over the lease life.

(L.O. 5) 11. A sales-type lease to the lessor results in removing the asset from the lessor's books. Income is earned at the time the lease is signed equal to the difference between the value of the lease and the carrying value of the leased asset on the lessor's books. Interest revenue is earned through time over the lease life.

(L.O. 6) 12. Since lessees capitalize only the residual values they guarantee but lessors capitalize all residual values, provisions for guarantees of the residual value by a third party can result in a lease accounted for as an operating lease by the lessee and as a capital lease by the lessor. This asymmetric result can also be obtained if the lessee uses a different (and higher) interest rate than the lessor.

(L.O. 7) 13. A sale-leaseback arrangement is an agreement in which the seller-lessee sells an asset and then leases the asset. The seller-lessee obtains cash while incurring a (tax deductible) lease payment. The buyer-lessor receives the lease payments, depreciates the asset for tax purposes, and also may deduct for taxes any interest on debt used to finance the asset purchase. The seller-lessee accounts for the transaction as a sale and for the lease as a capital or operating lease. The buyer-lessor accounts for the transaction as a purchase and the lease as a direct-financing lease or capital lease as appropriate.

(L.O. 8) 14. The portion of a lessee's lease liability typically reported as current is the decline in the present value of the total lease obligation that will occur during the operating period.

(L.O. 8) 15. Lease disclosure requirements for both lessees and lessors are extensive and include data on payments to be made and descriptions of lease agreements for both capital and operating leases.

REVIEW PROBLEM

◆

Orion leased a computer to the Lenox Silver Company January 1, 1991. The terms of the lease are:

 1. Lease term (fixed and noncancelable) . . . . 3 years
 2. Estimated economic life of the equipment . . . . 5 years
 3. Fair market value at lease inception $5,000
 4. Lessor's cost of asset $5,000
 5. Bargain purchase offer . . . . None
 6. Transfer of title . . . . No
 7. Guaranteed residual value by lessee
    (excess to lessee) 1/1/94 . . . . $2,000
 8. Lessee's normal depreciation method . . . . Straight line
 9. Lessee's incremental borrowing rate 11%
10. Executory costs . . . . None
11. Initial indirect costs . . . . None
12. Collectibility of rental payments . . . . Assured
13. Performance by lessor . . . . Complete
14. Annual rental (1st payment January 1, 1991) $1,620
15. Lessor's implicit interest rate . . . . Unknown
                                                              to lessee

16. Unguaranteed residual value
    (known only to lessor) . . . . None

Required:

1. Determine what type of lease this is for the lessee.
2. Determine what type of lease this is for the lessor.
3. Provide entries for the lessee and the lessor from January 1, 1991, through January 1, 1992.
4. Provide entries for the lessee and the lessor if the asset is disposed of for $2,100 by the lessee on January 1, 1994. Assume interest has been accrued on December 31.

SOLUTION

◆

1. Discounting the minimum lease payments, which include the guaranteed residual value of $2,000, yields:

   $1,620 (*PVAD*, 11%, 3) + $2,000 (*PV1*, 11%, 3) =
   $$\$1,620(2.71252) + \$2,000(.73119) = \$5,857$$

   The lease qualifies as a capital lease to the lessee since the present value of the minimum lease payments, $5,857, exceeds 90% of the fair value of the leased property at the time of the lease inception: criterion 4. It does not satisfy any of the first three criteria. In this case, the lessor's implicit rate could not be used because it is unknown to the lessee. But even if it were known (or were estimated, assuming the lessee knew there was no unguaranteed residual value) *and,* to be used by the lessee, it was lower than 11%, the present value of the minimum lease payments would be even greater. (Lower discount rates increase present values.) Thus, this lease would still qualify as a capital lease to the lessee.

2. The lessor records the lease at the asset's fair market value at the time of the lease's inception, $5,000. Since the asset's fair market equals the carrying cost of the asset on the lessor's books, there is no immediate profit on the transaction. Thus, this is a direct-financing lease to the lessor.

3. **Lessee entries:**

   January 1, 1991—Inception of lease:

Leased asset	5,000	
Lease liability		5,000

   January 1, 1991—First rent:

Lease liability	1,620	
Cash		1,620

The lessee is constrained to enter the lower of the discounted payments or the fair market value.

December 31, 1991—Accrual of interest:

Interest expense [.2455 × ($5,000 − $1,620)]   830
    Lease liability   830

For reporting the lessee must use the interest rate that equates the lease payments to the recorded value of the leased asset, here constrained to the market value of $5,000 since it is less than $5,857, the discounted minimum lease payments.

The required interest rate is 24.55% and is found by solving:

$$\$1,620 \ (PVAD \ i, \ 3) + \$2,000 \ (PV1, \ i, \ 3) = \$5,000.$$

December 31, 1991—To recognize depreciation expense:

Depreciation expense 1,000
    Accumulated depreciation   1,000
    [($5,000 − $2,000) ⅓]

Since the capital lease did not meet criterion 1 or 2, the asset is depreciated over the life of the lease.

January 1, 1992—Second rental payment:

Lease liability 1,620
    Cash   1,620

Lessor entries:

January 1, 1991—To record sale:

Lease receivable 5,000
    Asset   5,000

January 1, 1991—To record first payment:

Cash 1,620
    Lease receivable   1,620

December 31, 1991—To record interest earned:

Lease receivable   830
    Interest revenue   830

January 1, 1992—To record second payment:

Cash 1,620
    Lease receivable   1,620

4. Entries on disposal of asset:

Lessee:

January 1, 1994—Recognize disposal of asset:

Cash   100
Lease liability 2,000
Accumulated depreciation 3,000
    Leased asset   5,000
    Gain on disposition   100

The lessee is assumed to sell the asset for $2,100, remit $2,000 to the lessor, and retain the $100 excess.

Lessor:

January 1, 1994—Recognize receipt of payment:

Cash 2,000
     Lease receivable   2,000

    While the problem did not ask what entries would be made if the lease had been an operating lease, so as not to imply the answers to requirements (1) and (2), these entries are shown next for 1991 only.

Lessee:

January 1, 1991—To record the first payment:

Rent expense 1,620
     Cash   1,620

    Although the lessee is owed the rent service at this moment, the service will be fulfilled by year's end, and thus the amount may be debited to the expense now.

Lessor:

January 1, 1991—To record the first payment:

Cash 1,620
     Lease revenue   1,620

    Although the lessor has not earned the revenue on January 1, it will be earned by the end of the year and may be credited to revenue now. The lessor would also recognize depreciation at this time. Sufficient data to establish the depreciation amount is not available.

APPENDIX 18A: *Leases Involving Real Estate*

Leases that involve real estate (land and buildings) are subject to special accounting treatment. The discussion can be divided into three major subareas: leases involving only land, leases involving land and buildings, and leases involving equipment and real estate.

Leases Involving Land Only

A lease involving only land is accounted for as an *operating lease* by the *lessee* unless the lease meets criterion 1 (ownership is transferred) or criterion 2 (there is a BPO) in Exhibit 18–2. If the lease meets either criterion 1 or 2, it is treated as a capital lease by the lessee. Depreciation is not taken on the land since land normally does not depreciate. The Board's conclusion that, unless criterion 1 or 2 is met, a lease of land should be accounted for as operating leases, is based on the concept that the lease does not transfer substantially all the benefits and risks of ownership unless the lessee obtains title to the land directly or can do so through a BPO.

If the lease meets criterion 1 or 2 and title is transferred to the lessee, the *lessor* accounts for the lease as a sales-type capital lease if a dealer profit is involved (*SFAS No. 98*, par. 22). The two additional criteria for the lessor (the collectibility and uncertainty tests) are not applicable to a sales-type lease involving land. Accounting standards for sales of real estate already specify requirements relating to the completion of the lessor's earnings process in order that sales-type leases of real estate and real estate sales will be treated consistently.

If the lease satisfies criterion 1 or 2 and meets the collectibility and uncertainty test and if no dealer profit is involved, the lease is accounted for as a direct-financing lease (*SFAS No. 98.* par. 27). Finally, if neither of the situations applies, the lessor accounts for the lease as an operating lease. Criteria 3 and 4 do not apply to leases involving land since land has an unlimited life. Under unlimited life, the 75% criterion is not meaningful. Further, a lease meeting criterion 4 would in all probability also meet criterion 1.

Leases Involving Land and Buildings

In this case, and under the conditions for treating the lease of land as a capital lease (the lease meets criterion 1 or 2), the *lessee's* accounting is unchanged. The present value of the minimum lease payments is, however, apportioned between land and buildings according to their fair market value at the time of the lease's inception.

The *lessor,* on the contrary, treats the land and buildings as a single unit, using either a sales-type or direct-financing lease, as appropriate.

The accounting is different from that for leases involving only land when neither criterion 1 nor 2 is met but either criterion 3 *or* 4 *is* met. In such cases, the accounting is dependent on whether the proportion of the total combined value represented by land is *less than* 25%. If so, both the lessee and the lessor treat land and building as one unit and as a capital lease. In this case, the lessee depreciates the land and building together.

Separating the land and building portions of a joint lease is difficult. Hence, the Board relied on an arbitrary rule. If the value of the land equals or exceeds 25% of the total fair market value, the lessee and lessor treat each separately. The *lessor* accounts for the building as a sales-type or direct-financing lease and the land as an operating lease. The *lessee* accounts for the land as an operating lease and for the building as a capital lease. If none of the criteria (1 to 4) are met, the *lessee* and *lessor* uses operating-lease accounting.

The accounting for leases involving land and buildings is summarized and augmented with additional details in Exhibit 18A-1.

Leases Involving Equipment and Real Estate

When equipment is involved, the value of the equipment, estimated if necessary, should be separated and accounted for by the lessee and lessor using the methods discussed in the chapter. The remaining real estate is accounted for using the procedures described in the prior two subsections of this appendix. This situation commonly arises when a portion of a building or an entire building containing equipment is leased.

Leases Involving Only Part of a Building

If the cost and fair market value of the leased property are objectively determinable, both the lessee and lessor account for the lease as they would for a lease involving land and buildings. If either the cost or fair market value cannot be determined, the lessor accounts for the lease as an operating lease.

The lessee, however, accounts for the lease as a lease involving land and buildings if the fair market value can be objectively determined. If the fair market value cannot be objectively determined, the lease is capitalized only if it meets criterion 3 in Exhibit 18-2 (75% test), using the economic life applied to the building containing the leased premises. Otherwise, the lease is accounted for as an operating lease. Examples of such leases include facilities at airports, ports, and bus terminals.

APPENDIX 18B: Leveraged Leases

A **leveraged lease** is one in which the lessor uses borrowed capital to acquire assets that are then leased out to a business customer (lessee). That, however, is only a surface definition. Underneath, a leveraged lease is a complex leasing arrangement in which one or more lenders participate as third-party principals in a lease in addition to the lessor and lessee. It is also a completely different type of leasing in terms of motives. Leasing, in general, is an economically viable financial activity in which the lessor earns a return on capital invested in leases. In contrast, leveraged leasing is basically driven by tax benefits that accrue to high-income taxpayers who participate as lessors. Earning a competitive before-tax return on investment usually is of secondary importance to these taxpayer-lessors.

When viewed as a tax strategy rather than as a profit-making business activity, the key elements that make a leveraged lease arrangement work for the taxpayer-lessor are:

High interest expense during the early years of the lease due to a large unpaid loan principal balance.

EXHIBIT 18A-1   Accounting for Leases of Land and Buildings

I. Criterion 1 or 2 is satisfied (transfer of title or BPO):
    A. Lessee—capital lease (building and land separated):
        1. The present value of minimum lease payments allocated to land and buildings in proportion to their fair market values.
        2. Building(s) depreciated over estimated useful life.
    B. Lessor (building and land treated as one unit):
        1. Criterion 1 met:
            a) Sales-type lease if there is dealer profit.
            b) Direct-financing lease if there is no dealer profit and if the two additional lessor criteria (a and b) are met.*
            c) Operating lease if there is no dealer profit and if either of the two additional lessor criteria (a and b) is not met.
        2. Criterion 2 met:
            a) Direct-financing lease if there is no dealer profit and if the two additional lessor criteria (a and b) are met.
            b) Operating lease if there is no dealer profit and if either of the two additional lessor criteria (a and b) is not met.
II. Neither criterion 1 nor 2 is satisfied, and the fair market value of the land *is less than* 25% of the total fair market value of the leased property. The land and building are treated as a single unit with the building life used to apply criterion 3:
    A. Lessee:
        1. Capital lease if either criterion 3 or 4 is met. The land and building are recorded as a single unit and amortized over the lease term.
        2. Operating lease if neither criterion 3 or 4 is met.
    B. Lessor:
        1. Direct-financing or sales-type lease if either criterion 3 or 4 is met and the two additional lessor criteria are met, depending on whether or not there is a dealer profit.
        2. Operating lease if neither criterion 3 nor 4 is met or if either of the two additional lessor criteria is not met.
III. Neither criterion 1 nor 2 is satisfied, and the fair market value of the land equals or *exceeds* 25% of the total fair market value of the leased property.
    A. Lessor and lessee consider land and building separately for purposes of applying criteria 3 and 4. The segment of the minimum lease payments allocated to the land is the value of land divided by the appropriate present value factor. The remainder is allocated to buildings.
    B. Lessee:
        1. Capital lease if the building meets either criterion 3 or 4.
            a) The building is amortized over the lease term.
            b) The land is classified as an operating lease.
        2. Operating lease if the building meets neither criterion 3 or 4.
    C. Lessor:
        1. Building meets either criterion 3 or 4 and the two additional lessor criteria (a and b) are met.
            a) The building is classified as a direct-financing lease.
            b) The land is classified as an operating lease.
        2. Building meets neither criterion 3 nor 4 or it does not meet either of the two additional lessor criteria (a and b). Building and land classified as a single operating lease.

* Criteria a and b refer to the lessor's collectibility and uncertainty tests.
Source: *SFAS No. 13* (as amended), par. 26, and *SFAS No. 98*.

♦ Use of accelerated depreciation methods also results in higher expenses during the early years of the lease. (Virtually all leveraged leases are structured as direct-financing leases, meaning that depreciation passes to the lessee. However, for income tax reporting purposes, the taxpayer-lessor uses leased asset depreciation as a deductible item.)
♦ Level lease payments collected from the lessee result in income shortfalls (expenses exceed leasing revenue) during early years and the reverse during the later years of a lease.
♦ Although investment tax credits were eliminated by the Tax Reform Act of 1986, taxpayer-lessors engaged in leveraged leases initiated prior to 1986 are entitled to 10% tax credits on investments in tax-qualified business assets. Many pre-1986 leveraged leases remain in force today.

Thus, a taxpayer-lessor with high levels of taxable income from other sources is able to use losses, tax credits, and expenses from leveraged leasing operations to offset all or a portion of taxable income and thereby achieve tax savings. However, this is true of the early years only; during the later years when leasing revenue exceeds expenses, taxable income results.

Leveraged leases tend to be multimillion-dollar affairs, with many deals are valued in the billions. Some are so large that a number of financial institutions will form a lending syndicate to accommodate the size of the loans, which typically run as high as 80% of the value of the assets covered in the lease. Because of the high leverage factor, the lessor's investment in the lease is typically only 20% of the assets involved. However, if the assets covered in a leveraged lease are big-ticket items such as Boeing jumbo jets worth over $1 billion, 20% is a substantial amount, over $200 million in this case. For this reason, the taxpayer-lessor (also known as the *equity participant*) is sometimes not an individual or single company, but a limited partnership formed specifically for the purpose of engaging in leveraged leasing operations.

These limited partnerships normally consist of one or more general partners and a large pool of limited partners (public investors) who buy partnership interests in the deal. The same tax benefits that accrue to an individual taxpayer-lessor accrue to these partnerships, meaning that tax benefits are passed on to the limited partners (public investors).

Fundamental Characteristics of a Leveraged Lease

For the reasons outlined above, leveraged leases constitute a special category of leasing activity that, for accounting purposes, pertains *only* to lessors. Lessees involved in leveraged lease arrangements continue to report and account for these transactions in the usual manner—as capital leases in the vast majority of cases. Furthermore, many lessors (commercial leasing companies, in particular) routinely borrow cash from banks and other sources in order to acquire assets intended for the leasing market, but this fact does not qualify the transaction as a leveraged lease. Such borrowings are equivalent to short-term inventory-financing loans, common to most dealer and retailing businesses. To qualify as a leveraged lease, the following conditions must be met:

1. The lease must otherwise meet the definition of a direct-financing lease.
2. The lease must involve three parties: a lessee, lessor, and a long-term creditor. (The term *long-term creditor* is used to distinguish a lease financing participant from a lender extending short-term inventory and asset-acquisition financing loans.)
3. The financing provided by the long-term creditor must be nonrecourse as to the general credit of the lessor. (In the event of default by the lessor, the long-term creditor—lease-financing participant—has no claim against the lessor beyond the lease payments unremitted by the lessee and, in some case, repossession of the leased asset. No other assets or cash flows of the lessor may be attached by the lender, which is not the case with inventory and asset-acquisition type loans.)
4. The lessor's net investment in the lease must decline in the early years of the lease and rise during the later years. (High depreciation and interest expenses in the early years result in operating losses that diminish the lessor's equity in the lease. In later years, as depreciation and interest charges decrease, net investment is increased due to operating profits.)
5. In the case of leverage leases initiated prior to 1986 in which the lessor is entitled to a 10% investment tax credit, such tax credits must be deferred and allocated to income over the life of the lease. (For personal income tax purposes, the lessor applies the full amount of the tax credit against tax liabilities due for the tax year in which the leveraged lease transaction occurs. Any unused credits may be carried forward. But for leveraged lease accounting purposes, the amount of the credit is treated as described above.)

Unless one of the above conditions is not met, the transaction is deemed to be a regular direct-financing lease rather than a leveraged lease.

The Rights of the Lending Participant (Lender)

The lending participant's debt investment (loan) in a leverage lease is secured by a first lien on the leased property, by assignment of the lease, and by assignment of the lease payments from the lessee. This means that the lender has first priority on the leased property and the lease receivables carried by the lessor if timely payments of interest and loan principal are not made.

Protection Afforded Investors in Leveraged Leases

In instances where the lessor is a limited partnership and equity participation interests are sold to public investors, the SEC requires the use of an owner trustee as a precautionary measure. The *owner trustee* holds conditional title to the leased property and issues trust certificates evidencing each public investor's equity participation in the leased property. This is in lieu of an individual general partner–lessor holding title to the property and issuing equity participation certificates to outside investors. Owner trustees are also used in many private leveraged leasing deals in which two or more individuals, or corporations, engage in a leveraged lease transaction as joint equity participants (lessors).

Similarly, an *indenture trustee* frequently is used, this time to protect the interests of the lending participants, especially if a large number of lenders are involved. Sometimes, rather than soliciting lending participation interest from commercial banks and other lending institutions, the equity participant (lessor) may enlist the services of an investment banker. Most investment bankers are securities underwriters, who, in this case, underwrite the entire amount of the loan by issuing and selling debt participation certificates to either public investors or private institutional investors, or both. In such cases, an independent bank or trust company serves as an indenture trustee, safeguarding the interest of the debt investors. The trustee collects rental payments directly from the lessee, allocates each payment (typically 80% to the lending participants and 20% to the equity participants), and distributes them accordingly. If an owner trustee is involved, the equity participation portion of each rental payment is turned over to this trustee for redistribution to the equity participants (lessors).

Exhibit 18B–1 contains a cash flow diagram for a basic three-party leveraged lease. Exhibit 18B–2 repeats the cash flows for a leveraged lease in which an owner trustee and indenture trustee are used.

Leveraged Leasing Cash Flows from the Lessor's Viewpoint: An Example

On January 1, 1991, the lessor acquires for $1,000,000 an asset with a five-year useful life and no estimated residual value. The acquisition is financed by the lessor with cash of $200,000 and an $800,000, 12% loan payable in five equal payments of $221,928 beginning December 31, 1991. The lessor uses the sum-of-the-year's digits method of depreciation for book purposes. The lessor then leased the asset on January 1, 1991, for five years to the lessee for an annual lease payment of $275,000 payable yearly beginning December 31, 1991. The debt amortization schedule for the lessor and the schedule of cash flows are given in Exhibit 18B–3. A 40% tax rate is assumed for the lessor.

Cash Flows under Leveraged Leases

In a typical leveraged lease, the *lessor* has a net cash inflow during the early years of the lease, a net cash outflow in the later years, and a final receipt of cash if the leased asset has a residual value and is sold after the lease terminates. Early tax-deductible expenses are high because interest on the unpaid debt is high in the early years and because of accelerated depreciation. This combination, plus the investment tax credit (if available), produces tax benefits in the early years of the lease. These benefits create net cash inflows because of the reduction of tax that otherwise would be paid on income from other sources. In the later years, a reverse effect is experienced: lower interest and depreciation amounts cause taxable income to rise and tax payments to increase. However, due to the time value of money, the early cash inflows create an advantage in favor of leveraged leasing.

The cash-flow schedule in Exhibit 18B–3 shows the lessor's payments of $275,000 in column *a*. As shown in column *b*, the lessor depreciates the asset over a five-year life using an accelerated method with no estimated residual value. Thus, the first year's depreciation is $333,333. The lessor's total annual expense related to the lease is given in column *e*. It is composed of the annual depreciation and interest. Taxable income, consisting of annual

EXHIBIT 18B-1 Diagram of Basic Leveraged Lease Cash Flows

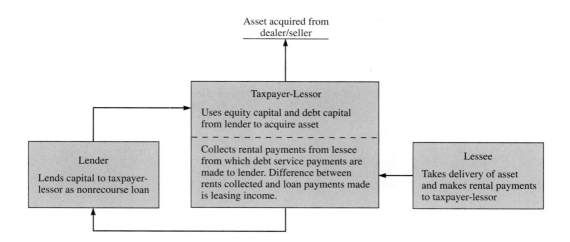

EXHIBIT 18B-2 Diagram of Leveraged Lease Cash Flow Employing Owner and Indenture Trustees

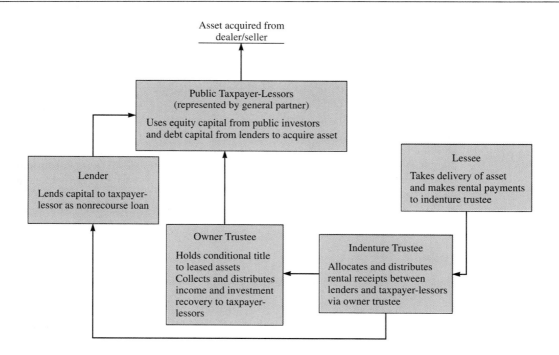

EXHIBIT 18B-3 Lessor's Loan Amortization and Cash Flow Schedules

Lessor's Debt Amortization Schedule

Year-end	(a) Cash Payment (Given)	(b) Interest Expense (12% of [d])	(c) Reduction of Principal (a) − (b)	(d) Unamortized Principal (d) − (c)
Jan. 1, 1991				$800,000
1991	$ 221,928	$ 96,000	$125,928	674,072
1992	221,928	80,889	141,039	533,033
1993	221,928	63,964	157,964	375,069
1994	221,928	45,008	176,920	198,149
1995	221,928	23,779	198,149	–0–
	$1,109,640	$309,640	$800,000	

Lessor's Cash Flow Schedule

Year-end	(a) Annual Cash Rentals (per Lease)	(b) Annual Depreciation Expense (SYD)	(c) Annual Cash Interest Paid	(d) Principal Reduction	(e) Total Expense (b) + (c)	(f) Taxable Income (Loss) (a) − (e)	(g) Tax-Saving (Expense) 40% of (f)	(h) Net Annual Cash Flow [(a) + (g)] −[(c) + (d)]
Jan. 1, 1991 . . . . . Initial investment								$(200,000)
1991	$ 275,000	$ 333,333	$ 96,000	$125,928	$ 429,333	$(154,333)	$ 61,733	114,805
1992	275,000	266,667	80,889	141,039	347,556	(72,556)	29,022	82,094
1993	275,000	200,000	63,964	157,964	263,964	11,036	(4,414)	48,658
1994	275,000	133,333	45,008	176,920	178,341	96,659	(38,664)	14,408
1995	275,000	66,667	23,779	198,149	90,446	184,554	(73,822)	(20,750)
	$1,375,000	$1,000,000	$309,640	$800,000	$1,309,640	$ 65,360	$(26,145)	$ 39,215

rentals minus annual expenses, is given in column *f*, and the related tax saving (expense) is given in column *g*. When the total in column *f* is a loss, the lessor experiences a tax saving of 40% of the amount of the loss because losses on the leveraged lease activities offset assumed income that otherwise would be taxable at 40%. Finally, the lessor's annual cashflow is shown in column *h*. Some elements of the cash flow are fixed. For example, the debt payments cause a fixed annual outflow of $221,928 (columns c + d), and the lease rents cause a fixed periodic inflow of $275,000. Column *h* shows the typical pattern of cash flows for a leveraged lease, positive in early years and negative in later years.

Accounting for Leveraged Leases

Leveraged leases create no special accounting problems for the *lessee*. The lessee accounts for a leveraged lease in a manner similar to nonleveraged operating or capital leases, depending on which is appropriate.

However, leveraged lease accounting for the *lessor* is unique and complex. Under *SFAS No. 13*, the annual income of the lessor from a leveraged lease is measured in such a way that annual income differs from after-tax income. The allocation of income in a particular year depends on the *net lease investment* during that year.

SFAS No. 13 defines the *net lease investment* of the lessor as:

◆ The rentals receivable under the leveraged lease.

◆ Plus any receivable for an investment tax credit to be realized.[32]

---

[32] If the investment tax credit is available, it is added to the net lease investment, less any deferral to future periods.

EXHIBIT 18B-4   Lessor's Allocation of Annual Cash Flows to Investment and Income

Year	Lessor's Net Investment at Beginning of Year (a)	Annual cash flow			
		Total (b)	Allocated to Income (c)	Allocated to Investment (d)	Pretax Income (e)
1991	$200,000	$114,805*	$22,680**	$ 92,125†	$37,792 §
1992	107,875‡	82,094	12,233	69,861	20,384
1993	38,014	48,658	4,311	44,347	7,184
1994	(6,333)	14,408	—	14,408	—
1995	(20,741)	(20,750)	—	(20,750)¶	—
		$239,315	$39,224	$200,000	$65,360

* See Exhibit 18B-3, column *h*. However, 1991 cash flow excludes the $200,000 investment in the leased asset.

** If Lessor's "net investment at beginning of year" is positive, cash flow allocated to income equals .1134 × Net investment at beginning of year. If "net investment at beginning of year" is negative, cash flow allocated to income equals zero. The allocation rate (11.34%) is solved iteratively until a rate is found that fully amortizes the lessor's net investment.

† Cash flow allocated to investment = total cash flow − cash flow allocated to income.

‡ Lessor's net investment at beginning of 1992 = lessor's net investment at beginning of 1991 − cash flow allocated to investment in 1991.

§ The allocation of cash flows to pretax income in 1991 is:

$$\$65,360 \times (\$22,680 \div \$39,224) = \$37,792$$

¶ Rounded. The rounding also causes the $39,224 figure to differ from the $39,215 total in column *h* of Exhibit 18B-3.

+ Plus any residual value of the leased property.
+ Minus lessor's nonrecourse debt on borrowing to acquire the leased property.
+ Minus unearned lease revenue.

Thus, using the example in Exhibit 18B-3, the net lease investment on January 1, 1991, is $200,000: the total rentals receivable ($275,000 × 5 years = $1,375,000), plus residual value of the property (0), minus lessor's total debt on the asset ($221,928 × 5 years = $1,109,640), minus unearned lease revenue ($65,360 = total pretax income given in column *f*).

SFAS No. 13 requires that a rate of return be computed on the net investment in years in which the net investment is positive such that, when applied to the net investment in those years, it will fully distribute income and amortize net investment. In each year, the difference between the net cash flow and the amount of income recognized, if any, increases or decreases the net investment balance. Computation of this rate of return requires the use of a computer. This allocation is shown in Exhibit 18B-4. The rate of return is 11.34% (computed iteratively). The annual cash flows (column *b*) are allocated, based on this rate, between amortization of net investment and income. For example, the 1991 allocation income (column *c*) is $22,680 ($200,000 × .1134). The remaining cash flow is assumed to reduce the net investment balance ($114,805 − $22,680 = $92,125 reduction). The net investment balance at the beginning of 1992 then is $107,875 ($200,000 − $92,125 = $107,875), as shown in column *a*. In years in which the net investment balance is negative, such as 1994, the entire cash flow for that year is allocated to the net investment balance and no income is recognized. The total cash flow allocated to investment sums to the initial net investment; thus, the sum of column *d* is $200,000. Similarly, the sum of column *c*, allocation to income equals total net income (except for a rounding error).

The remaining accounting problem is to allocate annual income to its component parts; that is, to pretax income and tax expense. This allocation is done on a proportionate basis. For example in 1991, pretax income (column *e*) is allocated $37,792 [total pretax income times 1991 allocation to income divided by total allocation to income: $65,360 × ($22,680 ÷ $39,224)]. Journal entries reflecting the 1991 allocations are shown in Exhibit 18B-5. The lease receivable beginning balance is recorded net of the corresponding liability of the lessor (i.e., $1,375,000 − $1,109,640 = $265,360).

EXHIBIT 18B-5   Lessor Journal Entries in 1991

January 1, 1991—Inception of the lease:

Lease receivable (net)	265,360	
Unearned lease revenue		65,360
Cash		200,000

Computations:
Gross lease receivable, $1,375,000 − gross liability, $1,109,640 = net lease receivable, $265,360.

Total pretax income, $65,360 = unearned lease revenue, $65,360.

December 31, 1991—Collection cf 1991 net rent:

Cash (net rent)	53,072	
Lease receivable		53,072

Computation:
Lease rental, $275,000 − debt payment, $221,928 = $53,072, net rent.

December 31, 1991—Recognition of 1991's pretax income:

Unearned lease revenue	37,792	
Income from leveraged lease (Exhibit 18B-4, col. [e])		37,792

December 31, 1991—Recognition of tax effect of leveraged lease:

Income tax payable (Exhibit 18B-3, col. g)	61,733	
Income tax expense ($37,792 × .40)	15,117	
Deferred income tax liability		76,850*

* Computation of deferred income tax:

Tax loss (Exhibit 18B-3, col. f)	$154,333
Pretax accounting income (Exhibit 18B-4, col. e)	37,792
Temporary difference	$192,125
Deferred tax liability ($192,195 × .40)	$ 76,850

APPENDIX 18C: *More on Tax Considerations*

Taxes have played a prominent role in the content of this chapter on leasing. Although this is not a course in taxation, a few additional remarks are appropriate since tax considerations are an important factor in many leasing arrangements. This is always true of leveraged lease investments made by taxpayer-lessors, and it is also true of many regular leasing arrangements between lessees and lessors as explained next.

For any number of reasons the *lessee* may be unable to use the tax benefits provided in purchasing an asset—namely, depreciation, interest on debt incurred in connection with the acquisition, and the investment tax credit when available. While such a company may be in the market to acquire new assets, it may be that the company is in a growth phase and has little or no taxable income against which tax benefits could be applied. Chances are that such a company has operating losses being carried forward from previous years. Also, such companies tend to be short on cash and must borrow heavily to finance new asset acquisitions. If so, the company has ample internal means for sheltering future taxable income; tax benefits from leasing would go to waste.

But tax benefits that the lessee can't use might be extremely valuable to some other company that has a large cash position and is reporting high levels of taxable income. Such a company is probably in the market for tax savings. The solution, of course, is to match the cash-poor company (in the market to acquire assets) with the cash-rich company (in the market for tax savings). Then the task is structuring a lease transaction that meets both parties' needs. The wealthy company with high taxable income becomes the lessor and retains the tax benefits that otherwise would be passed on to the lessee. The needy company benefits by negotiating lease rental terms below the going market rate. Generally, the lessor company is happy to accommodate the lessee company in exchange for retention of the tax benefits involved.

By allowing the use of accelerated depreciation methods such as MACRS (modified accelerated cost recovery systems), some accountants point out that the IRS makes tax incentives more attractive and thereby encourages leasing transactions. Similarly, the existence and extent to which the IRS allows investment tax credits to be taken also works in favor of leasing. These are just two examples of the many ways in which the federal government influences economic activity and promotes tax-oriented business transactions.

KEY TERMS

Bargain purchase option (BPO) (960)
Bargain renewal option (BRO) (961)
Capital lease (954)
Direct-financing lease (956)
Executory costs (982)
Implicit interest rate (963)
Initial direct costs (983)
Lease (953)
Lease term (971)
Lessee (953)

Lessee's incremental borrowing rate (971)
Lessor (953)
Leveraged lease (995)
Minimum lease payments (961)
Off-balance-sheet financing (954)
Operating lease (954)
Sale-leaseback (984)
Sales-type lease (956)
Unguaranteed residual value (974)

QUESTIONS

1. Match the lettered items immediately below with the numbered statements that follow by entering one letter in each blank space.

   A. Lessor; B. Capital lease; C. Operating lease; D. Lessee.
   _____ (1) Contract in which lessor finances property leased.
   _____ (2) Lender in a lease contract transaction.
   _____ (3) Tenant in a lease contract transaction.
   _____ (4) Type of lease that requires capitalization.
   _____ (5) Type of lease that does not require capitalization.
   _____ (6) Property owner in a lease contract transaction during the lease term.

   Questions (2) and (3) below are based on the following information (briefly explain your choices):

   Marne Company purchased a machine for leasing purposes on January 1, 1991, for $1,000,000. The machine has a 10-year life, no residual value, and will be depreciated on a straight-line basis. On March 1, 1991, Marne leased the machine to Dal Company for $400,000 a year for a five-year period ending February 28, 1996. During the year ended December 31, 1991, Marne incurred normal maintenance and other related expenses of $25,000 under the provisions of this assumed operating lease. Dal paid $40,000 to Marne on March 1, 1991.

2. Assuming an operating lease, what was the income before income taxes derived by Marne from this lease for the year ended December 31, 1991?
   a. $229,167.   c. $160,000.
   b. $291,667.   d. $225,000.
3. What was rent expense for Dal from this lease for the year ended December 31, 1991
   a. $225,000.   c. $400,000.
   b. $120,000.   d. $333,333.
4. Give the primary GAAP concepts of accounting for an operating lease by lessors and lessees.
5. Advance rental payments often are received under operating lease contracts that extend well beyond a single fiscal year. Give the acceptable accounting procedures that should be used for advance rentals.
6. What is meant by capitalization of a lease from the view of the lessee?
7. From a lessee's standpoint, leases are classified as capital or operating leases. What criteria are used to identify a capital lease?
8. From a lessor's view, a capital lease involves two types of leases. Identify the types and distinguish between them.

9. Briefly define the following terms related to capital leases (refer to the technical definitions):
   a. Lease term.
   b. Bargain purchase option.
   c. Bargain renewal option.
   d. Minimum lease payments from the standpoint of the lessee.
   e. Minimum lease payments from the standpoint of the lessor.
   f. Interest rate implicit in the lease.
10. How does a lessee determine what interest rate is appropriate for capitalization of a lease?
11. How does an unguaranteed residual value in a sales-type lease affect the lessor's accounting in recording the entries at date of inception of the lease?
12. Briefly explain how inclusion of a provision of residual value guaranteed by a third party in a capital lease can result in asymmetric accounting by lessor and lessee.
13. Define initial direct costs.
14. Define executory costs.
15. When computing annual depreciation, what residual value should the lessee use for a leased asset under a capital lease? Briefly explain each alternative.
16. What distinguishes leveraged leases from other leases? What pattern of cash flows can normally be expected in a leveraged lease? (Appendix 18B)

EXERCISES

E 18-1
Operating Lease: Leasehold Costs, Entries (L.O. 3)

Arrow Company signed an operating lease contract effective for five years from January 1, 1991. Arrow is to pay $40,000 at the start of the lease plus $6,000 monthly rentals throughout the lease term. During January 1991, Arrow spent $20,000 renovating the property leased and also built an addition to the leased property with the lessor's consent at a cost of $80,000. The estimated life of the addition is 20 years, and its residual value is zero. The lease contract does not contain a renewal option and may be terminated by the lessee with six months notice.

Required:

Give all entries on Arrow's books to reflect the renovation outlays, leasehold, and rental payments for 1991 and entries at the end of 1991, assuming Arrow's accounting year is the calendar year. The straight-line method of amortization is to be used.

E 18-2
Explain Distinctions: Capital versus Operating, and Direct-financing versus Sales-Type Leases (L.O. 1, 2)

Part A

Capital leases and operating leases are the two classifications of leases described in FASB pronouncements, from the standpoint of the lessee.

Required:

1. Describe how a capital lease would be accounted for by the lessee both at the inception of the lease and during the first year of the lease; assume the lease transfers ownership of the property to the lessee by the end of the lease term.
2. Describe how an operating lease would be accounted for by the lessee both at the inception of the lease and during the first year of the lease; assume equal monthly payments are made by the lessee at the beginning of each month of the lease. Do not discuss the criteria for distinguishing between capital leases and operating leases.

Part B

Sales-type leases and direct-financing leases are two of the classifications of leases described in FASB pronouncements, from the standpoint of the lessor.

Required:

Compare and contrast a sales-type lease with a direct-financing lease as to:

1. Net investment in the lease.
2. Recognition of interest revenue.
3. Manufacturer's or dealer's profit.

Do not discuss the criteria for distinguishing between the leases described above and operating leases.

E 18-3

Lease: Apply Lease Criteria, Entries for Lessor and Lessee

(L.O. 2, 4, 5)

Kim Leasing Company agreed with Lee Corporation to provide the latter with equipment under lease for a three-year period. The equipment cost Kim $40,000 and will have no residual value when the lease term ends. Kim expects to collect all rentals from Lee and has no material cost uncertainties. The carrying value of the equipment was $40,000 at the inception of the lease. The three equal annual rents (amount to be determined) are to be paid each January 1, starting January 1, 1991 (at which time the equipment was delivered). Lee has agreed to pay taxes, maintenance, and insurance throughout the lease term as well as any other "ownership" costs. Kim expects a 20% return (known to Lee). The accounting year of both companies ends December 31.

Required:

Round to the nearest dollar.

1. What kind of lease is this to Lee? To Kim?
2. Compute the annual rentals and prepare an amortization schedule reflecting the interest and principal elements of Lee's payments over the three-year term of the lease. Give all journal entries relating to the lease for Lee Corporation for 1991 including year-end adjusting entries.
3. Give all journal entries for Kim Leasing Company relating to the lease for 1991 including year-end adjusting entries.

E 18-4

Lease: Financing or Sales Type, Schedule, Entries for Lessor

(L.O. 2, 5)

Brown Company uses leases as a secondary means of selling its products. The company contracted with Blue Corporation to lease a machine to be used by Blue as an operational asset. The retail market value of the asset at the inception of the lease was $50,000; it cost Brown $40,000 and is carried in its inventory at that value. Payments of $11,231 are to be made by Blue at the end of each of the five quarters following inception of the lease. Brown's implicit interest rate is 4% per quarter, which is known by Blue. The lease qualifies as a capital lease for both parties.

Required:

Round to the nearest dollar.

1. Classify the lease showing how the $11,231 rental payment was computed and prepare an amortization schedule for use by Brown covering the five-quarter term of the lease.
2. Give Brown's journal entries at the inception of the lease and upon receipt of the first payment. Assume the first receipt coincides with the end of Brown's accounting year.

E 18-5

Lease: Financing or Sales Type, Schedule and Entries, Lessor and Lessee

(L.O. 2, 4, 5)

MPI Corporation (lessor) and JRD Company (lessee) agreed to a noncancelable lease. The following information is available regarding the lease terms and the leased asset:

a. MPI's cost of the leased asset, $60,000. The asset was new at lease inception date.
b. Lease term, four years, beginning January 1, 1991. Lease rental payments are made each January 1, beginning January 1, 1991.
c. Estimated useful life of leased asset, four years. Estimated residual value at end of lease, zero.
d. Sales price of leased asset on January 1, 1991, $66,000.
e. MPI's implicit interest rate, 15% on retail price (known to JRD).
f. MPI expects to collect all rentals from JRD, and there are no material cost uncertainties.

Required:

1. What kind of lease is this to MPI? To JRD?
2. Compute the annual lease rentals.
3. Prepare an amortization schedule for the lease.
4. Give the journal entries for both parties on January 1, 1991, and December 31, 1991. Do not make closing entries.

E 18-6

Lease: Analysis of Dealer's Profit or Loss

(L.O. 2, 4, 5)

Hardin Company is an equipment dealer that sometimes uses leasing as a means to sell its products. On January 1, 1991, Hardin leased equipment to Wesley Corporation. The lease term was four years, with annual lease payments of $6,769 to be paid on each December 31. The equipment has an estimated zero residual value at the end of the lease term. The equipment was carried on Hardin's accounts at a cost of $24,000. Hardin expects to collect all rentals from Wesley, and there were no material cost uncertainties at inception of the lease. The implicit interest rate on the lease was 11% on the selling price (known to Wesley).

Required:
1. What kind of lease is this to Hardin? to Wesley?
2. What is the cost of the equipment to Wesley?
3. What is the dealer's profit or loss recognized by Hardin?
4. Assume the implicit interest rate is 4% (not 11%). What is the dealer's profit or loss recognized by Hardin?
5. Give the entries (based on the 11% rate) at date of inception of the lease for each party.

E 18-7
Overview of Special Lease Cases: Provide Explanations
(L.O. 6, 8)

Select the best answer in each of the following. Justify each choice that you make.

1. On the first day of its accounting year. Lessor, Inc., leased certain property at an annual rental of $100,000 receivable at the beginning of each year for 10 years. The first payment was received immediately. The leased property, which is new, cost $550,000 and has an estimated useful life of 12 years and no residual value. Lessor's implicit rate is 12%. Lessor had no other costs associated with this lease. Lessor should have accounted for this lease as a sales-type lease but mistakenly treated the lease as an operating lease. What was the effect on net income during the first year of the lease by having treated this lease as an operating lease rathar than as a sales-type lease?
   a. No effect.
   b. Overstated.
   c. Understated.
   d. The effect depends on the accounting method selected for income tax purposes.
2. The appropriate valuation of leased assets under an operating lease on the balance sheet of a lessee is as follows:
   a. Zero.
   b. The absolute sum of the lease payments.
   c. The sum of the present values of the lease payments discounted at an appropriate rate.
   d. The market value of the asset at the date of the inception of the lease.
3. What are the three types of expenses that a lessee experiences with a capital lease?
   a. Lease expense, interest expense, amortization expense
   b. Interest expense, amortization expense, executory costs.
   c. Amortization expense, executory costs, lease expense.
   d. Executory costs, interest expense, lease expense.
4. When measuring the present value of future rentals to be capitalized in connection with a capital lease, identifiable payments to cover taxes, insurance, and maintenance should be accounted for as follows:
   a. Included with the future rentals to be capitalized.
   b. Excluded from future rentals to be capitalized.
   c. Capitalized, but at a different rate and recorded in a different account from that for future rentals.
   d. Capitalized, but at a different rate and during a different period from the rate and period used for the future rental payments.
5. GAAP requires that certain lease agreements be accounted for as purchases. The theoretical basis for this treatment is that a lease of this type:
   a. Effectively conveys most of the benefits and risks incident to the ownership of property.
   b. Is an example of form over substance.
   c. Provides the use of the leased asset to the lessee for a limited period of time.
   d. Must be recorded in accordance with the concept of cause and effect.
6. Your client constructed an office building at a cost of $500,000 and then sold this building to Jones for a large gain. The client leased it back from Jones for a stipulated annual rental. How should this gain be treated?
   a. Recognized in full as an ordinary item in the year of the transaction.
   b. Recognized in full as an extraordinary item in the year of the transaction.
   c. Amortized as an adjustment of the rental cost, an ordinary item, over the life of the lease.
   d. Amortized as an extraordinary item over the life of lease.

(AICPA adapted)

E 18–8
Direct Financing Lease with BPO: Schedule, Entries for Lessor
(L.O. 5, 6)

Lessor Jones and Lessee Smith contract for the lease of a machine for six rentals of $6,000 each. The first $6,000 rental is to be paid at the inception of the lease, and $6,000 is to be paid at the start of each of five quarters thereafter. They also agree that at the time of the sixth payment, for an added $6,930 bargain purchase option payment, Smith can buy the property. The interest rate is 2.5% per quarter. The lease qualifies as a direct financing lease.

Required:
Round to the nearest dollar.

1. Calculate the present value of the lease payments and prepare an amortization schedule for the lease covering the six-quarter term.
2. Give the lessor's entries at the inception of the lease and at the time of the sixth payment if the lessee exercises the purchase option. Assume a direct-financing lease.

E 18–9
Direct-Financing Lease with BPO
(L.O. 4, 5)

Flint Company leased a computer to Land Company for a five-year period. Flint paid $46,965 for the computer (estimated useful life five years, no residual value). The lease started on January 1, 1991, and qualifies as a direct financing lease to the lessor and as a capital lease to the lessee. Flint uses a target rate of return of 14% in all lease contracts. The first rental payment was on January 1, 1991, and the accounting periods end on December 31.

Required:

1. Compute the annual rental for the lessor and the amount to be capitalized for the lessee. The computer reverts to the lessor at the end of the lease term.
2. Now assume, instead, that the lease contract contains a BPO which states that Land Company can purchase the computer on December 31, 1994, for $14,000, at which time its estimated residual value is $17,500. Compute the annual rental for the lessor and the amount to be capitalized for the lessee. Show whether the BPO is really a bargain.
3. Give the entries at inception date under Requirements 1 and 2 for the lessor and lessee.

E 18–10
Financing Lease: Unguaranteed Residual Value, Schedules, Ordinary and Annuity Due
(L.O. 5)

The present value to a lessor of a lease on which the lessee is obligated to make a $20,000 payment at the end of each of the next three years and on which there is an unguaranteed residual value of $4,000 at the end of the lease term, is $49,133 if the lessor's implicit interest rate is 14%. The lease qualifies as a direct-financing lease.

Required:
Round amounts to the nearest dollar.

1. Prepare an amortization schedule for the lessor covering the three-year lease term.
2. Compute the present value of a similar lease; assume the lessor's implicit rate is 12%. Prepare an amortization schedule similar to the one required in (1) above.
3. Assume, instead, that each of the three $20,000 annual payments is paid at the beginning of each year, in advance, and that the $4,000 residual value is expected at the end of the lease term of three years. What is the present value of the lease payments at 14%? Prepare the lessor's amortization schedule for this lease.

E 18–11
Sales-Type Lease: Unguaranteed Residual Value, Inception Entries
(L.O. 2, 4, 5, 6)

On January 1, 1991, ABC Company signed a lease contract with Abel Company. The leased asset cost ABC $45,000 and had a normal selling price of $55,000. Three annual rentals, based on the selling price, are payable by Abel on January 1, beginning in 1991. The asset reverts to ABC at the end of the lease term, December 31, 1993, and is estimated to have an unguaranteed residual value on that date of $3,000. ABC's implicit interest rate is 12%, which is known to Abel.

Required:

1. What type of lease is this for ABC?
2. Compute the annual lease rentals.
3. Give the lessor's entry on January 1, 1991.
4. Give the lessee's entry on January 1, 1991.

E 18–12
Residual Value Guaranteed by Third Party: Lessor, Direct Financing; Lessee, Operating
(L.O. 2, 6)

Mike Leasing Company (lessor) and Ash Corporation (lessee) signed a four-year lease on January 1, 1991. The leased property cost Mike $50,000, which was also its carrying value at inception of the lease. The leased asset had an estimated useful life of six years and the property reverts to Mike at the end of the lease term. Lease payments of $12,830 are payable on January 1 of each year and were set to yield Mike a return of 12%, which was known to Ash. The estimated residual value at the end of the lease term is $10,000 and is guaranteed by a third party. The lease contains no bargain purchase option. Mike is reasonably certain of the collectibility of the lease rentals and there are no additional costs to be incurred. The lease qualifies as a direct-financing lease to the lessor, but an operating lease to the lessee.

Required:

1. What evidence supports this as a direct-financing lease for the lessor? Give Mike's journal entries at inception of the lease and to record the first lease payment.
2. What evidence supports this as an operating lease for Ash? Explain. Give Ash's journal entries at inception of the lease and to record the first lease payment.

E 18–13
Direct-Financing Lease: Residual Value Partially Guaranteed by the Lessee
(L.O. 4, 5, 6)

Davis Company leased a large copier to Gore Company for a three-year period. Davis paid $15,000 for the copier and immediately leased it on January 1, 1991 (estimated useful life four years and an estimated residual value at the end of the lease term of $3,000). Davis used an expected rate of return of 16% on cost (known by Gore). Because of inadequate maintenance the lessee agreed to guarantee two thirds (i.e., $2,000) of the residual value. The lease qualifies as a direct-financing lease for the lessor and a capital lease for the lessee. The lessee uses straight-line depreciation. The first lease payment is on January 1, 1991, and the accounting periods for both parties end on December 31. At the lease termination date, an independent appraiser provided an estimated residual value of $1,500. The lessee immediately paid the difference of $500 ($2,000 guaranteed residual value minus $1,500, the actual residual value).

Required:

1. Compute the minimum lease payment for the lessor and the amount to be capitalized by the lessee.
2. Give the entries for the lessor and lessee on January 1, 1991.
3. Give the entries for the lessor and lessee to record the lease termination.

E 18–14
Accounting for Executory Costs
(L.O. 4, 5, 6)

On January 1, 1991, Foxtrot leased a machine to Green on a three-year direct-financing lease to the lessor and a capital lease to the lessee. The machine cost the lessor $42,000 and was immediately placed on lease at a 12% target rate of return (known by both parties). The lease did not contain a BPO, and there is no residual value. The rentals are payable each year starting on January 1, 1991. The accounting periods end December 31. All executory costs are to be paid by the lessee. However, insurance coverage was provided, at a cost of $87 per year, under the lessor's blanket policy. This amount is billed each year along with the lease rental.

Required:

1. Compute the annual lease rental.
2. Give the entry for the lessor and lessee to record the inception of the lease (do not include the first rent payment).
3. Give the entry for the lessor and lessee to record the first rent payment.

E 18–15
Sale-Leaseback, Direct-Financing Lease
(L.O. 7)

Grumpy Grocery owns the building it uses; it has current carrying value on January 1, 1991, of $900,000, a 10-year remaining life, and no residual value. On this date it was sold to Investor Brown for cash for $1,000,000. Simultaneously, the two parties executed a 10-year direct-financing lease with a 12% implicit interest rate; each annual rent is payable on December 31 (end of their accounting periods).

Required:

1. Compute the annual rents to be paid by Grumpy to Brown.
2. Give the entries for the seller-lessee (Grumpy Grocery) for 1991. Use straight-line depreciation.

E 18–16
Operating Lease:
Amortization, Interest
Method
(L.O. 2, 3)

Valley Company paid $50,000 on January 1, 1991, to Hill Properties as an advance lease bonus to secure a three-year lease on premises it will occupy starting from that date. Additionally, $60,000 will be paid as rent on each December 31, throughout the term of the lease. The lease contains no specific renewal agreement. Valley's accounting period ends December 31. Hill will maintain the property and pay taxes and other ownership costs.

Required:
Round to the nearest dollar.

1. What type of lease contract is involved? Explain.
2. Develop an interest method amortization schedule using a 14% rate (assume an ordinary annuity).
3. What is Valley's total occupancy cost for 1991 under the interest method used in your response to (2) above? What is the total occupancy cost using the straight-line basis for 1991?
4. What lease-related items should Valley's financial statements report as of December 31, 1991, if the amortization schedule developed in (2) above is used?

E 18–17
Appendix 18B:
Leveraged Lease
(L.O. 10)

Lansing Leasing, Inc., leased a machine with a five-year useful life to Bart Company for a five-year period beginning January 1, 1991. Lansing acquired the machine at a cost of $250,000, paid $50,000 cash, and borrowed the remainder at 8% per annum. The loan agreement provides for four equal annual payments starting on December 31, 1991.

Bart agreed to pay five equal annual year-end rents of $64,273. Lansing will realize a 10% investment credit the first year and will depreciate the machine (which has no residual value) by using the double-declining balance (200% acceleration) method. Lansing has extensive income from other sources and pays income tax at an average rate of 40%; any losses on a single phase of its operations result in a 40% income tax saving.

Required:
Round to the nearest dollar.

1. Prepare a cash flow analysis similar to Exhibit 18B–3.
2. Give Lansing's journal entries at date of inception of the lease.
3. Give Bart's journal entries at date of inception of the lease.

PROBLEMS

P 18–1
Lease: Determine Type,
Entries for Lessor and
Lessee
(L.O. 2, 3)

Trump leases a limo to Ray Productions for four years on January 1, 1991, which requires equal annual payments on each January 1 and, in addition, a single lump-sum prepayment of $3,000. The leased asset, recently purchased new, cost the lessor $50,000. Estimated value of asset at end of lease term is $20,000.

The annual lease payments were computed to yield Trump a 12% yield (the implicit interest rate after considering residual value is known to Ray Productions). The leased asset has an eight-year life with zero residual value at the end of Year 8. There is no bargain purchase option, and the asset is retained by Trump at the end of the lease term. Depreciation will be on the straight-line basis. The accounting period for both lessor and lessee ends December 31.

Required:
1. Compute the annual lease payment.
2. What type of lease is this? Explain.
3. In parallel columns for the lessor and lessee, give the following:
   a. Entries at the inception of the lease, including the initial advance payment.
   b. Adjusting and closing entries for the year ended December 31, 1991. Use straight-line amortization for the prepayment.

P 18–2
Operating Lease: Down
Payment, Entries for Both
Parties
(L.O. 3, 8)

On July 1, 1991, Staley Company leased a small building and its site to West Company on a five-year contract. The lease provides for an advance rental of $5,000 plus an annual rental of $18,000 payable each July 1 starting in 1991. The lease can be terminated at any year end by the lessee with a six-month advance notice. There is no renewal agreement. On July 8, 1991, West Company spent $8,000 on internal changes and painting. Staley's accounts showed the following data on January 1, 1991: initial cost of the building, $125,000 (accumulated depreciation, $30,000); estimated remaining life, 15 years; and estimated residual value, $5,000. The accounting period for each company ends December 31.

Required:
1. Give the entries for the lessor and lessee for 1991, 1992, and through July 1, 1993. Both companies will use straight-line depreciation and amortization of the advance rental. Use reversing entries; closing entries not required.
2. Give the amounts that each party should report on their respective 1991 and 1992 income statements and balance sheets.

P 18–3
Direct-Financing Lease:
Ordinary versus Annuity
Due, Schedules, Entries
for Both Parties
(L.O. 4, 5)

On January 1, 1991, Armor Leasing Company leased to Hogg Service Company a new machine that cost $91,000. The lease is a direct-financing lease to Armor and a capital lease to Hogg. Hogg agrees to pay all executory costs and assume other risks and costs of ownership. Armor computed the periodic rents at an amount that will yield an annual return on cost of 10%, and the lessee, being aware of this rate, also uses it to record the lease and calculate interest expense. The property is expected to have no residual value at the end of the four-year lease term. There are no collection or cost uncertainties. Both lessor and lessee have accounting years ending December 31.

Required:
Round all amounts to the nearest dollar.

1. If the annual rents are payable at the end of each year, provide the following: (*a*) the amount of the periodic rental payments and (*b*) an amortization schedule for the lessor reflecting interest and recovery of investment throughout the four-year lease term.
2. Assume, instead, that the annual rentals are payable at the start of the lease and annually thereafter. Provide the answers to (*a*) and (*b*) that were required in (1) above.
3. Hogg depreciates all assets using the straight-line method. Give entries under (1) above for both lessor and lessee relating to the lease for 1991, including adjusting and closing entries.

P 18–4
Sales-Type Lease:
Amortization Schedules,
Entries for Both Parties
(L.O. 4, 5)

Key Company uses leases as a secondary means of selling it products. On January 1, 1991, it contracted with Lock Corporation to lease machinery for six years that had a sales price of $90,000 and that cost Key $60,000 (its carrying value in inventory). Equal annual lease payments of $18,786 are to be made each January 1, starting on January 1, 1991. Key's implicit interest rate, based on the sales price, is 10% (known to Lock). This lease qualifies as a capital lease for both parties. The accounting period for both companies ends on December 31.

Required:
Round to the nearest dollar.
1. Prepare an amortization schedule for Key and Lock covering the six-year lease term.
2. Give the lessor's and lessee's entries at the inception of the lease. The lessee uses straight-line depreciation and zero residual value of the asset after six years. Also, give the adjusting and closing entries for both parties at December 31, 1991.

P 18–5
Direct-Financing and
Sales-Type Leases
Compared: Entries for
Both Parties
(L.O. 4, 5)

On January 1, 1991, Sun Company leased to Marfa Corporation new equipment. The equipment cost Sun $38,000. The lease agreement specified that Marfa is to make five equal annual lease payments (on December 31, beginning December 31, 1991) to yield Sun a 14% return. The equipment has a five-year useful life with no residual value. Ownership of the leased asset transfers to Marfa at the end of the lease term. Marfa is aware of the implicit interest rate used by Sun. Straight-line depreciation will be used. Sun expects to collect all rentals from Marfa, and there are no material cost uncertainties at inception of the lease. The accounting period for both Sun and Marfa ends December 31.

Required:
1. If the equipment has a sales price of $42,000 on January 1, 1991, and the lease rentals are based on this amount, what type of lease is this to the lessor? To the lessee? Explain. Compute the annual rental payments and prepare an amortization schedule for the lessor and lessee. Give all journal entries associated with this lease for the lessor and the lessee for the year ended December 31, 1991, including adjusting and closing entries.

2. If the equipment has a cost or carrying value of $38,000 on January 1, 1991, and the lease rentals are based on this amount, what type of lease is this to the lessor? To the lessee? Explain. Compute the annual rental payments and prepare an amortization schedule for the lessor and the lessee. Give all journal entries associated with this lease for the lessor and the lessee for the year ended December 31, 1991, including adjusting and closing entries.

P 18-6

Direct-Financing Lease: Different Interest Rates Used by Lessor and Lessee, Entries (L.O. 4, 5, 8)

On January 1, 1991, Lessor Alexa leased a machine to Lessee Baker on a three-year lease that qualifies as a direct financing lease. The machine cost Alexa $240,000 immediately prior to the lease. The machine has a three-year estimated useful life and no residual value. The lessor used an 11% target rate of return. The three annual lease payments start on January 1, 1991. The lessee uses straight-line depreciation, will retain the machine at the end of the lease term, and has a borrowing rate of 10%. The lessee must use the lower of the two interest rates. The accounting period for each company ends on December 31.

Required:

1. Compute the equal annual rentals that the lessor will receive.
2. Prepare an amortization schedule for the lessor and give the related entries through December 31, 1991.
3. Compute the lease capitalization amount and prepare an amortization schedule for the lessee and give the related entries through December 31, 1991.
4. Complete the following 1991 comparative tabulation for the lessor and lessee and explain any differences:

Items	Lessor	Lessee
Income statement		
Interest revenue		
Interest expense		
Depreciation expense		
Balance sheet		
Lease receivable		
Lease liability		
Leased property		
Accumulated depreciation		

P 18-7

Sales-Type Lease: BPO, Entries for Both Parties (L.O. 4, 5, 6)

On January 1, 1991, lessor Ray and lessee Evans signed a four-year lease that qualifies as a sales-type lease. The equipment cost Ray $900,000 and the cash sale price is $1,400,000. The equipment has a six-year estimated useful life. Estimated residual values were the following: end of Year 4, $200,000, and end of Year 6, $80,000. The lease gives Evans on option to buy the equipment at the end of Year 4 for $150,000 cash. The lease requires four equal annual rents starting on January 1, 1991. Ray's expected rate of return on the lease is 15%, and the incremental borrowing rate of Evans is 16%. On December 31, 1994, the lessee exercises the purchase option, at which time a new estimate of residual value was $180,000.

Required:

1. Compute the annual rent and the amount the lessee should capitalize.
2. Prepare a lease amortization schedule for the lessor and lessee.
3. Give the entries for the lessor and lessee from the date of inception through the lease termination date.

P 18-8

COMPREHENSIVE PROBLEM
◆

Analysis to Classify Lease: Capital versus Operating, Unguaranteed Residual Value, Entries for Both Parties (L.O. 1, 2, 3, 4, 5, 6)

Lessor Sales Company and lessee Manufacturing Company agreed to a noncancelable lease. The following information is available regarding the lease terms and the leased asset:

a. Lessor's cost of the leased asset, $30,000. The asset was new at the inception of the lease term.
b. Lease term, four years starting January 1, 1992.
c. Estimated useful life of the leased asset, six years. Estimated residual value at end of six years, zero.
d. On January 1, 1992, estimated unguaranteed residual value of the leased asset one day after the end of the lease term is $4,000.
e. Depreciation method for the leased asset, straight-line.

f. Lessee's incremental borrowing rate on January 1, 1992, 18%. The lessee is considered a high-risk borrower.

g. Bank prime rate of interest on January 1, 1992, 10%.

h. Purchase option price of leased asset exercisable one day after the end of the lease term, $4,500.

i. Title to the leased asset retained by the lessor unless the purchase option is exercised.

j. Sales price of leased asset on January 1, 1992, $40,000.

k. Lessor's unreimbursable cost uncertainties, none.

l. Four annual lease rentals due on January 1 of each year during the lease term, with the first payment due at inception of the lease term, $11,643.

m. The accounting period for the lessor and lessee ends on December 31.

Both the lessor and lessee knew all of the above information.

Required:

Round to the nearest dollar.

1. What was the lessor's implicit interest rate in this lease?
2. What type of lease was this to the lessee? To the lessor? Explain.
3. In parallel columns for the lessor and lessee, record the following:
   a. Entry, or entries, at inception of the lease on January 1, 1992, if appropriate.
   b. Adjusting and closing entries on December 31, 1992.

P 18-9
Lease Classification:
Entries for Lessor and
Lessee
(L.O. 2, 4, 5)

The following data are available about a noncancelable lease that involves a leased asset that was new at the inception date of the lease term:

Lease term	6 years
Interest rate implicit in the lease	12%
Lessee's incremental borrowing rate	14%
Amount of each lease payment	$ 3,648
Lessor's cost of asset (market value)	$15,000
Lessee has no way of knowing the interest rate implicit in the lease.	
Each lease payment occurs at the end of each period, (i.e., an ordinary annuity).	
Unreimbursable cost uncertainties of lessor	None
Credit standing of lessee	Excellent
Depreciation method, if needed	Straight-line
Estimated useful life of asset	6 years
Estimated residual value at end of lease term	$–0–
Accounting period for both parties ends on December 31.	

Required:

Round to the nearest dollar.

1. What type of lease is this to the lessee? To the lessor? Explain.
2. Give entries in parallel columns for lessor and lessee to record:
   a. The inception of the lease on January 1, 1991.
   b. All entries needed at year-end, December 31, 1991, for both parties to record lease payment (receipt), interest, depreciation, including closing entries.

P 18-10
Direct-Financing Lease:
Unguaranteed Residual
Value, Entries for Lessor
(L.O. 5, 6)

Jinx, Incorporated, purchased a machine (for leasing purposes) on January 1, 1991, for $270,000. By prior agreement the machine was delivered to Pine Company (lessee) under a direct-financing lease whereby Pine paid the first lease rental of $73,516 on January 1, 1991, and agreed to pay three more such annual rentals.

At the end of the four-year lease term, the machine will revert to the lessor, at which time it is expected to have a residual value of $20,000 (none of which was guaranteed by the lessee). The lessor's implicit interest rate was 10% on cost.

Required:

Round amounts to the nearest dollar.

1. Show how the lessor computed the annual rental.
2. Prepare a lease amortization schedule for the lessor.

3. Give all of the entries for the lessor on the following dates:
   a. January 1, 1991—Purchase and other transactions.
   b. December 31, 1991—End of the accounting period.
   c. Year 1994—Return of the machine by the lessee at the termination of the lease. At this date the machine has an actual market value of $14,000 (instead of the $20,000 estimated residual value).
4. How would the lessor's entries differ at the end of the lease term if the actual market value of the machine turned out to be $23,000 (instead of the estimated residual value of $20,000)?

P 18–11

Capital Lease: Residual Value, Third-Party Guarantee, Schedules and Entries for Both Parties (L.O. 2, 4, 5, 6)

The following data are available regarding a noncancelable lease:

a. Lease term, five years, beginning January 1, 1991.
b. The leased property cost the lessor $400,000 on January 1, 1991.
c. Estimated useful life of the asset, six years; residual value at the end of the six-year useful life, $20,000.
d. On January 1, 1991, the estimated residual value of the leased asset at the end of the lease term, $50,000. This residual value is guaranteed in full by a third-party guarantor (not the lessee).
e. Depreciation method for the leased asset, straight-line.
f. No bargain purchase option available to the lessee. Ownership retained by lessor at the end of the lease term.
g. Five annual lease payments are payable on January 1 of each year (starting January 1, 1991) to yield the lessor a 14% return (implicit interest rate). Lessee does not know and cannot reliably estimate the lessor's yield rate. Lessee's incremental borrowing rate is 16%.
h. Lessor's unreimbursable cost uncertainties, none. Lessee's credit rating, excellent.
i. Lessor and lessee accounting year-end, December 31.

Required:

Round to the nearest dollar.

1. Compute the annual rentals by the lessor.
2. What type of lease is this to the lessor? To the lessee? Explain.
3. Prepare an amortization schedule for the lessor. Give the following entries for the lessor:
   a. At the inception of the lease and for the initial lease rental on January 1, 1991.
   b. Adjusting and closing on December 31, 1991.
4. Prepare an amortization schedule for the lessee. Give the following entries for the lessee:
   a. At the inception of the lease and for the initial lease rental on January 1, 1991.
   b. Adjusting and closing on December 31, 1991.

P 18–12

Direct-Financing Lease: Change in Residual Value, Amortization Schedule (L.O. 6)

On January 1, 1991 Kokomo Leasing Company leased equipment to a lessee for an eight-year term whereby $45,000 rents are payable each January 1, starting on January 1, 1991. The unguaranteed residual value of the equipment at the end of the lease term is $20,000. The interest rate implicit in the lease is 15%. The accounting period for both the lessor and lessee ends on December 31. The lease qualifies as a direct-financing lease.

Required:

Round to the nearest dollar.

1. Compute the initial investment value (i.e., cost to the lessor) of the leased property and the total amount of interest to be earned by Kokomo over the lease term.
2. Immediately after the fifth annual payment, the lease amortization schedule shows a lease receivable balance of $114,181. Prepare the amortization schedule for the lessor, using the value determined in (1) above to prove the correctness of that amount. For problem purposes, stop the amortization schedule after the January 1, 1995, payment.
3. Immediately after the fifth payment, Kokomo determined that the expected unguaranteed residual value of $20,000 probably will be zero. This change in accounting estimate will decrease the unrecovered investment value by the present value of the previously estimated residual value. Prepare the journal entry to record this change. After adjusting the January 1, 1995 receivable balance, complete the lease amortization schedule developed in (2) above from the $114,181 value in view of this new determination.

P 18-13
Sales-Type Lease:
Schedule, Entries for
Lessor
(L.O. 5, 6)

On December 31, 1991, a lessor leased a machine that cost $70,000. The machine was leased on January 1, 1992, for five years under a sales-type lease, which required annual payments of $28,199 at the end of each year. At inception of the lease, the sales value of the leased asset was $110,000. At the end of the lease term, the machine will revert to the lessor, at which time the estimated residual value will be $5,000 (none of which is guaranteed by the lessee). The lessor's implicit rate of interest was 10% on the investment.

Required:
Round amounts to the nearest dollar.

1. Show how the lessor computed the annual rental of $28,199.
2. Prepare a lease amortization schedule for the lessor.
3. Give the following entries for the lessor:
    a. To record acquisition of the machine on December 31, 1991.
    b. To record the inception of the lease on January 1, 1992.
    c. To record collection of the first rental and recognition of interest revenue on December 31, 1992 (end of the accounting period).
    d. To record, at termination of the lease on December 31, 1996, the last rental, interest revenue, and return of the asset, assuming the estimate of residual value is confirmed.
4. How would the lessor's entries differ at the end of the lease term assuming the market value of the returned machine was $4,000 (instead of the $5,000 estimated residual value)?

P 18-14
Sales-Type Lease:
Amortization Schedules,
Entries for Both Parties
(L.O. 2, 4, 5)

Lessor Company entered into a lease with Lessee Company on January 1, 1994. The following data relate to the leased asset and the lease agreement.

a. Asset leased—large construction crane.
b. Cost to Lessor, $150,000.
c. Estimated useful life, 10 years.
d. Estimated residual value at end of useful life, $10,000.
e. Lessor's normal selling price, $200,000.
f. Lease provisions:
    (1) Noncancelable; the asset will revert to Lessor at the end of the lease term.
    (2) Estimated residual value at end of lease term, $20,000 (none guaranteed).
    (3) Ownership does not transfer to Lessee by the end of the lease term.
    (4) No bargain purchase option is included.
    (5) Lease term, six years starting January 1, 1994.
    (6) Lease payment at each year-end, starting December 31, 1994, $43,329.
g. Lessor's implicit rate of return, 10% (assume Lessee knows this rate).
h. Lessee's incremental borrowing rate, 12% (assume this is evidence of a good credit rating).
i. Lessor has no material cost uncertainties.

Required:
Show computations and round to the nearest dollar.

1. What kind of lease was this to Lessee Company? Give the basis for your response.
2. What kind of lease was this to Lessor Company? Give the basis for your response.
3. For Lessor Company, give the entries to record (*a*) the lease at inception date and (*b*) the first rental.
4. For Lessee Company, give the entries to record (*a*) the lease at inception date and (*b*) the first rental.

P 18-15
Determine the Kind of
Lease, Schedule, Entries
for Both Parties
(L.O. 2, 4, 5, 8)

Lessor and lessee agreed to a noncancelable lease for which the following information is available:

a. Lessor's cost of the asset leased, $25,000. The asset was new at the inception of the lease term.
b. Lease term, four years starting January 1, 1993.
c. Estimated useful life of the leased asset, six years.
d. On January 1, 1993, lessor and lessee estimated that the residual value of the leased asset on the purchase option date (see [*h*] below) will be $6,000 and zero at the end of its useful life. The residual value is not guaranteed.

e. Depreciation method for the leased asset, straight-line.

f. Lessee's incremental borrowing rate, 10%. Lessee has an excellent credit rating.

g. Lessor's interest rate implicit in the lease, 10%.

h. Purchase option price of leased asset exercisable on January 2, 1996, $5,000.

i. Title to the leased asset retained by the lessor unless the purchase option is exercised.

j. Sale value of leased asset on January 1, 1993, $30,000.

k. Lessor's unreimbursable cost uncertainties, none.

l. Four annual lease rentals payable each January 1 during the lease term, with the first payment due at inception of the lease term, $7,526.

Required:

Round to the nearest dollar.

1. Show how the annual rental was computed.
2. Is this an operating lease or a capital lease to the lessee? Explain. Compute the lessee's capitalizable cost of the leased asset.
3. What type of lease is this to the lessor? Explain.
4. Prepare an amortization schedule. In parallel columns for the lessee and lessor, record the inception of the lease on January 1, 1993 (if appropriate), and the adjusting and closing entries on December 31, 1993.
5. Prepare the financial statement presentation of all lease-related accounts as they would appear in the financial statements of the lessee at December 31, 1993, for the year then ended. Disclosures are not required.

P 18-16
Direct-Financing Lease:
Executory Cost, Partially
Guaranteed Residual
Value, Entries
(L.O. 4, 5, 6)

Stockton Leasing Company (lessor) entered into a four-year noncancelable, direct financing lease with Acme Corporation (lessee) on January 1, 1991. The leased asset has a six-year life, with zero residual value at the end of the six years. On January 1, 1991, both lessor and lessee estimated the residual value of the asset at the end of the lease term to be $30,000, of which Acme guaranteed $20,000. The leased asset cost $500,000 (same as its market value). Lease payments are to be made on December 31 of eacy year, starting December 31, 1991, and are set to yield 16% to Stockton (implicit interest rate). This interest rate is known to Acme, which has an 18% incremental borrowing rate. Straight-line depreciation is used. Stockton agreed to pay annual executory costs of $3,000 and included this amount in the lease rentals. There is no bargain purchase option, and ownership is retained by Stockton at the end of the lease term. The accounting period for both companies ends on December 31.

Required:

Round to the nearest dollar.

1. Compute the annual lease rentals.
2. Prepare amortization schedules for the lessor and lessee.
3. Record the following for the lessor and lessee:
   a. Entry at the inception of the lease.
   b. Adjusting and closing entries at December 31, 1991.
4. Assuming that the actual residual value of the leased asset on December 31, 1994 (end of lease term) was $15,000, prepare entries for lessor and lessee on December 31, 1994, to record the return of the asset to the lessor.
5. Ignore (4). Assuming that the actual residual value of the leased asset on December 31, 1994 was $25,000, prepare entries for lessor and lessee on December 31, 1994, to record the return of the asset to the lessor.

P 18-17
Accounting for Initial
Direct Lease Costs
(L.O. 5)

On January 1, 1991, lessor Roth leased equipment to lessee Thomas. The equipment cost the lessor $400,000 and the lessor's expected rate of return was 15%. The three annual payments are to start on December 31, 1991. The lease has no BPO and there is no residual value. The lessor incurred, and paid, intitial indirect costs of $6,000 in consummating the lease. The lessor recorded these costs as a credit to cash and a debit to a temporary holding account called Initial Direct Leasing Costs. The rent payments were indirectly set to cover such costs.

Required:

1. Compute the annual rent (ordinary annuity basis) set by the lessor (where the rent includes the direct-leasing costs) assuming the following cases:

Case A

An operating lease.

Case B

A direct-financing lease.

Case C

A sales-type lease. The normal or regular selling price of the leased asset is $600,000.

2. Give the lessor's entries for (*a*) the inception of the lease and (*b*) the payments related to the lease at the end of the first year, for each case.
3. Give any entry needed for each case that the lessor should make during the first year for the initial direct costs. (The lessee's entries are unaffected.)

P 18–18
Sale-Leaseback:
Operating and Direct
Financing Leases
Compared
(L.O. 7)

On January 1, 1991, Supergrocery, Inc., sold the building currently used to Diversified Investors for $9,000,000, its current market value. Prior to the sale, the carrying value of the building was $7,000,000. The estimated remaining useful life of the building is 10 years, with no residual value at the time; straight-line depreciation is used.

On January 1, 1991, Supergrocery signed a 10-year noncancelable leaseback agreement that has a 15% implicit rate of return for the lessor. The lessee's incremental borrowing rate also is 15%. The annual rent payments start on January 1, 1991. During 1991, Supergrocery would pay $10,000 for executory costs (e.g., insurance, taxes, maintenance), if this transaction qualifies as a direct-financing lease. Alternatively, if this qualifies as an operating lease, this $10,000 would be paid by the buyer-lessor. For problem purposes only, two cases are assumed about the lease: Case A—an operating lease; Case B—a direct-financing lease.

Required:
For practical reasons give all amounts in $000s.

1. Compute the annual lease payments and the gain or loss on the sale of the building.
2. Give the 1991 entries for the seller-lessee and the buyer-lessor in parallel columns for Case A—operating lease.
3. (*a*) Prepare the lease amortization schedule through 1992 for Case B—direct-financing lease.
   (*b*) Give the 1991 entries for the seller-lessee and the buyer-lessor in parallel columns for Case B—direct-financing lease.

P 18–19
Operating Lease:
Advance Payment,
Ordinary Annuity Basis
(L.O. 3)

In lieu of making four $10,000 rent payments spaced at one-year intervals with the first payment due at the end of the first year of the lease term, the lessee and lessor agree that the lessee can make a lump-sum initial payment, the amount to be computed, at the start of the four-year lease term. This amount was calculated on the basis of an agreed 16% annual interest rate.

Required:
Round all amounts to the nearest dollar.

1. Compute the lump-sum initial payment amount.
2. On the assumption that the lessee amortizes the prepayment on a straight-line basis, give the lessee's entries to record the initial payment and year-end adjustments if the lease year and lessee accounting year coincide.

P 18–20
Operating Lease:
Advance Payment,
Annuity Due Basis
(L.O. 3)

A lessor and a lessee began negotiations that would have provided that the lessee pay six semiannual $8,000 rents for the use of property with the first payment to be at the beginning of the lease term. However, after agreeing that money was worth 14% per year at the time, the parties finally agreed that the lessee would instead pay $? at the outset and that this single advance payment would be in lieu of all other rents for the three-year term. Assume an operating lease.

Required:
Round to the nearest dollar.

1. Calculate the advance payment and prepare an amortization schedule covering the entire term of the lease.

2. Assume that the lessor and lessee amortize the advance payment computed in (1) above by the straight-line method. Give entries for both parties to record amortization at the end of the year if the lease year and accounting year of the parties coincide.

P 18–21
Appendix 18B:
Leveraged Lease: Debt
Amortization, Cash Flow,
Entries
(L.O. 10)

A lessor arranged financing of property leased to a lessee under a leveraged lease contract. The property cost the lessor $700,000 and was expected to have a five-year life with a zero residual value. It will be depreciated by the lessor using the SYD method. (A 10% investment tax credit realized by the lessor in the first year is assumed for instructional purposes). The lessor had other income in addition to this lease; all income was taxed at a rate of 40%, and any losses resulted in a 40% tax saving. The parties agreed on five annual rental payments of $175,000 at the end of each year for the use of the property.

The lessor paid $200,000 of the purchase price of the property and borrowed the remaining $500,000 at an annual interest rate of 10%. Five annual payments of $131,899 at the end of each year fully amortized the debt and payed all interest.

Required:
Round all amounts to the nearest dollar.

1. Prepare a debt amortization schedule, a cash flow schedule, and a schedule of allocation of cash flow to income and investment (similar to those in Exhibits 18B–3 and 18B–4) covering the entire lease term.
2. Prepare journal entries for the lessor for the first year of the lease.

(*Hint:* The rate of return required to fully amortize the lessor's net investment is 22.824%).

CASES

C 18–1
Implementing *SFAS No.*
***13*—Interest Rate**
(L.O. 6)

Pertinent provisions of *SFAS No. 13* concerning the interest rate to be used in capitalizing leases are cited below (italics added):

> A lessor shall compute the present value of the minimum lease payments using the *interest rate implicit in the lease.* . . . A lessee shall compute the present value of the minimum lease payments using his incremental borrowing rate . . . unless (*i*) it is practical for him to learn the implicit rate computed by the lessor, and (*ii*) the implicit rate computed by the lessor is less than the lessee's incremental borrowing rate. If both of these conditions are met, the lessee shall use the implicit rate.

Interest rate implicit in the lease is defined as the discount rate that, when applied to the minimum lease payments (excluding executory costs) and to the unguaranteed residual value of the property to the lessor, causes the present value at the start of the lease term to equal the market value of the property to the lessor at the inception of the lease. (There are some qualifications to this abstracted definition, but they are not important for present purposes.)

APB Opinion No. 21, which deals with the imputation of interest to receivables and payables, indicates that the choice of an interest rate "may be affected by the credit standing of the issuer, restrictive covenants, the collateral, payment and other terms pertaining to the debt, and, if appropriate, the tax consequences to the buyer and seller."

Required:
Evaluate the foregoing criteria in light of the following assertions:

1. Asking a lessor what interest rate is inherent in a lease transaction would be similar to asking a farmer what rate is implicit in the price the farmer can expect *now* for next fall's corn crop. There are varying degrees of risk in any operation having a distant future; the higher the farmer's future risks are thought to be, the higher the farmer will set his or her rate and, likewise, the lessor.
2. The assumption that a lease has an implicit interest rate, in many cases, represents circular reasoning in that the market value of the leased asset itself (i.e., the benchmark value used in determining the implicit rate) is determined by market forces. The value of the property stems from the rentals it will command rather than the rentals stemming from the value of the property.
3. One determinant of the implicit interest rate in a lease is the residual value of the property to be leased. This is a subjective judgment, which, depending on the property, can be substantially in error. Lessors will not disclose what this guess is.

C 18-2
Concern about Debt-
Equity Ratio and Third-
Party Residual Value
Guarantees; Ethics
(L.O. 1, 2, 8)

Speedware Corporation has entered into a debt agreement that restricts its debt-to-equity ratio to less than two to one. The corporation is planning to expand its facilities, which creates a need for additional financing. The board of directors is considering leasing the additional facilities but is concerned that leasing may violate its existing debt agreement; a violation would place the corporation in default. The potential lessor insists that the lease be structured such that it can be accounted for as a capital lease by the lessor (the lessor is a dealer and wants to recognize the dealer's profit on the transaction immediately). In addition, the lessor requires that the residual value of the leased asset be guaranteed when it reverts to the lessor at the end of the lease term. Speedware's board has asked you to analyze the following alternatives:

Alternative A—Speedware would enter into a lease that qualifies as a capital lease (to Speedware). If this alternative is selected, Speedware's reported debt-to-owners'-equity ratio would be 1.9, and its ability to issue debt in the future would be seriously constrained.

Alternative B—Speedware would enter into a lease and pay a third party to guarantee the residual value of the leased property. The lease would be structured such that it would qualify as an operating lease to Speedware and as a capital lease to the lessor. In this case, Speedware's reported debt-to-equity ratio would be unaffected by the lease contract.

Required:

Analyze and explain the consequences of each of the above alternatives. Do you see any ethical considerations?

C 18-3
Sherwin-Williams:
Analysis of Actual
Financial Statements
(L.O. 2, 3, 4, 8)

Answer the following questions using the financial statements of the Sherwin-Williams Company found at the end of this text.

Required:

1. Does The Sherwin-Williams Company have any capitalized leases? How do you know?
2. If the firm has capitalized leases, is the firm a lessee or lessor?
3. If the firm has capitalized leases, where do the liabilities appear on the balance sheet and in what amounts?
4. Does Sherwin-Williams have any operating leases? How do you know? How are these rentals accounted for by the firm.
5. What entries would Sherwin-Williams make to account for its leases during 1991, based on those leases currently on the books. (Ignore any executory costs.)
6. Does Sherwin-Williams lease a substantial portion of its buildings, machinery, and equipment under capital leases?
7. Assuming Sherwin-Williams depreciates its leased property using the same method as is used principally to depreciate its other fixed assets, what criterion (Exhibit 18–2) caused the company to capitalize these leases?

C H A P T E R
19

Accounting for Pensions

After you have studied this chapter, you will:

1. Be familiar with fundamental pension concepts.

2. Understand the basic nature of pension expense and be able to determine the components of pension expense not subject to delayed recognition.

3. Be able to distinguish among the ways of measuring pension liability: projected benefit obligation, accumulated benefit obligation, vested benefit obligation, and accrued pension cost.

4. Understand unrecognized pension cost amounts and their effect on pension expense.

5. Understand and be able to compute additional minimum pension liability.

6. Acquire a basic knowledge of accounting for postretirement benefits other than pensions. (Refer to Appendix 19A.)

7. Be familiar with pension plan settlements, curtailments, and termination benefits. (Refer to Appendix 19B.)

8. Be conversant with accounting for pension plans. (Refer to Appendix 19C.)

◆

INTRODUCTION
◆

Pension funds own 26% of the outstanding equity securities and 15% of taxable bonds in the United States; they hold a total $2.5 trillion in assets, according to the Employee Benefit Research Institute. In 1950, pension funds held less than 1% of total corporate equity.[1] Pension plans paid retirees $220 billion in 1988, 50% more than Social Security.[2] Pension funds exercise increasing power in corporate board rooms and in the securities markets.

The size of corporate pension funds reflects the substantial expense resulting from employers' promises to pay retiree pension benefits. This expense is a significant percentage of earnings for many corporations. For example, Chrysler's pension expense was 21.6% of pretax income in 1987, and Boeing's was 21.1% of pretax income in 1988.

A company promises to pay estimated retirement benefits in partial payment of services performed by its employees each year. How should the cost of benefits earned in a period be measured if payable at a much later date? Should the entire liability for promised benefits be recognized immediately? If not, are the financial statements misleading?

The need to estimate a variety of factors over a long time horizon compounds the difficulty of these questions. If future salaries are used to estimate pension benefits, should reported costs also reflect future salaries? How many employees will be working for the company 20 years from now? How long will they draw retirement benefits? To what extent can these estimates form a reliable basis for financial reporting? This chapter considers these and other issues in accounting for pensions.

◆

PENSION PLAN FUNDAMENTALS
◆

Since the early 1900s, public and private retirement programs have provided pension benefits for employees. These programs include social security, company retirement programs for employees, and tax-sheltered savings plans. Companies establish pension plans to increase employee motivation and productivity, reduce current demands for pay increases, comply with union demands, and be competitive in the labor market. Pension costs are a substantial percentage of total compensation costs, and pension benefits are a significant portion of total income for many retirees.

Through *pension plans,* employers agree to make payments into a fund for future retirement benefits, in return for current and past services. A plan *participant* is any current or former employee (and beneficiaries of these individuals) for whom the pension plan provides benefits. Pension plans provide participants with a degree of retirement security not otherwise possible. Pension plans also can provide insurance benefits at rates lower than those available to individuals. Pension plans discourage turnover because participants may lose a portion of their accumulated benefits if they change jobs.

Many pension plans conform to Internal Revenue Code requirements and qualify for the following tax advantages:

- Employers deduct from taxable income contributions to the pension fund, subject to certain limitations.
- Employers exclude pension fund earnings from taxable income.
- Employees exclude employer contributions from taxable income, subject to certain elections by the employee.
- Employees defer tax on benefits until after retirement.[3]

---

[1] *The Wall Street Journal,* May 15, 1990, p. A1.

[2] "Labor Letter," *The Wall Street Journal,* January 16, 1990 p. A1.

[3] Tax deferral bestows two benefits on employees. The pension fund grows much faster during the years of employment, and employees may be in a lower tax bracket when they retire.

Types of Pension Plans Employers generally establish one of two types of pension plans: **defined contribution** and **defined benefit** plans.[4] This chapter is primarily concerned with defined benefit plans.

In a defined contribution plan, the *contributions* are defined by formula or contract; the benefits are not specified. For example, some defined contribution plans require the employer to contribute an amount equal to a percentage of an employee's salary each month into an employee-directed investment fund. The employer makes no promise about the amount of retirement benefits. The employee bears the risk of pension fund performance in a defined contribution plan.

In contrast, the employer commits to specified retirement benefits in a defined benefit plan. The *benefits* are defined by a **pension benefit formula;** the contributions are not specified. The employer bears the risk of pension fund performance. Fund shortages caused by poor investment performance increase the employer's liability.

The variables in pension benefit formulas include number of qualified years of service credited to the employee, compensation levels, and age at retirement. An example of a *final-pay* pension benefit formula for a defined benefit plan is:

Annual benefit payment during retirement =
$$2.5\%(\text{Number of years service})(\text{Final salary})$$

An employee with a $100,000 final salary who retires after 25 years of service receives $62,500 (.025 × 25 × $100,000) each year of retirement. The annual benefit payment is a determinant of the investment required to satisfy the obligation and of the cost of the pension plan. The 2.5% term implies that 40 years of service must be rendered to achieve a pension equal to final salary.

Vesting of Benefits The right to receive earned pension benefits is **vested** when no longer contingent on continued employment. Most plans require a minimum employment term before benefits vest. Vesting provisions are especially important in a mobile labor force. Without vesting, workers who change jobs lose all their accumulated benefits. In some plans, vesting also guarantees benefits to the spouse of an employee who dies before retiring.

Pension Plan Funding A pension fund is an accumulation of cash and other assets restricted for the payment of retiree benefits. Funding sources include employer contributions, fund earnings, and employee contributions. Pension fund earnings generally supply a significant portion of total required funding. Pension plans are **contributory** or **noncontributory.** A plan is contributory if the employees must pay part of the funding needed to provide the specified benefits, or if the employees voluntarily make payments to increase retirement benefits.

Firms fund pension plans in three ways:

1. The firm maintains and administers the pension fund internally.
2. A bank or trust company, serving as the fund trustee, invests the employer contributions, makes retirement payments, and provides the employer with periodic information about the plan and investment performance.
3. The firm purchases a retirement annuity from an insurance company that accepts the responsibility for paying the pension benefits to the retirees.

The examples in this chapter assume an outside trustee. The trustee assumes ownership of the assets and bears the obligation for retirement payments. The trustee and employer are legally separate. Exhibit 19–1 summarizes the relationships among the parties in a pension plan when an outside trustee is used.

---

[4] In 1987, 70% of pension plan assets were held by defined benefit plans. See M. Warshawsky, *The Funding of Private Pension Plans,* Board of Governors of the Federal Reserve System, 1987, p. 6.

EXHIBIT 19-1   Relationships among Entities in a Pension Plan

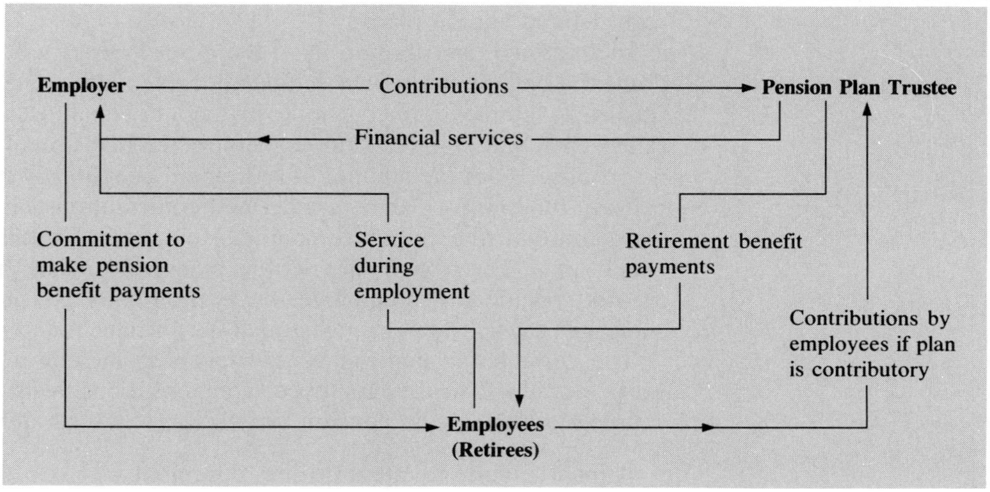

Defined benefit pension plans are fully funded or *overfunded* if the market value of plan assets equals or exceeds the actuarial present value of all benefits earned by participants. Otherwise the plan is *underfunded*. The tax law restricts the deductibility of payments to a pension plan if it is overfunded. Tax law, pension regulations, fund performance, current period pension benefits earned, general economic conditions, the pension agreement, and cash flow constraints are among the factors affecting the amount contributed each year by employers to pension funds.

Importance of Actuaries   Actuaries—professionals trained in a specific branch of mathematics and statistics—develop the estimates of future retirement benefit payments needed to compute the employer's pension expense and pension obligation. Actuaries use statistical models incorporating several variables including turnover, inflation, future compensation levels, life expectancy, the interest rate used for discounting benefit payments, final retirement age, and administrative costs.

The actuary works with the employer to develop the relevant historical data and expected changes in the employee population for this estimation process. Actuaries also give advice on the attributes of the plan most appropriate to an employer. Without the actuary, current pension accounting would not be possible.

Regulation of Private Pension Plan Funding   The Employees Retirement Income Security Act of 1974, as amended, known as **ERISA,** regulates the funding and administration of private (nongovernmental) pension plans. ERISA was enacted to alleviate many administrative and funding problems and to protect the pension benefits of employees. Before ERISA, underfunded pension plans were a major concern. Many employers funded plans on a pay-as-you-go basis, paying only those retirement benefits currently due.

ERISA sets minimum vesting and funding standards for private pension plans. Funding standards protect employee benefits by requiring that employers back benefit promises with assets. Employers are subject to fines and denial of tax deductibility for noncompliance. ERISA requires extensive reporting to regulatory authorities that evaluate the plan's funded status, and requires pension funds be audited by certified public accountants.

ERISA also created the Pension Benefit Guaranty Corporation (**PBGC**) to administer and make retirement payments for terminated plans. The PBGC is financed by premiums from sponsoring companies to provide some assurance that a minimum level of retirement funding is available if a plan is terminated. If a covered pension plan terminates with liabilities exceeding assets, the PBGC guarantees certain basic benefits, including vested benefits and cost of living adjustments effective before termination.

Minimum Vesting Standards   Under ERISA, employee benefits must be vested according to one of the following alternatives:[5]

1. 100% vesting of employer contributions after five years of service ("cliff" vesting).
2. The following schedule:

Years of Service	Percent Vested
3	20%
4	40
5	60
6	80
7 or more	100

For example, under the second alternative, 80% of an employee's promised pension benefits are vested after six years of service. Employee contributions to a pension plan vest immediately.

Minimum Funding Standards   The annual amount contributed by the employer to the pension fund must cover at least the benefits earned in the current year, adjusted for the effects of plan amendments and changes in assumptions. Congress amends ERISA frequently. Changes in vesting and funding standards after 1974 have generally increased the protection of employee benefits.

CONCEPT REVIEW

1. What is the main difference between defined contribution and defined benefit plans?
2. What role does a pension benefit formula play in a defined benefit pension plan?
3. How are employee interests in pension benefits protected by ERISA?

SUMMARY OF CURRENT PENSION ACCOUNTING

◆

Accounting for a defined *contribution* plan does not involve new measurement or recognition issues. The employer debits pension expense for the amount of the required contribution, credits cash for the amount paid and credits a liability for underpayments or debits a prepaid asset for overpayments.

The major issues encountered in pension acccounting involve defined *benefit* plans and include how to measure and recognize pension expense and pension liabilities.

Measuring Pension Expense in Defined Benefit Plans   Pension expense is measured under the concept of **attribution,** the process of assigning pension benefits to periods of employee service as defined by the pension benefit formula.[6] The measurement of

---

[5] *United States Code Annotated*, Title 29, Section 1053 (St. Paul, Minn.: West Publishing Company, 1989).

[6] The term *pension expense* is used to designate the pension cost recognized in a period. Manufacturing firms capitalize part of total periodic pension cost to inventory for the portion relating to manufacturing personnel.

pension expense takes into account the cost of pension benefits earned in the period, effects of previous over- or underfunding, return on the pension fund, and changes in the plan and underlying assumptions. The effects of these changes are recognized on a delayed basis.

Pension expense reflects future compensation levels if they are a factor in the benefit formula. However, only benefits attributable to service rendered through the reporting date are included in the measurement of pension expense and liabilities.

Recognizing Pension Liabilities   *SFAC No. 6* defines *liabilities* as follows:

> Liabilities are probable future sacrifices of economic benefits arising from present obligations of a particular entity to transfer assets or provide services to other entities in the future as a result of past transactions or events. (par. 35)

The obligation to pay retirement benefit payments is based on past service by employees and the pension agreement. The existence of a future pension obligation is evident, although the amount is not known with certainty.

However, many accountants maintain that the employer's pension liability is extinguished to the extent that the actuarial present value of future benefits is funded. Under this view, the sponsoring firm does not own the assets contributed to the fund, and has a liability only for underfunded pension benefits. This view is consistent with in-substance defeasance (see Chapter 16). The arrangement between the employer and trustee further supports this view. The trustee is a separate legal entity having title to the plan assets. Normally, the assets are restricted because the employer has access to the assets only on termination of the plan.

An alternative view holds that the employer extinguishes its liability only when benefit payments are made. This view requires recognition of the total obligation (present value of unpaid benefits) and pension fund assets in the balance sheet. Otherwise, the employer has significant off-balance-sheet debt, and employer assets are greatly understated. In addition, the economic substance, rather than the legal form, of the employer-trustee relationship suggests that the employer, rather than the trustee, is in debt to employees for pension benefits. The ability of the employer to terminate the plan and reclaim surplus assets supports this view. Furthermore, the employer is liable for any underfunded amounts.

The profession has adopted a modified version of the latter view. Both the fund asset balance and several liability measures are disclosed in the footnotes. But the FASB stopped short of recognizing the total liability and plan assets in the *accounts,* favoring instead footnote disclosure.

SFAS No. 87, "Employers' Accounting for Pensions   For many years, the pay-as-you-go approach to accounting for pensions provided an opportunity for income manipulation. Under this approach, pension expense equals the funding amount, which can be altered easily. *APB Opinion No. 8,* "Accounting for the Cost of Pension Plans," was the first pronouncement to *require* accrual accounting for pensions. This opinion was superseded by *SFAS No. 87,* which defines current pension accounting standards.[7]

SFAS No. 87 requires that periodic pension expense be recognized before the actual payment of benefits to retirees and significantly changes accounting for pensions in three ways:

- The recognized cost of a pension plan is directly related to the terms of the plan. The actuarial present value of benefits provides a standardized measure of pension expense.
- Employers recognize a liability equal to the underfunded obligation based on current compensation levels.

---

[7] *SFAS No. 87* applies to all pension plans whether written or implied. It does not apply to life and health benefits during employment or postemployment life insurance and health care benefits. The first appendix to this chapter discusses postretirement benefits other than pensions.

EXHIBIT 19-2   Information for Lone Pine Pension Plan and Employee Nicole Whitney

Pension plan: Noncontributory defined benefit plan
Pension plan inception: January 1, 1991
Date Nicole Whitney joins Lone Pine: January 1, 1991
Starting salary for Nicole: $45,000 per year
Nicole's age on January 1, 1991: 40
Nicole's expected retirement date: December 31, 2015 (25 years of employment service
  expected)
Nicole's expected salary at retirement: $150,000
Pension benefit formula:

   Annual retirement benefit payment = 2% (Number of service years)(Final salary)

Lone Pine vests 10% of benefits after the first year, 15% of benefits after the second year, then
  conforms to the present ERISA schedule (20% of total benefits vested after the third year and
  so forth)
Discount rate and expected long-term rate of return on pension plan assets (assume expected
  equals actual return): 10%
Nicole's expected retirement period: 10 years; payments are made at the end of each calendar
  year during retirement
Time line depicting service and retirement periods for Nicole:

	Service			**Retirement**	
1/1/1991	**Period**	1/1/2016		**Period**	12/31/2025
	25 years			10 years	

Contributions to pension plan   Retirement benefit payments
(funding) are made at   are made at the end of
the end of service years: retirement years:

First contribution: 12/31/1991   First payment: 12/31/2016
Last contribution: 12/31/2015   Last payment: 12/31/2025

♦ The *Statement* significantly expands disclosure. The principal additions to required disclosures are the pension liability based on the benefit formula, and plan
assets at fair value.

MEASURING PENSION EXPENSE AND PENSION OBLIGATIONS

♦

Let's consider the pension plan of the Lone Pine Corporation, a hypothetical
software development company. This example focuses on one employee, Nicole
Whitney, a software engineer, and develops the concepts of pension expense and
liability for pension benefits.[8] Exhibit 19–2 gives the initial data for the example.

Discount Rate   Employers use a *discount rate* when computing the actuarial present
value of benefits, pension expense, and the obligation of the employer under the
plan. The discount rate is the rate at which pension obligations *could be settled* if
sufficient funds were invested at that rate. The actuarial present value reflects not
only the time value of money but also factors that affect the probability of payment,
including life expectancy, turnover, and disability.

---

[8] In practice, the actuary analyzes data for the employee group and develops estimates of life expectancy, turnover, and
other factors. It is generally not possible to predict the benefits payable to an individual employee. However, the example
uses one individual to simplify the presentation and focus on the concepts. Actuarial models are beyond the scope of this
text.

SFAS No. 87 requires that the discount rate approximate the market interest rate. The employer changes the discount rate periodically to reflect changing economic conditions.[9] When choosing the discount rate, firms consider the following factors:

* Rates implicit in annuity contracts offered by insurance companies.
* Information on interest rates from the PBGC.
* Returns on high-quality fixed-income investments expected during the accumulation period.

Firms also consider the average age of employees. For example, the discount rate for a plan covering mainly retirees might reflect a portfolio of investments with shorter maturities than those of a plan covering a younger work force.[10]

Pension Expense   Pension expense is the *net cost* of six components. Net cost is one of the three fundamental aspects of previous pension accounting retained by *SFAS No. 87*.[11]

Pension expense components:

1. Service cost.
2. Interest cost.
3. Actual return on plan assets.
4. Amortization of prior service cost.
5. Gain or loss to the extent recognized.
6. Amortization of transition asset or liability.

Service Cost: Component 1 of Pension Expense

Service cost is the actuarial present value of pension benefits attributed to employee service in a period, based on the pension benefit formula. The service cost for Nicole in 1991 is computed below (see Exhibit 19–2):

$$\text{Annual retirement benefit earned by Nicole in 1991} = .02(1 \text{ service year})(\$150,000) = \$3,000$$

$$
\begin{aligned}
\text{Service cost, 1991} &= \text{Present value of benefit payments earned in 1991} \\
&= \$3,000\ (PVA,10\%,10^*)(PV1,10\%,24\dagger) \\
&= \$3,000(6.14457)(.10153) \\
&= \underline{\underline{\$1,872}}
\end{aligned}
$$

* Ten years of retirement payments.

† Retirement in 24 years, as of December 31, 1991.

Nicole *earned* a retirement benefit of $3,000 *per retirement year* by working for Lone Pine during 1991. To *receive* the entire benefit she must continue with Lone Pine until the benefits vest. According to the vesting schedule, Lone Pine guarantees Nicole $300 (10% × $3,000) per retirement year at the end of 1991; this guarantee is independent of whether she continues to work for Lone Pine.

---

[9] The average discount rate used by Fortune 500 companies in 1988 was 8.84%. 30% of firms changed the rate during 1988. Of those, a roughly equal number increased and decreased the discount rate. See *Deloitte & Touche Review*, February 12, 1990.

[10] Minor changes in discount rates can dramatically affect the measurement of the employer's obligation. For example, a 1% decrease in the discount rate can increase pension liabilities 10% to 15%. See "The Surplus Vanishes," *Forbes*, November 17, 1986, p. 94.

[11] The other two, *offsetting* and *delayed recognition*, are discussed later.

Service cost for Nicole in 1991 is $1,872, the investment required at 12/31/91 (the *measurement date*)[12] to settle the obligation for her future retirement payments *earned in 1991*. Service cost is not related to the amount contributed to the fund in 1991.[13]

For the first year *only* (assuming no amendments or transition gain or loss, and funding at the end of the year), pension expense equals service cost. No other components are involved. If Lone Pine contributes only $1,500 to the pension fund trustee because of liquidity problems,[14] the following entry records pension expense:

December 31, 1991—Record pension expense:

Pension expense	1,872	
Accrued pension cost		372
Cash		1,500

Accrued Pension Cost Account The $372 balance in the liability account, accrued pension cost, is the amount by which the pension plan is underfunded. If Lone Pine plans to increase funding in 1992 to cover the deficiency, the liability is classified as current.

If Lone Pine contributed $1,900 (rather than $1,500) to the fund in 1991, an asset account, prepaid pension cost, would be debited for $28, the amount by which the plan would be overfunded.[15] The balance in accrued or prepaid pension cost equals the difference between cumulative pension expense recognized to date and cumulative funding to date.

Employer Pension Obligations The **projected benefit obligation** (PBO) is the actuarial present value of the benefits attributed to employee service rendered to date, as measured by the benefit formula. Service cost *increases* PBO. Benefit payments *reduce* PBO.

PBO at the end of the first year of a pension plan (without amendments) equals service cost ($1,872 for Nicole) because service cost is also the present value of benefits earned in the first year. The FASB concluded that PBO is the most representationally faithful measure of the pension obligation because it is an estimate of a present obligation to make future cash payments as a result of past events. In this example, the benefit formula incorporates future salaries. Therefore, PBO also reflects future salaries. The going-concern assumption supports the use of future compensation levels in calculating PBO.[16]

SFAS No. 87 requires disclosure of two additional liability measures: **accumulated benefit obligation** (ABO) and **vested benefit obligation** (VBO). The computation for each is similar to PBO except that ABO is based on *current* salary levels,[17] and VBO is based on vested benefits. If the benefit formula does not incorporate future salary levels, ABO and PBO are *equal*. All three liability measures are disclosed in the footnotes to the financial statements.

---

[12] In order to allow sufficient time to gather information, *SFAS No. 87* allows the *measurement date*, the date at which pension assets and liabilities are measured, to fall within the three-month period before the balance sheet date.

[13] In practice, the determination of service cost considers productivity, seniority, promotion, turnover, life expectancy, and disability in the employee group.

[14] This amount is in violation of minimum funding standards under ERISA, but is used for instructional purposes. Waivers of minimum funding requirements are available.

[15] It is common for firms to report a pension asset. For example, IBM reported $551 million of prepaid pension cost in 1988 on its U.S. plans.

[16] The rate of assumed annual compensation increase for computing PBO most commonly used by a sample of 600 major companies in 1989 was 6%. See AICPA, *Accounting Trends & Techniques* (New York, 1990), p. 232.

[17] If the benefit formula considers an average of compensation levels, ABO reflects both past and current compensation levels.

ABO and VBO as of December 31, 1991, for Nicole are computed below:

Annual retirement benefit
earned by Nicole in 1991
based on *current* salary $= .02(1 \text{ service year})(\$45,000) = \$900$

$$ABO = \$900(PVA,10\%,10)(PV1,10\%,24)$$
$$= \$900(6.14457)(.10153)$$
$$= \underline{\$561}$$

Annual retirement benefit
earned by Nicole in 1991
based on *vested benefits* $= .02(1 \text{ service year})(\$45,000)(.10)* = \$90$

$$VBO = \$ 90(PVA,10\%,10)(PV1,10\%,24)$$
$$= \$ 90(6.14457)(.10153)$$
$$= \underline{56}$$

* Vesting percentage for first year.

If the benefit formula considers future compensation levels, the following relationship generally holds:

$$PBO > ABO > VBO$$

This relationship is illustrated below for Nicole:

Vested benefit obligation (VBO)	$ 56
Add nonvested benefit obligation	505
Accumulated benefit obligation (ABO)	561
Add effect of future compensation levels	1,311
Projected benefit obligation (PBO)	$1,872

PBO is the measure of the employer's obligation in a going concern, whereas ABO and VBO provide a measure of the employer's potential obligation if the plan is discontinued. Some accountants consider ABO a more *reliable* measure of the employer's obligation because it is based on definite compensation levels. Others believe that PBO is a more *relevant* measure because it uses compensation levels more likely to be in effect at retirement. The disclosure of several measures of the pension liability allows the financial statement reader to develop a comprehensive assessment of the employer's obligation.

Plan Assets   Plan assets are exclusively restricted for the payment of pension benefits. Except for plan terminations, the employer should not be able to access plan assets. Otherwise, a plan's funded status is uncertain. Plan assets include investments (primarily stocks, bonds, and other securities) and operational assets used in administering the pension fund.

Investment assets are valued at *fair market value* or *market-related value*. The fair market value is the amount realizable through a normal sale. Market-related value equals fair market value or a calculated value that recognizes changes in fair market value of plan investments in a systematic and rational manner over a period of not more than five years. The use of market-related value reduces the volatility of periodic pension expense.

Operational pension assets are valued at book value as shown in the records of the fund trustee.[18] The sum of the plan investments (at fair market value or market-

---

[18] Book value is used because there generally is no intent to sell these assets, fair market value may be difficult to obtain, and they are generally unavailable to pay pension benefits.

EXHIBIT 19-3   Reconciliation of Funded Status, Lone Pine Corporation, December 31, 1991

Projected benefit obligation	($1,872)
Plan assets at fair value	1,500
Underfunded PBO (funded status)	($ 372)
Balance in accrued pension cost	($ 372)

related value) and plan operational assets (at book value) is called *plan assets at fair value*. The trustee of the funding agency prepares an annual report showing the beginning balance in plan assets, all changes during the year, and the ending balance. For simplicity, this chapter assumes that the pension fund consists entirely of investments and that fair value and market-related value are equal.

Some companies contribute noncash assets to pension funds in an attempt to maintain their own liquidity levels. For example, USX and Wheeling-Pittsburgh issued preferred stock to their pension funds in lieu of cash. Diamond Shamrock provided its fund a royalty interest in its Texas oil and gas properties.[19]

Funded Status, 1991   The *funded status* of a plan is the difference between PBO and the plan assets at fair value and indicates whether the plan is under- or overfunded. It is the critical measure of a pension plan. Lone Pine's plan is underfunded because PBO exceeds the pension fund's fair value, as indicated in Exhibit 19–3.

At the end of 1991, the pension fund holds $1,500, the first contribution made by Lone Pine. PBO and fund assets describe separate characteristics of the pension plan and are not related. However, they have two attributes in common. Neither is recorded in the accounts of the employer, and both are reduced by benefit payments. Benefit payments are paid from plan assets and extinguish the employer's liability. They are recorded by the trustee rather than by the employer. The nonrecognition of PBO is an example of off-balance-sheet financing.

The disclosure of funded status is an example of *offsetting,* one of three fundamental aspects of prior pension accounting retained by *SFAS No. 87.* In this example, the plan's funded status equals the balance in the accrued pension cost account. Therefore, Lone Pine's plan assets are offset against PBO for balance sheet reporting. There are no reconciling items. Reconciling items are those subject to delayed recognition, illustrated in later examples.

Nonrecognition of PBO is controversial. The FASB was sensitive to concerns that recognition of PBO in the balance sheet would greatly increase many companies' debt levels. For example, the underfunded pension obligation of American Motors Corporation in 1984 was 148% of the total market value of its outstanding stock.

Interest Cost and Actual Return: Components 2 and 3 of Pension Expense, 1992

Refer to Exhibit 19–4 for information and pension calculations for 1992.

Interest Cost   *Interest cost,* the second component of pension expense, is the growth in PBO during a reporting period. At December 31, 1991, PBO equals $1,872. Therefore, interest cost for 1992 equals $187 ($1,872 × .10). The amount of the

---

[19] There is concern that equity securities and assets whose value is tied to the performance of the sponsoring company abrogate the fundamental arm's-length relationship between sponsor and employee. See "Pension Raiding, 1983 Style," *Forbes,* June 20, 1983, p. 130.

EXHIBIT 19-4   New Information and Initial Pension Calculations, Lone Pine Corporation, 1992

1992 compensation for Nicole: $47,250 (a 5% raise for 1992)
Estimated salary at retirement: $150,000 (unchanged)
Funding for 1992: $2,000
Service cost for 1992:

Annual retirement benefit earned by Nicole in 1992 = .02(1 service year)($150,000) = $3,000
$$\text{Service cost, 1992} = \$3,000 \ (PVA,10\%,10)(PV1,10\%,23^*)$$
$$= \$3,000(6.14457)(.11168) \qquad = \underline{\$2,059}$$

$$\text{PBO,12/31/92} = \$6,000\dagger(PVA,10\%,10)(PV1,10\%,23)$$
$$= \$6,000(6.14457)(.11168) \qquad = \underline{\$4,117}$$

Nicole's vested benefits: .02(2 years)($47,250)(.15) = $284
Nicole's benefits based on current salary: .02(2 years) $47,250 = $1,890

VBO [$284(PVA,10%,10)(PV1,10%,23)]	$ 195
Add nonvested benefit obligation	1,102
ABO [$1,890(PVA,10%,10)(PV1,10%,23)]	1,297
Add effect of future compensation levels	2,820
PBO	$4,117

* 23 years from 12/31/92 to retirement.

† Nicole has earned 2-years' of retirement benefits or $6,000 according to the formula: .02(2 years)$150,000 = $6,000.

liability at December 31, 1992, for Nicole's first year benefits *only* is $2,059, computed in two ways:

$$\$2,059 = \$1,872(1.10)$$

Or:

$$\$2,059 = \$3,000(PVA,10\%,10)(PV1,10\%,23)$$
$$= \$3,000(6.14457)(.11168)$$

Lone Pine must have $1,872 invested at *December 31, 1991,* to provide the benefits promised in 1991, and must have $2,059 invested at *December 31, 1992,* for the same benefits. The $187 difference is interest cost, the growth in PBO ($2,059 − $1,872). The current year service cost is not a part of interest cost.

PBO ($4,117 in Exhibit 19-4) is the present value of benefit payments earned through December 31, 1992. An alternative way to compute PBO highlights the relationship between certain pension expense components and PBO:

PBO, 12/31/92:

Service cost through 12/31/92 ($1,872 + $2,059)	$3,931
Interest cost through 12/31/92	187
Benefits paid to Nicole through 12/31/92	(0)
PBO, 12/31/92	$4,118*

*$1 discrepancy due to rounding of present value factors.

Actual Return on Plan Assets   Actual return on plan assets, the third component of pension expense, is the increase or decrease in plan assets at fair value, adjusted for contributions and benefit payments. The following equation shows the changes in the fund during a period:

Beginning fund balance
+ Actual return during the period
+ Employer contributions
− Benefit payments
= Ending fund balance

EXHIBIT 19-5   Reconciliation of Funded Status, Lone Pine Corporation, December 31, 1992

Projected benefit obligation	($4,118)
Plan assets at fair value	3,650
Underfunded PBO (funded status)	($ 468)
Balance in accrued pension cost	($ 468)

Actual return generally *reduces* pension expense by partially or wholly offsetting the interest cost component, and *increases* the pension fund.[20] Actual return on fund assets includes dividends and interest, and realized and unrealized changes in plan assets at fair value. Assume actual return is $150 in 1992.

Pension expense for 1992 is computed as follows:

Service cost, 1992	$2,059 (from Exhibit 19–4)
Interest cost, 1992	187
Actual return, 1992	(150)
Pension expense, 1992	$2,096

Lone Pine funds $2,000 in 1992 (Exhibit 19–4). Then the firm records the following entry to recognize pension expense:

December 31, 1992—Record pension expense:

Pension expense	2,096	
Accrued pension cost		96
Cash		2,000

Pension expense increased in 1992 because service cost reflects a shorter period to retirement, interest cost increases pension expense, and actual return is less than interest cost. The balance in accrued pension cost at December 31, 1992, is $468 ($372 from 1991 + $96 from 1992). The $96 increase represents an additional funding deficiency. Full funding required a contribution of $2,468 ($2,096 + $372 previous accrued pension cost balance) at the end of 1992.

Funding levels and pension expense are inversely related because actual return reduces pension expense. For example, if the plan were fully funded in 1991 ($1,872 contribution), pension expense in 1992 would be $2,059 (1992 service cost) because interest cost and actual return would exactly offset. Early full funding results in smaller subsequent pension expense.

Using the original information the fund balance at the end of 1992 is as follows:-

Fund balance, 1/1/92	$1,500
Actual return, 1992	150
Employer contributions, 1992	2,000
Benefits paid, 1992	(0)
Fund balance, 12/31/92	$3,650

Exhibit 19–5 shows the reconciliation of funded status for 1992. Relationships among the several new terms introduced in this section are summarized in Exhibit 19–6.

Pension Spreadsheet   The spreadsheet in Exhibit 19–7 brings together the reports of the actuary and trustee, emphasizes the relationship among pension variables, and reinforces certain pension relationships listed in Exhibit 19–6. For example, service cost and interest cost appear in the PBO and pension expense columns as additions. Actual return increases assets but is entered as a negative amount in the pension

---

[20] With sufficiently high return, pension expense can be negative (an earnings increase). For example, pension expense for IBM's U.S. plans in 1988 was a negative (credit) $55 million due to actual return of more than $2 billion.

EXHIBIT 19-6   Summary of Pension Relationships

	Effect On		
Item	**Pension Expense**	**Projected Benefit Obligation**	**Plan Assets**
Service cost	Increase	Increase	No effect
Interest cost	Increase	Increase	No effect
Actual return	Decrease	No effect	Increase
Contributions	No effect*	No effect	Increase
Benefit payments	No effect	Decrease	Decrease

* Contributions indirectly reduce future pension expense by increasing plan assets and, therefore, actual return.

EXHIBIT 19-7   Pension Spreadsheet

LONE PINE COMPANY
Pension Plan Spreadsheet, 1992

	PBO (Actuary)	Plan Assets (Trustee)	Pension Expense	Accrued Pension Cost
Beginning balances, 1992	$1,872	$1,500		($372)
Service cost	2,059		$2,059	
Interest cost	187		187	
Actual return		150	(150)	
Contributions		2,000		2,000
Benefits paid	0	0		
Ending balances:				
PBO	$4,118			
Plan assets		$3,650		
Underfunded PBO	$468			
Pension expense			$2,096	(2,096)
Accrued pension cost				$ (468)

expense column. The contribution is a positive entry in the assets column, yet is a decrease in the accrued pension cost column.

CONCEPT REVIEW

1. How is the benefit formula used in the calculation of service cost for a period?
2. Why are pension expense, service cost, and projected benefit obligation the same amount for the first year of Lone Pine's pension plan?
3. Why are the projected benefit obligation and plan assets not recorded in the accounts?

Expected Return of Plan Assets   Expected return on plan assets is derived by multiplying the *expected long-term rate of return on plan assets* by the fair value of plan assets at the beginning of the reporting period. Current earnings rates on the fund and rates expected in the future are considered when estimating this rate.[21] Expected return in 1992 for Lone Pine is $150 (.10 × $1,500). When expected and actual return differ, a gain or loss on the plan occurs. Later examples illustrate accounting for gains and losses. For Lone Pine, both return measures are equal.[22]

The discount rate and the expected long-term rate of return on plan assets are not necessarily equal. The rate of return chosen by the sponsor reflects the trade-off between risk and return. One employer might be willing to accept a higher degree of risk and demand a 12% expected rate of return. Another employer might prefer to accept a 9% expected rate of return with lower risk. Yet both employers could choose an 8% discount rate consistent with data from insurance companies or the PBGC. The discount rate reflects the rate at which the obligation could be settled. The rate of return more closely considers the investment strategy of the sponsoring firm.

Pension Expense Based on Funding Levels The belief that an exchange takes place between the employer and employee supports attribution as the basis for expense recognition under *SFAS No. 87*. The FASB rejected the *cost approach*, an alternative to *attribution*. The cost approach projects the estimated total benefit at retirement and determines the annual contribution (funding) necessary to provide that benefit. Under this approach, pension expense equals the necessary annual contribution. For the Nicole Whitney example, this approach recognizes only $208 of pension expense in 1991, computed below:

$$P(FVA,10\%,24) = \$3,000(PVA,10\%,10)$$
$$P(88.49733) = \$3,000(6.14457)$$

where:

P = the annual payment required to fulfill the expected retirement annuity.

P = $208

The left-hand side of the above equation is the accumulation of an annuity of $208 paid each year for 24 years, Nicole's remaining service period. That accumulation is necessary to fund the retirement annuity of $3,000 each year to Nicole. Lone Pine need only contribute $208 annually for 24 years to fulfill the benefits promised Nicole based on her service in 1991.

However, as Nicole provides more years of service, the necessary payment increases. For example, the required payment needed to fulfill the benefits earned in Nicole's last service year alone is $18,434 [computed as $3,000(PVA,10%,10)]! Furthermore, this amount is added to the required annual payments for earlier years of service. The cost approach would have provided an incentive to maintain very low funding levels early in the pension plan, to the possible detriment of the participants.

The cost approach focuses on financing, rather than on the accrual aspects of the pension plan. The attribution approach is more consistent with *SFAC No. 6,* which defines liabilities in terms of obligations. The employer's obligation for a defined benefit pension plan is determined by the benefit formula, rather than by the necessary funding amount.

Delayed recognition The last three components of pension expense result from delayed recognition of changes affecting pension obligations or assets. Delayed recognition is a fundamental aspect of current pension accounting. The changes are recognized in

---

[21] The long-term expected rate of return most commonly used by a sample of 600 major companies was 9%. See AICPA, *Accounting Trends & Techniques* (New York, 1990) p. 233.

[22] When expected and actual returns differ, pension expense ultimately reflects expected return. The discussion on the fifth component of pension expense addresses this aspect.

pension expense systematically over subsequent periods. The unamortized (unrecognized) amounts are carried forward to the next accounting period.

One effect of delayed recognition is that the balance in accrued pension cost does not equal the plan's funded status. Reconciling items are required in the funded status report. For example, an increase in PBO resulting from a plan amendment is recognized only gradually in pension expense. Therefore, the balance in accrued pension cost reflects only the portion of the increase in PBO amortized to date.

The primary purpose of delayed recognition is to reduce the volatility of pension reporting by spreading changes in the pension plan over a number of years. Delayed recognition increased the business community's acceptance of *SFAS No. 87*. However, delayed recognition increases the likelihood that the accrued pension cost of employers with grossly underfunded plans seriously understates the actual obligation. Therefore, when underfunded *ABO* exceeds accrued pension cost, an *additional minimum pension liability* is recognized. This requirement partially reduces the effects of delayed recognition and appeases those not favoring the use of future compensation levels for measuring pension expense. (ABO is based on *current and past* salary levels.) The remaining pension expense components and additional liability are discussed in the next sections.

Prior Service Cost and Component 4 of Pension Expense

Prior Service Cost (PSC) results from plan amendments granting employees and retirees pension benefits attributable to service rendered before the inception of the pension plan, or from amendments granting increased pension benefits attributable to service rendered before the amendment.

Retroactive increases in pension benefits are a common result of collective bargaining agreements. For example, if an employer initiates a pension plan in 1992, employees who started in 1980 suffer a severe injustice if not granted pension benefits for service rendered before 1992. Almost all plans recognize service rendered before the inception of the plan.[23]

PSC, the present value of increased benefits under the amendment, is an increase in PBO. An expanded expression for PBO follows:

$$
\begin{array}{rl}
 & \text{Sum of service cost to measurement date} \\
+ & \text{Sum of interest cost to measurement date} \\
+ & \text{PSC (present value at amendment date)} \\
- & \text{(Benefits paid to measurement date)} \\
\hline
= & \text{PBO at measurement date[24]}
\end{array}
$$

Assume that on January 1, 1992, Lone Pine Company (from Exhibit 19–2) amends its plan to award Nicole an additional *annual* $500 retirement benefit for service rendered in 1991. Nicole has 24 years of service remaining, and she is expected to draw 10 retirement payments. PSC is computed as follows:

PSC, 1/1/92 = Present value of increased benefits granted by amendment

$$= \$500(PVA,10\%,10)(PV1,10\%,24)$$
$$= \$500(6.14457)(.10153) = \underline{\underline{\$312}}$$

Employers who increase pension benefits attributable to prior service benefit in *future* periods from the resulting improved employee productivity and morale, reduced turnover, and reduced demand for pay raises. PSC is subject to delayed recognition and is amortized in periods after the grant, but is not recorded in an account.

---

[23] M. Warshawsky, *The Funding of Private Pension Plans*, Board of Governors of the Federal Reserve System, 1987, p. 3.

[24] PSC also increases interest cost because it increases PBO.

EXHIBIT 19-8   Information for Example

SIERRA COMPANY
Information for Example of PSC Amortization

Date of amendment: January 1, 1991
Amendment: Increased the benefits attributable to service performed before January 1, 1991 for all active employees
PSC: Present value of increased benefits at 1/1/91 is $48,000
Active employees, and remaining estimated service years at 1/1/91:
Jim, 1; Frank, 2; Susan, 2; Katherine, 3; Bill, 4
Schedule of employee-service years remaining at January 1, 1991:

Employee	Employee Service Years				
	1991	1992	1993	1994	Total
Jim	1				1
Frank*	1	1			2
Susan	1	1			2
Katherine	1	1	1		3
Bill	1	1	1	1	4
Service-years per fiscal year	5	4	2	1	12

Average service period: 12 total years/5 employees = 2.4 years.

* Frank has two years of service remaining: 1991 and 1992.

Amortization (recognition) of PSC is the fourth component of pension expense and generally *increases* pension expense.[25] PSC is amortized over the remaining service period of those employees active at the date of the amendment who are expected to receive benefits under the plan. Employees hired after that date do not affect the amortization. The number of years used for amortization is not subsequently changed except for a curtailment (discussed in the second appendix to this chapter). If most of a plan's participants are inactive, PSC is amortized over the remaining life expectancy of those participants. Amortization of PSC is limited to amounts known at the beginning of the year.

Methods of Amortizing PSC   *SFAS No. 87* allows two approaches to amortizing PSC. One is the *service method,* which allocates an equal amount of PSC to each employee service-year and results in declining amortization as employees retire. Another is the *straight-line* method, which amortizes PSC over the average service period and results in quicker amortization. Refer to Exhibit 19–8, which presents information for an example of both approaches.

Service Method   Under the service method, $5/12$ of total PSC, or $20,000 ($5/12 \times$ 48,000), is amortized in 1991. Five of the total 12 service years are rendered in 1991. Pension expense is increased by $20,000 in 1991. At the end of 1991, $28,000 of PSC remains unamortized ($48,000 − $20,000). The following table presents the amortization for each year:

Year	Amortization Recognized	Unrecognized PSC at 12/31
1991	$20,000 = $48,000($5/12$)	$28,000 = $48,000 − $20,000
1992	$16,000 = $48,000($4/12$)	$12,000 = $28,000 − $16,000
1993	$ 8,000 = $48,000($2/12$)	$ 4,000 = $12,000 − $ 8,000
1994	$ 4,000 = $48,000($1/12$)	$ 0 = $ 4,000 − $ 4,000

---

[25] A plan amendment can reduce PBO by reducing future benefits on a retroactive basis. The reduction is first used to reduce any existing unrecognized PSC. The amortization of the excess reduces pension expense.

EXHIBIT 19-9   Reconciliation of Funded Status

SIERRA COMPANY
Summary Pension Plan Information for
Funded Status Report,
December 31, 1991

PSC information applies from Exhibit 19-8, remaining data assumed
Unrecognized PSC, 12/31/91: $28,000
Service cost, 1991: $300,000
Interest cost, 1991: $80,000
Actual and expected return: $90,000
PBO, 12/31/91: $1,200,000 (includes PSC from 1/1/91 amendment)
Plan assets at fair value: $962,000
Accrued pension cost, 12/31/91: $210,000 cr. (after recording pension expense)

Pension expense, 1991:

Service cost	$300,000
Interest cost	80,000
Actual return	(90,000)
Amortization of PSC	20,000
Pension expense	$310,000

Reconciliation of funded status, 12/31/91:

Projected benefit obligation	($1,200,000)
Plan assets at fair value	962,000
Underfunded PBO (funded status)	(238,000)
Unrecognized PSC	28,000
Balance in accrued pension cost	($ 210,000)

Straight-Line Method   The *average* remaining service period for the employee group is 2.4 years, as indicated in Exhibit 19–8. The following table illustrates the results of the straight-line method:

Year	Amortization Recognized[26]	Unrecognized PSC at 12/31
1991	$20,000 = $48,000/2.4	$28,000 = $48,000 − $20,000
1992	$20,000 = $48,000/2.4	$ 8,000 = $28,000 − $20,000
1993	$ 8,000 (remaining)	0 = $ 8,000 − $ 8,000

This method amortizes PSC more quickly (2.4 years compared to 4 years under the service method) resulting in greater pension expense in early years. Although the method fully amortizes PSC before the last covered employee retires, frequent plan amendments may imply that the benefit period of each amendment is shorter than the entire service period of active employees.

The service method is conceptually preferable because it relates PSC to years of service as rendered. Early years receive a greater allocation. In addition, the benefits realized by the employer are greatest during the years immediately after the grant. More employees are working, and the motivational effect of the grant is at its peak soon after the award.

Reconcilation of Funded Status   Unrecognized PSC is a reconciling amount in the funded status report. Refer to Exhibit 19–9 for summary information about Sierra Company's pension plan and the reconciliation for 1991.

Sierra's plan is underfunded $238,000. However, $28,000 of PSC remains unrecognized. This amount has not been recognized in pension expense and therefore

---

[26] The two methods always prooduce the same amortization in the first year.

accrued pension cost does not yet reflect the $28,000 amount. The unrecognized PSC explains why funded status and accrued pension cost are unequal.

CONCEPT REVIEW

1. What are the two sources of prior service cost? How is it computed?
2. Explain the effect of prior service cost on the projected benefit obligation.
3. What is the rationale for amortizing prior service cost in current and future periods?

Gains and Losses and Component 5 of Pension Expense

Pension accounting is greatly dependent on estimates that must be updated as new information becomes available. For example, PBO reflects estimates of employee turnover. If turnover is greater than expected, PBO is reduced because the estimate of benefit payments is decreased.

Two Sources of Gains and Losses A pension *gain* occurs when (1) a change in actuarial estimate or experience decreases PBO or (2) actual return on plan assets exceeds expected return. The opposite holds true for pension *losses*. Pension gains *decrease* pension expense when recognized because gains reduce the cost of the pension plan to the sponsor. Pension losses similarly *increase* pension expense.

PBO gains and losses are subdivided further into (*a*) experience gains and losses and (*b*) actuarial gains and losses. An experience gain (loss) occurs when actual results are more (less) favorable than planned. For example, greater than expected turnover causes an experience gain. An actuarial gain (loss) occurs when changes in assumptions about future events reduce (increase) PBO. Increasing the discount rate reduces the present value of future payments and causes an actuarial gain.

In each accounting period, the actuary supplies information about PBO gains and losses, and the trustee supplies information about asset gains and losses. The gains and losses from both sources are combined to form a net gain or loss for accounting purposes. The employer amortizes the net gain or loss to periodic pension expense using a systematic and rational approach.

To illustrate the calculation of an actuarial loss, reconsider the Nicole Whitney example from Exhibit 19–4. In that example, Lone Pine used a 10% discount rate to compute PBO at 12/31/92 as follows:

$$PBO, \ 12/31/92 \ = \ \$6,000(PVA,10\%,10)(PV1,10\%,23)$$
$$= \ \$6,000(6.14457)(.11168) \ = \ \underline{\$4,117}$$

At the beginning of January 1993, on the advice of its actuary, Lone Pine reduces the discount rate to 8% based on changing market conditions. PBO is recalculated as follows:

$$PBO, \ 1/1/93 \ = \ \$6,000(PVA,8\%,10)(PV1,8\%,23)$$
$$= \ \$6,000(6.71008)(.17032) \ = \ \underline{\$6,857}$$

The resulting $2,740 actuarial loss is the difference between the original and adjusted PBO ($6,857 − $4,117).

As with PSC, unrecognized gains and losses are subject to delayed recognition. Gains and losses are subject to offset by future losses and gains. For example, future PBO increases from changing life expectancy and turnover can offset previous PBO decreases. Immediate recognition of gains and losses under the time period assumption does not necessarily provide the most relevant information about long-run pension costs. Immediate recognition of the huge losses suffered by many pension funds from the stock market's Black Monday (October 19, 1987) would have greatly increased pension expense for many firms. Within a relatively short time, the market recovered much of its loss.

Calculating Component 5   Gains and losses are combined to form one *net* unrecognized gain or loss at the beginning of each period. Component 5 of pension expense for a period consists of two elements:

Element 1: The difference between expected and actual return on plan assets for the period.

Element 2: Amortization of the net unrecognized gain or loss at the *beginning* of the period.

Although actual return is component 3 of pension expense, the result of including element 1 of component 5 in pension expense is to recognize *expected return* on plan assets, rather than actual return, in pension expense:

Actual return	(Component 3 of pension expense)
+ Expected return − actual return	(Element 1 of component 5 of pension expense)
= Expected return	

This relationship gives rise to two alternative approaches of computing pension expense. The first approach is to use actual return for component 3, and *both* elements of component 5. The second approach is to use expected return for component 3 and only element 2 of component 5. The second approach makes use of the above relationship. Actual return and element 1 combine to yield expected return, leaving only element 2 for the computation of component 5. Refer to Exhibit 19–10 for an example.

Pension expense reflects expected return because actual return in any one period does not represent the long-run return on the fund. This practice reduces the volatility of pension expense. Although *SFAS No. 87* requires disclosure of actual return as a component of pension expense, for simplicity the examples to follow use expected return as component 3 of pension expense, and only the amortization of net unrecognized gain or loss as component 5 (the second approach).

In Exhibit 19–10, the $2,000 excess of expected over actual return in 1991 is an unrecognized loss because plan assets increased less than expected. This amount becomes part of the net unrecognized gain or loss at the end of 1991. It is not amortized in 1991 because it did not occur at the beginning of 1991. The net unrecognized gain at January 1, 1992, subject to amortization in 1992 (and giving rise to element 2 of component 5) is:

Net unrecognized gain, 1/1/91 (Exhibit 19–10)	($21,000)
Amount recognized through amortization, 1991	7,000
Excess of expected over actual return, 1991 (loss)	2,000
Net unrecognized gain, 1/1/92	($12,000)

Amortization Methods   The example in Exhibit 19–10 assumed the amount of amortization of beginning net unrecognized gain in 1991 ($7,000). *SFAS No. 87* specifies minimum amortization of net unrecognized gain or loss if certain conditions are met. Alternatively, any systematic amortization method can be used if it amortizes at least the minimum amount, is applied consistently, and is disclosed.

Minimum Amortization   Amortization is not required if the net unrecognized gain or loss at the *beginning of the period* is within the **corridor**. The corridor bound or amount is 10% of the greater of PBO or fair value of plan assets at the *beginning of the period*. For example, if PBO were $20,000 and fair value of plan assets were $15,000, no amortization is required if the beginning net unrecognized gain or loss is $2,000 or less ($20,000 × .10). The width of the corridor in this case is actually 20% of PBO at the beginning of the period because the net unrecognized amount can vary from a

EXHIBIT 19-10   Component 5 and Two Ways to Compute Pension Expense: White Mountain Company, 1991

Service cost, 1991: $10,000
Interest cost, 1991:   8,000
Actual return on plan assets, 1991: $6,000
Expected long-term rate of return on plan assets: 8%
1991 beginning balance in plan assets at fair value: $100,000
Expected return, 1991: $8,000 ($100,000 × 8%)
Amortization of PSC, 1991: $17,000
Net unrecognized gain, 1/1/91: $21,000 (the remaining unamortized net gain from the two sources of gains and losses occurring before 1991)
Amortization of net unrecognized gain for 1991: $7,000 (this amount is assumed, and it meets the minimum requirements, discussed later)—this is element 2 of component 5

Pension Expense Using Actual Return for Component 3		Pension Expense Using Expected Return for Component 3	
Service cost	$10,000	Service cost	$10,000
Interest cost	8,000	Interest cost	8,000
Actual return	(6,000)	Expected return	(8,000)
Amortization of PSC	17,000	Amortization of PSC	17,000
Recognized gain	(9,000)*	Recognized gain	(7,000)†
Pension expense, 1991	$20,000	Pension expense, 1991	$20,000

* Expected return − actual return . . . . . . ($2,000)   (Element 1 decreases pension expense)
   Amortization of net unrecognized
      gain at 1/1/91 . . . . (7,000)   (Element 2 decreases pension expense)
   Recognized gain, component 5 . . . . ($9,000)

Actual return reduces pension expense by $6,000, but ultimately pension expense reflects *expected return* ($8,000). Therefore, element 1 of component 5 must decrease pension expense an additional $2,000.

† The difference between expected and actual return (Element 1) is automatically included by using *expected return* as component 3. Therefore, only element 2 of component 5 is listed ($7,000).

$2,000 loss to a $2,000 gain, a $4,000 difference, or 20% of PBO, without amortization being required.

If the beginning net unrecognized gain or loss exceeds the 10% corridor amount, the minimum amortization that must be recognized is the difference between the net unrecognized gain or loss and the 10% corridor amount, divided by the average remaining service period of active employees expected to receive benefits under the plan. If all or almost all of a plan's participants are inactive, the average remaining life expectancy of the inactive participants is used.

Alternative Amortization   A common alternative is straight-line amortization, which divides the beginning net unrecognized gain or loss by the average remaining service period. The denominator for both approaches, average remaining service life, is adjusted each year to reflect the changing nature of the employee group. Refer to Exhibit 19-11 for an illustration of both approaches for El Capitan Company.

El Capitan must amortize at least $1,500 of net loss as an increase to pension expense in 1992. Firms have an incentive to amortize large unrecognized gains faster than the minimum, and unrecognized losses at the minimum, to minimize pension expense. The chosen amortization method must be used consistently, however.

If El Capitan chooses minimum amortization, only a very small percentage of the net loss is recognized, allowing gains and losses to offset. For instance, the net unrecognized loss completely absorbs the PBO decrease (gain) in 1992. In many cases, because the corridor is so wide, no amortization is necessary. For example, if the unrecognized net loss on 1/1/92 is $14,000 or less, no amortization is required.[27]

---

[27] In the example, the unrecognized amount could vary from a $14,000 gain to a $14,000 loss (a $28,000 difference, or 20% of $140,000) without requiring amortization.

EXHIBIT 19-11   Two Approaches for Amortization of Beginning Net Unrecognized Gain or Loss: El Capitan Company

---

1991 Information (For simplicity, service cost, interest cost, and PSC are omitted.)

PBO, 1/1/91: $120,000
Fair value of plan assets, 1/1/91: $80,000
Expected long-term rate of return on plan assets: 10%
Expected return on plan assets: $80,000(.10) = $8,000
Actual return, 1991: $12,000
Net unrecognized gain or loss, 1/1/91: $0
Increase in PBO due to change in actuarial assumptions, determined on 12/31/91: $30,000
Average remaining service period of active employees expected to receive benefits under the plan: 8 years
1991 pension expense reflects:

Expected return	($8,000)	($80,000 × .10)
Amortization of net unrecognized gain or loss at beginning of year	0*	
Effect on pension expense	($8,000)	(decrease)

Net unrecognized loss, ending, 1991:

Net unrecognized gain or loss, 1/1/91	0
Loss due to PBO increase	$30,000
Actual return less expected return (gain) $12,000 − $8,000	(4,000)
Net unrecognized loss, 12/31/91	$26,000

1992 Information

PBO, 1/1/92: $140,000
Fair value of plan assets, 1/1/92: $95,000
Actual return on plan assets, 1992: $8,000
Decrease in PBO due to change in actuarial assumptions, determined on 12/31/92: $5,000

Minimum (corridor) amortization, 1992:

Net unrecognized loss, 1/1/92		$26,000	(from 1991)
PBO, 1/1/92	$140,000		
Plan assets, 1/1/92	95,000		
Greater of PBO and plan assets, 1/1/92	140,000		
Corridor amount: (.10 × $140,000)		14,000	
Amount subject to amortization		$12,000	
Minimum (corridor) amortization		$ 1,500	($12,000/8)

Straight-line amortization, 1992:

(Net unrecognized loss, 1/1/92)/8:	$ 3,250	($26,000/8)

Net unrecognized loss, ending (assume corridor amortization) 1992:

Net unrecognized loss, 12/31/91		$26,000
Expected return less actual return, 1992: .10($95,000) − $8,000	(loss)	1,500
PBO decrease, 1992	(gain)	(5,000)
Corridor amortization of net unrecognized loss		(1,500)
Net unrecognized loss, 12/31/92		$21,000†

1992 pension expense reflects (assume corridor amortization):

Expected return	($9,500)	($95,000 × .10)
Corridor amortization of beginning unrecognized loss	1,500	
Effect on pension expense	($8,000)	(decrease)

---

* No net unrecognized gain or loss at 1/1/91.

† Under straight-line amortization, this amount is $1,750 ($3,250 − $1,500) less, or $19,250.

It is possible for an unrecognized gain to offset completely the net unrecognized loss existing at the beginning of a period. If El Capitan's 1992 PBO decrease were $30,000 rather than $5,000, for example, 1993 would begin with an unrecognized net gain. Unrecognized gains and losses, therefore, are not fully amortized in the usual sense.

If the unrecognized gain or loss becomes excessively large, amortization is appropriate and required. PBO and plan assets are used to determine the corridor because gains and losses are changes in these values. Beginning-of-year balances for amortizations are used to reduce the complexity of the computation.

CONCEPT REVIEW

1. What is the rationale for delayed recognition of pension gains and losses?
2. Explain two different measures of the third component of pension expense and how they relate to the fifth component.
3. Explain corridor amortization and how it reduces volatility in pension expense.

Transition Amount and Component 6 of Pension Expense

To reduce the impact of the accounting changes brought about by *SFAS No. 87,* a phase-in period was established. Employers of all affected plans were to comply with the provisions of *SFAS No. 87* for reporting years beginning after December 15, 1986. Under *APB Opinion No. 8* (superseded by *SFAS No. 87*), employers frequently reported a pension asset or liability account similar to accrued or prepaid pension cost under *SFAS No. 87.* The *transition asset or liability* is a bridge between the two pronouncements.

The periodic amortization (under delayed recognition) of this amount is the sixth and final component of pension expense. The sixth component is unique because it results from a transition asset or liability that occurs only once, and after the transition asset or liability is fully amortized, the sixth component no longer appears in pension expense. The transition asset is also called transition gain; the transition liability is also called transition cost.

Transition Asset or Liability The transition asset or liability is the amount that equates the pension asset or liability balance reported under *APB Opinion No. 8* and the plan's funded status at transition:

$$\begin{array}{c} APB\ Opinion\ No.\ 8 \\ \text{account balance} \end{array} + \begin{array}{c} \text{Transition asset} \\ \text{or liability} \end{array} = PBO - \begin{array}{c} \text{Plan assets at} \\ \text{fair value} \end{array}$$

The transition asset or liability for firms with no pension account under *APB Opinion No. 8* at transition equals the plan's funded status at transition. The transition asset or liability affects neither PBO nor plan assets, and is not recognized immediately. The account balance under *APB Opinion No. 8* continues as the accrued or prepaid pension cost account under *SFAS No. 87.* Exhibit 19–12 presents information for several examples.

Example 1 The employer has a $30,000 underfunded plan (PBO − assets) at transition, but is reporting only a $10,000 liability. Therefore, a $20,000 transition liability is required to account for the difference between accrued pension cost ($10,000 liability) and funded status ($30,000 liability). (In the examples, the letter A denotes an asset; L denotes a liability):

$$\$10,000L + \text{Transition amount} = \$30,000L$$
$$\text{Transition amount} = \$30,000L - \$10,000L = \$20,000L$$

EXHIBIT 19-12   Data for Examples: Transition Asset or Liability—Transition Date: January 1, 1987

Amounts at Transition	Example 1	Example 2	Example 3
PBO	$200,000	$1,400,000	$426,000
Assets at fair value	170,000	1,600,000	300,000
APB Opinion No. 8			
asset (liability)	(10,000)	(150,000)	15,000

A T-account also can be used to determine the transition amount, shown in **bold face** type:

Underfunded PBO

APB Opinion No. 8 balance	10,000
Transition liability	**20,000**
Funded status	30,000

The transition amount reconciles funded status and the accrued or prepaid pension cost account at transition.

Example 2   In this example, the employer has an overfunded plan ($200,000 net asset) but is reporting a $150,000 liability (a bullish stock-market in recent years would contribute to such a situation). Therefore, a transition asset of $350,000 is required:

$$\$150,000L + \text{Transition amount} = \$200,000A$$
$$\text{Transition amount} = \$200,000A - \$150,000L = \$350,000A$$

Overfunded PBO

		APB Opinion No. 8 balance	150,000
Transition asset	**350,000**		
Funded status	200,000		

Example 3   In this example, the employer is reporting a $15,000 asset, yet has an underfunded plan. *APB Opinion No. 8* did not require recognition or disclosure of PBO. In certain instances, funding was ahead of expensing (hence the asset account), but the plan remained underfunded. The transition amount is therefore a $141,000 liability:

$$\$15,000A + \text{Transition amount} = \$126,000L$$
$$\text{Transition amount} = \$126,000L - \$15,000A = \$141,000L$$

Underfunded PBO

APB Opinion No. 8 balance	15,000		
		Transition liability	**141,000**
		Funded status	126,000

A transition liability is similar to PSC because it represents the cost of benefits promised *before* transition to *SFAS No. 87,* and often reflects unrecognized past retroactive grants. In the discussion on additional minimum pension liability to follow, the transition liability is treated as if it were unrecognized PSC.

Amortization of Transition Amount The amortization of a transition asset reduces pension expense; the opposite is true for a transition liability. In Example 1, the $10,000 pre-*SFAS No. 87* liability represents $10,000 of recognized, but unfunded, pension expense. The remaining $20,000 of underfunded liability is not yet recognized in expense. Delayed recognition requires amortization rather than immediate recognition. Therefore, pension expense is gradually increased to reflect the additional pension cost not yet recognized.

The transition asset or liability is amortized on a *straight-line basis* over the average remaining service period of employees expected to receive benefits under the plan, beginning in the transition year.[28] If the average period is less than 15 years, the employer can elect to use 15 years for amortization. This provision prevents excessively quick amortization for plans with a short service period. Otherwise, a plan with a four-year average remaining service period (for example) and large transition liability would experience a substantial increase in pension expense during the four years after transition.

In Example 3 ($141,000 transition liability), if the average remaining service period is 10 years, the employer increases 1987 pension expense by one of the following:

$$\text{Amortization based on 10 years:} \quad \$141,000/10 = \underline{\underline{\$14,100}}$$

$$\text{Amortization based on 15 years:} \quad \$141,000/15 = \underline{\underline{\$\ 9,400}}$$

To illustrate component 6 as an integral part of pension expense, the components of pension expense for a firm with the transition amount in Example 3 (using 10 years for amortization) are illustrated below (the remaining values are assumed):

Service cost	$67,000
Interest cost	19,000
Expected return on plan assets	(23,000)
Amortization of PSC	8,000
Amortization of net unrecognized gain	(12,000)
Amortization of unrecognized transition liability	14,100
Pension expense	$73,100

Rationale for Delayed Recognition of Transition Amount The unrecognized transition asset or liability includes some or all of the following amounts existing before transition: unrecognized costs of past retroactive plan amendments, the net unrecognized gain or loss, and the cumulative effect of past accounting standards that were different from *SFAS No. 87*. These factors combined to create large transition liabilities for many firms. Respondents to the exposure draft preceding *SFAS No. 87* argued that immediate recognition of both the liability and resulting expense would adversely affect the perception of these firms in the marketplace. This view was adopted even though delayed recognition runs counter to the retroactive treatment afforded the transition to most new accounting principles.

Yet amortization of transition *assets* is a contributing factor to the general *decline* in pension expense under *SFAS No. 87*. A study of 100 firms employing over 10 million people found that pension expense decreased an average of 64% for those firms adopting the new standard in 1986.[29] McDonnell Douglas's amortization of transition asset was $106 million in 1989, causing it to record $95 million of pension

---

[28] If all or almost all employees are inactive, the inactive participants' average remaining life expectancy is used for amortization.

[29] S. Bleiberg, "Less Than Zero" (in "Pension Fund Perspective"), *Financial Analysts Journal,* March–April, 1988 pp. 13–15.

income (that is, negative pension expense). Without amortization of the transition asset, the company would have recognized $11 million in pension expense.

CONCEPT REVIEW

1. Explain how the transition amount is computed.
2. What does the transition amount represent?
3. How is the transition asset or liability unique among the three pension amounts subject to delayed recognition?

ADDITIONAL MINIMUM PENSION LIABILITY

During the exposure draft phase of *SFAS No. 87,* there was considerable concern about underreporting of pension liabilities. As a compromise measure, *SFAS No. 87* requires recognition of an additional minimum pension liability under certain circumstances. The purpose of this requirement is to increase the *recognized* pension liability when a pension plan is grossly underfunded, and to reduce the volatility of reported pension liabilities. The term *additional* denotes an amount in excess of accrued pension cost. A separate journal entry records the additional minimum pension liability, if necessary, after recording the pension expense entry.

Total Minimum Liability The *total* minimum recognized pension liability is the excess of *ABO* (accumulated benefit obligation) over plan assets at fair value.[30] This amount is also called *underfunded ABO.* Use of ABO is another example of the compromise nature of *SFAS No. 87.* Although future compensation levels are used to compute service cost and pension expense, they are not used for computing the total minimum liability.

Total minimum liability also is an example of offsetting assets and liabilities. The liability is not settled and the employer has ultimate control over plan assets, yet neither is separately recognized.

Additional Minimum Pension Liability An additional minimum pension liability is recognized if total minimum liability exceeds accrued pension cost. For example, additional minimum pension liability for Washington Company at December 31, 1991 (after recording pension expense), is computed as follows (amounts assumed):

ABO	($100,000)
Plan assets at fair value	70,000
Total minimum liability	(30,000)
Balance, accrued pension cost (cr.)	(20,000)
Additional minimum pension liability	($ 10,000)

Washington must recognize $30,000 of total pension liability. Accrued pension cost accounts for $20,000. Therefore, an additional minimum pension liability of $10,000 is recorded. The offsetting debit is recorded in an intangible pension asset account. The intangible is presented with other intangible assets in the balance sheet. The maximum intangible balance is the sum of unrecognized PSC and unrecognized transition liability at the *end* of the year.[31] Excess amounts are debited to unrealized pension cost, a contra equity account.

[30] When market-related value and plan assets at fair value are not equal, plan assets at fair value is used to compute the total minimum liability. When assets exceed ABO, an additional asset is not recorded.

[31] The transition liability often is composed largely of retroactive grants made prior to the adoption of *SFAS No. 87.*

EXHIBIT 19-13   Additional Minimum Pension Liability

WASHINGTON COMPANY
Information for Years 1992–1994:
Continuation of Additional Minimum Pension Liability Example
(Amounts are after recording pension expense)

	Balances and Amounts at Year-End		
	1992	1993	1994
ABO	$130,000	$170,000	$190,000
Assets at fair value	120,000	135,000	185,000
(Accrued) prepaid pension cost	(5,000)	(12,000)	8,000
Unrecognized PSC	4,000	14,000*	12,000

* Result of a new amendment in 1993 (for simplicity, assume no unrecognized transition liability).

Extending the Washington Company example, assume that at the end of 1991, after recording pension expense, the firm has unrecognized PSC of $7,000 (but no transition liability) and no previous intangible pension asset or additional minimum pension liability. The entry to record additional minimum pension liability is:

December 31, 1991—To record additional minimum pension liability:

Intangible pension asset 7,000	
Unrealized pension cost 3,000	
Additional minimum pension liability	10,000

For financial reporting purposes, the additional minimum pension liability and accrued pension cost accounts are combined into one net pension liability. In this case, Washington discloses a net pension liability of $30,000 in its 1991 balance sheet. Separate accounts are maintained only for internal purposes.

Under one interpretation, the intangible asset is the present value of additional benefits to the firm from retroactive benefit grants to employees. Underfunded PSC causes much of the additional minimum pension liability, as reflected in ABO. In theory, the employer obtains long-term benefits from retroactive grants. The intangible reflects this benefit. The intangible is not amortized in the traditional manner, but is reduced as PSC is amortized.

The additional $3,000 recorded in unrealized pension cost represents pension costs not associated with retroactive grants and not yet recognized in pension expense. The requirement of an additional minimum pension liability in excess of unrecognized PSC and transition liability forces the $3,000 amount. Recognition of the additional $3,000 in pension expense would run counter to delayed recognition. The owners' equity account represents the change in the net worth of the company caused by the excess of the liability over the intangible.[32]

Adjusting the Accounts   In subsequent years, the necessary additional minimum pension liability balance determines whether the intangible asset is increased or decreased. Exhibit 19–13 gives information to continue the example.

1992   The relevant beginning balances from 1991 (previous example):

Additional minimum pension liability	$10,000
Intangible pension asset	7,000
Unrealized pension cost	3,000

---

[32] This account is similar to the contra owners' equity account used for decreases in market value below cost of marketable equity securities held as a long-term investment (see Chapter 14).

EXHIBIT 19-14   Additional Minimum Pension Liability

WASHINGTON COMPANY
Additional Minimum Pension Liability Example
Journal Entries for 1993 and 1994:

Balances and Amounts at Beginning of Year	1993	1994
Additional minimum pension liability	$5,000	$23,000
Intangible pension asset	4,000	14,000
Unrealized pension cost	1,000	9,000

Adjustment to Additional Minimum Pension Liability

ABO	($170,000)	($190,000)
Plan assets at fair value	135,000	185,000
Total minimum liability	(35,000)	(5,000)
Balance, (accrued) prepaid pension cost	(12,000)	8,000
Required balance, additional minimum pension liability	(23,000)	(13,000)*
Current balance, additional minimum pension liability	(5,000)	(23,000)
(Increase) decrease, additional minimum pension liability	($ 18,000)	$ 10,000
Balance in net pension liability, in balance sheet	$ 35,000	$ 5,000†

December 31, 1993—To record additional minimum pension liability:

Intangible pension asset	10,000	
Unrealized pension cost	8,000	
Additional minimum pension liability		18,000

December 31, 1994—To record additional minimum pension liability:

Additional minimum pension liability	10,000	
Intangible pension asset		2,000‡
Unrealized pension cost		8,000

* Net liability of $5,000 is required. Prepaid pension cost of $8,000 exists at this date. Therefore, $13,000 of additional minimum pension liability is required.

† It is possible to have a prepaid pension cost account and an additional minimum pension liability account. This could be caused, for example, by large unrecognized losses (PBO increases) or poor return on plan assets.

‡ Intangible balance is not to exceed the lower of unrecognized PSC ($12,000) or additional minimum pension liability ($13,000) at year-end. Therefore the intangible is reduced to $12,000.

The necessary adjustment to additional minimum pension liability is as follows:

ABO	($130,000)
Plan assets at fair value	120,000
Total minimum liability	(10,000)
Balance, accrued pension cost (cr.)	(5,000)
Required balance, additional minimum pension liability	(5,000)
Current balance, additional minimum pension liability	(10,000)
Required reduction, additional minimum pension liability	$ 5,000

December 31, 1992—To record additional minimum pension liability:

Additional minimum pension liability	5,000	
Intangible pension asset		3,000
Unrealized pension cost		2,000

The maximum balance in the intangible asset account is $4,000, the lower of unrecognized PSC ($4,000) and required balance in the additional minimum pension liability ($5,000). Thus, the intangible is reduced $3,000 to an ending balance of $4,000. The ending 1992 account balances are:

Additional minimum pension liability . . . . . $5,000 ($10,000 − $5,000)
Intangible pension asset . . . . 4,000 ($ 7,000 − $3,000)
Unrealized pension cost . . . . 1,000 ($ 3,000 − $2,000)

Washington reports a $10,000 net pension liability ($5,000 accrued pension cost plus $5,000 additional minimum pension liability) in its 1992 balance sheet. Exhibit 19–14 presents the results for 1993 and 1994.

CONCEPT REVIEW

1. Explain the relationship between total minimum liability and additional minimum pension liability.
2. What is the maximum intangible pension asset account balance?
3. Interpret unrealized pension cost.

COMPREHENSIVE CASE AND PENSION ISSUES

♦

This section presents a three-year case showing how pension accounts and unrecognized amounts change over time. A fifth column is added to the spreadsheet for the beginning and ending unrecognized amount balances, changes during the year, and amortizations.

On January 1, 1989, the Owens Valley Company makes the transition to *SFAS No. 87* for its noncontributory defined benefit pension plan. On that date, Owens Valley has a $10,000 accrued pension liability. Refer to Exhibit 19–15, which presents the required information for years 1989 through 1991. Exhibits 19–16 through 19–18 are the completed pension spreadsheets.

1989   The actuary supplies the beginning PBO, and the trustee's report is the source of plan assets at fair value. The employer provides the unrecognized pension cost and unrecognized transition liability amounts. The pension expense column has six entries corresponding to the six pension expense components. The last column, accrued or prepaid pension cost, starts with the beginning balance. Additional minimum pension liability is determined outside the spreadsheet.

For ease of illustration, expected return is used as component 3 of pension expense. Component 5 is the amortization of beginning unrecognized gain or loss. The beginning and ending balance in the unrecognized pension cost column is the net sum of all three unrecognized amounts. The beginning balance does not enter into the calculation of the ending balance. For example, the 1989 ending net balance, $8,333, is the net sum of the $1,000 unrecognized gain and $9,333 unrecognized transition liability (Exhibit 19–16). The ending balances of the three unrecognized amounts are netted to form the beginning balance of unrecognized pension cost for the next period.

Refer to Exhibit 19–16. The transition liability is amortized beginning in 1989 because the amount is known at the beginning of the year. The unrecognized $1,000 gain on assets is not amortized until 1990. Owens Valley records the following entry:

December 31, 1989—Record pension expense:

Pension expense 42,667
    Accrued pension cost 6,667
    Cash 36,000

The spreadsheet automatically reflects the reconciliation of funded status, both at the beginning and end of the period. At the beginning of 1989, the funded status

EXHIBIT 19-15   Information for Three-Year Pension Case

OWENS VALLEY COMPANY
Pension Plan Information

APB Opinion No. 8 accrued pension liability, 1/1/89: $10,000
Transition date: 1/1/89

From Actuary's Report	1989	1990	1991
Discount rate used by actuary	10%	10%	10%
Rate of compensation increase	6%	6%	6%
Average remaining service period of employees (years).	10	10	12
PBO, January 1	$100,000	$120,000	$194,000
Service cost	40,000	50,000	60,000
Interest cost (10% of PBO at Jan. 1)	10,000	14,000*	19,400
PSC (determined January 1)		20,000	
Actuarial loss (December 31)†		30,000	
Experience gain (December 31)‡			(12,000)
Benefit payments to retirees	(30,000)	(40,000)	(40,000)
PBO, December 31	$120,000	$194,000	$221,400
ABO, December 31	$ 96,000	167,000	177,000
VBO, December 31	42,000	67,000	125,000

From Trustee Report			
Expected long-term rate of return on plan assets	10%	9%	8%
Plan assets at fair value, January 1	$ 80,000	$ 95,000	$116,000
Actual return on plan assets	9,000	11,000	8,200
Contributions by Owens Valley (end of year)	36,000	50,000	55,000
Benefit payments to retirees (end of year)	(30,000)	(40,000)	(40,000)
Plan assets at fair value, December 31	$ 95,000	$116,000	$139,200
Expected return on plan assets (rate of return × beginning asset balance):	$ 8,000	$ 8,550	$ 9,280

Company Assumptions

The net unrecognized gain or loss is amortized on the straight-line basis.
Unrecognized PSC is amortized over the average remaining service period at date of grant.
Unrecognized net gain or loss is amortized over average remaining service period.
Transition amount is amortized over 15 years.

---

* Includes PSC determined 1/1/90: .10($120,000 + $20,000) = $14,000.

† Increase in life expectancy estimates.

‡ Increase in actual turnover, relative to previous expectations.

($20,000 liability) and the $10,000 accrued pension cost account are reconciled by the $10,000 transition liability. At the end of 1989, underfunded PBO ($25,000) less net unrecognized pension cost ($8,333) yields the ending accrued pension cost balance ($16,667).

No additional minimum pension liability is required at the end of 1989. Plan assets are nearly sufficient to cover ABO, as shown in the following schedule:

ABO, 12/31/89	$96,000
Plan assets at fair value, 12/31/89	95,000
Total minimum liability	1,000
Balance, accrued pension cost, 12/31/89	16,667*
Required additional minimum pension liability	$ 0

* $10,000 (bal. 1/1/89) + $6,667 (from above entry).

EXHIBIT 19-16 Spreadsheet

OWENS VALLEY COMPANY
Pension Plan Spreadsheet, 1989

Transition Liability, 1/1/89:

$$APB \text{ } Opinion \text{ } No. \text{ } 8 \text{ account} + \text{Transition amount} = \text{PBO} - \text{Plan assets}$$
$$\$10,000L + \text{Transition amount} = \$100,000 - \$80,000$$
$$\$10,000L + \text{Transition amount} = \$20,000L$$
$$\text{Transition amount} = \$10,000L$$

	PBO (Actuary)	Plan Assets (Trustee)	Unrecognized Pension Cost	Pension Expense	Accrued Pension Cost
Balances, 1/1/89	$100,000	$80,000	$10,000		($10,000)*
Service cost	$ 40,000			$40,000	
Interest cost	10,000			10,000	
Expected return				(8,000)	
Unrecognized loss:					
Beginning balance			0		
1989 amortization			0†		
Change from assets			G 1,000‡		
Ending balance			G 1,000		
Unrecognized transition liability:					
Beginning balance			L 10,000		
1989 amortization			(667)§	667	
Ending balance			L 9,333		
Actual return		9,000			
Contributions		36,000			36,000
Benefits paid	(30,000)	(30,000)			
Ending balances:					
PBO	$120,000				
Plan assets		$95,000			
Underfunded PBO	$25,000				
Unrecognized pension costs			$8,333‖		
Pension expense				$42,667	(42,667)
Accrued pension cost					($16,667)

Note: L = loss, liability or cost; G = gain or asset.

* Account balance under *APB Opinion No. 8*.

† No beginning unrecognized gain or loss; therefore, no amortization.

‡ Actual return ($9,000) − expected return ($8,000).

§ $10,000/15 = $667.

‖ $9,333 − $1,000

1990 Refer to Exhibit 19-17. The ending balances from 1989 carry over to 1990. The actuarial loss increases PBO and results in a net unrecognized loss at the end of 1990. The net unrecognized loss at the end of 1990 reflects the unamortized difference between actual and expected return in 1990. Component 5 of pension expense is restricted to amortization of the beginning $1,000 gain. Owens Valley records pension expense as follows:

December 31, 1990—Record pension expense:

Pension expense	58,017	
Accrued pension cost		8,017
Cash		50,000

EXHIBIT 19-17 Spreadsheet

OWENS VALLEY COMPANY
Pension Plan Spreadsheet, 1990

	PBO (Actuary)	Plan Assets (Trustee)	Unrecognized Pension Cost	Pension Expense	Accrued Pension Cost
Balances, 1/1/90	$120,000	$ 95,000	$ 8,333		($16,667)
Service cost	50,000			$50,000	
Interest cost	14,000			14,000	
Expected return				(8,550)	
Unrecognized PSC:					
Beginning balance	20,000		L 20,000		
1990 amortization			(2,000)*	2,000	
Ending balance			L 18,000		
Unrecognized loss:					
Beginning balance			G (1,000)		
1990 amortization			100†	(100)	
Change from assets			G (2,450)‡		
Actuarial loss	30,000		L 30,000		
Ending balance			L 26,650§		
Unrecognized transition liability:					
Beginning balance			L 9,333		
1990 amortization			(667)‖	667	
Ending balance			L 8,666		
Actual return		11,000			
Contributions		50,000			50,000
Benefits paid	(40,000)	(40,000)			
Ending balances:					
PBO	$194,000				
Plan assets		$116,000			
Underfunded PBO		$ 78,000			
Unrecognized pension costs			$53,316**		
Pension expense				$58,017	(58,017)
Accrued pension cost					($24,684)

Note: L = loss, liability or cost; G = gain or asset.

* ($20,000 beginning PSC)/(10 year service life at date of grant)

† ($1,000 unrecognized gain at 1/1/90) /10 = $100. Corridor amortization: 10% of greater of PBO, assets at 1/1/90 = .10($120,000) = $12,000. This amount exceeds the unrecognized gain; minimum amortization = 0. Owens amortizes unrecognized gains and losses on the straight-line basis rather than amortize the minimum amount.

‡ Actual return ($11,000) − expected return ($8,550) = $2,450G.

§ This is an example of beginning the year with a gain, ending with a loss.

‖ ($10,000 initial transition liability) /15 = $667.

** $18,000 + $26,650 + $8,666

Additional minimum pension liability is required in 1990:

ABO, 12/31/90	$167,000
Plan assets at fair value, 12/31/90	116,000
Total minimum liability	51,000
Balance, accrued pension cost, 12/31/90	24,684*
Required additional minimum pension liability	26,316
Current balance, additional minimum pension liability	0
Required increase, additional minimum pension liability	$ 26,316

* $24,684 = $16,667 (bal. 1/1/90) + $8,017 (from above entry).

The maximum intangible asset allowed, $26,666, is the sum of unrecognized PSC ($18,000) and unrecognized transition liability ($8,666) at the end of the year. This amount exceeds the required additional minimum pension liability; therefore, unrealized pension cost is not recorded. The following entry records the additional minimum pension liability:

December 31, 1990—Record additional minimum pension liability:

Intangible pension asset	26,316	
Additional minimum pension liability		26,316

The net pension liability reported in the balance sheet is $51,000.

1991 Refer to Exhibit 19–18. As a result of the spreadsheet analysis, Owens records the following entries at the end of 1991:

December 31, 1991—Record pension expense:

Pension expense	$75,008	
Accrued pension cost		20,008
Cash		55,000

December 31, 1991—Reduce additional minimum pension liability:

Additional minimum pension liability	26,316	
Intangible pension asset		26,316

The second entry, which reduces the additional minimum pension liability and intangible to zero, is based on the following schedule:

ABO, 12/31/91	$177,000
Plan assets at fair value, 12/31/91	139,200
Total minimum liability	37,800
Balance, accrued pension cost, 12/31/91	44,692*
Required additional minimum pension liability	0
Current balance, additional minimum pension liability	26,316
Required decrease, additional minimum pension liability	$ 26,316

* $44,692 = $24,684 (bal. 1/1/91) + $20,008 (from above entry).

Pension expense increased considerably in 1991 without a corresponding funding increase. Therefore, accrued pension cost increased enough to eliminate the need for the additional minimum pension liability.

Financial Statement Disclosures Owens Valley discloses the following account balances related to pensions in its financial statements. Long-term classification for pension liabilities is assumed. Owens Valley does not plan to increase funding in the near future.

	1989	1990	1991
Income statement:			
Pension expense (a component of an operating expense such as cost of goods sold, or wages and salaries)	$42,667	$58,017	$75,008
Balance sheet:			
Intangible assets: Intangible pension asset	0	26,316	0
Long-term liabilities: Net pension liability	16,667	51,000	44,692
Owners' equity: Unrecognized pension cost	0	0	0

EXHIBIT 19-18 Spreadsheet

OWENS VALLEY COMPANY
Pension Plan Spreadsheet, 1991

	PBO (Actuary)	Plan Assets (Trustee)	Unrecognized Pension Cost	Pension Expense	Accrued Pension Cost
Balances, 1/1/91	$194,000	$116,000	$53,316		($24,684)
Service cost	$60,000			$60,000	
Interest cost	19,400			19,400	
Expected return				(9,280)	
Unrecognized PSC:					
Beginning balance			L 18,000		
1991 amortization			(2,000)*	2,000	
Ending balance			L 16,000		
Unrecognized loss:					
Beginning balance			L 26,650		
1991 amortization			(2,221)†	2,221	
Change from assets			L 1,080‡		
Experience gain	(12,000)		G (12,000)		
Ending balance			L 13,509		
Unrecognized transition liability:					
Beginning balance			L 8,666		
1991 amortization			(667)§	667	
Ending balance			L 7,999		
Actual return		8,200			
Contributions		55,000			55,000
Benefits paid	(40,000)	(40,000)			
Ending balances:					
PBO	$221,400				
Plan assets		$139,200			
Underfunded PBO	$82,200				
Unrecognized pension costs . . .			$37,508 ‖		
Pension expense				$75,008	(75,008)
Accrued pension cost					($44,692)

Note: L = loss, liability or cost; G = gain or asset.

* ($20,000 beginning PSC)/(10 year service life at date of grant) = $2,000.

† $26,650/12 = $2,221. Corridor amortization: 10% of greater of PBO, assets at 1/1/91 = .10($194,000) = $19,400. Excess of unrealized loss over corridor threshold = $26,650 − $19,400 = $7,250. Minimum amortization = $7,250/12 = $604. Owens chooses to amortize more than the minimum.

‡ Expected return ($9,280) − actual return ($8,200) = $1,080 L.

§ ($10,000 initial transition liability)/15 = $667.

‖ $16,000 + $13,509 + $7,999

Required Footnote Disclosures for Defined Benefit Plans In addition to the required balance sheet and income statement account balances, *SFAS No. 87* specifies *five* categories of required disclosures for defined benefit plans. These are illustrated for Owens Valley by fiscal year. The spreadsheet provides most of the required quantitative information.

1. Description of the pension plan:
    a. Employees covered: all employees with at least one year of full-time employment.
    b. Type of benefit formula: defined benefit, final-pay formula—retirees are paid benefits based on years of service and final salary.
    c. Funding policy: annual contributions to approximate ERISA minimum standards are sent to the trustee. Basic investment policy: 55% equity securities, 30% debt securities, and 15% other investments. (Owens Valley does not meet the minimum standard in 1989 and 1991 because funding is less than service cost in those years.)
    d. Nature and effect of significant matters affecting comparability of information for all periods presented: none.

2. Amount of pension expense for each period with separate disclosure of service cost, interest cost, actual return on plan assets, and the net total of other components. (Actual return is a required disclosure. Therefore, both elements of component 5 appear in "net total of other components.")

	1989	1990	1991
Service cost	$40,000	$50,000	$60,000
Interest cost	10,000	14,000	19,400
Actual return on plan assets	(9,000)	(11,000)	(8,200)
Net total of other components	1,667*	5,017†	3,808‡
Pension expense	$42,667	$58,017	$75,008

Note: L = liability or loss; G = gain or asset.

* Component 5:		
Unrecognized gain (assets)		1,000 L[33]
Amortization of transition liability		667 L
		$1,667 L

† Amortization of PSC		$2,000 L
Component 5:		
Unrecognized gain (assets)	2,450 L	
Amortization, previous gain	100 G	2,350 L
Amortization of transition liability		667 L
		$5,017 L

‡ Amortization of PSC		$2,000 L
Component 5:		
Unrecognized loss (assets)	1,080 G	
Amortization, previous loss	2,221 L	1,141 L
Amortization of transition liability		667 L
		$3,808 L

3. A schedule reconciling the funded status of the plan with amounts reported in the employer's balance sheet showing separately (a) plan assets at fair value, (b) PBO, (c) unrecognized PSC, (d) amount of unrecognized net gain or loss, (e) unrecognized transition asset or liability, (f) additional minimum pension liability, and (g) the amount of net pension asset or liability recognized in the balance sheet.

---

[33] From the earlier discussion, the gain is listed as a loss in this schedule because actual return (component three) reduced pension expense by $1,000 more than expected return. To compensate, pension expense is increased by $1,000. Hence the loss.

	1989	1990	1991
Vested benefit obligation	($42,000)	($67,000)	($125,000)
Accumulated benefit obligation	(96,000)	(167,000)	(177,000)
Projected benefit obligation	(120,000)	(194,000)	(221,400)
Plan assets at fair value	95,000	116,000	139,200
Underfunded PBO (funded status)	(25,000)	(78,000)	(82,200)
Unrecognized PSC	0	18,000	16,000
Unrecognized (gain), loss	(1,000)	26,650	13,509
Unrecognized transition liability	9,333	8,666	7,999
Accrued pension cost	(16,667)	(24,684)	(44,692)
Additional minimum pension liability	0	(26,316)	0
Net pension liability, disclosed in balance sheet	($16,667)	($51,000)	($ 44,692)

4. The assumed weighted average discount rate (10% each year) and rate of compensation increase (6% each year) used to measure PBO, and the weighted average expected long-term rate of return on plan assets (10%, 9%, 8% from 1989 through 1991).

5. Amounts and types of employer securities included in plan assets (none).

Note disclosures provide information not recorded in the accounts and help compensate for the effects of delayed recognition. Information about funding policies helps users assess the future cash flow aspects of the plan. The disaggregation of pension expense clarifies the nature of pension cost. In particular, for most plans, pension expense does not equal the amount funded during the period or the increase in cost attributable to benefits earned in the period.

The breakdown of pension liabilities into PBO, ABO, VBO, and net pension liability allows a more comprehensive appraisal of the effect of pension liabilities on the riskiness of the employer. Disclosure of the assumptions under which pension expense and liabilities are measured also aids in the assessment of pension cost and obligation.

Other Pension Disclosures

Multiple Pension Plans   When an employer sponsors more than one plan, *SFAS No. 87* is applied separately to each. Unless the employer has the right to commingle funds, assets and liabilities of each plan are not offset.

Annuity Contracts   A *pension annuity contract* is a contract between an employer and an insurance company that unconditionally requires the insurance company to provide pension benefits for a fixed fee or premium. The contract must be irrevocable and transfer the risk of the pension plan to the insurance company. If the contract covers all the benefits for a service period, service cost equals the periodic contract cost. Benefits covered by contracts are excluded from the employer's pension liabilities, and annuity contracts are excluded from plan assets.

Multiemployer Plans   Many employers participate in a *multiemployer pension plan* in which contributions are commingled and used for retirees of all participating companies. Pension expense equals the required annual contribution to the plan. Liabilities are recognized only to the extent of unpaid contributions. Employers are required to disclose a description of the plan along with information on the benefits provided, and the effect of significant matters on comparability of information for all periods presented.

Disclosures for Defined Contribution Plans   The following disclosures are required for employers with defined contribution plans:
* A description of the plan, employee groups covered, basis for determining contributions, and information affecting the comparability of information for all periods presented.
* The amount of cost (expense) recognized during the period.

SFAS No. 87: A Compromise

SFAS No. 87 was adopted after lengthy debate. The four to three vote by the FASB reflects the controversial nature of the subject. The Board rejected the notion that the pension plan bears the obligation for pension benefits and retained the concept that plan assets are controlled by the employer. The FASB noted the frequent raiding of excess assets by employers as support for this view (see the next section for a discussion). However, the Board was unwilling to mandate recognition of PBO and assets in the balance sheet.

Certain board members believed the use of a market-related asset value and the expected rate of return allow too much flexibility in the measurement of pension expense. The resulting lack of comparability and uniformity runs counter to the objectives of *SFAS No. 87*. Other members noted the inconsistency of requiring an additional minimum pension liability but not permitting an additional pension asset.

The Board acknowledged that delayed recognition excludes current and relevant information from the employer's balance sheet. For most plans, underfunded PBO is not recognized in the balance sheet. The FASB concluded that immediate recognition of unrecognized pension amounts is impractical, and too great a departure from previous accounting principles. However, accrued pension cost, additional minimum pension liability, and expanded footnote disclosures mitigate (to a degree) the effects of delayed recognition. At a minimum, underfunded ABO is disclosed in the balance sheet. Furthermore, although delayed recognition reduces the volatility of pension expense, it does not affect disclosure of PBO or plan assets in the footnotes.

Certain reporting effects are unintended. For example, some plans with assets in excess of PBO disclose a liability. When the pension fund assets increase in value faster than expected, gains are recognized only on a delayed basis. Therefore, pension expense is larger than under immediate recognition of these gains. Under these circumstances, the firm might reduce its contributions, thereby increasing accrued pension cost. The gradual amortization of a transition asset adds to this effect.

The opportunities for income manipulation under *APB Opinion No. 8* are not completely eliminated by *SFAS No. 87*. Future salaries, the expected rate of return on plan assets, and the discount rate are variables that can be adjusted for desired income effect. For example, a study found that the profitability of a company and the rate used for discounting pension obligations are inversely related. Firms with lower profitability chose higher discount rates resulting in lower pension obligations.[34]

Although *SFAS No. 87* does not satisfy everyone, many believe that incremental progress is the best overall strategy for achieving quality accounting principles. Large-scale changes often are unacceptable to constituents. The FASB believes that pension accounting will continue to evolve.

---

[34] Z. Bodie, J. Light, R. Morck, and R. Taggart, Jr., "Corporate Pension Policy: An Empirical Investigation," *Financial Analysts Journal*, September–October 1985, pp. 10–16.

Pension Terminations and Asset Reversions

A pension asset reversion occurs when an employer with an overfunded pension plan withdraws excess assets for purposes other than paying pension benefits. A pension plan must be terminated, and accumulated employee benefits must be satisfied through payment or purchase of an insurance company annuity before assets are reverted.

Asset reversions were prevalent in the 1980s. The bull market increased the market value of many pension funds well beyond the pension obligation. Increases in interest rates lowered the cost of insurance company annuities purchased when plans were terminated and assets reverted. In certain cases, asset reversions supplied the cash needed to service the higher debt levels resulting from corporate takeovers.

In the period 1980 to 1989, 1,897 defined benefit pension plans, each with more than $1 million in excess assets, were terminated. The employer companies recovered $19.9 billion in excess assets after purchase of retirement annuities from insurance companies. Reversions reached a peak in 1985, during which 582 plans were reverted.[35] Asset reversions became a matter of public concern in the 1980s. Plan terminations reduced the number of healthy contributors to the Pension Benefit Guaranty Corporation. Legislation was introduced in Congress to limit asset reversions.

The fundamental question underlying asset reversions is: Who owns the excess—the sponsoring company or the employees? Those opposed to asset reversions argue that the fund belongs to the participants, and excess funds should be maintained as a cushion against leaner times. They maintain that reversions reduce the security of the plan and lower employee morale.[36] In addition, nonvested benefits become vested on termination, raising the ultimate cost of the pension plan by the amount of benefits that would otherwise be forfeited through normal turnover.

Those in favor of reversions argue that ERISA allows the employer to remove excess funds. Legally, the company's responsibility to employees ends when the employer extinguishes the liability by purchasing an annuity. In addition, investing the pension surplus in productive assets increases U.S. employment. Furthermore, restricting access to excess funds could contribute to a decline in the voluntary nature of pension plans. Employers can also reduce funding levels to offset the restrictions. A 1986 Department of Labor study of 97 pension-plan terminations found that no loss of benefits occurred to participants as a result of reversions.[37]

SUMMARY OF KEY POINTS

♦

(L.O. 1)   1. There are two basic types of pension plans. Employers bear the risk of providing the specified retirement benefit in a defined benefit plan. A benefit formula defines the amount of retirement benefit. Vested benefits are not contingent on future employment. The employer's responsibility ends with the contribution in defined contribution plans.

(L.O. 1)   2. An overfunded plan is one with assets in excess of the benefit obligation. In an underfunded plan, the pension obligation exceeds assets. ERISA and the PBGC play an important role in regulating pension plans and protecting employee

---

[35] "The Battle Over Pension Surpluses," *Nation's Business,* August 1989, pp. 66–67.

[36] "Overfunded Plans," *Financial Executive,* November, 1986, p. 29–30.

[37] "The Battle over Pension Surpluses," *Nation's Business,* August 1989, pp. 66–67.

benefits. The actuary provides much of the data for measuring pension expense and liabilities. The actuary uses present value analysis and estimates of life expectancy, turnover, retirement age, future compensation levels, interest rates, and other variables in measuring a plan's cost and obligations.

(L.O. 2) 3. Pension expense is based on attribution of benefits to periods of employee service as measured by the benefit formula. The six elements of pension expense are service cost, interest cost, actual return, amortization of prior service cost, gain or loss to the extent recognized, and amortization of unrecognized transition asset or liability.

(L.O. 2) 4. Service cost, component 1 of pension expense, is the actuarial present value of pension benefits attributed by the benefit formula to services rendered in a period. It is the increase in projected benefit obligation during the period, exclusive of plan amendments, interest cost, and gains or losses.

(L.O. 2) 5. Interest cost, component 2 of pension expense, is the growth in projected benefit obligation due to the passage of time. It is the product of the discount rate and beginning projected benefit obligation.

(L.O. 2) 6. Actual return on plan assets, component 3 of pension expense, generally reduces pension expense. Actual return, and employer and employee contributions are the sources of plan assets, measured at fair value. Actual return consists of interest, dividends, and realized and unrealized changes in fair value of plan assets.

(L.O. 3) 7. *SFAS No. 87* requires disclosure of three liability measures. Projected benefit obligation is the actuarial present value of all benefits attributed by the formula to employee service rendered to date using future compensation levels if incorporated by the benefit formula. Projected benefit obligation is the fundamental measure of the pension liability. The difference between projected benefit obligation and fair value of plan assets is the plan's funded status.

(L.O. 3) 8. Accumulated benefit obligation is the actuarial present value of all benefits attributed by the formula to employee service rendered to date, but is based on current compensation levels. Accumulated benefit obligation is one measure of the obligation if the plan is terminated. It is the basis for additional minimum pension liability.

(L.O. 3) 9. Vested benefit obligation is the actuarial present value of vested benefits. It is the investment required to satisfy all vested benefits.

(L.O. 3) 10. The change for the period in accrued or prepaid pension cost is the difference between the amount funded and pension expense. The balance in accrued or prepaid pension cost does not equal the plan's funded status except under very restrictive conditions.

(L.O. 4) 11. Prior service cost, gains and losses, and transition asset (or liability) are not recognized immediately in pension expense or recorded in balance sheet accounts. Rather, to reduce volatility in the measurement of pension expense and liabilities, they are gradually recognized through amortization.

(L.O. 4) 12. Prior service cost is the present value of benefits granted for service rendered before the plan's inception or before a plan amendment date. Gains and losses result from changes in projected benefit obligation and differences between actual and expected return. Transition asset or liability is the difference between the pension asset or liability under *APB Opinion No. 8* and the plan's funded status at the date of adopting *SFAS No. 87*.

(L.O. 4) 13. The reconciliation of funded status highlights the delayed recognition concept in pension accounting. The funded status is critically important for the evaluation of a pension plan. The reconciliation explains why the balance sheet account does not equal funded status, and it discloses the remaining unrecognized pension cost amounts.

(L.O. 5)   14. When accumulated benefit obligation exceeds plan assets at fair value, the employer must disclose this difference in the balance sheet as a liability. This is accomplished by combining additional minimum pension liability and accrued or prepaid pension cost. When the additional minimum pension liability is recorded, an intangible pension asset also is recorded.

(L.O. 6)   15. Postretirement benefits other than pensions include health and insurance coverage for retirees. Accounting for postretirement benefits is similar to accounting for pensions, although there are significant measurement and reporting differences.

(L.O. 7)   16. Pension plan settlements, curtailments, and termination benefits are events that require immediate recognition of gains or losses.

(L.O. 8)   17. Pension plans are subject to separate accounting and reporting guidelines. The value of accumulated benefits of participants is treated as the equity of the pension plan, and equals the plan assets at fair value less plan liabilities.

REVIEW PROBLEM
◆

Each of the following five independent cases illustrates a different aspect of pension accounting:

1. *Present value: computation of pension expense, projected benefit obligation, and accumulated benefit obligation.* Raymond is a participant in a pension plan. Information on the plan, and Raymond's involvement follow:

> Plan inception: 1/1/91
> Funding: $3,000 per year for the first 3 years (end of year payments)
> Raymonds's first day with the company: 1/1/91
> Raymond's expected service period: 20 years
> Raymond's expected final salary: $100,000
> Retirement period: 10 years
> Raymond's salary for 1991, 1992: $30,000
> Discount rate, expected return rate, actual return rate: 10%
> Pension benefit formula: Yearly benefit during retirement =
> (number of years worked) (final salary)/25

Required:

a. Compute pension expense for 1991.
b. Compute accumulated benefit obligation at 12/31/92.
c. Compute projected benefit obligation at 12/31/92.

2. *Six components of pension expense.* The following data relate to a defined benefit pension plan:

> PBO 1/1/91, not including any items below $20,000
> Actuary's discount rate 8%
> PSC from amendment dated 1/1/91 (10 years is
>   the amortization period) 10,000
> Unrecognized transition liability, original initial
>   value: $5,000 at 1/1/89, the transition date,
>   unrecognized amount at 1/1/91   4,000
> Gain from change in actuarial assumptions,
>   computed as of 1/1/91, straight-line
>   amortization, 15 year period   3,000
> Actual return on plan assets, 1991   2,000
> Fair value of plan assets 1/1/91 16,000
> Long-run expected rate of return on plan assets 10%
> Contributions to plan assets in 1991   4,000
> Benefits paid to retirees in 1991   5,000
> Service cost for 1991   9,000

Required:

a. Compute pension expense for 1991.

b. Compute PBO at 1/1/92.

c. Compute fair value of plan assets at 1/1/92.

3. *Unrecognized gains and losses*. Mountain Oak Company presents the following information related to its pension plan, for 1991, before recording pension expense.

Projected benefit obligation, 1/1/91	$300,000
Net unrecognized gain, 1/1/91	12,000
Actuarial loss, determined at 12/31/91	4,000
Plan assets at fair value, 1/1/91	280,000
Expected long-term rate of return	10%
Plan assets at fair value, 12/31/91	295,000
1991 contribution to pension fund	10,000
Benefits paid in 1991	15,000
Average remaining service period of employees	20 years
Projected benefit obligation, 12/31/91	325,000

Required:

a. Determine the amortization of the unrecognized gain for 1991, using (1) corridor or minimum amortization and (2) straight-line amortization based on average remaining service period.

b. Determine the unrecognized gain or loss at 1/1/92, assuming straight-line amortization.

c. Determine component 5 of pension expense, for 1991 (amortization of unrecognized gain, and difference between expected and actual return), assuming straight-line amortization.

d. For 1991, provide computations that illustrate that both actual and expected return lead to the same effect on pension expense; use the results from *c*. above.

e. Amortization of unrecognized gain or loss, for 1992, assuming straight-line amortization.

4. *Additional minimum pension liability*. At the end of 1991, after recording pension expense but before determining the change in additional minimum pension liability, Furnace Company has the following balances in its ledger accounts for its pension plan:

	12/31/91
Intangible pension asset	$ 6,000 dr.
Unrecognized pension cost	8,000 dr.
Accrued pension cost account	18,000 cr.
Additional minimum pension liability	14,000 cr.

Unrecognized PSC remaining at 12/31/91 is $4,000 after recognizing pension expense for 1991. Also at 12/31/91, PBO is $98,000, ABO is $72,000 and plan assets at fair value are $48,000.

Required:

Record the entry to adjust additional minimum pension liability.

5. *Transition asset or liability*. The following pension-related values are measured at date of transition to *SFAS No. 87:*

PBO	$100,000
ABO	60,000
Plan assets at fair value	80,000
APB Opinion No. 8 pension asset balance	30,000

Required:

Determine the transition asset or liability.

SOLUTION

◆

1. *a.* Benefit based on future salary levels, earned in 1991:

$$1(\$100,000)/25 = \$4,000$$

Pension expense, 1991 = Service cost, 1991 =
$\$4,000(PVA,10\%,10)(PV1,10\%,19) =$
$\$4,000(6.14457).16351 = \$4,019$

b. Benefits based on current salary levels, earned through 1992:

$$2(\$30,000)/25 = \$2,400$$

Accumulated benefit obligation =
$\$2,400(PVA,10\%,10)(PV1,10\%,18) =$
$\$2,400(6.14457)(.17986) = \$2,652$

c. Benefits based on future salary levels, earned through 1992:

$$2(\$100,000)/25 = \$8,000$$

Projected benefit obligation =
$\$8,000(PVA,10\%,10)(PV1,10\%,18) =$
$\$8,000(6.14457)(.17986) = \$8,841$

2. *a.* Pension expense, 1991:

Service cost	$ 9,000
Interest cost (.08 × $27,000)*	2,160
Expected return (.10 × $16,000)	(1,600)
Amortization of PSC $10,000/10	1,000
Amortization of unrecognized gain $3,000/15	(200)
Amortization of transition liability	500†
Pension expense, 1991	$10,860

* $27,000 = $20,000 + $10,000 (PSC) − $3,000 (gain).

† From the information given, ($5,000 − $4,000)/2.

b. PBO, 1/1/92:

PBO, 1/1/91	$20,000
PSC	10,000
Actuarial gain	(3,000)
Revised PBO, 1/1/91	27,000
Interest cost [.08($27,000)]	2,160
Service cost, 1991	9,000
Benefits paid, 1991	(5,000)
PBO, 1/1/92	$33,160

c. Plan assets at fair value, 1/1/92:

Plan assets at fair value, 1/1/91	$16,000
Actual return, 1991	2,000
Contributions, 1991	4,000
Benefits paid, 1991	(5,000)
Plan assets at fair value, 1/1/92	$17,000

3. *a.*

(1) $\dfrac{\$12,000 - 10\% \times \text{greater of } (\$300,000 \text{ or } \$280,000)}{20 \text{ years}}$ = corridor amortization

= $0 because the calculation yields a negative amount (there is no excess of unrecognized gain over the corridor).

(2) Straight-line amortization based on average service period = $12,000/20 = $600, decreases pension expense.

b.

$$\text{Expected return} = .10(\$280,000) = \$28,000$$

Actual return is determined as follows:

$$\$280,000 + \text{actual return} + \$10,000 - \$15,000 = \$295,000$$
$$\text{actual return} = \$20,000$$

Calculation of unrecognized loss at 1/1/92:

Unrecognized gain, 1/1/91	($12,000)
1991 amortization of unrecognized gain	600
Actuarial loss, 12/31/91	4,000
Excess of expected over actual return, 1991	8,000
Unrecognized loss, 1/1/92	$ 600

c. Component 5 of pension expense for 1991:

Excess of expected over actual return, 1991	($ 8,000)
Amortization of unrecognized gain	(600)
Net decrease in pension expense	($ 8,600)

(Because pension expense ultimately reflects expected return in any given year, and actual return is less than expected return, the first element of component 5 must reduce pension expense $8,000.)

d. Using actual return, the net effect on pension expense of items affecting gains and losses:

	Effect on 1991 Pension Expense
Actual return	($20,000)
Component 5 from *(c.)*	(8,600)
Net effect, decrease pension expense	($28,600)

Using expected return, the net effect on pension expense of items affecting gains and losses:

	Effect on 1991 Pension Expense
Expected return	($28,000)
Amortization of unrecognized gain	(600)
Net effect, decrease pension expense	($28,600)

e. Amortization of unrecognized loss in 1992 = $600/20 = $30, an increase in pension expense for 1992.

4. Determination of additional minimum pension liability:

ABO	($72,000)
Plan assets at fair value	48,000
Total minimum liability	(24,000)
Balance, accrued pension cost (cr.)	(18,000)
Required balance, additional minimum pension liability	(6,000)
Current balance, additional minimum pension liability	(14,000)
Required reduction, additional minimum pension liability	$ 8,000

December 31, 1991:

Additional minimum pension liability	8,000	
Unrealized pension cost		6,000
Intangible pension cost		2,000*

* Maximum intangible is $4,000, the amount of unrecognized PSC. Therefore, the intangible is reduced by $2,000.

5. The transition liability is $50,000:

Underfunded PBO			
APB Opinion No. 8 asset	30,000		
		Transition liability	**50,000**
		Funded status	20,000

APPENDIX 19A   *Accounting for Postretirement Benefits Other than Pensions*[38]

The FASB, in one of the most significant changes to accounting ever, issued a rule on post-retirement health benefits that could cut corporate profits by hundreds of billions of dollars.[39]

Nonpension postretirement benefits include all benefits, other than pensions, that an employer promises to provide retirees. Health care and other benefit costs are difficult to predict. Factors affecting postretirement benefit cost estimates include the variety of health care services needed by retirees, changes in technology and government reimbursement policies, the proportion of the retiree group covered by Medicare, geographical location, age, future pay increases, general health, and whether spouses and dependents are covered.

Nonpension postretirement benefits represent an increasingly significant obligation for many firms. The inflation in health care costs (in excess of general inflation), increased longevity, reductions in Medicare reimbursement, and an increase in the number of employees retiring early exacerbate the problem. Estimates of the total nonpension postretirement benefit obligation (at present value) for all U.S. firms range from $100 billion to $2 trillion. A survey by consulting firm William M. Mercer, Inc., found that 91% of companies with more than 5,000 workers offer postretirement health benefit plans.[40]

SFAS No. 106, "Employers' Accounting for Postretirement Benefits Other Than Pensions," issued December, 1990, significantly changes accounting for nonpension postretirement benefits. The statement requires accrual of the cost and obligation of other post-employment benefits as employees render the service necessary to receive their benefits.[41] The statement treats postretirement benefits as part of the compensation to employees for services rendered.

Most employers previously accounted for nonpension postretirement benefits on a pay-as-you-go cash basis, recognizing as expense only the payments made to retirees during a period. Consequently, both the expense and liability for benefits were significantly understated. This form of off-balance-sheet financing is no longer allowed under *SFAS No. 106.*[42]

The objectives of the *Statement* are to enhance the relevance and representational faithfulness of income and balance sheet reporting, and to improve user understanding in this area. The statement incorporates three fundamental aspects of pension accounting: delayed recognition, net cost, and offsetting. The FASB believes the new principles will improve the management of postretirement plans, improve the credibility of financial statements, and provide an incentive for firms to estimate benefits more accurately.

Scope of *SFAS No. 106*   *SFAS No. 106* applies to all postretirement benefits expected to be paid to current and former employees (and their spouses, dependents, and beneficiaries) other than pension benefits or life insurance benefits provided through a pension plan. These benefits include health care coverage, life insurance, tuition assistance, day care, legal services, and

---

[38] This appendix assumes knowledge of pension accounting, as discussed in this chapter. Accounting for nonpension postretirement benefits is similar to accounting for pensions in many respects.

[39] "FASB Issues Rule Change on Benefits," *The Wall Street Journal,* December 20, 1990, p. A3.

[40] "Now That Wasn't So Bad, Was It?," *Business Week,* December 2, 1991, p. 123.

[41] *SFAS No. 106* supersedes *SFAS No. 81,* "Disclosure of Postretirement Health Care and Life Insurance Benefits" (which required disclosures of the period cost of such plans but not recognition) and rescinds *FASB Technical Bulletin No. 87–1,* "Accounting for a Change in Method of Accounting for Certain Postretirement Benefits," which permitted a change to accrual accounting to be treated either as a change in estimate (prospective treatment) or as a cumulative effect of a change in accounting principle (immediate recognition in net income).

[42] *SFAS No. 106* is effective for fiscal years beginning after December 15, 1992; restatement of previously issued annual financial statements is not permitted.

EXHIBIT 19A-1   Factors Leading to Estimates of Future Payments to Retirees
                 under a Postretirement Health Care Plan

1. *Per capita claims cost by age:* the current cost of providing postretirement health care benefits for one year at each age plan participants are expected to receive benefits under the plan. Past and present claims data for the plan, or the experience of other employers or insurance companies and consultants if such data are unavailable, are used to determine these amounts.

2. *Health care cost trend rates:* assumptions about the annual rate of change of health care costs for the benefits provided by the plan. These assumptions include health care inflation, changes in utilization, technological advances, and health care status of participants.

3. *Assumed per capita claims cost by age:* the per capita claims cost by age adjusted for health care cost trend rates.

4. *Plan demographics:* the characteristics of the plan population, including geographical distribution, age, sex, and marital status.

5. *Future gross eligible charges:* assumed per capita claims cost adjusted by plan demographics.

6. *Net incurred claims cost by age:* the employer's share of the cost of providing postretirement health care. Net incurred claims cost equals future gross eligible charges reduced by expected Medicare reimbursement, expected employee contributions (cost sharing), and deductibles. The net incurred claims cost by age are the cash flow inputs into the actuarial present value models.

housing subsidies. However, for most employers, health care benefits are the most significant type. The *Statement* does not apply to accounting for similar benefits provided to active employees during the term of their employment, or to contracts for postemployment benefits for employees on an individual basis.[43]

SFAS No. 106 focuses on defined benefit postretirement plans. Benefits are defined in terms of specific monetary amounts or specific benefit coverage. Examples include coverage up to $200 per day for hospitalization, 70% of the cost of dental work, and complete (open-ended) health care coverage during retirement.

The *Statement* applies to unwritten as well as to contractual plans. The *substantive* plan is the basis for the accounting. The *Statement* presumes that an employer providing regular postretirement benefits in the past will continue to do so, whether or not an underlying contract exists.

Full Eligibility An employee is *fully eligible* for postretirement benefits when the employee renders the service necessary to receive all *expected* benefits. Full eligibility is attained by fulfilling age and service requirements, depending on the plan.

Some plans require both age (e.g., age 55) and service requirements (e.g., 20 years of service) to attain full eligibility. Other plans provide differential benefits that depend on age and service. Assume a plan promises 50% of full postretirement health care coverage for 15 years of service after age 40, 75% for 20 years service after age 40, and 100% for 25 years service after age 40. The full eligibility date for an employee hired at age 40 and *expected* to retire at age 63 is age 60, at which time the employee is eligible for 75% coverage during retirement. The full eligibility date for *pay-related* plans is generally the retirement date because benefits are based on final salary.

Service beyond the full eligibility date does not increase future benefits. However, if the employee continues to earn material benefits for each year of service until retirement date (such as in a pay-related plan), the full eligibility date is the retirement date.

Employer Obligations for Postretirement Benefit Plans

An employer's obligation under a postretirement benefit plan is the actuarial present value of expected future payments to retirees. The estimates of the amount and timing of payments for postretirement health care depend on several unique factors, listed in Exhibit 19A–1.

---

[43] *SFAS No. 106* amended APB Opinion No. 12 to require that the employer's obligation for the latter plans be accrued according to the terms of the contract.

EXHIBIT 19A-2   Determining Expected Postretirement Benefit Obligation and Accumulated Postretirement Benefit Obligation

Michael Reni works for a firm with a postretirement plan that provides health care benefits to employees who render 15 years of service and retire after age 60. Michael was hired January 1, 1972, just after turning age 35. He must serve 25 years to reach his full eligibility date, December 31, 1996.

Michael is expected to leave the firm at age 65 (at the end of 2001) and live to age 70. The first benefit payment ($3,000 in the table below) is expected to be paid December 31, 2002. Assume a 9% discount rate. The health benefit payments for Michael estimated at the measurement date, December 31, 1992 (age 56), follow:

Age	Expected Net Incurred Claims Cost by Age*	Present Value of Claims Cost at Age	
		56 (12/31/92)	60 (12/31/96)
66	$3,000	$1,267†	$1,789‡
67	3,500	1,356§	1,915‖
68	2,700	960	1,355
69	1,900	620	875
70	4,600	1,377	1,943
	Total present value	$5,580	$7,877

* Assume end-of-year payments; these amounts reflect anticipated health care cost trend rates, and the other factors listed in Exhibit 19A-1.

† $3,000($PV1,9\%,10$) = $3,000(.42241) = $1,267**

‡ $3,000($PV1,9\%,6$) = $3,000(.59627) = $1,789

§ $3,500($PV1,9\%,11$) = $3,500(.38753) = $1,356

‖ $3,500($PV1,9\%,7$) = $3,500(.54703) = $1,915

** The present value of the first benefit payment ($3,000) at 12/31/92, 10 years before payment, is $1,267.

At December 31, 1992:

Michael is 56 and has served 21 years, or $^{21}/_{25}$ of the period required for full eligibility.
EPBO = $5,580, the present value of payments expected under plan.
APBO = $5,580($^{21}/_{25}$) = $4,687

In addition to the factors in Exhibit 19A-1, the benefits under pay-related plans are affected by salary increases. The actuarial present value of benefit payments also incorporates estimates of turnover and life expectancy.

The discount rate used for present value purposes is based on the rate of return on high-quality fixed-income investments currently available to settle the obligation, and interest rates implied by contracts with third-party insurers.

The *expected postretirement benefit obligation* (EPBO) is the actuarial present value of future postretirement benefits *expected* to be paid. The *accumulated postretirement benefit obligation* (APBO) is the actuarial present value of future postretirement benefits attributed to an employee's service rendered to a particular date (*measurement date*). APBO is the more important liability measure for reporting purposes because it reflects service through a measurement date. Neither EPBO nor APBO are recognized as balance sheet liabilities, but APBO is disclosed in the footnotes.

Before the full eligibility date, APBO is the portion of the EPBO attributed to service rendered to that date. If the benefit formula includes expected salary increases, then both the APBO and EPBO reflect them.[44] On the full eligibility date, APBO and EPBO are equal. Refer to Exhibit 19A-2, which illustrates both liability measures.

In that exhibit, EPBO is $5,580 at December 31, 1992, because this amount is the present value of benefits expected to be paid, as of that date. An equal amount of EPBO for each employee is attributed to each year of service, from the date of hire to the full eligibility date,

---

[44] Therefore, APBO is more comparable to PBO than to ABO for pension plans. If the plan is pay related, APBO is affected by changes in future salary levels. Both APBO and PBO are based on service rendered to a measurement date.

unless the benefit formula attributes a disproportionate share of the benefits to early years of service.[45] Therefore, the APBO at December 31, 1992, a measurement date, reflects the portion of the total required period served, or $2\frac{1}{25}$ in Michael's case (Exhibit 19A–2).

Assuming no changes in expected health care costs, both EPBO and APBO equal $7,877 at December 31, 1996. At this date, Michael has served 25 years and is fully eligible for the benefits. These two obligation measures are reestimated at the end of each year until payments are no longer required, but remain equal.

Postretirement Benefit Expense

Postretirement benefit expense,[46] a current operating expense, is the cost of a postretirement benefit plan recognized in a reporting period.[47] The expense has six components, each with an interpretation similar to that for pensions:

1. Service cost.
2. Interest cost.
3. Actual return on plan assets.
4. Amortization of prior service cost.
5. Gains and losses to the extent recognized.
6. Amortization of transition asset or liability.

Service cost for a period is the actuarial present value of benefits attributed to service rendered by employees during the period. It is the portion of EPBO attributed to service in the period. Actuaries calculate service cost from the per capita claims cost and other information.

Interest cost is the increase in APBO during the period resulting from the passage of time, and it is obtained by multiplying beginning APBO by the discount rate.

The *actual return on plan assets* is the change in the fair value of plan assets during the period, adjusted for contributions and benefit payments. However, similar to pensions, the *expected return* on plan assets, found by multiplying the expected long-term rate of return by beginning plan assets at fair value, is the amount incorporated into periodic postretirement benefit expense.

Plan assets ordinarily cannot be withdrawn by the employer except when plan assets exceed obligations and the employer has taken steps to satisfy the obligations. The expected long-term rate of return on plan assets reflects the average rate of earnings expected on plan assets. In contrast to pensions, this return reflects a reduction for income tax because nonpension postretirement benefit funds are not tax-exempt.

When postretirement benefit expense and annual funding are not equal, accrued or prepaid postretirement benefit cost is recognized for the difference. For example, assume that postretirement benefit expense is $30,000 in the first year of a plan, and $20,000 is funded by contribution to the plan fund. The following entry records the expense and obligation.

To record annual postretirement benefit expense:

Postretirement benefit expense	30,000	
Accrued postretirement benefit cost		10,000
Cash		20,000

The $10,000 accrued postretirement benefit cost balance (a liability) represents recognized, but unfunded, postretirement benefit expense. The liability (or asset if overfunded) is classified as current or long-term depending on the expected period of payment (or reduction in future payment). Because prior service cost, gains and losses, and transition amount are subject to delayed recognition, the balance in accrued or prepaid postretirement benefit cost is generally not equal to the plan's funded status (difference between APBO and plan assets at fair value).

---

[45] Given the complexity of many plans, the FASB chose to attribute an equal amount of EPBO to each year of service, rather than to base attribution on the benefit formula. For example, a plan may define different benefits for different years of service and have multiple age and service requirements that must be met to attain eligibility for any benefit.

[46] The term *expense* rather than *cost* is used for instructional convenience. However, manufacturing firms capitalize the portion of cost relating to manufacturing personnel to an inventory account, pending sale.

[47] If the full eligibility date occurs before retirement, postretirement benefit expense is recognized only to the full eligibility date. However, the measurement of the obligation considers periods beyond that date because benefit payments do not commence until retirement.

Transition Obligation or Asset

The transition obligation or asset is the difference between the firm's accrued or prepaid postretirement benefit cost account (if any) and the plan's funded status, at the date of transition to *SFAS No. 106:*

$$\begin{bmatrix} \text{Accrued or prepaid} \\ \text{postretirement} \\ \text{benefit cost} \end{bmatrix} + \begin{bmatrix} \text{Transition} \\ \text{asset or} \\ \text{liability} \end{bmatrix} = \text{APBO} - \text{Plan assets at fair value}$$

For example, at transition, a plan with a $400,000 APBO and $210,000 in plan assets at fair value is underfunded by $190,000. If the firm recognized $100,000 of accrued postretirement benefit cost before transition, then the firm has a $90,000 transition liability (The letter L is used for liability and A for asset):

$$\$100,000 + \begin{bmatrix} \text{Transition} \\ \text{liability} \end{bmatrix} = \$400,000 - \$210,000$$

$$\begin{bmatrix} \text{Transition} \\ \text{liability} \end{bmatrix} = \$190,000 - \$100,000L = \$90,000L$$

The transition liability generally represents nonrecognition of service cost, interest cost, prior service cost, and net unrecognized losses before transition.

The transition amount can be recognized immediately (in the transition period, not in later periods) in net income as a cumulative effect of a change in accounting principle[48], or on a delayed basis as a component of postretirement benefit expense. If delayed recognition is elected, the transition amount is amortized on a straight-line basis over the average remaining service period of active plan participants. If that average is less than 20 years, the employer can elect to use 20 years for amortization.[49] If almost all plan participants are inactive, the average life expectancy of those participants is used for amortization.

Amortization of a transition liability increases postretirement benefit expense; the reverse is true for a transition asset. However, delayed recognition of the transition liability should not result in slower recognition of the postretirement obligation than under the pay-as-you-go approach. Therefore, after transition, if the cumulative benefit payments exceed the cumulative recognized postretirement benefit expense, additional amortization of the transition liability is recognized for the difference. An example later in this appendix illustrates this provision.

Accounting for the transition amount is of particular concern to employers. The transition liability is substantial for many firms which used the cash basis of accounting before transition.[50] For many firms, the transition liability equals APBO at transition because no plan assets or previously recognized balance sheet liability exists. Therefore, delayed recognition of the transition liability is consistent with delayed recognition of the entire obligation. For this reason, the FASB does not require recognition or disclosure of a *minimum liability* for postretirement benefits. Also, whereas the minimum liability for pensions approximates the statutory U.S. liability for vested benefits, no such statutory requirement exists for postretirement benefits.

Prior Service Cost

Prior service cost arises from plan amendments that attribute an increase in benefits to employee service rendered in prior periods. Amendments are granted on the assumption that the employer will realize future economic benefits. Therefore, the prior service cost (the increase in the APBO) is amortized by allocating an equal amount to each remaining year of service to the *full eligibility date* for each active plan participant. Consistent use of a more rapid amortization method, such as straight-line amortization, is allowed over the average

---

[48] The portion of the transition amount attributable to the effects of a plan initiation or benefit improvement adopted after December 21, 1990, is treated as prior service cost and excluded from the transition amount immediately recognized.

[49] In a field test of the exposure draft preceding *SFAS No. 106*, the FASB found that a majority of participating companies had an average remaining service period between 18 and 21 years.

[50] One study of 25 companies found that interest cost would average approximately 50% of postretirement benefit expense because the transition obligation is so large. See M. Akresh, B. Bald, and H. Dankner, "Results of OPEB Field Test Show Impact On Corporate Expenses," *Financial Executive*, July–August 1989, pp. 33–36.

EXHIBIT 19A-3 Amortization of Prior Service Cost

On January 1, 1994, a firm amended its postretirement benefit plan by increasing the benefits attributable to service performed before the amendment date. The accumulated postretirement benefit obligation increased $93,000 as a result (prior service cost). The remaining years of service for employees who have not yet reached full eligibility follow:

Number of Employees	Remaining Years to Full Eligibility at January 1, 1994	Total Service Years for Each Remaining Year to Full Eligibility					Total
		1994	1995	1996	1997	1998	
3	1	3*					3
6	2	6	6				12
9	3	9	9	9			27
4	4	4	4	4	4		16
7	5	7	7	7	7	7	35
29		29	26	20	11	7	93

Note: Average remaining years of service to full eligibility: 3.207 (93 total years/29 employees).
* Three employees have one remaining year to full eligibility.

Amortization under the two approaches for each year is as follows:

Amortization of Prior Service Cost

Year	Allocating an Equal Amount to Each Remaining Year to Full Eligibility	Using Average Remaining Years of Service to Full Eligibility
1994	$29,000 ($93,000 × 29/93)	$29,000 ($93,000/3.207)
1995	26,000 ($93,000 × 26/93)	29,000 ($93,000/3.207)
1996	20,000 ($93,000 × 20/93)	29,000 ($93,000/3.207)
1997	11,000 ($93,000 × 11/93)	6,000 (remaining)
1998	7,000 ($93,000 × 7/93)	
	$93,000	$93,000

remaining years of service to full eligibility for active participants. The amortization increases postretirement benefit expense. Employees who are already fully eligible for the increased benefits and employees hired after the amendment date are not included in the calculation. Refer to Exhibit 19A-3 for an example.

If most participants are fully eligible for the amended benefits, prior service cost is amortized over the remaining life expectancy of those plan participants. If an amendment *reduces* APBO, that reduction first is used to reduce any existing unrecognized prior service cost from previous amendments, then any unrecognized transition liability, and any remainder is amortized as in Exhibit 19A-3 (reduces postretirement benefit expense).

Gains and Losses

Gains and losses arise from changes in APBO resulting from changes in assumptions or from experience different from assumptions, and from differences between expected and actual return on plan assets. As in pensions, these gains and losses are allowed to cancel out to a considerable extent, before they are recognized in postretirement benefit expense.

Minimum (corridor) amortization of the net unrecognized gain or loss is the same for postretirement benefits and pensions. An example later in this appendix illustrates the computation. Any systematic amortization method can be used in lieu of the minimum if:
* The minimum is recognized when the alternative method results in a smaller amount.
* The method is applied consistently.
* The method is disclosed.

In contrast to pensions, immediate recognition of gains and losses also is allowed. However, the amount of any net gain exceeding a net loss previously recognized in income is first offset against any unrecognized transition liability, and the amount of any net loss in excess of a net gain previously recognized in income is first offset against any unrecognized transition asset.[51]

Therefore, the gain or loss component of postretirement benefit expense consists of these values:
* The difference between actual and expected return on plan assets for the current period.
* Any gain or loss immediately recognized at the discretion of the employer *or* amortization of net unrecognized gain or loss.
* Any gain or loss required to be immediately recognized.[52]

Three-Year Example of Postretirement Accounting

In this section, a three-year running example is presented to illustrate accounting for postretirement benefits. Refer to Exhibit 19A-4 for background information and first year results. Exhibits 19A-5 and 19A-6 illustrate the second and third years.

Required Disclosures   The following disclosures are required under *SFAS No. 106* for full disclosure of the postretirement benefit plan. The amounts for Waldorf Corporation (at December 31, 1995) are indicated, where relevant.
* A description of the substantive plan and planned changes, the employee groups covered, types of benefits provided, funding policy and types of assets held.
* The amount of postretirement benefit expense showing service cost, interest cost, actual return, amortization of transition amount, and the net of other components (1995 postretirement benefit expense, $84,104; service cost, $40,000; interest cost, $31,403; actual return, $5,000; amortization of transition liability, $10,000; net of other components, $7,701).
* A schedule reconciling the plan's funded status with amounts disclosed in the balance sheet (the 1995 reconciliation for Waldorf, is given in Exhibit 19A-6).
* The assumed health care cost trend rates used to measure the gross eligible charges for the next year, and a description of the direction and change in the trend rate.
* The weighted-average discount rate (9%) and rate of compensation increase (for pay-related plans) used to measure APBO, the expected long-term rate of return on plan assets (10%), and estimated income tax rates included in the rate of return.
* The effect of a 1% increase in the assumed health care cost trend rates for each future year on the sum of service cost and interest cost and on APBO.[53]

Recognition of Additional Amortization of Transition Liability

Although delayed recognition is allowed for the transition liability, *SFAS No. 106* does not allow cumulative postretirement benefit expense to be exceeded by cumulative benefit payments *as a result of delayed recognition*. Otherwise, the cumulative expense on a pay-as-you-go basis would exceed cumulative expense under the accrual basis. If this situation exists, then additional amortization of the transition liability is required.

Refer to Exhibit 19A-7, which uses some of the Waldorf Corporation results and illustrates an example of additional amortization.

---

[51] This provision was added to avoid recognizing gains (losses) before the underlying underfunded (overfunded) accumulated postretirement benefit obligation is recognized.

[52] If an employer forgives a retroactive adjustment of current or past-years' cost-sharing provisions relating to benefit costs already incurred by employees, or if an employer deviates from the provisions of the substantive plan to increase or decrease the employer's share of the benefit costs incurred in current or past periods, the effect is recognized immediately as a gain or loss.

[53] The reason for this requirement is that postretirement benefit costs are very sensitive to small changes in future health care costs. See H. Dankner and N. Ford, "Postemployment Benefits: Key Measurement Issues," *Financial Executive*, November–December 1987, pp. 24–27.

EXHIBIT 19A-4   Postretirement Benefit Expense and Liabilities

---

WALDORF CORPORATION
Background Information for Three-Year
Postretirement Benefit Accounting Example

Transition date: January 1, 1993
Average remaining service period of active plan participants: 12 years (assume this value remains constant throughout the example)
APBO, January 1, 1993: $200,000
Waldorf accounted for postretirement benefit costs on a pay-as-you-go basis before transition; consequently, no accrued or prepaid postretirement benefit cost account balance or postretirement benefit fund exists on January 1, 1993
Discount rate: 9%
Amortization period for unrecognized transition liability: 20 years (Waldorf chose the maximum period rather than 12 years)

1993: Service Cost, Interest Cost and Amortization of Transition Obligation

Information for 1993:
Waldorf created a postretirement benefit fund with a contribution on December 31, 1993: $35,000
Benefit payments (to retirees), December 31, 1993: $20,000
Service cost: $30,000

> *Postretirement benefit expense, 1993:*
> Service cost $30,000
> Interest cost ($200,000 × .09) 18,000
> Amortization of transition
>   liability ($200,000/20) 10,000*
> Postretirement benefit expense, 1993 . . . . . $58,000

> * If 12 years is used, the amortization is $16,667 ($200,000/12), causing postretirement benefit expense to increase to $64,667. If the entire unrecognized transition liability is recognized immediately, income is reduced by the resulting $200,000 cumulative effect of accounting change. Postretirement benefit expense is then $48,000.

To record 1993 postretirement benefit expense:

Postretirement benefit expense 58,000
    Accrued postretirement benefit cost   23,000
    Cash   35,000

Actual return is not a component of the expense because a benefit fund does not exist at the beginning of 1993. The following report reveals why the recognized liability ($23,000) does not equal the plan's funded status:

Reconciliation of Funded Status
December 31, 1993

APBO . . . . ($228,000)*
Plan assets at fair value . . . .   15,000†

Underfunded APBO (funded status) . . . . . (213,000)
Unrecognized transition liability . . . . 190,000‡

Accrued postretirement benefit cost . . . . . ($ 23,000)

* APBO, 1/1/93	$200,000	† Plan assets, 1/1/93	$	0
Service cost	30,000	Contributions		35,000
Interest cost	18,000	Benefit payments		(20,000)
Benefit payments	(20,000)	Plan assets, 12/31/93		$15,000
APBO, 12/31/93	$228,000			

‡ $200,000 beginning-of-year amount − $10,000 amortization.

The unrecognized transition liability is that part of APBO not yet recognized in expense, and therefore not yet recognized in accrued postretirement benefit cost.

WALDORF CORPORATION
1994: Plan Amendment, Amortization of Prior Service Cost
Actual and Expected Return on Plan Assets

Information for 1994:

On January 1, 1994, the plan is amended to increase benefits attributed to service performed before the amendment date; the amendment causes APBO to increase $60,000

Average remaining years of service to full eligibility for active plan participants: 10 years (Waldorf chooses the straight-line amortization method for prior service cost)

An increase in estimated health care cost trend rates at December 31, 1994 results in a $50,000 increase in APBO

Service cost: $30,000

Contribution to fund, December 31, 1994: $75,000

Benefit payments, December 31, 1994: $45,000

Expected rate of return on plan assets: 10%

Actual return on plan assets in 1994: $1,000

The plan amendment is a voluntary change in the provisions of the postretirement benefit plan. The change in the estimated health care costs is involuntary, and represents an unrecognized loss on the plan. Both events cause APBO to increase.

Postretirement benefit expense, 1994:

Service cost	$30,000
Interest cost ($228,000 + $60,000*) (.09)	25,920
Expected return ($15,000 × .10)	(1,500)
Amortization of prior service cost ($60,000/10)	6,000
Amortization of transition liability ($200,000/20)	10,000
Postretirement benefit expense, 1994	$70,420

* Prior service cost, determined at January 1, 1994.

Interest cost reflects the immediate increase in APBO caused by the plan amendment. The $50,000 loss does not affect interest cost in 1994, nor is it amortized in 1994, because it occurred at the end of the year. Expected return reduces postretirement benefit expense.

To record 1994 postretirement benefit expense:

Postretirement benefit expense	70,420	
Accrued postretirement benefit cost	4,580	
Cash		75,000

Waldorf contributed more to the fund than it recognized as expense during the year. Therefore, the accrued postretirement benefit cost account decreased $4,580 at the end of 1994. However, the unrecognized APBO increased significantly during the period. The unrecognized portion of this increase is represented by unrecognized prior service cost and the unrecognized loss, as shown in the funded status report:

Reconciliation of Funded Status
December 31, 1994

APBO	($348,920)*
Plan assets at fair value	46,000†
Underfunded APBO (funded status)	(302,920)
Unrecognized prior service cost	54,000‡
Unrecognized net loss	50,500§
Unrecognized transition obligation	180,000‖
Accrued postretirement benefit cost	($ 18,420)

* APBO, 1/1/94	$228,000		† Plan assets, 1/1/94	$15,000
Service cost	30,000		Contributions	75,000
Interest cost	25,920		Actual return	1,000
Prior service cost	60,000		Benefit payments	(45,000)
Loss on rate change	50,000		Plan assets, 12/31/94	$46,000
Benefit payments	(45,000)			
APBO, 12/31/94	$348,920			

‡ $60,000 beginning-of-year amount − $6,000 amortization.

§ $50,000 loss on rates + ($1,500 expected return − $1,000 actual return).

‖ $190,000 beginning-of-year amount − $10,000 amortization.

EXHIBIT 19A–6   Postretirement Benefit Expense and Liabilities

WALDORF CORPORATION
1995: Amortization of Unrecognized Loss

Information for 1995:
Service cost: $40,000
Contribution to fund, December 31, 1995: $80,000
Benefit payments, December 31, 1995: $60,000
Actual return on plan assets in 1995: $5,000
Waldorf recognizes minimum amortization of gains and losses:

Minimum (corridor) amortization:
Unrecognized net loss, 1/1/95:		$50,500
APBO, 1/1/95	$348,920	
Plan assets, 1/1/95	46,000	
Greater of APBO or plan assets, 1/1/95	348,920	
10% of greater of APBO or plan assets, 1/1/95		34,892
Amount in excess of corridor, subject to amortization		15,608
Amortization of net unrecognized loss, 1995 ($15,608/12)		$ 1,301

Postretirement benefit expense, 1995:
Service cost	$40,000
Interest cost ($348,920 × .09)	31,403
Expected return ($46,000 × .10)	(4,600)
Amortization of prior service cost ($60,000/10)	6,000
Amortization of net unrecognized loss	1,301
Amortization of transition liability ($200,000/20)	10,000
Postretirement benefit expense, 1995	$84,104

To record 1995 postretirement benefit expense:
Postretirement benefit expense	84,104	
Accrued postretirement benefit cost		4,104
Cash		80,000

The funded status report explains the $22,524 ($18,420 + $4,104) ending 1995 balance in accrued postretirement benefit cost:

Reconciliation of Funded Status
December 31, 1995

APBO	($360,323)*
Plan assets at fair value	71,000†
Underfunded APBO (funded status)	(289,323)
Unrecognized prior service cost	48,000‡
Unrecognized net loss	48,799§
Unrecognized transition obligation	170,000‖
Accrued postretirement benefit cost	($ 22,524)

*APBO, 1/1/95	$348,920	†Plan assets, 1/1/95	$46,000
Service cost	40,000	Contributions	80,000
Interest cost	31,403	Actual return	5,000
Benefit payments	(60,000)	Benefit payments	(60,000)
APBO, 12/31/95	$360,323	Plan assets, 12/31/95	$71,000

‡ $54,000 beginning-of-year amount − $6,000 amortization.

§ Unrecognized net loss, 1/1/95	$50,500
Amortization, 1995	(1,301)
Gain: actual return ($5,000) − expected return ($4,600)	(400)
Unrecognized net loss, 12/31/95	$48,799

‖ $180,000 beginning-of-year amount − $10,000 amortization.

EXHIBIT 19A-7   Additional Amortization of Transition Liability

Assume the following for the Waldorf corporation in 1996:

On January 1, 1996, the firm contributes $230,000 to the fund
At December 31, 1996, postretirement benefit expense before additional amortization of transition liability (but including the usual $10,000 amortization): $90,000
Benefit payments, December 31, 1996: $200,000

Schedule to Determine Additional Amortization and Final Postretirement Benefit Expense

Year	Postretirement Benefit Expense	Benefit Payments
1993	$58,000	$ 20,000
1994	70,420	45,000
1995	84,104	60,000
1996, before additional transition amortization	90,000	200,000
Cumulative benefit payments		325,000
Cumulative expense through 1996 before additional transition liability amortization	302,524 ⟶	(302,524)
Required additional amortization of transition liability		22,476
1996 expense before additional amortization of transition liability		90,000
Final 1996 postretirement benefit expense		$112,476
Unrecognized transition liability, 1/1/96		$170,000
Amortization of transition liability, 1996 ($10,000 + $22,476)		(32,476)
Unrecognized transition liability, 12/31/96, to be amortized over the remaining 16-year term (20 years − 4 years of amortization)		$137,524

Concerns About *SFAS No. 106*

Many observers voiced concern about the effect of *SFAS No. 106* on corporate income statements and balance sheets. According to one estimate, the accrual expense for some firms can exceed the cash basis expense by a factor of 43.[54] Actuaries estimate that the new requirement could reduce the net worth of General Motors by $16 to $24 billion (out of $28 billion), and erase Chrysler's retained earnings if the transition liability were recognized immediately.[55]

Firms anticipate a substantial one-time cost to set up the necessary systems for compliance. Some firms are considering reducing benefits, or have done so, in response to the new statement.[56] Others argue that the costs of providing the information exceeds the benefits, given the difficulty of predicting future health care costs.

Although accounting for pensions is very similar to that for other postretirement benefits,[57] the sensitivity of the results to changes in assumptions can be more significant for postretirement benefits. For example, employee turnover can completely erase postretirement benefits, whereas pension benefits might only be reduced. In addition, health care costs often increase dramatically with age, whereas pension benefit payments remain constant. Other postretirement benefits are reduced less than pension benefits by early retirement.

The FASB is sensitive to these concerns, but concluded that disclosure of estimates of the costs and obligations of postretirement benefits is more useful than failure to recognize any cost or obligation. In addition, the concerns about adverse stock market effects may be unfounded. The market is aware of these plans and analysts already make their own estimates of the costs and obligations of postretirement plans. Fears that debt covenants will be abrogated may be unfounded, given the time available before the statement becomes effective

[54] "New Benefits-Accounting Rule Yields Fresh Red Tape," *The Wall Street Journal*, January 29, 1991, p. B2.

[55] "Now That Wasn't So Bad, Was It?", *Business Week*, December 2, 1991, p. 123.

[56] "New Benefits-Accounting Rule Yields Fresh Red Tape," *op cit.*

[57] Accounting for settlements, curtailments, and termination benefits for postretirement benefits also are similar to pensions (see the next appendix).

to renegotiate debt contracts. Furthermore, some covenants provide that the accounting principle applicable at the issuance of debt be in effect during the entire debt term, for purposes of evaluating compliance with the covenant.

APPENDIX 19B: *Settlements and Curtailments of Defined Benefit Pension Plans and Termination Benefits*

Employers occasionally make changes to defined benefit pension plans that cause immediate recognition of certain amounts subject to delayed recognition under *SFAS No. 87*. *SFAS No. 88*, "Employers' Accounting for Settlements and Curtailments of Defined Benefit Pension Plans and for Termination Benefits," provides guidelines to account for these events. *SFAS No. 88* is based on the principles established in *SFAS No. 87*, and supersedes *SFAS No. 74*, "Accounting for Special Termination Benefits Paid to Employees."

For example, plan termination or a plant closing resulting in a signficant reduction in personnel can require immediate recognition of unrecognized pension amounts. Future benefit payments, and therefore the projected benefit obligation (PBO), are reduced. The rationale for delayed recognition no longer applies under these circumstances.

SFAS No. 88 applies to pension plan curtailments, pension plan settlements, and termination benefits. These are strategic changes in a pension plan, not to be confused with actuarial or experience gains and losses.

Pension Plan Settlements A **settlement** is an irrevocable transaction that relieves the employer (or the plan) of primary responsibility for a pension plan obligation, and that eliminates significant risk related to the obligation and assets used to effect the settlement.

Examples include lump-sum cash payments to replace future pension benefits and purchase of an annuity to cover pension benefits. Employers can partially or completely settle a plan. For example, an employer can settle only the vested benefits and continue the plan. Accumulation of resources in an investment for future payment of pension benefits does not constitute a settlement. The investment is reversible and does not relieve the employer of the pension obligation.

Pension Plan Curtailments A **curtailment** is an event that either reduces the number of expected years of future service of present employees or eliminates, for a significant number of employees, the accrual of defined benefits for some or all of their future services.

Curtailments can occur through termination of employee service earlier than expected, or through a business contraction. The termination or suspension of a plan is also a curtailment if employees do not earn additional defined benefits for future service. Curtailments often decrease PBO, causing a gain. If the benefit formula is based on projected final (or average-final) compensation levels, the curtailment reduces PBO because benefits are reduced. A curtailment also can increase PBO, causing a loss.

A settlement and curtailment can occur simultaneously. For example, a plan termination can cause both a curtailment and a settlement. The employer is relieved of the pension obligation, and there are no years of future service expected.

Termination Benefits **Termination benefits** include special termination benefits offered for only a short period of time or contractual termination benefits required by the pension plan only if a special event, such as a plant closing, occurs.

Termination benefits often are provided to employees when employment is terminated before their expected retirement dates. Termination benefits also are used to encourage employees to voluntarily retire or seek employment elsewhere. For example, US West, a Denver-based telecommunications firm, offered early-retirement incentives to 20,000 of its managers as part of a cost-cutting program. Pension payments were increased by 15% for five years or until age 65, whichever occurs first.[58]

Termination benefits are lump-sum payments, periodic future payments, or both. Termination benefits can be associated with a plan termination, although the two are not necessarily related.

---

[58] "US West to Set Pension Plan to Cut Costs," *The Wall Street Journal*, December 1, 1989, p. A6.

Accounting for Settlements

The partial or complete settlement of a pension plan reduces PBO. One justification for delayed recognition of gains and losses is to allow offsetting against future gains and losses. To the extent that PBO is settled, the ability of future gains and losses from changes in PBO and asset value to offset is eliminated. In addition, settlement of the PBO is viewed as the realization of the net gain or loss at date of settlement.

The maximum gain or loss recognized in a settlement is the net sum of unrecognized gain or loss and the unrecognized transition asset. The maximum gain or loss is recognized in full if the entire projected benefit obligation is settled. If only part of the PBO is settled, a pro rata portion of the maximum amount is recognized. For example, if 25% of the projected benefit obligation is settled, 25% of the maximum gain or loss is recognized.

Therefore, the recognized gain or loss equals:

$$\begin{bmatrix} \text{Pro rata portion of} \\ \text{PBO settled} \end{bmatrix} \times \begin{bmatrix} \text{Unrecognized net gain or loss } + \\ \text{Unrecognized transition asset} \end{bmatrix}$$

In this calculation, an unrecognized gain is added to the unrecognized transition asset, and an unrecognized loss is offset against the unrecognized transition asset. The unrecognized transition asset is included because the FASB considers transition assets more likely to result from gains before transition than from plan amendments (which usually increase PBO and cause losses). The gains represented by the transition asset can no longer be offset by PBO losses, to the extent of the settlement. Refer to Exhibit 19B-1 which supplies the information for a settlement example.

The maximum settlement gain Havasu can recognize is $400 ($200 unrecognized transition asset plus $200 unrecognized net gain). Havasu is settling 60% of its projected benefit obligation ($1,200/$2,000); therefore, the recognized gain is $240 ($400 × .60). Havasu records the gain as follows:

December 31, 1991—To record settlement gain:

```
Accrued pension cost  . . . . . . . . . . . . . . . . . . . . . . . . . . . . . 240
    Settlement gain  . . . . . . . . . . . . . . . . . . . . . . . . . . . . . .        240
```

Havasu reports the settlement gain as an operating gain. The debit to accrued pension cost reflects the realization of a previously unrecognized gain. Exhibit 19B-2 illustrates the effect of the settlement on the reconciliation schedule.

If Havasu reported an unrecognized net loss of $100 rather than the $200 net gain in its reconciliation schedule before settlement, the maximum gain allowed is $100 ($200 transition asset minus $100 unrecognized loss). In this case, only a $60 gain is recognized. The maximum gain or loss does not consider an unrecognized transition *liability*.

The Havasu settlement is not a termination because the plan continues. The assets and PBO are reduced by the settlement. The remaining unrecognized pension amounts are subject to amortization in future periods.

Accounting for Curtailments

Curtailments reduce the expected future service of some or all employees, and they increase or decrease PBO. The recognized curtailment gain or loss is the net sum of the following amounts (item 2 or item 3 below is present for any particular curtailment, but not both):

1. Loss from reduction in future service:

$$\begin{bmatrix} \text{Percent reduction in} \\ \text{future service} \end{bmatrix} \times \begin{bmatrix} \text{Unrecognized PSC } + \text{ Unrecognized} \\ \text{transition liability} \end{bmatrix}$$

2. PBO gain from curtailment reduced by the net unrecognized loss. If the net unrecognized loss exceeds the PBO gain, no PBO gain is recognized. If there is a net unrecognized gain, the entire PBO gain is recognized.
3. PBO loss from curtailment reduced by the net unrecognized gain. If the net unrecognized gain exceeds the PBO loss, no PBO loss is recognized. If there is a net unrecognized loss, the entire PBO loss is recognized.

For the purpose of computing Items 2 and 3, the net unrecognized transition asset is treated as an unrecognized gain. Therefore, the net unrecognized gain or loss includes any unrecog-

EXHIBIT 19B-1   Plan Settlement

HAVASU COMPANY
Accounting for Pension Plan Settlement
Data For Example

Reconciliation of funded status, December 31, 1991, after all adjusting entries are completed:

(Dollars in thousands)

Projected Benefit Obligation	($2,000)
Plan assets at fair value	2,100
Overfunded PBO	100
Unrecognized transition asset	(200)
Unrecognized net gain	(200)
Accrued pension cost	($ 300)
Vested benefit obligation	($1,200)

On December 31, 1991, Havasu settles the vested benefit obligation by purchasing with pension plan assets an annuity contract that transfers the obligation to an insurance company.

EXHIBIT 19B-2   Plan Settlement

HAVASU COMPANY
Analysis of the Effects of Pension Plan Settlement

(Dollars in thousands)	Before Settlement	Effects of Settlement	After Settlement
Projected benefit obligation	($2,000)	$1,200	($800)
Plan assets at fair value	2,100	(1,200)	$900
Overfunded PBO	100	0	100
Unrecognized transition asset	(200)	120*	(80)
Unrecognized net gain	(200)	120*	(80)
Accrued pension cost	($ 300)	240	($ 60)
Vested benefit obligation	($1,200)	1,200	$ 0

* 60% is recognized.

nized transition asset. For example, if the unrecognized transition asset is $100, it increases a net unrecognized gain of $200 to a total of $300, and reduces a net unrecognized loss of $200 to a net loss of $100. An unrecognized transition asset of $300 converts an unrecognized loss of $200 into a net unrecognized gain of $100. The rationale for including the unrecognized transition asset in the unrecognized gain or loss is the same as for its inclusion in the settlement gain or loss.

The timing of recognition depends on whether the curtailment causes a net gain or loss. If the net sum is a loss, it is recognized when it is probable that a curtailment is imminent and the effects are estimable. If the net sum is a gain, it is recognized when the related employees terminate or the curtailment occurs. This distinction between gains and losses is consistent with *SFAS No. 5,* "Accounting for Contingencies," which states that certain gains are not recognized until realized.

The first item, loss from reduction in future service, is included because a curtailment reduces future service but does not reduce the retirement benefits under retroactive grants. The total benefits to the firm from retroactive grants is therefore reduced, and immediate loss recognition is warranted. For example, if a curtailment eliminates half of the estimated remaining future years of service related to the prior service cost and transition liability, then the loss is half of the remaining unrecognized prior service and transition cost. The FASB

EXHIBIT 19B-3 Recognized PBO Gain and Loss, a Component of Total Curtailment Gain or Loss: Independent Cases

(Dollars in thousands)	Case A	Case B	Case C	Case D	Case E	Case F
PBO gain (loss)	$100	$100	$100	$(100)	$(100)	$(100)
Unrecognized net gain (loss)*	50	(50)	(120)	50	(50)	120
Net PBO gain (loss)	$100	$ 50	$ 0	(50)	$(100)	$ 0

* Includes any unrecognized transition asset.

The net PBO gain or loss determined above is netted against the loss from reduction in future service to determine the final curtailment gain or loss.

EXHIBIT 19B-4 Information for Cases

AMADOR COMPANY
Information for Two Independent Curtailment Cases

1. On January 1, 1991, Amador Company significantly reduces its operations and terminates a number of employees.
2. The curtailment reduces Amador's PBO by $500 and the expected future years of employee service by 50%.
3. Reconciliation of funded status for the two cases:

(Dollars in thousands)	Case I	Case II
Projected benefit obligation	$(1,000)	$(1,000)
Plan assets at fair value	1,100	900
(Underfunded) overfunded PBO	100	(100)
Unrecognized PSC	40	40
Unrecognized net (gain), loss	(150)	150
Unrecognized transition (asset), liability	(100)	90
(Accrued) prepaid pension cost	$ (110)	$ 180

considers a transition liability to be related primarily to retroactive grants before the adoption of *SFAS No. 87,* and therefore includes them as a determinant of the loss.

The PBO gain or loss (Items 2 and 3) is offset against the remaining unrecognized loss or gain because the change in PBO caused by the curtailment may not be independent of previously unrecognized gains and losses. A part of PBO, for example, may be related to actuarial assumptions concerning increases in compensation levels that produced a currently unrecognized loss. A reduction in future service levels (and therefore a PBO gain) caused by the curtailment is considered to reverse part of the previously unrecognized loss. Hence the offsetting of PBO gain (loss) with the unrecognized loss (gain).

Exhibit 19B-3 provides examples of computations leading to Items 2 and 3.

In Case A, the entire PBO gain is recognized because no unrecognized loss exists to reduce it. In Case C, the PBO gain is completely offset by the unrecognized loss and therefore does not contribute to curtailment gain or loss. In Case D, $50 of PBO loss remains unrecognized after offsetting against $50 of unrecognized gain. Exhibit 19B-4 provides information for the next two comprehensive examples, which include the loss from reduction in the future service (Item 1). Exhibits 19B-5 and 19B-6 illustrate the accounting for the curtailments.

In *Case II,* Amador recognizes a $285 gain from curtailment. This gain consists of the reduction in PBO without equivalent reduction in plan assets (the funded status is greatly

EXHIBIT 19B-5   Curtailment

AMADOR COMPANY
Accounting for Effects of Curtailment—*Case I*

($000)

(Item 1)   Loss from reduction in future service = .50*($40) . . . . $ 20
  (Transition asset does not contribute to this loss)

(Item 2)   Net PBO gain: the entire $500 PBO gain (reduction in PBO caused $(500)
  by curtailment) is recognized because Amador has a $250 net unrecognized
  gain ($100 unrecognized transition asset plus $150 unrecognized net gain)

Net curtailment gain . . . . $(480)

* Percent reduction in future service.

Effects on Reconciliation of Funded Status

(*Dollars in thousands*)	**Before Curtailment**	**Effects of Curtailment**	**After Curtailment**
Projected benefit obligation	$(1,000)	$500	$ (500)
Plan assets at fair value	1,100		1,100
(Underfunded) overfunded PBO	100		600
Unrecognized PSC	40	(20)**	20
Unrecognized net (gain), loss	(150)		(150)
Unrecognized transition (asset) liability	(100)		(100)
(Accrued) prepaid pension cost	$ (110)	$480	$ 370

** Reduced 50% by curtailment.

January 1, 1991—To record curtailment gain:

  Accrued pension cost 480
    Gain from curtailment   480

(The accrued pension cost liability is now prepaid pension cost.)

---

improved, reducing the need for future funding) *less* recognition of the portion of unrecognized PSC and transition liability having no future benefit, and *less* the realization of the offsetting net unrecognized loss against PBO gain.

In contrast to settlements, plan assets are often not affected by curtailments. In both situations, however, assuming continuation of the plan, the remaining unrecognized pension amounts are carried forward for future amortization.

Accounting for Termination Benefits

Employers who offer *special* termination benefits must recognize a loss and a related liability when the employees accept the offer, and termination benefits are estimable. Employers who provide *contractual* termination benefits must recognize a loss and a related liability when it is probable that employees are entitled to benefits and the amount is estimable. The cost of termination benefits includes lump-sum payments and the present value of any expected future payments. Termination benefits are paid from company assets or pension plan assets.

Refer to Exhibit 19B-7, which presents an example of termination benefits coupled with a curtailment. In this example, the portion of the loss due to termination benefits is the lump-sum payment of $250,000. The computation of curtailment loss is consistent with the previous examples. This example highlights the potential interaction of a curtailment and termination benefits. Both are based on a reduction of future service levels.

EXHIBIT 19B–6   Curtailment

AMADOR COMPANY
Accounting for Effects of Curtailment—*Case II*

(*Dollars in thousands*)

(*Item 1*)   Loss from reduction in future service:

.50* ($40 PSC + $90 transition liability) . . . . $ 65

(*Item 2*)   Net PBO gain: $500 − $150 net unrecognized loss . . . .   (350)

   (The transition liability does not affect the net unrecognized loss)

Net curtailment gain . . . .   ($285)

* Percent reduction in future service.

Effects on Reconciliation of Funded Status

(*Dollars in thousands*)	Before Curtailment	Effects of Curtailment	After Curtailment
Projected benefit obligation	$(1,000)	$500	$(500)
Plan assets at fair value	900		900
(Underfunded) overfunded PBO	(100)		400
Unrecognized PSC	40	(20)†	20
Unrecognized net (gain), loss	150	150 ‡	0
Unrecognized transition (asset) liability	90	(45)†	45
(Accrued) prepaid pension cost	$ 180	$285	$465

† reduced 50% by curtailment

‡ offset against PBO gain

January 1, 1991—To record curtailment gain:

    Prepaid pension cost   285
        Gain from curtailment   285

EXHIBIT 19B–7   Termination Benefits and Curtailment

REDWOOD COMPANY
Termination Benefits and Curtailment

1. On January 1, 1991, Redwood Company offers a $250,000 special cash termination benefit to certain employees for voluntary termination. The offer is accepted.
2. The portion of PBO based on expected future compensation levels of the terminated employees is $200,000. (The pension plan is not terminated.)
3. The portion of unrecognized transition liability related to the future service periods no longer expected is $300,000.
4. Redwood has an unrecognized gain of $600,000, but no unrecognized PSC, before the offer of termination benefits.

        Effects of curtailment:
            1. loss from reduction in future service: $300,000
            2. net PBO gain (100% recognized because
               Redwood has an unrecognized gain) . . . .   (200,000)

        Curtailment loss   100,000
        Effects of termination benefits (loss)   250,000

        Total loss recognized $350,000

January 1, 1991—To record curtailment and termination benefits:

    Loss on employee terminations   350,000
        Accrued pension cost   100,000
        Cash   250,000

EXHIBIT 19B-8 Settlement and Curtailment

RAINIER COMPANY
Plan Termination: Settlement and Curtailment

1. Reconciliation of funded status, December 31, 1991:

   Dollars in thousands
   Accumulated benefit obligation . . . . ($750)

   Projected benefit obligation . . . . ($950)
   Plan assets at fair value 1,050
   Overfunded PBO 100
   Unrecognized transition asset . . . . (100)
   Unrecognized net gain . . . . (150)
   Accrued pension cost . . . . ($150)

2. Plan termination date: January 1, 1992
3. Rainier settled the accumulated benefit obligation by purchasing insurance company annuity contracts, and withdrew excess assets. There is no successor plan.

Settlement and Curtailment, Plan Termination and Asset Reversion

Refer to Exhibit 19B–8 which provides information for a settlement and curtailment caused by a plan termination and asset reversion. The pension plan was not terminated in previous examples.

Rainier has a curtailment. PBO is reduced $200 (PBO − ABO) from the reduction in future services. Rainier also has a settlement because it no longer has responsibility for the pension plan as a result of an irrevocable action. Amounts are in thousands of dollars:

Effect of curtailment:

1. Effect of reduction in future service years . . . . $ 0
   (Rainier has no unrecognized PSC or transition liability) . . . . .
2. PBO gain (no unrecognized loss to offset) 200
   Curtailment gain $200

Gain on settlement:

100%($100 + $150): $250*

Total gain on termination $450

* (Percent of PBO settled) × (sum of unrecognized transition asset and unrecognized net gain).

January 1, 1992—To record termination of pension plan:

Cash 300*
Accrued pension cost 150
   Gain from plan termination 450
* Plan assets at fair value ($1,050) − ABO ($750).

Rainier takes advantage of an overfunded pension plan by satisfying the ABO and removing the excess assets ($300). Because the plan is terminated, future salary estimates are no longer relevant; payment of ABO satisfies the current obligation. Rainier's $450 gain includes the $300 cash withdrawn from the plan and reduction of accrued pension cost, which no longer represents a liability.

Disclosure of Settlements, Curtailments, and Termination Benefits

For settlements, curtailments, and termination benefits, the employer discloses a description of the event, and the amount of gain or loss recognized. The gain or loss from settlements, curtailments, or termination benefits directly related to the disposal of a business segment is included in the total gain or loss reported from discontinued operations (discussed in Chapter 4).

APPENDIX 19C: *Financial Reporting by Pension Plans*

Pension plans often use a trustee, maintain and operate assets, incur liabilities, and are subject to ERISA. The pension plan is an entity separate from the employer for reporting purposes. Reporting by plans was limited before 1976. Financial statements often consisted only of summary information about assets. Conformity with GAAP was often lacking. Pressure to require reporting of plans not covered by ERISA, the diversity of reporting practices, and the significance of pension assets and benefits prompted the FASB to consider reporting standards for pension plans. The resulting statement, *SFAS No. 35,* "Accounting and Reporting by Defined Benefit Pension Plans," establishes standards of financial accounting and reporting for the annual statements of the plan.[59]

The statement applies only to defined benefit pension plans, but is broad in scope. Most private and public pension plans are subject to *SFAS No. 35.* Plans expected to be terminated and government-sponsored social security plans are exempt. The financial statements of a pension plan are separate from those of the employer. Pension plan statements report on the amounts available for payment of benefits. Those interested in plan statements include pension plan participants, advisors to participants, investors and creditors of the employer, and the government.

The main objective of plan financial statements is to provide information useful in *assessing the present and future ability of the plan to pay benefits when due.* To fulfill this objective, information about assets and benefits must appear in plan financial statements.

Financial Statement Components

To accomplish the objective of plan financial statements, the following four categories of information, measured under the accrual basis of accounting, are required:

1. Net Assets Available for Benefits   This is the difference between a plan's assets and its liabilities. It represents the participants' equity, the amount available to plan participants. Participant benefits are not liabilities of the plan because the plan exists for the benefit of the employees. Liabilities include normal operating liabilities for plan operations.

The assets of a plan include contributions receivable from the employer (and employees if the plan is contributory), investments, and operating assets. Contributions receivable are included in assets if a formal commitment is made by the employer to make a future contribution. Investments are measured at fair value (not a forced or liquidation sale value).[60] Operating assets are measured at book value. These measurement principles are consistent with *SFAS No. 87.*

2. Changes during the Year in the Net Assets Available for Benefits   Minimum disclosures include:
* Net change in fair value for each significant class of investment.
* Investment income.
* Employer and participant contributions.
* Benefits paid.
* Administrative expenses.

This category provides a much more detailed picture of plan assets than is required of the employer.

3. The Actuarial Present Value of Accumulated Plan Benefits   Accumulated plan benefits are the future benefit payments attributable to employee service rendered, to the financial statement

---

[59] *SFAS No. 35* does not *require* financial statements to be prepared by the plan. Rather, it establishes principles applying to financial statements when they are prepared and purport to be in accordance with GAAP.

[60] This is a major departure from the historical cost principle, but it is particularly appropriate in light of the objective of financial statements for pension plans.

date, as measured under the plan's provisions. The present value of these benefits is another measure of the total obligation of the employer. This amount normally does not equal the reported liabilities under *SFAS No. 87,* but is most similar to the accumulated benefit obligation. The total actuarial value of accumulated benefits is disclosed as the sum of vested and nonvested benefits. Both the time value of money and probability of payment are considered in this measurement.

For example, if a plan provides an annual benefit of 1% of the average of the last three years' salaries per year of service, the accumulated pension benefit for an employee with 15 years of service is based on 15% (15 years × 1%) of the employee's average salary for the 3 years immediately *preceding* the date of the financial statements.

Current, rather than future, compensation levels are the primary input to accumulated benefits. This position is contradictory to that taken by *SFAS No. 87* with regard to compensation levels. Automatic cost-of-living adjustments reflecting the cost of past services are included in accumulated benefits, however.

Changes in actuarial assumptions and experience are treated as estimate changes. For example, if the discount rate used to measure the present value of benefits is decreased, the actuarial present value of accumulated benefits increases.

4. Information about Factors Causing Changes in the Actuarial Present Value of Accumulated Plan Benefits This category explains why the present value of accumulated benefits changed during the period and includes plan amendments, changes in actuarial assumptions, benefits earned in the period, and benefits paid. This information, coupled with the second category, facilitates an assessment of the plan's ability to pay benefits on a continuing basis, and supplements the disclosures as of a particular date (categories 1 and 3).

Format *SFAS No. 35* does not specify the format of plan financial statements. For example, a plan can present net asset and benefit information with equal prominence in separate financial statements or in the same financial statement. Changes in net assets available for benefits and changes in accumulated plan benefits can appear separately or together. The plan has no income statement because the financial statements describe the benefits, and the ability to pay benefits, rather than the increase in equity as a result of operations. However, information about investment earnings is included in changes in net assets available for benefits.

Additional required disclosures to supplement the financial statements include information about the following:
* The methods used to determine investment fair value.
* Assumptions used to determine the actuarial present value of accumulated benefits, including changes in assumptions.
* The plan agreement including vesting and benefit provisions.
* Plan amendments.
* Compliance with ERISA and PBGC.

Example of Financial Statement Disclosures

Exhibits 19C-1 through 19C-4 illustrate the required disclosures for pension plans. Other formats are acceptable.

The net assets available for benefits is the net of plan assets and plan liabilities (Exhibit 19C-1). Employee benefits are not listed as liabilities because they are the liability of the employer, not the plan.

The statement in Exhibit 19C-2 explains why net assets available increased or decreased. Investment income is broken down by appreciation in market value, interest, dividends and rent. Contributions also increase the assets available. Benefit payments are the main deduction. The $450,000 of contributions from employees includes the $300,000 receivable at year-end listed in the statement of net assets available for benefits. The end of year balance in net assets is the same value for the first two statements illustrated. The present value of accumulated pension benefits is presented in the next statement.

The term *liability* is not used in the statement in Exhibit 19C-3. The plan is not liable to participants. Rather, the present value of accumulated benefits is one measure of the unpaid benefits earned to date. The statement of net assets available for benefits and the statement of accumulated plan benefits are used to determine the plan's funded status (over- or under-funded using current compensation levels to determine the present value of benefits). Inyo

EXHIBIT 19C-1 Pension Plan Financial Statement

INYO COMPANY PENSION PLAN
Statement of Net Assets Available for Benefits
December 31, 1991

Assets

Investments at fair value:

U.S. government securities	$ 400,000	
Investments in corporate bonds	600,000	
Investments in common stock	1,900,000	
Mortgages	700,000	
Real estate	2,100,000	
		$5,700,000
Receivables:		
Employee contributions	300,000	
Accrued interest and dividends	90,000	
		390,000
Cash		250,000
Total assets		$6,340,000

Liabilities

Accounts payable	160,000	
Accrued payables	210,000	
Total liabilities		370,000
Net assets available for benefits		$5,970,000

EXHIBIT 19C-2 Pension Plan Financial Statement

INYO COMPANY PENSION PLAN
Statement of Changes in Net Assets Available for Benefits
For the Year Ended December 31, 1991

Investment income:		
Net appreciation in fair value, investments	$ 230,000	
Interest	100,000	
Dividends	150,000	
Rents	80,000	
	560,000	
Less: Investment expenses	30,000	
		$ 530,000
Contributions:		
Employer	1,500,000	
Employee	450,000	
		1,950,000
Total additions		2,480,000
Benefits	1,300,000	
Administrative expenses	450,000	
Total deductions		1,750,000
Net increase		730,000
Net assets available for benefits:		
Beginning of year		5,240,000
End of year		$5,970,000

EXHIBIT 19C-3   Pension Plan Financial Statement

INYO COMPANY PENSION PLAN
Statement of Accumulated Plan Benefits
December 31, 1991

Actuarial present value of accumulated plan benefits:
Vested benefits:

Of participants currently receiving payments	$1,100,000
Other participants	3,200,000
	4,300,000
Nonvested benefits	2,200,000
Total actuarial present value of accumulated plan benefits	$6,500,000 ←

EXHIBIT 19C-4   Pension Plan Financial Statement

INYO COMPANY PENSION PLAN
Statement of Changes in Accumulated Plan Benefits
For the Year Ended December 31, 1991

Actuarial present value of accumulated plan benefits, beginning of year		$4,900,000
Increase (decrease) during the year attributable to:		
Plan amendment (increase in benefit percentage)	470,000	
Change in actuarial assumption (increase in average assumed retirement age)	(560,000)	
Benefits earned in 1991	2,990,000	
Benefits paid in 1991	(1,300,000)	
Net increase		1,600,000
Actuarial present value of accumulated plan benefits, end of year . . .		$6,500,000 ←

Company's plan is underfunded $530,000 ($6,500,000 − $5,970,000) at December 31, 1991. This amount does not equal the funded status per *SFAS No. 87,* and it may not equal the difference between accumulated benefit obligation and fair value of plan assets.

The information about assets and benefits must reflect the same measurement date to provide meaningful information. *SFAS No. 35* allows stating accumulated benefits as of the beginning of the year to allow more time to complete the accounting. If this alternative is chosen, the statement of net assets available for benefits must also reflect this date, and the statement of changes in net assets available must reflect changes for the preceding year.

The final statement explains why the actuarial present value increased during 1991 (Exhibit 19C-4). The increase in benefit percentage affects all future retirement benefits and increases the accumulated benefit total. An increase in average retirement age decreases expected total benefits. Benefits paid reduce both the accumulated plan benefit and assets available. The ending actuarial value ($6,500,000) appears in the last two statements illustrated. Appropriate footnotes to fulfill the additional information requirements outlined above would accompany the financial statements.

The four pension plan statements illustrated above do not articulate as do a balance sheet and income statement. However, the second and fourth categories of required information explain the change from the previous period in the first and third categories, respectively. Pension plan financial statements provide information not available from the employer. Plan liabilities, net assets available for benefits, and benefits earned and paid during the year are examples. Furthermore, plan financial statements provide detailed information about actual return on fund assets and about plan expenses. By focusing on different aspects of the pension plan, pension plan financial statements and employers' pension disclosures supply a broad range of information for the assessment of a pension plan.

KEY TERMS

Accumulated benefit obligation (1027)	PBGC (1022)
Asset reversion (1056)	Pension benefit formula (1021)
Attribution (1023)	Prior service cost (1034)
Contributory pension plan (1021)	Projected benefit obligation (1027)
Corridor (1038)	Service cost (1026)
Curtailment (1073)	Settlement (1073)
Defined benefit pension plan (1021)	Termination benefits (1073)
Defined contribution pension plan (1021)	Vested benefit obligation (1027)
ERISA (1022)	Vested benefits (1021)
Noncontributory pension plan (1021)	

QUESTIONS

1. Distinguish between a defined contribution pension plan and a defined benefit pension plan.
2. Distinguish the three parties involved in accounting and reporting for a pension plan.
3. What are the primary actuarial factors related to a pension plan?
4. Explain the three funding approaches that the employer can use for pension plans.
5. Distinguish between a contributory pension plan and a noncontributory pension plan.
6. Employer X has a defined benefit pension plan. The estimated pension expense for 1991 is $100,000. Explain and give the 1991 journal entry for each of the following cases: Case A—X pays 100% of the pension expense; Case B—X pays 80% of the expense; Case C—X pays 120% of the expense.
7. Employee X will receive an annual pension benefit of $12,000 for five years, starting on December 31, 1990. Assuming an interest rate of 8%, how much must be in the pension fund on January 1, 1990? Explain why the answer is not $60,000.
8. Employer W must build a pension fund of $50,000 by December 31, 1995. Five equal annual payments are made into the fund starting on December 31, 1991. The fund will earn 8%. What is the amount of each payment? Explain why it is not $10,000.
9. Explain why pension accounting must be based on assumptions and estimates.
10. What is the pension benefit formula?
11. Explain the application of the matching principle in accounting for pensions.
12. What does attribution mean in pension accounting?
13. Three special features of pension accounting are (a) delayed recognition, (b) net cost, and (c) offsetting. Explain each feature.
14. What is the vested benefit obligation?
15. List and define the six components of net periodic pension expense.
16. Explain the additional minimum pension liability.
17. VW Company recorded an additional minimum pension liability as follows (000s):

Intangible pension asset	15
Unrealized pension cost	3
Additional minimum pension liability	18

Explain each line in the above entry.
18. Define and explain the projected benefit obligation (PBO).
19. What information would typically be found in the report from the trustee on plan assets?
20. Explain what is meant by the "underfunded (overfunded) PBO."
21. Explain the difference between the projected benefit obligation and the accumulated benefit obligation.
22. Explain the primary approaches for amortizing unrecognized pension costs.
23. Explain the purpose and application of the additional minimum pension liability. Illustrate

its computation with the following data: Prepaid pension cost, $10; accumulated benefit obligation, $300; and plan assets at fair value, $240.

24. In the case of the unrecognized pension costs, such as prior service cost, which are first incurred during 1991, amortization may or may not be appropriate at the end of 1991. Explain why.

25. Explain a pension plan curtailment.

26. Explain a pension plan settlement.

27. Explain termination benefits.

EXERCISES

E 19-1
Understanding Pension Terminology
(L.O. 1, 2)

Match the brief definitions with the terms by entering one letter in each space provided.

Terms	Brief Definition
____ 1. Projected benefit obligation	A. Amount reported as total pension expense for the period; has six components
____ 2. Expected return on plan assets	
____ 3. Amortization of gains and losses	B. Allocation to periodic expense of the cost of retroactive pension benefits
____ 4. Pension plan assets	
____ 5. Net periodic pension expense	C. Actuarial present value of all future pension benefits excluding the effects of expected future compensation levels
____ 6. Fair market value (of plan assets)	
____ 7. Amortization of prior service costs	
____ 8. ERISA (1974)	D. Employee Retirement Income Security Act of 1974
____ 9. Prepaid pension cost	
____ 10. Accumulated benefit obligation	E. Cost of future pension benefits earned during the current accounting period
____ 11. Interest cost	
____ 12. Discount rate	F. The interest rate used by the actuary to adjust for the time value of money
____ 13. Service cost (pensions)	
____ 14. Amortization of transition cost	G. Present value of the employee's benefits not contingent on remaining an employee
____ 15. Vested benefit obligation	
____ 16. Actual return on plan assets	H. Allocation to periodic expense of the difference between expected and actual return on plan assets and changes in actuarial assumptions.
	I. Cumulative fund assets plus unrecognized pension costs in excess of the PBO.
	J. Difference between plan assets at fair market value at the beginning and ending of the period minus contributions and plus distributions during the accounting period
	K. The value of plan assets between a willing buyer and a willing seller (not a forced sale)
	L. Attribution (allocation) to accounting periods of the costs recognized when *SFAS No. 87* is first applied
	M. Actuarial present value of all future pension benefits, including the effects of current and future compensation levels
	N. Projected benefit obligation at the beginning of the current accounting period multiplied by the actuary's discount rate
	O. Resources set aside to provide future pension benefits to retirees
	P. Beginning market-related value of pension plan assets multiplied by the expected rate of return on plan assets

E 19-2
Multiple Choice
(L.O. 2, 3, 4, 5)

Choose the best answer from among the multiple choice alternatives.

1. Service cost for 1991 for a pension plan whose pension benefit formula considers estimates of future compensation levels is:

   a. The present value of benefits earned by employees in 1991 based on current salary levels.

     b. The increase in ABO for 1991 less interest cost on the beginning balance in ABO.

     c. The nominal value of benefits earned by employees in 1991 based on future salary levels.

     d. The present value of benefits earned by employees in 1991 based on future salary levels.

2. The following statements describe some aspect of accounting for defined benefit pension plans. Choose the incorrect statement.

     a. When only the first three components of pension expense have occurred to date for a plan, and actual return has always equaled expected return, underfunded PBO at a reporting date equals the balance in the accrued pension liability.

     b. When only the first three components of pension expense have occurred to date for a plan, and actual return has always equaled expected return, pension expense reflects the true annual cost to the company of providing future benefits earned in the current period, assuming all the actuarial assumptions are correct.

     c. Because the last three components of pension expense are derived from amortizing initial present values on a straight-line or similar basis, the true total cost of these items is not reflected in pension expense.

     d. Pension expense can be negative.

3. Choose the correct relationship among off-balance-sheet values and values reported in a balance sheet, relative to a pension plan.

     a. Underfunded PBO less amortization of unrecognized PSC equals the balance in accrued pension cost.

     b. Unrecognized PSC is an item that reconciles the balance in accrued pension cost and overfunded PBO.

     c. Sum of pension expense to date = PBO.

     d. PBO − ABO = balance in accrued pension cost.

4. For external reporting purposes, assuming an underfunded ABO, the liability that must be reported in the balance sheet is:

     a. PBO − plan assets at fair value.

     b. Balance in accrued pension cost.

     c. The underfunded ABO.

     d. Additional minimum pension liability.

5. Choose the correct statement concerning amortization of unrecognized gain or loss:

     a. Some amortization must be recognized in a year that begins with a nonzero unrecognized gain or loss.

     b. The corridor is the maximum amortization allowed.

     c. The corridor amount for 1991 is 10% of the greater of these two December 31, 1991, values: PBO and plan assets at fair value.

     d. The amortization of an unrecognized gain yields a reduction in pension expense and a reduction in that unrecognized gain.

6. Defined contribution plans and defined benefit plans are two common types of pension plans. Choose the correct statement concerning these plans.

     a. The required annual contribution to the plan is determined by formula or contract in a defined contribution plan.

     b. Both plans provide the same retirement benefits.

     c. The retirement benefit is usually determinable well before retirement in a defined contribution plan.

     d. In both types of plans, pension expense is generally the amount funded during the year.

7. PBO and plan assets at fair value are two values critical to the determination of the financial status of defined benefit plans. Choose the correct statement regarding items to be included in each (none of these statements is necessarily complete).

     a. Ending PBO includes total service cost to date, interest cost to date, net initial unamortized actuarial gain or loss to date, and initial PSC.

     b. Ending PBO includes total service cost to date, interest cost to date, net initial unamortized actuarial gain or loss to date, initial PSC, and initial transition cost.

     c. Ending fair value of plan assets includes funding to date, expected return to date, reduced by benefits paid to date.

     d. Ending PBO includes service cost to date, gross differences between expected and actual returns to date, net initial unamortized actuarial gain or loss to date, less contributions to date.

8. Which of the following is not one of the six components of pension expense (or part of a component)?

a. Initial transition asset.
b. Amortization of unrecognized gain or loss.
c. Actual return on plan assets.
d. Growth (interest cost) in PBO since the beginning of the period.

E 19–3
Prepaid Pension Cost
(L.O. 2, 3)

Rico Corporation adopted a defined benefit pension plan on January 1, 1991. The plan does not provide any retroactive benefits for existing employees. The pension funding payment is made to the trustee on December 31 of each year. The following information is available for 1991 and 1992.

	1991	1992
Service cost	$150,000	$165,000
Funding payment (contribution)	170,000	185,000
Interest on projected benefit obligation		15,000
Actual return on plan assets		18,000

Required:

In its December 31, 1992, balance sheet, Rico should report what amount of prepaid pension cost? (Prepare the journal entry to record pension expense for 1992.)

(AICPA adapted)

E 19–4
Amortization of Transition Amount
(L.O. 4)

As of December 31, 1987, the projected benefit obligation and plan assets of a noncontributory defined benefit plan sponsored by Neeni, Inc., were:

Projected benefit obligation	$780,000
Plan assets at fair value	600,000

Neeni elected to apply the provisions of *SFAS No. 87* in its financial statements for the year ended December 31, 1988. As of December 31, 1987, all amounts accrued as net periodic pension cost had been contributed to the plan. The average remaining service period of active plan participants expected to receive benefits was estimated to be 10 years at the date of transition. Some participants' estimated service periods are 20 and 25 years.

Required:

To minimize 1988 pension expense, what amount of amortization of the transition amount should Neeni recognize?

(AICPA adapted)

E 19–5
Pension Plan, One Employee: Compute Funding Payment
(L.O. 2, 3)

Fisher Company initiated a noncontributory defined benefit pension plan on January 1, 1988. The accounting period ends December 31. This exercise relates to one employee, V. R. Able. The pension formula specifies that Able will receive five annual retirement benefits of $50,000 at the end of each year, starting on December 31, 1998. Fisher Company will fully fund the pension plan by contributing 10 equal annual amounts starting on December 31, 1988. The pension fund will earn 8% annual interest during Able's service period and 7% during the retirement (payment) period.

Required:

Compute the equal annual funding payment that must be made by Fisher Company.

E 19–6
Pension Plan, Five Employees; Compute Funding Payment
(L.O. 2, 3)

Plans are being made to fund the prospective pension benefits of a group of employees of Farr Company due to retire in nine years and to be paid in amounts from one to five years after retirement as below:

End of Year 1	$ 90,000
End of Year 2	50,000
End of Year 3	30,000
End of Year 4	15,000
End of Year 5	5,000
Thereafter	–0–
Total of pension payments	$190,000

Funds deposited with the pension fund trustee will earn 6% per annum. The pension plan contract calls for deposit of an amount sufficient to fund all of the expected payments from the fund by the date the employees retire.

Required:

Round amounts to nearest dollar.

1. Compute the amount required by the trustee on the employees' retirement date, assuming the first pension payment is one year after retirement, and prepare a proof schedule reflecting the 6% earnings on unused funds and pension payout by the trustee.
2. Assuming that eight equal payments are made to the trustee, with the last payment coinciding with the retirement date, compute the amount of the equal payment.

E 19–7
Understanding the PBO, Plan Assets, and Under- or Overfunding
(L.O. 2, 3)

BV Company has a noncontributory, defined benefit pension plan. Data available for 1991 were:

> Projected benefit obligation (PBO):
> Balance, January 1, 1991 . . . . $164,000
> Balance, December 31, 1991 214,000
>
> Plant assets (at fair value):
> Balance, January 1, 1991 . . . . $ 80,000
> Balance, December 31, 1991 140,000

Required:

1. How much did the PBO increase during 1991? Give five items that could have caused the PBO to change.
2. How much did the pension plan assets change during 1991? Give three items that could have caused the change in plan assets.
3. Compute the amount of the under (over) funded PBO at (*a*) January 1, 1991, and (*b*) December 31, 1991. Explain what these amounts mean.

E 19–8
Understanding the Relationships between the Actuary's Report and the Trustee's Report
(L.O. 2, 3, 4)

Below are listed items that are shown on the 1992 PBO actuary's report (AR) or the trustee's report, status of plan assets (TR). Enter one check mark to the left for each item to indicate the report on which each one would appear. However, if a single item appears in both reports enter two check marks. If the item does not appear on either report do not enter a check mark on that line.

AR	TR	Items (1992 unless Stated Otherwise)
———	———	1. December 31, 1991, ending pension obligation
———	———	2. Interest cost
———	———	3. Loss (gain) related to changes in actuarial assumptions
———	———	4. Unrecognized pension costs
———	———	5. Cash funding by the employer
———	———	6. Prior service cost (increase)
———	———	7. Net periodic pension expense
———	———	8. Actual return on plan assets
———	———	9. Accrued/prepaid pension costs
———	———	10. Under (over) funded PBO
———	———	11. December 31, 1991, balance of pension plan asset
———	———	12. Pension benefits paid to retirees
———	———	13. Transition cost (increase or decrease)
———	———	14. PBO balance, January 1, 1993
———	———	15. Expected return on plan assets
———	———	16. Pension plan assets, January 1, 1993
———	———	17. Service cost
———	———	18. Accumulated benefit obligation

E 19–9
Prepare Trustee's Report, Analysis, Prepare Employer's Entries
(L.O. 2, 3)

Mason Company has a noncontributory, defined benefit pension plan. On December 31, 1991 (end of the accounting period and the measurement date), information about the pension plan included the following:

a. Projected benefit obligation (actuary):

January 1, 1991	$ 40,000
Service cost	60,000
Interest cost	3,600
Pension benefits paid	(–0–)
December 31, 1991	$103,600

Interest (discount) rate used by actuary, 9%.

b. The trustee's report on plan assets showed a beginning balance of $50,000, cash received from the employer of $37,000, and an actual return and expected return on plan assets of $10,000.

c. Unamortized prior service cost, gains and losses, transition costs, and additional minimum pension liability—none (from company records).

Required:

1. Prepare the trustee's report on the status of the plan assets (i.e., listing of the beginning asset balance, changes and the ending balance).
2. Compute the amount of the underfunding (overfunding) of the PBO on the beginning and ending dates.
3. Give the 1991 entry for Mason Company to record net periodic pension expense.
4. Give the same entry, assuming cash funding of $55,000 (instead of $37,000).
5. Show how the interest of $3,600 was computed.

E 19–10
Compute Net Periodic Pension Expense and Under- or Overfunded PBO; Entries
(L.O. 2, 3)

The 1991 records of Jax Company provided the following data related to its noncontributory, defined benefit pension plan (amounts in $000s):

a. Projected benefit obligation (report of actuary):

Balance, January 1, 1991	$1,500
Service cost	600
Interest cost	120
Pension benefits paid	(200)
Balance, December 31, 1991	2,020

Discount rate used by actuary, 8%.

b. Plan assets at fair value (report of trustee):

Balance, January 1, 1991	$1,204
Actual return on plan assets	84
Contributions, 1991	508
Pension benefits paid, 1991	(200)
Balance, December 31, 1991	$1,596

Expected long-term rate of return on plan assets, 7%.

c. January 1, 1991, balance of unrecognized prior service cost, gains and losses, and transition cost, zero.

Required:

1. Compute 1991 net periodic pension expense. Show the correct amount for each of the six components.
2. Give the 1991 entry(s) for Jax Company to record pension expense and funding.
3. Compute the under- or overfunded PBO at the beginning and end of 1991.

E 19–11
Compute Net Periodic Pension Expense and Under- or Overfunding of the PBO; Entries
(L.O. 2, 3)

Fox Company has a noncontributory, defined benefit pension plan. On December 31, 1991 (end of the accounting period and measurement date), the following data were available:

a. Projected benefit obligation (actuary's report):

Balance, December 31, 1990	$180,000
Prior service cost (due to plan amendment on January 1, 1991)	20,000
Balance, January 1, 1991	200,000
Service cost	130,000
Interest cost	16,000
Pension benefits paid	(–0–)
Balance, December 31, 1991	$346,000

Interest (discount) rate used by actuary, 8%.

b. Funding report of the trustee:

Balance, January 1, 1991	$210,000
Actual return on plan assets*	10,000
Cash received from employer	100,000
Pension benefits paid to retirees	(–0–)
Balance, December 31, 1991	$320,000

* Same as the expected return.

Required:

1. Show how the interest cost was computed.
2. Compute net periodic pension expense. Assume prior service cost will be amortized over a 10-year average remaining service period. Show the correct amounts for each component.
3. Give the 1991 entry for Fox Company to record net periodic pension expense.
4. Give the same entry assuming cash funding from the employer of $142,000, and no other changes.
5. Compute the underfunding (overfunding) of the PBO for (3) and (4).

E 19-12

Compute Net Periodic Pension Expense and Under- or Overfunded PBO; Entries

(L.O. 2, 3)

New Company started a noncontributory, defined benefit pension plan on January 1, 1990. Data available for 1991 were as follows:

a. Projected benefit obligation, 1991 (actuary's report):

Balance, January 1, 1991	$60,000
Service cost	20,000
Interest cost (interest rate, 10%)	6,000
Prior service cost	–0–
Losses (gains) due to change in actuarial assumptions (amortization to start in 1992)	(4,000)
Pension benefits paid	(1,000)
Balance, December 31, 1991	$81,000

b. Status of fund assets (trustee's report):

Balance, January 1, 1991	$55,000
Actual earnings on plan assets (same as expected return)	5,000
Payments received from employer during 1991	30,000
Pension benefits paid	(1,000)
Balance, December 31, 1991	$89,000

c. Company records: Unamortized gain from 1990 due to changes in assumptions, $3,000 (this amount was included in the 1990 PBO). There are no gains or losses on plan assets. Unamortized (unrecognized) prior service cost and transition cost from 1990 are zero.

Required:

1. Compute net periodic pension expense for 1991 assuming the 1990 losses (gains) are amortized for 1991 over a 15-year average remaining service period.
2. Give the 1991 pension expense and funding entry for New Company.
3. Give the same entry assuming the 1991 cash payment by employer was $18,000 instead of $30,000.
4. Compute the under (over) funded PBO for (2) and (3).

E 19-13

Pension Spreadsheet: Underfunded and Accrued Pension Cost; Entries

(L.O. 2, 3, 4)

GEE Company has a defined benefit pension plan. At the end of the current reporting period, December 31, 1995, the following information was available:

a. Projected benefit obligation (actuary's report):

Balance, January 1, 1995	$600
Service cost	78
Interest cost ($600 × 7% actuary's rate)	42
Loss (gain) change in actuarial assumptions*	18
Pension benefits paid	(40)
Balance, December 31, 1995	$698

* Amortization to start in 1996.

b. Status of fund assets (trustee's report):

Balance, January 1, 1995	$500
Actual return on plan assets (same as expected)	30
Cash received from employer company	70
Pension benefits paid to retirees	(40)
Balance, December 31, 1995	$560

c. From company records, unamortized pension cost from prior years (amortize over a nine-year average remaining service period):

Transition cost	$ 18
Prior service cost	27
Losses (gains)	36
Total	$ 81

Required:

1. Set up and complete a spreadsheet or format of your choice to develop the pension data required at the end of 1995.
2. Give the employer's pension entry at December 31, 1995.

E 19–14
Pension Spreadsheet: Underfunded and Accrued Pension Cost; Entry (L.O. 2, 3, 4)

Avis Company has a defined benefit pension plan. At the end of the current reporting period, December 31, 1991, the following information was available:

a. Projected benefit obligation (actuary's report);

Balance, January 1, 1991	$750
Service cost	80
Interest cost ($750 × 10%, actuary's rate)	75
Loss (gain) change in actuarial assumptions*	(7)
Pension benefits paid	(34)
Balance, December 31, 1991	$864

* Amortization to start in 1992.

b. Status of fund assets (trustee's report):

Balance, January 1, 1991	$600
Actual return on plan assets (same as expected)	54
Cash received from employer company	150
Pension benefits paid to retirees	(34)
Balance, December 31, 1991	$770

c. From company records, unamortized pension cost from prior years (amortize over a 10-year average remaining service period):

Transition cost	$100
Prior service cost	30
Losses (gains)	(20)
Total	$110

Required:

1. Set up and complete a spreadsheet or format of your choice to develop the pension data required at the end of 1991.
2. Give the employer's pension entry at December 31, 1991.

E 19-15

Understanding Pension Accounting Terminology

(L.O. 2, 3, 4, 5)

Match the following items with the financial statements by entering the appropriate letter in each blank.

Items	Reported on the Financial Statements
_____ 1. Accumulated benefit obligation	A. Income statement expense
_____ 2. Unrealized pension cost	B. Income statement gains and losses
_____ 3. Unrecognized gains (losses)	C. Balance sheet assets
_____ 4. Additional minimum pension liability	D. Balance sheet liabilities
_____ 5. Unrecognized prior service cost	E. Balance sheet owners' equity
_____ 6. Pension benefits paid	F. None of the above
_____ 7. Expected return on pension plan assets	
_____ 8. Unrecognized transition cost	
_____ 9. Accrued pension cost	
_____ 10. Net periodic pension expense	
_____ 11. Vested benefit obligation	
_____ 12. Unfunded accumulated benefit obligation	
_____ 13. Pension plan assets at fair value	
_____ 14. Prepaid pension cost	
_____ 15. Pension plan assets used in operations of the plan (i.e., furniture and fixtures)	

E 19-16

Minimum Amortization of Unrecognized Losses or Gains

(L.O. 4)

TV Company is preparing the 1992 entry to record pension expense, funding, and the change in accrued/prepaid pension cost. The company has a noncontributory, defined benefit plan. The date is the end of the annual accounting year. The company has the reports of the actuary and the fund trustee. This is the second year after changing from *APB Opinion No. 8* to *SFAS No. 87* and *88*. The company is preparing a spreadsheet.

Concern has been expressed about the three unrecognized pension costs—transition, prior service, and gains and losses. The first two costs will be properly amortized based on the average remaining service period (currently 10 years). The concern in this exercise is about the amortization of losses and gains. Separate data maintained by the company showed the following at December 31, 1992:

Company record of unrecognized losses (gains):

	Case A	Case B
a. Losses (gains):		
Balance loss (gain) Jan. 1, 1992	$ 15,000	$ 8,000
Increase (decrease) during 1992	–0–	–0–
Total	15,000	8,000
Amortization during 1992*	?	?
Balance, December 31, 1992	$?	$?

* Included in pension expense.

	Case A	Case B
b. Additional data on January 1, 1992:		
Projected benefit obligation (actuary)	$100,000	$100,000
Plan assets at market-related value	80,000	80,000
Average remaining service years	10	10

Required:

For each case complete the above schedule using the minimum method. Show computations.

E 19-17

Unrecognized Gains and Losses

(L.O. 4)

On January 1, 1991, a company reported a $6,000 unrecognized gain in the informal record of its pension plan. During 1991, the following events occurred:

a. Actual return on plan assets was $8,000 and expected return was $10,000.

b. A gain of $4,000 was determined by the actuary at December 31, 1991, based on changes in actuarial assumptions.

The company amortizes unrecognized gains and losses on the straight-line basis over the average remaining service life of active employees (20 years). It does not recognize the minimum amortization. Further information on this plan follows:

	Values At	
	January 1, 1991	**December 31, 1991**
PBO	$50,000	$56,000
Fair value of plan assets	30,000	34,000

Required:

Compute amortization of unrecognized gain or loss for 1991 and 1992.

E 19-18

Transition Asset or Liability

(L.O. 4)

Maxfield Corporation made its transition to *SFAS No. 87* for its pension plan on January 1, 1991. At that date, its PBO was $120,000, and plan assets at fair value were $140,000. Accounting for pensions under *APB Opinion No. 8* produced an accrued pension liability of $30,000 as of January 1, 1991.

Required:

1. Determine the transition asset or liability for Maxfield on January 1, 1991.
2. If the transition item relates to an employee group with an average remaining service life of 10 years, how is pension expense in 1991 affected by the amortization of the item?

E 19-19

Apply Minimum Amortization of Unrecognized Losses or Gains

(L.O. 4)

West Corporation initiated a noncontributory, defined benefit pension plan on January 1, 1989, and applied the provisions of *SFAS No. 87*. Information is available for the reporting year ended December 31, 1991, for the following independent cases (amounts in $000s):

	Case A	Case B
Projected benefit obligation, January 1, 1991	$500	$700
Plan assets at fair value, January 1, 1991*	400	800
Unrecognized (gain) or loss, January 1, 1991	(50)	30
Average remaining service period of active employees	10 years	15 years

* Same as market-related value.

Required:

West uses the straight-line method, based on the average remaining service period of active employees, to amortize unrecognized gain or loss (subject to required minimum amortization).

1. Compute the amount of straight-line amortization of unrecognized gain or loss in each case. Round all amounts to the nearest $ thousand.
2. Verify that the amortization computed in (1) meets the minimum required amortization.

E 19-20

Minimum Pension Liability: Four Years; Entries

(L.O. 5)

Goode Corporation established a noncontributory, defined benefit pension plan for its employees in 1989. On January 1, 1992, Goode initially applied the provisions of *SFAS No. 87* related to the recognition of an additional minimum pension liability to its pension accounting. The following information is available for the reporting years ended December 31, 1995 (in $000s):

Items	1992	1993	1994	1995
Projected benefit obligation	$1,100	$1,500	$2,000	$2,500
Accumulated benefit obligation	900	1,050	1,400	1,900
Plan assets at fair value	800	1,100	1,300	1,400
(Accrued) prepaid pension cost	100	25	(90)	(180)
Unrecognized prior service cost	150	180	160	200

Required:

1. Compute the required additional minimum liability for each year, 1992 through 1995.
2. Give the entry to recognize the additional minimum liability for each year, 1992 through 1995.

E 19-21

Minimum Liability: Three Cases; Entries

(L.O. 5)

XY Company has a noncontributory, defined benefit pension plan. It is December 31, 1991, end of the accounting year and measurement date for the pension plan. The following is the data for three separate cases, as of the measurement dates (in $000s):

Items (at December 31, 1991)	Case A	Case B	Case C
a. Projected benefit obligation	$500	$500	$500
b. Accumulated benefit obligation	400	400	400
c. Vested benefit obligation	180	180	180
d. Pension plan assets at book value	275	275	275
e. Pension plan assets at fair value	300	420	300
f. (Accrued) prepaid pension cost	0	40	(10)
g. Unrecognized prior service cost	110	90	75

Required:

1. For each case, compute the "additional minimum pension liability" that should be reported.
2. For each case (a) explain whether a minimum liability must be reported and why, and (b) if yes, give the entry.

E 19–22
Prepare Pension Spreadsheet: Additional Minimum Pension Liability; Entries
(L.O. 2, 3, 4, 5)

Fox Company has a noncontributory, defined benefit pension plan. The following data are available at December 31, 1991, which is the end of the accounting period and the measurement date:

a. Projected benefit obligation (actuary):

Balance, January 1, 1991	$223,000
Service cost	80,000
Interest cost	?
Prior service cost	–0–
Losses (gains) due to changes in assumptions (begin amortizing in 1992)	8,000
Pension benefits paid	(30,000)
Balance, December 31, 1991	?

Average remaining service period, 10 years
Actuary's discount rate, 8%
Accumulated benefit obligation, $292,000.

b. Pension plan assets (trustee):

Balance, January 1, 1991, at fair value	$200,000
Contributions to the pension plan by Fox	70,000
Actual return on plan assets	10,000
Benefits paid to retirees	(30,000)
Balance, December 31, 1991, at fair value	$250,000

Long-term expected rate of return on plan assets, 7%

c. Other balances at December 31, 1991: Unrecognized pension costs (total), $3,000, only prior service has a balance; accrued pension cost, $20,000.

Required:

1. Prepare a spreadsheet or format of your choice to develop the required pension data.
2. Give the annual pension entry for Fox.
3. Compute the additional minimum pension liability and give the related entry.
4. Give the entry for the next year assuming additional minimum pension liability is $10,000.

E 19–23
Prepare Spreadsheet: Additional Minimum Pension Liability; Entries
(L.O. 2, 3, 4, 5)

Saxon Company has a noncontributory, defined benefit pension plan. The accounting period ends December 31, 1991 (also the pension measurement date). Pension plan data for 1991 are as follows:

a. Projected benefit obligation:

Balance, January 1, 1991	$5,000
Service cost	3,000
Interest cost	402
Loss (gain) due to change in actuarial assumptions, January 1, 1991	25*
Pension benefits paid	(60)
Balance, December 31, 1991	$8,367

Accumulated benefit obligation, $8,365.
Actuary's discount rate, 8%.
Average remaining service period, 10 years.

b. Pension plan assets:

Balance, January 1, 1991, at fair value	$4,000
Actual return; gain (expected return $160; 4%)	150
Contribution to the pension fund by Saxon	3,200
Benefits paid to retirees	(60)
Balance, December 31, 1991	$7,290

c. Company records:

(1) January 1, 1991, Unamortized amounts:

Unrecognized prior service cost	$ 500
Unrecognized gain/loss	300 (gain)
Unrecognized transition cost	200

(2) December 31, 1991 changes:

Unrecognized prior service cost	no change
Unrecognized (gain)/loss ($175−$150)	25
Unrecognized transition cost	no change
(3) (Accrued) prepaid pension cost at January 1, 1991	(600) cr.

* Begin amortizing in 1991

Amortize all unrecognized items over the average service period (for problem purposes).

Required:

1. Prepare a spreadsheet or other format of your choice for the pension plan for 1991.
2. Based on (1), give the December 31, 1991 entry to record pension expense and funding for Saxon.
3. Test to determine whether additional minimum pension liability is required. Show computations and give the related entry.
4. Give the related entry for the next year assuming the additional minimum pension liability is $200.

E 19–24
Appendix 19A: Postretirement Benefit Liabilities (L.O. 6)

At December 31, 1992, Gypsum, Inc., estimated the following net incurred claims costs for one of its employees, for each year of the employee's retirement period to which the plan applies:

At Age	Estimated Net Incurred Claims Cost by Age
64	$4,194
65	4,640
66	1,284
67	1,421
68	1,577

The postretirement plan of Gypsum provides no benefits after age 68. For full eligibility, an employee must serve 20 years. The employee in question is 51 years old at December 31, 1992, and has served 15 years at that date. The employee is expected to retire at age 63. Gypsum's discount rate for postretirement benefit accounting purposes is 8%.

Required:

1. Determine the expected postretirement benefit obligation and accumulated postretirement benefit obligation at December 31, 1992, for this employee.
2. Assuming the employee works another five years after December 31, 1992, and there are no changes in expected net incurred claims costs, determine the expected postretirement benefit obligation and accumulated postretirement benefit obligation at December 31, 1997, for this employee.

E 19–25
Appendix 19A: Full Eligibility Date and Attribution Period (L.O. 6)

The following situations relate to an employee's eligibility for postretirement benefits.

a. A postretirement benefit plan provides 25% of full postretirement health coverage in return for 15 years of service to the firm after age 30, 50% coverage for 25 years of service after age 30, and 100% (full) coverage for 35 years of service after age 30. What is the full eligibility date for an employee hired at age 25 if she is expected to retire at age 57? And what percentage of full coverage will she receive?

b. Another plan provides life insurance benefits to employees who serve 20 years and reach age 50. The benefit equals 30% of final salary. A 45-year-old employee who currently earns $100,000 has worked 15 years for the firm. He is expected to retire at age 65 and is expected to be earning $200,000 at that time. What is the full eligibility date for this employee?

c. Bob joined a firm at age 25. The firm has a postretirement benefit plan. Five years later, Tom joined the firm at age 30. The postretirement plan specifies that employees are eligible for full benefits after rendering 20 years of service after age 30. What are the full eligibility dates for Bob and Tom?

d. A postretirement plan promises 100% health care coverage for all employees who retire after age 62. It is expected that participants will have rendered an average of 15 years of service at age 62. What is the full eligibility date for a participant? What is the attribution period (the period to which the expected postretirement benefit obligation is assigned)?

Required:

Answer each question independently.

E 19-26
Appendix 19A:
Amortization of Prior
Service Cost
(L.O. 6)

A firm amended its postretirement plan on January 1, 1994, by increasing health care benefits attributable to service rendered by employees before the amendment date. The accumulated postretirement benefit obligation increased $90,000 (prior service cost). The three employees affected, and their remaining years to full eligibility, follow:

	Remaining Years to Full Eligibility at Date of Amendment (January 1, 1994)				
Employee	1994	1995	1996	1997	1998
Robert	1	1	1	1	1
Susan	1	1			
William	1	1	—	—	—
	3	3	1	1	1

The average remaining service period for all active plan participants is 10 years.

Required:

1. Determine the amortization of prior service cost for each remaining year to full eligibility by allocating an equal amount to each remaining year to full eligibility.
2. Determine the amortization of prior service cost for each remaining year to full eligibility using the average remaining years to full eligibility.

E 19-27
Appendix 19A: Transition
Item and Amortization
(L.O. 6)

The following cases relate to the transition to *SFAS No. 106* for postretirement benefit accounting. The average remaining service period for active plan participants is 15 years. Assume the firm does not choose to recognize the obligation or asset in income immediately.

	At Transition Date		
Case	Accumulated Postretirement Benefit obligation	Plan Assets at Fair Value	Balance Sheet Account: (Accrued) Prepaid Postretirement Benefit Cost
I	$100,000	$ 0	$ 0
II	100,000	200,000	30,000
III	100,000	50,000	(60,000)
IV	100,000	40,000	(40,000)

Required:

For each case, determine the two permitted annual amortization amounts for the unrecognized transition asset or liability.

E 19-28
Appendix 19B:
Understanding Pension
Accounting Terminology
(L.O. 7)

Match the following brief descriptions with the terminology by entering appropriate letters in the blanks.

Terminology	Brief Description
_____ 1. Curtailment	A. *SFAS No. 88* has the same transition date as this earlier statement
_____ 2. Accrued/prepaid pension cost	
_____ 3. Termination benefits	B. An irrevocable event (or transaction) that (1) relieves the employer of a primary pension obligation and (2) reduces the employer's risks
_____ 4. Settlement	
_____ 5. *SFAS No. 87*	
_____ 6. Interest expense	C. The effects of a curtailment gain or loss are recorded in this account
_____ 7. Loss, termination benefits	
_____ 8. None of the above	D. Special or contractual benefits paid to employees who retire early
	E. An event that either (1) reduces expected years of future service or (2) reduces the number of employees
	F. This account is debited when it is probable that early retirees will be entitled to special benefits and the amount can be reasonably estimated
	G. When termination benefits are paid over an extended time, this account must be periodically debited
	H. Vested benefit obligation—for pension benefits retained regardless of employment to retirement date

E 19-29

Appendix 19B: Pension Curtailment: Analysis; Entry (L.O. 7)

CT Company has a noncontributory, defined benefit pension plan. On June 1, 1991, the company reduced its operations and, as a consequence, terminated 150 of its regular employees. As of that date the actuary provided the following information ($000s):

	Total	Related to Terminations
Projected benefit obligation	$1,000	$100
Composed of the following:		
Accumulated benefit obligation:*		
Vested benefits	$ 700	$ 75
Nonvested benefits	200	15
Total	900	
Effect of projected future compensation levels	100	10
Total	$1,000	$100

* Excludes effect of projected future compensation levels.

There were no unrecognized losses or gains (*a*) at transition date or (*b*) after transition date.

Required:

1. Complete the following schedule:

Items	Curtailment		
	Before	Effects	After
PBO			
Composed of the following:			
Accumulated benefit obligation			
Vested benefits			
Nonvested benefits			
Total			
Effect of projected future compensation levels			
Total			

2. Give the entry to record the curtailment.

E 19–30
Appendix 19B:
Pension Settlement:
Analysis; Entry
(L.O. 7)

Stacy Company has a noncontributory, defined benefit pension plan. On December 31, 1991 (end of the accounting period and pension measurement date), the company settled its vested benefit obligation of $248. Settlement was made by purchasing, with pension plan assets, nonparticipating annuity contracts that cost $248. Relevant pension plan data on this date were (all amounts in $000s):

a. Actuary's report, December 31, 1991 (before the settlement):
Projected benefit obligation $400
Accumulated benefit obligation 300
Vested benefit obligation 248
Effects of projected future compensation levels 100

b. Trustee's report (before settlement):
Pension plan assets at fair value $415

c. Company records (before the settlement):
Unrecognized net assets at transition . . . . $ 50
Unrecognized net gain subsequent to transition 60
Accrued/prepaid pension cost (a credit) 95

Required:

1. What percent of the PBO was settled?
2. Complete an analysis of the pension plan settlement to determine its effects.
3. Give the entry to record the settlement.

E 19–31
Appendix 19B: Pension
Termination; Entries
(L.O. 7)

On January 1, 1991 (accounting period ends December 31), Fox Company reduced its payroll by terminating 40 employees. Each terminated employee was given (*a*) a lump-sum payment of $1,000 on January 1, 1991, and (*b*) six monthly payments of $100 starting on January 31, 1991. The payments were made from company assets. All of the terminated employees accepted the termination benefits as of January 1, 1991.

Required:

1. Compute the cost of the termination benefits as of January 1, 1991. Use a 2% interest rate, compounded monthly.
2. Give the following entries for Fox Company:
   (*a*) January 1 1991—to record the termination.
   (*b*) January 1, 1991—to record the lump-sum cash payment.
   (*c*) January 31, 1991—to record the first monthly payment.

PROBLEMS

P 19–1
Present Value: PBO
and ABO
(L.O. 3)

Felco company sponsors a pension plan with the following pension benefit formula:

Benefit paid at end of each year of retirement =
                         (number of years worked) (Annual salary at retirement)/25

Credit for service began January 1, 1981, Bob Johnson's first day with the company. Bob is expected to work a total of 30 years with an annual salary at retirement of $100,000. He is expected to draw 10 years of retirement benefits. The discount rate is 10%.

Required:

1. Compute PBO on January 1, 1991, if Bob's current salary is $30,000.
2. Compute ABO on January 1, 1991.

P 19–2
Prior Service Cost
Amortization
(L.O. 4)

On January 1, 1991, Oracle Company amended its pension plan by granting retroactive pension benefits for work performed prior to that date. The present value of those benefits was determined to be $100,000 at that date. The following employees expect to receive benefits under the plan, and they have the indicated expected number of years remaining in their careers at January 1, 1991:

Bob: three years.

Joe: five years.

Required:

Determine the amortization of prior service cost to be recognized in 1995 under:

1. The method that associates an equivalent amount of prior service cost to each service year.
2. The straight-line method based on the average remaining service period of employees.

P 19-3
Pension Expense
(L.O. 2. 4)

The following data relate to a pension plan:

PBO, 1/1/91	$30,000
Intitial total PSC awarded 1/1/89	10,000
(relates to an employee group with an average remaining service period of 10 years, use SL method)	
Initial total transition liability	8,000
(transition occurred 1/1/89, use SL method, 15 years)	
Discount rate	8%
Unrecognized gain (use SL method), 1/1/91	5,000
Service cost	7,000
Contributions	9,000
Expected return	2,000
Actual return	3,000
Average remaining service period	15 years

Required:

Provide the entry to record pension expense for 1991.

P 19-4
Unrecognized Gains and
Losses
(L.O. 4)

Information for a pension plan follows:

Unrecognized gain, 1/1/90	$ 2,000
Years used to amortize unrecognized gain or loss	10
Fair value of plan assets, 1/1/90	50,000
Expected rate of return on plan assets	12%
Fair value of plan assets, 12/31/90	55,000
1990 funding	10,000
Benefits paid in 1990	8,000
Actuarial loss computed 12/31/90	2,000

The SL method is used for all amortizations. The firm does not use the minimum amortization for unrecognized gains and losses.

Required:

Compute the net unrecognized gain or loss at January 1, 1991.

P 19-5
Pension Expense
(L.O. 2, 4)

The following information pertains to a pension plan for a company that always recognizes only the minimum amortization of unrecognized gains and losses.

Unrecognized gain or loss, 1/1/90	$ 0
PBO, 1/1/90, not considering items below	30,000
Discount rate	10%
Fair value of plan assets, 1/1/90	12,000
Initial PSC value, from a grant in 1986	20,000
Unrecognized PSC, 1/1/90	4,000
Average remaining service life of employees covered under initial PSC grant	10 years
Actuarial loss, 1/1/90	$ 6,000
Expected rate of return on fund assets	12%
Average remaining service life used to amortize unrecognized gain or loss	12 years
Service cost, 1990	$ 6,000
Service cost, 1991	7,000
Funding amount, end of 1990	8,000
Funding amount, end of 1991	10,000
Actual return on fund in 1990	900
Actual return on fund in 1991	1,200

No benefits were paid in either year.

Required:

Compute pension expense for 1990 and 1991.

P 19-6
Pension Spreadsheet:
Overfunded and Prepaid
Pension Cost; Entry
(L.O. 2, 3, 4)

Waters Company has a defined benefit pension plan. At the end of the current reporting period, December 31, 1991, the following information was available:

a. Projected benefit obligation (actuary's report):

Balance January 1, 1991	$75,000
Service cost	20,000
Interest cost ($75,000 × 10%, actuary's rate)	7,500
Loss (gain) change in actuarial assumptions*	(200)
Pension benefits paid	(21,000)
Balance, December 31, 1991	$81,300
Accumulated benefit obligation	$60,000
Vested benefit obligation	$20,000

Average remaining service period, 10 years.†

* At December 31, 1991.

† Assume this is appropriate for all amortizations.

b. Status of fund assets (trustee's report):

Balance, January 1, 1991	$80,000
Actual return on plan assets (same as expected)	8,000
Cash received from employer company	15,000
Pension benefits paid to retirees	(21,000)
Balance, December 31, 1991	$82,000

c. From company records—Unrecognized pension costs:

Transition cost	$ 5,000
Prior service cost	10,000
Losses (gains)	(1,000)
Total	$14,000
Accrued (prepaid) pension cost	($19,000)

Required:

1. Set up and complete a spreadsheet or other format of your choice to develop the pension data required at the end of 1991.
2. Give the employer's pension entry at December 31, 1991.

P 19-7
Prepare a Spreadsheet
and Respond to a Query
about the Use of Cash
(L.O. 2, 3, 4)

Stoney Company first applied the provisions of *SFAS No. 87* to its noncontributory, defined benefit program on January 1, 1991. The annual accounting period ends on December 31. Data about the pension plan for 1992 are given below.

a. Projected benefit obligation (actuary's report):

Balance January 1, 1992	$16,000
Service cost	1,920
Interest cost ($16,000 × 8% actuary's rate)	1,280
Loss (gain) change in actuarial assumptions*	660
Pension benefit paid to retirees	(1,600)
Balance, December 31, 1992	$18,260

* At December 31, 1992.

Accumulated benefit obligation	$16,000
Vested benefit obligation	6,000
Actuary's estimated discount rate	8%
Average remaining service period (assumed appropriate for all amortizations)	11 years

b. Status of fund assets (trustee's report):

Balance, January 1, 1992	$12,600
Actual return on plan assets	1,000
Cash received from employer company	3,000
Pension benefits paid to retirees	(1,600)
Balance, December 31, 1992	$15,000
Expected return on plan assets	$ 1,000

c. Company data of January 1, 1992:

Unrecognized transition cost	$ 660
Unrecognized prior service cost	1,980
Unrecognized losses (gains)	(440)
Total unrecognized	$ 2,200
(Accrued) prepaid pension cost	$ (1,200)

Required:

1. Prepare a pension spreadsheet or other format of your choice and give Stoney's 1992 journal entry for the pension plan.
2. The company president asked the following question: We paid $3,000 cash to the pension fund, but the pension liability was reduced by only $600. Why? Prepare your response with data and explanation.

P 19–8

Comparative Cases: Prepare Two Spreadsheets and Employer's Entry (L.O. 2, 3, 4)

Art Company first applied the provisions of *SFAS No. 87* to its noncontributory, defined pension plan in 1991. The annual accounting period ends December 31. Data about the pension plan for 1992 are given below for two comparative cases to emphasize how losses versus gains affect the results.

	Case A	Case B
a. Actuary's PBO Report at December 31, 1992:		
Projected benefit obligation (actuary's report):		
Balance, January 1, 1992	$500	$500
Service cost	100	100
Interest cost ($500 × 10%, actuary's rate)	50	50
Loss (gain) change in actuarial assumptions*	8	(8)
Pension benefits paid to retirees	(10)	(15)
Balance, December 31, 1992	$648	$627

* At December 31, 1992; amortizations start in 1993.

	Case A	Case B
Accumulated benefit obligation	$500	$484
Vested benefit obligation	$200	$184
Actuary's estimated interest rate	10%	10%
Average remaining service period†	8 years	8 years
b. Status of fund assets (trustee's report):		
Balance, January 1, 1992	$450	$450
Actual return on plan assets	20	20
Cash received from employer company	150	120
Pension benefits paid to retirees	(10)	(15)
Balance, December 31, 1992	$610	$575
Expected return on plan assets	$ 24	$ 25

† Assume eight years is appropriate for all amortizations.

	Case A	Case B
c. Company data on January 1, 1992:		
Unrecognized transition cost	$ 8	$ 8
Unrecognized prior service cost	16	16
Unrecognized losses (gains)*	24	(24)
Total unrecognized	$ 48	$-0-
(Accrued) prepaid pension cost	$ (2)	$(50)

* Due only to changes in actuarial assumptions.

Required:

Prepare a spreadsheet or other format of your choice and give the employer's journal entry for the pension plan for Case A and Case B. When preparing these two spreadsheets or formats, focus on the effects of losses versus gains.

P 19–9

Spreadsheet: Additional
Minimum Pension
Liability; Entries
(L.O. 2, 3, 4, 5)

Frazier Company has a noncontributory, defined benefit pension plan. The company must record its pension expense for the year ended December 31, 1991. The following data are available (in $000s):

a. Actuary's report: PBO

Balance, January 1, 1991	$300
Service cost	30
Interest cost (at 8%)	24
Lost (gain) actuarial changes*	10
Pension benefits paid to retirees	(100)
Balance, December 31, 1991	$264
Accumulated benefit obligation, end of 1991	$247

   * At December 31, 1991.

b. Fund trustee's report:

Balance, January 1, 1991 (at fair value)*	$200
Actual return on plan assets	18
Expected return on plan assets, 10%	
Payments received from Frazier	60
Pension benefits paid	(100)
Balance, December 31, 1991	$178

   * Same as market-related value.

c. Data from company records:

Unrecognized transition cost (January 1, 1991)	$ 27
Unrecognized prior service cost (January 1, 1991)	36
Unrecognized loss (January 1, 1991)	4
Total unrecognized	$ 67

Amortization periods, for problem purposes only:
Transition cost 9 years; prior service cost,
10 years; and losses (gains), 4 years.
(Accrued) prepaid pension cost, January 1, 1991, $(33).

Required:

1. Prepare a pension spreadsheet or other format of your choice and give the 1991 entry for Frazier Company.
2. Compute any additional minimum pension liability to be recorded for 1991 and give the related entry.
3. Give the related entry for 1992 assuming the ending balance of additional minimum pension liability for 1992 is $10.

P 19–10

Spreadsheet: Additional
Minimum Pension
Liability; Entries
(L.O. 2, 3, 4, 5)

Jacks Company has a noncontributory, defined benefit pension plan. The company will record its pension expense for the year ended December 31, 1991. The following data are available (in 000s):

a. Actuary's report: PBO

Balance, January 1, 1991	$300
Service cost	50
Interest cost (at 8%)	24
Loss (gain) actuarial changes (December 31, 1991)	(10)
Pension benefits paid to retirees	(124)
Balance, December 31, 1991	$240
Accumulated benefit obligation, end of 1991	$237

b. Fund trustee's report:

Balance, January 1, 1991 (at fair value)*	$170
Actual return on plan assets	27
Expected return on plan assets, 12%	
Payments received from Jacks	110
Pension benefits paid	(124)
Balance, December 31, 1991	$183

   * Same as market-related value.

c. Data from company records:

Unrecognized transition cost (January 1, 1991) . . . . $ 60
Unrecognized prior service cost (January 1, 1991) 40
Unrecognized loss (gain) (January 1, 1991) . . . . –0–

Total unrecognized $100

Average remaining service period is 10 years (for problem purposes use this for amortizing each of the three unrecognized pension costs).
(Accrued) prepaid pension cost, January 1, 1991, $30 accrued.

Required:

1. Prepare a pension spreadsheet or other format of your choice and give the 1991 entry for Jacks Company.
2. Compute any additional pension liability for 1991 and give the related entry.
3. Give the related entry for the next period, 1992, assuming the additional minimum liability required for 1992 is $40 and the amortization of PSC and transition cost is the same as in 1991.

P 19–11
Prepare Pension Spreadsheet and Additional Minimum Pension Liability for Two Consecutive Years
(L.O. 2, 3, 4, 5)

AAP Company has a noncontributory, defined benefit pension plan. This case focuses on the accounting required at December 31, 1991 and 1992, with emphasis on the PBO, plan assets, unrecognized pension costs, net periodic pension expense, accrued/prepaid pension cost and the additional minimum pension liability. The data for the two years are as follows (in $000s):

	1991	1992
a. Actuary's (PBO):		
Projected benefit obligation beginning	$1,700	$2,196
Service cost	180	210
Interest cost	136	198
Prior service cost	240	
Loss (gain), actuarial changes, December 31.	20	5
Loss (gain), plan assets		
Pension benefits paid	(80)	(125)
Projected benefit obligation, ending	$2,196	$2,484
Accumulated benefit obligation	$1,775	$2,109
Average remaining service period*	10 years	9 years
Actuary's interest rate	8%	9%

* For problem purposes, assume minimum amortization of unrecognized loss/gain does not apply; therefore, use these periods for all amortization.

b. Trustee's report (plan assets at fair value):†	1991	1992
Balance at beginning	$1,000	$1,210
Actual return on plan assets	90	110
Contribution from employer	200	440
Pension benefits paid to retirees	(80)	(125)
Balance at ending	$1,210	$1,635
Expected return on plan assets	10%	10%

† Same as market-related value.

c. AAP Company records:	1991	1992
Unrecognized cost at beginning:		
Prior service cost	$ –0–	$ 216
Transition cost	300	270
Loss (gain)	150	165
Total	$ 450	$ 651

Required:

1. Prepare a pension spreadsheet or format of your choice and give the related pension entry for AAP Company for (a) 1991 and (b) 1992.
2. Compute the additional minimum pension liability for 1991 and 1992 and give any related entry for (a) 1991 and (b) 1992. Also, give the 1992 ending balances in the three related accounts.

P 19-12
Additional Minimum Pension Liability
(L.O. 5)

The following information (amounts in $000's) applies to 1990 through 1992 for a pension plan. The sponsor has no balance in either the additional minimum pension liability or intangible pension asset at 1/1/90.

	1990	1991	1992
ABO at end of year	$40	$45	$60
Plan assets at fair value			
at end of year	30	31	48

The next two values are stated at the end of each year, after the pension expense entry, but before the entry to adjust additional minimum pension liability.

Balance in accrued pension			
cost (cr.)	4	7	9
Unrecognized PSC	4	3	2

Required:

Provide the entry adjusting additional minimum pension liability for each year. Assume that the maximum intangible balance is the lower of unrecognized PSC and balance in additional minimum pension liability.

P 19-13
Appendix 19A: Postretirement Benefit Expense and Funded Status
(L.O. 6)

The following information pertains to a firm with a postretirement benefit health care plan:

Transition date: January 1, 1993
Accumulated postretirement benefit liability at transition: $100,000
The firm has no plan assets or balance sheet account relating to the plan at transition
Discount rate: 12%
Amortization period for unrecognized transition liability: average remaining service period of active plan participants, 15 years
Service cost, 1993: $25,000
Contribution to benefit fund, December 31, 1993: $35,000
Benefit payments, December 31, 1993: $10,000

Required:

Provide the entry to record 1993 postretirement benefit expense, and the reconciliation of funded status and (accrued) prepaid postretirement benefit cost at December 31, 1993.

P 19-14
Appendix 19A: Postretirement Benefit Expense and Funded Status
(L.O. 6)

The December 31, 1994, reconciliation of funded status and accrued postretirement benefit cost for a firm with a postretirement benefit plan is:

APBO	$(224,000)
Plan assets at fair value	63,000
Underfunded APBO (funded status)	(161,000)
Unrecognized transition liability	61,000
Accrued postretirement benefit cost	$(100,000)

At the beginning of 1995, the plan was amended to increase future health care benefits for retirees. The increase is attributable to service performed before 1995. As a result, APBO increased $56,000. The discount rate is 12%, and the expected long-term rate of return on plan assets is 10%. There are 10 years remaining in the amortization period for the unrecognized transition liability. The average remaining years of service to full eligibility for active plan participants is 15 years.

Additional information for 1995:

Service cost	$50,000
Actual return on plan assets	6,000
Contributions (end-of-year)	75,000
Benefit payments (end-of-year)	85,000

Required:

Provide the entry to record 1995 postretirement benefit expense and the reconciliation of funded status and (accrued) prepaid postretirement benefit cost at December 31, 1995.

P 19–15

Appendix 19A: Postretirement Benefit Expense and Funded Status

(L.O. 6)

The December 31, 1996, reconciliation of funded status and accrued postretirement benefit cost, and additional information, for a firm with a postretirement benefit plan is:

APBO	($450,000)
Plan assets at fair value	125,000
Underfunded APBO (funded status)	(325,000)
Unrecognized prior service cost	48,000
Unrecognized net loss	62,000
Unrecognized transition liability	180,000
Accrued postretirement benefit cost	($ 35,000)

Additional information:

Expected return on plan assets: 10%
Discount rate: 8%
Remaining years to amortize prior service cost: 8
Average remaining service period: 10
Remaining years to amortize unrecognized transition liability: 18
The firm recognizes the minimum amortization of gains and losses
Service cost, 1997: $80,000
Actual return on plan assets, 1997: $30,000
APBO increased $100,000 on December 31, 1997 due to an increase in health care cost trend rates.
Contributions to fund, December 31, 1997: $100,000
Benefit payments, December 31, 1997: $80,000

Required:

Provide the entry to record 1997 postretirement benefit expense and the reconciliation of funded status and accrued (prepaid) postretirement benefit cost at December 31, 1997.

P 19–16

Appendix 19B: Pension Curtailment, Analysis, Entry

(L.O. 7)

Hardy Company experienced financial difficulties in 1991. In response, one action taken by Hardy's management was to offer special termination benefits to certain employees. Each employee was offered $10,000 in a lump-sum cash payment to resign. One hundred employees accepted the offer. The special termination benefits were paid from Hardy's assets, not from pension plan assets.

In addition, Hardy's pension plan obligation was curtailed. The amount of the reduction in Hardy's projected benefit obligation due to the curtailment was $500,000. None of this amount was vested; therefore, Hardy did not reduce pension plan assets. Expected future years of employee service was reduced by 25% due to the the curtailment. Details of Hardy's pension plan obligation, assets, and recognized and unrecognized amounts as of December 31, 1991 (termination date) are given below (amounts in thousands):

Projected benefit obligation (PBO)	($2,800)
Plan assets at fair value	2,000
	(800)
Add (deduct) unamortized items:	
Unrecognized transition cost	400
Unrecognized net gain	(200)
Unrecognized prior service cost	100
Accrued (prepaid) pension cost	$ (500)

Required:

1. Prepare an analysis of the effects of the curtailment. Show computations.
2. Give the entry to reflect the curtailment and special termination benefits.

P 19–17

Appendix 19B: Pension Curtailment, Analysis, Entries

(L.O. 7)

Casey Company has had a noncontributory, defined benefit pension plan for its employees since 1991. Faced with declining demand for its products, Casey reduced its operations in 1995. Because of the reduced level of operations, a number of employees were terminated, and Casey's pension obligations were curtailed. The impact of the curtailment was to reduce Casey's projected benefit obligation by $200,000 and the expected future years of employee service by 20% as of January 1, 1995. The following pension plan information is based on two independent cases as of January 1, 1995 (amounts in thousands):

	Case A	Case B
Projected benefit obligation (PBO)	($1,200)	($1,500)
Plan assets at fair value	1,000	2,000
	(200)	500
Add (deduct) unamortized items:		
Unrecognized transition cost (gain)	50	(80)
Unrecognized net (gain) loss	100	(120)
Unrecognized prior service cost	30	40
(Accrued) prepaid pension cost	($ 20)	$ 340

Required:

1. Prepare an analysis of the effects of the curtailment for each case. Show computations.
2. Give the entry to reflect the curtailment for each case.

P 19–18

Appendix 19B: Pension Settlement, Analysis; Entries (L.O. 7)

On December 31, 1991, Watson Corporation reduced its pension obligations by purchasing nonparticipating annuity contracts with pension plan assets. The annuity contracts were designed to provide Watson's employees with future pension benefits in return for a fixed payment of $500,000 by Watson. A summary of Watson's pension plan obligation, assets, and recognized and unrecognized components immediately before the settlement is given below for two independent cases (amounts in thousands):

	Case A	Case B
Projected benefit obligation (PBO)	($2,500)	($2,000)
Plan asset fair value	2,200	2,200
	(300)	200
Add (deduct) unamortized items:		
Unrecognized transition cost (gain)	50	(70)
Unrecognized net (gain) loss	120	(130)
Unrecognized prior service cost	40	40
(Accrued) prepaid pension cost	($ 90)	$ 40

Required:

1. Prepare an analysis of the effects of the settlement for each case. Show computations. Round to the nearest thousand. The analysis should have column headings as follows:

Item	Before Settlement	Effects of Settlement	After Settlement

2. Give the entry to reflect the settlement for each case.

P 19–19

Appendix 19C: Pension Plan Financial Statements (L.O. 8)

The following information (which is in no particular order) relates to the Bamson Company pension plan. Some of the values refer to account balances as of December 31, 1991. Others refer to changes in amounts during 1991:

Interest earned on plan investments	$ 20,000
Vested benefits:	
Of participants current receiving payments	80,000
Other participants	400,000
Investments at fair value	500,000
Cash	230,000
Accrued and account payables	440,000
Net appreciation in fair value, investments	50,000
Contributions:	
Employer	850,000
Employee	300,000
Change in actuarial assumption (decrease in average assumed retirement age)	60,000

Benefits paid	800,000
Nonvested benefits	200,000
Dividends	5,000
Investment expenses	10,000
Benefits earned	950,000
Administrative expenses	150,000
Employee contributions	200,000
Accrued interest and dividends	20,000

Required:

1. Prepare the statement of net assets available for benefits, statement of changes in net assets available for benefits, statement of accumulated plan benefits, and statement of changes in accumulated plan benefits, for the Bamson plan. Use the format suggested in Appendix 19C.
2. What does the total actuarial present value of accumulated plan benefits represent?
3. Is the plan over- or underfunded at December 31, 1991?
4. By how much has the plan changed its funded status during 1991?

P 19–20
Comprehensive Problem:

COMPREHENSIVE PROBLEM
♦

Prepare Pension Spreadsheet for Two Years with Corridor (Minimum) Amortization Test; Entries
(L.O. 2, 3, 4, 5)

Voss Company has a noncontributory, defined benefit pension plan for its employees. The data available at year-end for December 31, 1991 and 1992, are as follows ($000s):

	1991	1992
a. Actuary's report (PBO):		
Projected benefit obligation, beginning	$1,520	$1,752
Service cost	200	238
Interest cost	152	140
Prior service cost	20	13
Loss (gain), actuarial changes, December 31	10	6
Pension benefits paid	(150)	(170)
Projected benefit obligation, ending	$1,752	$1,979
Accumulated benefit obligation	$ 920	$1,000
Average remaining service period*	10 years	9 years

* For problem purposes use this for all unrecognized pension costs.

	1991	1992
b. Trustee's report (plan assets at fair value):		
Balance at beginning	$ 940	$1,084
Actual return on plan assets	84	92
Contributions from employer	210	320
Pension benefits paid to retirees	(150)	(170)
Balance at ending	$1,084	$1,326
Expected return on plan assets	10%	10%

	1991	1992
c. Voss Company records:		
Unrecognized costs at beginning:		
Prior service cost	$ 100	$ 110
Transition cost	40	36
Loss (gain)	182	184
Total	$ 322	$ 330

Required:

1. Prepare a spreadsheet or other format of your choice and give the related pension entry for Voss Company for (*a*) 1991 and (*b*) 1992. Use the straight-line method to amortize unrecognized gains and losses in your format. Also compute the minimum amortization.
2. Explain why additional minimum pension liability does not apply in this situation.
3. Provide the following footnote disclosures required by *SFAS No. 87* for both years: (*a*) the amount of pension expense for each period with separate disclosure of service cost, interest cost, actual return on plan assets, and net total of other components; and (*b*) the reconciliation of funded status.

CASES

**C 19-1
Is *SFAS No. 87*
Workable?
(L.O. 1-5)**

SFAS No. 87, "Employers' Accounting for Pensions," was one of the most controversial standards issued by the FASB, as illustrated by the following excerpts from an article in *The Wall Street Journal* about the *Standard* shortly before its release ("Accounting Proposal Troubles Firms," *The Wall Street Journal,* December 6, 1985, p. 6):

> Corporate financial executives are fuming about a controversial pension-accounting rule that the Financial Accounting Standards Board is expected to issue soon.
>
> They say the proposed rule is vexing on two counts: It would burden corporate balance sheets by placing a hefty new liability on the books, and it would make bottom-line financial results more volatile.
>
> The FASB sets the four-year phase-in period to cushion the rule's effects. But some financial executives in depressed smoke-stack industries argue that boosting liabilities simply by a bookkeeping change is like kicking them when they're down.

This debate continues unabated. For example, an interesting article in the *Financial Executive Magazine* (September/October 1987) contained an interesting dialogue in "Is FASB '87 Workable?" The dialogue was summarized as follows:

No!

1. The rule-making body of the accounting profession has issued the *Statement* despite objections by the overwhelming majority of their own profession, clients, and related professions. This is either admirable or foolish. Only time will tell.
2. The *Statement* is much too complex. Simpler solutions exist.
3. It does not accomplish its objectives of presenting a more meaningful measure of pension expense and introducing balance sheet items helpful to readers of financial statements.
4. The FASB based its decisions on conceptualizations, rather than on user needs.

The authors of the article continue with comments to support these statements.

Yes!

The four myths concerning the *Statement* are as follows:

1. *SFAS No. 87* represents bad accounting.
2. The new standards eliminate management's ability to tailor financial reporting to individual facts and circumstances.
3. The accounting and disclosure requirements do not provide the information that users need.
4. As a result of all of the above, corporate financial managers are badly served.

The authors of the article continue with comments to deflate these myths.

Required:

1. Discuss the requirements of *SFAS No. 87* that might cause concern to companies affected by the *Standard*. Give reasons why companies might be upset.
2. Be prepared to discuss this controversy, even including your opinion. Also, focus on delayed recognition and its implications.

**C 19-2
Appendix 19A:
Differences between
Accounting for Pensions
and Nonpension
Postretirement Benefits
(L.O. 6)**

Accounting for pensions is similar to accounting for nonpension postretirement benefits in many ways. However, there are some significant differences. List and discuss some of these differences and their financial statement effects.

C 19–3

Ethical Considerations and Opportunities for Managing Pension Expense and Liabilities (L.O. 2, 3, 4, 5)

You are the senior auditor for the audit of a client firm in considerable financial difficulty. In particular, debt covenants may be violated if liabilities are increased. In addition, the client's balance in retained earnings is minimal as a result of excessively high dividends and diminished earnings in the past several years.

The client firm is dominated by its CEO, a person who has worked his way up the ladder and has served the firm for 30 years. The CEO makes most of the major decisions in the firm. This person is the primary firm representative working with the audit staff. At present, there is no organized audit committee. The CEO is very aggressive with respect to earnings.

From the minutes, you have discovered that extreme emphasis has been placed on meeting earnings projections. Department officers have been fired for not meeting earnings goals for two successive years. The firm uses FIFO, straight-line depreciation, and other accounting techniques that reduce or delay expense recognition. The firm has resisted using the installment sales method for customers with questionable credit ratings.

You know that, through *Statement on Auditing Standards No. 53,* "The Auditor's Responsibility to Detect and Report Errors and Irregularities," part of your responsibility as an auditor is to develop an audit plan that is sensitive to audit risk. Audit risk is the probability that you may unknowingly fail to modify your audit report on financial statements that are materially misstated. Your audit plan should be designed to provide reasonable assurance that material errors and irregularities are detected.

Required:

You understand that the pressures faced by this firm may create incentives for unethical and fraudulent financial reporting. What aspects of pension accounting should you inspect with special care? What pension-related variables might be changed, and in what direction, to achieve reduced pension expense and liabilities? Include in your discussion reasons why you chose these variables.

C 19–4

Sherwin-Williams: Analysis of Actual Financial Statements (L.O. 2, 3, 4, 5, 6)

Refer to the 1990 financial statements of Sherwin-Williams that appear at the end of this text. Respond to the following questions concerning the firm's pension plans.

1. For the defined benefit plans, how large were plan assets relative to total assets listed in the balance sheet, at December 31, 1990?
2. For the defined benefit plans, how large was PBO relative to total liabilities listed in the balance sheet, at December 31, 1990?
3. Are the defined benefit plans under- or overfunded in the aggregate, and by what amount, at December 31, 1990?
4. Are most of the defined benefits vested at December 31, 1990?
5. Why was pension expense for defined benefit plans a credit in 1990?
6. Does the firm have an intangible pension asset at December 31, 1990?
7. Is the firm currently using accrual accounting for nonpension postretirement benefits?

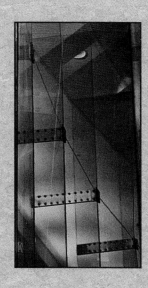

OWNERS' EQUITY

C H A P T E R
20

Corporations: Contributed Capital

LEARNING
OBJECTIVES
◆

After you have studied this chapter, you will:

1. Be able to describe the characteristics, advantages, and disadvantages of the corporate form of business organization.

2. Be familiar with different types of investments shareholders make in firms, and the various rights that attach to each.

3. Be able to describe and demonstrate accounting and reporting practices for the issuance of various forms of capital stock, for both cash transactions and non-cash transactions.

4. Understand the accounting and reporting practices for the issuance of subscription stock.

5. Understand the accounting and reporting practices for treasury stock, including both the cost method and the par value method.

6. Understand the accounting and reporting practices for the retirement of callable and redeemable stock, and for the conversion of convertible preferred stock.

◆

INTRODUCTION
◆

K ing World Productions, Inc., a profitable company, earned approximately $60 million in 1988. During 1988, however, the company purchased in the open market approximately $150 million worth of its own stock. As a result, the company reported a negative net worth of nearly $30 million. How, you might reasonably ask, can a perfectly healthy company (and King World is a healthy company) report its stockholders' equity in such a way that each common share appears to be a debt owed to the company in the amount of $1.20 per share?

The answer is that the firm is following GAAP in accounting for its transaction of acquiring its own shares, and the accounting result of this transaction makes it appear as if the firm were insolvent. As we will see, reacquired shares are reported in a contra account to stockholders' equity, and if enough shares are acquired at a sufficiently high price, the result is the situation described for King World Productions.

SFAC No. 3 defines **owners'** or **stockholders' equity** as the difference between the assets and liabilities of the entity. It is a residual interest and has no existence without the presence of assets. Owners' equity is not a claim on specific assets, but rather a claim on total assets after liabilities are recognized. As such, it is often called *net assets*. Stockholders' equity is the net contribution to the firm by owners, plus the firm's cumulative earnings that have been retained in the business, less any reacquisition of the company's own shares of stock.

Previous chapters focused the discussion on understanding the content and application of generally accepted accounting principles applied primarily to assets and liabilities. The principles covered are applicable to all forms of business organization, whether sole proprietorship, partnership, or corporation. However, because of the legal requirements and complex contracts that can be developed under the corporate form of organization, the accounting and reporting requirements for owners' equity for corporations are discussed in this separate chapter. The terms *stockholders' equity* or *shareholders' equity* will be used to refer to the owners' equity section of a corporation's financial statements.

The corporation is the dominant form of business organization measured in terms of total contributed capital invested in the U.S. economy. Moreover, several factors make it likely that the corporation will continue to grow and be the dominant form in the future:

1. The corporate form of business organization permits the accumulation of large amounts of capital in an organization and allow economies of scale to be achieved.
2. The corporate form of business organization limits the liability of the shareholders.
3. Ownership interests of corporations are generally more readily transferable than are those of other forms of business ownership.

This chapter concentrates on the transactions that affect contributed capital of the corporation. The next chapter covers the accounting and reporting issues that affect earnings retained in the organization.

◆

CONTRIBUTED CAPITAL AT FORMATION OF A CORPORATION
◆

Formation of a Corporation

In the United States, the incorporation process is prescribed by the laws of the specific state in which a corporation is organized. State law dictates the process because there are no federal incorporation laws. Most states have adopted many of the principles recommended in the Model Business Corporation Act. As a result, the corporate laws of the various states have many common provisions.

The laws of the various states have a significant impact on accounting for stockholders' equity. These laws specify such items as requirements for stock issuance, definition of legal capital, limitations on dividends, constraints on treasury stock, and provisions for the retirement of capital stock. It is impractical to include in this text the legal requirements of each state. Therefore, reasonable generalizations and typical situations are used to facilitate the discussion.

For most states, the incorporation process can be outlined as follows:

1. The articles of incorporation are prepared by the organizers to meet the legal requirements of the state. These articles specify such items as purpose of the business, location, names of the organizers, classes and numbers of shares of capital stock authorized, and the consideration to be paid in by the organizers for their respective shares. This must be done before the corporation begins operations.
2. The articles of incorporation are filed with a designated state official, usually the secretary of state.
3. When the articles of incorporation are approved, a corporate charter is issued by the state. The charter makes the articles of incorporation operative.
4. A board of directors is selected. It meets and approves (a) corporate bylaws to supplement, but not change, the provisions of the charter and (b) corporate officers.

Classification of Corporations

Corporations can be classified as follows:

1. **Public (government-owned) corporations:** corporations that perform governmental activities or are business operations owned by governmental bodies. Examples include the Tennessee Valley Authority, Federal Deposit Insurance Corporation, and municipal transit systems owned by local government agencies.
2. **Private corporations:** corporations that are privately owned by individuals or other nongovernmental units. Private corporations can be further classified:
   a. **Nonstock:** nonprofit organizations that do not issue shares of stock (such as colleges, churches, and charities).
   b. **Stock:** companies that issue shares of capital stock and operate to earn a profit. Private stock corporations can be further classified:
      (1) **Closed corporations** (nonpublic enterprises): stock is held by a few stockholders and is not available for purchase by the public. Generally, there are two types: (a) professional corporations, in which members of a legally recognized profession (e.g., medicine, law, accounting) form a corporation and membership is open only to members of the profession; and (b) a Subchapter S corporation established through Subchapter S of the Internal Revenue Code (S corporations can have no more than 35 shareholders, and have the advantage of avoiding the double taxation of open corporations). Unlike other forms of private corporations, professional corporations generally do not limit the liability of their owners.
      (2) **Open (publicly traded) corporations:** stock of the corporation is available for purchase by the public. It is generally widely held. Such open corporations are often classified as either (a) listed, meaning its shares are traded on an organized stock exchange (e.g., the New York Stock Exchange), or as (b) unlisted or over-the-counter (OTC), meaning the stock is traded in a market in which securities dealers buy and sell to the public.
      Many open corporations that are traded on stock exchanges and some that are traded over-the-counter have familiar names—General Motors, IBM, Exxon, Procter & Gamble. Many more are smaller and less well-known. Open corporations will be the focus of attention in this chapter, but

the principles to be covered apply to the other types of private, stock corporations.

Characteristics of Capital Stock

Shares of capital stock, represented by stock certificates, evidence ownership in a corporation. Shares may be bought, sold, or otherwise transferred by the stockholders without the consent of the corporation (unless there is an enforceable agreement not to do so). Ownership of shares usually entitles the holder to certain basic rights:

1. The right to influence the management of the corporation through participating and voting in stockholder meetings.
2. The right to participate in the earnings of the corporation through dividends declared by the board of directors.
3. The right to share in the distribution of assets of the corporation at liquidation or through liquidating dividends.
4. The right to purchase shares of common stock of the corporation on a pro rata basis when new issues are offered for sale. This preemptive right is designed to provide each stockholder the opportunity to maintain a proportional ownership in the corporation. Some corporations have withheld this preemptive right because of difficulties it creates when the corporation issues new stock.

The first three rights are the most basic, and generally hold in all states. The fourth right is less consistently required across states, and in some instances, it may not exist. These basic rights are shared proportionately by all stockholders of each class of stock unless the charter or bylaws (and as noted on the stock certificates) specifically provide otherwise. In the case of common stock, all holders enjoy the basic rights. When there are two or more classes of stock, the holders of the additional classes of stock usually have rights that are favorable or unfavorable compared with the rights of common stockholders.

Concepts and Definitions Fundamental to Corporate Equity Accounting

The fundamental concepts that underlie the accounting and reporting of stockholders' equity may be summarized as follows:

1. Separate legal entity—According to the law, a corporation is a nonpersonal entity that may own assets, owe debts, and conduct operations as an independent entity separate from each stockholder. Thus, it is a separate accounting entity, independent of the stockholders.[1]
2. Sources of stockholders' equity—The primary sources of stockholders' equity are organized, accounted for, and reported separately on the balance sheet to provide useful data for financial statement users. Sources of stockholders' equity include the following:
   a. **Contributed capital** (often referred to as *paid-in capital*):
      (1) Capital stock:
         (a) Preferred stock.
         (b) Common stock.
      (2) Other contributed capital or additional paid-in capital (an obsolete term, *capital surplus,* sometimes is used):

---

[1] The issue of what is a separate legal entity becomes more complex when one corporation is the majority shareholder of a second corporation, or when there are reciprocal holdings of shares. Complex ownership structures are covered in advanced accounting texts.

EXHIBIT 20–1   Stockholders' Equity Section of a Balance Sheet

Stockholders' Equity

Contributed capital:
Capital stock:

Preferred stock, 6%, par $10, cumulative and nonparticipating, 20,000 shares authorized; 15,000 issued and outstanding	$150,000	
Preferred stock subscribed, 100 shares	1,000	
Total preferred stock outstanding and subscribed	151,000	
Common stock nopar value, 10,000 shares authorized; 8,000 shares issued and outstanding, stated value $5	40,000	$191,000
Additional contributed capital*:		
In excess of par value, preferred stock	12,000	
In excess of stated value, common stock	3,000	
Donation of plant site	5,000	20,000
Total contributed capital		211,000
Retained earnings:†		
Appropriated for bond sinking fund	50,000	
Unappropriated	170,000	
Total retained earnings		220,000
Unrealized capital:		
Unrealized loss on long-term investments in marketable equity securities		(6,000)
Total stockholders' equity		$425,000

* The additional contributed capital accounts often are aggregated into a single amount on the balance sheet with detailed disclosure in the notes or a supporting schedule (see Exhibit 20–8).

† Total retained earnings often is reported on the balance sheet with disclosure of the appropriations in a supporting note.

    (*a*) From owners: Contributed capital in excess of par or stated value (sometimes called *premium on capital stock*) and contributed capital from treasury stock and stock retirement transactions.

    (*b*) From nonowners: Contributed capital from donation of assets.

  b. **Retained earnings:**

    (1) Unappropriated retained earnings.

    (2) Appropriated retained earnings (sometimes inappropriately called *reserves*). This term is defined and discussed further in the next chapter.

  c. Unrealized capital—Defined in a later section.

Exhibit 20–1 illustrates a typical stockholders' equity section in a balance sheet. The stockholders' equity is reported by source; that is, contributed capital, retained earnings, and an unrealized capital item—unrealized loss on long-term investments in equity securities.

3. Issuance of capital stock—The issuance of capital stock is recorded in conformity with the *cost principle*. That is, the issue price recorded should be the cash consideration received plus the market value of all noncash consideration received.

4. Sale and repurchase of shares—Transactions of a corporation involving the sale, purchase, or resale of its own shares do not directly affect periodic net income. When shares are issued, any difference between the market value of the consideration received and the par or stated value of the shares sold, purchased, or resold is recorded as an adjustment to an additional contributed (paid-in) capital account.

5. Equity versus debt—Stockholders' equity should be clearly separated from the liabilities of the corporation.

6. Form of business organization—Aside from owners' equity, the accounting and reporting for a business are not affected in principle by its status as a corporation, partnership, or sole proprietorship. The legal form of a business can, however, materially influence the financial consequences of various decisions for the business. Even so, the principles are consistent across alternative forms of business entity.

7. Terminology—The word *capital* has different meanings in accounting, finance, and the business world. For example, capital sometimes is used to mean total owners' equity. For precision and clarity, this text uses capital to identify that portion of stockholders' equity that relates to capital stock, including additional contributed capital. It excludes retained earnings and unrealized capital (gains or losses) on long-term investments in equity securities. The generic terms *contributed capital* and *paid-in capital* are used interchangeably. The following additional definitions for various types of capital stock are necessary to facilitate discussion:

1. **Authorized capital stock**—the number of shares of stock that can be issued legally, as specified in the charter of the corporation.
2. **Issued capital stock**—the number of shares of authorized capital stock that have been issued to stockholders to date.
3. **Unissued capital stock**—the number of shares of authorized capital stock that have not been issued; that is, the difference between authorized and issued shares.
4. **Outstanding capital stock**—the number of shares issued, less the number of shares repurchased and held as treasury stock.
5. **Treasury stock**—shares once issued and later reacquired by the corporation and that are still held by the corporation; that is, the difference between issued shares and outstanding shares.
6. **Subscribed capital stock**—unissued shares of stock set aside to meet subscription contracts (i.e., shares sold on credit and not yet paid for). Subscribed stock usually is not issued until the subscription price is paid in full. Subscribed shares of voting stock confer voting rights unless the subscription agreement specifies otherwise.

Advantages and Disadvantages of the Corporate Form of Organization

The corporate form of business has both advantages and disadvantages when compared with partnerships and sole proprietorships. The primary advantages are:

1. Limited liability—The liability of each stockholder is limited to his or her proportionate share of investment in total shareholders' equity. In cases of dissolution or insolvency, stockholders may lose an amount limited to their investment, or the legal capital of the shares they own, whichever is greater.
2. Capital accumulation—Large accumulations of funds from investors with diverse investment objectives are possible, as well as access to the investment market (e.g., stock exchanges). This allows a firm to invest large amounts in capital equipment or other capital investments in order to achieve manufacturing or other efficiencies, and generally to take advantage of economies of scale activities that might not be affordable by partnerships or proprietorships.
3. Ease of ownership transfer—Continuity, transfer, expansion, and contraction of ownership interests are facilitated.

The primary disadvantages of the corporate form of business are:

1. Increased taxation—Corporate earnings are subject to double taxation. They are taxed first as earned by the corporation, and again after distribuiton in the form of dividends to stockholders. Also, there have been times in the past when the corporate tax rate was significantly higher than the individual tax rate, which can result in a high overall rate of taxation.

2. Difficulties of control—the large size and impersonal nature of a corporation may cause problems in stockholders' control of the corporation. Since ownership is usually separated from management and can become quite dispersed, owners may be unable to exercise active and frequent control over management actions. There can be difficulties of communication. Owners may have difficulty gaining and understanding information about the extensive activities of the firm.

CONCEPT REVIEW

1. How is a public corporation different from a private corporation? How is an open corporation different from a closed corporation? What type of corporation may not have the characteristic of limited liability?
2. Explain the differences between authorized stock, issued stock, outstanding stock, subscribed stock, and treasury stock.
3. Most corporations will have two primary sources of stockholders' equity. What are they? How are they distinguished on the balance sheet?

FEATURES OF EQUITY SECURITIES

The term *equity security* refers to all of the classifications of capital stock issued by corporations. These are usually divided into two basic types of stock: common and preferred. More than one class of common or preferred stock may be issued by a corporation, and the contractual characteristics of each specific type can vary greatly. Indeed, in the extreme, some preferred stock has many of the characteristics of debt.

In this section, the different features or contractual rights that may be attached to an issue of common or preferred stock are discussed first. Then the accounting requirements for equity securities with various features, regardless of whether they are common or preferred stock, are presented.

Par Value Stock

The laws of each state provide for the issuance of **par value stock;** that is, shares of stock with a designated dollar amount per share as stated in the corporate charter and printed on the face of the stock certificates. Either common or preferred stock may be issued at par.

Par value stock sold initially at less than par is issued at a *discount*. Par value stock sold initially above par is issued at a *premium*. A discount liability protects creditors and holds the original stockholders liable unless the liability is contractually transferred to subsequent stockholders. Today, the issuance of par value stock at a discount is illegal in most states.[2]

In the early history of corporations in the United States, only par value stock was authorized. Because the owners of a corporation were not personally liable to the corporation's creditors, statutes allowing only par value stock were intended to afford a measure of protection to creditors. In this respect, the courts tended to hold that stockholders of a corporation who paid less than par value for their stock could be assessed an additional amount equal to the discount if it was deemed necessary to satisfy creditors' claims.

---

[2] Despite laws that forbid issuance of par value stock at a discount, it sometimes happens de facto when promoters and others receive shares of stock in exchange for noncash assets or services that are overvalued.

Par value has no particular relationship to market value. However, par value has some significance in most states. In the case of insolvency, stockholders cannot be held personally liable to creditors if the par value of all outstanding shares was fully paid in (or an equivalent amount of retained earnings was capitalized as in a stock dividend). Par value establishes the minimum amount of owners' equity the law requires to be contributed by shareholders to the firm when the shares are initially issued. Also, par value is often the basis on which preferred dividends are declared. To avoid a real or implied discount, many corporations use a low par value, such as $1 per share, and sell the stock at a much higher price.

Nopar Stock

Nopar stock was first permitted by statute in New York in 1912. Since then, the authorization of stock without par value has become so widespread that today practically all states permit its issuance. True **nopar stock** is so designated in the charter and does not carry a stated or assigned value per share. However, the laws of some states authorize the issuance of nopar stock with a *stated* or *assigned* value per share. The stated or assigned value is established permanently by the corporate directors and is included in the bylaws of the corporation. Most companies use a stated value for nopar stock.

The use of an assigned or stated value makes nopar stock equivalent to par value stock for accounting purposes. Both common and preferred stock may be represented by nopar shares. The chief advantages claimed for nopar stock are that (1) a contingent liability of stockholders for stock discount is avoided, and (2) in some jurisdictions, there is less tax on nopar shares. The chief disadvantage of nopar stock is that some taxing bodies levy high franchise tax (another form of a state tax) and other taxes (e.g. registration taxes) on nopar stock.

Legal Capital

Legal capital is that portion of stockholders' equity, specified by the laws of the state in which the corporation receives its charter, that must be contributed to the firm at the issuance of shares. Generally it cannot be distributed to shareholders (except on liquidation). In the case of par value stock, legal capital is specified in most states as the par value of the issued or outstanding shares, including subscribed shares.[3] In the case of nopar stock, legal capital is (1) the full amount paid in at issuance if it is true nopar stock, or (2) the stated or assigned value per share as initially established by the corporate directors if it is other than true nopar stock. In some states, preferred stock is not included in legal capital.

Maintenance of legal capital means that a corporation must refrain from paying dividends when the effect would be to impair legal capital. This provides a measure of protection for the creditors. In some states, treasury stock cannot be purchased when such expenditures would exceed retained earnings. In other states, the limit is the same as for cash dividends. Legal capital also can be impaired as a result of operating losses.

Common Stock

Common stock is the primary issue of shares, and it normally carries all of the basic rights listed earlier. When there is only one class of stock, all of the shares are common stock (whether so designated or not).

---

[3] Whether legal capital at a specific date is based on shares issued or shares outstanding depends upon the laws of incorporation of the state. It appears that using outstanding shares as a basis is prevalent, particularly when there is a treasury stock restriction on retained earnings.

The common stockholders are the residual owners of the corporation. As such, their position is more risky than the positions of creditors and preferred stockholders. The corporation owes its creditors legally enforceable principal and interest amounts on specified dates, and preferred shares usually specify a priority for them to dividend and liquidation amounts per share. Consequently, the common stockholders are exposed to the risks and benefits of corporate success or failure because their right to cash flows comes after creditor and preferred stockholder claims have been met.

Although common stock usually is voting stock, some corporations have issued two (or more) classes of common stock: one class has voting rights (often identified as Class A); and a second or more classes (Class B and other classes), that is nonvoting. When two (or more) classes of common stock are issued, the Class B stock usually is traded publicly, while the Class A stock is often held by a small group (e.g., "the family") and traded privately. This arrangement permits control by a small group (a protection against takeovers) and at the same time, allows access to capital markets.

Preferred Stock

Preferred stock confers *preferences* or specifies differences that distinguish it from common stock. The most common preference is a priority claim on dividends, usually at a stated rate or amount. In exchange for this preference, the preferred stockholders often sacrifice their voting rights and their rights to dividends beyond the stated rate or amount. In general, these preferences and differences may involve one or more of the following rights:

1. Voting.
2. Dividends.
   a. Cumulative or noncumulative.
   b. Nonparticipating, partially participating, or fully participating with common stockholders in dividends in excess of the stated preferred dividend.
3. Assets in liquidation.
4. Convertibility to other securities.
5. Call features, under specified conditions.
6. Redemption.

Preferred stock usually is *par value* stock, and its dividend preference is expressed as a percentage of par. For example, 6% preferred stock has a dividend of 6% of the par value of each share. This preference does not guarantee a dividend but means that when the corporation declares a dividend, preferred stockholders must get a 6% preferred dividend before common stockholders receive any dividends. In the case of nopar preferred stock, the dividend preference is expressed as a specific dollar amount per share, such as $5 per preferred share.

Voting Privileges on Preferred Stock   Because the right to vote is a basic right, preferred stockholders have full voting rights unless specifically prohibited in the charter. A nonvoting specification for preferred stock represents a negative preference. Preferred stock often is nonvoting because it is used to obtain resources without diluting the voting strength of the common stock.

Cumulative Dividend Preferences on Preferred Stock   The **cumulative dividend preference** on preferred stock provides that dividends not declared in a given year accumulate at the preference rate for the stock. This accumulated amount must be paid in full when dividends are declared in a later year before dividends can be paid on the common stock. If dividends are not declared in a given year, they are said to have been passed and are called *dividends in arrears* on the cumulative preferred stock. If only a part of the preferred stock dividend is met for any years, the remainder of the cumulative dividend is in arrears. Cumulative preferred stock normally carries the right, in dissolution of the corporation, to dividends in arrears to the extent the corporation has retained earnings. However, different provisions for dividends in arrears may be stipulated in the charter and bylaws.

When the charter is silent as to the cumulative feature, most courts have ruled that preferred stock dividends are cumulative. In this text, assume preferred stock is cumulative unless stated otherwise. *APB Opinion No. 9* (par. 35) states: "When cumulative preferred dividends are in arrears, the per share and aggregate amounts thereof should be disclosed." Dividends in arrears are recorded with a memo entry and are disclosed in notes to the financial statements. They are not recorded as liabilities until they are declared.

Noncumulative preferred stock provides that dividends not declared (i.e., dividends "passed") for any prior year or years are lost permanently by the preferred stockholders. As a result, the noncumulative feature has a negative effect for the preferred stock investor. Noncumulative preferred stock is seldom issued.

Participating Dividend Preferences on Preferred Stock   There are several types of **participating dividend preferences** on preferred stock. *Nonparticipating* preferred stock limits the dividends for any year to the specified dividend preference (plus any dividends in arrears if preference is cumulative). For example, 5% preferred stock, par $10, noncumulative, nonparticipating, would limit the holder to a $.50 dividend per share in any one year.

Partially participating preferred stock provides that the preferred stockholders participate above the preferential rate on a *pro rata basis* in dividend declarations with the common stockholders. However, this participation is limited to an additional rate, which is specified in the charter and on the stock certificate. For example, a corporation may issue 5% preferred stock with participation up to a total of 7%. In this case, participation privileges with the common stockholders would be limited to an additional 2% above the 5% preference.

Fully participating preferred stock means that the preferred stockholders have a preference for the current year at a stated preference rate and will also share on a pro rata basis in any dividends declared beyond the preference rate. For example, 5% preferred stock, par $10, fully participating, would receive its 5% preference (i.e., $.50 per share) plus a pro rata share (based on the total par or stated value of the common and preferred stock) of any excess dividends after the common stockholders have received a "matching" amount (i.e., 5% of the par or stated value of the common stock in this case). Most preferred stock is not fully participating.

The following five cases illustrate various combinations of cumulative/noncumulative rights and of participating/nonparticipating rights. Assume the following capital structure for all the cases (the contractual rights of the preferred shareholders will vary case by case):[4]

> Preferred stock, 5%, $10 par, 10,000 shares issued and outstanding $100,000
> Common stock, $5 par, 40,000 shares issued and outstanding 200,000

Case A   Cash dividends of $28,000 are declared. The preferred stock is *cumulative* and *nonparticipating,* and dividends are in arrears for the two preceding years.

	Preferred	Common
Step 1: Preferred dividends in arrears ($100,000 × .05 × 2 years)	$10,000	
Step 2: Preferred, current dividends ($100,000 × .05)	5,000	
Step 3: Balance of declared dividends to common ($28,000 − $15,000)		$13,000
	$15,000	$13,000

Case A shows the allocation of dividend payments as required by the rights attached

---

[4] Dividends are discussed substantively in Chapter 21. Cases A, B, C, D, and E are given here only to help illustrate the definition and features of preferred stock. The declaration of a dividend is much more involved than merely selecting a total amount.

to the preferred stock. First, payment of dividends in arrears is made. Next, current preferred dividends are paid. The remainder, no matter how large or small, accrues to the common shareholders.

Case B Cash dividends of $28,000 are declared. The preferred stock is *noncumulative* and *nonparticipating*. No dividends have been paid in the past two years.

	Preferred	Common
Step 1: Preferred, current dividends ($100,000 × .05)	$5,000	
Step 2: Balance of declared dividends to common ($28,000 − $5,000)		$23,000
	$5,000	$23,000

Since the preferred stock is noncumulative, there are no dividends in arrears even though dividends have been passed for two prior years.

Case C Cash dividends of $28,000 are declared. The preferred stock is *noncumulative* and *partially participating,* up to an additional 4%.

	Preferred	Common
Step 1: Preferred, current dividends ($100,000 × .05)	$5,000	
Step 2: Common, current dividends (matching) ($200,000 × .05)		$10,000
Step 3: Allocation up to limit of participation:		
Preferred ($100,000 × .04)	4,000	
Common ($200,000 × .04)		8,000
Step 4: Balance of declared dividends to common ($28,000 − $27,000)		1,000
	$9,000	$19,000

In the above example, the dividends declared were sufficient to pay dividends to preferred shareholders up to the limit of their participation and still have enough to pay the common shareholders a matching amount. If the amount of dividends declared was not sufficient (in this example, when dividends declared are less than $27,000), the dividends after Step 2 are allocated proportionately between the preferred and common shareholders.

Case D Cash dividends of $21,000 are declared. The preferred stock is *noncumulative* and *partially participating,* up to an additional 4%.

	Preferred	Common
Step 1: Preferred, current dividends ($100,000 × .05)	$5,000	
Step 2: Common, current dividends, matching ($200,000 × .05)		$10,000
Step 3: Allocation of remainder of $6,000 based on relative total par value:		
Preferred ($100,000/$300,000 × $6,000)	2,000	
Common ($200,000/$300,000 × $6,000)		4,000
	$7,000	$14,000

After Step 2, $6,000 remains to be allocated to preferred and common stockholders. This amount is allocated in proportion to the total par value of each class of stock.

Case E Cash dividends of $28,000 are declared. The preferred stock is *cumulative* and *fully participating*. Dividends are in arrears for the preceding two years:

	Preferred	Common
Step 1: Preferred, dividends in arrears ($100,000 × .05 × 2 years)	$10,000	
Step 2: Preferred, current dividends ($100,000 × .05)	5,000	
Step 3: Common, current dividends, matching ($200,000 × .05)		$10,000
Step 4: Allocation of remainder of $3,000 based on total par value:		
Preferred ($100,000/$300,000 × $3,000)	1,000	
Common ($200,000/$300,000 × $3,000)		2,000
	$16,000	$12,000

In Cases C, D, and E, common stockholders begin to receive a matching allocation when the basic dividend preference for the preferred shares has been satisfied. Once participation begins, the dividends are allocated based on the total par value of the class of stock. If either the common or preferred stock is nopar and the preferred stock has participating privileges (partial or full), a specified dollar amount per share must be established in the charter to replace the percent and par value for the participation matching computations. For example, assume the following capital structure for a firm:

Preferred stock, 5%, $10 par, 10,000 shares outstanding $100,000
Common stock, nopar, 40,000 shares outstanding 200,000

The preferred shares are *cumulative* and *fully participating*. Dividends are in arrears for the preceding two years. The common stock shares have a dividend participation value of $4 per share specified in the charter. Dividends in the amount of $49,000 are declared in the current year.

	Preferred	Common
Step 1: Preferred, dividends in arrears ($100,000 × .05 × 2 years) . .	$10,000	
Step 2: Preferred, current dividends ($100,000 × .05)	5,000	
Step 3: Common, matching (40,000 shares × $4 × .05)		$ 8,000
Step 4: Allocation of remainder of $26,000 based on allocation bases:		
Preferred ($100,000/($100,000 + $160,000) × $26,000)	10,000	
Common ($160,000/($100,000 + $160,000) × $26,000)		16,000
	$25,000	$24,000

After the dividends in arrears and the current period preferred dividends are deducted from the total amount declared, $34,000 in dividends remain to be allocated to preferred and common shareholders. The matching participation of common shareholders (related to the current-year preferred dividends) is computed, based on the participation share value of $4, to be 40,000 shares times $4 per share times the dividend rate of 5%, or a total of $8,000. The remaining dividend amount of $26,000 (the original $49,000 less the $23,000 allocated through Step 3) is allocated to each shareholder group based on allocation bases, with the common share participation valued again at $4 per share.

Asset Preference on Preferred Stock Preferred stock that has a liquidation preference provides that the preferred stockholders, in case of corporate dissolution, have a priority on the assets of the corporation up to the par value or other stated amount per share. Often the asset preference is higher than the par or stated value. When it is satisfied, the remainder of the assets are distributed to the common stockholders. *APB Opinion No. 10* (par 10) requires that "the liquidation preference of the preferred stock be disclosed in the equity section of the balance sheet in the aggregate . . . rather than on a per share basis or by disclosure in notes."

Preferred Stock Convertible to Other Securities Preferred stock may carry a *convertibility* provision. At the option of the preferred stockholder, the preferred shares owned may be exchanged for (converted to) other securities, usually common stock. Because the conversion privilege offers the preferred stockholder the option of holding the original preferred stock or converting it to another specified security, convertible preferred stock is favored by investors. Convertibility privileges should be disclosed in the financial statements (tabular portion or notes) of the issuing corporation.

Callable Preferred Stock Preferred stock may be *callable,* which means that, at the issuer's option, the preferred stock can be called in for cancellation at a specified price and date(s). When callable stock is called by the issuer, the stockholder has no option but to forward the stock (usually through a stockbroker) to the issuer and receive payment as specified in the call agreement. All dividends in arrears on cumulative stock must be paid prior to the call date. The call price usually is above par and sometimes above the original issue price. *APB Opinion No. 10* (par 11) states that the corporation should disclose "on the face of the balance sheet or in notes pertaining thereto, the aggregate or per share amounts at which preferred shares may be called."

Redeemable Preferred Stock Recently, some corporations have issued **redeemable preferred stock,** preferred stock with the unique feature of *redemption.* This stock allows either (1) mandatory redemption at a specified date and price or (2) redemption at the option of the shareholder, who has a right to redeem the shares at a specified date and redemption price. The latter feature allows the shareholder to sell the shares back to the issuing corporation, and the issuing corporation must purchase them. With mandatory redemption, the corporation must redeem all shares of the issue at the specified date and price. Preferred shares that are not redeemable or are redeemable solely at the option of the issuer are viewed as *nonredeemable preferred shares* by the SEC.[5]

Redeemable preferred shares have financial characteristics of both debt and equity. They are similar to debt in that they either must be retired or refunded at the option of the holder at a specified date. On the other hand they have several characteristics of equity securities:

1. If a dividend is passed, the shareholder does not have the right to initiate default proceedings as would a debt holder whose interest payments were passed.
2. Redeemable preferred shares are subordinate to debt in the event of liquidation.

Some accountants believe that preferred stock with extensive characteristics of debt should be reported as debt rather than as stockholders' equity. Preferred stock with mandatory redemption has increased in popularity over the past decade. Such stock carries with it a commitment to use the firm's future cash flows to redeem the preferred stock, and as such is more like debt than equity. However, current GAAP does not directly recognize any preferred stock as debt[6] The SEC does, however, have a rule prohibiting the inclusion of redeemable preferred stock in the general category of stockholders' equity.[7] That is, amounts for redeemable preferred stock, nonredeemable preferred stock, and common stock cannot be combined in financial statements filed with the SEC.

The authors expect increasing pressure on the FASB to change its requirements so that such issues are accounted for as debt rather than as equity. Such a change would be consistent with the SEC's position. *Accounting Series Release No. 268* (Washington, D.C.: SEC, July 1979) requires that the redeemable preferred stock amount be reported immediately before stockholders' equity. Exhibit 20–2 is an illustration of the reporting and disclosure of redeemable preferred stocks by BFGoodrich Company in 1988. The redeemable preferred stock is not included in stockholders' equity; it is reported as a separate item after liabilities and before shareholders' equity.

If redeemable preferred stock is debt, why don't corporations just issue debt in the first place? From the issuing firm's perspective, preferred dividends are not tax deductible, whereas interest payments normally would be. The answer may lie in the use of the debt-to-equity ratio or other similar measures of debt capacity in debt agreements and covenants. Debt covenants are usually based on financial statements

---

[5] *Securities and Exchange Commission Release No. 33-6097* (Washington, D.C.: SEC, July 27, 1979).

[6] Several accounting standards have distinguished between redeemable and nonredeemable preferred stock. *SFAS No. 12* excludes redeemable preferred stock from the definition of *equity security,* and *SFAS No. 47* requires the same disclosures for capital stock redeemable at fixed or determinable prices as for long-term debt.

[7] *SEC Release No. 33-6097.*

EXHIBIT 20-2   Disclosures of Redeemable Preferred Stock, The BFGoodrich Company

	December 31	
(In Millions of Dollars)	1988	1987
Redeemable preferred stocks	$ 11.3	$ 14.4
Shareholders' equity:		
$3.50 cumulative convertible preferred stock:		
Series D (stated at involuntary liquidation value of $50 per share) 2,200,000 shares issued and outstanding	110.0	110.0
Common stock—$5 par value:		
Authorized 10,000,000 shares; issued 25,554,627 shares	127.8	127.8
Additional capital	382.9	382.2
Income retained in the business	548.9	405.3
Cumulative unrealized translation adjustments	(2.6)	(19.8)
Common stock held in treasury, at cost (352,396 shares in 1988 and 417,511 shares in 1987)	(12.4)	(14.6)
Total shareholders' equity	$1,154.6	$990.0

Abridged Notes to Consolidated Financial Statements

(Dollars in millions, except per share amounts)
Note Q: Preferred Stock

There are 10,000,000 authorized shares of Series Preferred Stock—$1 par value. Shares of Series Preferred Stock which have been redeemed are deemed retired and extinguished and may not be reissued. As of December 31, 1988, 534,174 shares of Series Perferred Stock have been redeemed. The Board of Directors establishes and designates the series and fixes the number of shares and the relative rights, preferences and limitations of the respective series of the Series Preferred Stock.

Whenever dividends on Cumulative Series Preferred Stock are in arrears six quarters or more, holders of such stock (voting as a class) have the right to elect two Directors of the Company until all cumulative dividends have been paid.

Dividends on outstanding Series Preferred Stock must be declared and paid or set apart for payment, and funds required for sinking-fund payments, if any, on Series Preferred Stock must be paid or set apart for payment before any dividends may be paid or set apart for payment on the Common Stock.

Redeemable Preferred Stock—Series A (stated at involuntary liquidation value of $100 per share): BFGoodrich has issued 250,000 shares of $7.85 Cumulative Preferred Stock, Series A. In order to comply with sinking-fund requirements, each year on August 15, BFGoodrich must redeem 12,500 shares of the Series A Stock. The redemption price is $100 per share, plus dividends accrued at the redemption date. BFGoodrich may redeem, at such price, up to an additional 12,500 shares in each year. The sinking-fund requirements may also be satisfied with shares acquired on the open market. At December 31, 1988 and 1987, BFGoodrich held 12,050 and 12,500 shares, respectively, for future sinking-fund requirements. After giving effect to the shares held for future sinking-fund requirements, there were 112,950, 125,000, and 150,000 shares of Series A Stock outstanding at December 31, 1988, 1987 and 1986, respectively. The aggregate amount of redemption requirement for the Series A Stock is $.1 for 1989 and $1.3 in each of the years 1990, 1991, 1992, and 1993.

Redeemable Preferred Stock—Series B (stated at involuntary liquidation value of $10 per share): BFGoodrich had issued 372,383 shares of $.975 Cumulative Preferred Stock, Series B. Sinking-fund requirements required BFGoodrich to redeem 30,000 shares of the Series B Stock on July 15 of each year at a redemption price of $10 per share, plus dividends accrued at the redemption date. On July 15, 1988, BFGoodrich redeemed the 192,838 outstanding shares of Series B Cumulative Preferred Stock at $10.24 per share plus accrued dividends.

prepared according to GAAP. A borrower might prevent a debt covenant violation by issuing redeemable preferred stock instead of straight debt.

A second incentive is the desire to raise capital at rates below the market rate of interest. Corporate buyers are willing to accept a dividend rate on redeemable preferred stock which is less than the market rate of interest because corporations can exclude 85% of their dividend income from taxable income. No such exclusion is available for interest income.

The accounting for preferred stock issues that are, in substance, debt is a topic on the FASB agenda under the general heading of "financial instruments." If the amount of redeemable preferred stock issued continues to increase, the FASB can be expected to issue pronouncements clarifying when such issues must be accounted for as debt, and whether the dividend payments related to these issues should be treated as an expense on the income statement.

CONCEPT REVIEW

1. What are the fundamental differences between common stock and preferred stock?
2. Why would a firm issue redeemable preferred stock?
3. A firm has issued and outstanding 1,000 shares of $100 par, cumulative, nonparticipating shares of 5% preferred stock, and 20,000 shares of $5 par common stock. Dividends are in arrears for the past year (not including the current year). The board of directors of the firm declares dividends of $25,000 to be paid to shareholders at the end of the fiscal year. How will the $25,000 be shared between the preferred and common shareholders?

ACCOUNTING FOR STOCK ISSUANCE AND RELATED TRANSACTIONS
◆

Accounting for the Issuance of Par Value Stock

Accounting for stockholders' equity emphasizes the source of capital investment. If a corporation has more than one class of stock, separate accounts should be maintained for each class. If there is only one class of stock, an account titled "capital stock" usually is used. In cases where there are two or more classes of stock, account titles such as "common stock," "preferred stock, 5%," and "common stock, nopar" are used. The additional (or other) capital stock accounts represent the remaining contributed capital of the corporation. The sequence of transactions related to the issuance of stock is:

1. Authorization of shares.
2. Sale for cash or subscriptions (i.e., the sale of shares on credit).
3. Collections on subscriptions (when applicable).
4. Issuance of the shares.

Authorization   The charter authorization to issue a specified number of shares may be recorded as a memo entry in the general journal and in the ledger account by the following notation:

Common stock—Par value $10 per share
(authorized 50,000 shares)

Par Value Stock Issued for Cash   When stock is issued, a stock certificate, specifying the number of shares represented, is prepared for each stockholder. An entry reflecting the number of shares held by each stockholder is made in the stockholder ledger, a subsidiary ledger of the capital stock account.

In most cases, capital stock is sold and issued for cash rather than on a subscription (i.e., credit) basis. The issuance of 10,000 shares of common stock, par $10, for cash of $10.20 per share would be recorded as follows:

Cash	102,000	
Common stock, par $10 (10,000 shares)		100,000
Contributed capital in excess of par, common stock		2,000

The common stock account is credited for the par value of the stock issued. The excess over par is credited to an account descriptively named "contributed capital in excess of par" or "additional paid-in capital" to record the source in detail. If par value stock is sold at a discount (i.e., less than par), a negative stockholders' equity account, discount on common (or preferred) stock, should be debited for the amount of the discount.

Accounting for the Issuance of Nopar Stock

Various state statutes permit either of two types of nopar stock, *true* nopar stock and *stated value* nopar stock. Therefore, some variation exists in accounting.

Authorization of nopar stock may be recorded by notation as shown for par value stock. With nopar stock, most states require that the total number of shares authorized be shown on each stock certificate, in addition to the customary imprint of the number of shares represented by that particular stock certificate.

True nopar stock, when sold, is recorded as a credit to the capital stock account in conformity with the legal requirements of the state of incorporation. Thus, if the state's statute provides that all proceeds represent legal capital, then the capital stock account should be credited for the full amount received. If the statutes establish a minimum amount per share, then at least this amount should be credited to the capital stock account and any remainder credited to an account labeled "contributed capital in excess of stated value." Without legal requirements, the total amount received should be credited to the nopar capital stock account. In this case, no contributed capital in excess of par (or additional paid-in capital) is recorded.

Nopar stock with a stated (or assigned) value is accounted for in the same manner as for par value stock. The stated value places the nopar stock on essentially the same basis as par value stock. The amount of the sale (issue) price in excess of stated value should be credited to an account with a descriptive title such as "contributed (or additional paid-in) capital in excess of stated value, nopar common stock."

Capital Stock Sold on a Subscription Basis

During the organization of a corporation, prospective stockholders may sign a contract to purchase a specified number of shares on credit, with payment due at one or more specified future dates. A corporation may also sell its capital stock on credit after incorporation. Such contractual agreements are known as stock subscriptions, and the stock involved is called subscribed capital stock. When a legal contract is involved, accounting recognition must be given to these transactions. The agreed or contractual purchase price is debited to stock subscriptions receivable. Capital stock subscribed is credited for the par, stated, or assigned amount per share. The difference is credited to contributed capital in excess of par (or stated value) as though the subscriber had paid for the subscribed shares in full.

To illustrate, assume 120 shares of Bee Corporation common stock, par $10, are subscribed for at $12 by J. Doe. The total is payable in three installments. The entry by Bee Corporation would be as follows:

Stock subscriptions receivable—Common stock (Doe) 1,440*
    Common stock subscribed, par $10 (120 shares)   1,200
    Contributed capital in excess of par, common stock   240
   * Payable in three installments of $480 each.

The premium is recorded when the subscription is recorded, rather than later when the cash is collected. In this way, the legal claim (the stock subscription receivable) the corporation has on the subscriber is recognized. Like capital leases, this is an example of recognition of an executory contract.

The credit balance in common stock subscribed reflects the corporation's obligation to issue the 120 shares on fulfillment of the terms of the agreement by the subscriber. This account is reported on the balance sheet similar to the related capital stock account (see Exhibit 20-1). There are two ways to present stock subscriptions receivable. Some argue it should be classified as a current asset if the corporation expects current collection. Otherwise, it is reported as a noncurrent asset under the category "other assets."

Others argue it should be treated as a contra account to stockholders' equity, and offset against the common stock subscribed account in the stockholders' equity section of the balance sheet. In support of this view, it is not possible in many states to obtain a judgment against a subscriber for failure to pay the unpaid balance of a subscription receivable. Because of the risk of uncollectibility, the SEC requires the contra equity approach. This is the preferred treatment.

In some cases, subscription contracts call for installment payments. In such cases, separate "call" accounts may be set up for each installment. If the corporation has a number of subscriptions, it is usually desirable to maintain a subscribers' ledger as a subsidiary record to the stock subscriptions receivable account, similar to that maintained for trade accounts receivable.

Collections on stock subscriptions receivable may be in cash, property, or services. The appropriate account is debited, and subscriptions receivable is credited. If a noncash asset or a service is received, the amount recorded would be based on the market value of that asset or service.

Stock certificates sometimes are not issued until the subscription price is paid in full. Using the last example, when the final collection of $480 is received, the issuer makes two entries as follows:

To record the collection:

```
Cash . . . . . . . . . . . . . . . . . . . . . . . . . . . . . . . . . . . . .   480
      Stock subscriptions receivable—Common stock (Doe)  . . . . .            480
```

To record issuance of the stock:

```
Common stock subscribed  . . . . . . . . . . . . . . . . . . . . . . . 1,200
      Common stock, par $10 (120 shares) . . . . . . . . . . . . . . .       1,200
```

Accounting for cash sales and for stock subscriptions of true nopar stock and stated value nopar stock are illustrated and compared in Exhibit 20-3.

Default on Subscriptions When a subscriber defaults after partial fulfillment of the subscription contract, certain complexities arise. In case of default, the corporation may decide to (1) return all payments received to the subscriber; (2) issue shares equivalent to the number paid for in full, rather than the total number subscribed; or (3) simply keep the monies received. The first two options involve no disadvantage to the subscriber. The third option is usually not done, although state statutes generally do not prevent it. However, the laws of most states cover the contingency where the corporation elects the third alternative. Such laws vary considerably; two contrasting provisions are as follows:

1. The subscribed stock is forfeited, and all payments made by the defaulting subscriber are forfeited by the subscriber. Therefore, the forfeited amount is credited to the contributed capital of the corporation. Further, the corporation is free to resell the shares. Provisions of this type favor the corporation and seldom occur. To illustrate, refer to Bee Corporation and J. Doe, presented earlier, and assume one

EXHIBIT 20-3   Entries for Sales and Subscriptions for Nopar Stock

Case Data and Accounts	Stated Value Stock*		True Nopar Value Stock	
1. To record authorization of 10,000 shares of nopar stock:				
Notation—10,000 shares of nopar common stock authorized	Stated value, $5		No stated value	
2. To record cash sale and issuance of 5,000 shares at $6:				
Cash	30,000		30,000	
Common stock, nopar, stated value $5		25,000		
Common stock, nopar				30,000
Contributed capital in excess of stated value, nopar				
common stock		5,000		
3. To record subscription taken for 5,000 shares at $6; 20% collected in cash:				
Cash (5,000 × $6 × .20)	6,000		6,000	
Stock subscriptions receivable, nopar common stock	24,000		24,000	
Nopar common stock subscribed (5,000 shares)		25,000		30,000
Contributed capital in excess of stated value, nopar				
common stock		5,000		
4. To record collection of subscription receivable and issuance of				
all of the subscribed shares:				
Cash	24,000		24,000	
Stock subscriptions receivable, nopar common stock		24,000		24,000
Nopar common stock subscribed	25,000		30,000	
Common stock, nopar, stated value $5 (5,000 shares)		25,000		
Common stock, nopar (5,000 shares)				30,000

* Essentially the same as for par value stock.

$480 payment has been made by Doe prior to default. All related account balances would be removed as follows:

Common stock subscribed (120 shares)	1,200	
Contributed capital in excess of par, common stock	240	
Subscriptions receivable (Doe)		960
Contributed capital from defaulted subscriptions		
(amount paid in by Doe)		480

Essentially the corporation receives a contribution of $480 to stockholders' equity.

2. The stock is forfeited, and the corporation must resell the stock under a lien whereby the original subscriber must be reimbursed for the amount that the net receipts for the stock (i.e., the total cash collected from both the subscriber and subsequent resale of the stock to another investor, less the cost incurred by the corporation in making the later sale) exceed the original subscription price. To avoid an incentive to default, the refund to the defaulting subscriber cannot exceed the amount paid to the date of default less resale costs. Exhibit 20-4 illustrates the accounting under this provision.

Noncash Sale of Capital Stock

Corporations sometimes issue capital stock for noncash assets. For example, *The Wall Street Journal* recently reported that Butterfield Equities Corporation privately placed 1.8 million shares of its new preferred stock and 100,000 new common shares, primarily in exchange for real estate. A private placement occurs when an issuer of securities arranges to sell an issue to a limited number of specific buyers; the issue is not sold in a public market. Usually, a private placement can occur without the issuer meeting all the public disclosure requirements of a public offering.

EXHIBIT 20-4   Default on Stock Subscriptions—Shares Resold under Lien

1. Bee Corporation received from Subscriber Doe a subscription for 120 shares of common stock, par $10, at $12 per share:

   Stock subscription receivable, common stock
   (120 shares × $12) 1,440
       Common stock subscribed, par $10 (120 shares × $10) 1,200
       Contributed capital in excess of par, common stock
       (120 shares × $2) 240

2. Bee Corporation received a $480 installment on the subscription from Subscriber Doe:

   Cash 480
       Stock subscription receivable, common stock 480

3. Subscriber Doe defaults on the subscription. Bee Corporation records the default under the lien provision:

   Common stock subscribed, par $10 (120 shares) 1,200
   Contributed capital in excess of par, common stock 240
       Stock subscription receivable, common stock
       ($1,440–$480) 960
       Payable to Subscriber Doe (pending resale of formerly
       subscribed shares) 480

4. Bee Corporation resells the formerly subscribed shares for $15 per share. Bee Corporation pays the cost of resale, $50, and debits this amount to the payable to Subscriber Doe account.

   Resale of shares:
       Cash [(120 shares × $15) − $50] 1,750
       Payable to Subscriber Doe (resale costs)   50
           Common stock, par $10 (120 shares) 1,200
           Contributed capital in excess of par, common stock
           (120 shares × $15 = $1,800) − $1,200 600

5. BT Corporation pays stipulated amount to Subscriber Doe:

   Payable to Subscriber Doe* 430
       Cash 430

* Computation:
  Amount to be paid to Subscriber Doe based on lien provisions:
    Net receipts for the stock:
      Cash collected from Subscriber Doe . . . . $ 480
      Cash collected from resale of shares 1,800
      Less: Cost of resale . . . .   (50)
        Net receipts $2,230
    Original subscription price 1,440
    Remainder payable to Subscriber Doe, subject to limitation . . . . $ 790

    Limitation—total actual payments made by Subscriber Doe, less resale costs
    (i.e., $480 − $50) . . . . $ 430

  Therefore, pay $430 to Subscriber Doe.

When a corporation issues its capital stock for noncash assets or services or to settle debt, the current market value of the stock issued or the noncash consideration received, whichever is the most reliably determinable, is used to record the transaction.[8] If the current market value of either the capital stock issued or the noncash consideration received cannot be reliably determined, appraised values are used.

[8] AICPA, *APB Opinion No. 16,* "Business Combinations" (New York, 1970), par. 67; and *FASB Technical Bulletin 84-1* (Norwalk, Conn., 1984), par 7.

Further, if market values or appraisals are not reliably determinable, the values must be established by the governing authority of the company (i.e., the board of directors). If a reliable market value for the capital stock is established within a reasonable time after a noncash sale of the stock, then the appraised value set by the corporation's governing authority which was originally recorded may be revised.

The issuance of capital stock for noncash considerations sometimes involves questionable valuations. Some companies have disavowed market values and independent appraisals in order to permit the governing authority of the company to set arbitrary values in these noncash transactions. In some such cases, these companies seem to be motivated to overvalue the assets received, and as a consequence, overvalue stockholders' equity. This condition is often referred to as *watered stock*. The value of the resources received for the issued stock is less than (i.e., watered down) the value of the stock issued. On the other hand, some companies are motivated to undervalue the assets received. As a consequence, they understate stockholders' equity—a condition often called secret reserves. Secret reserves are also created by depreciating or amortizing a properly recorded asset over a period less than its useful life.

Special Sales of Capital Stock

A corporation usually sells each class of its capital stock separately. However, a corporation may sell two or more classes of its capital stock for one lump-sum amount (often referred to as a *basket sale*). In addition, a corporation may issue two or more classes of its capital stock in exchange for a noncash consideration.

When two or more classes of securities are sold and issued for a single lump sum, the total proceeds must be allocated logically among the several classes of securities. Two methods used in such situations are (1) the *proportional method,* in which the lump sum received is allocated proportionately among the classes of stock on the basis of the relative market value of each security, and (2) the *incremental method,* in which the market value of one security is used as a basis for the security and the remainder of the lump sum is allocated to the other class of security.

The method selected should produce the most reliable results based upon the data available. To illustrate, assume Vax Corporation issued 1,000 shares of common stock, par $10, and 500 shares of preferred stock, par $8, in three different situations as follows. In each case, the issuance does not affect market values.

Situation 1—Proportional Method Applied   The common stock was selling at $40 per share and the preferred at $20. Assume the total cash received was $48,000. Because reliable market values are available, the proportional method is preferable as a basis for allocating the lump-sum amount as follows:

Proportional allocation:		
Market value of common (1,000 shares × $40)	$40,000	(⅘)
Market value of preferred (500 shares × $20)	10,000	(⅕)
Total market value	$50,000	(5/5)

Allocation of the lump-sum sale price of $48,000:

Common stock ($48,000 × ⅘)	$38,400
Preferred stock ($48,000 × ⅕)	9,600
Total	$48,000

The journal entry to record the issuance:

Cash	48,000	
Common stock, par $10 (1,000 shares)		10,000
Preferred stock, par $8 (500 shares)		4,000

Contributed capital in excess of par, common ($38,400 − $10,000)	28,400
Contributed capital in excess of par, preferred ($9,600 − $4,000)	5,600

Situation 2—Incremental Method Applied The common stock of Vax Corporation was selling at $40; a market for the preferred stock has not been established. Because there is no market for the preferred stock, the market value of the common must be used as a basis for the following entry:

Cash 48,000	
Common stock, par $10 (1,000 shares)	10,000
Preferred stock, par $8 (500 shares)	4,000
Contributed capital in excess of par, common	
[1,000 shares × ($40 − $10)]	30,000
Contributed capital in excess of par, preferred (remainder) . .	4,000

Situation 3—There is No Established Market for Either Class of Stock, Neither Proportional Method nor Incremental Method of Allocation Can Be Used In this case, an arbitrary allocation is used. In the absence of any other logical basis, a *temporary* allocation may be made on the basis of relative par values. Should a market value be established for one of the securities in the near future, a correcting entry based on such value would be made. The entry to record the temporary allocation on the basis of relative par values would be similar to that shown for Situation 1, but the apportionment of the $48,000 lump-sum amount would be based on the relative par values of the two securities as follows:

$$\text{Common stock } (\$10,000 \div \$14,000) \times \$48,000 = \underline{\$34,286}$$

$$\text{Preferred stock } (\$4,000 \div \$14,000) \times \$48,000 = \underline{\underline{\$13,714}}$$

Assessments on Capital Stock

Some states permit the issuance of *assessable stock* if the charter includes this provision. Also in some states, under certain conditions, the board of directors may assess the stockholders a certain amount per share, even though the stock is not identified as assessable stock. However, such an assessment usually requires stockholder approval. A stock assessment is the collection of cash from each stockholder in proportion to the shares held without the issuance of additional stock. Stock assessments may be used when a corporation needs cash, is facing insolvency, or when the stock originally was issued at a discount. If the stock was originally issued at a discount, the assessment (up to the amount of the discount) should be credited to the discount account. If no stock discount is carried in the accounts, the credit is to a contributed capital account with an appropriate title such as "contributed capital from stock assessments."

Except in small companies, stock assessments are not often used. To the extent that such assessments are required to be paid, the feature of limited liability has been removed or at least reduced. Very few firms issue assessable stock. There would be reduced interest by investors to own such stock, especially if investors felt they would have little direct control over the firm.

Stock Issue Costs

Corporations often incur substantial expenditures with major issues of capital stock. These expenditures include registration fees, underwriter commissions, attorney and accountant fees, printing costs, clerical costs, and promotional costs. These expenditures are called *stock issue costs*. While stock issue costs are usually not large compared with the total funds received, they are large enough to require careful accounting. Two methods of accounting for stock issue costs are used:

1. *Offset method*—Under this method, stock issue costs are treated as a reduction of the amount received from the sale of the related capital stock. The rationale to support this method is that these are one-time costs that cannot be reasonably assigned to future periodic revenues, and that the net cash received is the actual issue price of the stock. Under this method, stock issue costs are debited to contributed capital in excess of par. A practical problem arises when the stock issue costs are greater than the amount by which the issue price exceeds the par value of the issued stock. If this is the case, the stock is accounted for as having been issued at a discount. The buyers of the stock, however, have no liability as long as their payment to the corporation is equal to or greater than the legal capital (i.e., the par value of the stock issued).

2. *Deferred charge method*—Under this method, stock issue costs are recorded as a deferred charge, and are then amortized over a reasonable period. The argument for this method is that these costs create an intangible asset that contributes to the earning of future revenues. They are allocated against future periodic revenues in conformity with the matching principle.

Although the offset method dominates in practice, both methods are used. After the issuance of capital stock, costs required to maintain stockholder records, transfer costs, and dividend payment costs (clerical only) are expensed when incurred.

Unrealized Capital

Unrealized capital is another category of stockholders' equity. Conceptually, it involves increments (i.e., increases) and decrements (i.e., decreases) in stockholders' equity.

Unrealized capital increases (i.e., a credit balance) is not widely used as a category of stockholders' equity. It arises when assets are written up to market value from historical cost. Because of rather strict adherence to the cost principle and conservatism, assets rarely are written up from cost to market value. Exceptions can be found in the financial statements of companies in particular industries, such as insurance and investment companies. GAAP allows these industries to account for their investments at market value. These companies adjust their investment portfolios to market value periodically. An upward adjustment of the asset account (i.e., a debit entry) requires an offsetting credit to either revenue, gain, or an unrealized capital account. Generally, the credit is to a revenue account for these firms, because investing in the securities of other firms is a normal part of operations.

The write-up of operational (fixed) assets to appraisal (i.e., estimated market) value was discussed briefly in Chapter 13 with respect to discovery value of natural resources. Except for certain specified assets such as farm products, natural resources, and investments of financial institutions, current GAAP does not permit the write-up of assets to market value. However, if such a write-up is credited to an unrealized capital account, any credit balance in the account would be reported as a separate, positive item of owners' equity, rather than as part of income.

Unrealized capital decreases (i.e., a debit balance) is a contra, or negative, amount in stockholders' equity. It arises when assets are written down under special circumstances. Unrealized capital decrements are recorded with some frequency. For example, *SFAS No. 12*, "Accounting for Certain Marketable Securities," requires the recording of an "unrealized loss on long-term investment in equity securities." This unrealized capital decrement on long-term investments must be reported as a contra item in stockholders' equity, as discussed in Chapter 14.

CONCEPT REVIEW

1. When capital stock is sold on a subscription basis, what are the arguments for and against accounting for the stock subscription receivable as an asset?
2. Why is the transaction in (1) recorded at all?
3. A bundle or unit of securities consisting of one share of common stock and one share of new-issue preferred stock is sold for $50. There is a current market price for the firm's publicly traded common stock, but not for the preferred stock. Describe how to account for the issue.

ACCOUNTING FOR REACQUISITION OF STOCK
◆

Treasury Stock

The statutes of most states permit a corporation to purchase its own stock after it has been issued, subject to specified limitations. Treasury stock is a corporation's own stock (preferred or common) that (1) has been issued, (2) is reacquired by the issuing corporation, and (3) has not been resold or formally retired. The purchase of treasury stock does not reduce the number of *issued* shares, but does reduce the number of outstanding shares. Treasury shares subsequently may be resold, or, in some cases, retired.

In general, treasury stock is acquired for the following reasons:

1. To use for employee stock options, bonus plans, and direct sale to employees.
2. To establish a market for the company's stock. This is an often cited reason.
3. To use the shares acquired to purchase other securities or assets.
4. To use the shares acquired for a stock dividend.
5. To increase earnings per share by reducing the number of shares outstanding.
6. To buyout one or more particular stockholders and to thwart takeover attempts.
7. To reduce dividend payments by reducing the number of shares outstanding.

Accounting Trends & Techniques, 1990, reports that 390 of the 600 corporations surveyed disclosed treasury stock. These data indicate the prevalence of the purchase and sale of treasury stock, which almost always is common stock. For example, the 1988 annual report of General Signal Corporation revealed the company repurchased over 9.5 million of its own common stock shares in 1988. The data is given in Exhibit 20–5.

By purchasing approximately one third of its outstanding shares of common stock, General Signal Corporation substantially reduced its size ($491 million has been paid to shareholders), substantially increased its leverage (by reducing shareholders' equity), and concentrated ownership of the firm with the remaining shareholders. One reason a firm might take this action is to discourage other firms or investor groups from attempting a takeover of the firm.

The purchase of treasury stock decreases both assets and stockholders' equity, whereas a sale of treasury stock increases both assets and stockholders' equity. Treasury stock may be obtained by purchase, by settlement of an obligation, or through donation. Treasury stock usually does not carry voting, dividend, preemptive, or liquidation rights. Treasury stock is not an asset. It is accounted for as a contra account to stockholders' equity. Treasury stock transactions do not affect the income statement. Treasury stock transactions may cause retained earnings to decrease, but seldom to increase.

EXHIBIT 20-5   Disclosure of Repurchase of Stock: General Signal Corporation

(*In thousands of dollars*)	1988	1987
Shareholders' equity (notes 6 through 9):		
Common stock, par value $1 per share; authorized 75,000,000 shares; issued 30,737,505 in 1988, 29,584,000 in 1987	$ 41,842	$ 40,692
Additional paid-in capital	295,916	236,818
Retained earnings	705,226	731,000
Cumulative translation adjustments	(2,062)	(12,662)
	$1,040,922	$995,848
Common stock in treasury, at cost; 11,677,913 shares in 1988, 2,112,379 shares in 1987	(579,876)	(88,697)
Total shareholders' equity	$ 461,046	$907,151

Note 6 to the financial statements provides the following additional information:

Treasury stock:

Number of Shares	1988	1987	1986
Balance at beginning of year	2,112,379	732,202	600,322
Common stock reacquired*	9,585,274	1,380,578	132,296
Common stock issued under the company's incentive compensation plan	(19,740)	(401)	(416)
Balance at end of year	11,677,913	2,112,379	732,202

* Includes the repurchase of 9,572,627 shares in December 1988 pursuant to the company's tender offer to shareholders, as well as the repurchase of 1,355,900 and 116,400 shares on the open market in 1987 and 1986, respectively, in connection with the company's share repurchase program. The remaining shares were reacquired in connection with the company's stock option plans.

Self-tender offer:

On November 17, 1988, the company commenced a "Dutch Auction" self-tender offer to shareholders for the repurchase of nine million shares of its own common stock, subject to increase at the company's discretion. Under the terms of the offer, shareholders were invited to tender their shares by December 15, 1988, at prices ranging from $44 to $51 per share as specified by each shareholder.

At the conclusion of the offer, approximately 10.9 million shares had been tendered, of which the company repurchased 9,572,627 shares at $51 per share for a total cost of approximately $491 million, including legal and financial consulting fees. The total shares repurchased represent approximately one third of the outstanding shares at that date.

Companies must exercise extreme care in transactions involving their own stock (including treasury stock) because of the opportunity the corporation (and its management) has to use the insider information to the detriment of a stockholder from whom the corporation is acquiring, or to whom the corporation is selling, its own stock. For example, an oil company (or members of its management) with inside knowledge of a profitable oil discovery could withhold the news and acquire stock at a low market price. Alternatively, a company could withhold bad news and sell its own stock (including treasury stock) at an artificially high market price. The latter action would unfairly deprive the purchasing stockholder of the excess cash paid for the stock. For these reasons, the securities laws (particularly Rules 10b-5 and 10b-6 of the Securities and Exchange Act of 1934) prohibit corporations from engaging in deceptive conduct, including acts related to transactions involving their own stock. Both of the above examples are prohibited.

The repurchase by a corporation of shares of its own capital stock poses a conceptual question about its classification. Should treasury stock be accounted for as an asset (i.e., an investment in equity securities) or as a contraction of the stockholders' equity of the corporation? Although treasury stock has some of the attributes of an asset, it is viewed conceptually in accounting as a reduction of stockholder's equity for these reasons:

1. A corporation cannot own itself.
2. The purchase of treasury stock is a payment to the selling stockholders for their investment interest in the corporation.
3. Treasury stock is essentially the same as the unissued stock of the corporation. Unissued stock is not an asset; it cannot be voted and earns no dividends.
4. Treasury stock may be formally retired by the corporation. When this is done, the number of shares issued is reduced.

Recording and Reporting Treasury Stock Transactions

Two methods are used to account for treasury stock:

1. Cost method (one-transaction concept).
2. Par value method (dual-transaction concept).

Both of these methods are accepted. While they yield different results for individual accounts within the stockholders' equity section of the balance sheet, the total amount of stockholders' equity is the same under both methods.

Cost Method   The cost method sometimes is referred to as the one-transaction concept because the purchase and subsequent sale of the treasury stock are viewed as one transaction with two parts. First, at acquisition, the cost of the treasury stock is debited to a contra stockholders' equity account called "treasury stock." Separate treasury stock accounts are established for each class of stock, with an offsetting credit to cash or the consideration used to acquire the stock. At date of subsequent resale, the treasury stock account is credited for the cost of the treasury stock. When treasury stock is acquired at different costs, specific shares may be identified. Otherwise, a FIFO or average cost per share must be used to determine the credit to the treasury stock account (at cost) at resale date.

When treasury stock is sold (usually a debit to cash) for an amount greater than its acquisition cost, the difference is credited to a contributed capital account titled, "Contributed capital from treasury stock transactions." If treasury stock is sold for an amount less than its acquisition cost, the difference is debited to the account called "contributed capital from treasury stock transactions." If, however, the balance in that account is insufficient to absorb all of the debit, the excess is debited to retained earnings (similar to a dividend being paid to the stockholder). *FASB Technical Bulletin 85–6* specifies that when treasury stock is purchased for a price significantly in excess of market price, such as in a tender offer to combat a take-over attempt, the current market price is used as cost.

The journal entries and reporting under the cost method are illustrated in Exhibit 20–6 (this exhibit also presents a comparison with the par value method). Under the cost method, the treasury stock account at the end of the accounting period is reported as an unallocated reduction of the total amount of owners' equity, as shown in Exhibit 20–6 (see the section titled "Financial Statement Reporting"). Under the cost method, the original contributed capital accounts are unaffected. Instead, the account Contributed capital from treasury stock transactions is used (retained earnings may be affected upon resale).

Par Value Method   The par value method sometimes is called the dual-transaction concept because it views the purchase and sale of treasury stock as two independent and separate transactions. The two objectives of the par value method:

EXHIBIT 20-6   Recording and Reporting Treasury Stock—Cost and Par Value Methods Compared

Case Data (Initial Sale of Stock)

To record the initial sale and issuance of 10,000 shares of common stock, par $25, at $26 per share:

Cash (10,000 shares × $26)	260,000	
Common stock, par $25 (10,000 shares)		250,000
Contributed capital in excess of par,		
common stock (10,000 shares × $1)		10,000

Entries to Record Treasury Stock Transactions

Cost Method	**Par Value Method**

1. Acquisition—To record the acquisition of 2,000 shares of treasury common stock at $28 per share:

Cost Method			Par Value Method		
Treasury stock, common stock:			Treasury stock, common stock		
(2,000 shares × $28)	56,000		(2,000 shares × par, $25)	50,000	
Cash		56,000	Contributed capital in excess		
			of par, common stock (at $1)	2,000	
			Contributed capital from		
			treasury stock transactions,		
			common stock	–0–*	
			Retained earnings	4,000	
			Cash		56,000

* There is no credit balance to absorb a debit, thus the remaining $4,000 is debited to retained earnings. Alternatively, if the 2,000 shares had been acquired for $46,000, Contributed capital from treasury stock transactions would be credited for $6,000.

2. Sale—To record sale of 500 shares of the treasury stock at $30 per share (above cost and above par):

Cost Method			Par Value Method		
Cash (500 shares × $30)	15,000		Cash (500 shares × $30)	15,000	
Treasury stock, common stock			Treasury stock, common stock		
(500 shares × cost, $28)		14,000	(500 shares × par, $25)		12,500
Contributed capital from			Contributed capital in excess		
treasury stock transactions,			of par, common stock		2,500
common stock*		1,000			

* If this sale had been at cost ($28 per share), no entry would have been made to contributed capital from treasury stock transactions, common stock.

3. Sale—To record the sale of another 500 shares of the treasury stock stock at $19 per share (below cost and below par, which would be an unusual occurrence):

Cost Method			Par Value Method		
Cash (500 shares × $19)	9,500		Cash (500 shares × $19)	9,500	
Contributed capital from			Contributed capital from		
treasury stock transactions,			treasury stock transactions,		
common stock‡	1,000		common stock†	–0–	
Retained earnings	3,500		Retained earnings	3,000	
Treasury stock, common stock			Treasury stock, common stock		
(500 shares × cost, $28)		14,000	(500 shares × par, $25)		12,500

‡ Debit limited to the credit balance in this account (Entry 2); any remainder is debited to retained earnings.

† Debit limited to the credit balance in this account, which is zero, because there were no prior purchases of treasury stock below original issue price. Any remainder is debited to retained earnings.

1. At date of acquisition of treasury stock—To make a final accounting with the retiring stockholder and to adjust the capital accounts on a "constructive stock retirement" basis.
2. At date of resale of treasury stock—To record the sale in essentially the same manner as for the sale and issuance of unissued stock.

EXHIBIT 20-6   (*concluded*)

Financial Statement Reporting (after All the Above Transactions)

Cost Method		Par Value Method	
Contributed capital:		Contributed capital:	
Common stock, par $25, authorized 50,000 shares, issued 10,000 shares	$250,000	Common stock, par $25, authorized 50,000 shares, issued 10,000 shares	$250,000
Contributed capital in excess of par, common stock	10,000	Less: Treasury stock, 1,000 shares at par, $25	(25,000)
Total contributed capital	$260,000	Total common stock outstanding, 9,000 shares	225,000
Retained earnings ($40,000* − $3,500)	36,500	Contributed capital in excess of par, common stock ($10,000 − $2,000 + $2,500)	10,500
Total contributed capital and retained earnings	$296,500	Contributed capital from treasury stock transactions, common stock	-0-
Less: Treasury stock, 1,000 shares at cost, $28	28,000	Total contributed capital	$235,500
Total stockholders' equity	$268,500	Retained earnings ($40,000* − $4,000 − $3,000)	33,000
		Total stockholders' equity	$268,500
* Balance assumed.		* Balance assumed.	

To accomplish these two objectives, the treasury stock acount is carried at the par or stated value per share (thus the designation *par value method*). Accounting for treasury stock under the par value method is described below.

Date of Acquisition   The acquisition of the stock for cash is recorded as a credit to cash for the price paid and a debit to treasury stock for the par value (in the case of par value stock), stated value (in the case of nopar stock with a stated value), or average amount previously credited to the capital stock account (in the case of true nopar stock). Also, contributed capital in excess of par is debited for the proportionate amount of any excess over par or stated value that was paid by the stockholders when the shares originally were issued. If a debit or credit balance still remains, this excess is allocated as follows:

1. When the acquisition cost of the treasury shares is more than the original issue amount paid in by the original stockholder (i.e., there is a debit difference to be allocated):
   a. Step 1—debit contributed capital from treasury stock transactions (to the extent needed, but not in excess of any credit balance in that account from the same class of stock).
   b. Step 2—allocate any remainder as a debit to retained earnings. The purpose of this step allocation is to maintain a distinction among the sources of contributed capital.
   In lieu of the above step allocation, *APB Opinion No. 6* (par. 12a) states that "the excess [debit difference] may be [debited] entirely to retained earnings in recognition of the fact that a corporation can always capitalize or allocate retained earnings for such purposes." Companies are reluctant to debit retained earnings for two reasons: to "protect" their cumulative earnings amount and to declare dividends in the future.
2. When the acquisition cost of the treasury stock is less than the original issue amount paid in by the retiring stockholders, the excess should be credited in full to Contributed capital from treasury stock transactions.

Application of the par value method and the cost method of accounting for the acquisition of treasury stock is illustrated in Exhibit 20–6.

Date of Resale   Under the par value method, the entry for resale of treasury stock is essentially the same as the entry for original sale (see exception below). Cash is debited for the amount of cash received, and treasury stock is credited for the par value, stated value, or average paid in (in the case of true nopar stock). If the sale price (the debit to cash) of the treasury stock is more than its par value, stated value, or average paid in for nopar stock originally, the full amount of the difference should be credited to contributed capital in excess of par. If the sale price of the treasury stock is less than its par value, stated value, or average paid in for nopar stock, the usual debit is to contributed capital from treasury stock transactions. If the credit balance in that account cannot absorb the difference, the remainder is debited to retained earnings. Some accountants prefer to debit the full amount to retained earnings. This approach is acceptable; it does not cause a GAAP problem. However, most companies would prefer not to debit retained earnings.

The basic difference between the cost and par value methods when treasury stock is sold is shown in Exhibit 20–6 under "Entries to Record Treasury Stock Transactions." The section titled "Financial Statement Reporting" shows how the two methods report treasury stock. The par value method is viewed as conceptually preferable because it maintains a "source of capital" reporting, and treasury stock is reported as a negative element of contributed capital. By contrast, under the cost method, treasury stock is reported as an unallocated negative element of total stockholders' equity. Nevertheless, probably due to its relative simplicity, the cost method is used more often. Of the 420 companies reporting treasury stock in *Accounting Trends & Techniques, 1990,* 393 companies used the cost method, while only 27 companies used the par value method.

Accounting for Nopar Treasury Stock   Nopar stock having a stated or assigned value per share is accounted for as illustrated for par stock under each of the two methods. The stated or assigned value per share is treated as if it were par. With true nopar stock, the cost method almost always is used because it can be applied exactly the same way as the cost method for par value stock. If the par value method is used for nopar stock, the average paid-in amount is substituted for par value.

Stock Received by Donation   Stockholders occasionally donate shares of a corporation back to the corporation. In the past this such donated stock was credited to a new contributed capital account called **donated capital** at its market value at the date of receipt. You may encounter a stockholders' equity account identified as donated capital. The stock received was treated as treasury stock unless it was formally retired. As treasury stock, it is accounted for using either the cost method or the par value method as was described earlier and illustrated in Exhibit 20-6.

A 1990 *Exposure Draft* entitled "Accounting for Contributions Received and Contributions Made, and Capitalization of Works of Art, Historical Treasures, and Similar Assets" is expected to change the accounting for donated capital stock. Rather than credit a donated capital account for the amount of the contribution, the amount will be recorded as a revenue or gain and will be included in income for the period. The donated stock will continue to be identified as treasury stock. This topic is discussed further in Chapter 11 under the heading "Donated Assets." As of this date the above *Exposure Draft* has not been issued as an *SFAS*. Your authors, however, anticipate that a *Standard* will be issued that follows the substance of the *Exposure Draft*. For end-of-chapter material, treat any donated capital as a revenue or gain item at its fair market value, and include it as a part of treasury stock.

Example   Assume Snow Company has 10,000 shares of $10 par common stock issued and outstanding. On May 15, a stockholder donates 1,000 shares of her stock to the

Company. On that date the market price of the stock is $15 per share. Snow Company plans to resell the donated shares in the near future, and uses the cost method to account for treasury stock.

The entry Snow Company would make, under the *Exposure Draft* requirements, would be:

```
Treasury stock  . . . . . . . . . . . . . . . . . . . . . . . . . . . .  15,000
     Gain from receipt of donated stock  . . . . . . . . . . . . . .           15,000
```

Suppose Snow sold the donated stock on June 15 for $17 per share. The entry to record the resale of the donated shares is the same as the sale of any treasury stock:

```
Cash  . . . . . . . . . . . . . . . . . . . . . . . . . . . . . . . .  17,000
     Treasury stock . . . . . . . . . . . . . . . . . . . . . . . . .          15,000
     Contributed stock from treasury
        stock transactions, common . . . . . . . . . . . . . . . . .            2,000
```

The receipt of donated capital shares is a rare event for most corporations. There are no examples of this transaction in the three most recent issues of *Accounting Trends & Techniques*. Corporations are more frequently the recipient of other types of donated assets (such as land upon which to build a plant), and the accounting requirements for these types of donations are covered in detail in Chapter 11.

Formal Retirement of Treasury Stock

A corporation may constructively retire treasury shares (by amending the charter) and have the shares revert to an unauthorized (i.e., not subject to resale or reissuance) status. It may also retire the treasury stock and return it to the unissued status. When treasury stock is retired, the treasury stock account is credited, and all capital account balances related to the treasury shares, including contributed capital from treasury stock transactions, are reduced (i.e., debited) on a proportional basis. Any difference, if a credit, is recorded in contributed capital from stock retirement; if a debit, retained earnings is reduced.

To demonstrate a retirement of treasury stock, assume General Signal Corporation plans to retire the 9,572,627 shares it acquired in its self-tender offer of December 1988 (see Exhibit 20–5 for a description of the transaction). These shares were acquired at a cost of $491 million and are accounted for using the cost method. To retire the shares, the common stock account is debited for the par values of the shares being retired, which equals $9,572,627. Additional paid-in capital is debited a proportionate share of the paid-in capital balance. The amount to be debited is the number of shares being retired divided by the number of shares issued, times the additional paid-in capital balance: $(9,572,627/30,737,505) \times \$295,916,000$, or $92,157,561. The remainder of the cost of $491 million less the amounts debited to common stock and additional paid-in capital, or $389,269,812, is debited to retained earnings. The entry is:

```
Common stock, par value $1  . . . . . . . . . . . . . .    9,572,627
Additional paid-in capital . . . . . . . . . . . . . . . .   92,157,561
Retained earnings . . . . . . . . . . . . . . . . . . . .  389,269,812
     Treasury stock at cost . . . . . . . . . . . . . . . .             491,000,000
```

The retirement of the stock does not affect the net balance in stockholders' equity, but it does reduce the number of shares accounted for as issued. It also signals to investors that the firm is not going to resell the retired shares on the stock market.

Restriction of Retained Earnings for Treasury Stock

When treasury stock is purchased, assets (usually cash) of the corporation are disbursed to the owners of the particular shares purchased. If a corporation has a free hand, it is not difficult to perceive how creditor interests (or the interests of another class of stockholders) may be jeopardized through the distribution of corporate assets via treasury stock purchases from selected stockholders, even though legal capital may be technically maintained. To prevent such situations, some states have a law that limits the amount of treasury stock that may be held at any one time to a specified amount. This limit is usually the total amount of retained earnings. This provision has the effect of requiring a restriction (often called an *appropriation*) of retained earnings equivalent to the cost of treasury stock held to reduce the amount of retained earnings that may be used for dividends until the treasury shares are resold. The restriction is based upon the cost of the treasury stock held, whether the cost method or the par value method is used to account for treasury stock. Also, debt covenants often limit the amount of treasury stock a corporation may purchase. Some states impose no limits on treasury stock. Such is apparently the case for King World Productions, Inc., the example used in the opening of this chapter, where the cost of treasury stock was greater than the total amount recorded in the stockholders' equity accounts.

Retained earnings restrictions (i.e., appropriations) related to treasury stock usually are reported by a disclosure note in the financial statements. Alternatively, formal appropriation entries may be recorded and reported as discussed in the following chapter.

Formal Retirement of Callable and Redeemable Stock

Callable preferred stock provides the issuing corporation the option, after a certain date, to call in the shares at a specified price for formal retirement. In contrast, *redeemable* stock provides that at the option of the stockholder and under certain conditions, the shares tendered by the stockholders will be retired at a specified price per share. The exercise of the call or redemption option usually involves acquisition and formal retirement of the stock by the issuing corporation. The call or redemption price is at or above par and usually is above the original issue price. Shares called or redeemed have the status of unissued shares. They are not classified as treasury stock.

When callable or redeemable stock is acquired and formally retired, cash is credited, and all capital balances relating to the specific shares are removed from the accounts. Any remaining debit difference is recorded in retained earnings as a de facto dividend. Any remaining credit difference is credited to a contributed capital account, such as Contributed capital from retirement of stock. If the preferred stock is cumulative and there are dividends in arrears, such dividends must be paid and debited to retained earnings at the date of the call or redemption.

With respect to disclosure of callable and redeemable stock, *APB Opinion No. 10* (par. 10) states that "any liquidation preference of the stock be disclosed in the equity section of the balance sheet in the aggregate, either parenthetically or 'in short' rather than on a per share basis or by disclosure in notes." Amounts of cumulative preferred dividends in arrears also should be disclosed. Also, *SFAS No. 47* (par. 10) states that the balance sheet should disclose "the amount of redemption requirements for all issues of capital stock that are redeemable at fixed or determinable prices on fixed or determinable dates, separately by issue or combined."

To illustrate, assume a corporation had 2,500 shares of 5% callable preferred stock (par value $100) outstanding, $250,000; contributed capital in excess of par, preferred stock, $10,000; and retained earnings, $45,000. Assume the corporation called and formally retired all of the preferred stock. Three different assumptions as to the call and retirement are illustrated below.

Assumption 1   The preferred stock is noncumulative and callable at the original issue price of $104 per share.

```
Preferred stock (2,500 shares at par, $100)  . . . . . . . . . . . .  250,000
Contributed capital in excess of par, preferred stock
  ($4 per share)  . . . . . . . . . . . . . . . . . . . . . . . . . . . . . .   10,000
    Cash (2,500 shares × $104)  . . . . . . . . . . . . . . . . . .              260,000
```

Assumption 2   The preferred stock is noncumulative and callable at $110 per share—$6 per share above the original issue price of $104.

```
Preferred stock (2,500 shares at par, $100)  . . . . . . . . . . . .  250,000
Contributed capital in excess of par, preferred stock
  ($4 per share)  . . . . . . . . . . . . . . . . . . . . . . . . . . . . . .   10,000
Retained earnings . . . . . . . . . . . . . . . . . . . . . . . . . . . . .   15,000
    Cash (2,500 shares × $110)  . . . . . . . . . . . . . . . . . .              275,000
```

Assumption 3   The preferred stock is cumulative; three years' dividends are in arrears. The stock is callable at $101. The dividends in arrears must be paid:
To recognize payment of dividends in arrears:

```
Retained earnings ($250,000 × .05 × 3 years)  . . . . . . . . . .   37,500
    Cash  . . . . . . . . . . . . . . . . . . . . . . . . . . . . . . . . . .                37,500
```

Note: If half of the shares were called, the above entry would record $18,750, and the cumulative dividends on the remaining shares of preferred stock also would have to be paid and recorded.

To record the retirement of called preferred shares:

```
Preferred stock (2,500 shares at par, $100)  . . . . . . . . . . . .  250,000
Contributed capital in excess of par, preferred stock
  ($4 per share)  . . . . . . . . . . . . . . . . . . . . . . . . . . . . . .   10,000
    Contributed capital from retirement of preferred stock
      [($104 − $101) × 2,500 share]  . . . . . . . . . . . . . . . .              7,500
    Cash (2,500 shares × $101)  . . . . . . . . . . . . . . . . . .              252,500
```

If true nopar *stock* is formally retired, the average price per share originally credited to the stock account is removed from the capital stock account, cash is credited, and any net debit or credit is accounted for as illustrated above. If nopar stock with a stated or assigned value is retired, the procedures illustrated above for par value stock are followed.

CONCEPT REVIEW

1. Describe two methods of accounting for treasury stock. How do they differ with respect to how amounts in the individual contributed capital accounts in the stockholders' equity section of the balance sheet are treated?
2. What effect does choosing one method over the other have on the total balance reported in stockholders' equity?
3. A firm receives as a donation from a stockholder the shares of its $100 par value common shares. At the time the shares are received, they have a market value of $140 per share. The shares were originally issued for $110 per share. Describe three methods of accounting for this transaction.

ACCOUNTING FOR CONVERSIONS, CHANGES IN PAR VALUE, AND CONTRIBUTED CAPITAL

Conversion of Convertible Preferred Stock

Similar to the issuance of convertible bonds, discussed in Chapter 16, corporations sometimes issue convertible preferred stock. This stock gives the stockholder an option, within a specified time period, to exchange the convertible preferred shares held for other classes of capital stock, usually common stock, at a specified rate. The accounting treatment for conversion of preferred stock is analogous to that for convertible bonds. The converted shares usually are formally retired when received by the corporation. Conversion privileges require the issuing corporation to set aside a sufficient number of units of the other security to fulfill the conversion privileges until they are exercised or expire.

At date of conversion, all account balances related to the converted shares are removed, and the new shares issued are recorded at their par or stated value. Any credit difference is recorded in an appropriately designated contributed capital account (e.g., "Contributed capital from conversion of preferred stock). If there is a debit difference, retained earnings are reduced. To illustrate three typical cases, assume the following data, and that the converted stock is formally retired:

Preferred stock, convertible, noncumulative, par $2, shares outstanding, 100,000	$200,000
Contributed capital in excess of par, preferred stock	20,000
Common stock, par $1, shares authorized, 500,000; shares outstanding, 150,000	150,000
Contributed capital in excess of par, common stock	50,000

Case 1   The conversion privilege specifies the issuance of one share of common stock for each share of preferred stock. Assume stockholders turn in 10,000 shares of preferred stock for conversion.

Preferred stock (10,000 shares at par, $2)	20,000	
Contributed capital in excess of par, preferred stock ($20,000 ÷ 100,000 shares = $.20 per share)	2,000	
Common stock (10,000 shares at par, $1)		10,000
Contributed capital from conversion of preferred stock		12,000

Case 2   The conversion privilege specifies the issuance of two shares of common stock for each share of preferred stock. Stockholders turn in 10,000 shares of preferred stock for conversion.

Preferred stock (10,000 shares at par, $2)	20,000	
Contributed capital in excess of par, preferred stock ($.20 per share)	2,000	
Common stock (20,000 shares at par, $1)		20,000
Contributed capital from conversion of preferred stock		2,000

Case 3   The conversion privilege specifies the issuance of three shares of common stock for each share of preferred stock. Stockholders turn in 10,000 shares of preferred stock for conversion.

Preferred stock (10,000 shares at par, $2)	20,000	
Contributed capital in excess of par, preferred stock ($.20 per share)	2,000	
Retained earnings	8,000	
Common stock (30,000 shares at par, $1)		30,000

Conversion of bonds for capital stock was discussed in Chapter 16.

Changing Par Value

Companies sometimes desire to increase the number of shares outstanding. One reason to do this is to reduce the market price per share, which often increases the market activity of the shares. One way to increase the number of shares outstanding is to reduce the par value per share and issue additional shares on a pro rata basis to shareholders with the end result that total legal capital is unchanged but more shares are outstanding. A corporation, if it conforms with the applicable state laws, may amend the charter and bylaws to change the par value (and/or the number of authorized shares) of one or more classes of authorized stock. Par value stock may be called in, formally retired, and replaced with nopar stock or stock of a different

EXHIBIT 20–7 Some Transactions that May Affect Additional Contributed Capital

Decreases Additional Contributed Capital	Increases Additional Contributed Capital
1. Issuance of stock below par or stated value.	1. Issuance of stock above par or stated value.
2. Sale of treasury stock below cost, cost method.	2. Sale of treasury stock above cost, cost method.
3. Acquisition and/or sale of treasury stock above par and/or average paid in originally, par value method.	3. Acquisition and/or sale of treasury stock below par and/or average paid in originally, par value method.
4. Conversion of convertible preferred stock.	4. Receipt of donated treasury stock or donated assets.
5. Retirement of callable or redeemable preferred stock.	5. Conversion of convertible preferred stock.
6. Payment of a liquidating dividend (Introduced in Retaining earnings chapter).	6. Retirement of callable or redeemable preferred stock.
7. Quasi reorganizations (Introduced in Retaining earnings chapter).	7. Conversion of convertible bonds (Introduced in chapter 16).
	8. Distribution of a stock dividend (Introduced in Retaining earnings chapter).

par value; conversely, nopar stock may be replaced with par value stock. (This is not allowed in all states.)

To record changes in par value, all capital account balances that relate to the old stock retired are removed from the accounts and the new stock issued is recorded. If an additional credit is needed, an appropriately designated contributed capital account is credited; if an additional debit is needed, retained earnings is debited. The entries are similar to those illustrated above for recording the conversion of convertible preferred stock.

A stock split is a special case involving a change in par value. In a stock split, the par value per share is reduced and the number of shares outstanding is increased proportionately. Therefore, the balance in the capital stock account is unchanged. Only a memorandum entry in the original stock account is needed to reflect the new par value per share and the number of shares outstanding after the split. Stock splits are covered in the next chapter.

Additional Contributed Capital

Legal capital, defined earlier, is recorded in the specific capital stock accounts—common stock and preferred stock. All **additional contributed capital** [often called *additional paid-in capital,* or *paid-in capital in excess of par (or stated value)*] is recorded in appropriately designated additional (or other) contributed capital accounts.

Contributed capital does not include retained earnings or unrealized capital. No operating or extraordinary gains and losses or prior period adjustments may be recorded as contributed capital. Additional contributed capital is created by a number of events that involve the corporation and its stockholders. Several accounts for additional contributed (or additional paid-in) capital were introduced in this chapter. Exhibit 20–7 summarizes some of the transactions that may cause increases or decreases in additional contributed capital.

Corporations often report increases and decreases in additional contributed capital accounts. For example, numerous changes as reported by Betz Laboratories, Inc., over a three-year period are shown in Exhibit 20–8. Several of these changes, including those related to stock plans and unearned compensation, are covered in the next chapter. Unrealized loss on investments relates to accounting for long-term investments in marketable equity securities and was covered in Chapter 14. Foreign currency translation adjustments are beyond the scope of this text.

EXHIBIT 20-8   Disclosure Schedule of Common Shareholders' Equity

BETZ LABORATORIES, INC.
Consolidated Statements of Common Shareholders' Equity

	Year Ended December 31		
	1989	**1988**	**1987**
Common shares:			
Balance at beginning of year	$ 1,686,829	$ 1,687,556	$ 1,688,466
Shares cancelled through stock plans (1989—9,106 shares; 1988—7,269 shares; 1987—9,100 shares)	(911)	(727)	(910)
Balance at end of year	$ 1,685,918	$ 1,686,829	$ 1,687,556
Capital in excess of par value of shares:			
Balance at beginning of year	$ 47,439,034	$ 43,236,226	$ 39,128,915
Tax effects relating to stock plans	621,473	684,481	291,889
Shares issued through stock plans	3,988,013	3,518,327	3,815,422
Balance at end of year	$ 52,048,520	$ 47,439,034	$ 43,236,226
Retained earnings:			
Balance at beginning of year	$242,517,683	$219,384,949	$202,044,397
Net earnings for the year	55,860,044	48,385,076	40,633,789
Common dividends declared (per share: 1989-$1.83; 1988—$1.64; 1987—$1.49)	(27,133,933)	(25,252,162)	(23,293,237)
Preferred dividends declared ($8.00 per share)	(4,000,000)	—	—
Tax benefit related to ESOP preferred dividends	1,480,000	—	—
Balance at end of year	$268,723,974	$242,517,863	$219,384,949
Treasury shares:			
Balance at beginning of year	$ 50,663,483	$ 53,056,016	$ 29,478,624
Purchases: (1989—1,366,800 shares; 1987—610,000 shares)	78,133,614	—	36,361,800
Reissue of shares to stock plans: (1989—152,053 shares; 1988—145,002 shares; 1987—168,752 shares)	(2,550,866)	(2,392,533)	(2,784,408)
Balance at end of year	$126,246,231	$ 50,663,483	$ 53,056,016
Unearned compensation:			
Balance at beginning of year	$ 11,281,685	$ 9,493,514	$ 7,468,733
New grants	3,807,118	5,356,264	4,635,445
Amounts expensed during the year	(3,523,722)	(3,568,093)	(2,610,664)
Balance at end of year	$ 11,565,081	$ 11,281,685	$ 9,493,514
Unrealized loss on investments:			
Balance at beginning of year	$ 3,588,168	$ —	$ —
Unrealized decline in value of investments	452,387	3,588,168	—
Balance at end of year	$ 4,040,555	$ 3,588,168	$ —
Foreign currency translation adjustments:			
Balance at beginning of year	$ (4,462,812)	$ (3,436,329)	$ 1,874,311
Current-year adjustments	2,203,722	(1,026,483)	(5,310,640)
Balance at end of year	$ (2,259,090)	$ (4,462,812)	$ (3,436,329)

CONCEPT REVIEW

1. Describe the basic accounting when preferred stock is converted.
2. Why would a company elect to change the par value of its stock?
3. What capital stock items are included in contributed capital? What items are excluded?

SUMMARY OF KEY POINTS

(L.O. 1) 1. For corporations, owners' equity is called *stockholders' equity* or *shareholders' equity*. Claims to ownership are represented by shares of stock. Different types of claims are represented by shares of stock with differing contractual rights for the holder. Shareholders' equity arises from two sources: contributed capital and capital arising from earnings of the corporation not paid out to shareholders. The latter is called *retained earnings*.

(L.O. 1) 2. The principal advantages of the corporate form of organization over proprietorships and partnerships include (1) separation of ownership and management so that large amounts of capital can be acquired and (2) limited liability for the shareholders. The principal disadvantage of the corporate form is the likelihood of double taxation. The earnings of the corporation are normally taxed, and dividends received by shareholders, which are distributions of after-tax corporate earnings, are also taxed.

(L.O. 2) 3. Two basic types of stock are common stock and preferred stock. Common stock generally has the residual claim and the residual risk of the corporation. Preferred stock has one or more contractually specified preferences over common stock. These preferences involve one or more of the following rights: voting rights, dividend rights, preference in liquidation rights, conversion rights, call rights, and redemption rights.

(L.O. 2) 4. Preferred stock features can vary from one extreme, where the stock has almost the same risks and opportunity for returns as common stock, to the opposite extreme, where the risks and returns are such that the stock is essentially a form of debt. An example of the former would be convertible, fully participating, noncumulative preferred stock. The latter would be represented by cumulative preferred stock that is redeemable at the option of the holder.

(L.O. 3) 5. Authorized stock is the total number of shares that legally can be issued. The term *issued shares* refers to the number of shares that have been sold or otherwise issued to shareholders. Treasury stock is shares that were issued and have been reacquired by the corporation. Outstanding shares equal issued shares less treasury shares. Subscribed stock is unissued shares that are to be used to meet executed subscription contracts. Subscription contracts are legal contracts between the corporation and a purchaser of shares, stating the number of shares the purchaser has agreed to purchase, the agreed price, and the period of payment for the shares.

(L.O. 3) 6. Par value stock generally establishes the legal capital amount that stockholders must contribute to the corporation when the shares are issued. Since capital stock almost always sells for a premium over par value, par value has little economic meaning. When shares are sold and issued by the corporation, par value is used to record the stock issuance in the stock account specific to the type of stock issued. Any proceeds received in excess of par value are recorded in an additional paid-in capital account, also called capital in excess of par (for the specific type of stock issued).

(L.O.3) 7. Nopar value, whether for preferred stock or common stock, is accounted for at issuance by first crediting the appropriate capital stock account with the stated value if there is one, otherwise with an amount required by state law. Any additional amount is credited to an additional paid-in capital account.

(L.O. 3) 8. When a corporation issues stock for assets or for services rendered to the corporation, often the accounting problem is determining the appropriate amount at which to record the transaction. The most reliably determinable side of the transaction, whether it is the market value of the shares issued or the current market value of the asset or service received, is used to record the transaction.

(L.O. 1)   9. Stock issue costs are either offset against the proceeds received, resulting in lower net proceeds being recorded in stockholders' equity, or are treated as a deferred charge on the balance sheet. The deferred charge is amortized over future periods. Both methods are acceptable under GAAP, but the offset method is the more commonly used method.

(L.O. 4)   10. Stock subscriptions are contractual agreements specifying a certain number of shares that are to be acquired by specified buyers. The subscribed stock receivable account is generally not viewed as an asset of the corporation. It is treated as a contra to stockholders' equity.

(L.O. 5)   11. Treasury stock is accounted for either by the cost method or by the par value method. Both are acceptable. Both have the same effect on total stockholders' equity, but result in different amounts being recorded in the various accounts within the stockholders' equity section. The cost method is the more commonly used method.

(L.O. 5)   12. When the cost method of accounting for treasury stock is used, the acquisition cost of the stock acquired is debited to a contra stockholders' equity account titled "treasury stock, at cost." When the stock is resold, the difference between the acquisition price and the resale price is debited or credited as appropriate to an additional paid-in capital account, or debited to retained earnings if necessary.

(L.O. 5)   13. When the par value method of accounting for treasury stock is used, the transaction effectively treats the acquired stock as being retired. The appropriate stock account is debited at the par value of the stock, and any additional amount is debited to the additional paid-in capital account. When the shares are resold, the sale is treated in the same manner as the sale and issuance of unissued stock.

(L.O. 6)   14. When shares are retired, either through the call feature, redeemable feature, or simply retirement through treasury stock acquisitions, all capital balances relating to the specific stock are removed. Any remaining balance is either debited to retained earnings as a de facto dividend or is credited to an additional paid-in capital account.

(L.O. 6)   15. Upon conversion of convertible preferred stock, all account balances related to the converted shares are removed, and newly issued shares are recorded first at par value. Any difference is either debited to retained earnings or credited to an appropriate additional paid-in account.

REVIEW PROBLEM

◆

On January 2, 1991, Fleury Corporation was chartered in the state of Delaware. It was authorized to issue 100,000 shares of $5 par value common stock, and 10,000 shares of $100 par value, cumulative, and nonparticipating preferred stock. During the year 1991 the firm completed the following transactions:

Jan. 8   Accepted subscriptions for 40,000 shares of common stock at $12 per share. Down payment on the subscribed stock totaled $150,000.

     30   Issued 4,000 shares of preferred stock in exchange for the following assets: machinery with a fair value market value of $35,000, a factory with a fair market value of $110,000, and land with an appraised market value of $295,000.

Apr. 25   Collected the balance of the subscription receivable and issued the shares.

Jun. 30   Purchased 2,200 shares of common stock at $18 per share. Use the cost method to account for treasury stock.

Sep. 20   Sold the 2,200 shares of treasury stock at $21 per share.

Dec. 31   Closed the income summary to retained earnings. The income for the period was $88,000.

Required:

1. Prepare the journal entries to record the above transactions up to closing the books on December 31.
2. Prepare the stockholders' equity section of the balance sheet for Fleury Corporation for December 31, 1991.

SOLUTION

◆

Jan. 8: Account for subscription of common stock:

Cash	150,000	
Stock subscription receivable	330,000	
Common stock subscribed		200,000
Additional paid-in capital, common		280,000

Jan. 30: Issue preferred stock in exchange for assets:

Machinery	35,000	
Factory	110,000	
Land	295,000	
Preferred stock, $100 par		400,000
Additional paid-in capital, preferred stock		40,000

Note: Since there is no market price established for the preferred shares prior to this transaction, the transaction is recorded at the fair market values of the assets received.

April 25: Record receipt of cash for subscribed stock and issuance of stock:

Cash	330,000	
Stock subscription receivable		330,000
Common stock subscribed	200,000	
Common stock, $10 par		200,000

June 30: Record acquisition of treasury stock:

Treasury stock, at cost	39,600	
Cash		39,600

Sept. 20: Record sale of treasury stock:

Cash	46,200	
Treasury stock, at cost		39,600
Additional paid-in capital from treasury stock transactions		6,600

Dec. 31: To close income summary to retained earnings:

Income summary	88,000	
Retained earnings		88,000

2. Prepare the stockholders' equity seciton of the balance sheet for Fleury Corporation for December 31, 1991.

FLEURY CORPORATION
Stockholders' Equity
At December 31, 1991

Contributed Capital:	
Common stock, $5 par value (100,000 shares authorized; 40,000 shares issued)	$200,000
Preferred stock, $100 par value (10,000 shares authorized; 4,000 shares issued)	400,000
Additional paid-in capital, common stock	280,000
Additional paid-in capital, preferred stock	40,000
Additional paid-in capital, treasury stock transactions	6,600
Retained earnings	88,000
Total stockholders' equity	$1,014,600

For financial reporting purposes, the various "additional paid-in capital" accounts are often aggregated and reported as one item, additional paid-in capital.

KEY TERMS

Additional contributed capital (1145)	Par value stock (1119)
Authorized capital stock (1118)	Participating dividend preferences (1122)
Common stock (1120)	Preferred stock (1121)
Contributed capital (1116)	Redeemable preferred stock (1125)
Cumulative dividend preference (1121)	Retained earnings (1117)
Donated capital (1140)	Stockholders' equity (1114)
Issued capital stock (1118)	Subscribed capital stock (1118)
Legal capital (1120)	Treasury stock (1118)
Nopar stock (1120)	Unissued capital stock (1118)
Outstanding capital stock (1118)	Unrealized capital (1134)

QUESTIONS

1. Define public, private, open, closed, and publicly traded corporations.
2. What are four basic rights of stockholders? How may one or more of these rights be withheld from the stockholders?
3. Explain each of the following: authorized capital stock, issued capital stock, unissued capital stock, outstanding capital stock, subscribed capital stock, and treasury stock.
4. In accounting for corporate capital, explain what it means to report by source, and the significance of doing so.
5. Explain how the cost principle relates to the issuance of capital stock.
6. Define the term *capital* as it is usually applied in accounting.
7. Define legal capital in the general sense.
8. Distinguish between par and nopar stock.
9. Distinguish between common and preferred stock.
10. Explain the difference between cumulative and noncumulative preferred stock.
11. Explain the difference between nonparticipating, partially participating, and fully participating preferred stock.
12. Explain asset preference as it relates to preferred stock.
13. Distinguish between callable and redeemable preferred stock.
14. Under what circumstances should stock subscriptions receivable be reported (a) as a current asset, (b) as a noncurrent asset, and (c) as a deduction in the stockholders' equity section of the balance sheet?
15. How should premium and discount on capital stock be accounted for and reported?
16. How are assets valued when shares of stock are given in payment for these assets?
17. Briefly explain the two methods of accounting for stock issue costs.
18. What is the difference between unrealized capital increases and unrealized capital decreases? How might each arise?
19. Define treasury stock.
20. What is the effect on assets, liabilities, and stockholders' equity of (a) the purchase of treasury stock and (b) the sale of treasury stock?
21. Explain the theoretical difference between the one-transaction concept and the dual-transaction concept in accounting for treasury stock.
22. Total owners' equity is not affected by the use of the cost or par value methods of accounting for treasury stock yet some components of owners' equity are affected. Is this statement correct? Explain.
23. Why have many states limited purchases of treasury stock to the amount reported as retained earnings? How may the restriction on retained earnings be removed?
24. In recording treasury stock transactions, explain why gains are recorded in a contributed capital account, whereas losses may involve a debit to retained earnings.
25. How is treasury stock reported on the balance sheet (a) under the cost method and (b) under the par value method?
26. How do you record stock donated back to the corporation?
27. When treasury stock is formally retired, retained earnings may be affected. Explain how this situation may occur.

EXERCISES

E 20–1
Stock Issuance: Effects on the Balance Sheet
(L.O. 3)

NIC Corporation received a charter authorizing 200,000 shares of $5 par value stock. During the first year, 120,000 shares were sold at $8 per share. One thousand additional shares were issued in payment for legal fees. At the end of the first year, reported net income was $46,000. Dividends of $20,000 were paid on the last day of the year. Liabilities at the year-end amounted to $60,000.

Required:

Complete the following tabulation (show calculations); state any assumptions that you make.

Items	Amount	Assumptions
a. Total assets	$	
b. Owners' equity	$	
c. Contributed capital	$	
d. Issued capital stock	$	
e. Outstanding capital stock	$	
f. Unissued capital stock	$	
g. Treasury stock	$	

E 20–2
Prepare Stockholders' Equity, Two Classes of Stock, and Subscribed Stock
(L.O. 2, 3, 4)

The charter of RAE Corporation authorized 100,000 shares of nopar common stock and 20,000 shares of 6%, cumulative and nonparticipating preferred stock, par value $10 per share. Stock issued to date: 40,000 shares of common sold at $220,000 and 10,000 shares of preferred stock sold at $21 per share. In addition, subscriptions for 2,000 shares of preferred have been taken, and 30% of the purchase price of $21 has been collected. The stock will be issued upon collection in full. The retained earnings balance is $288,000. At year-end, there was a $10,000 unrealized loss on long-term investments in equity securities.

Required:
Prepare the stockholders' equity section of the balance sheet.

E 20–3
Prepare Stockholders' Equity: Subscriptions, Donation, and Unrealized Loss
(L.O. 2, 3, 4)

Prepare, in good form, the stockholders' equity section of the balance sheet for Warren Corporation.

Retained earnings	$ 390,000
Premium on common stock	40,000
Preferred stock subscribed, but not yet issued (3,000 shares)	30,000
Preferred stock, 6%, par $10, authorized 25,000 shares (15,000 shares issued)	150,000
Common stock, par $20, authorized 500,000 shares (110,000 shares issued)	2,200,000
Stock subscriptions receivable, preferred	4,000
Donation of plant site	50,000
Premium on preferred stock	30,000
Unrealized loss on long-term investment in equity securities	10,000

E 20–4
Analysis of Stockholders' Equity: Prepare Statement
(L.O. 2, 3, 4)

The following data were provided by the accounts of Mitar Corporation at December 31, 1993:

Subscriptions receivable (noncurrent)	$ 5,000
Retained earnings, 1/1/1993	450,000
Capital stock, par ?, authorized 100,000 shares	500,000
Future site for office (donated to Mitar)	15,000
Capital stock subscribed, 1,000 shares (to be issued upon collection in full)	10,000
Premium on capital stock	200,000
Subscriptions receivable, capital stock (due in three months)	2,000
Bonds payable	100,000
Net income for 1993 (not included in retained earnings above)	95,000
Dividends declared and paid during 1993	40,000

Required:

1. Respond to the following (state any assumptions that you made):
   a. Total retained earnings at end of 1993 is . . . . $_____
   b. Retained earnings on 1/1/1993 was . . . . $_____
   c. Number of shares outstanding is . . . . $_____
   d. Legal capital is . . . . $_____
   e. Total stockholders' equity is . . . . $_____
   f. Number of shares issued is . . . . _____

g. Average selling price per share including any shares subscribed was . . . . $\rule{1.5cm}{0.4pt}$

h. Number of shares sold including any shares subscribed was . . . . $\rule{1.5cm}{0.4pt}$

i. Par value per share is . . . . $\rule{1.5cm}{0.4pt}$

2. Prepare the stockholders' equity section of the balance sheet at December 31, 1993. Use good form, complete with respect to details.

E 20-5
Compute Dividends: Preferred Stock, Cumulative and Partially Particpating
(L.O. 2, 3)

Darby Corporation has the following stock outstanding:

Preferred, 6%, par $10, cumulative and partially participating up to an additional 2%; outstanding, 5,000 shares. No dividends were declared during the prior two years.

Common stock, nopar, outstanding, 10,000 shares; participating matching dividend, $1.50 per share.

The board of directors has just declared a total cash dividend of $33,000.

Required:

You have been requested to complete the following journal entry to record the dividend declaration (show computations):

Dividends declared, preferred stock* . . . . $\rule{1cm}{0.4pt}$
Dividends declared, common stock* . . . . $\rule{1cm}{0.4pt}$
     Dividends payable . . . . $\rule{1cm}{0.4pt}$

* To be closed to retained earnings.

E 20-6
Compute Dividends: Preferred Stock, Six Cases
(L.O. 2, 3)

Able Corporation has the following stock outstanding:

Common, $50 par value—6,000 shares.

Preferred, 6%, $100 par value—1,000 shares.

Required:

Compute the amount of dividends payable in total and per share on the common and preferred stock for each separate case:

Case A

Preferred is noncumulative and nonparticipating; dividends declared, $20,000.

Case B

Preferred is cumulative and nonparticipating; two years in arrears; dividends declared, $34,000.

Case C

Preferred is noncumulative and fully participating; dividends declared, $24,000.

Case D

Preferred is noncumulative and fully participating; dividends declared, $40,000.

Case E

Preferred is cumulative and partially participating up to an additional 3%; three years in arrears; dividends declared, $60,000.

Case F

Preferred is cumulative and fully participating; two years in arrears; dividends declared, $50,000.

E 20-7
Compute Dividends: Preferred Stock, A Legal Constraint
(L.O. 2, 3)

Polaris Corporation has the following account balances:

Common stock, par $5, 40,000 shares outstanding	$200,000
Preferred stock, par $20, 9% cumulative and nonparticipating,	
5,000 shares outstanding	100,000
Contributed capital in excess of par:	
Common	80,000
Preferred	15,000
Retained earnings (total cash dividends limited to the balance in retained	
earnings; no dividends were paid during the two prior years)	220,000

Required:

Show computations.
1. The average issue price per share for (*a*) common was $_____ and (*b*) preferred was $_____.
2. Compute dividends for each class of stock under each of the following proposals:
   a. The dividend declaration is $50,000.
   b. The dividend declaration specifies that (1) the same amount of dividends per share will be paid for each class of stock, and (2) all preferences of the preferred stock are met. Does this situation pose a problem? Explain.

E 20-8
Stock Issuance: Par Value and Nopar Value, Subscriptions
(L.O. 4)

Vanguard Corporation received a charter authorizing the issuance of 200,000 shares of common stock. Give the journal entries in parallel columns for the following transactions during the first year, assuming Case A—true nopar stock; and Case B—par value of $5 per share.

a. To record authorization (memorandum).
b. Sold 100,000 shares at $7; collected in full and issued the shares.
c. Received subscriptions for 10,000 shares at $7 per share; collected 60% of the subscription price. The stock will not be issued until collection is in full.
d. Issued 200 shares to an attorney in payment for legal fees related to the charter. Use the deferred-charge method.
e. Issued 10,000 shares and in addition paid $190,000 cash in total payment for a building.
f. Collected balance on subscriptions receivable in (*c*).

State and justify any assumptions you make. Assume all transactions occurred within a short time span.

E 20-9
Stock Issuance: Nopar with Stated Value versus True Nopar, Subscriptions
(L.O. 2, 4)

The charter of Rainier Corporation authorized the issuance of 400,000 shares of nopar common stock. Give journal entries for the following transactions, assuming Case A—the board of directors set a stated value of $1 per share; and Case B—the stock is true nopar. Set up two pairs of columns so that Case A is to the left and Case B is to the right. Explain and justify any assumptions that you make. Assume all transactions occurred within a short time span.

a. Authorization recognized (memorandum).
b. Sold 150,000 shares at $5 and collected in full; the shares were issued.
c. Received subscriptions for 12,000 shares at $5 per share; collected 40% of the subscription price. The shares will be issued upon collection in full.
d. Issued 500 shares for legal services related to the charter. Use the deferred charge method.
e. Issued 2,000 shares and in addition paid $80,000 cash for some used machinery.
f. Collected balance of subscriptions in (*c*).

E 20-10
Stock Issuance: Subscriptions, Default
(L.O. 4)

The charter of Maly Corporation authorized 100,000 shares of $10 par value common stock. A. B. Cook subscribed for 500 shares at $25 per share, paying $2,500 down, the balance to be paid $1,000 per month. The stock will not be issued until collection in full. After paying for three months, Cook defaulted. Six months later, the corporation sold the stock for $33 per share.

Required:
1. Give all journal entries related to the 500 shares originally subscribed for by Cook, assuming Maly refunded all collections made to date of default.
2. Give the journal entry for the default, assuming shares equivalent to the collections were issued to Cook (at $25 per share). Also give the entry for the sale of the remaining shares at $33 six months later.
3. Give the journal entries, assuming:
   a. The stock is true nopar.
   b. The subscriber paid in full as scheduled over the 10-month period.

E 20-11
Noncash Sale of Stock: Three Cases
(L.O. 3)

The charter for Kay Manufacturing Corporation authorized 100,000 shares of common stock ($10 par value) and 10,000 shares of preferred stock ($50 par value). The company issued 600 shares of its common and 100 shares of its preferred stock for used machinery.

Required:

For each separate situation, give the entry to record the purchase of the machinery, assuming the following: Case A—the common stock currently is selling at $70 and the preferred at $80; Case B—the common stock has been selling at $70, and there have been no recent sales of the preferred stock, and no reliable value can be placed on the used machinery; and Case C—there is no current market price for either class of stock (however, the machinery has been independently appraised at $44,000).

State and justify any assumptions made.

E 20–12

Common and Preferred Stock Issued: Four Transactions

(L.O. 2, 3)

The charter of Varna Company authorized 10,000 shares of common stock, par $20, and 10,000 shares of preferred stock, par $10. The following transactions were completed. Assume each is completely independent.

a. Sold 200 shares of common and 100 shares of preferred stock for a lump sum of $6,150. The common had been selling during the current week at $25 per share, and the preferred at $12 per share.

b. Issued 90 shares of preferred stock for some used equipment. The equipment had been appraised at $1,200; the book value shown by the seller was $600. A reliable market value on the preferred stock has not been established.

c. A 10% assessment on par value was voted on both the common and preferred when 6,000 shares of common and 4,000 shares of preferred were outstanding. The assessment was collected in full.

d. Sold 300 shares of common and 200 shares of preferred stock in one transaction for a total cash price of $10,000. The common recently had been selling at $26; there were no recent sales of the preferred.

Required:

Give the journal entry for each transaction. State and justify any assumptions that you make.

E 20–13

Changes in Stockholders' Equity: An Overview

(L.O. 3)

Each numbered item in the tabulation given below changes the amount of owners' equity. Some affect retained earnings (a) directly and appear on the retained earnings statement, (b) others affect retained earnings indirectly because they are reported on the income statement, and (c) others are not reported on either statement.

Item	(a)	(b)	(c)
1. Donation of a plant site to the company			
2. Purchased treasury stock (cost method)			
3. Declaration of cash dividend payable next period			
4. Unrealized loss on marketable securities			
5. Sale of additional common stock of the corporation			
6. Sold the company's capital stock on credit			
7. Corrected an accounting error (expense) from a prior period			
8. Default on a stock subscription			
9. Collected a stock assessment			
10. Restricted retained earnings by making an entry equal to the cost of treasury stock purchased			
11. Exchanged the corporation's capital stock for land			
12. Investors tendered their convertible preferred stock for the common stock of the corporation			

Required:

Indicate with a check mark where each of the numbered items should be reported. Be prepared to discuss any questionable items.

E 20-14
Treasury Stock, Cost Method: Entries and Reporting (L.O. 5)

Automatic Tire Corporation had outstanding 10,000 shares of preferred stock, par value $10, and 10,000 shares of nopar common stock sold initially for $20 per share. Contributed capital in excess of par on the preferred stock amounted to $40,000; the retained earnings balance was $81,600. The corporation purchased 200 shares of its preferred at $25 per share and 500 shares of its common at $30 per share. Subsequently, 100 shares of the common treasury stock were sold for $26 per share.

Required:

1. Give entries to record the treasury stock transactions, assuming the cost method is used.
2. Prepare the resulting stockholders' equity section of the balance sheet subsequent to the above transactions.

E 20-15
Treasury Stock, Par Value Method: Entries and Account Balances (L.O. 5)

Alaska Corporation had the following stock outstanding:

Common stock, nopar, 20,000 shares (originally sold at $15) $300,000
Preferred stock, par $10, 6,000 shares (originally sold at $25) 60,000

The following treasury stock transactions were completed:

a. Purchased 50 shares of the common stock at $17 per share.
b. Purchased 20 shares of the preferred stock at $27.
c. Sold 30 shares of the common stock at $14.
d. Sold 10 shares of the preferred stock at $35.

Required:

1. Give entries for all of the above transactions, assuming the par value method is used for treasury stock.
2. Give resulting balances in each stockholders' equity account; assume a beginning balance in retained earnings of $80,000.

E 20-16
Treasury Stock, Cost and Par Value Methods Compared: Entries and Account Balances (L.O. 5)

On January 1, 1991, Johnson Soap Corporation issued 10,000 shares of $20 par value common stock at $50 per share. On January 15, 1994, Simon purchased 50 shares of its own common stock at $55 per share. On March 1, 1994, 20 of the treasury shares were resold at $58. The balance in retained earnings was $25,000 prior to these transactions.

Required:

1. Give all entries indicated in parallel columns, assuming application of (*a*) the cost method and (*b*) the par value method.
2. Give the resulting balance in each one of the stockholders' equity accounts for each method.

E 20-17
Treasury Stock: Analysis and Entries

During 1992, Crown Corporation had several changes in stockholders' equity. The comparative balance sheets for 1991 and 1992 reflected the following amounts in stockholders' equity:

	Balances December 31	
	1991	1992
Common stock, par $10, issued	$600,000*	$700,000†
Contributed capital in excess of par	180,000	230,000
Contributed capital, treasury stock transactions		1,000
Retained earnings	120,000	146,000
Treasury stock	18,000	1,400

* Includes 1,000 shares of treasury stock.

† Includes 100 shares of treasury stock (the 1,000 shares held at the end of 1991 were sold, and the 100 shares held at the end of 1992 were purchased during 1992).

Required:

1. What method was used to account for treasury stock? Explain the basis for your conclusion.
2. Give the required entry for each transaction that affected stockholders' equity during 1992. Show how you determine the amounts used in each entry.

E 20–18
Treasury Stock:
Reporting, Restrictions,
Cost and Par Value
Methods Compared
(L.O. 5)

The records of Pincoff Corporation at December 31, 1991, showed the following, assuming the cost method was used for treasury stock:

Assets	$139,000
Liabilities	32,000
Stockholders' equity:	
Common stock, par $10, 7,000 shares	70,000
Treasury stock, 1,000 shares (at cost)	17,000
Contributed capital in excess of par	14,000
Retained earnings	40,000

Required:

Prepare balance sheets (including any disclosure notes) for the corporation with special emphasis on the stockholders' equity section assuming the state law places a restriction on retained earnings equal to the cost of treasury stock held if:

1. The cost method is used.
2. The par value method is used. *Hint:* Certain of the above account balances must be modified for the par value method.

PROBLEMS

P 20–1
Stockholders' Equity:
Donation, Appropriation,
and Unrealized Capital
(L.O. 2, 3)

Use appropriate information from the data given below to prepare the stockholders' equity section of a balance sheet for Croton Corporation.

Stock subscriptions receivable, preferred stock	$ 8,000
Retained earnings appropriated for bond sinking fund	40,000
Unrealized capital increment per appraisal of natural resources (discovery value)	44,000
Preferred stock, 6%, authorized 1,000 shares, par $100 per share,	
cumulative and fully participating	90,000
Bonds payable, 7%	200,000
Common stock, nopar, 5,000 shares authorized and outstanding	250,000
Donation of future plant site (to Croton)	6,000
Premium on preferred stock	15,000
Discount on bonds payable	1,000
Retained earnings	250,000
Preferred stock subscribed (to be issued upon collection in full)	10,000
Unrealized loss on long-term investments in equity securities	5,000

P 20–2
Entries and Reporting,
Par and Nopar,
Subscriptions, and
Unrealized Loss
(L.O. 2, 3, 4)

Don Corporation was granted a charter that authorized 10,000 shares of 6% preferred stock, par value $10 per share, and 100,000 shares of common stock, nopar value. No stated or assigned value was identified with the common stock. During the first year, the following transactions occurred:

a. 20,000 shares of common stock were sold for cash at $12 per share.
b. 2,000 shares of preferred stock were sold for cash at $25 per share.
c. Subscriptions were received for 2,000 shares of preferred stock at $25 per share; 20% was received as a down payment, and the balance was payable in two equal installments. The shares will be issued upon collection in full.
d. 5,000 shares of common stock, 500 shares of preferred stock, and $37,500 cash were given as payment for a small plant that the company needed. This plant originally cost $40,000 and had a depreciated value on the books of the selling company of $20,000. Assume the prior market price per share did not change.
e. The first installment on the preferred subscriptions was collected.

Required:

1. Give journal entries to record the above transactions. State and justify any assumptions you made.
2. Prepare the stockholders' equity section of the balance sheet at year-end. Retained earnings at the end of the year amounted to $121,500. There was a $10,000 balance in the account labeled "unrealized loss on long-term investments in equity securities."

P 20–3

Subscription and Default under Two Assumptions: Entries

(L.O. 4)

Ace Corporation was issued a charter that authorized 500,000 shares of $5 par value common stock. A. B. Rye subscribed for 10,000 shares at $20 per share and paid a 30% cash down payment. The remaining 70% was payable in four equal quarterly amounts. After paying the first quarterly amount, Rye defaulted. The stock is issuable at date of full payment.

Required:

1. Give the journal entries to record (*a*) the subscription and (*b*) collection of the first quarterly payment.
2. Assumption A—Give the journal entries to record (*a*) the default by Rye and the issuance to Rye of shares equivalent to the cash paid by Rye and (*b*) the sale one month later of the remaining subscribed shares to another party for cash at $22 per share (the cost of reselling was 40 cents per share).
3. Assumption B—Give the journal entries to record (*a*) the default by Rye and (*b*) the resale one month later under lien of all of the subscribed shares to another party for cash at $22 per share (the cost of reselling was 40 cents per share), including any cash refunded to Rye.

P 20–4

Entries and Reporting: Subscriptions, Noncash Sale

(L.O. 3, 4)

The charter of Day Corporation, a manufacturing business, authorized 300,000 shares of common stock, nopar value, and 50,000 shares of 6% preferred stock, which is cumulative and nonparticipating with par value per share of $10. During the early part of the first year, the following transactions occurred:

a. Each of the six individuals subscribed to 1,000 shares of Day Corporation common at $18 per share and 500 shares of the preferred at $12 per share. Half the subscription price was paid, and half the subscribed shares issued.
b. Another individual purchased 500 shares of Day common and 100 shares of preferred stock, paying $9,280 cash.
c. One of the stockholders purchased a used machine for $40,000 and immediately transferred it to the corporation for 2,000 shares of common stock, 200 shares of preferred stock, and a one-year, 15% interest-bearing note for $8,000.
d. The investors paid the subscriptions, and the remaining stock was issued.

Required:

1. Give all journal entries indicated for Day Corporation.
2. Prepare the stockholders' equity section of the balance sheet. Assume retained earnings of $53,320 at year-end.

P 20–5

Entries and Reporting: Subscriptions, Noncash Sale—Par, Nopar, and Stated Value Compared

(L.O. 2, 3, 4)

The charter for Wiley Corporation authorized 500,000 shares of common stock. During the first year of operations, the following transactions affected stockholders' equity:

a. Immediately after incorporation, the corporation sold 400,000 shares of its capital stock at $10 per share; collected cash.
b. Immediately after incorporation, Wiley received a subscription for 10,000 shares of capital stock from one individual at $10 per share. It collected 40% of the subscription, and the balance is due at the end of one year. The shares will be issued upon collection in full.
c. Near year-end, Wiley exchanged 6,000 shares of capital stock for a plant site. The site was carried on the books of the seller at $25,000, and it had been independently appraised within the past month at $70,000. The market value of the stock is $10 per share.
d. Wiley collected $12,000 on the subscription in (*b*).

Required:

1. Give journal entries for the above transactions, assuming: Case A—Par value stock, $4 par value per share. Case B—True nopar value stock. Case C—Nopar value stock with a

stated value of $2 per share. Set up parallel amount columns for each case. State and justify any assumptions you make.

2. Prepare the stockholders' equity section of the balance sheet at the end of the first year for each case. Assume a $94,000 ending balance in the retained earnings account, a reserve for bond sinking fund of $27,000, and unrealized loss on long-term equity investments of $11,000.

P 20–6
Entries and Reporting: Par and Nopar, Subscriptions, and Deferred Charge
(L.O. 4)

The charter of Koke Corporation authorized the issuance of 20,000 shares of 6% cumulative, nonparticipating preferred stock, par $10 per share, and 100,000 shares of common stock, nopar value. During the first year of operations, the following transactions affecting stockholders' equity were completed:

a. The company sold 9,000 shares of the preferred stock at $25 per share for cash; the stock was issued.

b. Subscriptions were received for an additional 1,000 shares of preferred stock at $25 per share; 20% was collected, the balance is to be paid in four equal installments; the stock will be issued upon collection in full.

c. Each of the three promoters was issued 1,000 shares of common stock (only the common stock has voting privileges) at $20 per share; each paid one fifth in cash. The remainder was considered to be appropriate reimbursement for promotional activities; the shares were issued. Use the deferred-charge method.

d. An individual purchased 100 shares of preferred and 100 shares of common stock and paid a single sum of $4,400. The stock was issued. Assume a current market price of $25 for the preferred stock and that, at this date, no current market price for the common was established.

e. Collected cash from the subscribers in (b) for the first installment.

f. Koke issued 5,000 shares of common stock for a used plant. The plant had been independently appraised during the past month at $110,000 and was reported by the seller at a book value of $60,000. Assume, that, at this date, no current market price for the common was established.

Required:

1. Prepare journal entries to record these transactions. State and justify any assumptions you make.

2. Prepare the stockholders' equity section of the balance sheet; assume retained earnings at year-end of $32,200 and an unrealized loss on long-term investment in equity securities of $6,600.

P 20–7
Reconstruct Entries Based on Stockholders' Equity
(L.O. 3)

The stockholders' equity section of the balance sheet for the Star Corporation at the end of its first accounting year was reported as follows:

Contributed capital:
  Capital stock:
    Preferred, 6%, cumulative, nonparticipating, $100 par
      value, redeemable at $125 per share, authorized 5,000
      shares; issued and outstanding 4,185 shares . . . . $ 418,500
    Preferred stock subscribed, 465 shares (J. Doe) . . . .   46,500 $ 465,000

    Common stock, stated value $8 per share, authorized
      1,500,000 shares; issued and outstanding 954,000 shares 7,632,000
    Common stock subscribed, 106,000 shares   848,000   8,480,000

  Other contributed capital:
    In excess of par, preferred   15,000
    In excess of stated value, common   21,200   36,200

Retained earnings   110,000

Total stockholders' equity $9,091,200

Required:

Prepare journal entries during the first year as indicated by the above report. Use the memorandum approach to record the authorization and assume that all stock was purchased through subscriptions under terms of 30% cash down payment and 70% payable six months later. Also assume that of the 70%, all but 10% of the subscribers had paid in full by year-end. Shares are not issued until collection in full from the subscriber.

P 20–8
Compute Dividends;
Five Cases
(L.O. 3)

The charter of Ace Corporation authorized 5,000 shares of 6% preferred stock, par value $20 per share, and 8,000 shares of common stock, par value $50 per share. All of the authorized shares have been issued. In a five-year period, annual dividends paid were: $4,000, $40,000, $32,000, $5,000, and $36,000, respectively.

Required:

Prepare a tabulation (including computations) of the amount of dividends that would be paid to each class of stock for each year under the following separate cases: Case A—Preferred stock is noncumulative and nonparticipating; Case B—Preferred stock is cumulative and nonparticipating; Case C—Preferred stock is noncumulative and fully participating; Case D—Preferred stock is cumulative and fully participating; Case E—Preferred stock is cumulative and partially participating up to an additional 2%; assume the dividend for Year 5 was $42,000 instead of $36,000.

P 20–9
Treasury Stock, Cost and
Par Value Methods
Compared: Entries and
Account Balances
(L.O. 5)

At January 1, 1991, the records of Frazer Corporation provided the following:

Capital stock, par $10, 60,000 shares outstanding	$600,000
Contributed capital in excess of par	240,000
Retained earnings	160,000

During the year, the following transactions affecting stockholders' equity were recorded:

a. Purchased 500 shares of treasury stock at $20 per share.
b. Purchased 500 shares of treasury stock at $22 per share.
c. Sold 600 shares of treasury stock at $25.
d. Net income for 1991 was $45,000.

The state law places a restriction on retained earnings equal to the cost of treasury stock held.

Required:

1. Give entries for the initial issuance of stock and for each of the above transactions, in parallel columns, assuming application of (*a*) the cost method and (*b*) the par value method. Assume FIFO flow for treasury stock.
2. Give the resulting balances in each capital account. Include any required disclosure note related to the treasury stock.

P 20–10
Treasury and Donated
Stock, Cost Method:
Entries and Stockholders'
Equity
(L.O. 5)

Monet Corporation had 30,000 shares of $10 par value capital stock authorized, of which 20,000 shares were issued three years ago at $15 per share. During the current year, the corporation received 500 shares of the capital stock as a bequest from a deceased stockholder; in addition (at approximately the same date), 1,000 shares were purchased by Monet at $14 per share. State law places a restriction on retained earnings equal to the cost of treasury stock held. At the end of the year, a cash dividend of 85 cents per share was paid; prior to the dividend, retained earnings amounted to $40,000.

Required:

1. Prepare entries to record all of the transactions; assume that the cost method for recording treasury stock is used. Record the donated stock at its market value.
2. Prepare the stockholders' equity section of the balance sheet at year-end and include any required disclosure notes related to the treasury stock.

P 20–11
Treasury Stock Retired:
Entries, and Cost and Par
Value Compared
(L.O. 5)

The records for Maryville, Inc., provided the following data on stockholders' equity:

a. Preferred stock, par $50, issued 2,000 shares.
b. Preferred treasury stock, 200 shares (cost $54 per share).
c. Premium on preferred stock at original issue, $2 per share.
d. Common stock, par $100, issued 3,000 shares.
e. Common treasury stock, 300 shares (cost $98 per share).
f. Premium on common stock at original issue, $3 per share.

The stockholders voted to retire all of the treasury stock immediately and to purchase for retirement another 400 shares of common stock that could be purchased currently at $125 per share.

Required:

Give entries in parallel columns for the following transactions, assuming application of the (*a*) cost method and (*b*) par value method:

1. Purchase of the 400 shares of outstanding common stock and their immediate retirement. This transaction does not affect treasury stock.
2. Retirement of all of the treasury shares. Give separate entries for the preferred and common stock.

P 20–12

Treasury Stock: Entries and Reporting, Cost and Par Value Methods Compared

(L.O. 5)

Fibber Corporation reported the following summarized data prior to the transactions given below:

Assets	$660,000
Less: Liabilities	100,000
	$560,000
Stockholders' equity:	
Preferred stock, $10 par	$300,000
Common stock, $5 par	150,000
Contributed capital in excess of par, preferred stock	30,000
Retained earnings	80,000
	$560,000

The state law places a restriction on the retained earnings equal to the cost of treasury stock held.

The following transactions affecting stockholders' equity were recorded:

a. Purchased preferred as treasury stock, 600 shares at $15.
b. Purchased common as treasury stock, 1,000 shares at $20.
c. Sold preferred treasury stock, 100 shares at $17.
d. Sold common treasury stock, 400 shares at $14.

Required:

1. Give entries in parallel columns for these treasury stock transactions assuming application of (*a*) the cost method and (*b*) the par value method.
2. Prepare the resulting balance sheet for each method with emphasis on stockholders' equity. Include any required note disclosure.

P 20–13

Exchange of Old Shares for New Shares: Entries for Seven Cases

(L.O. 6)

Rather Corporation had authorized an outstanding 100,000 shares of capital stock, par value $2 per share. The stockholders approved the exchange of two new shares for each share of the old stock.

Required:

Give the journal entries to record the change under each of the following independent cases (assume a sufficient balance in retained earnings):

Case A

The old stock was sold at par, and the new stock was nopar stock with no stated or assigned value.

Case B

The old stock was sold at a premium of $3 per share, and the new stock was nopar stock with a stated value of $2 per share.

Case C

The old stock was sold at a premium of $1.50 per share, and the new stock was nopar stock with a stated value of $2 per share.

Case D

The old stock was sold at par, and the new stock was nopar stock with a stated value of $1.50 per share.

Case E

The old stock originally was sold at a premium of $1.50 per share, and the new stock was $1 par value.

Case F

The old stock was sold at a premium of $3 per share, and the new stock was nopar stock with no stated or assigned value.

Case G

The old stock was sold at a premium of $1 per share, and the new stock was nopar stock with no stated or assigned value.

P 20–14

COMPREHENSIVE PROBLEM
◆

Preferred and Common
Stock Transactions,
Treasury Stock
Transactions
(L.O. 2, 3, 5)

At the end of 1992, the comparative balance sheets for Sandford Corporation reported the following stockholders' equity amounts:

	Balance December 31	
	1991	1992
Preferred stock, par $10, shares authorized 20,000	$150,000	$200,000
Common stock, nopar, shares authorized 100,000; issued (near the end of 1991), 30,000; 1992, 31,000	210,000	218,000
Contributed capital in excess of par, preferred stock	74,000	155,600
Treasury stock, preferred	2,000	1,000
Treasury stock, common	2,100	3,500 *
Retained earnings	60,074	97,974 †

Restriction on retained earnings at the end of 1991 equal to the cost of treasury shares held: Preferred stock, $5,124; common stock, $1,950 (300 shares).

* Increased by 200 shares during 1992 at $8 per share.

† No dividends were declared during 1992.

Required:

1. What method is being used to account for the treasury stock? Explain.
2. At the end of 1991, what had been the average selling price per share (by the corporation) of (*a*) the preferred and (*b*) common shares?
3. Complete the following tabulation for the treasury stock held at December 31, 1991 (show computations):

	Number of Treasury Shares Held	Average Cost per Share
Preferred	———	———
Common	———	———

4. How many shares were outstanding at December 31, 1991, for (*a*) preferred and (*b*) common?
5. What was the total amount of stockholders' equity at December 31, 1991?
6. Give the required entry for each transaction that affected stockholders' equity during 1992 (exclude consideration of net income). The preferred stock sold for $26 per share in 1992.
7. Explain the reasons for a possible disclosure concerning treasury stock sometimes required by state laws.

CASES

C 20–1
Conceptual: Classification
of Treasury Stock
(L.O. 5)

Arguments are made that treasury stock is an asset because it is purchased, owned, and paid for in cash like any other asset. Further, as with other assets, it can be sold for cash at any time in an established market. Conclusion: because treasury stock has the overriding attributes of an asset, it should be reported and classified on the balance sheet as an asset.

Required:

1. Assuming you have no GAAP constraints to consider, how do you think treasury stock should be classified?
2. Justify your position indicated in (1) above.
3. Assume the issuing company has a bond sinking fund being accumulated to retire outstanding bonds payable at maturity date. It is administered by an independent outside trustee in

accordance with the bond agreement. Assume the sinking fund investments include stock of the issuing company. How should that particular stock be classified? Explain the basis for your conclusions.

C 20-2

Issuance of Capital Stock to Organizers: Valuation (L.O. 3)

C. Banfield, an engineer, developed a special safety device to be installed in backyard swimming pools; when turned on, it would set off an alarm if anything should fall into the water. Over a two-year period, Banfield's spare time was spent developing and testing the device. After receiving a patent, three of Banfield's friends, including a lawyer, considered plans to produce and market the device. Accordingly, a charter was obtained, which authorized 200,000 shares of $10 par value stock. Each of the four organizers contributed $20,000, and each received in return 2,000 shares of stock. They also agree that, for other consideration, each would receive 5,000 additional shares. The remaining shares were to be held as unissued stock. Each organizer made a proposal concerning how the additional 5,000 shares would be paid for. These individual proposals were made independently; then the group considered them as a package. The four proposals were as follows:

Banfield: The patent would be turned over to the corporation as payment for the 5,000 shares. An independent appraisal of the patent could not be obtained.

Lawyer: 1,000 shares would be received for legal services already rendered during organization, 1,000 shares would be received as advance payment for legal retainer fees for the next three years, and the balance would be paid for in cash at par.

Friend No. 2: A small building, suitable for operations, would be given to the corporation for the 5,000 shares of stock. It was estimated that $20,000 would be needed for renovation prior to use. The owner estimates that the market value of the building is $750,000 and there is a $580,000 loan on it to be assumed by the corporation.

Friend No. 3: To pay $10,000 cash on the stock and to give a 12% (the going rate) interest-bearing note for the total price of $40,000 (subscriptions receivable) to be paid out of dividends over the next five years.

Required:

You have been engaged as an independent CPA to advise the group. Specifically, you have been asked the following questions:

1. How would the above proposals be recorded in the accounts? Assess the valuation basis for each, including alternatives.
2. What are your recommendations for an agreement that would be equitable to each organizer? Explain the basis for such recommendations.

C 20-3

A Reporting Issue Concerning Preferred Stock: Equity versus Debt (L.O. 2)

Onray Corporation reported the following items on its balance sheet dated December 31, 1992:

Liabilities:
Long-term note payable, 12% interest payable each June 30
and December 31 (maturity date December 31, 1997) . . . . $ 500,000
Stockholders' equity:
Common stock, nopar   6,000,000
Preferred stock, par $100, nonvoting, 9% cumulative,
nonparticipating, and mandatory redemption at
par no later than December 31, 1997, 4,000 shares
authorized and outstanding   400,000
Retained earnings   800,000

Required:

1. Critically evaluate the reporting classifications applied by Onray. Did Onray violate current GAAP? Explain.
2. Disregarding all current accounting rules, how do you think Onray should report the four items shown above? Explain why.

C 20-4

Equity versus Debt Agreements: Asset Purchased (L.O. 2)

Ellis Corporation purchased equipment (cash price of $144,000) for $107,000 cash and a promise to deliver an indeterminate number of shares of its $5 par common stock, with a market value of $15,000, on January 1 of each year for the next four years. Hence, $60,000 in "market value" of shares will be required to discharge the $37,000 balance due on the equipment.

The corporation then acquired 5,000 shares of its own stock (which became treasury shares) in the expectation that the market value of the stock would increase substantially before the delivery date.

Required:

1. Discuss the propriety of recording the equipment at the following values:
   a. $107,000 (the cash payment).
   b. $144,000 (the cash price of the equipment).
   c. $167,000 (the $107,000 cash payment + the $60,000 market value of treasury stock that must be transferred to the vendor in order to settle the obligation according to the terms of the agreement). Assume an ordinary annuity.

2. Discuss the arguments for treating the balance due as the following:
   a. A liability.
   b. Treasury stock subscribed.

3. Assuming that legal requirements do not affect the decisions, discuss the arguments for treating the corporation's treasury shares as follows:
   a. An asset awaiting ultimate disposition.
   b. A capital element awaiting ultimate disposition.

(AICPA adapted)

C 20-5
Conceptual: Debt versus Equity Securities Used to Purchase an Asset
(L.O. 2)

On January 1, 1991, Crefax Corporation purchased a tract of land, for long-term use as a possible future plant site, in exchange for $50,000 cash plus a five-year note with no interest, even though the current interest for similar debt is 15%. The note is to be paid in $20,000 annual amounts; the first $20,000 is due one year from the date of the land purchase, and the last $20,000 is due at the end of five years. The note also specifies (quite unusually) that instead of being payable in cash, each $20,000 annual amount is to be settled by issuance of 20,000 shares of Crefax common stock, par $1, to the holder of the note. On the date land was purchased, the market value of the stock set aside to be issued on the five dates by Crefax Corporation was $180,000.

Required:

1. Develop and explain the basis for the journal entry that Crefax should make on January 1, 1991.
2. Give, and explain the basis for, the entry or entries that Crefax should make on December 31, 1991.
3. Explain how the following items should be reported on the 1991 financial statements of Crefax Corporation: (*a*) interest expense, (*b*) land, (*c*) debt, and (*d*) contributed capital.

C 20-6
Sherwin-Williams: Analysis of Actual Financial Statements

The 1990 annual report of Sherwin-Williams is shown in an appendix at the end of the book. You are to respond to the following questions related to 1990 unless stated otherwise:

a. What types of capital stock does the company use? Give the par value per share.
b. At the end of 1990, how many shares were (1) authorized, (2) issued, (3) held as treasury stock, (4) unissued, and (5) outstanding.
c. What is the average amount of capital in excess of par value for the shares outstanding at the end of 1990?
d. What overall percentage of total capital (total assets) was provided by stockholders at the end of 1990?
e. What percentage of the shares of common stock issued was held as treasury stock at the end of 1990?
f. What was the ratio of 1990 earnings to the dividends declared?
g. Explain the changes in authorized capital stock in 1990.
h. Explain the changes in treasury stock during 1990.
i. Explain why no preferred stock is reported on the 1990 balance sheet.
j. What was the percentage change in the balance of retained earnings from December 31, 1988, through December 31, 1990?

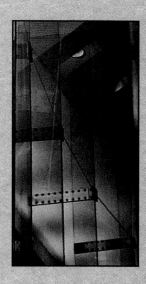

C H A P T E R

21

Corporations: Retained Earnings and Stock Options

LEARNING OBJECTIVES

◆

After you have studied this chapter, you will:

1. Understand the nature of dividends and retained earnings.

2. Be familiar with accounting for cash dividends, property dividends, liquidating dividends, and scrip dividends.

3. Know how to account for stock dividends and stock splits.

4. Understand appropriations of retained earnings and how they are reported.

5. Be familiar with the appropriate accounting and reporting standards for a variety of stock options plans, stock rights, and warrants.

6. Understand the nature of and accounting treatment for stock appreciation rights.

7. Appreciate what a quasi reorganization is, when it is appropriate, and the accounting procedures that are applied in a quasi reorganization (refer to the Appendix).

◆

T he 1990 annual report of Kimberly-Clark Corporation shows that nearly 95% of its stockholders' equity is accounted for by one item—retained earnings:

	December 31	
(Amounts in thousands)	**1990**	**1989**
Stockholders' equity:		
Common stock—$1.25 par value—authorized		
300.0 million shares, issued 81.0 million shares	$ 101.2	$ 101.2
Additional paid-in capital	129.5	134.3
Common stock held in treasury—1.0 million and		
.3 million shares at December 31, 1990 and 1989, respectively	(66.8)	(14.5)
Unrealized currency translation adjustments	(34.2)	(50.7)
Retained earnings	2,130.0	1,915.5
Total stockholders' equity	$2,259.7	$2,085.5

Since its inception, Kimberly-Clark has retained over $2.1 billion of earnings. Why did the company do this? Were shareholders likely to have been upset that these earnings were not distributed to them in the form of dividends? What did the company do with these retained earnings? If management wanted to distribute these earnings by declaring $2.1 billion as dividends at December 31, 1990, is it likely they would have been able to do so?

When a corporation earns a profit, management of the corporation advises the board of directors on two alternative uses of the earnings:

1. Reinvest the earnings in assets of the firm.
2. Distribute the earnings to shareholders in the form of a dividend.

If the company has investment and growth opportunities in which it expects to earn profits in the future, management may well advise that the earnings be retained and used as a source of capital for financing the investment opportunities. Retaining earnings is a very common way for a firm to provide capital for the growth of the firm. Kimberly-Clark has financed a very large portion of its growth over the years by retaining its earnings and reinvesting them in the business. Generally, investors are not disappointed to have a firm retain earnings and reinvest them in the business, so long as the investment earns a high return. Once the earnings are reinvested, however, they are generally not available for distribution to shareholders. For example, the $2.1 billion in retained earnings for Kimberly-Clark could not easily be distributed to shareholders—the earnings have been invested in property and equipment, in inventory and accounts receivable, and other forms of assets. Most of these assets would have to be liquidated to raise the cash needed to distribute a $2 billion dividend. If the decision is to reinvest earnings in the business, the financial statements reflect the reinvestment as a claim by shareholders in the form of retained earnings.

When the decision is to pay out the earnings as a dividend, some form of asset, usually cash, is distributed. Cash dividends depend on the corporation's having both retained earnings and cash (or some other asset) available for distribution to shareholders. Another form of dividend, stock dividends, can also be declared. When stock dividends are declared, the company is essentially signaling to shareholders its intention to permanently retain the earnings. This portion of retained earnings is transferred to the contributed capital portion of stockholders' equity.

The purpose of this chapter is to discuss the application of the concepts and procedures used in measuring, recording, and reporting retained earnings. The procedures for declaring and paying dividends are also covered, as well as the accounting procedures for stock rights and stock options. The discussion begins with retained earnings and the various transactions that affect retained earnings. The chapter then discusses the rationale for, and the accounting treatment of, stock rights and stock options.

◆

CHARACTERISTICS OF RETAINED EARNINGS

◆

Retained earnings represent the firm's accumulated net income or net loss, (including prior period adjustments), less accumulated cash dividends, property dividends, stock dividends, and other amounts transferred to the contributed capital accounts. If the accumulated losses and distributions of retained earnings exceed the accumulated gains, a *deficit* will exist (i.e., a debit balance) in retained earnings.

As explained in the previous chapter, a distinction is maintained between *contributed* or *paid-in capital* and *retained earnings*. These two categories constitute the primary sources of total stockholders' equity. Total retained earnings may include two subcategories: appropriated or restricted retained earnings, and unappropriated retained earnings. When these two categories are recorded separately in the accounts, the retained earnings account (if not designated otherwise) represents the *unappropriated* portion of retained earnings (i.e., it has not been set aside, appropriated, or restricted for specific reasons). The second category, *appropriated* retained earnings, includes specially designated amounts in separate accounts, such as retained earnings appropriated for bond sinking fund, or retained earnings appropriated for the cost of treasury stock. Reporting appropriated and unappropriated retained earnings is discussed later in this chapter.

Items that increase and decrease retained earnings can be summarized as follows:

Retained Earnings

Decreases (Debits)	Increases (Credits)
◆ Net loss (including extraordinary losses) ◆ Prior period adjustments (correction of accounting errors of prior periods) ◆ Cash dividends ◆ Property dividends ◆ Scrip dividends ◆ Stock dividends ◆ Treasury stock and stock retirement transactions	◆ Net income (including extraordinary gains) ◆ Prior period adjustments (correction of accounting errors of prior periods) ◆ Removal of deficit by quasi reorganization

NATURE OF DIVIDENDS

◆

Dividends are distributions of cash, noncash assets, or the corporation's stock to stockholders in proportion to the number of shares of each class of stock held by each stockholder. Dividends result in a credit to the account that represents the item distributed (cash, noncash asset, or capital stock) and a debit to retained earnings (some exceptions are explained later). The following types of dividends are encountered:

1. Most common:
   a. Cash dividends (cash disbursed).
   b. Property dividends (noncash assets disbursed).
   c. Stock dividends (corporation's own stock distributed).

2. Special:
   a. Liquidating dividends (return of contributed capital).
   b. Scrip dividend (creation of a liability by declaring a dividend to be paid at a specific future date).

For a number of economic, legal, and contractual reasons, corporations are not required to pay dividends. It is very rare that all of a firm's earnings are distributed as dividends. Instead of paying a dividend, the corporation may want to do one or more of the following:

1. Conserve cash for other immediate uses.
2. Expand, grow, and modernize by investing in new assets when income is earned.
3. Provide a cushion of resources to minimize the effect of recessions and other unforeseen contingencies.

Furthermore, some state laws and bond covenants place restrictions on the amount of retained earnings that may be used for cash and property dividends. These constraints recognize that cash and property dividends result in (1) a disbursement of assets and (2) a reduction in retained earnings by the same amount. Cash and property dividends cannot be paid without this dual effect. Aside from this effect, however, there is no particular relationship between retained earnings and any specific asset.

Relevant Dividend Dates

Prior to payment, dividends must be formally *declared* by the board of directors of the corporation. Four dates are important in accounting for dividends: (1) date of declaration, (2) date of record, (3) ex-dividend date, and (4) date of payment.

Date of Declaration   On this date, the corporation's board of directors formally approves and announces the dividend declaration. In the case of a cash or property dividend, the declaration is recorded on this date as a debit to retained earnings and a credit to dividends payable. In the absence of fraud or illegality, the courts have held that formal declaration of a cash, property, or liability (i.e., scrip) dividend constitutes an enforceable contract between the corporation and the stockholders. Therefore, on the dividend declaration date, such dividends are recorded, and a liability, dividends payable, is recognized.

In the case of a stock dividend, no distribution of corporate assets is directly or indirectly involved. Therefore, the courts have held that a stock dividend declaration is revocable up to the date of issuance. Because there is no liability, no entry is required on the declaration date. However, accountants sometimes prefer to make an entry on the declaration date to recognize the intention to issue additional stock. When an entry is made, stock dividends distributable is credited. This account is reported as a subsection of retained earnings.[1]

Date of Record   This date is selected by the board of directors and is stated in the declaration. Usually it follows the declaration date by two to three weeks. The date of record is the date on which the list of stockholders of record is prepared. Individuals holding stock at this date, as shown in the corporation stockholders' record, receive the dividend, regardless of sales or purchases of stock after this date. No entry is made in the accounts on this date. The period between the declaration and record dates is needed to allow sufficient time to prepare the list of shareholders.

---

[1] See the subsequent section on stock dividends. In the case of cash dividends, if the declaration date and payment date are in the same accounting period, there would be no reason to make an entry in the accounts on the declaration date.

Ex-Dividend Date Conceptually, the ex-dividend date is the day after the date of record, when shares are traded without the right to receive the declared dividends. However, to provide time for transfer of the stock, the stock exchanges advance the effective ex-dividend date by three or four days. Thus, one who holds the stock on the day prior to the stipulated ex-dividend date receives the dividend, and one who buys shares on and after the ex-dividend date will not receive the dividend.

Between the declaration date and the ex-dividend date, the market price of the stock includes the dividend. On the stipulated ex-dividend date, the price of the stock usually drops because the recipient of the dividend already has been identified, and succeeding owners of the stock will not receive that particular dividend. Thus, under the revenue principle, dividend revenue is earned on the declaration date and not on the date of record, the ex-dividend date, or the date of payment. The importance of the ex-dividend date is evidenced by a continuing section, "Dividend News," in *The Wall Street Journal*. This section of the *Journal* lists stocks that are ex-dividends effective as of the publication date.

Date of Payment This date also is determined by the board of directors, and usually is stated in the declaration. The date of payment typically follows the declaration date by four to six weeks. At the date of payment of cash or property dividends, the liability recorded at date of declaration is debited and the appropriate asset account is credited. A stock dividend distribution usually is recorded on the date of its issuance, as is illustrated in a subsequent section.

A cash or property dividend is a nonreciprocal transfer. A nonreciprocal transfer is defined as a transfer of assets or services in one direction; that is, either from a corporation to its owners (or another enterprise), or from owners or another entity to the corporation, with no assets or services coming from the other direction. Cash and property dividends are not paid on treasury stock.

Legality of Dividends

States require that there be sufficient retained earnings (in some states augmented by elements of contributed capital) before dividends can be declared. Identification of the specific elements of stockholders' equity that are available for cash, property, and stock dividends, respectively, would require study of the laws of each state. However, at least two provisions appear to be uniform. First, dividends may not be paid from *legal capital* (usually represented in the capital stock accounts—par value, stated value, and average paid-in on nopar stock. Second, retained earnings are available for dividends unless there is a contractual or statutory restriction. Beyond these two provisions, numerous variations exist, depending upon the particular state statutes and the type of dividend, including:

1. All contributed capital, other than legal capital, is available for dividends.
2. Specified items of contributed capital, other than legal capital, are available for dividends.
3. Contributed capital, other than legal capital, is available for dividends on preferred stock but not on common stock.
4. Unrealized capital is not available for any kind of dividends.
5. Unrealized capital is available for stock dividends only.
6. Debits to the additional contributed capital accounts and a deficit in retained earnings must be restored before payment of any dividends.
7. Dividends debited to retained earnings must not reduce the retained earnings balance below the cost of treasury stock held.

The accountant has a responsibility when the legality or accounting treament of dividends is at issue to ensure that such matters are referred to an attorney and that the financial statments disclose all material facts concerning such dividends.

TYPES OF DIVIDENDS
◆

Cash Dividends

Cash dividends are the usual form of distributions to stockholders. Before a cash dividend can be paid to common shareholders, any preference dividends (including those in arrears) must be paid to preferred stockholders.

To illustrate a cash dividend, assume the following announcement is made: The board of directors of Bass Company, at their meeting on January 20, 1992, declared a dividend of 50 cents per share, payable March 20, 1992 to stockholders of record on March 1, 1992. Assume that 10,000 shares of nopar capital stock are outstanding.

At date of declaration (January 20, 1992):

```
Retained earnings* (10,000 shares × $.50) . . . . . . . . . . . . . .  5,000
    Cash dividends payable  . . . . . . . . . . . . . . . . . . . . . . .         5,000
```
* Or cash dividends declared, which is later closed to retained earnings.

At date of record (March 1, 1992):
No entry. The list of dividend recipients is prepared as of this date.
At date of payment (March 20, 1992):

```
Cash dividends payable . . . . . . . . . . . . . . . . . . . . . . . . .  5,000
    Cash  . . . . . . . . . . . . . . . . . . . . . . . . . . . . . . . .         5,000
```

The account cash dividends payable is reported on the balance sheet as a current liability if the duration of the dividend liability fits the definition of a current liability; otherwise, it is a long-term liability.

Property Dividends

Corporations occasionally pay dividends with noncash assets. Such dividends are called **property dividends** or **dividends in kind.** The property may be securities of other companies held by the corporation, real estate, merchandise, or any other noncash asset designated by the board of directors. A property dividend is recorded at the current market value of the assets transferred in conformity with *APB Opinion No. 29,* "Accounting for Non-Monetary Transactions." When the corporation's book value of the property to be distributed as the dividend is different from its market value on the declaration date, the corporation must recognize a gain or loss on disposal of the asset as of the declaration date. Most property dividends are paid with the securities of other companies that are held by the dividend-issuing corporation as an investment. This kind of property dividend avoids the problem of indivisibility of units that would occur with most other noncash assets.

An alternative transaction to a property dividend is called a **spin-off.** In a spin-off, the shares of a wholly or substantially owned subsidiary are distributed to shareholders. The shareholders would then own the subsidiary directly, rather than indirectly through the corporation. When a transaction is a spin-off, it is usually valued at the book value of the spun-off organization, not at the market value.

The following excerpt from the disclosure notes in the 1988 financial report of Sun Company, Inc., describes a spin-off.

> On November 1, 1988, the Company distributed on a pro rata basis to holders of its issued and outstanding common stock substantially all of the issued and outstanding shares of common stock of Sun E&P Co., with no consideration being paid by such holders of Sun Company Stock. Each holder of Sun Company common stock on October 14, 1988, the record date for the Distribution, received one share of common stock of Sun E&P Co. for each share of Sun Company common stock owned.

> The Distribution has been accounted for as a "spin-off" with a pro rata reduction in Sun's earnings employed in the business . . . in an aggregate amount equivalent to the stockholders' equity of Sun E&P.

The statement of changes in stockholders' equity shows a debit to retained earnings of $1,458 million, which is labeled as "distribution of Sun E&P Co. common stock." This debit entry indicates that the book value of the distributed stock was $1,458 million. The entries to record the transaction would be as follows:

At the declaration date:

Retained earnings		
(Distribution of Sun E&P Co. common stock) . . .	1,458,000,000	
Property dividend payable		1,458,000,000

At the distribution date (November 1, 1988):

Property dividend payable	1,458,000,000	
Investment in stock of Sun E&P Co.		1,458,000,000

Suppose this transaction were to be accounted for as a property dividend, as described earlier. To illustrate the accounting entries, assume Sun Company had acquired and currently recorded its interest in Sun E&P at $1,458 million, but that the current market value of the Sun E&P common shares to be distributed was $1,800 million. This latter amount could be determined easily if the shares of Sun E&P were publicly traded. If the transaction is to be treated as a property dividend, Sun Company must recognize the gain in market value over book value ($1,800 million less $1,458 million, or $342 million) before recording the distribution:

At the declaration date:

Investment in stock of Sun E&P Co.	342,000,000	
Gain on disposal of investment		342,000,000
Retained earnings	1,800,000,000	
Property dividend payable		1,800,000,000

At the distribution (payment) date:

Property dividend payable	1,800,000,000	
Investment in stock of Sun E&P Co.		1,800,000,000

The balance sheet of the parent company (Sun Company in this example) is unaffected by whether the transaction is treated as a spin-off or as a straight property dividend, assuming there are no taxes on the gain. The income statement for the year of the transaction, however, will reflect the amount of the gain if the transaction is treated as a property dividend. There are tax reasons for preferring the spin-off treatment over the property dividend treatment. Under a spin-off, the transaction can be tax-free, whereas there may well be tax ramifications if the gain to market value is recognized. But since tax reporting can differ from financial reporting, there is no apparent reason to prefer one treatment over the other for financial reporting except for the expediency of using the same method for both book and tax purposes. In recent years there have been a number of corporate spin-offs, but there are few examples of property dividends for major corporations.

Liquidating Dividends

Distributions that are a return of the amount received when stock was issued rather than assets accquired through earnings are called **liquidating dividends.** Owners' equity accounts other than retained earnings are debited. Any dividend that is not based on retained earnings is a liquidating dividend to the extent that it is not debited to retained earnings. Liquidating dividends may be either intentional or unintentional.

Intentional liquidating dividends occur when the board of directors knowingly declares dividends that will, in effect, represent a return of investment, in whole or in part, to the stockholders, for example when a corporation is reducing its permanent capital. In most states, intentional liquidating dividends are not legal until creditors' claims have been met.

Mining companies sometimes pay dividends on the basis of earnings plus the amount of the deduction for depletion. Such a dividend would be an intentional liquidating dividend equal to the amount of depletion. A company might pay such a liquidating dividend when it is exploiting a nonreplaceable asset. Stockholders should be informed of the portion of any dividend that represents a return of capital. The liquidation portion of the dividend is not income to the investor and usually is not taxable to stockholders as income. Rather it reduces the cost basis of the stock investment.

In accounting for liquidating dividends, a contributed capital account, rather than retained earnings, is debited because a portion of contributed capital is returned. Rather than debiting the capital stock accounts, as would be done if shares were being retired, other contributed capital accounts, such as the "in excess of par" accounts, may be debited. In some cases, it may be desirable to set up a special account, "capital repayment," which would be reported as a deduction (contra account) in the contributed capital section of the balance sheet. For example, assume Dako Corporation declared a cash dividend of $40,000 and informed the stockholders that 75% of it was a liquidating dividend. The entries would be as follows:

At declaration date:

Retained earnings ($40,000 × .25)	10,000	
Capital repayment ($40,000 × .75)	30,000	
Dividends payable		40,000

At payment date:

Dividends payable	40,000	
Cash		40,000

Unintentional liquidating dividends can occur when the balance of retained earnings is overstated because of an overstatement of income, and dividends are declared and paid. For example, any error that overstated revenue or understated expense would cause retained earnings to be overstated. In such cases, if reported retained earnings (prior to correction) were used in full for dividends, part of the dividend would be a liquidating dividend. Unintentional liquidating dividends paid, and later discovered, would require an entry to correct the retained earnings account and any other affected accounts.

Scrip Dividends

Sometimes a corporation that has a temporary cash shortage will declare a dividend to maintain its continuing dividend policy by issuing a **scrip dividend.** A scrip dividend (also called a *liability dividend*) occurs when the board of directors declares a dividend and issues promissory notes, called *scrip,* to the stockholders. This declaration generally means that a comparatively long time (e.g., six months or one year) will elapse between the declaration and payment dates. In most cases, scrip dividends are declared when a corporation has sufficient retained earnings as a basis for dividends, but is short of cash. A stockholder may hold the scrip until the due date and collect the dividend, or sell the scrip to a financial institution to obtain immediate cash. When scrip is used, the due date and rate of interest are specified. Scrip usually is payable at a specified future date. The interest period usually is specified as the time from the declaration date to the payment date. However, if the dividend is payable as part cash and part scrip, the interest period usually starts on the dividend payment date. A scrip dividend is recorded by a debit to retained earnings and a credit to a liability account titled "scrip dividends payable." On payment, the liability account is debited and the cash account is credited. Because interest paid on a scrip dividend is not a part of the dividend, any interest payments should be debited to interest expense. In other respects, accounting for a scrip dividend is the same as for a cash dividend.

Assume DVX Corporation declared a 1992 dividend of 25 cents per share on its 200,000 outstanding shares of nopar capital stock. Scrip was issued in full for the dividend that specified a 10% interest rate and a maturity date six months after declaration date.

At declaration date:

Retained earnings (20,000 × $.25)	50,000	
Scrip dividends payable		50,000

At scrip payment date (six months after declaration date):

Scrip dividends payable	50,000	
Interest expense ($50,000 × .10 × $\frac{6}{12}$)	2,500	
Cash		52,500

Stock Dividends

A **stock dividend** is a proportional distribution to stockholders of additional shares of the corporation's common or preferred stock. A stock dividend does not change the assets, liabilities, or total stockholders' equity of the issuing corporation, nor does it change the proportionate ownership of any stockholder. A stock dividend merely increases the number of stock certificates or shares that represent the same proportion of ownership as before the stock dividend. A stock dividend is usually accompanied by a transfer of an amount from retained earnings to the contributed capital accounts (capital stock and contributed capital in excess of par). Therefore, it changes the internal account balances of stockholders' equity between contributed capital and retained earnings.

A stock dividend may be issued from either treasury stock or unissued stock. When a stock dividend is of the same class as that held by the recipients, it is called an *ordinary* stock dividend. When a class of stock other than the one already held by the recipients is issued, such a dividend is called a *special* stock dividend (e.g., preferred shares issued to the common stockholders).

Several reasons exist for a company to issue a stock dividend, including:

1. To indicate that the firm plans to permanently retain a portion of earnings in the business by capitalizing it. The effect of a stock dividend, through a debit to retained earnings and offsetting credits to permanent capital accounts, is to raise the contributed (and legal) capital and thereby shelter the new legal capital from future declarations of cash or property dividends.
2. To continue dividend distributions without disbursing assets (usually cash) that may be needed for operations. This action may be motivated by a desire to please stockholders who may be willing to accept a stock dividend representing accumulated earnings because they can sell these additional shares. Ordinary stock dividends are not subject to income tax to stockholders. Instead, they reduce the investment cost per share to the investor.
3. To increase the number of shares outstanding, which reduces the market price per share and which, in turn, leads to increased trading of shares in the market. This is a frequent and important reason for the issuance of stock dividends. Small investors are viewed as being able to afford investments in equity securities if the unit cost is low. Stock dividends also reduce earnings per share.

Accounting Issues Related to Ordinary Stock Dividends   The three primary issues in accounting for stock dividends are the amounts that should be recognized, the accounts and dates that should be used, and the manner of disclosure in the financial statements.

Accountants disagree about the amounts that should be used in recognizing stock dividends. The basic issue, aside from the availability of retained earnings and shares of unissued stock or treasury stock, is whether the stock issued for the dividend should be recorded at market value, at par or stated value, or at some other value.

A stock dividend usually is based on the availability of retained earnings. The question is what amount of retained earnings to capitalize as contributed capital. State laws and GAAP do not establish a specific amount. Therefore, the board of directors has the authority to determine the amount to be capitalized, subject to certain legal and contractual constraints. State laws vary as to whether additional contributed capital can also be used as a basis for stock dividends, and as to the minimum amount of retained earnings that must be capitalized for a stock dividend. With respect to the use of additional contributed capital as a basis for a stock dividend, a few states permit any type of additional contributed capital to be used, other states prohibit its use, while still others only permit the use of additional contributed capital in excess of the par or stated value of the stock. Regarding the *minimum* amount that must be capitalized from whatever source, the statutory minimum in most states is par or stated value. If the stock is true nopar, the minimum amount is the average amount per share originally paid in.

Because of the lack of agreement about whether to capitalize the market value or just the par value for stock dividends, the AICPA Committee on Accounting Procedures in *ARB No. 43*, reaffirmed two distinct situations affecting the amount of retained earnings to capitalize for an ordinary stock dividend:

Situation 1—Small Stock Dividend, Market Value Method   When the proportion of the additional shares issued is "small" in relation to the total shares previously outstanding, the *current market value* of the additional shares should be capitalized. Small is defined as less than 20% to 25% of the outstanding shares. The market value of the stock dividend is measured on the basis of the market price per share immediately after the stock dividend is issued. The Committee on Accounting Procedures of the AICPA rationalized this position as follows:

> Many recipients of stock dividends look upon them as distributions of corporate earnings and usually in an amount equivalent to the [market] value of the additional shares recieved. Furthermore, it is to be presumed that such views of recipients are materially strengthened in those instances, which are by far the most numerous, where the issuances are so small in comparison with the shares previously outstanding that they do not have any apparent effect upon the share market price and, consequently, the market value of the shares previously held remains substantially unchanged. The committee therefore believes that where these circumstances exist the corporation should in the public interest account for the transaction by transferring from [retained earnings] to the category of permanent capitalization . . . an amount equal to the [market] value of the additional shares issued [i.e., the market value immediately after issuance].[2]

Situation 2—Large Stock Dividend, Par Value Method   When the proportion of the additional shares issued is large in relation to the total shares previously outstanding (more than 20% to 25%), no less than the legal minimum (usually par, or stated value, or average paid in for nopar stock) should be capitalized. If the stock dividend is between 20% and 25%, judgment is required based on the situation. The Committee, giving the appearance of a political compromise, continued the rationalization as follows:

---

[2] AICPA, *Accounting Research Bulletin No. 43*, "Restatement and Revision of *Accounting Research Bulletins*" Nos. 1–42 (New York, 1953), Chapter 7, Sec. B, par. 10.

Where the number of additional shares issued as a stock dividend is so great that it has, or may reasonably be expected to have, the effect of materially reducing the share market value, the committee believes that the implications and possible constructions discussed in the [above quotation] are not likely to exist. . . .
Consequently, the committee considers that under such circumstances there is no need to capitalize [retained earnings], other than to the extent occasioned by legal requirements.[3]

Although *ARB No. 43* was intended to settle the issue for GAAP purposes, the disagreement continues. Strong arguments are made for the par value method because (1) legal capital is preserved; (2) the corporation's assets, liabilities, and total stockholders' equity are not changed; and (3) stockholders' proportionate ownership is not changed. Arguments based on market value lack persuasive validity partly because of measurement problems. However, it is generally recognized that if a company doubles the number of shares outstanding by issuing a stock dividend, the competitive market price will fall to one half its previous level, absent any other market factors.

Recording a Stock Dividend   A stock dividend is recorded as a debit to retained earnings and a credit to common stock. In addition to the "large" and "small" dividend distinction discussed above, accountants disagree about whether market price (when used) should be determined at the declaration or the issuance date. When market value is used, any excess of that price above par or stated value must be measured. This excess cannot be measured prior to knowing what date to use. *ARB No. 43*, Chapter 7, par. 10, specifies that for a small stock dividend, market value at issuance date must be used. Since that source uses the word *issuance* exclusively throughout (declaration is never mentioned), many accountants believe that market value at issuance date (if used) also applies to a large stock dividend. However, such a belief is not supported by subsequent interpretations.

The declaration of a stock dividend is revocable prior to issuance date. Given this fact and the market-price measurement date problem discussed above, many accountants do not make an originating journal entry on the declaration date. Rather, they make the originating journal entry on the issuance date. If an originating entry is made on the declaration date, it is made at the par value amount, then "adjusted" to market value on the issuance date when market value is known. Whether the originating entry is made on the declaration date or the issuance date, a disclosure note is needed for financial statements prepared between these two dates. Given these considerations, either recording approach can be used with the same results. This result is demonstrated as follows:

Declaration date: Suppose a 10% common stock dividend is declared on 100,000 shares of $1 par common stock issued and outstanding; market price immediately after issuance is $5 per share:

	Originating Entry Date:	
	Declaration	**Issuance**
Declaration date (par value used):		
Retained earnings 10,000		None
Stock dividends distributable*	10,000	
* Reported as a credit under stockholders' equity until issuance.	Also use disclosure note	Use disclosure note
Issuance date (record transaction at market price):		
Retained earnings 40,000		50,000
Stock dividends distributable 10,000		
Common stock	10,000	10,000
Contributed capital in excess		
of par (or stated) value	40,000	40,000

[3] Ibid.

The differences between these two approaches are trival; either one satisfies GAAP in all respects.

CONCEPT REVIEW

1. What four dates are important in accounting for dividends? What does each represent?
2. What is a liquidating dividend? How is a liquidating dividend accounted for?
3. Describe two alternative methods of recording stock dividends. Under what circumstances is each used?

Special Stock Dividends

In the case of *special* stock dividends, such as a stock dividend consisting of preferred stock issued to common stockholders, the market value of the dividend (i.e., the preferred) shares should be capitalized by the issuing corporation. Issuance of the dividend shares usually would not be expected to have much impact, if any, on the market value of the common stock. In this instance, stockholders would appear to receive a dividend equal to the market value of the dividend shares received.

In 1989, Texaco Inc. declared a special dividend to common shareholders. The dividend was described in the Notes as follows:

> The Special Dividend is to consist of $3.00 cash per share of Common Stock and $1.00 stated value of a new series of non-voting variable rate cumulative preferred stock of the Company (the "Series C Preferred Stock") per share of Common Stock. The Company intends to set the terms of the Series C Preferred Stock so that it will trade, on a fully distributed basis, at its stated value.
>
> Since the market value of the preferred stock is to be the stated value, the issuance of the preferred shares would be recorded as a debit to retained earnings at $1.00 times the number of shares issued, and as a credit to Series C preferred stock.

Exhibit 21–1 provides examples of the issuance of ordinary and special stock dividends: Case A—a small stock dividend, market value method; Case B—a large stock dividend, par value method; and Case C—a special stock dividend.

An important aspect of stock dividends is the amount of retained earnings transferred to contributed capital. This transfer reflects the company's commitment to permanently retain this amount of earnings by making them unavailable for dividends. For many corporations, a significant amount of their contributed capital came from capitalizing retained earnings. The reported retained earnings of these companies is less than the actual total accumulated earnings, minus cash and property dividends paid, over the life of the corporation because such transfers have been made.

Dividends and Treasury Stock

Cash dividends are not paid on treasury stock; such a transaction would involve the corporation transferring assets to itself. Stock dividends, however, may be paid on treasury stock in certain situations. Some states prohibit the issuing of stock dividends on treasury stock. Even though some state statutes allow the issuing of stock dividends on treasury stock, not all corporations do so. The decision depends, in part, on why the treasury stock is held. If the treasury stock is held primarily in connection with a stock option plan, the corporation may issue a stock dividend on the treasury stock. This is done because stock options are usually adjusted for stock dividends and stock splits. Issuing stock dividends on the firm's treasury stock

EXHIBIT 21-1   Stock Dividend Entries: Small Dividend, Large Dividend, Special Dividend

---

Data Prior to the Dividend (Same for each Case)

Preferred stock, par value $20, 10,000 shares authorized	
5,000 shares outstanding	$100,000
Common stock, par value $10, 20,000 shares authorized,	
10,000 shares outstanding	100,000
Contributed capital in excess of par, preferred stock	10,000
Contributed capital in excess of par, common stock	15,000
Retained earnings	150,000
Total stockholders' equity	$375,000

Market price per share immediately before issuance of dividend shares:
Preferred, $25; Common, $24.

Stock Dividend Entry at Date of Issuance of Dividend Shares (Each Situation Is Independent)

Case A—A small stock dividend, market value method: A 10% common stock dividend is declared on the common stock. The stock dividend is capitalized at market value.

Retained earnings (10,000 × .10) $24	24,000	
Common stock, par $10 (1,000 shares)		10,000
Contributed capital in excess of par, common stock		14,000

Case B—A large stock dividend, par value method: A 50% common stock dividend is declared on the common stock. The market value per share drops immediately to $16. The stock dividend is capitalized at par value.

Retained earnings (5,000 shares at par, $10)	50,000	
Common stock, par $10 (5,000 shares)		50,000

Case C—A special stock dividend: A 20% common stock dividend is issued to both common and preferred stockholders. The market price per share does not change appreciably after issuance from $24.

Retained earnings, (3,000 shares* × $24)	72,000	
Common stock, par $10 (3,000 shares)		30,000
Contributed capital in excess of par, common stock		42,000

* (10,000 + 5,000 shares) × 20% = 3,000 shares.

---

allows the firm to maintain its position with regard to the number of shares available when stock options are exercised. However, unless treasury stock is held for a specific purpose such as the issuance of stock options, the firm will seldom issue stock dividends on treasury stock.

Treasury stock may be used for the issuance of a stock dividend. If treasury stock is used for this purpose, the stock dividend should be recorded as a debit to retained earnings (or other appropriate account) for the market value of the treasury stock issued and a credit to treasury stock for the book value of the treasury stock issued. Any difference is debited or credited to an appropriate additional contributed capital account. If additional contributed capital is insufficient to make up any debt difference, the excess should be debited to retained earnings.

Fractional Share Rights

When a small stock dividend is issued, not all shareholders are going to own exactly the number of shares needed to receive whole shares. For example, when a firm issues a 5% stock dividend and a shareholder owns 30 shares, the stockholder is entitled to 1½ shares (30 × .05). When this happens, the firm can issue **fractional share rights** for portions of shares to which individual shareholders are entitled.

To demonstrate, suppose Moon Company has 1,000,000 outstanding shares of common stock, par $5. Moon issues a 5% stock dividend. The market value of the common shares before the stock dividend is $80 per share. The number of shares to be issued as the stock dividend is 5% of the number of shares outstanding, or 50,000 shares. Suppose the firm's shareholder ownership is such that 42,000 whole or complete shares can be issued. The firm would issue fractional share rights for the remaining shares to be issued. Each fractional share right would entitle the holder to acquire one twentieth of a share. Since there are 8,000 shares yet to be issued, there would be 8,000 times 20, or 160,000 fractional share rights issued. A market would develop for the fractional share rights, with each having a market value of approximately one twentieth of a whole share ($80/20), or $4. Shareholders could buy or sell fractional share rights to the point where whole shares can be acquired. A holder would turn in 20 fractional share rights to receive 1 share of common stock.

The entries for recording the issuance of the above stock dividend and fractional share rights would be as follows:

To record the 42,000 shares issued as a stock dividend (at market value):

```
Retained earnings (42,000 × $80)  . . . . . . . . . . . . . . 3,360,000
     Common stock, at par (42,000 × $5) . . . . . . . . . . .              210,000
     Additional paid-in capital (42,000 × $75) . . . . . . . .            3,150,000
```

To record the issuance of 160,000 fractional share rights:

```
Retained earnings (8,000 × $80) . . . . . . . . . . . . . .  640,000
     Common stock fractional share rights  . . . . . . . . .              640,000
```

Common stock fractional share rights is an account included in paid-in capital. When rights are turned in to the company for redemption in common shares, the common stock fractional share rights account is debited, and common stock, as well as additional paid-in capital (if needed), is credited. Suppose, for example, that 2,000 fractional share rights are turned in for 100 shares of common stock. The entry to record the transaction would be:

```
Common stock fractional share rights (2,000 × $4)  . . . . .    8,000
     Common stock, $5 par (100 shares) . . . . . . . . . . .                  500
     Additional paid-in capital . . . . . . . . . . . . . . . . .            7,500
```

An alternative to the issuance of fractional share rights is to pay cash to shareholders for the fractional shares to which they are entitled. For example, suppose a shareholder of Moon Company owns 30 shares of common stock; the shareholder is entitled to 1½ shares when the 5% stock dividend is issued. The firm would sell enough shares in the market to represent fractional ownership, then distribute the proceeds to shareholders, as appropriate. Thus, Moon would sell 8,000 shares at a market price of $80:

```
Cash . . . . . . . . . . . . . . . . . . . . . . . . . . . . . . 640,000
     Common stock, $5 par (8,000 shares) . . . . . . . . . . .               40,000
     Additional paid-in capital . . . . . . . . . . . . . . . . .           600,000
```

Shareholders with fractional share holdings would receive a cash dividend in lieu of fractional share rights. Thus the above shareholder would receive one share from the firm, and a cash payment of $40 ($80 per share × .5 shares), representing the value of the one-half share at current market value. The entry to record the cash payment is a debit to retained earnings and a credit to cash. This procedure is simpler for the stockholder, as there is no need to buy or sell fractional shares. After all fractional share rights are redeemed, the stockholders' equity accounts have the same balance regardless of which procedure is followed.

STOCK SPLITS

♦

A **stock split** is a change in the number of shares outstanding accompanied by an offsetting change in the par or stated value per share. A stock split is implemented by either calling in all of the old shares and concurrently issuing the split shares, or by issuing the additional split shares with notification to the stockholder of the change in par or stated value per share of all shares. The primary purpose of a stock split is to increase the number of shares outstanding and decrease the market price per share. In turn, this will often increase the market activity of the stock, and may cause prices to rise. By increasing the number of shares outstanding, the stock split also reduces earnings per share. In a *pure* stock split, no accounting entry is needed because there is no change in the dollar amounts in the capital stock accounts, additional contributed capital, or retained earnings. Instead, the increase in the number of shares is exactly counterbalanced by a proportional reduction in the par or stated value per share. Therefore, in a pure stock split, the following dollar amounts are not changed: (1) capital stock accounts, (2) additional contributed capital accounts, (3) retained earnings, and (4) total stockholders' equity. The following items are changed: (1) par or stated value per share and (2) shares issued, outstanding, in treasury, and subscribed.

To illustrate a two for one, pure *stock split,* (two new shares for each old share called in) and to compare it with a 100% *stock dividend* (one additional share for each share already outstanding), assume Split Corporation is authorized to issue 200,000 shares of common stock, par $10, of which 40,000 shares were issued initially at par, and retained earnings has a current balance of $450,000. The different effects of a 100% stock dividend and a two for one stock split are contrasted below:

Split Corporation—Stock Dividend and Stock Split Compared

Transaction	Shares Outstanding		Par Per Share		Prior to Stock Dividend or Stock Split	100% Stock Dividend	2 for 1 Stock Split
Initial issue	40,000	×	$10	=	$400,000		
100% stock dividend;	80,000	×	10	=		$800,000*	
two for one stock split	80,000	×	5	=			$400,000
Total contributed capital					400,000	800,000*	400,000
Retained earnings					450,000	50,000	450,000
Total stockholders' equity					$850,000	$850,000	$850,000

* Retained earnings capitalized: 40,000 shares × $10 = $400,000. Entry: Debit retained earnings $400,000; credit contributed capital accounts $400,000.

The stock dividend capitalizes retained earnings as contributed capital. The stock split, however, does not. Total stockholders' equity was unchanged by either the stock dividend or the stock split.

The example above described a pure, normal stock split. During the past several years, some stock splits have been issued that did not exactly maintain the offsetting relationship between the split shares and the change in the par or stated value per share, such as a two for one split on $10 par value stock and a reduction of par value per share to $6 rather than to $5. Such a transaction is a combined stock split and stock dividend. Also, some financial statements inappropriately refer to a stock dividend as a stock split. *ARB No. 43* uses the phrase "stock split affected in the form of a dividend" to describe large stock dividends; this may be a source of confusion.

A reverse stock split decreases the number of shares. A reverse stock split involves a proportional increase in the par or stated value per share, and reduction in the number of shares issued and outstanding. A one new share for every two held is an example of a reverse split.

APPROPRIATIONS AND RESTRICTIONS OF RETAINED EARNINGS

◆

Appropriated retained earnings are the result of discretionary management action. *Restricted* retained earnings are the result of a legal contract or law. In either case, **appropriated retained earnings** and **restricted retained earnings** involve a constraint on a specified portion of accumulated earnings for a specific purpose. Such specific appropriations and restrictions nevertheless represent a part of total retained earnings. Thus, retained earnings can comprise two subcategories: (1) appropriated and restricted retained earnings and (2) unappropriated retained earnings.[4]

Appropriations and restrictions of retained earnings usually are recorded as debits to the retained earnings account and credits to descriptively designated *appropriation or restriction of retained earnings* accounts. This approach is a convenient way to provide information for reporting and disclosing appropriations and restrictions. Some companies will inappropriately use the term *reserve* in the titles of appropriation and restriction accounts, such as "reserve for retained earnings invested in the business." For reporting purposes on the financial statements, the appropriations and restrictions may be reported by any one of three ways:

1. Report each appropriation and restriction as a separate item on the statement of retained earnings.
2. Report appropriations and restrictions parenthetically on the statement of retained earnings.
3. Disclose appropriations and restrictions in the notes to the financial statements.

When the need for an appropriation or restriction no longer exists, the appropriated balance is returned to the unappropriated retained earnings account. This is done by making an entry reversing the one that initially set up the appropriation.

Retained earnings are appropriated and restricted primarily to protect the cash position of the corporation by reducing the amount of cash dividends that otherwise might be paid. Appropriations and restrictions of retained earnings arise in the following situations:

1. To fulfill a legal requirement, as in the case of a state law required restriction on retained earnings equivalent to the cost of treasury stock held.
2. To fulfill a contractual agreement, as in the case of a debt covenant that stipulates a restriction on the use of retained earnings for dividends that would result in the disbursement of assets.
3. To report a discretionary appropriation made by the board of directors to constrain a specified portion of retained earnings as an aspect of financial planning.
4. To report a discretionary appropriation by the board of directors of a specified portion of retained earnings in anticipation of possible future losses.

The appropriation or restriction of retained earnings made by transferring an amount from retained earnings to an appropriated retained earnings account has no effect on assets, liabilities, or total stockholders' equity. An appropriation is a "clerical" identification. The appropriation does not set aside specific assets such as cash. This effect would occur only if, as a separate action, cash is set aside in a separate fund, such as a bond sinking fund.

Since dividends are issued at the discretion of the board of directors, the primary purpose of appropriations is to communicate to statement users that management does not feel the appropriated amounts are available for dividends. Since the allowable amount of dividends is reduced, less dividends are paid and cash is conserved.

---

[4] Accountants traditionally use the term *appropriation of retained earnings* to include both appropriations and restrictions. These terms are used here in this traditional way, but ultimately it is important to know whether the retained earnings are appropriated or restricted.

EXHIBIT 21-2   Retained Earnings Statement: Reporting Prior Period Adjustments
and Appropriations

Basic Case Data (May Corporation)

1. For the year ended December 31, 1993, May Corporation reported:
   a. Retained earnings balance, December 31, 1992, $158,000.
   b. Net income, $52,000.
   c. Dividends declared and paid, $30,000.
2. During 1993, it was discovered that 1992 depreciation expense was understated by $20,000 (the applicable tax rate during 1992 was 30%). An amended tax return was submitted for 1992.

Reporting Retained Earnings

MAY CORPORATION

Retained Earnings Statement
For Year Ended December 31, 1993

Balance in retained earnings, 12/31/1992	$158,000
Prior period adjustment (a debit);	
Correction of accounting error in 1992, net of $6,000 income tax	
saving (see Note 4)	(14,000)
Balance in retained earnings, 12/31/1992 as corrected	144,000
Add: Net income for 1993	52,000
Total	196,000
Deduct: Dividends for 1993	(30,000)
Balance in retained earnings, 12/31/1993 (see Note 5)	$166,000

Note 4: During, 1992, the company inadvertently understated depreciation expense by $20,000. This accounting error caused an overstatement of the reported income of 1992, and of the balance in retained earnings at December 31, 1992, by $14,000, which reflects the $6,000 tax effect of the error. The error was detected and corrected during 1993 by debiting retained earnings for a prior period adjustment in the aftertax amount of $14,000. To correct other affected accounts, an income tax receivable was set up for the $6,000 tax saving and accumulated depreciation was increased by $20,000.

Note 5: Appropriations and restrictions:

Appropriation for investment in plant	$ 35,000
Restriction for cost of treasury stock	25,000
Unappropriated retained earnings	106,000
Total retained earnings	$166,000

Once an appropriation or restriction is returned to unappropriated retained earnings, the full amount once again becomes available for dividends.

REPORTING RETAINED EARNINGS
♦

Under GAAP, the retained earnings statement should include:

1. Beginning balance of retained earnings.
2. Restatement of beginning balance for prior period adjustments.
3. Restatement of beginning balance for retroactive types of accounting changes.
4. Net income or loss for the period.
5. Dividends.
6. Appropriations and restrictions of retained earnings.
7. Adjustments made pursuant to a quasi reorganization.
8. Ending balance of retained earnings.

Exhibit 21–2 illustrates the reporting of all the above items except for (3) and (7). The appendix to this chapter discusses quasi reorganizations.

CONCEPT REVIEW

1. When might it be appropriate to issue a stock dividend on treasury stock?
2. What is a stock split and when, if ever, does a stock split affect the retained earnings of the firm?
3. What are restricted retained earnings? What are appropriated retained earnings? Why would management want to appropriate a portion of the firm's retained earnings?

STOCK RIGHTS AND WARRANTS

Corporations often issue **stock rights** that provide the holder with an option to acquire a specified number of shares of capital stock in the corporation under prescribed conditions and within a stated future time period. When rights are issued to *current stockholders,* the corporation issues *one stock right for each share of stock owned.* These rights are often similar to the fractional share rights in that it may require more than one right to acquire an additional share of stock.

Evidence of ownership of one or more stock rights is a certificate called a *stock warrant.* Stock rights sometimes are referred to simply as stock warrants. A stock warrant typically specifies (1) the number of rights represented by the warrant, (2) the option price (which may be zero) per share of the specified stock, (3) the number of rights required to obtain a share of the stock, (4) the expiration date of the rights, and (5) instructions for exercising the rights. When more than one right is required to obtain one share of stock in the future, the rights represent fractional shares and are called *fractional share rights.*

Three dates are important regarding stock rights: (1) *announcement date* of the rights offering, (2) *issuance date* of the rights, and (3) *expiration date* of the rights. Between the announcement date and the issuance date of the rights, the related stock will sell *rights on.* Rights on means the price of the stock includes the value of the rights because the stock and the rights are not separable during that period of time. After the issuance date and until expiration of the rights, the shares and rights sell separately. That is, the shares sell *ex rights* during this period of time. The *rights* will have a separate price.

Stock rights received by a stockholder may be (1) exercised by purchasing additional shares of the specified stock from the corporation, (2) sold at the market value of the rights, or (3) allowed to lapse on the expiration date.

Corporations issue stock rights and options for the following reasons:

1. To give existing stockholders the first chance to buy additional shares when the corporation decides to raise additional equity capital by selling a large number of unissued shares. This is the preexemptive right.
2. As compensation to outsiders (such as underwriters, promoters, and professionals) for services provided to the corporation.
3. To represent fractional shares when a stock dividend is declared and issued. The option price for these rights is zero (discussed under fractional shares earlier in this chapter).
4. As additional compensation to officers and other employees of the corporation. These rights often are referred to as **stock options** or stock incentive plans (discussed later in this chapter).
5. To enhance the marketability of other securities issued by the corporation. These rights include issuing common stock rights with convertible bonds (discussed and illustrated in Chapter 16).

ACCOUNTING FOR STOCK RIGHTS AND WARRANTS

♦

The issuance of stock rights raises accounting issues for both the recipient and the issuing corporation. Stock rights received on corporate stock held by an investor have no additional cost. Therefore, the current carrying value of the shares already owned is allocated by the investor between the original shares and the rights received, based on the current market values of each. Accounting for rights received by investors is discussed in Chapter 14.

Accounting for stock rights by the issuing corporation involves either a memorandum entry or a regular journal entry on each of the three relevant dates defined above: (1) announcement date, (2) issuance date, and (3) expiration date. The accounting under the first two of the five reasons for issuing stock rights listed in the previous section are discussed next. The accounting for stock options is covered later in this chapter.

Reason 1—Issuance of Stock Rights Related to a Planned Sale (Primarily to Existing Stockholders) of Unissued Stock   In this case, stock rights are issued in advance of the planned sale date to give current stockholders the opportunity to maintain their proportional share of ownership in the firm. These are preemptive rights.

Case data:

	Amount
Sax Corporation account balances prior to the decision to issue rights:	
Common stock, par $10, authorized 100,000 shares, issued and outstanding 30,000 shares	$300,000
Additional paid-in capital, common stock	150,000
Retained earnings	70,000

Decision of Sax Corporation:
* To increase the outstanding shares by 50% (issue 15,000 additional shares).
* Issue price per share to current stockholders—$30 plus two stock rights.
* Announcement date: January 1, 1993.
* Issue date for rights: March 1, 1993.
* Expiration date for rights: September 1, 1993.
* Market prices:

Rights—Between issuance and expiration dates, average $5 per right.

Stock—At announcement date, $30 per share.

Stock—At issue date, $32 per share.

Stock—At expiration date, $34 per share.

Journal entries by Sax Corporation:

January 1, 1993—Announcement date—no entry because the transaction is not completed.

March 1, 1993—Issuance date—memorandum only, because there is no inflow of resources. There is only a commitment to issue shares contingent upon the future actions of the party holding the rights. The memo expresses that commitment:

Memo—Issued 30,000 stock rights to current stockholders for 15,000 shares of stock to be sold. Each share will be sold for $30 cash plus the receipt of two stock rights. After September 1, 1993, all outstanding rights will expire, and the remaining shares will be sold in the market at the then-current market price.

July 1, 1993—Exercise date—1,000 stock rights exercised by one stockholder. There is now a completed transaction. An entry is required:

```
Cash (1,000 rights ÷ 2 = 500 shares) × $30 . . . . . . . . . . . . 15,000
       Common stock, par $10 (500 shares) . . . . . . . . . . . . . .          5,000
       Additional paid-in capital, common stock . . . . . . . . . . .         10,000
```

Reason 2—Compensation to Outsiders   Management sometimes wishes to conserve cash during the early part of a firm's life. Therefore, management may issue shares as payment for professional services. In some instances, stock rights rather than shares, are issued.

Assume the same data as in Case 1. In addition, a decision was made by Sax to issue Larry Brown 100 stock rights that specified a $30 option price. The rights were issued as payment for legal services. The rights were issued on March 1, 1993, expire on December 31, 1993, and were exercised by Brown on July 1, 1993. At the time of issuance of the stock rights, assume the market value of the stock was $35. The required journal entries are:

March 1, 1993—Issue date (payment of a liability is a completed transaction):

```
Expense (legal services) . . . . . . . . . . . . . . . . . . . . . . . .       250
   Stock rights outstanding
   (100 rights ÷ 2 = 50 shares × $35–$30) . . . . . . . . . . .                   250
```

Brown was awarded the right to acquire for $30 each shares having a market value of $35, thus his compensation is $5 for each of the shares he can acquire with his rights, or $250.

July 1, 1993—Exercise date:

```
Cash (50 shares × $30) . . . . . . . . . . . . . . . . . . . . . . . . .     1,500
Stock rights outstanding (for 50 shares × $5) . . . . . . . . . . . .         250
   Common stock, par $10 (50 shares) . . . . . . . . . . . . . .                  500
   Additional paid-in capital, common stock
   ($35 − $10) × 50 shares . . . . . . . . . . . . . . . . . . . . . .            1,250
```

During the period the stock rights are outstanding, the account labeled "stock rights outstanding" should be reported under stockholders' equity as a credit item along with the capital stock account to which it relates.

STOCK OPTION INCENTIVE PLANS

♦

The accounting for stock option plans (reason 5) is complex and merits a separate section. Corporations often establish stock option plans whereby shares of stock in the company are issued to employees over a period of time. For example, 556 of the 600 companies reported in *Accounting Trends & Techniques, 1990,* disclosed stock option plans. The purposes of stock option plans vary across firms. They may be used to help recruit and retain outstanding employees, to encourage ownership in the company by employees, and to obtain additional resources from equity owners. Often stock options (represented by stock rights) are granted to a particular group of employees to purchase common stock over an extended period of time as a form of additional compensation to encourage superior performance.

Plans for the issuance of capital stock to employees are designated with a variety of terms, none of which has been accorded standard usage. For instance, Hewlett-Packard Company refers to its plan simply as a "stock option plan." Kimberley-Clark Corporation refers to its plan as a "equity participation plan." The Sherwin-Williams Company has a stock incentive program consisting of stock appreciation rights, stock options, and a restricted stock purchase plan. In stock option plans, the issuing corporation is designated as the *grantor,* and the employee recipient is designated as the *grantee.*

The most important characteristic of a stock option plan from an accounting perspective is whether the plan causes additional expense to the company. Thus, for accounting purposes, a distinction is made between two categories of stock option incentive plans for employees:

1. *Noncompensatory plans*—These plans specify the issuance of company stock to employees at a price that is not significantly less than the market price. Under such plans, there is no additional cost to the company and no additional compensation to the employee. An example of a noncompensatory plan is the employee stock purchase plan of International Business Machine Corporation. IBM disclosed the elements of its plans in the notes to its 1989 annual report:

> The employees stock purchase plan enables employees who are not participants in a stock option plan to purchase IBM capital stock through payroll deduction up to 10% of eligible compensation. The price an employee pays for a share of stock is 85% of the average market price on the date the employee has accumulated enough money to buy a share. During 1989 employees purchased 7,292,894 shares, all of which were treasury shares for which $687 million was paid to IBM.

There would be no income or expense effects with the above plan.

2. *Compensatory plan*—These plans involve both compensation expense to the grantor and compensation income to the grantee. Such plans usually specify the issuance of company stock to designated employees at a set price per share (to be paid by the employee) that is significantly less than the current market price of the stock at measurement date (defined later). In some cases, the employee receives the stock under specified conditions at no cost.

Accounting for stock options granted to employees is governed by *ARB No. 43* (Chapter 13B), as amended and supplemented by *APB Opinion No. 25,* "Accounting for Stock Issued to Employees," and *FASB Interpretation No. 28,* "Accounting for Stock Appreciation Rights and Other Variable Stock Option or Award Plans." The following discussion is based on these pronouncements.

Accounting for Noncompensatory Stock Option Plans

Noncompensatory stock options involve no expense to the company and no compensation to the employees. Therefore, they cause no special accounting problems. *APB Opinion No. 25* (par. 7) defines a noncompensatory stock plan as one that possesses all of the following four characteristics:

1. Substantially all full-time employees meeting limited employment criteria are included.
2. The stock is offered to eligible employees either equally or is based on a uniform percentage of salary or wages.
3. The time permitted for exercise of an option or purchase right is limited to a reasonable period.
4. The discount from the market price of the stock is no greater than would be reasonable in an offer of stock to current stockholders or others. Discounts up to 15% are permitted in actual practice.

Accounting for a noncompensatory stock option plan involves recording the issuance of the stock in conformity with the *cost principle*. The option price per share is the issue price. To illustrate accounting for noncompensatory stock options, assume Straw Company has a *stock purchase plan*. Straw's employees may acquire stock from the company at 96% of (a discount of 4% from) the market price through payroll deductions. Suppose the firm has a monthly employee payroll of $90,000, and employees have authorized 8% for stock purchases. Typical entries for this noncompensatory plan, including the $7,200 of voluntary payroll deductions for employee stock purchases, would be (amounts assumed):

1. To record the monthly payroll of $90,000 and related deductions:

Salary and wage expense 90,000
    Withholding income tax payable   18,400
    Payroll taxes payable   6,500
    Liability—employee stock purchase plan*   7,200
    Cash (or salary and wages payable)   57,900

* Per payroll deductions authorized in advance by employees ($90,000 × .08).

2. To record issuance of the required number of shares to employees (market price per share, $18.75):

Liability—employee stock purchase plan 7,200
    Capital stock, par $15 (400 shares)*   6,000
    Contributed capital in excess of par   1,200

* $7,200 ÷ ($18.75 × .96) = 400 shares.

Accounting for Compensatory Stock Option Incentive Plans for Employees

A stock option plan for employees that does not meet all four of the characteristics of a noncompensatory plan must be classified and accounted for as a compensatory stock option incentive plan. A compensatory stock option incentive plan for employees almost always involves an expense to the grantor corporation in addition to the regular wage and salary expense and additional compensation income to the grantee. In some instances the option price might be greater than the market price of the stock on the measurement date; in these instances no compensation (or expense) is recorded.

Accounting for compensatory stock option plans requires application of the *cost principle* to measure and record the total amount of compensation cost during the relevant service period and application of the *matching principle* to allocate the total compensation cost as periodic expense throughout the service period of the grantee (from date of grant).

The numerous types of compensatory stock option plans that exist include a wide range of diverse and complex specifications. The measurement, recording, and reporting reflect that complexity. For this reason, the related APB and FASB pronouncements are often detailed. The discussions and illustrations that follow present the basic distinctions and recording requirements that must be used for all plans. For practical reasons, comprehensive discussion of all possible types of plans in the wide range of compensatory plans is not undertaken here.

The various stock option incentive plans can be classified as follows:

1. *Stock options*—Stock options give the grantee the right to buy a specified number of shares of the common stock of the grantor (the issuing company) at a specified price per share.
2. *Stock appreciation rights* (SARs)—Stock appreciation rights provide a cash bonus to the employee based upon the change in the market value of the specified shares of capital stock from the date of grant to the exercise date.
3. *Combination plans*—Typical combination plans give the employee the option to select one alternative from among two or more alternatives, such as to select either stock options or cash (SARs).

To account for any stock option plan, five basic questions must be resolved. To illustrate resolution of these basic questions, a simplified stock option plan for Abat Corporation is presented in Exhibit 21–3.

EXHIBIT 21-3   Data for Compensatory Stock Option Plan—Abat Corporation

Plan Specifications and Actual Data for Stock Option Transactions

1. Abat Corporation—plan specifications—executive stock options:
   a. Options approved for each of 10 designated executives.
   b. 5,000 shares of common stock, par $5, for each executive.
   c. Nontransferable, exercisable 5 years after grant and prior to expiration date, which is 10 years from date of grant. Exercise of option requires continuing employment to date exercised.
   d. Option price, $20 per share.
2. On January 1, 1992, an executive covered by the plan (I. Goode), was granted an option for 5,000 shares:
   a. For services to be performed from date of grant to the earliest possible exercise date (this also is the vesting date) at December 31, 1996 (approximately equal services each year).*
   b. At January 1,1992, the quoted market price was $30 per share.
   c. The option was exercised by I. Goode on December 31, 1996, when the quoted market price per share was $60 (the stock price experienced steady increases from 1992 through 1996).

* The vesting date is important because on that date the employee can exercise the option to acquire the stock with no constraints as to continued employment or disposition of the shares.

Question 1: Is the plan compensatory?

Any plan that fails to meet any one of the four characteristics listed earlier for a noncompensatory plan is classified as a compensatory plan.

- Abat Corporation's plan is compensatory because, according to the data given in Exhibt 21-3, it does *not* meet all four of the criteria for a *noncompensatory* plan. The plan is limited to 10 executives (not substantially all of the full-time employees), and the discount from the market price of the stock is 33⅓%, that is ($30 − $20) ÷ $30. Discounts associated with noncompensatory plans range no higher than 15%. Either factor makes the plan compensatory.

Question 2: When should the total compensation cost be measured?

Conceptually, total compensation cost should be measured when the grantor forgoes alternative uses (e.g., sale) of the optioned shares. This date is called the *measurement date* under GAAP, as specified by *APB Opinion No. 25* (par. 10). It is "the first date on which are known both (1) the number of shares that an individual employee is entitled to receive and (2) the option price . . . if any." Both of these specifications are necessary to measure total compensation cost. The measurement date is usually the *date of grant*. However, a compensation plan may allow both the number of shares and the option price to be determined at a later date. If this is the case the measurement date is the first date when both facts are known.

- For Abat Corporation, the measurement date is the date of grant. On that date, January 1, 1992, both (1) the number of optioned shares (5,000) and (2) the option price per share ($20) are known (see Exhibit 21-3).

Question 3: What is the amount of total compensation cost?

Total compensation cost for Goode is determined on the measurement date to be the difference between the market value of the stock on that date and the option price per share, multiplied by the number of optioned shares.[5] If the market value of the stock is less than the option price on the measurement date, no compensation cost is recorded. *APB Opinion No. 25* states that "if the quoted market price is

---

[5] Conceptually, compensation cost should be the market value of stock rights (not the shares themselves). Because the value of the stock rights cannot be known (since there is no market in these options), the difference between the market price and the option price per share is used as a substitute valuation.

unavailable, the best estimate of the market value of the stock should be used to measure compensation.''

* For Abat Corporation (Exhibit 21–3), total compensation cost on the measurement date (date of grant, January 1, 1992) was $50,000. That is, the market value of the stock on measurement date, $30, minus option price, $20, times optioned shares, 5,000, equals $50,000.

Question 4: To what service period should the total compensation cost be assigned as periodic expense?

Under the matching principle, total compensation cost should be allocated as periodic expense over a service period that extends from the date of grant to the date on which the employee has no further service obligations or constraints imposed by the stock option incentive plan. Usually the service period will end at the first date that the option is exercisable (the vesting date). From that date forward, if the option is exercised, the employee controls the disposition of the shares. Sometimes the compensation plan specifies the service period. If the termination of the service period is not known at the date of grant, the grantor must use a ''best estimate.'' The assignment of total compensation cost to period expense must begin in the first year and extend through the end of the service period. The service period is not reduced in length by early exercise of the options. When estimates of the service period are used, revisions are accounted for as ''changes in accounting estimate.''

* For Abat Corporation, the total compensation cost of $50,000 should be allocated as expense equally to each year of the five-year service period from date of grant (January 1, 1992) to the first exercise date (December 31, 1996). Executive Goode is required to work full time for the company during that period.

Question 5: What journal entries should be made by the grantor?

The journal entries to record the effects of a compensatory stock option plan will vary depending upon whether the measurement date is on or after the date of grant.

Measurement Date on Date of Grant   If the measurement date is the *date of grant,* the number of optioned shares, the option price, and the market price of the stock are known at that date. Therefore, total compensation cost can be computed. Total compensation cost is recorded on the date of grant as a debit to deferred compensation cost and a credit to executive stock options outstanding. As of the grant date, these two accounts are reported on the balance sheet under stockholders' equity, as follows:

> Contributed capital:
> Executive stock options outstanding $50,000
> Less: Deferred compensation cost . . . . . . (50,000)   –0–

Deferred compensation cost is subtracted from executive stock options outstanding because the stock options have been issued to the employee and the stock has not been issued. However, the employee has not yet earned the stock options; and consequently, no owners' equity has been created for the unearned stock options.[6]

For each subsequent period in the employee's service period, total compensation cost is allocated on a straight-line basis. Straight-line allocation is used because it is reasonable to assume that the employee will provide equal service each period.

Exhibit 21–4 illustrates accounting for Abat Corporation when the measurement date is the grant date. The exhibit gives the entries required (1) on the measurement

---

[6] *APB Opinion No. 25* (par. 14) also states (italics added): ''If stock is issued in a plan before some or all of the services are performed, part of the consideration recorded for the stock issued is unearned compensation and should be shown as a *separate reduction of stockholders' equity.* The unearned compensation should be accounted for as expense of the period or periods in which the employee performs service.''

EXHIBIT 21-4   Accounting for Compensatory Stock Options, Abat Corporation—Measurement
Date Is Date of Grant

Case Data–See Exhibit 21–3.

Entries of Abat Corporation for Stock Option Transactions of Executive Goode

1. January 1, 1992—date of grant; to record total deferred compensation cost and the issuance
   of stock options to Executive Goode:

Deferred compensation cost [($30 − $20) × 5,000 shares] . . .	50,000	
Executive stock options outstanding (for 5,000 shares of common stock)		50,000

2. December 31, 1992 through 1996—to record the annual allocation of deferred compensation
   cost to compensation expense (equal amount for each of the five years):

Compensation expense	10,000	
Deferred compensation cost		10,000

   $50,000 ÷ 5 years = $10,000 per year (straight line because
   approximately equal services each year).

3. December 31, 1996—exercise date, to record the stock rights tendered by Executive Goode
   and the issuance of the 5,000 shares:

Cash (5,000 shares × $20 option price)	100,000	
Executive stock options outstanding (for 5,000 shares)	50,000	
Common stock, par $5 (5,000 shares)		25,000
Contributed capital in excess of par, common stock		125,000

Reporting in the Financial Statements of 1992

Income Statement:
Expenses:

Compensation expense	$ 10,000

Balance Sheet:

Stockholders' Equity

Contributed capital:

Common stock, par $5, authorized 500,000 shares, issued and outstanding 200,000 shares (assumed)		$1,000,000
Executive stock options outstanding (for 5,000 shares of common stock)	$50,000	
Less: Deferred compensation cost	$40,000	10,000
Other contributed capital (etc.)	(not illustrated)	

Note: For additional disclosures required, see the last section of this chapter.

date, (2) at each year-end to record the assignment of periodic expense, and (3) on
the exercise date for the stock option granted to Goode. The related reporting is also
presented. This exhibit should be studied carefully. It is coordinated with the above
discussion.

Note in Exhibit 21–4 that the actual compensation received by the grantee,
Goode, was ($60 − $20) × 5,000 shares, or $200,000. The total compensation
expense reported by the grantor, Abat Corporation, was ($30 − $20) × 5,000 shares,
or $50,000. This comparison shows a major reason for the popularity of stock option
incentive plans. The plans provide incentives for management to maximize future
stock price, since they benefit directly from price increases. The plans provide for
compensation in excess of the expense recognized on the books when the stock price
rises. Employees covered by the plans have incentives to work to raise the firm's
stock price.

EXHIBIT 21-5   Accounting for Compensatory Stock Options, Abat Corporation—Measurement Date Subsequent to Date of Grant

Case Data

1. Basic data as given in Exhibit 21–3, but the option price is unspecified.
2. Date of grant to Executive Jones—January 1, 1992:
   a. A stock option for 5,000 shares of common stock, par $5, is granted to Executive Jones, exercisable after 5 years from date of grant and within 10 years from date of grant, at which time the option expires.
   b. Option price—to be established on December 31, 1994, by reducing the basic option price of $20 by the percentage increase in net income for 1992 through 1994 (a three-year period).
   c. Additional compensation will be for services to be rendered from date of grant, January 1, 1992, to the first exercise date, December 31, 1996, assuming approximately equal services each year.
   d. Market price per share of stock on date of grant, $20.
3. Estimates made on December 31, 1992, and December 31, 1993, of the amounts for December 31, 1994, measurement date:
   a. Estimated percentage increase in net income for 1992 through December 31, 1994: 15%.
   b. Resulting estimated option price on December 31, 1993, measurement date: $20 × (1 − .15) = $17 per share.
   c. Market price estimated for December 31, 1994, measurement date: for 1992, use the actual market price on December 31, 1992—$22 per share; for 1993, use the actual market price on December 31, 1993—$24 per share.
4. Actual amounts on December 31, 1994, the measurement date:
   a. Percentage increase in net income for 1994 through December 31, 1994: 10%.
   b. Resulting actual option price: $20 × (1 − .10) = $18 per share.
   c. Market price per share of stock quoted on December 31, 1994: $28.
5. December 31, 1996—Executive Jones exercised the option on December 31, 1996, when the quoted price per share was $60.

Entries of Abat Corporation for Stock Option Transactions of Executive Jones

1. January 1, 1992 (date of grant to Executive Jones):
   No entry—measurement and recording of compensation expense will begin on December 31, 1992, and will be based on estimated amounts until the measurement date.
2. December 31, 1992—end of period; to record stock options and compensation earned by Executive Jones during 1992—based on estimated future market price (use actual current market price, $22) and estimated future option price (i.e., $17):

Deferred compensation cost, estimated		
[($22 − $17) × 5,000 shares]	25,000	
Executive stock options outstanding		25,000
Compensation expense [straight-line		
($25,000 ÷ 5 years) = $5,000 per year]	5,000	
Deferred compensation cost		5,000

3. December 31, 1993—end of period; to record stock options and compensation earned by Executive Jones during 1993—based on estimated future market price (use actual current market price, $24) and estimated future option price (i.e., $17):

Deferred compensation cost		
[($24 − $17) × 5,000 shares = $35,000] − $25,000	10,000	
Executive stock options outstanding		10,000
Compensation expense*	9,000	
Deferred compensation cost		9,000

	Per Year
* [($24 − $17 = $7) × (5,000 shares) = $35,000)] ÷ 5 years =	$7,000
Add catch-up for 1992 ($7,000 − $5,000) = ...	2,000
Total	$9,000

Measurement Date after Date of Grant   If on the date of grant either the number of optioned shares or option price is not known, or if the appropriate market price is not known, total compensation expense cannot be computed. If this is the case, the measurement date must be after the date of grant. Nevertheless, periodic compensation expense must be recorded for each service year from the date of grant. Therefore, between the date of grant and the later measurement date, best estimates of total compensation cost must be used for accounting purposes. At the end of each service year from the date of grant to the later measurement date, the best estimate must be revised. This revision is done by using the latest year-end price of the stock. The

EXHIBIT 21-5 *(concluded)*

Entries of AB Corporation for Stock Option Transaction of Executive Jones *(concluded):*

4. December 31, 1994—*measurement date;* to record stock options and compensation earned by Executive Jones during 1994—based on actual current market price of $28 and actual option price of $18 on the measurement date:

Deferred compensation cost	15,000	
Executive stock options outstanding		
[($28 − $18) × 5,000 = $50,000]		
− $25,000 − $10,000		15,000
Compensation expense*	16,000	
Deferred compensation cost		16,000

	Per Year
* [($28 − $18 = $10) × (5,000 shares) = $50,000 ÷ 5 years =	$10,000
Add catch-up for 1992 ($10,000 − $5,000)	5,000
Add catch-up for 1993 ($10,000 − $9,000)	1,000
Total	$16,000

5. December 31, 1993. and 1996—end of period; to record compensation earned by Executive Jones during 1995, and 1996:

Compensation expense*	10,000	
Deferred compensation cost		10,000

* [($28 − $18 = $10) × 5,000 shares = $50,000)] ÷ 5 years = $10,000.

6. December 31, 1996—*exercise date;* to record the stock rights tendered by Executive K and the issuance of the 5,000 shares:

Cash ($18 × 5,000 shares)	90,000	
Executive stock options outstanding (for 5,000 shares)	50,000	
Common stock, par $5 (5,000 shares)		25,000
Additional paid-in capital, common stock		115,000

Reporting on 1993 and 1994 Financial Statements

	1993		1994	
Income Statement:				
Compensation expense		$ 9,000		$ 16,000
Balance Sheet:				
Contributed capital:				
Common stock, par $5, authorized 500,000 shares;				
issued and outstanding 80,000 shares (assumed)		400,000		400,000
Executive stock options outstanding (for 5,000 shares);				
see Note X	$35,000*		$50,000‡	
Less: Deferred compensation expense	(21,000)†	14,000	(20,000)‖	30,000
Other contributed capital, etc. (not illustrated)				

* $25,000 + $10,000 = $35,000

† ($25,000 − $5,000) + ($10,000 − $9,000) = $21,000.

‡ $35,000 + $15,000 = $50,000.

‖ $21,000 (from 1993) + $15,000 − $16,000 = $20,000.

year-end stock price is considered to be the new best estimate.[7] Also, new estimates may have to be made for either the number of optioned shares or the option price or both. These changes in estimates represent the new "best estimate." Although changes in accounting estimates normally are spread prospectively over the current and future periods, *FASB Interpretation No. 28,* Appendix B, illustrates use of the

---

[7] *FASB Interpretation No. 28,* "Accounting for Stock Appreciation Rights and Other Variable Stock Option or Award Plans" (Norwalk, Conn., December 1978). There is some misunderstanding of this interpretation because in par. 18 it prescribes "prospective application" (which is how a change in estimate is treated), but in Appendix B the catch-up (retroactive approach) is illustrated. The change in estimate approach spreads the catch-up amounts over the remaining periods on a straight-line basis. The change in estimate approach appears to be conceptually and practically preferable, especially when significant increases followed by significant decreases in market prices occur. The catch-up method is used in these illustrations.

catch-up method. Application of the catch-up method means that when the estimated stock price changes, the amount recorded in the prior year must be updated in full in the current year with a catch-up amount.

Exhibit 21–5 illustrates the accounting for Abat Corporation when the measurement date is later than the date of grant. This exhibit gives the changes assumed in the option plan, and shows the entries at (1) date of grant, January 1, 1992, (2) year-end to record periodic expense (for the periods of service between the grant date and the later measurement date for which the estimates were made), and (3) exercise date. In this example the measurement date is the first date that the options can be exercised, December 31, 1994. The exhibit also illustrates the related financial reporting. Abat Corporation had to estimate total compensation cost at the end of 1992 and 1993, and then subsequently determines the actual amount at the end of 1994 (the measurement date). To compute estimated total compensation expense at the end of 1992 and 1993, Abat had to use (a) the year-end market price of the stock as the best estimate of future stock price, and (b) a best estimate for the option price. The expense amounts for 1993 and 1994 were computed using the catch-up method.

Lapse of Stock Options

Employee stock options outstanding may be allowed to lapse due to:

1. Failure of an employee to fulfill the option obligations due to severance, disability, or death. Such situations should be accounted for as a change in accounting estimates in conformity with *APB Opinion No. 20*. Two items should be removed: the credit balance relating to the particular lapsed option carried in the stock options outstanding account, and any related debit balance carried in the deferred compensation cost account. The difference should be accounted for as a reduction of compensation expense in the period of forfeiture (*APB Opinion No. 25, par. 15*).
2. Failure to exercise because the option price of the stock is higher than the quoted market price of the stock. In this case, it would not be rational to exercise the options. In this situation the employee has fulfilled the obligations of the option plan. However, the options lapsed on December 31, 2001. For example, assume Executive Jones (Exhibit 21–5) did not exercise the stock rights by December 31, 2001. All compensation expense has been recorded. However, there is a remaining credit balance of $50,000 in executive stock options outstanding. What should be the disposition of this balance on the date of lapse, December 31, 2001? *APB Opinion No. 25* and *FASB Interpretation No. 28* are silent on this specific situation.

Two approaches to account for the remaining credit balance are used in practice:

1. Transfer the credit balance of executive stock options outstanding to an appropriately designated account, such as "contributed capital from lapsed stock options." This approach increases permanent capital by the amount of compensation expense. Conceptually, the employee is making a contribution to permanent capital.
2. Allocate the credit balance of executive stock options outstanding to compensation expense of the current period and a reasonable number of future periods as a change in estimate. This approach does not assume that the employee made a contribution to permanent capital. Rather, it assumes that the prior debits to compensation expense (which decreased retained earnings) should be corrected as a change in estimate. This method increases retained earnings rather than permanent capital. Also, some accountants believe that *FASB Interpretation No. 28* (par. 5) applies: "If all parts of the grant or award are forfeited or

cancelled, accrued compensation expense shall be adjusted by decreasing compensation expense in that period.''

STOCK APPRECIATION RIGHTS

Stock appreciation rights were developed primarily to provide cash incentives to employees and to take advantage of favorable income tax provisions. These plans involve the issuance of stock appreciation rights (SARs) that, upon exercise, require the grantor to pay cash (in some cases, either cash or common stock) to the grantee. The amount of cash to be paid is based on the difference between the grant price and the market price of the company's common stock on exercise date.

From the point of view of the employee, stock appreciation rights have two potential advantages over stock options. First, with SARs the employee does not have to purchase shares of stock as is required with stock options. If a large number of shares are involved, amassing the cash necessary to exercise a stock option may be difficult for the employee. Second, the difference between the market price and the exercise price for the newly acquired shares is considered taxable income for the employee when the shares are acquired. The employee must have the resources to pay this income tax, which presents another cash flow problem, especially if the employee plans to hold the newly acquired shares. SARs do not require the employee to acquire shares. Rather, cash is paid to the employee based on the increase in share price. As with stock options, this receipt of cash is immediately considered taxable income for the employee, but the employee has the cash just received as a resource with which to pay the income tax.

SAR plans involve dates similar to stock option incentive plans—grant date, measurement date, exercise date, and year-ends during the the service period. Total compensation cost must be allocated to years within the service period (from date of grant). Neither the market price nor the exercise date is known in advance; estimates must be used each year to record annual compensation expense. Also, because cash will be paid, an account titled, ''stock appreciation plan liability'' replaces the executive stock options outstanding account that typically is used with stock incentive plans.[8]

To illustrate accounting for SARs, the following simplified example is presented:

Example On January 1, 1991, Soker Corporation began a stock appreciation rights plan. Soker specified that for each stock appreciation right (SAR), the grantee will receive cash for the difference between the market value per share of the company's common stock on the date the SARs are exercised and the market price per share on the measurement date, which is the date the SARs are granted. The rights require continuing employment and may be exercised at any time between the end of the fourth year after the grant date and the expiration date. The rights expire at the end of the sixth year after the grant date, or when employment is terminated, whichever is earlier. The service period is from the grant date to the earliest exercise date (i.e., the vesting date), or in this case, four years.

On January 1, 1992, the company's common stock has a market price $10 per share, and Executive Anne Killian is granted 5,000 SARs under the above incentive plan. Killian exercises the SARs on December 31, 1995. Relevant year-end market prices of Soker common stock are:

---

[8] The entries used for stock option incentive plans usually are set up on the deferral basis (see Exhibit 21-5). In contrast, SARs usually are set up on the accrual basis as illustrated here. Either approach may be used in either situation because the entries can be made so that their net effects (but not detailed effects) are the same.

Year-end	Price per Share
1992	$11.00
1993	13.50
1994	12.00
1995	14.00

First, a determination must be made as to whether this a compensatory plan or a noncompensatory plan. Since the plan does not apply to all employees, it is a compensatory plan. Therefore, the plan will create compensation expense for the grantor and additional compensation income for the grantee. Next, the earliest possible measurement date must be determined in order to establish a service period. Since the earliest exercise date is four years after the grant date, the service period is four years, and the earliest measurement date is December 31, 1995. Since this is the date that Killian exercises the SARs, the total actual compensation is computed to be 5,000 SARs times the difference between the price on the exercise date ($14 per share) less the price on the grant date ($10 per share), or 5,000 × (14 − 10) equals $20,000.

To compute the compensation expense for each year, the year-end market price of common stock and the portion of the service period that has expired need to be known. With this information, the total amount of compensation expense that must be accrued to the end of the currrent year can be computed. This amount is labeled stock appreciation rights liability:

$$\begin{bmatrix} \text{Stock appreciation} \\ \text{rights liability} \\ \text{(to date)} \end{bmatrix} = \begin{bmatrix} \text{No. of} \\ \text{SARs} \\ \text{granted} \end{bmatrix} \times \begin{bmatrix} \text{(Market price/} \\ \text{share at end} \\ \text{of current} \\ \text{year)} \end{bmatrix} - \begin{bmatrix} \text{(Market price/} \\ \text{share at} \\ \text{grant date)} \end{bmatrix} \times \begin{bmatrix} \text{Percent of} \\ \text{period of} \\ \text{service} \\ \text{completed} \end{bmatrix}$$

After computing the amount to be accrued as the SAR liability at the end of the current year, the current year compensation expense equals the accrual at the end of the current year less the accrual at the end of the prior year. A schedule of these computations for the Soker Company example of granting 5,000 SARs to Killian is as follows:

(1) Year	(2) Year-end Market Price	(3) Difference from Grant Date Price	(4) Aggregate Compensation To Date (Col. 3 × 5,000 SARs Granted)	(5) Percent Accrued (Percent of Service Period Expired)	(6) SAR Liability Accrued to Year-end (Col. 4 × Col. 5)	(7) Annual Compensation Expense (Ending Liability minus Prior Year Liability)
1992	$11.00	$1.00	$ 5,000	25%	$ 1,250	$ 1,250
1993	$13.50	$3.50	$17,500	50%	$ 8,750	$ 7,500
1994	$12.00	$2.00	$10,000	75%	$ 7,500	$(1,250)
1995	$14.00	$4.00	$20,000	100%	$20,000	$12,500

The annual compensation expense equals the SAR liability at the end of the current year less the SAR liability at the end of the prior year. When the market price of common stock declines, as it does in this example in 1994, the total accrued liability is reduced. In 1994, there will be a credit to compensation expense and a debit entry to the SAR liability. In the extreme event that the market price falls below the market price at the grant date, the stock appreciation plan liability account would be reduced to zero with an offsetting credit to compensation expense.

The journal entries to record the compensation expense resulting from the SARs for the four years would be:

1992:

Compensation expense	1,250	
Stock appreciation plan liability		1,250

1993:

Compensation expense	7,500	
Stock appreciation plan liability		7,500

1994:

Stock appreciation plan liability	1,250	
Compensation expense		1,250

1995:

Compensation expense	12,500	
Stock appreciation plan liability		12,500

The methods of accounting prescribed by the authoritative pronouncements for stock option incentive plans and stock appreciation rights plans are inconsistent. SARs compute total compensation expense based on market price at the exercise date; whereas stock options use the first possible measurement date. With essentially the same economic effects, stock option plans and SAR plans report significantly different (1) total compensation expense, (2) patterns of compensation expense for each year in the service period, and (3) amounts and items on the balance sheet.

ADDITIONAL DISCLOSURES REQUIRED FOR STOCK OPTION PLANS (NONCOMPENSATORY AND COMPENSATORY)

ARB No. 43 (Chapter 13B, par. 15) requires grantor companies to disclose certain information about their stock option plans. The purpose of these disclosures is to inform existing and potential investors and creditors of the company's obligation to make such shares available to employees under existing option plans. This information would be important, for example, to an investor contemplating the purchase of a controlling interest in the company. Based on the *full-disclosure principle,* the required disclosures are:

1. The status of the option plan at the end of the period.
2. The number of shares under option.
3. The option price(s).
4. The number of shares into which options are exercisable.
5. The number of shares exercised during the period and the option price thereof.

SUMMARY OF KEY POINTS

(L.O. 1) 1. Retained earnings, also occasionally called *earnings invested in the business,* represent the accumulated net income or net loss and prior period adjustments of a corporation, less the sum of dividends declared since the inception of the corporation and adjustments for stock retirement as well as treasury stock transactions.

(L.O. 1) 2. Retained earnings are unappropriated unless appropriated for a specific purpose.

(L.O. 2) 3. Dividends are distributions to the stockholders of cash, noncash assets, or the corporation's own stock in proportion to the number of outstanding shares held by each stockholder.

(L.O. 2)   4. The relevant dates for dividends are:
   a. The declaration date—the date the corporation's board of directors formally announces the dividend declaration,
   b. The date of record—the date on which the list of stockholders of record will be prepared,
   c. The ex-dividend date—the date after the date of record at which the shares of stock will trade without the right to receive the declared dividend, and
   d. The date of payment—that date upon which payment of cash or property dividends to the list of stockholders of record actually occurs.

(L.O. 2)   5. The declaration of dividends, other than stock dividends, by the board of directors creates a liability for the corporation as of the date of declaration.

(L.O. 2)   6. Liquidating dividends are a return of capital rather than a return on capital. They represent a reduction of the paid-in capital of the corporation.

(L.O. 2)   7. Scrip dividends are a declaration of an intention by the corporation to pay a cash dividend at some specified date in the future. Scrip, in the form a promissory note, is issued by the corporation to shareholders at the date of declaration. Interest expense accrues on the scrip dividend between the declaration date and the payment date.

(L.O. 3)   8. Stock dividends are proportional issuances of additional shares of stock in lieu of other forms of distributions of cash or noncash property to shareholders. Small stock dividends, those less than 20 to 25%, are recorded at the market value of the stock just before the stock dividend declaration. Large stock dividends, those in excess of 20 to 25 percent, are recorded at par or legal capital amounts.

(L.O. 3)   9. A stock split is a change in the number of shares outstanding accompanied by an offsetting change in the par or stated value per share.

(L.O. 4)   10. Appropriations of retained earnings are the result of management action to constrain a portion of retained earnings for some specific purpose. Restrictions of retained earnings result from contractual or legal agreements wherein a portion of retained earnings cannot be paid out in dividends.

(L.O. 5)   11. Stock rights are privileges awarded to various individuals or shareholders to acquire a specified number of shares at a specified price during a specified period of time.

(L.O. 5)   12. Many corporations have stock option incentive plans for employees. Such plans are either compensatory or noncompensatory. If the plans are compensatory, they result in compensation expense for the grantor and income for the grantee. Noncompensatory plans do not result in compensation expense to the grantor or income to the grantee.

(L.O. 5)   13. Noncompensatory plans must have several characteristics:
   a. Substantially all employees must be included.
   b. Stock is offered to all eligible employees either equally or based on a percentage of salary or wages.
   c. The time for exercising the option is of reasonable length.
   d. The discount on the purchase price is small, generally 15% or less.

(L.O. 5)   14. Compensation expense for stock options is allocated over the service period from the grant date to the date at which the employee has no further service obligations or constraints by the stock option plan. For any given time span within the service period, the best estimate of total compensation expense is used to determine the expense allocation. As this estimate changes from period to period, a catch-up method is used to determine the current period allocation.

(L.O. 6)   15. Stock appreciation rights require the grantor to pay cash or common stock to the grantee based on the difference between the grant price and the market price of the common stock on the exercise date. SARs are usually compensatory, and as such they result in compensation expense for the corporation.

(L.O. 7) 16. A quasi reorganization is a procedure in which a corporation, usually one that has a deficit in retained earnings, can establish a new basis of accounting for its assets, liabilities, and stockholders' equity, and in the process have a fresh accounting start with a retained earnings balance of zero immediately after the quasi reorganization.

REVIEW PROBLEM
◆

The Gilmore Company has the following stockholders' equity section as of December 31, 1991:

Stockholders' Equity

Preferred stock, $100 par, 8% cumulative, voting, 10,000 shares issued and outstanding	$1,000,000
Common stock, $20 par, 100,000 shares authorized, 70,000 shares issued and outstanding	1,400,000
Additional paid-in capital	800,000
Total paid-in capital	3,200,000
Retained earnings	3,000,000
Total stockholders' equity	$6,200,000

There are no dividends in arrears on the preferred shares.

1. Earnings during 1992 total $600,000. The board of directors declares a cash dividend totaling $280,000 to be paid as appropriate to preferred and common shareholders. Later, a stock dividend of 10% is declared on common stock. The market value of common stock is $68 per share on the date the stock dividend is declared.

2. In order to familiarize stockholders with one of the company's new products, the board declares a property dividend of one ounce of a new perfume the company produces for every share of outstanding common stock (before the above stock dividend). The cost of the perfume is 60 cents per ounce, and has a wholesale market value of $1 per ounce. Any gain or loss on this transaction is already included in the earnings reported above.

3. Subsequent to the end of 1992 and the above transactions, the board declares a three-for-two stock split. With the split the number of shares authorized to be issued is increased to 150,000. At the date of the stock split the market value of common stock is $75 per share.

Required:

1. Show all computations and entries to record the above transactions.
2. Show the stockholders' equity section as of December 31, 1992.

SOLUTION
◆

1. Computations and entries for cash and stock dividends:

a. To close the 1992 earnings to retained earnings:

Income summary	600,000	
Retained earnings		600,000

b. To compute and record cash dividends payable to preferred and common shareholders:

Total amount of dividends to be paid	$280,000
Preferred shareholder dividends ($1,000,000 × .08)	80,000
Common stock dividends	$200,000

The entry to record dividends payable:

```
Retained earnings . . . . . . . . . . . . . . . . . . . . . . . . . . 280,000
    Dividends payable (preferred)  . . . . . . . . . . . . . . . .          80,000
    Dividends payable (common)   . . . . . . . . . . . . . . . .         200,000
```

c. To compute and record stock dividend:

The number of shares to be issued as a stock dividend is:

$$70,000 \text{ shares outstanding} \times .10 = 7,000 \text{ shares.}$$

Since the stock dividend is less than 20%, it is to be recorded at market value. The amount to be capitalized as permanent capital is:

$$7,000 \text{ shares} \times \$68 \text{ per share} = \$476,000$$

The entry is:

```
Retained earnings . . . . . . . . . . . . . . . . . . . . . . . . . . 476,000
    Common stock (at par) (7,000 × $20) . . . . . . . . . . . .         140,000
    Additional paid-in capital . . . . . . . . . . . . . . . . . . . .         336,000
```

2. Computations and entries to record the property dividend:

The property dividend is to be recorded at market value, with the gain being recorded for the amount by which the market value of the perfume exceeds the book value:

```
Market value of property dividend (70,000 × $1.00) . . . . . $70,000
Cost of property dividend (70,000 × $.60) . . . . . . . . . . .  42,000
Gain on disposal of inventory . . . . . . . . . . . . . . . . . . $28,000
```

The entries to record the property dividend are:

a. Record the gain when dividend declared:

```
Inventory held for property dividend . . . . . . . . . . . . . . . 70,000
    Intentory, at cost  . . . . . . . . . . . . . . . . . . . . . . . .          42,000
    Gain on disposal of inventory  . . . . . . . . . . . . . . . .          28,000
```

b. Record declaration of dividend:

```
Retained earnings . . . . . . . . . . . . . . . . . . . . . . . . . . 70,000
    Property dividend payable  . . . . . . . . . . . . . . . . . . .          70,000
```

c. When property dividend is distributed:

```
Property dividend payable . . . . . . . . . . . . . . . . . . . . . 70,000
    Inventory held for property dividend  . . . . . . . . . . . .          70,000
```

3. The three-for-two stock split occurs after all the above transactions; therefore, the number of common shares to be split is 70,000 plus the 10% stock dividend (7,000 shares), or a total of 77,000 shares with a par value totaling $1.54 million. Every two shares outstanding will become three new shares; hence, there will be 77,000 times (3/2), or 115,500 new shares outstanding after the split. The new par value of a share is:

$$\$1.54 \text{ million (the amount in the par value of outstanding shares)} \div$$
$$115,500 \text{ new shares outstanding} = \$13.33 \text{ per share}$$

This new par value can also be determined by noting that each existing share with a par value of $20 becomes one and one-half new shares. The $20 in par value is allocated to the one and one-half new shares, or each share has a new par value of $20/1.5, or $13.33 per share.

The entry to record the stock split:

Common stock ($20 par) 1,540,000
    Common stock ($13.33 par)   1,540,000

There is no change in paid-in capital and no capitalization of retained earnings for this transaction.

The Gilmore Company has the following stockholders' equity section as of December 31, 1992:

Stockholders' Equity

Preferred stock, $100 par, 8% cumulative, voting,
    10,000 shares issued and outstanding $1,000,000
Common stock, $13.33 par, 150,000 shares authorized,
    115,500 shares issued and outstanding 1,540,000
Additional paid-in capital 1,136,000
Total paid in capital 3,676,000
Retained earnings 2,774,000
Total stockholders' equity $6,450,000

The retained earnings balance is determined as follows:

Retained earnings

Cash dividend	280,000	3,000,000	Beg. bal.
Stock dividend	476,000	600,000	1992 Earnings
Property dividend	70,000		
		2,774,000	End. bal.

APPENDIX :   *Quasi Reorganizations*

If a corporation has sustained heavy losses over an extended period of time and a significant *deficit* in retained earnings, and if there are unrealistic carrying values for the assets, a quasi reorganization may be desirable.

Quasi reorganization is a procedure whereby a corporation, without formal court proceedings of dissolution, can establish a new basis for accounting for assets, liabilities, and stockholders' equity. In effect, a quasi reorganization is an accounting reorganization in which a fresh start is reflected in the accounts with respect to certain assets, liabilities, legal capital, and retained earnings.

The Committee on Accounting Procedure of the AICPA recognizes the procedure, provided it is properly safeguarded.[9] The Securities and Exchange Commission also recognized quasi reorganization and listed certain associated safeguards or conditions:

1. Retained earnings immediately after the quasi reorganization must be zero.
2. Upon completion of the quasi reorganization, no deficit shall remain in any corporate capital account.
3. The effects of the whole procedure shall be made known to all stockholders entitled to vote and appropriate approval in advance obtained from them.
4. A fair and conservative balance sheet shall be presented as of the date of the reorganization, and the readjustment of values should be reasonably complete in order to obviate as far as possible future readjustments of like nature.[10]

---

[9] *ARB No. 43*, Chapter 7, Section A.
[10] Securities and Exchange Commission, *Accounting Series Release 25*.

EXHIBIT 21A-1   Accounting for Quasi Reorganization

Case Data

1. Balance sheets at January 1, 1992, immediately prior to quasi reorganization:

Current assets	$ 200,000
Operational assets	1,300,000
	$1,500,000
Liabilities	$ 300,000
Capital stock	1,500,000
Contributed capital in excess of par	100,000
Retained earnings	(400,000)
	$1,500,000

2. The inventories are overvalued by $50,000, and the carrying value of the operational assets should be reduced by $350,000.

Entries and Balances

Accounts	Balance before Quasi Reorganization	Entries to Record Quasi Reorganization*		Balance after Quasi Reorganization
Current assets	$ 200,000		(a) $ 50,000	$ 150,000
Operational assets	1,300,000		(b) 350,000	950,000
Total assets	$1,500,000			$1,100,000
Liabilities	$ 300,000			$ 300,000
Capital stock	1,500,000	(d) $700,000		800,000
Contributed capital in excess of par	100,000	(c) 100,000		–0–
Retained earnings	(400,000)	(a) 50,000 (b) 350,000	(c) 100,000 (d) 700,000	(Note 1)
Total liabilities and stockholders' equity	$1,500,000			$1,100,000

Note 1 (on balance sheet): Retained earnings represents accumulations since January 1, 1992, at which time a $400,000 deficit was eliminated as a result of a quasi reorganization.

* Explanation of entries:
  (a) To write down a current asset (inventory) by $50,000.
  (b) To write down an operational asset by $350,000.
  (c) To write off contributed capital in excess of par as a partial offset to the deficit in retained earnings, $100,000.
  (d) To bring retained earnings up to a zero balance and to restate legal capital by the same amount (i.e., $400,000 + $50,000 + $350,000 − $100,000 = $700,000). This leaves legal capital at $800,000, the amount necessary to reconcile the basic accounting model after quasi-reorganization. Legal capital can be restated by (1) reducing par value per share (requires a charter change) or (2) reducing the shares outstanding (no charter change required).

The accounting guidelines to record a quasi reorganization are (1) the recorded values relating to relevant assets are restated; (2) the capital accounts (and occasionally the liabilities) are restated, and the retained earnings account is restated to a zero balance; and (3) the corporate entity itself is unchanged.[11] Subsequent to a quasi reorganization, there must be full disclosure on the financial statements for the year of reorganization of the reorganization procedure and its effects. Also, the retained earnings amount must be "dated" for a period of 3 to 10 years after the reorganization date, as illustrated in Note 1 of Exhibit 21A-1.

In the data presented in Exhibit 21A-1, the company could consider two alternatives. First, the corporation could be *dissolved,* pay creditors, and then form a new corporation. The new corporation would receive the remaining assets and report their total amount as the stockholders' equity of the new corporation.

---

[11] For a detailed treatment of quasi reorganization, see J. Schindler, *Quasi Reorganization* in Michigan Business Studies, vol. 13, no. 5 (Ann Arbor: Bureau of Business Research, University of Michigan, 1958).

Alternatively, the corporation may undergo a *quasi reorganization* (without dissolution). This alternative would be less cumbersome and less expensive than legal reorganization. By complying with the conditions set forth above, including creditor and stockholder approval, the quasi reorganization can be effected without paying off the creditors at this time. The entries needed are reflected in Exhibit 21A–1. The exhibit also shows the restated balance sheet amounts immediately after the quasi reorganization. The quasi reorganization restatements of specific account balances are transferred to retained earnings. Retained earnings is then restated to a zero balance, and legal capital is reduced accordingly.

In general, a quasi reorganization is justified when (1) a large deficit from operations exists, (2) it is approved by the stockholders and creditors, (3) the cost basis of accounting for operational assets becomes unrealistic in terms of going-concern values,[12] (4) a break in continuity of the historical cost basis is needed so that realistic financial reporting is possible, (5) the retained earnings balance is inadequate to absorb the decrease in going-concern asset values, and (6) a fresh start in the accounting sense, appears to be desirable or advantageous to all parties who are concerned with the corporation. A quasi reorganization, by approval of the creditors and stockholders, usually is supervised by a court to assure adequate protection of the interests of all parties. Because legal capital, as measured in the accounts, is reduced in a quasi reorganization, all concerned parties seek equity through court supervison to avoid future litigation.

KEY TERMS

Appropriated retained earnings (1180)	Spin-off (1170)
Fractional share rights (1177)	Stock appreciation rights (1193)
Liquidating dividend (1171)	Stock dividend (1173)
Property dividend (1170)	Stock option (1182)
Restricted retained earnings (1180)	Stock rights (1182)
Retained earnings (1167)	Stock split (1179)
Scrip dividend (1172)	

QUESTIONS

1. Explain what an appropriation of retained earnings is, and why it is done.
2. What are the principal sources and uses of retained earnings?
3. Differentiate between total retained earnings and the balance of the retained earnings account.
4. What are the four important dates relative to dividends? Explain the significance of each.
5. Distinguish between cash dividends, property dividends, and liability or scrip dividends.
6. What is a liquidating dividend? What are the responsibilities of the accountant with respect to such dividends?
7. Explain the difference between intentional and unintentional liquidating dividends.
8. What is the difference between a cash or property dividend and a stock dividend?
9. When property dividends are declared and paid, a loss or gain often must be reported. Explain this statement.
10. Explain how interest paid on a liability or scrip dividend is recorded.
11. Contrast the effects of a stock dividend (declared and issued) versus a cash dividend (declared and paid) on assets, liabilities, and total stockholders' equity.
12. Contrast the effects of a typical small stock dividend (declared and issued) versus a typical cash dividend (declared and paid) on the components of stockholders' equity.

---

[12] The AICPA *Technical Aids* (CCH, sec. 4220.01) states: "Thus, the official statements of the SEC and the APB can be interpreted as indicating that a quasi-reorganization, if otherwise appropriate, could result in a write-up as well as a write-down of assets." *APB Opinion No. 6*, (par. 17) states: "The Board is of the opinion that property, plant and equipment should not be written up by an entity to reflect appraisal, market or current values which are above cost. This statement is not intended to change the accounting practice followed in connection with quasi-reorganizations or reorganizations."

Also, restructure of debt that sometimes occurs in a quasi reorganization does not come under the provisions of *APB Opinion No. 26* or *SFAS No. 15* (debt restructure is discussed in Chapter 16).

13. Explain why the amount of retained earnings reported on the balance sheet often is not the net amount of all accumulated earnings (and losses) less all accumulated cash and property dividends.
14. Distinguish between a stock dividend and a pure stock split.
15. What are the primary reasons for appropriating and for restricting retained earnings?
16. Explain the distinction between (a) a bond sinking fund and (b) an appropriation of retained earnings for a bond sinking fund.
17. What items are properly reported on the statement of retained earnings?
18. Is the following statement correct? "Retained earnings was reduced by the $10,000 appropriated for plant expansion." Explain.
19. Does a bond sinking fund cause a restriction on retained earnings? Explain.
20. What is the difference between stock rights and stock warrants?
21. Can stock rights usually be bought and sold? Explain.
22. List the three important dates with respect to stock rights. When will the related stock sell (a) rights on and (b) ex rights?
23. List the five primary situations when stock rights are used.
24. Explain how the following account should be reported: "Stock rights outstanding (for 100 shares), $3,000."
25. Stock option incentive plans for employees may be either noncompensatory or compensatory. Briefly explain each.
26. Give the two primary accounting principles that underlie the accounting for compensatory stock option incentive plans for employees. Also, identify their application.
27. What is the measurement date for a compensatory stock option incentive plan? Why is it sometimes later than the date of grant?
28. What is the amount of total compensation expense in a stock option plan?
29. Why are estimates necessary when the measurement date is later than the date of grant of a compensatory stock option?
30. What are stock appreciation rights?

EXERCISES

E 21-1
Overview:
Subclassifications of
Stockholders' Equity
(L.O. 1)

Stockholders' equity has the following subclassifications:

A. Capital stock.
B. Additional contributed capital (excluding donated capital).
C. Donated capital.
D. Retained earnings.
E. Retained earnings appropriated.
F. Unrealized capital.

Match each item below with the letter above that corresponds to its proper classification within stockholders' equity. Use NA if the above classifications are not applicable (give explanations if needed):

1.＿＿＿Net loss.
2.＿＿＿Restriction on retained earnings.
3.＿＿＿Goodwill.
4.＿＿＿Extraordinary item.
5.＿＿＿Cash dividends declared, not paid.
6.＿＿＿Bond sinking fund.
7.＿＿＿Treasury stock, cost method.
8.＿＿＿Plant site given by Twin City.
9.＿＿＿Net income.
10.＿＿＿Correction of accounting error.
11.＿＿＿Legal capital.
12.＿＿＿Premium on capital stock.
13.＿＿＿Subscribed stock.
14.＿＿＿Stock dividends declared, but not issued.
15.＿＿＿Prior period adjustment.

E 21-2
Property Dividend
Recorded: Common and
Preferred Stock
(L.O. 2)

The records of Frost Corporation showed the following at the end of 1993:

Preferred stock, 6% cumulative, nonparticipating, par $20 . . . . $200,000
Common stock, nopar value (50,000 shares issued and outstanding) 240,000
Contributed capital in excess of par, preferred stock 30,000
Retained earnings 125,000
Investment in stock of Ace Corporation (500 shares at cost) 10,000

The preferred stock has dividends in arrears for 1991 and 1992. On January 15, 1993 the board of directors approved the following resolution: "The 1993 dividend, to stockholders of record on February 1, 1993, shall be 6% on the preferrred stock and $1.00 per share on the common stock; the dividends in arrears are to be paid on March 1, 1993, by issuing a property dividend using the requisite amount of Ace Corporation stock. All current dividends for 1993 are to be paid in cash on March 1, 1993." On January 15, 1993, the stock of Ace Corporation was selling at $60 per share, on February 1, at $61 per share, and at $62 on March 1, 1993.

Required:

1. Compute the amount of the dividends to be paid to each class of stockholders, including the number of shares of Ace Corporation stock and the amount of cash required by the declaration. Assume that divisibility of the shares of Ace Corporation poses no problem.
2. Give journal entries to record all aspects of the dividend declaration and its subsequent payment.

E 21-3
Cash Dividend Recorded: Error in Retained Earnings
(L.O. 1, 2)

On November 1, 1994, Toni Corporation declared the 1994 cash dividend of $1.50 per share on its 20,000 outstanding shares of common stock (par $1, originally sold at $10 per share). The dividend is payable on January 5, 1995, to its stockholders of record as of December 30, 1994. On declaration date, the balance in the retained earnings account was $23,000; this balance had not been corrected for a $3,000 overstatement of the 1993 net income (caused by an understatement of 1993 depreciation expense). The annual accounting period ends December 31.

Required:

1. Give all entries required for the declaration and payment in full of the dividend as declared. Include any additional disclosure notes.
2. Were any problems posed by this cash dividend? Explain.

E 21-4
Cash Dividend Recorded: Return of Capital and Entries
(L.O. 2)

On December 1, 1992, the board of directors of Jax Mining Company declared the maximum cash dividend permitted by state law. The company had never declared a dividend prior to this time. There were 100 stockholders, each holding 200 shares of stock with a par value of $5 per share. The laws of the state provide that "dividends may be paid equal to all accumulated profits prior to the depletion amount." Retained earnings showed a correct balance of $60,000; depletion for the year amounted to $12,000 (accumulated depletion was $20,000). The dividend was payable 60 days after declaration date.

Required:

1. Give all entries related to the dividend through the payment date.
2. What special notification, if any, should be given the stockholders?
3. What items related to the dividend declaration would be reported on a balance sheet dated December 31, 1992, assuming net income for 1992 of $15,000 (included in the $60,000 balance of retained earnings given above)? Write any note that may be needed to fully disclose the dividend.

E 21-5
Cash and Scrip Dividend: Entries
(L.O. 2)

On September 1, 1994, Fox Corporation declared a cash dividend of $2 per share on its 400,000 outstanding shares of common stock (par $1). The dividend is payable on December 1, 1994, to stockholders of record as of October 1, 1994, as follows: one-fourth cash and the balance with scrip, which will be paid on June 30, 1995, plus 12% annual interest starting on the cash payment date. The annual accounting period ends December 31. The amount in the retained earnings account is adequate for payment of the dividend.

Required:

Give all required journal entries, through final payment, directly related to this dividend.

E 21-6
Stock Dividend Recorded: Dates Cross Two Periods
(L.O. 3)

The records of Round Corporation showed the following balances on November 1, 1992:

Capital stock, par $10	$300,000
Contributed capital in excess of par	102,000
Retained earnings	200,000

On November 5, 1992, the board of directors declared a stock dividend to the stockholders of record as of December 20, 1992, of one additional share for each five shares already outstanding; issue date, January 10, 1993. The market value of the stock immediately after the issuance was $18 per share. The annual accounting period ends December 31.

Required:

1. Give entries in parallel columns for the stock dividend assuming, for problem purposes, *Case A*—market value is capitalized; *Case B*—par value is capitalized; and *Case C*—average paid in is capitalized.
2. Explain when each value should be used.
3. With respect to the stock dividend, what should be reported on the balance sheet at December 31, 1992, assuming no intervening dividend transactions?

E 21-7
Stock Dividend with
Fractional Share Rights:
Entries and Reporting
(L.O. 3)

The accounts of Amick Corporation provide the following data at December 31, 1993:

Capital stock, par $5, authorized shares 100,000, issued and
  outstanding 20,000 shares $100,000
Contributed capital in excess of par   80,000
Retained earnings   150,000

On May 1, 1994, the board of directors of Amick Corporation declared a 50% stock dividend (i.e., for each two shares already outstanding, one additional share is to be issued) to be issued on June 1, 1994. The stock dividend is to be capitalized at the average of contributed capital per share at December 31, 1993.

On June 1, 1994, all of the required shares were issued for the stock dividend except for those required by 1,300 fractional share rights (representing 650 full shares) issued.

On December 1, 1994, the company honored 1,000 of the fractional share rights by issuing the requisite number of shares. The remaining fractional share rights were still outstanding at the end of 1994.

Required:

1. Give the required entries by Amick Corporation at each of the following dates:
   a. May 1, 1994.
   b. June 1, 1994.
   c. December 1, 1994.
2. Prepare the stockholders' equity section of the balance sheet at December 31, 1994, assuming net income for 1994 was $30,000.
3. Assume instead that the fractional share rights specified (*a*) that two such rights could be turned in for one share of stock without cost or (*b*) that each right could be turned in for $2.50 cash. As a result, 900 rights were turned in for shares, 200 rights for cash, and the remainder lapsed. Give the entry to record the ultimate disposition of all the fractional share rights.

E 21-8
Stock Dividend and Stock
Split: Effects Compared
(L.O. 3)

Bailey Corporation has the following stockholders' equity:

Capital stock, par $12, 20,000 shares outstanding $240,000
Contributed capital in excess of par   70,000
Retained earnings   500,000
  Total stockholders' equity $810,000

The corporation decided to triple the number of shares currently outstanding (to 60,000 shares) by taking one of the following alternative and independent actions:
a. Issue a 200% (2-for-1) stock dividend (40,000 additional shares) and capitalize retained earnings on the basis of par value.
b. Issue a pure (3-for-1; that is, 3 new shares issued for each old share replaced) stock split by changing par value per share proportionately.
c. Issue a (3-for-1) stock split and change the par value per share to $5.

Required:

1. Give the journal entry that should be made for each alternative action. If none is necessary, explain why. On the stock splits, the old shares are called in, and the new shares are issued to replace them.

2. For each alternative, prepare a schedule that reflects the stockholders' equity immediately after the change. For this requirement, complete the following schedule, which is designed to compare the effects of the three alternative actions:

Item	Before Change	Stock Dividend	Pure Stock Split (Par $4)	Stock Split (Par $5)
Shares/par value				
Capital stock	$	$	$	$
Additional paid-in capital in excess of par				
Total contributed capital				
Retained earnings				
Total stockholders' equity	$	$	$	$

Be prepared to explain and compare the effects among the four columns in the above schedule.

E 21-9
Appropriations and Restrictions of Retained Earnings: Entries (L.O. 4)

Watters Corporation carries separate accounts for appropriations and restrictions of retained earnings. One such account is entitled "reserve for profits invested in operational assets, $420,000." Capital stock outstanding, par value $20, amounted to $400,000.

The company had bonds payable outstanding of $200,000. The following accounts were also carried: bond sinking fund, $100,000; and bond sinking fund reserve, $100,000.

The board of directors voted a 10% stock dividend and directed that the market value of the stock, $130 per share, be capitalized, using as a basis "the reserves for profits invested in operational assets" to the extent possible.

Required:

Give entries for the following, using preferable titles:

1. To originally establish the reserve related to fixed (operational) assets.
2. To record the issuance of the stock dividend.
3. To originally establish the bond sinking fund.
4. To originally establish the reserve for the bond sinking fund.
5. To record payment of the bonds, assuming the bond sinking fund and the reserve each have a balance of $180,000 at retirement date.

E 21-10
Prepare Comparative Income Statements and Retained Earnings Statements (L.O. 1)

Using the simplified data for Fey Corporation given below, construct comparative statements of (1) income (single step) and (2) retained earnings for 1991 and 1992. Assume all amounts are material, annual data, and an average tax rate of 40% on all items. Disregard EPS.

	1991	1992
Current items (pretax):		
a. Sales	$110,000	$120,000
b. Cost of goods sold	45,000	50,000
c. Expenses	25,000	29,000
d. Extraordinary gain	3,000	
e. Extraordinary loss		6,000
f. Dividends declared and paid	12,000	10,000
g. Appropriation for profits invested in operational assets	10,000	
h. Prior period adjustment—correction of accounting error made in prior period; income tax was understated and no additional tax effect	2,200	
Beginning balances:		
Unappropriated retained earnings	130,000	?
Appropriation for profits invested in operational assets	–0–	?

E 21–11
Stock Sale—Stock Rights Issued, Some Lapses: Entries
(L.O. 5)

Lytle Corporation has outstanding 50,000 shares of common stock, par $5. On January 15, 1991, the company announced its decision to sell an additional 25,000 shares of unissued common stock at $15 per share and to give the current stockholders first chance to buy shares proportionally equivalent to the number now held. To facilitate this plan, on February 1, 1991, each stockholder was issued one right for each common share currently held. Two rights must be submitted to acquire one additional share for $15. Rights not exercised lapse on June 30, 1991.

Required:

Give any entry or memorandum that should be made in the accounts of Lytle Corporation on each of the following dates:

1. January 15, 1991, the date of the announcement.
2. February 1, 1991, issuance of all the rights. At this date, the stock of Lytle Corporation was quoted on the market at $12.50 per share.
3. June 27, 1991, exercise by current stockholders of 98% of the rights issued.
4. June 30, 1991, the remaining rights outstanding lapsed because of the deadline.

E 21–12
Employee Stock Purchase Plan—Compensatory or Noncompensatory? Entries
(L.O. 5)

Davis Corporation has a stock purchase plan with the following provisions:

> Each full-time employee, with a minimum of one year's service, may acquire, from Davis Corporation, its common stock, par $10, through payroll deductions at 10% below the market price on the date selected by the employee for a stock purchase (i.e., the exercise date). The exercise decision must be made within one year from the payroll deduction date.

Employee L. Adam signed a payroll decuction form on January 1, 1993, for $60 per month. At that date, the market price of the stock was $27. Assume a monthly salary of $2,000 and other payroll deductions in the aggregate of 18%. At the end of 1993, Adam requested that stock be purchased equal to the amount accumulated to Adam's credit. At that date, the market price of the stock was $25.

Required:

1. Is this a compensatory plan? If so, how much should be recorded as additional compensation for Adam? Explain.
2. How many shares will Adam acquire for the 1993 deductions? Show computations.
3. Give entries to record (*a*) one monthly payroll and (*b*) issuance of the shares for the year, assuming unissued shares are used.

E 21–13
Stock Incentive Plan: Compensatory? Analysis and Entries
(L.O. 5)

Rex Corporaton is authorized to issue 300,000 shares of common stock, par $1, of which 140,000 shares have been issued. The corporation initiated a stock bonus plan during 1991 for designated managers. Each manager will receive stock options to purchase 1,000 shares of Rex common stock, if still employed by the company, any time after two years from the date of grant, January 1, 1991. The rights are nontransferable and expire immediately after December 31, 1995. The option price is $20 per share; the market price on date of grant was $24. The services will be rendered approximately equally over the five-year period ending December 31, 1995. Assume Roger Roe is a manager who receives the stock options on January 1, 1991.

Required:

1. Is this a noncompensatory plan? Explain.
2. What is the measurement date? Explain.
3. What is the amount of total compensation cost for manager Roe?
4. Over what period should this compensation cost be assigned as expense? How much should be assigned to 1991 and 1992. Explain.
5. What entry should be made on the date of grant to manager Roe?
6. What entry should be made on December 31, 1991 for manager Roe?
7. Give the entry to record the exercise of the option by manager Roe on December 31, 1995, when the market price of the common stock was $80 per share.
8. How much actual "incentive pay" did manager Roe receive? How much additional compensation expense did Rex Corporation report?

E 21-14
Performance Option Plan:
Measurement Date?
Analysis and Entries
(L.O. 5)

In October 1991, Meno Corporation announced a stock option incentive plan for its six top executives. The plan provided each executive 3,000 stock options for Meno's common stock, par $1, at a standard option price of $36 per share reduced by the percentage increase in EPS from December 31, 1991, to December 31, 1993. The rights are nontransferable and are exercisable three years after the grant date and prior to five years from the grant date. Continuing employment is required through exercise date, and the service period ends on the first possible exercise date.

On January 1, 1992, Executive Smith was granted 3,000 options when the market price was $30 per share. On December 31, 1992, Meno's management believed that the EPS increase would be met and that Smith would exercise her options at the first exercise date. By December 31, 1993, Meno's EPS had increased by 20%. On December 31, 1993, Meno's stock was selling at $40. For simplification, assume total compensation cost at the end of 1992 was estimated to be $24,000.

Smith exercised her option on December 31, 1994, when the market price of the stock was $60 per share.

Required:

1. Is this a compensatory plan? Explain.
2. What date is the measurement date? Explain.
3. What is total compensation cost?
4. What is the service period? Explain.
5. Explain how total compensation cost is allocated to periodic expense in this situation.
6. Give all entries related to executive Smith's stock option.
7. How much actual "incentive pay" did Smith receive? How much additional compensation expense did Meno Corporation report?

E 21-15
Stock Appreciation
Rights: Analysis,
Estimates, and Entries
(L.O. 7)

On January 1, 1991, Kelly Corporation established a stock appreciation rights plan that offers to selected executives rights (SARs) that can be redeemed for cash equal to the difference between the market price of the company's common stock at grant date and market price at the first exercise date. The rights can be exercised three years from grant date and expire four years from grant date or when employment is terminated, if earlier. The service period is considered to be three years because exercise is expected (highly probable) to occur on December 31, 1993.

Executive Brown was granted 2,000 SARs on January 1, 1991 (when the common stock price was $20) and exercised the rights on December 31, 1993. Relevant market prices at year-end on Kelly common stock: 1991, $23; 1992, $27; 1993, $30; and 1994, $26.

Required:

1. Answer the following questions:
   a. Is this plan compensatory? _____ Yes _____ No
   b. The measurement date is _____.
   c. The service period is _____.
   d. Total compensation cost is $_____.
   e. Total cash paid by grantor to grantee is $_____
2. Give the appropriate journal entries from January 1, 1991, through December 31, 1993.

E 21-16
Stock Incentive Plan—
Lapse of Rights: Analysis
and Entries
(L.O. 5)

Stacy Corporation offers a stock option incentive plan that it granted to six of its top executives. During the second year from date of grant, but prior to the permissible exercise date, one of the six executives resigned and accepted employment with a competitor. In accordance with the provisions of the incentive plan, the stock option for the resigned executive lapsed. At the date of lapse, the relevant account balance for all six executives combined: deferred compensation expense, $225,000; and executive stock options outstanding, $300,000. The service period extends for three more years, including the second year.

Required:

1. Briefly explain what accounting treatment should be accorded the one sixth of these balances that relate to the one resigned executive.
2. Give all journal entrties directly related to the lapsed options.

PROBLEMS

P 21-1
Analysis and Correction of Stockholders' Equity: Entries
(L.O. 1)

Careless Corporation was organized on January 1, 1991, and began operations immediately. Unfortunately, the company hired an incompetent bookkeeper. For the years 1991 through 1993, the bookkeeper presented an annual balance sheet that reported only one amount for stockholders' equity: 1991, $137,700; 1992, $156,600; and 1993, $185,000. Also, the condensed income statement reported as follows: 1991, net loss, $17,500; 1992, net profit, $12,000; and 1993, net profit, $40,930 (cumulative earnings of $35,430). Based on the $35,430, the president has recommended to the board of directors that a cash dividend of $35,000 be declared and paid during January 1994. The outside director on the board has objected on the basis that the company's financial statements contain major errors (there has never been an audit). You have been engaged to clarify the situation. The single stockholders' equity account, provided by the bookkeeper, appeared as follows:

Stockholders' Equity

1991 Stock issue costs	1,300	1991	Common stock, par $5,	
1991 Net loss	17,500		20,000 shares issued	160,000
1992 Bought 100 shares of company stock from unhappy stockholder Doe	700	1992	Net profit (including $10,000 land write-up to appraisal)	22,000
Depreciation expense* (1991, $1,500; 1992, $1,700; 1993, $2,300)	5,500	1992	Common stock, 200 shares issued	1,800
Cash shortages* (1991, $2,000; 1992, $2,500; 1993, $500)	5,000	1993	Sold 30 of the Doe shares	270
1993 Cash loan to the company president	10,000	1993	Net profit	40,930
	40,000			225,000

* Recorded but not shown on the income statement as expense.

Required:

Based upon the concerns of the outside director, you must address three major questions:

1. What amount of retained earnings would be available to support a cash dividend? (Assume the above figures have been found to be arithmetically accurate and that there is no change in income tax.)
2. Based on your calculations in requirement 1, what journal entries should be made for declaration, and later payment, of the full amount available as a cash dividend?
3. What entry, prior to the dividend entries in requirement 2, is necessary (a) to close the above single stockholders' equity account and (b) to record the various components of stockholders' equity in separate accounts? Use the cost method for treasury stock and the offset method for stock issue costs.

P 21-2
Dividend of Property and Scrip: Entries
(L.O. 2)

On June 1, 1995, Ward Corporation had outstanding 10,000 shares of capital stock, par value $10 per share. The shares were held by 10 stockholders, each having an equal number of shares. The retained earnings account showed a credit balance of $60,000, although the company was short of cash. The company owned 20,000 shares (2%) of the stock of Carson Corporation that had been purchased as a long-term investment for $20,000. The current market value of this stock is $1.25 per share. On June 1, 1995, the board of directors of Ward Corporation declared a dividend of $4 per share "to be paid with the Carson stock 30 days after declaration date and scrip to be issued for the difference. The scrip will be payable at the end of 12 months from payment date of the property dividend and will earn 12% interest per annum." The accounting period ends December 31.

Required:

1. Give all entries related to the dividends through date of payment of the scrip.
2. Illustrate how all items related to the dividend declaration should be reported by Ward on (a) the balance sheet and (b) income statement at the end of 1985, including any notes needed for full disclosure (i.e., write the notes as they should appear in the statements).

P 21-3
Common and Preferred
Dividends: Property
and Scrip
(L.O. 2)

The summarized balance sheet at December 31, 1994, for Saxon Corporation is shown below.

Cash	$ 28,000
Receivables	36,000
Inventory	110,000
Long-term investment, 4,000 shares (4%) of Mita Corporation stock at cost	6,000
Operational assets (net)	80,000
Other assets	10,000
Total	$270,000
Current liabilities	$ 26,000
Bonds payable	50,000
Preferred stock, 6%, par $10, cumulative	20,000
Common stock, nopar (5,000 shares)	100,000
Contributed capital in excess of par, preferred	5,000
Retained earnings	69,000
Total	$270,000

The dividends on preferred stock are three years in arrears (excluding the current year, 1995). On November 1, 1995, the board of directors of Saxon declared dividends, payment date December 1, as follows:

a. Preferred stock: all dividends in arrears plus the current year dividend; payment to be made by transferring the requisite number of shares of Mita stock at its current market value of $5 per share.

b. Common stock: $4 per share for the current year; payment to be made by transferring the remainder of the Mita stock and issuing a scrip dividend for the balance. The scrip will earn 10% annual interest. The scrip, including interest, will be paid at the end of five months from date of declaration.

Required:

1. Compute the amount of dividends payable on each class of stock and the amount of the scrip dividend.
2. Give entries to record the transfer of the Mita stock and the issuance of the scrip dividend. Use separate accounts for the common and preferred stock.
3. Give the adjusting entry at December 31, 1995, for the interest on the scrip dividend.
4. Give the entry to record payment of the scrip dividend and interest on April 30, 1996.
5. Prepare the stockholders' equity section of the balance sheet as of December 31, 1995. Assume reported net income of $26,000 for 1995 (does not yet include the interest on the scrip dividend and gain on disposal of Mita stock; assume no change in income tax expense for these items).

P 21-4
Cash and Stock
Dividends—Fractional
Shares: Entries and
Reporting
(L.O. 2, 3)

On December 31, 1991, the accounts for Akers Corporation showed the following balances:

Stockholders' Equity

Preferred stock, 7%, par value $25, noncumulative, authorized 10,000 shares, outstanding 8,000 shares	$200,000
Common stock, nopar, stated value $10, authorized 20,000 shares, outstanding 12,000 shares	120,000
Additional paid-in capital, preferred	15,000
Additional paid-in capital, common	30,000
Retained earnings	175,000

During 1992, the following transactions, in order of date, were recorded relating to the capital accounts:

a. Apr. 1 A stock dividend was issued whereby (1) each holder of 10 preferred shares received 1 share of common stock and (2) each holder of 6 shares of common stock received 1 additional share of common. The market price of the common stock was $15 per share immediately after issuance of the stock dividend. In issuing the stock dividend, 2,700 shares of common stock and 1,000 fractional share rights were issued. Each fractional share right represents one tenth of a share of stock.

b. Nov. 1   All of the rights were redeemed except 100, which remained outstanding.

c. Dec. 15   A 7% cash dividend on the preferred shares and a $1.00 per share dividend on the common shares were declared and paid.

d. Dec. 31   Reported net income was $70,000.

Required:

1. Give the journal entries for each of the above transactions during 1992.
2. Prepare the stockholders' equity section of the balance sheet at December 31, 1992.
3. Assume Akers paid cash to the stockholders in lieu of issuing fractional share rights. The cash distribution was based on the market value of $15 per common share. Give the entry on April 1, 1992, to record the dividend transaction. What would be the total stockholders' equity of Akers Corporation on December 31, 1992, in this situation if all other factors remain as they were given above?

P 21–5

Property and Scrip Dividends—Fractional Shares: Entries and Reporting
(L.O. 2, 3)

Dawn Corporation records reflect the following data at the end of 1992:

Current assets	$ 167,000
Operational assets (net)	960,000
Other assets	300,000
Long-term investment in AC Corp. stock (5,000 shares at cost)	5,000
	$1,432,000
Current liabilities	$ 60,000
Long-term liabilities	100,000
Preferred stock, 6%, par $100	300,000
Common stock, nopar, 100,000 shares outstanding	800,000
Contributed capital in excess of par, preferred	12,000
Retained earnings	160,000
	$1,432,000

To date, 3,000 shares of the preferred stock (6%, $100 par value, cumulative, nonparticipating) have been issued. Authorized shares were as follows: common, 200,000; preferred, 3,000. No dividends were declared or paid for 1992. During the subsequent two years, the following transactions affected stockholders' equity:

1993:

a. Feb. 1   Declared and immediately issued one share of the AC Corporation stock for each share of preferred stock as a property dividend to pay the dividends in arrears from 1992 to date. The current market value of the AC stock was $3.50 per share. In addition, a cash dividend was paid to complete payment of the dividends in arrears.

b. Oct. 1   Declared and immediately issued scrip dividends amounting to 6% on the preferred and $1.00 per share on the common stock. Interest on the scrip is 7% per year (maturity date, September 30, 1994).

c. Dec. 31   Reported 1993 net income was $150,000, including all effects of the above transactions.

1994

d. Sept. 30   Paid the scrip dividends including 7% per annum interest for 12 months.

e. Nov. 1   Declared and issued a stock dividend, payable in common stock to holders of both preferred and common stock. The preferred holders are to receive "value" equivalent to 6%, and the common holders are to receive one share for each five shares held. The "value" and the amount to be capitalized per share as a debit to retained earnings is the market value. The price per share of the common stock immediately after the stock dividend was $1.50. Issued the stock dividend in full to the preferred. Fractional share rights for 500 shares (i.e., 2,500 rights) were issued to common stockholders.

f. Dec. 1   The fractional rights specified that five such rights could be turned in for one share of common stock. On this basis, 1,800 of the outstanding fractional share rights were turned in. The remaining 700 rights remain outstanding.

g. Dec. 31 Reported 1993 net income was $95,000, including all effects of the above transactions.

Required:

1. Give the journal entries for each of the above transactions (round to the nearest dollar).
2. Prepare the stockholders' equity section of the balance sheet at December 31, 1994, after recognition of the above transactions.

P 21–6
Retained Earnings—
Appropriations and
Restrictions: Reporting
(L.O. 4)

The following annual data were taken from the records of Yen Corporation at December 31, 1990 (assume all amounts are material; the items in parentheses are credit balances):

Current items (pretax):
a. Sales revenue . . . . $(450,000)
b. Cost of goods sold 230,000
c. Expenses 85,000
d. Extraordinary loss 30,000
e. Stock dividend issued 80,000
f. Cash dividend declared and paid 25,000
g. Correction of accounting error involving understatement
   of income tax expense from prior period
   (not subject to income tax) 8,000
h. Current restriction for bond sinking fund 10,000
i. Current appropriation for plant expansion 40,000

Income Taxes:
Assume an average income tax rate of 40% on all items except the prior period adjustment.

Retained earnings balances, debit (credit), January 1, 1990:
j. Unappropriated retained earnings . . . . $(120,000)
k. Restriction for bond sinking fund . . . . (20,000)
l. Appropriation for plant expansion . . . . (60,000)

Required:

1. Prepare a single-step income statement for the year ended December 31, 1990. Disregard EPS.
2. Prepare a statement of retained earnings for the year ended December 31, 1990, that separately discloses each restriction on total retained earnings.
3. Give any entries related to the appropriations and restrictions that would have been made, assuming subdivisions of retained earnings are recorded in separate accounts.
4. Assume Yen Corporation set up a bond sinking fund to pay off the bonds payable at maturity. Also assume the bonds ($200,000 principal) mature when the bond sinking fund has a balance of $194,000 and that the restriction for bond sinking fund has a balance of $190,000. Give all related entries to record the bond payment at maturity date (assume all interest has already been paid).

P 21–7
Comparative Retained
Earnings: Appropriations
and Reporting
(L.O. 4)

Fumer Corporation records provided the following annual data at December 31, 1992, and 1993 (assume all amounts are material):

	1992	1993
Current items (pretax):		
a. Sales revenue	$240,000	$260,000
b. Cost of goods sold	134,000	143,000
c. Expenses	71,000	77,000
d. Extraordinary loss	7,000	2,000
e. Cash dividend declared and paid	20,000	
f. Stock dividend issued		30,000
g. Restriction for bond sinking fund	10,000	10,000
h. Increase in bond sinking fund	10,000	10,000
i. Prior period adjustment—error correction,		
salary expense understated	6,000	
j. Income taxes—assume an average rate of 45% on all items		
including extraordinary items and prior period adjustments.		

	1992	1993
Balances, January 1:		
k. Restriction for bond sinking fund	70,000	?
l. Unappropriated retained earnings	160,000	?
m. Appropriation for plant expansion	65,000	?
n. Bonds sinking fund	75,000	?
o. Bonds payable	100,000	?

Required:

1. Prepare a single-step income statement for years 1992 and 1993. Common stock outstanding, 10,000 shares.
2. Prepare a comparative statement of retained earnings for the years 1992 and 1993 that sets out separately each of the restrictions and appropriations of retained earnings.

P 21–8

COMPREHENSIVE PROBLEM
♦

Analysis and Correction
of Retained Earnings
Account
(L.O. 2, 3, 4)

Perkins Corporation is undergoing an audit. The books show an account entitled "surplus," which is reproduced below, covering a five-year period, January 1, 1992, to December 31, 1996.

Credits

1992–1995	Net income carried to surplus	$ 800,000
1992	Offset with debit to goodwill—authorized by management	50,000
12/31/1993	Contributed capital in excess of par	6,000
1/1/1994	Correction of prior accounting error*	2,000
1/1/1994	Donation to company—operational asset	5,000
3/31/1994	Refund of prior years' income taxes due to carryback of a 1993 net operating loss to 1992	9,000
7/1/1995	Reduction in capital stock from par value, $100, to par value, $50, with no change in number of shares outstanding (10,000); approved by stockholders	500,000
12/31/1996	Net income, 1996	170,000
		$1,542,000

* Not included in net income 1992–1995.

Debits

1992–1995	Cash dividends declared	$ 520,000
12/31/1992	To reserve for bond sinking fund (required annually 1991–1993)	20,000
12/31/1994	Reserve for bond sinking fund	20,000
12/31/1995	Reserve for bond sinking fund	20,000
9/1/1996	50% stock dividend	250,000
		$ 830,000

Required:

1. The above account is to be closed and replaced with appropriate accounts. Complete a worksheet analysis of the above account to reflect the correct account balances and the corrections needed. It is suggested that the worksheet carry the following columns: (*a*) surplus account per books; (*b*) net income, 1996; (*c*) corrected unappropriated retained earnings, December 31, 1996; and (*d*) columns for debits and credits to any other specific accounts needed.
2. Give the entry or entries to close this account as of December 31, 1996, and to set up appropriate accounts in its place.

(AICPA adapted)

P 21–9
Incentive Stock Plan—
Overview, No
Complexities: Entries
and Reporting
(L.O. 5)

Proctor Corporation is authorized to issue 400,000 shares of common stock, par $5, of which 160,000 are outstanding; issue price $8 per share. On January 1, 1991, the company initiated a stock incentive plan for certain executives. The plan provides for each qualified executive to receive an option for 4,000 shares of the common stock. Subject to continued employment, the option is exercisable at any time after four years and prior to expiration, which is five years from the date of grant. The options are nontransferable, and the specified option price is $60 per share. The option is considered to be additional compensation, prorated equally for the period from the date of grant to the first exercise (vesting) date, which is four years. On January 1, 1991, J. Doe, the company president, was granted an option under the plan when the market price of the stock was $71. Doe exercised the option on December 28, 1995, when the market price of the stock was $90 per share.

Required:

1. Is this a compensatory plan? Explain.
2. What is the measurement date? Explain.
3. What is the amount of the total compensation to Doe?
4. Over what period should Doe's compensation be assigned as expense? How much should be assigned to 1991? to 1992? Explain.
5. Give appropriate entries on the following dates for Doe's option (if none, explain why):
   a. Date of grant.
   b. Measurement date.
   c. End of each year, starting on December 31, 1991.
   d. Exercise date.
6. Show how Doe's option would affect the income statement and balance sheet at the end of 1991 and 1992.
7. What were the amounts of (*a*) actual incentive pay "earned" by Doe and (*b*) the total additional compensation expense reported by Proctor Corporation?

P 21-10
Stock Incentive Plan—
Measurement and Grant
Dates Different: Entries
and Reporting
(L.O. 5)

Manford Corporation has 100,000 shares of common stock, par $20, authorized, of which 40,000 shares are outstanding. The company has a stock option plan that provides the following:

a. Each qualified manager shall receive on January 1, an option for a computed number of shares of common stock at a computed option price per share. The computation of the number of option shares and the option price shall be made three years after the option is granted and will be related to the increase in net income over the three-year period. The plan provides additional compensation for qualified managers for services to be performed approximately equally during the years 1991 to 1995.

b. The options are nontransferable and must be exercised not earlier than three years, and not later than five years, from date of grant. Employment with the company is required through the exercise date.

On January 1, 1991, an option was granted to J. Dean, the controller. At that date, the common stock was quoted on the market at $50 per share. Assume Dean exercised the option near the end of 1995, when the price of the stock was $90. The following additional information is available:

	Estimates Made 12/31/91 of What the Amount Would Be on 12/31/93*	Actual Amount on 12/31/93
Number of shares optioned	500	510
Option price	$60	$62
Market price per share	$67†	$71

* Estimate at 12/31/92 same as estimate at 12/31/91

† Estimate of future market price, based on actual market price on 12/31/91.

Required:

1. Is this a compensatory plan? Explain.
2. When is the measurement date? Explain.
3. Over what period should total compensation expense for Dean be assigned?
4. Give appropriate entries (related to Dean) for the following dates (if none, explain why):
   a. Date of grant.
   b. End of 1991 and 1992.
   c. Measurement date.
   d. End of 1993, 1994, and 1995.
   e. Exercise date.
5. Show how Dean's option would affect the income statements and balance sheets for 1992 and 1993.
6. How much actual incentive compensation did Dean "earn"? How much compensation expense did Manford Corporation report?

P 21–11
Stock Incentive Plan—
Dates of Grant and
Measurement Different:
Entries and Reporting
(L.O. 5)

Huber Corporation is authorized to issue 200,000 shares of common stock, par $10, of which 75,000 shares have been issued. On January 1, 1992, the corporation initiated a stock option plan for its three top managers. The plan provides that each manager will receive an option to purchase, no later than December 31, 1996, 2,000 shares of the common stock at a base option price of $48, which will be adjusted for changes in earnings per share (EPS); it requires continued employment through the actual exercise date. The option price is to be established on December 31, 1994, and will be based on changes in EPS. EPS for 1991 was $2. The option price will be established at the end of 1994 as follows:

> The option price per share will be the basic option price of $48 multiplied by the additive inverse of the percentage change (i.e., 1 minus the % of change) in EPS from December 31, 1991 through 1994.

The options are nontransferable and expire on December 31, 1996. The stock was quoted at $45 per share on the market on January 1, 1992. On December 31, 1992, the management made what they consider to be realistic estimates that EPS would increase steadily to $3.20 at December 31, 1992, and that the stock price would be $46 per share on that date; this latter estimate was based upon the actual market price of the stock on December 31, 1992, which was $46. These estimates were not revised in 1993 because the actual market price of the stock was very close to $46 on December 31, 1993, and EPS expectations remained the same. EPS on December 31, 1994, actually turned out to be $3, and the actual market price of the stock was $47.

The president received the options with the option price unknown on January 1, 1992. The service period was established to be five years (1992 through 1996). Assume the president exercised the option on December 31, 1996, when the market price of the stock was $64.

Required:

1. Is this a compensatory plan? Explain.
2. What is the measurement date? Explain.
3. Over what period should total compensation cost for the president be assigned?
4. Give appropriate entries (related to the president) on the following dates (if none, explain why):
   a. Date of grant.
   b. End of 1992 and 1993.
   c. Measurement date.
   d. End of 1994, 1995, and 1996.
   e. Exercise date.
5. Show how the president's option would affect the income statement and balance sheet for 1993 and 1994.
6. What were the amounts of (*a*) additional compensation expense reported by the grantor and (*b*) the actual incentive compensation "earned" by the grantee?

P 21–12
Stock Appreciation
Rights: Analysis, Entries
(L.O. 6)

Delphi Corporation has just employed a new president with the following compensation package: (1) salary, $200,000 per year (minimum employment period, three years); (2) an annual bonus of 10% of the dollar increase in accrual basis income before extraordinary items; and (3) 10,000 stock appreciation rights (SARs) tied to the market price of Delphi's common stock. This problem focuses on the SARs granted to the new president on January 1, 1992, when the market price per share was $30. Four other executives also participate in this SAR plan.

The SAR plan specifies that each SAR will earn for the grantee cash equal to the difference between the market price of Delphi's common stock on the grant date and on the exercise date. The SARs may be exercised at any time after the end of the fourth year from the grant date, and they expire at the end of the fifth year from the grant date, or at date of termination of employment, if before the end of the fifth year. The service period is from the grant date to the expected (a high probability) exercise (i.e., vesting) date, December 31, 1995.

The president exercised the SARs on January 4, 1996, when the market price per share was $40. Relevent year-end market price of Delphi's common stock; 1992, $33; 1993, $38; 1994, $38; 1995, $40; and January 4, 1996, $40. The accounting period ends December 31.

Required:

1. Respond to the following questions:
   a. Is this plan compensatory? Why?
   b. What is the measurement date? Explain.

c. What is total compensation cost?

d. What is the service period? Explain.

e. How is total compensation expense allocated to annual periodic expense?

2. Give all entries related to the SARs granted to the president from the grant date through the exercise date.

P 21-13

COMPREHENSIVE PROBLEM
◆

An Overview of
Stockholders' Equity
Chapters
(L.O. 2, 3, 4, 5)

Howard Corporation is a publicly owned company whose shares are traded on a national stock exchange. At December 31, 1992, Howard had 25,000,000 shares of $10 par value common stock authorized, of which 15,000,000 shares were issued and 14,000,000 shares were outstanding.

The stockholders' equity accounts at December 31, 1992, had the following balances:

Common stock	$150,000,000
Contributed capital in excess of par	80,000,000
Retained earnings	50,000,000
Treasury stock (at cost)	18,000,000

During 1993, Howard had the following transactions:

a. On February 1, 1993, a secondary distribution of 2,000,000 shares of $10 par value common stock was completed. The stock was sold to the public at $18 per share, net of issue costs.

b. On February 15, 1993, Howard issued, at $110 per share, 100,000 shares of $100 par value, 8% cumulative preferred stock with 100,000 detachable warrants. Each warrant contained one right, which with $20 could be exchanged for one share of $10 par value common stock. On February 15, 1993, the market price for one stock right was $1.

c. On March 1, 1993, Howard reacquired 20,000 shares of its common stock for $18.50 per share. Howard uses the cost method to account for treasury stock.

d. On March 15, 1993, when the common stock was trading for $21 per share, a major stockholder donated 10,000 shares, which are appropriately recorded as treasury stock.

e. On March 31, 1993, Howard declared a semiannual cash dividend on common stock of 10 cents per share, payable on April 30, 1993, to stockholders of record on April 10, 1993. The appropriate state law prohibits cash dividends on treasury stock.

f. On April 15, 1993, when the market price of the stock rights was $2 each and the market price of the common stock was $22 per share, 30,000 stock rights were exercised. Howard issued new shares to settle the transaction.

g. On April 30, 1993, employees exercised 100,000 options that were granted in 1991 under a noncompensatory stock option plan. When the options were granted, each option had a preemptive right and entitled the employee to purchase one share of common stock for $20 per share. On April 30, 1993, the market price of the common stock was $23 per share. Howard issued new shares to settle the transaction.

h. On May 31, 1993, when the market price of the common stock was $23 per share, Howard declared a 5% stock dividend distributable on July 1, 1993, to stockholders of record on June 1, 1993. Immediately after issuance of the dividend shares, the market price of the common stock was $20.

i. On June 30, 1993, Howard sold the 20,000 treasury shares reacquired on March 1, 1993, and an additional 280,000 treasury shares costing $5,600,000 that were on hand at the beginning of the year. The selling price was $25 per share.

j. On September 30, 1993, Howard declared a semiannual cash dividend on common stock of 10 cents per share and the yearly dividend on preferred stock, both payable on October 30, 1993, to stockholders of record on October 10, 1993. The appropriate state law prohibits cash dividends on treasury stock.

k. On December 31, 1993, the remaining outstanding rights expired.

l. Net income for 1993 was $25,000,000.

Required:

Prepare a schedule to be used to summarize, for each transaction, the changes in Howard's stockholders' equity accounts for 1993. The columns on this schedule should have the following 11 headings:

Date of transaction (or beginning date); common stock—number of shares; common stock—amount; preferred stock—number of shares; preferred stock—amount; common stock warrants—number of rights; common stock warrants—amount; additional contributed capital (including contributed capital in excess of par, etc.); retained earnings; treasury stock—number of shares; and treasury stock—cost amount.

(AICPA adapted)

P 21-14
Appendix—Quasi
Reorganization: Entries
and Reporting
(L.O. 7)

The following account balances were shown on the books of Overton Corporation at December 31, 1991:

Noncumulative preferred stock, 5% par $100, 2,000
  shares outstanding $200,000
Common stock, par $50, 5,000 shares outstanding   250,000
Retained earnings (deficit) . . . .   (45,000)

At a stockholders' meeting (including holders of preferred shares) the following actions related to a quasi reorganization were decided upon:

a. Amendment to the charter shall be obtained authorizing a total of 5,000 shares of preferred stock, 6%, par $100 per share, cumulative; and 40,000 shares of nopar common stock.
b. All outstanding stock shall be returned in exchange for the new stock as follows:
  (1) For each share of the old preferred stock, one share of new preferred. Purchased for cash at par 20 shares of old preferred stock from a dissatisfied stockholder. All the remainder was exchanged.
  (2) For each share of the old common stock, two shares of the new common stock; the credit to the nopar stock account shall be at an amount that creates a credit balance in contributed capital from conversion sufficient exactly to eliminate the deficit in retained earnings. All of the old common shares were exchanged.
c. The retained earnings deficit shall be written off against the credit created by the conversion of the common stock. The above actions were subsequently approved by Overton's creditors.

During the ensuing year, 1992, the following additional transactions and events were completed:

d. Sold 200 shares of the new preferred stock at $112 per share.
e. The company issued 1,200 shares of nopar common stock in payment for a patent tentatively valued by the seller at $20,000. (The current market value of a share of the common stock was $15.)
f. The company sold 50 shares of nopar common stock at $19 per share, receiving cash. Overton also issued 100, $1,000 bonds at 102; one share of common stock, as a bonus, was given with each bond.
g. At the end of 1992, the board of directors met and was informed that the new income before deductions for bonuses to officers was $100,000. The directors approved the following actions:
  (1) 500 shares of nopar common stock (from authorized but unissued shares) shall be issued to the officers as a bonus (at no cost to the officers). The market price of a nopar common share on this date was $16.
  (2) Declared and paid cash dividends (for one year) on the preferred stock outstanding.

Required:

1. Prepare journal entries to record the above transactions, including the quasi reorganization.
2. Prepare the stockholders' equity section of the balance sheet after all of the above transactions were recorded.

P 21-15
Appendix—Quasi
Reorganization: Entries
and Reporting
(L.O. 7)

During the last five years, Norwood Corporation experienced severe losses. A new president has been tentatively employed who is confident the company can be saved from bankruptcy (and dissolution). Working with an independent CPA, the new president has proposed a quasi reorganization with the constraints that (a) the capital structure must be changed to eliminate the deficit in retained earnings and (b) it must be approved by the stockholders and creditors. The Norwood board of directors approved the prosposal and submitted it to a vote of the stockholders and obtained approval of the creditors.

Prior to quasi reorganization, Norwood's balance sheet (summarized) reflected the following:

Cash	$ 20,000
Accounts receivable	94,000
Allowance for doubtful accounts	(4,000)
Inventory	150,000
Operational assets	800,000
Accumulated depreciation	(300,000)
Deferred charges	40,000
	$800,000
Current liabilities	$150,000
Long-term liabilities	240,000
Common stock, par $50	500,000
Preferred stock, par $100	100,000
Contributed capital in excess of par, preferred stock	30,000
Retained earnings, deficit	(220,000)
	$800,000

The quasi reorganization proposal, as approved by the stockholders and creditors, provided the following:

a. To adequately provide for probable losses on accounts receivable, increase the allowance to $6,000.
b. Write down the inventory to $100,000 because of obsolete and damaged goods.
c. Reduce the book value of the operational assets to $400,000 by increasing accumulated depreciation.
d. With the agreement of the creditors, reduce all liabilities by 5%.
e. Reduce the par value of the preferred shares to $60.
f. Eliminate the contributed capital in excess of par on the preferred stock.
g. Call in the old common stock and issue a new common stock, nopar. Set up a new nopar common stock account reduced by the amount needed to adjust retained earnings to zero.

Required:
1. Give a separate entry for each of the above changes.
2. Prepare a balance sheet immediately after the quasi reorganization.

CASES

C 21-1
Recommendations about Dividends
(L.O. 1, 2)

Tranor Corporation's accounts on January 1, showed the following balances (summarized):

Cash	$ 35,000
Other current assets	25,000
Operational assets (net)	235,000
Other assets	55,000
	$350,000
Current liabilities	$ 30,000
Long-term liabilities	60,000
Capital stock, par $10 (20,000 shares)	200,000
Contributed capital in excess of par	10,000
Retained earnings	50,000
	$350,000

The board of directors is considering a cash dividend, and you have been requested to provide assistance as an independent CPA. The following questions have been referred to you:

a. What is the maximum amount of cash dividends that can be paid on January 1? Explain.
b. Approximately what amount of dividends would you recommend based upon the data from the accounts? Explain.

c. Give the entries that should be made assuming that a $26,000 cash dividend is declared, with the following dates specified: (a) declaration date, (b) record date, and (c) payment date.

d. Assuming a balance sheet is prepared between declaration date and payment date, how should the dividend declaration be reported?

C 21-2
Financial Shares: Analysis
(L.O. 3)

Tudor Corporation made the following entry to record the final disposition of all fractional share rights issued in connection with a small stock dividend:

Fractional share rights outstanding	3,750	
Common stock, par $10		2,000
Contributed capital, lapsed stock rights		1,250
Cash		500

Required:

1. What dispositions were made of the total of the fractional share rights, as evidenced by the above entry? State specifically what the stockholders did with their fractional share rights to dispose of them.
2. On what date would Tudor have known the number of fractional share rights it would have to issue as a part of the stock dividend distribution?
3. How would the above entry be altered if the stock dividend had been large instead of small?

C 21-3
Should the Board of Directors Declare a Dividend?
(L.O. 1, 2, 3)

Drake Company was started in 1975 to manufacture a wide range of plastic products from three basic components. The company was originally owned by 23 stockholders; however, in 1985 the capital structure was expanded considerably, at which time preferred stock was issued. The preferred is nonvoting, cumulative, nonparticipating, 6% stock. The company has experienced a substantial growth in business over the years. This growth was due to two principal factors: (a) the dynamic management and (b) geographic location. The firm served a rapidly expanding area with relatively few regionally situated competitors.

The December 31, 1990, audited balance sheet showed the following (summarized):

Cash	$ 11,000		Current liabilities	$ 38,000
Other current assets	76,000		Long-term notes payable	60,000
Investment in K Co. stock				
(at cost)	30,000		Preferred stock, par $100	
Plant and equipment (net)	310,000		(500 shares)*	50,000
Intangible assets	15,000		Common stock, $15 par value	
Other assets	8,000		(10,000 shares)*	150,000
	$450,000		Premium on preferred stock	2,000
			Retained earnings	25,000
			Profits invested in plant	125,000
				$450,000

* Authorized shares—preferred, 2,000; common, 20,000.

The board of directors has not declared a dividend since organization; instead, the profits were used to expand the company. This decision was based on the facts that the original capital was small and there was a decision to limit the number of stockholders. At the present time, the common stock is held by slightly fewer than 50 individuals. Each of these individuals also owns preferred shares; their total holdings approximate 46% of the outstanding preferred. The preferred was issued at the time of the capital expansion.

The board of directors had been planning to declare a dividend during the early part of 1991, payable June 30. However, the cash position as shown by the balance sheet has raised serious doubts about the advisability of a dividend in 1991. The president has explained that most of the cash will be needed shortly to pay for inventory already purchased.

The company has a chief accountant but no controller. The board relies on an outside CPA for advice concerning financial management. The CPA was asked to advise about the contemplated dividend declaration. Four of the seven members of the board felt very strongly that some kind of dividend must be declared and paid, and that all stockholders "should get something."

Required:

You have been asked to analyze the situation and make whatever dividend proposals that appear to be worthy of consideration by the board. Present amounts to support your recommendations in a form suitable for consideration by the board in reaching a decision. Provide the basis for your proposals and indicate any preferences that you may have.

C 21–4 Relates to the Appendix: Quasi Reorganization (L.O. 7)	Marks Corporation, a medium-size manufacturer, has experienced operating losses for the past five years. Although operations for the current year ended also resulted in a loss, several important changes made the fourth quarter a profitable one; as a result, future operations of the company are expected to be profitable.

The treasurer suggested a quasi reorganization to (*a*) eliminate the accumulated deficit of $325,000 in retained earnings, (*b*) write up the $600,000 cost of operating land and buildings to their current market value of $800,000, and (*c*) set up an asset of $175,000 representing the estimated future tax benefit of the losses accumulated to date.

Required:

1. What are the characteristics of a quasi reorganization? (That is, of what does it consist?)
2. List the conditions under which a quasi reorganization generally would be justified.
3. Discuss the propriety of the treasurer's proposals to do the following:
    a. Eliminate the deficit of $325,000.
    b. Write up the value of the operating land and buildings of $600,000 to their current market value.
    c. Set up an asset of $175,000 representing the future tax benefit of the losses accumulated to date.

(AICPA adapted)

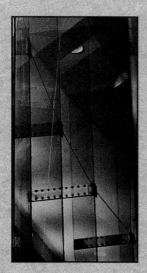

C H A P T E R

22

Earnings per Share

LEARNING OBJECTIVES

♦

After you have studied this chapter, you will:

1. Understand why financial statement users pay close attention to a company's reported earnings per share (EPS) and why EPS is difficult to interpret.

2. Know how to calculate EPS for companies with simple capital structures.

3. Be able to define primary EPS (PEPS) and know how and when to apply PEPS to companies with complex capital structures.

4. Be able to define fully diluted EPS (FDEPS) and know how and when to apply FDEPS to companies with complex capital structures.

5. Know how to apply the treasury stock method to computations involving stock options, rights, and warrants.

6. Know how to apply the "if-converted" method to convertible securities.

7. Be able to classify securities as either common stock equivalents (CSEs) or other dilutive securities for purposes of computing primary and fully diluted EPS. This objective includes using the effective-yield test to determine whether a convertible security should be included when computing either primary or fully diluted EPS.

8. Know how to test for dilution/antidilution (D/A) in calculating EPS when multiple dilutive/antidilutive securities are present.

9. Be able to apply the treasury stock method on a quarterly basis. (Refer to the appendix.)

♦

INTRODUCTION

♦

Earnings per share (EPS) is an important factor for many investors' investment decisions. From the viewpoint of the average investor with no management or employment ties to the company, a publicly traded corporation's reported earnings per share may well be all that matters. Earnings per share values appear to these investors to correlate highly with the market price of the company's common stock. Given the importance of EPS figures to investors, it should come as no surprise that the FASB, the SEC, and other investment regulatory agencies are concerned with how this corporate financial statistic is calculated.

When the CFO (chief financial officer) for a large corporation talks of steps being taken to better manage the company's financial performance, the executive is often referring to:

♦ Different assumptions made in both calculating the dollar amount of earnings and how these dollars are classified and allocated before they are finally reported as after-tax income. Net income after taxes is the base for EPS computations.

♦ Different techniques for adjusting either net income after taxes or the number of shares over which the net income is spread in computing EPS. Adjusting the dollar base and number of shares over which it is spread changes the reported EPS figure(s).

The principles followed in reporting net income components on the income statement were one of the topics covered in Chapter 4. To an extent, this chapter contains a reprise of that information, presented in conjunction with how to apply and evaluate various techniques for computing EPS.

To emphasize the importance of EPS computations, consider the waves of forced mergers and hostile takeovers that marked the corporate finance world of the 1980s. Back then, it often seemed as though there were only two types of companies in the United States: corporate predators and corporate takeover targets.

To ward off predators, target companies resorted to two survival strategies involving EPS. One approach was to alter EPS by contracting the number of common shares outstanding. This approach automatically raised EPS and the market price of the remaining outstanding shares. This increase, it was hoped, would make it too expensive for a predator to pursue a takeover. Alternatively, some takeover target companies took the opposite route. They deliberately diluted their EPS, in an attempt to drive down the market price of their common stock to the point where a predator would be afraid to attempt a takeover. (Actually, the banks and other lenders that were financing these takeovers were the ones to back away from such situations. Because the target company's common stock was pledged as collateral for takeover financing, the lower the market price, the less takeover financing capital was available.)

In implementing the first strategy (contracting the number of shares outstanding and raising EPS), takeover target companies needed to find ways to buy back their stock from the public without using only debt to finance the buy-back. Debt decreases net income (due to increased interest expense) and lowers EPS, thereby partially defeating the purpose of the buy-back.

Shearson Lehman Hutton—a major brokerage house and investment banking firm—devised a plan for target companies to use in buying back large blocks of their shares without having to make a cash tender offer to the shareholders. Shearson's plan called for the target company to issue *unbundled stock units* (USUs) in lieu of cash offers.

With USUs, for each share of common stock surrendered, the shareholder received the following:

♦ A bond sold (at a discount from par value) that paid annual interest equal to the annual dividend paid on the common stock being surrendered. Thus, the shareholder did not forfeit current investment income. Moreover, the issuing company did not commit to any increase in cash outflow.

* A share of hybrid preferred stock (featuring a variable dividend payout), providing the surrendering shareholder with assurance of additional income equal to any and all future increases in the declared dividends paid on the remaining common stock outstanding. Again, the issuing company did not commit to any extra payout beyond what would have been paid had the common stock not been bought back.
* A common stock warrant with an exercise price equal to the par value (maturity value) of the bond. Thus, the surrendering stockholder had the option to reacquire shares in the company (at no loss in value) at the bond maturity date, at which time the hostile takeover threat was expected to have passed.

The objective of this maneuvering is for the number of common shares outstanding to decline substantially, shifting a large portion the company's equity capitalization away from common stock to preferred stock and debt capitalization—but without altering the company's present and projected cash flows in any material way. As a result, with net income constant and the number of common shares outstanding reduced significantly, EPS rises dramatically. If the market price of the stock rises as expected, meaning that the price-earnings (PE) ratio remains as it was before issuing the USUs (and overall market conditions do not turn adverse), the takeover attempt will likely be thwarted.

Battling corporate takeovers is but one example of financial situations in which EPS computations play a part. EPS computations are complex, and the accounting rules governing these computations are extensive. Indeed, there are entire books written on the subject of EPS and the intricacies involved in its calculation.[1] This chapter covers the major EPS-related accounting rules and practices and the logic behind them.

♦

FUNDAMENTALS OF EARNINGS PER SHARE

Prior to 1960, reporting earnings per share was left to the discretion of company management. Emphasis at that time tended to be on raw dollar earnings rather than on EPS; thus, there was a bias in favor of large corporations over smaller companies, purely on the basis of dollar volume. Another earnings measurement system was needed—one that compensated for the fact that even though big corporations are capable of generating dollar earnings that dwarf a smaller company's net income, a smaller company might offer the investor the better investment return on a per share basis: that is, EPS.

Significance of EPS

Earnings per share applies only to common stock, the basic equity investment medium that all corporations use to raise business capital. Over 110 million Americans own common stock either directly, through an intermediary such as a mutual

---

[1] *APB Opinion No. 15* is the primary pronouncement governing the computation of EPS for publicly held corporations. This pronouncement is supplemented by a 186-page interpretation: J, Ball, *Computing Earnings per Share, AICPA, Unofficial Accounting Interpretations of APB Opinion 15. SFAS No. 21,* "Suspension of the Reporting of Earnings per Share and Segment Information by Nonpublic Enterprises" (Norwalk, Conn., April 1978), suspended the EPS reporting requirement for most closely held corporations.

fund or insurance company, or by participating in employer-sponsored profit-sharing and pension programs.

Common stock investors, and the brokers, advisors, and analysts who support them, evaluate companies and often make decisions to buy, sell, or hold (or sometimes to sell short) based on the company's EPS and the stock's current PE ratio. The PE ratio gives the number of times the stock's market price exceeds the company's last reported EPS figure. Thus, if a company is reporting an EPS of $3.25 and the market price of the stock is quoted at 48¾, it means the stock is selling at 15 times earnings ($48.75 ÷ $3.25 = 15).

The significance of PE ratios becomes clear if the same company reported increased earnings per share of $3.50, up 25 cents from the last earnings report. All other factors remaining the same, the stock can be expected to advance in market price to about $52.50, which is a $3.75 rise in price (or $375 profit per 100 shares). At a market price of $52.50, the stock once again is selling at 15 times earnings ($52.50 ÷ $3.50 = 15).[2]

The point is that market prices are sensitive to trends in EPS figures. Because of the profit and loss ramifications that can ensue, EPS figures should be computed using procedures designed to prevent accidental or deliberate overstatement and understatement. There are several common causes of misstatements in published reports:

- Failure to deduct cash dividends on preferred stock from total earnings to determine earnings available to common stockholders. This error overstates the net-income after-tax figure on which EPS is based.
- Failure to account for additional issues of stock (or retirement of outstanding stock) during the accounting period on a weighted-average basis. This error results in distortions that lead to inappropriate comparisons of EPS between both yearly accounting periods and between interim earnings reporting periods.
- Failure to account for stock dividends and splits on a retroactive basis for the full year in which such distributions are made. This error also distorts comparisons of EPS between periods in which the number of outstanding shares is different.

In addition, shareholders of a firm's common stock should be kept informed about any possible dilution of EPS figures due to the existence of convertible securities, corporate stock options, warrants, subscription rights, and corporate commitments to issue common stock at some point in the future. Such matters must be reported to the present shareholders as follows:

1. *Unconditional conversions and exercises:* those cases in which an increase in the number of common shares outstanding may occur at any time and without restriction, at the discretion of the security holder or benefactor of a corporate commitment. In making current-period earnings evaluations and projecting earnings trends from today's base point, common stockholders should assume that all unconditional conversions and exercises have, in fact, already taken place and that reported EPS figures reflect all such imminent conversions and exercises.

2. *Conditional conversions and exercises:* those situations in which an increase in the number of common shares outstanding may occur at some future date if certain conditions are met. For EPS reporting purposes, conditional conversions and exercises are reported differently depending on whether the conditions have been met or not. In making earnings per share projections, and for contingency planning purposes, stockholders should be kept advised of all conditional events that may reduce (dilute) EPS.

---

[2] Rather than remain constant, PE ratios are in fact quite elastic. They tend to expand in response to positive developments in the expectation that future earnings will show improvement, and they contract in response to negative developments in the expectation of still lower earnings in the future. Also, the response of PE ratios to general market conditions is independent of a given company's earnings outlook. PEs tend to expand during bull markets and contract during bear markets.

A fundamental objective of EPS calculations is to show the worst-case, lowest EPS possible. In this regard, the approach reflects the *conservatism principle*.

Basic Calculations for Earnings per Share

The issuance of common stock and preferred stock provides a corporation with permanent capital that the company uses to generate economic wealth. This wealth is reported in the form of after-tax income available to the shareholders, both common and preferred. These resources are either paid out to the shareholders or retained by the company for reinvestment and generation of more wealth. However, preferred stockholders do not share in the wealth retained by the company. Like bondholders, they are paid a return on their investments in the form of dividends rather than interest payments. Preferred stock is also similar to bonds in that both are senior securities. In terms of dividend payouts, this means the preferred shareholders have priority over the common shareholders.

Therefore, the calculation of EPS (which pertains to common stock only) is based on the total wealth generated by a company during a particular accounting period, less the amount of dividends accruing over the period to the preferred stockholders. Expressed as a formula, EPS is computed as:

$$\text{EPS} = \frac{\text{Net Income After Tax} - \text{Preferred Dividends}}{\text{Weighted Average of Outstanding Common Shares}}$$

For example, if a company has 300,000 (weighted-average) common shares outstanding (the term *weighted-average* will be explained shortly), 50,000 shares of preferred stock outstanding paying $10 a share, and has net income after taxes $2 million, EPS would be $5, computed as follows:

$$\$5 = \frac{\$2,000,000 - 50,000(\$10)}{300,000}.$$

If dividends equal to current period earnings were paid on each share of common stock outstanding for the entire year, each share would entitle the holder to receive $5.

Cumulative Preferred Dividends   In deducting preferred dividends from net income after taxes, all preferred dividends declared for the accounting period are deducted. This applies to both cumulative and noncumulative preferred issues. With cumulative preferred stock, if current-period dividends have not been declared by management, an amount equal to the dividends must still be deducted from net after-tax income. With noncumulative preferred, only declared dividends are deducted.

Most preferred stock issues carry the provision that either the dividend must be earned from current operations or else it may be omitted—however, if it is a cumulative preferred issue, the dividend is carried in arrears. Unpaid cumulative preferred dividends must be paid before current common dividends are paid, which is why they are deducted from current-period net after-tax income even though undeclared. In addition, for EPS purposes, undeclared cumulative dividends are deducted even if such deductions convert a net income to a net loss or increase the net loss already calculated.[3]

Additional Stock Issues and Stock Retirements: Weighted-Average Computations   Corporations sometimes issue additional common stock, either as public offerings or privately in conjunction with the exercise of corporate stock options and warrants to purchase stock. A corporation may also buy back blocks of its outstanding common stock to

---

[3] Only this year's cumulative, but undeclared, dividend is deducted from current-period income (or added to the current-period loss). Prior years' undeclared cumulative dividends are not deducted in calculating the current year's EPS.

be held either as treasury shares or for permanent retirement. These changes in the number of common shares outstanding must be taken into consideration when calculating EPS for the accounting period in which such changes occur because they change the assets on which the firm earns. Weighted-average computation techniques are used to accommodate these changes.

For example, assume that a company reported EPS of $3 for 1991, computed on the basis of net after-tax income of $300,000 and 100,000 common shares outstanding (with no preferred stock outstanding). During the next year, on October 1, 1992, the company issues an additional 50,000 shares. At the end of 1992, net income after taxes of $337,500 is reported for the full year, with 150,000 shares outstanding. What should the company report as its EPS figure for 1992?

* If the company uses the end-of-year share count of 150,000, EPS is $2.25 ($337,500 ÷ 150,000), which is a drop of 75 cents per share from last year's $3 level. The market price of the stock could drop in response to such negative news.
* If the old shares-outstanding figure of 100,000 is used, EPS would be $3.375 ($337,500 ÷ 100,000), up 37.5 cents from last year.
* If a simple average of shares outstanding during the year is used (100,000 + 150,000 ÷ 2 = 125,000), EPS would be $2.70 ($337,500 ÷ 125,000), again down from last year's $3 level.

All the above answers are wrong. The correct calculation requires use of a weighted-average schedule accommodating the fact that 100,000 shares were outstanding for nine months (January through September) and 150,000 shares were outstanding for three months (October through December). The firm only had the money from the new issue for ⅓ of a year. The correct EPS figure in this case is $3:

Inclusive Dates	Shares Outstanding	Months Outstanding	Weighted Shares Outstanding (Share-Months)
January–September	100,000	9	900,000
October–December	150,000	3	450,000
		12	1,350,000

Weighted-average number of shares outstanding is 112,500 = (1,350,000 ÷ 12) and EPS is $3 = (337,500 ÷ 112,500), the same as in the prior year.

To further illustrate the weighted-average computation process, assume the following changes in common stock outstanding:

	Transaction	Shares Issued (Retired)	Total Shares Outstanding
Jan. 1:	Balance outstanding	100,000	100,000
Mar. 1:	Additional stock issued	25,000	125,000
May 1:	Stock purchased for treasury	(50,000)	75,000
July 1:	Additional stock issued	100,000	175,000
Sept.1:	Additional stock issued	25,000	200,000

Based on the above transaction information, the following weighted-average schedule would be developed:

Inclusive Dates	Shares Outstanding	Months Outstanding	Weighted Shares Outstanding
Jan.–Feb.	100,000	2	200,000
March–April	125,000	2	250,000
May–June	75,000	2	150,000
July–Aug.	175,000	2	350,000
Sept.–Dec.	200,000	4	800,000
		12	1,750,000

Weighted-average number of shares outstanding is 145,833 = (1,750,000 ÷ 12).

Stock Dividends, Splits, and Reverse Splits (Retroactive Adjustments)   Stock dividends and stock splits are unlike the issuance of new stock in that the issuance of new stock generates additional capital for the company, but stock splits and dividends do not. Similarly, stock retirements reduce the company's capital, but reverse splits do not. There is no infusion of cash or other assets from the shareholders when shares are issued as dividends or in connection with stock splits; rather, these actions merely increase the shares outstanding, while reverse splits merely reduce the number of shares. Because no change in dollar capitalization takes place, there is no need to make weighted-average computations for stock dividends and splits.

Shares issued as dividend stock or split shares are treated as subdivisions of the shares already outstanding. (Reverse splits are considered as contractions in the number of shares previously outstanding.) As such, stock dividends and splits are taken into consideration by adjusting the number of shares outstanding *retroactively* to when the firm began. For example, if a company has 100,000 common shares outstanding as of January 1 and declares a 3-for-1 stock split on May 1, for EPS purposes at the end of the year, the number of shares considered would be 300,000 shares outstanding for the entire year. If net income after taxes were $600,000 in this case, EPS on 300,000 shares outstanding at the end of the year would be $2, which is the same as an EPS of $6 on 100,000 shares outstanding before the split. For comparability, reported EPS figures for prior years are also adjusted for the split.

EPS computations for stock dividends and splits are more involved when they occur during the same accounting period in which new shares are issued or share retirements occur. In such cases, new-issue shares and retirements must be calculated using a weighted-average schedule, and then stock dividends must be applied retroactively in proportion to the number of shares outstanding at various points during the accounting period. Thus, changes in shares outstanding (issuances and retirements) occurring *before* stock dividends or splits are adjusted for any dividend or split.

To illustrate, assume the following hypothetical case facts related to the common stock account of Cloverleaf Dairy for the year ended December 31, 1991:

	Transaction	Shares Issued or (Retired)	Total Shares Outstanding
Jan. 1:	Balance outstanding	10,000	10,000
Apr. 1:	Additional stock issued	1,000	11,000
June 1:	100% stock dividend paid	11,000	22,000
Sept. 1:	Additional stock issued	2,000	24,000

The weighted-average schedule shown in Exhibit 22–1 gives an accounting of how the 100% stock dividend is applied retroactively to January 1, and how the weighted-average number of common stock outstanding for the year is computed.

Weighted-average schedules can be compiled with greater precision based on "share-days" rather than "share-months," as in Exhibit 22–1. To illustrate this point and to gain greater familiarity with weighted-average schedules when share changes occur due to additional issue and share-retirement transactions, and when stock dividend and splits also take place, consider the following events for the Zap Construction Company:

	Transaction	Shares Issued or (Retired)	Total Outstanding
Jan. 1:	Balance outstanding	100,000	100,000
Feb. 25:	5% stock dividend distributed	5,000	105,000
Mar. 21:	Treasury stock bought	(525)	104,475
Oct. 9:	Additional stock issued	10,000	114,475
Nov. 21:	2-for-1 stock split	114,475	228,950

Exhibit 22–2 shows the weighted-average schedule for an accounting of how the 5% stock dividend on February 25 and the 2-for-1 stock split on November 21 are both

EXHIBIT 22-1   Computation of Weighted-Average Number of Shares of Common Stock Outstanding When Stock Dividends or Stock Splits Occur: Cloverleaf Dairy

Inclusive Dates	Actual Shares Outstanding	Retroactive Restatement for 100% Stock Dividend on June 1		Equivalent Shares Outstanding	Months Outstanding		Weighted Shares Outstanding (Share-Months)
Jan. 1–March 31	10,000	× 2	=	20,000	× 3	=	60,000
April 1–May 31	11,000	× 2	=	22,000	× 2	=	44,000
June 1–August 31	22,000*		=	22,000	× 3	=	66,000
Sept. 1–Dec. 31	24,000*		=	24,000	× 4	=	96,000
Totals					12		266,000

Weighted-average number of shares outstanding: 266,000 ÷ 12 = 22,167.

* These numbers already include the stock dividend.

EXHIBIT 22-2   Computation of the Weighted-Average Common Shares Outstanding Involving a Stock Dividend, Treasury Stock, and a Stock Split: Zap Construction

Inclusive Dates	Actual Shares Outstanding	Retroactive Restatement		Equivalent Shares Outstanding	Days Outstanding		Weighted Shares Outstanding (Share-Days)
		Stock Dividend	Stock Split				
Jan. 1–Feb. 24	100,000	× 1.05	× 2 =	210,000	× 55	=	11,550,000
Feb. 25–Mar. 20	105,000*		× 2 =	210,000	× 24	=	5,040,000
Mar. 21–Oct. 8	104,475*		× 2 =	208,950	× 202	=	42,207,900
Oct. 9–Nov. 20	114,475*		× 2 =	228,950	× 43	=	9,844,850
Nov. 21–Dec. 31	228,950†		=	228,950	× 41	=	9,386,950
Totals					365		78,029,700

Weighted-average number of common shares outstanding: 78,029,700 ÷ 365 = 213,780.

* Already includes the effect of the stock dividend.

† Already includes the effect of the stock dividend and the stock split.

applied retroactively to January 1 on a "share-day" basis. Exhibit 22–2 also illustrates how a weighted-average number of common stock shares outstanding for the year is computed using share-days. As shown in Exhibit 22–2, the 5% stock dividend on February 25 required retroactive restatement of the 100,000 actual shares outstanding between January 1 and February 24 to 105,000 shares. Then the 2-for-1 stock split distributed later in the year was applied retroactively to the shares outstanding during the same January 1 to February 24 period—including the 5% dividend shares. The result of these two retroactive restatements is 210,000 shares as reported under the Equivalent Shares Outstanding column. The resulting "share-days" figure for this 55-day period is 11,550,000 share-days (210,000 shares × 55 days).

EPS Restatements in Conjunction with Comparative Income Statements   In reporting EPS figures in comparative financial statements, a weighted-average schedule of changes in capitalization plus retroactive restatements of stock dividends and splits (if any) is also needed. The schedule preparation process is essentially the same as that shown in Exhibit 22–1 and 22–2. However, EPS figures for each year shown (or other accounting period length) reflect all stock dividends and splits since the firm started operations. In this manner, all stock dividends and splits are automatically taken into account when computing EPS figures for prior years. This procedure avoids the need to manually restate share amounts outstanding for these prior years.

CONCEPT REVIEW

1. Why are preferred dividends deducted from net income after taxes for EPS computation purposes?
2. When a stock dividend is distributed, why is the resulting increase in shares outstanding considered to be in effect for the entire year?
3. If additional shares of common stock are issued and sold to the public for cash midway through the current accounting period, what impact does this transaction have on EPS for the current period?

CAPITAL STRUCTURE EFFECTS ON COMPUTING EPS

Types of Capital Structures

APB Opinion No. 15 identifies two types of capital structures—simple and complex—and prescribes different EPS disclosure requirements for each. The basic distinction between simple and complex capital structures is the presence of potentially dilutive securities.

1. **Simple capital structure**—A firm has a simple capital structure if the stockholders' equity consists only of common stock or if no potentially dilutive securities exist that on their conversion or exercise could dilute (decrease) earnings per common share.[4] For simple capital structures, *APB Opinion No. 15* prescribes a single EPS presentation (amounts assumed):[5]

   > Earnings per common share:
   > Income before cumulative effect of accounting change $1.50
   > Cumulative effect of accounting change . . . . (.11)
   > Net income $1.39

   When a simple capital structure exists, *APB Opinion No. 15* calls the reported EPS figure simply *earnings (or net income) per common share*. Since it is easy to be confused about whether a calculation is for earnings per common share (appropriate for simple capital structure) or for either primary or fully diluted earnings per common share (appropriate for a complex capital structure), the term **basic EPS** is used in this text to identify the calculation for a simple capital structure.

2. **Complex capital structure**—A complex capital structure includes all capital structures except those described above as simple. The firm has a complex capital structure if it has outstanding convertible securities or rights that are potentially dilutive. Dilutive securities that may increase the outstanding shares of common stock include convertible preferred stock; convertible bonds; contingent common stock issues; stock rights, stock options; and other securities that provide for the

---

[4] This category includes capital structures involving only common stock and nonconvertible preferred stock for example.

[5] *APB Opinion No. 15* does not require EPS amounts for extraordinary items. These amounts may be deduced by taking the difference between EPS for income before extraordinary items and EPS for net income. EPS figures are required for income before extraordinary items, net income (par 13), and for the cumulative effect of an accounting change (*APB 20*, par. 20). When discontinued operations and extraordinary items are reported, it is desirable to add additional lines to the EPS presentation.

conversion into or purchase of common stock. For complex capital structures, *APB Opinion No. 15* prescribes a dual EPS presentation that reports the dilutive effects. Two EPS amounts are reported: primary and fully diluted EPS (PEPS and FDEPS). The term *earnings per common share* should not be used without the appropriate qualifier when the dual presentation is called for. (These qualifiers *primary* and *fully diluted* are explained later in this chapter.)

To illustrate the reporting (amounts assumed):

	Primary EPS	Fully Diluted EPS
Income before extraordinary items	$1.40	$1.25
Extraordinary loss	(.10)	(.09)
Net income	$1.30	$1.16

APB Opinion No. 15 provides relief from the complex calculations required under complex capital structures if the dilution effect of other securities is small. (This additional consideration, called the *3% test,* is discussed later in this chapter.)

Basically, earnings per share (EPS) is the ratio of income to average outstanding common shares. EPS is computed by dividing the periodic income associated with common stock by the average number of common shares outstanding during the period. However, depending on the corporation's capital structure, income and average number of shares often must be adjusted for certain items. *APB Opinion No. 15* provides specific guidelines concerning these adjustments. One basic guideline is that when either the denominator or numerator is changed, the other one must also be changed if there are any related effects.

Computing EPS with a Simple Capital Structure

A simple capital structure is one that includes only common stock or common stock and nonconvertible securities. EPS figures are required for income before extraordinary items, the cumulative effect of a change in accounting principle, and net income.

Exhibit 22–3 shows the computation of basic EPS for a simple capital structure involving nonconvertible cumulative preferred stock, based on the following data for the Framis Corporation.

	Shares
Capital stock:	
Common stock, par $1, outstanding on January 1, 1991	90,000
Common stock: Sold and issued May 1, 1991	6,000
Preferred stock, par $20, 6% (cumulative, nonconvertible) outstanding on January 1, 1991	2,500

Income data for the year ending December 31, 1991:	
Net income before extraordinary items	$124,000
Extraordinary gain (net of tax)	$ 10,000
Net income	$134,000

If net income for Framis Corp., before extraordinary items were a negative $124,000 (other facts unchanged), the three EPS figures calculated in Exhibit 22–3 would be: − $1.35, $0.11, and − $1.24, respectively.

Computing EPS for a Complex Capital Structure

Corporations with complex capital structures, that is, those that do not meet the definition of a simple capital structure, must present two sets of EPS figures with equal prominence on the income statement. *APB Opinion No. 15* describes these two sets of EPS figures as primary and fully diluted EPS.

EXHIBIT 22-3 Basic EPS Computations for a Simple Capital Structure with Nonconvertible Preferred Stock: Framis Corporation

1. For the numerator (income): preferred dividend claim, for the current year only.

$50,000 (total par value; 2,500 shares × $20) × .06 = $3,000

2. For the denominator (shares): computation of weighted-average number of common shares outstanding during 1991:

Inclusive Dates	Actual Shares Outstanding	Months Outstanding	Weighted Shares Outstanding
Jan. 1–Apr. 30, shares outstanding	90,000	× 4 =	360,000
May 1, sold additional shares	6,000		
May 1–Dec. 31, shares outstanding	96,000	× 8 =	768,000
Dec. 31, shares outstanding	96,000		
Totals		12	1,128,000

Weighted-average number of shares outstanding during 1991: 1,128,000 ÷ 12 = 94,000.

Earnings per Common Share

Earnings per common share outstanding:
Income before extraordinary items:
  ($124,000 − $3,000 = $121,000) ÷ 94,000 share $1.29
  Extraordinary gain: $10,000 ÷ 94,000 shares .11
  Net income: ($124,000 − $3,000 + $10,000) ÷ 94,000 shares $1.40

1. **Primary EPS** is based on the outstanding common shares plus dilutive common stock equivalents (CSEs). **Common stock equivalents** are securities that are likely to be converted to common stock or represent likely issuances of common stock. They are treated as if they are equivalent to common shares.
2. **Fully diluted EPS** reflects the *maximum dilution* of EPS that would have occurred if all contingent issuances of common stock that would individually reduce EPS had taken place at the beginning of the period (or time of issuance of the convertible security, if later). Therefore, fully diluted EPS includes the effects of common shares, CSEs, and any other dilutive securities.

The EPS relationships among simple and complex capital structures are shown in Exhibit 22–4.

The 3% Test *APB Opinion No. 15* recognizes the complexity required for EPS calculations by providing relief if the impact of the calculations is small. Often the fact that the impact of the dilutive securities will be small can be ascertained by inspection or using simple calculations. Any reduction of less than 3% in the aggregate to EPS from dilutive securities need not be considered as dilution and, hence, need not be reported. This is **the 3% test.** Essentially, this test is a materiality test. The test is applied in practice to the net income figure and is done twice. First, EPS ignoring all dilutive securities (basic EPS) is compared to primary EPS, and then the same test is made between basic EPS and fully diluted EPS. If either difference is at least 3%, presentation of both primary EPS and fully diluted EPS, appropriately titled, is required. For example, suppose a firm's calculations yield basic EPS of $1.00, primary EPS of $.98 and fully diluted EPS of $.97. The firm must report both primary and fully diluted EPS because the calculation of fully diluted EPS indicates dilution of at least 3%: ($1.00 − $.97) ÷ $1.00 ≥ .03.

Dilutive and Antidilutive Securities The distinction between dilutive and antidilutive securities is critical to computing EPS in complex structures.

EXHIBIT 22–4   Relationship between Simple Capital Structure Basic EPS and Complex Structure Primary EPS
and Fully Diluted EPS

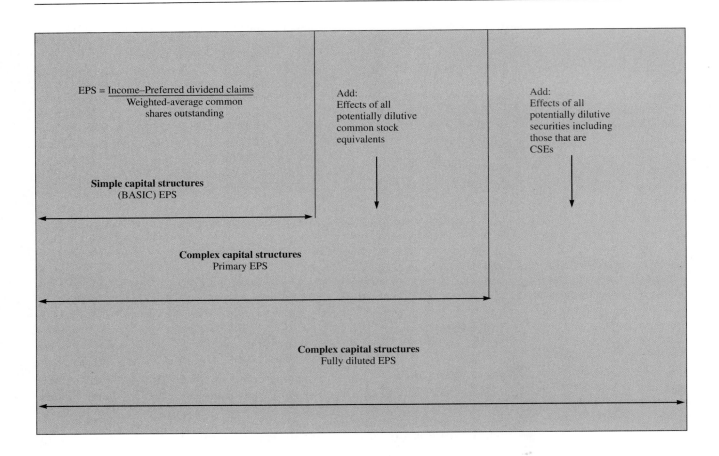

Dilutive securities are those securities whose inclusion in earnings per share computations would decrease the EPS figure computed excluding these same securities. (If earnings per share is negative, this means increasing the loss per share.)

Antidilutive securities are those securities whose inclusion in earnings per share computations would increase the EPS figure computed excluding these same securities. (If earnings per share is negative, this means decreasing the loss per share.) Antidilutive securities are never included in either primary or fully diluted EPS computations (except for very unusual cases not covered in this text).

The test for dilution versus antidilution should be based on the higher of net income or income before extraordinary items. Thus, for example if an extraordinary loss is reported, the income figure before extraordinary items is used. This procedure allows for a greater dilution of EPS.

> ## CONCEPT REVIEW
>
> 1. How does a simple capital structure differ from a complex capital structure?
> 2. What is the purpose of the 3% test and how does it work?
> 3. What is an antidilutive security?

SECURITIES AND PURCHASE CONTRACTS: BASIC EFFECTS ON EPS

When a firm is considered to have a complex capital structure, the calculation to make is primary earnings per share (PEPS). The first step in this calculation is to determine which potentially dilutive securities are defined as *common stock equivalents* (CSEs). A CSE is an equity contract or convertible security that is treated as common stock when computing EPS. To determine whether a potentially dilutive security is a CSE and to compute the number of equivalent shares for EPS purposes, separate consideration must be given to both equity contracts and convertible securities:

- *Equity contracts*—common stock rights, options, warrants, and other common stock purchase contracts, and subscribed common stock, if not fully paid.
- *Convertible securities*—securities convertible to common shares such as convertible preferred stock and convertible bonds.
- *Contingent common stock*—common stock issued upon the occurrence of a stipulated future event.

If either an equity contract or a convertible security is classified as a dilutive CSE, it is assumed to have been converted to common stock at the beginning of the current reporting period if it was outstanding at that time, or otherwise at its issuance date during this period. The number of shares is included in computing both primary and fully diluted EPS. Equity contracts and convertible securities are considered separately here because their effects on the computation of EPS are different. If the security is not considered a CSE, it is included only in computing FDEPS, and then only if dilutive.

Equity Contracts

Common stock rights, options, subscribed stock, and other common stock purchase contracts, have two effects, if exercise is assumed. First, they would increase the number of common shares outstanding and, hence, the denominator of the EPS calculation. Second, exercise of these equity contracts increases the firm's cash because their exercise typically requires a cash payment by the investor.

The additional cash could be used for several purposes, including:

- To acquire productive assets that would be used to increase earnings and, hence, the numerator of the EPS calculation.
- To retire nonconvertible debt, which would increase income (by reducing interest expense) and, hence, increase EPS.
- To pay extra dividends on common stock, which would have no effect on EPS.
- To buy back outstanding common stock for the treasury, which would reduce the impact of the conversion on EPS.[6]

Since the assumed conversion of the equity contract did not in fact occur, an assumption must be made about how any cash received would be used. *APB Opinion No. 15* specifies that all firms will assume the funds would be used to repurchase common shares. This choice results in a consistent treatment across firms and, thereby, increases comparability. The method specified is called the **treasury stock method.** Thus, to compute the increase in the number of common shares caused by the *as-if* exercise of the equity contracts, the treasury stock method assumes that the

---

[6] Treasury stock constitutes shares purchased by a company in open market transactions. Treasury shares remain part of the company's capitalization, but they are no longer outstanding shares. Thus, neither are dividends paid on these shares, nor are they used in EPS computations. Treasury shares become outstanding shares once again when they are sold or otherwise distributed to the public, typically in conjunction with corporate stock option programs.

firm would apply any cash proceeds from exercise of the contract to the purchase of common stock for the treasury.

Treasury Stock Method   The **treasury stock method** is used to calculate increases in common stock outstanding when options or warrants are treated *as if* exercised. This method is an accounting convention based on the assumption that the shares are sold by a company in conjunction with the exercise of an option or warrant, and the proceeds are used to repurchase shares for the treasury. The convention takes into account the dollar amount (exercise proceeds) collected by the company from the holder of the option or other security. The exercise proceeds are then assumed to be used to acquire treasury stock, partially replacing the shares sold, by purchasing stock in the open market at the current market price. The net increase in shares outstanding is the difference between the shares sold in conjunction with the exercise of the options and the shares assumed to be reacquired for the treasury via open market transactions.

When corporate stock options or warrants can be exchanged for common stock, two prices must be considered: the fixed *exercise price* or subscription price (also referred to as the *strike price*) at the time the holder of the security is entitled to purchase stock from the company, and the current price of the stock in the open market, which varies.[7]

If the current market price for a company's common stock is higher than the exercise price of an option or warrant, the security is said to "be in the money." When an option or warrant is in the money, it is advantageous for the holder to exercise it. Exercising such a security causes an increase in the number of common shares outstanding, with no corresponding increase in net income under the treasury stock method; thus EPS declines. However, for primary and fully diluted EPS computation purposes, the increase in shares outstanding will not equal the number of common shares underlying the option, right, or warrant due to the shares assumed reacquired under the treasury stock method.

Exhibit 22–5 illustrates hypothetical stock option exercise scenarios involving 1,000 shares of stock at various exercise prices. Selecting line 3, for example, the holders of this option have the right to purchase 1,000 shares of common stock from the company at the exercise price of $30 per share, which is $20 below the market value of $50 (column *e*). In exercising this option, the holders are assumed to pay $30,000 to the company in exchange for 1,000 shares of company stock. Then the company is assumed to use the $30,000 to buy stock in the open market at $50 a share to partially replace the common stock issued. In this case, 600 shares are bought as shown in column *f*. Thus, the net increase in outstanding shares is 400 shares.

Line 5 in Exhibit 22–5 illustrates the case where the exercise price ($50) is equal to the market price. There is no increase in common stock outstanding (for EPS computation purposes) in this instance because the company would use the $50,000 exercise price to buy back in the open market the same amount of shares sold via the exercise of the option.

The incremental increase (or decrease) in the number of common shares outstanding as the result of the exercise of an option or warrant can be found using this formula:

$$\left[\frac{\text{Market price} - \text{Exercise price}}{\text{Market price}} \right] \left[\begin{matrix} \text{Number of} \\ \text{shares} \\ \text{exercised} \\ \text{(sold)} \end{matrix} \right] = \begin{matrix} \text{Increase (decrease)} \\ \text{in shares outstanding} \end{matrix}$$

---

[7] The term *strike price* is more commonly used in conjunction with securities option contracts traded on the Chicago Board Options Exchange, American Stock Exchange, and other regulated securities markets. These publicly traded option contracts are high-leverage trading vehicles, typically used as an alternative to buying and selling shares in the open market. As such, securities option contracts should not be confused with corporate stock options.

EXHIBIT 22-5   Treasury Stock Method for Computing Net Increase in Common Stock Outstanding

	(a) Common Shares Underlying Option Contract	× Contract Exercise Price	= (c) Exercise Proceeds Collected by Company	÷ (d) Current Open Market Stock Price	= (e) Open Market Shares Bought Back by Company Using Exercise Proceeds	(f) Net Increase in Shares Outstanding: Column (a) less (e) for EPS Computation Only
1.	1,000	$10	$10,000	$50	200	800
2.	1,000	$20	$20,000	$50	400	600
3.	1,000	$30	$30,000	$50	600	400
4.	1,000	$40	$40,000	$50	800	200
5.	1,000	$50	$50,000	$50	1,000	0
6.	1,000	$60	$60,000	$50	1,200	(200)

For example, according to the data shown on line 1 of Exhibit 22–5, if 1,000 shares are exercised at $10 per share when the market price is $50, the net increase in common stock outstanding will be 800 shares, computed as:

$$\left(\frac{\$50 - \$10}{\$50}\right)(1,000) = 800.$$

This is the same figure given in column f.

Antidilutive Options, and Rights, and Warrants   If the fixed exercise or subscription price is higher than the current market price, stock options, rights, and warrants are antidilutive. As such, they are not included in EPS computations. Line 6 of Exhibit 22–5 illustrates this case. The option's exercise price is $60, which is $10 higher than the $50 market price. It is not likely the options would be exercised. If this option were considered exercised, the company would collect $60,000 from the option holder in exchange for 1,000 shares of treasury stock, but the $60,000 could be used to buy 1,200 treasury replacement shares in an open market transaction ($60,000 ÷ $50 market price).[8]

The net effect of this sale/buy back transaction is a 200 share decrease in common stock outstanding. Since common stock outstanding is decreased without a corresponding decrease in net income, EPS will increase. This result makes the option antidilutive under the treasury stock method. Antidilutive securities are never used in computing EPS.

The 20% Limit on Treasury Stock Buy-Back Transactions   In Exhibit 22–5, various amounts of common stock were bought back at $50 (the current market price) to replace treasury shares sold in conjunction with the exercise of stock options. In theory, working with a set market price is reasonable, but if a large number of shares is involved, using a set market price is unrealisitic; the size of the purchase transaction would likely drive the market price higher, rendering the $50 used in the EPS computation invalid.

For this reason, the maximum number of shares presumed to be bought back in the open market for treasury stock replacement purposes must not exceed 20% of the common shares outstanding at the end of the period.

To illustrate, assume the following data applies to the Sandie Corporation:
* The number of shares outstanding at the end of the period is 210,000.
* The weighted average of common shares outstanding is 200,000, and net income after taxes is $500,000. There is no preferred stock.

---

[8] The actual exercise of an option (or any other equity-equivalent security) when the exercise price is above the current market price is rarely encountered since the option holder would immediately sustain a loss.

♦ Stock options (outstanding for the entire year) equal to 100,000 shares are exercisable at a price of $40 per share; the appropriate market price to use under the treasury stock method is $50.

♦ For EPS computation purposes, the assumed exercise would require the issue of 100,000 shares to the option holders, with the company receiving $4 million in exchange.

♦ The $4 million could be used to buy 80,000 shares in the open market ($4,000,000 ÷ $50) were it not for the 20% limit.

♦ Instead, the maximum number of shares allowed to be bought back in the open market is 42,000 shares (210,000 × .20), at a total cost of $2.1 million.

♦ Thus, the net increase in common shares outstanding for EPS computation purposes in this case is 58,000 shares (100,000 shares issued less the 42,000 shares bought back).

♦ This leaves $1.9 million ($4 million − $2.1 million) of excess proceeds.

The excess exercise proceeds not applied to open market stock purchases are treated *as if* they were used first to retire short- or long-term debt,[9] and if this does not exhaust these funds, then to invest in government securities or commercial paper. In this situation, the interest on any debt treated as if it were retired must be added back to net income on a net-of-tax basis. If the debt is assumed to be retired, then there would be no interest on the debt (an expense), and taxes would be higher since the company would not have the interest deduction available. (The numerator of the EPS calculation is affected only if the 20% limit is exceeded.)

To continue with the example, assume the following debt (outstanding the full year) is reported on the company's balance sheet:

Current liabilities
    Short-term 6% interest-bearing notes payable . . . . . $ 800,000
Noncurrent liabilities:
    Long-term 7% mortgage bonds $2,000,000

To determine how the remaining $1.9 million would be used, it is necesssary to establish whether as-if retirement of the short or long-term debt provides a lower EPS number.[10] Retiring short-term debt increases income by less than retiring long-term debt in this case, because the interest on the short-term debt is lower. Assuming a 40% tax rate, the addition to net income for the Framis Corporation is .06($800,000)(1 − .4) + .07 ($1,100,000)(1 − .4) = $75,000. (All the 6% debt is treated as if retired, and $1,100,000 = $1,900,000 − $800,000 of the 7% debt.) Sandie would report an EPS before extraordinary items of ($500,000 + $75,000) ÷ (200,000 + 58,000), or $2.23. EPS before this computation was $500,000 ÷ 200,000, or $2.50.[11]

Below is a summary of the procedures and calculations under the 20% limitation:

1. Determine the EPS figure before considering options or warrants. The result is $2.50 = $500,000 ÷ 200,000.

2. Determine if the potential dilution exceeds 20% of the outstanding common stock at the end of the period. The result is:

$$\frac{\$50 - \$40}{\$50} [100,000] = 80,000$$

This exceeds 42,000 = .20(210,000)

---

[9] To comply with the spirit of *APB Opinion No. 15,* the choice among several qualifying securities at this step should be made in such a way that the lowest possible EPS is reported.

[10] Nonconvertible debt should be considered before convertible debt. Convertible debt will usually dilute EPS and, hence, should not typically be retired by this process.

[11] If the computation using the 20% limit were to increase EPS, the securities would be antidilutive and the options should not be treated as if exercised.

3. Establish the amount of debt that is available to be considered as if retired and the funds that would be available if the options were converted. The result is $2.8 million of debt and $1.9 million of funds.

4. Treat the debt as if retired so as to obtain the maximum dilution in EPS (i.e., in order of the interest rate, lowest rate first). The result is to consider the 6% debt first.

5. Compute the after-tax effect on income from the retirement and add it to the numerator of the EPS calculation. The result is:

$$[.06\ (\$80,000)\ +\ .07\ (\$1,100,000)]\ [1-\text{tax rate}]$$

This equals $75,000 using a 40% tax rate. An entire year's interest is used since the debt was outstanding for the entire year.

6. Determine the total shares outstanding if conversion had taken place. The result is $200,000 + (100,000 - .2(210,000)) = 258,000$.

7. Compute the revised EPS, $(\$500,000 + \$75,000) \div 258,000 = \$2.23$, and report this number if it is less than the EPS number in Step 1 (subject to the 3% rule).

To alter the example, suppose that only $.5 million of 7% bonds were outstanding. Under this change, both debt issues would be treated as retired. The remaining $600,000 of proceeds would then be assumed invested in government securities (U.S. Treasury bills, normally). The purpose in treating the excess exercise proceeds first as debt reductions and then as an investment in government securities (if the excess proceeds extend that far) is that net income after taxes is increased less by interest savings on debt reductions than by the tax exempt incremental interest income from government securities.

Suppose that U.S. Treasury bills earned a 5% return. This would add $30,000 to income since U.S. Treasury bills are tax exempt. The new computation of EPS yields $2.25:

$$\frac{\$500,000\ +\ .06(\$800,000)(1-.4)\ +\ .07(\$500,000)(1-.4)\ +\ \$30,000}{200,000\ +\ 58,000}\ =\ \$2.25$$

Impact of Changes in Market Prices   Because stock prices in the open market fluctuate, it is possible for stock options, rights, and warrants to be classified as dilutive (market price above the exercise price) during one accounting period and antidilutive (market price below the exercise price) during the next period. This fact creates additional computational problems when EPS calculations cover a period longer than a quarter. The issue is covered in the appendix. It is fair to say that market price fluctuations and the ensuing impact on potentially dilutive EPS computations make for tedious, time-consuming detail work in preparing EPS figures.

Convertible Securities

Convertible securities—convertible bonds and convertible preferred stocks—are dilutive if, when the common shares for which they are exchangeable are included in EPS computations, such inclusion causes a decrease in the EPS figure. The same securities are antidilutive if inclusion of the shares resulting from conversion produces an increase in EPS.

The If-Converted Method   The **if-converted method** is used to determine whether a convertible security is dilutive based on the impact of the converted shares on EPS. As with the treasury stock method used for options and warrants, the if-converted method is a hypothetical calculation used for EPS computation purposes only. The premises for the if-converted method are:

1. The securities being tested for their dilutive impact on EPS are assumed to have been converted at the beginning of the current accounting period or at date of

issue during the current period, if later. If a new issue of convertible securities is sold at any point during the current year, the number of as-if conversion shares is weighted by the period over which the new shares are outstanding.[12] The number of total shares used in computing EPS, therefore, includes both the weighted average of common shares then outstanding plus the conversion shares.

2. The interest expense incurred on convertible bonds is eliminated if the bonds are considered converted into common stock, as are the dividends paid on convertible preferred issues. Thus, for EPS computation purposes, net income after-tax is adjusted upward to include interest expense savings (net of any tax effect) and preferred dividend savings (which are not subject to a tax effect adjustment since dividends are paid from after-tax earnings).

Exhibit 22–6 illustrates the computations for a convertible bond debenture issue of 10,000 debentures each with a face value of $100. The debentures are convertible at the rate of two common shares per $100 debenture, yielding a total of 20,000 common shares. A 33% tax rate is assumed for illustrative purposes, and the calculations are made for several different interest rates varying from 4% up to 12%. The debenture is assumed to be outstanding at the start of the accounting period.

For the debenture shown in Exhibit 22–6, if the interest rate paid on the bond is 4%, the annual interest expense would be $40,000. For EPS computation purposes, this amount is added back to income, but only after the tax effect is taken into consideration. In this case, the assumed income tax rate is 33%, which means that if $40,000 were actually added back to income, the tax liability on the added income would be $13,200 (column *d*), leaving a net increase of $26,800 (column *e*).

The middle columns (*f, g, h*) display the information needed to compute EPS based on the common stock outstanding, *exclusive* of the conversion shares. The net after-tax income is $600,000, the number of common shares outstanding is 200,000 and, therefore, EPS is $3.00.

The columns on the right (*i, j, k*), show the computation of EPS, taking into account the increase in income (column *e*) and the 20,000 increase in common stock outstanding that would occur if the bonds are converted. In the first instance, EPS would decline to $2.85 (column *k*) from $3.00 (column *h*). Thus, this convertible bond issue at 4% interest is dilutive and would be included in EPS computations.

Line 4 of Exhibit 22–6 describes the same bond issue, but this time with an interest rate of 10%. Tracing line 4 to the right reveals that if these bonds were converted, EPS would increase to $3.03 from $3.00. Thus, these bonds would be antidilutive. Antidilutive securities are not included in any reported EPS computations, and hence this computation would not be reported. Thus reported EPS would be $3.00.

Exhibit 22–7 illustrates the effect of conversion for a convertible preferred stock. The example assumes 10,000 shares of $100 convertible preferred, convertible at the rate of two common shares for every $100 preferred share, yielding 20,000 shares. The preferred stock is assumed to be outstanding at the start of the accounting period. Two dividend rates, expressed as a percentage of the $100 per share value, are illustrated.

In Exhibit 22–7, the preferred issue of 10,000 shares ($100 par) is convertible into common shares. Each preferred share is equal to two common shares, or 20,000 total common shares (10,000 × 2). If the preferred stock paid a 4% dividend ($4 a share), the full amunt of the $40,000 dividend payout would be added to the $600,000 after-tax income reported in column *f*. There is no tax effect because dividends (unlike interest payments) are paid from after-tax income. In this instance, assuming conversion, the 4% preferred issue would cause a decline in EPS to $2.91 from $3.00. Thus, the issue is dilutive and would be included in EPS computations. In the case of the

---

[12] The partial year is used since it is only during this period that the firm would have additional resources provided by the cash received upon conversion with which to earn.

EXHIBIT 22-6   Schedule of If Converted Method Test Computations for Convertible Bonds

		Convertible Bond Information			Unadjusted Common Stock Information			Adjusted Common Stock Information		
(a)	(b)	(c)	(d)	(e)	(f)	(g)	(h)	(i)	(j)	(k)
Interest Rate	Principle × Amount =	Interest Expense –	33% Tax Effect =	After-Tax Income Adjustment	After-Tax Income Unadjusted ÷	Average Shares Outstanding =	EPS Unadjusted	After-Tax Income Adjusted* ÷	Adjusted Shares Outstanding =	Adjusted EPS
1. .04	× 1,000,000 =	$ 40,000 –	$13,200 =	$26,800	$600,000 ÷	200,000 =	$3.00	$626,800 ÷	220,000 =	$2.85
2. .06	× 1,000,000 =	$ 60,000 –	$19,800 =	$40,200	$600,000 ÷	200,000 =	$3.00	$640,200 ÷	220,000 =	$2.91
3. .08	× 1,000,000 =	$ 80,000 –	$26,400 =	$53,600	$600,000 ÷	200,000 =	$3.00	$653,600 ÷	220,000 =	$2.97
4. .10	× 1,000,000 =	$100,000 –	$33,000 =	$67,000	$600,000 ÷	200,000 =	$3.00	$667,000 ÷	220,000 =	$3.03
5. .12	× 1,000,000 =	$120,000 –	$39,600 =	$80,400	$600,000 ÷	200,000 =	$3.00	$680,400 ÷	220,000 =	$3.09

* Columns e + f.

EXHIBIT 22-7   Schedule of If-Converted Method Test Computations for Preferred Stock

		Convertible Preferred Stock Information			Unadjusted Common Stock Information			Adjusted Common Stock Information		
(a)	(b)	(c)	(d)	(e)	(f)	(g)	(h)	(i)	(j)	(k)
Dividend* Rate	Total Preferred × Par Value =	Dividends Declared –	33% Tax Effect =	After-Tax Income Adjustment	After-Tax Income Unadjusted ÷	Average Shares Outstanding =	EPS Unadjusted	Adjusted After-Tax Income† ÷	Shares Outstanding =	Adjusted EPS
.04	× 1,000,000 =	$ 40,000	None	$ 40,000	$600,000 ÷	200,000 =	$3.00	$640,000 ÷	220,000 =	$2.91
.10	× 1,000,000 =	$100,000	None	$100,000	$600,000 ÷	200,000 =	$3.00	$700,000 ÷	220,000 =	$3.18

* The .04 and .10 dividend rates are equivalent to a $4 and $10 dividend per share ($50 par value), respectively.

† Columns e + f.

same convertible preferred issue, but with a dividend rate of 10% ($10 a share), conversion would increase EPS to $3.18 from $3.00. Thus, this issue is antidilutive and would not be included in EPS computations.

Contingent Common Stock Issues

In addition to potentially dilutive options, rights, and convertible securities, EPS may also be subject to dilution due to the existence of *contingent stock issue agreements*. Normally, such agreements come about in conjunction with corporate acquisitions, buy outs, and business combinations. This result is especially true if the acquiring company's offer includes an exchange of stock (acquired company's shares exchanged for shares in the acquiring company). Sometimes, during the acquisition negotiations the acquiring company offers the acquired company's shareholders the equivalent of bonus shares as an inducement to close the deal.

These bonus shares in the acquiring company are referred to as *contingent-issue shares*. These shares will be issued and distributed to the acquired company shareholders at some point in the future, contingent on the profit performance of the acquired company. Normally, contingent issue shares are issued gratis to the acquired company's shareholders (increasing the number of common shares outstanding). Thus, they are dilutive and would be included in EPS computations.

However, in certain instances, the contingent shares have a purchase price attached to them, typically set far below the price of the stock in the open market at the time the acquisition is negotiated. In such cases, potentially dilutive contingent-issue agreements are treated as corporate option stock for EPS computation purposes. Dilution, therefore, is determined using the treasury stock method.[13]

CONCEPT REVIEW

1. What is the purpose of the if-converted method?
2. What modification is required in the treasury stock method if more than 20% of the outstanding stock is to be purchased?
3. Describe how a potentially dilutive convertible debenture would alter the reporting of EPS.

COMPUTING PRIMARY AND FULLY DILUTED EPS

♦

If a company's capital structure is complex, it must use a dual presentation format to disclose primary EPS and fully diluted EPS. However, relief is provided, as discussed before, if potentially dilutive securities are present but their impact on EPS is less than 3% of the EPS figure computed excluding such securities.

Primary EPS and Common Stock Equivalents

Primary EPS calculates earning per share on the basis of common shares presently outstanding plus common stock equivalents. Common stock equivalents are equity contracts, contingent shares, or convertible securities that are treated as outstanding common shares in computing EPS. Common stock equivalents include three categories of securities:

---

[13] In the event of adverse market price fluctuations, contingent-issue shares might conceivably be antidilutive—if market value declines below the equivalent of the contingent-issue shares' exercise price.

* Corporate options and rights—provided exercise of the security may be made at the discretion of the security holder any point within five years of the EPS reporting date.
* Convertible securities—debentures (bonds) and preferred stocks—provided they meet the 66⅔% effective-yield test explained in detail below. In addition, convertible securities must be exchangeable for common stock at any point within five years of the EPS reporting date.
* Contingent common stock issues in which the earnings level that triggers the issuance of such shares is set at or below the current year's earnings level.

Fully Diluted EPS and Other Dilutive Securities

Fully dilutive EPS calculates earnings per share on the basis of common shares presently outstanding plus common stock equivalents and other dilutive securities. Other dilutive securities include:

* Corporate stock options, subscription rights, and stock warrants that are dilutive, but are not considered common stock equivalents because their exercise feature is not available until after 5 years. Instead, these securities are exercisable within 5 to 10 years from the EPS reporting date.
* Convertible securities that are dilutive, but do not meet the 66⅔% effective-yield test, explained in detail below. Also included are convertible securities that are eligible for conversion within 5 to 10 years from the EPS reporting date.
* Contingent common stock issues in which the earnings level that triggers the issuance of such shares is set above the current year's earnings level.

The relationships between primary EPS and fully diluted EPS, both of which are required if a company's capital structure is complex, and basic EPS which is reported for a simple capital structure are presented in Exhibit 22–4. As shown in this exhibit, primary EPS includes all common stock equivalents, while fully diluted EPS includes both common stock equivalents and other dilutive securities. FDEPS therefore provides a more conservative figure based on the as-if conversion of still additional securities.

The Effect of Corporate Stock Options and Rights

Generally, options, rights, and warrants, are dilutive when the exercise price is below the market price. However, this may not be the case when, for example, special requirements are included in the option contract that involve either the application of the proceeds to retire debt or other securities, or that require the tendering of debt at exercise. When dilutive they are included in primary EPS computations.

In applying the treasury stock method, the market price is a key factor used to determine whether the security is dilutive or antidilutive and, if dilutive, the hypothetical increase in the number of shares outstanding. To be classified as dilutive, the following criterion must be met:

Market price of dilutive security criterion: Under *APB Opinion No. 15,* the market price used in applying the treasury stock method must be higher than the exercise price for substantially all of three consecutive months, with the latest month being the last month of the accounting period for which the EPS computation is being made. The term *substantially* is taken to mean 11 of the 13 weeks in the quarter.

The above three-consecutive-months qualifier coincides with the fact that EPS computations are normally made quarterly in conjunction with interim financial reporting.

When computing the incremental increase in common shares under the treasury stock method in conjunction with primary EPS calculations, the average market price of the common stock over the course of the accounting period is used (quarterly reporting is assumed). This approach contrasts with the fully diluted EPS computation in which the higher of the average market price or closing market price for the quarter is used. The additional shares of stock must be weighted by the fraction of the period during which the options are outstanding and dilutive.

The Effect of Convertible Securities

Convertible debentures (bonds) and convertible preferred stocks are common stock equivalents (CSEs) if they are found to meet the following criterion:

Effective-yield test: The effective-yield test is used to establish whether a convertible security is a common stock equivalent. Convertible securities are classified as common stock equivalents if the effective yield to the security holder *at the time of the security's issuance* is substantially below the yield available on similar securities of the issuer without the conversion feature. This criterion has been interpreted in *SFAS No. 85* to mean that a convertible security—whether bond or preferred stock—is a common stock equivalent if at the time of issuance it has an *effective yield* that is *less than 66⅔%* of the average yield on Aa corporate bonds with similar characteristics but without the conversion option.[14]

If the above effective-yield test is met the convertible security is classified as a CSE and is used in computing primary EPS. If this test is not met, the security is classified as "other dilutive securities" and used in computing fully diluted EPS only. Under the effective-yield test, a convertible security is classified as a CSE or not when issued. Thereafter its classification does not change.

Effective yield must not be confused with a bond's stated interest rate or a preferred stock's stated dividend rate. Only when a bond or preferred stock issue is offered for sale at par value does the yield equal the stated interest or dividend rate. If a bond or preferred stock issue if offered for sale at a premium over par value, its yield will be less than the stated interest or dividend rate. The opposite is true if the security is offered at a discount from par value as shown in Exhibit 22–8.

Exhibit 22–8 illustrates the effective-yield test for a \$1,000 par-value, 10-year, 6% interest paid semiannually, convertible bond offered to the public at several selling prices when the average yield on similar corporate Aa bonds is 9%. When this bond is issued and sold at an initial discount price of \$900 per \$1,000 par value (line 2), the effective yield is 7.4% (column *d*): found by solving \$900 = \$30 (PVA, *i*, 20) + \$1,000 (PV1, *i*, 20) for *i*. Comparing the effective yield to the benchmark yield for Aa corporate bonds (column *e*) proves that the convertible bond's effective yield is equal to 82% of the 9% Aa corporate bond yield in this case. Since 82% exceeds 66⅔%, this convertible bond is not considered to be a CSE and is not included in primary EPS computations. This bond would be classified as an "other dilutive security" and used only in the computation of fully diluted EPS, if dilutive.

Suppose, alternatively, that the bond is being issued and sold at an initial premium price of \$1,100 per \$1,000 par value (line 4). Because of the price premium, the effective yield at 4.7% is only 52% of the 9% yield on Aa corporate bonds of similar maturity. This time, the convertible bond would be classified as a CSE and would be included in the primary EPS computation, if dilutive.

With convertible preferred issues, the same type of schedule can be developed to determine if the effective yield (the annual dividend divided by the issue price) is less

---

[14] If the security does not have a stated maturity date, the effective yield is the security's stated annual interest or dividend payment divided by its market price at issue. If there is no market price available, the test should be based on the fair value of the security. If there is a scheduled change in the interest or dividend rate during the first five years after issue, the lowest scheduled rate should be used.

EXHIBIT 22-8   Schedule of Effective Yields on a $1,000, 10 Year, Six Percent, Convertible Bond versus Aa Corporate Bond Yield

(a) Public Offering Price	(b) Stated Interest Rate	(c) Annual Cash Yield	(d) Effective* Yield	(e) Yield Aa Corporate Bonds	(f) Convertible Bond Effective Yield as a Percent of Aa Corporate Bond Yield	(g) Decision
$800 (discount)	6%	$60	9.1%	9%	101%	Other dilutive security
$900 (discount)	6%	$60	7.4%	9%	82%	Other dilutive security
$1,000 (at par)	6%	$60	6.0%	9%	67%	Other dilutive security
$1,100 (premium)	6%	$60	4.7%	9%	52%	Common stock equivalent
$1,200 (premium)	6%	$60	3.6%	9%	40%	Common stock equivalent

* The discount rate that equates the cash payments of interest semiannually of $30 and a final payment of $1,000 at the end of year ten to the public offering price.

than 66⅔% of the Aa corporate yield, in which case the issue would be classified as a CSE and included in primary EPS, if dilutive. Otherwise the preferred stock would be classified as other dilutive securities and used only in the computation of fully diluted EPS.

Admittedly, use of the Aa corporate yield as a benchmark is arbitrary, as is the 66⅔% demarcation line for classifying convertible bonds and preferred stock issues as either common stock equivalents or other dilutive securities. The logic, however, is fairly easy to understand: If a convertible security is priced to yield a return to the holder that is reasonably close to the return for nonconvertible, straight-debt securities, then the conversion feature is deemed to be subordinate to the security's ability to generate current income. For this reason, conversion of the security is less likely. Such a security is classified as an other dilutive security and is used only in fully diluted EPS computations. However, if a convertible security is priced to yield a return that is substantially below the yield on nonconvertible straight-debt issues, the conversion feature is deemed to be the dominant appeal to the investor, and current income is secondary. This security is classified as a CSE and included in primary EPS because conversion to common stock is likely to occur. The 66⅔% figure is arbitrarily used to make this judgment.

However, there is a flaw in the above logic. If market prices change after the security has been issued, current effective yields will also change. But reclassification of the security is not allowed. Thus, convertible securities initially classified as CSEs will continue to be CSEs even though conversion to common stock is not likely because the yield has risen sufficiently.

In 1985, *SFAS No. 85* changed the test to its present effective yield basis. Prior to that time, the ratio of the annual cash yield (at stated interest rate) to the issue price was used in determining whether or not a convertible security was classified as a CSE. The reason for this change was that low coupon rates and zero coupon bonds caused these issues to be classified as CSEs when there was never any intention of holders converting the issues.

The Effect of Contingent Common Stock

As described earlier, contingent common stock issues are sometimes used in conjunction with corporate acquisitions, buy-outs, and business combinations. The issuance of the contingent common stock (which increases the number of shares outstanding) is dependent on a future event such as the ability of the acquired company to meet target net income goals set by the management of the acquiring company. When the target net income level is reached or exceeded, the shareholders of the acquired company will receive additional shares of the acquiring company's common stock.

EXHIBIT 22-9   Complex Capital Structure—Components of Primary EPS and Fully Diluted EPS

Dual Presentation of EPS for Complex Capital Structure

Primary EPS	Fully Diluted EPS
Include all common stock equivalents as detailed below.	Include all common stock equivalents and all other potentially dilutive securities as detailed below.
Stock options and rights: If dilutive (using treasury stock method) and exercisable within five years	**Stock options, rights, and warrants:** If dilutive (using treasury stock method) and exercisable within 10 years
Convertible securities: If dilutive (using if-converted method) and the effective yield is less than 66⅔% of the Aa corporate bond yield at time of issuance and exercisable within five years	**Convertible securities:** If dilutive (using if-converted method) and exercisable within 10 years
Contingent common stock issues: If dilutive and the contingent goal is met for the current period	**Contingent common stock issues:** If dilutive and the contingent goal is not met for the current period

If the target net income level is set at or below the acquired company's current period net income level, the contingent stock issue is treated as a CSE and is used in computing both primary and fully diluted EPS. If the target level is set above the acquired company's current period net income level, the contingent stock issue is treated as other dilutive securities and is used in computing fully diluted EPS only.

Exhibit 22–9 offers a summary of components used in computing primary EPS and fully diluted EPS for companies having complex capital structures.

CONCEPT REVIEW

1. Describe how the interest rate test is used to classify a convertible security as a common stock equivalent.
2. If a convertible preferred is considered to be a common stock equivalent, what impact does this have on the EPS calculation assuming the conversion effect is dilutive?
3. When are contingent shares considered in computing primary EPS?

PRIMARY AND FULLY DILUTED EPS COMPUTATIONS ILLUSTRATED

The example used here is an extension of the Framis Corporation. The initial data is repeated below and the additional data is given next.

Initial Data: Framis Corporation

	Shares
Capital stock:	
Common stock, par $1, outstanding on January 1, 1991	90,000
Common stock, sold and issued May 1, 1991	6,000
Preferred stock, par $20, 6% (cumulative nonconvertible)	
outstanding on January 1, 1991	2,500
Income data for year ending December 31, 1991:	
Net income before extraordinary items	$124,000
Net extraordinary gain	$ 10,000
Net income	$134,000

Additional Data: Framis Corporation

1. Stock rights entitle stockholders to purchase 2,000 common shares for $20 per share. The market price of the shares has averaged $25 over the current accounting period and has exceeded $20 over the last three months. The market price per share was $24 on December 31, 1991. The rights have been outstanding for the entire accounting period.
2. Convertible preferred, no par, with a $7 annual dividend per share. The stock is cumulative and each preferred share is convertible into eight shares of common. The stock has been outstanding over the entire accounting period. One thousand shares issued at $108 per share are outstanding.
3. Series A convertible bonds, $200,000 outstanding, 8% interest payable annually. Each $1,000 bond is convertible into 30 shares of common. The bonds were issued at par and were outstanding over the entire year.
4. Series B convertible bonds, $500,000 outstanding, 10% interest payable annually. Each $1,000 bond is convertible into 50 shares of common. The bonds were issued at par and were outstanding over the entire year.

The corporate Aa bond rate was 12.6% when each of these securities was issued. A 40% tax rate is assumed for illustration. The conversion feature is exercisable within five years for all securities, and the lowest interest or dividend rate is the one given. (The calculations are based on a yearly period and not all of the complexities discussed in the chapter are covered.)

Computing Primary Earnings per Share

Determining the Number of CSE Shares   The rights are CSEs. The use of the treasury stock method to establish the number of common stock equivalent shares for the Framis Corporations stock rights yields 400 shares:

	Shares
Shares that would be issued upon exercise of rights	2,000
Cash proceeds if rights were exercised, 2,000 rights × $20 (option price) = $40,000.	
Treasury stock shares that could be purchased: $40,000 ÷ $25 at the average market price	(1,600)
Common stock equivalent shares (incremental number of common shares that would be outstanding for PEPS)	400

The determination of CSE status for each convertible issue is established in Exhibit 22–10. The number of common stock equivalent shares under the if converted method is determined in Exhibit 22–11. No computation is necessary in Exhibit 22–11 for the Series B preferred since this security is determined not to be a CSE in Exhibit 22–10.

While the number of CSE shares has now been established, the calculation of PEPS requires further elaboration. A series of steps must be followed with the set of qualifying securities to produce the lowest (most conservative) PEPS number. This procedure, called the dilution-antidilution (D/A) method. The idea is that while all of, say, three securities appear to lower basic EPS, it can be the case that after two securities are considered, the third actually increases EPS. The D/A method provides a way to avoid the effort needed to calculate EPS for all possible combinations needed to find the lowest EPS value.[15]

The Dilution-Antidilution (D/A) Method   The **dilution-antidilution (D/A) method** is used only with complex capital structures and, hence, only in the computation of primary and fully diluted EPS. To attain the maximum dilutive effect, *APB Opinion No. 15* requires that all antidilutive securities be excluded and all dilutive securities be

---

[15] Without some short-cut method, a company with *n* convertible securities needs to make 2^n calculations to identify the lowest EPS amount. With the short-cut method, only *n* calculations are needed. See S. Davidson and R. Weil, "A Shortcut in Computing Earnings per Share," *Journal of Accountancy*, December 1975, pp. 45–47.

EXHIBIT 22-10   Convertible Securities—Interest Rate Test to Identify CSEs: Framis Corporation

	Effective Rate	Decision
1. Aa bond interest rate times ⅔ for comparison		
12.6% × ⅔	8.4%	
2. Effective yield on convertible securities:		
a. Convertible preferred stock, issued at		
$108: Dividend $7 ÷ $108	6.5%	Less than 8.4: CSE
b. Series A convertible bonds payable,		
issued at par:	8.0%*	Less than 8.4: CSE
c. Series B convertible bonds payable,		
issued at par:	10.0%*	Greater than 8.4: not CSE

* The effective rate equals the stated rate because the bonds were issued at par.

EXHIBIT 22-11   Convertible Securities CSEs—If Converted Method: Framis Corporation

	Common Shares if Converted
Convertible securities that qualify as CSEs (See Exhibit 22–10):	
1. Convertible preferred stock (1,000 × 8)	8,000
2. Series A convertible bonds payable (200 × 30)	6,000

included in computing both primary EPS (if a CSE) and fully diluted EPS. Footnote 8 to *APB Opinion No. 15* identifies one exception to this general rule:

> The presence of a common stock equivalent or other dilutive securities together with income from continuing operations and extraordinary items may result in diluting one of the per share amounts which are required to be disclosed on the face of the income statement—i.e., . . . income before extraordinary items, . . . and net income —while increasing another. In such a case, the common stock equivalent or other dilutive securities should be recognized for all computations even though they have an antidilutive effect on one of the per share amounts.

Because of this provision, the D/A test should be made on the *higher* of income before extraordinary items or net income. If the lower amount were used, a security could be labeled incorrectly as antidilutive. The D/A method must be applied at two levels in EPS computations:

1. For primary EPS—A test based on CSEs only.
2. For fully diluted EPS—A test based on all potentially dilutive securities including all CSEs and non-CSEs.

At this point, the discussion is to illustrate primary EPS, so only the level 1 computation above is discussed. Computation 2 is discussed later in conjunction with fully diluted EPS.

When there is more than one CSE security (as in this case), the D/A effect of a security can depend on the order in which the securities are tested for dilution. As a result, all possible combinations of the securities should be tested. The combination yielding the lowest EPS amount would be selected for use in computing primary EPS. If there are many securities to consider, this process can be lengthy. The D/A method provides a shortcut approach. The steps for the D/A method are shown in Exhibit 22–12 and applied to compute primary EPS for Framis in Exhibit 22–13.

Primary EPS for the Framis Corporation is $1.28. In calculating primary EPS, the series A convertible bonds are antidilutive and, hence, excluded from the computation. This fact is known immediately since $1.60 exceeds the $1.31 EPS amount calculated in step 3. However, suppose the ratio for the series A convertible bonds were $1.29. The Series A convertibles would still be antidilutive and should be excluded, but this fact would not be known until the convertible preferred were used to reduce EPS from $1.31 to $1.28, a figure below the assumed $1.29 ratio. This is the situation the D/A method is designed to catch.

Computing Fully Diluted Earnings per Share

APB Opinion No. 15 requires companies to present fully diluted EPS, which is the level of EPS the company would report if all its dilutive outstanding equity contracts and convertible securities were assumed to be converted to common stock. Thus, in addition to CSE securities whose conversion to common stock was assumed for computation of primary EPS, computation of fully diluted EPS also must consider convertible securities that were not classified as CSEs. The purpose of doing so is to show the most conservative EPS amount.

For the Framis Corporation, only one potentially dilutive security (the Series B convertible bonds payable) does not qualify as a CSE. Therefore, in conducting the D/A test for fully diluted EPS, the Series B convertible bonds payable, in addition to the two CSE securities, also must be considered. For fully diluted EPS, the D/A test must reconsider the two convertible securities classified as CSEs for computing primary EPS because a security that was dilutive for primary EPS may be anti-dilutive for fully diluted EPS due to the effect of any other securities that are not CSEs.

Referring back to Exhibit 22–12, a sixth step is added to compute fully diluted EPS:

6. For fully diluted EPS, again perform Step 4 for any additional dilutive securities, starting with the same tentative EPS amount computed in Step 3. This time, however, the comparison of D/A ratio amounts and initial EPS amounts in Step 5 involves all convertible securities (CSEs and non-CSEs). The D/A test for fully diluted EPS is complete when an antidilutive security is found. Fully diluted EPS is the last EPS amount computed.

Steps 1 through 3 are identical for primary EPS and fully diluted EPS. In Step 4 for fully diluted EPS, the D/A ratio is now required for the Series B convertible bonds which were not CSEs. The additional ratio is shown below along with the D/A ratios calculated in Exhibit 22–13 and the new ranking.

	Ratio	Rank Order
a. Convertible preferred	$ .88	1
b. Series A convertible bonds	1.60	3
c. Series B convertible bonds		
[($500,000 × .1 × .60) ÷ (500 × 50)]	1.20	2

Inclusion of the Series B convertible bonds changes the rank order. Because its ratio is lower, the Series B convertible bonds are considered before the Series A convert-

EXHIBIT 22-12   Dilution/Antidilution (D/A) Method for Primary EPS: Framis Corporation

1. Determine net income to common stockholders, (net income minus all preferred dividend claims for the current year).
2. Determine whether equity contracts (e.g., options or warrants) are dilutive.
3. Compute a tentative EPS value based upon net income to common stockholders and assuming the conversion of all dilutive equity contracts to common stock.* "Income to common stockholders" used in this computation should be the higher of income before extraordinary items or net income. (Use of the higher amount increases the probability of identifying a dilutive security.)
4. Compute the D/A ratio for each convertible security. Then rank the respective D/A ratio amounts from lowest to highest.
   The D/A ratio for each convertible security is computed as follows:

$$\text{D/A ratio} = \frac{\text{Effect of assumed conversion on numerator of EPS}}{\text{Effect of assumed conversion on denominator of EPS}} = \frac{\text{Interest expense (net of tax) or preferred dividend amount}}{\text{Number of common shares into which the security can be converted}}$$

5. For primary EPS, consider only convertible securities that are CSEs:
   a. Compare the lowest D/A ratio to the tentative EPS as computed in Step 3. This comparison determines whether this first convertible security is dilutive or antidilutive. The security is dilutive if its D/A ratio is less than tentative EPS. It is antidilutive if its D/A ratio is greater than tentative EPS. If dilutive, assume conversion of the security to common stock and compute a new tentative EPS. Compare this new tentative EPS with the next larger D/A ratio. Repeat this process until an antidilutive security is found or until the list of convertible securities is used.
   b. If the security is antidilutive, the D/A test for primary EPS is complete. All remaining CSEs have higher D/A ratios and, hence, are also antidilutive.
   c. Primary EPS is the last EPS amount computed in Step 5a.

* Equity contracts are treated differently from convertible securities. The common shares associated with dilutive equity contracts are included in the computation of tentative EPS because equity contracts usually directly affect (reduce) only the denominator of the EPS computation. In contrast, the assumed conversion of convertible securities affects both the numerator and the denominator.

EXHIBIT 22-13   D/A Method Used to Calculate Primary EPS: Framis Corporation

1. Net income to common stockholders [$134,000 − ($50,000 × .06) − (1,000 shares × $7)] = $124,000. Basic EPS = $124,000 ÷ (90,000 + 6000 (8/12)) = $1.32.
2. Stock rights are dilutive because they increase the number of shares of common stock (denominator) used to compute EPS by 400 shares.
3. Tentative EPS [$124,000 ÷ 94,400 shares (90,000 shares + 6,000 (8/12) + 400 shares)] = $1.31.
4. D/A ratios of all convertible CSE securities.   **Rank Order**
   a. Convertible preferred stock [(1,000 shares × $7) ÷ 8,000 shares] .... $ .88   1
   b. Series A convertible bonds [($200,000 × .08 × .60) ÷ 6,000 shares]* $1.60   2
5. Primary EPS—comparison of D/A ratio to the tentative EPS calculated in Step 3.
   a. Convertible preferred stock is dilutive because the D/A ratio ($0.88) is less than the tentative EPS is obtained ($1.31); a new tentative EPS [$124,000 + (1,000 × $7)] ÷ (94,400 + 8,000 shares) = $1.28.
   b. Series A convertible bonds are antidilutive because the D/A ratio ($1.60) is more than the new tentative EPS ($1.28) calculated in Step 5a.
   c. Therefore, the primary EPS for net income is $1.28

* The .60 multiplier is 1 minus the tax rate.

EXHIBIT 22-14   D/A Method Used to Calculate Fully Diluted EPS: Framis Corporation: Step 6

a. Convertible preferred stock is dilutive because the D/A ratio amount ($0.88) is less than the tentative EPS ($1.31); the new tentative EPS is the same as in Step 5*a* (Exhibit 22-13), $1.28.

b. Series B convertible bonds are dilutive because the D/A ratio amount ($1.20) is less than the new tentative EPS ($1.28); the new tentative EPS is now changed to [$124,000 + (1,000 × $7) + ($500,000 × .10 × .60* = $161,000)] ÷ (94,000 + 400 + 8,000 + 25,000 shares = 127,400 shares) = $1.26.

c. Series A convertible bonds are antidilutive because the D/A ratio ($1.60) is more than the new tentative EPS ($1.26).

d. Therefore, fully diluted EPS for net income is $1.26

* (1 − tax rate) = (1 − .4).

ible bonds in computing fully diluted EPS. The D/A method for the computation of fully diluted EPS for Framis is presented in Exhibit 22-14.

The Series A convertible bonds are also antidilutive for fully diluted EPS. The stock rights are included in each computation because they are dilutive when the common stock price exceeds the option price. The 3% test is now applied to determine if a dual presentation of EPS is required. Basic EPS for the extended Framis Corporation example is $124,000 ÷ 94,000 = $1.32. If the dilution for either primary or fully diluted EPS is at least 3%, both primary EPS and fully diluted EPS must be reported. The criterion is exceeded and both are reported.

Exhibit 22-15 shows how the amounts obtained in the prior calculations are brought together to compute primary and fully diluted EPS. Consistency between the denominator and numerator is maintained throughout.

Primary EPS (on Net Income)

$$\frac{\$134,000 - \$3,000 - \$7,000 + \$0 + \$7,000}{94,000 + 400 + 8,000} = \frac{\$131,000}{102,400} = \$1.28$$

with columns: Net Income to Common / Stock Rights / Convertible Preferred CSE

Fully Diluted EPS (on Net Income)

$$\frac{\$134,000 - \$3,000 - \$7,000 + \$0 + \$7,000 + \$30,000}{94,000 + 400 + 8,000 + 25,000} = \frac{\$161,000}{127,400} = \$1.26$$

with columns: Net income to Common / Stock Rights / Convertible Preferred CSE / Series B Convertible Bond (Non-CSE)

Fully Diluted EPS and the Treasury Stock Method: A Complexity   Most of the computations for fully diluted EPS, including the number of if-converted shares to add to the denominator and the amount of interest (net of tax) to add back to the numerator of the EPS computation, are the same as in the computation of primary EPS. However, in applying the treasury stock method to equity contracts to compute fully diluted EPS, the ending market price per share of stock is substituted for the average market price used for primary EPS if the ending market price is higher. Thus, when the ending market price is higher, fully diluted EPS is reduced below primary EPS by use of the treasury stock method because less treasury stock can be purchased at the higher price.[16]

[16] The calculation can be involved and is discussed in more detail in the appendix. This complexity was not present in the Framis example because the ending market price was below the average price.

EXHIBIT 22-15   Primary and Fully Diluted EPS (Complex Capital Structure): Framis Corporation

---

Primary EPS

	$\dfrac{\text{Numerator}}{\text{Denominator}}$	= EPS
Income before extraordinary items	$\dfrac{\$124,000^a - \$3,000^b}{94,000^c + 400^d + 8,000^e} = \dfrac{\$121,000}{102,400}$	$= \$1.18$
Extraordinary gain:	$\dfrac{\$10,000^f}{102,400}$	$= \underline{.10}$
Net income:	$\dfrac{\$134,000^g - \$3,000^b}{102,400} = \dfrac{\$131,000}{102,400}$	$= \underline{\underline{\$1.28}}$

Note: Series B convertible bonds were excluded because they were not CSEs based on the interest rate test (Exhibit 22-10). Series A convertible bonds were excluded because they were antidilutive (Exhibit 22-13).

[a]Income before extraordinary items.

[b]Dividend claim of nonconvertible preferred stock ($50,000 × .06).

[c]Average number of common shares actually outstanding during the year [90,000 + 6,000 (8/12)].

[d]CSE shares from stock rights.

[e]CSE shares from convertible preferred stock (1,000 × 8).

[f]Extraordinary gain.

[g]Net income.

Fully Diluted EPS

		= EPS
Income before extraordinary items:	$\dfrac{\$124,000 - \$3,000^a + \$30,000^b}{94,000 + 400^a + 8,000^a + 25,000^c} = \dfrac{\$151,000}{127,400}$	$= \$1.18$
Extraordinary gain:	$\dfrac{\$10,000}{127,400}$	$= \underline{.08}$
Net income:	$\dfrac{\$151,000 + \$10,000}{127,400} = \dfrac{\$161,000}{127,400}$	$= \underline{\underline{\$1.26}}$

Note: Fully diluted EPS includes average common shares actually outstanding, all dilutive CSEs, and all other common shares that could be issued from dilutive securities (series B convertible bonds which are not CSEs, but are dilutive; Exhibits 22-10 and 22-14).

[a]In this example, the CSE securities which are dilutive for primary EPS are also dilutive for fully diluted EPS.

[b]Interest expense (net of income tax) on Series B convertible bonds, ($500,000 × .10 × .60 = $30,000); added back because it is deducted to compute net income.

[c]The if-converted shares from Series B convertible bonds are not CSEs but they are dilutive.

Exhibit 22–16 provides a simplified overview of EPS calculations (e.g., neither the 20% rule nor the effect of a higher end-of-period stock market price is included under the treasury stock method).

CONCEPT REVIEW

1. What steps are necessary to compute primary EPS under the D/A method?
2. What additional step is necessary to compute fully diluted EPS under the D/A method?
3. For the Framis Corporation, is it necessary to report both primary EPS and fully diluted EPS? Why or why not?

EXHIBIT 22-16 Overview of EPS Computations (Simplified).

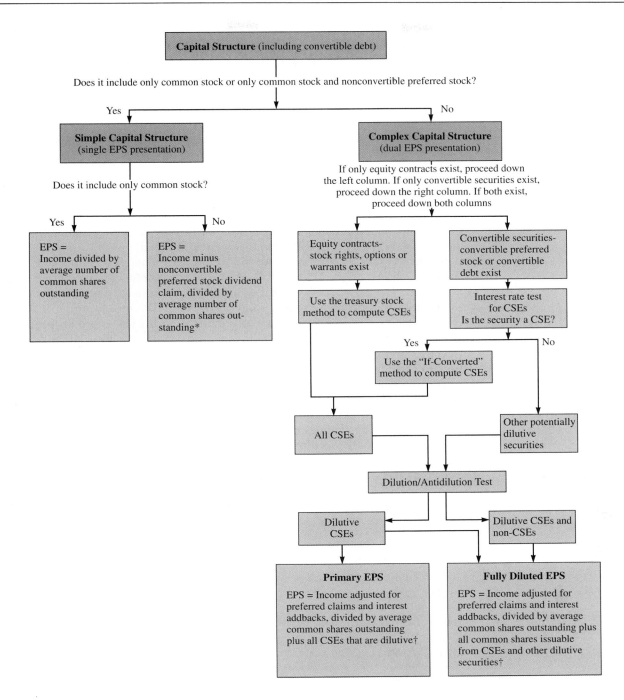

* If the preferred stock is cumulative, deduct the dividends for the current year whether declared or not; if noncumulative, deduct for current year only if declared during the current year.

† If the dilution for primary EPS or fully diluted EPS is at least 3%, both primary EPS and fully diluted EPS are reported.

ADDITIONAL ISSUES IN EPS COMPUTATIONS
♦

Reporting Earnings per Share

APB Opinion No. 15, as amended by *SFAS No. 21,* requires that EPS data be "shown on the face of the income statement" for all periods presented by "publicly held" corporations. In addition, the following information should also be disclosed (paraphrased from *APB Opinion 15,* par. 19 to 21):

* A description, in summary form, that explains the rights and privileges of the various securities outstanding.
* A schedule or note to explain the basis upon which both primary and fully diluted EPS are calculated.
* All assumptions and any resulting adjustments used in calculating the EPS data.
* The number of shares issued upon conversion, exercise, or satisfaction of equity contracts during at least the most recent annual accounting period and any subsequent interim period presented.
* Computations and reconciliations as needed to provide a clear understanding of the manner in which the EPS amounts were computed.

The income statement presentation of the EPS for the extended Framis Corporation example is shown in Exhibit 22–17. Framis Corporation has a complex capital structure involving both CSE securities and other potentially dilutive securities. In this case, it must report both primary and fully diluted EPS unless the 3% test is met. (If Framis Corporation did not have any dilutive securities, it would report EPS assuming no dilution. In this case, Framis would report only basic EPS.)

Because the 3% test is not met, for either primary EPS or fully diluted EPS, Framis Corporation reports both primary and fully diluted EPS. Reporting EPS for income from continuing operations, income before extraordinary items, for the effect of any accounting principle change, and for net income is required. Reporting is optional for both extraordinary items and discontinued operations. Cumulative effects of accounting changes must be shown.

The reporting of EPS is illustrated below for Overseas Shipholding Group, Inc., which has a simple capital structure, and for Boise Cascade Corporation and subsidiaries, which has a complex capital structure.

OVERSEAS SHIPHOLDING GROUP, INC.

	1989	1988	1987
Per share amounts—Note L:			
Net income	$1.46	$1.29	$ .98
Cash dividends declared and paid	$ .50	$ .357	$ .357

Note L—Common Stock, Stock Options and Per Share Amounts:

In October 1989, the Company's Board of Directors authorized a nonqualified stock option plan covering 400,000 of the Company's shares held in its treasury. Options were granted to certain officers of the Company and a subsidiary for the purchase of all the shares covered by the plan, at $13.50 per share, which was less than the fair market value at the date of grant; 10% of the options vest and become exercisable on each December 31 commencing in 1990.

Net income per share is based on the weighted average number of common shares outstanding during each year, 35,697,842 shares (1989), 36,008,000 shares (1988) and 36,126,075 shares (1987), adjusted to reflect the 7-for-5 stock split declared in February 1989. Cash dividends declared and paid per share have also been adjusted for the stock split. The aforementioned stock options have not been included in the computations of net income per share since their effect thereon would not be material.

As of December 31, 1988, paid-in additional capital was charged and common stock credited, retroactively, with the aggregate par value ($10,326,000) of the shares issued in conection with the stock split (based on the number of shares issued at that date). The reduction in paid-in additional capital in 1989 resulted from cash paid in lieu of fractional shares.

EXHIBIT 22-17 Reporting EPS for a Complex Capital Structure—Framis Corporation

---

FRAMIS CORPORATION
Income Statement (partial)
For the Year Ended December 31, 1991

Income before extraordinary items	$124,000
Extraordinary gain (net of income taxes of $6,667)	10,000
Net income	$134,000

Earnings per share (Note X):

	Primary	Fully Diluted
Income before extraordinary items	$1.18	$1.18
Extraordinary gain (net of tax)	.10	.08
Net income	$1.28	$1.26

Notes to the financial statements:

Note X. EPS amounts were computed in conformity with the provisions of *APB Opinion No. 15*, Primary EPS included all dilutive common stock equivalents, based on stock rights and options outstanding (using the treasury stock method), plus those based on convertible securities (using the if-converted method). Fully diluted EPS includes all additional common shares that would be issued for all convertible securities that are dilutive, thus, it represents maximum dilution.

The outstanding stock rights, convertible preferred stock, and Series A convertible bonds payable are determined to be common stock equivalents; however, the Series A convertible bonds have antidilutive effects on both primary and fully diluted EPS and, accordingly, are excluded from consideration as common stock in all EPS computations. The Series B convertible bonds, although not common stock equivalents, are included in the computation of fully diluted amounts. The income amounts are adjusted for the interest (net of income taxes) effects of these securities.

The rights and privileges of the stock rights and the convertible securities are explained in the notes related to those items (refer to the balance sheet).

No shares were issued during the past two years for exercise of stock rights or conversion of convertible securities.

BOISE CASCADE CORPORATION AND SUBSIDIARIES

	1989	1988	1987
Net income per common share (Note 1):			
Primary	$6.19	$6.34	$3.70
Fully diluted	$5.70	$6.15	$3.64

The accompanying notes are an integral part of these financial statements.

Notes to Financial Statements

1. Summary of Significant Accounting Policies

■ *Net Income Per Common Share.* Net income per common share was determined by dividing net income, as adjusted below, by applicable shares outstanding:

	Year Ended December 31		
(*In Thousands*)	1989	1988	1987
Net income as reported:	$267,580	$289,120	$182,990
Preferred dividends declared	(6,943)	(2,333)	(7,050)
Primary income	260,637	286,787	175,940
Assumed conversions:			
Preferred dividends eliminated	6,943	2,333	7,050
Interest on 7% debentures eliminated	4,467	2,992	—
Supplemental ESOP contribution	(4,571)	—	—
Fully diluted income	$267,476	$292,112	$182,990
Average number of common shares:			
Primary	42,100	45,232	47,546
Fully diluted	46,943	47,481	50,219

Notes to the financial statements (see next page)

EXHIBIT 22-17 (concluded)

Primary income excludes preferred dividends, net of a tax benefit applicable to dividends on the Company's Series D ESOP (employees stock ownership plan) preferred stock. The Series D ESOP preferred stock was issued in July 1989. To determine fully diluted income, dividends and interest, net of applicable taxes if any, have been added back to primary income to reflect assumed conversions. Fully diluted income was reduced by the amount of additional after-tax contributions that the Company would be required to make to its ESOP if the Series D ESOP preferred shares were converted to common stock. Primary average shares include common shares outstanding and common stock equivalents, primarily stock options. In addition to common and common equivalent shares, fully diluted average shares include common shares that would be issuable upon conversion of the Company's convertible securities.

A reporting question relating to EPS concerns what should be done if primary EPS (or fully diluted EPS) for income before the cumulative effect of an accounting change is antidilutive while the figure for net income is dilutive when compared to basic EPS. The answer is that when one of the two figures is dilutive, both calculations are reported. In other words, antidilutive securities are *not* excluded from one EPS computation if the effect is dilutive for the other calculation.

For illustration, assume a loss plus an extraordinary gain yield the following results

	Basic EPS	Primary EPS
Income before effect of accounting change	$(.80)	$(.40)
Accounting change	1.80	1.15
Net income	1.00	.75

In this case, primary EPS should be reported for both income (before the accounting change) and for net income since the net income primary EPS figure is dilutive. This is true even though the result for income (before the accounting change) is antidilutive.

Effect of Stock Dividends and Stock Splits with Stock Rights and Convertible Securities

When a company issues additional shares of common stock in a stock dividend or a stock split at the time it has stock rights or convertible securities outstanding, the number of shares of common stock represented by the stock rights or convertible securities, as used in EPS computations, must be adjusted for the effect of the stock dividend or split. For example, assume that Framis Corporation split its common stock two for one after May 1, 1991 when it last issued stock. In this case, the numbers of shares of common stock represented by the outstanding stock rights and convertible securities of Framis would be doubled, as shown in Exhibit 22-18. The numbers of shares of common stock, given in Exhibit 22-18, would be used in all EPS-related computations.

Application of the Treasury Stock Method to Fully Diluted EPS

In applying the treasury stock method to compute primary EPS, the average market price of the stock always is used. In contrast, for computing fully diluted EPS, the ending market price per share of stock is substituted for the average market price per share if the ending market price is higher. This reduces fully diluted EPS below primary EPS by use of the treasury stock method.

To show the effect of a higher end-of-period (versus average) price of common stock subject to stock rights or other stock purchase contracts, assume the price of the common stock of Framis Corporation at December 31 is $40 per share rather than $24 (average for the year is $25). This change would not affect primary EPS. However, it would decrease fully diluted EPS because it would increase the number

EXHIBIT 22-18 Effect of a Stock Split on Convertible Securities: Framis Corporation

Security	Number of Common Shares Used in EPS Computations before 2-for-1 Stock Split	Effect of 2-for-1 Stock Split		Number of Common Shares Used in EPS Computations after 2-for-1 Stock Split
1. Weighted average number of common shares (Exhibit 22–3)	94,000	× 2	=	188,000
2. Stock rights	400	× 2	=	800
3. Convertible preferred stock	8,000	× 2	=	16,000
4. Series A convertible bonds payable	6,000	× 2	=	12,000
5. Series B convertible bonds payable	25,000	× 2	=	50,000

of shares of common stock added to the denominator in the fully diluted EPS computation, as shown next:

Number of CSE shares represented by stock rights for primary EPS . . 400
Number of shares represented by stock rights for fully diluted EPS 1,000*

* Computation:
Shares that would be issued upon exercise of rights 2,000
Cash proceeds if rights were exercised:
  2,000 rights × $20 (option price) = $40,000.
Less: Treasury stock that could be purchased at year-end market price:
  $40,000 ÷ $40 (market price) . . . . (1,000)

Common shares added to denominator in fully diluted EPS computation 1,000

With the above change, Framis Corporation's fully diluted EPS would be computed using 1,000 common stock equivalent shares added to the denominator of the EPS computation (instead of the 400 shares used for computing primary EPS).

Application of Interest Rate Test and If-Converted Method to Convertible Debt Securities Issued at a Premium or Discount

Debt securities, including those that are convertible, are often issued at a premium or a discount. When there is a premium or discount, the effective yield on the debt securities is different from their stated interest rate. Therefore, the interest rate test used to determine whether convertible debt securities are CSEs must be based on their effective yield, taking into account the premium or discount on issue of the convertible debt. Also, the D/A ratio used to identify dilutive securities must be based on the net-of-tax interest expense on the convertible debt, including any related amortization of premium or discount recorded as part of the interest expense on the bonds. Finally, if the convertible debt is dilutive, the net-of-tax interest add-back to the numerator in the EPS computation must include the effect of amortization of the premium or discount.

To show the effect of premium or discount amortization on EPS computations, assume the Series B convertible bonds payable of Framis Corporation were 10-year bonds and were issued to yield 8% instead of 10% (the stated interest rate). The total issue price would then be $567,953 instead of par.[17] Because the effective yield of 8% is less than two thirds of the assumed Aa bond rate (.126 × ⅔ = .084), the Series B

---

[17] $500,000 (PV1, 4%, 20) + $25,000 (PVA, 4%, 20) = $500,000 (.45639) + $25,000 (13.59033) = $567,953. Interest is paid semi annually.

convertible bonds are CSEs. The interest effect of the bonds on primary EPS would be computed based on the effective interest rate applied to the net carrying value of the bonds each period if the interest method of amortization were used. If the straight-line method of amortization were used, the yearly interest effect would be:

Cash interest ($500,000 × .10) $50,000
Amortization of premium (straight-line):
   Issue price $567,953 − $500,000 = $67,953 premium
   Premium amortization ($67,953 ÷ 10 years) 6,795
Pretax interest expense 56,795
Multiply by the effect of the tax rate (1 − .40 = .60) . . . . . . × .60
Interest effect $34,077

The interest effect would be included in the numerator of primary (and/or fully diluted) EPS computations assuming Series B convertible bonds are dilutive.

A Final Comment

Despite the inordinate attention given to these numbers in the financial press and, hence, the concerns on management's part over these numbers, it is extraordinarily difficult to evaluate just what these numbers mean. For example, does either the magnitude or trend of EPS values indicate the effectiveness with which management uses the resources entrusted to its care?

A firm's asset structure changes through operations and through acquisitions, making comparisons over time difficult at best. Reported EPS is not simply the earnings per share of common stock outstanding. Instead, weighted averages are used, and some securities (bonds and preferred) may be considered as if converted to common. Further, common stock equivalents are not necessarily more likely to be converted into common stock than non-CSEs. Moreover, firms may engage in activities merely to influence the year's EPS figures. One firm sold off some of its extensive land holdings each year so that the gain on sale allowed it to achieve a constant EPS growth rate. The felt need by some firms to attain their own EPS goals and those of analysts adds to the pressures. Thus one well-known firm has reported nearly 60 years now of quarterly increase in EPS. The firm considers it necessary to report continued increases.

EPS calculations are extensive, and their meaning is sufficiently questionable that many accountants believe the reliance placed on them is unwarranted. Further, using EPS as an important element in a firm's goal structure contributes to a short-term management attitude that can be detrimental to the long-term productivity and financial health of the firm.

Nevertheless, EPS computations are regularly reported and anxiously awaited by stockholders, financial pundits, and management. Therefore, knowledge of how EPS is calculated is essential if intelligent use is to be made of the resulting figures.

CONCEPT REVIEW

1. What income amounts must also be reported in EPS form?
2. How are stock dividends and splits handled in EPS computations when they occur during the accounting period?
3. What additional complexity is introduced when the market price of the stock at the end of the accounting period exceeds the average market price over the accounting period and both exceed the exercise price?

SUMMARY OF KEY POINTS

◆

(L.O. 1)   1. Earnings per share figures are watched closely by investors and by regulators because they have an important impact on the movement of stock market prices.

(L.O. 2)   2. The computation of EPS is based on whether a firm has a simple or complex capital structure. Simple capital structures do not involve common stock equivalents or other potentially dilutive securities.

(L.O. 2)   3. The EPS calculation divides return to common by the weighted average of the outstanding common shares. For simple capital structures this result is called basic EPS in this text.

(L.O. 3, 7)   4. Common stock equivalents (CSEs) include options, other equity contracts, and convertible securities whose effective yield at time of issue is less than two thirds of the return on corporate Aa bonds. Primary EPS recognizes the impact of treating these securities as additional outstanding shares if their inclusion reduces basic EPS (i.e., they are dilutive). In making this calculation, any impact the conversion would have on income to common (the deletion of preferred dividends or interest net of tax) must be recognized in the numerator of the EPS calculation.

(L.O. 4)   5. Convertible securities that are not common stock equivalents but that are dilutive are considered in addition to CSEs in computing fully diluted EPS.

(L.O. 5)   6. The treasury stock method is used to establish the impact of dilutive options on the denominator of the EPS calculation. The number of shares resulting from the assumed exercise of the options is reduced by using the funds obtained on exercise to purchase shares in the market at the period's average market price. (The year-end price, if higher, is used for fully diluted EPS).

(L.O. 8)   7. The effective-yield test is used to determine if a convertible bond or preferred stock is a CSE.

(L.O. 8)   8. The efficient procedure for calculating primary and fully dilutive EPS is the dilutive antidilutive (D/A) method. This method assures that antidilutive securities do not inadvertently lead to an increase in reported EPS.

(L.O. 9)   9. The EPS calculations required to use the treasury stock method on a quarterly basis are complex and extensive.

REVIEW PROBLEM

◆

1. A company with 100,000 shares of common stock at the start of the year declares a 3-for-1 stock split halfway through the year and, the next day, issues 200,000 new shares in conjunction with the acquisition of a new plant. What is the effect on EPS?

2. On March 31 when the corporate Aa bond rate is 15%, the company issues:

   a. 10,000 shares of nonconvertible, noncumulative preferred paying a $10 dividend per share. The firm receives $1,000,000.

   b. $500,000 of 9% convertible bonds are issued at par. Each $100 bond is convertible into 2 shares of common.

   If the company reports on a calendar year basis, what is the impact on primary EPS, assuming any common stock equivalents are dilutive?

3. Assume in (2) that the convertible bonds have warrants attached that allow holders immediately to subscribe to one common share for each bond at $25 per share. The average market price of the stock during the period over which the options are exercisable was $40. What is the effect on primary EPS?

4. Suppose in (3) that the stock price at the end of the year is $50. What impact is there on fully diluted EPS?

5. Suppose in (2) that the corporate bond rate on March 31 was 12%. What would the effect on EPS be?

SOLUTION

◆

1. The effect is entirely on the denominator. The stock split means that 300,000 shares are now outstanding. Since no new assets are involved, the 300,000 shares are assumed to be outstanding the entire year. The issue of 200,000 shares for the

new plant, is outstanding for only half the year since only during this period does management have additional assets on which to earn. The denominator for all reported EPS calculations in this year's report is:

$$300,000 + 1/2(200,000) = 400,000$$

2. The nonconvertible preferred is not a potentially dilutive security. The only effect for all EPS calculations is to subtract the dividend from net income. Thus, $10(10,000) 3/4 = $75,000 is subtracted from the numerator in all of this year's EPS calculations. The preferred dividend is only paid this year for three fourths of the year, April 1 to December 31.

   The 9% convertible bond is a CSE since $.09 < 2/3(.15)$. Hence, for this year's primary EPS, the bond is treated as if converted. Since it is dilutive, the effects of assumed conversion are as follows:

   Add to the numerator: $.09($500,000)(3/4)(1 - t)$.

   Add to the denominator: $2($500,000 \div $100)(3/4)$.

   The convertible bond is outstanding for only three fourths of the year and results in a change in the outstanding debt and stock if converted.

3. The warrants affect only the denominator and are CSEs since they are immediately exercisable. The effect on this year's primary EPS is obtained using the treasury stock method. The number of shares added to the denominator in the calculation of this year's primary EPS is:

$$3/4\{($500,000 \div $100) - [$25($500,000 \div $100)] \div $40\}$$
$$= 3/4(5,000 - 3,125) = 1,406 \text{ shares}$$

   The warrants are only outstanding for three fourths of the year.

4. The effect on fully diluted EPS is obtained using the end-of-period stock price since it exceeds the average stock price. The effect on the denominator is to add:

$$3/4[5,000 - $25(5,000) \div $50] = 1,875 \text{ shares}$$

5. In this case, the convertible bonds are not CSEs since $.09 > 2/3(.12)$. Therefore, they are not considered in calculating primary EPS. For fully diluted EPS, the bonds are considered if their effect is dilutive. If dilutive, the additions to the numerator and denominator of the EPS calculation are identical to those given in the answer to Question 2.

APPENDIX: *Using the Treasury Stock Method*

EPS is reported for any period for which net income is reported. However, if the treasury stock method is in use and the reporting period exceeds three months, a separate computation is made for each quarter for which the options are outstanding and for which a dilutive effect is present.

For example, assume that a firm had 25,000 shares of common outstanding for the year and also had granted options at the end of the first quarter that resulted under the treasury stock method in:

1st quarter:	No incremental shares (options not issued):
2nd quarter:	500 incremental shares.
3rd quarter:	No incremental shares (effect antidilutive due to market price).
4th quarter:	1,100 incremental shares.

The weighted average of shares for primary EPS would be 25,400:

$$\frac{25,000 + 25,500 + 25,000 + 26,100}{4}$$

To compute fully diluted EPS, an addition to the shares computed above is required if, under the treasury stock method, the stock price at the end of the quarter exceeds the average price used to compute primary EPS.

Consider the following example: Stock options are outstanding to obtain 5,000 shares of common at an exercise price of $10 per share. The average and ending market prices are as follows:[18]

	Average Market Price	Ending Market Price
First quarter	$11.11	$12.00
Second quarter	9.75	11.00
Third quarter	13.89	14.00
Fourth quarter	12.50	13.00

For primary EPS, the calculation of the incremental shares to reflect the dilutive effect is:

First quarter:	$5,000 - (5,000 \times \$10) \div \$11.11 =$	500
Second quarter:	Antidilutive	0
Third quarter:	$5,000 - (5,000 \times \$10) \div \$13.89 =$	1,400
Fourth quarter:	$5,000 - (5,000 \times \$10) \div \$12.50 =$	1,000
Incremental shares:	$(500 + 0 + 1,400 + 1,000) \div 4 =$	725

For fully diluted EPS, the calculation of the incremental shares to reflect the additional dilution is:

First quarter:	$5,000 - (5,000 \times \$10) \div \$12.00 =$	833
Second quarter:	$5,000 - (5,000 \times \$10) \div \$11.00 =$	455
Third quarter:	$5,000 - (5,000 \times \$10) \div \$14.00 =$	1,429
Fourth quarter:	$5,000 - (5,000 \times \$10) \div \$13.00 =$	1,154
Incremental shares:	$(833 + 455 + 1,429 + 1,154) \div 4 =$	968

If the ending market price in the fourth quarter had been $12.00, the computation of fully diluted EPS would have used the $12.50 average market price value.

When options are exercised during a quarter, the treasury stock method is applied to those shares for the portion of the period up to the exercise date. For primary EPS, the average market price during the period up to the exercise date is used. Incremental shares are weighted for the period outstanding but not exercised. (Exercised shares are weighted by the period outstanding.) For fully diluted EPS, however, the computation for the period prior to exercise is based on the market price of the common at the exercise date if the options were exercised regardless of whether the results are dilutive or antidilutive.

When the price of the stock fluctuates above and below the exercise price during the quarter, it becomes difficult to ascertain if the average market price exceeds the exercise price "for substantially all of the three consecutive months with the last month being the last month of the period." The FASB has ruled that if the market price is above the exercise price for 11 of the 13 weeks in the quarter, the options or warrants are assumed to be CSEs. A simple average of daily or weekly closing prices can be used to compute the average price.

KEY TERMS

Antidilutive securities (1232)
Basic EPS (1229)
Common stock equivalents (1231)
Complex capital structure (1229)
Dilution/Antidilution (D/A) method (1245)
Dilutive securities (1232)
Effective-yield test (1242)

Fully diluted EPS (1231)
If-converted method (1237)
Primary EPS (1231)
Simple capital structure (1229)
The 3% test (1231)
Treasury stock method (1233)

QUESTIONS

1. What is the basic difference in EPS computations and reporting between a simple capital structure and a complex capital structure?
2. What is a common stock equivalent? How do common stock equivalents affect EPS computations?

---

[18] See FASB, *Accounting Standards. Original Pronouncements Issued through June 1973* (Homewood, Ill.: Richard D. Irwin, 1987), pp. 426–28.

3. What is the 3% materiality rule in EPS computations and how is it used?
4. Contrast primary EPS and fully diluted EPS.
5. Explain the treasury stock method.
6. What is the interest rate test and when is it used?
7. What is the difference between a dilutive security and an antidilutive security? Why is the distinction important in EPS computations?
8. A company split its common stock 2 for 1 on June 30 of its accounting year ended December 31. Before the split, there were 4,000 shares of common stock outstanding. How many shares of common stock should be used in computing EPS? How many shares of common stock should be used in computing a comparative EPS amount for the preceding year?
9. Explain why nonconvertible securities do not cause a complex capital structure, while convertible securities do cause a complex capital structure.
10. Explain why and when dividends on nonconvertible preferred stock must be subtracted from income to compute EPS in both simple and complex capital structures.
11. Suppose that a common stock equivalent, together with the presence of extraordinary items, causes one of the per share amounts that must be reported to be dilutive while the other per share amounts that must be reported to increase. What reporting is required?
12. Suppose a convertible bond is considered to be a common stock equivalent under the interest rate test. What additional calculations must be made to establish the impact on EPS?
13. What is the D/A method and why is it useful?
14. What are contingent shares and do they need to be considered in figuring EPS?

EXERCISES

E 22-1
Analyze the Capital Structure: Average Shares, Compute EPS (L.O. 2)

At the end of 1991 the records of Nickle Corporation reflected the following:

Common stock, par $5, authorized 500,000 shares:	
Outstanding 1/1/1991, 300,000 shares	$1,500,000
Sold and issued 4/1/1991, 2,000 shares	10,000
Issued 10% stock dividend, 9/30/1991, 30,200 shares	151,000
Preferred stock, 6%, par $10, nonconvertible, noncumulative, authorized 50,000	
shares, outstanding during year, 20,000 shares	200,000
Contributed capital in excess of par, common stock	180,000
Contributed capital in excess of par, preferred stock	100,000
Retained earnings (after the effects of current preferred dividends declared	
during 1991)	640,000
Bonds payable, 6½%, nonconvertible	1,000,000
Income before extraordinary items	182,000
Extraordinary loss (net of tax)	(18,000)
Net income	164,000
Average income tax rate, 40%.	

Required:

1. Is this a simple or complex capital structure? Explain.
2. What kind of EPS presentation is required? Explain.
3. Compute the required EPS amounts (show computations).
4. Compute the required EPS amounts, assuming the preferred is cumulative.

E 22-2
Analyze the Capital Structure: Average Shares, Compute EPS (L.O. 2)

The records for Potter Corporation, at the end of 1991, reflected the following:

Common stock, nopar, authorized 500,000 shares:	
Outstanding at beginning of year, 100,000 shares	$200,000
Sold and issued during the year, September 1, 3,000 shares	8,000
Preferred stock, 9%, par $10, nonconvertible, cumulative, authorized 20,000 shares,	
outstanding during the year, 6,000 shares	60,000
Contributed capital in excess of par, preferred stock	5,000
Retained earnings	150,000
Bonds payable, 6½%, nonconvertible	400,000
Income before extraordinary items	130,000

Extraordinary gain (net of tax)   20,000
Net income   150,000

Required:

1. Is this a simple or complex capital structure? Explain.
2. What kind of EPS presentation is required? Explain.
3. Compute the required EPS amounts (show computations).
4. Compute the required EPS amounts, assuming the preferred stock is noncumulative, the current year's dividend has not been declared, and the preceding year's dividend was passed (i.e., not declared).

E 22-3

Compute EPS for Three Years: Stock Dividend and Split

(L.O. 2)

Rambo Corporation's accounting year ends on December 31. During these three recent years, its common shares outstanding changed as follows:

	1993	1992	1991
Shares outstanding, January 1	150,000	120,000	100,000
Sale of shares, 4/1/1991			20,000
25% stock dividend, 7/1/1992		30,000	
2-for-1 stock split, 7/1/1993	150,000 *		
Shares sold, 10/1/1993	50,000		
Shares outstanding, December 31	350,000	150,000	120,000
Net income	$375,000	$330,000	$299,000

* For each share turned in, two new shares were issued so that the shares doubled.

Required:

1. For purposes of calculating EPS at the end of each year, for each year independently, determine the number of shares outstanding.
2. For purposes of calculating EPS at the end of 1993, when comparative statements are being prepared on a three-year basis, determine the number of shares outstanding for each year.
3. Compute EPS for each year based on year computations in (2).

E 22-4

Analyze the Capital Structure: Stock Dividend, Compute EPS

(L.O. 2)

At the end of 1991 the records of Alert Corporation showed the following:

Common stock, nopar, authorized 250,000 shares:
  Outstanding 1/1/1991, 84,000 shares $420,000
  Purchased treasury shares 4/1/1991, 4,000 shares (at cost) . . . .   (92,000)
  Issued a 100% stock dividend on 12/1/1991 on outstanding shares
  (80,000 additional shares).

Preferred stock, par $10:
  Class A, 6% nonconvertible, noncumulative, outstanding 20,000 shares   200,000
  Class B, 8%, nonconvertible, cumulative, outstanding 40,000 shares   400,000
Contributed capital in excess of par, preferred stock   200,000
Retained earnings (no dividends declared in 1991)   570,000
Bonds payable, 7%, nonconvertible   120,000
Income before extraordinary items   360,000
Extraordinary gain (net of tax)   24,000
Net income   384,000
Average income tax rate, 40%.

Required:

1. Is this a simple or complex capital structure? Explain.
2. What kind of EPS presentation is required? Explain.
3. Compute the required EPS amounts (show computations).

E 22-5

Compute Primary EPS: Different Kinds of Gains and Losses

(L.O. 3)

To illustrate EPS reporting for various combinations of gains and losses, assume 1,000 weighted-average shares of common stock for primary EPS are outstanding for the five cases given below.

Items	Case A (All Gains)	Case B (All Losses)	Case C (Mixed)	Case D (Mixed)	Case E (Mixed)	Case F (Mixed)
Income (loss)	$10,000	$(10,000)	$10,000	$(10,000)	$(10,000)	$10,000
Extraordinary items (loss)	6,000	(6,000)	(6,000)	6,000	6,000	(6,000)
Discontinued operations (loss)	3,000	(3,000)	(3,000)	3,000	(3,000)	(6,000)
Net income (loss)	$19,000	$(19,000)	$ 1,000	$ (1,000)	$ (7,000)	$ (2,000)

Required:

Compute primary EPS.

E 22-6
The 3% Materiality Test and Dilution Effects
(L.O. 3, 7)

Refer to Exercise 22-5: If the weighted-average number of shares outstanding for basic EPS were 800, should basic EPS be reported instead of primary EPS in any of the five cases? If so, in which one(s)?

E 22-7
Computing and Reporting Fully Diluted EPS: Different Kinds of Gains and Losses
(L.O. 4)

Using the data in 22-5, assume a complex capital structure and that the weighted-average number of shares outstanding for fully diluted EPS is 1,500 and that the income and loss amounts are $12,000 instead of $10,000 for Cases A to F. In Case F assume an EO gain of $9,000.

Required:

1. Compute FDEPS for each case.
2. Give a proof for each result in Requirement 1.
3. Assuming dilution compared to basic EPS exceeds 3% in all cases where the FDEPS is less than basic EPS, what EPS numbers would the company report?
4. Suppose that extraordinary items produced a gain of $9,000 in Case D. What is the proper reporting?

E 22-8
Complex Capital Structure and Reporting EPS
(L.O. 3, 4)

The Ratelli Company has the following situation:

Operating income	$(1,000,000)
Extraordinary item	2,000,000
Net income	$1,000,000

Shares Outstanding:

For basic EPS	1,000,000
For primary EPS	1,200,000
For fully-diluted EPS	1,500,000

Income adjustments to be made to:

	Operating Income	Net Income
For primary EPS	$100,000	$100,000
For fully-diluted EPS	$200,000*	$200,000*

* For fully diluted EPS, the $200,000 replaces rather than adds to the $100,000.

Required:

What EPS figures would Ratelli report? What are their values?

E 22-9
Complex Capital Structure and Reporting EPS under the 3% Materiality Test
(L.O. 3, 4)

The Jones Company faces the following situation:

Operating income	$1,000,000
Extraordinary item	(20,000)
Net income	$980,000

Shares Outstanding:

For basic EPS	1,000,000
For primary EPS	1,060,000
For fully-diluted EPS	1,100,000

Income adjustments to be made to:

	Operating Income	Net Income
For primary EPS	$50,000	$50,000
For fully-diluted EPS	$80,000*	$80,000*

* For fully diluted EPS, the $80,000 replaces rather than adds to the $50,000.

Required:

What EPS figures would Jones Company report? What are their values?

E 22-10
Contingent Shares and Computing EPS
(L.O. 3, 4)

In 1991, Xonacs acquired Realtest Service. The acquisition agreement included a commitment by Xonacs to the shareholders of Realtest that if 1992 net income exceeded $250,000, an additional 50,000 shares of Xonacs stock would be issued to the shareholders in 1993. Realtest's net income in 1991 was $250,000.

Required:

1. Must Xonacs recognize the contingent shares in its 1991 EPS calculations?
2. Suppose Realtest's earnings in 1991 were $200,000. Would your answer be different?

E 22-11
Options and the Computation of EPS
(L.O. 3, 4, 5, 6)

Caball Inc. had a net income of $600,000. During the year in question, 160,000 shares were outstanding on average. During the year, Caball's common stock sold at an average market price of $50, but at year's end it was selling for $70. In addition, Caball had 20,000 options outstanding to purchase a total of 20,000 shares at $25 for each option exercised.

Required:

1. Are the options dilutive?
2. Compute primary and fully diluted EPS.

E 22-12
Convertible Bonds and the Calculation of Primary and Fully Diluted EPS
(L.O. 1, 2, 6, 7)

Shaffer Corporation issued 100, $1,000, 10% convertible bonds in 1989. Each bond is convertible into 100 shares of common. At the time the bonds were issued, the average Aa corporate bond yield was 12%. Shaffer's net income for 1991 is $1,824,000 ($3,040,000 before tax). If you consider all factors except convertible bonds, average common shares outstanding for 1991 are:

PEPS: 1,010,000.

FDEPS: 1,033,000.

Required:

1. Compute PEPS.
2. Compute FDEPS.
3. How would you answer (1) and (2) if the bonds were issued July 1, 1991?
4. How would the answers to (1) and (2) change if half the bonds were converted July 1, 1991?

E 22-13
Analyze Capital Structure: Stock Split, Convertible Securities, Compute EPS
(L.O. 3, 4, 6, 7)

At the end of 1991, the records of Ruso Corporation reflected the following:

Common stock, nopar, authorized 250,000 shares; issued and outstanding throughout the period to 12/1/1991, 60,000 shares. A stock split issued 12/1/1991 doubled outstanding shares	$840,000
Preferred stock, 5%, par $10, nonconvertible, cumulative, nonparticipating, shares authorized, issued, and outstanding during year, 10,000 shares	100,000
Contributed capital in excess of par, preferred stock	30,000
Retained earnings (no cash or property dividends declared during year)	570,000
Bonds payable, 8%, issued 1/1/1991, each $1,000 bond is convertible into 60 shares of common stock after the stock split on 12/1/1991 (bonds initially sold at par)	200,000

Income before extraordinary items 86,000
Extraordinary loss . . . . (14,000)
Net income 72,000
Average income tax rate, 30%.
Aa bond interest rate (at date of issuance of bonds), 15%.

Required:

1. Is this a simple or complex capital structure? Explain.
2. What kind of EPS presentation is required? Explain.
3. Compute the required EPS amounts (show computations, rounded to two decimal places, and assume all amounts are material).

E 22–14

Analyze Capital Structure: Nonconvertible Preferred, Stock Rights, Compute EPS

(L.O. 3, 4, 5, 6)

The records of Thermal Corporation as of December 31, 1991, showed:

Common stock, par $10, authorized 400,000 shares, issued and
  outstanding during 1991, 200,000 shares $2,000,000
Contributed capital in excess of par, common stock 300,000
Common stock rights outstanding (for 20,000 shares of common stock) 200,000
Preferred stock, 8%, par $100, nonconvertible, cumulative:
  authorized, 40,000 shares, outstanding during 1991, 10,000 shares 1,000,000
Contributed capital in excess of par, preferred stock 400,000
Retained earnings 7,000,000
Net income (no extraordinary items) 2,000,000

Additional data: Common stock rights issued on April 1, 1991; option price, $15 per share; average market price of common stock during the period (i.e., 4/1/1991–12/31/1991) the rights were outstanding, $25; market price of common stock on 12/31/1991, $28.

Required:

1. Is this a simple or complex capital structure? Explain.
2. Prepare the required EPS presentation for 1991. Show all computations. Disregard the optional 3% materiality test.

E 22–15

Analyze Capital Structure: Stock Rights, Preferred Stock, Compute EPS

(L.O. 3, 4, 5, 6, 7, 8)

At the end of 1991 the records of Wolverine Corporation reflected the following:

Common stock, par $10; authorized 100,000 shares; issued and outstanding
  throughout the year, 50,000 shares $500,000
Stock rights outstanding (all year for 10,000 shares of common stock at
  $15 per share) 100,000
Preferred stock, par $50, 7%, cumulative, convertible into common stock share
  for share, authorized, 10,000 shares; issued and outstanding throughout
  year, 2,000 shares 100,000
Contributed capital in excess of par, common stock 80,000
Retained earnings (no dividends declared during the year) 470,000
Bonds payable, 10%, nonconvertible 150,000
Income before extraordinary items 85,000
Extraordinary gain (net of tax) 35,000
Net income 120,000
Average income tax rate, 30%.
Average market price of the common stock during 1991, $25 per share.
Market price of common stock on 12/31/1991, $22 per share.
Aa bond interest rate at date of issuance of preferred stock, 10%.

Required:

1. Is this a simple or complex capital structure? Explain.
2. What kind of EPS presentation is required? Explain.
3. Compute the required EPS amounts (show computations and assume all amounts are material).

PROBLEMS

P 22-1
Analyze Capital
Structure: Stock
Dividend, Convertible
Securities, Compute EPS
(L.O. 3, 4, 6, 7, 8)

At the end of 1991, the records of Johnson Corporation showed:

Common stock, nopar, authorized 400,000 shares:
Outstanding 1/1/1991, 200,000 shares	$1,650,000
Treasury shares acquired 6/1/1991, 1,000 shares (at cost)	(15,000)
Stock dividend issued, 11/1/1991, 19,900 shares	
(10%, one additional share for each 10 shares outstanding)	398,000
Preferred stock, 4%, par $20, noncumulative, nonconvertible, authorized,	
issued, and outstanding throughout the year, 10,000 shares	200,000
Contributed capital in excess of par, preferred stock	75,000
Retained earnings (no cash or property dividends declared during 1991)	942,000
Bonds payable, Series A, 7%, each $1,000 bond is convertible	
to 20 shares of common stock after stock dividend	
(bonds issued at par)	50,000
Bonds payable, Series B, 6%, each $1,000 bond is convertible	
to 57 shares of common stock after stock dividend	
(bonds issued at par)	400,000
Income before extraordinary gain	380,000
Extraordinary gain (net of tax)	15,000
Net income	395,000

Average income tax rate for 1991, 30%.
Aa bond interest rate at date of issuance of: 7% bonds, 15%; 6% bonds, 9%.
Both bond series were issued prior to January 1, 1991.

Required:

1. Is this a simple or complex capital structure? Explain.
2. Prepare the EPS presentation with all supporting computations.

P 22-2
Analyze Capital
Structure: Stock Rights
and Convertible
Securities, Compute EPS
(L.O. 3, 4, 5, 6, 7, 8)

Jiffie Corporation is developing its EPS presentation at December 31, 1991. The records of the company provide the following information:

Liabilities

Convertible bonds payable, 7% (each $1,000 bond is convertible	
to 100 shares of common stock)	$150,000

Stockholders' Equity

Common stock, nopar, authorized 100,000 shares:	
Outstanding 1/1/1991, 59,000 shares	214,000
Sold and issued 10,000 shares on 4/1/1991	40,000
Common stock rights outstanding (all year for 4,000 shares	
of common stock)	16,000
Preferred stock, par $10, 6%, cumulative, convertible	
(each share is convertible into ½ of 1 share of common stock),	
authorized 10,000 shares, outstanding	
during 1991, 5,000 shares	50,000
Contributed capital in excess of par, preferred stock	15,000
Retained earnings	452,000
Income before extraordinary items	110,000
Extraordinary gain (net of tax)	20,000
Net income	130,000

Additional data:

a. Stock rights—option price, $4 per share; average market price of the common stock during 1991, $6; market price of common stock on 12/31/1991, $7.
b. Convertible bonds—issue price, par.
c. Aa bond interest rate on dates of issuance of all convertible securities, 8%.
d. Average income tax rate, 30%.

Required:

1. Is this a simple or complex capital structure? Explain.
2. What kind of EPS presentation is required? Explain.

3. Prepare the required EPS presentation for 1991. Show all computations.
4. Were there any antidilutive securities? How was this determined?
5. How should antidilutive securities be treated in the computations of EPS? Why?

P 22–3
Complex Capital Structure—Partial Year, 20% Rule, Compute EPS for Two Alternatives
(L.O. 3, 4, 5, 6)

Falcon Company has a compensatory stock option plan under which options to buy 255,000 common shares were issued in 1991. These options are exercisable during 1992 and 1993 at $16 per share. In 1992, Falcon reported net income of $500,000; the company's capital structure remained unchanged that year.

Outstanding stock consists of 1 million common shares, which traded at an average price of $20 per share throughout 1992. The company's long-term debt consists of a $2,500,000 bond issue sold at par, which pays 12% annual interest and was outstanding throughout 1992. Falcon had no other indebtedness. Falcon's average income tax rate is 30%.

Required:

1. Compute primary EPS for 1992.
2. Suppose the facts given above are modified as follows: Falcon issued the stock options on July 1, 1992. The per share market price of Falcon's stock averaged $20 throughout the last quarter of 1992. Compute primary EPS for 1992. Ignore the 3% materiality rule.

P 22–4
Analyze Capital Structure: Convertible Bonds Sold at a Premium, Compute EPS
(L.O. 3, 4, 6, 7, 8)

At the end of 1991, the records of Mathias Corporation reflected the following information:

Common stock, nopar, authorized 500,000 shares:	
Outstanding 1/1/1991, 150,000 shares	256,000
Sold and issued on 8/1/1991, 15,000 shares	30,000
Bonds payable, 6% convertible	100,000
Premium on bonds payable	9,200
Retained earnings	900,000
Net income (no extraordinary items)	360,000

The convertible bonds were issued on July 1, 1991 to yield 4.03%. The Aa corporate bond interest rate was 10%. Each $1,000 bond is convertible to 20 shares of common stock. Premium amortization related to the bonds during 1991 was $800. Mathias's average income tax rate during 1991 was 40%.

Required:

1. Is this a simple or complex capital structure? Explain.
2. Prepare the required EPS presentation for 1991. Show all computations. Disregard the optional 3% materiality test.

P 22–5
Analyze Capital Structure: Stock Warrants, Nonconvertible Securities, Compute EPS
(L.O. 3, 4, 5, 6, 7, 8)

The records of Jefferson Corporation reflected the following data at the end of 1991:

Liabilities

Bonds payable, 5%, convertible (each $1,000 bond is convertible to 40 shares of common stock)	$150,000

Stockholders' Equity

Common stock, par $2 authorized 400,000 shares:	
Outstanding 1/1/1991, 150,000 shares	300,000
Sold and issued on 10/1/1991 20,000 shares	40,000
Common stock warrants outstanding (all year for 6,000 shares)	12,000
Preferred stock, 6% par $5 nonconvertible, cumulative; authorized 100,000 shares; outstanding during 1991, 20,000 shares	100,000
Contributed capital in excess of par, common stock	375,000
Contributed capital in excess of par, preferred stock	45,000
Retained earnings	280,000
Income before extraordinary items	170,000
Extraordinary loss (net of tax)	(20,000)
Net income	150,000

Additional data:

a. Stock warrants—option price, $3 per share; average market price of common stock during 1991, $3.60 per share; market price of common stock on 12/31/1991, $3.50 per share.

b. Convertible bonds—issue price, par; Aa bond interest rate at date of issuance of the bonds was 9%.

c. Average income tax rate, 30%.

Required:

1. Is this a simple or complex capital structure? Explain.
2. What kind of EPS presentation is required? Explain.
3. Prepare the required EPS presentation for 1991. Show all computations. Disregard the optional 3% materiality test.
4. Were there any antidilutive securities? How was this determined?
5. How should antidilutive securities be treated in EPS computations? Why?

P 22–6

Analyze Capital Structure: Stock Dividend, Convertible Securities, Compute EPS

(L.O. 3, 4, 6, 7, 8)

At the end of 1991, the records of Luholtz Corporation reflected the following:

Common stock, nopar, authorized 500,000 shares; issued and outstanding throughout period, 100,000 shares	$680,000
Stock dividend issued, 12/31/1991, 50,000 shares (not included in the 100,000 shares above)	340,000
Retained earnings (aftereffect of dividends on all shares)	500,000
Bonds payable, 4½%; each $1,000 bond is convertible to 80 shares of common stock after the stock dividend (bonds issued at par)	100,000
Bonds payable, 6½%; each $1,000 bond is convertible to 90 shares of common stock after the stock dividend (bonds issued at par)	300,000
Income before extraordinary items	210,000
Extraordinary gain	12,000
Net income	222,000
Average income tax rate, 40%.	
Aa bond interest rate at date of issuance: 4½% bonds, 8%; 6½% bonds, 9%.	

Required:

1. Is this a simple or complex capital structure? Explain.
2. What kind of EPS presentation is required? Explain. Disregard the optional 3% materiality test.
3. Compute the required EPS amounts (show computations, rounded to two decimal places, and assume all amounts are material).

P 22–7

Computing a Loss per Share

(L.O. 3, 4, 6, 7)

Cooper Corporation's financial statements at December 31, 1992, reported:

Accrued interest payable	$ 1,000
Long-term notes payable, 10%, due in 1995	50,000
Bonds payable, 7%; each $1,000 of face value is convertible into 90 shares of common stock; bonds mature in 2004	800,000
Preferred stock, 5%, nonconvertible, cumulative, par value $100	250,000
Common stock, par value $5	700,000
Common stock rights outstanding all year entitling holders to acquire 40,000 shares of common stock at $9 per share	200,000
Net loss for 1992	125,000

Additional data:

a. During 1992, 1,000 shares of preferred stock were issued at par on July 1. Dividends are paid semiannually, on May 31 and November 30. Declaration precedes payment by three weeks. On newly issued shares, dividends are prorated from issue date.

b. Aa bond rate of interest was 8% when the convertible bonds were issued at par.

c. Average market price of common stock during 1992 was $10; market price per share of common stock on 12/31/1992 was $10.

d. Cooper's income tax rate is 30%.

e. Cooper earned taxable income of $400,000 during 1989 to 1991.

Required:

Compute the EPS amount that Cooper should report on the income statement for 1992. Show all computations.

P 22-8
Compute Average Number of Shares Outstanding and EPS
(L.O. 2, 3, 4, 5, 6)

Zolar Corporation reported earnings per share of $22,875,000 ÷ 10,500,000 = $2.18 based on the following data:

Net income	$22,875,000
Common shares:	
January 1, 1991	12,000,000
December 31, 1991	9,000,000
Average number of shares outstanding	10,500,000

After examining Zolar's records, you note that Zolar acquired and retired 4 million shares on April 1, 1991, and issued 1,000,000 shares to satisfy all employee options outstanding on September 30, 1991. No equity securities besides common are outstanding, and Zolar has no convertible securities or other options outstanding.

Required:

1. Is Zolar's EPS calculation correct or not? Explain.
2. Revise the EPS figure if you think it is in error.
3. Suppose the facts above are altered thus:
    a. An additional 500,000 options allowing holders to subscribe to 500,000 shares at $25 a share are outstanding all of 1991. The average stock price during the year is $30. The year-end price is $27.
    b. Zolar has outstanding 100,000 shares of $100 par, 5% cumulative preferred, issued to yield 5% on 7/9/85 when the Aa bond rate was 10%. The dividend was paid in 1991.
   What changes are required in the EPS calculations for primary and fully diluted EPS?

P 22-9
Determine Capital Structure; Calculate and Report of EPS
(L.O. 3, 4)

Davidson Corporation had a net operating income from operations of $5.60 million for 1991. Davidson also settled legal claims of $1.00 million, which it shows as an extraordinary item of $.74 million after tax. Davidson also reported a $1.23 million after-tax loss on the disposal of its textile subsidiary. Davidson uses a calendar year reporting period.

Davidson's capital structure consists of:

Preferred: 100,000 shares of $100 par, 8% cumulative
nonconvertible preferred issued in 1985.
The dividend was passed this year.

Common: Outstanding 1/1/91,
4,271,865 shares, $1 par.
Dividends of 25 cents per share were paid in 1991.
On July 1, 1991, a 2-for-1 stock split was declared and the shares issued.

Required:

1. What type of capital structure does Davidson have (simple or complex)?
2. Compute and label the relevant EPS figures.
3. Must the EPS figures for the law settlement and discontinued operations be reported?

P 22-10
Compute Primary and Fully Diluted EPS
(L.O. 2, 3, 4, 6, 7, 8)

Zorbas Inc. needs to establish its EPS figures for its 1991 reports. The following information is available to Deb Its, Zorba's controller:

a. Net income (before tax = $50 million) $30 million.
b. Common stock (20 million shares authorized; 15 million shares outstanding January 1, 1991).
c. Cumulative convertible preferred stock (2 million shares issued August 1, 1988, and outstanding January 1, 1991). Issued at $50 a share with a yearly $4 dividend paid semiannually June 30 and December 31. The stock is convertible on a share-for-share basis adjusted automatically for any stock dividends or splits. The Aa bond rate at the time of issue was 10%.
d. March 1, 1991: Half the preferred was converted to common.
e. April 1, 1991: Zorbas declared a 10% stock dividend.
f. July 1: One million shares of stock were issued in the acquisition of the Tande Corporation. The stock's market value at this time was $15 a share.

g. October 1: Zorbas purchased and retired 600,000 shares of its common stock for $700,000.
h. All preferred dividends were declared and paid.

Required:

1. Establish the number of shares to be used in computing primary EPS for 1991.
2. Establish the number of shares to be used in computing fully diluted EPS for 1991.
3. Compute primary EPS.
4. Compute fully diluted EPS.
5. What additional considerations are required if Zorbas had issued convertible debt?

P 22-11
Approximate Test for the Number of Incremental Shares When Only Options and Warrants Are Present
(L.O. 5)

When options and warrants are present, the treasury stock method may produce additional common stock equivalents. In this case, if the number of additional common shares assumed to be issued exceeds 3% of the outstanding shares, the expression:

$$\left[\frac{\text{Market price—Exercise price}}{\text{Market price}}\right] \text{Number of shares on exercise} = N[(M—E)/M]$$

approximates the number of incremental shares that will result using the treasury stock method.

Required:

1. Develop this formula from the discussion of the treasury stock method in the chapter.
2. When should the test not be used to give a final answer? Give two situations.
3. Why is the test an approximate test?

P 22-12
Disclosure of EPS Figures
(L.O. 3, 4)

Four captions that might be used in selecting a title for the EPS figures are these:

A. Earnings per common share.
B. Earnings per common share—assuming no dilution (where dilutive securities exist).
C. Earnings per common share—assuming full dilution.
D. Earnings per common share and common equivalent share (where common equivalent shares exist).

Common Stock Equivalents Present	Other Potentially Dilutive Securities Present	Appropriate Presentation		
		Simple (Basic) EPS Caption	Dual	
			PEPS Caption	FDEPS Caption
1. No*	No			
2. No*	Dilutive			
3. No*	Antidilutive			
4. Dilutive	No			
5. Dilutive	Dilutive	—	D	C
6. Dilutive	Antidilutive			
7. Antidilutive	No*			
8. Antidilutive	Dilutive			
9. Antidilutive	Antidulutive			

* Or dilution is less than 3%.

Required:

1. Restrict yourself to these four titles. Which appears to be the most appropriate presentation for each of the nine cases in the table? The answer to (5) is given as an example.
2. In which cases are primary EPS and fully diluted EPS the same?
3. Indicate cases in which additional footnote disclosure should be given.

P 22–13

Appendix: Computing the
Average Market Price of
Common Stock

(L.O. 9)

The treasury stock method requires that an average market price for the common be established. This average can be calculated in several ways. The two most commonly used computations based on the weekly prices for a three month period are provided following the basic data.

Basic Data: Three-Month Stock Price Data

	Week	High	Low	Close	Shares Traded
Month 1	1	21	19	20	300
	2	24	20	23	700
	3	24	22	22	500
	4	23	21	21	500
Month 2	5	26	22	23	1,000
	6	27	23	26	1,200
	7	29	27	28	1,500
	8	31	29	31	2,000
Month 3	9	28	26	26	2,500
	10	26	22	23	1,500
	11	24	22	22	1,000
	12	22	20	21	800
	13	20	20	20	500

1. A simple average of monthly prices is normally adequate unless prices fluctuate greatly, in which case weekly (or even daily) prices are preferable.
2. The average of the market's closing price, used consistently, is satisfactory unless, again, prices fluctuate widely, in which case an average of the high and low prices for the period would be preferable.

Required:

1. Compute a simple average price for the three-month period using monthly close prices.
2. Compute a simple average for the three-month period using the averages of the weekly high-low prices.
3. Which of the two methods' seems most appropriate in this case? Why?

P 22–14

Appendix: Application of
Treasury Stock Method
for Options

(L.O. 9)

The Elax Company has 200,000 common shares outstanding along with 20,000 options that are exercisable at $40 per share. Each option allows the holder to obtain one share upon exercise. The market prices for the common over the last three years were:

	Year 1		Year 2		Year 3	
Quarter	Average	Ending	Average	Ending	Average	Ending
1	36	44	48	50	40	36
2	40*	42	44	42	36	44
3	44	38	40	38	48	42
4	48	46	36	34	44	50

* Assume market prices exceeded $40 for substantially all of the previous quarter.

Required:

Compute the number of incremental shares for primary and fully diluted EPS for each quarter.

P 22–15

COMPREHENSIVE PROBLEM
♦

(L.O. 1–8)

The following facts pertain to Purdue Company:

Year Ended 12/31/91

From the income statement:
Net Income $10,300,000

From the balance sheet:
Long-term debt:
10% convertible debentures, due October 1, 2000 . . . . $10,000,000

Stockholders' equity (Note 1):
Convertible voting preferred stock of $1 par value, 20-cent
cumulative dividend. Authorized, 600,000 shares;
issued and outstanding, 600,000. Liquidation value $22 per share,
aggregating $13,200,000   600,000
Common stock of $1 par value per share; authorized,
5,000,000 shares; issued and outstanding 3,300,000   3,300,000

Note 1
The 20-cent convertible preferred stock is callable by the company after March 31, 1990, at $53 per share. Each share is convertible into one share of common stock.

Warrants to acquire 500,000 shares of the company's stock at $60 per share were outstanding at the end of 1991.

Other Information:

a. The average market value of the common stock during 1991 was:

	Average	Closing
First quarter	$50	
Second quarter	$60	
Third quarter	$70	
Fourth quarter	$70	72

b. Cash dividends of 12½ cents per common share were declared and paid for each quarter of 1991.
c. 10% convertible debentures with a principal amount of $10,000,000 due October 1, 2000, were sold for cash at a price of $98 on October 1, 1990. Each $100 debenture is convertible into two shares of common stock. At issuance, the rate on corporate Aa bonds was 15%. Discount is amortized on a straight line basis.
d. The 600,000 shares of convertible preferred stock were issued for assets in a purchase transaction of April 1, 1991. The annual dividend on each share of this convertible preferred stock is 20-cents. Each share is convertible into one share of common stock. The market value of the convertible preferred stock was $53 at the time of issuance. The rate on corporate Aa bonds was 15.5%.
e. Warrants to buy 500,000 shares of common stock at $60 per share for a period of five years were issued along with the convertible preferred stock mentioned in (d).
f. 3.3 million shares of common stock were outstanding at the end of 1990. There have been no conversions or warrants exercised in 1991.
g. An average tax rate of 40% is assumed.

Required:

1. Determine if CSEs exist and if so, compute the number of CSE shares.
2. Calculate basic EPS.
3. Calculate primary EPS.
4. Calculate fully diluted EPS.

CASES

C 22–1
Importance of EPS
Figures
(L.O. 1)

On July 24, 1990, the Financial Accounting Standards Advisory Council (FASAC) met with SEC Commissioner Philip Lochner and SEC Chief Accountant Edward Coulson to discuss the effect of accounting standards on U.S. competitiveness. At that meeting, Mr. Dennis Dammerman, senior vice president for finance of General Electric Company and a member of FASAC, stated: "The chief executive officers of America, right or wrong, get their report card at least once a quarter and it's generally called earnings per share and that report card reflects accounting."

What relevance do you believe this statement has to America's competitive strengths and why do you think the issue was raised with FASAC?

C 22–2
The Logic for Some EPS
Calculations
(L.O. 1)

Many people believe earnings per share is the single most salient fact most financial statement readers examine. Together with earnings, it is also the most commonly reported statistic about a company's yearly activities. Discuss the following issues:

Required:
1. If a convertible debenture exists:
   a. When is it considered a CSE? Why?
   b. If it reduces EPS to consider it (as if) converted, what calculations need to be made?
2. In applying the treasury stock method:
   a. How is the method used if the number of shares repurchased exceeds 20% of the outstanding common shares?
   b. Why must firms use the (as if) funds generated to repurchase common shares for the treasury?
3. If a 10% stock dividend is issued half way through the year, how many additional shares are added to the denominator of the EPS calculation? Does the answer change if the same number of shares are issued for cash? Why?

C 22–3
Sherwin-Williams:
Analysis of Actual
Financial Statements
(L.O. 1–8)

This problem refers to the financial statements for the Sherwin-Williams Company given at the end of this book.
1. What EPS value did Sherwin-Williams report for 1990?
2. What EPS would Sherwin-Williams have reported in 1990 if it had not been for the information given in Note 2 to the financial statements? Did the stock split on February 20, 1991, alter the 1989 EPS figure reported by Sherwin-Williams in its 1990 statement?
3. Does Sherwin-Williams have any convertible securities? Does it have any stock options outstanding on December 31, 1990?
4. If your answer to (3) is yes, are any of these securities CSEs? If so, which securities? How many shares of common were they equivalent to in 1990?
5. Does Sherwin-Williams have a simple or complex capital structure? If complex, why is only one EPS number reported and what is it?
6. Show that the 6.25% debenture issue was dilutive. Why wasn't it treated as a CSE?
7. Was the price of Sherwin-Williams stock higher on December 31, 1990, than the average market price used to calculate the additional shares outstanding under the treasury stock method? How do you know?

SPECIAL
TOPICS

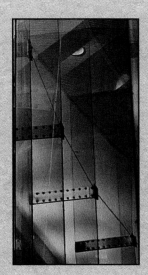

C H A P T E R

23

Statement of Cash Flows

**LEARNING
OBJECTIVES**

◆

After you have studied this chapter, you will:

1. Recognize the usefulness of the statement of cash flows.

2. Know the main provisions of *SFAS No. 95*, "Statement of Cash Flows."

3. Be able to analyze transactions to identify disclosures in the statement of cash flows.

4. Know how to prepare a statement of cash flows by analyzing transactions.

5. Be familiar with the spreadsheet approach to preparing a statement of cash flows.

6. Be familiar with the T-account approach to preparing a statement of cash flows. (Refer to the appendix at the end of the chapter.)

◆

INTRODUCTION
◆

Phillips Petroleum Company reported earnings of $219 million in 1989, yet received $1.65 billion more cash from receivables and other operating sources than it paid for operating costs. Why was net cash flow from operations so much larger than earnings? The statement of cash flows reveals the answer. Phillips recognized depreciation and other *noncash* expenses that reduced earnings but did not affect cash flow. These and other amounts listed in the statement of cash flows explain why earnings and cash flows are not the same.

In 1984, investors purchased Disney Production stock for $60 per share. Yet Disney's EPS were less than $1 at the time. Why did these investors pay so much for these shares? They did because Disney was generating tremendous cash flow. As one analyst put it, "It's cash flow that services debt, pays dividends, [and] maintains and expands plant and equipment."[1]

Investors and creditors use current cash flow information to project future business cash flows. The statement of cash flows also provides information not disclosed in the income statement, balance sheet, or footnotes. For example, how much did IBM spend on software development? What was Boeing's cash outlay for a Canadian aircraft company? How much did General Motors spend on capital expenditures? These amounts are listed in the nonoperating sections of the statement of cash flows.

This chapter discusses the use and preparation of the statement of cash flows. Cash flow information is an integral part of the total information package provided by a complete set of financial statements. Some of the topics considered in previous chapters are used to illustrate the principles developed in this chapter.

◆

CASH FLOW REPORTING: DEVELOPMENT AND USEFULNESS
◆

The statement of cash flows (SCF) is a report listing cash inflows and outflows by meaningful categories. The statement explains the change in cash during the period. This chapter illustrates several statements (see Exhibit 23–1).

The accounting profession did not always require firms to present a cash flow statement. A brief chronology of events leading to the statement of cash flows follows:

* Before 1961: Firms voluntarily disclose *funds flow statements,* which report sources and uses of working capital (current assets less current liabilities) and present partial operating, financing, and investing activity information. Funds flow statements exhibit a variety of titles, format, content, and terminology.
* 1961: *Accounting Research Study No. 2,* "Cash Flow Analysis and the Funds Statement," commissioned by the AICPA, recommends that a funds statement be required. The study emphasizes that the balance sheet and income statement together do not provide a complete reporting of all changes in resources.
* 1963: *APB Opinion No. 3,* "The Statement of Source and Application of Funds," recommends but does not require a funds statement.
* 1971: *APB Opinion No. 19,* "Reporting Changes in Financial Position" requires the *statement of changes in financial position,* a funds statement allowing several funds definitions including working capital, cash, and others.[2]
* 1984: *SFAC No. 5,* "Recognition and Measurement in Financial Statements of Business Enterprises," states that a full set of financial statements should show the cash flows for the period.

---

[1] "Confusing Flows the Cash Flow," *Forbes,* April 7, 1986, pp. 72–75.

[2] Most firms initially chose working capital. The statement explained why working capital increased or decreased during the period, but did not explain the change in cash.

EXHIBIT 23-1   Statement of Cash Flows

SIMPLE COMPANY
Statements of Cash Flows, Direct and Indirect Methods
For the Year Ended December 31, 1991
(in thousands)

Direct Method Statement of Cash Flows

Cash flows from operating activities:		
Cash received from customers	$ 58	
Payments to employees	(26)	
Payments for administrative and selling		
activities	(12)	
Net cash inflow from operating activities		$20
Cash flows from investing activities:		
Cash paid for acquisition of plant assets	$(30)	
Cash received from sale of plant assets	21	
Net cash outflow from investing activities		(9)
Cash flows from financing activities:		
Cash received from long-term debt issuance	$ 40	
Cash paid on long-term debt (principal only)	(46)	
Cash paid for treasury stock purchased	(8)	
Cash paid for dividends	(11)	
Cash received from sale of common stock	48	
Net cash inflow from financing activities		23
Effect of foreign exchange rates on cash		0*
Net increase in cash and cash equivalents during 1991		34
Cash and cash equivalents, January 1, 1991		42
Cash and cash equivalents, December 31, 1991		$76

Indirect Method Statement of Cash Flows

Cash flows from operating activities:		
Net income	$22	
Add (deduct) to reconcile net income to		
net operating cash inflow:		
Accounts receivable increase	(8)	
Salaries payable increase	2	
Depreciation expense	4	
Net cash inflow from operating activities		$20
Cash flows from investing activities:		
Cash paid for acquisition of plant assets	$(30)	
Cash received from sale of plant assets	21	
Net cash outflow from investing activities		(9)
Cash flows from financing activities:		
Cash received from long-term debt issuance	$ 40	
Cash paid on long-term debt (principal only)	(46)	
Cash paid for treasury stock purchased	(8)	
Cash paid for dividends	(11)	
Cash received from sale of common stock	48	
Net cash inflow from financing activities		23
Effect of foreign exchange rates on cash		0*
Net increase in cash and cash equivalents during 1991		34
Cash and cash equivalents, January 1, 1991		42
Cash and cash equivalents, December 31, 1991		$76

---

* Effects of foreign currency exchange rate changes are listed here for firms with foreign operations or transactions in foreign currencies. The effect of exchange rate changes on foreign currencies held is not a cash flow, but affects the change in the cash balance, as measured in dollars, during the period. Advanced accounting courses discuss foreign currency issues in detail.

◆ 1987: *SFAS No. 95,* "Statement of Cash Flows," supersedes *APB Opinion No. 19* and requires the SCF whenever a balance sheet and income statement are reported.[3] Separate disclosure of operating, investing, and financing cash flows is required.

The development of the SCF is an excellent example of how the accounting profession reacted to suggestions by user groups about how to improve financial reporting.

The Trend toward Cash Flows

Between 1980 and 1986, the percentage of 600 surveyed firms defining funds as cash in the statement of changes in financial position grew from 10% to 66%.[4] Investors and creditors found cash flow information increasingly valuable for assessing a firm's liquidity and risk.[5] Several organizations, including the Financial Executives Institute, encouraged companies to use the cash-basis statement of changes in financial position.

Increased Business Risk   Beginning in the mid-1970s, an increase in business failures and suits against auditors for not adequately warning of those failures were factors contributing to an increased interest in cash flow information. An increasing bankruptcy rate, as well as general economic indicators, supported an assessment of a general increase in risk. For example, the average current ratio of U.S. manufacturing firms fell from 2.67 to 1.71 between 1947 and 1979, suggesting a general deterioration in financial condition.[6]

The W. T. Grant bankruptcy demonstrates the potential use of cash flow information for assessing risk. W. T. Grant, one of the nation's larger retailers in 1974, filed for bankruptcy in 1975. In 1973, Grant's common stock was selling for 20 times its earnings per share, a high level by historical standards. Grant's income and working capital provided by operations were positive from 1966 through 1974. The company paid regular dividends from 1966 through 1974.

However, during the decade before bankruptcy, the company generated almost no cash from *operations*.[7] Except for two years in which operating net cash flow was minimal, operations consumed, rather than provided, cash during the period 1966 to 1974. The decline in operating cash flows preceded bankruptcy by a decade. Those investors acting on cash flow information, rather than income and other traditional financial ratios, avoided losses.[8]

Previous Funds Statements   The lack of uniformity in format and content of funds statements and the variety of fund definitions also contributed to increased interest in cash flow information. In addition, a strong working capital position does not necessarily imply a strong cash flow. A firm with healthy working capital, but also having large inventories, prepaids, and receivables, might be in a weak cash position. Working capital increases are not necessarily available to pay debts. The W. T. Grant case is an example.

---

[3] Interim reports and nonprofit organizations are exempt. *SFAS No. 102,* which amends *SFAS No. 95,* exempts defined benefit pension plans and investment companies subject to certain requirements.

[4] AICPA, *Accounting Trends & Techniques*—1987 (New York), p. 109. Also, the 1984 edition reflected a threefold increase in the number of firms categorizing cash flows into operating, investing, and financing from the year before.

[5] Louis Harris and Associates, *A Study of the Attitudes Toward and an Assessment of the Financial Accounting Standards Board,* (Stamford Conn., April 1980, p. 13) found 67% of those interviewed rated cash flow information as highly important.

[6] FASB, *Reporting Funds Flows, Liquidity, and Financial Flexibility, Discussion Memorandum,* Norwalk, Conn., 1980, par. 27.

[7] Payments for operating expenses exceeded collections from receivables and other operating sources.

[8] J. Largay and C. Stickney, "Cash Flows, Ratio Analysis and the W. T. Grant Company Bankruptcy," *Financial Analysts Journal,* July–August, 1980, p. 51.

Differences between Cash and Accrual Accounting   Another factor in the trend toward cash flow reporting was the increased complexity of financial accounting principles. Accounting pronouncements on leases, pensions, foreign exchange, tax allocation, and investments, have increased the complexity of financial statements. Determining the relationship between accrual earnings and cash flow is now more difficult for many financial statement users.

Accrual accounting matches efforts (costs) and results (revenues). The timing of receipts from sales or of payments for raw materials and labor does not affect the timing of normal recognition of sales and expenses. Financial statement users are interested in earnings information because in the long run, profits determine the success of a company. Net income reflects changes in general financial position, rather than immediate cash consequences.

But in the short run, many financial statement users are interested in cash flow. For example, will the borrower produce sufficient cash to pay its liabilities? Business creditors are especially interested in the historical record of cash inflows and outflows, for the same reasons that a person's credit history and cash income are important in home mortgage lending. Some lenders point to the emphasis on accrual accounting as the reason for their preference for cash flow information.[9]

Usefulness of Cash Flow Information

Many financial statement readers use cash flow in making their decisions and recommendations. Some investors avoid companies without **free cash flow,** variously defined but generally connoting cash remaining after necessary operating and capital expenditures, and debt service payments are covered.[10] Free cash flow can be used to repurchase stock, pay dividends, expand, acquire other businesses, or invest in debt and equity securities. If free cash flow is negative, the deficiency must be financed with additional debt or equity funding.

The trend of cash flows over several periods allows an assessment of **financial flexibility,** the ability to alter the amount and timing of cash flows to enable a response to unexpected needs and opportunities. For example, a firm able to raise additional capital in the debt and equity markets, to sell nonoperating assets, and to increase cash inflows by increasing efficiency and lowering costs is financially flexible. Healthy operating cash flows provide the basis for most other cash flows and imply financial flexibility.

When Moody's Investors Service Inc. reviewed Chrysler Corporation for a possible downgrade of its debt rating, it was concerned about financial flexibility:

> The review comes in the wake of "recent management defections" and reflects Moody's concerns about the automaker's "financial flexibility," to compete in an increasingly competitive market.[11]

Cash flow information helps users to understand the relationship between income and cash flow and to predict similar cash flows. For example, the trend of net cash inflow from operations is useful for predicting future operating cash flows, in the aggregate and by component. Cash flow information provides feedback about past decisions. What effects are previous investment decisions having on cash flows? How were capital expenditures financed? How much debt was retired?

Cash flow information also helps explain changes in balance sheet accounts. For example, why did long-term debt increase $100,000? There are many possible causes. Did the change involve cash? Cash flow reporting provides answers to these questions and yields information about investing and financing activities.

---

9 "Where's the Cash?" *Forbes,* April 8, 1985, p. 120.

10 "Earnings, Schmernings—Look at Cash," *Business Week,* July 24, 1989, p. 57.

11 "Moody's Considers Downgrading Debt of Chrysler Corporation," *The Wall Street Journal,* June 14, 1990, p. A3.

A study of 491 financial statement users sponsored by the Financial Executives Research Foundation found funds flow information useful for the following purposes:[12]

Assessments by Investors and Creditors of	Uses within the Firm
Ability to finance operations	Cash forecasting
Ability to pay dividends	Monitoring liquidity and changes
Ability to pay interest	in financial position
Cash consequences of deferred taxes	Budgeting
Liquidity	Strategic planning
Ability to adapt to changing	Evaluating operating
conditions	performance
The quality of earnings	Monitoring working capital and
A firm's general performance	fixed-asset investments

The same purposes are served by cash flow information.

THE STATEMENT OF CASH FLOWS AND REQUIREMENTS OF *SFAS NO. 95*

♦

The purpose of the SCF is to provide relevant information about cash receipts and disbursements. The SCF is designed to help users assess the following factors:

1. A firm's ability to generate cash flows.
2. A firm's ability to meet its obligations.
3. The reasons for differences between income and associated cash flows.
4. The effect of cash and noncash investing and financing activities on a firm's financial position.

By listing cash flows in meaningful categories and disclosing significant noncash investing and financing activities, the SCF details the cash consequences of operations and the changes in balance sheet accounts arising from investing and financing activities.

Exhibit 23–1 presented the SCF for Simple Company, an example used later to illustrate statement preparation. **Cash equivalents**—highly liquid, short-term securities readily convertible into cash—are the reporting basis for the SCF. Cash and cash equivalents are normally combined for balance sheet reporting. The exhibit shows both the *direct method* and *indirect method* both allowed under SFAS No. 95. Firms report the SCF using only one of these methods of presentation.

The SCF categorizes Simple Company's 1991 cash flows into operating, investing, and financing categories. The reasons *why* cash and cash equivalents increased $34 during 1991 is explained by the SCF. The difference between operating inflows and outflows is **net cash inflow (outflow) from operating activities.** Simple Company generated $20 from operations in 1991. This subtotal is an important factor in investor assessments of future cash flows. Cash flow from operations is necessary for debt servicing, capital expenditures, dividend payments, and other cash outflows. SFAS No. 95 does not require inflows to be listed before outflows.

The operating activity section in each statement in Exhibit 23–1 is boxed to emphasize the major difference between the two methods. The **direct method,** given first, lists the actual operating cash flows resulting in net cash inflow from operating activities. The **indirect method,** given second, derives net cash inflow from operating activities by adjusting net income for items whose cash flow and income effect are not equal. For example, depreciation expense reduced income $4 but caused no cash outflow. The investing and financing activities sections are identical for both methods.

The operating section of the indirect method SCF in Exhibit 23–1 lists income, net operating cash flow, and amounts reconciling the two. For Simple Company, these

[12] Seed III and Arthur D. Little, Inc., Financial Executives Research Foundation, *The Funds Statement: Structure and Use*, (Morristown, 1984).

two amounts are similar ($22 and $20, respectively). For many other firms (for example, Phillips Petroleum mentioned in the introduction), these two amounts are vastly different. This SCF section explains the difference between earnings and operating cash flows. For firms using the *direct* method, a supporting schedule equivalent to the operating activities section under the *indirect* method also is a required disclosure. This schedule is called the reconciliation of net income and operating cash flows.

Except for the operating section of the indirect method, each line-item in the SCF describes a cash flow. The change in cash for the period from the comparative balance sheets equals the change disclosed in the SCF. Through the double-entry accounting system, the change in cash is algebraically equal to the net change in all other accounts.

A firm can experience a cash decrease during the year yet generate considerable income and operating cash flow. The explanation is found in the SCF. Large investing cash outflows for equipment or investments, or large financing cash outflows for debt retirement or dividend payments would explain the cash decrease.

Cash and Cash Equivalents

SFAS No. 95 standardized the definition of the term *funds* by requiring that the SCF explain the change in cash and cash equivalents. Cash includes only those items immediately available to pay obligations. Cash equivalents are short-term, highly liquid investments with two additional characteristics:

1. They are readily convertible to known amounts of cash.
2. They are so near maturity that there is insignificant risk of market value fluctuation from interest rate changes.

Generally, only investments with an *original* maturity (to the purchasing firm) of three months or less qualify as cash equivalents under this definition. For example, a two-year U.S. Treasury note purchased three months before maturity is a cash equivalent because it is readily convertible into a known amount of cash and is very near maturity. However, the same note purchased four months before maturity is not, and does not become a cash equivalent one month later because its original maturity to the purchaser is four months.

Examples of securities that can qualify as cash equivalents are Treasury bonds, notes and bills,[13] money market funds, and commercial paper. An investment in equity securities cannot be a cash equivalent because it has no maturity date and is not convertible into a known (unchanging) amount of cash. The values of stocks change frequently.

Cash equivalents are merged with cash for SCF purposes because a security that fulfills the criteria for cash equivalents is economically equivalent to cash. Their known value is not likely to change significantly, and they are readily convertible to cash. Cash also has these characteristics. The three-month rule minimizes the risk of security price fluctuation from changes in interest rates and usually ensures that the face (or recorded value if different) of the investment is essentially equal to its market value during the holding period.

The assessment of a firm's cash flows would be incomplete without considering cash equivalents. Typically, firms invest a substantial portion of idle cash in cash-equivalent securities to earn a return higher than is available from savings accounts. Furthermore, purchases and sales of cash equivalents are a normal part of cash management practices.

Purchases of cash equivalents and sales of cash equivalents at book vaue are not reported in the SCF because they do not change total cash and cash equivalents. For

---

[13] Treasury bills have maturities of one year or less and constitute the largest component of the money market, the market for short-term debt. Treasury notes have maturity periods of 2 to 10 years. Treasury bonds have maturity periods exceeding 10 years.

example purchasing $20,000 of cash equivalents for cash does not change total cash and cash equivalents.

SFAS No. 95 requires reporting the change in cash and cash equivalents as an item that reconciles the beginning and ending balances of cash and cash equivalents. The bottom portion of both statements in Exhibit 23–1 illustrate this reconciliation. Simple Company's net increase in cash and cash equivalents ($34) equals the net sum of net operating cash inflow ($20), net investment cash outflow ($9) and net financing cash inflow ($23). This increase is added to the beginning cash and cash equivalents balance ($42), yielding the ending balance ($76).

A firm need not classify as cash equivalents all securities fulfilling the definition. Many companies invest in cash equivalents as long-term investments, rolling large quantities of securities over as they mature. Such securities are part of a larger pool of investment securities appropriately treated as other investments. *SFAS No. 95* requires disclosure of the policy relative to classification of securities as cash equivalents. Changes in that policy are retroactive accounting principle changes. *SFAS No. 95* also requires that the beginning and ending cash and cash equivalent amounts disclosed in the SCF reflect those shown in the balance sheet. This requirement restricts balance sheet classification of securities as cash equivalents to those fulfilling the *SFAS No. 95* definition.

The 1989 annual report of Harley-Davidson, Inc., discloses the firm's policy on cash equivalents:

> The Company considers all highly liquid investments purchased with an original maturity of three months or less to be cash equivalents.

For the remainder of this chapter, the term *cash* is used to describe both cash and cash equivalents unless there is a need to distinguish between the two.

Three Cash Flow Categories

All cash inflows and outflows are classified into one of the following categories:

1. Operating.
2. Investing.
3. Financing.

Classification of cash flows is important for evaluating past cash flows and predicting future flows. For example, the ability of a firm to generate a positive cash flow from operations is critical to its survival. A firm cannot indefinitely sell fixed assets or incur additional debt without successful operations. The three categories above allow the user to distinguish between repetitive, on-going activities and long-term, strategic changes. An uncategorized list would be less easily understood.

Operating Cash Flows Operating cash flows are those not defined as investing or financing activities.[14] Operating cash flows include:

Inflows:	Outflows:
Receipts from customers.[15]	Payments to suppliers.
Interest received.	Payments to employees.
Dividends received.	Interest payments (net of amounts capitalized).
Income tax refunds.	
Refunds from suppliers.	Income and other tax payments.

---

[14] *SFAS No. 95*, par. 21.

[15] Includes receipts of principal amounts from both short and long-term receivables from the sale of goods and services.

Inflows:

Other receipts related to income producing activities such as revenues received in advance.

Receipts from lawsuits.

Insurance proceeds from health, life, and business interruption insurance.

Outflows:

Other payments related to income producing activities, including prepayments.

Charitable contributions.

Payments on lawsuits.[16]

Principal payments on long- and short-term loans from suppliers.[17]

Payments on operating leases.

Pension fund contributions.

Payments for fines and penalties.

The association of a cash flow with income is the primary criterion for classifying the flow as operating. For example, interest received and paid, and dividends received are associated with expenses or revenues. All income tax payments are operating cash outflows, including those resulting from extraordinary items, discontinued operations, accounting changes and prior period adjustments.

Cash flows from other transactions that may at first appear to be investing or financing flows are classified as operating if related to the main business activity. For example, if a real estate developer acquires land for subdivision, improvement, and resale as individual lots, then the cash payment used to purchase the land is appropriately classified as operating. In this case, land is similar to inventory in other types of businesses.

The direct method lists the actual operating cash flows resulting in net operating cash flow. Simple Company (Exhibit 23–1, direct method) received $58 from customers, paid $26 to employees, and paid $12 for administrative and selling expenses. Sales and expenses, the accrual counterparts to these receipts and payments, are listed in the income statement. A comparison of the income statement and the SCF reveals the degree to which cash flows lead or lag revenue and expense recognition. The indirect method determines net operating cash flow *indirectly,* but does not list the individual operating cash flows.

Investing Cash Flows Investing cash flows are related to long-term strategic activities and investments in securities, real estate, and other ventures. These cash flows are usually associated with transactions involving long-term assets and are important for identifying a firm's growth plans. Capital expenditures and acquisitions of subsidiaries are important strategic decisions for a firm. The typical cash flows under this classification are:

Inflows:

Proceeds from plant asset sales.

Proceeds from sales of debt and equity securities of other firms (not cash equivalents, both short- and long-term).

Collections of principal amounts of loans except for loans to customers from the sale of goods and services.

Proceeds from sale of real estate.

Outflows:

Payments to purchase plant assets.

Payments for investments in debt and equity securities of other firms (not cash equivalents, both short- and long-term).

Loans made to other parties.

Payments to purchase real estate.

Payments for capitalized interest (increases plant assets).

---

[16] However, the cost of a successful legal defense of a patent is capitalized to patents and therefore is treated as an investing cash outflow.

[17] Suppliers provide the raw materials for the firm's business. Principal payments are considered a necessary cost of operations regardless of the term of the loan.

Inflows:

Casualty insurance proceeds
(related to involuntary
disposal of plant assets).

Outflows:

Downpayments, advance payments,
and other payments before or
soon after purchase of plant assets
(subsequent principal payments on
debt financing are financing
cash outflows).

The difference between the investing cash inflows and outflows is the *net cash inflow (outflow) from investing activities*. For example, Simple Company (Exhibit 23–1) received $21 from plant asset sales, and paid $30 for capital expenditures. The net cash *outflow* from investing activities is $9, indicating that Simple Company applied more cash in this area than it received.

A fundamental distinction between operating and investing cash outflows is the anticipated benefit period. Inventory purchases are considered operating cash outflows because the benefits from inventory sales are expected in the short run. Benefits from plant assets are long-run in nature and provide benefits for many periods.

Gains and losses from discontinued operations and transactions producing extraordinary gains and losses are often associated with investing cash flows. For example, the sale of assets from discontinued operations produces an investing inflow. The gains and losses from extraordinary items and discontinued operations appear as adjustments to net income in the reconciliation of net income and operating cash flows but are not cash flows. Examples of these disclosures are given in later sections of the chapter.

For most firms, cash flows from purchases and sales of investments in securities are investing cash flows. However, banks and securities dealers that carry securities at market value in a trading account[18] for resale classify flows from purchases and sales of securities as operating.[19] Such securities are considered inventory to a dealer because they are held for resale and generally are turned over quickly. Cash flows from sales of securities to customers are therefore operational for those businesses. These activities also are the principal source of income to the dealer.[20]

Financing Cash Flows   This category describes how the firm obtained capital from creditors (other than suppliers) and investors, and repayments of those amounts. Typically, long-term debt or owners' equity accounts are involved in the transactions giving rise to these cash flows. Examples of financing cash flows include:

Inflows:

Proceeds from stock issuance.

Proceeds from bond issuance.

Proceeds from debt incurred for
specific investing activities.

Outflows:

Payments to purchase treasury stock.

Payments to retire bonds.

Dividends paid to shareholders.

Principal payments on loans from
financial institutions.

---

[18] Securities held in a trading account by a securities dealer are held principally for resale to customers. Both fixed-income and equity securities can be held in a trading account. The typical holding period is very short, sometimes only a few hours.

[19] See *SFAS No. 102*, "Statement of Cash Flows—Exemption of Certain Enterprises and Classification of Cash Flows from Certain Securities Acquired For Resale."

[20] Furthermore, cash receipts and payments associated with loans purchased for resale and held for short periods are also classified as operating if the loans are carried at market, or the lower of cost or market. If these securities are not held for resale to customers, associated cash flows are classified as investing.

Inflows:

Proceeds from loans from financial institutions.[21]

Outflows:

Principal payments on capital leases.

Principal payments on debt used to purchase operating assets financed by dealers or third parties.

The difference between the financing cash inflows and outflows is the *net cash inflow (outflow) from financing activities.* For example, Simple Company (Exhibit 23–1) was active in the financing area in 1991. The company sold common stock and incurred new long-term debt for a total $88 cash inflow. Simple Company retired long-term debt, purchased treasury stock, and paid dividends to its shareholders. The company netted $23 from financing activities.

Noncash Activities

Explaining significant investing and financing activities is one of the objectives of the SCF. To assist fulfilling this objective, *SFAS No. 95* requires that significant noncash investing and financing activities be disclosed in a supporting schedule or in the footnotes, clearly identifying them as noncash transactions.

Some noncash transactions are economically similar to cash transactions. For example, settling a $50,000 debt by issuing stock with a $50,000 fair market has the same effect as issuing the stock for cash and using the proceeds to settle the debt. This transaction is disclosed in a schedule appended to the SCF as follows:

> Stock with a $50,000 fair market value was issued in payment of $50,000 of long-term debt.

The disclosure of transactions with both cash and noncash components must identify both components. The cash flow also is disclosed in the SCF. The footnote or supporting schedule discloses both components. For example, if a plant asset costing $400,000 is acquired by paying $100,000 cash and issuing a $300,000 long-term note, the SCF discloses the $100,000 cash payment as an investing cash outflow and references a footnote or supporting schedule. The supporting schedule would be:

> A plant asset was acquired as follows:
> Cost of asset acquired $400,000
> Cash paid 100,000
> Long-term note issued $300,000

Common noncash transactions include:

Bond retirement by issuing stock.
Conversion of bonds to stock.
Conversion of preferred stock to common stock.
Settlement of debt by transferring noncash assets.
Bond refunding.
Receipt of donated property.
Incurrence of capitalized lease obligations.

The 1989 annual report of H. J. Heinz Company provides an example of a noncash investing transaction:

---

[21] Regardless of the use of the proceeds, borrowings from financial institutions are financing cash flows. The proceeds of a bank loan is a financing cash inflow even if it is used to buy inventory. If the firm finances the inventory purchase with the supplier however, repayment of the loan is an operating outflow.

Supplemental Cash Flow Information
In January 1989, the company issued 1.2 million shares of common stock in exchange for its 7¼% convertible subordinated debentures due 2015. As a result, long-term debt was reduced by $34.7 million.

SFAS No. 95 provides no guidance on disclosure of events such as retained earnings appropriations, stock dividends, and stock splits issued and received. These transactions typically were not disclosed in prior funds statements because they did not represent significant financing activities or changes in capital structure.

Gross and Net Cash Flows

To maximize the information content of cash flow disclosures, *SFAS No. 95* generally requires that firms report gross cash flows. Cash flows are grouped by similar type. For example, an SCF line-item titled "Purchase of plant assets . . . $120,000" can represent several individual asset purchases. However, the effects of fundamentally different transactions are not netted. For example, the proceeds from bond issuances cannot be netted against payments to retire other bond issues.

The requirement to report cash flows at gross ensures better cash flow reporting of individual or similar transactions. Netting different types of cash flows would obscure the very information the SCF is designed to disclose.

However, *SFAS No. 95* allows netting in certain situations:
* Transactions involving only cash and cash equivalents.
* Operating activities under the indirect method.
* Demand deposits of a bank, customer accounts of a broker-dealer, and other items that the firm holds or pays cash for on behalf of its customers.
* Investments, loans receivable, and debt if turnover is quick, amounts are large, and maturities are at most three months.

For these transactions, gross reporting is considered unnecessary to the understanding of the nature of the cash flows.[22]

Cash Flow per Share

Some financial statement users compute **cash flow per share,** an amount defined in several ways. One common definition is net operating cash flow divided by weighted average common shares outstanding during the year. *SFAS No. 95 prohibits* disclosure of statistics so labeled in financial statements, except for contractually determined cash flow per share values.

The FASB concluded that allowing disclosure of cash flow per share amounts would cause confusion with earnings per share and might imply an amount available for cash dividends.

CONCEPT REVIEW

1. How is the interest portion of a payment on a capital lease classified in the SCF? How is the principal portion classified?
2. Why are noncash activities disclosed?
3. Why does the reporting basis for the SCF include cash equivalents?

---

[22] *SFAS No. 104,* which amends *SFAS No. 95,* allows banks, savings institutions, and credit unions to report certain cash flows net or gross.

PREPARING THE SCF

◆

The next several sections of the chapter are devoted to analyzing transactions and preparing the SCF. Learning to prepare the SCF provides an opportunity to review and integrate your financial accounting knowledge.

Several approaches for preparing the SCF are used in practice. The objective of each is to identify, through analysis of transactions:

* The operating, investing, and financing cash flows.
* Significant noncash investing and financing transactions.
* Items which reconcile income and net operating cash flow.

This chapter demonstrates three approaches for preparation:

* A format-free approach, which uses no specific format for analysis.
* A spreadsheet approach.
* A T-account approach (appendix).

The spreadsheet and T-account approaches are popular formats for manipulating information. Although the spreadsheet dominates in industry and public accounting, many preparers combine features from several approaches. T-accounts are often used in all three approaches to isolate the effects of transactions on specific accounts during the reporting period. To begin, the format-free approach is presented.

Format-Free Approach, Direct Method, Simple Company

Exhibit 23–2 gives the background information leading to the Simple Company SCFs (Exhibit 23–1). This section discusses how to prepare the *direct* SCF, using the Simple Company information, under the format-free approach. This approach is appropriate for companies with small numbers of transactions and accounts, and is useful for explaining transaction analysis.

Sources of Information To identify amounts for disclosure in the SCF, the information sources are searched for data relating to the period's transactions. Journal entries often are reconstructed to identify the components of transactions more clearly. The following information sources are searched, in the order indicated, for information about items to place into the SCF or supporting schedules:

1. The income statement yields information about noncash gains and losses, depreciation, and operating revenues and expenses helpful in determining operating cash flows. Additional information and the comparative balance sheets are consulted for related data.
2. The additional information (including the retained earnings statement or owners' equity statement) yields data on transactions such as debt issuance and retirement, stock transactions, and extraordinary items.
3. The remaining comparative balance sheet account changes not yet explained suggest additional transactions for analysis.

As cash flows are identified, they are placed into one of the three cash flow categories. For example, if the firm purchased land during the year for $200,000, the cash outflow is placed into the investing activities section. Noncash transactions are placed into a supporting schedule. Amounts reconciling income and net operating cash flow are discussed in a later section on the *indirect* method.

Refer back to Exhibit 23–2 for information as transactions are analyzed, and to Exhibit 23–3, which repeats the Simple Company *direct* method SCF, as cash flows are identified. Also, as transactions are analyzed, keep track of the balance sheet account changes that are explained. The income statement accounts are analyzed first.

EXHIBIT 23-2   Case Information

SIMPLE COMPANY
Case Data for Preparing the Statements of Cash Flow
Illustrated in Exhibit 23-1, 3 and 4
(in thousands)

A. Income statement for the year ended 12/31/1991:

Sales (all on credit)	$66
Salaries expense	(28)
Depreciation expense	(4)
Administrative and selling expenses (excluding salaries)	(12)
Net income	$22

B. Comparative Balance Sheets

	12/31/1990	12/31/1991
Cash (no cash equivalents)	$ 42	$ 76
Accounts receivable	31	39
Plant assets	82	81
Accumulated depreciation	(20)	(14)
Total assets	$135	$182
Salaries payable	$ 3	$ 5
Notes payable, long-term	46	40
Common stock, par $10	61	101
Contributed capital in excess of par	9	17
Treasury stock	0	(8)
Retained earnings	16	27
Total liabilities and stockholders' equity	$135	$182

C. Additional information:

1. Plant assets account:
   (a) Purchased plant assets for cash, $30.
   (b) Sold old plant assets for $21 cash; recorded as follows (at book value):

Cash	21	
Accumulated depreciation	10	
Plant assets		31

2. Long-term notes payable account:
   Borrowed cash, $40.
   Payments on note principal, $46.
3. Treasury stock account—Purchased treasury stock for $8 cash.
4. Retained earnings statement:

Balance, 1/1/1991	$16
Net income for 1991	22
Cash dividend paid in cash at end of 1991	(11)
Balance, 12/31/1991	$27

5. Issued common stock for $48 cash.

Transaction Analysis for the Direct Method SCF

Income Statement Accounts   Amounts are expressed in thousands of dollars.

1. *Sales.* Credit sales ($66) increase accounts receivable. A quick scan of additional information indicates no related data (for example, a write-off might be listed in additional information and would be considered here).

The related cash flow is collections on accounts receivable. This amount can be derived in several ways. If Simple Company's accounting system permits, the total cash receipts amount is obtained from the cash receipts journal. Alternatively, an analysis of accounts receivable reveals collections on account. The following T-

EXHIBIT 23-3   Statement of Cash Flows, Direct Method

SIMPLE COMPANY
Statement of Cash Flows, Direct Method
For the Year Ended December 31, 1991
(in thousands)

Italic letters refer to the text discussion.

Cash flows from operating activities:
(*a*) Cash received from customers $58
(*b*) Payments to employees . . . . (26)
(*c*) Payments for administrative and selling activities . . . . (12)

      Net cash inflow from operating activities $20

Cash flows from investing activities:
(*d*) Cash paid for acquisition of plant assets . . . . $(30)
(*e*) Cash received from sale of plant assets 21

      Net cash outflow from investing activities . . . . (9)

Cash flows from financing activities:
(*f*) Cash received from long-term debt issuance $40
(*g*) Cash paid on long-term debt (principal only) . . . . (46)
(*h*) Cash paid for treasury stock purchased . . . . (8)
(*i*) Cash paid for dividends . . . . (11)
(*j*) Cash received from sale of common stock 48

      Net cash inflow from financing activities   23
Effect of foreign exchange rates on cash 0

Net increase in cash and cash equivalents during 1991 34
Cash and cash equivalents, January 1, 1991 42

Cash and cash equivalents, December 31, 1991 . . . . $76

---

account illustrates transactions in summary form, leading to the identification of collections on accounts receivable.

Accounts Receivable

Bal. 1/1/91	31		
Sales in 1991	66	58	*Cash collections*
Bal. 12/31/91	39		*in 1991 (derived)*

In lieu of the T-account, the following expression allows conversion of the accrual information (sales) to the cash-basis (collections on account):[23]

$$\text{Cash collections} = \text{Accrual-basis revenue} \begin{array}{l} + \text{ Decrease in associated receivable} \\ - \text{ Increase in associated receivable} \end{array}$$

$58 customer collections = $66 sales − $8 accounts receivable increase

Either way, the resulting disclosure in the SCF is:

Operating inflow (*a*) (Exhibit 23–3): Collections received from customers $58.

---

[23] These and other expressions facilitate preparation and embody the same logic as the use of the T-account. The emphasis is on the relationships among transactions and account balances, rather than on the expression.

2. *Salaries expense.* Salaries expense ($28), is related to salaries payable, which increased $2 during 1991. No additional information applies. The related cash flow is salary payments, determined in two ways as follows:

Salaries Payable

		Bal. 1/1/91	3
Salary payments *(derived)*	26	Salaries expense	28
		Bal. 12/31/91	5

$$\text{Cash payment} = \text{Accrual-basis expense} \quad \begin{array}{l} + \text{ Decrease in associated payable} \\ - \text{ Increase in associated payable} \end{array}$$

$26 salary payments = $28 salaries expense − $2 salaries payable increase

Operating outflow (*b*) (Exhibit 23–3): Payments to employees ($26).

3. *Depreciation expense.* Depreciation expense ($4) is not a cash flow; therefore, there is no disclosure in the direct method SCF, although this amount will appear in the reconciliation of net income and net operating cash flow.

4. *Administrative and selling expenses.* There is no related additional information or balance sheet account. Therefore, the cash and accrual amounts are the same for this expense.

Operating outflow (*c*) (Exhibit 23–3): Payments for administrative and selling activities $(12).

All income statement accounts now are analyzed, and the second source of information is considered.

Additional Information

1. Simple Company purchased plant assets for $30 cash. This is an investing cash outflow.

Investing outflow (*d*) (Exhibit 23–3): Cash paid for acquisition of plant assets ($30).

Simple Company also sold plant assets; the reconstructed entry is illustrated in the additional information, Exhibit 23–2. The $21 proceeds is an investing cash inflow.

Investing inflow (*e*) (Exhibit 23–3): Cash received from sale of plant assets $21.

The two transactions listed in this item of additional information help explain the changes in accumulated depreciation and plant assets accounts during 1991.

2. Simple Company borrowed $40 cash (financing cash inflow) and paid $46 principal (financing cash outflow) on its long-term notes payable.

Financing inflow (*f*) (Exhibit 23–3): Cash received from long-term debt issuance $40.

Financing outflow (*g*) (Exhibit 23–3): Cash paid on long-term debt (principal only) ($46).

3. The treasury stock purchase is a financing outflow.

Financing outflow (*h*) (Exhibit 23–3): Cash paid for treasury stock purchased ($8).

4. The retained earnings statement reveals $11 dividends declared and paid in 1991, a financing cash outflow. There is no dividends payable account, meaning all dividends declared were paid.

Financing outflow (*i*) (Exhibit 23–3): Cash paid for dividends ($11).

5. The last item is common stock issuance for $48, a financing cash outflow.

Financing inflow (*j*) (Exhibit 23–3): Cash received from sale of common stock $48.

At this point, all additional information is incorporated, and the last information source is considered.

All balance sheet account changes are explained by the transaction analysis. Therefore, there are no further items to disclose in the SCF. For example, plant assets decreased by $1 in 1991. This is explained by the $30 purchase, and sale of assets originally costing $31. Accumulated depreciation decreased $6, which equals depreciation expense (increase $4) less the decrease from equipment disposal ($10). The retained earnings $11 increase is explained by net income (increase $22) less dividends ($11).

Completing the Direct Method SCF   All cash flows are identified and classified as operating, investing, or financing. To complete the SCF, the change in cash (increase $34) and the beginning and ending cash balances are entered as shown in Exhibit 23–3. The net increase in cash from the SCF ($34) agrees with the cash account balance change.

Additional Examples of Operating Cash Flows—Direct Method

The Simple Company example focused on the order of information search and transaction analysis. Before turning to the indirect method, this section provides additional examples of determining operating cash flows.

Deferred Revenues   Determining the cash receipts related to deferred revenues such as unearned rent revenue is accomplished through transaction analysis with the T-account, or with a formula. The analysis follows the same reasoning applied to the accrual revenues and expenses of Simple Company.

$$\text{Cash collections} = \text{Accrual-basis revenue} \quad \begin{array}{l} + \text{ Increase in associated} \\ \quad \text{deferred revenue} \\ \\ - \text{ Decrease in associated} \\ \quad \text{deferred revenue} \end{array}$$

For example, assume a firm reported $12,000 in fee revenue and a $2,000 decrease in unearned fee revenue:

$10,000 fees collected = $12,000 fee − $2,000 decrease in unearned revenue   fee revenue

Using T-accounts, and reconstructing the summary transactions also explains the result:

Unearned Fee Revenue		
Decrease	2,000	
Revenue earned	12,000	*Fees collected (derived)* *10,000*

Some accountants in practice prefer to reconstruct full summary worksheet journal entries to determine the cash flow. In this example, the first entry is:

Unearned fee revenue 12,000
    Fee revenue   12,000

The second entry is implied by the first and the decrease in the unearned fee revenue account:

Cash 10,000
    Unearned fee revenue   10,000

Fees collected is an *operating inflow*.

Prepaid Assets   The expression used to determine cash payments related to prepaids is:

$$\begin{array}{rl} & +\text{ Increase in associated} \\ & \quad\text{prepaid} \\ \text{Cash payment} = \text{Accrual-basis} & \\ \quad\text{expense} & \\ & -\text{ Decrease in associated} \\ & \quad\text{prepaid} \end{array}$$

For example, assume a firm reported $4,000 rent expense and a $1,000 increase in prepaid rent. Applying the above expression, cash payments is determined as follows:

$$\begin{array}{rl} \$5,000 \text{ cash paid for rent} = \$4,000 \text{ rent} & + \$1,000 \text{ increase in} \\ \text{expense} & \quad\text{prepaid insurance} \end{array}$$

Rent payments exceed rent expense because prepaid rent increased during the period. Rent payments is an *operating outflow*. The T-account analysis also can be applied.

Payments for Inventory Purchases   Purchases of inventory are normally made on account. Therefore, accounts payable, cost of goods sold, and inventory are analyzed to determine the associated cash flow:

$$\begin{array}{rl} & +\text{ Inventory increase} \\ \text{Cash paid for} \quad = \text{Cost of} & -\text{ Inventory decrease} \\ \text{inventory purchases} \quad \text{goods sold} & +\text{ Accounts payable} \\ & \quad\text{decrease} \\ & -\text{ Accounts payable} \\ & \quad\text{increase} \end{array}$$

An inventory increase implies a cash outflow exceeding cost of goods sold. Therefore, the increase is added to derive cash payments. An accounts payable increase implies purchases exceed payments. Therefore, the increase is subtracted to derive cash payments. Assume that cost of goods sold is $10,000 for the year, accounts payable increased $3,000, and inventory increased $2,000. Payments for inventory purchases is therefore determined as follows:

$$\begin{array}{lll} \$9,000 \text{ cash paid} = \$10,000 \text{ cost of} & + \$2,000 \text{ inventory} & - \$3,000 \\ \text{for purchases} \quad\quad \text{goods sold} & \quad\text{increase} & \quad\text{accounts payable} \\ & & \quad\text{increase} \end{array}$$

A T-account analysis is particularly useful for deriving cash flows when more than one account is involved:

Inventory

Increase	2,000		
Purchases (derived)	12,000	Cost of goods sold	10,000

Accounts Payable

		Increase	3,000
Cash payments (derived)	9,000	Purchases (from inventory)	12,000

This analysis assumed that accounts payable is used only for inventory purchases. Payments for inventory purchases is an *operating outflow*.

Format-Free Approach, Indirect Method, Simple Company

The investing and financing sections of the indirect and direct method SCFs are identical. Therefore, this section discusses only the *operating section* for the indirect method and uses the Simple Company as an example. The operating section of the indirect method SCF begins with net income, and discloses the items that reconcile net income and net operating cash flow (see Exhibit 23–4, which repeats the Simple Company indirect SCF). The indirect method SCF does *not* disclose the individual operating cash flows.

The reconciliation of net income and operating cash flows is another approach to converting accrual income to cash-basis income. However, this analysis generally does not seek to uncover the operating cash flows. Rather, the search is for amounts that explain why net income is not equal to net operating cash flow. These amounts are called reconciling adjustments. The order of information search used in the direct method also is used in the indirect method.

Depreciation expense is an example of a reconciling adjustment. In the Simple Company example, net income is reduced by $4 depreciation expense in 1991. Depreciation is a noncash expense. However, the indirect method operating section *begins* with net income. Therefore, the $4 depreciation expense must be added to net income as a reconciling adjustment to avoid understating net operating cash flow (see Exhibit 23–4).

The following generalization is useful for determining reconciling adjustments:

*If a transaction's effect on **operating** cash flow is not equal to its effect on net income, a reconciling adjustment is needed for the difference.*

The income effect plus or minus the adjustment yields the operating cash flow effect. In the depreciation expense example, the effect on operating cash flow (zero) is not equal to the income effect (decrease $4). Therefore, a reconciling adjustment of $4 (increase) is required.

Refer to Exhibit 23–2 for information as transactions are analyzed, and to Exhibit 23–4, the *indirect method* SCF, as reconciling amounts are identified.

Transaction Analysis for the Indirect Method SCF

Income Statement Accounts   All amounts are expressed in thousands of dollars.

1. *Sales.* Credit sales ($66) increased accounts receivable, yet accounts receivable increased a net of $8, implying $58 of collections on account. Therefore, the net income effect (increase $66) exceeds the operating cash flow effect (increase $58), necessitating an $8 reconciling adjustment. The $8 accounts receivable increase is *subtrated* from net income to remove the excess of accrual revenue over cash received from net income, *adjustment (a)* in Exhibit 23–4.

EXHIBIT 23-4 Statement of Cash Flows, Indirect Method

SIMPLE COMPANY
Statement of Cash Flows, Indirect Method
For the Year Ended December 31, 1991
(in thousands)

Italic letters refer to the text discussion.

Cash flows from operating activities:

Net income		$22
Add (deduct) to reconcile net income to net operating cash inflow:		
(a) Accounts receivable increase	(8)	
(b) Salaries payable increase	2	
(c) Depreciation expense	4	
Net cash inflow from operating activities		$20
Cash flows from investing activities:		
Cash paid for acquisition of plant assets	$(30)	
Cash received from sale of plant assets	21	
Net cash outflow from investing activities		(9)
Cash flows from financing activities:		
Cash received from long-term debt issuance	$40	
Cash paid on long-term debt (principal only)	(46)	
Cash paid for treasury stock purchased	(8)	
Cash paid for dividends	(11)	
Cash received from sale of common stock	48	
Net cash inflow from financing activities		23
Effect of foreign exchange rates on cash		0
Net increase in cash and cash equivalents during 1991		34
Cash and cash equivalents, January 1, 1991		42
Cash and cash equivalents, December 31, 1991		$76

---

2. *Salaries expense.* Salaries expense ($28) increased salaries payable, yet salaries payable increased a net of $2, implying $26 of salary payments. The net income effect (decrease $28) exceeds the operating cash flow effect (decrease $26). Therefore, the $2 increase in salaries payable is *added* to net income to offset the excess of accrual expense deducted over salary payments made, *adjustment* (b) in Exhibit 23-4.

3. *Depreciation expense.* As discussed before, the $4 expense is *added* to net income, *adjustment* (c) in Exhibit 23-4.

4. *Administrative and selling expenses.* There is no related additional information or balance sheet account, and the cash payments equal the accrual expense. Therefore, no reconciling adjustment is needed.

Additional Information None of the items in additional information affect net income or operating cash flow. Therefore, no additional reconciling adjustments are required. (The investing and financing cash flows are identified and entered as under the direct method.)

Comparative Balance Sheets After completing the investing and financing sections of the SCF, all balance sheet account balance changes are explained. After entering the change in cash for the period, and the beginning and ending cash balances, the indirect method SCF is complete.

EXHIBIT 23-5 Reconciling Adjustments for Net Income and Net Operating Cash Flows

1. Adjustments for changes in *working capital* accounts related to operations (accounts receivable, inventory, prepaids, interest receivable, accounts payable, interest payable, income taxes payable, short-term payables to suppliers and others):*

| | Change in Account Balance during Year | |
	Increase	Decrease
Current asset	*Subtract* increase from net income	*Add* decrease to net income
Current liability	*Add* increase to net income	*Subtract* decrease from net income

The following working capital accounts are excluded from this category of adjustment:

  * Cash and cash equivalents (the SCF is explaining the net change in this fund).
  * Short-term investments (associated cash flows are investing).
  * Dividends payable (dividend payments are financing).
  * Short-term payables to financial institutions (associated cash flows are financing).

2. Noncash expenses, including depreciation, depletion, amortization of intangibles and amortization of discount on bonds payable, are *added* to net income as reconciling adjustments because they do not cause cash to decrease.
  Also *add* to income:

  * Increase in deferred tax liability.
  * Negative investment revenue from equity-method investments.
  * Amortization of premium on bond investments.
  * Unrealized loss on short-term marketable equity securities.†
  * Dividends received from equity-method investments.

3. Noncash revenues, including investment revenue from equity-method investments, and revenues realized by receipt of noncash resources (settlement of liabilities, receipt of long-term assets for services) are *subtracted* from income because they do not cause cash to increase.
  Also *subtract* from income:

  * Amortization of premium on bonds payable.
  * Amortization of discount on bond investments.
  * Decrease in deferred tax liability.

4. Noncash gains are *subtracted* from net income, and noncash losses are *added* to net income. Gains and losses on disposals of plant assets, extraordinary gains and losses on casualties and bond retirements, and gains and losses from discontinued operations are examples.

* *Long-term* payables to suppliers for inventory purchases and other operating activities also are included in this type of adjustment.

† There is no adjustment for unrealized loss on long-term marketable securities under the LCM method because the unrealized loss reduces owners' equity, rather than net income.

Additional Examples of Reconciling Adjustments

Refer to Exhibit 23–5 for common reconciling adjustments.[24] In this section, several of these reconciling adjustments are discussed in detail.

Changes in Operating Working Capital Accounts   The Simple Company case provides two examples of this type of adjustment: the increase in accounts receivable (subtracted from net income) and the increase in salaries payable (added to net income).

---

[24] Most adjustments are not cash flows. An exception is dividends received from equity method investments, illustrated later in the chapter.

These adjustments are required because the operating cash effect is not equal to the income effect. The table in Exhibit 23-5 applies only to working capital accounts associated with operations. Changes in working capital accounts such as dividends payable are not related to operating cash flows.

Amortization of Bond Discount Information pertaining to bond discount is found in additional information or in the comparative balance sheets. An example entry amortizing bond discount appears below.

To recognize interest expense and amortize bond discount (amounts assumed):

Interest expense	12,000	
Discount on bonds payable		2,000
Cash		10,000

Interest expense reduces income $12,000, yet only $10,000 cash was paid. Therefore, the $2,000 amortization is added to income in the reconciliation. Amortization of bond premium is subtracted from net income.

Noncash Revenues Revenues recognized on collection of noncash resources or in settlement of liabilities are subtracted from net income because they provide no cash. The income statement is the source of information for these revenues. For example, assume a firm extinguishes a $10,000 long-term note payable by performing a service for the creditor as recorded in the following entry.

To record service revenue (amounts assumed):

Long-term note payable	10,000	
Service revenue		10,000

The income effect ($10,000) exceeds the operating cash flow effect (zero); therefore, the $10,000 revenue is subtracted from income.

Gain on Sale of Land The income statement (or additional information) is the information source for these items. The following entry records such a gain.

To record sale of land (amounts assumed):

Cash	200,000	
Land (cost)		150,000
Gain on sale of land		50,000

The $200,000 proceeds is an investing cash inflow. This cash flow completely explains the cash consequences of the transaction. However, net income reflects the $50,000 gain and consequently overstates net operating cash flow by that amount. The gain does not represent an additional cash inflow, nor is it related to operations. Therefore, the $50,000 gain is subtracted from net income in the reconciliation.

Comparison of Direct and Indirect Methods

The investing and financing sections of both methods are identical. However, the direct method SCF and related disclosures supply all the information found in the indirect method SCF, and more. The direct method SCF and related disclosures provide more information by supplying *both* of the following:
* The individual operating cash flows within the statement.
* Reconciliation of income and operating cash flows in a supporting schedule.

The indirect method provides *only* the reconciliation, which appears in the operating section of the SCF or in a supporting schedule. In effect, an indirect method SCF is prepared whenever a direct method SCF and related disclosures are prepared. Exhibit 23-6 illustrates the required reconciliation of income and operating cash

EXHIBIT 23-6   Reconciliation of Income and Operating Cash Flow

---

SIMPLE COMPANY

Reconciliation of Net Income and Operating Cash Flows:
Supporting Schedule to the _Direct Method_ SCF

Reconciliation of Net Income and Operating Cash Flows (in thousands)

Net income	$22
Add (deduct) to reconcile net income to net cash inflow:	
Accounts receivable increase	(8)
Salaries payable increase	2
Depreciation expense	4
Net cash flow from operating activities	$20

EXHIBIT 23-7   Disclosure Requirements of _SFAS No. 95_

Operating cash flows, in SCF
  Minimum breakdown of reporting for operating cash flows:
    Collections from customers (including lessees, licensees)
    Interest and dividends received
    Other operating receipts
    Payments to employees and suppliers of all goods and services
    Interest payments, net of amounts capitalized
    Income tax payments
    Other operating payments
Reconciliation of net income and net operating cash flow in supporting
  schedule

Investing cash flows, in SCF
Financing cash flows, in SCF
Minimum breakdown of reporting for reconciliation (reconciling items to be
  clearly identified as such to avoid inference that they are cash flows):
    Change in receivables related to operations
    Change in inventories
    Change in payables related to operations
    Other categories including amortization, depreciation, and noncash gains
      and losses
Noncash investing and financing activities disclosure
Cash and cash equivalents: the change during the period reconciles beginning
  and ending balances; policy regarding securities included in cash
  equivalents is disclosed

Disclose income tax payments and interest payments (net of amounts
  capitalized), in schedule or notes
Reconciliation of net income and net operating cash flow in SCF, or disclose
  in one line the net operating cash flow in the SCF with supporting schedule
  showing detail

Key:
  Required under the direct method: •••••••••••
  Required under the indirect method: ★★★★★★★★★★★

---

flows for Simple Company under the direct method. The reconciliation is _identical_ to the operating section of Simple Company's SCF under the indirect method (Exhibit 23-4).

Disclosure Requirements of *SFAS No. 95*

Exhibit 23–7 presents the disclosure requirements for both the direct and indirect methods. The exhibit's middle area illustrates the considerable overlap between the two methods.

The FASB was concerned with the lack of operating cash flow reporting under the indirect method and, therefore, required disclosure of interest and income tax payments. The minimum reconciliation items under the indirect method allow users to approximate certain operating cash flows when used with income statement information.

The Spreadsheet Approach

Spreadsheets are frequently used for preparing the SCF. A spreadsheet is a computerized columnar format for analyzing transactions and identifying SCF disclosures.

The spreadsheet approach:

* Provides an organized format for documenting the preparation process for subsequent analysis, review and evaluation (spreadsheets are often used in legal proceedings by CPA firms to substantiate their work).
* Provides several proofs of accuracy.
* Formally keeps track of the changes in balance sheet accounts and ensures that all account changes are explained.

The spreadsheet is the most involved format for preparing the SCF, and a certain amount of practice is required for proficiency. For complex preparation problems, however, the benefits of the spreadsheet are worth the extra effort. Even so, no format, spreadsheet or otherwise, eliminates the need to analyze transactions carefully.

The spreadsheet developed for the accounting cycle in Chapter 3, resulting in the income statement and balance sheet, cannot be used for the SCF. Preparation of the SCF requires information beyond the ending adjusted ledger account balances.[25] Several different spreadsheet formats are currently in use, and most are variations on a common theme. The spreadsheet format used in this chapter is concise and results in simultaneous preparation of both direct and indirect method SCFs.[26]

Although the spreadsheet and format-free approaches use the same order of information search and logic for identifying disclosure items, the speadsheet formalizes the process. In many cases, a transaction entry is reconstructed and entered into the spreadsheet to explain changes in account balances. These entries are not formally recorded; they are used only for spreadsheet purposes.

Refer to Exhibit 23–8, which illustrates the complete spreadsheet for the Simple Company. As cash flows are located, they are entered into one of the cash flow activity sections in the lower half of the spreadsheet. Inflows are debits (a cash inflow is a debit to cash), outflows are credits (a cash outflow is a credit to cash). The corresponding debit or credit is entered into the appropriate balance sheet account in the upper half of the worksheet. For example, the spreadsheet entry corresponding to the purchase of plant assets for $30 is entry (*f*). The debit of $30 helps to explain the change in plant assets in the upper half, and the credit of $30 appears in the investing section of the worksheet—a cash outflow—in the lower half.

In the *operating* activities section, the debit and credit *columns* reflect the reconciliation of income and net operating cash flow. These columns are labeled "indirect method" because the entries in these columns are used for the operating section

---

[25] If it did not, the SCF would simply repeat the information in the balance sheet and income statements.

[26] This format is adapted from an article by W. Collins that appeared in the "Practitioners Forum" of the *Journal of Accountancy*, May 1990, p. 124.

EXHIBIT 23-8 Spreadsheet Approach

SIMPLE COMPANY
Spreadsheet for Direct and Indirect Method SCF
For the Year Ended December 31, 1991
(in thousands)

Italic letters refer to the text discussion.

Comparative Balance Sheets	12/31/90	Dr.		Cr.		12/31/91
Cash	42	(m)	34			76
Accounts receivable	31	(b)	8			39
Plant assets	82	(f)	30	31	(g)	81
Accumulated depreciation	(20)	(g)	10	4	(d)	(14)
Total assets	135					182
Salaries payable	3			2	(c)	5
Notes payable	46	(i)	46	40	(h)	40
Common stock	61			40	(l)	101
Contributed capital in excess of par	9			8	(l)	17
Treasury stock		(j)	8			(8)
Retained earnings	16	(k)	11	22	(a)	27
Total liabilities and owners' equity	135					182
Total changes				147	147	

Adjustments Leading to SCF

		Indirect Method Dr.		Indirect Method Cr.		Direct Method (Operations)
Operating activities:						
Net income	22	(a)	22			
Sales	66			8	(b)	58 customer collections
Salary expense	28	(c)	2			26 salary payments
Depreciation	4	(d)	4			
Administrative and selling	12				(e)	12 payments
Investing activities:						
Purchase plant assets				30	(f)	
Sale of plant assets		(g)	21			
Financing activities:						
Issue notes payable for cash		(h)	40			
Payments on notes payable				46	(i)	
Purchase treasury stock				8	(j)	
Dividends paid				11	(k)	
Issue common stock		(l)	48			
				103		
Net cash increase				34	(m)	
			137	137		

under the indirect method. Debit adjustments are added to net income, and credits are subtracted in the reconciliation. Going across *rows,* the debits and credits adjust the accrual revenue or expense to yield the operating cash flow for the direct method. The process is complete when all balance sheet account changes are explained. The information from the three activity sections is transferred to the direct method or indirect method SCFs.

Spreadsheet Approach, The Simple Company Example

The explanation for each cash flow and reconciling adjustment mirrors the format-free approach (the italic letters, however, do not correspond). Except for entering net income first, the information sources are searched in the usual order. Refer to Exhibit 23–8 for each spreadsheet entry.

Amounts are in thousands:

(a) The $22 debit (net income, implying cash increase) in the operating section of the indirect method columns begins the reconciliation schedule. Net income is the starting figure for net operating cash flow. The credit partially explains the change in retained earnings. Net income is not a cash flow and is not extended to the direct method columns.

(b) The $8 debit explains the increase in accounts receivable. In the indirect method columns (the reconciliation), the $8 credit is subtracted from net income. Increases in operating current assets are subtracted from net income. The credit also is subtracted from sales to yield cash collected from customers, under the direct method. When used as adjustments across rows, credits result in cash decreases (either a decrease in a cash inflow as in this item, or an increase in a cash outflow). The direct method column lists the $58 operating cash inflow.

(c) The $2 credit explains the increase in salaries payable. The debit (indirect method columns) increases net income because an operating payable increased. The debit also adjusts salaries expense to yield cash paid to employees. When used as adjustments across rows, debits result in cash increases (either an increase in a cash inflow, or a decrease in a cash outflow as in this item). The direct method column lists the $26 operating cash outflow.

(d) Depreciation affects only the reconciliation (indirect method columns). This spreadsheet entry is the first to reconstruct an actual journal entry. The $4 credit explains part of the accumulated depreciation change, and the debit implies an addition to net income for the reconciliation.

(e) This is not a formal spreadsheet entry because no balance sheet account requires explanation. Administrative and selling expenses were paid entirely in cash. No reconciling item appears, but the direct method column lists the $12 operating cash outflow.

(f) At this point, the operating section is complete; both methods now use only the indirect method columns. The $30 debit for plant asset purchase in this reconstructed journal entry helps explain the change in plant assets. The investing section lists the credit, or cash outflow.

(g) This reconstructed entry records the removal of $10 accumulated depreciation on disposal, removes the $31 original asset cost, and records the $21 investing cash inflow.

(h) The $40 credit of this reconstructed entry records the issuance of a long-term note payable. The financing section records the debit, or cash inflow.

(i) The $46 debit of this reconstructed entry records the decrease or principal payment for the long-term note. The financing section records the credit, or cash outflow.

(j) The reconstructed entry to record the treasury stock purchase includes an $8 debit, which completely explains the treasury stock account change, and the credit (outflow) listed in the financing section of the spreadsheet.

(k) The reconstructed entry to record dividends paid results in the $11 credit (cash outflow) listed in the financing section.

(l) The stock issue is the only transaction affecting common stock. The reconstructed entry explains that account change, with a $48 debit (cash inflow) in the financing section.

(*m*) This is a balancing entry, not a reconstructed journal entry. At this point, all balance sheet account changes except cash are explained, and all relevant information is incorporated. The $34 debit explains the cash change, and the $34 credit reconciles the cash credit change total with the cash debit change total.

The three operating cash flows (direct method column) are transferred to the direct method SCF (Exhibit 23–3). The three reconciling items (indirect method columns) are transferred to the operating section of indirect method SCF, *and* to the reconciliation for the direct method. The two investing cash flows and five financing cash flows are transferred to both direct and indirect method SCFs. The spreadsheet easily accommodates either method.

The spreadsheet affords Simple Company several accuracy checks. The changes in all balance sheet accounts are explained. The debit and credit balance sheet change column totals agree ($147), although this amount is meaningful only for checking purposes. Entry (*m*), the $34 cash change, reconciles the total of cash increases and decreases. Furthermore, the net operating cash flow ($20) agrees for both methods. Disagreement of these two totals is a common problem when first learning the spreadsheet approach. Finally, the cash ledger account change equals the change listed in the SCF.

CONCEPT REVIEW

1. Explain why a gain on sale of equipment is subtracted in the reconciliation of income and operating cash flows.
2. Why is depreciation added in the reconciliation?
3. Why is an accounts receivable increase subtracted in the reconciliation?

ANALYZING MORE COMPLEX SITUATIONS
◆

The purpose of the Simple Company example is to emphasize preparation of a complete SCF. Before turning to a comprehensive example, this section considers more involved transactions on an individual basis. Firms report the SCF under the direct *or* the indirect method, not both. However, to provide a complete discussion, the remaining sections present the appropriate disclosures for both methods.

Dividends   When the amounts of dividends declared and paid are equal, the financing activities section discloses dividends declared and paid as a cash outflow. Frequently however, dividends are declared in one period, and paid in the next. For example, assume comparative balance sheets disclose the following:

	1991	1992
Dividends payable	$40,000	$60,000

Assume also that $70,000 of dividends were declared during 1992. The amount of dividends paid is derived as follows:

Dividends Payable

	Beginning balance	40,000
Dividends paid (derived) *50,000*	Dividends declared	70,000
	Ending balance	60,000

Although dividends payable is a current liability, it is not related to operations. Therefore, its change is not shown in the reconciliation of income and operating cash flow. The following disclosure is required:

Direct and indirect methods: Financing cash outflow, $50,000 dividends paid.

Some accountants maintain that unpaid dividends are a significant financing activity. Under this view, the firm in this example reports $60,000 unpaid dividends in the noncash activity schedule of the SCF.

Cumulative Effect of an Accounting Change   This type of accounting change generally does not affect cash. For example, a change from accelerated depreciation to straight-line depreciation increases net income (cumulative effect account) and increases net plant assets, but does not affect cash. Therefore, the cumulative effect is a reconciling adjustment.

For example, Kellogg Company changed its method of accounting for income taxes in 1989, increasing income $48.1 million. Kellogg included the following disclosure in the operating section of its 1989 SCF, indirect method:

> (*In millions*)
> Cumulative effect of accounting change . . . . . ($48.1)

This accounting change supplied no cash and is subtracted from net income.

Cash Surrender Value of Life Insurance   The cash surrender value of an insurance policy increases with time. As premiums are paid, a portion is applied to the insured's surrender account. The surrender value is the amount payable upon termination of the policy, and is classified as an investment. Consider the following entry:

To record insurance premium payment:

> Cash surrender value of life insurance 2,000
> Life insurance expense 18,000
>   Cash   20,000

In this case, $2,000 of the $20,000 premium is applied to the surrender value of the policy.

Direct method: Operating cash outflow, insurance premiums, $20,000.

Indirect method and reconciliation for direct method: Subtract $2,000, the increase in surrender value, from net income.

Operating cash flows decreased $20,000, yet earnings decreased only $18,000 (insurance expense). Therefore, the difference is subtracted from earnings in the reconciliation.[27]

Rowe Furniture Corporation in 1989 included the following subtraction adjustment in the reconciliation, supporting its direct method SCF:

(*In thousands*)	1989	1988	1987
Increase in cash surrender value of insurance policies	($150)	($128)	($253)

Sale of Cash Equivalents   Cash equivalents are often sold at face value. No disclosure in the SCF is warranted because the total of cash and cash equivalents is not changed

---

[27] A completely different disclosure is arguable, considering that the surrender value is an investment:

Direct and indirect methods: Operating cash outflow, $18,000 insurance premiums; investing cash outflow, $2,000 increase in cash surrender value.

There is no reconciliation adjustment under this treatment. Most firms probably use the text disclosure, treating the entire transaction as operating.

by the sale. A gain or loss on sale requires disclosure, however. Assume that $50,000 (cost) of cash equivalents are sold for $52,000, resulting in a $2,000 gain. The gain equals the increase in cash and cash equivalents.

Direct method: Operating cash inflow, gain on sale of cash equivalents, $2,000.

Indirect method and reconciliation for direct method: No adjustment is necessary because the operating cash effect ($2,000) is reflected in income ($2,000 gain).

Transactions involving only cash and cash equivalents are considered operating activities rather than investment activities.[28]

Sale of Short-Term Investment (Not Cash Equivalent) For both the direct and indirect methods, the proceeds from the sale of short-term investments other than cash equivalents is an investing cash inflow. Any gain or loss from sale is a reconciliation adjustment. For example, the sale of $24,000 (cost) of short-term investments in common stock for $21,000 is disclosed in the SCF as follows:

Direct and indirect methods: Investing cash inflow, sale of short-term investments, $21,000; add the $3,000 loss on sale of investments in the reconciliation.

The $3,000 loss reduces income, but does not cause a cash outflow. Therefore, the loss is added back to income.

Capital Leases The increase in a lessee's long-term assets and liabilities resulting from lease capitalization is a significant investing and financing activity. Lease payments consist of interest (an operating payment) and principal (a financing payment). For example, assume that on January 1, 1991, a lease requiring five equal annual payments of $31,656 due each December 31 is capitalized at 10%. The entries to record the lease and first lease payment follow:

January 1, 1991—To record capital lease:

Leased property	120,000	
Lease liability		120,000*

* $31,656(PVA,10\%,5) = \$31,656(3.79079)$.

December 31, 1991—To record first lease payment:

Interest expense (.10 × $120,000)	12,000	
Lease liability	19,656	
Cash		31,656

Direct and indirect methods: Operating cash outflow, interest payment, $12,000;[29] financing cash outflow, principal payment on capital lease, $19,656; noncash supplementary schedule, asset acquired under capitalized lease, $120,000.

Income Taxes, Current and Deferred Income tax expense on income from continuing operations is recorded in income taxes payable and a deferred tax account. Assume the following information:

	1991	1992
From comparative balance sheets:		
Income taxes payable	$20,000	$27,000
Deferred taxes (long-term)	18,000	23,000
Income tax expense for 1992: $45,000		
Assume no net reversals of temporary differences.		

---

[28] *SFAS No. 95*, pars. 16, 21.

[29] Indirect method discloses this amount in a supporting schedule.

The reconstructed entries for taxes are as follows:

To record income tax expense:

```
Income tax expense  . . . . . . . . . . . . . . . . . . . . . . .   45,000
     Deferred income tax liability ($23,000 − $18,000) . . . . . .          5,000
     Income taxes payable . . . . . . . . . . . . . . . . . . . .         40,000
```

To record income tax payments:

```
Income taxes payable ($20,000 + $40,000 − $27,000) . . . . . .   33,000
     Cash  . . . . . . . . . . . . . . . . . . . . . . . . . . .         33,000
```

Income tax expense reduces income $45,000, yet cash from operations is reduced only $33,000, a $12,000 difference. As indicated in Exhibit 23–5, both the $7,000 income taxes payable increase and $5,000 deferred tax increase are added in the reconciliation of income and net operating cash flow. Together, the two adjustments provide $12,000 of reconciliation adjustments, which explains the difference between income and net operating cash flows. Collapsing the above two entries into one clarifies these conclusions:

Combined entry:

```
Income tax expense  . . . . . . . . . . . . . . . . . . . . . . .   45,000
     Deferred taxes . . . . . . . . . . . . . . . . . . . . . . .          5,000
     Income taxes payable . . . . . . . . . . . . . . . . . . . .          7,000
     Cash  . . . . . . . . . . . . . . . . . . . . . . . . . . .         33,000
```

The combined entry reveals that increases in deferred taxes and income taxes payable completely explain the difference between income tax expense and the tax paid. Reconstruction of entries is helpful whenever the SCF disclosures are not readily apparent. The following disclosures are required in the SCF:

Direct method: Operating cash outflow, tax payments, $33,000.

Indirect method and reconciliation for direct method: Add $7,000 income taxes payable increase and $5,000 deferred taxes increase to net income. Disclose income tax payments, $33,000, in a supporting schedule for the indirect method.

Equity Method of Accounting for Investments   Under the equity method, the investor records its share of investee earnings as an increase in the investment and investment revenue accounts. Dividends received, an operating cash inflow, decreases the investment. For example, assume Emmet Company owns 30% of Sandoval Company. Sandoval earned $400,000 and paid $300,000 in dividends the current year. Emmet records the following entries:

To record Emmet's share of Sandoval income:

```
Investment in stock (.30 × $400,000)  . . . . . . . . . . . . . .  120,000
     Investment revenue . . . . . . . . . . . . . . . . . . . . .        120,000
```

To record dividends received:

```
Cash (.30 × $300,000) . . . . . . . . . . . . . . . . . . . . . .   90,000
     Investment in stock . . . . . . . . . . . . . . . . . . . .         90,000
```

Investment revenue increases income, but not cash. Dividends received is an operating cash inflow. The SCF disclosures are as follows:

Direct method: Operating cash inflow, dividends received from investment, $90,000.

Indirect method and reconciliation for direct method: Subtract $120,000 investment revenue from net income, add $90,000 dividends received to net income.

The second reconciliation adjustment, $90,000 dividends received, is necessary because net income does not reflect dividends under the equity method, thereby understating operating cash inflow. Alternatively, one net adjustment can be made: subtract from net income the excess of investment revenue over dividends, $30,000.

Honeywell, Inc., disclosed the following in its 1989 reconciliation (in millions):

	1989
Equity income, net of dividends received	$(30.2)

Honeywell uses the net disclosure alternative. In 1989, the company subtracts investment earnings because its share of investee income exceeds dividends received.

Short-Term and Long-Term Notes Payable to Suppliers   Inventory purchases financed by the supplier are operating activities. The principal payments on both short- and long-term notes to suppliers are operating cash outflows. For example, if notes payable to suppliers increased from $10,000 to $15,000 during the year, and if $25,000 was paid on account during the year, the following disclosures are required:

Direct method: Operating cash outflow, payments to suppliers, $25,000.

Indirect method and reconciliation for direct method: Add increase in notes payable to suppliers, $5,000 (short- or long-term).

Short-Term and Long-Term Notes Payable to Banks   Principal payments on loans from financial institutions, whether short or long-term, are financing cash flows. Assume that notes payable to banks increased from $10,000 to $15,000 during the year, and that $25,000 was paid on loans during the year. This implies that $30,000 was received on loans from banks during the year. The following disclosures are required:

Direct and indirect methods: Financing cash inflow, borrowings from banks, $30,000; financing cash outflow, principal payments on borrowings from banks, $25,000.

There is no reconciliation adjustment because income is unaffected.

Accounts Receivable, Bad Debts, and Write-offs   The Simple Company example did not include bad debts or receivable write-offs. In general, the following disclosures are made for accounts receivable:

Direct method: Operating cash inflow, collections from customers on account.

Indirect method and reconciliation for direct method: Either adjust net income for the change in *net* accounts receivable, or adjust net income for the change in *gross* accounts receivable *before* write-offs, and add bad debt expense to net income.

The following example illustrates these generalizations. This is another situation where reconstructing transactions is helpful:

	1991	**1992**
From comparative balance sheets:		
Accounts receivable	$600,000	$175,000
Allowance for doubtful accounts	20,000	35,000
During 1992:		
Bad debt expense, $40,000		
Accounts written off, $25,000		
Collections on account, $1,400,000		
Sales on account, $1,000,000		

Accounts Receivable

Beg. bal.	600,000		
Sales	1,000,000	Collections	1,400,000
		Write-offs	25,000
End. bal	175,000		

Allowance for Doubtful Accounts

		Beg. bal	20,000
Write-offs	25,000	Bad debt expense	40,000
		End. bal	35,000

Net accounts receivable, 12/31/91 $600,000 − $20,000 = $580,000
Net accounts receivable, 12/31/92 $175,000 − $35,000 = 140,000
Decrease in net accounts receivable $440,000

Change in gross accounts receivable before write-offs:

Sales ($1,000,000) − Collections ($1,400,000) = $400,000 decrease

Net income effect:

Sales ($1,000,000) − Bad debt expense ($40,000) = $960,000 increase

Required SCF disclosures:

Direct method: Operating cash inflow, collections from customers on account, $1,400,000.

Indirect method and reconciliation for direct method: Either add net accounts receivable decrease of $440,000 to net income, or add gross accounts receivable decrease of $400,000, and add bad debt expense of $40,000 to net income.

Both reconciliation alternatives yield a net $440,000 addition reconciling adjustment. When this $440,000 adjustment is added to net income, it combines with the $960,000 income effect from transactions involving accounts receivable to yield the $1,400,000 cash inflow.

Extraordinary Items   Extraordinary items generally are not cash flows, but they do affect income. Therefore, they often are adjustments to net income in the reconciliation in their pretax amounts. The cash flow associated with the transaction giving rise to the extraordinary item is usually classified as investing or financing. Tax payments (or reductions in payments) resulting from extraordinary items are operating cash flows. The adjustment for the change in income taxes payable automatically includes the tax effects of extraordinary items.

For example, assume a company retires a bond issue before maturity by paying $330,000, excluding accrued interest. The firm recognizes a $20,000 extraordinary gain before tax ($4,000 tax effect) on the retirement. The following are the SCF disclosures:

Direct and indirect methods: Financing cash outflow, bond retirement, $330,000; subtract the $20,000 extraordinary gain in the reconciliation.

Total income tax payments, which include payments on the extraordinary gain, are disclosed in the operating section of the direct method SCF and in a supporting schedule for the indirect method. The reconciliation also shows an adjustment for the change in income taxes payable, which reflects the tax effect on the extraordinary gain.

Schlumberger Limited included the following disclosures in its 1989 indirect method SCF:

Cash flows from operating activities:
   Extraordinary gain (subtracted from net income) . . . . . ($21,500,000)

Cash flows from investing activities:
   Proceeds from extraordinary item   50,151,000

SCF disclosures for discontinued operations are similar to those for extraordinary items. McCormick & Company, Inc., disclosed the following in its 1989 indirect method SCF:

Cash flows from operating activities:
  Gain on sale of discontinued real estate
    operations (subtracted from net income) . . . . ($83,000,000)
Cash flows from investing activities:
  Proceeds from sale of discontinued
    real estate operations   139,230,000

CONCEPT REVIEW

1. What is the effect on cash and cash equivalents of selling cash equivalents at a $3,000 loss?
2. Explain how transactions giving rise to extraordinary items are disclosed in the SCF.
3. Explain why dividends received from equity method investments are added in the reconciliation.

COMPREHENSIVE EXAMPLE, THE COMPLEX COMPANY

◆

This section provides a longer, more involved example of preparing a complete SCF. The spreadsheet approach is used to determine both the direct and indirect method SCFs in this example. Example 23–9 furnishes the case data for Complex Company. Refer to Exhibit 23–10, the complete spreadsheet, as transactions are analyzed.

Income Statement Accounts   The accounts are analyzed in order of appearance in the statement. Amounts are in thousands of dollars:

(a) $15 net income begins the reconciliation of net income and net operating cash flows.

(b) Reconciliation: gross $3 accounts receivable decrease (related to sales and services) is added to net income. Bad debt expense is a separate adjustment, in (i).

Direct method: cash collections exceed sales by $3 because accounts receivable decreased $3. In terms of the spreadsheet, the $96 sales (initial cash inflow estimate) is increased by the $3 entry in the debit column (a debit to cash increases cash), yielding the $99 cash inflow.

(c) Reconciliation: no adjustment for $1 dividends on short-term investments is necessary because the increase in net income equals the cash inflow.

Direct method: $1 dividends is an operating cash inflow.

(d) Reconciliation: subtract the $3 gain on sale of plant assets.

Both methods: using related additional information, proceeds on sale of plant assets ($15) is an investing cash inflow. The related changes in plant assets and

EXHIBIT 23-9   Case Information

COMPLEX COMPANY
Case Data for Preparing the Statements of Cash Flow
(in thousands)

Income Statement, 1991

Revenues and gains:

Sales and services	$96
Dividends (Xenon Corp.)	1
Gain on sale of plant assets	3
Gain on sale of cash equivalents	2

Expenses:

Cost of goods sold	(42)
Depreciation expense	(8)
Bad debt expense	(3)
Interest expense (on bonds)	(5)
Remaining expenses	(13)
Income tax expense (continuing operations)	(9)
Income before extraordinary items and discontinued operations	22
Discontinued operations, gain $10 (tax expense, $3)	7
Extraordinary loss, land condemnation $20 (tax saving, $6)	(14)
Net income	$15

Comparative Balance Sheets, December 31, 1991:

Items	12/31/1990	12/31/1991
Cash	$ 30	$ 61
Cash equivalents	6	0
Total	36	61
Investment, short term (stock of Xenon Corp.)	12	17
Accounts receivable	32	29
Allowance for doubtful accounts	(2)	(5)
Inventory (perpetual system)	30	37
Prepaid insurance	4	2
Land	60	41
Plant assets	80	96
Accumulated depreciation	(20)	(26)
Other assets (includes discontinued operations, $13)	35	22
Total assets	$267	$274
Accounts payable	$ 26	$ 30
Interest payable	2	1
Income tax payable	11	4
Notes payable, long-term	0	10
Bonds payable	80	60
Unamortized bond discount	(3)	(2)
Common stock, nopar	100	130
Retained earnings	51	41
Total liabilities and stockholders' equity	$267	$274

---

accumulated depreciation are entered. These amounts serve to partially explain the account balance changes.

(*e*) Reconciliation: no adjustment is needed for the gain on sale of cash equivalents because the $2 gain equals the cash increase.

Direct method: the gain is a $2 operating cash inflow.

EXHIBIT 23–9 (*concluded*)

COMPLEX COMPANY
Case Data for Preparing the Statements of Cash Flow
(in thousands)

Additional Information

1. Sold cash equivalents in January, 1991 for $8 cash.
2. Cash borrowed on long-term note at the end of 1991, $10.
3. Retained earnings statement, year ended December 31, 1991:

Beginning balance	$51
Net income for 1991	15
Cash dividend declared and paid in 1991	(15)
Stock dividend issued in 1991 (capitalize par value)	(10)
Ending balance	$41

	Asset	Accumulated Depreciation
4. Plant asset account:		
Beginning balance	$80	$20 credit
Disposal of asset (for cash, $15)	(14)	(2)
Acquisition of new asset (machine)*	30	
Depreciation		8
Ending balance	$96	$26

* Paid cash $10 and issued common stock in full settlement, $20 (market value).

	Bonds	Discount, Unamortized balance
5. Bonds payable account:		
Beginning balance	$80	$3 debit
Discount amortization for 1991		(1)
Bonds retired at end of 1991 at face value	(20)	
Ending balance	$60	$2

6. Land account:

Beginning balance	$60
Sale due to condemnation (extraordinary loss); cash received in full payment, $40	(60)
Land acquisition (paid cash, $41)	41
Ending balance	$41

7. Discontinued operations:
    Closed out a segment completely by selling all related assets
    for cash $23. The $13 cost of these assets is included in the account
    other assets. Assume no accumulated depreciation.

8. Income tax payable account:

Beginning balance		$11
Additions for current income taxes:		
Tax on continuing operations	$9	
Extraordinary loss ($20), tax saving	(6)	
Discontinued operations ($10), tax expense	3	
Increase in payable (net)		6
Cash payments made during 1991		(13)
Ending balance		$ 4

EXHIBIT 23-10   Spreadsheet

COMPLEX COMPANY
Spreadsheet for Direct and Indirect Method SCF
For the Year Ended December 31, 1991
(in thousands)

Comparative Balance Sheets	12/31/90	Dr.		Cr.		12/31/91
Cash	30	(v) 31				61
Cash equivalents	6			6 (v)		
Investment in Xenon	12	(u) 5				17
Accounts receivable	32			3 (b)		29
Allowance for doubtful accounts	(2)			3 (i)		(5)
Inventory	30	(g) 7				37
Prepaid insurance	4			2 (k)		2
Land	60	(t) 41		60 (n)		41
Plant assets	80	(r) 30		14 (d)		96
Accumulated depreciation	(20)	(d) 2		8 (h)		(26)
Other assets	35			13 (m)		22
Total assets	267					274
Accounts payable	26			4 (f)		30
Interest payable	2	(j) 1				1
Income taxes payable	11	(l) 7				4
Notes payable				10 (o)		10
Bonds payable	80	(s) 20				60
Unamortized bond discount	(3)			1 (j)		(2)
Common stock	100			10 (q)		130
				20 (r)		
Retained earnings	51	(p) 15		15 (a)		41
		(q) 10				
Total liabilities and owners' equity	267					274
Total changes		169		169		

(*f*), (*g*) Reconciliation: the adjustments related to cost of goods sold include the $4 accounts payable increase added to net income, and $7 inventory increase subtracted from net income.

Direct method: in terms of the spreadsheet, the $42 cost of goods sold (initial cash outflow estimate) is decreased by the $4 entry in the debit column (a debit to cash increases cash or decreases the cash outflow) and is increased by the $7 credit entry (a credit to cash increases the cash outflow).

(*h*) Reconciliaton: $8 depreciation is added to net income.

(*i*) Reconciliation: $3 bad debt expense is added to net income. Alternatively, the reconciliation adjustments in (*b*) and (*i*) can be combined into one adjustment for the decrease in net accounts receivable: add $6.

(*j*) Reconciliation: subtract the $1 interest payable decrease (related to interest expense), and add the $1 amortization of bond discount.

Direct method: $5 operating cash outflow. A summary entry explains this outflow, and the changes in relevant accounts.

Interest expense	5	
Interest payable	1	
Unamortized bond discount		1
Cash (derived)		5

EXHIBIT 23–10 (*concluded*)

COMPLEX COMPANY

Spreadsheet for Direct and Indirect Method SCF
For the Year Ended December 31, 1991
(in thousands)

Adjustments leading to SCF

Italic letters refer to the text discussion.

		Indirect Method				Direct Method (Operations)
		Dr.		Cr.		
Operating Activities:						
Net income	15	(a)	15			
Sales and services	96	(b)	3		99	customer collections
Dividends	1			(c)	1	dividends received
Gain, sale of plant asset	3			3 (d)		
Gain on sale of cash equivalents	2			(e)	2	cash equivalent sale
Cost of goods sold	42	(f)	4	7 (g)	45	payments to suppliers
Depreciation	8	(h)	8			
Bad debt expense	3	(i)	3			
Interest expense	5	(j)	1	1 (j)	5	interest payments
Remaining expenses	13	(k)	2		11	payments for other expenses
Income tax expense	9			7 (l)	16	tax payments
Gain on discontinued operations	10			10 (m)		
Less tax	3				3	increase tax payments
Extraordinary loss	20	(n)	20			
Less tax savings	6				6	reduce tax payments
Investing activities:						
Sale of plant assets		(d)	15			
Proceeds from sale of discontinued assets		(m)	23			
Proceeds from condemnation		(n)	40			
Purchase of plant assets				10 (r)		
Acquisition of land				41 (t)		
Purchase of Xenon stock				5 (u)		
Financing activities:						
Issue long-term note		(o)	10			
Dividend payment				15 (p)		
Bond retirement				20 (s)		
				119		
Net increase in cash & cash equivalents				25 (v)		
			144	144		

(*k*) Reconciliation: add the $2 prepaid insurance decrease (the only balance sheet account related to remaining expenses).

Direct method: the $11 cash payment equals the $13 remaining expenses less the $2 decrease in prepaid insurance.

(*l*) Reconciliation: subtract the $7 income tax payable decrease (related to income tax expense).

Direct method: $16 income tax payment exceeds $9 income tax expense by the $7 income tax payable decrease. This is an initial tax payment amount, adjusted by the tax related to the extraordinary loss and discontinued operations gain (see m next).

(*m*) Reconciliation: subtract the $10 gain from discontinued operations.

Both methods: using related additional information, the $23 proceeds from sale of assets from discontinued operations is an investing cash inflow. The original cost of assets is entered into the spreadsheet.

Direct method: the $3 tax on the gain increases tax payments.

(*n*) Reconciliation: add the $20 extraordinary loss to net income.

Both methods: using related additional information, the $40 proceeds from sale of land due to condemnation is an investing cash inflow. The original cost of land is entered into the spreadsheet.

Direct method: the $6 tax savings reduces tax payments. Total tax payments equal $13 ($16 tax payments on continuing operations plus $3 on discontinued operations less $6 on extraordinary loss).

Additional Information   The additional information not already incorporated into the spreadsheet is analyzed in order of appearance in Exhibit 23-9:

(*o*) Both methods: financing cash inflow, $10 proceeds from issuing long-term note.
(*p*) Both methods: financing cash outflow, $15 dividend payments.
(*q*) Stock dividends are not disclosed in the SCF.
(*r*) Both methods: investing cash outflow, $10 payment to purchase plant assets. Note A to the SCF (Exhibit 23–11) describes the noncash aspects of the acquisition: issuance of $20 of common stock for the remaining portion of the purchase price.
(*s*) Both methods: financing cash outflow, $20 payment to retire bonds.
(*t*) Both methods: investing cash outflow, $41 payment to acquire land.

Remaining Unexplained Balance Sheet Accounts

(*u*) At this point, all additional information is incorporated, and all balance sheet account changes are explained except for investment in the Xenon stock which increased $5 during 1991. This implies a purchase of additional stock.

Both methods: investing cash outflow, $5 payment to acquire Xenon stock.

(*v*) Balancing entry: cash increased $31 during 1991, and cash equivalents decreased $6. The net increase in cash and cash equivalents is therefore $25. This amount reconciles total cash increases and total cash decreases.

The spreadsheet is totaled to confirm its accuracy. The direct method SCF is prepared by transferring the operating cash flows in the direct method columns of the spreadsheet to the operating activities section of the SCF. The investing and financing cash flows are transferred to their respective sections in the SCF. The complete direct method SCF is illustrated in Exhibit 23–11, which also shows the noncash footnote or schedule.

The reconciliation of net income and net operating cash flow for both methods is prepared by transferring the 12 reconciling adjustments from the indirect method columns in the operating section of the spreadsheet. The reconciliation appears in Exhibit 23–12. To prepare the indirect method SCF (not illustrated), replace the operating section of the direct method SCF with the reconciliation. The policy for cash equivalents and the supporting schedule for income tax payments and interest payments for the indirect method also are not illustrated.

EXHIBIT 23-11   Statement of Cash Flows

COMPLEX COMPANY

Statement of Cash Fows, Direct Method
For the Year Ended December 31, 1991
(in thousands)

Cash flows from operating activities:		
Cash inflows:		
From customers	$99	
From dividends received on short-term investments	1	
From gain on cash equivalents sold	2	
Cash outflows:		
Paid to suppliers (for cost of goods sold)	(45)	
Paid for interest	(5)	
Paid for remaining expenses	(11)	
Paid for income taxes	(13)	
Net cash inflow from operating activities		$28
Cash flows from investing activities:		
Cash inflows:		
From sale of plant assets	15	
From discontinued operations	23	
From sale of land (condemnation)	40	
Cash outflows:		
Paid for plant assets (Note A)	(10)	
Paid for purchase of land	(41)	
Paid for purchase of investment in Xenon	(5)	
Net cash inflow from investing activities		22
Cash flows from financing activities:		
Cash inflows:		
Borrowing on long-term note	10	
Cash outflows:		
Paid cash dividend	(15)	
Payment on bond principal	(20)	
Net cash outflow for financing activities		(25)
Net increase in cash and cash equivalents during 1991		25
Cash and cash equivalents, January 1, 1991		36
Cash and cash equivalents, December 31, 1991		$61

Note A: The company purchased an operational asset (machine); payment was in cash and the company's common stock as follows:

Cash paid	$10
Common stock issued	20
Total asset cost recorded	$30

ISSUES IN CASH FLOW REPORTING
◆

Cash or Accrual Information

Several researchers have focused on the relative usefulness of cash flow versus accrual information. For example, in one study of 98 firms, the authors found that cash flow information increases the overall information content of financial statements.[30] In another study, investigators found evidence to suggest that in assessing a

---

[30] R. Bowen, D. Burgstahler, and L. Daley, "The Incremental Information Content of Accrual Versus Cash Flows," *Accounting Review,* October 1987, pp. 723–47.

EXHIBIT 23-12   Reconciliation

COMPLEX COMPANY	
Reconciliation of Net Income to Net Cash Inflow	
(Outflow) from Operating Activities	
For the Year Ended December 31, 1991	
(in thousands)	
Net income (accrual basis, from income statement)	$15
Add (deduct) to reconcile net income to net cash flow from operating activities:	
Accounts receivable decrease	3
Gain on sale of operational assets	(3)
Inventory increase	(7)
Accounts payable increase	4
Depreciation expense	8
Bad debt expense	3
Interest payable decrease	(1)
Amortization of bond discount	1
Prepaid insurance decrease	2
Income tax payable decrease	(7)
Discontinued operations, gain (pretax)	(10)
Extraordinary loss (pretax)	20
Net cash inflow from operating activities	$28

firm's risk, cash flow variables supply information in addition to that provided by earnings information alone.[31]

However, other researchers have reported less favorable predictive results for cash flow. For example, in a study of 290 companies, the authors found that operating cash flow data over a five-year period was not a good discriminator between healthy firms and firms that declared bankruptcy.[32] The authors found that accrual measures, including traditional financial accounting ratios, were more accurate predictors of business failure.

One reason that firms with poor operating cash flows can survive for an extended period is the willingness of creditors to renegotiate and restructure debt. Massey-Ferguson and International Harvester (now Navistar) are examples.[33] Also, growing companies often have negative cash flow because they invest heavily in capital expenditures.

Neither accrual nor cash flow information alone is sufficient for a complete understanding of a company's performance. The relationship between revenues and cash inflows and between expenses and cash outflows can be understood only by studying both types of information. As such, the SCF provides one input to that understanding.

Classification of Cash Flows

Net cash flow from operating activities includes only amounts classified as operating. Historically, accountants have viewed operating activities as those that are repetitive in nature and that are related to income-producing activities. In *SFAS No.*

---

[31] B. Ismail and M. Kim, "On the Association of Cash Flow Variables with Market Risk: Further Evidence," *Accounting Review,* January 1989, pp. 125–36.

[32] C. Casey and N. Bartczak, "Cash Flow—It's Not the Bottom Line," *Harvard Business Review,* July–August 1984, p. 61.

[33] Ibid.

95, the FASB chose association with earnings as the criterion for classifying a cash flow as operating. Consequently, net cash flow from operating activities may reflect amounts that are nonrepetitive and that result from investing and financing activities.

For example, all income tax payments are classified as operating cash outflows. However, this results in classifying taxes on gains and losses from extraordinary items, discontinued operations, and plant asset disposals as operating. The FASB concluded that the cost of requiring allocation of income tax payments among the three cash flow categories exceeded its benefit.

Interest received and paid, and dividends received also are classified as operating. An alternative view maintains that interest and dividends *received* result from lending money and investing in stock, which are investing activities. Interest *paid* results from incurring debt, a financing activity. This issue is related to the decision to classify all income tax payments as operational. If these amounts were classified as financing, then the associated income tax also would be classified as financing.

The FASB stated that a distinction must be made between return *of* investment (return of principal) and return *on* investment (interest and dividends). Return on investment is a component of income. The Board decided that inclusion in income is a stronger argument than association with a previous investing transaction, for classifying return on investment. In addition, the Board noted that generally all firms reported interest received and paid as an operating fund flow in the statement of changes in financial position, which preceded the SCF. Also, under both direct and indirect methods, interest and income tax payments must be disclosed and can therefore be reclassified by the user.

Principal payments on long-term notes to suppliers also are classified as operating. An alternative view maintains that these flows are actually investing cash inflows. Under this view, the operating classification is inconsistent with that of payments on notes to financial institutions and other creditors.

Direct or Indirect Method

Is the additional information disclosed under the direct method worth its cost? The direct method discloses the actual operating cash flows, which may be more useful than aggregate net cash flow from operating activities or reconciling adjustments for predicting future net operating cash flow. The indirect method does not report collections from sales and other operating cash inflows that analysts need to assess cash-generating ability.

The direct method reports the three categories consistently. Cash flows are presented in all three cash flow categories. The user of the indirect method receives only indirect information concerning operating cash flows, but direct information for investing and financing activities. Banker respondents to the exposure draft preceding *SFAS No. 95* overwhelmingly favored the direct method. However, according to one study, 82% of surveyed CPAs favored the indirect method.[34] Familiarity and previous use in the statement of changes in financial position contributed to the overall preference for the indirect method by preparers.

The FASB recommends the direct method. However, after considerable controversy, the Board decided to permit either method. Tradition played a part in the FASB's decision. The indirect method of reporting fund flows was used for more than four decades. Industry has more experience with the indirect method, and it is less costly. Ledger account balances provide most of the reconciling adjustments. Also, financial statement users can approximate operating cash flows from the reconciliation and income statement and balance sheet accounts.

---

[34] C. Gibson, T. Klammer, and S. Reed, "The Cash Flow Statement," *CPA Journal,* November, 1986, pp. 18–38.

Many companies reported that their accounting systems do not readily provide gross operating cash receipts and payments.[35] Furthermore, companies are very reluctant to divulge more information than required, especially about cash flows. Only 3% of 600 surveyed companies used the direct method in 1989.[36] Thus far, creditors are unable to persuade their corporate clients to use the direct method.

CONCEPT REVIEW

1. Why is interest received classified as operating?
2. Explain how all the information found in an indirect method SCF is present in the direct method SCF and related disclosures.
3. Why are all income tax payments classified as operating?

SUMMARY OF KEY POINTS

♦

(L.O. 1)   1. Cash flow information is used to predict future cash flows, to assess liquidity, to assess the ability of a firm to pay dividends and extinguish obligations, to assess the ability of a firm to adapt to changes in the business environment, and for other purposes.

(L.O. 1)   2. The SCF is one of three required financial statements. The primary purpose of the SCF is to provide relevant information about cash receipts and disbursements.

(L.O. 2)   3. Cash and cash equivalents is the reporting basis for the SCF. Cash equivalents are investments readily convertible into a known amount of cash and with an original maturity of three months or less.

(L.O. 2)   4. Cash flows fall into three categories. Operating flows are those associated with the earnings process. Investing flows describe the long-term purposes to which cash is applied, and the proceeds from sale of long-term assets. Financing flows describe the sources of short- and long-term financing other than operations, repayments of short and long-term liabilities not related to operations, and equities.

(L.O. 2)   5. *SFAS No. 95* permits two different methods or formats for preparing the SCF: the direct and indirect methods. These methods differ only with respect to cash flows from operating activities. The direct method reports the operating cash flows. The indirect method reports adjustments that reconcile net income and net cash flow. Investing and financing activities are reported in exactly the same way under the two methods.

(L.O. 2)   6. The reconciliation of net income and net operating cash flow is required for both methods. The operating activity sections of both the direct and indirect SCFs convert accrual income to cash-basis income, the net cash flow from operations.

(L.O. 2)   7. Significant noncash transactions are disclosed in a supplementary schedule in order to complete the description of investing and financing activities.

(L.O. 3)   8. There are many approaches to preparing the SCF. The same objective applies to

---

[35] *SFAS No. 95,* par. 109.

[36] AICPA, *Accounting Trends & Techniques*—1990 (New York, 1990), p. 350.

all: analyze transactions to identify all cash flows, reconciling items, and non-cash transactions.

(L.O. 4) 9. The format-free approach to preparing the SCF emphasizes transaction analysis and uses no particular format. The sources of information for cash flows are the income statement, additional information, and comparative balance sheets.

(L.O. 5) 10. The spreadsheet is an organized format for preparing the SCF. Both the direct and indirect method SCFs can be prepared with the same spreadsheet.

(L.O. 6) 11. The T-account approach to preparing the SCF is an alternative to the spreadsheet approach and is particularly useful for companies with a limited number of transactions.

REVIEW PROBLEM

♦

The Phillies Company prepared the following information relevant to its 1992 SCF:

	12/31/91	12/31/92
Comparative Balance Sheets:		
Cash	$200,000	$ 62,000
Accounts receivable, net	60,000	80,000
Inventory	12,000	20,000
Prepaids	6,000	10,000
Equipment, net	300,000	500,000
Patent	90,000	70,000
Total assets	$668,000	$742,000
Accounts payable	$ 40,000	$ 60,000
Salaries payable	60,000	50,000
Interest payable	6,000	9,000
Income tax payable	12,000	20,000
Mortgage payable	120,000	110,000
Bonds payable	200,000	100,000
Premium on bonds payable	8,000	3,000
Common stock, no par	150,000	170,000
Retained earnings	72,000	220,000
Total liabilities & owners' equity	$668,000	$742,000

Income statement accounts, 1992:

Sales	$820,000
Cost of goods sold	(380,000)
Depreciation expense	(100,000)
Amortization of patent	(20,000)
Other expenses	(46,000)
Gain, excess of insurance proceeds over book value of equipment destroyed	10,000
Interest expense	(22,000)
Income tax expense	(72,000)
Extraordinary loss, bond retirement, net of $1,000 tax	(2,000)
Net income	$188,000

Additional information:
1. Phillies declared $40,000 of dividends in 1992.
2. Equipment (cost: $100,000; accumulated depreciation $60,000) was destroyed by fire. Proceeds from insurance: $50,000.
3. Bonds were retired on January 1, 1992 at 107. Applicable taxes: $1,000.

Required:

Prepare the 1992 SCF for Phillies; use the direct method. The spreadsheet is used to illustrate the solution. You may also use the format-free or T-account approaches (see appendix).

SOLUTION
♦

Spreadsheet

Comparative Balance Sheets	12/31/91	Dr.	Cr.	12/31/92
Cash	200,000		138,000 (*q*)	62,000
Accounts receivable, net	60,000 (*b*)	20,000		80,000
Inventory	12,000 (*c*)	8,000		20,000
Prepaids	6,000 (*g*)	4,000		10,000
Equipment, net	300,000 (*h*)	60,000	100,000 (*e*)	500,000
	(*n*)	340,000	100,000 (*h*)	
Patent	90,000		20,000 (*f*)	70,000
Total assets	$668,000			$742,000
Accounts payable	40,000		20,000 (*d*)	60,000
Salaries payable	60,000 (*g*)	10,000		50,000
Interest payable	6,000		3,000 (*i*)	9,000
Income tax payable	12,000		8,000 (*k*)	20,000
Mortgage payable	120,000 (*o*)	10,000		110,000
Bonds payable	200,000 (*l*)	100,000		100,000
Premium on bonds payable	8,000 (*l*)	4,000		3,000
	(*j*)	1,000		
Common stock, no par	150,000		20,000 (*p*)	170,000
Retained earnings	72,000 (*m*)	40,000	188,000 (*a*)	220,000
Total liabilities . . . . and owners' equity	$668,000			$742,000
Total changes		597,000	597,000	

			Indirect Method		Direct Method (Operations)
Adjustments Leading to SCF			**Dr.**	**Cr.**	
Operating activities:					
Net income	188,000	(*a*)	188,000		
Sales	820,000			20,000 (*b*)	800,000
					customer collections
Cost of goods sold	380,000	(*d*)	20,000	8,000 (*c*)	368,000
					payments to suppliers
Depreciation expense	100,000	(*e*)	100,000		
Amortization of patent	20,000	(*f*)	20,000		
Other expenses	46,000			14,000 (*g*)	60,000
					other operating payments
Gain on equipment	10,000			10,000 (*h*)	
Interest expense	22,000	(*i*)	3,000	1,000 (*j*)	20,000
					interest payments
Income tax expense	72,000	(*k*)	8,000		64,000
					tax payments
Extraordinary loss	3,000	(*l*)	3,000		
Tax	1,000				1,000
					reduce tax payments
Investing activities:					
Insurance proceeds, equipment		(*h*)	50,000		
Purchase of equipment				340,000 (*n*)	
Financing activities:					
Retirement of bonds				107,000 (*l*)	
Dividends paid				40,000 (*m*)	
Principal payment, mortgage				10,000 (*o*)	
Issue stock		(*p*)	20,000		
			412,000		
Net cash decrease		(*q*)	138,000		
			550,000	550,000	

Explanations for spreadsheet entries:

(a) Net income.
(b) Accounts receivable increase.
(c) Inventory increase.
(d) Accounts payable increase.
(e) Depreciation expense.
(f) Amortization of patent.
(g) Prepaids increase, and salaries payable decrease (related to other expenses).
(h) Equipment fire—gain is subtracted from income because the investing cash inflow completely explains the cash effect. The original cost and accumulated depreciation are removed from the net equipment account.
(i) Interest payable increase.
(j) Amortization of bond premium in 1992—one half the premium was removed from the accounts at the beginning of the year upon retirement of one half the bond issue. The remaining $1,000 decrease in bond premium is amortization.
(k) Increase in income taxes payable.
(l) Extraordinary loss does not decrease cash, yet it decreased net income. The associated tax reduction decreases the initial amount of tax payment computed after entry (k).

Entry to record the bond retirement, January 1, 1992:

Bonds payable	100,000	
Bond premium (½ of $8,000)	4,000	
Extraordinary loss	3,000	
Cash (1.07 × $100,000)		107,000

(m) Dividends declared equal dividends paid (no dividends payable account).
(n) There remained a $340,000 unexplained increase in net equipment after all available information was incorporated.
(o) Decrease in mortgage payable implies a principal payment, in the absence of other information.
(p) Increase in common stock implies issuance of additional shares, in the absence of other information.
(q) Net cash decrease (to balance).

PHILLIES COMPANY
Statement of Cash Flows
For the Year Ended December 31, 1992

Cash flows from operating activities:		
Collections from customers	$800,000	
Payments to suppliers	(368,000)	
Other payments	(60,000)	
Interest payments	(20,000)	
Tax payments	(63,000)	
Net cash inflow from operating activities		$289,000
Cash flows from investing activities:		
Insurance proceeds—equipment fire	50,000	
Purchase of equipment	(340,000)	
Net cash outflow from investing activities		(290,000)
Cash flows from financing activities:		
Bond retirement	(107,000)	
Dividends paid	(40,000)	
Principal payment, mortgage	(10,000)	
Issue stock	20,000	
Net cash outflow from financing activities		(137,000)
Net cash decrease		(138,000)
Cash and cash equivalents, January 1, 1992		200,000
Cash and cash equivalents, December 31, 1992		$62,000

Reconciliation of Net Income and Net Cash Inflow from Operating Activities

Net income	$188,000
Reconciling items:	
Accounts receivable, increase	(20,000)
Accounts payable increase	20,000
Inventory increase	(8,000)
Depreciation	100,000
Patent amortization	20,000
Salaries payable decrease	(10,000)
Prepaids increase	(4,000)
Gain on equipment fire	(10,000)
Interest payable increase	3,000
Amortization of bond premium	(1,000)
Income taxes payable increase	8,000
Extraordinary loss	3,000
Net cash inflow from operating activities	$289,000

APPENDIX   *The T-Account Approach to Preparing the SCF*

The T-Account approach is similar to the spreadsheet approach. The same logic, order of information search, and reconstructed journal entries are used. The T-account approach enters the reconstructed entries directly into a complete set of T-accounts that summarizes the actual ledger accounts. The T-accounts replace the columnar format of the spreadsheet. The actual ledger accounts are not affected by the preparation process.

The T-account approach is particularly efficient for companies with relatively few transactions when there are time constraints, and when there is no need to review or retain working papers. Some preparers use T-accounts only for cash, plant assets, retained earnings, and other active accounts, and use the format-free approach for less involved transactions.

The cash T-account accumulates all changes in cash and is divided into three sections corresponding to the three cash flow categories in the SCF. In the direct method, reconciling items are placed into a schedule as encountered. The T-accounts are not used for these items. Alternatively, a second cash T-account can be used for reconciling items. This second T-account is the same T-account used in the indirect method.

The beginning and ending balances of all accounts are used in the direct method to better focus on the operating cash flows. Under the indirect method, the reconciling items for operating activities are placed directly into the T-accounts. Only the balance sheet accounts are needed because the changes in operational working capital accounts, rather than cash flows, are used in the operating activities section. The indirect method works with the changes in accounts during the period.

The SCF is prepared directly from the entries in the cash account. The process is complete when all account balance changes are explained. The Simple Company data in Exhibit 23–2 is used to illustrate the T-account approach for the direct and indirect methods. Lower-case italic letters indicate the order of the T-account entries. The explanations for each entry parallel those of the format-free and spreadsheet approaches discussed in the chapter (although the letters do not correspond between the different approaches).

T-Accounts for Simple Company, Direct Method

The process begins with the income statement. Sales, entry (*a*), is posted to both accounts receivable and sales. Customer collections is the amount that balances accounts receivable. This amount is posted to the cash account, which accumulates all cash flows by category. The explanations for the remaining entries follow the chapter discussion for Simple Company, direct method (amounts in thousands).

Cash

1/1/91 balance		42		
Operating Activities			Operating Activities	
(b)	Customer collections	58	(d) Salary payments	26
			(f) Payments for administrative and selling expenses	12
		58		38
Investing Activities			Investing Activities	
(h)	Sale of plant assets	21	(g) Purchase of equipment	30
		21		30
Financing Activities			Financing Activities	
(i)	Issue long-term note	40	(j) Principal payment on note	46
(m)	Issue stock	48	(k) Purchase treasury stock	8
			(l) Dividend payments	11
		88		65
12/31/91 balance		76		

Balance Sheet Accounts

Accounts Receivable

1/1/91 balance		31		
(a)	Sales	66	(b) Customer collections	58
12/31/91 balance		39		

Plant Assets

1/1/91 balance		82		
(g)	Equipment purchase	30	(h) Sale of plant assets	31
12/31/91 balance		81		

Accumulated Depreciation

			1/1/91 balance	20
(h)	Sale of plant assets	10	(e) Depreciation expense	4
			12/31/91 balance	14

Salaries Payable

			1/1/91 balance	3
(d)	Salary payments	26	(c) Salary expense	28
			12/31/91 balance	5

Notes Payable

			1/1/91 balance	46
(j)	Principal payment	46	(i) Issue note	40
			12/31/91 balance	40

Common Stock

			1/1/91 balance	61
			(m) Issue stock	40
			12/31/91 balance	101

Contributed Capital in Excess of Par

	1/1/91 balance	9
	(*m*) Issue stock	8
	12/31/91 balance	17

Treasury Stock

1/1/91 balance	0
(*k*) Purchase treasury stock	8
12/31/91 balance	8

Retained Earnings

		1/1/91 balance	16
(*l*) Dividend payments	11	Net income (to balance)*	22
		12/31/91	27

* Alternatively, separate closing entries can be made for each income statement account, posting directly to the retained earnings account.

Income Statement Accounts

Sales

	(*a*) Sales	66

Salaries Expense

(*c*) Salaries expense	28

Depreciation Expense

(*e*) Depreciation expense	4

Administrative and Selling Expense

(*f*) Administrative and selling expense	12

The SCF is prepared by transferring the cash flow information in the cash account to the statement. The complete statement is shown in Exhibit 23–3.

T-Accounts for Simple Company, Indirect Method

The indirect method focuses on the change in operating working capital accounts, noncash expenses, and other items to determine the operating activities section of the SCF. The first entry (*a*) places net income into the cash account, operating activities section. The next item from the income statement is (*b*), depreciation expense. Depreciation expense is added to income in the cash account. The explanations for the remaining entries follow the chapter discussion for Simple Company, indirect method.

Cash

1/1/91 balance	42		
Operating Activities		Operating Activities:	
(a) Net income	22	(c) Accounts receivable increase	8
(b) Depreciation expense	4		
(d) Salary payable increase	2		
	28		8
Investing Activities:		Investing Activities:	
(f) Sale of plant assets	21	(e) Purchase of equipment	30
	21		30
Financing Activities:		Financing Activities:	
(g) Issue long-term note	40	(h) Principal payment on note	46
(k) Issue stock	48	(i) Purchase treasury stock	8
		(j) Dividend payments	11
	88		65
12/31/91 balance	76		

Balance Sheet Accounts

Accounts Receivable

Net increase	8		
(c) Increase	8		

Plant Assets

		Net decrease	1
(e) Equipment purchase	30	(f) Sale of plant assets	31

Accumulated Depreciation

		Net increase	6
(f) Sale of plant assets	10	(b) Depreciation expense	4

Salaries Payable

		Net increase	2
		(d) Increase	2

Notes Payable

Net decrease	6		
(h) Principal payment	46	(g) Issue note	40

Common Stock

		Net increase	40
		(k) Issue stock	40

Contributed Capital in Excess of Par

		Net increase	8
		(k) Issue stock	8

Treasury Stock

Net increase		8	
(i) Purchase treasury stock		8	

Retained Earnings

			Net increase	11
(j) Dividend payments	11	(a)	Net income	22

The SCF is prepared by transferring the cash flow information and income adjustments in the cash account to the statement. The complete statement is shown in Exhibit 23–4 in the chapter.

KEY TERMS

Cash equivalents (1280)
Cash flow per share (1286)
Direct method (1280)
Financial flexibility (1279)

Free cash flow (1279)
Indirect method (1280)
Net cash inflow (outflow) from operating activities (1280)

QUESTIONS

1. Compare the purposes of the balance sheet, income statement, and statement of cash flows.
2. Explain the basic difference between the three activities reported in the SCF—operating, investing, financing.
3. List three major cash inflows and three major cash outflows under (a) operating activities, (b) investing activities, and (c) financing activities.
4. Define a noncash investing activity. Give an example of each of the two possible cases.
5. Define a noncash financing activity. Give an example of each of the two possible cases.
6. Define a cash equivalent for SCF purposes.
7. What policy must a company adopt about cash equivalents? What accounting procedure must the company follow if the policy is changed?
8. Explain the basic difference between the direct and indirect methods of reporting on the SCF. Use net income $5,000, sales revenue, $100,000, and an increase of accounts receivable, $10,000, to illustrate the basic difference. Which method provides the most relevant information to investors and creditors?
9. Explain why cash paid during the period for purchases and for salaries is not specifically reported on the SCF, indirect method, as cash outflows.
10. Explain why a $50,000 increase in inventory during the year must be considered when developing disclosures for operating activities under both the direct and indirect methods.
11. What three reconciling amounts must be reported at the bottom of the SCF? Which one must agree with a key amount in another financial statement. Use assumed amounts for illustrative purposes.
12. One of the criticisms of the SCF, indirect method, is that it does not report each of the three activities consistently. Explain the basis for this argument.
13. Explain why an adjustment must be made to compute cash flow from operating activities for depreciation expense, bad debt expense, and amortization of intangibles (e.g., patents, copyrights, franchises, goodwill, and bond discount or premium).
14. Explain why gains and losses reported on the income statement usually must be omitted (or removed) from operating activities to compute cash flow from operating activities.
15. X Corporation's records showed the following: sales, $80,000, and accounts receivable decrease, $10,000, after the write-off of a $3,000 bad debt. Assuming the direct method, compute the cash inflow from customers.
16. Explain the two ways that the SCF, indirect method, can be designed to report cash flows from operating activities.
17. Why are cash and cash equivalents grouped together for purposes of the SCF even though cash equivalents are not actually cash?
18. Why is a two year Treasury note purchased three months before maturity a cash equivalent for SCF purposes, yet the same security purchased one year before maturity is not?

19. If the intent is to hold an investment in common stock less than three months, why is the investment not a cash equivalent?
20. Is there an inconsistency in the classification of dividends received, and dividends paid, in the SCF. Discuss.
21. How is a lease payment (after inception) on a capital lease classified in the SCF?

EXERCISES

E 23-1
SCF: Terminology,
Format, and
Requirements

Two lists are given below—key terms and brief descriptions. You are to match the descriptions with the terms by entering one letter in each blank to the left.

Key Terms	Brief Description
_____ 1. Fundamental purpose of the SCF.	A. Net cash increase (decrease), beginning balance, and ending balance.
_____ 2. Basic components of the SCF.	B. Cash flows related to obtained cash for the enterprise.
_____ 3. Three reconciling lines at the bottom of the SCF.	C. Cash flows primarily related to the income statement.
_____ 4. Must be disclosed in a separate SCF schedule.	D. Financial statements shall not report this ratio.
_____ 5. Cash flows from operating activities.	E. Includes highly liquid investments, but not all short-term investments.
_____ 6. Cash flow per share.	F. Cash flows from three activities: operating, investing, and financing.
_____ 7. SCF, direct method.	G. Add (deduct) to adjust net income to net cash flows.
_____ 8. This amount must agree with the change in cash.	H. Noncash investing and financing activities.
_____ 9. Cash flows from investing activities.	I. Two approaches to develop the SCF.
_____ 10. This is a special item on the SCF.	J. To help investors, creditors, etc., to assess future cash flows.
_____ 11. SCF, indirect method.	K. Cash flows related to obtaining productive facilities and other noncash assets.
_____ 12. T-account and spreadsheet.	L. Report cash flows for each major revenue and expense.
_____ 13. Cash equivalents.	M. Effect of foreign exchange rates on cash.
_____ 14. Cash flows from financing activities.	N. Net increase (decrease) in cash during the period.
_____ 15. This item on the SCF, indirect method, must be clearly identified as a reconciliation.	O. Does not report cash flows for revenues and expenses, but reconciles net income with cash flows.

E 23-2
SCF: Cash Flow Analysis
of Sales
(L.O. 3)

The records of ZZ Company showed sales revenue of $100,000 (on the income statement) and a change in the balance of accounts receivable. To demonstrate the effect of changes in accounts receivable on cash inflows from customers, five independent cases are used. Complete the following tabulation for each independent case:

Case	Sales Revenue (from Income Statement)	Accounts Receivable Increase (Decrease)	Computations	Cash Inflow
A	$100,000	$ –0–		
B	100,000	10,000		
C	100,000	(10,000)		
D	100,000	9,000*		
E	100,000	(9,000)*		

* Includes the effect of a $1,000 write-off of an uncollectible account.

E 23-3
SCF: Cash Flow Analysis
of Cost of Goods Sold
(L.O. 3)

The records of Atlas Company showed cost of goods sold (on the income statement) of $60,000 and a change in the inventory and accounts payable balances. To demonstrate the effect of these changes on cash outflow for cost of goods sold (i.e., payments to suppliers), eight independent cases are used. Complete the following tabulation for each case:

Case	Cost of Goods Sold	Inventory Increase (Decrease)	Accounts Payable Increase (Decrease)	Computations	Cash Outflow*
A	$60,000	$-0-	$-0-		
B	60,000	6,000	-0-		
C	60,000	(6,000)	-0-		
D	60,000	-0-	4,000		
E	60,000	-0-	(4,000)		
F	60,000	6,000	4,000		
G	60,000	(6,000)	(4,000)		
H	60,000	(6,000)	(6,000)		

* This is the amount of cash paid during the current period for past and current purchases.

E 23-4
SCF: Direct Method:
Analysis of Cash Inflows
and Outflows
(L.O. 3)

The records of Easie Company provided the following data:

a. Sales revenue, $95,000; accounts receivable decreased, $5,000.
b. Cost of goods sold, $42,000; inventory decreased, $3,000; accounts payable, no change.
c. Wage expense, $16,000; wages payable decreased, $1,500.
d. Depreciation expense, $4,000.
e. Purchased productive asset for $18,000; paid one third down and gave a two-year, interest-bearing note for the balance.
f. Borrowed $20,000 cash on a note payable.
g. Sold an old operational asset for $3,000 cash; original cost, $10,000; accumulated depreciation, $9,000.
h. Paid a $2,500 note payable (principal).
i. Paid a cash dividend, $4,000.

Required:
For each of the above transactions give (a) its SCF activity (operating, investing, financing) and (b) the SCF (direct method) inflow or outflow amount. Also, give any disclosure schedules required.

E 23-5
Transaction Analysis
(L.O. 3)

You are requested by the controller of a large company to determine the appropriate disclosure for the following transactions in the SCF. Assume all adjusting entries were recorded.

a. The company wrote off a $2,000 account. During the year, gross accounts receivable increased $50,000, and the allowance for doubtful accounts increased $5,000. All sales ($300,000) are on account.
b. Pension expense is $50,000; the balance of accrued pension cost (cr.) increased $12,000.
c. Deferred tax (cr. balance, long-term) increased $40,000; no net reversals occurred during the year.
d. $10,000 of interest was capitalized. Interest expense is $50,000. There is no change in interest payable.
e. The company sold short-term investments (cash equivalents) at a $2,000 gain, proceeds $8,000.

f. The company sold short-term investments (not cash equivalents) at a $2,000 gain, proceeds $8,000.

Required:

Indicate the complete disclosure of each item in the SCF under the (*a*) direct method and (*b*) indirect method.

E 23–6
Cash Flow Categories:
Transaction Analysis
(L.O. 3)

Denton Corporation's balance sheet accounts as of December 31, 1991 and 1992, and information relating to 1992 activities are presented below.

	December 31	
	1992	1991
Assets:		
Cash	$ 230,000	$ 100,000
Short-term investments	300,000	-----
Accounts receivable (net)	510,000	510,000
Inventory	680,000	600,000
Long-term investments	200,000	300,000
Plant assets	1,700,000	1,000,000
Accumulated depreciation	(450,000)	(450,000)
Goodwill	90,000	100,000
Total assets	$3,260,000	$2,160,000
Liabilities and stockholders' equity:		
Accounts payable and accrued liabilities	$ 825,000	$ 720,000
Short-term debt to financial institutions	325,000	-----
Common stock, $10 par	800,000	700,000
Additional paid-in capital	370,000	250,000
Retained earnings	940,000	490,000
Total liabilities and stockholders' equity	$3,260,000	$2,160,000

Information relating to 1992 activities:

* Net income for 1992 was $690,000.
* Cash dividends of $240,000 were declared and paid in 1992.
* Equipment costing $400,000 and having a carrying amount of $150,000 was sold in 1992 for $150,000.
* A long-term investment was sold in 1992 for $135,000. There were no other transactions affecting long-term investments in 1992.
* 10,000 shares of common stock were issued in 1992 for $22 per share.
* Short-term investments consist of treasury bills maturing on 6/30/93.

Required:

Determine the following for Denton for 1992:

1. Net cash provided by operating activities.
2. Net cash used in investing activities.
3. Net cash provided by financing activities.

(AICPA adapted)

E 23–7
SCF, Direct Method
(L.O. 4)

The following data were provided by the accounting records of SM Company at year-end, December 31, 1992:

Income Statement

Sales	$70,000
Cost of goods sold	(42,000)
Depreciation expense	(5,000)
Remaining expenses	(18,000)
Gain on sale of investments	3,000
Loss on sale of operational assets	(1,000)
Net income	$ 7,000

Comparative Balance Sheet

Debits	December 31 1991	December 31 1992	Increase (Decrease)
Cash	$ 34,000	$ 33,500	$ (500)
Accounts receivable (net)	12,000	17,000	5,000
Inventory	16,000	14,000	(2,000)
Long-term investments	6,000		(6,000)
Operational assets	80,000	98,000	18,000
Treasury stock		11,500	11,500
Total debits	$148,000	$174,000	$26,000

Credits			
Accumulated depreciation . . .	$ 48,000	$ 39,000	$(9,000)
Accounts payable	19,000	12,000	(7,000)
Bonds payable	10,000	30,000	20,000
Common stock, nopar	50,000	65,000	15,000
Retained earnings	21,000	28,000	7,000
Total credits	$148,000	$174,000	$26,000

Analysis of selected accounts and transactions:

a. Sold operational assets for $6,000 cash; cost, $21,000, and two-thirds depreciated (the loss or gain is not an extraordinary item).
b. Purchased operational assets for cash, $9,000.
c. Purchased operational assets; exchanged unissued bonds payable of $30,000 in payment.
d. Sold the long-term investments for $9,000 cash, net of tax (assume the gain or loss is an extraordinary item).
e. Purchased treasury stock for cash, $11,500.
f. Retired bonds payable at maturity date by issuing common stock, $10,000.
g. Sold unissued common stock for cash, $5,000.

Required:
Prepare the SCF, direct method.

E 23–8
SCF, Direct Method
(L.O. 2)

The accounting records of Pall-Mall Company provided the following data:

Income Statement for year ended December 31, 1992

Sales	$300,000
Cost of goods sold	(180,000)
Depreciation expense	(4,000)
Remaining expenses	(64,000)
Net income	$ 52,000

Comparative Balance Sheets

Debits	December 31 1991	December 31 1992	Increase (Decrease)
Cash	$ 8,000	$ 34,000	$26,000
Accounts receivable (net)	10,000	18,000	8,000
Inventory	20,000	24,000	4,000
Investment, long-term	4,000		(4,000)
Operational assets	60,000	94,000	34,000
Total debits	$102,000	$170,000	$68,000

Credits

Accumulated depreciation	$ 10,000	$ 14,000	$ 4,000
Accounts payable	6,000	10,000	4,000
Notes payable, short term (nontrade)	8,000	6,000	(2,000)
Notes payable, long term	20,000	36,000	16,000
Common stock, nopar	50,000	80,000	30,000
Retained earnings	8,000	24,000	16,000
Total credits	$102,000	$170,000	$68,000

Analysis of selected accounts and transactions:

a. Sold the long-term investment at cost, for cash.
b. Declared and paid a cash dividend of $14,000.
c. Purchased operational assets that cost $34,000; gave a $24,000 long-term note payable and paid $10,000 cash.
d. Paid an $8,000 long-term note payable by issuing common stock; market value, $8,000.
e. Issued a stock dividend, $22,000.

Required:
Prepare the SCF, direct method.

E 23–9
SCF, Indirect Method:
Prepare the Reconciliation
for Operating Activities
(L.O. 4)

The data given below were provided by the accounting records of Darby Company. Prepare the reconciliation of net income with cash flow from operations for inclusion in the SCF, indirect method.

Net income (accrual basis), $40,000.

Depreciation expense, $8,000.

Decrease in wages payable, $1,200.

Decrease in trade accounts receivable, $1,800.

Increase in merchandise inventory, $2,500.

Amortization of patent, $100.

Increase in long-term liabilities, $10,000.

Sale of capital stock for cash, $25,000.

Amortization of premium on bonds payable, $200.

Accounts payable increase, $4,000.

Stock dividend issued, $10,000.

E 23–10
SCF, Indirect Method:
Prepare the Reconciliation
for Operating Activities
(L.O. 4)

The data given below were provided by the accounting records of Sileo Company. Prepare the reconciliation of net income with cash flow from operating activities for inclusion in the SCF, indirect method.

Net income (accrual basis), $50,000.

Depreciation expense, $6,000.

Increase in wages payable, $1,000.

Increase in trade accounts receivable, $1,800.

Decrease in merchandise inventory, $2,300.

Amortization of patent, $200.

Decrease in long-term liabilities, $10,000.

Sale of capital stock for cash, $25,000.

Amortization of discount on bonds payable, $300.

E 23-11
SCF, Direct Method:
Optional Spreadsheet
(L.O. 5)

Analysis of accounts: (*a*) purchased an operational asset, $60,000, issued capital stock in full payment; (*b*) purchased a long-term investment for cash, $20,000; (*c*) paid cash dividend, $20,000; (*d*) sold operational asset for $10,000 cash (cost, $36,000; accumulated depreciation, $32,000); and (*e*) sold capital stock, 1,000 shares at $11 per share cash.

Item	Balances 12/31/1991	Analysis		Balances 12/31/1992
		Debit	Credit	
Income Statement accounts:				
Sales			240,000	
Cost of goods sold		96,000		
Depreciation		12,000		
Wage expense		44,000		
Income tax expense		20,000		
Interest expense		14,000		
Remaining expenses		4,600		
Gain on sale of operational asset			6,000	
Net income		55,400		
Balance Sheet accounts:				
Cash	39,000			63,800
Accounts receivable (net)	68,000			68,000
Merchandise inventory	156,000			170,000
Investments, long term				20,000
Operating, plant & equipment	337,000			361,000
Total	600,000			682,800
Accumulated depreciation	88,000			68,000
Accounts payable	42,000			38,000
Wages payable	3,000			1,000
Income taxes payable	4,000			7,000
Bonds payable	200,000			200,000
Premium on bonds payable	8,000			7,400
Common stock, nopar	240,000			311,000
Retained earnings	15,000			50,400
Total	600,000			682,800

Required:

Prepare the SCF, direct method. (The solution to this exercise features an optional spreadsheet.)

E 23-12
SCF, Direct Method:
Optional Spreadsheet
(L.O. 5)

Analysis of accounts: (*a*) retired bonds, paid $40,000 cash; (*b*) bought long-term investment, $20,000 cash; (*c*) purchased operational asset, $14,000 cash; (*d*) purchased short-term investment, $6,000 cash; (*e*) paid cash dividend, $8,000; and (*f*) issued capital stock, 1,000 shares at $19 cash per share.

Item	Balances 12/31/1991	Analysis Debit	Analysis Credit	Balances 12/31/1992
Income Statement accounts:				
Sales			208,000	
Cost of goods sold		110,000		
Depreciation expense		16,000		
Patent amortization		600		
Remaining expenses		35,400		
Net income		46,000		
Balance Sheet accounts:				
Cash	30,000			43,000
Investment, short term				6,000
Accounts receivable	34,000			42,000
Inventory (perpetual)	20,000			30,000
Investments, long-term				20,000
Property, plant, and equipment	120,000			118,000
Patent (net)	6,000			5,400
Other assets	14,000			14,000
Total	224,000			278,400
Accounts payable	24,000			44,000
Accrued expenses payable				17,400
Bonds payable	80,000			40,000
Common stock, par $10	70,000			80,000
Contributed capital in excess of par				9,000
Retained earnings	50,000			88,000
Total	224,000			278,400

Required:

Prepare the SCF, direct method. (The solution to this exercise features an optional spreadsheet.)

E 23-13
SCF, Direct Method:
Optional Spreadsheet
(L.O. 5)

Shown below are the income statement, comparative balance sheets, and additional information useful in preparing the 1992 SCF for Sells Company.

Income statement for year ended December 31, 1992:

Net sales		$300,000
Cost of goods sold		80,000
Gross margin		220,000
Depreciation expense	$45,000	
Amortization	2,000	
Other expenses	44,000	
Interest expense	3,000	
Income tax expense	65,000	159,000
Net income		$ 61,000

	December 31, 1991	December 31, 1992
Comparative balance sheets:		
Cash	$ 16,000	$ 32,000
Accounts receivable	56,000	52,000
Allowance for doubtful accounts	(6,000)	(5,000)
Other receivables	3,000	2,000
Inventory	30,000	32,000
Equipment	80,000	77,000
Accumulated depreciation	(6,000)	(5,000)
Intangibles, net	55,000	53,000
Total assets	$228,000	$238,000
Accounts payable	50,000	60,000
Income taxes payable	70,000	50,000
Interest payable	2,000	1,000
Bonds payable	32,000	
Discount on bonds payable	(2,000)	
Common stock, no par	70,000	80,000
Retained earnings	6,000	47,000
Total liabilities and owners' equity	$228,000	$238,000

Additional information:

1. $20,000 of dividends were declared in 1992.
2. Equipment costing $66,000 with a book value of $20,000, was sold at book value. New equipment was also purchased; common stock was issued in partial payment.
3. The bonds were retired at book value; $500 of bond discount was amortized in 1992.

Required:

Prepare the 1992 SCF, direct method, for Sells Company. (The solution to this exercise features an optional spreadsheet.)

E 23–14
T-Account Approach,
Direct Method (Appendix)
(L.O. 6)

Required:

Using the information from E 23–7, prepare the SCF, direct method, using the T-account approach.

PROBLEMS

P 23–1
Correcting Erroneous
Cash Flow Statement
(L.O. 2)

The accountant for Mentor Company prepared the following cash flow statement and additional information.

MENTOR COMPANY
Cash Flow Statement
December 31, 1991

Cash inflows:		
Net income (loss)	$(20,000)	
Extraordinary gain on bond retirement	10,000	
Dividends received on equity method investment	40,000	
Issue stock	60,000	
Total cash inflows		$ 90,000
Cash outflows:		
Market value of bonds retired	80,000	
Cost of treasury stock acquired	16,000	
Dividends paid	25,000	
Acquisition of property, plant, and equipment	30,000	
Issuance of bonds for real estate	43,000	
Total cash outflows		194,000
Net cash decrease during 1991		$(104,000)

The accountant was sure that cash decreased $104,000 during 1991, but was not quite sure that all relevant information was incorporated into the statement. Also, the accountant admitted knowing very little about cash flow statements. Therefore, the accountant made available the additional information:

Beginning cash balance	$204,000
Depreciation	35,000
Amortization of premium on bonds	5,000
Gain on equipment sale (not extraordinary)	4,000
Stock dividend declared and distributed	20,000
Mentor's share of income from equity method investment	65,000
Retained earnings appropriation	15,000

The following accounts changed by the amount noted, during 1992:

Increased	**Decreased**
Accounts payable, $18,000	Prepaids, $6,000
Revenue received in advance	Inventory, $5,000
(current liability), $7,000	
Accounts receivable, $20,000	

Required:

Using the above information, prepare a revised SCF, indirect method. Assume all values are correct in both the statement and additional information. Ignore taxes.

P 23–2
SCF, Direct Method
(L.O. 4)

The records of Easy Trading Company provided the following information for the year ended December 31, 1992:

Income statement, 1992:

Sales revenue	$80,000
Cost of goods sold	(35,000)
Depreciation expense	(5,000)
Bad debts expense	(1,000)
Insurance expense	(1,000)
Interest expense	(2,000)
Salaries and wages expense	(12,000)
Income tax expense	(3,000)
Remaining expenses	(13,000)
Loss on sale of operational assets	(2,000)
Net income	$ 6,000

Balance sheet:	1/1/1991	12/31/1991
Cash	$ 15,000	$ 31,000
Accounts receivable	30,000	28,500
Allowance for doubtful accounts	(1,500)	(2,000)
Inventory	10,000	15,000
Prepaid insurance	2,400	1,400
Operational assets	80,000	81,000
Accumulated depreciation	(20,000)	(16,000)
Land	40,100	81,100
Total	$156,000	$220,000
Accounts payable	$ 10,000	$ 11,000
Wages payable	2,000	1,000
Interest payable		1,000
Notes payable, long term	20,000	46,000
Common stock, nopar	100,000	136,000
Retained earnings	24,000	25,000
Total	$156,000	$220,000

a. Wrote off $500 accounts receivable as uncollectible.
b. Sold operational asset for $4,000 cash (cost, $15,000; accumulated depreciation, $9,000).

c. Issued common stock for $5,000 cash.

d. Declared and paid a cash dividend, $5,000.

e. Purchased land, $20,000 cash.

f. Acquired land for $21,000 and issued common stock as payment in full.

g. Acquired operational assets, cost $16,000; issued a $16,000, three-year, interest-bearing note payable.

h. Paid a $10,000 long-term note installment by issuing common stock to the creditor.

i. Borrowed cash on long-term note, $20,000.

Required:

Prepare the SCF, direct method.

P 23–3
SCF, Indirect Method
(L.O. 4)

This problem uses the data given in P 23–2. No additional information is needed.

Required:

Prepare the SCF, indirect method.

P 23–4
SCF, Indirect Method
(L.O. 4)

The income statement and balance sheet of Kenwood Company and a related analysis are given below.

KENWOOD COMPANY
Income Statement
For the Year Ended December 31, 1992

Sales revenue	$1,000,000
Expenses and losses:	
Cost of goods sold	560,000
Salaries and wages	190,000
Depreciation	20,000
Patent amortization	3,000
Loss on sale of equipment	4,000
Interest expense	16,000
Miscellaneous expenses	8,000
Total expenses	801,000
Income before income taxes and extraordinary item	199,000
Income tax expense (including tax on the EO gain)*	90,000
Income before extraordinary item	109,000
Extraordinary item—gain on early extinguishment of long-term bonds payable ($10,000* income tax)	12,000†
Net income	$121,000

* Total income tax, $90,000.

† $12,000 is the amount before tax.

Analysis of selected accounts and transactions:

a. On February 2, 1992, Kenwood issued a 10% stock dividend to stockholders of record on January 15, 1992. The market price per share of the common stock on February 2, 1992, was $15.

b. On March 1, 1992, Kenwood issued 3,800 shares of common stock for land. The common stock had a current market value of approximately $40,000 on March 1, 1992.

c. On April 15, 1992, Kenwood repurchased its long-term bonds payable with a face value of $50,000 for cash. The gain of $22,000 was correctly reported as an extraordinary item on the income statement because this early extinguishment of the bonds payable occurred prior to their maturity date (12/31/2001).

d. On June 30, 1992, Kenwood sold equipment that cost $53,000, with a book value of $23,000, for $19,000 cash.

e. On September 30, 1992, Kenwood declared and paid a 4 cents per share cash dividend to stockholders of record on August 1, 1992.

f. On October 10, 1992, Kenwood purchased land for $85,000 cash.

KENWOOD COMPANY
Comparative Balance Sheets

Assets	December 31	
	1992	1991
Current assets:		
Cash	$ 100,000	$ 90,000
Accounts receivable (net of allowance for doubtful accounts of $10,000 and $8,000, respectively)	210,000	140,000
Inventory	260,000	220,000
Total current assets	570,000	450,000
Land	325,000	200,000
Plant and equipment	580,000	633,000
Less: Accumulated depreciation	(90,000)	(100,000)
Patents	30,000	33,000
Total assets	$1,415,000	$1,216,000

Liabilities and Stockholders' Equity	December 31	
	1992	1991
Liabilities:		
Current liabilities:		
Accounts payable	$ 260,000	$ 200,000
Salaries and wages payable	200,000	210,000
Income tax payable	140,000	100,000
Total current liabilities	600,000	510,000
Bonds payable (due 12/15/2001)	130,000	180,000
Total liabilities	730,000	690,000
Stockholders' equity:		
Common stock, par value $5, authorized 100,000 shares, issued and outstanding 50,000 and 42,000 shares, respectively	250,000	210,000
Additional paid-in capital	233,000	170,000
Retained earnings	202,000	146,000
Total stockholders' equity	685,000	526,000
Total liabilities and stockholders' equity	$1,415,000	$1,216,000

Required:

Prepare the SCF, indirect method.

(AICPA adapted)

P 23–5
SCF, Direct Method
(L.O. 4)

This problem uses the data given in P 23–4. No additional information is needed.

Required:
Prepare the SCF, direct method.

P 23–6
SCF, Direct Method:
Optional Spreadsheet
(L.O. 5)

At December 31, 1992, the following data for Lincoln Company were available:

Balance Sheet:

	December 31 1991	December 31 1992	Increase (Decrease)
Debits			
Cash	$ 8,000	$ 22,000	$14,000
Accounts receivable (net)	18,000	24,000	6,000
Inventory	16,000	10,000	(6,000)
Long-term investments	4,000		(4,000)
Plant	60,000	60,000	
Equipment	40,000	44,000	4,000
Land	20,000	80,000	60,000
Patents	16,000	14,000	(2,000)
	$182,000	$254,000	$72,000
Credits			
Accumulated depreciation—plant	$ 14,000	$ 20,000	$ 6,000
Accumulated depreciation—equipment	20,000	16,000	(4,000)
Accounts payable	16,000	4,000	(12,000)
Wages payable	2,000		(2,000)
Notes payable, long term	20,000	38,000	18,000
Common stock, nopar	100,000	150,000	50,000
Retained earnings	10,000	26,000	16,000
	$182,000	$254,000	$72,000

Income Statement

Sales revenue	$180,000
Cost of goods sold	(110,000)
Depreciation expense, plant	(6,000)
Depreciation expense, equipment	(4,000)
Patent amortization	(2,000)
Remaining expenses	(40,000)
Loss on sale of equipment	(2,000)
Income tax expense (including tax on EO gain)	(8,000)
Income from continuing operations	8,000
Extraordinary item: gain on sale of long-term investment (amount before tax)	16,000
Net income	$24,000

Analysis of selected accounts and entries:

a. At the end of the year, sold equipment that cost $16,000 (50% depreciated) for $6,000 cash (this was not an extraordinary item).
b. Purchased land that cost $20,000; paid $4,000 cash, gave long-term note for the balance.
c. Paid $8,000 to retire long-term note payable at maturity.
d. Sold $20,000 common stock at par.
e. Purchased equipment costing $20,000; paid half in cash, balance due in three years (interest-bearing note).
f. Issued 3,000 shares of common stock, market value $30,000, for land that cost $40,000; the balance was paid in cash.
g. Sold the long-term investments for $20,000 cash.
h. Declared and paid dividends, $8,000.

Required:

Prepare the SCF, direct method. (The solution to this problem features an optional spreadsheet.)

P 23–7
SCF, Indirect Method
(L.O. 4)

This problem uses the data given in P 23–6. No additional information is needed.

Required:

Prepare the SCF, indirect method.

P 23–8
SCF, Direct Method:
Optional Spreadsheet
(L.O. 5)

The records of ABE Company provided the following data for the accounting year ended December 31, 1992:

Comparative Balance Sheets, December 31, 1992:

	12/31/1991	12/31/1992	Increase (Decrease)
Debits			
Cash	$ 30,000	$ 69,000	$39,000
Investment, short term (X Co. stock)	10,000	8,000	(2,000)
Accounts receivable	56,000	86,000	30,000
Inventory	20,000	30,000	10,000
Prepaid interest (expense)		2,000	2,000
Land	60,000	25,000	(35,000)
Machinery	80,000	90,000	10,000
Other assets	29,000	39,000	10,000
Discount on bonds payable	1,000	900	(100)
Total debits	$286,000	$349,900	$63,900
Credits			
Allowance for doubtful accounts	$ 6,000	$ 7,000	$ 1,000
Accumulated depreciation	20,000	26,900	6,900
Accounts payable	33,000	45,000	12,000
Salaries payable	5,000	2,000	(3,000)
Income taxes payable	2,000	8,000	6,000
Bonds payable	70,000	55,000	(15,000)
Common stock, nopar	100,000	131,000	31,000
Preferred stock, nopar	20,000	30,000	10,000
Retained earnings	30,000	45,000	15,000
Total credits	$286,000	$349,900	$63,900

Income Statement

Sales revenue	$180,000
Cost of goods sold	(90,000)
Depreciation expense	(6,900)
Bad debt expense	(1,000)
Salaries	(32,900)
Interest expense	(6,100)
Remaining expenses	(4,000)
Income tax expense*	(12,100)
Gain on sale of land, condemnation (income tax, $5,400)	18,000 †
Loss on bond retirement (tax saving, $300)	(1,000)†
Net income	$ 44,000

* Total income tax, $12,100, including the effects of additional tax on the gain and the tax saving on the loss.

† These amounts are pretax.

Analysis of selected accounts and transaction:

a. Issued bonds payable for cash, $5,000.

b. Sold land due to condemnation for $53,000 cash; book value, $35,000; extraordinary item.

c. Purchased machinery for cash, $10,000.

d. Purchased short-term investments for cash, $2,000.

e. Declared a property dividend on the preferred stock and paid it with a short-term investment (X Company stock); market value and carrying value are the same, $4,000.

f. Prior to maturity date, retired $20,000 bonds payable by issuing common stock; the common stock had a market value of $21,000.

g. Acquired other assets by issuing preferred stock with a market value of $10,000.

h. Retained earnings statement:

Balance, January 1, 1992	$30,000
Net income for 1992	44,000
Dividends paid, cash	(15,000)
Stock dividend issued, common stock	(10,000)
Property dividend, X Company stock	(4,000)
Balance, December 31, 1992	$45,000

Required:

Prepare the SCF, direct method. (The solution to this problem features an optional spreadsheet.)

P 23–9
SCF, Indirect Method:
(L.O. 4)

This problem uses the data given in P 23–8. No additional information is needed.

Required:

Prepare the SCF, indirect method.

P 23–10
T-Account Approach,
Indirect Method
(Appendix)
(L.O. 6)

Required:

Using the information from P 23–2, prepare the SCF, indirect method, using the T-account approach.

P 23–11
SCF, Indirect Method:
Optional Spreadsheet
(L.O. 5)

The income statement, balance sheet, and analysis of selected accounts of Summer Company are given below.

Balance Sheet

	12/31/1991	12/31/1992	Increase (Decrease)
Debits			
Cash plus short-term investments*	$ 80,000	$ 89,800	$ 9,800
Accounts receivable (net)	120,000	105,000	(15,000)
Merchandise inventory (perpetual)	360,000	283,200	(76,800)
Prepaid insurance	4,800	2,400	(2,400)
Investments, long term	60,000		(60,000)
Land	20,000	76,800	56,800
Plant assets	500,000	518,000	18,000
Patent (net)	3,200	2,800	(400)
	$1,148,000	$1,078,000	$(70,000)

* Cash equivalents

	12/31/1991	12/31/1992	Increase (Decrease)
Credits			
Accumulated depreciation	$130,000	$158,000	$ 28,000
Accounts payable	100,000	106,000	6,000
Wages payable	4,000	3,000	(1,000)
Income taxes payable	18,000	26,800	8,800
Bonds payable	200,000	100,000	(100,000)
Premium on bonds payable	10,000	3,400	(6,600)
Common stock, par $10	600,000	612,000	12,000
Contributed capital in excess of par	30,000	36,000	6,000
Retained earnings	56,000	32,800	(23,200)
	$1,148,000	$1,078,000	$(70,000)

Income Statement, 1992

Sales revenue	$800,000
Cost of goods sold	(448,800)
Depreciation expense	(28,000)
Patent amortization	(400)
Remaining expenses (including interest)	(292,800)
Extraordinary gain	20,000*
Net income	$ 50,000

* Amount is before income tax; the income tax on the gain is reflected in the amount for remaining expenses.

Analysis of selected accounts and entries:

a. Purchased operational asset; cost, $18,000; payment by issuing 1,200 shares of stock.
b. Payment at maturity date to retire bonds payable, $100,000.
c. Sold the long-term investments for $80,000.
d. Purchased land, $56,800; paid cash.
e.

Retained earnings, beginning balance	$56,000
Prior period adjustment, income tax, paid in 1992	(13,200)
Net income, 1992	50,000
Cash dividend paid	(60,000)
Ending balance	$32,800

Required:

Prepare the SCF, indirect method. (The solution to this problem features an optional spreadsheet.)

P 23–12

COMPREHENSIVE PROBLEM
♦

SCF, Direct Method,
Optional Spreadsheet
(L.O. 2, 3, 4, 5)

The comparative balance sheets and incomes statement for Gamme Company follow:

	12/31/91	12/31/92
Comparative balance sheets:		
Cash	$ 35,000	$ 49,582
Cash equivalents	20,000	10,000
Short-term investments in equity securities, LCM, net	8,000	4,000
Accounts receivable	50,000	75,000
Allowance for doubtful accounts	(2,000)	(3,000)
Inventory	120,000	40,000
Prepaid insurance	20,000	30,000
Long-term investment, equity	40,000	45,000
Land	250,000	350,000
Equipment	100,000	130,000
Leased building		75,816
Accumulated depreciation (including leased building)	(50,000)	(80,000)
Intangible assets, net	45,000	35,000
Total assets	$636,000	$761,398
Accounts payable	40,000	70,000
Income tax payable	5,000	8,000
Dividends payable	6,000	12,000
Lease liability, long-term		63,398
Deferred taxes	20,000	25,000
Mortgage payable		80,000
Note payable		100,000
Bonds payable	180,000	
Unamortized bond discount	(12,000)	
Common stock	300,000	300,000
Retained earnings	97,000	103,000
Total liabilities and owners' equity	$636,000	$761,398

Income statement, 1992:

Sales		$620,000
Cost of goods sold		400,000
Gross margin		220,000
Bad debt expense	(18,000)	
Interest expense	(23,000)	
Depreciation	(42,000)	
Amortization of intangibles	(10,000)	
Other expenses	(85,000)	
Gain on sale of short-term investments	3,000	
Unrealized loss on short-term investments	(1,000)	
Gain on equipment sale	7,000	
Investment revenue	30,000	
Income tax expense (continuing operations)	(20,000)	(159,000)
Income before extraordinary item		61,000
Extraordinary gain, bond retirement, net of $5,000 tax		15,000
Net income		$ 76,000

Additional information about events in 1992:

1. On January 1, 1992, the market value of the portfolio of short-term investments in equity securities exceeded cost. During 1992, investments costing $3,000 were sold for $6,000. No securities were purchased during 1992. At December 31, 1992, the market value of the portfolio is $4,000.
2. Cash equivalents were continually purchased and sold at cost. No gains or losses were incurred.
3. $20,000 of accounts receivable were written off in 1992, and $3,000 was collected on an account written off in 1990. All sales are on account.
4. The long-term equity investment represents a 25% interest in Wickens Company. During 1992, Wickens paid $100,000 of dividends and earned $120,000.
5. At the end of 1992, Gamme acquired land for $100,000 by assuming an $80,000 mortgage and paying the balance in cash.
6. Equipment (cost, $20,000; book value, $8,000) was sold for $15,000.
7. Gamme started and completed construction of equipment for its own use in 1992. The cost of the finished equipment, $50,000, includes $5,000 of capitalized interest.
8. Gamme entered into a capital lease on January 1, 1992. The interest rate used to capitalize the lease is 10%. Equal annual payments of $20,000 are due each December 31 for five years.
9. The bonds were retired before maturity at a $20,000 gain, before taxes. Applicable taxes, $5,000; discount amortized in 1992, $4,000.
10. There were no net reversals of temporary tax differences in 1992.
11. Gamme declared $70,000 of dividends in 1992.

Required:

Prepare the 1992 SCF, direct method, Gamme Company. (The solution to this problem features an optional spreadsheet.)

CASES

C 23-1
SCF: Direct or Indirect?
(L.O. 2)

During the FASB deliberations on the SCF, there was considerable debate and disagreement about the direct and indirect methods of reporting operational activities on the SCF. There was pressure on the Board from various groups. The following quotations from *SFAS No. 95* paragraphs suggest the diversity of views:

107. The principal advantage of the direct method is that it shows operating cash receipts and payments. Knowledge of the specific sources of operating cash receipts and the purposes for which operating cash payments were made in past periods may be useful in estimating future operating cash flows. The relative amounts of major classes of revenues and expenses and their

relationship to other items in the financial statements are presumed to be more useful than information only about their arithmetic sum—net income—in assessing enterprise performance.
108. The principal advantage of the indirect method is that it focuses on the differences between net income and net cash flow from operating activities.
109. Many providers of financial statements have said that it would be costly for their companies to report gross operating cash receipts and payments. They said that they do not presently collect information in a manner that will allow them to determine amounts such as cash received from customers or cash paid to suppliers directly from their accounting systems.
111. A majority of respondents to the Exposure Draft asked the Board to require use of the direct method. Those respondents, most of whom were commercial lenders, generally said that amounts of operating cash receipts and payments are particularly important in assessing an enterprise's external borrowing needs and its ability to repay borrowings. They indicated that creditors are more exposed to fluctuations in net cash flow from operating activities than to fluctuations in net income and that information on the amounts of operating cash receipts and payments is important in assessing those fluctuations in net cash flow from operating activities. They also pointed out that the direct method is more consistent with the objective of a statement of cash flows—to provide information about cash receipts and cash payments—than the indirect method, which does not report operating cash receipts and payments.

As a basis for your analysis of the two methods, make appropriate check marks on each line in the following overview.

	Reported On		
	SCF method		
Cash Inflows and Outflows (and Related Changes)	**Direct***	**Indirect**	**Comparative Balance Sheet**
1. Cash inflow from sales			
2. Cash inflow from services			
3. Cash inflow from interest			
4. Cash inflow from dividend received			
5. Accounts receivable increase or decrease			
6. Interest receivable increase or decrease			
7. Payments to suppliers (cash purchases)			
8. Inventory increase or decrease			
9. Accounts payable increase or decrease			
10. Payments for salaries and wages			
11. Wages and salaries payable increase or decrease			
12. Payments for income tax			
13. Income taxes payable increase or decrease			
14. Net income			
15. Net cash flow from operating activities			
16. Investing activities			
17. Financing activities			
18. Net increase or decrease in cash during the period			
19. Cash, beginning balance			
20. Cash, ending balance			

* Statement only, and not the reconciliation.

Required:

Consider the above comments and your checkoff responses. Prepare an outline of the advantages of each method and be prepared to discuss both your outline and your responses in the checkoff overview.

C 23–2
Ethical Considerations:
Interpretation of the SCF
(L.O. 1)

Honore Company has competed for many years in product lines that recently experienced a great increase in global competition. These products have long been dominated by U.S. firms. Honore has no foreign operations and few personnel with experience in international trade. Honore has made few product changes in recent years and is not actively engaged in product innovation or research and development.

The following informaton is selected from the company's financial statements and notes for the period 1989 to 1991 (in thousands):

	1989	1990	1991
Net income	$50,000	$30,000	$10,000
Net accounts receivable (ending)	40,000	12,000	6,000
Inventory (ending)	19,000	14,000	7,000
Net cash inflow from operations	15,000	7,000	4,500
Capital expenditures	9,000	7,000	6,000
Proceeds from sale of plant assets	15,000	10,000	18,000
Net gain on sales of plant assets and net extraordinary gains	16,000	12,000	15,000

The company:
* Recently negotiated with banks to extend payment terms on short-term loans.
* Has maintained very low levels of accounts payable during this period.
* Has significant investments in corporate bonds (interest revenue on bonds in 1992 is $3,000).
* Paid no dividends during this period.
* Issued no stock or bonds during this period.

HONORE COMPANY
Statement of Cash Flows
For the Year Ended December 31, 1992
(in thousands)

Cash flows from operating activities:		
Net income	7,000	
Items reconciling net income and net cash inflow from operating activities		
Accounts receivable decrease	1,000	
Inventory decrease	1,500	
Extraordinary loss, building fire	8,000	
Dividends received (equity investment)	6,000	
Investment revenue (equity investment)	(10,000)	
Gains on sales of plant assets	(14,000)	
Depreciation, amortization	4,000	
Net cash inflow from operating activities		$ 3,500
Cash flows from investing activities:		
Purchase of plant assets	(4,000)	
Insurance proceeds on building fire	20,000	
Sale of plant assets	25,000	
Purchase of corporate bonds	(5,000)	
Purchase of corporate stocks	(10,000)	
Net cash inflow from investing activities		26,000
Cash flows from financing activities:		
Principal payments on short-term notes to financial institutions	(15,000)	
Purchase of treasury stock	(6,000)	
Net cash outflow from financing activities		(21,000)
Net cash increase		8,500
Beginning cash balance		12,000
Ending cash balance		$20,500

Required:

Provide an interpretation of the SCF in light of Honore's situation. Weigh ethical considerations in terms of company strategy and financial disclosure.

C 23-3
Sherwin-Williams:
Analysis of Actual
Financial Statements
(L.O. 2, 3)

Refer to the 1990 financial statements of Sherwin-Williams that appear at the end of this text. Respond to the following questions concerning the statement of cash flows.

1. Is the statement of cash flows for Sherwin-Williams prepared under the direct or indirect method?
2. Provide an estimate of cash receipts on sales for 1990.
3. Provide an estimate of cash payments to suppliers for goods and services in 1990.
4. Were all 1990 declared dividends paid in 1990?
5. What is the company's policy with respect to classification of investments fulfilling the definition of cash equivalent for SFAS No. 95?
6. Did the firm fulfill the requirement to disclose certain operating cash flows?

C H A P T E R
24

Accounting Changes and Error Corrections

♦

INTRODUCTION
♦

For years, General Motors Corporation used shorter useful lives to depreciate its plant assets than its competitors. In 1987, the company abruptly increased those estimates. The change decreased depreciation and increased income but did not increase cash inflow. McDonnell Douglas Corporation changed its method of accounting for income taxes in 1989, thus raising its net income from $40 million to $219 million, a 448% increase.

Accounting changes often substantially affect the bottom line, but changes made strictly for financial accounting purposes usually do not affect cash flows. Disclosures about accounting changes affect assessments of the quality of earnings. Comparative financial statements, not considered in detail until this chapter, are particularly important for this purpose.

Some observers believe that the major motivation for accounting changes is to achieve a specific reporting objective. These objectives include increasing income for better access to capital markets, improving bonuses for management, enhancing compliance with debt covenants, and reducing earnings volatility. But how do accounting changes affect consistency, comparability, and public confidence in the reporting process? Should companies be allowed to restate previously published financial statements for reasons other than to correct errors?

Imagine an investor examining the 1991 income statement of a prominent engineering and construction company reporting $100 million in construction revenue and $25 million net income. A year later the 1992 report discloses a change in the method of accounting for long-term construction contracts. The company retroactively applies the change to the 1991 statements reported with the 1992 statements. The change restates 1991 revenue to $40 million and net income to $7 million. Was the investor misled in 1991? Is it time to sell stock in this company?

This chapter considers the issues underlying accounting changes and the methods of reporting them. The reporting principles governing accounting changes apply to most of the topics covered in previous chapters of this text. Many accounting methods can be changed, and accounting estimates are always subject to change. This chapter also discusses the rationale for the reporting principles and illustrates accounting for error corrections.

♦

ACCOUNTING CHANGES: REPORTING ISSUES AND APPROACHES
♦

Accounting changes are made for many reasons. In recent years, several new FASB pronouncements have required changes in accounting principles. For example, since 1985, the FASB has issued statements affecting the accounting for pensions and other postemployment benefits, changing prices, regulated enterprises, business combinations, the statement of cash flows, and income taxes.

Firms also change accounting principles to adapt to changing macroeconomic conditions. For example, increasing tax burdens provide an incentive for firms to change to LIFO for tax purposes, and therefore for accounting purposes, when prices rise.[1] LIFO expenses the most recent (and highest priced) purchases, causing income and taxes to decline. New information and changing internal circumstances are additional factors contributing to the need for accounting changes. For example,

---

[1] The income tax requirement that a firm report income under LIFO for financial reporting purposes if LIFO is used for tax purposes is known as the *LIFO conformity rule*.

technological change and obsolescence often necessitate revisions in the useful lives of plant assets, and hence depreciation expense.

Unfortunately, accounting changes obscure the impact of net income for casual financial statement users. For example, General Electric reported 1987 earnings of $2.9 billion, a considerable increase over 1986. However, before accounting changes involving deferred taxes and inventory, income was $2.1 billion. The accounting change supplied 28% of GE's income. Critics charge that accounting changes undermine the usefulness and credibility of financial statements because the changes affect income, but not the value of the firm.

Before 1971, firms reported accounting changes in a variety of ways. Increases in income caused by accounting changes often were treated as gains in the income statement, while decreases were reported as corrections to retained earnings. Firms often recognized accounting changes that reduced net income in periods of poor operating performance to avoid reducing income in better times.

To enhance consistency and comparability, confidence in financial reporting, and full disclosure, the Accounting Principles Board issued *Opinion No. 20, "Accounting Changes,"* (1971). This opinion, as amended, allows firms to change accounting methods and estimates only under certain conditions, and narrows the reporting alternatives available to the firm.

The essential issues in reporting accounting changes are:

- Whether to restate prior period financial statements to reflect the new principle or estimate.
- Whether to recognize the effect of the change on prior years' income as an adjustment to current net income, or to the beginning retained earnings balance in the year of the change.

The reporting principles applied to accounting changes vary depending on the type of change.

Types of Accounting Changes

APB Opinion No. 20 defines three types of **accounting change** and specifies the treatment of corrections of errors in previously issued financial statements.

Accounting changes:

1. A **change in accounting principle** is a change from one generally accepted accounting principle to another. A change from straight-line to declining-balance depreciation is an example.
2. A **change in accounting estimate** is a change from one good faith estimate to another, justified by new information or conditions. A change in the estimated useful life or estimated residual value of a depreciable asset is an example.
3. A **change in reporting entity** (a special category of accounting principle change classified separately for purposes of *APB Opinion No. 20*) results in financial statements of a different reporting entity. Substituting consolidated statements for individual company financial statements is an example.

Corrections of errors affecting the income of prior periods require special treatment. The discovery and correction in 1991 of overstated depreciation recorded in 1989 is an example. Errors are distinct from estimate changes. Estimate changes result from new information; error corrections require only information known at the time of the error. *APB Opinion No. 20* does not classify error corrections as accounting changes. However, reporting principles similar to those for certain accounting changes apply to error corrections, and that is why they are covered in this chapter.

Objectives of Reporting for Accounting Changes

Relevance Maintaining the *relevance* of financial accounting information in light of new information and changing circumstances is one objective of reporting for accounting changes. In certain instances, an accounting change can improve the relevance of reported information. For example, generally increasing inventory prices may prompt a change to the LIFO method of accounting for inventories, which matches more recent inventory costs against sales.

Consistency   Maintaining *consistency* is a second objective of reporting for accounting changes. Consistency, the conformity of accounting principles and procedures across periods, makes accounting information more useful by facilitating an understanding of information and relationships across time periods and firms. Financial statement users expect consistent application of accounting principles.

Comparability, the quality of information enabling users to identify similarities and differences between two sets of reports, is related to consistency. Information is more useful if it can be compared to similar data of the same firm for different time periods and with similar data from other firms. For example, to determine whether $2 million of net income for a firm is a favorable result, previous income from the same firm and income from other firms are consulted.

Consistency is a necessary but not a sufficient condition for comparability. For example, significant inflation reduces the comparability of sales revenue over time even though the same recognition method is used consistently. If different accounting methods are used in consecutive reporting periods, comparability suffers. Consistency and comparability are secondary qualities of accounting information that increase relevance and reliability, the primary qualities.

The increase in the number of new FASB pronouncements contributes to the perception that the comparability of financial statements has decreased: "One of the FASB's original missions was to foster more comparability, and they've just made it worse. Nowadays, unless you're a sophisticated portfolio manager, you can just forget about having comparability."[2]

However, consistency and comparability do not guarantee relevance and reliability, and should not prevent necessary change. "And you can't blame the accountants, either, unless you think accountants should stop trying to discover more accurate ways of describing the financial health of a company."[3]

Public Confidence   Maintaining *public confidence* in the financial reporting process is a third objective. Inconsistent use of accounting principles, disparity between disclosures and underlying firm value, and restatement of previously published financial statements erodes confidence. Once published, many users expect that, except for error corrections, financial statements are final. "If companies were forever changing their earnings retroactively, investors would quickly lose whatever faith they once had in financial reports."[4]

Meeting these three objectives simultaneously is difficult. Allowing the application of a new accounting method to current and future periods is in conflict with the consistency objective. Restating previously issued financial statements to reflect a new accounting method results in comparative statements based on the same accounting principles, but is in conflict with the public's expectation that previous financial statements should not be changed.

However, the disclosure requirements of *APB Opinion No. 20* attempt to satisfy these objectives. The APB appealed to the need to maintain public confidence when it decided that previous financial statements should not be restated for most accounting principle changes. But to promote consistency, prior period income as measured under the new accounting principle also is disclosed for most principle changes. Other accounting principle changes are applied retroactively by restating the prior statements (discussed in a later section).

---

[2] "Solutions, Anyone?" *Forbes,* April 18, 1988, p. 72.

[3] Ibid.

[4] "Add a Dash of Cumulative Catch-up," *Forbes,* June 6, 1983, p. 98.

Approaches to Reporting Accounting Changes

This section briefly describes the three approaches for recognizing and reporting accounting changes. The application of each to specific accounting changes is specified by *APB Opinion No. 20,* which also applies to summaries of financial information appearing in annual reports.

1. Current Approach This reporting approach recognizes the cumulative difference ("catch-up" adjustment) between the expense or revenue under the old and new accounting principles to the beginning of the current period.[5] This amount is disclosed net of tax effect in the income statement between extraordinary items and net income in an account titled **cumulative effect of change in accounting principle.** Prior financial statements shown comparatively with the current period are not restated. **Pro forma income** amounts (income computed under the new accounting principle) are disclosed in the footnotes for each year presented.[6]

For example, Ansel Company changes its depreciation method from double-declining balance (DDB) to straight-line (SL) in 1991 and applies the current approach. Applying SL to years before 1991 results in $500,000 *less* depreciation than actually recognized under DDB in those years. Ignoring income taxes, Ansel records the following journal entry:

To record accounting principle change, 1991:

Accumulated depreciation	500,000	
Cumulative effect of change in accounting principle		500,000

The cumulative effect of change in accounting principle increases *1991* income. The accumulated depreciation balance after this entry reflects the use of SL to January 1, 1991. Ansel reports the 1989–1991 results in its 1991 annual report and does not restate account balances for 1989 or 1990. However, pro forma income amounts, recomputed under the SL method for 1989 and 1990, are disclosed. The 1991 results reflect the SL method and the 1991 ending retained earnings balance reflects application of the *new* principle.

The APB concluded that most accounting principle changes should be reported under the current approach. The pro forma amounts support the consistency objective and furnish a trend in income computed under the same (new) method, for all periods presented.

2. Retroactive Approach This reporting approach restates all prior financial statements presented on a comparative basis to conform to the new principle. The cumulative income difference (net of tax), computed as in the current approach, adjusts the current beginning *retained earnings* balance. The change does not affect current income. Pro forma disclosures are not included because prior years are restated.

Assume that Ansel Company changes its accounting method for long-term construction contracts in 1991 from the completed-contract method to the percentage-of-completion method, and applies the retroactive approach. Total income before tax actually recognized in past years under the completed contract method is $1 million, but under the percentage of completion method would be $2.5 million.

Ignoring income taxes, Ansel records the following journal entry:

To record accounting principle change, 1991:

Construction in process inventory	1,500,000	
Retained earnings, adjustment for accounting change . .		1,500,000

---

[5] Throughout this chapter, the *current* reporting period is the period in which an accounting change or error correction is made.

[6] Pro forma financial statements and amounts show the effect of transactions, conditions, or principles that have not yet occurred or been applied. They are as-if amounts.

The beginning 1991 retained earnings balance is increased by $1.5 million to reflect earnings under percentage of completion to January 1, 1991. All relevant account balances in the 1989 and 1990 statements are restated to conform to percentage of completion. Construction-in-process inventory reflects the increased profit recognized on long-term contracts and 1991 income reflects the percentage-of-completion method.

The APB concluded that for some accounting principle changes, the advantages of retroactive restatement outweigh the disadvantages.[7] The retroactive approach applies one accounting principle consistently to all periods presented. Prior year income effects are not recognized in current income. The effect of the change on income for all periods presented is disclosed.

3. Prospective Approach This reporting approach applies revised accounting *estimates* to current and future periods affected by the change.[8] Prior financial statements remain unchanged, and no cumulative effect on prior years' income is computed. Estimate changes are the most common accounting change. Estimates, by their nature, are subject to error and require periodic revision over time. Firms are expected to report financial statements that reflect the most current information.

Assume that in 1991, Springfield Company changes its estimate of useful life and residual value for equipment costing $440,000 and purchased January 1, 1989. The original useful life and residual value estimates are 10 years and $40,000, respectively. Springfield revises the remaining useful life and residual value estimates to five years and $0. The estimate changes reflect technological obsolescence. Springfield uses straight-line depreciation.

The new salvage value and remaining useful life estimates are applied to the book value of the equipment remaining at the beginning of 1991:

Original cost, January 1, 1989	$440,000
Depreciation per year: ($440,000 − $40,000)/10 = $40,000	
Accumulated depreciation, January 1, 1991 [2($40,000)]	80,000
Book value, January 1, 1991	$360,000
Depreciation, 1991: $360,000/5 =	$ 72,000

Depreciation in 1991 and subsequent years reflects the new estimates. Springfield discloses the effect of the estimate change on 1991 income and repeats unchanged the 1989 and 1990 financial statements in its 1991 annual report.

The prospective approach supports the notion that good faith estimates using all available information are valid until conditions change. The new estimates are not applied to the results of previous periods because the information supporting the estimate change was not available or applicable until the current period. Although the results of previous periods reflect different estimates, disclosing the effect of the change on current income partially offsets the reduced consistency.

CONCEPT REVIEW

1. How does the current approach maintain a measure of consistency in financial reporting?
2. Why are estimate changes treated prospectively?
3. Explain the major differences between the current and retroactive approaches.

---

[7] *APB Opinion No. 20*, par. 27.

[8] This approach also is referred to as the *current and prospective* approach.

EXHIBIT 24–1 Summary of Accounting Changes and Reporting Approaches

Type of Accounting Change or Error Correction	Reporting Approach Required	Summary of the Approach	
		Catch-up Adjustment Identified With	Comparative Statements (Results of Prior Years)
Accounting changes: 1. Changes in accounting principles: a. Most principle changes.*	Current	Income statement	Prior year's results remain unchanged (pro forma income disclosed).
b. Specified exceptions.	Retroactive	Retained earnings	Prior year's results restated to new principle.
2. Changes in accounting estimates.	Prospective	Catch-up adjustment not computed or reported	Prior year's results remain unchanged. New estimates applied prospectively.
3. Changes in reporting entity.	Retroactive	None†	Prior years' results restated.
Accounting errors affecting income of prior years.	Retroactive	Retained earnings (a prior period adjustment)	Prior years' results correctly restated.

* The change to LIFO typically does not require reporting a cumulative effect of a change in accounting principle, but is otherwise treated as a current-type change.

† Discussed in advanced accounting courses.

General Applicability of the Three Approaches

Exhibit 24–1 summarizes the applicability of the three approaches to accounting changes. Changes in accounting principles, estimates, and error corrections often are made during the closing process. However, entries to record accounting principle changes and error corrections affecting prior years are made *as of the beginning* of the current year. The current year's results reflect the new principle or estimate for the entire year because the accounts are not yet closed. The entries to record the change are not affected by the number of prior years shown comparatively with the current period.

The cumulative effect on prior years' income under the current and retroactive approaches, and prior period adjustments (for errors), are disclosed in the financial statements net-of-tax. Intraperiod tax allocation separates the tax effects on these three items from tax on income from continuing operations. Extraordinary items and discontinued operations are handled similarly.

Justification for Accounting Changes

Firms cannot arbitrarily change accounting principles. Under *APB Opinion No. 20,* only changes that improve financial reporting are permitted (emphasis added).

> The presumption that an entity should not change an accounting principle may be overcome *only* if the enterprise justifies the use of an alternative acceptable accounting principle on the basis that it is *preferable.* However, a method of accounting that was previously adopted for a type of transaction or event which is being terminated or which was a single, nonrecurring event in the past should not be changed. *The burden of justifying other changes rests with the entity proposing the change.* (par. 16).

The nature of the change and its justification are disclosed. The justification should clearly explain why the new principle is preferable. Improved matching of expenses and revenues, enhanced asset valuation, and compliance with a new reporting standard are common justifications. For example, a firm can justify its change from the completed-contract method to the percentage-of-completion method by citing improved reliability of total construction cost estimates.

A FASB statement creating a new accounting principle, expressing a preference for a particular accounting principle, or rejecting a previous principle is sufficient support for a change in accounting principle. In addition, specialized accounting and reporting principles and practices are specified in *AICPA Statements of Position (SOP)* and *Guides on Accounting and Auditing Matters* as preferable principles for justifying a change in accounting principle.[9] The FASB has not yet deliberated on these issues, which primarily apply to special industry practices. For example, *SOP 79-1* concerns accounting for municipal bond funds, an area for which no *SFAS* yet exists.

A firm making an accounting principle change in conformance with an *AICPA SOP* should report the change as specified in the *SOP*. If the *SOP* does not specify how to report the change, *APB Opinion No. 20* guidelines apply.[10]

In addition to the preferability requirement, the *audit report* for a firm is modified to reflect an accounting principle change which materially affects the financial statements. If the auditor is in agreement with the change, and if the change is to an acceptable method, the modficiation is informational only. If not, or if management has not sufficiently justified the change, the auditor qualifies the report for lack of conformity with GAAP.[11]

Comparative Statements

Annual reports generally include financial statements for the current year and for one or two previous years for comparative purposes. Comparative financial statements increase the usefulness of annual reports by increasing the quantity of information available and by establishing a base against which the current results can be compared. This dynamic portrayal is more useful for predictions than single-year statements because it indicates whether reported accounting data is increasing or decreasing.

Comparative financial statements are recommended under GAAP,[12] and the SEC requires firms under its jurisdiction to report more than one year's data. Creditors also typically require comparative financial statements for lending purposes. The next three sections use comparative statements to illustrate the three approaches to accounting changes in detail.

REPORTING ACCOUNTING PRINCIPLE CHANGES: CURRENT APPROACH

♦

Accounting principles include methods, techniques, or procedures applied to transactions or information for purposes of measurement, recognition, or disclosure. When a firm makes a change in accounting principle, it substitutes one generally accepted accounting principle for another. Examples include changing from FIFO to the weighted-average method, and straight-line to accelerated depreciation.[13]

Accounting principle changes also include less obvious modifications in measurement and reporting. For example, under *FASB Interpretation No. 1,* "Accounting

---

[9] *SFAS No. 32,* "Specialized Accounting and Reporting Principles and Practices in AICPA Statements of Position and Guides on Accounting and Auditing Matters," and *SFAS No. 83,* "Designation of AICPA Guides and Statement of Position on Accounting by Brokers and Dealers in Securities, by Employee Benefit Plans, and By Banks as Preferable for Purposes of Applying *APB Opinion No. 20.*"

[10] *FASB Interpretation No. 20,* "Reporting Accounting Changes under AICPA Statements of Position."

[11] AICPA, *Statement on Auditing Standards No. 58,* "The Auditors Standard Report" (New York, 1988).

[12] AICPA, "Restatement and Revision of Accounting Research Bulletins Nos. 1–42" *Accounting Research Bulletin No. 43,* (New York, 1953), Chapter 2, Section A, par. 2.

[13] Changes in accounting principle also include changes in method of application. For example, a change in the application of LCM from an individual-item basis to an aggregate basis for inventory is an accounting principle change.

Changes Related to the Cost of Inventory," a change in the composition of inventory cost is an accounting change. In a second example, Hyde Athletic Industries included the following footnote related to a change in inventory accounting in its 1989 annual report.

> In the fourth quarter of 1989, the Company changed its method of accounting for the costs of inventory by capitalizing certain inventory procurement and other indirect production costs, effective January 1, 1989. Previously, these costs were charged to expense in the period incurred rather than included in cost of sales in the period in which the merchandise was sold. The Company believes that this new method is preferable because it provides a better matching of costs with related revenues.

The procedures for accounting changes are applied only to existing assets and liabilities and to those that would exist under a new accounting principle. The required disclosures are limited to the financial statements presented on a comparative basis.

Although the following appear similar to accounting changes, thay are *not* so considered under *APB Opinion No. 20:*

1. Initial adoption of an accounting principle for new transactions or for transactions that were previously immaterial. An example is immaterial prepaid advertising costs that were previously expensed but that are now capitalized because the advertising program is expanded.
2. Adopting an accounting principle to a new group of assets or liabilities. For example, a firm begins applying accelerated depreciation to new equipment but continues to use straight-line depreciation for old equipment.
3. A change from an inappropriate accounting principle to an allowed method. For example, switching from capitalizing research and development costs to immediate expensing is an error correction.
4. A *planned* change to straight-line depreciation from accelerated depreciation, at a particular future date to avoid over-depreciating plant assets.
5. A change in accounting principle that cannot be distinguished from a change in accounting estimate is generally treated as a change in estimate:

> For example, a company may change from deferring and amortizing a cost to recording it as an expense when incurred because future benefits of the cost have become doubtful. The new accounting method is adopted, therefore, in partial or complete recognition of the change in estimated future benefits. The effect of the change in accounting principle is inseparable from the effect of the change in accounting estimate. Changes of this type are often related to the continuing process of obtaining additional information and revising estimates and are therefore considered as changes in estimates. (*APB Opinion No. 20,* par. 11)

The current approach applies to all accounting principle changes *except* those subject to the retroactive approach (the specified exceptions).

Reporting Guidelines: Current Approach

The following guidelines are followed when reporting an accounting principle change subject to the current approach.

1. Prior year financial statements reported on a comparative basis remain unchanged.
2. The cumulative income difference between the two methods for all affected prior periods is disclosed between extraordinary items and net income, net of tax. The entry to record the cumulative effect involves a real account (e.g., accumulated depreciation or inventory), and often an income tax account.[14]

---

[14] If the change also is made for tax purposes, income taxes payable or receivable is recorded, and an amended tax return is filed. If not, a change in a deferred income tax account is recorded. In most cases, changes are not made for both purposes.

3. The effects of the new principle on current year's income before extraordinary items and on net income (and related per share amounts) are disclosed.
4. Pro forma income before extraordinary items and net income (and related per share amounts) are disclosed on the face of the income statement (or noted prominently and cross-referenced) for all prior periods presented and the current year as if the new accounting principle were in effect during those periods. If only the current period is presented, the actual and pro forma amounts for the immediately preceding period and the current period are disclosed.
5. The new principle is applied as of the beginning of the current year. The current year's financial statements reflect the new principle; the prior years' statements reflect the old principle.
6. Future annual reports repeat the disclosures until the year of change is no longer presented.

Refer to Exhibit 24–2 which presents case information for a detailed example of the current approach applied to a change in depreciation method. In that exhibit, the cumulative income difference before tax ($37,600) also represents the difference in the accumulated depreciation balance between the two methods. If the DDB method were used during the previous three years, the accumulated depreciation balance would be $97,600 at the end of 1990. The following entries are made in 1991 to record the accounting change, and depreciation expense:

As of January 1, 1991: To record accounting change:

Cumulative effect of change in accounting principle, depreciation	22,560	
Deferred income tax ($37,600 × .40)	15,040	
Accumulated depreciation		37,600

December 31, 1991—To record depreciation expense (DDB):

Depreciation expense ($200,000 − $97,600) .20	20,480	
Accumulated depreciation		20,480

The cumulative effect account[15] is similar to a loss or expense in this instance, and reduces income $22,560 because DDB recognizes depreciation expense faster than SL during the asset's early years. Depreciation expense for 1991 reflects the DDB method.

The entry to record the accounting change decreases the deferred income tax liability. The accounting change increases book depreciation before January 1, 1991; book depreciation after that date decreases. Therefore, future differences between book and tax depreciation are decreased. Under these conditions, deferred tax liabilities are reduced. Exhibit 24–3 illustrates the comparative financial statements and related disclosures.

Exhibit 24–3 shows the 1990 statements under the old method (SL) and the 1991 statements under the new method (DDB). The ending accumulated depreciation balance and depreciation expense for 1990 reflect SL, yet the corresponding 1991 amounts reflect DDB. This lack of consistency is somewhat offset by the pro forma disclosures.

Pro forma income before extraordinary items is always equal to its actual counterpart in the current year (1991) because both values reflect the new method. Pro forma net income for the current year is always the reported net income plus or minus the cumulative effect. If DDB were used previously, there would be no cumulative effect. Therefore, 1991 pro forma income equals actual net income *plus* the cumulative effect because the cumulative effect *reduced* actual income.

---

[15] The cumulative effect of change in accounting principle is an example of the type of item that would be included in comprehensive income, but not earnings. (*SFAC No. 5,* par. 42)

EXHIBIT 24-2   Change in Depreciation Method: Application of Current Approach:
Case Information for Sunrise Company

1. In 1991, Sunrise Company changes from straight-line (SL) depreciation to double-declining balance (DDB) for financial reporting purposes. The new method affects machinery purchased January 1, 1988, costing $200,000. The machinery has no salvage value; its estimated useful life is 10 years. The reporting year ends December 31. A 40% tax rate is assumed.
2. Sunrise reports 1990 and 1991 results on a comparative basis. Summary financial information for both years follows. (The order of years presented facilitates the discussion; normally the most recent statements begin to the left.)

	Reported in 1990	1991 Trial Balance Prior to Accounting Change and Depreciation
Balance sheet, December 31:		
Assets (not detailed)	$700,000	$823,400
Machinery	200,000	200,000
Accumulated depreciation (straight-line)	(60,000)	(60,000)
Total	$840,000	
Liabilities (including deferred income tax)	$340,000	$291,112
Contributed capital (100,000 shares)	300,000	300,000
Retained earnings	200,000	200,000
Total	$840,000	
Income statement, year ended December 31:		
Revenues	$700,000	$770,000
Expenses (includes 40% income tax)	(550,000)	(607,712)
Depreciation expense	(20,000)	
Income before extraordinary items	130,000	
Extraordinary gain (loss), net of tax	(6,000)	10,000
Net income	$124,000	
Earnings per share:		
Income before extraordinary items	$1.30	
Extraordinary gain (loss)	(.06)	
Net income	$1.24	

Analysis of the Accounting Change

1. This is a change in accounting principle (not a specified exception); the current approach must be applied.
2. Computation of the catch-up adjustment:

From SL depreciation: depreciation recorded to date for years 1988–1990 ($200,000 × .10 × 3 years)		$60,000
To DDB depreciation: depreciation that would have been recorded under DDB:		
1988: $200,000 × .20*	$40,000	
1989: ($200,000 − $40,000) × .20	32,000	
1990: ($200,000 − $40,000 − $32,000) × .20	25,600	97,600
Catch-up adjustment—increase in accumulated depreciation to DDB basis (pretax), (1988–1990)		$37,600
Catch-up adjustment, net of tax [$37,600 × (1.00 − .40)]		$22,560

* .20 = ²/₁₀ years.

The footnote describes the change, its justification, and the effect on 1991 income. These disclosures supplement the pro forma disclosures and help users understand the change. W. H. Brady Company used the current approach to report an accounting principle change in its 1989 income statement. Both the cumulative effect and pro forma amounts are illustrated (per share amounts are omitted):

EXHIBIT 24–3   Sunrise Company's Comparative Financial Statements and Related Disclosures

	1990—From Prior Year; No Change	1991—Based on New Principle; DDB
Balance Sheet:		
Assets	$700,000	$823,400
Machinery (cost)	200,000	200,000
Accumulated depreciation (SL)	(60,000)	
DDB: ($60,000 + $37,600 + $20,480)		(118,080)
Total	$840,000	$905,320
Liabilities (1991: $291,112 − $15,040 − $8,192*)	$340,000	$267,880
Contributed capital (100,000 shares)	300,000	300,000
Retained earnings	200,000	
1991: ($200,000 + income, $137,440 see income statement below)		337,440
Total	$840,000	$905,320

* Tax effect of 1991 depreciation: $20,480(.40)

	1990—From Prior Year; No Change	1991—Based on New Principle; DDB
Income statement:		
Revenues	$700,000	$770,000
Expenses (including 40% income tax)	(550,000)	(DB) (599,520)†
Depreciation expense . . . . (SL)	(20,000)	(DB) (20,480)
Income before extraordinary items and accounting change	130,000	150,000
Extraordinary gain (loss), net of tax	(6,000)	10,000
Cumulative effect of accounting change		(22,560)
Net income	$124,000	$137,440

† $607,712 − $8,192 (tax effect of depreciation)

	1990—From Prior Year; No Change	1991—Based on New Principle; DDB
Earnings per share (100,000 shares):		
Income before extraordinary items	$1.30	$1.50
Extraordinary items	(.06)	.10
Effect of accounting change		(.23)
Net income	$1.24	$1.37

Pro Forma Income under DDB

	1990—From Prior Year; No Change	1991—Based on New Principle; DDB
Income before extraordinary items and accounting change:		
1990: $130,000 − [($25,600, DDB − $20,000, SL) × .60]	$126,640	
1991: No change; as above		$150,000
Earnings per share	$1.27	$1.50
Net income:		
1990: ($124,000 − [($25,600, DDB − $20,000, SL) × .60]	$120,640	
1991: ($137,440 net income above + $22,560 catch-up)		$160,000
Earnings per share	$1.21	$1.60

Note: As of the beginning of 1991, the company changed from the straight-line method to double-declining balance for depreciation. In management's opinion, the new method better measures income. The effect of the change on 1991 results is to increase depreciation expense and decrease net income before extraordinary items $480 before tax ($288 after tax and less than $.01 per share), and decrease net income $22,848 ($22,560 cumulative effect plus $288 after tax depreciation increase, or $.23 per share.)

(in thousands)	**1989**
Earnings before extraordinary item and cumulative effect of change in accounting method	$ 9,875
Extraordinary item	4,625
Earnings before cumulative effect of change in accounting method	14,500
Cumulative effect on prior years of change in method of accounting for catalog costs (Note A)	1,233
Net earnings	$15,733
Pro forma amount assuming the new accounting method is applied retroactively.	
Earnings before extraordinary item and cumulative effect of change in accounting method	$ 9,875
Net earnings	$14,500

Portions of Note A follow:

> During the fiscal year ended July 31, 1989, the Company changed its method of accounting for catalog costs from one which expensed catalog publication and development costs as incurred, to a method under which such costs are initially capitalized and amortized over the estimated useful lives of the publications (generally between 4 and 14 months). The change was made in order to better match expenses with revenues and to prevent the timing of purchasing decisions from impacting the results of operations.

Direct and Indirect Effects of Changes in Accounting Principle

Many firms that change accounting principles under the current approach report both direct and indirect effects. The *direct* effects of the change are those adjustments made to account balances and earnings amounts to reflect the new principle. The Sunrise Company example illustrated the direct effects only.

Had the new accounting principle been in effect in prior years, certain nondiscretionary items based on earnings, including bonus arrangements and royalties, would have been different. These are the *indirect* effects of the accounting principle change. For example, Sunrise's depreciation change decreased 1990 net income $3,360 on a pro forma basis ($124,000 − $120,640). If Sunrise's executive compensation arrangement includes a bonus based on income, the 1990 bonus would be less under the new method.

The cumulative effect account reflects only direct effects unless the indirect effects are actually recorded.[16] The pro forma amounts reflect both direct and indirect effects. Therefore, the pro forma income amounts reflect the assumed bonuses and royalties under the new method even though such amounts did not occur in the past. Income tax is applied to both direct and indirect effects.

The direct and indirect effects may interact. For example, if Sunrise granted a bonus based on income, the accounting change caused Sunrise's 1990 calculated bonus to decrease because income decreased. The decreased bonus in turn serves to increase 1990 income on a pro forma basis, partially offsetting the effect of the accounting change.

Cumulative Effect of Change Not Determinable

The cumulative income difference for prior years' income between the old and new methods is occasionally too costly to determine. In this case, the reporting requirements are reduced to the following:

1. Disclose the effect of the change on income before extraordinary items and net income (and related per share amounts) for the current year only.
2. Disclose the nature and justification for the change.
3. Explain why the cumulative effect and pro forma amounts are not disclosed.

Generally, firms that change to the LIFO method report only the reduced disclosures because reconstructing LIFO inventory layers is prohibitively expensive or impossible. Past costs and purchase prices necessary to reconstruct inventory layers typically are unavailable. For example, a firm whose annual unit production exceeded unit sales each year during the last decade requires cost information dating back 10 years to make the change under the current approach.

Instead, the beginning inventory balance in the current year serves as the base layer or beginning balance for LIFO. The current year's financial statements use LIFO. If the firm produces more than it sells in the current year, the entire base year layer remains in ending inventory.

Quaker Oats Company adopted LIFO but was unable to prepare the customary disclosures normally required under the current approach. The following footnote appeared in the company's 1989 annual report:

---

[16] Whether the firm retroactively adjusts the actual bonus or royalty payments based on an accounting change depends on the underlying agreement.

Effective July 1, 1988, the Company adopted the LIFO cost flow assumption for valuing the majority of remaining U.S. Grocery Products inventories. The Company believes that the use of the LIFO method better matches current costs with current revenues. The cumulative effect of this change on retained earnings at the beginning of the year is not determinable, nor are the pro forma effects of retroactive application of LIFO to prior years. The effect of this change on fiscal 1989 was to decrease net income by $16.0 million, or $.20 per share.

CONCEPT REVIEW

1. Verify that the effect of Sunrise's accounting change on income before extraordinary items in 1991 is $288 (see footnote to Exhibit 24–3).
2. Explain how the cumulative effect of a change in accounting principle is computed.
3. How are the following current year (year of change) pro forma amounts computed: net income before extraordinary items and net income?

REPORTING ACCOUNTING PRINCIPLE CHANGES: RETROACTIVE APPROACH
◆

The accounting principle changes subject to the retroactive approach often create catch-up amounts that would greatly increase income if the current approach were applied. The sheer size of the resulting income difference for these specified exceptions argues for the retroactive approach.

The following changes in accounting principle are reported under the *retroactive approach* rather than the current approach:

1. A change from the LIFO inventory method to another inventory method.
2. A change in the method of accounting for long-term construction contracts (from percentage-of-completion to completed-contract or vice versa).
3. A change to or from the full-cost method in extractive industries.
4. The retroactive approach *may* be applied to all changes in accounting principle made in conjunction with the initial public offering of equity securities for obtaining additional equity capital, effecting a business combination, or registering securities. This exemption from the current approach is available only once (*APB Opinion No. 20*, par. 29).
5. A change from retirement/replacement accounting to depreciation accounting for railroad track structures.
6. A change to a principle required by a new SFAS or recommended by an *AICPA SOP*, which requires retroactive application.
7. A change to the equity method.[17]

Changes in reporting entity and prior period adjustments, both discussed in later sections, also are reported under the retroactive approach.

For some firms, the *change from LIFO* to FIFO would cause serious distortion in income under the current approach. LIFO layers can be many years or even decades old. FIFO would recognize in income the old (lower) cost layers, rather than the more recent (higher) cost layers expensed under LIFO, resulting in a potentially large increase in income.

The methods allowed for long-term *construction contracts and natural resource exploration costs* are among the accounting principles that produce the greatest income differences. The percentage-of-completion method gradually recognizes income on long-term construction projects. The completed-contract method recog-

---

[17] *APB Opinion No. 18*, "The Equity Method of Accounting for Investments in Common Stock," par. 19 (*m*).

nizes no income until the project is complete. Substantial differences also occur between immediate expensing of unsuccessful exploration efforts (successful-efforts method) and gradual amortization (full costing).

The use of completed contract for financial reporting may gradually diminish because its use for tax purposes has been significantly restricted in recent years. The frequency of accounting changes involving long-term construction contracts therefore may also be reduced in the future.

The APB concluded, for *initial public offerings of equity securities,* that retroactively restating financial statements for periods before the first public share offering better serves the investing public. The same accounting principles are applied to all presented statements to allow meaningful comparisons. No loss in public confidence occurs because the statements were not previously issued.

Regulatory changes resulted in the requirement that changes *by railroads to depreciation accounting* be applied retroactively. Beginning in 1983, railroads were required to depreciate railroad track structures in reports to the Interstate Commerce Commission. Many railroads adopted the practice for general-purpose financial reporting. The FASB concluded, in *SFAS No. 73,* "Reporting a Change in Accounting for Railroad Track Structures," that the comparability advantages of retroactive restatement outweigh the disadvantages for this accounting change. Analysts at the time expected a general increase of 20% to 30% in railroad net income as a result of the change.[18]

Most recent *SFAS*s require that *mandatory accounting changes be made retroactively* when first applying the statement. In this way, the FASB reinforces consistency as an important quality of accounting information. For example, *SFAS No. 48,* "Revenue Recognition When Right of Return Exists," requires retroactive application when first adopted. This category of accounting change is involuntary, in contrast to the other changes discussed.

The equity method is controversial because it allows the investor to recognize its share of investee income before receiving dividends. A *change to the equity method* can affect investor income materially because undistributed investee net income from many previous years is immediately recognized by the investor. This change is sometimes categorized as a change in reporting entity.

Reporting Guidelines: Retroactive Approach

The following guidelines are followed when reporting an accounting principle change subject to the retroactive approach.

1. Prior year financial statements reported on a comparative basis are restated to conform to the new accounting principle. All affected account balances are restated. Therefore, all periods presented reflect the new accounting principle.
2. The cumulative income difference between the two methods for all affected prior periods is recorded as an adjustment to the beginning retained earnings balance for the current period, net of tax. The entry to record the cumulative adjustment involves a real account and often an income tax account.
3. For each year presented in the retained earnings statement, the beginning retained earnings balance is adjusted by the after-tax effect of the change attributable to prior years (whether or not presented). The adjustment for the current year (only) equals the recorded cumulative adjustment in (2) above.
4. The effects on income before extraordinary items and on net income (and related per share amounts) are disclosed for all periods presented (if affected by the change).
5. Subsequent financial statements need not repeat the disclosures.

See Exhibit 24–4, which presents the case data for a change from LIFO to FIFO.

---

[18] "Add a Dash of Cumulative Catch-up," *Forbes,* June 6, 1983, p. 98.

EXHIBIT 24–4   Application of Retroactive Approach—Case Information for Sunset Company:
Change from LIFO to FIFO

1. In 1991, Sunset Company changes its inventory cost method from LIFO to FIFO for financial reporting and tax purposes. The reporting year ends on December 31, and the average
income tax rate is 40%.
2. To provide data for the change, a computer run reflected the following selected data:

	1990		1991—Year of Change	
Item	FIFO	LIFO*	FIFO*	LIFO
a. Beginning inventory	$47,000	$ 45,000	$ 60,000	$50,000
b. Ending inventory	60,000	50,000	80,000	68,000
c. Income before extraordinary items (after tax)			160,000	176,000
d. Retained earnings, beginning balance			86,000	
e. Extraordinary gains (losses), net of tax			3,000	(2,000)
f. Dividends declared and paid			80,000	88,000
g. Common shares outstanding all year			100,000	100,000

* Reporting method in 1990 and 1991 respectively.

Analysis of the Accounting Change

The change from LIFO to FIFO, a retroactive change, affects 1990 and 1991. The
effect on both years must be determined, as well as the overall change to the
beginning of both years, to fulfill the reporting requirements.

Effect of the Accounting Change on Pretax Income

To the beginning of 1990

$47,000 (FIFO) − $45,000 (LIFO) = $2,000 ($1,200 after tax)

(FIFO pretax income is higher by $2,000 through December 31, 1989, because $2,000 less cost of
goods sold is recognized.)

To the beginning of 1991

$60,000 (FIFO) − $50,000 (LIFO) = $10,000 ($6,000 after tax)

(FIFO pretax income is higher by $10,000 through December 31, 1990, because $10,000 less cost of
goods sold is recognized.)

For 1990

Beginning inventory effect:
  FIFO has higher beginning inventory, higher cost of
  goods sold, lower income, $47,000 − $45,000 = ($2,000)
Ending inventory effect:
  FIFO has higher ending inventory, lower cost of
  goods sold, higher income, $60,000 − $50,000 = 10,000

  Change to FIFO increases 1990 pretax income $8,000 ($4,800 after tax)

For 1991:

Beginning inventory effect:
  FIFO has higher beginning inventory, higher cost of
  goods sold, lower income, $60,000 − $50,000 = ($10,000)
Ending inventory effect:
  FIFO has higher ending inventory, lower cost of
  goods sold, higher income, $80,000 − $68,000 = 12,000

  Change to FIFO increases 1991 pretax income $2,000 ($1,200 after tax)

When computing the income effect of an inventory change to a particular date (the first two computations above), only the *ending* inventory amounts need be considered. The inventory cost flow assumptions do not affect purchases, and no beginning inventory existed when the firm was organized. The first two effects are the adjustments to the beginning retained earnings balances, shown comparatively. The $10,000 effect on pretax income to the beginning of 1991 *is* the pretax cumulative difference recognized in 1991, the year of change.

When computing the effect for individual years (the last two computations above), *both* beginning and ending inventories are considered because both affect cost of goods sold. These amounts are needed for the footnote describing the income effect for each year presented.

As of January 1, 1991—To record accounting change:

Inventory	10,000	
Income taxes payable ($10,000 × .40)		4,000
Retained earnings, adjustment for accounting change		6,000

The total pretax income increase from changing to FIFO for all years before January 1, 1991, is $10,000. This amount is also the difference between ending 1990 inventories under the two methods ($60,000 − $50,000). The $4,000 increase in taxes reflects the tax on profits avoided by using LIFO in the past. After adjusting for the $6,000 increase, beginning 1991 retained earnings reflects FIFO. The 1991 income statement does not reflect this cumulative catch-up amount because the change from LIFO is a retroactive change.

Refer to Exhibit 24–5 which shows the 1990 and 1991 comparative statements. The 1990 statements are restated to reflect FIFO, although they originally were reported under LIFO. Some firms title the retained earnings adjustment "cumulative effect of accounting change."

The comparative statements reflect the FIFO method after restating the 1990 results. Net income for 1990 is increased $4,800, and the 1990 balance sheet discloses ending inventory under FIFO, not LIFO.

The retained earnings statements for both years contain a cumulative adjustment, because income *before* both 1990 and 1991 is affected by the change. The $1,200 adjustment to the beginning 1990 retained earnings balance accounts for the income effect on all years before 1990. The $6,000 adjustment to the beginning 1991 balance accounts for the income effect on all years before 1991, and equals the amount in the entry to record the accounting change. As such, the $6,000 amount *includes* the $1,200. The 1991 adjustment equals the effect on all years before 1990 ($1,200) plus the effect on 1990 ($4,800). The adjustments in the retained earnings statements thus overlap.

The beginning retained earnings balance is not adjusted if prior years are not affected. For example, assume that the years 1991 to 1995 are shown comparatively, but only the years 1992 to 1995 are affected by a retroactive accounting principle change. The beginning retained earnings balances for 1993 to 1995 are adjusted. No retained earnings adjustment is needed for 1992 because 1992 net income is adjusted for the change, and no year before 1992 is affected.

In the Sunset Company retained earnings statement, the ending 1990 retained earnings balance ($175,000) does not equal the beginning 1991 retained earnings balance as previously reported ($169,000) for two reasons:
- Income for 1990 now reflects the change to FIFO.
- The beginning 1990 retained earnings balance as restated also reflects the change to FIFO.

But the $175,000 ending 1990 balance equals the 1991 beginning balance *as restated*. In general, the restated ending balance for any year equals the next year's beginning restated balance.

EXHIBIT 24-5   Abbreviated Comparative Financial Statements—Change from LIFO to FIFO for Sunset Company

	1990 FIFO Basis	1991 FIFO Basis
Balance sheet:		
Inventory (FIFO)	$ 60,000	$ 80,000
Income statement:		
Income before extraordinary items	$164,800*	$176,000
Extraordinary item, net of tax	3,000	$ (2,000)
Net income	$167,800	$174,000
Earnings per share (100,000 shares):		
Income before extraordinary items	$1.65	$1.76
Extraordinary items	.03	(.02)
Net income	$1.68	$1.74
Retained earnings statement:		
Beginning balance, as previously stated	$ 86,000	$169,000†
Add: Adjustment for accounting change net of $800 and $4,000 tax	1,200	6,000
Beginning balance as restated	87,200	175,000
Add: Net income (from above)	167,800	174,000
Deduct: Dividends declared and paid	(80,000)	(88,000)
Ending balance	$175,000	$261,000

Note: During 1991 the company changed from LIFO to FIFO for inventory accounting purposes because FIFO more realistically measures net income. The change increased 1990 net income $4,800 ($.048 per share). The change increased 1991 net income $1,200 ($.012 per share). The 1990 statements are restated to reflect the change.

* $164,800 = $160,000 + $4,800 (after-tax increase in 1990 income due to accounting change).

† $169,800 = ending 1990 retained earnings under LIFO
= $86,000 + $160,000 + $3,000 − $80,000
(All from Exhibit 24–4 under 1990 LIFO column.)

An alternative to overlapping adjustments is sometimes used, which adjusts only the *earliest* beginning retained earnings balance shown if previous years are affected by the change. Under this alternative, Sunset discloses:

	1990	1991
Retained earnings statement:		
Beginning balance	$ 86,000	
Add: Adjustment for accounting change	1,200	
Beginning balance as restated	87,200	$175,000
Add: Net income	167,800	174,000
Deduct: Dividends declared and paid	(80,000)	(88,000)
Ending balance	$175,000	$261,000

The authors prefer the first approach because it discloses the previously reported retained earnings balance for each year, and the adjustment for the current year equals the total adjustment to retained earnings for the change (recognized in the entry to record the change). This approach also has authoritative support.

The 1988 Westinghouse Electric Corporation annual report illustrates two retroactive accounting changes and exemplifies the overlapping adjustments to retained earnings:

WESTINGHOUSE ELECTRIC CORPORATION
Retained Earnings Statement
For the Years Ended December 31, 1986, 1987, and 1988
(in millions)

	1988	1987	1986
Balance at beginning of year, as previously reported	$4,441.6	$3,937.3	$3,470.7
Adjustment for the cumulative effect on prior years of applying the new method of accounting for:			
Loan origination fees	(32.1)	(18.0)	(13.5)
Income taxes	(317.7)	(493.4)	—
Balance at beginning of year, as adjusted	4,091.8	3,425.9	3,457.2
Net income	822.8	900.5	172.9
Dividends	(278.0)	(234.6)	(204.2)
Balance at end of year	$4,636.6	$4,091.8	$3,425.9

The related footnotes explain the two changes:

> In 1988, the corporation retroactively adopted the requirements of a new accounting standard which requires the amortization of income related to non-refundable loan fees over the life of the loan instead of recognition at time of loan origination. The retroactive application of the new standard resulted in a decrease in net income of $5.7 million ($.04 per share), $14.1 million ($.10 per share) and $4.5 million ($.03 per share) in 1988, 1987, and 1986.

> The Corporation adopted *SFAS No. 96,* "Accounting for Income Taxes," retroactively to January 1, 1986. The effect of adopting *SFAS No. 96* on net income was an increase of $58.8 million ($.40 per share) in 1988, an increase of $175.7 million ($1.21 per share) in 1987 and a decrease of $493.4 million ($3.24 per share) in 1986. Certain amounts in these financial statements have been restated as a result of this accounting change.

CONCEPT REVIEW

1. How is the entry to record an accounting principle change under the retroactive approach different from the entry for the current approach?
2. Why are pro forma income amounts not necessary under the retroactive approach?
3. Explain how the adjustments to the beginning comparative retained earnings balances are computed under the retroactive approach.

REPORTING ACCOUNTING ESTIMATE CHANGES: PROSPECTIVE APPROACH
♦

Accounting estimates are necessary when future events that affect current measurement and disclosure are not known with certainty. Examples include estimated uncollectible accounts, estimated useful lives and residual values of plant assets, and estimated turnover and mortality in accounting for pensions. Estimates result from judgments based on specific assumptions and projections concerning future events.

As time passes, new information often becomes available prompting an improvement of the original estimate. When estimates are revised, no entry is needed to record the change because prior years are not affected.[19] A change in an estimate not made in good faith or one which did not consider all the relevant information at the time is treated as an error.

Reporting Guidelines: Prospective Approach (Estimate Changes)

The following guidelines are followed when reporting an accounting estimate change.

1. The estimate change affects the reporting for the current and future periods only.
2. Prior year statements shown on a comparative basis are not restated.
3. The effects of the change on income before extraordinary items and on net income (and related per share amounts) for the current period are disclosed for a change in estimate affecting future periods. For changes affecting only the current period (e.g., a change in expected uncollectible accounts), this disclosure is not required, although is recommended if material.
4. The new estimate is applied as of the beginning of the current period, generally based on the book value of the relevant real account remaining at that time.
5. No entry is made for prior year effects; only the normal current year entry incorporating the new estimate is made.
6. Future years, if affected by the change, continue to use the new estimate.

Estimate Change Affecting Only the Current Year

Assume that during the first two years of Tenaya Company's operations, the actual and estimated uncollectible account receivable rate varied widely as collection experience was gained and credit policies matured. At the end of the third year (1991), Tenaya changed its estimated uncollectible percentage, applied to the ending gross accounts receivable balance, from 2% to 4%. This increase reflects a recent upturn in delinquent accounts.

Tenaya's December 31, 1991, unadjusted trial balance contained the following information:

Accounts receivable $300,000
Allowance for doubtful accounts . . . . .   5,000 (dr. balance)

The debit balance in the allowance account reflects the unexpectedly high rate of write-offs. Tenaya records the following entry to recognize uncollectible accounts:

December 31, 1991: To record estimated uncollectible accounts:

Bad debt expense (.04 × $300,000 + $5,000) 17,000
Allowance for doubtful accounts   17,000

This entry reflects the estimate change for 1991. A similar change is possible in subsequent years. Under the old estimate, bad debt expense would be $11,000 (.02 × $300,000 + $5,000). The following footnote is typical (assuming a material effect on income):

> In 1991, the Company changed its estimate of uncollectible accounts to provide a better estimate of net realizable accounts receivable. Net income in 1991 declined $4,200 [after 30% income tax, .70($17,000 − $11,000)] or $.42 per share, based on 10,000 shares outstanding, as a result of the change.

---

[19] However, estimate changes often affect deferred taxes in current and future periods by changing the amounts of future expected temporary differences, necessitating an adjustment to the tax accrual entry.

Estimate Change Affecting Current and Future Years

Assume that equipment with no residual value and a 10-year useful life was purchased by LeMond Company for $120,000 on January 1, 1991. On the basis of new information available during 1995, a 12-year total useful life appears more realistic. In addition, the estimated residual value is now $8,000. LeMond uses straight-line depreciation.

The book value of the machine on January 1, 1995, represents a new starting point for subsequent depreciation:

Original cost	$120,000
Depreciation through December 31, 1994 ($120,000/10)4 years	48,000
Book value, January 1, 1995	$ 72,000
Annual depreciation beginning in 1995 ($72,000 − $8,000)/(12–4)	$ 8,000

December 31, 1995: To record depreciation expense:

Depreciation expense	8,000	
Accumulated depreciation		8,000

LeMond reports the following in its 1994–1995 comparative financial statements:

	1994	1995
Income statement:		
Depreciation expense	$ 12,000	$ 8,000
Balance sheet:		
Machine	120,000	120,000
Accumulated depreciation	(48,000)	(56,000)*
Net book value	$ 72,000	$ 64,000

* $56,000 = $48,000 + $8,000 (1995 depreciation).

The following footnote would be appropriate:

In 1995, the company changed its estimate of useful life and residual value on major equipment. This change was made in response to new information about the benefits to be derived from the equipment, and estimated residual value. Net income increased $2,800 [after 30% tax, .70($12,000 − $8,000)] as a result of the change, or $.28 per share based on 10,000 shares outstanding.

The 1994 statements reflect the old estimates and the 1995 statements reflect the new. The inconsistency is unavoidable because conditions have changed. Future years continue to use the new estimates until the asset is sold or until further new information becomes available, requiring another estimate change.

The 1989 financial statements of Baker-Hughes Inc. give the following example of disclosures for a change in accounting estimate from actual practice:

During 1989, the Company revised the estimated remaining useful lives of certain rental tools and equipment to more closely reflect expected remaining lives. The effect of this change in accounting estimate resulted in an increase in the Company's income before extraordinary item of $2,220,000.

CONCEPT REVIEW

1. If the estimated useful life of equipment is reduced and residual value is not changed, what is the effect on annual depreciation?
2. Explain how book value is used when changing the estimated useful life of a plant asset.
3. If an estimate was not made in good faith, how is the change in estimate treated?

CHANGES IN REPORTING ENTITY

Changes in reporting entity result in financial statements that, in effect, are those of a different reporting entity. This category is limited mainly to:

* Reporting consolidated or combined statements in place of individual company statements.
* Reporting the effects of changing the composition of the consolidated group.
* Reporting the effects of changing the composition of the group of companies included in combined financial statements.

To allow meaningful comparisons across reporting periods, the retroactive approach is applied to these changes. The results of all prior periods presented are restated as if the present consolidated group contained the current combination of entities during those periods. In addition, the nature and justification for the change are reported, as well as the effect on income before extraordinary items, net income, and related per share amounts for all periods presented. Subsequent financial statements need not repeat the disclosures. Advanced accounting courses discuss consolidations in detail.

SUMMARY OF ACCOUNTING CHANGES

The three approaches to reporting accounting changes have certain similarities. Each approach includes disclosures designed to reduce the loss in consistency caused by the accounting change. The current and retroactive approaches recognize the effect of the change on prior years' income directly in the accounts, and either change prior statements presented comparatively or add disclosures related to them. The pro forma amounts under the current approach and the restated net income amounts under the retroactive approach supply the same *income* information. All three approaches disclose the effect of the change on current income. Exhibit 24–6 is a summary of accounting principle and estimate changes, and the three accounting approaches.

ACCOUNTING CHANGES: AN EVALUATION

APB Opinion No. 20 was not endorsed by the entire APB. Some members believed that all accounting principle changes should be applied retroactively. The cumulative income effect of the change is not relevant to current income measurement in their view. They, and others, were worried about the effect on comparability:

> It is the worst of all worlds. Not only is the current year incompatible with past years, the change rips the current year's figures away from any link with reality. Why such a ridiculous method? "I think some members of the APB felt the catch-up method would be punitive and would reduce the number of capricious accounting changes," says Price Waterhouse partner Raymond Lauver.[20]

In addition, Board members feared that allowing alternative approaches to reporting accounting principle changes would dilute public confidence to a greater extent than would requiring retroactive restatement for all principle changes.

Certain board members contended that once an income item is reported, it is final. Changes should be made only prospectively, except for error corrections. Furthermore, they argued that the *Opinion* as written tends to increase the frequency of changes, especially if the cumulative effect increases net income.

Others argued that the cumulative effect on prior years' income cannot be computed accurately. Certain accounting principles influence operating decisions and pricing. These effects cannot be approximated simply by the arithmetic effect of the

---

[20] "Add a Dash of Cumulative Catch-up," *Forbes*, June 6, 1983, p. 98. Mr. Lauver later served as a member of the FASB.

EXHIBIT 24-6   Accounting Changes and Reporting Approaches: Summary Table

Attribute	Estimate Change	Most Accounting Principle Changes	Specified Accounting Principle Changes, Prior Period Adjustments
Accounting approach	Prospective	Current	Retroactive
Entry to record effect of change on prior years' income	None	Recognize cumulative effect in current income	Cumulative effect adjusts beginning retained earnings balance
Restate prior statements	No	No	Yes
Pro forma income disclosures	No	Yes	No
Report effect of change on net income	Yes, current period only	Yes, current period only	Yes, for all years presented and affected
Repeat disclosures in subsequent statements	Continue to use new estimates	Yes	No
Consistency maintained by	Disclosing effect on net income	Disclosing pro forma amounts	Restating prior statements
Confidence in reporting process maintained by	Leaving prior statements unchanged	Leaving prior statements unchanged	Disclosing effect on net income

new accounting principle on net income. Also, evidence suggests that accounting changes reduce the predictive ability of accounting information. For example, one study found that the accuracy of analysts' earnings forecasts declined when accounting changes were made.[21]

The variety of reporting approaches reflects disagreement concerning which method provides the most useful information. Future deliberations by the FASB on this issue may consider in greater depth the motivations for making changes. Why do firms choose specific accounting principles, and later make accounting changes?

Motivations for Accounting Changes

Many explanations are advanced to explain initial accounting method choices and later changes. The following factors are traditionally cited as motivations for accounting method choices:

* To adhere to established firm practice.
* To conform to industry practice.
* To minimize accounting costs.
* To correspond with tax accounting.
* To maximize income and facilitate capital formation.
* To report the most advantageous accounting ratios—particularly, rates of return and ratios involving debt.
* To achieve the closest match between reporting and economic reality (the "best" method).

[21] J. Elliot and D. Philbrick, "Accounting Changes and Earnings Predictability," *The Accounting Review,* January, 1990, pp. 157–74.

It is likely that some firms base accounting changes on one or more of these factors. However, researchers are finding additional factors which explain accounting choices. Their findings suggest that changes in accounting methods may not always be made to improve accounting measurement. For example, why did "entire industries switch from accelerated to straight-line depreciation without changing their tax depreciation methods"?[22] One theory holds that accounting choices are made to achieve objectives such as increased bonus compensation, compliance with debt covenants, and reduction in government interference.[23]

The findings of many studies of accounting principle choice are consistent with the notion that firms with bonus plans based on earnings choose accounting methods that increase current income.[24] Even if no structured bonus agreement exists, some managements may choose techniques and make accounting changes to increase income because an implicit link exists between income and increased compensation. Furthermore, a study of bonus agreements found that if earnings are not expected to reach the minimum income level necessary to achieve a bonus, managers tend to recognize discretionary losses, including plant asset write-downs (the big bath, Chapter 12).[25] Future years are thus relieved of these losses.

Debt covenants requiring minimum income levels provide another incentive for methods that report higher income. For example, Control Data Corporation, which was suffering from a general downturn in the computer industry, was required by its creditors to report positive net earnings for the four quarters ending March 31, 1989.[26] A change to a method that increases current income is desirable under these circumstances. In addition, increases in income ease the burden imposed by debt covenants that stipulate minimum retained earnings balances.

The theory does not imply a unilateral preference for standards that increase net income, however. Evidence suggests that larger firms are more likely than smaller firms to reduce reported income in an attempt to avoid antitrust and other regulatory restrictions.[27] Reduced income may lessen media exposure and scrutiny by regulators, politicians, and labor unions. Larger firms tended to favor the proposed general price level–adjusted disclosures in the FASB's exposure draft "Reporting the Effects of General Price-Level Changes in Financial Statements" (1974). The draft proposed that earnings recomputed on an inflation-adjusted basis be disclosed. These disclosures dramatically reduced earnings in many cases. Researchers believe that large firms favored the proposed standard because their cash flows would remain unaffected, yet the firms would be perceived as less successful and therefore less susceptible to governmental interference and public disapproval.

Income Smoothing

Income smoothing, also known as *earnings management, cooking the books,* and *paper entrepreneurialism,* is the reputed practice of choosing accounting methods and making accounting principle changes to produce a specified income level or trend. In particular, reducing the volatility of income and reporting relatively gradual and continual increases in income are alleged to be common company goals. The

---

[22] R. Watts and J. Zimmerman, "Positive Accounting Theory: A 10-Year Perspective," *The Accounting Review,* January, 1990, p. 132.

[23] Ibid., p. 150.

[24] See R. Watts and J. Zimmerman, *Positive Accounting Theory* (Englewood Cliffs, N.J.: Prentice-Hall, 1986), Chapter 11.

[25] P. Healy, "The Effect of Bonus Schemes on Accounting Decisions," *Journal of Accounting & Economics,* April 1985, pp. 85–107.

[26] "Control Data Is Considering Asset Sales to Satisfy Bankers' Profit Covenants," *The Wall Street Journal,* April 7, 1989, p. A4.

[27] For example, see M. Zmijewski and R. Hagerman, "An Income Strategy Approach to the Positive Theory of Accounting Standard Setting/Choice," *Journal of Accounting & Economics,* August 1981, pp. 129–49.

implicit assumption is that the investing public values a smooth and predictable income trend. Investors perceive an erratic earnings trend as more risky than a smooth trend.

> McDonald's numbers, like its food, have long been synonymous with predictability. For 101 consecutive quarters, the burger behemoth reported record results. So last Friday, when second-quarter earnings came in just a penny a share below Wall Street expectations, it was like getting a Big Mac without the pickle.[28]

The French cosmetics company L'Oreal ("I'm Worth It") did not like to draw attention to a large increase in earnings:

> This year, for example, when L'Oreal realized that a big capital gain had pushed its 1989 net profit up 43%, it didn't boast. It tried to hide the gain. It announced that net profit had gone up 17.3%—the growth rate before capital gains. Reporters had to hunt through annual report tables to find what many companies would have considered good news.[29]

To smooth income, firms must increase reported earnings during a downturn and decrease reported earnings during particularly prosperous times. Excessively high income often invites unfriendly press, government intervention, and increased demands for dividends. Furthermore, large income increases are difficult to sustain, and they create increased expectations.

Stock Prices and Economic Consequences

Many firms seek to avoid the unfavorable economic consequences of lowered earnings and choose methods that increase income. Unfavorable economic consequences include lowered stock prices, higher borrowing costs, and noncompliance with debt covenants. However, research suggests that stock prices usually do not react to the changes in earnings caused by accounting changes unless those changes cause a change in the firm's cash flows, through tax or indirect effects. Indirect effects include changes in bonuses, royalties, and other arrangements based on income, and changes in borrowing costs and regulation.

In spite of the evidence however, some firms continue to manage income to avoid earnings reductions. For example, a study of 163 firms found that companies exhibiting financial stress (potential insolvency) made almost twice as many accounting changes as a control group of healthy firms, and over four times as many changes which increased net income or another measure of financial performance and position.[30]

During the exposure draft phase of a new accounting standard, firms make their views on the proposed standard known to the FASB. The controversy over accounting for oil exploration costs provides an example of efforts made by firms to influence accounting standards. *SFAS No. 19,* "Financial Accounting and Reporting by Oil and Gas Producing Companies" (1977), required the successful efforts method, which capitalizes exploration costs only for successful wells. All other exploration costs are immediately expensed. Small and medium-size oil companies lobbied the FASB, stating that their income would be drastically reduced under the standard, thus impairing their ability to raise capital. These firms were using the full-cost method, which allows capitalizing all exploration costs, with subsequent expensing through cost of goods sold.

---

[28] "McDonald's, Its Profit Predictability Shaken, Should Add Innovation to Menu, Analysts Say," *The Wall Street Journal,* July 26, 1990, p. C2.

[29] "L'Oreal's Preference Is to Shun Publicity," *The Wall Street Journal,* May 11, 1990, p. A7.

[30] K. Schwartz, "Accounting Changes by Corporations Facing Possible Insolvency, *Journal of Accounting, Auditing and Finance,* Fall 1982, pp. 32–43.

They claimed that the FASB's ruling would have the effect of rendering their reported earnings meaningless, of impeding their access to the capital markets and ultimately of reducing their ability to be competitive in their own exploration arena.[31]

Their lobbying efforts contributed to the reversal of *SFAS No. 19*. Following the SEC's permission to use either method, the FASB suspended its requirement to use the successful efforts method in *SFAS No. 25*, "Suspension of Certain Accounting Requirements for Oil and Gas Producing Companies" (1979).

CORRECTION OF ACCOUNTING ERRORS

♦

An accounting error occurs when a transaction or event is recorded incorrectly or is not recorded. For example:

1. Use of an inappropriate or unacceptable accounting principle, and mistakes in applying GAAP are errors. For example, if LCM is used to account for an investment when the equity method is appropriate, an error occurs. Changing from an unacceptable accounting principle, or one incorrectly applied, to a generally accepted one is an error correction.
2. Intentional use of an unrealistic accounting estimate, or gross negligence in making estimates are errors. For example, adopting an unrealistic depreciation rate requires an error correction.
3. Misstating or misclassifying an account balance are errors.
4. Delay in, or failure to recognize, accruals, deferrals and other transactions are errors. For example, Oracle Systems Corporation, a software development firm, recorded $15 million of revenue (6% of total revenue) in the wrong quarter of 1988.[32]
5. Arithmetic mistakes are errors.
6. Fraud or gross negligence in financial reporting are errors.

Material errors are not a common occurrence. Larger firms discover most material errors before completing the financial statements. However, smaller firms cannot afford the internal controls found in large companies.

The following (shortened and paraphrased) footnote to the 1987 financial statements of Matrix Science Corporation highlights the variety of errors made in practice.

> In August 1987, it became known that the Company recorded sales prior to the shipment of goods. It was determined that substantial amounts of credit memorandums, primarily for customer returns, had not been processed in a timely manner. These practices involved the former president, executive vice president and chief financial officer who resigned their positions. The results of the ensuing investigation concluded that the sales recording and credit memo practices resulted in the incorrect recording of sales. Accordingly, the financial statements for 1982 through 1986 have been restated.

Classification of Accounting Errors

Accounting and reporting for error corrections depends on these factors:
* Whether the error affects prior financial statements.
* Whether the error affects prior net income.
* Whether the error counterbalances (automatically self-corrects) within two accounting periods.

---

[31] "Storm Brewing over Oil Accounts," *The Wall Street Journal*, February 22, 1978, p. 22.

[32] "Oracle Systems Posts 1.3% Rise in 3rd-Quarter Net," *The Wall Street Journal*, March 28, 1990, p. C15.

* When the error was made and is discovered.[33]
* The periods presented in the comparative financial statements.

To facilitate the discussion, errors are classified as follows:

I. Errors that occur and are discovered in the same accounting period.
II. Errors that occur in one accounting period and are discovered in a later accounting period.
   A. Errors affecting prior period financial statements but not income.
   B. Errors affecting prior period net income.
      1. Counterbalancing errors.
      2. Noncounterbalancing errors.

Errors That Occur and Are Discovered in the Same Accounting Period This type of error does not affect prior financial statements and is corrected by reversing the incorrect entry and then recording the correct entry or by making a single correcting entry designed to correct the account balances. For example, assume that the collection of $4,000 cash in advance from a customer is credited to a revenue account as $400:

Incorrect entry:

Cash	400	
Revenue		400

The correcting entry, when combined with the incorrect entry, yields the correct ending balance for all affected accounts.[34]

Correcting entry:

Cash	3,600	
Revenue	400	
Unearned revenue		4,000

After this entry is recorded as part of the adjusting process, cash, revenue, and unearned revenue are correctly stated.

Errors Affecting Prior Financial Statements but Not Income This type of error involves incorrect classification of permanent or temporary accounts. Neglecting to classify the current portion of a long-term liability as current is an example. Another example is crediting a gain rather than revenue. Neither error affects prior years' income.

APB Opinion No. 20 requires that previously issued statements that contain errors and are presented with the current period statements be corrected. Applying the retroactive approach to these is not complex because income is not affected. An entry reclassifying any current accounts affected is recorded. A footnote discloses the nature of the error.

Errors Affecting Prior Period Net Income (Counterbalancing) An accounting error is a **counterbalancing error** if it self-corrects over a two-year period. The income for the period of error is misstated as is the income of the second period, but in the opposite direction. Many errors that affect both the income statement and balance sheet are self-correcting over a two-year period.[35]

---

[33] In the examples to follow, errors are discovered before closing the books in the year of discovery, and before preparing the financial statements.

[34] A useful way to determine the correcting entry is as follows: incorrect entry + correcting entry = correct entry.

[35] Practically all errors eventually counterbalance, but many require more than two years to reverse. For example, a depreciation error on an operational asset self-corrects at disposal. However, a more meaningful classification is achieved when the term is restricted to a two-year cycle.

For example, assume 1990 ending inventory is overstated $4,000 through an arithmetic error in applying unit costs to inventory items. The error causes the following effects, assuming a 30% tax rate:

		Effect of Error On		
	1990		**1991**	
Beginning inventory	Unaffected		Overstated	$4,000
Ending inventory	Overstated	$4,000	Unaffected	
Cost of goods sold	Understated	$4,000	Overstated	$4,000
Pretax income	Overstated	$4,000	Understated	$4,000
Income tax expense (30%)	Overstated	$1,200	Understated	$1,200
Net income (70%)	Overstated	$2,800	Understated	$2,800
Ending retained earnings	Overstated	$2,800	Unaffected	

The inventory error is a counterbalancing error because the overstatement of 1990 income and ending retained earnings is offset by the understatement of 1991 income. Ending 1991 retained earnings is automatically corrected, as is the inventory account.

The counterbalancing feature does not imply correct financial statements, however. If the 1991 report presents both years comparatively, all the above errors (under or overstatements) remain in the statements if not corrected. For example, net income for both years is in error. In addition, if the income tax rate changes in 1991, the effects of the error do not completely counterbalance. Assume the tax rate changes to 40% in 1991. Then, in 1991, beginning inventory and pretax income are misstated by $4,000, but income tax expense and payable are now understated $1,600 ($4,000 × .40). Net income is understated by $2,400. Therefore, 1991 ending retained earnings remains overstated $400 ($2,800 overstatement in 1990 − $2,400 understatement in 1991).

Discovery after Self-Correction   Counterbalancing errors discovered two or more years after the year of error do not require a correcting entry. For example, if the above 1990 ending inventory error is discovered in 1992 (assume the original 30% tax rate), no correcting entry is required because all relevant 1992 beginning account balances are correct. The ending balances of inventory and retained earnings are no longer affected, and the temporary account balances (containing errors) were closed at the end of 1991. However, the financial statements for 1990 and 1991 are restated if presented.

Discovery before Self-Correction   In contrast, if counterbalancing errors are discovered during the second year of the two-year cycle, a correcting entry is required. If the error in the inventory example is discovered in 1991, an entry is recorded that corrects the beginning 1991 retained earnings balance for the effect of the 1990 error (assume the original 30% tax rate):

As of January 1, 1991, to correct error made in 1990:

Prior period adjustment, inventory correction	2,800	
Income tax receivable	1,200*	
Inventory		4,000

* Assuming 1990 income tax is paid.

A **prior period adjustment** is the after-tax adjustment required to correct an error in prior period income ($2,800 in our example). This account is closed to retained earnings and revises the beginning retained earnings balance in the discovery year. The errors in the 1990–1991 comparative statements are corrected under the retroactive approach. Income tax receivable is debited because the error was made for both accounting and tax purposes.

The accounts involved in counterbalancing errors include inventories, prepayments and deferrals, and accruals. Inventory errors involve omitting, miscounting and misclassifying items, nonrecording of purchases, and costing errors. Errors involving prepayments and deferrals are caused by failing to recognize the expirations applicable to the current year. Because accruals precede cash flows, accrual errors are caused by failing to recognize expense and revenue accruals.

Errors Affecting Prior Period Net Income (Noncounterbalancing) An accounting error is not counterbalancing if it does not automatically self-correct within two consecutive accounting periods. The error continues to affect account balances for a longer period. One or more balance sheet accounts remain in error.

Over- or understating depreciation expense is an example of a noncounterbalancing error. The accumulated depreciation and retained earnings balances are in error until corrected or until the asset is sold or fully depreciated.

Another example is the immediate expensing of a large purchase of plant assets. The effects include incorrect asset balances, expense amounts, and retained earnings until corrected or until the asset is sold or fully depreciated. Correcting a noncounterbalancing error usually requires a prior period adjustment.

Reporting Guidelines: Prior Period Adjustments

The previous examples of errors affecting prior net income applied the retroactive approach. The general reporting guidelines for the retroactive approach as applied to errors affecting prior period income are listed below:[36]

1. Prior year financial statements presented are shown on a restated basis, without error.
2. The cumulative after-tax effect of the error on prior years' income is recorded as a prior period adjustment to the beginning retained earnings balance in the current (discovery) period.[37] The entry also involves other real accounts with incorrect balances, and often an income tax account.[38]
3. For each year presented in the retained earnings statement, the beginning retained earnings balance is adjusted by the after-tax effect of the error attributable to prior years (whether or not presented). The adjustment for the current year (only) equals the recorded prior period adjustment in (2) above.[39]
4. The nature of the error, and its effect on income before extraordinary items and on net income (and related per share amounts), is disclosed for all periods presented (if affected).
5. Subsequent financial statements need not repeat the disclosures (there is no need to continue drawing attention to a corrected error).

Analysis and Reporting—Example with Comparative Statements

Refer to Exhibit 24–7, which presents the case data for an example of error correction with comparative statements.

---

[36] There are only minor differences between applying the retroactive approach to the previously discussed specified accounting principle changes and to error corrections.

[37] There is one exception already illustrated: the discovery of a counterbalancing error after self-correction requires no entry for correction.

[38] An accounting error need not necessarily imply a tax error. Furthermore, if an error is made for both accounting and tax, the effects on income may be different. For example if a plant asset is not depreciated, the depreciation errors are not the same for the two systems if different depreciation methods are used in each.

[39] If the beginning retained earnings balance is correct because the error counterbalanced in the past, no adjustment is reported in that year.

EXHIBIT 24-7   Case Information: Error Correction for Emory Company

1. The accounting records of Emory Company reflect the following data:

	1990	1991
Sales revenue	$450,000	$480,000
Cost of goods sold	(300,000)	(310,000)
Depreciation expense	(20,000)	(25,000)
Remaining expenses	(55,000)	(65,000)
Income tax (40% average rate)	(30,000)	(32,000)
Net income (for year ended December 31)	$ 45,000	$ 48,000
Balance in retained earnings, January 1	$135,000	$165,000
Dividends declared and paid	15,000	17,000

2. During June 1991, the company discovers that depreciation expense for 1989 and 1990 was understated each year by $5,000 for both accounting and income tax purposes;* total pretax understatement, $10,000. Depreciation for 1991 is correct.

* Assume Emory uses the same depreciation method for accounting and tax purposes.

The error overstates January 1, 1991, retained earnings by $6,000, the total after-tax effect on 1989 and 1990 income ($10,000 × .60). This is not a counterbalancing error. The following entry is required for correction:

As of January 1, 1991:

Prior period adjustment, depreciation correction	6,000	
Income tax receivable (amended return)	4,000	
Accumulated depreciation		10,000

The entry corrects all account balances stated incorrectly as of January 1, 1991. The prior period adjustment is closed to retained earnings, thus correcting the beginning balance. Refer to Exhibit 24–8, which shows the corrected comparative statements for 1990 and 1991.

The corrected 1990 statements reflect error-free account balances. Depreciation expense, income tax expense, net income, and beginning retained earnings are corrected. Income tax expense is decreased because pretax income decreased as a result of the error correction. The error did not affect 1991.

The adjustments to the beginning retained earnings balances overlap, as in accounting principle changes under the retroactive approach. The 1991 adjustment ($6,000), the amount from the correcting entry, accounts for both 1989 and 1990 effects and therefore *includes* the 1989 adjustment ($3,000). Both adjustments *decrease* retained earnings because income was overstated.

The American Building Maintenance Company provides an example of a prior period adjustment from practice. The company prepared comparative statements of owners' equity, rather than retained earning statements, in 1988. American chose to use the nonoverlapping format. Only the 1985 retained earnings balance was adjusted in the statement.

(in thousands)	Common Stock	Additional Capital	Retained Earnings (Restated)
Balance, October 31, 1985, as previously reported	$37	$13,670	$50,356
Prior period adjustment			(9,397)
Balance, October 31, 1985, as restated	37	13,670	40,959

EXHIBIT 24-8 Emory Company's Corrected Comparative Income and Retained Earnings Statements

	1990	1991
Comparative income statements:		
Sales revenue	$450,000	$480,000
Cost of goods sold	(300,000)	(310,000)
Depreciation expense	(25,000)*	(25,000)
Remaining expenses	(55,000)	(65,000)
Income tax expense	(28,000)†	(32,000)
Net income	$ 42,000	$ 48,000
Comparative retained earnings statements:		
Beginning balance, as previously stated	$135,000	$165,000
Prior period adjustment, depreciation, net of $2,000 ($5,000 × .40) and $4,000 ($10,000 × .40) tax	(3,000)	(6,000)
Beginning balance, as restated	132,000	159,000
Net income	42,000	48,000
Dividends declared and paid	(15,000)	(17,000)
Ending balance	$159,000	$190,000

Note: Prior period adjustment: in 1991, the company discovered that depreciation expense for 1989 and 1990 were understated. Accordingly, the 1990 statement is restated. The error overstated net income $3,000 after tax ($.03 per share, based on 100,000 shares outstanding) in both years.

* $25,000 = $20,000 + $5,000 error correction.

† $28,000 = $30,000 − ($5,000 × .40).

Portions of American Building's related footnote follow:

> Based on an analysis of insurance claims, the Company has determined that in certain prior years the effect of claims incurred but not reported was not considered, resulting in an understatement of insurance expense and accrued insurance claims. As a result, the Company has restated net income for 1986 and retained earnings as of October 31, 1985, 1986 and 1987 to provide for increased insurance claims.

CONCEPT REVIEW

1. If an error is discovered after it counterbalances, why must certain account balances in comparative statements be corrected?
2. What is a prior period adjustment?
3. Do all errors require prior period adjustments?

The All-Inclusive Concept of Income and Prior Period Adjustments

Most profit and loss items are disclosed in the income statement. *SFAC No. 6* defines comprehensive income as the net of all changes in equity except those resulting from investments by, and distributions to, owners. Although a few items other than transactions with owners are currently excluded from earnings, income measurement continues to evolve toward a more all-inclusive concept.

The following are some of the items excluded from income:

* Certain changes in the market value of long-term marketable equity securities (affects owners' equity).

* The effect on prior year's income of accounting principle changes under the retroactive approach (adjusts retained earnings).
* Certain foreign currency translation adjustments.
* Changes in the market value of investments in special industries.
* *Prior period adjustments*.

   SFAS No. 16, "Prior Period Adjustments," as amended by *SFAS No. 109*, "Accounting for Income Taxes," considerably narrowed the definition of prior period adjustment to include only errors affecting prior period income.[40]

At one time, however, prior period adjustments included items such as income tax adjustments of prior years and the costs and proceeds of lawsuits initiated in prior years. If an item fulfilled the criteria of *APB Opinion No. 9*, "Reporting the Results of Operations," it was excluded from current income.

Errors are caused by misusing or omitting information known at the time the error was committed. The prior statements *could have* reflected the correct information. For example, all the information to correctly report 1989 depreciation is present in 1989. Therefore, the correction of the error should not affect income of years other than 1989, even if discovered after 1989. A prior period adjustment, which adjusts retained earnings, is consistent with this rationale.

Other items previously included in prior period adjustments are not measurable until later periods. For example, the cost of a lawsuit brought in 1989 and concluded in 1991 is not known until 1991. Therefore, it is reasonable to reflect the cost in 1991 income.

The FASB concluded that the all-inclusive concept is less confusing than allowing special treatment for some profit and loss items and not for others. To reinforce its stance, the FASB reviewed approximately 6,000 annual reports of the mid 1970s and found that items reported as prior period adjustments (before *SFAS No. 16*) were not sufficiently different from items included in net income to warrant treatment as prior period adjustments.

Correcting Entries and Analysis

The number and variety of possible errors is unlimited. This section illustrates additional examples of errors and focuses on correcting entries. A spreadsheet is introduced as an analytical tool for correcting several errors simultaneously. The following five situations for Coe Company include both counterbalancing and non-counterbalancing errors. To focus on the recognition of prior period adjustments, income taxes are ignored.

Situation 1 *Error in both purchases and inventory*. Coe purchases $2,000 of inventory in 1991 but records the purchase in 1992 when paid. Coe did not include the goods in the 1991 ending inventory although they were on hand at December 31, 1991.

   Case A: Coe discovers the error in 1992.

   Analysis: In 1991, both purchases and ending inventory are understated by the same amount. Therefore, because they have opposite effects on cost of goods sold and income, 1991 income is correctly stated. However, the ending 1991 inventory and payables balances are understated $2,000. Also, both beginning inventory and purchases for 1992 are in error. The 1991 statements are restated.

Correcting entry in 1992:

```
Inventory . . . . . . . . . . . . . . . . . . . . . . . . . . . . . . . . . . . . . 2,000
    Purchases . . . . . . . . . . . . . . . . . . . . . . . . . . . . . . . . . .        2,000
```

   Case B: Coe discovers the error in 1993.

---

[40] *SFAS No. 16* included a second item in the definition, and *SFAS No. 109* subsequently removed that item.

Analysis: At the beginning of 1993, all account balances are correct. Neither 1991 nor 1992 income was misstated. Therefore, no correcting entry is needed in 1993. The 1991 and 1992 financial statements are restated.

Situation 2 *Error in prepaid expense.* Coe acquires a five-year fire insurance policy on January 1, 1991, pays the entire $500 premium, and debits insurance expense in 1991. Coe does not make an adjusting entry to recognize prepaid insurance at the end of 1991.

Case A: Coe discovers the error in 1992.

Analysis: In 1991, insurance expense is overstated and income understated by $400 ($500 expense recognized less $100 correct expense). At the end of 1991, both prepaid insurance and retained earnings are understated by $400. The 1991 statements are restated.

Correcting entry in 1992:

Prepaid insurance (1993–1995)	300	
Insurance expense (1992)	100	
Prior period adjustment, insurance correction		400

Case B: Coe discovers the error in 1993.

Analysis: The error in beginning 1993 retained earnings is now only $300, because at January 1, 1993, $200 of insurance expense should have been recognized (1991 and 1992), but $500 was recognized. (Eventually, this error self-corrects.) The 1991 and 1992 statements are restated.

Correcting entry in 1993:

Prepaid insurance (1994–1995)	200	
Insurance expense (1993)	100	
Prior period adjustment, insurance correction		300

Situation 3 *Error in accrued expense.* Coe fails to record $100 accrued property tax payable for 1991. Coe pays the tax early in 1992 and records an expense at that time.

Case A: Coe discovers the error in 1992.

Analysis: In 1991, property tax expense is understated and income overstated. Also, liabilities are understated by $100. Property tax expense for 1992 is overstated by $100. The 1992 payables balance is correct because taxes were paid in 1992. The 1991 statements are restated.

Correcting entry in 1992:

Prior period adjustment, property tax correction	100	
Property tax expense		100

Case B: Coe discovers the error in 1993.

Analysis: The errors counterbalanced in 1992 because 1991 income is overstated and 1992 income is understated by the same amount. No correcting entry is needed for 1993. The 1991 and 1992 statements are restated.

Situation 4 *Error in revenue earned but not yet collected.* Coe fails to accrue $75 interest receivable earned to the end of 1991. Coe collects the interest in 1992 and records revenue at that time.

Case A: Coe discovers the error in 1992.

Analysis: In 1991, interest revenue, net income and receivables are understated. In 1992, interest revenue is overstated. 1992 receivables are correctly stated because the interest was collected. The 1991 statements are restated.

Correcting entry in 1992:

Interest revenue	75	
Prior period adjustment, interest revenue correction		75

Case B: Coe discovers the error in 1993.

Analysis: The error counterbalanced in 1992 because 1991 income is understated and 1992 income is overstated by the same amount. No correcting entry is needed in 1993. The 1991 and 1992 statements are restated.

Situation 5 *Error in capitalizing an asset.* On January 1, 1991, Coe pays $500 for ordinary repairs and debits the machinery account. Depreciation is 10% per year.

Case A: Coe discovers the error in 1992.

Analysis: For 1991, repair expense is understated and depreciation expense over-stated. Also, income is overstated by the difference. Assets and retained earnings are overstated by $450 [$500 − (.10 × $500)]. The 1991 statements are restated.

Correcting entry in 1992:

Accumulated depreciation ($500 × .10)	50	
Prior period adjustment, repair expense	450	
Machinery		500

Case B: Coe discovers the error in 1993.

Analysis: Retained earnings is overstated $400 because $500 expense should have been recognized but only $100 depreciation is recognized by the end of 1992. The 1991 and 1992 statements are restated.

Correcting entry in 1993:

Accumulated depreciation ($500 × .10 × 2)	100	
Prior period adjustment, repair expense	400	
Machinery		500

Spreadsheet Techniques for Correcting Errors

Individual errors can be analyzed and corrected without a spreadsheet. However, when errors are numerous and complicated, a spreadsheet approach often is helpful. In addition, several immaterial errors can cause a material income effect in the aggregate. The spreadsheet facilitates the analysis of errors and their effects. Errors that cancel each other are easily identified. One compound entry corrects all the errors at the end of the period. In the remainder of this section, two popular formats for error correction spreadsheets are highlighted.

Refer to Exhibit 24–9, which illustrates a case example and the first spreadsheet format. This spreadsheet is useful for computing correct income for each of several periods and for providing data to record correcting entries.

In Exhibit 24–9, the counterbalancing errors are those that self-correct in two years. For example, 1991 Error *a* understates prepaid rent, overstates rent expense, and understates income. The opposite effects automatically occur in 1992, counter-balancing the 1991 errors. Each adjacent pair of equal numbers with opposite signs in the income columns represents a counterbalancing error. No correcting entry is needed for these errors in 1994.

The errors requiring correction in 1994 are those that did not counterbalance *because* they were discovered in the second year of the cycle (1994), or those that do not counterbalance in two years. These errors are 1993 Errors *a* to *d* and Error *e* for all years (depreciation). For example, 1993 Error *b* overstates 1993 income because rent was recognized as revenue in error. This error is discovered in 1994, requiring restatement of the 1993 statements and correction of the accounts for 1994.

The following 1994 entry corrects these errors.[41]

---

[41] A separate correcting entry could be made for each error with the same result.

EXHIBIT 24–9   Spreadsheet to Correct Net Income: Juniper Company

Case Data

1. The first audit of Juniper Company covering years 1991, 1992, and 1993, discovered the following errors in 1994:

Error	1991	1992	1993
a. Prepaid rent for the next year incorrectly recognized as rent expense at year-end	$100	$300	$400
b. Rent revenue collected one year in advance incorrectly recognized as revenue at year-end	300	500	100
c. Wage expense incurred but not accrued at year-end (recognized when paid in the next period)	600	800	500
d. Rent revenue earned but not collected or recognized at year-end (recognized when collected in the next period)	500	400	600
e. Depreciation expense understated	200	200	200

2. Reported pretax income, uncorrected for the above errors: 1991, $5,000; 1992, $7,000; and 1993, $6,000. The accounting year ends December 31.

Spreadsheet to Compute Correct Income at Each Year-End

	Income		
Item	1991	1992	1993
Reported income (pretax)	$5,000	$7,000	$6,000
Corrections:			
a. Prepaid rent not recognized as asset:			
1991	+100	−100	
1992		+300	−300
1993			+400*
b. Rent revenue collected in advance not recognized as liability:			
1991	−300	+300	
1992		−500	+500
1993			−100*
c. Accrued wages not recognized in:			
1991	−600	+600	
1992		−800	+800
1993			−500*
d. Accrued rent revenue not recognized in:			
1991	+500	−500	
1992		+400	−400
1993			+600*
e. Depreciation understated:			
1991	−200*		
1992		−200*	
1993			−200*
Correct income (pretax)	$4,500	$6,500	$6,800

* See correcting entry, 1994.

As of January 1,1994:

Prepaid rent	400*	
Rent receivable	600‡	
Prior period adjustment, error correction	200¶	
Rent revenue collected in advance		100**
Accrued wages payable		500†
Accumulated depreciation		600§

* Error *a*, prepaid rent understated at 12/31/93.
** Error *b*, rent revenue collected in advance understated at 12/31/93.
† Error *c*, wages payable understated at 12/31/93.
‡ Error *d*, rent receivable understated at 12/31/93.
§ Error *e*, accumulated depreciation understated at 12/31/93 (3 years).
¶ The net effect of errors on retained earnings before 1994:

	Prior Year Income Effect Under- (Over-) Statement
1993 rent expense overstated	$ 400
1993 rent revenue overstated	(100)
1993 wage expense understated	(500)
1993 rent revenue understated	600
1991–1993 depreciation expense understated	(600)
Net overstatement of prior year's income	$(200)

Four accounts in the correcting entry are involved in the following entries during 1994, assuming the errors are discovered early in 1994.

Rent expense	400		(when incurred)
Prepaid rent		400	
Rent revenue collected in advance	100		(when earned)
Rent revenue		100	
Accrued wages payable	500		(when paid)
Cash		500	
Cash	600		(when received)
Rent receivable		600	

Depreciation expense also is recorded for the correct amount in 1994, $200 more than in previous years.

Errors often are discovered during the closing process. Correction requires recasting the incorrect account balances to develop the correct income statement, balance sheet, and retained earnings statement. Refer to Exhibit 24–10, which shows the second spreadsheet format designed for this purpose. This spreadsheet was illustrated in Chapter 3 for use with adjusting entries.

For example, Entry *a* corrects the overstatement of beginning inventory by reducing beginning inventory and retained earnings through a prior period adjustment. In total, four errors affected prior years' income (see Entries *a, d, f,* and *g*). Entry *g* corrects the understatement of prior years' depreciation that overstated income in prior years.

The entries made in the second set of columns, Correcting and Adjusting Entries, are journalized and posted. The spreadsheet permits a complete analysis before formally recording the adjustments in the accounts.

The appendix extends the discussion of error analysis by considering the preparation of financial statements from incomplete records.

SUMMARY OF KEY POINTS

(L.O. 1) 1. Firms change accounting principles and estimates to adapt to changing economic conditions and new accounting principles, to improve financial reporting, and to fulfill other reporting objectives. Major reporting considerations include the effect of changes on consistency, public confidence in financial reporting, and the need to adapt to changing environments. Financial reporting of accounting changes emphasizes comparability, consistency, and full disclosure.

(L.O. 2) 2. Accounting changes include changes in accounting principle, changes in estimate, and changes in reporting entity. An accounting error is an erroneous recording (or omission) of a transaction, but is not classified as an accounting change.

(L.O. 3) 3. Most accounting principle changes are reported under the current approach; specified exceptions are reported under the retroactive approach. Estimate changes are reported under the prospective approach. Errors affecting prior years' income are reported under the retroactive approach.

(L.O. 4) 4. The current approach recognizes the cumulative effect of the change on prior years' income as a separate item in the income statement for the year of the

EXHIBIT 24-10   Spreadsheet to Correct Income Statement, Balance Sheet, and Retained Earnings Statement

Case Data

Uncorrected and unadjusted trial balance at December 31, 1992 is shown in first column of the spreadsheet.

Additional data:

a. Merchandise inventory, December 31, 1991, overstated, $4,000 (periodic inventory).

b. Prepaid advertising of $2,000 at December 31, 1992, not recorded. It was charged to selling expenses.

c. Prepaid insurance of $2,000 at December 31, 1992, not recognized because the entire premium, paid on December 31, 1992, was debited to general expense.

d. Accrued sales salaries of $1,000 at December 31, 1991, not recorded.

e. Accrued utilities expense of $1,000 at December 31, 1992, not recorded (classify as general expense).

f. No provision was made for doubtful accounts—the amounts should have been: 1991, $1,000, and 1992, $3,000 (classify as general expense).

g. Depreciation expense not recorded prior to 1992, $15,000; 1992, $5,000 (classify as general expense).

h. Cash shortage at end of 1992, $1,000 (classify as general expense).

i. Premium on capital stock is included in the amount credited to the capital stock account.

j. 1992 ending inventory correctly determined, $32,000. The firm does not recognize cost of goods sold in a separate account.

Spreadsheet to Correct Income Statement, Balance Sheet, and Retained Earnings Statement

Account	Uncorrected Trial Balance Debit	Uncorrected Trial Balance Credit	Correcting and Adjusting Entries Debit	Correcting and Adjusting Entries Credit	Income Statement Debit	Income Statement Credit	Retained Earnings Statement Debit	Retained Earnings Statement Credit	Balance Sheet Debit	Balance Sheet Credit
Cash	9,000			(h) 1,000					8,000	
Receivables	20,000								20,000	
Allowance for doubtful accounts .				(f) 4,000						4,000
Inventory, beginning	30,000			(a) 4,000	26,000					
Equipment	60,000			(g) 20,000					60,000	
Accumulated depreciation										20,000
Accounts payable		5,000								5,000
Capital stock, par $10, 7,500 shares outstanding		76,000	(i) 1,000							75,000
Retained earnings, beginning . . .		25,000						25,000		
Prior period adjustments Inventory (CGS) correction . .			(a) 4,000				4,000			
Salary expense correction (1991)			(d) 1,000				1,000			
Bad debt expense correction . .			(f) 1,000				1,000			
Depreciation expense correction			(g) 15,000				15,000			
Sales revenue		130,000				130,000				
Purchases	90,000				90,000					
Selling expenses	17,000			(b) 2,000 (d) 1,000	14,000					
General expenses	10,000		(e) 1,000 (f) 3,000 (g) 5,000 (h) 1,000	(c) 2,000	18,000					
	236,000	236,000								
Prepaid advertising			(b) 2,000						2,000	
Prepaid insurance			(c) 2,000						2,000	
Utilities payable				(e) 1,000						1,000
Inventory, ending						(j) 32,000			(j) 32,000	
Contributed capital in excess of par				(i) 1,000						1,000
Net income					14,000			14,000		
Retained earnings balance							18,000			18,000
			36,000	36,000	162,000	162,000	39,000	39,000	124,000	124,000

change between extraordinary items and net income. Also, pro forma income amounts for all prior years' presented are reported as if the new principle were applied in those periods.

(L.O. 5)   5. The retroactive approach recognizes the cumulative effect of the change on prior years' income as an adjustment to the beginning balance in retained earnings in the year of the change. The beginning balance in retained earnings for all years shown comparatively is adjusted by the effect of the change attributable to previous years.

(L.O. 6)   6. Only current and future reporting periods are affected by estimate changes. No cumulative catch-up amount is recognized. In many cases, the book value of the affected account at the beginning of the current year is the starting amount to which new estimates are applied.

(L.O. 7)   7. The net effect of an error on prior year's income is recorded and reported as a prior period adjustment to the beginning retained earnings balance. Accounting errors are counterbalancing if they self-correct over two consecutive reporting periods, such as an error in the ending inventory. Noncounterbalancing errors such as errors in depreciation do not self-correct in two reporting periods.

(L.O. 8)   8. Financial statements can be prepared from incomplete records by an analysis of source documents and other evidence.

REVIEW PROBLEM
◆

The following cases are independent.

1. Change in Estimated Useful Life and Residual Value. Phelps Company purchases equipment on January 1, 1990, for $36,000 and decides to use the sum-of-years digits method for depreciation. The equipment has a residual value of $6,000 and useful life of three years. On July 1, 1991, Phelps decides that the machine has an original total useful life of four years and $3,000 salvage value.

Required:
What is depreciation in 1991?

2. Retroactive Change in Accounting Principle. Rhein Company changes its method of accounting for long-term construction contracts from the percentage-of-completion method to the completed-contract method in 1992. Income for the years affected by the change appear below (ignore income taxes):

Year	Percentage of Completion	Completed Contract
1990	$400	$200
1991	300	150
1992	500	200

Required:
If comparative financial statements for 1991 and 1992 are shown, what are the adjustments to the January 1 balances of retained earnings for 1991 and 1992?

3. Current-Type Change in Accounting Principle. Gear Company records $2,000 of depreciation under the sum-of-years digits method (SYD) in 1991, the firm's first year of operations. In 1992, the firm decides to change to straight-line (SL) for accounting purposes. If SL were used in 1991, depreciation would have been $1,500. Depreciation in 1992: SYD, $2,200; SL, $1,800. The tax rate is 30%. Net income from continuing operations before tax and before deducting depreciation in 1992 is $12,000.

Required:

Provide the 1992 entry to record this change and calculate 1992 net income and 1992 pro forma net income.

4. Error Correction and Prior Period Adjustment. Helms Company purchases a delivery truck for $12,000 on January 1, 1990. Helms expects to use the truck only two years and sell it for $4,000. The accountant is instructed to use straight-line depreciation but neglects to record any depreciation in 1990. Rather, the accountant charges the entire cost to delivery expense in 1990. The controller discovers the error late in 1991.

Required:

Provide the 1991 entries to record depreciation and the error correction, and indicate the amounts of the prior period adjustments appearing in the 1990 and 1991 comparative retained earnings statements. The tax rate is 30%.

5. Error Correction, Prior Period Adjustment, and Comparative Statements. On July 1, 1991, a full year's insurance premium of $2,400, covering the period July 1, 1991, to June 30, 1992, was paid and debited to insurance expense. Assume:
* A calendar-fiscal year.
* January 1, 1991, retained earnings is $20,000.
* 1991 reported net income (assuming the error is not discovered) is $22,800.
* 1992 net income (assuming the error is not discovered) is $30,000.
* 1993 net income is $40,000.

Required:

a. List the effects of the error on affected accounts and on net income in 1991 and 1992, assuming no adjusting entry is made on December 31, 1991.
b. Prepare the entry to record the error if discovered in 1991.
c. Prepare the entry to record the error if discovered in 1992, and the 1991 and 1992 comparative retained earnings statements.
d. Prepare the entry (if needed) to record the error if discovered in 1993, and the 1992 and 1993 comparative retained earnings statements.

SOLUTION

◆

1.

$$\text{Book value, January 1, 1991} = \$36,000 - (\$36,000 - \$6,000)3/6$$
$$= \$21,000$$
$$\text{1991 depreciation} = (\$21,000 - \$3,000)3/6 = \$9,000$$

(Three years remain in the asset's useful life on January 1, 1991.)

2. The adjustment for the change in accounting principle for the 1991 retained earnings statement is the effect of the change for all years before 1991: $200 decrease (dr.) ($400 − $200). For 1992, this amount is a $350 decrease (dr.) ($400 + $300) − ($200 + $150). These amounts decrease the balance in retained earnings as previously reported.

3.

1992 entry to record accounting change:

Accumulated depreciation	500	
Cumulative effect of change in accounting principle, depreciation ($2,000 − $1,500).70		350
Deferred income tax		150

1992 net income:

Net income before tax, depreciation, and cumulative effect	$12,000
Depreciation expense (SL)	(1,800)
Net income from continuing operations before tax	10,200
Income tax expense (30%)	(3,060)
Net income from continuing operations	7,140
Cumulative effect of accounting change	350
Net income	$ 7,490

1992 pro forma net income is $7,140. If SL were used in previous years, there would be no cumulative effect, and 1992 results reflect SL depreciation.

4.

1991 entry to record error correction:

Equipment	12,000	
Prior period adjustment, depreciation $8,000 × .70		5,600
Income taxes payable $8,000 × .30		2,400
Accumulated depreciation ($12,000 − $4,000)/2		4,000

Pretax income for 1990 is understated $8,000 ($12,000 erroneous delivery expense less $4,000 omitted depreciation).

1991 entry to record depreciation:

Depreciation expense	4,000	
Accumulated depreciation		4,000

Only the 1991 retained earnings statement reports a prior period adjustment ($5,600 cr.). This is the effect of the error on income in years before 1991. The 1990 statement does not report a prior period adjustment because years before 1990 are not affected by the error.

5. *a.*

Effects of Error If Not Discovered

	1991	1992
Insurance expense	+ $1,200	− $1,200
Ending prepaid insurance	− 1,200	no effect
Net income	− 1,200	+ 1,200
Ending retained earnings	− 1,200	is now correct

Note: − = understated; + = overstated.

b. **If Discover Error in 1991**

Prepaid insurance	1,200	
Insurance expense		1,200

c. **If Discover Error in 1992**

Insurance expense	1,200	
Prior period adjustment		1,200

	1991	1992
Retained earnings, Jan. 1, as previously stated	$20,000	$42,800†
Prior period adjustment	0*	1,200
Retained earnings, Jan. 1, as adjusted	20,000	44,000
Net income	24,000**	28,800‡
Retained earnings, Dec. 31	$44,000	$72,800

 * No year before 1991 was affected by the error.

** Correct 1991 net income = $22,800 + $1,200 = $24,000.

† This balance reflects erroneous 1991 income:

$42,800 = $20,000 + $22,800.

‡ $30,000 erroneous income − $1,200 (1992 income was overstated).

d. No entry is needed because the error counterbalanced.

	1992	1993
Retained earnings, Jan. 1, as previously stated	$42,800*a*	$72,800*c*
Prior period adjustment	1,200*b*	0
Retained earnings, Jan. 1, as adjusted	44,000	72,800
Net income	28,800	40,000
Retained earnings, Dec. 31	$72,800	$112,800

a $20,000 + $22,800.

b To correct the error's effect on 1991 net income.

c Equals the ending adjusted retained earnings from 1992 because by January 1,

1993, the error has counterbalanced.

APPENDIX : *Preparation of Financial Statements from Single-Entry and Other Incomplete Records*

Large businesses generally maintain a record of all transactions in the double-entry accounting system. However, many small businesses, sole proprietorships, nonprofit organizations, and persons acting in a fiduciary capacity as administrators or executors of estates maintain only a single-entry system with minimum transaction detail. In some cases only records of cash, accounts receivable, accounts payable, and taxes paid are maintained. Records of operational assets, inventories, expenses, revenues, and other elements usually considered essential in an accounting system are not maintained.

Single-entry records are used for simplicity and are less expensive to maintain than double-entry systems. However, single-entry record keeping usually is inadequate except for low-volume operations. Some of the more important disadvantages of single-entry systems are:

1. Effective planning and control of business operations are diminished because account balances are unavailable.
2. Single-entry records do not provide the built-in check against clerical errors inherent in a double-entry system.
3. Internal transactions, such as depreciation and other adjusting entries often are not recorded.
4. Omission of information from the financial statements is more likely.
5. Detection of theft and other losses is less likely.

However, the incomplete account record and supplemental transaction data often are the basis for a reasonably complete income statement and balance sheet. The procedures are illustrated in the next set of examples.

Balance Sheet Preparation from Single-Entry Records

Identification and measurement of assets and liabilities are essential to preparing the balance sheet from incomplete records. Canceled checks, receipts, bills of sale, papers transferring title to real estate, and other such records supply information about the cost of operational assets. Depreciation is based on original cost. The amount of merchandise, supplies, and other inventories on hand is obtained by actual count. If original cost cannot be determined, merchandise and supplies are recorded at current replacement cost.

Similarly, the amounts of notes payable are obtained from source documents, memoranda, correspondence, and consultation with creditors. Invoices from suppliers support accounts payable.

Exhibit 24A–1 illustrates preparation of the balance sheet and computation of income from incomplete records. Owners' equity is determined by subtracting total liabilities from total assets. Net income is the difference between ending and beginning owners' equity, adjusted for owner investments and withdrawals.

The following schedule shows the computation of net income when investments or withdrawals occur during the period (all other amounts assumed):

	Computation if There Was	
	Income	**A Loss**
Owner's equity, end of period	$8,000	$5,500
Owner's equity, beginning of period	7,100	6,300
Change increase (decrease)	900	(800)
Add: Withdrawals during period	1,200	1,000
	2,100	200
Deduct: Additional investments during period	500	300
Income (loss) for period	$1,600	$ (100)

Income Statement Preparation from Incomplete Data

Interested financial statement users at times request information about the components of net income. Banks and other credit grantors usually request a statement describing the results of

---

EXHIBIT 24A-1   Preparing a Balance Sheet and Computing Net Income from Incomplete Records

---

Case Data

1. Brown Company was organized by A. A. Brown on January 1, 1991; on this date the owner invested $4,500 cash in the business. During 1991, no formal records were kept.
2. Additional data for 1991:
   a. December 31, cash on hand and on deposit, $2,345–from count of cash and bank statement.
   b. December 31, merchandise inventory, $1,550–count made by Brown, costed at current replacement cost because purchase invoices were not available.
   c. Office and store equipment acquired on January 1, 1991, $500—from invoice found in the files.
   d. Brown agreed that a depreciation rate of 5% per annum, with no material amount of residual value, was reasonable.
   e. Note receivable, dated December 31, 1991, $50—this note, signed by a customer for goods purchased, was in the files.
   f. December 31, accounts receivable, $90—Brown maintained a charge book that listed four customers as owing a total of $90; Brown was positive that the bills were outstanding. You called the customers for verification.
   g. December 31, accounts payable, $240—The unpaid invoices file contained two invoices that totaled to this amount; Brown assured you that they were the only unpaid invoices.

Balance Sheet Prepared from Incomplete Data

BROWN COMPANY
Balance Sheet
At December 31, 1991

Assets			**Liabilities**	
Current assets:			Current liabilities:	
Cash	$2,345		Accounts payable	$ 240
Accounts receivable	90		Long-term liabilities	0
Notes receivable, trade	50		Total liabilities	240
Merchandise inventory	1,550		**Owner's Equity**	
Total current assets	4,035			
			A. A. Brown, proprietorship capital	
Property and equipment:			($4,510 − $240)	4,270
Office and store equipment $500			Total liabilities and owner's equity	$4,510
Less: Accumulated depreciation 25	475			
Total assets	$4,510			

Income (Loss) Computed

BROWN COMPANY
Computation of Net Loss
For the Year Ended December 31, 1991

Owner's equity, January 1, 1991	$4,500
Owner's equity, December 31, 1991	4,270
Net loss for period	$ 230

EXHIBIT 24A-2   Preparing the Income Statement from Incomplete Data

Case Data

	1991			1991
	Jan. 1	Dec. 31		
Account balances:			Analysis of bank statements:	
Accounts and trade notes receivable (no doubtful accounts)	$35,000	$48,000	Bank overdraft, 1/1/1991	$ 2,800
Inventory (from physical count)	6,900	8,700	Deposits during year: Collections on account	42,000
Building and equipment (appraised at estimated cost less depreciation)	17,000	17,400	Additional capital contributions by owner	10,000
Prepaid expenses (from memoranda)	100	110	Checks drawn during year for:	
Accounts payable (from files)	8,100	9,200	Purchases (goods for resale)	26,000
Notes payable (for equipment, from files)		500	Expenses	6,000
Cash on hand (from cash register)	60	110	Salaries of employees	7,000
Liability for accrued expenses (from memoranda)	120	150	Withdrawals by owner	3,000
Salaries paid		7,000	Purchase of equipment	340

Income Statement Items

1. Sales revenue:

Accounts and trade notes receivable, 12/31/91	$48,000
Cash collected from customers and deposited	42,000
Increase of cash on hand ($110 − $60)	50
Less: Accounts and trade notes receivable, 1/1/1991	(35,000)
Sales revenue for the year, 1991	$55,050

2. Purchases:

Accounts and trade notes payable, 12/31/1991	$ 9,200
Payments to creditors for purchases	26,000
Less: Accounts payable, 1/1/1991	(8,100)
Purchases for the year, 1991	$27,100

3. Depreciation expense:

Net balance of buildings and equipment, 1/1/1991	$17,000
Purchases of equipment during 1991	
By issue of note payable	500
By cash payment	340
Balance before depreciation	17,840
Less: Net balance on 12/31/1991 (after 1991 depreciation)	(17,400)
Depreciation expense for the year, 1991	$ 440

4. Remaining expenses:

Expenses paid in cash during 1991		$ 6,000
Add: Expenses accrued on 12/31/1991		150
Prepaid expenses on 1/1/1991		100
Total		6,250
Deduct: Expenses accrued on 1/1/1991	$120	
Prepaid expenses on 12/31/1991	110	(230)
Other expenses for the year, 1991		$ 6,020

Income Statement
For Year Ended December 31, 1991

Sales revenue (Item 1)		$55,050
Cost of goods sold:		
Inventory, 1/1/1991 (given)	$ 6,900	
Purchases (Item 2)	27,100	
Goods available for sale	34,000	
Less inventory, 12/31/1991 (given)	8,700	
Cost of goods sold		25,300
Gross margin on sales		29,750
Less: Expenses:		
Depreciation (Item 3)	440	
Other expenses (Item 4)	6,020	
Salaries (given)	7,000	13,460
Net income		$16,290

EXHIBIT 24A-3   Spreadsheet to Develop Account Balances Based on Incomplete Records

Case Data

1. Main Company has been in business two years and has kept only incomplete records. An accountant prepared a balance sheet at December 31, 1991, and a balance sheet has been completed by "inventorying all assets and liabilities at December 31, 1992." These balance sheet accounts are entered on the spreadsheet.
2. Additional data for 1992, developed in various ways as follows:
   a. Main kept no record of cash receipts and disbursements, but an analysis of canceled checks provided the following summary of payments: accounts payable, $71,000; expenses, $20,700; and purchase of equipment, $3,700. No checks appeared to be outstanding.
   b. Main stated that $100 cash was withdrawn regularly each week from the cash register for personal use. No record was made of these personal withdrawals.
   c. The $5,000 bank loan was for one year, the note was dated July 1, 1992, and 6% interest was deducted from the face amount (cash proceeds, $4,700).
   d. Main stated that equipment listed in the January 1 balance sheet at $900 was sold for $620 cash.
   e. The bank reported that it had credited Main with $4,000 during the year for customers' notes that Main left for collection.
   f. One $400 note on hand December 31, 1992, was past due and appeared worthless. Therefore, this note was not included in the $3,000 notes receivable listed in the December 31, 1992, balance sheet. Assume no allowance for doubtful accounts; bad debts are written off directly to expense because of immateriality.

Spreadsheet

Account	Beginning balances 1/1/1992	Spreadsheet Entries Debit	Spreadsheet Entries Credit	Income Statement	Ending balances 12/31/1992
Accounts with debit balances:					
Cash	10,000	(c) 4,700 (d) 620 (e) 4,000 (h) 103,280	(a) 95,400 (b) 5,200		22,000
Notes receivable	5,000	(g) 2,400	(e) 4,000 (f) 400		3,000
Accounts receivable	61,000	(i) 112,680	(g) 2,400 (h) 103,280		68,000
Inventories	25,000	(j) 27,000	(j) 25,000		27,000
Prepaid expenses	500	(c) 150 (k) 50	(k) 500		200
Furniture and equipment (net)	10,600	(a) 3,700	(d) 900 (l) 1,000		12,400
Expenses		(a) 20,700 (k) 500 (n) 650	(k) 50 (n) 800	21,000	
Interest expense		(c) 150		150	
Loss on sale of equipment		(d) 280		280	
Loss on worthless note		(f) 400		400	
Depreciation expense		(l) 1,000		1,000	
Purchases		(m) 77,000		77,000	
Net income		(o) 14,850		14,850	
	112,100			114,680	132,600
Accounts with credit balances:					
Bank loan payable			(c) 5,000		5,000
Accounts payable	30,000	(a) 71,000	(m) 77,000		36,000
Accrued expenses payable	800	(n) 800	(n) 650		650
Main, owner's equity	81,300	(b) 5,200	(o) 14,850		90,950
Sales revenue			(i) 112,680	112,680	
Income summary (inventory change)		(j) 25,000	(j) 27,000	2,000	
	112,100	476,110	476,110	114,680	132,600

EXHIBIT 24A-3 (*concluded*)

Explanation of Entries on Spreadsheet (Main Company)

a. To record cash payments shown by analysis of canceled checks.

b. To record Main's cash withdrawals of $100 per week for 52 weeks.

c. To record bank loan of $5,000 less $300 interest of which $150 was prepaid as of December 31, 1992.

d. To record sale of equipment (cost less depreciation, $900) for $620 cash.

e. To record $4,000 notes receivable collected by bank.

f. To record write-off of bad note, $400.

g. To record notes from customers, computed as follows (data taken directly from spreadsheet).

Notes collected	$ 4,000
Note written off	400
Notes on hand, 12/31/1992	3,000
	7,400
Less: Notes on hand, 1/1/1992	5,000
Notes receivable (received on accounts)	$ 2,400

h. Cash collected from customers from data shown in the cash account on the spreadsheet:

Cash paid out ($95,400 + $5,200)	$100,600
Cash balance, 12/31/1992	22,000
	122,600
Cash collected from all sources other than from customers: ($4,700 + $620 + $4,000)	9,320
	113,280
Less: Cash balance, 1/1/1992	10,000
Cash collected from customers	$103,280

i. Sales are computed by finding the only "missing entry" in **accounts receivable,** which is for sales on account. (Balance in notes receivable has already been reconciled on the spreadsheet.)

Note received on account (Item g)	$ 2,400
Cash collected from customers (Item h)	103,280
Ending balance of accounts receivable	68,000
Total	173,680
Less: January 1 balance	61,000
Total debits for the year (sales revenue)	$112,680

j. To close the January 1 inventory and to record the December 31 inventory (to income summary).

k. To adjust the balance of prepaid expenses and to increase the prepaid expense balance as of December 31 to $200 as given.

l. To set up the depreciation expense for the period. All entries have been made in the furniture and equipment account on the spreadsheet except the 1992 depreciation credit. Depreciation is computed as follows:

Furniture and equipment, 1/1/1992	$ 10,600
Equiment purchased	3,700
	14,300
Less: Equipment sold	900
	13,400
Less: Balance of furniture and equipment, 12/31/1992	12,400
Depreciation expense for the period	$ 1,000

m. Purchases are computed by finding the missing entry in accounts payable on the spreadsheet as follows:

Payments on accounts payable	$ 71,000
Balance of accounts payable, 12/31/1992	36,000
	107,000
Less: Accounts payable, 1/1/1992	30,000
Purchases for the period	$ 77,000

n. To transfer the beginning balance ($800) of accrued expenses payable to expense and to record accrued expenses payable as of December 31. Note that Entry a on the spreadsheet transfers all of the expenses paid in cash during 1992 to the expense account. As a result, the beginning and ending balances of accrued expense payable, respectively, are entered in the expense account. This avoids counting the expenses accrued at year-end as expenses twice.

o. To close net income to owner's equity. The net income is computed by analyzing the changes in capital from January 1 to December 31, 1992, as illustrated previously, or by extending the balances in the temporary accounts to the Income Statement column and then computing the difference between the debits and credits. One computation serves as a check on the other.

operations. The Internal Revenue Service requires detailed information about taxable revenues and deductible expenses.

It is possible to prepare an itemized income statement from single-entry records and supplemental data without converting to double-entry form. Much of the needed detail is obtained through an analysis of the cash receipts and disbursement records. This process is illustrated in Exhibit 24A-2.

The preceding example (Exhibit 24A-2) suggests the need for a spreadsheet approach to reduce clerical work and minimize errors and omissions. A spreadsheet recognizes each group of transactions in debit-credit form and provides several internal checks for accuracy. Written explanations and computations support the spreadsheet entries. Exhibit 24A-3 illustrates such a spreadsheet designed to develop the income statement and balance sheet.

KEY TERMS

Accounting change (1347)
Change in accounting estimate (1347)
Change in accounting principle (1347)
Change in reporting entity (1347)
Counterbalancing error (1371)

Cumulative effect of change in accounting principle (1349)
Income smoothing (1368)
Prior period adjustment (1372)
Pro forma net income (1349)

QUESTIONS

1. Distinguish among the following: (*a*) change in principle, (*b*) change in estimate, (*c*) change in reporting entity, and (*d*) accounting error.
2. What are the three basic ways to account for the effects of accounting changes and error corrections?
3. Complete the following schedule:

Method of Reflecting the Effect*

	(1) _____	(2) _____	(3) _____
a. Change in estimate	_____	_____	_____
b. Change in principle	_____	_____	_____
c. Correction of error	_____	_____	_____

* Identify these three captions; then enter appropriate check on each line.

4. What are pro forma statements? Why are they used for some accounting changes?
5. Explain the basic difference between an accounting change and an error correction.
6. Why are the effects of changes from LIFO to other inventory flow methods accounted for retroactively when changes to LIFO from another method are reflected as changes in the income of the year the change is made?
7. Other than changing from LIFO to another inventory flow method (which must be reflected retroactively), what other types of accounting changes must be accorded retroactive treatment rather than being accounted for using the current approach?
8. *APB Opinion No. 20* deals with three types of accounting changes in addition to error corrections. The three types of accounting changes involve (*a*) principles, (*b*) estimates, and (*c*) reporting entities. Using these letters and (*d*) for error corrections, identify each of the following types of change:
   (1) A lessor discovers during the term of a capital lease that an estimated material unguaranteed residual value of the leased property has probably become zero.
   (2) A corporation with foreign subsidiaries has used the cost method of accounting for its investments in the subsidiary companies since they were acquired because economic conditions in the countries in which the subsidiary companies operate have been unstable and exchange of foreign currency into dollars has been restricted. Under changed, improved conditions, it has become feasible for the controlling entity to prepare consolidated statements instead, thereby eliminating the foreign investment account from the balance sheet of the corporation.
   (3) After 5 years of use, an asset originally estimated to have a 15-year life is now to be depreciated on the basis of a 20-year life.
   (4) Because of inability to estimate reliably, a contractor began business using the completed-contract method. Now that reliable estimates can be made, the percentage-of-completion method is adopted.
   (5) Office equipment purchased last year is discovered to have been debited to office expense when acquired. Appropriate accounting is to be applied at the discovery date.
   (6) A company that has been using the FIFO inventory method is changing to LIFO.
   (7) A company that used 1% of sales to estimate its bad debt expense discovers losses are running higher than expected and changes to 2½%.

9. How is the book value of a plant asset at the begining of the year of a change in estimated life used in the accounting for the change?
10. Explain why (*a*) net income before extraordinary items in the year of a current type accounting principle change equals its pro forma counterpart, and (*b*) why net income does not equal its pro forma counterpart.
11. What is the difference between a counterbalancing and a noncounterbalancing error? Why is the distinction significant in the analysis of errors?

12. Complete the schedule below by entering a plus to indicate overstatement, a minus to indicate understatement, and a zero for no effect.

	Effect of Error On			
	Net Income	Assets	Liabilities	Owners' Equity
a. Ending inventory for 1991 understated:				
1991 financial statements	_____	_____	_____	_____
1992 financial statements	_____	_____	_____	_____
b. Ending inventory for 1992 overstated:				
1992 financial statements	_____	_____	_____	_____
1993 financial statements	_____	_____	_____	_____
c. Failed to record depreciation in 1991:				
1991 financial statements	_____	_____	_____	_____
1992 financial statements	_____	_____	_____	_____
d. Failed to record a liability resulting from revenue collected in advance at end of 1991; instead, credited revenue in full erroneously:				
1991 financial statements	_____	_____	_____	_____
1992 financial statements	_____	_____	_____	_____

13. Give two examples of each of the following types of errors:
    a. Affects the income statement only.
    b. Affects the balance sheet only.
    c. Affects both income statement and balance sheet.
14. A company failed to accrue $12,000 of wages at the end of 1991. Explain (*a*) why the discovery of the error in 1992, after the issuance of the 1991 statements, requires a correcting entry, and (*b*) why discovery of the error in 1993, after the issuance of the 1992 statements, does not require a correcting entry.

EXERCISES

E 24–1
Conflicting Issues in Accounting Changes
(L.O. 1)

Consistency, comparability, and the need to maintain public confidence in the financial reporting process (defined in terms of the expectation that prior financial statements not be changed except for error) are conflicting objectives.

Required:

Briefly discuss the extent to which the three approaches to accounting changes (current, retroactive, and prospective) fulfill these objectives.

E 24–2
Multiple Choice: Accounting Changes
(L.O. 2, 3)

Choose the correct answer to each question.

1. Which of the following is a change in accounting principle?
   a. Correction of an error using the retroactive approach.
   b. Change from an incorrect method to a correct method.
   c. Change in the application of an accounting principle.
   d. Change in the number of total expected service miles for depreciating a truck.
2. Which of the following is not the type of accounting change that reports a cumulative effect in the income statement?
   a. Change to the successful-efforts method of accounting for natural resources.
   b. Change to LIFO for a firm in its second year and that is able to reconstruct LIFO inventory layers.
   c. Change in depreciation method.
   d. Change in method of amortizing bond discount.
3. Retroactive accounting treatment is used for which of the following:
   a. Correcting errors and making estimate changes.
   b. Changing to LIFO and correcting errors affecting income of prior years.
   c. Changing to the completed-contract method of accounting for long-term contracts.
   d. Correcting errors affecting prior years' income, but only if those prior years are disclosed on a comparative basis with the current year.
4. A company changed from percentage of completion (PC) to completed contract (CC) for financial accounting purposes during 1992. Therefore:

    a. Beginning January 1, 1992, CC should be used for construction accounting, and the difference between the income under the two methods for years before 1992 is disclosed in the 1992 income statement.

    b. Beginning January 1, 1992, CC should be used for construction accounting, but no entry is made for the effects of the change on years before 1992.

    c. Beginning January 1, 1992, CC should be used for construction accounting, and the difference between the income under the two methods for years before 1992 is an adjustment to the January 1, 1992, retained earnings balance.

    d. Pro forma income amounts are disclosed in a schedule to the income statement for all years before 1992 shown in the 1992 annual report.

5. Choose the correct statement concerning comparative financial statements.
    a. They are required by the APB.
    b. They are required by the SEC.
    c. The number of statements presented comparatively affects the recorded amount of a cumulative effect of a change in accounting principle.
    d. Firms generally do not disclose more than one year because financial statement users already have access to the reports of previous years.

6. One of the advantages of the current, or cumulative effect type change is:
    a. Consistency is maintained.
    b. Prior years' income effects do not affect income in the year of change.
    c. The statements of previous years shown comparatively do not disclose any information about the effect of the change in those previous years.
    d. Prior years' financial statements are not altered.

7. Pro forma income numbers:
    a. Somewhat reduce the loss of comparability inherent in current, or cumulative effect type, accounting principle changes.
    b. Are required only for the year of change.
    c. Are required for changes in estimates.
    d. Equal the effect of the accounting change on income for each year shown.

8. Pro forma net income for the year of a change in accounting principle equals:
    a. Net income for the year of change.
    b. Net income for the year of change under the new method.
    c. Net income before extraordinary items for the year of change.
    d. Net income before cumulative effect of changes in accounting principle for the year of change.

E 24-3

Overview: Types of Accounting Changes and Errors

(L.O. 2, 3)

Analyze each case and enter a one letter code under each column (type and approach) to indicate the basic accounting for each case.

	Type	Approach
	P = Principle	
	E = Estimate	C = Current
	R = Entity	R = Retroactive
Case (Event or Transaction)	AE = Error	P = Prospective
1. Recorded expense, $870; should be $780.	_____	_____
2. Changed useful life of a machine.	_____	_____
3. Changed from single company to consolidated financial statements.	_____	_____
4. Changed from straight-line to accelerated depreciation.	_____	_____
5. Change in residual value of an intangible operational asset.	_____	_____
6. Changed from cash basis to accrual basis in accounting for bad debts.	_____	_____
7. Changed from percentage completion to completed contract for long-term construction contracts.	_____	_____
8. Changed from LIFO to FIFO for inventory.	_____	_____
9. Changed to a new accounting principle required by the FASB.	_____	_____

E 24-4

Change in Depreciation Method: Entries and Reporting

(L.O. 4)

Gunnard Company changed from double-declining-balance depreciation (DDB) to the straight-line method (SL) for both accounting and tax purposes in 1991. Had SL been used before 1991, total depreciation for all prior years would be $10,000 less than under DDB. Gunnard discloses 1990 and 1991 results comparatively in its 1991 annual report. The tax rate is 30% in both years. Assume a calendar fiscal year.

Depreciation expense for 1990 and 1991 under both methods:

	SL	DDB
1990	$2,000	$3,000
1991	2,000	2,500

Additional information for Gunnard:

	1990	1991
Revenues	$40,000	$60,000
Expenses other than depreciation and tax	25,000	30,000
Extraordinary loss after tax		3,500

Required:
1. Prepare the 1991 entry(ies) for depreciation and the accounting change.
2. Prepare the comparative income statements and include disclosures related to the accounting change.

E 24–5
Change in Estimated Useful Life and Salvage Value for a Plant Asset
(L.O. 6)

Bellico Company, which has a calendar fiscal year, purchased its only depreciable plant asset on January 1, 1991, which has the following characteristics:

Original cost	$10,000
Estimated residual value	1,000
Estimated useful life	three years
Depreciation method	sum-of-years'-digits

In 1992, Bellico increased the estimated residual value to $2,000, and increased the total estimated useful life to five years for financial accounting purposes. Additional information:

	1991	1992
Revenue	$ 40,000	$50,000
Expenses other than depreciation and tax	25,000	30,000
Extraordinary loss before tax		5,000
Tax rate	30%	30%
Common shares outstanding entire year	100,000	100,000

Required:
1. Provide the 1992 entry(ies) for depreciation and the ending 1992 accumulated depreciation balance.
2. Provide the comparative 1991 and 1992 income statements, including disclosures related to the accounting change.

E 24–6
Change in Estimated Useful Life: Entries, Reporting
(L.O. 6)

Stacy Corporation has been depreciating equipment over a 10-year life on a straight-line basis. The equipment, which cost $24,000, was purchased on January 1, 1991. The equipment has an estimated residual value of $6,000. On the basis of experience since acquisition, the management has decided to depreciate it over a total life of 14 years instead of 10, with no change in the estimated residual value. The change is to be effective on January 1, 1995. The annual financial statements are prepared on a comparative basis (1994 and 1995 are presented). 1994 and 1995 income before depreciation and accounting changes for 1994 and 1995 were $49,800, and $52,800, respectively. Disregard income tax considerations.

Required:
1. Identify the type of accounting change involved and analyze the effects of the change. Which approach should be used—current, prospective, or retroactive? Explain.
2. Prepare the entry, or entries, to appropriately reflect the change in the accounts for 1995, the year of the change.
3. Illustrate how the change should be reported on the 1995 financial statements, which are accompanied by the 1994 results for comparative purposes (shares of common stock outstanding, 100,000).

E 24–7
Change in Estimated Useful Life: Entries, Reporting
(L.O. 6)

On January 1, 1991, Darvis Company purchased a machine that cost $80,000. The estimated useful life was 12 years with an estimated residual value of $8,000. Starting on January 1, 1996, the company revised its estimates as follows: total useful life, 18 years; total residual value, $5,800. The company uses straight-line depreciation, and the reporting period ends December 31.

Required:

1. What kind of accounting change is this? How should it be accounted for—current, retroactive, or prospective? Explain.
2. Give all entries required in 1995 and 1996 related to this case. Disregard income tax considerations.
3. Show what related 1995 and 1996 amounts should be reported in the comparative financial statements.

E 24-8

Change in Depreciation Method: Entries, Reporting

(L.O. 6)

Bite Corporation has been depreciating equipment over a 10-year life using the SYD method. The equipment was acquired January 1, 1991, and cost $68,000 (estimated residual value, $13,000). The company decided to change to straight-line depreciation, effective the beginning of 1995, with no change in the estimated useful life or the residual value. The annual accounting period ends December 31. The annual financial statements are prepared on a comparative basis (1994 and 1995 are presented). Income before depreciation and prior to giving effect to this change was 1994, $55,000, and 1995, $57,500. Shares of stock outstanding were 100,000. Disregard income tax considerations.

Required:

1. Identify the type of accounting change involved and analyze the effects of the change. Which approach should be used—current, prospective or retroactive? Explain.
2. Prepare the entry, or entries, to appropriately reflect the change in the accounts in 1995, the year of the change, including the 1995 adjusting entry.
3. Show how the change should be reported on the 1995 financial statements, which include 1994 results for comparative purposes.

E 24-9

Change SYD Depreciation to Straight-Line and Change Useful Life: Entries

(L.O. 4)

XY Sales Company has made several accounting changes to improve the matching of expenses with revenue. Assume it is the end of 1991, and that the accounting period ends on December 31. The books have not been adjusted or closed at the end of 1991. Among the changes were the following:

a. Machinery that cost $25,000 (estimated useful life 10 years, residual value $3,000) has been depreciated using the SYD method. Early in the eighth year (1991), it was decided to change to straight-line depreciation (with no change in residual value or estimated life).
b. A patent that cost $8,500 is being amortized over its legal life of 17 years. Early in the 6th year (1991) since its acquisition, it was decided that the economic benefits would not last longer than 13 years from date of acquisition.

Required:

1. For each of the above situations, identify the type of accounting change that was involved, and briefly explain how it should be accounted for.
2. Give the appropriate entry to record the change and the 1991 adjusting entry in each instance. Show computations and disregard income tax considerations. If no entry is required in a particular instance, explain why.

E 24-10

Change from LIFO to FIFO: Entries, Reporting

(L.O. 5)

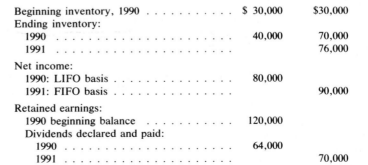

On January 1, 1991, Baker Company decided to change the inventory costing method used from LIFO to FIFO. The annual reporting period ends on December 31. The average income tax rate is 30%. The following related data were developed:

	LIFO Basis	FIFO Basis
Beginning inventory, 1990	$ 30,000	$30,000
Ending inventory:		
1990	40,000	70,000
1991		76,000
Net income:		
1990: LIFO basis	80,000	
1991: FIFO basis		90,000
Retained earnings:		
1990 beginning balance	120,000	
Dividends declared and paid:		
1990	64,000	
1991		70,000
Common shares outstanding, 10,000.		

Required:

1. Identify the type of accounting change involved. Which approach should be used—current, prospective, or retroactive? Explain.
2. Give the entry(ies) to record the effect of the change, assuming the change was made only for accounting purposes.
3. Complete the following schedule:

	FIFO Basis	
	1990	**1991**
Comparative balance sheet:		
Inventory	$	$
Retained earnings		
Comparative income statement		
Net income:		
1990		
1991		
Earnings per share		
Retained earnings statement:		
Beginning balance		
Cumulative effect of accounting change		
Beginning balance restated		
Net income		
Dividends declared and paid		
Ending balance		

E 24-11

Analysis of Seven Errors: Correcting Entries, Correct Pretax Income (L.O. 7)

The 1991 income statement of Burke Corporation has just been tentatively completed. It reflects pretax income for 1991 of $85,000. The accounts have not been closed for the year ended December 31, 1991. A review of the company's files and records revealed the following errors that have not been corrected:

a. Patent amortization of $3,000 per year was not recorded in 1990 and 1991.
b. The 1989 ending inventory was overstated by $4,000.
c. Machinery acquired on January 1, 1987, at a cost of $26,000, is being depreciated on the straight-line method over 10 years. The good faith estimate of its residual value of $6,000 has not been included in the computation of depreciation expense.
d. Accrued wages of $1,500 at December 31, 1990, were not recognized.
e. A $1,000 cash shortage during 1991 was debited to retained earnings.
f. Ordinary repairs on the machinery in (*c*) above of $7,000, incurred during January 1991, were debited to the machinery account.
g. During 1991, treasury stock that cost $8,000 was sold for $11,000. The difference was credited to extraordinary gain. The company uses the cost method to account for treasury stock.

Required:

1. Give the correcting entry, if needed, for each of the above errors. Explain the basis and show computations for each item. Ignore income tax considerations.
2. Compute the correct pretax income amount for 1991. Set up an appropriate schedule that reflects each change and the "Correct 1991 pretax income."

E 24-12

Analysis of Four Errors: Correcting Entries and Correct Pretax Income (L.O. 7)

Travis Corporation has just completed its financial statements for the reporting year ended December 31, 1995. The pretax income amount is $160,000. The accounts have not been closed for December 31, 1995. Further consideration and review of the records revealed the following items related to the 1995 statements:

a. On January 1, 1991, a machine was acquired that cost $10,000. The estimated useful life was 10 years, and the residual value was $2,000. At the time of acquisition, the full cost of the machine was incorrectly debited to the land account. Use straight-line depreciation.
b. On January 1, 1993, a long-term investment of $18,000 was made by purchasing a $20,000, 8% bond of XT Corporation. The investment account was debited for $18,000. Each year, starting on December 31, 1993, the company has recognized and reported investment revenue on these bonds of $1,600. The bonds mature in 10 years from date of purchase. Assume any amortization would be straight line and the net method is used to record the investment.

c. The 1994 ending inventory was overstated by $7,000 (periodic inventory system).

d. An $11,000 credit purchase of merchandise occurred on December 18, 1994. Because the merchandise was on hand on December 31, 1994, it was included in the 1994 ending inventory. The purchase was recorded on January 18, 1995, when the invoice was paid.

Required:

1. Prepare any correcting and adjusting entries that should be made on December 31, 1995, and reported on the 1995 income statement. Ignore income tax.
2. Compute the correct income for 1995. Set up an appropriate schedule that reflects each change and the "Correct pretax income, 1995."

E 24-13
Error, Comparative Statements, Correcting Entry and Reporting (L.O. 7)

Bar Corporation had never been audited prior to December 31, 1994, the current year. Prior to the arrival of the auditor, the company accountant prepared comparative financial statements showing the results of 1993 and 1994. The accounts for 1994 have not been closed. The auditors discovered that an invoice dated January 1991 for $9,000 (paid in cash at the time) was debited to 1991 operating expenses, although it was for the purchase of equipment. The equipment has an estimated useful life of 10 years and no estimated residual value.

Reported incomes reflected on the financial statements prepared by the company (prior to discovery of the error) were: 1991, $11,000; 1992, $22,000; 1993, $30,000; and 1994, $33,000. Shares of common stock outstanding, 100,000. Disregard income tax considerations, and assume Bar uses straight-line depreciation.

Required:

1. Identify the type of change or correction involved and analyze the effects of the change or correction, as appropriate.
2. Give the entry, or entries, to appropriately record the change or correction in the accounts for 1994, the year of the change.
3. Show how the change or correction should be reported on the 1994 comparative financial statements.

E 24-14
Four Errors: Corrections Before and After Closing Entries (L.O. 7)

Give the journal entries needed to correct the accounts, and the subsequent adjusting entry, for each of the errors described below assuming (*a*) the errors were discovered on December 31, 1992, before the books were adjusted or closed, and (*b*) the errors were discovered in January 1993 (after the books for 1992 were adjusted and closed). Assume each item is material. Disregard income tax considerations.

a. Merchandise that cost $12,000 was received on December 28, 1991, and was included in the ending inventory of 1991, but the credit purchase was not recorded in the purchases journal until January 13, 1992.

b. An entry was made on December 30, 1992, to write-off of organization expense as follows (assume only one year's amortization was justified for 1992; amortization per year, $2,000):

General expense 10,000
    Deferred organization expense   10,000

c. Discount of $6,600 on a long-term bond investment purchased on May 1, 1991, was written off directly and in full to retained earnings on that date. These bonds mature on July 1, 2000. Use straight-line amortization.

d. Machinery that cost $1,800 was purchased and debited in full to repair expense on June 30, 1991. The depreciation rate on machinery is 10% per year on cost (no residual value; depreciation is calculated on the number of months held).

E 24-15
Errors, Prior Years Adjustments Not Recorded and Entries to Correct for Current Year (L.O. 7)

You are auditing the accounts of Sun Merchandising Corporation for the year ended December 31, 1992. You discover that the adjustments made in the previous audit for the year 1991 were not entered in the accounts by Sun's bookkeeper; therefore, the accounts are not in agreement with the audited amounts as of December 31, 1991. The following adjustments were included in the 1991 audit report.

a. Invoices for merchandise purchased on credit in December 1991, were not entered on the books until payment of $6,000 was made in January 1992. The merchandise was not included in the December 31, 1991, inventory. The company uses a periodic inventory system.

b. Invoices for merchandise received on credit in December 1991 were not recorded in the accounts until payment was made in January 1992; the goods were included in the 1991 ending inventory, $9,000.

c. Allowance for doubtful accounts for 1991 was understated by $1,000 because bad debt expense in 1991 was not recorded.

d. Selling expense for 1991 was not recorded in the accounts until paid in January 1992, $2,500.

e. Accrued wages of $2,000 at December 31, 1991, were not recorded in the accounts until paid in January 1992.

f. Prepaid insurance at December 31, 1991, was understated by $300 because this amount was included in 1991 expense. The insurance policy expires on December 31, 1992.

g. Income tax expense of $1,200 for the last part of the year ended December 31, 1991 was not recorded until paid in January 1992.

h. Depreciation of $4,500 was not recorded for 1991.

Required:

You have the uncorrected and unadjusted trial balance dated December 31, 1992. Give the journal entry for each of the above items that should be made to the trial balance before using it for further 1992 audit purposes.

E 24–16
Analysis of Four
Accounts: Compute
Correct Ending Balances
(L.O. 7)

The accounts and financial statements of Slo Company have never been audited. A preliminary examination has shown numerous errors. Also, the files and supporting documentation are not available in some cases and unclear in others. As a consequence, you have been asked to compute the ending 1992 balances of the four accounts identified below based on the data given. Each item is independent of the others. Show computations.

a. Wage expense, $_____ .
   Data: Amount paid during 1992, $15,000; accrued on December 31, 1991, $1,000; and accrued on December 31, 1992, $2,000.

b. Rent revenue, $_____ .
   Data: Amount collected during 1992, $8,000; unearned (collected in advance), $500 on December 31, 1991, and $300 on December 31, 1992; earned but not collected, $200 on December 31, 1991, and $600 on December 31, 1992.

c. Sales revenue, $_____ .
   Data: Cash account, balance, December 31, 1991, $26,000; balance, December 31, 1992, $33,000; and total disbursements for 1992, $39,000. All cash receipts were from customers. Accounts receivable: balance, December 31, 1991, $40,160; and balance, December 31, 1992, $59,000. Accounts written off during 1992 as uncollectible, $960.

d. Purchases (net cash discounts), $_____ .
   Data: Accounts payable balance on December 31, 1991, $28,320, and on December 31, 1992, $33,000; payments made on accounts during 1992, $46,000. Credit purchases are recorded net of cash discount whether taken or not.

E 24–17
Incomplete Records:
Worksheet to Develop
Income Statement and
Balance Sheet (Appendix)
(L.O. 8)

On January 2, 1991, Star Retail Company was organized. During 1991, the company paid trade creditors $49,062 in cash and had an ending inventory per count (FIFO basis) of $9,563. Balances available on December 31, 1991, were the following: accounts payable, $16,125; expenses, $2,450 (no depreciation); M. Lane (sole proprietor), capital (representing beginning balance of cash on January 2, 1991), $45,000; accounts receivable, $13,188; and sales, $50,000. There were no withdrawals. All sales and purchases were on credit. The company is not subject to income tax.

Required:

1. Complete a worksheet to develop a correct income statement and balance sheet. Use a format similar to the following:

Accounts	Balance Sheet Jan. 2, 1991	Spreadsheet Entries		Income Statement	Balance Sheet Dec. 31, 1991
		Debit	Credit		
Cash					
Accounts receivable					
Purchases					
Expenses					
Accounts payable					
M. Lane, capital					
Sales revenue					
Income summary					
Net gain (loss)					

2. Prepare a proof of the ending cash balance.

PROBLEMS

P 24–1

Multiple Choice: Accounting Changes (L.O. 3, 4, 5, 6)

Choose the correct answer to each of the following questions.

1. Immutable Company changed from the sum-of-years digits method (SYD) to the straight line method (SL) of depreciation in 1992. Depreciation under each method for the years affected follows:

Year	SYD	SL
1989	$200	$150
1990	240	160
1991	600	450
1992	450	500

Ignoring taxes, Immutable reports which of the following amounts in a cumulative effect of change in accounting principle in 1992?
   a. $280 cr.
   b. $230 cr.
   c. $ 50 dr.
   d. $320 dr.

2. Quick Company changed depreciation methods for accounting purposes and correctly computed a cumulative effect before tax of $600 (reduces income). The tax rate is 30%. The entry to record the change in accounting principle includes:
   a. Cr. accumulated depreciation $420.
   b. Dr. deferred income tax $180.
   c. Dr. income taxes payable $420.
   d. Dr. cumulative effect $600.

3. Fido Dog Food Company changed its method of accounting for inventory from LIFO to FIFO in 1992 for both tax and financial accounting purposes. The 1991 ending inventory was $40,000 under LIFO, and $55,000 under FIFO. Fido discloses 1991 and 1992 results comparatively. The tax rate is 30%. The entry to record the change in accounting principle includes:
   a. Cr. inventory $15,000.
   b. Cr. retained earnings $10,500.
   c. Cr. cumulative effect of change in accounting principle $10,500.
   d. Insufficient information.

4. An asset purchased January 1, 1991, costing $10,000 with a 10-year useful life and no salvage value was depreciated under the straight-line method during its first three years. During 1994, the total useful life was reestimated to be 17 years. What is depreciation in 1995?
   a. $462
   b. $412.
   c. $464.
   d. $500.

5. A company made a retroactive accounting change in 1992. Only the net incomes of 1991 and 1992 were affected. Therefore, the comparative retained earnings statements featuring both years disclose which of the following?
   a. A cumulative effect adjusting the January 1, 1991, retained earnings balance.
   b. A cumulative effect adjusting the January 1, 1991, and 1992 retained earnings balances.
   c. A cumulative effect adjusting the January 1, 1992, retained earnings balance.
   d. No cumulative effect.

P 24-2

Change from Declining-Balance to Straight-Line Depreciation: Entries and Reporting

(L.O. 4)

On January 1, 1991, KLM Corporation purchased equipment that cost $23,000; the estimated useful life was 10 years with no estimated residual value. The company uses 200% declining-balance depreciation; however, at the start of 1996, the company decided to switch to straight-line depreciation (no change in useful life or residual value). At December 31, 1995, the annual financial statements reported the following correct amounts:

> Depreciation expense (DB) . . . . $ 1,884*
> Accumulated depreciation (DB) 15,463
> Shares of common stock outstanding, 10,000.
>
> * 1996, $1,507.

Net income before depreciation and before the effects of the accounting change was 1995, $40,000; and 1996, $47,000. Disregard income tax considerations.

Required:

1. What type of accounting change is this? What approach should be used—current, prospective, or retroactive? Explain.
2. Prepare the 1996 (i.e., the year of change) entries to appropriately reflect the change; also prepare the 1996 adjusting entry.
3. Show how the change and the amount of depreciation should be reported on the 1996 comparative balance sheet, including any required pro forma disclosure.

P 24-3

Change from Straight-Line to SYD: Income Tax, Entries and Reporting

(L.O. 4)

CRT Company purchased a machine on January 1, 1991, for $240,000. At the date of acquisition, the machine had an estimated useful life of 10 years with an estimated residual value of $20,000. The machine is being depreciated on a straight-line basis for financial reporting purposes, but for income tax purposes, an accelerated method is used because of its cash flow advantage.

On January 1, 1994, CRT changed, for financial reporting purposes, to an accelerated method of depreciation for this machine (with no change in estimated useful life or residual value). The accelerated depreciation amounts: 1991, $40,000; 1992, $36,000; 1993, $32,000; and 1994, $28,000. The annual accounting period ends December 31. The annual financial statements are presented on a comparative basis (1993 and 1994 presented). CRT has an average income tax rate of 40%. Pretax income before depreciation and prior to giving effect to this change was 1993, $90,000; and 1994, $98,000. There are 10,000 shares of common stock outstanding.

Required:

1. Identify the type of accounting change involved. Which approach should be used—current, prospective, or retroactive? Explain.
2. Give the entry to appropriately reflect the accounting change in 1994, the year of change, including the 1994 adjusting entry. Debit deferred income tax.
3. Show how the change should be reported on the 1994 comparative balance sheet (1993 and 1994).
4. Prepare the comparative income statements for 1993 and 1994, starting with pretax income before depreciation and prior to the effects of the change.

P 24-4

Change in Method of Accounting for Natural Resources: Entries and Reporting

(L.O. 5)

In 1994, Digger Oil Company changes its method of accounting for oil exploration costs from the successful-efforts method (SE) to the full-costing method (FC), for financial reporting. Digger has been in operation since January 1991.

Pretax income under each method:

	SE	FC
1991	$ 5,000	$15,000
1992	22,000	25,000
1993	25,000	35,000
1994	40,000	60,000

Digger reports the results of years 1992 to 1994 in its 1994 annual report and has a calendar fiscal year. The tax rate is 30%.

Additional information:

	1991	1992	1993	1994
Ending retained earnings (SE basis)	$18,000	$23,000	$31,000	
Dividends declared	9,000	10,400	9,500	18,000

Required:

1. Prepare the entry in 1994 to record the accounting change. Use natural resources as the depletable asset. For simplicity, assume the difference in accounting for exploration costs accounts for the entire income difference in all years.
2. Prepare the comparative retained earnings statements.

P 24–5
Change from Completed Contract to Percentage of Completion: Entries and Reporting
(L.O. 5)

Modern Construction Company began operations on January 1, 1991. During 1991 and 1992, the company used the completed-contract (CC) basis to account for its long-term construction contracts for financial reporting purposes.

At the start of 1993, the company changed to the percentage-of-completion (PC) basis. The following data are available:

	1991		1992		1993	
Income (net of 30% income tax)	$140,000 (CC)		$240,000 (CC)		$370,000 (PC)	
Dividends	–0–		100,000		180,000	
Retained earnings (ending balance)	140,000 (CC)		280,000 (CC)			
	CC	PC	CC	PC	CC	PC
Inventory of construction in process, net of billings (ending balance)	$300,000	$330,000	$500,000	$700,000	$560,000	$720,000

Shares outstanding, 100,000.

Required:

1. Identify the type of accounting change involved. How should it be accounted for—current, retroactive, prospective? Explain.
2. Give the entry on January 1, 1993, to record this accounting change in 1993 (net of income tax).
3. Show how the following should be reported on the 1992 and 1993 comparative:
   a. Balance sheet—inventory of construction in process and ending balance of retained earnings.
   b. Income statement—starting with income before extraordinary items.
   c. Retained earnings statement—starting with beginning balance (CC). The ending 1993 balance of retained earnings is $610,000.

P 24–6
Two Assets: Useful Life and Residual Value Changed, Entries and Reporting
(L.O. 6)

On January 1, 1991, TV Company purchased a machine that cost $78,000 with an estimated useful life of 20 years and an estimated residual value of $8,000. Starting on January 1, 1998, the company revised its estimates to 16 years for total life and $9,000 for residual value.

The company also owns a patent that cost $34,000 when acquired on January 1, 1995. It is being amortized over its legal life of 17 years (no residual value). On January 1, 1998, the patent is estimated to have a total useful life of only 13 years (no residual value). The company uses the straight-line method for both of these assets. The annual reporting period ends December 31. Disregard income tax considerations.

Required:

1. What kinds of accounting changes are involved? How should each change be accounted for—current, retroactive, or prospective? Explain.
2. Give all entries required in 1997 and 1998 related to these changes.

3. Show what amounts related to these changes should be reported on the comparative 1998 income statement and balance sheet.

P 24-7
Eight Errors: Analysis and Correction, Entries
(L.O. 7)

General Sales Company recently was acquired by a new owner who has decided to clean up the prior accounting records during the current reporting period, which ends December 31, 1989. The accounts have been partially adjusted but not closed for 1989. The following additional items have been discovered:

a. The merchandise inventory at December 31, 1988, was overstated by $10,000 (periodic inventory system).

b. During January 1987, extraordinary repairs on machinery were debited to repair expense; the $15,000 should have been debited to machinery, which is being depreciated 15% per year on cost (no residual value).

c. A patent that cost $9,350 has been amortized (straight-line) for the past 7 years (excluding 1989) over its legal life of 17 years. It is now clear that its economic life will not be more than 12 years from the initial acquisition date.

d. At the end of 1988, sales revenue collected in advance of $3,000 was included in 1988 sales revenue. It was earned in 1989.

e. Paid $8,000 during January 1987 for ordinary repairs on a machine that was acquired during January 1987. The repairs were erroneously capitalized. The machine has an estimated life of five years and no residual value. Assume straight-line depreciation.

f. The rate used for bad debts has been ½% of credit sales, which has proven to be too low; therefore, for 1988 and thereafter, the rate used will be 1% of credit sales. The amount of the expense recorded per year under the old rate was 1987, $800; and 1988, $1,000 (the amount for 1989 has not been entered in the accounts because the adjusting entries have not been made). Credit sales for 1989 exceeded 1988 credit sales by 20%.

g. During January 1987, a five-year insurance premium of $750 was paid, which was debited in full to insurance expense at that time.

h. At the end of 1988, accrued wages payable of $1,800 were not recorded; they were first recorded when paid early in 1989. Unpaid wages at the end of 1989 were $2,100.

Required:

1. For each of the above items, identify if it is an error correction or an accounting change and briefly explain how each should be accounted for.
2. Give the appropriate pretax entry to record any change or correction and give any adjusting entry needed in each instance at the end of 1989. Show computations. If no entry is needed, explain why.

P 24-8
Error: Depreciation, Income Tax and Correcting Entries
(L.O. 7)

On January 3, 1991, Young Sales Company purchased a machine that cost $30,000. Although the machine has an estimated useful life of 10 years and an estimated residual value of $6,000, it was debited to expense when acquired. It is now December 1994, and the error has been discovered. The average income tax rate is 30%, and straight-line depreciation is used.

Required:

1. Give the entry to correct the accounts at the end of 1994 assuming the books have not yet been closed for 1994. Also give the adjusting entry for depreciation for 1994. The income tax return was correct and there was no deferred income tax related to this transaction.
2. Assume instead that the income tax return also was incorrect because of this error; therefore, additional income tax must be paid, including a 10% penalty for each year an amount of tax was underpaid, less 10% each year on any amount of tax that was overpaid. Give the entry to correct the accounts, including the income tax effects, at the end of 1994, and the adjusting entry for depreciation for 1994. Round amounts to the nearest dollar.

P 24-9
Error Correction: Entry and Reporting
(L.O. 7)

In 1994, Arrow Company, a calendar fiscal year company, discovered that depreciation expense was erroneously overstated $1,000 in both 1992 and 1993, for financial reporting purposes. The tax rate is 30%.

Additional information:

	1993	1994
Beginning retained earnings, as previously reported	$18,000	—
Net income (as previously reported for 1993)	16,000	$18,000
Dividends declared	6,000	8,000

Required:
1. Record the entry in 1994 to correct the error.
2. Provide the comparative retained earnings statements for 1993 and 1994, including any required footnote disclosure.

P 24–10
Errors: Worksheet to Correct Pretax Income and Entries
(L.O. 7)

L. Long established a retail business in 1991. Early in 1994, Long entered into negotiations with S. Short with the intent to form a partnership. You have been asked by Long and Short to check Long's books for the past three years to help Short evaluate the earnings potential of the business.

The net incomes reported on statements submitted to you were as follows:

| | Year Ending 12/31 | | |
	1991	1992	1993
Income, pretax	$9,000	$10,109	$8,840

During the examination of the accounts, you found the data given below:

| | For Year Ended Dec. 31 | | |
	1991	1992	1993
Omissions from the books:			
a. Accrued expenses at end of year	$2,160	$2,094	$4,624
b. Earned (uncollected) revenue at end of year	200	—	—
c. Prepaid expenses at end of year	902	1,210	1,406
d. Unearned revenue (collected in advance) at end of year	—	610	—
Goods in transit at end of year omitted from inventory:			
e. Purchase for which the entry had been made (ownership passed)	—	2,610	—
f. Purchase for which the entry had not been made (ownership not passed)	—	—	1,710

Other points requiring consideration:
g. On January 1, 1993, sold operational equipment for $4,500 that originally cost $5,000 on January 1, 1991. Cash was debited for $4,500 and equipment was credited for $4,500. The asset sold was depreciated in 1991 and 1992 but not 1993 on the basis of a 10-year life and no residual value.
h. No allowance for bad debts has been set up. An analysis of accounts receivable as of December 31, 1993, indicates that the allowance account should have a balance of $2,000, of which $500 relates to 1991, $700 to 1992, and $800 to 1993.

Required:
1. You have decided to set up a worksheet to correct net income for each of the three years. Use column headings similar to those in the above tabulation and analyze each item separately.
2. Give the correcting entry, if any, for each item that should be made on date of discovery (that is, early 1994). For each item, code the entries with the letters given for each item in the above data.

(AICPA adapted)

P 24–11
Incomplete Records: Worksheet to Develop Income Statement and Balance Sheet (Appendix)
(L.O. 8)

Stanley Company has maintained single-entry records. In applying for a much-needed loan, a set of financial statements was required. An analysis of the records for 1991 provided the following data:

Cash receipts:
Cash sales	$130,000
Collections on credit sales	43,000
Collections on trade notes	1,000
Purchase allowances	1,500
Miscellaneous revenue	250

Cash payments:

Cash purchases	84,500
Payments to trade creditors	34,100
Payment on mortgage on 7/1/1991 plus prepayment of one year's interest of $1,020 to 7/1/1992	4,020
Sales commissions	7,200
Rent expense	2,400
General expenses (including interest)	14,590
Other operating expenses	29,800
Sales returns ($3,000 including $1,000 cash)	1,000
Insurance (renewal three-year premium, April 1)	468
Operational assets purchased	1,500

	Balances	
	1/1/1991	**12/31/1991**
Cash	$14,100	$10,172
Accounts receivable	13,000	18,000
Trade notes receivable	2,000	1,500
Inventory	10,000	18,400
Prepaid insurance	39	?
Prepaid interest expense	600	510
Trade accounts payable	26,500	23,800
Income taxes payable		1,984
Accrued operating expenses payable	600	400
Operational assets (net)	35,400	33,290
Other assets	11,861	11,861
Common stock	40,000	40,000
Mortgage payable (6%, dated 7/1/1990)	20,000	?

No operational assets were sold during the year.

Required:

Prepare a worksheet to provide data for a detailed income statement for 1991 and a balance sheet at the end of 1991. Show how the amounts for the various entries were developed. *Suggestions:* Set up columns for Balances, January 1, 1991; Spreadsheet Entries—Debit and Credit; Income Statement; and Balance Sheet, December 31, 1991.

P 24-12
Incomplete Records: Analysis to Compute Income (Appendix) (L.O. 8)

The following data were taken from the records of Rooster's Sporting Goods Store:

	Balances	
	1/1/1991	**12/31/1991**
Accounts receivable	$ 2,300	$ 3,900
Notes receivable (trade)	1,500	2,000
Interest receivable	90	70
Prepaid interest on notes payable	75	60
Inventory	9,255	10,400
Prepaid expenses (operating)	100	130
Store equipment (net)	8,500	8,600
Other assets	—	500
Accounts payable	1,700	1,900
Notes payable (trade)	11,000	11,500
Notes payable (equipment)	—	500
Accrued interest payable	40	30
Accrued expenses (operating) payable	170	210
Interest revenue collected in advance	30	40

Analysis of the checkbook, canceled checks, deposit slips, and bank statements provided the following summary for the year:

Balance, 1/1/1991		$ 4,200
Cash receipts:		
Cash sales	$23,000	
On accounts receivable	7,600	
On notes receivable	1,000	
Interest revenue	160	31,760
Cash disbursements:		
Cash purchases	11,800	
On accounts payable	2,400	
On notes payable (trade)	500	
Interest expense	560	
Operating expenses	14,130	
Miscellaneous nonoperating expenses	970	
Other assets purchased	500	
Withdrawals by Rooster	2,400	(33,260)
Balance, 12/31/1991		$ 2,700

Required:

1. Compute income by analyzing the changes in the owner's equity account.
2. Prepare a detailed income statement with supporting schedules; show computations.

P 24–13

COMPREHENSIVE PROBLEM
♦

Multiple Accounting Changes—Entries and Reporting
(L.O. 4, 6, 7)

The year 1991 was not a good one for Zealand Company accountants. The company made several financial accounting changes that year.

First, the company changed the total useful life from 20 years to 13 years on an asset purchased January 1, 1988, for $350,000. The asset was originally expected to be sold for $50,000 at the end of its useful life, but that amount was also changed in 1991 to $200,000. Zealand applies the straight-line method of depreciation to this asset.

Second, the company changed from FIFO to LIFO, but is unable to recreate LIFO inventory layers. The FIFO 1991 beginning and ending inventories are $30,000 and $45,000. Under LIFO, the 1991 ending inventory is $35,000. The company expects LIFO to render income numbers more useful for prediction, given inflation.

Third, the company changed to the straight-line method from the sum-of-years'-digits method on equipment purchased for $650,000 on January 1, 1987. The equipment has a $100,000 residual value and 10-year useful life. These values were not changed. The change in depreciation method was made to provide a better measure of expired equipment cost because the annual benefits derived from the asset have been relatively constant.

Fourth, an error in amortizing patents was discovered in 1991. Patents costing $510,000 on January 1, 1989, were amortized over their legal life (17 years). The accountant neglected to obtain an estimate of the patent's economic life, which totals only 5 years.

Additional information: Zealand is a calendar fiscal year company, is subject to a 30% tax rate, and has had 10,000 shares of common stock outstanding since 1986.

	1990 (Previously Published)	1991
Beginning retained earnings	$319,000	—
Income before extraordinary items, after tax	220,000	$325,000*
Extraordinary gain, net of tax		10,000
Dividends declared	50,000	70,000

* This is the correct reported amount and includes the appropriate amounts related to the accounting changes.

Required:

1. Record the entries in 1991 necessary to make the accounting changes.
2. Prepare the 1990 and 1991 comparative income statements (lower portion) and retained earnings statements, including footnote disclosures for the accounting changes.

CASES

C 24–1
Analysis of Three Accounting Changes
(L.O. 2, 3)

A business entity may change its method of accounting for certain items. The change may be classified as a change in accounting principle, accounting estimate, or reporting entity. Listed below are three independent, unrelated situations.

Situation 1:

Able Company determined that the depreciable lives currently used for its operational assets were too long to best match the cost of using the assets with the revenue produced. At the beginning of the current year, the company decided to reduce the depreciable lives of all its existing operational assets by five years.

Situation 2:

On December 31, 1991, Baker Company owned 51% of the voting stock of Allen Company. At that time Baker reported its investment using the cost method due to political uncertainties in the country in which Allen was located. On January 2, 1992, the management of Baker Company was satisfied that the political uncertainties had been resolved and the assets of the company were in no danger of nationalization. Accordingly, Baker will prepare consolidated financial statements for Baker and Allen for the year ended December 31, 1992.

Situation 3:

Charlie Company decided in January 1992 to adopt the straight-line method of depreciation for plant equipment. The straight-line method will be used for new acquisitions as well as for previously acquired plant equipment for which depreciation in the past has been provided on a declining-balance basis (DB).

Required:

For each of the situations described above, provide the information indicated below:
1. Type of accounting change.
2. Manner of reporting the change under current GAAP, including a discussion, for Situations 1 and 3 only, of how amounts are computed.
3. Effect of the change on the balance sheet and income statement (Situations 1 and 3 only).
4. Note disclosures which would be necessary.

(AICPA adapted)

C 24-2
Ethical Considerations: Accounting Changes
(L.O. 1)

In 1982, RTE Corporation more than doubled its EPS by changing depreciation methods. In justifying the change, the controller said: "We realized that, compared to our competitors, our conservative method of depreciation might have hurt us with investors because of its negative impact on net earnings." ("Double Standard," *Forbes,* November 22, 1982, p. 178).

Although difficult to prove, there is considerable evidence that accounting changes are made for reasons other than improved financial reporting. GAAP is flexible in the initial selection of accounting methods and in making subsequent changes. However, *APB Opinion No. 20* specifically requires that only changes to preferable accounting methods be made.

Required:

Comment on the appropriateness of making accounting changes to fulfill financial reporting objectives. Consider the relevant ethical issues in your response.

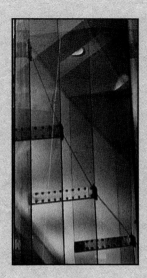

C H A P T E R

25

Financial Statement Analysis and Changing Prices

After you have studied this chapter, you will:

1. Understand the importance and limitations of financial statement information in the evaluation of investment opportunities.

2. Be able to perform vertical (within years) and horizontal (across years) comparative percentage analyses.

3. Know how to calculate a number of ratios used in financial statement analysis and interpret the results.

4. Understand the limitations of ratio analysis.

5. Be aware of the concept of capital market efficiency and what it implies for financial statement analysis.

6. Be aware of the effects of price changes on historical cost financial statements.

7. Understand the advantages and disadvantages of general and specific price level–adjusted financial statements.

8. Be able to adjust financial statements for general price level changes (historical cost–constant dollar model).

9. Know how to adjust financial statements for specific price level changes (current cost–nominal dollar and current cost–constant dollar models.)

◆

INTRODUCTION
◆

The Du Pont Company and Merck recently concluded an arrangement in which Du Pont would market a new drug using Merck's distribution network. Merck, in turn, would receive the advantages of Du Pont's extensive R&D capabilities. Before entering the joint venture, both companies investigated the operational and financial health of their potential partner. Similar analyses occur before firms agree to merge, make acquisitions, conclude contracts with suppliers, grant credit, and enter into leasing agreements.

Financial statements are an important source of information for these decisions. But financial statement data is only a part of the information set consulted by the parties involved. Financial statement information must be supplemented with information from other sources, including company management, investment advisors, trade associations, business periodicals, government agencies, and other materials distributed by and about the company. These latter sources are important because they disclose certain information often on a more timely basis than the published financial statements.

For example, unreported litigation and liabilities can threaten the profit potential of a company. Sources such as *The Wall Street Journal* provide timely disclosure of such facts. For instance, in early 1987, Loral Corporation was considering a $640 million purchase of Goodyear Aerospace. Until approached by a reporter, Loral Chairman Bernard Schwartz was unaware of the size of the potential health care costs Loral would face from Goodyear's 3,800 current retirees. Estimates of this liability ranged upwards of $30 million over the next 20 years. Schwartz is alleged to have said, "It is not an issue that has come to my attention. . . . This may have been handled at a different level." In a separate situation, Armco's buyout value dropped by 10% ($10,000,000) after last-minute negotiations uncovered a similar "liability."[1]

The use of financial statements is not restricted to the actions and plans of other firms. Financial institutions examine these statements to ascertain credit risk. Lawyers and other professional groups do so to assure their fees will be paid. Government agencies scrutinize financial reports in regard to excess profits, as they have done with the oil and gas industry, as well as for potential antitrust violations. Labor unions seek information on the ability of firms to grant wage and work concessions. Communities examine these reports for evidence of good citizenship. Finally, current and potential investors and, in particular, those in the securities industry who advise them, seek to evaluate the attractiveness of alternative investments.[2]

Decisions relating to businesses are particularly influenced by economic considerations, with earnings, financial position, and cash flows being especially significant factors. An entity's financial statements that span several reporting periods and include selected long-term trend data are sources of relevant economic information. One of the primary objectives of financial statement analysis is to identify and assess major changes in trends, amounts, and relationships. Investigation and evaluation of the reasons underlying those changes are particularly important. Recognition of turning points can provide an early warning of a significant change in the future success or failure of the business.

Financial statements are organized summaries of the extensive activities of a business. For example, the published financial statements of a large corporation, such as General Motors, Exxon, or IBM, usually contain from 10 to 15 printed pages, including the supporting notes. It is difficult to imagine the number of transactions, the critical accounting decisions, and the details summarized in these

---

[1] Reported in "The Silent Killer," *Forbes*, February 23, 1987, p. 112.

[2] The notion here is to seek undervalued firms which is the basis of what is termed *fundamental analysis*. See B. Graham, D. Dodd, and S. Cottle, *Security Analysis: Principles and Techniques*, 5th ed. (New York: McGraw-Hill, 1987). Some comments on this approach and a different point of view are given later in this chapter.

few pages. Summarization inevitably reduces the amount of information available. On the other hand, excessive detail is undesirable because statement users experience time constraints and difficulties in assimilating a mass of data (called *information overload*).

The analysis and interpretation of financial statements is enhanced if users understand the meaning and purpose of the information. As *SFAC No. 1* states:

> The information should be comprehensible to those who have a reasonable understanding of businesses and economic activities and are willing to study the information with reasonable diligence. (par. 34)

♦

OVERVIEW OF FINANCIAL STATEMENT ANALYSIS
♦

Financial statement analysis is an organized approach for extracting information relevant to particular decisions from the financial statements. The thrust of financial statement analysis in a particular situation is determined by the decision(s) being contemplated. This chapter considers analytical and interpretative approaches widely used by decision makers. The analysis and interpretation of financial statements involves the following phases, usually done in this order:

1. Examine the auditors' report.
2. Analyze the statement of accounting policies included in the notes to the financial statements.
3. Examine the financial statements as a whole, including notes and supporting schedules.
4. Apply analytical approaches such as the following:
   a. Analysis of comparative statements.
   b. Horizontal and vertical percentage analysis.
   c. Ratio (proportional) analysis.
5. Search for important supplemental information.

Examine the Auditors' Report (Phase 1)

Expert financial analysts often suggest that in evaluating financial statements, the first basic step is a careful examination of the auditors' report (also called the *Report of the Independent Certified Public Accountants*). The auditors' report is important because it provides the analyst with an independent and professional opinion about the degree to which the representations in the financial statements comply with GAAP. Also, the auditor's report calls attention to all major concerns the auditors have as a result of their intensive examination.

The most favorable auditor's report is an **unqualified (clean) opinion,** in which the auditor states that the financial statements present the company's position and results of operations in conformity with generally accepted accounting principles. Because most statements receive an unqualified opinion, the analyst must seek the information relevant to the particular questions of interest elsewhere.

Under certain conditions, including material uncertainties and inconsistent application of accounting principles, the auditor's unqualified report is modified to draw attention to the particular circumstances. Modifications of this kind are common and can be important. An explanatory paragraph is added to highlight the uncertainty or inconsistency. However, the opinion remains unqualified. In the last paragraph of the following unqualified audit report modified for an uncertainty, the auditors of Mack Trucks, Inc., explain their concern about the future viability of the company:

INDEPENDENT AUDITORS' REPORT
The Board of Directors
Mack Trucks, Inc.:

We have audited the consolidated balance sheets of Mack Trucks, Inc., and consolidated subsidiaries as of December 31, 1989 and 1988, and the related consolidated statements of income (loss), cash flows and changes in shareholders' equity for each of the three years in the period ended December 31, 1989. These financial statements are the responsibility of the Company's management. Our responsibility is to express an opinion on these financial statements based on our audits.

We conducted our audits in accordance with generally accepted auditing standards. Those standards require that we plan and perform the audit to obtain reasonable assurance about whether the financial statements are free of material misstatement. An audit includes examining, on a test basis, evidence supporting the amounts and disclosures in the financial statements. An audit also includes assessing the accounting principles used and significant estimates made by management, as well as evaluating the overall financial statement presentation. We believe that our audits provide a reasonable basis for our opinion.

In our opinion, such consolidated financial statements present fairly, in all material respects, the financial position of the companies at December 31, 1989 and 1988, and the results of their operations and their cash flows for each of the three years in the period ended December 31, 1989, in conformity with generally accepted accounting principles.

The consolidated financial statements have been prepared assuming the Company will continue as a going concern. As discussed in Note 1 to the financial statements, the liquidity of the Company has been adversely affected by recurring losses from operations, and the Company was in default under certain of its loan covenants at December 31, 1989, all of which raise substantial doubt about the Company's ability to continue as a going concern in its present form. Management's plans concerning these matters are also described in Note 1. The financial statements do not include any adjustments that might result from the outcome of this uncertainty.

Instead of an unqualified opinion, the auditor can give a *qualified* opinion, an *adverse* opinion, or a *disclaimer* of opinion about the financial statements. Each of these unfavorable opinions must include an explanation by the auditor of the factors underlying the decision for the opinion. These unfavorable opinions alert the statement user to major problem areas in the company that should be investigated. An unfavorable auditors' opinion can cause the SEC or the stock exchanges to stop public trading of the company's stock. This action can have a serious effect on the financial interests of investors. Such opinions are unusual for major firms.[3]

Analyze the Statement of Accounting Policies (Phase 2)

Accounting must accommodate a wide variety of circumstances. Although accounting principles and their implementation are prescribed primarily by the *ARBs, APB Opinions, FASB Statements* and by precedent, there is considerable room for judgment by the reporting entity.

In keeping with the *full-disclosure principle, APB Opinion No. 22,* "Disclosure of Accounting Policies," states that "information about the accounting policies adopted by a reporting entity is essential for financial statement users" (par. 8). Accounting policies are the specific policies and methods adopted by a company for preparation of its financial statements. The *Opinion* requires that a statement of these policies be provided either in the notes or, preferably, "in a separate *Summary of Significant Accounting Policies* preceding the notes to the financial statements or as the initial note" (par. 15).

---

[3] There were no such opinions for the 600 firms covered in AICPA's annual *Accounting Trends & Techniques* survey (1990).

The summary must disclose all important accounting policies. These policies include selections from among acceptable reporting alternatives, accounting policies peculiar to the industry, and unusual or innovative applications of generally accepted accounting principles. Examples include the basis for consolidated statements, depreciation and amortization methods, inventory costing and valuation, translation of foreign currencies, revenue recognition on long-term construction contracts, franchising, and leasing.

The information in the statement of accounting policies is fundamental to understanding, interpreting, and evaluating the information reported in the financial statements. This information is particularly useful in evaluating the credibility of the statements and the reliability of reported earnings, and in comparing data across companies, industries, and reporting periods.

Integrative Examination of Financial Statements (Phase 3)

After the auditor's opinion and summary of accounting policies are examined, the evaluation and interpretive process continues with a careful study of the financial statements in their entirety. This phase of the analysis involves an integrative study of each statement to gain an overall perspective and to identify major strengths and weaknesses. This study also identifies unusual changes, such as turning points in the trends of sales revenue, expenses, income, asset structure, liabilities, capital structure, and cash flow.

The overall examination should include a review of all the statements and footnotes. Consideration of the notes as a separate activity is not particularly fruitful because a specific note usually is informative only in the context of the related statement item. The position of the accounting profession is that the disclosure notes are an integral part of the financial statements.

Concurrent with, or after, the overall examination of the financial statements under review, analysts find it helpful to apply some of the analytical techniques discussed in the next section.

CONCEPT REVIEW

1. Give an example of a circumstance that would not qualify an auditor's opinion, but that should be considered when making an investment decision.
2. What are the five phases used in the analysis and interpretation of financial statements?
3. What information is included in the statement of significant accounting policies?

COMPARATIVE FINANCIAL STATEMENTS AND PERCENTAGE ANALYSIS (PHASE 4a, 4b)

Various approaches are used to enhance the analysis and communication of the information in financial statements:
* Comparative financial statements.
* Percentage analysis.
* Ratio analysis.
* Graphic presentations and special tabulations.
* Subclassifications of information on the statements.
* Supplementary information in separate schedules and notes to the statements.

This section considers comparative statements and percentage analysis; the following section discusses ratio analysis.

EXHIBIT 25-1   Vertical Analysis: Merck & Co. Consolidated Balance Sheet

MERCK & CO., INC., AND SUBSIDIARIES
Consolidated Balance Sheets
With Vertical Percentage Analysis
December 31, 1988 and 1989

($ in millions)	1989 Amount	1989 %	1988 Amount	1988 %
Assets				
Current assets:				
Cash and cash equivalents	$ 685.1	10	$ 854.0	14
Short-term investments	458.4	7	696.0	11
Accounts receivable	1,265.6	19	1,022.8	16
Inventories	779.7	11	657.7	11
Prepaid expenses and taxes	221.0	3	158.8	3
Total current assets	3,409.8	50	3,389.3	55
Property, plant, and equipment, at cost:				
Land	162.1	2	130.5	2
Buildings	1,129.1	17	1,038.1	17
Machinery, equipment, and office furnishings	2,417.2	36	2,224.8	36
Construction in progress	285.5	4	197.1	4
Total property, plant, and equipment	3,993.9	59	3,590.5	59
Less: Allowance for depreciation	1,701.4	25	1,519.8	25
Net property, plant, and equipment	2,292.5	34	2,070.7	34
Investments	737.2	11	402.9	7
Other assets	317.2	5	264.6	4
Total Assets	$6,756.7	100	$6,127.5	100
Liabilities and Stockholders' Equity				
Current liabilities:				
Accounts payable and accrued liabilities	$ 937.2	14	$ 832.9	14
Loans payable	327.3	5	458.8	7
Income taxes payable	464.8	7	470.5	8
Dividends payable	178.0	3	146.8	2
Total current liabilities	1,907.3	29	1,909.0	31
Long-term debt	117.8	2	142.8	2
Deferred income taxes and noncurrent liabilities	701.1	10	676.2	11
Minority interests	509.9	7	543.7	9
Stockholders' equity:				
Common stock:				
Authorized—900,000,000 shares				
Issued—455,524,308 shares	152.4	2	145.4	2
Retained earnings	5,394.2	80	4,580.3	75
	5,546.6	82	4,725.7	77
Less treasury stock, at cost:				
60,116,101 shares—1989				
58,784,163 shares—1988	2,026.0	30	1,869.9	30
Total stockholders' equity	3,520.6	52	2,855.8	47
Total liabilities and stockholders' equity	$6,756.7	100	$6,127.5	100

Comparative Financial Statements (Phase 4a)

Comparative financial statements present financial information for the current period and for one or more past periods in a way that facilitates comparison. Complete financial statements for the current and one or two immediately preceding periods often are presented in annual reports. In addition, selected financial statement data for several preceding periods are reported in summary fashion. Firms often include

EXHIBIT 25-2 Vertical Analysis: Merck & Co. Consolidated Income Statement

MERCK & CO., INC., AND SUBSIDIARIES
Consolidated Income Statements
With Vertical Percentage Analysis
Years Ended December 31, 1987, 1988, and 1989

($ in millions except per share amounts)	1989 Amount	%	1988 Amount	%	1987 Amount	%
Sales	$6,550.5	100	$5,939.5	100	$5,061.3	100
Costs and expenses:						
Materials and production	1,550.3	24	1,526.1	26	1,444.3	28
Marketing and administrative	2,013.4	31	1,877.8	31	1,682.1	32
Research and development	750.5	11	668.8	11	565.7	11
Other (income) expense, net	(46.7)	(1)	(4.2)	—	(36.0)	1
Total costs and expenses	4,267.5	65	4,068.5	68	3,656.1	72
Income before taxes	2,283.0	35	1,871.0	31	1,405.2	28
Taxes on income	787.6	12	664.2	11	498.8	10
Net income	$1,495.4	23	$1,206.8	20	$ 906.4	18
Earnings per share of common stock*	$3.78		$3.05		$2.23	

* No percentage is calculated since amounts are per share.

earnings, capital expenditures, dividends, total assets, and working capital in these long-term summaries. The summaries are particularly relevant for financial statement analysis. An example is provided in the Sherwin-Williams annual report found at the end of this text.

The annual financial statements for the current year give only a limited view of the successes and failures of a company. In contrast, the long-term summaries (5 to 10 years) provide a broad overview of the company's financial past and clues about the firm's future. In this regard, even the results of one or two years provide only a limited picture of the company's potential.

Percentage Analysis of Financial Statements (Phase 4*b*)

Conversion of financial statement amounts to percentages reveals proportionate relationships that are difficult to perceive from dollar amounts alone. Conversion of dollar amounts involves dividing one amount by another; the result is expressed as a percentage or ratio.

Analysts and other users typically rely on two variations of percentage analysis called vertical analysis and horizontal analysis. **Vertical analysis** (also called *common-size analysis*) expresses each item on a particular financial statement as a percentage of one specific item, called the *base* amount. Vertical analysis emphasizes proportional relationships *within* each reporting period, rather than *between* reporting periods.

The base amount (the denominator) for the balance sheet is total assets, and each individual account balance (the numerator) is expressed as a percentage of total assets. For the income statement, the base amount is net revenue.

Exhibits 25–1 and 25–2 illustrate vertical percentage analysis for the balance sheet and income statement of Merck & Co. Placing the various items for the two periods side by side in two columns facilitates comparison. Both the dollar amounts and vertical percentages are developed for each reporting year. The percentage columns in the exhibits do not add to 100% because there are intermediate totals in the statements.

EXHIBIT 25-3   Horizontal Analysis: Merck & Co. Consolidated Income Statement

MERCK & CO., INC., AND SUBSIDIARIES
Consolidated Income Statements
With Horizontal Percentage Analysis
Years Ended December 31, 1987, 1988, and 1989

($ in millions except per share amounts)	1989	Percentage Change from 1987	1988	Percentage Change from 1987	1987
Sales	$6,550.5	29	$5,939.5	17	$5,061.3
Costs and expenses:					
Materials and production	1,550.3	7	1,526.1	6	1,444.3
Marketing and administrative	2,013.4	20	1,877.8	12	1,682.1
Research and development	750.5	33	668.8	18	565.7
Other (income) expense, net	(46.7)	30	(4.2)	(88)	(36.0)
Total costs and expenses	4,267.5	17	4,068.5	11	3,656.1
Income before taxes	2,283.0	62	1,871.0	33	1,405.2
Taxes on income	787.6	58	664.2	33	498.8
Net income	$1,495.4	65	$1,206.8	33	$ 906.4
Earnings per share of common stock	$3.78	70	$3.05	37	$2.23

A cursory examination of the balance sheet percentages shows that Merck's stockholders' equity rose as a percentage of total assets from 47% to 52%. This result is supported by the increase in net income for 1989. Merck's income statements suggest that an increase in revenues and a decrease in certain operating costs as a percent of revenue have contributed to its increased earnings.

Horizontal analysis involves the use of percentages to measure the change from one year (the base) to one or more following years. Horizontal analysis emphasizes proportional relationships *between* reporting periods, rather than *within* reporting periods. For example, Merck's cash and cash equivalents decreased from $854 million in 1988 to $685.1 million in 1989, a decline of 20% [($685.1 − $854)/$854].

Exhibit 25-3 illustrates the use of horizontal percentage analysis on Merck's consolidated income statements. The percentage changes are calculated by dividing the amount of increase or decrease in each item from the base year (1987) amount, by the base year amount. For example, 1988 sales increased 17% over 1987 sales [($5,939.5 − $5,061.3)/$5,061.3]. Horizontal analysis is applied to the balance sheet and to the statement of cash flows in exactly the same manner.

Items involving relatively large dollar amounts should be scrutinized more carefully than other items. For example, sales for Merck involve billions of dollars, while several expenses are much less. A small change in sales can be more significant than a larger change in a smaller item. Horizontal analysis is not restricted to the two or three years reported in the balance sheet and income statement. Merck provides a multiyear summary (10 years) of selected financial data in its annual report, as is common for many firms.

CONCEPT REVIEW

1. How are the calculations for vertical analysis performed?
2. How are the calculations for horizontal analysis performed?
3. What is the difference in the comparisons made between vertical and horizontal analysis?

RATIO ANALYSIS (PHASE 4c)

◆

Ratio analysis involves measuring the proportional relationship between two or more financial statement items. For example, the *current ratio,* the ratio of current assets to current liabilities, is one way of analyzing a company's working capital position. According to Merck's 1989 balance sheet:

Total current assets . . . . $3,409.8 million
Total current liabilities . . . . . 1,907.3 million
Working capital . . . . $1,502.5 million

The amount of working capital standing alone is a useful figure; however, expressing it as a ratio adds insight to this relationship. The current ratio based on the above amounts is 1.79:

$$\text{Current ratio} = \frac{\text{Current assets}}{\text{Current liabilities}} = \frac{\$3,409.8}{\$1,907.3} = 1.79$$

Merck had $1.79 of current assets for each $1 of current liabilities at the end of 1989.

Ratio analysis is helpful when the proportional relationship between the selected factors assists in the interpretation of the individual absolute amounts. In view of the large number of ratios that could be computed, it is important for analysis purposes to select those amounts that involve relevant relationships. For example, the relationship between bad debt expense and credit sales generally is more meaningful than the relationship between bad debt expense and total sales (including cash sales).

Ratios are more helpful if used comparatively, rather than in isolation. A firm's ratios for different time periods should be compared, and its ratios should be compared to those of other firms involved in similar activities. Several investment services, including Moody's Investor Services and Standard & Poor's, supply industry data against which to compare the ratios for individual firms. In addition, the purposes for which the ratios are to be used must be considered. Investors, managers, and creditors encounter different kinds of problems and decisions. Therefore, different sets of ratios are meaningful to each group. In a later section, the usefulness and limitations of ratio analysis are discussed at length.

Because a complete study of ratio analysis is beyond the scope of this text, only representative ratios having general application are discussed.[4] The analyses selected for discussion cover ratios that measure the following:

1. Liquidity (solvency).
2. Efficiency (activity).
3. Equity position and coverage.
4. Profitability.

The discussion uses the financial statement data for Merck given in Exhibits 25-1 and 25-2. To assess whether a ratio indicates a favorable or unfavorable condition, the firm's history, industry norms, and other factors must be considered. Therefore, such an assessment for Merck is not attempted for several of the ratios discussed in the following sections.

Ratios that Measure Liquidity (Solvency)

Ratios in this category are designed measure a firm's ability to pay its obligations. Ratios often used to measure liquidity are summarized in Exhibit 25-4.

---

[4] There is no single "generally accepted" method of computing specific ratios or of determining the values to be used in their computation. The formulas presented in this chapter reflect only one approach. For a more detailed list of ratios, see J. Palmer, "Technical Consulting Practice Aid No. 3," *Financial Ratio Analysis,* New York: AICPA, 1983.

EXHIBIT 25-4   Ratios that Measure Liquidity (Solvency)

Ratio	Formula for Computation	Summary of Significance
1. Current (or working capital) ratio.	$\dfrac{\text{Current assets}}{\text{Current liabilities}}$	Test of short-term liquidity. Indicates ability to meet current obligations from current assets as a going concern. Measure of adequacy of working capital.
2. Acid-test (or quick) ratio.	$\dfrac{\text{Quick assets}}{\text{Current liabilities}}$	A more severe test of immediate liquidity than the current ratio. Tests ability to meet sudden demands upon liquid current assets, particularly cash.
3. Working capital to total assets.	$\dfrac{\text{Working capital}}{\text{Total assets}}$	Indicates relative liquidity of total assets and distribution of resources employed as to liquidity.
4. Defensive-interval ratio	$\dfrac{\text{Quick assets}}{\substack{\text{Projected daily} \\ \text{operational expenditures}}}$	Length of time in days the firm can operate on its present liquid resources.

Current Ratio   This ratio (computed as 1.79 previously for Merck) has a long history as an index of short-term liquidity. According to accounting historians, it is the first financial ratio developed.[5] The ratio measures the ability of the business to meet the maturing claims of its creditors from current operating assets. The amount of working capital and the related ratio have a direct impact on the amount of short-term credit that can be obtained. The minimum acceptable current ratio is unique to the industry in which the business operates, and even to the business itself in light of its operating and financial characteristics. For example, a ratio of 2.11 may be adequate in one situation, but too low or too high in another.[6]

The current ratio is only one measure or index of ability to meet short-term obligations and must be interpreted carefully. For example, a high current ratio can result from overstocking inventory. The ratio also is influenced by the inventory cost flow method used. A business can have a high current ratio even though it has a cash deficit. Furthermore, a high current ratio can indicate excess funds that should be invested or used for other purposes.[7]

Acid-Test (or Quick) Ratio   This ratio is used as a test of *immediate liquidity* and equals *quick assets* divided by current liabilities. Quick assets include cash, accounts receivable, short-term notes receivable, and short-term investments in marketable securities. These assets represent funds readily available for paying current obligations. By contrast, quick assets exclude other current assets such as inventories and prepayments. Inventories must be sold and collection made before cash is available for paying obligations. In many cases, particularly for raw materials and work-in-process inventories, the marketability of the inventory involves considerable uncertainty regarding ultimate conversion to cash. Also, prepayments generally do not represent liquid resources because they represent claims to services or goods, rather than to cash.

Traditionally, an acid-test ratio of 1 to 1 (a rule of thumb standard) is considered desirable. As with the current ratio, the acid-test ratio for a particular company must be evaluated in terms of industry characteristics and business considerations. Merck's acid-test ratio for 1989 is:

---

[5] W. Cooper and Y. Ijiri, *Kohler's Dictionary for Accountants*, 6th ed. (Englewood Cliffs, N.J.: Prentice-Hall, 1983), p. 146.

[6] A popular rule of thumb is that the current ratio should be at least 2.00. According to this rule, having twice the current assets as current liabilities implies sufficient resources to pay current liabilities as they come due.

[7] The term *fund* is used in a general sense in this chapter and includes cash, cash equivalents, other securities that are readily converted into cash, and working capital. The term is not limited to cash and cash equivalents.

$$\frac{\text{Quick assets}}{\text{Total current liabilities}} = \frac{\$685.1 + \$458.4 + \$1,265.6}{\$1,907.3} = 1.26$$

Merck could liquidate its current debt without requiring additional debt financing and without relying on the sale of its existing inventory, assuming collection of its receivables in a reasonably short period of time.

Working Capital to Total Assets The ratio of working capital to total assets is a generalized expression of the distribution and liquidity of the assets employed after current liabilities are deducted from current assets. Merck's working capital to total assets ratio for 1989 is:

$$\frac{\text{Working capital}}{\text{Total assets}} = \frac{\$3,409.8 - \$1,907.3}{\$6,756.7} = .22$$

An excessively high ratio might indicate excess cash, an inability to collect receivables, or overstocking of inventory, whereas a low ratio indicates a weakness in the current position.

Defensive-Interval Ratio Relating current or quick assets to current liabilities presumes these assets are expected to be used to pay existing current liabilities. An alternative, favored in some quarters, is a measure of how long the firm can operate using only its present liquid resources. This measure is the ratio of the firm's defensive assets (quick assets) to projected daily expenditures for production, distribution, and administration. Merck's defensive-interval ratio for 1989 is:

$$\frac{\text{Defensive assets (quick assets)}}{\text{Projected daily operational expenditures}} = \frac{\$685.1 + \$458.4 + \$1,265.6}{(\$1,550.3 + \$2,013.4)/365}$$
$$= 247 \text{ days}$$

Merck's ratio appears quite substantial. Operating funds from future operations should arrive long before current liquid assets are exhausted. Research and development expense, excluded from the ratio, reflects an activity that could be curtailed or eliminated if Merck encounters severely adverse business conditions.

Ratios that Measure Efficiency (Activity)

Efficiency measures provide another way of evaluating liquidity. In fact, these measures were developed in part to complement the previously discussed liquidity measures. More generally, the efficiency measures provide information about how effectively the firm is using its assets. Exhibit 25–5 lists six efficiency ratios.

Accounts Receivable Turnover and Age of Accounts Receivable The ability to quickly convert credit sales (accounts receivable) into cash is an important objective of cash management programs. The balance in trade receivables is related to the credit sales for the period and to the credit terms. The first two ratios in Exhibit 25–5 provide important insights into the efficiency of a firm's credit and collection activities. Assuming all Merck's 1989 sales are on credit,[8] these two ratios are computed as follows:

$$\text{Accounts receivable turnover} = \frac{\text{Net credit sales}}{\text{Average accounts receivable (net)}}$$

$$\frac{\$6,550.5}{(\$1,265.6 + \$1,022.8)/2} = \frac{\$6,550.5}{\$1,144.2} = 5.72 \text{ times}$$

---

[8] In many cases, the financial statement user must use total sales for this ratio because the breakdown of sales into cash and credit sales is not available.

EXHIBIT 25-5   Ratios that Measure Efficiency (Activity)

Ratio	Formula for Computation	Summary of Significance
1. Accounts receivable turnover.	$\dfrac{\text{Net credit sales}}{\text{Average trade receivables (net)}}$	Efficiency of credit policies and collection of trade accounts and notes.
2. Age of accounts receivable.	$\dfrac{365 \text{ (days)}}{\text{Accounts receivable turnover}}$	Average number of days to collect trade receivables.
3. Inventory turnover.	$\dfrac{\text{Cost of goods sold}}{\text{Average inventory}}$	Indicates average number of times inventory was "turned over," or sold, during the period. Indicates possible over- or understocking.
4. Working capital turnover.	$\dfrac{\text{Net sales}}{\text{Average working capital}}$	Indicates the effectiveness with which average working capital was used to generate sales.
5. Asset turnover.	$\dfrac{\text{Net sales}}{\text{Average total assets}}$	Indicates efficiency of asset utilization.
6. Net cash flow to current liabilities.	$\dfrac{\text{Net cash flow from operations}}{\text{Current liabilities}}$	Indicates ability to pay current liabilities.

$$\text{Age of accounts receivable} = \frac{365 \text{ (days)}}{\text{Accounts receivable turnover}}$$

$$= \frac{365}{5.72} = 63.8 \text{ average days to collect}$$

The numerator of accounts receivable turnover is net credit sales, which encompasses the entire reporting period. Therefore, the denominator uses the *average* accounts receivable, a more representative value for the amount of accounts receivable outstanding during the period than either beginning or ending accounts receivable.

Accounts receivable were generated and collected ("turned over") 5.72 times during 1989. On average, receivables required 63.8 days to collect—a relatively long term for collection. It is assumed that all sales were on credit. If Merck actually experienced cash sales, turnover decreases and the age of receivables increases. An age of accounts receivable closer to one month would reflect traditional industry credit terms requiring payment of the net invoice within 30 days of sale to avoid interest charges.[9]

The example raises computational issues:

* Should the total of cash and credit sales, or credit sales only, be used in the computation? Because only credit sales give rise to accounts receivable, a more stable and meaningful ratio results if only credit sales are used. Otherwise, a shift in the proportion of cash to credit sales affects the ratio, even though collection experience is unchanged.

* Should the ending balance in receivables or average receivables be used? The *average monthly* receivables balance eliminates seasonal influences. Ideally, the average is determined by adding the 13 monthly balances (January 1 and January 31 through December 31) of trade accounts and trade notes receivable and dividing by 13. In the absence of monthly balances, the average of the annual beginning and ending balance is used (with a potentially significant loss of information).

---

[9] Some analysts prefer to use 250 (5-day workweek) or 300 (6-day workweek) days as an approximation of the number of business days in the year. Using fewer days would improve Merck's figure somewhat.

♦ Receivables should be net of the allowance for doubtful accounts. The amounts used in the Merck example were net amounts.

♦ Trade notes receivable should be included in average receivables.

Inventory Turnover   The inventory turnover ratio expresses the relationship between cost of goods sold and the average inventory balance. Merck's inventory turnover for 1989 is:

$$\frac{\text{Cost of goods sold}}{\text{Average inventory}} = \frac{\$1,550.3}{(\$779.7 + \$657.7)/2} = 2.16 \text{ times}$$

The result indicates that Merck turns its inventory into sales about twice a year. Care must be taken when using aggregate financial statement amounts, however. For example, inventories can include items used internally by the firm for administrative and research purposes.

Accepting the inventory turnover figure at face value, the number of days supply of inventory held by Merck on average is 169 days (365/2.16).[10] Inventory turnover varies across industries and businesses. For example, grocery stores experience high inventory turnover, whereas antique dealers' experience is just the opposite. The turnover ratio represents an average across all inventory items and does not reflect necessarily the rate for individual items. Thus, a grocery store with an average turnover of 20 will have items on the shelves that have not turned over for a three-month period. Furthermore, this ratio is influenced by the inventory costing method used, which also affects comparisons among companies. For example, when inventory prices are rising, companies using LIFO will tend to have higher turnover rates than those using other cost flow methods, because cost of goods sold reflects higher priced goods.

Profitability is directly related to inventory turnover. To illustrate, assume that the inventory turnover is 12 (cost of goods sold, $1,200,000/average inventory, $100,000) and that the company realizes gross profit of $1,000 each time the $100,000 investment in inventory turns over. A $12,000 gross profit is indicated. Now assume another company is identical in every respect except that its inventory turnover is 6. The second company has a $6,000 profit on a similar $100,000 inventory investment, half that of the first company.

With respect to all inventories, turnover computations based on appropriate *unit* data (both numerator and denominator), when practicable, provide more reliable results than those based on dollar amounts. Unit-based computations, generally possible only for internal purposes, avoid the problems brought about by cost-flow assumptions and inflation.

Working Capital Turnover   Working capital has a functional relationship to sales revenue through accounts receivable, inventory, and cash. Therefore, the ratio of sales revenue to working capital is used as a measure of the effectiveness of a company's use of working capital to generate revenue. Merck's working capital turnover ratio for 1989 is:

$$\frac{\text{Net sales}}{\text{Average working capital}} =$$

$$\frac{\$6,550.5}{[(\$3,409.8 - \$1,907.3) + (\$3,389.3 - \$1,909.0)]/2} = 4.39 \text{ times}$$

Merck is generating approximately $4.39 of sales for each $1 of working capital employed in the business.

----

[10] This ratio is analogous to the age of accounts receivable. One measure of the length of a firm's operating cycle is the age of accounts receivable plus the number of days supply of inventory: 232.8 days (63.8 + 169) for Merck.

Asset Turnover   This ratio is calculated by dividing net sales by average total assets. The asset turnover ratio extends the idea of efficient use of working capital to all assets. Unfortunately, the ratio is larger for firms using older, more fully depreciated assets. When used to evaluate performance, the ratio discourages replacement of older, inefficient assets. Merck's asset turnover ratio for 1989 is:

$$\frac{\text{Net sales}}{\text{Average total assets}} = \frac{\$6,550.5}{(\$6,756.7 + \$6,127.5)/2} = 1.02 \text{ times}$$

Merck is generating approximately \$1 of sales for each \$1 of assets employed in the business per year. Because of its limitations, the asset turnover ratio should be used with care and only in conjunction with other related measures.

Net Cash Flow to Current Liabilities   This ratio indicates the ability of the firm to cover its current liabilities. It is placed in this category of ratios (efficiency or activity measures) because its numerator is net cash flow from operations, rather than a balance sheet amount. Merck's net cash flow from operations is \$1,380.7, obtained from its 1989 statement of cash flows (not reproduced here). Therefore, Merck's net cash flow to current liabilities ratio for 1989 is:

$$\frac{\text{Net cash flow from operations}}{\text{Current liabilities}} = \frac{\$1,380.7}{\$1,907.3} = .72$$

In 1989, Merck's operating activities provided 72% of the cash required to liquidate its ending current liabilities.

Ratios that Measure Equity Position and Coverage

Exhibit 25–6 summarizes five ratios used to measure equity and coverage relationships. The balance sheet reports the two basic sources of funds used by a business: owners' equity and creditor's equity (debt). The relationship between these two different types of equities is measured because it reflects the financial strength of the business. In particular, the long-term solvency of a business and its potential capacity to generate and obtain investment resources are affected by the proportion of debt to equity.

The first two ratios in Exhibit 25–6 focus on the amount of resources provided by creditors relative to the amount provided by owners. Because debt and equity capital have significantly different characteristics, the relationship between debt and owners' equity is important. Debt requires the payment of interest at specific intervals. In addition, the principal must be paid at maturity. Interest on debt is an expense and is tax deductible. In contrast, owners' equity does not have a maturity date. Dividends are paid only if earnings have accumulated and dividends are declared. A dividend is not an expense and is not tax deductible. These ratios are closely monitored by interested parties.

Debt to Equity Ratio   This equity ratio is the most widely used ratio in this category because it provides a direct reading of the relationship between debt and owners' equity. Merck's debt to equity ratio for 1989 is:

$$\frac{\text{Total liabilities}}{\text{Total owners' equity}} = \frac{\$6,756.7 - \$3,520.6}{\$3,520.6} = .92$$

The owners are providing about the same level of resources as the creditors. Again, care must be taken when interpreting this number. The recorded value for debt is usually much closer to market value than is the case with stockholders' equity amounts, since the latter reflects the values when the equity securities were issued and when income was earned.

EXHIBIT 25-6   Ratios that Measure Equity Position and Coverage

Ratio	Formula for Computation	Summary of Significance
1. Debt to equity.	Total liabilities / Owners' equity	Measures the balance between resources provided by creditors and resources provided by owners (including retained earnings).
2. Debt to total assets.	Total liabilities / Total assets	Proportion of assets provided by creditors. Extent of leverage.
3. Book value per share of common stock.	Common stock equity / Number of outstanding common shares	Number of dollars of common equity (at book value) per share of common stock outstanding at year-end.
4. Times interest earned.	Income before taxes and interest / Interest charges	Income available to cover interest.
5. Cash flow per share.	Net cash flow from operations / Number of outstanding common shares	Measures cash generated on a per-share basis (common shares outstanding at year-end).

Debt to Total Assets   This ratio measures the relationship between debt and total assets. Therefore, it represents the percentage of total resources provided by creditors. Merck's 1989 ratio is:

$$\frac{\text{Total debt}}{\text{Total assets}} = \frac{(\$6,756.7 - \$3,520.6)}{\$6,756.7} = .48$$

The creditors provided 48% of the total assets, and the shareholders (and earnings) provided the remaining 52%.

Book Value per Share of Common Stock   Book value per share of common stock is computed by dividing total common stockholders' equity by the number of common shares outstanding at year-end. When more than one class of stock is outstanding, total stockholders' equity is allocated among the various classes according to the legal and statutory claims that are effective in case of liquidation of the company. The usual case requires an allocation based on the preferential rights of the preferred stockholders. Liquidating, cumulative, and participating preferences must be included in the computation.

Merck does not face the problem of multiple classes of stock and carries no preferred. Hence Merck's 1989 book value ratio is:

$$\frac{\text{Common stock equity}}{\text{Number of outstanding common shares}} = \frac{\$3,520.6}{455.5 - 60.1} = \frac{\$8.90 \text{ per}}{\text{share}}$$

At the end of 1989, Merck has 455.5 million common shares issued, including 60.1 million treasury shares. Book value per share considers only the *outstanding* common shares.

To further illustrate the adjustments necessary in a more complex situation, assume Merck has outstanding 10 million shares of 8%, $1 par cumulative preferred stock. Assume further that this stock has a *liquidation preference* of $3 per share, and at December 31, 1989, preferred dividends are in arrears for two years (including

1989). Computation of book value per common share at December 31, 1989, yields (all share and dollar amounts in millions):

Total stockholders' equity		$3,520.6
Allocation to preferred stock:		
Liquidation value (10* shares × $3)	$30.0	
Cumulative dividends		
in arrears (10 shares × .08 × 2 years)	1.6	
Total allocated to preferred stock equity		$31.6
Balance applicable to common stock equity		$3,489.0
Book value per share of common stock [$3,489/(455.5 − 60.1)]		$8.82

* 10 million shares.

Although often computed, book value per share of common stock has limited usefulness. This value has little, if any, correlation to the market value per share of common stock. Some investors view with interest a stock that has a book value significantly in excess of its market price because this may suggest a good buy. Under the cost and matching principles and because of conservatism, the total assets of a business, particularly during a period of rising prices, have book values considerably below market values.

Times Interest Earned   This ratio is computed by dividing income before taxes and interest by interest charges (including capitalized interest). The ratio indicates how many times interest charges are covered by available income. Merck's 1989 interest coverage ratio is:

$$\frac{\text{Income before taxes and interest}}{\text{Interest charges}} = \frac{\$1,495.4 + \$787.6 + \$53.2^*}{\$53.2}$$

$$= 43.91 \text{ times}$$

* Interest is given in Note 6 to Merck's financial statements (not reproduced here).

To understand why interest and taxes are added in the numerator, reconsider the above situation but assume interest expense were 43.91 times larger than the amount reported. In this case, pretax income would be zero and no income tax would be recognized:

Reported pretax 1989 income (reflects $53.2 interest)	$2,283
Additional interest [(43.91 × $53.2) − $53.2]	$2,283
Pretax and after-tax income	$ 0

Therefore, pretax income covered interest expense 43.91 times in 1989. Merck appears to have no problem covering its interest charges.

Cash Flow per Share   Various measures of cash flow per share are computed by financial statement users. These measures are receiving increased attention, partly due to the inclusion of cash flow statements in the annual report. The measure chosen for discussion in this text relates net cash flow from operations to the number of common shares outstanding at year-end. For Merck, in 1989, this ratio is:

$$\frac{\text{Net cash flow from operations}}{\text{Number of outstanding common shares}} = \frac{\$1,380.7^*}{455.5 - 60.1} = \$3.49$$

* From Merck's statement of cash flows, not reproduced here.

This measure should be interpreted with extreme caution. It represents neither the cash flowing through the firm per share nor the cash available to the common shareholders per share. Under *SFAS No. 95,* "Statement of Cash Flows," firms are not permitted to disclose cash flow per share amounts in the financial statements. However, if sufficient cash were available after other commitments, Merck could pay $3.49 in dividends per share from cash generated from operations.

EXHIBIT 25-7 Ratios that Measure Profitability

Ratio	Formula for Computation	Summary of Significance
1. Profit margin on sales	$\dfrac{\text{Income*}}{\text{Net sales}}$	Indicates net profitability of each dollar of sales revenue.
2. Return on investment: *a.* On total assets.	$\dfrac{\text{Income plus interest expense (after tax)}}{\text{Average total assets†}}$	Rate earned on all resources used. Measures earnings on all investments provided by owners and creditors.
b. On owners' equity.	$\dfrac{\text{Income}}{\text{Average owners' equity}}$	Rate earned on resources provided by owners (excludes creditors). Measures earnings accruing to the owners.
3. Earnings per share of common stock (EPS).	$\dfrac{\text{Income associated with common stock}}{\text{Common shares outstanding}}$	Income earned on each share of common stock. Indicates ability to pay dividends and to grow from within.
4. Price-earnings ratio.	$\dfrac{\text{Market price per share}}{\text{Earnings per share}}$	Reflects the relationship between the latest earnings per share amount and the current market price per share; provides a rough measure of how the market values one share of stock.
5. Dividend payout ratio. *a.* Based on income to common.	$\dfrac{\text{Cash dividends to common stock}}{\text{Income less preferred dividends}}$	Measures the percent of income that is represented by cash dividends to common.
b. Based on market price of common.	$\dfrac{\text{Cash dividends per common share}}{\text{Market price per share}}$	Provides a rough estimate of the rate of return per share of stock.

* Income before extraordinary items, rather than net income, usually is preferable. The inclusion of extraordinary gains and losses is misleading because they are unusual and infrequent.

† The denominator as used here is also referred to as total liabilities plus owners' equity, total equities, and total investment.

Ratios that Measure Profitability

Many investors are more interested in a company's income statement than in its balance sheet. This is because a company can continue to expand, develop, generate positive cash inflows, and pay attractive dividends when its long-term earnings record is favorable and appears likely to continue in the future. Consequently, ratio analysis related to profitability is given considerable attention by both investors and creditors. Exhibit 25–7 summarizes several ratios that are widely used to help assess the earnings and cash flow strengths of a business.

Profit Margin on Sales   This ratio is widely used as an index of profitability. It represents the percentage of net sales remaining after all expenses are recognized. Merck's 1989 profit margin on sales is healthy and is computed as follows:

$$\frac{\text{Income}}{\text{Net sales}} = \frac{\$1,495.4}{\$6,550.5} = .23$$

Merck kept (as income) 23% of its sales. The remainder went to cover expenses.

However, one significant factor related to profitability, the total amount of assets used to earn income, is given no consideration in the ratio. To illustrate, assume the accounts of a firm showed the following data: income, $20,000; net sales, $200,000; and total assets $1,000,000. In this case the profit margin on sales appears to be quite high at 10% ($20,000/$200,000). However, when earnings performance is measured by the 2% return on total assets ($20,000/$1,000,000), it appears to be low. Thus, the profit margin ratio has value primarily for evaluation of trends and for comparison with industry and competitor statistics.

Return on Investment   Many accountants consider return on total assets to be the single most important ratio because it incorporates both earnings and investment. Return on any investment is computed by dividing the income earned from that investment by the investment at risk to earn the income.

The broad concept of return on investment has two important applications for a single business entity:

* Evaluating proposed capital additions and other investments on the basis of projected cash flows.[11]
* Measuring the annual rate of return earned on the total assets employed during the period; this analysis is based on accrual accounting results (book values) for each accounting period standing alone.

The discussion in this section relates to the latter application. With an income measure in the numerator, return on the investment for a business is computed on the basis of either average total assets or average total owners' equity (Items 2a and 2b in Exhibit 25–7).

Financial analysts use the two return ratios together to measure *financial leverage* (also called **trading on the equity**). Financial leverage is the effect of borrowing at a higher or lower rate of interest than the rate of return earned on total assets. To illustrate, if a business can borrow at 8% and earn 12% on the funds borrowed, the financial leverage is *positive*. In contrast, if the borrowing rate is 12% and the earnings rate is 8%, the financial leverage is *negative*. Businesses borrow in anticipation of positive financial leverage.

To illustrate the computation of return on total assets, return on owners' equity, and financial leverage, the following data for Merck is restated for convenience (figures in millions):

	1989	1988
Balance Sheet:		
Total assets	$6,756.7	$6,127.5
Total liabilities	$3,236.1	$3,271.7
Total stockholders' equity	$3,520.6	$2,855.8
Income statement:		
Total revenues (pretax)	$6,550.5	
Total expenses (pretax and before interest expense)($4,267.5 − $53.2*)	(4,214.3)	
Interest expense (pretax)	(53.2)	
Pretax income	2,283.0	
Income tax†	(787.6)	
Net income	$1,495.4	

* Interest is given in Note 6 to Merck's financial statements.

† The approximate effective income tax rate is 34.5% ($787.6/$2,283).

Merck's *return on total assets* for 1989 is:

$$\frac{\text{Income} + \text{interest expense after tax}}{\text{Average total assets}} = \frac{\$1,495.4 + \$53.2(1 - .345)}{(\$6,756.7 + \$6,127.5)/2}$$
$$= .24$$

Interest expense (net of income tax) is added back to net income because interest is paid to creditors of the entity. Because the denominator includes the resources provided by both creditors and owners, the numerator must include the return on both types of equities. Therefore, the numerator reflects earnings computed before

---

[11] For a fundamental discussion, see H. Bierman, and S. Smidt, *The Capital Budgeting Decision*, 7th Edition/1988 (New York: Macmillan) or J. Van Horne, *Financial Management and Policy*, (Englewood Cliffs, N.J.: Prentice-Hall, 1987).

these returns. Income before extraordinary items usually should be used to avoid any distortion from nonrecurring and unusual items.

Return on total assets measures the profitability of the total assets available to the business. The ratio indicates the efficiency with which management used the *total* available resources to earn income. A more general return-on-assets measurement, defined as the ratio of income and average total assets,[12] can be expressed as the product of profit margin on sales and asset turnover:

$$\frac{\text{Income}}{\text{Average total assets}} = \frac{\text{Income}}{\text{Net sales}} \times \frac{\text{Net sales}}{\text{Average total assets}}$$

Therefore, the return on total assets can be increased with a larger profit margin on sales or a higher asset turnover. Increased asset turnover can be accomplished by increasing the turnover of assets such as inventory and accounts receivable.

Merck's *return on owners' equity* for 1989 is:

$$\frac{\text{Income}}{\text{Average stockholders' equity}} = \frac{\$1,495.4}{(\$3,520.6 + \$2,855.8)/2} = .47$$

Return on owners' equity measures the return that accrues to the stockholders *after* the interest paid to the creditors is deducted. It does not measure the efficiency with which total resources are used, but rather the *residual return* to the owners on their investment in the business.

The difference between return on owners' equity and return on total assets is financial leverage. The only difference between these two percentages is the effect of debt. The financial leverage for Merck in 1989 is a positive 23% (47% − 24%). The 23% positive effect in favor of owners' equity resulted because the company earned a higher rate of return on total assets than the after-tax rate of interest paid for borrowed resources. Without debt, the rate on total assets equals the rate on owners' equity.

Earnings per Share of Common Stock   This ratio relates income to the average number of common shares outstanding. It reduces income (or loss) to a per share basis. Merck's 1989 EPS of $3.78 appears in the income statement (Exhibit 25–2).[13]

Price-Earnings Ratio (P-E Ratio)   This ratio, sometimes called the *multiple,* is frequently used by analysts and investors for evaluating stock prices because it relates the earnings of the business to the *current market price* of the stock. This ratio changes each time the market price of the stock changes. Years ago, multiples of 20 or more were not unusual; however, multiples in the range of 5 to 15 currently are more common. The multiple usually should be computed on the basis of EPS before extraordinary items. Merck's price-earnings ratio for 1989 (based on Merck's end-of-year market price per share of common stock of about $78) is:

$$\frac{\text{Market price per share}}{\text{Earnings per share}} = \frac{\$78}{\$3.78} = 20.6$$

Merck's P-E ratio is quite high. The primary weakness of this ratio is that only at the end of the fiscal year are the numerator and denominator measured as of the same date. The P-E ratio often is computed during the year using the EPS amount from the most recent financial statements. However, some investment services compensate for this problem to a degree by using a moving quarterly average.

Dividend Payout Ratio   Exhibit 25–7 shows two variations for computing this ratio. The first (5a) relates cash dividends declared on common stock during the reporting

---

[12] This more general measurement does not add back after-tax interest and is presented only to illustrate the disaggregation of return on assets into two other ratios previously discussed.

[13] A previous chapter provided a complete discussion of EPS calculations.

period to the income *available to common stockholders* for that period. This ratio measures the percentage of income that is distributed as cash dividends. For Merck, this ratio for 1989 is:

$$\frac{\text{Cash dividends to common stock}}{\text{Income}} = \frac{\$681.5^*}{\$1,495.5} = .46$$

* Dividends were derived from Merck's statement of cash flows (not reproduced here).

Had there been preferred stock outstanding, the preferred dividends for 1989 would be subtracted from net income before computing the payout ratio. The primary weakness of this ratio is the timing mismatch between the numerator (the dividend declaration date) and the denominator (the end of the reporting period).

The second variation of the ratio (*5b*) relates cash dividends per common share to the ending *market price* of the stock. The ratio gives investors a rough estimate of the return *based on the current market price* of the stock.[14] This ratio for Merck in 1989 is:

$$\frac{\text{Cash dividends per common share}}{\text{Market price of common stock}} = \frac{\$681.5/(455.5 - 60.1)}{\$78} = .02$$

Shareholders receiving dividends in 1989 earned roughly 2% on their investment, measured at the end-of-year market price. One disadvantage of this ratio is the timing mismatch between the numerator (the dividend declaration date) and the denominator (the market price date). Another disadvantage is that investors who purchased Merck stock years ago would more likely compute a payout ratio based on the cost of their investment.

CONCEPT REVIEW

1. What are the four classifications of ratios discussed?
2. What issue does each try to address?
3. What additional value is obtained by examining these ratios over time and across similar firms?

INTERPRETATION AND USE OF RATIOS (PHASE 5)

Ratio analysis of financial statements is used widely along with more sophisticated techniques for making investment and credit decisions. Ratios communicate some aspects of the economic situation of an entity better than the absolute amounts reported in the financial statements. A major disadvantage of ratio analysis, based on financial statement data, is that book values rather than market values are used in many of the computations. Nevertheless, empirical studies demonstrate that the traditional financial ratios are associated with the process by which stock prices are formed.[15]

---

[14] Price appreciation, another component of total return, is not measured by this ratio.

[15] W. Beaver, P. Kettler, and M. Scholes, "The Association between Market Determined and Accounting Determined Risk Measures," *The Accounting Review*, October 1970, pp. 654–82. For an extension of this work, see W. Beaver and J. Manegold, "The Association between Market-Determined and Accounting-Determined Measures of Systematic Risk: Some Further Evidence," *Journal of Financial and Quantitative Analysis*, June 1975, pp. 235–84.

Financial ratios have been used successfully in prediction models to project whether a business would fail.[16] Thus, it is not surprising that financial and bank lending officers make wide use of ratio analysis in evaluating the future economic prospects of individual companies.

Ratios covering periods of more than one year represent average conditions. Therefore, they must be interpreted in light of the smoothing effect inherent in any average. Annual ratios viewed over an extended period of time can signal important *turning points,* either favorable or unfavorable, concerning future economic prospects for the business. However, a ratio for a single period does not always convey a clear message.

A primary problem confronting the statement user is the evaluation of ratios. For example, is an inventory turnover ratio of 12 good or bad? In determining what constitutes a favorable or unfavorable ratio for a particular business, comparisons are necessary:

* Compare the ratios for the current year with those of preceding years for the company. Comparisons of selected ratios for the company over a period of 5 to 10 years often are included in the published financial statements.
* Compare the ratios for the company with budgeted or standard ratios developed internally by the company. Unfortunately, this kind of comparison seldom is possible for external statement users.
* Compare the company's ratios with those of its competitors. The published financial reports of competitors, however, do not always provide information that makes this comparison feasible, given differences in accounting policy among firms.
* Compare the company's ratios with ratios for the industry in which the company operates.

Industry statistics can be obtained from:

* Industry trade associations—Major industries support one or more trade associations that collect and publish financial statistics about the industry.
* Bureaus of business research at universities—Many major universities collect, analyze, and publish a wide range of regional statistics on local industries and businesses.
* Governmental agencies—Agencies that deal directly with business often publish, or have available as a matter of public record, financial information about industries and individual companies. The more prominent ones are the U.S. Department of Commerce, the U.S. Department of the Treasury, and the Securities and Exchange Commission.
* Commercial sources, including Robert Morris Associates and Dun & Bradstreet.

Despite the wide use of ratio analysis, this technique has a number of limitations. Because of these limitations, ratios must be interpreted with some skepticism. Some of the important limitations are:

* Large percentage changes based on small base values typically are not meaningful. Percentages based on negative base figures need to be carefully considered to avoid misinterpretation.
* Ratios represent average conditions that existed in the *past*; they are based on historical data that incorporate all the peculiarities of the past.
* The method of computing each ratio is not standardized. Therefore, the computations (and, hence, the results) can be influenced by data selection choices. Except for EPS, ratios are not subject to audit.

---

[16] E. Altman, "Financial Ratios, Discriminant Analysis, and the Prediction of Corporate Bankruptcy," *Journal of Finance,* September 1968, pp. 589–609; E. Deakin, "A Discriminant Analysis of Predictors of Business Failure," *Journal of Accounting Research,* Spring 1972, pp. 167–79; and R. Libby, "Accounting Ratios and the Prediction of Business Failure: Some Behavioral Evidence, *Journal of Accounting Research,* Spring 1975, pp. 150–61.

- The choice of accounting methods affects ratios. For example, previous chapters have indicated the significant effects on financial statement amounts of such alternatives as FIFO versus LIFO and straight-line versus accelerated depreciation.
- Changes in accounting estimates and principles (such as a change from FIFO to LIFO) affect the ratios for the year of change.
- It is necessary to adjust the data for the effects of unusual or nonrecurring items and extraordinary items where material.
- Most ratios are based on historical book values. Therefore, they reflect neither changes in price level nor current market values.[17]
- Comparisons among companies are difficult. Each company has different operating characteristics including product lines, methods of operation, size, methods of financing, and geographical location. The use of different accounting methods obscures inter-firm comparisons. This is perhaps the most often voiced criticism of ratio analysis. In addition, the failure to adjust historical values for inflation also makes comparisons difficult. The techniques needed to adjust for price level changes are explored in depth in the next major section of this chapter.
- The **efficient market theory** states that all investors have access to the same data and can compute the same ratios. Studies have shown that the market very quickly absorbs publicly available information.[18] As a result, it is extremely difficult to consistently earn above-average returns on stock investments by relying only on publicly available information. Thus, *excessive reliance* on ratio analysis, or any analysis based upon publicly available information, must consider this limitation.

The issue in the latter limitation is to what extent fundamental analysis—as advocated in Graham, Dodd, and Cottle (see footnote 2) and which uses ratio analysis, in large part, to discover undervalued stocks—is refuted by the efficient market theory. Let's consider this issue in greater detail.

The Capital Market Approach

Fundamental analysis attempts to identify under- (or over-) valued stocks by establishing the stock's *intrinsic* value: the value justified by the economic characteristics of the investment. These characteristics include the stock's dividend record, its earnings history, and other factors available in the public record. The analysis also extends to private information not generally available, including the health of key employees and future business prospects. While any knowledge related to the *riskiness* of a particular investment is considered, there is no formal means of evaluating risk.

Those who support the capital market approach relate the expected return on an investment to the risk level assumed if the stock is purchased. The *expected return*, measured by the ratio of expected dividends plus appreciation to the security's price at the start of the period, is higher the greater the risk. Risk, in turn, can be conceptualized as the potential variability in return. Risk is composed of two components, **systematic risk** and **unsystematic risk.** Systematic risk is the average expected change in a security's return for a unit change in the return on a market portfolio of securities. This measure is known as the security's *beta,* a relative risk measure.

To illustrate, consider a stock traded on the New York Stock Exchange (NYSE) with a beta of 2. If a measure of the NYSE market's return (e.g., the S&P 500 Stock Index) rises (falls) by 10%, then the stock is expected to rise (fall), on average, by

---

[17] For example, the introduction to Chapter 14 noted that Corning Glass reported an investment in Owens Corning Fiberglass recorded at $5 million on its balance sheet when this highly liquid asset is worth more than $200 million.

[18] For a summary of this evidence, see W. Beaver, *Financial Reporting: An Accounting Revolution* (Englewood Cliffs, N.J.: Prentice Hall, 1981); and T. Dyckman and D. Morse, *Efficient Capital Markets and Accounting: A Critical Analysis* (Englewood Cliffs, N.J.: Prentice-Hall, 1986). An interesting example of an inefficiency in the market is documented in G. Foster, "Briloff and the Capital Market," *Journal of Accounting Research,* Spring 1979, pp. 262–74.

20% (2 × .10). The important fact is that the risk measure is related to the change in a portfolio of investments.

The second aspect of risk is the unsystematic portion, which does not vary in any predictable way. Unsystematic risk is random. But the investor is fortunate because this risk can be overcome (diversified away) by investing in a portfolio of stocks that can average out the random element. Moreover, it is easy to diversify a stock portfolio.

Since unsystematic risk can be eliminated, the investor can select investments based on their effect on the portfolio held. If the portfolio is of sufficient size and represents major markets, 10 stocks selected across industries is sufficient to remove essentially all of the unsystematic risk.

Capital market efficiency proponents believe that searching for under- or over-valued stocks using fundamental analysis and charting stock prices is a fruitless exercise. The issue of concern instead should be how the riskiness of the particular investment interacts with risk of the investor's current portfolio.

The debate between these alternative approaches continues. The authors believe that the truth lies somewhere between the extremes. While capital market analysis has given us a better understanding of how risk should be evaluated and measured, additional work needs to be done. Moreover, not all investments are traded in well-organized markets. Highly efficient markets rely in part on those who analyze financial information in search of bargains (fundamental analysis). And most important investment decisions rely on additional data beyond that contained in financial reports. Different decisions place different weights across financial data.[19]

Financial statement analysis should be considered in a broader context, namely, as an integral part of an information system designed to provide firm-related data for decision markers.[20] Investors need to search for information to supplement the financial statements. Investors should seek objective data concerning the company—its operations, policies, competitive position, the quality of the management, and other nonquantitative information. Brokerage firms and security analysts gather and disseminate this type of information. Periodic reports by listed companies filed with the SEC are available. They provide considerable information not included in the annual financial statements.

The financial press is a source of timely financial information. Examples of financial publications include *Fortune, Barrons, The Wall Street Journal, Business Week, Forbes,* and various industry publications. These publications are available in most libraries. The last chapter in this text discusses further sources of information beyond the financial statements.

CONCEPT REVIEW

1. What are the major limitations to ratio analysis?
2. What relevance does the idea of efficient capital markets have for financial statement analysis?
3. Where could you look for additional information to supplement the financial statements?

---

[19] J. Patton, "Ratio Analysis and Efficient Markets in Introductory Financial Accounting," *The Accounting Review,* July 1982, pp. 626–30.

[20] See B. Lev, *Financial Statement Analysis: A New Approach* (Englewood Cliffs, N.J.: Prentice-Hall, 1974); and G. Foster, *Financial Statement Analysis* (Englewood Cliffs, N.J.: Prentice-Hall, 1986).

FINANCIAL REPORTING AND CHANGING PRICES

♦

The accounting profession endorses historical cost (HC) as the basis for financial statements. Generally, historical cost financial statement elements are not adjusted for price changes. The historical cost accounting model provides reliable and relevant information when prices are stable.

Historical cost statements are reliable because they are based on objectively verifiable information. However, critics charge that historical cost statements fail to reflect current and relevant information when prices change. Some financial analysts make adjustments for changing prices when calculating ratios discussed in the preceding part of this chapter.

Historical cost financial statements are constructed under the assumption that the dollar is a stable unit of money measurement. This unit is called the **nominal dollar** (ND), one that is not adjusted for changing prices. Historical cost financial statements are stated in nominal dollar terms. The stable unit assumption ignores inflation,[21] and its eroding effect on the purchasing power of the dollar. Historical cost financial statements combine assets and liabilities measured in units of different purchasing power. For example, if total assets includes equipment purchased in 1980 and buildings constructed in 1990, how is the dollar amount of total assets interpreted?

The **constant dollar** (CD), or dollar of constant purchasing power, is the result of adjusting nominal dollars for inflation. For example, assume that $1,000 is invested in a bank account at the beginning of the year. The bank account pays 5% interest. During the year, the inflation rate also is 5%. At the end of the year the account balance is $1,050. The account increased 50 nominal dollars. However, its CD value is not changed. The purchasing power of $1,050 at the end of the year is equivalent to $1,000 at the beginning of the year ($1,000 × 1.05 = $1,050). The investor cannot purchase any more goods and services at the end of the year than at the beginning, assuming the price of all goods and services increased at the rate of inflation. The interest earned exactly offset the effects of inflation on your purchasing power.

Price increases cause reported income for many firms to overstate real or distributable earnings because expenses do not reflect the cost of replacing inventory and plant assets consumed in operations. Assume that a $40,000 plant asset purchased several years ago now costs $160,000 to replace in its present condition. Earnings based on historical cost depreciation overstate the amount available for reinvestment, because the cost to replace the assets has increased substantially. If the company distributes all its reported earnings in dividends, it does not retain sufficient funds for eventual replacement of capacity.

One source estimates that at least one fourth of all major firms paid dividends exceeding inflation-adjusted earnings in the late 1970s.[22] In 1981, total operating earnings for 29 of the Dow 30 industrial companies, adjusted for changes in the prices of specific assets, declined from $31 billion to $13.8 billion. AT&T's 1982 earnings dropped from $6.9 billion to $50 *million,* after adjusting for inflation. Exxon's $4.2 billion historical cost income turned into a $.3 billion *loss* when converted to a current cost basis![23] Which income measurement is more useful to investors and creditors?

The significant inflationary trend during the late 1970s and early 1980s prompted calls for supplementary information on the impact of changing prices on financial statements, and for a change in the accounting model. Historical cost statements were criticized for overstating profits and assets, concealing capital erosion, and invalidating trend and other analyses dependent on a reasonably constant dollar.

---

[21] Because inflation has been pervasive, this discussion illustrates rising prices. However, the concepts discussed also apply to times of generally declining prices (deflation).

[22] "Living Off Capital," *Forbes,* November 10, 1980, p. 232.

[23] "Out of Sight, Out of Mind?" *Forbes,* July 4, 1983, p. 133.

Proponents of this view charged that the historical cost model placed too much emphasis on reliability at the expense of relevance.

The profession recommended supplementary information on the effect of price changes beginning in 1963. Only during the period from 1979 to 1986 were such disclosures required for general financial statement reporting, and only for large companies. *SFAS No. 89,* "Financial Reporting and Changing Prices," removed those disclosure requirements. The FASB presently only recommends the disclosure of this information. The profession has never required that the primary financial statements be restated for price level changes.

General Price Level Changes—Inflation

The price of most goods and services change over time. Changes in supply and demand, technology, quality differences, acquisition and production costs, and government regulations are factors that affect prices. However, the price changes of *specific* goods and services are not necessarily related. For example, in the past, automobile prices generally increased while the prices of consumer electronics products declined. Real estate prices fluctuate according to supply and demand factors, and the strength of the local economy. Although prices in general have increased, certain locales have experienced significant declines in real estate prices.

General price level (GPL) indices report the *general* change in prices. A general price level index is a weighted average of the prices of a representative group or "market basket" of goods and services. The average is set to a base number (e.g., 100) for a particular year. The average for all other years is measured in relation to the base year. Increases in general price level indices define inflation; decreases define deflation.

An example of a GPL index is the **Consumer Price Index for All Urban Consumers** (CPI-U), which is published monthly by the U.S. Department of Labor. This index is based on the prices of food, clothing, housing, fuel, drugs, transportation costs, health care, and other goods and services for everyday living. The base year (1967) weighted average is set to 100. Other general price level indices in wide use are the Gross National Product Implicit Price Deflator, and the Wholesale Price Index.[24] The FASB recommends the CPI-U for financial statement purposes. Exhibit 25–8 lists the CPI-U for a representative period.

For example, in 1950 the group of goods and services used in the CPI-U cost only 72.1% of the cost in 1967. The inflation rate for a period is the percentage change in the CPI-U. Inflation in 1980, a year of very high inflation by U.S. standards, was 13.5%:

$$\frac{\text{CPI-U (1980)} - \text{CPI-U (1979)}}{\text{CPI-U (1979)}} = \frac{247.0 - 217.7}{217.7} = 13.5\%$$

Although small compared to some other countries, the compounded effect of U.S. inflation can be substantial over a period of years. From 1976 through 1990, the CPI-U increased a total of 130% [(391.4 − 170.5)/170.5]. A $10,000 starting salary in 1976 is equivalent to $23,000 in 1990. In addition to the compounding effect of annual inflation, many U.S. corporations have significant operations in countries experiencing much higher inflation rates. The effects of inflation on financial statements can be significant.

Changes in general price level indices and general purchasing power are inversely related. As inflation increases, general purchasing power decreases. For example, in 1990 the purchasing power of the dollar was only 25.5% of that in 1967 (100/391.4). Inflation is an important factor in lending decisions. During times of inflation, creditors lend dollars worth more than those received later in return. Therefore, the

---

[24] No general price level index is perfectly applicable to all individuals or businesses because each purchases a different mix of products and services.

EXHIBIT 25-8   Consumer Price Index for All Urban Consumers (CPI-U)

Year	Annual Average CPI-U Index	Annual Inflation Rate	Year	Annual Average CPI-U Index	Annual Inflation Rate
1950	72.1	—	1980	247.0	13.5%
1955	80.2	2.2%	1981	272.3	10.2
1960	88.7	2.0	1982	288.6	6.0
1965	94.5	1.3	1983	297.4	3.0
1967	**100.0**	2.9	1984	311.1	4.6
1970	116.3	5.2	1985	322.2	3.6
1975	161.2	9.1	1986	328.4	1.9
1976	170.5	5.8	1987	340.4	3.7
1977	181.5	6.5	1988	354.3	4.1
1978	195.3	7.6	1989	371.3	4.8
1979	217.7	11.5	1990	391.4	5.4

interest rate charged includes a component to compensate for this loss. During highly inflationary times, a substantial portion of the interest rate charged by lenders represents compensation for expected inflation.

Restatement of Historical Cost Amounts to Constant Dollars   Many accountants believe that historical cost statements restated to dollars of constant purchasing power improve relevance and comparability. The following formula converts the historical cost/nominal dollar (HC/ND) amounts reported in financial statements in conformance with GAAP, to historical cost/constant dollar (HC/CD) amounts:

$$\text{HC/CD amount} = \text{HC/ND amount} \times \frac{\text{GPL index at end of period}}{\text{GPL index at transaction date}}$$

For example, the \$100,000 cost of equipment purchased when the general price level index[25] was 200 is equivalent in purchasing power terms to \$125,000 at the end of a year for which the general price level index is 250:

$$\$125,000 = \$100,000(250/200)$$

The \$100,000 amount reflects the general price level index of 200, at the date of purchase. This purchasing power denomination cancels with the 200 index in the denominator of the formula ratio, leaving dollars measured in the numerator index.

The resulting HC/CD amount is not necessarily equal to the replacement cost of the equipment, a specific price. Rather, the purchasing power sacrifice made to purchase the equipment when the general price level index was 200 is identical to a sacrifice of \$125,000 when the general price level index is 250. Converting financial statement elements to constant dollars increases comparability because all amounts reflect the same purchasing power. HC/CD restatement is not a departure from historical cost. The restatement only adjusts for changes in the measuring unit.

Monetary and Nonmonetary Items   A financial statement element is classified as a **monetary item** or a nonmonetary item. Monetary assets are money, or claims to receive a fixed amount of dollars. Monetary liabilities are obligations to pay fixed amounts of dollars. These amounts do not change as market prices change. By contrast, **nonmonetary items** are not stated in fixed dollar amounts.

Monetary items include cash, accounts receivable and payable, bonds payable, and most other liabilities. For example a \$4,000 account payable is a claim on exactly

---

[25] Throughout this chapter, assumed general price level indices rather than actual CPI-U indices are used to facilitate computations.

$4,000 cash, regardless of inflation during the term of the payable. Neither inflation nor deflation affects the number of dollars to be received or paid for a monetary item, although inflation erodes the purchasing power of these dollars. Restatement of monetary items to end-of-year constant dollars is not necessary because such items are already stated in end-of-year dollars.

Items which do not fulfill the definition of a monetary item are classified as nonmonetary items.[26] The market value of nonmonetary items is subject to change. Nonmonetary items include inventories, operational assets, investments in stock, and common stock outstanding. Some liabilities also are nonmonetary. For example, a $4,000 estimated warranty liability will probably cost more or less than $4,000 to service. Nonmonetary items are restated to constant dollars as shown in the previous equipment example.

Revenues, expenses, gains, and losses are treated as nonmonetary items. *SFAS No. 89* (par. 96) lists most monetary and nonmonetary items. Several are listed as either monetary or nonmonetary, depending on management intent or the nature of the item.

Purchasing Power Gains and Losses During deflation or inflation, a holder of *monetary* items incurs a **purchasing power gain or loss.** For example, if $10,000 cash is held during a period in which the general price level increases 10%, a $1,000 purchasing power loss is incurred for that period. The cash is worth less at the end of the period because prices in general increased. For the purchasing power to remain the same, $11,000 must be held at the end of the period ($10,000 × 1.10). The $1,000 purchasing power loss is measured in end-of-period dollars.

If $10,000 is owed during the same period, then a $1,000 purchasing power gain is experienced because a smaller purchasing power sacrifice is required at the end of the period to extinguish the liability. Income statements restated for inflation include the net purchasing power gain or loss.

The magnitude of purchasing power gains and losses depends on the amount and mix of monetary items held and on the rate of inflation. Relative to many other countries, inflation in the U.S. has been moderate. For example, Brazil's compounded inflation rate between 1985 and 1990 was 1,000,000%. On average, items costing $1 in 1985 cost $10,000 in 1990.[27] However, many Brazilians benefitted from this hyperinflation. For example, the real cost of payments on mortgages became negligible reflecting enormous purchasing power gains from holding monetary liabilities: "By the end, he was paying the equivalent of a mere $6.50 per month. 'It was costing them more than that to send me the mortgage bill.'"[28]

Refer to Exhibit 25–9 which shows the computation of a purchasing power loss using both monetary assets and liabilities. Perk Company (Exhibit 25–9) began 1991 with a net monetary asset position and increased its holdings of net monetary assets during a period of inflation. Its purchasing power was eroded in 1991 because its actual net monetary asset amount ($25,000) was less than that required to keep pace with inflation ($28,364). The increase in net monetary items during 1991 is the result of income-producing activities as well as investing and financing activities that affected monetary items. The increase is restated to ending constant dollars by the ratio 240/220 because the changes in monetary items occurred evenly during 1991.

Holding *nonmonetary* items during inflationary times does not cause a purchasing power change. Purchasing power gains and losses are defined only for monetary

---

[26] The distinction is not always easily made. An amount reported for bonds payable expected to be extinguished early is a nonmonetary item because the market value fluctuates as interest rates change. Bonds expected to be held to maturity are monetary because the maturity amount is fixed.

[27] "Brazil's Efforts to Curb Inflation Face Hurdle. A Lot of People Like It," *The Wall Street Journal*, March 29, 1991, p. A1.

[28] Ibid.

EXHIBIT 25-9   Perk Company's Computation of Purchasing Power Loss

	January 1, 1991	December 31, 1991
Monetary assets	$20,000	$40,000
Monetary liabilities	10,000	15,000
Net monetary assets	$10,000	$25,000

General price level indices:

January 1, 1991	200
Average, 1991	220
December 31, 1991	240

Changes in monetary items occurred evenly throughout 1991.

Computation of purchasing power loss:

	Nominal Dollars	Restatement Ratio	Constant Dollars*
Net monetary assets, 1/1/91	$10,000	240/200	$12,000
Increase in net monetary assets, 1991	15,000	240/220	16,364
Net monetary assets required at 12/31/91 to keep pace with inflation			28,364
Net monetary assets, 12/31/91	$25,000		25,000
Purchasing power loss, 1991			$ 3,364

* At December 31, 1991.

items. The percentage change in specific prices of nonmonetary items may be different in amount and direction from inflation during the same period.

Specific Price Changes

Because inflation and specific price changes are not necessarily correlated, many accountants maintain that financial statements restated for changes in specific prices yield information more relevant for predicting income and cash flow than inflation-adjusted statements. The result of specific price restatement is a measure of current value. Current value is a departure from historical cost.

The current value of an asset is its value at the present time. Current value depends on the expected disposition of the item. Three alternative measures of current value are present value, exit value, and entry value (current cost).

An asset's *present value* is the discounted amount of its expected future net cash receipts. This amount is a measure of the economic value of the asset. Although theoretically appealing, the estimated present value is not considered reliable for most assets. Uncertainty of cash flows, interaction among assets, and the need to specify the appropriate discount rate render this alternative impractical in most situations.

If the firm plans to sell the asset, its *exit value* is the most appropriate measure of current value. The net amount a firm expects to realize from the sale of an asset through normal sale channels is its net realizable value. Published price lists and offers from buyers are reliable sources of exit values for assets.

The *entry value* of an asset is an estimate of its **current cost** (CC) in its present condition. Entry value can be the cost to either purchase or produce the item. Entry and exit value can differ appreciably. Entry value is consistent with the going concern assumption and the need to periodically replace assets. Exit value is relevant for planned liquidations. The FASB chose entry value as the most appropriate measure of current value.

A firm experiences an unrealized gain or loss when the current cost of an asset increases or decreases. For example, if land purchased for $40,000 at the beginning of the year costs $60,000 at the end of the year, the unrealized holding gain is

$20,000, the increase in current cost. This gain usually is not equal to the effect of inflation.

Current invoice prices, vendor price lists, and standard manufacturing costs are sources of direct price (current cost) information. Specific price indices also are employed to estimate current cost. Firms can use externally published indices relevant to specific assets, or they can develop indices internally. For example, some lumber firms estimate the current cost of lumber by applying industry price indices, which measure the change in lumber costs, to the historical cost of the lumber. The use of specific indices is less costly than obtaining the direct price of each individual item.

CONCEPT REVIEW

1. How is inflation measured?
2. Explain what is meant by a general price level–adjusted amount for land purchased several years ago. Is the amount the current cost of land?
3. Explain why a firm holding a monetary debt experiences a purchasing power gain during a period of inflation.

ALTERNATIVE MODELS OF ACCOUNTING FOR CHANGING PRICES

◆

There are several ways to adjust financial statements for price changes. The main issue is whether to maintain the historical cost basis or to report current cost. A secondary question is whether nominal dollars or constant dollars are more appropriate. These alternatives combine to form four alternative accounting models for financial reporting listed in Exhibit 25–10.

The HC/ND model, required by GAAP for primary financial statements, does not adjust for price level changes. The HC/CD model retains historical cost as the costing basis, but restates amounts to constant dollars by using the general price level restatement ratio. The CC/ND model reports current costs without adjusting for changes in the purchasing power of the dollar. The CC/CD model also reports current costs but in dollars of constant purchasing power. General price level adjustments restate amounts for changes in the value of the dollar and are appropriate for both the historical cost and current cost bases.

The following basic example of the four models emphasizes the advantages and disadvantages of each. Later sections give expanded illustrations of the HC/CD and CC/CD models.

Assumptions for the example:

1. Aido Company purchases inventory costing $8,000 on January 1, 1992. The general price level index is 120 on this date.
2. Aido sells the inventory on December 31, 1992, for $13,000. On this date, the cost to replace the inventory is $11,000, and the general price level index is 150. Assume no other expenses or transactions.

Historical Cost/Nominal Dollar

The 1992 HC/ND (GAAP) income statement for Aido follows:

Sales	$13,000
Cost of goods sold	8,000
Net income	$ 5,000

Aido must replace inventory to stay in business, assuming no major changes in operations or markets. The $13,000 cash received from the sale covers the replace-

EXHIBIT 25-10   Four Models for Financial Reporting

Costing Basis	Measurement Units	
	Nominal Dollars	**Constant Dollars**
Historical Cost	Historical Cost/ Nominal Dollar (HC/ND)	Historical Cost/ Constant Dollar (HC/CD)
Current Cost	Current Cost/ Nominal Dollar (CC/ND)	Current Cost/ Constant Dollar (CC/CD)

ment of the inventory ($11,000 at current cost) and leaves $2,000 for dividends. If Aido intends to replace the inventory and distribute all $5,000 of historical cost income as dividends, the firm must use $3,000 of funds earned previously or obtain the additional funds from the capital markets. Under these circumstances, the HC/ND model overstates **distributable income,** the amount that can be paid without eroding capital. The use of historical cost depreciation (not illustrated) causes an additional overstatement of distributable income, by understating the amount of resources that must be retained for eventual replacement of plant assets.

If Aido continued to hold the inventory at the end of 1992, the balance sheet would disclose $8,000 of inventory. This amount understates the inventory's current value. On a larger scale, this undervaluation can seriously affect assessments of firm value. In addition, the balance sheet reports assets measured in dollars of different purchasing power.

The income statement also reflects this problem. Net income is the difference between sales, measured when the general price level was 150, while the cost of goods sold is measured when the general price level was 120. Net income is difficult to interpret under these conditions.

Increases in the general price level index also distort rates of return involving plant assets. The historical cost model understates the current cost of the denominator, average total assets. The use of historical cost depreciation also overstates the numerator. Both factors serve to overstate the ratios. A study of companies disclosing constant dollar and current cost information found that average return on investment (operating income divided by net assets) based on the HC/ND model was 14.3% in 1981. However, it was only 2.9% and 2.5% on the HC/CD and CC/CD models, respectively.[29]

Although the HC/ND model does not directly adjust for price changes, some disclosures and reported account balances reflect current costs. For example, the lower-of-cost-or-market method applied to inventory and investments requires write-down to market if cost exceeds market value. Also, write-downs of assets to market are permitted for permanent declines in the value of plant assets and investments, and in quasi reorganizations.

Historical Cost/Constant Dollar

The 1992 HC/CD income statement for Aido follows:

Sales	$13,000	
Cost of goods sold	10,000	$8,000(150/120)
Net income	$ 3,000	

---

[29] K. Evans and R. Freeman, "*Statement 33* Disclosures Confirm Profit Illusion in Primary Statements," *FASB Viewpoints* (Norwalk, Conn.: FASB, June 1983).

This reporting basis maintains historical cost; it changes only the measuring unit and reports all account balances in dollars that have the same purchasing power. The adjustment for the general price level change between the purchase and sale of inventory results in restating inventory to $10,000. This amount is equivalent in purchasing power to $8,000 when the inventory was purchased. Sales occurred at the end of 1992: therefore, the reported amount equals the HC/CD amount.

Net income under HC/CD is less than its HC/ND counterpart because cost of goods sold now reflects inflation. To the extent that inflation and specific price level changes are correlated, HC/CD income is an improvement over HC/ND. However, HC/CD income does not necesssarily reflect distributable income ($2,000).

If Aido continued to hold the inventory at the end of 1992, the general price level–adjusted balance sheet would disclose $10,000 of inventory. This amount is closer to current cost ($11,000) than is the $8,000 amount reported under HC/ND. For Aido to maintain its purchasing power, the inventory must be worth $10,000. All nonmonetary balance sheet items are adjusted to the ending general price level index, resulting in a common measuring unit that improves comparability and understandability. Monetary items automatically reflect the ending general price level index.

HC/CD maintains the historical cost basis and is significantly less costly than either current cost model because general price level indices are readily available and relatively easy to apply. The model is objective and reliable, eliminates the effect of inflation, and can reduce the incentive to use accounting methods that partially compensate for inflation. These methods include LIFO and accelerated depreciation. Furthermore, the net purchasing power gain or loss is reported as an element of income (illustrated in a later comprehensive example) to disclose the economic effect of holding monetary items during inflation.

Current Cost/Nominal Dollar

This model is better understood by using a two-period example with the following information:

1. Aido Company purchases inventory on January 1, 1991, for $6,000 when the general price level index was 100.
2. At January 1, 1992, Aido still holds the inventory. On this date, the current cost of the inventory is $8,000 and the general price level index is 120.
3. Aido sells the inventory on December 31, 1992, for $13,000. On this date, the current cost to replace the inventory is $11,000, and the general price level index is 150. Assume no other expenses or transactions.

Item 1 adds to the data originally given; the rest remains unchanged. The 1991 and 1992 CC/ND income statements for Aido follow:

	1991	1992
Sales . . . . $	0	$13,000
Cost of goods sold		
at CC	0	11,000
CC operating income	0	2,000
Realized holding gain	0	5,000 †
Realized income	0	7,000
Unrealized holding		
gain (loss)	2,000 *	(2,000)‡
CC net income	$2,000	$5,000

* $8,000 − $6,000, the increase in current cost during 1991.

† $11,000 − $6,000, the realized increase in current cost during the period the inventory was held (1991 and 1992).

‡ The portion of the realized holding gain recognized in 1991.

The holding gain in 1991 is unrealized because the inventory was not sold in 1991.[30] Yet the income statement under this model recognizes the increase in the value of the inventory. Current cost operating income for 1992 is the amount that is earned by operations and that can be distributed without eroding capital. This amount is the real increase in value of the firm, the value added to the inventory. Current cost operating income reflects the current cost of expenses and sales, and is useful for predicting future current cost operating income. Ultimately, operations must provide sufficient resources for replacement of inventory and other assets consumed in operations.

The $5,000 realized holding gain represents the majority of the HC/ND earnings of $7,000 ($13,000 − $6,000) in 1992. The CC/ND model separates total 1992 income into distributable operating income and holding gain. The entire holding gain is realized in 1992 because the inventory was sold in this period. The portion of the 1992 realized holding gain recognized in 1991 is subtracted in 1992 to avoid double counting. Total CC/ND realized income is the sum of realized holding gain and current cost operating income which equals HC/ND income ($7,000).

The 1991 balance sheet reports $8,000 of inventory at current cost. If Aido continued to hold the inventory at the end of 1992, the balance sheet would report the inventory at $11,000 (current cost). All other assets and liabilities would also reflect current cost. The current cost of depreciable assets is reduced by depreciation based on current cost.

CC/ND is appealing because it reports operating income only after allowing for the maintenance of physical capital, and it uses specific prices rather than general price level indices. Proponents of the CC/ND model argue that CC/ND income is an improved basis for predicting income and cash flows, for computing income tax, for determining dividends and for use in wage disputes. The model distinguishes returns *of* invested physical capital ($11,000) from returns *on* physical capital ($2,000).

There is some disagreement with the premise that HC/ND income generally is overstated during inflationary times. Although the model does not consider the current cost of existing capacity, many firms are able to raise prices during inflation to offset increased costs. American Medical International makes this point in the Management Discussion and Analysis section of its 1989 annual report:

> Although a significant portion of the Company's operating costs are subject to inflationary increases, the Company believes that through price increases and the management of operating costs, the effects of inflation on future operating margins should be minimal.

Also, maintaining existing capital is not an appropriate strategy for certain companies. For example, firms in the motion picture and natural resources industries typically do not replace existing assets. Furthermore, current cost income does not reflect the effect of debt financing of plant assets. Debt is a hedge against inflation because it is repaid with cheaper dollars.

The high cost and questionable reliability of current cost estimates are disadvantages of the current cost models. The FASB defines the current cost of plant assets as the cost of acquiring the service potential supplied by existing assets.[31] Considerable judgment is required to estimate current cost for many assets. Adjustments are made for differences in useful life, output capacity, and operating costs. Most firms use external specific price indices to estimate current costs. A study of these indices found that current cost is often overstated, resulting in underestimated CC/ND earnings.[32] Another study found that the time requirements for complying with

---

[30] For assets acquired during the year, beginning CC equals HC at acquisition. For assets sold during the year, ending CC is the CC on the date sold.

[31] *SFAS No. 89*, par. 18.

[32] K. Shriver, "An Empirical Examination of the Potential Measurement Error in Current Cost Data," *The Accounting Review*, January 1987, pp. 79–96.

SFAS No. 33, "Financial Reporting and Changing Prices," which required both HC/CD and CC/CD disclosures, ranged from 100 to 4,800 hours annually.[33] A substantial portion of this effort was spent estimating current cost.

However, many believe that the CC/ND model is a considerable improvement over the previous two models. Unfortunately, it fails to separate the effects of inflation and the real change in the inventory's current cost. For example, Aido's wealth did not increase $2,000 in 1991 because the general purchasing power of the dollar declined that year. The income statement under the CC/ND model reflects dollars of several different purchasing power levels. *SFAS No. 89* does not recommend the CC/ND model, and requires that current cost be restated to dollars of constant purchasing power if the recommended disclosures are presented. The next section briefly illustrates the resulting CC/CD model.

Current Cost/Constant Dollar

To illustrate this model, assume the original one-period data (1992 only). The 1992 CC/CD income statement for Aido would be:

Sales	$13,000
Cost of goods sold at CC	11,000
CC operating income	2,000
Realized holding gain, net of inflation	1,000 *
CC net income	$3,000

* Computation of holding gain, net of inflation:

Increase in current cost of inventory, $11,000 − $8,000	$3,000
Effect of inflation, $8,000(150–120)/120	2,000
Increase in current cost of inventory, net of inflation	$1,000

This model adjusts current cost for inflation and reports the holding gain in constant dollars. Inflation accounts for $2,000 of the increase in current cost. In this example, the specific price of inventory increased faster than the general rate of inflation.

If Aido continued to hold the inventory at the end of 1992, the balance sheet would report $11,000 at current cost. The balance sheet reports assets at current cost, measured in end-of-period constant dollars.

The CC/CD model has many of the same advantages and disadvantages as the CC/ND model, especially as regards capital maintenance. All financial statement items are stated in terms of the same purchasing power, enhancing comparability. This model is discussed at greater length in a comprehensive example.

History and Usefulness of Price Level-Adjusted Financial Statements

Accounting for price changes is one of the most controversial issues in the history of the profession. A brief chronology of important events pertaining to this issue follows:

1963: *Accounting Research Study No. 6,* "Reporting the Financial Effects of Price Level Changes," recommends supplementary disclosure of inflation effects (HC/CD).

1969: *Accounting Principles Board Statement No. 3,* "Financial Statements Restated for General Price Level Changes," states that HC/CD financial statements

---

[33] R. Perry and J. Searfoss, "Eleven Companies' Approach to Changing Prices as of December 31, 1981," Memorandum to FASB, Touche Ross, 1982.

present useful information but are not required for fair presentation of financial statements at this time.

1974: *Exposure Draft,* "Financial Reporting in Units of General Purchasing Power," suggests that financial statements include supplementary information on an HC/CD basis. The FASB withdraws the *Exposure Draft* after a field-test, citing lack of understanding by users and preparers, and their conclusion that costs exceed benefits.

1976: *SEC Accounting Series Release (ASR) No. 190,* "Disclosures of Certain Replacement Cost Data," requires in the 10-K annual report supplementary replacement cost (specific price) disclosures about inventories, operational assets, cost of goods sold, and depreciation for large publicly held companies. This is the first time companies are *required* to present financial statement information adjusted for price level changes.

1979: *SFAS No. 33,* "Financial Reporting and Changing Prices," requires large companies to disclose both HC/CD and CC/CD supplementary information. The primary financial statements are not affected. Publicly held companies that reported more than $125 million of inventories and tangible operational assets, or $1 billion of total assets, were subject to *SFAS No. 33.* This statement is issued as an experiment to determine the usefulness of price level–adjusted information. The FASB pledges a review within five years. The SEC withdraws *ASR No. 190.*

1980–1982: FASB issues several *SFASs* modifying the disclosure requirements for special industries.

1982–1984: FASB eliminates HC/CD disclosure requirements because the reporting of two methods detracts from the usefulness of the information. The FASB concludes that CC/CD is more useful. *SFAS No. 70* (1982) eliminates the HC/CD disclosure requirement for firms not using the dollar as the functional currency, and *SFAS No. 82* (1984) eliminates HC/CD disclosures for all other firms.

1983: The FASB surveys financial statement users, preparers, and auditors about *SFAS No. 33* requirements. Both the number of users and extent of use is found to be limited. Most respondents to a subsequent *Exposure Draft* (1984) recommend revocation of the requirements.

1986: *SFAS No. 89,* "Financial Reporting and Changing Prices," supersedes prior *SFASs* on this topic and revokes *SFAS No. 33* requirements, but continues to recommend supplementary disclosure of price change effects. *SFAS No. 89* includes an extensive appendix providing guidance on preparing the disclosures. The disclosures, *no longer mandatory,* include both HC/CD and CC/CD adjusted information (discussed in a later section).

The profession has run full circle—from recommending price level adjustments, to requiring them, and now back to recommending them only. The profession's level of concern with the issue of price level–adjusted financial statements is related to the rate of inflation. For example, the increased interest in required disclosures developed in the 1970s, a period of increasing inflation (see Exhibit 25–8), culminating in *SFAS No. 33* in 1979, a year in which inflation was 11.5%. Then, in the mid-1980s, inflation subsided, as did the interest in inflation disclosures.

SFAS No. 89, which revoked the requirement to disclose price level–adjusted financial statement information, was approved by a four-to-three vote. Dissenting Board members believed that the issue of accounting for changing price levels is one of the most important to face the profession and argued that the requirements should remain in force. They maintain that *SFAS No. 33* was the beginning of a larger project that should be completed, and that five years is not sufficient for proper evaluation.

Are price level–adjusted financial statements useful? Although complete agreement is not possible on such an issue, a substantial body of research suggests that the disclosures required in *SFAS No. 33* added almost no incremental information beyond that supplied by HC/ND earnings. Furthermore, use of the information was minimal.

> In fact, Wall Street has never really paid much attention to the numbers at all. Arthur Young recently surveyed financial analysts to see whether they use the information, which, although unaudited, is included in large companies' annual reports. Only about half the analysts reported that they use the data at all. And cynics say even that estimate is inflated by analysts embarrassed to admit they are ignoring any corporate data.[34]

Several factors contributed to the repeal of *SFAS No. 33*. The statement was adopted in 1979, during the height of U.S. inflation. However, the inflation rate declined significantly after 1981, the last year of double-digit inflation. Many firms maintained that the costs of complying with *SFAS No. 33* greatly outweighed the benefit.

Many respondents to the FASB survey and exposure drafts complained that the requirements were too complex. Others indicated that a complete set of adjusted financial statements would improve the usefulness of the disclosures. Requiring that they be audited would enhance the quality of the disclosures. In addition, governmental (SEC) interest in continuing the requirements diminished.

Most studies of these disclosures found insufficient justification for requiring them.[35] A few studies found information content in price level–adjusted disclosures, but the preponderance of work suggests that the disclosures, at least in the form required by *SFAS No. 33*, were not worth the cost.[36]

Few companies voluntarily report the information recommended by *SFAS No. 89*.[37] However, those subject to SEC reporting requirements must comment on any material effects of general and specific price level changes on the financial statements. For example GATX, a major manufacturer of capital equipment for transportation, storage, and processing of materials, included the following in the financial review section of its 1989 annual report:

> GATX finances substantially all of its fixed assets with long-term debt which effectively hedges against the impact of inflation on depreciation expense. Further, most of these assets are on lease to customers. Such leases cover varying periods of time but, importantly, upon renewal permit GATX to address the impact of inflation.

A minority view holds that price level–adjusted information is worth its cost. Some U.S. firms with operations in countries experiencing high inflation rates use inflation–adjusted accounting for internal purposes. For example, FMC Corporation extensively used price level-adjusted financial information for its subsidiaries in Brazil, Argentina, and Mexico.[38]

Although many firms complained about the cost of complying with *SFAS No. 33*, others approved of the requirements and used them to advocate lower corporate tax rates and to justify lower dividends. Significantly reduced inflation-adjusted earnings were used as an argument for reduced government interference in general.

---

[34] "Out of Sight, Out of Mind?" *Forbes*, July 4, 1983, p. 133.

[35] See for example, B. Ro, "The Disclosure of Replacement Cost Accounting Data and Its Effect on Transaction Volume," *The Accounting Review*, January 1981, pp. 70–84, which suggests that the *ASR No. 190* disclosures had no effect on trading volume. W. Beaver and W. Landsman, *Incremental Information Content of Statement 33 Disclosures* (Norwalk, Conn.: FASB, 1983); W. Beaver and S. Ryan, "How Well Do *Statement No. 33* Earnings Explain Stock Returns," *Financial Analysts Journal*, September–October 1985, pp. 66–71; and J. Ketz, "Are Constant Dollar Disclosures Informative?" *Financial Analysts Journal*, March–April 1983, pp. 52–55, found little or no incremental information content over HC earnings.

[36] See E. Noreen and J. Sepe, "Market Reactions to Accounting Policy Deliberations: The Inflation Accounting Case," *The Accounting Review*, April 1981, pp. 253–269; and G. Lobo and I. Song, "The Incremental Information in *SFAS No. 33* Income Disclosures over HC Income and Its Cash and Accrual Components," *The Accounting Review*, April 1989, pp. 329–343.

[37] For example, none of the 600 companies surveyed in the 1990 edition of *Accounting Trends & Techniques* (AICPA, New York) chose to voluntarily disclose general or specific price level–adjusted financial statement information.

[38] "Experiment Abandoned?" *Forbes*, November 18, 1985, p. 218.

The lack of interest in price level disclosures may be due in part to an inability to understand and use the information. Users might benefit from a longer adjustment period. Improvement in the format and substance of the disclosures is possible. If significant inflation rates return, the long process of developing pronouncements to effectively address price level changes could be repeated. Accounting systems will be recreated, but the continuity of data will be lost. The Board stated that it will continue to consider the complex issues surrounding the financial statement effects of price changes.

CONCEPT REVIEW

1. Why are certain current cost amounts restated to constant dollars in the CC/CD model?
2. How does current cost operating income measure whether physical capital is maintained?
3. Prepare an argument against requiring price level–adjusted financial statements.

COMPREHENSIVE ILLUSTRATION: HC/CD FINANCIAL STATEMENTS

◆

Preparation of complete HC/CD financial statements requires restating all nonmonetary items to the general price level index at the end of the year, and computing the purchasing power gain or loss on monetary items. The purchasing power gain or loss is a component of HC/CD earnings.

HC/CD statements can be prepared as of any date. The following example uses the end-of-year general price level as the measure of constant dollars because it is the most current and requires no adjustment for monetary items. The alternative—the average-of-year general price level—alleviates the need to adjust many revenue and expense items that occur evenly throughout the year.[39]

Monetary items are restated when amounts from HC/CD statements of prior years are rolled forward to current year constant dollars,[40] and when HC/CD statements are restated to the average general price level index for the year, if this alternative is chosen. Restating monetary items does not imply that their fixed value has changed. Rather, *any* constant dollar amount must reflect the general price level index as of the statement date. These two situations are not illustrated because they do not change the procedures. However, the end-of-chapter material gives examples.

Exhibit 25–11 presents the HC/ND (GAAP) financial statements, general price level indices, and additional data to illustrate preparation of HC/CD statements for Phog Company. This data supports Exhibits 25–12 through 25–14. In these exhibits, M refers to monetary items, and NM to nonmonetary items.

HC/CD Balance Sheet   Exhibit 25–12 presents the HC/CD balance sheet. The objective of restating the HC/ND balance sheet for general price level changes is to report historical cost assets, liabilities, and owners' equity at their constant dollar equivalents.

---

[39] *SFAS No. 89*, par. 8, recommends use of either average or ending CPI-U as the measure of constant purchasing power.

[40] Comparative financial statements are restated to the ending general price level index of the most recent year using the restatement ratio: (ending GPL index for most recent year ÷ ending GPL index for the year reported comparatively).

EXHIBIT 25-11   Phog Company Case Data for Preparing HC/CD Financial Statements

General Price Level Indices and Ratios

Date	GPL Index
1/1/1986	127
3/31/1987	138
12/31/1990	147
3/31/1991	149
6/30/1991	151
9/30/1991	154
12/31/1991	159

Period

Average, 4th quarter 1990	146
Average, 4th quarter 1991	157
Average, full year 1991	152

Summary of Transactions During 1991

a. Sales of $144,000 were made evenly during the year (assume all on credit).

b. Purchases of $85,000 were made evenly during the year (assume all on credit).

c. The equipment is depreciated 4% per year with no residual value; the equipment was purchased on January 1, 1986, when the GPL index was 127.

d. The long-term investment in common stock of Smith Company was acquired for $25,000 on March 31, 1987, when the GPL index was 138. On December 30, 1991, when the GPL index was 159, half of these shares (i.e., cost of $12,500) were sold for $15,000 cash.

e. General expenses (including interest) of $20,000 were accrued and paid evenly during the year.

f. Collections on accounts receivable, $135,000, were made evenly during the year.

g. Payments on accounts payable, $80,000, were made evenly during the year.

h. A $10,000 cash dividend was declared at midyear when the GPL index was 151. It was paid one month later.

i. The parking garage was acquired January 1, 1991, when the GPL index was 147; issued 12% note payable, $50,000 to finance the purchase; interest is paid quarterly.

j. The parking garage is depreciated 4% per year with no residual value.

k. Issued common stock for cash on September 30, 1991, when the GPL index was 154; cash received, $60,000. The initial $100,000 of common stock was issued on January 1, 1986, when the GPL index was 127.

l. Income tax of $10,000 was accrued evenly during the year. For instructional convenience, assume that all of it will be paid in 1992.

m. The December 31, 1991, inventory was $25,000 (FIFO basis; LCM = cost).

n. Ending 1990 retained earnings on a HC/CD basis is $43,604.

(Exhibit continued on next page.)

Monetary Items   Because monetary items are stated in terms of the December 31, 1991, general price level index, their HC/ND and HC/CD amounts are the same.

Nonmonetary Items   The restatement ratio for each nonmonetary item uses the ending 1991 general price level index (159) as the numerator and the general price level index at transaction date as the denominator. For example, Phog purchased the ending inventory evenly during the fourth quarter during which the average general price level index was 157. Therefore, the restatement ratio is 159/157.

Phog first issued common stock on January 1, 1986, when the general price level index was 127. Phog subsequently issued additional stock on September 30, 1991, when the general price level index was 154. The two issuances are restated separately as shown in the second note of Exhibit 25-12.

EXHIBIT 25-11   *(concluded)*

Comparative Balance Sheets,
HC/ND at December 31, 1991

	12/31/1991 HC/ND (from Books)	12/31/1990 HC/ND (from Books)
Assets		
M Cash	$136,000	$ 36,000
M Accounts receivable (net)	33,000	24,000
NM Inventory (FIFO)	25,000	20,000
NM Investment in common stock	12,500	25,000
NM Equipment	100,000	100,000
NM Accumulated depreciation, equipment	(24,000)	(20,000)
NM Parking garage	50,000	—
NM Accumulated depreciation, parking garage	(2,000)	—
Total assets	$330,500	$185,000
Liabilities		
M Accounts payable	$ 45,000	$ 40,000
M Income tax payable	10,000	—
M Note payable, 12%	50,000	—
Stockholders' Equity		
NM Common stock, nopar	160,000	100,000
NM Retained earnings	65,500	45,000
Total liabilities and stockholders' equity	$330,500	$185,000

M = Monetary item.

Nm = Nonmonetary item.

Income Statement
HC/ND, for the Year Ended December 31, 1991
(All Items are NM)

	HC/ND (from Books)
Sales revenue	$144,000
Gain on sale of investment	2,500
Total revenues and gains	146,500
Cost of goods sold*	80,000
General expenses (including interest)	20,000
Depreciation expense, equipment	4,000
Depreciation expense, garage	2,000
Income tax expense	10,000
Total expenses	116,000
Net income	$ 30,500

* Cost of goods sold (FIFO):	
Inventory, beginning (1/1/1991)	$ 20,000
Purchases (all on credit)	85,000
Goods available for sale	105,000
Inventory, ending (12/31/1991)	(25,000)
Cost of goods sold	$ 80,000

Retained Earnings Statement
HC/ND, for the Year Ended December 31, 1991
(All Items Are NM)

Beginning balance, January 1, 1991	$ 45,000
Add: Net income for 1991	30,500
Deduct: Dividends declared during 1991	(10,000)
Ending balance, December 31, 1991	$ 65,500

EXHIBIT 25-12 Phog Company HC/CD Restated Balance Sheet

Summary of Acquisition Dates and GPL Index Values for Nonmonetary Items

a. Ending 1990 and 1991 inventories were acquired evenly throughout the fourth quarter; GPL indices, 146 and 157.

b. Investment in common stock of Smith Company was acquired March 31, 1987; GPL index, 138.

c. Equipment was acquired on January 1, 1986; GPL index, 127.

d. Accumulated depreciation, equipment, restated on same basis as related asset account.

e. Parking garage was acquired on January 1, 1991; GPL index, 147.

f. Accumulated depreciation, parking garage, restated on same basis as related asset account.

g. Original issue of common stock, $100,000, on January 1, 1986; GPL index, 127. Subsequent issuance of common stock, $60,000, on September 30, 1991; GPL index 154.

HC/CD Balance Sheet
At December 31, 1991

	HC/ND (from Books)	CD Restatement Ratio*	HC/CD
Assets			
Cash	$136,000	Monetary	$136,000
Accounts receivable (net)	33,000	Monetary	33,000
Inventory	25,000	159/157	25,325
Investment in common stock	12,500	159/138	14,400
Equipment	100,000	159/127	125,200
Accumulated depreciation, equipment	(24,000)	159/127	(30,048)
Parking garage	50,000	159/147	54,100
Accumulated depreciation, parking garage	(2,000)	159/147	(2,164)
Total assets	$330,500		$355,813
Liabilities			
Accounts payable	$ 45,000	Monetary	$ 45,000
Income tax payable	10,000	Monetary	10,000
Note payable, 12%	50,000	Monetary	50,000
Stockholders' Equity			
Common stock, nopar	160,000	†	187,120
Retained earnings	65,500	Bal. amt.	63,693‡
Total liabilities and stockholders' equity	$330,500		$355,813

* The CD restatement ratios are rounded to three decimals and then applied to the HC/ND amounts.

† Original common stock restatement (GPL index at issuance, 127):

$100,000 × (159/127) $125,200

1991 common stock issuance restatement (GPL index at issuance, 154):

$60,000 × (159/154) 61,920

Common stock restated in CDs $187,120

‡ See also Exhibit 25-14

HC/CD retained earnings is a balancing amount in Exhibit 25-12. Exhibit 25-14, illustrating the restated income and retained earnings statements, proves the ending $63,693 balance.

Purchasing Power Gain or Loss   Phog reported $60,000 of monetary assets ($36,000 cash and $24,000 accounts receivable) and $40,000 of monetary liabilities (accounts payable) at the beginning of 1991 (Exhibit 25-11). Therefore, Phog started 1991 in a $20,000 net monetary asset position. During the year, Phog completed transactions affecting monetary assets and liabilities.

The beginning net monetary asset amount, plus the increases and minus the decreases in HC/ND net monetary assets that occurred during the year, equals the ending HC/ND net monetary asset (or net monetary liability) amount. Exhibit 25-13

EXHIBIT 25-13   Phog Company Purchasing Power Loss for Year Ended December 31, 1991

	HC/ND	CD Restatement Ratio*	HC/CD
Net monetary items—increases (decreases):			
1. Total beginning net monetary assets	$ 20,000†	159/147	$ 21,640
2. Increases in net monetary assets during 1991 from:			
Sales revenue	144,000	159/152	150,624
Sale of investment	15,000	159/159	15,000
Sale and issuance of common stock	60,000	159/154	61,920
3. Decreases in net monetary assets during 1991 from:			
Purchases	(85,000)	159/152	(88,910)
General expenses (including interest)	(20,000)	159/152	(20,920)
Income tax expense	(10,000)	159/152	(10,460)
Cash dividends declared‡	(10,000)	159/151	(10,530)
Parking garage acquisition	(50,000)	159/147	(54,100)
4. Total ending net monetary assets:			
HC	$ 64,000§		
HC/CD			$ 64,264
5. Purchasing power gain (loss) on net monetary items; to income statement, HC, $64,000 − HC/CD, $64,264; a positive remainder is a gain and a negative remainder is a loss:			$ (264)

* The CD restatement ratios are rounded to three decimals and then applied to the HC/ND amounts.

† Computation from 1990 balance sheet: cash, $36,000 + accounts receivable, $24,000 − accounts payable, $40,000 = $20,000 (may be positive or negative; positive in this case).

‡ Declaration date, not payment date, is relevant to the CD restatement of cash dividends because on declaration date, the entity incurs a monetary liability and, hence, decreases net monetary assets. Subsequent payment has no effect on net monetary assets because payment involves monetary items only.

§ Computation from 1991 balance sheet; cash, $136,000 + accounts receivable, $33,000 − accounts payable, $45,000 − income tax payable, $10,000 − note payable, $50,000 = $64,000.

shows that the ending HC/ND net monetary asset amount is $64,000. To determine the effect of inflation on purchasing power, this amount is compared to its counterpart restated for inflation.

The general price level–adjusted ending net monetary asset amount is computed by restating the beginning HC/ND net monetary asset balance and all changes in monetary items during the year, to the ending general price level index.[41] These adjustments are performed individually because the changes in monetary items did not occur simultaneously. Sales of goods and services, operational assets, and common stock cause net monetary assets to increase. In contrast, purchases, expenses, declaration of dividends, and acquisitions of nonmonetary assets cause net monetary assets to decrease.

Exhibit 25–13 shows that the general price level–adjusted counterpart to the ending HC/ND net monetary assets equals $64,264. If Phog holds $64,264 in net monetary assets, its position kept pace with inflation. But monetary items, by definition, cannot keep pace with inflation because they are fixed in amount. Phog has only $64,000 of net monetary assets. Hence, Phog incurred a $264 purchasing power loss in 1991. This amount is placed into the HC/CD income statement (shown in Exhibit 25–14) to follow.

In general, maintaining a net monetary asset position during inflation results in a purchasing power loss; holding a net monetary liability position produces a gain

---

[41] If the accounts affected by revenue and expense recognition are monetary (such as cash, accounts receivable), then they are considered in the purchasing power gain or loss. If not (e.g. depreciation), they do not affect the purchasing power gain or loss.

EXHIBIT 25-14 Phog Company HC/CD Restated Income Statement and Retained Earnings
Statement for Year Ended December 31, 1991

HC/CD Income Statement	HC/ND (from Books)	CD Restatement Ratio*	HC/CD
Sales revenue	$144,000	159/152	$150,624
Gain on sale of investment	2,500	†	600
Total revenues and gains	146,500		151,224
Cost of goods sold	80,000	‡	85,365
General expenses (including interest)	20,000	159/152	20,920
Depreciation expense, equipment	4,000	159/127	5,008
Depreciation expense, garage	2,000	159/147	2,164
Income tax expense	10,000	159/152	10,460
Total expenses	116,000		123,917
Net income	$ 30,500		
HC/CD income before purchasing power loss on net monetary items			27,307
Purchasing power loss on net monetary items (Exhibit 25-13)			(264)
HC/CD income			$ 27,043

* The CD restatement ratios are rounded to three decimals and then
applied to the HC/ND amounts

† Entry to record sale of investment (12/30/1991):

Cash	15,000	159/159	15,000
Investment in common stock ($25,000 ÷ 2)	12,500	159/138	14,400
Gain on sale of investment	2,500	Bal. amt.	600

‡ Cost of goods sold:

Inventory 1/1/1991	$ 20,000	159/146	$ 21,780
Purchases	85,000	159/152	88,910
Goods available for sale	105,000		110,690
Inventory, 12/31/1991 (Exhibit 25-11)	$(25,000)	159/157	(25,325)
Cost of goods sold	$ 80,000		$ 85,365

HC/CD Retained Earnings Statement

	HC/CD
Beginning balance January 1, 1991, HC/CD balance from prior year, ($43,604 × 159/147)	$47,180
Add: Net income for 1991 (above)	27,043
Deduct: Dividends, 1991 ($10,000 × 159/151)	(10,530)
Ending balance, December 31, 1991	$63,693

during inflation. During inflation, if the restated ending net monetary asset balance exceeds the actual net monetary asset balance (Phog's situation), a purchasing power loss occurs. Suppose Phog began the year in a net monetary liability position. During inflation, if the restated ending net monetary liability balance exceeds the actual ending net monetary liability balance, a purchasing power gain occurs. Here, the company has less net monetary debt than if its position kept pace with inflation.[42]

HC/CD Income Statement   The objective of restating the historical cost income statement for general price level changes is to report the historical cost revenues, expenses, gains, and losses at their ending 1991 constant dollar equivalents. The restatement

---

[42] If a company begins a period with net monetary assets and ends with net monetary liabilities, it is helpful to convert the beginning asset position to a negative liability position to facilitate the computation. For example, a $10,000 net monetary asset position is equivalent to a negative $10,000 net monetary liability position.

procedure is the same as that applied to the balance sheet. Exhibit 25–14 illustrates the procedure.

For example, *sales* were recognized evenly during 1991. Therefore, the restatement ratio is the ending general price level index divided by the average general price level index for the year.[43]

To restate the *gain on sale of investment,* the components of the HC/ND entry recording the gain are restated as shown in the first note of Exhibit 25–14. The HC/ND amount of the investment is restated by the ratio of 159/138 because the general price level index at date of acquisition, March 31, 1987, was 138. The resulting HC/CD gain of $600 is the increase in the value of the investment account after restating the amounts to a constant dollar basis. The adjusted gain is considerably less than the reported gain because of inflation.

Cost of goods sold requires multiple HC/CD restatements as shown in the second note of Exhibit 25–14. Based on the FIFO assumption, Phog acquired the beginning inventory during the fourth quarter of the preceding year, when the average general price level index was 146. Therefore, it is restated by the constant dollar ratio 159/146. Because the purchases were made evenly during 1991, the average general price level index of 152 is used. Based on the FIFO assumption, Phog acquired ending inventory evenly during the fourth quarter of 1991, when the average general price level index was 157. This amount is restated by the ratio, 159/157.

If Phog used LIFO, the denominators of the general price level restatement ratios applied to beginning and ending inventory would be the general price level indices for the purchase dates. In some cases, those dates are in the distant past. If Phog used the average cost method for inventory, the denominators of the constant dollar ratios for beginning and ending inventory would be the average general price level indices for 1990 and 1991, respectively. Purchases are not affected by the inventory cost flow method.

The restatement ratios for *general expenses* and *income tax expense* reflect the average general price level index (152) because these expenses occurred evenly during the year. Restated *depreciation expense* is computed separately because the two plant assets were acquired on different dates. The restatement ratios reflect the acquisition dates (127 and 147).

HC/CD Retained Earnings Statement   Exhibit 25–14 also illustrates this statement. The ending 1990 HC/CD retained earnings amount, $43,604 (given), is restated to reflect the general price level index at December 31, 1991. That amount represents the ending balance resulting from the general price level–restatement process in *1990.* The ratio 159/147 restates that amount of end-of-1991 constant dollars. Next, HC/CD net income is added. Then dividends are restated by using the mid-year general price level index (151) because dividends were declared in the middle of the year. The ending $63,693 balance proves the retained earnings balancing amount used in the balance sheet (Exhibit 25–12).

Recap   The HC/CD statements report higher total assets and lower retained earnings and income, relative to the HC/ND statements. Total assets increased on a constant dollar basis because the general price level index increased. This effect is most pronounced for equipment and other older assets.

Restatement of revenues and expenses caused HC/CD earnings to fall below HC/ND earnings because expenses increased more than revenues and gains as a result of general price level restatement. HC/ND cost of goods sold and depreciation were significantly less than the restated amounts. In addition, restatement reduced

---

[43] Items that experience numerous transactions during the reporting period, such as sales revenue, often are assumed to occur evenly throughout the period. This assumption provides a practical basis for using an average general price level index value for the denominator in the restatement ratio.

the gain on sale of investment, and the purchasing power loss decreased HC/CD earnings.

The HC/CD balance sheet most probably does not reflect the current value of a firm's assets, nor does the HC/CD income statement likely reflect the real increase in wealth, after providing for capital maintenance. While HC/CD earnings are adjusted for changes in purchasing power, maintenance of general purchasing power does not imply maintenance of physical capital. Hence the value of CC/CD statements. The last example addresses these concerns.

COMPREHENSIVE ILLUSTRATION: CC/CD FINANCIAL STATEMENTS

This illustration is in the context of the *SFAS No. 89* guidelines as applied to a complete set of financial statements. The FASB does not discourage other forms of disclosure. These guidelines apply only if a reporting firm chooses to disclose price-adjusted financial statement information.

Objectives of the CC/CD Model   The objective of the CC/CD balance sheet is to report the lower of current cost or net recoverable amount of each asset or asset group.[44] This objective is consistent with conservatism. The objective of the CC/CD income statement is to report distributable income, in constant dollars.

Current Cost   The FASB defines current cost in terms of reacquiring existing assets:

Inventory: current cost is the cost of purchasing or producing an inventory item, including an overhead allowance.

Plant assets: current cost is the cost of acquiring the same service potential, as measured by operating costs and physical output capacity, of existing assets. The following measurement alternatives are allowed: (1) cost of a new asset having the same service potential as the used asset when it was new less depreciation, (2) cost of a used asset of the same age and condition, and (3) cost of a new asset with different service potential, adjusted for the difference in service potential due to differences in useful life, output capacity, nature of service, and operating costs.

Price quotations for individual assets, specific price indices for groups of similar assets, and standard manufacturing costs are used to compute current cost.

Overview   Comprehensive CC/CD statements include an income statement, retained earning statement, and balance sheet. Preparation of CC/CD financial statements involves measurement of the current cost of each financial statement item and restatement of all current cost amounts to end-of-period constant dollars. The purchasing power gain or loss is reported as a component of earnings, as in HC/CD statements. Other HC/CD information also is presented. Thus, the comprehensive CC/CD model includes amounts representing other measurement models. In addition, the change in the current cost of the nonmonetary items, net of inflation, is reported as a component of CC/CD comprehensive income. This amount, along with the purchasing power gain or loss, is computed before completing the income statement.

For this example, Exhibit 25–15 supplements Exhibit 25–11 (from the previous HC/CD Phog Company example) with current cost information.

CC/CD Balance Sheet   Exhibit 25–16 presents the CC/CD balance sheet stated in constant dollars at December 31, 1991. The reported amounts of monetary items agree

---

[44] The net recoverable amount for an asset is the net cash amount expected to be obtained from use or sale.

EXHIBIT 25-15   Phog Company Current Cost Information for CC/CD Restated Financial Statements

HC/ND transaction and financial statement data, and general price level indices are given in Exhibit 25-11.

Item	Source of CC Data	Current Cost
December 31, 1990:		Current cost
Assets (beginning balances):		(in CDs of 1/1/1991)
Inventory	From prior period, 1990	$ 20,500
Investment in common stock of Smith Company	From prior period, 1990	33,000
Equipment	From prior period, 1990	175,000
Retained earnings (credit)	From prior period, 1990	97,788
December 31, 1991:		Current cost
Assets (ending balances):		(in CDs of 12/31/1991)
Inventory	Suppliers' price lists	$ 26,000
Investment in common stock	Quoted market price	15,000
Equipment (acquired 1/1/1986)	Indexed, specific	196,000
Parking garage (acquired 1/1/1991)	Professional appraisal	56,000
During 1991 (revenues and expenses occurred		Current cost
evenly throughout the year):		(in average CDs of 1991)
Sales revenue	HC, Exhibit 25-11	$144,000
Cost of goods sold	Suppliers' price lists	86,000
General expenses (including interest)	HC, Exhibit 25-11	20,000
Income tax expense	HC, Exhibit 25-11	10,000

EXHIBIT 25-16   Phog Company CC/CD Balance Sheet at December 31, 1991

	Source (Exhibit)	CC/CD (in CDs of 12/31/1991)
Assets		
M Cash	25-11	$136,000
M Accounts receivable (net)	25-11	33,000
NM Inventory	25-15	26,000
NM Investment in common stock of Smith Co.	25-15	15,000
NM Equipment	25-15	196,000
NM Accumulated depreciation, equipment	See text	(47,040)
Parking garage	25-15	56,000
NM Accumulated depreciation, parking garage	See text	(2,240)
Total assets		$412,720
Liabilities		
M Accounts payable	25-11	$ 45,000
M Income tax payable	25-11	10,000
M Note payable, 12%	25-11	50,000
Stockholders' Equity		
NM Common stock, nopar	25-12	187,120
NM Retained earnings	Bal. amt.	120,600
Total liabilities and stockholders' equity		$412,720

M = monetary item.
NM = nonmonetary item.

with the HC/CD balance sheet because they are stated at ending constant dollars. The ending current costs for most nonmonetary items are given in Exhibit 25–15. In practice, a considerable amount of effort is required to estimate these values. For example, a specific price level index was used to determine the current cost of equipment, which increased from $175,000 to $196,000 during 1991. These amounts reflect the condition and utility of the equipment at the measurement dates.

The accumulated depreciation amounts reflect the percentage of depreciation recognized for HC/ND. The equipment is depreciated 24% ($24,000 HC depreciation/$100,000 HC). Therefore, $47,040 (.24 × $196,000) of accumulated depreciation, based on current cost, is reported at December 31, 1991. For the parking garage, the amounts are as follows: 4% depreciated ($2,000/$50,000) based on historical cost, $2,240 accumulated depreciation based on current cost (.04 × $56,000).

The CC/CD amount for common stock is the HC/ND amount restated to end-of-period dollars, which agrees with the amount in the HC/CD balance sheet. The common stock account, representing a previous cash investment, has no specific price. Retained earnings is computed as a balancing amount, but is proven after deriving CC/CD earnings.

Change in Current Cost of Nonmonetary Items, Net of Inflation   The CC/CD statements are stated in terms of constant dollars. Therefore, the holding gains or losses reported in CC/CD earnings are the changes in specific prices of nonmonetary items *after* removing the effects of general price level changes. Exhibit 25–17 shows how to separate these two effects.

The previous discussion of the four models for financial reporting included an example of this computation applied to inventory (see the CC/CD example for Aido Company). Exhibit 25–17 illustrates the same computation for Phog. The reasoning underlying the computations is similar to that of the purchasing power gain or loss on net monetary assets. Changes in the current cost amount of each nonmonetary asset are analyzed using the beginning balance, additions, and deductions during the period to derive the ending balance.

For *inventory,* the total increase in nominal current cost during the year is the difference between the actual ending current cost amount ($26,000), and the computed ending current cost nominal amount ($19,500). The Current Cost at Transaction Date column in the exhibit supplies the computed ending nominal current cost amount, which would also be the actual ending current cost amount if specific prices remained constant. The total nominal current cost increase is $6,500.

The nominal current cost increase is separated into an inflation effect and a specific price change effect. By restating each amount in the Current Cost at Transaction Date column to ending constant dollars, the expected ending current cost amount in constant dollars is derived, $21,135. This is the ending inventory balance Phog would have if inventory had kept exact pace with inflation. The effect of inflation during the period is the difference between this restated figure, $21,135, and the computed ending nominal current cost amount, $19,500. This difference, $1,635, is the part of the total $6,500 current cost increase attributable to inflation. The remainder, $4,865, is the increase in current cost exclusive of inflation.

This amount, $4,865, is the holding gain for inventory, exclusive of changes in the general price level index, reported in the CC/CD income statement. The increase in specific prices of inventory exceeded inflation.

Current cost depreciation for *equipment* and *parking garage*, a component of the computed ending nominal current cost amount for plant assets, is found using the following formula:

$$\text{CC depreciation} = \text{Depreciation rate} \times \text{Average CC during period based on HC}$$

Nonmonetary Assets	Source	CC at Transaction Date	Restated to CDs*	CC at 12/31/1991
Inventory:				
Beginning balance	25–15	$ 20,500	159/147 = $ 22,181	
Add—purchases during 1991	25–11	85,000	159/152 = 88,910	
Deduct—cost of goods sold for 1991	25–15	(86,000)	159/152 = (89,956)	
1. Ending inventory at CC at transaction dates.		$ 19,500		
2. Ending inventory at CC restated to CDs.			$ 21,135	
3. Ending inventory at year-end CC.	23–15			$ 26,000

Changes in CC during 1991:

Total increase (decrease) in CC (3 − 1) . . . . $26,000 − $19,500 = $6,500

Change in CC due to inflation (2 − 1) . . . . $21,135 − $19,500 = $1,635
Change in CC, net of inflation (3 − 2) . . . . $26,000 − $21,135 = $4,865

Investment in common stock of Smith Co.:				
Beginning balance	25–15	$ 33,000	159/147 = $ 35,706	
Add—acquisitions—none				
Deduct—sale on 12/30/1991, at CC when sold	25–11	(15,000)	159/159 = (15,000)	
1. Ending balance at CC at transaction dates.		$ 18,000		
2. Ending balance at CC restated to CDs.			$ 20,706	
3. Ending balance at year-end CC.	25–15			$ 15,000

Changes in CC during 1991:

Total increase (decrease) in CC (3 − 1) . . . . $15,000 − $18,000 = $(3,000)

Change in CC due to inflation (2 − 1) . . . . $20,706 − $18,000 = $ 2,706
Change in CC, net of inflation (3 − 2) . . . . $15,000 − $20,706 = $(5,706)

Equipment:				
Beginning balance (net of depreciation)	25–15	$140,000†	159/147 = $151,480	
Add—acquisitions—none				
Deduct—depreciation during 1991	See text	(7,420)	159/152 = (7,761)	
1. Ending balance at CC at transaction dates.		$132,580)		
2. Ending balance at CC restated to CDs.			$143,719	
3. Ending balance at year-end CC.	25–15			$148,960‡

Changes in CC during 1991:

Total increase (decrease) in CC (3 − 1) . . . . $148,960 − $132,580 = $16,380

Change in CC due to inflation (2 − 1) . . . . $143,719 − $132,580 = $11,139
Change in CC, net of inflation (3 − 2) . . . . $148,960 − $143,719 = $ 5,241

Parking garage:				
Beginning balance (net of depreciation)	25–15	$ –0–		$ –0–
Add—acquisition on 1/1/1991, CC at acquisition date	25–11	50,000	159/147 = 54,100	
Deduct—depreciation during 1991	See text	(2,120)	159/152 = (2,218)	
1. Ending balance at CC at transaction dates.		$ 47,880		
2. Ending balance at CC restated to CDs.			$ 51,882	
3. Ending balance at year-end CC.	25–15			$ 53,760§

Changes in CC during 1991:

Total increase (decrease) in CC (3 − 1) . . . . $53,760 − $47,880 = $5,880

Change in CC due to inflation (2 − 1) . . . . $51,882 − $47,880 = $4,002
Change in CC, net of inflation (3 − 2) . . . . $53,760 − $51,882 = $1,878

* The CD restatement ratios are rounded to three decimals and then applied to the CC/ND amounts.

† At 1/1/91, the equipment was 20% depreciated (see Exhibit 25–11; $20,000 HC accumulated depreciation, $100,000 HC). $140,000 = $175,000 × .80

‡ At 12/31/91, the equipment was 24% depreciated (see Exhibit 25–11; $24,000 HC accumulated depreciation, $100,000 HC). $148,960 = $196,000 × .76

§ At 12/31/91, the parking garage was 4% depreciated (see Exhibit 25–11; $2,000 HC accumulated depreciation, $50,000 HC). $53,760 = $56,000 × .96

For equipment,   = ($4,000/$100,000) × ($175,000 + $196,000)/2
CC depreciation

                 = $7,420

For parking garage, = ($2,000/$50,000) × ($50,000 + $56,000)/2
CC depreciation

                 = $2,120

This formula bases current cost depreciation on the *average* current cost associated with the period. The parking garage was purchased in 1991. Therefore, its beginning current cost equals its purchase price. These current cost depreciation amounts are reported in the CC/CD income statement, Exhibit 25–18. Current cost depreciation expense as computed above reflects average 1991 constant dollars. Therefore, these amounts are restated to ending constant dollars in the income statement, and are used for computing the change in current cost net of inflation.

The remaining computations for the investment in common stock, equipment, and parking garage follow the format applied to inventory. Both the equipment and parking garage experienced current cost changes in excess of inflation. However, the current cost of the investment in common stock declined in 1991 from $33,000 to $30,000 (half the investment shares were sold on December 30, 1991). Because the general price level increased during 1991, the change in current cost, net of general inflation, was a negative $5,706.

At the bottom of Exhibit 25–18, the total change in current cost of nonmonetary assets, the change in current cost due to inflation, and the change in current cost net of inflation are aggregated. For Phog Company during 1991, the total change in current cost, net of general inflation, is $6,278. This amount is carried to the CC/CD income statement.

The inclusion of this net holding gain in earnings is consistent with the all-inclusive concept of income. Furthermore, the holding gains represent increases in the value of the firm. However, this view is not universally accepted.[45] Others maintain that unrealized holding gains do not represent distributable income.

CC/CD Income Statement and Retained Earnings Statement   The last steps are to prepare the CC/CD income and retained earning statements. The purchasing power loss is carried from the HC/CD income statement. The CC/CD income statement is presented in Exhibit 25–18, and the CC/CD retained earnings statement in Exhibit 25–19.

Sales revenue, general expenses, and *income tax expense* are reported at the amounts appearing in the HC/CD income statement because these amounts involve only monetary items.

Cost of goods sold and *depreciation expense* involve nonmonetary assets. Supplier price lists were consulted to determine current cost of goods sold (see Exhibit 25–15). Depreciation expense is based on the historical cost depreciation rate applied to the average current cost of depreciable assets, as illustrated in the previous section.

No *gain on sale of the investment in common stock* of Smith Company is reported because the sale proceeds, $15,000, equals the current cost of the investment sold at the date of sale. The current cost of marketable common stock is the quoted market price of the shares. However, Phog suffered a $5,706 loss, the decline in current cost measured in ending constant dollars. This amount is part of the aggregate change in current cost of nonmonetary items, net of inflation.

---

[45] For example, see R. Samuelson, "Should Replacement Cost Changes Be Included in Income?" *The Accounting Review,* April 1980 pp. 254–268.

EXHIBIT 25-18   Phog Company CC/CD Income Statement for Year Ended December 31, 1991

	Source (Exhibit)	CC Nominal Dollars	CD Restatement Ratio*	CC/CD (in CDs of 12/31/1991)
Revenues and gains:				
Sales revenue	25–11	$144,000	159/152	$150,624
Expenses and losses:				
Cost of goods sold	25–15	86,000	159/152	(89,956)
General expenses (including interest)	25–15	20,000	159/152	(20,920)
Depreciation expense, equipment	25–17	7,420	159/152	(7,761)
Depreciation expense, parking garage	25–17	2,120	159/152	(2,218)
Income tax expense	25–15	10,000	159/152	(10,460)
CC/CD income from continuing operations				19,309
Purchasing power gain (loss) on net monetary items	25–13			(264)
Total change in CC of nonmonetary items	See table below		$25,760	
Change in CC of NM items due to general inflation	See table below		19,482	
Change in CC of NM items, net of general inflation	See table below			6,278
CC/CD comprehensive income				$25,323

Summary of Nonmonetary Price Changes, from Exhibit 25–17

Nonmonetary	Change in CC Total	Change in CC Due to General Inflation	Change in CC Net of General Inflation
Inventory	$ 6,500	$ 1,635	$4,865
Investment in common stock of Smith Co.	(3,000)	2,706	(5,706)
Equipment	16,380	11,139	5,241
Parking garage	5,880	4,002	1,878
Total	$25,760	$19,482	$6,278

M = monetary item.

NM = nonmonetary item.

* The CD restatement ratios are rounded to three decimals and then applied to the CC/ND amounts.

EXHIBIT 25-19   Phog Company CC/CD Retained Earnings Statement

CC/CD Retained Earnings Statement (also a Proof of Accuracy)
For Year Ended December 31, 1991
(Stated in CDs of December 31, 1991)

	CC/CD (in CDs of 12/31/1991*)
Retained earnings, 1/1/1991 (from prior year, Exhibit 25–15; $97,788 × 159/147)	$105,807
Add: CC/CD income (Exhibit 25–18)	25,323
Deduct: CC/CD dividends 1991 ($10,000 × 159/151)	(10,530)
CC/CD retained earnings, 12/31/1991	$120,600

* The CD restatement ratios are rounded to three decimals and then applied to the CC/ND amounts.

All the current cost revenue and expense items are multiplied by the constant dollar restatement ratio, 159/152, to restate each item from average 1991 dollars to constant dollars of December 31, 1991.

Income from continuing operations for Phog, $19,309, is the difference between current cost revenues and expenses. The remaining two items contributing to comprehensive CC/CD income are the purchasing power loss, taken from Exhibit 25–13, and the increase in current cost of nonmonetary items, net of inflation.

The beginning current cost balance in *retained earnings,* $97,788, is restated to ending constant dollars. Comprehensive CC/CD income is added to it, and restated dividends are deducted. The result is ending CC/CD retained earnings, stated in terms of ending constant dollars. This amount proves the balancing amount presented in the balance sheet.

Recap CC/CD income from continuing operations is useful for assessing the future net cash flows of an enterprise and for predicting distributable income because it deducts the current cost of assets consumed in production. CC/CD income from continuing operations is considerably less than HC/ND (GAAP) income, implying that Phog's reported earnings overstates distributable income.

The increase or decrease in the current cost of nonmonetary assets held represents a change in the value of the firm. The separation of CC/CD comprehensive income into its operating and holding components is useful for predicting the future net cash flows of the entity. Operating and holding activities are inherently different.

The CC/CD balance sheet presents assets, liabilities, and stockholders' equity at current cost. This presentation gives users an estimate of the amount required currently to replace the entity's assets in their present condition. It also helps investors and others to estimate the value of a company.

FASB Suggested Disclosure Requirements for Changing Prices

SFAS No. 89 emphasizes the CC/CD model, but includes other measurements in its minimum *recommended* (not required) disclosures, which follow:

1. Five-year comparison of the following HC/CD items, in either average-of-year or end-of-year units of constant purchasing power: total revenue, income from operations, purchasing power gain or loss, excess of change in current cost of assets over inflation, foreign currency translation adjustment, net assets, income from operations per share, and cash dividends.
2. Additional disclosures for the current year if income from continuing operations on a CC/CD basis differs materially from its GAAP counterpart:
   a. An estimate of income from continuing operations on a CC/CD basis achieved by restating cost of goods sold, depreciation, depletion, and amortization.
   b. Purchasing power gain or loss.
   c. Ending CC/CD amount (or lower recoverable amount) of inventory and plant assets.
   d. Change in current cost (or lower recoverable amount) of inventory and plant assets, net of inflation.
   e. The aggregate foreign currency translation adjustment.

SFAS No. 89 gives examples of the minimum disclosure recommendations. The comprehensive illustration described here exceeds the minimum for most items.

CONCEPT REVIEW

1. Why are monetary items not adjusted to the ending general price level index?
2. Why is the purchasing power gain or loss included in both HC/CD and CC/CD earnings?
3. Explain how to compute the change in the current cost of an asset, net of inflation. Why is this amount included as a component of CC/CD earnings?

SUMMARY OF KEY POINTS

(L.O. 1)   1. A major objective of financial statement analysis is to identify and assess major changes in trends, amounts, and relationships.

(L.O. 1)   2. An important first step in financial statement analysis is a careful examination of the auditor's report for any departures from GAAP.

(L.O. 2)   3. Horizontal analysis is particularly useful in revealing trends. However, it is important to be sure that changed circumstances do not render the comparisons inappropriate.

(L.O. 3)   4. Ratios can be classified into liquidity, efficiency, coverage, and profitability categories. Several ratios should be examined in each category before conclusions are attempted. Implications for ratios in other categories should also be considered.

(L.O. 4)   5. Great care should be exercised before drawing conclusions from either earnings per share or cash flow per share.

(L.O. 4)   6. The major disadvantage of ratio analysis is that the values used are almost always book values rather than market values. Company comparisons also are hazardous due to different business conditions and accounting techniques in use.

(L.O. 5)   7. To the extent capital markets are efficient, the information contained in ratios can be expected to be reflected quickly in market prices.

(L.O. 5)   8. Any serious analysis of a firm should search beyond the financial reports for additional information. Financial statement evaluation is an integral part of a broader information system designed to provide data for decisions.

(L.O. 6)   9. The alleged effects of price level changes on historical cost financial statements include overstatement of earnings and assets, and capital erosion.

(L.O. 7)   10. There are two types of price level changes: general and specific. Changes in general price level indices measure inflation; specific prices and indices measure the change in the prices of specific goods and services. Restating historical cost amounts for changes in the general price level results in reports measured in dollars of constant purchasing power.

(L.O. 7)   11. Monetary items are cash or claims to cash, and obligations to pay cash, which are fixed in dollar amount. Holding monetary items during times of general price level changes results in a purchasing power gain or loss. This amount is a component of general price level–adjusted earnings.

(L.O. 7)   12. Nonmonetary items are not fixed in dollar terms. Holding gains and losses, resulting from holding nonmonetary items during times of specific price level changes, are included in earnings adjusted for specific price changes.

(L.O. 7)   13. The FASB recommends current cost, the cost to replace an asset in its present condition and utility, as the appropriate measure of current value and for computing specific price changes.

(L.O. 7)   14. Three alternative models for adjusting financial statements for price level changes are proposed: historical cost/constant dollar (HC/CD), current cost/ nominal dollar (CC/ND), and current cost/constant dollar (CC/CD).

(L.O. 8)   15. The HC/CD model adjusts financial statement items to dollars of constant purchasing power, and maintains the historical cost basis.

(L.O. 9)   16. The CC/ND model reports all financial statement items at current cost, without adjusting for general price level changes. The CC/CD adjusts for general price level changes. The current cost models separate earnings into operating (distributable) and holding components. This separation may enhance prediction of earnings and cash flows and may help maintain physical capital.

REVIEW PROBLEM

This review problem consists of two unrelated parts, A and B.

PART A

This part is based on the 1989 balance sheet and income statement for GEOTEK Industries, Inc., and subsidiaries, an actual firm.

GEOTEK INDUSTRIES, INC., AND SUBSIDIARIES
Consolidated Balance Sheet
December 31, 1989
(*in thousands except per share data*)

Current assets:

Cash and equivalents	$	895
Marketable securities		525
Receivables (net)		2,773
Inventories		3,368
Costs in excess of billings		152
Prepaid expenses		400
Total	$	8,113

Property and equipment less $931 of accumulated depreciation		4,542
Intangibles less amortization		10,490
Other assets		452
Total	$	23,597

Current Liabilities:

Accounts and notes payable	$	4,112
Current maturities of long-term debt		777
Government advances		738
Estimated contract losses		651
Accrued payroll and payroll taxes		1,067
Other current liabilities		1,042
Total	$	8,387
Long-term debt		2,596

Shareholders Equity:

Preferred $.01 par value		9
Common $.01 par value		24
Capital in excess of par		19,864
Accumulated deficit		(7,283)
Total	$	23,597

GEOTEK INDUSTRIES, INC., AND SUBSIDIARIES
Income Statement
Year Ended December 31, 1989
(*in thousands except per share data*)

Revenues:

Net sales	$	15,538
Interest		343
Total	$	15,881

Costs and expenses:

Cost of goods sold		12,945
Research and development		1,267
Marketing		502
General administrative		2,925
Interest		301
Amortization of intangibles		491
Total	$	18,431

(Loss) from continuing operations before taxes		(2,550)
Foreign income tax		2
(Loss) from continuing operations		(2,552)
(Loss) from discontinued operation		(476)
Net loss		($3,028)

Weighted average number of common shares outstanding	1,838

Per common share:

Loss from continuing operations	($1.43)
Loss from discontinued operations	(.26)
Net loss	($1.69)

Required:

Answer the following questions (amounts are in $ thousands).

1. Compute the following for GEOTEK:
   a. Current ratio.
   b. Inventory turnover (GEOTEK's 1988 inventories were $2,850).
   c. Accounts receivable turnover (GEOTEK's 1988 receivables were $1,849).
   d. Debt to equity.
   e. Times interest earned.

2. Comment on GEOTEK's profitability ratios.
3. What additional ratios could you calculate if you had the rest of the 1988 figures from GEOTEK's balance sheet and income statement?
4. What additional data would you like to have before rendering an opinion concerning the health of this company (a) from the company's annual report and (b) from other sources?

PART B

Quality Transport Company transfers freight from its home office in Tuscon, Arizona, to cities throughout the United States. Thus, it is a service-oriented enterprise and has no merchandise inventory. On January 1, 1991, the HC/ND balance sheet of Quality Transport follows:

QUALITY TRANSPORT COMPANY
Balance Sheet
January 1, 1991

Assets

Cash and receivables	$12,000
Trucks	80,000
Accumulated depreciation	(–0–)
	$92,000

Liabilities and Owners' Equity

Current liabilities	$10,000
Long-term liabilities	30,000
Owners' equity	52,000
	$92,000

Assume for simplicity that all revenues and all expenses occur evenly during the year. The trucks are new on January 1, 1991, are expected to remain in service for five years, and will be depreciated on a straight-line basis with no estimated residual value. GPL indexes were 100 at January 1, 1991, 102 at February 15, 1991, 104 for the average of 1991, and 108 at December 31, 1991. Current cost (CC) of the trucks at December 31, 1991, was $88,000 before deducting accumulated depreciation.

Transactions for 1991 included the following:

1. Payment on February 15, 1991, of the $10,000 beginning balance of current liabilities.
2. Service revenue of $100,000, of which $70,000 is collected in cash.
3. Depreciation of $16,000.
4. Other expenses of $75,000, of which $35,000 is unpaid at December 31, 1991. The $35,000 of liabilities are current.

Required (round all CD restatement ratios to three decimals):

1. Prepare the CC/CD (CDs as of December 31, 1991) balance sheet of Quality Transport Company at December 31, 1991.
2. Prepare the CC/CD (CDs as of December 31, 1991) income statement for Quality Transport Company for the year ended December 31, 1991.

SOLUTION

◆

PART A

1. *a.* Current ratio:

$$\frac{\$8,113}{\$8,387} = .97$$

b. Inventory turnover:

$$\frac{\$12,945}{(\$3,368 + \$2,850)/2} = 4.16$$

c. Accounts receivable turnover (assuming all sales on credit):

$$\frac{\$15,538}{(\$2,773 + \$1,849)/2} = 6.72$$

d. Debt to equity:

$$\frac{(\$8,387 + \$2,596)}{\$19,864 + \$24 + 9 - \$7,283} = .87$$

e. Times interest earned:

$$\frac{-\$2,552 + \$301}{301} < 0$$

2. The profit margin on sales, return on total assets and owners' equity, and EPS are all negative. The price-earnings ratio is not meaningful given that EPS is negative. While you cannot be sure from the data given, you might expect, as was the case, no dividends were paid. Thus, the dividend payout ratios are zero.

3. Liquidity ratios: All ratios can be calculated from the figures given. Efficiency ratios: working capital turnover, asset turnover.

   To compute the ratio of net cash flow to current liabilities, the statement of cash flows is needed. The cash flow could be approximated from the data given. Cash flow per share also requires this information.

4. Here are some suggestions. The list is not exhaustive. From the company's annual report:

   a. Data from prior years, so trends can be observed (horizontal analysis.)

   b. The president's letter, which may give some clue to the potential future profitability of the firm.

   c. The statement of cash flows to indicate whether this aspect of the business is healthy. This statement would also allow calculation of additional ratios.

   d. The footnotes to detail the accounting principles used and to explain the items on the statements as well as give more detail.

   e. Segment data describing the nature of GEOTEK's business and its profitability.

   f. The auditors report.

   From other sources:

   a. Strength of the industry (electronics) and of GEOTEK's customers.

   b. Quality of GEOTEK's management, employee talent, marketing network, and R&D activities (new products and patents).

   c. Reputation for quality, ability to meet deadlines, and flexibility of manufacturing operations.

PART B

1.

QUALITY TRANSPORT COMPANY
CC/CD Balance Sheet
At December 31, 1991

Cash and receivables	$ 62,000*	Current liabilities	
Trucks	88,000	($10,000 − $10,000 +	
		$35,000)	35,000
Accumulated depreciation		Long-term liabilities	30,000
($88,000 ÷ 5)	(17,600)	Owners' equity (balancing	
		amount)	67,400†
Total	$132,400	Total	$132,400

* $12,000 − $10,000 + $100,000 − $40,000 = $62,000.

† ($52,000 × 108/100 = $56,160) + $11,240 (CC/CD earnings) = $67,400.

2.

QUALITY TRANSPORT COMPANY
CC/CD Income Statement
For the Year Ended December 31, 1991

Service revenue ($100,000 × 108/104)		$103,800
Expenses:		
Depreciation ($16,800* × 108/104)		(17,438)
Other ($75,000 × 108/104)		(77,850)
Operating income		8,512
Purchasing power gain on net monetary items (see computation below)		1,290
Increase in current cost of trucks (see computation below)	$7,200	
Increase due to general inflation (see computation below)	(5,762)	
Excess of CC over inflation (see computation below)		1,438
CC/CD comprehensive income		$ 11,240

* ($80,000 + $88,000) ÷ 2 = $84,000; $84,000 ÷ 5 = $16,800.

QUALITY TRANSPORT COMPANY
Purchasing Power Gain (Loss) on Net Monetary Items
For the Year Ended December 31, 1991

Monetary Items—Increases (Decreases)	HC	CD Restatement Ratio	HC/CD
Total beginning net monetary assets	$(28,000)	108/100	$(30,240)
Increases during 1991 from:			
Sales revenue	100,000	108/104	103,800
Decreases during 1991 from:			
Other expenses	(75,000)	108/104	(77,850)
Total ending net monetary assets:			
HC	$ (3,000)		
GPL restated			$ (4,290)
Purchasing power gain on net monetary items [− $3,000 − (− $4,290)]			$ 1,290

QUALITY TRANSPORT COMPANY
Change in the CC of Trucks
For the Year Ended December 31, 1991

	CC at Transaction Date	CD Restatement Ratio	CC/CD (in CDs of Dec. 31, 1991)
Beginning balance (net of depreciation)	$80,000	108/100	$86,400
Additions—none	—		—
Deductions—depreciation during 1991	(16,800)	108/104	(17,438)
Ending balance at CC when the transactions occurred	63,200		68,962
Ending balance at CC of Dec. 31, 1991 (net) ($88,000 − $17,600)	70,400	108/108	70,400
Total increase in CC ($70,400 − $63,200)	$ 7,200		
Increase in CC due to general inflation ($68,962 − $63,200)		$5,762	
Increase in CC net of general inflation ($70,400 − $68,962), gain			$ 1,438

KEY TERMS

Constant dollar (1430)
Consumer Price Index for All Urban
   Consumers (1431)
Current cost (1434)
Distributable income (1436)
Efficient market theory (1428)
General price level (1431)
Horizontal analysis (1414)
Monetary item (1432)

Nominal dollar (1430)
Nonmonetary item (1432)
Purchasing power gain or loss (1433)
Ratio analysis (1415)
Systematic risk (1428)
Trading on the equity (1424)
Unqualified (clean) opinion (1409)
Unsystematic risk (1428)
Vertical analysis (1413)

QUESTIONS

1. Why is the past financial record of a company important to statement users? What is meant by a turning point?
2. Explain why financial analysts and others, in analyzing financial statements, examine the auditors' report and the summary of accounting policies.
3. Explain why the notes to the financial statements should be read carefully when analyzing financial statements. Why are long-term summaries considered important to statement users?
4. Distinguish between vertical and horizontal analyses. Briefly explain the importance of each.
5. What is meant by ratio analysis? Why is it important in the analysis of financial statements?
6. Distinguish between the current ratio and the quick (acid-test) ratio. What purpose does each serve?
7. Current assets and current liabilities for two companies with the same amount of working capital are summarized below. Evaluate their relative liquidity positions.

	X Company	Y Company
Current assets	$200,000	$800,000
Current liabilities	100,000	700,000
Working capital	$100,000	$100,000

8. X Corporation's receivables average age is 24.3 days. Interpret this figure. What is the accounts receivable turnover ratio? What does it reveal?

9. Y Corporation has an inventory turnover of 9; interpret this figure. What is the average number of days of supply?

10. Explain and illustrate the effect of financial leverage.

11. Compute and explain the meaning of the book value per share of common stock of the Craft Manufacturing Company, assuming the following data are available:

Preferred stock, par $100, 6%, cumulative, nonparticipating, 200 shares
issued and outstanding, liquidation value is par . . . . $ 20,000
Common stock, par value $10, 10,000 shares issued and outstanding 100,000
Retained earnings 7,000
(Three years' dividends in arrears on preferred stock including current year.)

12. Explain how a company with debt financing can have a leverage factor that is (*a*) positive, (*b*) negative, and (*c*) zero.

13. Explain the return on total assets. Why is it an important measure of profitability?

14. What is meant by the price-earnings multiple? Why is it considered important?

15. What are the principal limitations in using ratios?

16. What is the price phenomenon known as inflation? What is the opposite phenomenon called? How would each affect you if you received an equal amount from an educational trust fund set up by your parents 20 years ago?

17. "When prices are going up, they all go up; when they drop, they all drop." Comment on this statement.

18. What indexes measure changes in the general purchasing power of the U.S. dollar? What index has been prescribed for preparation of CD financial statements?

19. Among sales, cost of goods sold, salaries, and depreciation expense, during a period of rapidly changing prices, which would most nearly be at the current price basis under the conventional historical cost (HC) model, and which would not be on a current price basis? Give reasons for your response.

20. When prices are changing rapidly, why may financial statements prepared on the HC basis be deficient in some respects?

21. When general prices are rising and depreciation expense is computed on the conventional HC basis, what is likely to be true with respect to the availability of resources that would be required for replacement of the depreciable assets?

22. Under the CD restatement approach, financial statement items are classified as monetary or nonmonetary. Briefly, by which criterion can these two categories be distinguished?

23. Indicate, with explanations where necessary, whether the following items are monetary or nomonetary: (*a*) stocks held as investments, (*b*) bonds held as investments, (*c*) deposits in domestic banks, (*d*) merchandise inventory, (*e*) accounts and notes receivable, (*f*) machinery and equipment, (*g*) accounts and notes payable, (*h*) preferred stock, (*i*) retained earnings, and (*j*) deferred credit related to income taxes.

24. During its most recent accounting period, XY Company had a larger balance of cash and receivables than monetary liabilities; general prices rose steadily. Would this condition cause a purchasing power gain or loss on net monetary items? Explain.

25. If prices rise steadily over an extended period of time, indicate whether the following items would cause a purchasing power gain, a purchasing power loss, or neither purchasing power gain nor loss on net monetary items:
   a. Maintaining a balance in a checking account.
   b. Owing bonds payable.
   c. Owning land.
   d. Amortizing goodwill.
   e. Holding common treasury stock.

26. Which item below is the valuation basis used in conventional HC financial statements?
   a. Market value.
   b. Original cost.
   c. Replacement cost.
   d. A mixture of costs and values.
   e. None of the above.

27. A company begins the fiscal year with a $10,000 net monetary asset position, has an even outflow of monetary assets of $25,000 during the year, and ends the year with a net monetary liability position of $15,000. If the GPL index is 120 at the beginning of the year, 125 average for the year, and 132 at the end of the year, what is the purchasing power gain or loss during the year?

28. "The HC/CD accounting model changes the unit of measure but retains the attribute measured relative to the conventional accounting model, whereas CC/CD changes both the attribute measured and the unit of measurement." Evaluate this statement.
29. What are the advantages and disadvantages of CC/CD reporting in relation to HC/CD reporting?
30. Why are increases or decreases in the current costs of nonmonetary assets in CC reporting defined in relation to the GPL?
31. How does the recognition of increases or decreases in the CC of nonmonetary assets under the CC/CD model affect the ability of an entity to "manipulate its earnings" by selling selected assets that have increased or decreased in value?
32. Distinguish between the current cost and replacement cost of an asset.
33. How does the net realizable value, or recoverable amount, of an asset affect current cost accounting?
34. The current cost of land is $50,000 on January 1, 1991, and $55,000 on December 31, 1991. If the GPL index was 100 and 110 on January 1 and December 31, respectively, what was the increase in the current cost of land, net of inflation, during 1991 (stated in dollars as of December 31, 1991)?
35. Assume that in Question 34 the GPL index remained unchanged during 1991; it was 100 on January 1, 1991, and December 31, 1991. What was the increase in the current cost of land, net of inflation, during 1991 (stated in dollars as of December 31, 1991)?

EXERCISES

E 25-1
Horizontal and Vertical Analysis: Income Statement
(L.O. 2)

Beathard Trading Company's income statements (condensed) for two years are shown below.

	December 31	
	1990	**1991**
Gross sales	$272,700	$303,000
Returns	(2,700)	(3,000)
	270,000	300,000
Cost of goods sold	(135,000)	(180,000)
Gross margin	135,000	120,000
Expenses:		
Selling	(67,500)	(69,000)
Administrative (including income taxes)	(37,800)	(33,000)
Interest (net of interest revenue)	(2,700)	3,000
Net income before extraordinary items	27,000	21,000
Extraordinary gain (loss), net of tax	5,400	(3,000)
Net income	$ 32,400	$ 18,000
Shares of common stock outstanding	10,000	10,000

Required:

1. Prepare a multiple-step comparative income statement including a vertical percentage analysis. Round to the nearest percent.
2. Prepare a single-step income statement, including horizontal percentage analysis. Round to the nearest percent.

E 25-2
Horizontal and Vertical Analysis: Balance Sheet
(L.O. 2)

Levy Company's balance sheet (condensed and unclassified) for two years is shown below.

	December 31	
	1990	**1991**
Cash	$12,000	$ 26,000
Accounts receivable (net)	20,000	19,000
Inventory (FIFO, LCM)	32,000	40,000
Prepaid expenses	2,000	1,000
Funds and investments (at cost)	18,000	22,000
Operational assets	120,000	126,000
Accumulated depreciation	(28,000)	(45,000)
Intangible assets	4,000	11,000
Total	$180,000	$200,000

| | December 31 | |
	1990	1991
Accounts payable	$ 30,000	$ 15,000
Remaining current liabilities	10,000	10,000
Long-term mortgage payable	40,000	33,000
Common stock, par $5	50,000	60,000
Contributed capital in excess of par	20,000	40,000
Retained earnings	30,000	42,000
Total	$180,000	$200,000

Required:

1. Prepare a comparative balance sheet in good form, including a vertical percentage analysis. Round to the nearest percent.
2. Prepare a comparative balance sheet, in good form, including a horizontal percentage analysis. Round to the nearest percent.

E 25-3
Analysis of Working Capital
(L.O. 3)

The following data were taken from the financial statements of Walker Company.

	1991	1992
Current assets:		
Cash	$ 30,000	$ 40,000
Short-term investments	10,000	10,000
Trade accounts receivable (net)	60,000	70,000
Notes receivable	6,000	2,000
Inventory	150,000	170,000
Prepaid expenses	4,000	2,000
Current liabilities	90,000	120,000

Required:

Based on the above data, compute (*a*) the amount of working capital, (*b*) the current ratio, and (*c*) the acid-test ratio for each year. Evaluate each ratio and compare the results of the two reporting periods. Round to the nearest percent.

E 25-4
Ratio Analysis of Current Assets: Significance
(L.O. 3)

The condensed financial data given below were taken from the annual financial statements of Conlan Corporation:

	1990	1991	1992
Current assets (including inventory)	$200,000	$240,000	$280,000
Current liabilities	150,000	160,000	140,000
Cash sales	800,000	780,000	820,000
Credit sales	200,000	280,000	250,000
Cost of goods sold	560,000	585,000	600,000
Inventory (ending)	120,000	140,000	100,000
Quick assets	80,000	80,000	112,000
Accounts receivable (net)	60,000	64,000	61,000
Total assets (net)	1,000,000	1,200,000	1,400,000

Required:

1. Based on the above data, calculate the following ratios for 1991 and 1992; use 365 days for computation purposes. Round to one decimal point (e.g., ratios, 5.2 and percents, 8.4%). Also, briefly explain the significance of each ratio listed. Use the following format:

Ratio	1991	1992	Significance

  a. Current ratio.
  b. Acid-test ratio.
  c. Working capital to total assets.
  d. Accounts receivable turnover.
  e. Age of accounts receivable.
  f. Inventory turnover.
  g. Days' supply in inventory.
  h. Working capital turnover.

2. Evaluate the overall results of the computations including trends.

E 25-5
Ratio Analysis of
Inventory and
Receivables: Assess
Results
(L.O. 3)

The following data were taken from the financial statements of Infante Company:

	1990	1991	1992
Sales—cash	$190,000	$200,000	$220,000
Sales—credit	100,000	120,000	130,000
Average receivables	25,000	34,000	50,000
Average inventory	60,000	70,000	80,000
Cost of goods sold	180,000	190,000	200,000

Required:

1. Prepare a ratio analysis (including turnover and days) of (*a*) inventory and (*b*) receivables. Use 365 days. Credit terms are 2/10, n/30. Round to one decimal place and whole days. Also, briefly explain the significance of each ratio. Use the following format:

Year   Turnover Ratio   Days   Significance

2. Assess possible impacts of any trends that your analysis indicates relative to (*a*) inventory and (*b*) receivables.

E 25-6
Compute Book Value per
Share: Common and
Preferred Stock
(L.O. 3)

Mandarich Manufacturing Corporation's balance sheet showed the following as of December 31, 1991:

Total liabilities	$100,000
Preferred stock, 6%, par value $50 per share	200,000
Common stock, nopar, 30,000 shares outstanding	360,000
Contributed capital in excess of par, preferred stock	40,000
Retained earnings	90,000

Required:

Compute the book value per share of common stock under each of the following independent assumptions:

1. None of the preferred shares have been issued.
2. Preferred is noncumulative and nonparticipating; liquidation preference value of preferred is par.
3. Preferred is cumulative and nonparticipating (three years' dividends in arrears, including current year); liquidation value of preferred is par.
4. Preferred has a liquidation value of $60 per share and is noncumulative and nonparticipating.
5. Preferred has a liquidation value of $60 per share and is noncumulative and nonparticipating, and the retained earnings account shows a deficit of $30,000, instead of the $90,000 credit balance shown above.

E 25-7
Compute and Explain
Profitability Ratios
(L.O. 3)

The 1992 comparative financial statements for Testaverde Corporation reports the following data:

	1990	1991	1992
Sales revenue	$12,000,000	$13,000,000	$14,000,000
Net income	100,000	120,000	100,000
Interest expense, net of income tax	10,000	12,000	20,000
Stockholders' equity	1,400,000	1,450,000	1,460,000
Total assets	3,500,000	3,500,000	3,700,000
Market value per share	$66	$72	$44
Shares of common stock outstanding	20,000	20,000	25,000

Required:

1. Based on the above financial data, compute the following ratios for 1991 and 1992: (*a*) profit margin on sales, (*b*) return on total assets, (*c*) return on owners' equity, (*d*) the leverage effect, (*e*) basic EPS, and (*f*) price-earnings ratio. Carry computations to two decimal places (e.g., ratios, 5.22 and percents 8.43%.)
2. As an investor in the common stock of Testaverde, which ratio would you prefer as a single measure of profitability? Why?
3. Explain any significant trends that appear to be developing.

E 25–8
Compute and Assess Profitability Ratios for Five Years
(L.O. 3)

The following data relate to the Peete Printing Company:

	1988	1989	1990	1991	1992
Net income	$ 12,000	$ 15,000	$ 25,000	$ 30,000	$ 40,000
Interest expense (net of tax)	1,000	1,200	2,000	2,200	3,000
Sales revenue	120,000	140,000	180,000	230,000	260,000
Total assets	50,000	72,000	110,000	160,000	190,000
Total liabilities	25,000	30,000	40,000	70,000	80,000

Required:

1. For each of the five years, compute (*a*) the profit margin on sales, (*b*) the return on owners' equity, (*c*) the return on total assets, and (*d*) the financial leverage effect. Round to the nearest percentage.
2. Based on Requirement 1, assess the five-year trend of earnings reflected in the income statement.

E 25–9
Four Financial Reporting Models
(L.O. 6, 7)

Nicky Company purchased land for $200,000 on January 1, 1990. Near the end of 1990, Nicky received several offers from other firms to purchase the land. The bids are all within $1,000 of the average $250,000 bid. Other, similar plots of land in the vicinity have sold for amounts very close to $250,000 in the recent past. Nicky decided not to sell. General price-level indices are as follows: January 1, 1990, 100; December 31, 1990, 110.

Required:

Discuss how each of the four models for financial reporting discussed in the text (HC/ND, HC/CD, CC/ND, CC/CD) would report the above information. Include income statement and balance sheet effects in your discussion, as well as general advantages and disadvantages of each approach.

E 25–10
Overview Questions about HC/CD Disclosures
(L.O. 7)

Select the best answer in each of the following. Give the basis for your response.

1. In preparing HC/CD financial statements, monetary items consist of:
   a. Cash items plus all receivables with a fixed maturity date.
   b. Cash, other assets expected to be converted into cash, and current liabilities.
   c. Assets and liabilities whose amounts are fixed by contract or otherwise in terms of dollars, regardless of price level changes.
   d. Assets and liabilities classified as current on the balance sheet.
   e. None of the above.
2. In preparing HC/CD financial statements, a nonmonetary item would include:
   a. Accounts payable in cash.
   b. Long-term bonds payable.
   c. Accounts receivable.
   d. Allowance for doubtful accounts.
   e. None of the above.
3. An accountant who recommends the restatement of financial statements for GPL changes should *not* support this recommendation by stating that:
   a. Purchasing power gains and losses should be recognized.
   b. Historical dollars are not comparable to present-day dollars.
   c. The conversion of asset costs to a constant dollar basis is a useful extension of the original cost basis of asset valuation.
   d. Assets should be valued at their replacement cost.
4. During a period of deflation, an entity usually would have the greatest gain in general purchasing power by holding:
   a. Cash.
   b. Plant and equipment.
   c. Accounts payable.
   d. Mortgages payable.
   e. None of the above.
5. CD restatement of HC financial statements to reflect GPL changes reports nonmonetary assets at:
   a. Lower of cost or market (LCM).
   b. Current appraisal values.
   c. Costs adjusted for purchasing power changes.

    d. Current replacement cost.

    e. None of the above.

6. An unacceptable practice for reporting HC/CD information is:

    a. The inclusion of general purchasing power gains and losses on monetary items in the price level income statement.

    b. The inclusion of extraordinary gains and losses in the HC/CD income statement.

    c. The use of charts, ratios, and narrative information.

    d. The use of specific price indexes to restate inventories, plant, and equipment.

    e. None of the above.

             (AICPA adapted)

E 25–11

Analysis of HC Statement Items: Comparability

(L.O. 6, 7)

Some items on conventional historical cost basis financial statements are expressed in current period dollars (or nearly so), while other items are normally expressed in dollars of prior periods.

Required:

1. Name the principal balance sheet items that probably would not be expressed in current period dollars. If any part of your answer depends on the accounting procedures employed, explain.

2. Name the principal items in the income statement that likely would not be expressed in current period dollars (or nearly so). If any part of your answer depends on the accounting procedures used, explain.

3. Name the principal items in the statement of cash flows, indirect method, that probably would not be expressed in current period dollars. If any part of your answer depends on the accounting procedures used, explain.

             (AICPA adapted)

E 25–12

Analysis of GPL Index Numbers: Investment

(L.O. 7)

Becker Corporation sold one third of its long-term investment in the common stock of another company (carried at cost) and made the entry shown in Column A below:

	Column A	Column B
Cash 62,000		62,000
Investment in stock	50,000	57,500
Gain on sale of investment	12,000	4,500

In preparing HC/CD statements, the transaction of Column A was restated as shown in Column B.

Required:

Round restatement ratios to five decimal places.

1. If the GPL index was 138 when the transaction recorded above occurred, what was the GPL index when the stock was acquired? Show computations.

2. Assume the remaining two thirds of the stock is sold later for $120,000 when the GPL index is 147. Give entries paralleling those above in Columns A and B.

3. If the stock prices and GPL index values given were unchanged, what other factors, if any, would cause entries reflected in Columns A and B to differ at the time of either the first or second sale?

E 25–13

HC/CD of Individual Items on the Balance Sheet and Income Statement

(L.O. 8)

Bertrand Company is preparing financial statements on the HC/CD basis. Selected data are as follows:

a. GPL index data: 1/1/1987, 115; 12/31/1987, 120; 6/30/1988, 126; 12/31/1990, 168; Average for 1991, 174; 12/31/1991, 180.

b. Property, plant and equipment acquisition and depreciation data.

    (1) Land acquired January 1, 1987, at a cost of $90,000.

    (2) Building acquired December 31, 1987, at a cost of $120,000; by year-end, 1990 and 1991, respectively, accumulated depreciation on the building amounted to $44,000 and $48,000.

    (3) Equipment costing $168,000 was acquired June 30, 1988; by December 31, 1990, accumulated depreciation amounted to $109,200; depreciation recorded for 1991 was $8,400.

c. Monetary items: At the start of 1991, total monetary assets amounted to $120,000, while total monetary liabilities amounted to $180,000. At the end of 1991, total monetary assets amounted to $140,000, while total monetary liabilities were $190,000.

Required:

Use the numbers below for identification and compute the amounts for each numbered item. Round CD restatement ratios to five decimal places.

A. On the HC/CD balance sheet as of December 31, 1991, carrying values for each would be:
   1. Land.
   2. Building (gross amount).
   3. Accumulated depreciation—building.
   4. Original equipment (gross amount).
   5. New equipment (gross amount).
   6. Accumulated depreciation on equipment (original).
   7. Accumulated depreciation on equipment (new).
   8. Total monetary assets.
   9. Total monetary liabilities.
B. On the HC/CD income statement for the year ended December 31, 1991, amounts reported would be:
   10. Depreciation expense (original equipment).
   11. Depreciation expense (new equipment).
   12. Depreciation expense (building).
   13. Sales revenue (if sales of $400,000 were made evenly throughout 1991).

E 25–14
HC/CD Restatement,
Seven Questions:
an Overview
(L.O. 7, 8)

Select the best answer in each of the following questions. Items are independent of one another except when otherwise indicated. Give the basis, including computations, for your choice.

The following information is applicable to Items 1 through 3:

Equipment purchased for $120,000 on January 1, 1989, when the price index was 100, was sold on December 31, 1991, at a price of $85,000. The equipment originally was expected to last six years with no residual value and was depreciated on a straight-line basis. The GPL index at the end of 1989 was 125; 1990, 150; and 1991, 175.

1. HC/CD (CDs as of December 31, 1989) financial statements prepared at the end of 1989 would include:
   a. Equipment, $150,000; accumulated depreciation, $25,000; and no gain or loss.
   b. Equipment, $150,000; accumulated depreciation, $25,000; and a gain, $30,000.
   c. Equipment, $150,000; accumulated depreciation, $20,000; and a gain, $30,000.
   d. Equipment, $120,000; accumulated depreciation, $20,000; and a gain, $30,000.
   e. None of the above.
2. HC/CD (CDs as of December 31, 1990) financial statements prepared at the end of 1990 should include depreciation expense of:
   a. $35,000.   *d.* $20,000.
   b. $30,000.   *e.* None of the above.
   c. $25,000.
3. The HC/CD (CDs as of December 31, 1991) income statement prepared at the end of 1991 should include:
   a. A gain of $35,000.   *d.* A loss of $5,000.
   b. A gain of $25,000.   *e.* None of the above.
   c. No gain or loss.
4. If land were purchased at a cost of $20,000 in January 1989 when the GPL index was 120 and sold in December 1993 when the GPL index was 150, the selling price that would result in no gain or loss on a HC/CD basis would be:
   a. $30,000.   *d.* $16,000.
   b. $24,000.   *e.* None of the above.
   c. $20,000.
5. If land were purchased in 1989 for $100,000 when the GPL index was 100 and sold at the end of 1995 for $160,000 when the GPL index was 170, the HC/CD (CDs as of the end of 1995) income statement for 1995 would show:
   a. A purchasing power gain of $70,000 and a loss on sale of land of $10,000.
   b. A gain on sale of land of $60,000.

    c. A purchasing power loss of $10,000.

    d. A loss on sale of land of $10,000.

    e. None of the above.

6. If the base year is 1989 (when the GPL index = 100) and land is purchased for $50,000 in 1991 when the GPL index is 108.5, the cost of the land restated to 1989 general purchasing power (rounded to the nearest whole dollar) would be:

    a. $54,250.   *d.* $45,750.

    b. $50,000.   *e.* None of the above.

    c. $46,083.

7. Assume the same facts as in (6). The cost of the land restated to December 31, 1995, general purchasing power when the GPL index was 119.2 (rounded to the nearest whole dollar) would be:

    a. $59,600.   *d.* $45,512.

    b. $54,931.   *e.* None of the above.

    c. $46,083.

(AICPA adapted)

E 25–15
HC/CD, Nine Questions:
an Overview
(L.O. 6, 7)

Select the best answer in each of the following. Give the basis for your response.

1. The valuation basis used in HC financial statements is:

    a. Market value.

    b. Original cost.

    c. Replacement cost.

    d. A mixture of costs and values.

    e. None of the above.

2. When preparing HC/CD financial statements, it would not be appropriate to use:

    a. Cost or market, whichever is lower, in the valuation of inventories.

    b. Replacement cost in the valuation of plant assets.

    c. The HC basis in reporting income tax expense.

    d. The actual amounts payable in reporting liabilities on the balance sheet.

    e. Any of the above.

3. Gains and losses on nonmonetary assets usually are reported in HC financial statements when the items are sold. Gains and losses on the sale of nonmonetary assets should be reported in HC/CD financial statements:

    a. In the same period, but the amount will probably differ.

    b. In the same period and the same amount.

    c. Over the life of the nonmonetary asset.

    d. Partly over the life of the nonmonetary asset and the remainder when the asset is sold.

    e. None of the above.

4. A practice of presenting HC/CD information that is not acceptable is the:

    a. Use of charts, ratios, and narrative information.

    b. Use of GPL indexes to restate inventories, plant, and equipment.

    c. Inclusion of purchasing power gains and losses on monetary items in the HC/CD income statement.

    d. Inclusion of extraordinary gains and losses in the HC/CD income statement.

    e. None of the above.

5. For purposes of restating financial statements for changes in the general level of prices, monetary items consist of:

    a. Assets and liabilities whose amounts are fixed by contract or otherwise in terms of dollars regardless of price level changes.

    b. Assets and liabilities that are classified as current on the balance sheet.

    c. Cash items plus all receivables with a fixed maturity date.

    d. Cash, other assets expected to be converted into cash, and current liabilities.

6. Following are four observations regarding the amounts reported in HC/CD financial statements. Which observation is valid?

    a. The HC/CD amount reported for an asset usually approximates its current market value.

    b. The HC/CD amounts are not departures from historical cost.

    c. When inventory increases and prices are rising, last-in first-out (LIFO) inventory accounting has the same effect on financial statements as HC/CD amounts.

    d. When inventory remains constant and prices are rising, LIFO inventory accounting has the same effect on financial statements as HC/CD amounts.

Items 7, 8, and 9 are based on the following information. The general price level index at the end of each of the following years was as follows: 1987, 100; 1988, 110; 1989, 115; 1990, 120; and 1991, 140.

7. In December 1990, Russel Corporation purchased land for $300,000. The land was held until December 1991, when it was sold for $400,000. The HC/CD (CDs as of December 31, 1991) income statement for the year ended December 31, 1991, should include how much gain or loss on this sale?
   a. $20,000 loss.   c. $50,000 gain.
   b. $20,000 purchasing power loss.   d. $100,000 gain.

8. On January 1, 1988, the Silver Company purchased equipment for $300,000. The equipment was being depreciated over an estimated life of 10 years on the straight-line method, with no estimated residual value. On December 31, 1991, the equipment was sold for $200,000. The HC/CD (CDs as of December 31, 1991) income statement for the year ended December 31, 1991, should include how much gain or loss from this sale?
   a. $10,600 loss.   c. $20,000 gain.
   b. $16,000 gain.   d. $52,000 loss.

9. An analysis of the Gallant Corporation's Machinery and Equipment account as of December 31, 1991, follows:

Machinery and equipment:	
Acquired in December 1988	$400,000
Acquired in December 1990	100,000
Balance	$500,000

Accumulated depreciation:	
On equipment acquired in December 1988	$160,000
On equipment acquired in December 1990	20,000
Balance	$180,000

An HC/CD (CDs as of December 31, 1991) balance sheet prepared as of December 31, 1991, should include machinery and equipment net of accumulated depreciation of:
   a. $284,848.   c. $398,788.
   b. $360,000.   d. $448,000.

(AICPA adapted)

E 25-16
Analysis of Purchasing Power Gain or Loss on Monetary Items
(L.O. 7, 8)

An incomplete computation of purchasing power gain or loss on net monetary items is given below.

	HC	HC/CD
Total beginning excess of monetary assets over monetary liabilities	$121,000	$132,000
Increases during the year:		
Sales revenue	$287,500	$300,000
Sale of common stock	106,200	108,000
Total increases	$393,700	$408,000
Decreases during the year:		
Purchases	$197,800	$206,400
Expenses	33,120	34,560
Cash dividend declared	20,000	20,000
Total decreases	$250,920	$260,960

Additional data: Sales, purchases, and expenses occurred evenly throughout the year. The GPL index at year-end was 120.

Required:
Support each answer; show how it was derived.

1. What was the index value when the period began?
2. What was the average index value for the year?

3. What was the index value when the stock was sold?
4. Assuming prices rose steadily, when was the dividend declared?
5. What was the purchasing power gain or loss on net monetary items?

E 25-17
CC/CD: Analysis of
Inventory and Cost of
Goods Sold
(L.O. 9)

The following information is available regarding the inventory of Spruce Corporation:

	HC	CC (at Transaction or Balance Date)
January 1, 1991, balance	$ 90,000	$100,000
Purchases during 1991	600,000	600,000
December 31, 1991, balance	164,000	190,000

Purchases were made evenly during 1991. Merchandise that sold evenly during 1991 had an average current cost of $50 per unit (10,800 units sold). GPL index information during 1991 was: January 1, 1991, 100; Average for 1991, 115; December 31, 1991, 132.

Required:
Round ratios to three decimal places.

1. Set up and complete a schedule of inventory changes in the current cost (CC) of inventory and compute (*a*) total increase in CC, (*b*) increase in CC due to general inflation, and (*c*) decrease in CC net of general inflation. *Suggestion:* set up three column headings: CC at transaction or balance date, CC restatement ratio, and CC/CD (in CDs as of 12/31/1991). Also indicate what items would be reported on the CC/CD financial statements.
2. Assume the CC/CD income from continuing operations is $80,000 and the purchasing power loss on net monetary items is $24,000. Complete the CC/CD income statement for Spruce Corporation.

E 25-18
CC/CD: Analysis of
Equipment
(L.O. 9)

Wood Company acquired equipment on January 1, 1988, at a cost of $100,000. On December 31, 1990, the current cost of the equipment was $140,000, and on December 31, 1991, the current cost was $170,000. Both current cost amounts are estimated before deducting associated accumulated depreciation. The equipment is being depreciated on a straight-line basis over a 10-year period with no residual value. GPL index data are as follows: January 1, 1988, 105; December 31, 1990, 120; December 31, 1991, 128; 1991 average, 124.

Required:
Round all CD restatement ratios to three decimal places.

1. Compute the CC of the equipment, net of accumulated depreciation, on December 31, 1990, and December 31, 1991.
2. Compute CC depreciation expense for 1991.
3. Compute for equipment 1991: (*a*) the total change in CC and (*b*) the change in CC due to general inflation at December 31, 1991. Set up captions for CC at transaction or balance date, CD restatement ratio, and CC/CD.
4. Assume the CC/CD income from continuing operations is $95,000 and the purchasing power loss on net monetary items is $11,000. Complete the CC/CD income statement for Wood Company.

E 25-19
CC/CD: FIFO versus
LIFO
(L.O. 9)

Signal Corporation purchased all of the shares of Flag Corporation (it will be a subsidiary) on January 1, 1991, at a cost of $150,000. Flag Corporation had cash and receivables of $10,000; finished goods inventory, $50,000; building, $125,000, with accumulated depreciation, $60,000; and land, $15,000. All amounts reflect the HC basis. Flag Corporation had no liabilities at the time of the acquisition, and the GPL index was 109.

It is now December 31, 1991, and the GPL index is 122. The December 31, 1991, balance sheet data of the purchased company are as follows, with HC and CC/CD data in comparative form:

FLAG CORPORATION
Balance Sheet—HC and CC/CD
December 31, 1991

	HC	CC/CD
Cash and receivables	$ 15,000	$ 15,000
Finished goods inventory	65,000	75,000
Building	125,000	150,000
Accumulated depreciation, building	(65,000)	(78,000)
Land	10,000	30,000
Total assets	$150,000	$192,000
Liabilities	$ 25,000	$ 30,000
Owners' equity	125,000	162,000
Total equities	$150,000	$192,000

Required:

1. Which item on the CC/CD balance sheet is reported incorrectly? Why?
2. Does the fact that CC data are presented for the building mean that the building could be sold on December 31, 1991, for $150,000? for $72,000? Explain.
3. Which inventory method (i.e., LIFO, FIFO, average, etc.) would yield an ending inventory cost closest to the CC/CD amount? for cost of goods sold?

E 25-20
CC/CD: Analysis of Changes in Land Costs (L.O. 9)

Waco Development Corporation acquired land on January 1, 1987, for $1,000,000. On June 30, 1991, half of the land was sold for $1,600,000. The following current cost data regarding the land are available:

	CC of Land	GPL Index
January 1, 1991	$2,800,000	150
June 30, 1991		162
1991—average		160
December 31, 1991	1,700,000*	171

*After sale of land.

Required:
Round all CD restatement ratios to three decimal places.

1. Compute for land the 1991 change in CC as follows: (*a*) total, (*b*) due to general inflation, and (*c*) net of general inflation (in average CDs of 1991). Set up column headings for CC at transaction or balance date, CD restatement ratio, and CC/CD.
2. Assume the CC/CD income from continuing operations is $1,600,000 and that the purchasing power loss on net monetary items is $30,000. Complete the CC/CD income statement for Waco Development Corporation.

PROBLEMS

P 25-1
Compute and Evaluate Ratios: Current Position, Equity Position, and Operating Results for Three Years (L.O. 3)

The financial statements of Larkin Manufacturing Company for a three-year period:

	1990	1991	1992
Total assets	$2,000,000	$2,040,000	$1,940,000
Total current assets	368,000	450,000	480,000
Total current liabilities	230,000	150,000	150,000
Operational assets (net)	1,248,000	1,257,600	1,260,000
Total liabilities	1,090,000	1,110,000	900,000
Common stock (par value $100)	600,000	600,000	700,000
Retained earnings	310,000	330,000	340,000
Sales revenue (net)	6,600,000	7,000,000	7,100,000
Net income (after tax)	50,000	70,000	40,000
Interest expense (net of tax)	34,000	38,000	30,000

Required:
Round to one decimal place.

1. Based on the above data, compute the following ratios for each year.
   a. Current ratio.
   b. Working capital turnover.
   Evaluate the current position. What additional information do you need to adequately evaluate the current position? Explain.
2. Based on the above data, compute the following ratios to measure the equity position:
   a. Debt to equity.
   b. Debt to total assets.
   c. Book value per share of common stock.
   Evaluate the equity position. What additional information do you need to adequately evaluate the equity position? Explain.
3. Based on the above data, compute the following ratios to measure profitability and leverage:
   a. Profit margin on sales.
   b. Return on average total assets.
   c. Return on average owners' equity.
   d. Effect of financial leverage.
   Evaluate the operating results and financial leverage.

P 25-2
Compute, Interpret, and Evaluate Three Equity Ratios
(L.O. 3)

The balance sheet for two similar companies reflected the following:

	Company A	Company B
Current liabilities	$ 30,000	$ 30,000
Long-term liabilities	30,000	230,000
Stockholders' equity:		
Common stock, par $5	170,000	46,000
Preferred stock, par $10	50,000	20,000
Contributed capital in excess of par, common	20,000	4,000
Retained earnings	60,000	30,000
Net income, included in the above retained earnings		
amount (less taxes 40%)	50,000	20,000

Required:

1. Compute the first two ratios listed in Exhibit 25-6 that measure equity position. Interpret the result.
2. Compute the leverage effect for each company. The average interest rate on total liabilities is 10% for both companies.
3. Interpret and evaluate the situation for each company.

P 25-3
Ratios to Measure Operating Results: Evaluate Implications
(L.O. 3)

The following annual data were taken from the records of McKeon Trading Corporation:

	1989	1990	1991	1992	1993
Sales revenue	$400,000	$420,000	$450,000	$440,000	$490,000
Net income	15,000	16,000	20,000	5,000	40,000
Total assets	200,000*	220,000	230,000	240,000	250,000
Owners' equity	100,000*	110,000	120,000	115,000	140,000
Market price per common share	20	20	33	14	60
Dividends per common share	4	4	4	1	5
Capital stock outstanding (shares)	4,000	4,000	4,000	3,900	3,800
Interest expense (net of tax)	4,000	4,500	4,600	5,000	4,100

* The beginning balance was the same as this year-end balance.

Required:

Compute the ratios that measure profitability and compute leverage for the years 1990, 1991, 1992, and 1993. Immediately following each ratio, evaluate and comment on the results (e.g., trends, problems, and favorable/unfavorable implications).

P 25–4

Leverage, Sell Capital Stock versus Debt: Analyze

(L.O. 3)

Boggs Corporation is considering building a second plant at a cost of $600,000. The management is considering two alternatives to obtain the funds: (a) sell additional common stock or (b) issue $600,000 five-year bonds payable at 10% interest. The management believes that the bonds can be sold at par (for $600,000) and the stock at $10 per share.

The balance sheet (before the new financing) reflected the following:

Liabilities . . . . None
Common stock, nopar $300,000
Retained earnings 100,000
Average income for past several years (net of tax) 30,000

The average income tax rate is 40%. Average dividends per share have been 50 cents per share per year. Expected increase in pretax income (excluding interest expense) from the new plant, $100,000 per year.

Required:

1. Prepare an analysis to show (a) expected income after the addition, (b) cash flows from the company to prospective owners of the new capital, and (c) the leverage advantage or disadvantage to the present stockholders of issuing the bonds to obtain the financing.
2. What are the principal arguments for and against issuing the bonds (as opposed to selling the common stock)?

P 25–5

Prepare HC/CD Balance Sheet, Income Statement, and Retained Earnings Statement

(L.O. 8)

The items reflected in the September 30 trial balance, given below, were acquired when the relevant GPL index was 105.0 except for capital stock, which was 105.2377 (to avoid rounding error).

Cash	$ 27,235	
Land	79,085	
Accounts payable		$ 2,570
Capital stock		100,000
Retained earnings		3,750*
	$106,320	$106,320

* HC/CD on this date, $4,165.

The following transactions were computed during the first quarter of the current accounting year.

Date	GPL Index	Data
Oct. 1	110	Purchased machinery costing $9,600 on account.
15	120	Paid for machinery purchased on October 1.
31	135	Billed customers for services rendered, $8,000.
Nov. 15	140	Paid $1,230 of the initial liability balance.
30	145	Collected half of the billed revenue.
Dec. 10	150	Paid general expense of $5,700.
31	160	Recorded three months' depreciation on machinery, which has a five-year life with no residual value.

Required:

1. Enter the initial balances and then record the transactions for the first quarter directly into ledger accounts; also include, in parentheses, the GPL index number prevailing when each transaction occurred.
2. As of the close of the quarter, prepare the balance sheet and income statement on the HC basis and the HC/CD (CDs as of December 31) basis using the GPL index number procedures illustrated in the chapter. Show calculation of the purchasing power gain or loss on net monetary items. Prepare a retained earnings statement at HC and HC/CD (the HC/CD beginning balance is $6,058). No average index value for the period is given. Therefore, it will be necessary to apply to each transaction a specific CD restatement ratio. For example, if a $360 transaction occurred when the index was 120, in December 31 terms, this would convert to $360 × 160/120 = $480. Round all calculations to the nearest dollar.

P 25-6
HC/CD, Six Analytical
Questions: an Overview
(L.O. 7)

Select the best answer in each of the following. Justify your choices.

1. A company was formed on January 1, 1990. Selected balances from its HC balance sheet at December 31, 1990, were as follows:

Accounts receivable	$ 70,000
Accounts payable	60,000
Long-term debt	110,000
Common stock	100,000

At what amounts should these selected accounts be shown in an HC/CD (CDs as of December 31, 1990) balance sheet at December 31, 1990, if the general price level index was 100 at December 31, 1989, and 110 at December 31, 1990?

	Accounts Receivable	Accounts Payable	Long-Term Debt	Common Stock
a.	$70,000	$60,000	$110,000	$100,000
b.	70,000	60,000	110,000	110,000
c.	70,000	60,000	121,000	110,000
d.	77,000	66,000	121,000	110,000

2. Baker Company reported sales of $2,000,000 in 1990 and $3,000,000 in 1991, made evenly throughout each year. The GPL index during 1989 remained constant at 100, and at the end of 1990 and 1991 it was 102 and 104, respectively. What should Baker report as sales revenue for 1991, restated for CD (in CDs as of the end of 1991) changes?
   a. $3,000,000.   c. $3,058,821.
   b. $3,029,126.   d. $3,120,000.

3. On January 2, 1991, the Mannix Corporation mortgaged one of its properties as collateral for a $1,000,000, 12%, five-year loan. The mortgage note payable was interest-bearing, and the interest rate was realistic. During 1991, the GPL increased evenly, resulting in a 5% rise for the year.
   In preparing an HC/CD (CDs as of the end of 1991) balance sheet at the end of 1991, at what amount should Mannix report the five-year mortgage note?
   a. $950,000.   c. $1,025,000.
   b. $1,000,000.   d. $1,050,000.

4. The HC balance sheet of Post Company showed the original cost of depreciable assets as $5,000,000 at December 31, 1989, and $6,000,000 at December 31, 1990. These asset costs are being depreciated on a straight-line basis over a 10-year period with no residual value. Acquisitions of $1,000,000 were made on January 1, 1990. A full year's depreciation was taken in the year of acquisition.
   Post presents HC/CD financial statements as supplemental information to its HC financial statements. The December 31, 1989, depreciable assets balance (before accumulated depreciation) restated to reflect December 31, 1990, purchasing power was $5,800,000. What amount of depreciation expense should be shown in the HC/CD (CDs as of December 31, 1990) income statement for 1990 if the GPL index was 100 at December 31, 1989, and 110 at December 31, 1990?
   a. $600,000.   c. $670,000.
   b. $660,000.   d. $690,000.

5. If a constant unit of measurement during a period of inflation is used, the general purchasing power of the dollar in which some expenses are measured (for assets systematically allocated among several accounting periods) may differ significantly from the general purchasing power of the dollar in which revenue is measured. Which of the following accounting procedures minimizes this effect?
   a. Allowance method of accounting for bad debts.
   b. Income tax allocation.
   c. Accelerated depreciation.
   d. Valuing inventory at the LCM.

6. Land was purchased for $20,000 when the GPL index was 115. When the index was 138, the land was sold for $25,000. Ignoring taxes on the transaction, the landowner, for having bought and sold the land, is economically (i.e., in terms of purchasing power):
   a. Worse off.
   b. Better off.
   c. In the same position.

P 25-7
HC/CD, Six Analytical
Questions: an Overview
(L.O. 7)

Select the best answer in each of the following. Justify your choices. For questions 1 to 4 below, use the following GPL data (round CD restatement ratios to three decimals): 12/31/1989, 165; 3/31/1990, 171; 6/30/1990, 175; 9/30/1990, 180; 12/31/1990, 186; 3/31/1991, 190; 6/30/1991, 194; 9/30/1991, 198; 12/31/1991, 201.

1. On January 1, 1990, P Corporation had as its only asset $14,000 in cash (no liabilities). On March 31, 1990, P Corporation paid $10,000 for a machine that will have a 10-year life and no residual value. On September 30, 1990, P Corporation purchased merchandise inventory on account for $2,000. At an even rate during the three months ended December 31, 1990, P Corporation paid off the $2,000 on the inventory and sold half the inventory for $1,300 cash. If these are the only transactions P Corporation entered into during 1990, the company will report for 1990 (in terms of CDs as of 12/31/1990) a purchasing power gain or loss on net monetary items of:
   a. Loss of $730.   *c.* Gain of $730.
   b. Loss of $852.   *d.* Gain of $852.

2. Assume that P Corporation's January 1, 1990, owners' equity consisted of capital stock of $14,000. On its HC/CD (CDs as of 12/31/1990) income statement for the year ended December 31, 1990, P Corporation will report net income (loss)—ignoring the purchasing power gain or loss on net monetary items—of:
   a. $(552).   *c.* $(510).
   b. $(528).   *d.* $506.

3. On its December 31, 1990, HC/CD (CDs as of 12/31/1990) balance sheet P Corporation will report cash of:
   a. $3,300.   *c.* $2,570.
   b. $4,160.   *d.* $5,808.

4. You are in the process of preparing the 1991, HC/CD financial statements (assume that you have been given the necessary transaction data involving revenues and expenses for 1991). In particular, you are now rolling forward the January 1, 1991, HC balance sheet in order to obtain the January 1, 1991, HC/CD owners' equity balance stated in December 31, 1991, dollars—as a test of the accuracy of your other HC/CD restatements. Assuming that the beginning cash balance arose on the beginning date, the correct January 1, 1991, owners' equity stated in December 31, 1991, dollars would be.
   a. $14,394.   *d.* $15,950.
   b. $14,644.   *e.* None of the above.
   c. $15,554.

5. Under HC/CD reporting, purchasing power gains are earned during inflation on:
   a. Net monetary assets.   *c.* Nonmonetary assets.
   b. Net monetary liabilities.   *d.* Nonmonetary liabilities.

6. Which of the following items is a nonmonetary item?
   a. Marketable securities—bonds to be held to maturity.
   b. Accounts receivable.
   c. Accounts payable.
   d. Preferred stock stated at liquidation value.
   e. Unearned revenue.

P 25-8
HC/CD Financial
Statements
(L.O. 8)

Wagner Company prepared the following comparative balance sheets (HC basis) at the close of its 10th year of operations (1991):

	December 31	
	1990	**1991**
Cash	$ 75,000	$101,000
Receivables (net)	215,000	195,000
Inventory	135,000	127,000
Land	150,000	150,000
Building	240,000	240,000
Accumulated depreciation, building	(56,000)	(64,000)
Machinery	225,000	280,000
Accumulated depreciation, machinery	(115,000)	(137,500)
Total	$869,000	$891,500

	December 31	
	1990	1991
Current liabilities	$124,000	$137,000
Long-term liabilities	75,000	81,000
Bonds payable	60,000	60,000
Common stock	350,000	350,000
Retained earnings	260,000*	263,500
Total	$869,000	$891,500

* At HC/CD on this date, $277,070.

In 1982, when the GPL index was 104, the common stock was issued and the land was purchased. The building was acquired early in 1984 when the GPL index was 107; it has an estimated 30-year life and no residual value and is depreciated on a straight-line basis. Machinery is depreciated 10% per year on cost with no residual value. The first machine was purchased at a cost of $50,000 in 1983 when the GPL index was 106; a second machine was acquired for $100,000 in 1985 when the index was 108.5; a third machine was purchased in 1989 when the index was 117. A full year's depreciation is taken in the year of acquisition unless the purchase is at year-end. At year-end 1991, machinery costing $55,000 was acquired.

On January 2, 1991, an $85,000 dividend was declared and paid when the GPL index was 121. Assume the beginning inventory was acquired when the GPL index was 107; the ending inventory should be restated to CDs on the assumption the index was 125 when it was purchased.

Sales, operating expenses, income taxes, and purchases occurred evenly during 1991. Relevant GPL index data (aside from that already given) are as follows: 12/31/1990, 121; 12/31/1991, 127; Average for 1991, 125. The income statement (HC basis) for the year 1991 was as follows:

Sales revenue		$1,275,000
Cost of goods sold:		
Inventory, January 1	$135,000	
Purchases	850,000	
Goods available	985,000	
Inventory, December 31	127,000	
Cost of goods sold		858,000
Gross margin		417,000
Expenses:		
Operating (excluding depreciation)	210,000	
Depreciation, building	8,000	
Depreciation, machinery	22,500	240,500
Income before taxes		176,500
Income tax expense		88,000
Net income		$ 88,500

Required:

Prepare an income statement for 1991 and a balance sheet as of December 31, 1991, on an HC/CD (CDs as of December 31, 1991) basis. Round all CD restatement ratios to three decimals. Show computations of the purchasing power gain or loss on net monetary items. Prepare a proof of retained earnings.

P 25–9
HC/CD: Analyze
Equipment Accounts for
Three Years and Compute
Purchasing Power Gain or
Loss on Monetary Items
(L.O. 8)

Cutter Retail Corporation was organized during 1988. Cutter's management has decided to supplement its December 31, 1991, HC financial statements with HC/CD financial statements. The following trial balance (HC basis) and additional information have been furnished:

CUTTER RETAIL CORPORATION
Trial Balance
December 31, 1991

	Debit	Credit
Cash and receivables (net)	$ 270,000	
Short-term investments (common stock)	200,000	
Inventory	220,000	
Equipment	325,000	
Accumulated depreciation, equipment		$ 82,000
Accounts payable		150,000
6% first-mortgage bonds, due 2009		250,000
Common stock, $10 par		500,000
Retained earnings, 12/31/1990	23,000	
Sales revenue		950,000
Cost of goods sold	754,000	
Depreciation	32,500	
Other operating expenses including interest	107,500	
	$1,932,000	$1,932,000

a. Monetary assets (cash and receivables) exceeded monetary liabilities (accounts payable and bonds payable) by $222,500 at December 31, 1990.

b. Purchases ($920,000 in 1991) and sales are made evenly throughout the year.

c. Depreciation is computed on a straight-line basis, with a full year's depreciation being taken in the year of acquisition and none in the year of retirement. The depreciation rate is 10%, and no residual value is anticipated. Acquisitions and retirements have been made evenly over each year, and the retirements in 1991 consisted of assets purchased during 1989 that were scrapped. An analysis of the equipment account reveals the following:

Year	Beginning Balance	Additions	Retirements	Ending Balance
1989	—	$275,000	—	$275,000
1990	$275,000	5,000	—	280,000
1991	280,000	75,000	$30,000	325,000

d. The bonds were issued in 1989, and the short-term investment in common stock was purchased evenly over 1991. Other operating expenses, including interest, are assumed to be incurred evenly throughout the year.

e. Assume the values of the GPL index were as follows:

Annual Averages	GPL Index	Quarterly Averages	GPL Index
1988	113.9	1990, 4th	123.5
1989	116.8	1991, 1st	124.9
1990	121.8	2d	126.1
1991	126.7	3d	127.3
		4th and year-end	128.5

Required:

Round CD statement ratios to three decimals.

1. Prepare a schedule to convert the equipment account balance at December 31, 1991, from HC to HC/CD (CDs as of 12/31/1991) amounts.

2. Prepare a schedule to analyze, at HC, the equipment—accumulated depreciation account for the year 1991.

3. Prepare a schedule to analyze, at HC/CD (CDs as of 12/31/1991), the equipment—accumulated depreciation account for the year 1991.

4. Prepare a schedule to compute Cutter's purchasing power gain or loss on its net monetary items for 1991 (ignore income tax implications).

(AICPA adapted)

P 25–10
CC/CD: Analyze Fleet of Trucks, Income Statement
(L.O. 9)

Brown Hauling Company maintains a fleet of trucks for use in its business. Information regarding the acquisition dates and cost of these trucks is provided below:

Total Cost	Date Acquired	GPL Index
$80,000	January 1, 1988	100
60,000	January 1, 1989	115
50,000	June 30, 1990	125

Trucks are depreciated on a straight-line basis over a five-year life with residual value estimated to be zero. The acquisition on June 30, 1990, was depreciated for one half of a year in 1990.

A schedule of the current cost of the trucks (before deducting accumulated depreciation) is given below as of January 1, 1991, and December 31, 1991:

Trucks Acquired In	CC on 1/1/1991	CC on 12/31/1991
1988	$100,000	$125,000
1989	80,000	90,000
1990	60,000	80,000

Additional GPL index data are as follows: January 1, 1991, 130; 1991—average, 135; December 31, 1991, 140.

Required:

1. Compute the current cost of the trucks, net of accumulated depreciation, on January 1, 1991, and December 31, 1991.
2. Compute 1991 depreciation expense for the trucks on a current cost basis.
3. Prepare a schedule that shows (*a*) the total 1991 change in CC, (*b*) the change in CC, due to general inflation, and (*c*) the change in CC, net of general inflation (in CDs as of 12/31/1991). Set up column headings for CC at transaction or balance date, CD restatement ratio, and CC/CD.
4. Assume the CC/CD income from continuing operations is $150,000 and the purchasing power loss on net monetary items is $12,000. Complete the CC/CD income statement for Brown Company.

P 25–11
CC/CD: Analysis of Inventory, Income Statement
(L.O. 9)

The following information regarding the historical and current cost of Control Corporation's inventory is available:

	HC	CC*
January 1, 1990, inventory	$ 10,000	$ 10,000
1990 purchases	100,000	100,000
1990 cost of goods sold	80,000	90,000
December 31, 1990, inventory	30,000	50,000
1991 purchases	120,000	120,000
1991 cost of goods sold	95,000	115,000
December 31, 1991, inventory	55,000	75,000

* Current cost at transaction or balance date.

GPL index data are as follows: January 1, 1990, 110; 1990—average, 118; December 31, 1990, 125; 1991—average, 132; December 31, 1991, 140. Sales and purchases occurred evenly during 1990 and 1991.

Required:

Round all CD restatement ratios to three decimal places.

1. Prepare a schedule of the total 1990 change in CC, change in CC due to general inflation, and change in CC, net of general inflation (in average CDs of 1990) for inventory. Set up three column headings, CC at transaction or balance date, CD restatement ratio, and CC/CD.
2. Assume the CC/CD income from continuing operations is $80,000 and that the purchasing power loss on net monetary items is $10,000. Complete the CC/CD income statement for 1990 for Control Company.

3. Prepare a schedule of the total 1991 change in CC, change in CC due to general inflation, and change in CC, net of general inflation (in average CDs of 1991) for inventory. Set up three column headings, CC at transaction or balance date, CD restatement ratio, and CC/CD.
4. Assume the CC/CD income from continuing operations is $90,000 and that the purchasing power gain on net monetary items is $7,000. Complete the CC/CD income statement for 1991 for Control Company.
5. Does the cost flow assumption used for inventory (i.e., LIFO, FIFO) affect the computation of changes in current cost? Explain.

P 25–12
CC/CD: Analysis of Equipment CC Changes and Income
(L.O. 9)

The following information regarding the historical and current cost of equipment for Weller Corporation is available:

Date of Acquisition (Retirement)	Original Cost	CC on 12/31/1989	CC on 12/31/1990	CC on 12/31/1991
1/1/1989	$100,000	$140,000	$160,000	$110,000*
6/30/1989	80,000	120,000	145,000	170,000
1/1/1990	40,000		50,000	64,000
1/1/1991	50,000			55,000
12/31/1991	(60,000)			
Total	$210,000	$260,000	$355,000	$399,000

* After retirement on 12/31/1991.

When equipment was sold on December 31, 1991, it had a CC (before deducting accumulated depreciation) of $70,000. Equipment is depreciated over a 10-year life, with an estimated residual value of zero. GPL index data are: January 1, 1989, 108; June 30, 1989, 112; December 31, 1989, 120; December 31, 1990, 135; 1990 average, 128; December 31, 1991, 150; 1991 average, 142.

Required:
Round all CD restatement ratios to three decimals.

1. Compute depreciation expense on a CC basis for 1990 (in average CDs for 1990) and 1991 (in average CDs for 1991).
2. Compute the CC of equipment, net of accumulated depreciation, on the following dates:
   a. December 31, 1989 (in CDs as of 12/31/1989).
   b. December 31, 1990 (in CDs as of 12/31/1990).
   c. December 31, 1991 (in CDs as of 12/31/1991).
3. Prepare a schedule for equipment of the total change in CC, change in CC due to general inflation, and change in CC, net of general inflation for:
   a. 1990 (in CDs as of 12/31/1990).
   b. 1991 (in CDs as of 12/31/1991).
4. Assume the 1991 CC/CD income from continuing operations is $350,000 and that the purchasing power loss on net monetary items is $22,000. Complete the 1991 CC/CD income statement for Weller Corporation.

P 25–13

COMPREHENSIVE PROBLEM
◆

Prepare CC/CD Financial Statements
(L.O. 6, 7, 8, 9)

Palmer Company prepared the following comparative balance sheet (HC/ND basis) at the close of its 10th year of operations (1991):

	December 31	
	1990	1991
Cash	$ 60,000	$101,000
Receivables (net)	175,000	195,000
Inventory	135,000	127,000
Land	150,000	150,000
Building	240,000	240,000
Accumulated depreciation, building	(48,000)	(56,000)
Machinery	280,000	280,000
Accumulated depreciation, machinery	(196,000)	(224,000)
Total	$796,000	$813,000

| | December 31 | |
	1990	1991
Current liabilities	$124,000	$137,000
Long-term liabilities	75,000	81,000
Bonds payable	60,000	60,000
Common stock	350,000	350,000
Retained earnings	187,000	185,000
Total	$796,000	$813,000

In 1982, when the GPL index was 104, the common stock was issued, and the land was purchased. The building was acquired late in 1984 when the GPL index was 107; it has an estimated 30-year life and no residual value and is depreciated on a straight-line basis. Machinery is depreciated 10% per year on cost with no residual value. The machinery was purchased late in 1983 when the GPL index was 106.

On January 2, 1991, an $85,000 dividend was declared and paid. Sales, operating expenses, income taxes, and purchases occurred evenly during 1991. Relevant GPL index data (aside from that already given) are as follows: 12/31/1990, 121; 12/31/1991, 127; Average for 1991, 125.

The income statement (HC basis) for the year 1991 was as follows:

Sales revenue		$1,275,000
Cost of goods sold:		
Inventory, January 1	$135,000	
Purchases	850,000	
Goods available	985,000	
Inventory, December 31	127,000	
Total cost of goods sold		858,000
Gross margin		417,000
Expenses:		
Operating, excluding depreciation	210,000	
Depreciation, building	8,000	
Depreciation, machinery	28,000	246,000
Income before taxes		171,000
Income tax expense		88,000
Net income		$ 83,000

Current cost data are as follows:

| | December 31 | |
	1990	1991
Nonmonetary assets (in CDs of the balance sheet date):		
Inventory	$160,000	$135,000
Land	185,000	200,000
Building	270,000	270,000
Accumulated depreciation, building	(54,000)	(63,000)
Machinery	300,000	330,000
Accumulated depreciation, machinery	(210,000)	(264,000)
Retained earnings (credit) from prior period	220,000	
Expenses (in average of CDs of 1991):		
Cost of goods sold		$897,000
Depreciation expense, building		9,000
Depreciation expense, machinery		31,500
Sales revenue and all other expenses		Same as HC/ND

Required:

Round all CD restatements ratios to three decimals.

1. Prepare the CC/CD (CDs as of 12/31/1991) balance sheet for the company at December 31, 1991.

2. Prepare the single-step CC/CD (CDs as of 12/31/1991) income statement for the company for the year ended December 31, 1991, with all supporting computations.
3. Prove the accuracy of the CC/CD ending balance of retained earnings.

CASES

C 25–1

Recommend Which Company's Stock Should Be Purchased: Ratio Analysis
(L.O. 3)

Investor Bob is considering investing $100,000 cash in the common stock of either Company A or Company B. The two companies are in the same industry, but in different regions of the country. The following summarized data were taken from the annual audited financial statements (in thousands):

	Company A	Company B
Income Statement:		
Sales revenue	$4,000	$ 9,400
Cost of goods sold	(2,160)	(5,640)
Operating expenses	(500)	(1,710)
Interest expense	(90)	(350)
Income tax expense	(500)	(680)
Extraordinary gain (loss), net of tax	(110)	350
Net income	$ 640	$ 1,370
Balance sheet		
Current assets	$1,000	$ 4,000
Operational assets	4,500	19,000
Accumulated depreciation	(1,500)	(7,000)
Investments, long term (cost)	400	100
Other assets	600	7,900
Total	$5,000	$24,000
Current liabilities	$ 900	$ 2,000
Long-term liabilities	100	1,800
Capital stock, par $1	3,000	18,000
Retained earnings	1,000	2,200
Total	$5,000	$24,000
Additional data for current year:		
Quick assets	$ 400	$ 500
Average income tax rate	42%	40%
Market price of stock—none, sold only in local market.		

After examining the data given above, Investor Bob has tentatively expressed a strong preference for Company B because (*a*) it is larger, (*b*) it has almost five times as much in total assets, (*c*) net income as a percent of sales is virtually identical, and (*d*) it earned more than twice as much as A. Bob has asked you to confirm the soundness of his tentative decision by analyzing the data available.

Because the only information now available to you is given above, a comparative analysis seems appropriate as a start.

Required:

1. Prepare your analysis and support it with comments related to each ratio computed.
2. Based only upon your analysis, prepare your recommendation to Bob, which is limited to consideration of these two companies. Give a brief to-the-point summary of the basis for your recommendation.

C 25–2

What Investors Want from the Annual Report
(L.O. 1, 5)

This case is adapted from a special article by Ned Reynolds, senior vice president in the financial relations division of Hill & Knowlton Inc., in *The Wall Street Journal,* January 19, 1988. The article posed a provocative issue related to the stock market crash of 1987.

American companies spend an estimated $2 billion a year on annual reports to shareholders. But their message often falls on deaf ears, research suggests.

A survey conducted by Hill & Knowlton Inc. asked a sample of individual investors where they got their best investment information. Only 3% named the annual report—1% less than those who cited friends and relatives.

The author correctly states that companies traditionally view the annual report as an opportunity to radiate optimism, not to report failings. The author then posed the following issue:

> But since the October market crash, which dealt investor confidence a severe blow, companies need to think seriously about enlisting the annual report as a natural way of getting investors to trust them.

The Hill & Knowlton survey asked questions about how credible do investors find annual reports. Comments received, such as the following presented a bleak view:
* "Annual reports hide too much. They don't tell the entire truth," (California investor.)
* "They are not dependable." (New York investor.)
* "The annual report is little more than a piece of advertising," (St. Louis securities analyst.)
* "I think annuals are much too biased." (Los Angeles investor.)
* "I believe they lie in these reports." (Wisconsin investor.)

Author Reynolds then states:

> Nonetheless, the annual report is the best shot a publicly held company has all year to speak directly to investors. The report is a powerful platform for management to persuade investors to buy or hold the company's stock. That's exactly what an annual report should be doing if it is earning its keep.
>
> To succeed, an annual report must answer the investor's gut question: "What's in it for me?"—a question that ought to be displayed on the wall of every preparer of annual reports.

The research findings pinpointed the investors' complaints about annual reports:

Credibility. Investors complain that annual reports are too promotional. The reports play down negatives, investors say, and present only management's viewpoint. Some investors distrust what they read in annual reports.

Business segments. Annual reports often fail to adequately show or explain information about a company's various business segments, investors say.

Detail. Contrary to a common view, the majority of investors do not believe annual reports are too detailed. In fact, investors are eager for more facts in annuals—provided they are relevant.

The Future. Investors believe annual reports fail to tell them what management is doing to build the shareholder's investment.

Clarity. The investors criticize companies for using stilted wording and "technicalese" in their annual reports. They want to hear from companies in clear, straightforward language.

The author concludes the article as follows:

> It is unlikely that during the October market debacle investors cooly scrutinized company annual reports before calling their brokers. But perhaps many investors might think twice about unloading their positions if management seizes the opportunity in its next annual report to foster an underlying sense of confidence by credibly answering that essential question: "What's in it for me?"

Required:
1. Be prepared to suggest ways that might be used by companies to resolve each of the five complaints.
2. Prepare notes to support your suggestions.

C 25–3
HC/ND versus HC/CD
Financial Statements
(L.O. 7)

The primary financial statements of U.S. companies are currently prepared on a stable-dollar assumption (historical cost) even though the general purchasing power of the dollar has declined considerably because of inflation in recent years. To account for this changing value of the dollar, many accountants argue that financial statements should be restated for general price level changes. Three independent, unrelated statements regarding HC/CD financial statements follow. Each statement contains some fallacious reasoning.

Statement I: The accounting profession has not seriously considered HC/CD financial statements before because the rate of inflation usually has been so small from year to year that the restatements would have been immaterial in amount. HC/CD financial statements represent a departure from the historical cost basis of accounting. Financial statements should be prepared from facts, not estimates.

Statement II: If financial statements were restated for GPL changes, depreciation expense in the earnings statement would permit the recovery of dollars of current purchasing power and thereby equal the cost of new assets to replace the old ones. GPL restated (i.e., HC/CD) data would yield balance sheet amounts closely approximating current values. Furthermore, management can make better decisions if HC/CD financial statements are published.

Statement III: When restating financial data for GPL changes, a distinction must be made between monetary and nonmonetary assets and liabilities, which, under the HC basis of accounting, have been identified as "current" and "noncurrent." When using the HC basis of accounting, no purchasing power gain or loss on net monetary assets is recognized in the accounting process. But when financial statements are restated for GPL changes, a purchasing power gain or loss will be recognized on monetary and nonmonetary items.

Required:

Evaluate each of the independent statements and identify the areas of fallacious reasoning in each. Explain why the reasoning is incorrect. Complete your discussion of each statement before proceeding to the next statement.

(AICPA adapted)

C 25–4
CC/CD Comprehensive Income
(L.O. 7)

In this chapter, changes in the current costs of nonmonetary assets are presented as elements of CC/CD comprehensive income (i.e., on the income statement). Many accountants favor reporting these current cost changes as a direct element of owners' equity, bypassing the income statement. The issue has not been resolved.

Required:

List and discuss arguments for reporting the changes in the current cost of nonmonetary assets on the income statement versus reporting them as separate elements of owners' equity on the balance sheet. List and discuss arguments for reporting the current cost changes on nonmonetary assets as separate elements of owners' equity on the balance sheet.

C 25–5
HC/CD versus CC/CD
(L.O. 7)

Checker Corporation, a manufacturer with large investments in property, plant, and equipment, began operations in 1940. The company's history has been one of expansion in sales, production, and physical facilities. Recently, some concern has been expressed that the HC financial statements do not provide sufficient information for decisions by investors. After consideration of proposals for various types of supplementary financial statements to be included in the 1988 annual report, management has decided to present an HC/CD balance sheet as of December 31, 1988, and an HC/CD income statement and retained earnings statement for 1988.

Required:

1. On what basis can it be contended that Checker's HC financial statements should be restated for changes in the general price level (GPL)?
2. Distinguish between HC/CD financial statements and CC/CD financial statements.
3. Distinguish between monetary and nonmonetary assets and liabilities as the terms are used in the HC/CD reporting model. Give examples of each.
4. Outline the procedures Checker should follow in preparing the proposed HC/CD statements.
5. Indicate the major similarities and differences between the proposed HC/CD statements and the corresponding HC statements.
6. Assuming that in the future Checker will want to present comparative HC/CD statements, can the 1988 HC/CD statements be presented in 1989 without adjustment? Explain.

(AICPA adapted)

C 25–6
Sherwin-Williams: Analysis of Actual Financial Statements
(L.O. 3, 4)

Using the Sherwin-Williams annual report for 1990 found at the end of this text, compute as many of the ratios for 1990 given in this chapter as possible and render an opinion on the financial strength of the company.

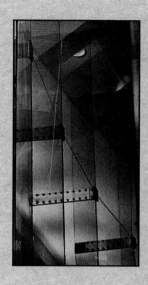

26

Special Topics

Disclosures, Interim Reporting, and Segment Reporting

LEARNING
OBJECTIVES
◆

After you have studied this chapter, you will:

1. Understand the problem of standards overload and some actions that might be undertaken to relieve the problem.

2. Understand why some accounting disclosures are not required for some firms.

3. Understand the financial disclosures required in the SEC Form 10-K report, and the rationale for and components of the Summary of Significant Accounting Policies.

4. Be familiar with the alternative concepts that may be applied in preparing interim reports and how to select the appropriate concept.

5. Understand the rationale and implementation requirements for segment reporting disclosures.

◆

INTRODUCTION
◆

Imagine you own a successful small business that produces and sells a variety of souvenirs for your university or college and for others like it in your geographical area. Your firm either produces or subcontracts production of football pennants, key chains, tie clasps, coffee cups, and similar products that are sold to area retailers. As your business grows, you find you need additional capital. You go to your bank and apply for a loan. The loan officer at the bank asks for the financial statements for your business and indicates they must be prepared in accordance with generally accepted accounting principles.

Now take another look at the inside front and inside back covers of this text, where there is a list of the pronouncements with which you must comply if your financial statements are going to be prepared in accordance with GAAP. You might note that your authors have written several hundred pages of text attempting to explain and teach the application of these various standards. At this point, you may begin to wonder whether it's worth it for your small business to comply with all the standards the various policy-making bodies have established. Indeed, the cost of total compliance with the rules of GAAP may be greater than the loan you wish to obtain!

This, in a nutshell, is the problem of **standards overload**. *Standards overload* is a term sometimes used by managements of firms to describe the financial reporting burden they have because of current accounting standards. A related and in many ways similar issue, **information overload**, essentially views the problem from the perspective of the user of the statements. Under this perspective the issue becomes: Why report all this information when it is likely that much of it will be of little or no relevance to most financial statement readers? More valuable information becomes buried—and perhaps even overlooked—by requiring information that the financial statement reader will not use.

In this chapter, the standards overload problem, the related information overload problem, and the trade-off that is involved between full disclosure and overload are discussed. SEC financial reporting requirements are outlined, and the issue of fradulent reporting is considered. Also covered are two reporting issues whose treatment for large, publicly held firms is different from what is required for non-public companies. These issues are providing interim financial reports to users, and providing information on the various types of businesses that a firm is pursuing.

◆

STANDARDS OVERLOAD AND FULL DISCLOSURE
◆

Generally, GAAP rules and standards apply equally to all reporting companies, regardless of the size of the reporting company.[1] The financial burden that smaller firms incur in complying with these rules and standards gives rise to what has been termed *the standards overload problem*.

The issue, then, is whether all the standards, practices, and disclosures of GAAP should apply equally to all firms regardless of size, ownership structure, and type of business. Specifically, should small or closely held companies be required to follow the same standards as widely held, large national and international corporations?

---

[1] Firms that are not required to present financial statements to public investors or creditors (because they are privately held and because creditors do not require financial statements) can use measurement standards and procedures that are not GAAP. Frequently, creditors such as banks will require the firm to submit financial statements prepared in accordance with GAAP measurement rules but will not require as much overall note disclosure as would otherwise be required under GAAP.

EXHIBIT 26–1   Types and Sources of Information Useful for Investment, Credit, and Similar Decisions

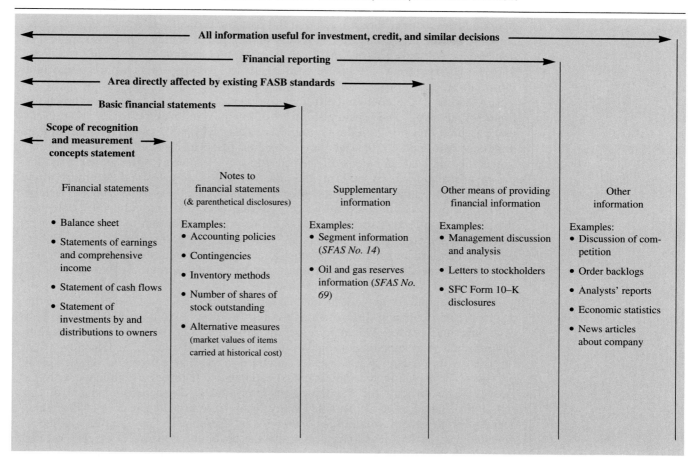

This issue is controversial. The Financial Accounting Standards Board has, in some instances, limited the applicability of some *Standards* to publicly held companies. Two such areas are (1) interim reporting and (2) segment reporting. Both of these topics are discussed in this chapter.

Consider this issue briefly from what might be the opposite perspective. It is extremely difficult, if not impossible, to present all the information about a firm essential for decision making in a balance sheet, income statement, statement of cash flows, and statement of stockholders' equity. With *Statement of Financial Accounting Concepts No. 5,* the FASB outlined the various types of information beyond financial statement information used in the various investment, credit, and similar decisions. The basic framework of the different types of information is presented in Exhibit 26–1.

Many in the business community and in the accounting profession are concerned about the ever increasing number and complexity of authoritative accounting pronouncements. Some of this concern focuses on the problem that smaller companies believe the cost of compliance with the standards is not cost-effective. This is the essence of the standards overload argument: the FASB is requiring accounting practices that are too costly for smaller firms to afford. At other times, even large corporations become concerned and express resistance to complex and potentially costly-to-implement standards. An example is the segment reporting requirements of *SFAS No. 14.* This *Statement,* discussed later in this chapter, generated considerable concern by many firms, large and small alike, about the costs and difficulties of implementation, and the potential benefits from its application. The arguments against such *Standards* often have both a standards overload and an information overload perspective. Firms argue that the cost and difficulty of compliance with the standard are too high compared with their perception of benefit. They also argue that compliance will only confuse the financial statement user because it is of little or no value, and requiring disclosure will tend to obscure other more important information.

In Chapter 2, the conceptual framework was presented as the underpinning for financial reporting. The primary objective of financial reporting is to provide present and potential investors, creditors, and other users with information that is useful in making investment, credit, and other decisions. The primary source of such information is the financial statements of the reporting entities. Many different users groups desire information about the firm, and different groups may desire different information. The conceptual framework, however, suggests that *general-purpose financial statements* prepared in conformity with generally accepted accounting principles are the most cost-effective way to provide the desired information to the various user groups. In an attempt to make such statements as comprehensive as possible, ensuring they are informative in a wide range of decisions settings, the tendency has been to require disclosure of virtually any piece of information that may be of interest to users of financial statements.

The conceptual framework includes a **full-disclosure principle,** which calls for the disclosure of all financial information that has the potential to influence the judgment of an informed reader. This requirement is subject to a cost-benefit evaluation, but making such an evaluation is usually difficult. The FASB often hears from firms that the cost of implementing a particular standard is too high relative to the benefit it provides. Firms will include specific cost estimates in their correspondence with the Board. More difficult for the Board to determine is the benefit to users of the required disclosures. For example, many firms have argued the cost of providing segment reporting information far outweighs its usefulness. Thus, until a method is developed to better measure and quantify the costs and benefits of disclosure, the Board will continue to be subject to the argument that requiring various disclosures results in standards overload and information overload.

There has been a substantial increase in the amount of required disclosures in the past two decades. Most of the *Standards* issued by the FASB require various disclosures in addition to providing guidance on accepted methods of measurement. This trend is expected to continue, although perhaps less rapidly than in recent years. There are many reasons for the increased disclosure requirements. Perhaps most important is the increasing complexity of business transactions, and the difficulty of distilling them into simple accounting transactions. An example is the increasingly complex financial instruments that have been used in recent years, primarily as tools in business acquisitions and mergers and in risk management. These instruments often have many of the characteristics of both debt and equity. Increased disclosure in the notes to the financial statements is one way to provide readers with detailed information on the specific debt and equity characteristics of the particular financial instrument.

Another reason for increased disclosure is rooted in the desire by many in society and government to better monitor and control the activities of large public corporations. Thus, government regulations require increased disclosure regarding items like management compensation, insider trading transactions, related party transactions, environmental issues, and potentially illegal activities. Many of these disclosures are required by the SEC, but the accounting profession must implement and respond to them. In the following sections we review major categories of expanded financial reporting and disclosure not covered under specific topics earlier in this text. First, a brief review of the SEC's financial reporting requirements is presented.

CONCEPT REVIEW

1. Define *standards overload*. Why is it a problem? What are some possible solutions to the problem?
2. What is the full-disclosure principle? How does it relate to standards overload and information overload?
3. Define *information overload*. How does it relate to the full disclosure principle? What are some possible solutions to the problem?

FINANCIAL REPORTING REQUIREMENTS OF THE SEC

♦

The Securities and Exchange Commission (SEC) is a governmental agency created in 1934 to administer various securities acts under powers provided by Congress in the Securities Act of 1933 and the Securities Exchange Act of 1934. Congress established the SEC for the purpose of regulating the disclosures of significant financial information by companies issuing publicly traded securities. Although the SEC has delegated much authority for prescribing the accounting principles and reporting practices for companies affected by SEC regulations to the FASB, the SEC continues to have legal responsibility and final authority in these matters.

The SEC is administered from its headquarters in Washington, D. C. by five commissioners. It is organized into several administrative offices, four divisions, and nine regional offices. The Office of the Chief Accountant is responsible for providing the SEC with advice concerning accounting and auditing. The Office of the Chief Accountant provides assistance in establishing administrative policies regarding accounting matters, and is directly responsible for the *Regulation S-X* (which establishes the form and content of financial statements filed with the SEC). The Chief Accountant is also responsible for the *Financial Reporting Releases (FRRs)* (these releases were called *Accounting Series Releases (ASRs)* prior to 1982). *FRR*s and *ASR*s prescribe accounting principles for reporting companies.

The Division of Corporate Finance also plays a major role in financial reporting. In particular, this division is responsible for both assisting in establishing reporting standards other than those dealing directly with financial statements, and for compliance with the standards. This division is also responsible for reviewing submitted financial reports.

Companies are required to file many forms and reports at various times with the SEC, but two of particular importance to financial reporting are:

♦ *Form 10-K.*
♦ *Form 10-Q.*

The Form 10-K is the annual report, including all financial reporting information, required to be submitted to the SEC. The Form 10-Q is the required quarterly report. The 10-Q is based on the Form 10-K and contains much of the same information, although usually in more summarized form. Only the Form 10-K is discussed in this text.

Form 10-K

The Form 10-K must be filed with the SEC within 90 days of a company's fiscal year-end. The form is organized into four major parts, each of which must provide information on specified topics, or items. Part II is especially relevant to accounting because all five items required in Part II must also be included in the company's annual report to shareholders. The items included in Part II are listed below:

Item No.	Heading	Description
5	Market for Common Stock	Identification of market(s) where corporation common stock is traded, including number of shares, frequency of trading, amounts of dividends.
6	Selected Financial Data	Five-year summary, including net sales, income (loss) from continuing operations, EPS, total assets, cash dividends, and long-term obligations.
7	Management Discussion and Analysis	Discussion of liquidity, capital resources, results of operations, and impact of inflation as needed to understand the company's financial condition, change in financial condition, and operating results.
8	Financial Statements and Supplementary Data	Consolidated financial statements, including balance sheets for two years, income statements, cash flow statements, and statements of changes in stockholders' equity for three years, and related notes. Also, selected quarterly data and the auditor's opinion.
9	Disagreements on Accounting Disclosures	If and when auditors are changed due to disagreements on accounting principles, a description of the disagreement and summary of the effects on the financial statements.

Exhibit 26–2 lists additional items of disclosure required in the Form 10-K that are not required to be included in the annual report to stockholders. However, companies often include many of these items in the annual report. The Sherwin-Williams 1990 annual report is an example; its format is modeled around the Form 10-K format.

Many of the items identified in Part II of the Form 10-K are self-explanatory and have been discussed in other sections and chapters of this text. There are some straightforward disclosure requirements. For example, firms must provide financial statement users with information on where the company's securities are traded. Item 6, Selected Financial Data, provides statement readers with a 5-year historical record on key financial variables. Many firms provide a 10-year summary. Item 8 relates to the financial statements and related notes, plus the Auditor's Opinion. These items are the primary focus of an annual report to shareholders. Items 7 and 9 require additional explanation.

Management Discussion and Analysis (MDA)

This item is a discussion, prepared by management, of the company's financial condition, change in financial condition, and results of operations for the periods presented in the report. The MDA is intended to give the reader a look at the company from the perspective of management. The MDA is forward-looking and deals with near-term and long-term analysis. The SEC's *Regulation S-K* and *Financial Reporting Release No. 36* provide guidance for MDA disclosures. Basically, firms must provide information regarding liquidity, capital resources, and the results of operations, and information needed to understand the financial condition and changes in financial condition. Some disclosures are required, others are encouraged but are voluntary. The voluntary disclosures are of a more forward-looking nature, involving anticipations of trends or events. The MDA is not required to be audited by the independent auditor. An example of an MDA is presented in Exhibit 26–3. This exhibit presents only the "revenues" portion of the MDA in Whirlpool's 1990 Annual Report. The complete Whirlpool MDA covers six pages.

EXHIBIT 26-2 Form 10-K Required Disclosures (Excluding Part II Disclosures)

Item No.	Heading	Description
1	Business	History and description of business, recent developments, principal products and services, major industry segments.
2	Properties	Locations and general descriptions of plants and other physical properties.
3	Legal Proceedings	Description of pending legal proceedings, principal parties to the proceedings, dates, allegations, and relief sought.
4	Voting Matters	Description of matters submitted to voting shareholders for approval.
PART III		
10	Directors and Officers	Names, ages, and positions of directors and officers.
11	Executive Compensation	Salaries, stock options, and other benefits for corporate officers and selected others.
12	Security Ownership	List of beneficial owners and management owners of corporate securities.
13	Certain Relationships	Description of transactions with managers and related parties, and for certain other business relationships.
PART IV		
14	Exhibits, Schedules and Reports	Detailed supporting schedules, often specified in *Regulation S-K*. Examples are marketable securities; property, plant, and equipment (including accumulated depreciation); short-term borrowings; and a listing of subsidiaries.
15	Signatures	The report must be signed by the chief executive officer, the chief financial officer, and a majority of the board of directors.

Disagreements on Accounting Disclosures

Accounting Trends & Techniques does not provide examples of these disclosures; thus, it is difficult to estimate how frequently they do occur. Our experience suggests that they are rare, in part because firm managements and their auditors work hard to find an appropriate middle ground or compromise position that both find acceptable when a possible area of disagreement arises. When a compromise position is reached, disclosure is not required. A disagreement disclosure occurs only when there is no solution to a disagreement between management and the auditor. In this case, the financial statements are prepared and disclosures made that are contrary to the wishes of one party.

NOTES TO FINANCIAL STATEMENTS
◆

Notes to the financial statements are an integral part of the financial statements. They are audited by the outside auditor, and must be included for the statements to be complete. Notes provide quantitative and verbal descriptive explanations of various items included (or not included) in the body of the statements that are deemed to be potentially meaningful to users. Information can be provided in qualitative terms, and readers can then make their own assessments of the potential quantitative ramifications of the information presented. Notes sometimes take on a complex and highly technical nature, and in many instances they provide very valuable information.

EXHIBIT 26-3   Excerpt from Management Discussion and Analysis: Whirlpool 1990 Annual Report

Results of Operations

The consolidated statements of earnings summarize Whirlpool operating results for the last 3 years. This section of Management's Discussion highlights the main factors affecting the changes in operating results during the 3-year period.

The accompanying financial statements include supplemental consolidating data reflecting the Company's investment in Whirlpool Financial Corporation accounted for on the equity method rather than as a consolidated subsidiary. Management believes this presentation provides additional useful information about the manufacturing and financial services businesses.

Revenues

Revenues were $6.6 billion in 1990, an increase of 5% over 1989 primarily due to the effects of strengthening European currencies relative to the dollar. The North American market was adversely affected by a recession in Canada, low room air conditioner sales and a severe second half slow-down across the major appliance industry. Unit volumes decreased 1% reflecting a continued decline in Kenmore brand products sales partially offset by increases in Whirlpool and KitchenAid brand product sales. Growth continued in Roper brand products launched in 1989 and the Estate brand was introduced in 1990. North American industry shipments are expected to continue to decline in 1991. European unit volumes were flat in 1990 compared to 1989 as strong German Bauknecht brand product sales were offset by a substantial decrease in microwave sales and difficult economic conditions in the United Kingdom. European industry shipments are expected to be flat in 1991 in a very competitive market. Financial services revenue improved significantly compared to 1989 due to improved performance across all businesses except middle market leasing which the Company exited in 1989.

Revenues for 1989 were $6.3 billion and included Whirlpool International's European operations for the first time. Europe showed unit gains of 3%; however, North American unit volume for 1989 was under competitive pressures and was 6% lower than 1988. The unit volume decline was represented primarily by refrigerator and freezer product categories resulting from a reduction in orders from the Company's largest single customer, the Company having discontinued its participation in segments of the freezer business, and a general slowdown across the major appliance industry. The refrigerator business was also adversely affected by cost and quality issues. Partially offsetting these factors were the continued growth of the KitchenAid brand volume and the launch of Roper brand products. For the most part, the decline in unit volume was offset by the effects of appliance price increases and an increase in financial services revenue resulting from improved performance across most businesses including the impact of new business initiatives in commercial lending (e.g., recapitalizations and acquisition funding) and aerospace financing (e.g., operating leases, subordinated loans, guarantee of pre-delivery payments, and asset value guarantees).

Revenues by Business Unit

(Millions of dollars)	1990	1989	1988
Whirlpool International	$2,156	$1,777	$ —
Whirlpool Appliance Group	1,834	1,738	1,678
Kenmore Appliance Group	1,078	1,208	1,447
KitchenAid Appliance Group	420	360	308
Inglis Limited	335	344	357
Whirlpool Overseas Corporation	220	—	—
Whirlpool Financial Corporation	218	163	136
Service, export (1989 and 1988) and other, including the elimination of intercompany transactions	362	699	495
	$6,623	$6,289	$4,421

Whirlpool Overseas Corporation (WOC) was formed in 1990 to conduct and expand existing marketing and industrial activities outside of North America and Europe. WOC revenues were included in Whirlpool International and export prior to 1990. Pro forma net revenues would have been $6.3 billion for 1988 including Whirlpool International net revenues of $1.9 billion.

Often the first note to the financial statements is a summary of significant accounting policies and consists of information on the accounting standards and procedures used to prepare the financial statements. The disclosure of this information is required by *APB Opinion No. 22*, although it does not necessarily have to be reported in the format of a note.

Summary of Significant Accounting Policies

Knowing the various accounting policies used in generating a set of financial statements is essential to developing an understanding of the specific figures presented in the statements. Knowing, for example, that a firm is using the LIFO method of inventory valuation rather than the FIFO method provides the reader with a basis for

EXHIBIT 26-4 Summary of Significant Accounting Policies: Honeywell Inc.
1990 Annual Report

Note 1—Accounting Policies

Consolidation The consolidated financial statements and accompanying data include Honeywell Inc. and subsidiaries. All material transactions between companies are eliminiated.

Sales Product sales are recorded when title is passed to the customer. This usually occurs at the time of delivery or acceptance. Sales under long-term contracts are recorded on the percentage-of-completion method measured on the cost to cost basis for engineering-type contracts and the units of delivery basis for production-type contracts. Provisions for anticipated losses on long-term contracts are recorded in full when they become evident.

Income Taxes Income taxes are accounted for in accordance with *Financial Accounting Standard No. 96*. Tax credits are included in income as a reduction of the income tax provision in the year the credits are realized for tax purposes.

Earnings Per Common Share Earnings per common share are based on the average number of common shares outstanding during the year.

Statement of Cash Flows Cash equivalents are all highly liquid, temporary cash investments purchased with a maturity of three months or less.
    Cash flows from contracts used to hedge cash dividend payments from subsidiaries are classified as part of the effect of exchange rate changes on cash.

Inventories Inventories are valued at the lower of cost or market. Cost is determined using the weighted-average method. Market is based on net realizable value.
    Payments received from customers relating to the uncompleted portion of contracts are deducted from applicable inventories.

Investments Investments in companies owned 20 to 50 percent are accounted for using the equity method.

Property Property is carried at cost and depreciated over estimated useful lives primarily using the straight-line method.

Intangibles Intangibles are carried at cost and amortized using the straight-line method over their estimated useful lives of not more than 40 years for goodwill, from 4 to 17 years for patents, licenses and trademarks, and from 4 to 24 years for software and other intangibles. Intangibles also include the asset resulting from recognition of the defined benefit pension plan minimum liability, which is amortized as part of net periodic pension cost.

---

interpreting both the inventory value and the cost of goods sold amount found in the financial statements.

APB Opinion No. 22 requires the disclosure of accounting policies used by the firm to present the financial position, cash flows, and results of operations in accordance with GAAP. Accounting policies include specific accounting principles and the methods of applying these principles. A description of all significant accounting policies is required to be included as an integral part of the financial statements. In general, the disclosure should reflect important judgments by management relating to the appropriateness of principles for revenue recognition and for the allocation of asset costs to current and future periods. More specifically, the disclosures must include those accounting principles and methods that involve the following factors:
* A selection from existing acceptable alternatives.
* Principles and methods particular to the industry.
* Unusual or innovative applications of GAAP.

A summary of significant accounting policies is presented either as a separate section or as the first note to the financial statements. An example of such a disclosure is found in Exhibit 26-4. The specific items found in this disclosure will vary from firm to firm. Looking more closely at the specific disclosures made by Honeywell Inc, the summary includes a discussion under the sales disclosure on how revenues are measured, including information on how the percentage of completion is determined for long-term contracts. Honeywell also describes how it accounts for income taxes and how it defines cash and cash equivalents, discloses the fact that it uses principally straight-line methods for depreciating property, uses the weighted-average method for determining inventory cost, and employs a lower-of-cost-or-market method for valuing inventories. The note also provides information on the amortization periods used for different types of intangible assets.

Different firms will cover different items in the summary of significant accounting policies section of the financial statements. In general, the information contained the summary is valuable to the reader in interpreting the reported amounts in the financial statements.

Other Notes to Financial Statements

Following the summary of significant accounting policies, there are a number of disclosures in the form of notes to the financial statements. Many are disclosures required by various accounting *Standards* covered earlier in this text. The specific details of what is required by any given *Standard* has been covered when the *Standard* was discussed. Some of the more common notes are summarized below:

1. *Accounts receivable.* This note often breaks down the accounts receivable balance into components such as accounts receivable, notes receivable, accrued interest, and allowance for doubtful accounts.

2. *Inventories.* This note usually identifies the inventory valuation method being used for various portions of inventory, and whether lower of cost or market is being used. Other disclosures may include whether a LIFO liquidation (voluntary or involuntary) has occurred, purchase agreements, inventory pledged for collateral, product financing arrangements, and related party transactions involving inventory.

3. *Property, plant, and equipment.* This note usually includes a breakdown of property, plant, and equipment into various categories (land, buildings, machinery and equipment, construction in progress, etc.). The note also usually discloses amounts of accumulated depreciation, amounts of capitalized interest, pledges, liens, and other commitments. If not disclosed elsewhere, the methods of depreciation and estimated useful lives of major categories of assets are disclosed here.

4. *Various creditor disclosures.* Often one or more notes provide information on the nature of various creditor claims on the firm. These notes may include a more detailed breakdown of the various types of current liability claims (e.g., accounts payable, wages and other employee obligations, current lease obligations, etc.) and details on the types of long-term debt claims. Recall that the firm is required to disclose the aggregate amounts of maturities and sinking-fund requirements for long-term borrowings for each of the next five years.

5. *Equity disclosures.* These notes often disclose information regarding outstanding stock options, convertible debt and preferred stock, redeemable stock, and many specific equity transactions occurring during the reporting period. If there are restrictions that affect the amount of earnings available for dividends, these are disclosed.

6. *Other important liability disclosures.* Extensive disclosures are required for leases, pensions, and deferred taxes. The specific requirements for these disclosures have been covered in detail in the chapters covering these topics. These disclosures can be very important. They can provide very valuable information on possible off-balance-sheet obligations and commitments, future financing needs, and implications for the future cash flows of the firms.

7. *Other notes.* Changes in accounting estimates, changes in accounting principles, and corrections of errors all require specified disclosures. Likewise, significant

events or transactions that occur subsequent to the balance sheet date but before the financial statements are issued are disclosed in the notes as subsequent events.

The Sherwin-Williams financial statements included in the appendix of this text gives another example of the notes found in a typical set of financial statements.

Special Transactions and Events

Most of the disclosures presented above have been discussed in greater detail in earlier chapters. Some transactions and events are sufficiently unusual and sensitive that they create especially difficult reporting problems for the firm. These include:
• Related party transactions.
• Errors and irregularities.
• Illegal acts.

The accountant has the problem of balancing the rights of the reporting entity and the rights of the potential users of the financial statements. There is some guidance on this issue for each of the above items.

Related Party Transactions   When a firm engages in transactions where one of the transacting parties has the ability to significantly influence the policies of the other, or when a nontransacting third party has the ability to influence the policies of the transacting parties, the transaction is termed a **related party transaction.** Such transactions cannot be assumed to be an arm's-length transaction because the conditions necessary for a competitive, free-market interaction are not likely to be present. Examples of related parties transactions include transactions between:
• A firm and its principal owners, management, members of families of owners or management, or its affiliates.
• A parent firm and its subsidiaries.
• Subsidiaries of a common parent firm.
• A firm and the trusts it controls or manages for the benefit of employees.
   SFAS No. 57 requires the following disclosures for related party transactions:
• The nature of the relationship(s) involved.
• A description of the transaction, including transactions in which no amounts or nominal amounts were involved, for each period for which income statements are presented.
• The dollar amounts of transactions for each period for which income statements are presented.
• Any amounts due to or from related parties as of the balance sheet date, and the terms and manner of settlement planned.
   An example of a related party disclosure note is found in Exhibit 26–5.

Errors and Irregularities   The accounting for errors is discussed in an earlier chapter. Errors are defined as "incorrect recording and reporting of the facts about the business that existed at the time an event or transaction was recorded." They are, essentially, unintentional mistakes. Irregularities, however, are intentional distortions of the financial statements. Irregularities should be corrected in the same manner as errors, but in many ways irregularities are more serious problems than errors. The problem of irregularities and other attempts by management to intentionally mislead readers of financial statements was of sufficient concern that a national commission was appointed to study the problem and recommend actions for dealing with it.[2] This issue is discussed in a later section of this chapter.

---

[2] National Commission on Fraudulent Financial Reporting, *Report of the National Commission on Fraudulent Financial Reporting* (Washington, D.C.: 1987).

EXHIBIT 26-5   A Related Party Disclosure: DSC Communications Corporation 1988 Annual Report

Related Parties

During the third quarter of 1986, the Company sold switching equipment to a finance company whose president is a member of the Company's Board of Directors for notes receivable of $1,800,000. At December 31, 1988, the unpaid balance of the notes receivable totaled $411,000. The notes receivable are payable over periods ranging from four to five years and bear interest of approximately 8%. The Company believes the terms of the sale were comparable to those available from unrelated parties.

The parent of the finance company discussed above leases certain office and manufacturing facilities to the Company and constructed a facility for the Company in 1985. The facility cost approximately $17,200,000. Rental expense on leases with the affiliates amounted to $1,855,000 in 1988, $1,988,000 in 1987, and $1,815,000 in 1986, with future minimum lease payments amounting to $3,242,000 at December 31, 1988.

During 1988, the Company purchased 90,000 shares of its outstanding common stock from a member of the Board of Directors at the existing market price at the date of the transaction.

The Company has an agreement to pay consulting fees, which amounted to $200,000 in 1988 and $183,000 in 1987, to a member of the Company's Board of Directors.

Illegal Acts Items such as illegal political contributions, bribes, kickbacks, and other violations of statutes and regulations constitute **illegal acts.** Congress enacted the Foreign Corrupt Practices Act of 1977 largely to stop these illegal acts and to require their disclosure when discovered. The Foreign Corrupt Practices Act has affected business practices, as well as the accounting profession. The auditor must ensure complete disclosure of relevant information when an illegal act is discovered. For example, if the auditor discovers that revenue is the result of an illegal act such as bribery, the amount must be disclosed, along with all the known facts about the bribe.

Firms are often involved in related party transactions such as those found in Exhibit 26-5. Much less frequently, however, is a firm involved in irregularities or illegal acts. Because of the violation of either laws, regulations, or even deliberate violation of accounting standards and principles, and because they are undertaken with full knowledge that they are intended to deceive, these items are very serious.

Fraudulent Financial Reporting

While rare, there are from time to time instances of fraudulent financial reporting, defined as "intentional or reckless, whether act or omission, that results in materially misleading financial statements." This definition is from the *Report of the National Commission on Fraudulent Financial Reporting* that was issued by the Commission in 1987. The Commission was chaired by James Treadway, and the report is often referred to as the *Treadway Report*. The report provides useful information on the causes of fraudulent financial reporting, and suggests way to prevent it.

Briefly, fraudulent financial reporting can generally be traced to the existence of conditions in either the internal environment of the firm such, as poor internal control, or to the external environment, such as poor industry or overall business conditions. Extreme pressures on management, such as a major decline in revenue, unrealistic profit or other performance goals, or bonus plans that depend on short-term performance can also lead to fraudulent financial reporting.

The opportunity for management to engage in fraudulent financial reporting is present under the following circumstances:

• The board of directors or an audit committee of the board does not carefully review the reporting process.

+ The firm has engaged in unusual or complicated transactions.
+ Poor systems of internal control are in place.
+ Internal audit staffs are small or poorly trained and underfunded.
+ There is extensive need for judgment in making accounting estimates.

The ethical climate or culture of an organization can either contribute to or inhibit fraudulent financial reporting. The attitude top management conveys toward issues of honesty and truthful reporting influences the actions of other managers in the organization who are in positions to engage in fraudulent reporting.

The accounting profession is faced with a problem of, first, trying to prevent fraudulent financial reporting and, second, determining responsibility when it occurs. The AICPA's Audit Standards Board is constantly considering standards for prevention and detection of fraudulent reporting. A number of new auditing standards have been issued in response to recommendations of the Treadway Report. The SEC also requires disclosures, such as the item on disagreements on accounting disclosures, in an attempt to prevent the issuance of potentially misleading financial statements.

Auditors' responsibility for detection of fraudulent reporting is not fully resolved. The accounting profession is generally of the opinion that it is not the responsibility of the auditor to detect fraud, beyond what can be detected with the diligent application of generally accepted auditing standards. In litigation, however, the auditor is often included among the parties being sued. The issue revolves around what the auditor should have detected in the audit, and what is beyond the scope of detection through normal procedures. The legal system will continue to play a leading role in defining the auditors' responsibility in this area.

CONCEPT REVIEW

1. Describe what we might expect to find in a summary of significant accounting policies. Why is this summary important?
2. What are the disclosures required for a related parties transaction?
3. Under what kinds of circumstances might fraudulent financial reporting occur?

INTERIM REPORTS
◆

The accounting period used throughout this text, and which is required for financial reporting, is the fiscal year of the firm. Annual financial statements, however, do not generally provide the most timely information for investors. Users of financial statements usually cannot wait until the end of the fiscal year of the firm to make decisions. **Interim reports** are often presented by firms to provide more timely information. Usually, such data are presented on a quarterly basis, although nothing prevents a firm from reporting more frequently.

Reporting more frequently than on a fiscal year basis gives rise to a new set of financial reporting problems. For example, many retailers do a large percentage of their business in the holiday season in the fourth quarter. Results of the fourth quarter often determine whether the firm will make a profit. In preparing quarterly reports for such a firm, the accountant must decide which costs to expense in the first three quarters, and which costs are more appropriately capitalized and expensed in the fourth quarter.

APB Opinion No. 28, "Interim Financial Reporting," was issued in 1973 to provide guidance on how to prepare interim financial reports, if a firm should decide to prepare them. *APB Opinion No. 28* does not require firms to prepare interim financial statements. There is no specific requirement for interim or quarterly reporting in GAAP. However, the SEC requires the Form 10-Q be completed and filed for publicly traded companies, and various exchanges require listed firms to prepare interim financial reports for public distribution.

Interim financial statements do not need to be complete. They may consist of only summarized financial data. If a firm elects to present only summarized financial data, however, the following data should be reported, at a minimum:
* Sales, income taxes, and net income.
* Disposal of a segment of a business and extraordinary, and unusual or infrequently occurring items.
* Primary and fully diluted earnings per share.
* Seasonal revenue, costs, or expenses.
* Significant changes in estimates or provisions for income taxes.
* Changes in accounting principles or estimates.
* Significant changes in financial position.

Underlying Concepts of Interim Reporting   Preparing interim reports presents difficulties because of a number of factors, including the following:
* Seasonality of revenues, costs, and expenses.
* Major costs that occur only in one interim period but benefit other interim periods within the same reporting year.
* Seasonality of production activities.
* Extraordinary items and accounting changes that occur in one interim period.
* Selection of appropriate income tax rates for each interim period.
* LIFO inventory that is liquidated during one or more interim periods but that is expected to be restored before the end of the reporting year.

There are two opposing views on how to treat the interim period:

1. *Discrete view.* Each interim period is viewed as a basic reporting period. It stands alone and separate without being considered as a part of a longer (i.e., annual) reporting period. Under this view, revenue and expense recognition, accruals, and deferrals for the interim period follow the same principles and procedures as for an annual period, and there would be no interim-period allocations. Thus, an expense incurred in one interim period usually would not be allocated to other interim periods.

2. *Integral-part view.* Each interim period is viewed as an integral part of the annual reporting period. Under this view, revenue and expense recognition, deferrals, and accruals are affected by judgments made at the end of each interim period about the results of operations for the remainder of the reporting period. Thus, an expense incurred in one interim period may be allocated among other interim periods within the reporting year.

Between these two points of view, *APB Opinion No. 28* states that "each interim period should be viewed primarily as an integral part of the annual period." The *Opinion* does, however, make some practical concessions on this point.

Guidelines for Preparing Interim Financial Reports   *APB No. Opinion 28* gives the following guidelines for preparing interim reports:

1. In general, the accounting principles and practices used by the firm in preparing its annual financial statements should be used for interim reports, with certain modifications (discussed below).
2. Revenue from products and services sold should be recognized as earning during the interim period on the same basis as followed for the annual period.
3. Costs and expenses for interim periods are classified as follows:
   a. Costs that are directly associated with interim revenue are reported in the interim period.
   b. Costs and expenses that are not directly associated with interim revenue must be allocated to interim periods on a reasonable basis.

Costs Directly Associated with Revenue The discrete view is used to report revenue. Costs directly associated with revenue, such as cost of goods sold, wages, salaries, fringe benefits, and warranties, should be expensed in the interim period in which the related revenue is recognized, with the following exceptions and disclosure:

1. Use of the gross margin method (discussed in Chapter 10) for computing costs of goods sold must be disclosed.
2. If LIFO is used and inventory is liquidated during an interim period and is expected to be restored by year-end, cost of goods sold for the interim period should be debited for the anticipated replacement cost of the number of units liquidated and an estimated liability account should be credited.
3. Declines in inventory value, unless temporary, should not be deferred to future interim periods; recovery in later interim periods should be recognized as gains, but not in excess of the previously recognized losses.

Costs Not Directly Associated with Revenue All costs not directly associated with revenue should be accounted and reported for interim periods as follows:

1. Recognize cost as an expense in the interim period in which it was incurred, or allocate the cost among interim periods based on an estimate of time expired, benefit received, or activity associated with the periods.
2. Arbitrary allocation of such costs should not be made. If any costs cannot be reasonably allocated, they should be assigned to the interim period in which they were incurred.
3. Gains and losses that arise in any interim period should be recognized in the interim period in which they arise if they would not normally be deferred at year-end.
4. Income tax expense for each interim period should be based on an estimate of the annual rate as made at the end of each quarter. The income tax expense for the current interim period is the difference between the income tax expense computed on year-to-date income from operations and the total income tax expense reported on prior interim reports for the fiscal year.

Unusual or infrequently occurring items and extraordinary items should be recognized in the interim period in which they occur. Similarly, contingent losses not directly associated with revenue and the related liabilities should be recognized in the interim period in which they occur. Accounting changes are accounted for and reported in essentially the same manner as in annual periods.

Interim Reporting Illustrated Assume the following data is for the first quarter (ended March 31, 1994) for the Gilmore Corporation:

Selected Items	Amount
Sales of products and services	$500,000
Interest revenue	1,000
Extraordinary loss	15,000
Correction of 1993 accounting error (credit)	6,000
Cost of goods sold	241,000
Operating assets, cost (10-year remaining useful life,	
no residual value, straight-line)	480,000
Salary and wage expense	89,000
Inventory allowance change, LCM (temporary)	4,000
Advertising expense (benefits first and second	
quarters equally)	18,000
Annual property tax for 1994 (estimated)	12,000
Contribution to United Fund for 1994	6,000
Shipping expense	7,000
Unusual loss	4,000
Retained earnings, 12/31/93	100,000
Estimated average annual income tax rate, 30%;	
reporting period ends December 31; 30,000	
common shares outstanding	

EXHIBIT 26-6   Interim (Quarterly) Income Statement and Statement of Retained Earnings for Gilmore Corporation.

GILMORE CORPORATION
Income Satement
For Quarter Ending March 31, 1994

Revenues:

Sales of products and services	$500,000
Interest revenue	1,000
Total Revenue	501,000

Expenses:

Cost of goods sold	241,000
Salaries and wages	89,000
Depreciation expense ($480,000 ÷ 10)(3/12)	12,000
Inventory decline, LCM	–0–
Advertising expense	9,000
Contributions	6,000
Property tax expense	3,000
Shipping expense	7,000
Unusual loss	4,000
Income tax expense*	39,000
Total expenses	410,000
Income before extraordinary item	91,000
Extraordinary loss (net of $4,500 income tax)	10,500
Net income	$ 80,500

Earnings per share (30,000 common shares outstanding):

Income before extraordinary items ($91,000/30,000 shares)	$3.03
Extraordinary loss ($10,500/30,000)	(.35)
Net income ($80,500/30,000)	$2.68

Retained Earnings Statement
For Quarter Ending March 31, 1994

Beginning balance (given)	$100,000
Prior period adjustment, error correction ($6,000 × .70)	4,200
Balance, as adjusted	104,200
Net income	80,500
Ending balance	$184,700

* (Revenues − Expenses).30 = ($501,000 − $371,000).30 = $39,000

Exhibit 26–6 illustrates the quarterly interim statement that meets the reporting requirements of *APB Opinion No. 28*. The report provides that the distinctions are maintained between costs directly related to interim revenue and other costs not directly related to interim revenue. Both sales of products and interest revenue are direct and thus recognized in full in the interim period. Cost of goods sold and salaries and wages are recognized in full since they relate directly to the revenues recognized. Depreciation expense is allocated based on time, hence is computed as ($480,000/10 years) × (3/12), or $12,000 for the quarter. There is no recognition of the inventory decline since it is viewed as temporary. Had the decline been viewed as permanent, the full amount would have been recorded as an expense in the current interim period. Advertising expense is allocated over the two periods expected to benefit from this item. The remaining $9,000 of advertising outlay is capitalized as an asset on the interim balance sheet. Similarly, the property tax item is allocated equally to each of the four quarters: ($12,000 × 1/4) equals $3,000 allocated to each quarter. The contribution is accrued as expense for the quarter since it is not related to operations and there is no reasonable basis for allocation. Finally, the shipping expense and unusual loss are both recognized as expenses in the current quarter. The estimate of the annual tax rate is used to determine income tax expense for the interim period. The income statement shows intraperiod tax

EXHIBIT 26-7   Third-Quarter 1990 Interim Report: The Sherwin-Williams Company.

Statements of Consolidated Income (Unaudited)

(in thousands of dollars, except per share data)	Three Months Ended September 30,		Nine Months Ended September 30,	
	1990	1989	1990	1989
Net sales	$ 638,532	$ 595,983	$1,749,377	$1,644,748
Costs and expenses:				
Operating expenses	567,215	533,823	1,596,024	1,510,329
Interest expense	2,677	3,217	7,951	9,910
Interest and net investment income	(1,374)	(3,593)	(7,862)	(8,748)
Other	(1,989)	(2,461)	(1,929)	(5,968)
	566,529	530,986	1,594,184	1,505,523
Income before income taxes	72,003	64,997	155,193	139,225
Income taxes	25,257	23,399	53,542	50,121
Net income	$ 46,746	$ 41,598	$ 101,651	$ 89,104
Income per share	$ 1.07	$ 0.96	$ 2.34	$ 2.07
Average shares and equivalents outstanding	43,573,780	43,298,259	43,494,426	43,118,643

During June, 1990, the Company sold Lyons Transportation Lines, Inc., and acquired for cash the Krylon and Illinois Bronze aerosol paints and coatings businesses of Borden, Inc. The net effect of these transactions did not significantly affect consolidated operating results for the third quarter or nine months ended September 30, 1990.

Consolidated Financial Position (Unaudited)

(in thousands of dollars)	September 30,	
	1990	1989
Current assets	$777,568	$827,314
Current liabilities	(417,536)	(409,981)
Working capital	360,032	417,333
Net property, plant, and equipment	363,734	350,220
Deferred pension assets	152,269	144,675
Other assets	154,868	24,170
Long-term debt	(110,516)	(127,818)
Other long-term liabilities	(171,162)	(145,284)
Shareholders' equity	$749,225	$663,296

allocation of the total income tax expense of $34,500—$39,000 to continuing operations, and a $4,500 tax savings with the extraordinary loss.

Exhibits 26–7 and 26–8 contain the third-quarter interim financial statements for Sherwin-Williams. These statements are discussed in more detail after the topic of segment reporting is covered. Since the interim statements contain information on business segments, it is useful to integrate the discussion of that topic and the general principles of interim reporting in one discussion of the Sherwin-Williams interim report.

Interim reporting standards are in a stage of infancy. While *APB Opinion No. 28* provides some guidance, many issues remain. It is our view that as information processing costs continue to decrease, the effect will be an increasing demand for and less resistance to interim financial reporting. A related issue will be the auditor's role in interim reporting. Most auditors are reluctant to express an opinion on interim financial statements because the data are subjective and involve more estimation and allocation than is required for annual reports. On the other hand, more users of

EXHIBIT 26-8   Segment Information in Third-Quarter 1990 Interim Report: The Sherwin-Williams Company

Selected Financial Information (Unaudited)

(in thousands of dollars)	Nine Months Ended September 30,	
	1990	**1989**
Depreciation and amortization	$32,987	$30,465
Capital expenditures	48,090	48,852
Cash dividends	24,656	22,536

Business Segments (Unaudited)

	Three Months Ended September 30,			
(in thousands of dollars)	**1990**		**1989**	
	Net External Sales	Operating Profit	Net External Sales	Operating Profit
Paint Stores	$ 411,667	$ 33,639	$ 391,957	$ 33,588
Coatings	223,230	45,524	200,697	38,772
Other	3,635	1,110	3,329	1,518
Segment totals	$ 638,532	80,273	$ 595,983	73,878
Corporate expenses—net		(8,270)		(8,881)
Income before income taxes . . .		$ 72,003		$ 64,997

	Nine Months Ended September 30,			
(in thousands of dollars)	**1990**		**1989**	
	Net External Sales	Operating Profit	Net External Sales	Operating Profit
Paint Stores	$1,110,564	$ 61,953	$1,041,639	$60,448
Coatings	628,144	113,323	593,227	100,531
Other	10,669	1,692	9,882	3,508
Segment totals	$1,749,377	176,968	$1,644,748	164,487
Corporate expenses—net		(21,775)		(25,262)
Income before income taxes . . .		$155,193		$139,225

financial statements will want the auditor to provide assurance that the published data are accurate and in accordance with generally accepted accounting standards. Interim reports are becoming increasingly important as a valuable source of information for investors.

CONCEPT REVIEW

1. Explain the difference between the discrete view and the integral-part view of accounting measurement in interim reporting.
2. Suppose a firm that operates a ski resort is preparing to issue a second-quarter interim report. The firm has just completed a $100,000 advertising campaign, which it expects to generate revenues in the third and fourth quarters. How would this item be accounted for under the discrete view? Under the integral-part view?
3. Provide two examples of costs not directly associated with revenues.

SEGMENT REPORTING
♦

Many large firms engage in more than one line of business. Indeed, many smaller corporations have diversified operations in more than one industry. In the past, investors seeking to assess the relative attractiveness of the capital stock of a diversified company were faced with the difficult task of analyzing and interpreting company financial reports that reported only aggregated data with little or no information on the performance of the various lines of business.

For example, suppose the General Electric Company (GE) is being analyzed as a possible investment. GE identifies the following lines of business in its 1990 Annual Report:

Business	Brief Description
♦ Aerospace	Electronics, automated test systems, avionic systems, military vehicle equipment, spacecraft radar
♦ Aircraft engines	Including replacement parts for commercial and military aircraft
♦ Appliances	Refrigerators, ranges, laundry equipment, room air conditioners, dishwashers, microwave ovens.
♦ Broadcasting	Primarily the National Broadcasting Company (NBC)
♦ Industrial	Lighting products, electrical distribution equipment motors, transportation systems
♦ Materials	Engineered plastics, silicones, superabrasives, laminates
♦ Power systems	Products for the generation, transmission, and distribution of electricity
♦ Technical	Medical systems, communications and information services
♦ Financing	Loans for time sales, revolving credit, inventory financing
♦ Insurance	Property and casualty reinsurer
♦ Securities	Investment banking, securities trading

In its annual report, GE goes into even more detail in describing its various businesses. It is apparent from the above, however, that GE is in a wide range of businesses. GE produces and sells products ranging from light bulbs to household appliances to aircraft engines. GE owns and operates a major television network and a major finance company. Demand for the many products and services will differ depending on economic conditions and other characteristics of the economy. For example, consumers are likely to buy light bulbs during bad economic times as well as good. Consumers must also have kitchen ranges and refrigerators. During a recession, however, consumers are more likely to delay purchases of consumer durables such as refrigerators and ranges, especially if their current range and refrigerator are working or can be repaired at a reasonable cost. Thus, the condition of the economy is more likely to affect the demand for consumer durables than for consumer nondurables like light bulbs. The demand for air travel and the related demand for aircraft engines is also likely to be responsive to changing economic conditions. The increased uncertainty about the future price of petroleum products in late 1990 (caused by the Iraqi invasion of Kuwait), for example, caused several airlines to postpone planned acquisitions of new aircraft. If the increased price of fuel was passed on to travelers in the form of increased air fares, there would be reduced demand for air travel. Further, the success at NBC may depend more on the programming success of the network relative to its major competitors than on explicit economic conditions.

Stated differently, each of the businesses discussed above possesses different risk characteristics. Investors who know the relative proportions of company resources committed to operations in the various businesses, and the success the company has experienced in each business, are in a better position to make informed decisions than investors using only aggregate data for the company.

This line of reasoning is the basis for *SFAS No. 14,* "Financial Reporting for Segments of a Business Enterprise," issued by the FASB in December 1976. A segment of a business is a subdivision in the business that derives revenue from individual products or services that represent significant parts of the overall business. In addition, segment reporting applies to each major customer that provides 10% or more of the company revenue, and to foreign operations (if they provide 10% or more of the company revenue or use 10% or more of the company's identifiable assets).

In part because so many firms objected to segment reporting, the FASB modified the applicability of *SFAS No. 14* in three important ways:

1. *SFAS No. 18* was issued in November 1977 and provided that segment reporting was not required for interim periods.
2. *SFAS No. 21* was issued in April 1978; it suspended the requirement of reporting segment information by a **nonpublic company**.[3] *SFAS No. 21* defines nonpublic companies as all companies except those whose debt or equity securities are traded on a domestic or foreign exchange or in any over-the-counter market, or that is required to file financial statements with the Securities and Exchange Commission.
3. *SFAS No. 30*, issued in August of 1979, amended *SFAS No. 14* with respect to disclosure required of sales to foreign or domestic governments.

These modifications to the original *Standard* can be viewed in part as a response to the standards overload issue mentioned earlier. The main reporting provisions of *SFAS No. 14,* as amended by the above *Standards,* follow.

Definition of Reportable Segments

SFAS No. 14 provides general guidance on defining reportable segments by suggesting that management:
* Identify the individual products or services from which the enterprise derives its revenue.
* Group those products or services into industry segments by common products or services, common production processes, or common markets or marketing methods.
* Select those industry segments that are significant with respect to the enterprise as a whole.

The *Standard* goes on to specify criteria for a subunit. If any one of these criteria is met, that subunit is defined as a reportable industry segment:
* The subunit's revenue is 10% or more of the combined revenue segments of the entity.
* The absolute amount of its operating profit or loss is 10% or more of the greater, in absolute amount, of either of the following:
  a. The combined operating profit of all industry segments of the entity that did not incur an operating loss.
  b. The combined operating loss of all industry segments of the entity that incurred an operating loss.
* The subunit's identifiable assets are 10% or more of the combined identifiable assets of all industry segments (of the entity).

The following must be reported for each reportable industry segment so defined:
* Segment revenue.
* Segment operating income or loss.
* Identifiable segment assets.
* Other related disclosures:
  a. The aggregate amount of depreciation, depletion, and amortization expense,

---

[3] *SFAS No. 21* also eliminated the requirement that earnings per share (EPS) be reported by nonpublic companies.

b. The amount of capital expenditures during the period (i.e., additions to property, plant, and equipment),

c. The company's equity in the net income and investment in unconsolidated subsidiaries and other equity investees whose operations are vertically integrated with the segment, including disclosure of the geographic area in which that investee operates,

d. The effect on the segment of all changes in accounting principle.[4]

Segment revenue includes all product and service sales to unaffiliated customers (i.e., customers outside the enterprise), intersegment sales, and interest on segment trade receivables. Segment revenue does not include interest revenue on loans to other segments. Intersegment sales are sales between the various industry segments identified for the company.

The segment's operating income or loss is segment revenue (as defined above) less all segment operating expenses. Operating expenses for a segment include the following:

1. Operating expenses that are directly related to a segment's revenue.
2. Operating expenses incurred by the company that can be "allocated on a reasonable basis" to a segment(s) for whose benefit those expenses were incurred.

None of the following can be added or deducted in computing the operating income or loss of a segment: (1) company revenues not derived from the segment, (2) general company expenses, (3) interest expenses, (4) income taxes, (5) equity in income of unconsolidated subsidiaries or other equity investees, (6) extraordinary items, (7) minority interests in income, and (8) cumulative effect of an accounting change.

Identifiable segment assets include both the tangible and intangible identifiable assets of the segment that are used exclusively by the segment or jointly by two or more segments (allocated on a reasonable basis). Asset valuation accounts, such as allowance for doubtful accounts and accumulated depreciation, must also be included. Assets that cannot be included are those used for general company purposes and loans or advances to other segments.

Additional Disclosures Required *SFAS No. 14* also requires disclosures regarding major customers and foreign operations, a requirement independent of that for industry segment reporting. If 10% or more of a firm's revenue is from sales to any single customer, the amount of the revenue and the customer identity must be disclosed. A single customer includes a group of firms under common control, or a federal, state, local or foreign government. A firm must report revenues, operating income or loss, and identifiable assets for each foreign operation if either revenue from foreign operations is 10% or more of the combined revenue of all segments of the entity, or identifiable assets of the entity's foreign operations are 10% or more of the combined identifiable assets of the entity.

The Sherwin-Williams interim report for the third quarter of 1990 is found in Exhibits 26-7 and 26-8. Exhibit 26-7 is the basic interim report information, and Exhibit 26-8 contains the reported segment information. The various schedules and statements presented are marked as "unaudited." The firm's public accountants audit only the annual financial statements. Sherwin-Williams presents comparative data for the third quarter for 1989 and 1990, and also for the first nine months of each year. Several observations can be made based on Exhibit 26-7:

• Sales, income before income taxes, and net income have increased in 1990, both in

---

[4] Vertical integration refers to the complementary nature of a parent and its subsidiaries' product lines whereby one supplies inputs to the other. An example of vertical integration would be General Motors and Libby-Owens-Ford or Fisher Body. Another example would be American Telephone and Telegraph and Western Electric (which builds telephones for AT&T).

EXHIBIT 26-9   Segment Reporting Example: The Boeing Company

Note 13—Industry Segment Information

The Company operates primarily in three industries: (1) Commercial Transportation Products and Services, (2) Military Transportation Products and Related Systems and (3) Missiles and Space. Operations in the commercial transportation segment principally involve development, production and marketing of commercial aircraft and providing related support services mainly to commercial customers. Operations in Military Transportation Products and Related Systems involve research, development, production and modification of such products primarily for the U.S. Government and also for foreign governments. Missiles and Space operations primarily involve research, development and production of various strategic and tactical missiles and space exploration products, principally for the U.S. Government.

Foreign sales by geographic area, consisting principally of export sales consisted of:

Year ended December 31,	1989	1988	1987
Europe	$ 5,429	$3,187	$2,337
Asia	3,213	2,470	2,877
Oceania	1,164	651	280
Western Hemisphere	888	1,140	649
Africa	327	401	143
	$11,021	$7,849	$6,286

Military sales were approximately 8%, 15% and 8% of total sales in Europe for 1989, 1988 and 1987, respectively. Military sales were approximately 5%, 9% and 22% of total sales in Asia for 1989, 1988 and 1987, respectively. Exclusive of these amounts, sales of Military Transportation Products and Missiles and Space were principally to the U.S. Government.

Financial information by segment for the three years ended December 31, 1989, is summarized below. Revenues consist of sales plus other income applicable to the respective segments. Corporate income consists principally of interest income from corporate investments. Corporate expense consists of interest on debt and other general corporate expenses. Corporate assets consist principally of cash and short-term investments.

Year ended December 31,	1989	1988	1987
Revenues:			
Commercial transportation products and services	$14,305	$11,369	$ 9,827
Military transportation products and related systems	3,962	3,668	3,979
Missiles and space	1,467	1,457	1,063
Other industries	542	468	636
Operating revenues	20,276	16,962	15,505
Corporate income	347	378	308
Total revenues	$20,623	$17,340	$15,813
Operating profit:			
Commercial transportation products and services	$1,165	$ 585	$ 352
Military transportation products and related systems	(559)	(95)	60
Missiles and space	85	124	119
Other industries	26	(28)	(34)
Operating profit	717	586	497
Corporate income	347	378	308
Corporate expense	(142)	(144)	(147)
Earnings before taxes	$ 922	$ 820	$ 658

the most recent quarter (the three months ending September 30), and over the three quarters of the fiscal year.

◆ Sherwin-Williams does not appear to be a seasonal business—sales in the third quarter ($638,532) are just over one third (actually 36.5%) of the three quarter total ($1,749,377).

However, nearly one half of the net income over three quarters is recorded in the

EXHIBIT 26-9   *(concluded)*

Identifiable assets at December 31:			
Commercial transportation products and services	$ 6,675	$ 4,558	$ 5,170
Military transportation products and related systems	3,367	2,923	2,846
Missiles and space	911	684	548
Other industries	329	319	362
	11,282	8,484	8,926
Corporate	1,996	4,124	3,640
Consolidated assets	$13,278	$12,608	$12,566
Depreciation:			
Commercial transportation products and services	$ 242	$ 243	$ 218
Military transportation products and related systems	208	188	170
Missiles and space	72	52	42
Capital expenditures, net:			
Commercial transportation products and services	$ 612	$ 326	$ 286
Military transportation products and related systems	506	241	316
Missiles and space	155	62	72

third quarter ($46,746 in the third quarter, compared to $101,651 for the nine months). This is largely because operating expenses were a smaller percentage of sales in the third quarter (88.8%) than they are for the nine-month period (91.2%). Moreover, this result is similar to the result shown for 1989. The reasons why gross margin increased during the third quarter are not apparent.

The segment reporting data reveals differing success in the various lines of businesses reported. While the firm's largest segment is paint stores, the segments for coatings and other are more profitable. The largest increases in profit are from the coatings segment.

A further example of segment reporting is given in Exhibit 26-9. This exhibit presents the note from the Boeing financial statements that is the firm's disclosure on industry segment information. Boeing uses category of customer (commercial or government) to develop its segments. Both the commercial transportation and the military transportation segments are primarily producing and marketing aircraft and related products. However, much of the marketing effort and the opportunities for profit, and indeed even the risk undertaken by the company, differ between these two markets.

The note also provides the required breakdown of foreign sales by geographic region. Finally, the note provides information on major customers by noting the amount of military sales for the various geographic regions.

CONCEPT REVIEW

1. Why might users of financial statements find segment reporting useful? How might it affect their decision making?
2. The apparels segment of a diversified company has a loss of $12 million. Five other segments have operating profits (losses) of $34 million, ($57 million), $48 million, $15 million, and ($73 million). Based only on this information, must this segment be separately reported? Why or why not?
3. Under what conditions is segment reporting not required?

SUMMARY OF KEY POINTS

(L.O. 1, 2)   1. There are two related concepts that argue for a decrease in the amount of information disclosed in financial statements. First, the notion of *standards overload* maintains there are too many complex and costly-to-implement standards. The notion is that costly standards place an unfair, or at least uneconomic financial burden on some firms, primarily smaller firms. The related notion of *information overload* essentially argues that some information that is required to be disclosed is of little or no value to readers, and thus it is not cost-effective to prepare and report such information.

(L.O. 1, 2)   2. The offsetting notion to the above two concepts is the principle of *full disclosure*. This principle calls for the disclosure of any financial information that is potentially of sufficient significance that it can influence the judgment of an informed reader.

(L.O. 3)   3. The SEC is the final authority for determining reporting standards for publicly traded companies. The Form 10-K is the primary annual financial report publicly traded companies must file with the SEC.

(L.O. 3)   4. Notes to financial statements are an integral part of the statements. Financial statements are incomplete if they do not contain the appropriate note disclosures.

(L.O. 3)   5. *APB Opinion No. 22* requires firms to include in the financial statements a summary of significant accounting policies. The disclosure must include a description of the selections made from existing acceptable alternatives, the principles and methods of accounting measurement particular to the industry, and any unusual or innovative application of GAAP.

(L.O. 3)   6. There are special disclosure requirements for related party transactions, errors and irregularities, and illegal acts.

(L.O. 4)   7. Interim reports are not generally required except by some stock exchanges. If they are presented, however, they should be prepared using the same accounting policies used for annual reports. The interim report can contain summary information that is less comprehensive than that presented in an annual financial statement. The information required for an interim report is specified in *APB Opinion No. 28*.

(L.O. 4)   8. *APB Opinion No. 28* primarily requires the integral-part view in preparing interim reports. This view results in allocations of items between interim periods that are not normally allocated across fiscal periods in annual financial statements.

(L.O. 5)   9. *SFAS No. 14* requires that publicly held firms operating in multiple businesses report various information on the activities of segments meeting qualifying criteria.

(L.O. 5)   10. If one or more of the following criteria are met by an industry segment, it must be reported as a separate segment: (a) the segment revenue is 10% or more of the combined revenue of the firm, (b) the segment assets are 10% or more of the combined assets of the firm, or (c) the absolute amount of the operating profit or loss of a segment is 10% or more of the greater of the absolute total of all industry segment operating profits or the absolute total of all industry segment operating losses.

(L.O. 5)   11. *SFAS No. 14* requires disclosure of segment information for foreign operations if revenues or assets are 10% or more of the comparable item for the entire entity.

(L.O. 5)   12. Segment reporting is not required for nonpublic firms.

KEY TERMS

Full-disclosure principle (p. 1488)	Nonpublic company (p. 1504)
Illegal acts (p. 1496)	Related party transaction (p. 1495)
Information overload (p. 1486)	Standards overload (p. 1486)
Interim reports (p. 1497)	

QUESTIONS

1. What is standards overload? Why is it a problem?
2. What is information overload? Why is it a problem?
3. What is the full disclosure principle? Why has note disclosure increased substantially over the past decade?
4. What is the purpose of notes to the financial statements?
5. What is the purpose of the Securities and Exchange Commission? Which specific offices and divisions are concerned with accounting matters?
6. What is the Form 10-K? What firms must prepare a Form 10-K? When must the Form 10-K be filed? What information items must be included in the Form 10-K?
7. What is interim reporting? Why is it potentially important?
8. What is the difference between the discrete view and the integral-part view of interim financial reporting periods?
9. Should income statement items that are separately classified, such as extraordinary items, be prorated over interim reporting periods or recognized in a single interim period?
10. What is the basic rationale for requiring segment reporting? What are the arguments against segment reporting?
11. *SFAS No. 14* requires disclosures in three areas: lines of business, foreign operations, and major customers. Are these three areas independent of each other? When might they be? When might they not be?
12. What is the difference, if any, between the terms *industry segment* and *reportable segment?* Explain how each is determined.
13. Define the following: identifiable assets, intersegment sales, and segment operating income or loss.
14. In recent years, many firms regulated by the SEC have included a management discussion and analysis section in the annual report to shareholders. Describe what is included in the MDA section.
15. What are the accounting policies of a company? What, if any, are the requirements for disclosing information about accounting policies?
16. What must a firm disclose about related party transactions?
17. Briefly describe the alternative tests for determining a reportable segment.
18. What items are required to be included in both the Form 10-K and the annual report to shareholders?
19. At a minimum, what information items should be included in an interim financial report?

EXERCISES

E26-1 Interim Reporting (L.O. 4)

In January 1992, management of Clip Inc. estimates that its year-end bonus to executives will be $500,000 for 1992. The amount paid in 1991 was $440,000. The final determination of the amount to be paid is made at the conclusion of the fiscal year.

Required

Determine the amount, if any, of bonus expense that should be reflected in Clip's quarterly income statement for the three months ending March 31, 1992. Justify and explain your answer.

E26-2 Interim Reporting (L.O. 4)

In September 1991, Crystal Mountain Ski Resorts spent $300,000 advertising for the coming ski season. The ski season lasts from October through the following March, with business expected to be spread evenly over this period. The fiscal year for Crystal Mountain ends March 31, 1992.

Required:

Determine the amount of expense that should be included in Crystal Mountain's interim financial statements for September 30 and for December 31, 1991. Justify and explain your answer.

E26-3 Interim Reporting (L.O. 4)

The Proctor Company reported income before income taxes of $100,000 and $150,000 in the first two quarters 1992. Management's estimate of the annual effective tax rate was 35% at the end of the first quarter, and 30% at the end of the second quarter.

Required:

Determine the income tax expense for the first two quarters of 1992.

E26-4 Segment Reporting: Major Customer Disclosure (L.O. 5)

Montgomery Company made sales in 1992 to customers as follows:

California Company	$16,000,000
Oregon Inc.	8,000,000
Montana Corp.	5,000,000
Arizona Company	4,000,000
Texas Inc.	3,000,000
Domestic governments	19,000,000
Foreign governments	14,500,000
Other sales	40,000,000

Additional information:

a. Other sales includes sales to many customers, none of which exceeds $1,000,000.

b. Oregon Inc. and Arizona Company are both subsidiaries of Utah Incorporated. Direct sales to Utah total $1,000,000 and are included in other sales.

c. Sales to domestic governments include $14,000,000 to federal governmental agencies, with the remainder to local governmental agencies.

d. Sales to foreign governments include $8,500,000 in sales to the Canadian government, with the remainder to various other foreign governments, none more than $1,000,000.

Required:

Determine the major customer disclosures that Montgomery must make in accordance with *SFAS No. 14.* Explain and justify your answer.

E 26-5 Segments: Prepare Income Statement and Balance Sheet (L.O. 5)

Big Company has two segments of its operations that qualify as identifiable segments. The revenues of the specialty products segment approximate 11% of total revenues, and the identifiable net assets of the services segment approximate 17% of total identifiable assets. Relevant pretax data for 1992 are as follows (in thousands):

	Specialty	Services	Company*
Revenues	$1,350	$ 975	$9,760
Direct expenses	800	400	6,000
Companywide expenses (allocable)			1,800†
General company expenses (not allocable)			1,385
Identifiable assets‡ (net of depreciation)	250	1,200	5,600
Income tax rate, 40%.			

* Excludes the segment amounts.

† Allocate on the basis of direct expense ratios.

‡ None used jointly.

Required:

1. Prepare the income statement for the company. Use three columns: Specialty Segment, Services Segment, and Total Company. Show computations.
2. Show what amounts should be reported on the balance sheet for identifiable assets for each segment and total company.

E26-6 Identify Reporting Segments: Give Basis (L.O. 5)

Keefe Corporation has expanded rapidly, and segment reporting has become an accounting issue. The following situations are under consideration (in millions):

Situation	Revenues	Operating profit	Identifiable assets
1. Product Group A	$28	$5	$15
2. Foreign Operation—SA	27	4	14
3. Single Customer X	30	5	
4. Foreign Operation—ME	28	6	16
5. Product Group B	29	4	15

Situation	Revenues	Operating profit	Identifiable assets
6. Single Customer Y	28	6	
7. Product Group C	30	7	13

Additional data:
(in millions)

   a. Combined operating profit of all industry segments (no operating losses) . . . . . . $ 50
   b. Combined identifiable assets of all industry segments 160
   c. Combined revenue of all segments of the entity 300

Required:

Select those segments, foreign operations, and customers that Keefe Corporation should report in accordance with *SFAS No. 14*. Explain the basis for your decision in each situation.

E26–7 Interim Reporting: Application of Guidelines (L.O. 4)

In the context of interim reporting, items may be (*a*) recognized in the interim statements of the current interim period, (*b*) recognized in the current interim period but require special disclosure, (*c*) deferred in their entirety (i.e., not recognized until some later interim period, or not at all), or (*d*) amortized or accrued (i.e., recognized partly in the current interim period and partly in subsequent interim periods). A number of items are listed below that require a decision on how they should be incorporated on interim statements. Match the letters given above with the numbered items given below to indicate how each item should be incorporated on the interim statements.

1. Salaries allocable to services rendered during the current period.
2. Inventories estimated by use of the gross margin method.
3. Temporary declines in market value of inventories.
4. Short-term stock investment gains from recoveries of market value (not in excess of previously recognized market declines).
5. Materials and wages allocable to products sold this period.
6. Costs benefiting two or more interim periods.
7. Increase in gross margin due to liquidation of a layer of LIFO base inventory expected to be replenished by year-end.
8. Quantity discounts allowed to customers based upon annual volume of their purchases.
9. Contingencies and other uncertainties that may affect fairness of presentation.
10. Income tax on income of first quarter where total income for the first quarter puts the company in a low tax bracket; subsequent operations are expected to be sufficiently profitable that by end of second quarter and thereafter taxable income of company will be in a higher bracket.

E26–8 Industry Segment Disclosure (L.O. 5)

Operating profit and loss figures for the seven industries in which the Sheets Company operates are as follows:

	1992 Operating Profit (Loss)
Industry 1	$1,075,000
Industry 2	200,000
Industry 3	550,000
Industry 4	(208,000)
Industry 5	(18,000)
Industry 6	5,000
Industry 7	(2,000)
	$1,602,000

Required:

Identify those industries that meet the operating profit or loss criteria to be a reportable segment for 1992.

PROBLEMS

P 26–1 Segment Reporting (L.O. 5)

Study the industry segment data as abstracted from the 1990 FMC Corporation annual report presented below.

FMC Corporation Segment Information

(in millions)

	Year Ended December 31		
	1990	**1989**	**1988**
Sales:			
Industrial chemicals	$1,029.6	$ 975.9	$ 914.0
Performance chemicals	594.4	565.6	521.0
Precious metals	187.7	190.2	175.7
Defense systems	1,067.2	900.3	945.7
Machinery and equipment	845.5	783.0	734.1
Eliminations	(2.2)	(0.5)	(3.6)
Total	$3,722.2	$3,414.5	$3,286.9
Income (loss) before income taxes:			
Industrial chemicals	$ 106.9	$ 137.7	$ 146.9
Performance chemcials	84.8	88.0	76.8
Precious metals*	81.3	100.9	93.3
Defense systems	96.8	47.3	54.2
Machinery and equipment	52.0	28.3	11.7
Operating profit	421.8	402.2	382.9
Net interest expense	(128.1)	(133.7)	(148.4)
Gain on FMC Gold Company sale of stock	—	—	—
Corporate and other	(101.8)	(86.2)	(84.7)
Unusual items	19.5	36.0	39.7
Total	$ 211.4	$ 218.3	$ 189.5
Identifiable assets:			
Industrial chemicals	$1,048.3	$ 931.5	$ 842.3
Performance chemicals	420.9	397.4	391.2
Precious metals	157.4	99.3	102.5
Defense systems	444.7	502.9	492.4
Machinery and equipment	495.2	459.3	450.8
Eliminations	—	—	(0.1)
Subtotal	2,566.5	2,390.4	2,279.1
Corporate and other	392.7	428.6	469.7
Total	$2,959.2	$2,819.0	$2,748.8

* Includes 100% of FMC Gold Company's income before income taxes of $49.0 million in 1990, $60.7 million in 1989, and $82.7 million in 1988, and the effects of the FMC Corporation hedging program. Minority shareholder interests since the initial public offering in June 1987 are included in Corporate and other.

Required:

1. For the 1990 data, identify the reporting criteria met for each reported segment.
2. For 1990, which segment earns the largest return on assets? Which segment earns the largest return on sales?
3. Suppose the precious metals segment operating profit were reduced by $49.0 million. Would this continue to be a reportable segment? Why or why not? If FMC had additional businesses, none of which by itself required reporting as a segment, how would the above industry segment data report be changed?
4. Repeat questions 1 and 2 using the 1988 data.

P26–2 Interim Reporting (L.O. 4)

APB Opinion No. 28, "Interim Financial Reporting" states that "each interim period should be viewed primarily as an integral part of an annual period." It goes on to state:

> In general, the results for each interim period should be based on the accounting principles and practices used by an enterprise in the preparation of its latest annual financial statements unless a change in an accounting practice or policy has been adopted in the current year.

However, the [APB] concluded that certain accounting principles and practices followed for annual reporting purposes may require modification at interim reporting dates so that the reported results for the interim period may better relate to the results of operations for the annual period.

Required:

Below are six independent cases on how accounting facts might be reported on a company's interim financial reports. State whether the proposed method would be acceptable under generally accepted accounting principles applicable to interim financial data. Support your answer with a brief explanation.

1. Cup Company management was reasonably certain it would have an employee strike in the third quarter. As a result, it shipped heavily during the second quarter but plans to defer the recognition of the sales in excess of the normal sales. The deferred sales will be recognized as sales in the third quarter, when the strike is in progress. Management thinks this is more representative of normal second and third quarter operations.
2. Glass Company takes a physical inventory at year-end for annual financial statement purposes. Inventory and cost of sales reported in interim quarterly statements are based on estimated gross profit rates because a physical inventory would result in a temporary shutdown of operations. Glass Company has reliable perpetual inventory records.
3. Taylor Company is planning to report one fourth of its annual pension expense each quarter.
4. Temple Company wrote down inventory to reflect lower of cost or market in the first quarter of 1992. At year-end, the market exceeds the original acquisition cost of this inventory. Consequently, management plans to write the inventory back up to its original cost as a year-end adjustment.
5. Tall Company realized a large gain on the sale of investments at the beginning of the second quarter. The company wants to report one third of the gain in each of the remaining quarters.
6. Dill Company has estimated its annual audit fee. Management plans to prorate this expense equally over the four quarters.

(CMA adapted)

P26–3 Interim Reporting (L.O. 4)

The Dunn Manufacturing Company budgeted activities for 1992 as follows:

	Amount
Net sales (1,000,000 units)	$6,000,000
Cost of goods sold	(3,600,000)
Gross margin	$2,400,000
Selling, general, and administrative expenses	(1,400,000)
Operating earnings	$1,000,000
Nonoperating income	100,000
Earnings before income taxes	$1,100,000
Estimated income taxes (current and deferred)	(385,000)
Net earnings	$ 715,000
Earnings per share of common stock	$7.15

Dunn has operated profitably for many years and has experienced a seasonal pattern of sales volume and production. Sales volume for 1992 is expected to follow a quarterly pattern of 10%, 20%, 35%, and 35% because of the seasonality of the industry. Due to production and storage capacity limitations, it is expected that production will follow a pattern of 20%, 25%, 30%, and 25% during the four quarters of 1992.

At the end of the first quarter of 1992, the controller of Dunn has prepared and issued the following interim report for public release:

	Amount
Net sales (100,000 units)	$ 600,000
Cost of goods sold	(360,000)
Gross margin	$ 240,000
Selling, general, and administrative expenses	(290,000)
Operating loss	$ (50,000)
Loss from warehouse fire	(175,000)
Loss before income taxes	$(225,000)
Estimated income taxes	0
Net loss	$(225,000)
Loss per share of common stock	($2.25)

The following additional information is available for the first quarter just completed, but was not included in the public information released:

a. The company uses a standard cost system in which standards are set at currently attainable levels on an annual basis. At the end of the first quarter, there was underapplied fixed factory overhead (volume variance) of $50,000 that was treated as an asset at the end of the quarter. Production during the quarter was 200,000 units, of which 100,000 were sold.

b. The selling, general, and administrative expenses were budgeted on a basis of $1,000,000 fixed expenses for the year plus 40 cents of variable expenses per unit of sales.

c. The warehouse fire loss met the conditions of an extraordinary loss. The warehouse had an undepreciated cost of $475,000 and $300,000 was recovered from insurance on the warehouse. No other gains or losses are anticipated this year from similar events or transactions, nor has Dunn had any similar losses in preceding years. The full loss will be deductible as an ordinary loss for income tax purposes.

d. The effective income tax rate, for federal and state taxes combined, is expected to average 35% of earnings before income taxes during 1992. There are no permanent differences between pretax accounting income and taxable income.

e. Earnings per share were computed on the basis of 100,000 shares of capital stock outstanding. Dunn has only one class of stock issued, no long-term debt outstanding, and no stock option plan.

Required:

1. Do you agree and approve of the way Dunn has prepared its interim income statement? Why or why not?
2. Identify any weaknesses in form and content of Dunn's interim report without reference to the additional information.
3. Without reference to the specific situation described previously, what are the standards of disclosure for interim financial data (published interim financial reports) for publicly traded companies? Explain.

CASES

C26–1
Segment Reporting
(L.O. 5)

Many financial analysts and professional accountants argue that firms should report segment data, while many managers argue strongly against such disclosures.

a. Outline reasons for requiring financial reporting by segments.
b. Outline reasons against requiring financial reporting by segments.
c. Outline the accounting difficulties in implementing segment reporting.

C26–2
Interim Reporting
(L.O. 4)

The unaudited quarterly financial statements issued by many corporations are prepared on the same basis as annual statements, with some minor exceptions.

a. Under what circumstances would there be a difference between the basis used to prepare interim statements and that for annual statements?
b. Why are there problems in using interim statements to predict annual income?
c. How might quarterly income be affected by the behavior of costs incurred in a repairs and maintenance of manufacturing equipment account?

C26–3
Sherwin-Williams:
Analysis of Actual
Financial Statements

Complete the following schedule for Sherwin-Williams for 1990:

Product class	Sales		Operating Profit		Assets	
	Amount	%	Amount	%	Amount	%
Paint stores						
Coatings						
Other						
Combined						
Interclass						
Unallocated expenses						
Consolidated		100%		100%		100%

Explain what each reported segment includes.

Sherwin-Williams
1990 Annual Report

Management's Discussion and Analysis of Financial Condition and Results of Operations

Highlights of 1990

- Effective June 1, 1990, the Company sold Lyons Transportation Lines, Inc. (LTL).

- Effective June 25, 1990, the Company acquired certain assets of the Krylon and Illinois Bronze aerosol paints and coatings businesses of Borden, Inc.

- Effective October 27, 1990, the Company acquired certain assets of the U.S. consumer paint business of DeSoto, Inc.

- During 1990, debt activity included the prepayment of certain outstanding debt with a total weighted-average annual interest rate of 10.04 percent and certain new borrowings that have a total weighted-average annual interest rate of 9.02 percent.

- The Company entered into an agreement with Sears, Roebuck & Co. for the supply of paint products previously supplied by DeSoto.

- New point-of-sale devices were in place in every store.

Earnings Per Common Share
Dollars.

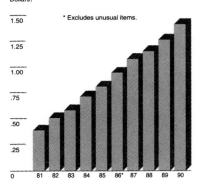

Financial Condition - 1990

Our current ratio dropped slightly, from 2.0 in 1989 and 1988 to 1.9 in 1990, primarily due to a decrease of $103.1 million in cash, cash equivalents and short-term investments as a result of acquisitions ($207.0 million), payments of debt ($33.7 million), and payments of cash dividends ($32.9 million). These decreases in cash were partially offset by proceeds from disposals of assets ($27.4 million) and from issuance of debt ($49.0 million). Accounts receivable ($24.3 million), inventories ($46.9 million), other current assets ($10.4 million), and accounts payable ($26.9 million) all increased primarily due to acquisitions, partially offset by the disposition of LTL. The decrease in the current portion of long-term debt was primarily due to the January 1990 payment of $15.8 million outstanding principal of the 10.50 percent

promissory notes. Other accruals decreased primarily as a result of current year costs and adjustments made to prior accruals.

Working Capital as a % of Sales
Percent

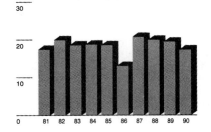

Property, plant and equipment increased from 1989 by capital expenditures of $64.3 million and acquired assets of $9.2 million, partially offset by the disposition of $8.8 million of LTL assets. Capital expenditures represent principally the cost of opening or remodeling paint stores, the installation of point-of-sale devices, and the continued upgrade of equipment at manufacturing, distribution, and research facilities. There were no significant acquisitions in 1989. During 1988, our principal acquisition was the purchase of certain assets of Western Automotive Finishes, Inc., an automotive paint manufacturer and distributor. Capital expenditures in 1988 were principally for the cost of opening or remodeling paint stores and constructing three warehouses to replace the Dayton, Ohio warehouse destroyed by fire in May, 1987. We do not anticipate the need for any external financing to support our capital programs.

The primary impacts on noncurrent assets and liabilities were the acquisitions, debt proceeds and debt repayments. The purchase of intangibles and goodwill accounted for the majority of the $122 million increase in intangibles and other assets. Other long-term liabilities were affected by provisions for the costs of programs related to environmental protection and control in 1990, 1989 and 1988. These provisions were more than offset in 1990 by reclassifications to current liabilities.

Despite the significant cash outlay for acquisitions in 1990, total debt increased by a net of only $15.3 million. During 1990, in addition to prepaying the outstanding principal of the 10.50 percent promissory notes, we exercised our option to prepay $7.6 million of 9.375 percent promissory notes, together representing a weighted-average annual interest rate of 10.04 percent. In October 1990, we incurred long-term borrowings of $12.5 million at 8.861 percent annual interest for 5 years and $12.5 million at 9.478 percent for 10 years under our credit agreement with The Sherwin-Williams Company Salaried

Employees' Retirement Trust. In addition, in December 1990, we completed the sale of $15 million in 8.78 percent annual interest promissory notes which are due in 1993. The new debt, taken as a whole, represents a weighted-average annual interest rate of 9.02 percent. We utilized short-term borrowings for brief periods during the third quarter of 1990, and we may need to utilize insignificant amounts of short-term borrowings briefly during the first half of 1991 to help finance working capital. However, once into the peak selling season, sufficient cash flows should be generated from operations to return to an investment position.

To complement our current outstanding debt, we have arranged significant additional financing flexibility. A shelf registration permits the Company to issue up to $200 million of unsecured debt securities; however, there is no guarantee that an offering thereunder would be successful or on terms acceptable to the Company. During 1990, the Company terminated a subsidiary's commercial paper program and established a similar commercial paper program in the name of the Company in the amount of $280 million. The Company also has in place a $280 million revolving credit agreement with a group of banks. There were no borrowings outstanding under any of these financing arrangements at December 31, 1990, 1989 or 1988. See Note 9 to the consolidated financial statements for a complete description of long-term debt.

Capitalization
Dollars in Millions

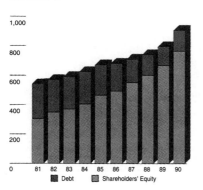

With the net increase in total debt of $15.3 million, we still improved our debt-to-capitalization ratio to 15.6 percent at the end of 1990 compared to 15.8 percent in 1989 and 18.6 percent in 1988. Our debt-to-capitalization ratio has steadily improved since 1978 as a result of increased profitability, planned debt reductions, and the conversion of debentures into common stock.

We acquire our own stock for general corporate purposes and, depending on our cash position and market conditions, we may purchase additional shares of stock in the future.

At a meeting held February 20, 1991, the board of directors declared a quarterly dividend of $.105 per share and a two-for-one stock split. (See Note 2 to the consolidated financial statements.) This dividend represents the twelfth consecutive increase and a compounded rate of increase of 37 percent since the dividend was reinstated in 1979. The 1990 quarterly dividend of $.095 per share marked the eleventh consecutive year that the dividend approximated our payout ratio target of 30 percent of trailing annual earnings.

The jury verdict and judgment for $31.1 million which was entered against the Company during 1989 were withdrawn by the Court in 1990 and the matter was settled for an undisclosed amount. The settlement agreement has been accepted by the Court and is subject to a protective order.

During the period 1987 - 1990, the Company and certain other companies were named defendants in a number of lawsuits arising from the manufacture and sale of lead pigments that were allegedly used in the manufacture of lead paints. It is possible that additional lawsuits may be filed against the Company in the future with similar allegations. The various existing lawsuits seek damages for personal injuries and property damages, along with costs incurred to abate the lead related paint from buildings. The Company believes that such lawsuits are without merit and is vigorously defending them. The Company does not believe that any potential liability ultimately determined to be attributable to the Company arising out of such lawsuits will have a material adverse effect on the Company's business or financial condition.

The Company is presently involved in several proceedings involving potential liability for the clean up of environmental waste sites. The Company continues to assess its potential liability with respect to these sites. This assessment is based upon, among other factors, the number of parties involved with respect to any given site, the nature of the wastes involved and the volumetric contribution which may be attributed to the Company. The Company does not believe that any potential liability ultimately determined to be attributable to the Company will have a material adverse effect on the Company's business or financial condition.

Results of Operations - 1990 vs 1989

Consolidated net sales increased 6.7 percent to $2.27 billion as all segments improved sales during the year. Sales in 1990 were impacted by the acquisitions of Krylon and DeSoto and the divestiture of LTL. Adjusting for these transactions, consolidated net sales increased 5.7 percent. The Paint Stores Segment had a 6.5 percent sales increase, despite economic problems encountered particularly in the northeastern part of the country. Comparable-store sales increased 6.2 percent in 1990. Sales of paint products increased 9.9 percent, while gallons sold increased 7.3 percent. The increase in sales of paint was partially offset by sales declines in wall-covering, floorcovering and window treatments. Sales of the Coatings Segment increased 7.1 percent, primarily in the

Consumer and Sprayon Divisions. The Consumer Division showed strong increases in the Dutch Boy group, as these products were sold nationally in all Sears locations beginning in the first quarter of 1990. The Consumer Division also included two months of DeSoto sales. Sprayon's sales included six months of Krylon sales, which more than offset soft applicator sales. After adjusting for the acquisitions and divestiture made in 1990, the Coatings Segment's sales gain was 4.1 percent. Sales for the Other Segment increased 3.9 percent from 1989.

Sales
Dollars in Millions

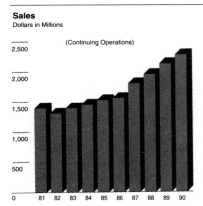

Consolidated gross profit dollars increased 9.5 percent during the year, as we experienced volume gains, price increases and a slowing in the escalation of most raw material costs. Consolidated gross margins were 41.0 percent in 1990 compared to 40.0 percent in 1989. In the last several months of the year, increasing oil prices began creating some raw material cost pressures, particularly in the Automotive, Transportation Services, and Chemical Coatings Divisions of the Coatings Segment. However, given the situation in the Middle East and fluctuating oil prices, we are unable to predict the effect oil prices might have on raw material costs and gross margins in 1991.

Consolidated selling, general and administrative expenses increased as a percent of sales to 32.9 percent from 32.2 percent in 1989. The addition of new stores in 1990 and increased promotional expenses were primarily responsible for the increase in SG&A expenses in the Paint Stores Segment. Amortization of intangible assets and goodwill recorded in the purchase of Krylon was the primary reason for the increase in SG&A expenses in the Coatings Segment.

Consolidated operating profits increased 10.0 percent in 1990. The Paint Stores Segment's operating profits decreased 5.3 percent, primarily due to special credits included in 1989's profits. Adjusting for these special credits in 1989, operating profit of the Paint Stores Segment increased 7.8 percent. The Coatings Segment's operating profit increased 7.8 percent as most raw material costs began to stabilize. The operating profits of the Other Segment increased due primarily to the absence of provisions established for the disposition of certain unprofitable non-retail properties in 1989. Corporate expenses decreased from 1989 as a result of changes in various provisions and other items which are not directly associated with or allocable to any operating segment. Refer to pages 4 through 9 for a more thorough discussion of Business Segment Information.

Interest expense decreased 17.1 percent during 1990 due to the continued reduction of long-term debt for most of 1990. Interest coverage improved to 18.2 times in 1990 compared to 13.9 times in 1989. Our fixed charge coverage, which is calculated using interest and rent expense, was 3.0 times in 1990. Decreased interest expense and increased profitability more than offset the increase in rent expense, resulting in the slightly higher fixed charge coverage from 2.9 times in 1989. We expect interest expense to increase slightly in 1991 as a result of additional borrowings.

Profits
Dollars in Millions

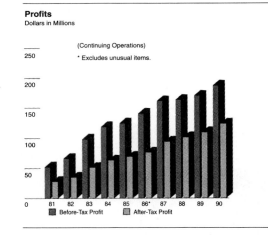

Interest and net investment income decreased 26.4 percent to $10.1 million due to lower investment levels as a result of the use of cash and short-term investments for acquisitions. Other income decreased $2.0 million primarily due to larger provisions for environmental protection and control and losses on disposals of certain assets. These increased expenses were partially offset by a net credit for the disposition and termination of operations as a result of adjustments made to prior accruals. (See Note 6 to the consolidated financial statements.) Net income increased 12.6 percent to $122.7 million and net income per share increased 11.9 percent to $1.41.

Our financial position and results of operations may be affected beginning in 1992 by Financial Accounting Standards Board Statement No. 96, "Accounting for Income Taxes", because of the lower rates adopted in the Tax Reform Act of 1986, and in 1993 by Financial Accounting Standards Board Statement No. 106, "Employers' Accounting for Postretirement Benefits Other than Pensions." The Company has not yet completed all the complex analyses required to estimate the impact of the new Statements. Based on preliminary information currently available, it appears that Statement No. 96 will have a favorable effect on the Company's tax expense by reducing the rate at which deferred taxes are recognized and that Statement No.106 will have a detrimental effect on profits due to the unrecorded liability and expense of accruing for future benefits due employees and retirees.

Return on Sales, Assets, and Equity
Percent

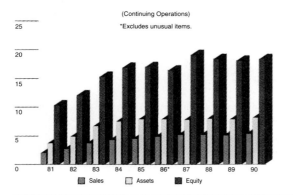

(Continuing Operations)
*Excludes unusual items.

Results of Operations - 1989 vs 1988

Consolidated net sales increased 8.9 percent. We improved our market share again in 1989 as gallons sold increased at a faster pace than the paint industry in general. The sales increase in 1989 was primarily due to price increases and, to a lesser extent, volume gains. The Paint Stores Segment had a 7.7 percent sales increase, despite continued sluggish retail sales and competitive price pressures. Comparable store sales gains were 7.5 percent. The sale of paint products, due to strong painter and contractor sales, increased 13.6 percent in 1989. Decreased sales of non-paint products, which are primarily retail sales, partially offset the paint products sales increase. The Coatings Segment had an 11.2 percent increase in 1989 sales, primarily in the Consumer and Automotive Divisions. The Consumer Division experienced strong increases in the Kem-Tone® and private label lines, while the Automotive Division showed strong increases in the Sherwin-Williams® product line, along with added sales from Western Automotive Finishes paint products, a company which was acquired in 1988. Sales for the Other Segment were flat in comparison to 1988.

Consolidated gross profit dollars increased 11.1 percent during 1989 as a result of volume gains and price increases. The increase was partially offset by continued raw material cost increases, resulting in gross margins of 40.0 percent in 1989 compared to 39.2 percent in 1988.

Consolidated selling, general and administrative expenses increased in dollars in 1989, but remained flat with 1988 at 32.2 percent of sales. The addition of new stores in 1989 and the annualization of stores opened in 1988, which resulted in additional expenses, along with increased promotional activities in the Paint Stores Segment, were primarily responsible for the increased selling, general and administrative expenses.

Consolidated operating profits increased in comparison with 1988 primarily due to a 30 percent increase in the Paint Stores Segment's operating profits due primarily to a reduction of 1988's profits by provisions established for the closing of certain unprofitable stores. Excluding special charges and credits in 1989 and 1988, operating profits in the Paint Stores Segment rose 7.7 percent for 1989. The operating profits of the Coatings Segment increased only 1.6 percent in 1989 due to the gain realized on the sale of BAPCO in 1988. Excluding the net gain, the operating profits of the Coatings Segment increased over 16.0 percent for the year. Coatings Segment operating profit improved due to price increases implemented during 1989 to cover the increasing costs of certain raw materials, especially titanium dioxide, that had caused lower operating profits in 1988. The operating profits of the Other Segment decreased due to provisions established for the disposition of certain unprofitable non-retail properties. Corporate expenses increased in 1989 when compared to 1988 as a result of changes in various provisions and other items which are not directly associated with or allocable to any operating segment.

Interest expense decreased 7.7 percent during 1989 because of the continued reduction in outstanding long-term debt. Interest coverage improved to 13.9 times in 1989 compared to 12.4 times in 1988. Our fixed charge coverage, which is calculated using interest and rent expense, was 2.9 times in 1989. Decreased interest expense and increased profitability more than offset the increase in rent expense, resulting in a slightly higher fixed charge coverage from 1988's level of 2.8 times.

Interest and net investment income increased 8.3 percent in 1989 to $13.8 million, as the Company had higher investment levels and higher yields than in 1988. Other income decreased $22.7 million due to the absence of gains on the sale of the Company's interest in BAPCO and the realization of certain long-term assets which were recognized in 1988. A reduced income tax rate decreased income tax expense for 1989. Net income increased 7.8 percent to $108.9 million and net income per share increased 9.6 percent to $1.26.

Financial Summary

Millions of dollars, except per share data

The Sherwin-Williams Company and Subsidiaries

Years ended December 31,	1990	1989	1988	1987	1986	1985	1984	1983	1982	1981
Operations										
Net sales	$ 2,267	$ 2,123	$ 1,950	$ 1,801	$ 1,558	$ 1,526	$ 1,454	$ 1,397	$ 1,312	$ 1,399
Cost of goods sold	1,338	1,275	1,187	1,067	922	916	900	897	881	976
Selling and administrative expenses	745	686	629	579	488	464	425	391	356	365
Interest expense	11	13	14	18	19	18	18	16	16	17
Income from continuing operations before income taxes	187	170	163	161	140*	124	118	98	66	52
Income taxes	64	61	62	67	64*	55	55	47	31	24
Income from continuing operations	123	109	101	94	76*	69	63	51	35	28
Net income	123	109	101	97	86*	75	65	55	43	31
Net cash flow provided by operations	155	171	40	85	95	102	126	100	124	51
Financial Position										
Inventories	$ 373	$ 326	$ 323	$ 281	$ 410	$ 367	$ 338	$ 332	$ 299	$ 335
Accounts receivable - net	230	206	196	176	158	155	149	137	131	132
Working capital	392	413	388	373	301	358	336	335	329	297
Property, plant and equipment - net	373	359	333	289	318	291	268	235	246	240
Total assets	1,504	1,375	1,259	1,210	1,207	1,108	1,043	970	902	864
Long-term debt	138	105	130	141	178	191	206	205	209	230
Common shareholders' equity	764	668	601	550	492	465	404	370	334	284
Total shareholders' equity	764	668	601	550	492	465	404	371	349	305
Per Common Share Data (A)										
Average shares and equivalents (thousands)	87,056	86,326	87,830	89,676	91,570	92,444	91,699	95,278	83,613	79,269
Book value	$ 8.77	$ 7.73	$ 6.85	$ 6.13	$ 5.37	$ 5.03	$ 4.41	$ 3.89	$ 4.17	$ 3.85
Income from continuing operations	1.41	1.26	1.15	1.05	.83	.74	.68	.54	.42	.35
Net income	1.41	1.26	1.15	1.08	.94	.81	.71	.58	.51	.40
Cash dividends	.38	.35	.32	.28	.25	.23	.19	.15	.125	.10
Financial Ratios										
Return on sales	5.4%	5.1%	5.2%	5.2%	4.9%*	4.5%	4.3%	3.7%	2.7%	2.0%
Asset turnover	1.5x	1.5x	1.6x	1.7x	1.7x	1.8x	1.8x	1.9x	1.8x	1.8x
Return on assets	8.2%	7.9%	8.0%	7.8%	7.9%*	7.9%	7.5%	6.7%	4.9%	3.7%
Return on equity (B):										
From continuing operations	18.4%	18.1%	18.4%	19.1%	16.4%	17.0%	16.9%	15.3%	12.1%	10.3%
From total operations	18.4%	18.1%	18.4%	19.6%	18.6%*	18.5%	17.6%	16.6%	14.8%	11.6%
Dividend payout ratio	26.8%	27.6%	27.7%	25.7%	26.2%*	28.2%	26.5%	25.1%	25.0%	26.1%
Debt to capitalization	15.6%	15.8%	18.6%	22.2%	27.6%	30.5%	35.0%	37.1%	38.6%	43.6%
Current ratio	1.9	2.0	2.0	2.0	1.7	1.9	1.9	2.0	2.1	2.0
Times interest earned (C)	18.2x	13.9x	12.4x	10.1x	8.5x*	7.9x	7.6x	7.0x	5.2x	4.1x
Working capital to sales	17.3%	19.4%	19.9%	20.7%	13.0%	18.5%	18.7%	18.5%	19.9%	17.4%
Effective income tax rate	34.5%	36.0%	38.0%	41.8%	45.5%*	44.5%	46.9%	47.9%	46.5%	46.5%
General										
Capital expenditures	$ 64	$ 67	$ 72	$ 57	$ 64	$ 75	$ 59	$ 52	$ 48	$ 43
Total technical expenditures	38	37	32	28	26	23	26	23	24	25
Advertising	106	84	84	73	62	62	57	51	42	40
Depreciation and amortization	45	42	37	32	27	24	23	23	22	22
Shareholders of record:										
Preferred	—	—	—	—	—	—	—	40	557	750
Common	12,012	12,230	12,606	12,327	11,936	11,384	9,777	9,641	8,590	8,858
Number of employees	16,397	16,726	16,607	15,901	13,706	12,970	13,092	13,172	14,297	15,879
Sales per employee (thousands)	$ 138	$ 127	$ 117	$ 113	$ 114	$ 118	$ 111	$ 106	$ 92	$ 88
Sales per dollar of assets	1.51	1.54	1.55	1.49	1.61	1.74	1.74	1.83	1.82	1.87

* In 1986, unusual items, which increased income from continuing operations and net income by $19,595,000 ($.22 per share), are excluded. Includes continuing operations only for the years 1981 through 1987.

(A) All common share amounts and per share data reflect the effect of the stock split described in Note 2 to the consolidated financial statements.

(B) Based on common shareholders' equity at beginning of year.

(C) Ratio of pre-tax income from continuing operations before interest expense to interest expense.

This summary should be read in conjuction with the financial statements and notes on pages 16-28 of this report.

14

Report of Management

Shareholders
The Sherwin-Williams Company

We have prepared the accompanying consolidated financial statements and related information included herein for the years ended December 31, 1990, 1989 and 1988. The primary responsibility for the integrity of the financial information rests with management. This information is prepared in accordance with generally accepted accounting principles, based upon our best estimates and judgments and giving due consideration to materiality.

The Company maintains accounting and control systems which are designed to provide reasonable assurance that assets are safeguarded from loss or unauthorized use and which produce records adequate for preparation of financial information. There are limits inherent in all systems of internal control based on the recognition that the cost of such systems should not exceed the benefits to be derived. We believe our system provides this appropriate balance.

The board of directors pursues its responsibility for these financial statements through the Audit Committee, composed exclusively of outside directors. The committee meets periodically with management, internal auditors and our independent auditors to discuss the adequacy of financial controls, the quality of financial reporting and the nature, extent and results of the audit effort. Both the internal auditors and independent auditors have private and confidential access to the Audit Committee at all times.

J. G. Breen	T. R. Miklich	J. L. Ault
Chairman and Chief Executive Officer	Senior Vice President - Finance and Chief Financial Officer	Vice President - Corporate Controller

---

Report of Independent Auditors

Shareholders and Board of Directors
The Sherwin-Williams Company
Cleveland, Ohio

We have audited the consolidated financial statements of The Sherwin-Williams Company and subsidiaries listed in Item 14(a) of the Index on page 33. These financial statements are the responsibility of management. Our responsibility is to express an opinion on these financial statements based on our audits.

We conducted our audits in accordance with generally accepted auditing standards. Those standards require that we plan and perform the audit to obtain reasonable assurance about whether the financial statements are free of material misstatement. An audit includes examining, on a test basis, evidence supporting the amounts and disclosures in the financial statements. An audit also includes assessing the accounting principles used and significant estimates made by management, as well as evaluating the overall financial statement presentation. We believe that our audits provide a reasonable basis for our opinion.

In our opinion, the consolidated financial statements listed in Item 14(a) of the Index present fairly, in all material respects, the consolidated financial position of The Sherwin-Williams Company and subsidiaries at December 31, 1990, 1989 and 1988, and the consolidated results of their operations and their cash flows for each of the three years in the period ended December 31, 1990, in conformity with generally accepted accounting principles.

Cleveland, Ohio
January 23, 1991, except for Note 2,
as to which the date is February 20, 1991

Ernst & Young

Statements of Consolidated Income
Thousands of dollars, except per share data

The Sherwin-Williams Company and Subsidiaries

Years ended December 31,	1990	1989	1988
Net sales	$2,266,732	$2,123,483	$1,950,474
Costs and expenses:			
Cost of goods sold	1,337,942	1,275,119	1,186,846
Selling, general and administrative expenses	745,651	685,645	628,574
Interest expense	10,902	13,149	14,253
Interest and net investment income	(10,159)	(13,810)	(12,752)
Other	(4,881)	(6,831)	(29,487)
	2,079,455	1,953,272	1,787,434
Income before income taxes	187,277	170,211	163,040
Income taxes	64,611	61,276	61,960
Net income	$ 122,666	$ 108,935	$ 101,080
Net income per share*	$ 1.41	$ 1.26	$ 1.15

* Per share data reflects the effect of the stock split described in Note 2.
  See notes to consolidated financial statements.

Consolidated Balance Sheets
Thousands of dollars

The Sherwin-Williams Company and Subsidiaries

December 31,	1990	1989	1988
Assets			
Current assets:			
Cash and cash equivalents	$ 95,977	$ 132,214	$ 69,838
Short-term investments	3,000	69,904	84,403
Accounts receivable, less allowance	229,926	205,661	195,726
Inventories:			
Finished goods	317,117	278,220	271,978
Work in process and raw materials	56,221	48,231	51,019
	373,338	326,451	322,997
Other current assets	122,027	111,621	93,174
Total current assets	824,268	845,851	766,138
Deferred pension assets	157,038	142,738	135,821
Intangibles and other assets	149,740	27,541	24,152
Property, plant and equipment:			
Land	41,913	36,748	35,206
Buildings	194,969	191,540	186,721
Machinery and equipment	432,271	404,156	365,834
Construction in progress	18,705	14,294	11,757
	687,858	646,738	599,518
Less allowances for depreciation and amortization	314,508	287,873	266,920
	373,350	358,865	332,598
Total assets	$1,504,396	$1,374,995	$1,258,709
Liabilities and Shareholders' Equity			
Current liabilities:			
Accounts payable	$ 202,855	$ 176,003	$ 160,844
Compensation and taxes withheld	56,477	52,954	49,055
Current portion of long-term debt	2,691	20,492	7,018
Other accruals	145,249	157,829	142,756
Accrued taxes	24,910	26,030	18,316
Total current liabilities	432,182	433,308	377,989
Long-term debt	137,999	104,952	129,604
Deferred income taxes	98,036	93,622	92,242
Other long-term liabilities	72,475	75,480	57,623
Shareholders' equity:			
Common stock — $1.00 par value*:			
86,738,836, 86,253,754, and 86,081,504 shares outstanding at December 31, 1990, 1989, and 1988, respectively	48,759	48,482	47,939
Other capital	150,661	142,999	132,621
Retained earnings	712,233	621,750	552,764
Cumulative foreign currency translation adjustment	(15,269)	(14,194)	(13,218)
Treasury stock, at cost	(132,680)	(131,404)	(118,855)
Total shareholders' equity	763,704	667,633	601,251
Total liabilities and shareholders' equity	$1,504,396	$1,374,995	$1,258,709

* Common share amounts reflect the effect of the stock split described in Note 2.
See notes to consolidated financial statements.

Statements of Consolidated Cash Flows
Thousands of dollars

The Sherwin-Williams Company and Subsidiaries

Years ended December 31,	1990	1989	1988
Operations			
Net income	$122,666	$108,935	$101,080
Non-cash adjustments:			
Depreciation and amortization	44,507	41,951	36,865
Deferred income tax expense	(90)	(395)	2,751
Provisions for disposition of operations	(2,221)	7,155	23,316
Funded employee benefits incurred	—	—	6,707
Amortization of intangible assets	7,007	2,299	2,199
Increase in deferred pension asset	(13,798)	(12,695)	(13,872)
Other	5,497	15,831	9,935
Change in current items-net:			
Increase in accounts receivable	(30,632)	(8,432)	(15,293)
Increase in inventories	(7,400)	(799)	(36,577)
Increase in accounts payable	29,511	15,159	2,019
Increase (decrease) in accrued taxes	(1,018)	7,714	(8,535)
Other current items	19,007	7,344	(8,409)
Gains on disposals of assets	—	—	(42,358)
Costs incurred for dispositions of operations	(6,120)	(8,594)	(12,423)
Other	(12,195)	(4,705)	(7,473)
Net operating cash	154,721	170,768	39,932
Investing			
Capital expenditures	(64,351)	(66,933)	(71,551)
Short-term investments	66,904	14,499	53,847
Acquisitions of assets	(207,025)	(4,725)	(18,162)
Proceeds from disposals of assets	27,412	—	55,453
Contribution to employee benefit fund	(467)	(5,432)	—
Other	(1,648)	(2,454)	3,032
Net investing cash	(179,175)	(65,045)	22,619
Financing			
Proceeds from issuance of debt	49,061	2,087	—
Payments of long-term debt	(33,730)	(13,201)	(13,926)
Payments of cash dividends	(32,890)	(30,081)	(27,956)
Purchases of stock for treasury	(1,276)	(12,549)	(25,618)
Other	7,052	10,397	4,507
Net financing cash	(11,783)	(43,347)	(62,993)
Net increase (decrease) in cash and cash equivalents	(36,237)	62,376	(442)
Cash and cash equivalents at beginning of year	132,214	69,838	70,280
Cash and cash equivalents at end of year	$ 95,977	$132,214	$ 69,838
Taxes paid on income	$ 65,720	$ 51,641	$ 62,578
Interest paid on debt	11,015	12,990	14,471

See notes to consolidated financial statements.

Statements of Consolidated Shareholders' Equity

Thousands of dollars

The Sherwin-Williams Company and Subsidiaries

	Common Stock	Other Capital	Retained Earnings	Cumulative Translation Adjustment	Treasury Stock
Balance at January 1, 1988	$ 47,603	$127,164	$479,640	$ (12,689)	$ (92,033)
Treasury stock acquired	—	—	—	—	(25,618)
Stock issued	336	5,457	—	—	(1,204)
Net income	—	—	101,080	—	—
Cash dividends — $.32 per share*	—	—	(27,956)	—	—
Current year translation adjustment	—	—	—	(529)	—
Balance at December 31, 1988	47,939	132,621	552,764	(13,218)	(118,855)
Treasury stock acquired	—	—	—	—	(10,484)
Stock issued	543	10,378	—	—	(2,065)
Net income	—	—	108,935	—	—
Cash dividends — $.35 per share*	—	—	(30,081)	—	—
Unfunded pension losses - net of taxes	—	—	(9,868)	—	—
Current year translation adjustment	—	—	—	(976)	—
Balance at December 31, 1989	48,482	142,999	621,750	(14,194)	(131,404)
Stock issued	**277**	**7,662**	—	—	**(1,276)**
Net income	—	—	**122,666**	—	—
Cash dividends — $.38 per share*	—	—	**(32,890)**	—	—
Reduction in unfunded pension losses - net of taxes	—	—	**707**	—	—
Current year translation adjustment	—	—	—	**(1,075)**	—
Balance at December 31, 1990	**$ 48,759**	**$150,661**	**$712,233**	**$ (15,269)**	**$(132,680)**

* Per share data reflects the effect of the stock split described in Note 2.
  See notes to consolidated financial statements.

Notes to Consolidated Financial Statements

The Sherwin-Williams Company and Subsidiaries

Years ended December 31, 1990, 1989 and 1988

Note 1 — Significant Accounting Policies

Consolidation. The consolidated financial statements include all significant majority-owned subsidiaries. Inter-company accounts and transactions have been eliminated.

Cash Flows. The Company considers all highly liquid investments with a maturity of three months or less when purchased to be cash equivalents. Short-term investments are stated at cost, which approximates market value.

Property, plant and equipment. Property, plant and equipment is stated on the basis of cost. Depreciation is provided principally by the straight-line method. The major classes of assets and ranges of depreciation rates are as follows:

Buildings	2% - 6 ⅔ %
Machinery and equipment	4% - 20%
Furniture and fixtures	5% - 20%
Automobiles and trucks	10% - 33 ⅓ %

Intangibles. Intangible assets, net of accumulated amortization, were $126,976,000, $12,879,000, and $13,909,000 at December 31, 1990, 1989 and 1988, respectively. These assets are amortized by the straight-line method over the expected period of benefit.

Research and development costs. Research and development costs were $19,442,000, $18,058,000, and $16,705,000 for 1990, 1989 and 1988, respectively.

Net income per share. Net income per share was computed based on the average number of shares and share equivalents outstanding during the year after adjustment for the effect of the two-for-one stock split.

Reclassification. Certain amounts in the 1989 and 1988 financial statements have been reclassified to conform with the 1990 presentation.

Note 2 — Stock Split

On February 20, 1991, the Company's board of directors authorized a two-for-one split of the common stock effected in the form of a 100 percent stock dividend to be distributed on or about March 29, 1991, to holders of record on March 4, 1991. Accordingly, all numbers of common shares and per share data have been restated to reflect the stock split. The par value of the additional shares of common stock issued in connection with the stock split will be credited to common stock and a like amount charged to other capital in 1991.

Note 3 — Business Segments

Business segment information appears on pages 4, 5, 6, 7, 8, and 9 of this report.

Note 4 — Acquisitions

Effective June 25, 1990, the Company acquired certain assets of the Krylon and Illinois Bronze aerosol paints and coatings businesses of Borden, Inc. for a total cost, as defined by Accounting Principles Board Opinion No. 16, of $137,510,000. The assets acquired were principally inventory and intangible assets. The excess of the cost over the fair value of the net assets acquired is being amortized over 40 years by the straight-line method.

Effective October 27, 1990, the Company acquired certain assets, primarily property, plant and equipment, and inventory, of the U. S. consumer paint business of DeSoto, Inc. for a total cost, as defined by Accounting Principles Board Opinion No. 16, of $67,940,000. Also effective October 27, 1990, the Company sold certain rights and interests in particular assets of the Chicago Heights, Illinois plant of DeSoto, Inc. for approximately book value.

The Company has accounted for the above acquisitions under the purchase method and, accordingly, the results of operations of the acquired businesses have been included in the statements of consolidated income since the respective dates of acquisition. The purchase price for each of the acquisitions has been allocated to the net assets acquired based on the fair market value determined by independent appraisals.

The following summarized unaudited pro forma financial information assumes the above acquisitions occurred on January 1 of each respective year.

| Thousands of dollars, except per share data | Years ended December 31, | |
	1990	1989
Net sales	$2,475,243	$2,396,974
Net income	$ 110,190	$ 98,681
Income per share	$ 1.27	$ 1.14

The above amounts are not necessarily indicative of the results which would have occurred had the acquisitions been made on January 1 of each respective period or of future results of the combined companies under the ownership and operation of the Company.

During the three year period ended December 31, 1990, the Company purchased various automotive paint distributors, as well as certain paint manufacturers. Assets purchased consisted primarily of accounts receivable, inventory and property, plant and equipment. The results of operations of these businesses since the dates of acquisition were not material to consolidated results.

Note 5 — Inventories

Inventories are stated at the lower of cost or market. Cost is determined principally on the last-in, first-out (LIFO) method which provides a better matching of current costs and revenues. The following presents the effect on inventories, net income and net income per share had the Company used the FIFO and average cost methods of inventory valuation adjusted for income taxes at the statutory rate and assuming no other adjustments. This information is presented to enable the reader to make comparisons with companies using the FIFO method of inventory valuation.

Thousands of dollars, except per share data	Years ended December 31,		
	1990	1989	1988
Percentage of total inventories on LIFO	97%	96%	96%
Excess of FIFO and average cost over LIFO	$81,205	$68,967	$56,138
Decrease in net income due to LIFO	(8,077)	(8,471)	(11,180)
Decrease in net income per share due to LIFO	(.10)	(.10)	(.13)

Note 6 — Other Costs and Expenses

A summary of significant items included in other costs and expenses is as follows:

Thousands of dollars	Years ended December 31,		
	1990	1989	1988
Dividend and royalty income	$(5,975)	$(6,046)	$(7,128)
Losses (gains) on disposals of assets	458	(3,299)	(30,179)
Realization of full value of assets	—	(500)	(14,176)
Provisions for environmental protection and control	8,300	5,900	12,000
Provisions for disposition and termination of operations (see Note 7)	(5,430)	3,405	13,716
Equity income	—	—	(3,263)
Miscellaneous	(2,234)	(6,291)	(457)
	$ (4,881)	$ (6,831)	$(29,487)

During the three years ended December 31, 1990, provisions for environmental protection and control reflect the increased cost of continued compliance with environmental regulations. During 1988, gains from the realization of certain long-term assets with little book value and from the sale of the Company's interest in BAPCO, a Canadian partnership, were recognized.

Note 7 — Disposition and Termination of Operations

The Company is continually re-evaluating its operating facilities with regard to the long-term strategic goals established by management and the board of directors. Operating facilities which are not expected to contribute to the Company's future plans are closed or sold.

At the time of the decision to close or sell certain plants, warehouses, stores or other operating units, provisions to reduce property, plant and equipment to their estimated net realizable values are included in other costs and expenses. Similarly, provisions to reduce all other assets to their estimated net realizable values and for the estimated related costs for severance pay, shutdown expenses and future operating losses to disposal date are included in cost of goods sold. Adjustments to such accruals as disposition occurs are included in other costs and expenses.

In 1990, management provided for the closing of certain warehouses and other operating facilities. Adjustments to prior accruals reflect primarily the decreased ongoing costs of certain previously sold facilities, resulting in a net credit to other costs and expenses. The provisions for 1988 included approximately $10,000,000 for the reduction of assets and closing costs of certain unprofitable retail paint stores.

A summary of the financial data related to the closing or sale of the facilities, expected to be completed by 1992, is as follows:

Thousands of dollars	**1990**	1989	1988
Beginning accrual — January 1	$53,812	$55,251	$44,358
Provisions included in cost of goods sold	3,209	3,750	9,600
Provisions and adjustments to prior accruals included in costs and expenses - other	(5,430)	3,405	13,716
Total provision (credit)	(2,221)	7,155	23,316
Actual costs incurred	(6,120)	(8,594)	(12,423)
Ending accrual — December 31	$45,471	$53,812	$55,251
Net after-tax provision (credit)	$ (1,466)	$ 4,772	$15,388
Net after-tax provision (credit) per share	$ (.02)	$ .06	$ .18

Note 8 — Employee Benefits

Substantially all employees of the Company participate in noncontributory defined benefit or defined contribution pension plans. Defined benefit plans covering salaried employees provide benefits that are based primarily on years of service and employees' compensation. Defined benefit plans covering hourly employees generally provide benefits of stated amounts for each year of service. Multiemployer plans are primarily defined benefit plans which provide benefits of stated amounts for union employees.

The Company's funding policy for defined benefit plans is to fund at least the minimum annual contribution required by applicable regulations. Recommended funding for the hourly defined benefit pension plans is actuarially calculated to properly amortize unfunded liabilities during the period of active service to meet the cost of benefits upon retirement. Current benefits paid to retirees primarily offset earnings of plan assets. A change in actuarial assumptions at December 31, 1989 increased the projected benefit obligation, the effect of which is being amortized over future periods.

At December 31, 1989, certain accounting changes were required by Financial Accounting Standards Board Statement No. 87, first adopted by the Company in 1986. The effect of these changes resulted in the recording of a minimum liability for the hourly defined benefit pension plan in long-term liabilities. At December 31, 1990, the minimum liability was partially offset by a noncurrent asset of $844,000.

The pension credit for defined benefit plans and its components was as follows:

Thousands of dollars	Years ended December 31,		
	1990	1989	1988
Service cost	$ 2,934	$ 3,279	$ 2,972
Interest cost	7,940	8,100	7,409
Actual return on plan assets	(14,709)	(24,176)	(14,362)
Net amortization and deferral	(7,934)	1,185	(8,941)
Net pension credit	$(11,769)	$(11,612)	$(12,922)

The Company's annual contribution for its defined contribution pension plans, which is based on a level percentage of compensation for covered employees, offset the pension credit by $14,500,000 for 1990, $13,600,000 for 1989 and $11,650,000 for 1988.

In addition to providing pension benefits, the Company provides certain health care and life insurance benefits under company-sponsored plans for retired employees. Substantially all of the Company's employees who are not members of a collective bargaining unit are eligible for these benefits upon retirement. The cost of these benefits for both active and retired employees is recognized as claims are incurred and amounted to $34,063,000, $29,259,000 and $31,903,000 for 1990, 1989 and 1988, respectively.

There were 13,236, 13,202 and 12,646 active employees and 4,263, 4,217 and 4,240 retired employees entitled to receive benefits under these plans as of December 31, 1990, 1989 and 1988, respectively.

The Company also has a fund to provide for payment of health care benefits of certain qualified employees. Contributions of $25,000,000, $26,000,000 and $18,000,000 were made to the fund in 1990, 1989 and 1988, respectively. Distributions from the fund amounted to $27,290,000 in 1990, $25,930,000 in 1989 and $21,771,000 in 1988.

Based on the latest actuarial information available, the following table sets forth the funded status and amounts recognized in the Company's consolidated balance sheets for the defined benefit pension plans:

Thousands of dollars	December 31,		
	1990	1989	1988
Actuarial present value of benefit obligations:			
Vested benefit obligation	$(86,090)	$ (89,894)	$(63,191)
Accumulated benefit obligation	$(87,255)	$ (91,713)	$(66,005)
Projected benefit obligation	$(99,224)	$(103,457)	$(87,175)
Plan assets at fair value:			
Salaried employees' plans	190,012	183,535	166,879
Hourly employees' plan	52,491	53,264	52,388
	242,503	236,799	219,267
Plan assets in excess of (less than) projected benefit obligation:			
Salaried employees' plans	155,247	143,998	133,533
Hourly employees' plan	(11,968)	(10,656)	(1,441)
	143,279	133,342	132,092
Unrecognized net asset at January 1, 1986, net of amortization	(24,473)	(27,395)	(30,317)
Unrecognized prior service cost	987	502	195
Unrecognized net loss	40,701	40,983	32,901
Adjustment required to recognize minimum liability for hourly employees' plan	(14,724)	(15,294)	—
Net pension assets	$145,770	$132,138	$134,871
Net pension assets recognized in the consolidated balance sheets:			
Deferred pension assets	$157,038	$142,738	$135,821
Minimum liability included in long-term liabilities	(9,448)	(9,516)	—
Accrued pension liability included in current liabilities	(1,820)	(1,084)	(950)
	$145,770	$132,138	$134,871
Assumptions used in determining actuarial present value of plan benefit obligations:			
Discount rate	8.5%	8.5%	9.25%
Weighted-average rate of increase in future compensation levels	5.0%	5.0%	7.0%
Assumed long-term rate of return on plan assets	10.0%	10.0%	10.0%

Plan assets consist primarily of cash, equity and fixed income securities.

The cost of multiemployer and foreign plans charged to income was immaterial for the three years ended December 31, 1990.

Note 9 — Long-Term Debt

Thousands of dollars	Due Date	Sinking Fund/Interim Payments Amount	Commence	Amount in Treasury December 31, 1990	1989	1988	Amount Outstanding Net of Treasury December 31, 1990	1989	1988
9.875% Debentures	2016	$5,000	2007	—	—	—	$ 50,000	$ 50,000	$ 50,000
5.45% Debentures	1992	2,000	Payable currently	$ 3,872	$ 2,894	$ 4,894	10,128	13,106	13,106
6.25% Convertible Subordinated Debentures (Convertible into common stock at $2.875 a share)	1995	2,000	Payable currently	9,521	9,521	9,521	341	425	490
9.45% Debentures	1999	2,000	Payable currently	4,909	4,598	4,798	23,091	25,402	27,202
9.375% Promissory Notes	—	—	—	—	—	—	—	7,575	13,425
10.50% Promissory Notes	—	—	—	—	—	—	—	—	18,027
8.78% Promissory Notes	1993	5,000	1992	—	—	—	15,000	—	—
8.861% Promissory Notes	1995	—	—	—	—	—	12,500	—	—
9.478% Promissory Notes	2000	—	—	—	—	—	12,500	—	—
6.25% to 8.31% Industrial Revenue Bonds	Through 2005	Varies	Payable currently	—	—	—	7,175	2,200	2,270
8% to 12% Mortgage Notes secured by certain land and buildings, and other	Through 2005	Varies	Payable currently	—	—	—	6,673	5,312	3,360
Obligations under capital leases — less current portion of $376 in 1990, $423 in 1989 and $471 in 1988							591	932	1,724
				$18,302	$17,013	$19,213	$137,999	$104,952	$129,604

On January 31, 1990, the Company exercised its option to prepay the outstanding principal of $15,768,000 for the 10.50% promissory notes and on December 21, 1990 exercised its option to prepay the outstanding principal of $10,900,000 for the 9.375% promissory notes.

During 1990, the Company completed the sale of $15,000,000 in 8.78% promissory notes due in 1993. The note agreement includes certain restrictive covenants regarding the working capital ratio and net worth.

Under a credit agreement with The Sherwin-Williams Company Salaried Employees' Retirement Trust, the Company may borrow up to the lesser of $65,000,000 or 25% of the assets of the trust until October 9, 1992. Revolving credit amounts outstanding can be converted into five-year term, ten-year term or six-year installment loans at any time. The Company completed a $12,500,000 five-year term and a $12,500,000 ten-year term borrowing under this credit agreement in 1990. The credit agreement includes certain restrictive covenants regarding working capital levels and the working capital ratio.

At December 31, 1990, the Company had no borrowings outstanding under any of the following financing arrangements.

Under a credit agreement with a group of twelve banks, the Company may borrow up to $280,000,000 until June 22, 1992. Amounts outstanding under the agreement may be converted into two-year term loans at any time. The credit agreement includes certain restrictive covenants regarding the working capital ratio. There are no compensating balance requirements.

During 1990, the Company terminated a commercial paper program which had been established for Sherwin-Williams Development Corporation, under which $100,000,000 aggregate principal amount of unsecured short-term notes could be issued, and established a similar commercial paper program in the name of the Company in the amount of $280,000,000.

Under a shelf registration with the Securities and Exchange Commission covering $200,000,000 of unsecured debt securities with maturities ranging from nine months to thirty years, the Company may issue securities from time to time in one or more series and will offer the securities on terms determined at the time of sale.

The Company has sufficient debentures in treasury to satisfy most sinking fund requirements of public debenture issues through 1992. Maturities of long-term debt, exclusive of capital lease obligations and after the above-mentioned reduction for sinking fund requirements to be satisfied from debentures on deposit with the trustee, are as follows for the next five years:

1991—$ 2,315,000
1992—$19,604,000
1993—$12,852,000
1994—$ 3,221,000
1995—$15,783,000

Interest expense on long-term debt amounted to $10,444,980, $12,703,000 and $13,501,000 for 1990, 1989 and 1988, respectively. There were no interest charges capitalized during the periods presented.

Note 10 — Leases

The Company leases stores, warehouses, office space and equipment. Renewal options are available on the majority of leases and, under certain conditions, options exist to purchase properties. In some instances, store leases require the payment of contingent rentals based on sales in excess of specified minimums. Certain properties are subleased with various expiration dates. Property, plant and equipment includes the following amounts for capital leases, which are amortized by the straight-line method over the lease term:

Thousands of dollars	1990	December 31, 1989	1988
Buildings	$ 3,639	$ 4,309	$ 6,001
Machinery and Equipment	404	168	168
	4,043	4,477	6,169
Less allowance for amortization	3,373	3,724	4,987
	$ 670	$ 753	$ 1,182

Rental expense for operating leases was $80,501,000, $78,843,000 and $76,656,000 for 1990, 1989 and 1988,

respectively. Contingent rentals included in rent expense were $7,293,000 in 1990, $7,234,000 in 1989 and $6,659,000 in 1988. Rental income, as lessor, from real estate leasing activities and sublease rental income for all years presented was not significant.

Following is a schedule, by year and in the aggregate, of future minimum lease payments under capital leases and noncancelable operating leases having initial or remaining terms in excess of one year at December 31, 1990:

Thousands of dollars	Capital Leases	Operating Leases
1991	$ 532	$ 51,390
1992	271	44,620
1993	120	36,101
1994	114	29,444
1995	81	21,663
Later years	277	33,255
Total minimum lease payments	$ 1,395	$216,473
Amount representing interest	(310)	
Executory costs	(118)	
Present value of net minimum lease payments	$ 967	

Note 11 — Capital Stock

	$1.00 Common Stock	
	Shares in Treasury	Shares Outstanding Net of Treasury
Balance at January 1, 1988	7,760,248	87,446,120
Stock issued upon:		
Exercise of stock options	88,252	555,298
Conversion of 6.25% Convertible Subordinated Debentures	—	28,506
Treasury stock acquired	1,948,420	(1,948,420)
Balance at December 31, 1988	9,796,920	86,081,504
Stock issued upon:		
Exercise of stock options	140,620	760,396
Restricted stock grants	—	163,000
Conversion of 6.25% Convertible Subordinated Debentures	—	22,254
Treasury stock acquired	773,400	(773,400)
Balance at December 31, 1989	10,710,940	86,253,754
Stock issued upon:		
Exercise of stock options	68,322	455,526
Conversion of 6.25% Convertible Subordinated Debentures	—	29,556
Balance at December 31, 1990	10,779,262	86,738,836

All common share amounts reflect the effect of the stock split described in Note 2.

An aggregate of 6,563,590, 7,117,002 and 4,203,280 shares of stock at December 31, 1990, 1989 and 1988, respectively, were reserved for conversion of convertible subordinated debentures, future grants of restricted stock, and exercise and future grants of stock options. At December 31, 1990, there were 200,000,000 shares of common stock and 30,000,000 shares of serial preferred stock authorized for issuance.

The Company has a shareholders rights plan which designates 1,000,000 shares of the authorized serial preferred stock as cumulative redeemable serial preferred stock which may be issued if the Company becomes the target of coercive and unfair takeover tactics.

Note 12 — Stock Purchase and Option Plans

All common share amounts reflect the effect of the stock split described in Note 2.

As of December 31, 1990, 8,733 employees participated through regular payroll deductions in the Company's Employee Stock Purchase and Savings Plan. The Company's contribution charged to income amounted to $13,519,000, $13,622,000 and $10,048,000 for 1990, 1989 and 1988, respectively. Additionally, the Company made contributions on behalf of participating employees, which represent salary reductions for income tax purposes, amounting to $6,107,000 in 1990, $5,658,000 in 1989 and $5,005,000 in 1988.

At December 31, 1990, there were 12,638,572 shares of the Company's stock being held by this plan, representing 15% of the total number of shares outstanding. Shares of company stock credited to each member's account under the plan are voted by the trustee under confidential instructions from each individual plan member. Shares for which no instructions are received are voted by the trustee in the same proportion as those for which instructions are received.

The Company's stock plan permits the granting of stock options, stock appreciation rights, and restricted stock to eligible employees. Non-qualified and incentive stock options have been granted to certain officers and key employees under the current and previous plans at prices not less than fair market value of the shares at the date of grant. The options generally become exercisable to the extent of one-third of the optioned shares for each full year of employment following the date of grant and generally expire ten years after the date of grant. Restricted stock grants for 163,000 shares were awarded in 1989 to certain officers and key employees which require four years of continuous employment from the date of grant before receiving the shares without restriction. The number of shares to be received without restriction is based on the Company's performance relative to a peer group of companies. Unamortized deferred compensation expense with respect to the restricted stock amounted to $1,783,878 at December 31, 1990 and $2,341,000 at December 31, 1989 and is being amortized over the four-year vesting period. Deferred compensation expense during 1990 aggregated $801,703 and aggregated $460,000 in 1989. No stock appreciation rights have been granted.

	1990		1989		1988	
	Shares	Aggregate Price	Shares	Aggregate Price	Shares	Aggregate Price
Stock Option Plans:						
Options outstanding beginning of year	2,623,516	$33,798,774	2,932,944	$34,484,313	3,398,808	$36,745,180
Granted	590,400	9,816,200	671,800	9,048,213	348,400	4,674,675
Exercised	(523,848)	(6,112,226)	(901,016)	(8,565,348)	(643,550)	(4,753,719)
Canceled	(73,916)	(1,047,932)	(80,212)	(1,168,404)	(170,714)	(2,181,823)
Options outstanding end of year	2,616,152	$36,454,816	2,623,516	$33,798,774	2,932,944	$34,484,313
Exercisable	1,528,962		1,591,158		1,612,050	
Reserved for future grants	3,829,060		4,345,544		1,100,132	

Note 13 — Income Taxes

Thousands of dollars	Years ended December 31,		
	1990	1989	1988
The components of income before income taxes consist of the following:			
Domestic	$178,647	$159,352	$118,178
Foreign	8,630	10,859	44,862
Total income before income taxes	$187,277	$170,211	$163,040
The components of income tax expense are as follows:			
Current:			
Federal	$52,991	$50,956	$36,777
State and Local	10,000	9,000	8,500
Foreign	1,710	1,715	13,932
	64,701	61,671	59,209
Deferred	(90)	(395)	2,751
Total income tax expense	$64,611	$61,276	$61,960

The Company has recognized the deferred income tax liabilities and benefits resulting from timing differences between financial and tax accounting, relating primarily to depreciation, deferred employee benefit items and other valuation allowances. It is the Company's intention to reinvest undistributed earnings of foreign subsidiaries; accordingly, no deferred income taxes have been provided thereon. At December 31, 1990, such undistributed earnings amounted to $4,705,602.

The source and deferred tax effect of timing differences are as follows:

Thousands of dollars	Years ended December 31,		
	1990	1989	1988
Depreciation	$ 104	$ 3,020	$ 3,425
Dispositions, terminations and other similar items	2,596	(1,954)	(2,630)
Deferred employee benefit items	(745)	5,915	1,419
Other items (each less than 5% of the computed "expected" tax amount)	(2,045)	(7,376)	537
	$ (90)	$ (395)	$ 2,751

A reconciliation of the statutory federal income tax rate and the effective tax rate follow:

	Years ended December 31,		
	1990	1989	1988
Statutory tax rate	34.0%	34.0%	34.0%
Effect of:			
State and local taxes	3.5	3.5	3.4
Other - net	(3.0)	(1.5)	.6
Effective tax rate	34.5%	36.0%	38.0%

Note 14 — Quarterly Data (Unaudited)

Quarterly Stock Prices and Dividends*

1990	Quarter	High	Low	Dividend	1989	Quarter	High	Low	Dividend
	1st	$ 18 ¼	$ 15 ⅜	$ .095		1st	$ 13 ⅞	$ 12 ½	$ .0875
	2nd	20 ⅛	17 ¼	$ .095		2nd	15 ½	13 ⅜	.0875
	3rd	21 ⅛	15 ⅛	$ .095		3rd	17 ⅞	14 ⅝	.0875
	4th	19 ⅞	15 ½	$ .095		4th	17 ½	15 ¾	.0875

Summary of Quarterly Results of Operations

Thousands of dollars, except per share data

Year	Quarter	Net Sales	Gross Profit	Net Income	Net Income Per Share*
1990	1st	$499,460	$193,171	$ 9,995	$ .11
	2nd	611,385	253,215	44,910	.51
	3rd	638,532	263,238	46,746	.54
	4th	517,355	219,166	21,015	.25
1989	1st	$464,781	$176,740	$ 8,810	$ .10
	2nd	583,984	237,620	38,696	.45
	3rd	595,983	240,196	41,598	.48
	4th	478,735	193,808	19,831	.23

* Per share data reflects the effect of the stock split described in Note 2.

1990

Fourth quarter adjustments increased net income by $2,690,000 ($.03 per share). This increase was due primarily to year-end inventory adjustments of $6,906,000 ($.08 per share) and a net credit for disposition and termination of certain operations of $1,466,000 ($.02 per share) which were partially offset by provisions for environmental protection and control and other year-end adjustments of $5,683,000 ($.07 per share).

1989

Fourth quarter adjustments increased net income by $8,250,000 ($.10 per share). This increase was due primarily to a reduction of prior quarters' LIFO expense and year-end inventory adjustments of $15,915,000 ($.19 per share) which were partially offset by provisions of $4,722,000 ($.06 per share) for the disposition and termination of certain operations, and other year-end adjustments of $2,943,000 ($.04 per share).

Note 15 — Real Estate Subsidiary

Sherwin-Williams Development Corporation, a wholly-owned subsidiary, and certain of its affiliates (SWDC) acquire, develop, lease, and manage properties for the Company and others. As required by Financial Accounting Standards Board Statement No. 94, SWDC is included in the consolidated financial statements. Total revenue includes intersegment revenue of $12,663,000, $10,058,000, and $9,575,000 in 1990, 1989 and 1988, respectively, which is eliminated in consolidation with the parent.

Summarized financial data for SWDC is as follows:

Thousands of dollars	December 31, **1990**	1989	1988
Property, plant and equipment — net	$106,768	$99,063	$88,871
Current assets	469	670	1,053
Other noncurrent assets	625	718	817
Long-term debt	58,136	53,225	53,615
Current liabilities	2,652	2,062	3,125
Other noncurrent liabilities	5,676	5,415	4,781
Due to parent	35,286	35,130	19,916
Total revenue	$ 16,678	$14,162	$15,414
Interest expense	5,279	5,306	5,156
Total expenses — net	13,674	11,545	11,191
Net income	1,968	1,714	2,883

Note 16 — Financial Schedules
Property, Plant and Equipment (10-K, Schedules V and VI)

Additions and retirements of property, plant and equipment were as follows:

Thousands of dollars	Beginning Balance	Additions	Retirements	Other Changes	Ending Balance
1990					
Land	$ 36,748	$ 4,470	$ 53	$ 748	$ 41,913
Buildings	191,540	11,574	960	(7,185)	194,969
Machinery and equipment	404,156	43,968	16,319	466	432,271
Construction in progress	14,294	4,339	—	72	18,705
	$646,738	$64,351	$17,332	$ (5,899)	$687,858
1989					
Land	$ 35,206	$ 1,841	$ 307	$ 8	$ 36,748
Buildings	186,721	8,322	1,749	(1,754)	191,540
Machinery and equipment	365,834	54,232	15,870	(40)	404,156
Construction in progress	11,757	2,538	—	(1)	14,294
	$599,518	$66,933	$17,926	$ (1,787)	$646,738
1988					
Land	$ 32,069	$ 3,005	$ 518	$ 650	$ 35,206
Buildings	159,478	22,038	1,632	6,837	186,721
Machinery and equipment	324,498	46,414	12,057	6,979	365,834
Construction in progress	11,663	94	—	—	11,757
	$527,708	$71,551	$14,207	$14,466	$599,518

Other changes consist primarily of acquisitions and dispositions in 1990 and acquisitions in 1988.

Total accumulated depreciation and amortization of property, plant and equipment were as follows:

Thousands of dollars	Beginning Balance	Additions	Retirements	Other Changes	Ending Balance
1990					
Buildings	$ 62,843	$ 7,422	$ 769	$(4,951)	$ 64,545
Machinery and equipment	211,662	37,085	12,302	(845)	235,600
Other	13,368	—	—	995	14,363
	$287,873	$44,507	$13,071	$(4,801)	$314,508
1989					
Buildings	$ 57,638	$ 7,651	$ 1,019	$(1,427)	$ 62,843
Machinery and equipment	190,511	34,300	13,295	146	211,662
Other	18,771	—	—	(5,403)	13,368
	$266,920	$41,951	$14,314	$(6,684)	$287,873
1988					
Buildings	$ 53,665	$ 6,713	$ 1,266	$(1,474)	$ 57,638
Machinery and equipment	166,939	30,152	8,779	2,199	190,511
Other	18,242	—	—	529	18,771
	$238,846	$36,865	$10,045	$ 1,254	$266,920

Other changes consist primarily of dispositions in 1990 and provisions for dispositions in 1989 and 1988.

Note 16 — Financial Schedules (Continued)

Valuation and Qualifying Accounts and Reserves (10-K, Schedule VIII)

Changes in the allowance for doubtful accounts are as follows:

Thousands of dollars	Years ended December 31, 1990	1989	1988
Beginning balance	$ 2,261	$ 2,737	$ 2,820
Bad debt expense	11,584	9,430	7,535
Net uncollectible accounts written off	(11,362)	(9,906)	(7,618)
Ending balance	$ 2,483	$ 2,261	$ 2,737

Activity related to other assets:

Thousands of dollars	Years ended December 31, 1990	1989	1988
Beginning balance	$ 27,541	$24,152	$42,153
Charges to expense	(7,007)	(3,822)	(10,595)
Asset additions (deductions)	129,206	7,211	(7,406)
Ending balance	$149,740	$27,541	$24,152

Charges to expense consist primarily of amortization of intangibles in 1990, 1989 and 1988 and funded employee benefits in 1988. Asset additions (deductions) consist primarily of the acquisition of intangibles and goodwill in 1990, the purchase of long-term investments and reclassifications in 1989, and the sale of the partnership interest in BAPCO in 1988.

Activity related to other long-term liabilities:

Thousands of dollars	Years ended December 31, 1990	1989	1988
Beginning balance	$75,480	$57,623	$42,482
Charges to expense	6,429	14,745	16,378
Accrual additions (deductions)	(9,434)	3,112	(1,237)
Ending balance	$72,475	$75,480	$57,623

Charges to expense consist primarily of adjustments to estimated liabilities and deferred compensation. Accrual additions (deductions) consist primarily of balance sheet reclassifications and adjustments of environmental and other long-term accruals.

Short-Term Borrowings (10-K, Schedule IX)

Thousands of dollars	Years ended December 31, 1990	1989	1988
Notes payable to banks at December 31	$ 559	$ 431	$ 362
Weighted-average interest rate at December 31	31.5%	28.0%	19.8%
Maximum amount outstanding at any month-end	$ 751	$ 735	$ 484
Average amount outstanding during the period	$ 395	$ 587	$ 284
Weighted-average interest rate during the period	33.4%	21.0%	16.9%

Short-term borrowings are included in accounts payable on the balance sheets. Borrowings for 1990 relate solely to certain foreign subsidiaries at rates prevailing in those countries.

The average amount outstanding is the total of month-end outstanding balances divided by twelve.

The weighted-average interest rate is the actual interest on short-term debt divided by average short-term debt outstanding.

Supplementary Income Statement Information (10-K, Schedule X)

Thousands of dollars	Years ended December 31, 1990	1989	1988
Maintenance and repairs	$ 25,274	$25,442	$26,351
Advertising costs	106,461	84,465	84,043

Amounts for depreciation and amortization of intangible assets, preoperating costs and similar deferrals, taxes other than payroll and income taxes, and royalties are not presented because such amounts are each less than 1% of total net sales.

Computation of Net Income Per Share (Exhibit 11, Form 10-K)*
Thousands of dollars, except per share data

	December 31,		
	1990	1989	1988
Fully Diluted			
Average shares outstanding	86,560,437	85,954,145	87,354,494
Options — treasury stock method	503,898	548,504	475,348
Assumed conversion of 6.25% Convertible Subordinated Debentures	132,638	156,146	182,956
Average fully diluted shares	87,196,973	86,658,795	88,012,798
Net income	$122,666	$108,935	$101,080
Add 6.25% Convertible Subordinated Debentures interest net of tax	16	18	20
Net income applicable to fully diluted shares	$122,682	$108,953	$101,100
Net income per share	$ 1.41	$ 1.26	$ 1.15
Primary			
Average shares outstanding	86,560,437	85,954,145	87,354,494
Options — treasury stock method	495,382	372,194	475,348
Average shares and equivalents	87,055,819	86,326,339	87,829,842
Net income applicable to shares and equivalents	$122,666	$108,935	$101,080
Net income per share	$ 1.41	$ 1.26	$ 1.15

* All common share amounts and per share data reflect the effect of the stock split described in Note 2 to the consolidated financial statements.

Business Segments

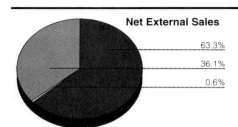

Net External Sales

63.3%
36.1%
0.6%

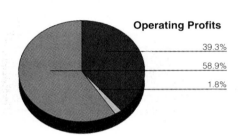

Operating Profits

39.3%
58.9%
1.8%

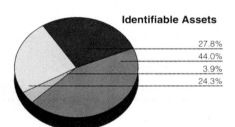

Identifiable Assets

27.8%
44.0%
3.9%
24.3%

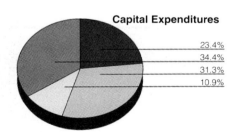

Capital Expenditures

23.4%
34.4%
31.3%
10.9%

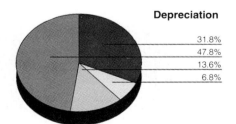

Depreciation

31.8%
47.8%
13.6%
6.8%

Millions of dollars

Years ended December 31,	1990	1989	1988
Net External Sales			
Paint Stores	$1,434	$1,346	$1,250
Coatings	819	764	687
Other	14	13	13
Segment totals	$2,267	$2,123	$1,950
Operating Profits			
Paint Stores	$ 86	$ 91	$ 70
Coatings	129	120	118
Other	4	(3)	6
Segment totals	219	208	194
Corporate expenses-net	(32)	(38)	(31)
Income from continuing operations before income taxes	$ 187	$ 170	$ 163
Identifiable Assets			
Paint Stores	$ 418	$ 393	$ 426
Coatings	662	480	457
Other	58	49	47
Segment totals	1,138	922	930
Corporate	366	453	329
Discontinued Operations	—	—	—
Consolidated totals	$1,504	$1,375	$1,259
Capital Expenditures			
Paint Stores	$ 15	$ 27	$ 15
Coatings	22	26	39
Other	20	10	8
Segment totals	57	63	62
Corporate	7	4	10
Discontinued Operations	—	—	—
Consolidated totals	$ 64	$ 67	$ 72
Depreciation			
Paint Stores	$ 14	$ 13	$ 11
Coatings	21	21	18
Other	6	5	4
Segment totals	41	39	33
Corporate	3	3	4
Continuing operations totals	$ 44	$ 42	$ 37
Operating Margins			
Paint Stores	6.0%	6.8%	5.6%
Coatings	9.8%	10.0%	10.8%
Other	13.8%	(11.1%)	25.5%
Segment totals	7.9%	8.1%	8.2%

Paint Stores
Coatings
Other
Corporate

Intersegment Transfers

	1990	1989	1988	1987	1986	1985	1984	1983	1982	1981
Coatings	$492	$442	$401	$368	$331	$314	$287	$271	$233	$261
All other segments	15	14	12	7	6	5	4	29	30	35
Segment totals	$507	$456	$413	$375	$337	$319	$291	$300	$263	$296

The Sherwin-Williams Company and Subsidiaries

	1987	1986	1985	1984	1983	1982	1981
	$1,158	$1,009	$ 931	$ 850	$ 724	$ 621	$ 616
	635	544	566	513	485	491	554
	8	5	39	91	188	200	229
	$1,801	$1,558	$1,526	$1,454	$1,397	$1,312	$1,399
	$ 82	$ 91*	$ 64	$ 56	$ 29	$ 14	$ 16
	104	129*	94	77	89	78	57
	5	—	3	10	10	11	8
	191	220	161	143	128	103	81
	(30)	(46)*	(37)	(25)	(29)	(37)	(29)
	$ 161	$ 174*	$ 124	$ 118	$ 99	$ 66	$ 52
	$ 367	$ 303	$ 283	$ 249	$ 197	$ 152	$ 167
	401	351	331	305	300	277	304
	43	46	38	63	67	142	145
	811	700	652	617	564	571	616
	399	257	224	217	203	155	75
	—	250	232	209	203	176	173
	$1,210	$1,207	$1,108	$1,043	$ 970	$ 902	$ 864
	$ 15	$ 12	$ 16	$ 16	$ 7	$ 6	$ 10
	29	21	24	15	12	9	10
	6	13	16	13	22	24	20
	50	46	56	44	41	39	40
	5	4	8	2	2	4	2
	2	14	11	13	9	5	1
	$ 57	$ 64	$ 75	$ 59	$ 52	$ 48	$ 43
	$ 10	$ 9	$ 8	$ 7	$ 6	$ 5	$ 6
	16	12	11	9	8	8	8
	3	2	3	5	8	7	6
	29	23	22	21	22	20	20
	3	4	2	2	1	2	2
	$ 32	$ 27	$ 24	$ 23	$ 23	$ 22	$ 22
	7.1%	9.0%	6.9%	6.6%	4.0%	2.2%	2.6%
	10.4%	14.8%	10.8%	9.6%	11.8%	10.7%	6.9%
	33.9%	(2.4%)	5.9%	10.7%	4.8%	5.0%	3.0%
	8.8%	11.6%	8.7%	8.2%	7.6%	6.5%	4.8%

* Operating profits in 1986 include net credits of $21,179,000 for Paint Stores and $30,023,000 for Coatings and a charge of ($17,417,000) for Corporate from unusual items.

Effect of LIFO

	Year of Adoption	Decrease (Increase) in Income From Continuing Operations									
		1990	1989	1988	1987	1986	1985	1984	1983	1982	1981
Paint Stores	1980	$ 6	$ 6	$ 4	$(2)	$(1)	—	$(1)	—	$ 2	$ 5
Coatings	1980	6	7	14	3	(5)	$ 1	4	$(1)	1	13
Other	1979	—	—	—	—	—	—	(1)	(2)	(3)	2
Segment totals		$12	$13	$18	$ 1	$(6)	$ 1	$ 2	$(3)	$—	$20

Notes to Segment Tables

The Other Segment consists of real estate leasing activities which began in 1982, the Chemicals Division which was disposed of in June 1985, and the Sherwin-Williams Container Corporation which was disposed of during November 1983.

Net external sales, operating profits, depreciation, and operating margins include continuing operations only for the years 1981 through 1987.

Operating profit is total revenue, including realized profit on intersegment transfers, less operating costs and expenses. Adjusting for special credits in 1989 and special charges in 1988, operating profit of the Paint Stores Segment increased 7.8 percent from 1989 to 1990 and 7.7 percent from 1988 to 1989. During 1984, a change in intersegment transfer values resulted in increased operating profit for the Paint Stores Segment while the Coatings Segment's operating profit declined due to the effects of the reduced transfer values. Corporate expenses include interest which is unrelated to real estate leasing activities, certain provisions for disposition and termination of operations which are not directly associated with or allocable to any operating segment, and other adjustments.

Identifiable assets are those directly identified with each segment's operations. Corporate assets consist primarily of cash, investments, headquarters property, plant and equipment, and certain property under capital leases.

The operating margin for each segment is based upon total external sales and intersegment transfers. Intersegment transfers are accounted for at values comparable to normal unaffiliated customer sales.

Export sales, sales of foreign subsidiaries and sales to any individual customer were each less than 10% of consolidated sales to unaffiliated customers during all years presented.

Our business segments offer customers quality products such as those bearing the registered trademarks Sherwin-Williams®, Dutch Boy®, Martin-Senour®, Kem-Tone®, Acme®, Rogers®, Western Automotive Finishes , Glas-Clad®, Perma-Clad®, Dupli-Color®, Krylon®, Color Works®, Illinois Bronze®, ProMar® 200, Dutch Boy SUPER®, Dutch Boy DIRT FIGHTER®, and others. Other quality paint products are offered under the trademark of SuperPaint™

INDEX

◆

ARB No.	Date Issued	Title
82	Nov. 1984	Financial Reporting and Changing Prices: Elimination of Certain Disclosures (an amendment of *FASB Statement 33*)
83	Mar. 1985	Designation of AICPA Guides and Statement of Position on Accounting by Brokers and Dealers in Securities, by Employee Benefit Plans, and by Banks as Preferable for Purposes of Applying *APB Opinion 20* (an amendment of *FASB Statement 32* and *APB Opinion 30*, and a recission of *FASB Interpretation 10*)
84	Mar. 1985	Induced Conversions of Convertible Debt (an amendment of *APB Opinion 26*)
85	Mar. 1985	Yield Test for Determining whether a Convertible Security Is a Common Stock Equivalent (an amendment of *APB Opinion 15*)
86	Aug. 1985	Accounting for the Costs of Computer Software to Be Sold, Leased, or Otherwise Marketed
87	Dec. 1985	Employers' Accounting for Pensions
88	Dec. 1985	Employers' Accounting for Settlements and Curtailments of Defined Benefit Pension Plans and for Termination of Benefits
89	Dec. 1986	Financial Reporting and Changing Prices
90	Dec. 1986	Regulated Enterprises: Accounting for Abandonments and Disallowances of Plant Costs (an amendment of *FASB Statement 71*)
91	Dec. 1986	Accounting for Nonrefundable Fees and Costs Associated with Originating or Acquiring Loans and Initial Direct Costs of Leases (an amendment of *FASB Statements 13, 60,* and *65,* and a recission of *FASB Statement 17*)
92	Aug. 1987	Regulated Enterprises—Accounting for Phase-In Plans (an amendment of *FASB Statement 71*)
93	Aug. 1987	Recognition of Depreciation by Not-for-Profit Organizations
94	Oct. 1987	Consolidation of All Majority-Owned Subsidiaries (an amendment of *ARB 51,* with related amendments of *APB Opinion 18* and *ARB 43,* Chapter 12)
95	Nov. 1987	Statement of Cash Flows
96	Dec. 1987	Accounting for Income Taxes
97	Dec. 1987	Accounting and Reporting by Insurance Enterprises for Certain Long-Duration Contracts and for Realized Gains and Losses from the Sale of Investments
98	May 1988	Accounting for Leases: Sale-Leaseback Transactions involving Real Estate; Definition of the Lease Term; Initial Direct Costs of Direct Financing Leases (an amendment of *FASB Statements 13, 66,* and *91,* and a recission of *FASB Statement 26* and *Technical Bulletin 79–11*)
99	Sept. 1988	Deferral of the Effective Date of Recognition of Depreciation by Not-for-Profit Organizations (an amendment of *FASB Statement No. 93*)
100	Dec. 1988	Accounting for Income Taxes—Deferral of the Effective Date of FASB Statement No. 96 (an amendment of *FASB Statement No. 96*)
101	Dec. 1988	Regulated Enterprises—Accounting for the Discontinuation of Application of *FASB Statement No. 71*
102	Feb. 1989	Statement of Cash Flows—Exemption of Certain Enterprises and Classification of Cash Flows from Certain Securities Acquired for Resale (an amendment of *FASB Statement No. 95*)
103	Dec. 1989	Accounting for Income Taxes—Deferral of the Effective Date of *FASB Statement No. 96* (an amendment of *FASB Statement No. 96*)
104	Dec. 1989	Statement of Cash Flows—Net Reporting of Certain Cash Receipts and Cash Payments and Classification of Cash Flows from Hedging Transactions (an amendment of *FASB Statement No. 95*)
105	Mar. 1990	Disclosure of Information about Financial Instruments with Off-Balance-Sheet Risk and Financial Instruments with Concentrations of Credit Risk
106	Dec. 1990	Employers' Accounting for Postretirement Benefits Other Than Pensions
	Jun. 1991	Proposed Statement of Financial Accounting Standards: Accounting for Income Taxes (Exposure Draft)

INT No.		**Financial Accounting Standards Board (FASB)** *Interpretations* (1974–85)
1	June 1974	Accounting Changes Related to the Cost of Inventory
2	June 1974	Imputing Interest on Debt Arrangements Made under the Federal Bankruptcy Act
3	Dec. 1974	Accounting for the Cost of Pension Plans Subject to the Employment Retirement Income Security Act of 1974
4	Feb. 1975	Applicability of *FASB Statement 2* to Business Combinations Accounted for by the Purchase Method
5	Feb. 1975	Applicability of *FASB Statement 2* to Development Stage Enterprises
6	Feb. 1975	Applicability of *FASB Statement 2* to Computer Software
7	Oct. 1975	Applying *FASB Statement 7* in Financial Statements of Established Operating Enterprises
8	Jan. 1976	Classification of a Short-Term Obligation Repaid Prior to Being Replaced by a Long-Term Security
9	Feb. 1976	Applying *APB Opinions 16* and *17* When a Savings and Loan Association or a Similar Institution Is Acquired in a Business Combination Accounted for by the Purchase Method
10	Sept. 1976	Application of *FASB Statement 12* to Personal Financial Statements
11	Sept. 1976	Changes in Market Value after the Balance Sheet Date
12	Sept. 1976	Accounting for Previously Established Allowance Accounts
13	Sept. 1976	Consolidation of a Parent and Its Subsidiaries Having Different Balance Sheet Dates
14	Sept. 1976	Reasonable Estimation of the Amount of a Loss

No.	Date Issued	Title
15	Sept. 1976	Translation of Unamortized Policy Acquisition Costs by a Stock Life Insurance Company
16	Feb. 1977	Clarification of Definitions and Accounting for Marketable Equity Securities That Become Nonmarketable
17	Feb. 1977	Applying the Lower of Cost or Market Rule in Translated Financial Statements
18	Mar. 1977	Accounting for Income Taxes in Interim Periods
19	Oct. 1977	Lessee Guarantee of the Residual Value of Leased Property
20	Nov. 1977	Reporting Accounting Changes under AICPA Statements of Position
21	Apr. 1978	Accounting for Leases in a Business Combination
22	Apr. 1978	Applicability of Indefinite Reversal Criteria to Timing Differences
23	Aug. 1978	Leases of Certain Property Owned by a Governmental Unit or Authority
24	Sept. 1978	Leases Involving Only Part of a Building
25	Sept. 1978	Accounting for an Unused Investment Tax Credit
26	Sept. 1978	Accounting for Purchase of a Leased Asset by the Lessee during the Term of the Lease
27	Nov. 1978	Accounting for Loss on a Sublease
28	Dec. 1978	Accounting for Stock Appreciation Rights and Other Variable Stock Option or Award Plans
29	Feb. 1979	Reporting Tax Benefits Realized on Disposition of Investments in Certain Subsidiaries and Other Investees
30	Sept. 1979	Accounting for Involuntary Conversions of Nonmonetary Assets to Monetary Assets
31	Feb. 1980	Treatment of Stock Compensation Plans in EPS Computations
32	Mar. 1980	Application of Percentage Limitations in Recognizing Investment Tax Credit
33	Aug. 1980	Applying *FASB Statement 34* to Oil and Gas Producing Operations Accounted for by the Full Cost Method
34	Mar. 1981	Disclosure of Indirect Guarantees of Indebtedness of Others
35	May 1981	Criteria for Applying the Equity Method of Accounting for Investments in Common Stock
36	Oct. 1981	Accounting for Exploration Wells in Progress at the End of a Period
37	July 1983	Accounting for Translation Adjustments upon Sale of Part of an Investment in a Foreign Entity
38	Aug. 1984	Determining the Measurement Date for Stock Options, Purchase, and Award Plans Involving Junior Stock

TB No.		**Financial Accounting Standards Board (FASB)** *Technical Bulletins* (1979–87)
79–1	Dec. 1979	Purpose and Scope of FASB Technical Bulletins and Procedures for Issuance—To Provide Guidance Concerning the Application of Official Pronouncements of the FASB, APB, and ARBs
79–2	Dec. 1979	Computer Software Costs
79–3	Dec. 1979	Subjective Acceleration Clauses in Long-Term Debt Agreements
79–4	Dec. 1979	Segment Reporting of Puerto Rican Operations
79–5	Dec. 1979	Meaning of the Term "Customer" as It Applies to Facilities
79–6	Dec. 1979	Valuation Allowances Following Debt Restructure
79–7	Dec. 1979	Recoveries of a Previous Writedown under a Troubled Debt Restructuring Involving a Modification of Terms
79–8	Dec. 1979	Applicability of *FASB Statements 21* and *33* to Certain Brokers and Dealers in Securities
79–9	Dec. 1979	Accounting in Interim Periods for Changes in Income Tax Rates
79–10	Dec. 1979	Fiscal Funding Clauses in Lease Agreements
79–11	Dec. 1979	Effect of a Penalty on the Term of a Lease
79–12	Dec. 1979	Interest Rate Used in Calculating the Present Value of Minimum Lease Payments
79–13	Dec. 1979	Applicability of *FASB Statement 13* to Current Value Financial Statements
79–14	Dec. 1979	Upward Adjustment of Guaranteed Residual Values
79–15	Dec. 1979	Accounting for Loss on a Sublease Not Involving the Disposal of a Segment
79–16	Dec. 1979	Effect of a Change in Income Tax Rate on the Accounting for Leveraged Leases
79–17	Dec. 1979	Reporting Cumulative Effect Adjustment from Retroactive Application of *FASB Statement 13*
79–18	Dec. 1979	Transition Requirement of Certain FASB Amendments and Interpretations of *FASB Statement 13*
79–19	Dec. 1979	Investor's Accounting for Unrealized Losses on Marketable Securities Owned by an Equity Method Investee
80–1	Dec. 1980	Early Extinguishment of Debt through Exchange for Common or Preferred Stock
81–1	Feb. 1981	Disclosure of Interest Rate Futures Contracts and Forward and Standby Contracts
81–2	Feb. 1981	Accounting for Unused Investment Tax Credits Acquired in a Business Combination Accounted for by the Purchase Method
81–3	Feb. 1981	Multiemployer Pension Plan Amendments Act of 1980
84–4	Feb. 1981	Classification as Monetary or Nonmonetary Items
81–5	Feb. 1981	Offsetting Interest Cost to Be Capitalized with Interest Income
81–6	Nov. 1981	Applicability of *FASB Statement 15* to Debtors in Bankruptcy Situations
82–1	Jan. 1982	Disclosure of the Sale or Purchase of Tax Benefits through Tax Leases
82–2	Mar. 1982	Accounting for the Conversion of Stock Options into Stock Incentive Plans as a Result of the Economic Recovery Tax Act of 1981
83–1	July 1983	Accounting for the Reduction in the Tax Basis of an Asset Caused by the Investment Tax Credit
84–1	Mar. 1984	Accounting for Stock Issued to Acquire the Results of a Research and Development Arrangement